Get Started

MyLab and Mastering for Blackboard Learn Students

March 21, 2013

Contents

Get started

Your Pearson MyLab and Mastering course is delivered inside Blackboard Learn at your college. The first time you access the MyLab and Mastering course, you need to enter the Blackboard course and then click a link to access Pearson and create an account. After the first time, you only need to sign in to Blackboard; you will not need to sign in to Pearson again.

Your instructor can direct you to the MyLab and Mastering links in Blackboard Learn to get you started.

The order in which you must enter the Blackboard course, register for the Pearson course, and then enter the MyLab and Mastering course is:

1. Enter your Blackboard course.

2. Register and pay for your Pearson course.

3. Access your Pearson course through Blackboard Learn.

If you need it, there is also a troubleshooting topic to help you through any errors you might see when logging in and getting started with your course.

View the pdf file as online Help

Click Get started as a Help file to view this guide as online help topics.

See also:

Course accounts and access | Operating systems and browsers

Course accounts and access

To access your course, you need the following:

- A Blackboard account.

- A Pearson account. If you do not already have a Pearson account, you are asked to create one on the registration page when you click a MyLab and Mastering link in your Blackboard course.

  Note: If you have previously registered for a Pearson MyLab and Mastering account from a Blackboard Learn course, you **must** use the same Pearson account when enrolling in additional MyLab and Mastering courses from Blackboard Learn. You cannot link a new Pearson account to your existing Blackboard Learn account.

- An access code for your MyLab or Mastering product. Alternatively, you can purchase access with a credit card when you register.

Note: In most cases, you can get temporary access to MyLab and Mastering for up to 17 days when you register through your Blackboard Learn course. If temporary access is available, you will see a link for Temporary Access when you register.

If you are enrolled in more than one Blackboard Learn course, you need to sign in once to each course and register with your access code or pay for each course.

You do not need to enter a course ID during registration. This is different from other MyLab and Mastering courses which do require you to provide this information.

Operating systems and browsers

Check the browser and operating system requirements on the MyLab and Mastering website for your MyLab and Mastering product's supported operating systems and browsers.

1. Enter your Blackboard course

Always go into your Blackboard Learn course first. Then, from the Blackboard course, register and enter the Pearson MyLab and Mastering course.

When you enter your Blackboard course, you will see links to your MyLab and Mastering course. The first time you click a MyLab and Mastering link, you are automatically taken through the Pearson registration process. Use the procedure below to sign in to Blackboard and access the MyLab and Mastering course links.

To sign in for the first time:

1. Sign in to Blackboard Learn and enter your Blackboard course.

2. Click **Tools** in the left navigation bar.

3. Click **Pearson's MyLab / Mastering** on the Tools page.

    The Pearson's MyLab and Mastering page is now displayed. The top area of the page lists the links into the MyLab and Mastering course. The lower area displays the course's Support Tools.

4. Click any course link in the top area of the page.

    The End-User License Agreement and Privacy Policy is displayed.

5. Continue with the procedure in 2. Register and pay for your Pearson course.

2. Register and pay for your Pearson course

You register and pay for your Pearson course the first time you click a MyLab and Mastering course link from within your Blackboard Learn course.

The Pearson registration process requires that you do one of the following:

- Use an access code that you already purchased with the textbook or a separate kit

- Purchase access online using a credit card or PayPal

- Request temporary access (If you're waiting for financial aid and can't pay immediately, you can access the full set of features in your instructor's online course without payment for 17 days. The temporary access option enables you to start your coursework and avoid missing deadlines set by your instructor.)

To register and pay for your Pearson MyLab and Mastering course:

1. Complete the procedure in 1. Enter your Blackboard course.

   The End-User License Agreement and Privacy Policy is displayed.

2. Review the agreement and policy and click **I Accept**.

   The MyLab and Mastering Register page is displayed, and it shows the name of the MyLab and Mastering course on the right. This is the Pearson name for your MyLab and Mastering course, and it may not be the same as the Blackboard course's name.

   > **Important!** If you are prompted to enter a **course ID**, cancel the procedure. Next, enter the Blackboard course and click a Pearson link as described in 1. Enter your Blackboard course. Then continue with this procedure.

3. Do one of the following:

   - If you already have a Pearson account, enter your Pearson username and password.

     Note: If you have previously registered for a Pearson MyLab and Mastering account from a Blackboard Learn course, you **must** use the same Pearson account when enrolling in additional MyLab and Mastering courses from Blackboard Learn. You cannot link a new Pearson account to your existing Blackboard Learn account.

   - If you do not have a Pearson account, click **Create** to create one. Then follow the screen prompts to set up an account.

   You are now prompted for an access code, payment, or request for temporary access.

4. Do one of the following:

   Enter an access code

   a. Click **Access Code**.

      The Access Code page is displayed.

   b. Enter the access code and click **Finish**.

   Pay for access now

   a. Under **Use a Credit Card or PayPal**, click the button displaying the price you're going to pay.

   b. Enter your payment information. For assistance, click the **Help** button on the payment screen.

Request temporary access

a. Click **Get temporary access without payment for 17 days** at the bottom of the Register page.

b. Click **Yes** to complete your request.

When your registration is complete, the Your Done page is displayed and you get a confirmation email. Click **Go to Your Course** to enter the course immediately.

Important: For all future access to the course, make sure to enter it through Blackboard. See 3. Access your Pearson course through Blackboard Learn.

3. Access your Pearson course through Blackboard Learn

After you have registered for the Pearson course, you return to it through Blackboard Learn.

The links to the MyLab and Mastering course are on both the Tools and Content pages in Blackboard. Which page you use is up to you. However, the Tools page also has links to the course's Support Tools.

To access your Pearson MyLab and Mastering course from the Tools page:

1. Enter your Blackboard course.

2. Click **Tools** in the left navigation bar.

3. Click **Pearson's MyLab / Mastering** on the Tools page.

   Pearson's MyLab and Mastering page is now displayed. The first link goes to your MyLab and Mastering course's home page. The following links are to specific course components, such as Homework, Tests, or Study Plan. The lower area of the page displays the course's Support Tools.

   Tip: When you click a course home link, you enter the MyLab and Mastering course on its home page and have access to all available course components and navigation.

4. Click the link for the course component you want to enter.

   The course component opens in a new window or browser tab.

To access links from the Content page:

1. Enter your Blackboard Learn course.

2. Click any content area in the left navigation bar.

   If you are not sure what content areas are or where the Pearson links are placed, ask your instructor.

   The **Pearson** icon is to the left of all MyLab and Mastering content links.

3. Click the link for the course component you want to enter.

   Tip: When you click a course home link, you enter the MyLab and Mastering course on its home page and have access to all available course components and navigation.

   The course component—such as Homework, Tests, or Study Plan—opens in a new window or browser tab.

Get more help

When you enter the MyLab and Mastering course on its home page, you can use the links in the top right corner to access:

- Help & Support — Opens a window with links to the MyLab and Mastering course's online Student Help and other support resources.

- Account — Provides access to your Pearson account so you can edit your personal information.

- Sign Out — Ends your Pearson session. Signing out prevents the next user of the computer from accessing your MyLab and Mastering course. This does not sign you out of your Blackboard course.

Tip: If you call Pearson Support, you can shorten the process by telling them you are using MyLab and Mastering for Blackboard Learn.

Go to http://pearsonmylabandmastering.com to find tours to get started and other support resources.

See also:

Troubleshoot logging in and getting started

Troubleshoot logging in and getting started

The following are issues and errors you might encounter when logging in and linking your courses using MyLab and Mastering for Blackboard Learn. Click an issue's or error's link for a description of what it might mean and the resolution.

Note: If you have previously registered for a Pearson MyLab and Mastering account from a Blackboard Learn course, you **must** use the same Pearson account when enrolling in additional MyLab and Mastering courses from Blackboard Learn. You cannot link a new Pearson account to your existing Blackboard Learn account.

I cannot sign into MyLab / Mastering when I attempt to link my account.

What this might mean:

You might be using an incorrect username and password.

Resolution:

Make sure you use your Pearson account username and password (not your Blackboard username and password).

If you have forgotten your Pearson username or password, click **Forgot your username or password?** and Pearson will email you this information. Or, if you are not sure if you have a Pearson account, click **Not sure if you have a Pearson account?** and Pearson will inform you if you have an account.

If you do not have a Pearson account, you can create one by clicking **Create**.

Your accounts were not linked.

What this might mean:

You might be using an incorrect username and password.

Resolution:

Make sure you use your Pearson account username and password (not your Blackboard username and password).

If you have forgotten your Pearson username or password, click **Forgot your username or password?** and Pearson will email you this information. Or, if you are not sure if you have a Pearson account, click **Not sure if you have a Pearson account?** and Pearson will inform you if you have an account.

If you do not have a Pearson account, you can create one by clicking **Create**.

For additional information, see the following Pearson 24/7 Knowledge Base article: http://247pearsoned.custhelp.com/app/answers/detail/a_id/10791

bbErrNoSuchCourse

What this might mean:

You are trying to access your MyLab and Mastering course before Pearson has finished creating your instructor's course.

Resolution:

If your instructor informs you that the course is set up but you still get the error message when you try to access it, contact Pearson's 24/7 Technical Support at http://247pearsoned.custhelp.com/app/answers/list/kw/+Bb/

We are sorry; your course did not load properly.

What this might mean:

You are trying to access your MyLab and Mastering course before Pearson has finished creating your instructor's course.

Resolution:

If your instructor informs you that the course is set up but you still get the error message when you try to access it, contact Pearson's 24/7 Technical Support at http://247pearsoned.custhelp.com/app/answers/list/kw/+Bb/

An error occurred while processing the request.

What this might mean:

You are trying to access your MyLab and Mastering course before Pearson has finished creating your instructor's course.

Resolution:

If your instructor informs you that the course is set up but you still get the error message when you try to access it, contact Pearson's 24/7 Technical Support at http://247pearsoned.custhelp.com/app/answers/list/kw/+Bb/

Error: The link you have accessed is currently unavailable. If this problem persists please contact your site administrator.
Root cause: Exception in executeEvent

What this might mean:

You are trying to access your MyLab and Mastering course before Pearson has finished creating your instructor's course.

Resolution:

If your instructor informs you that the course is set up but you still get the error message when you try to access it, contact Pearson's 24/7 Technical Support at http://247pearsoned.custhelp.com/app/answers/list/kw/+Bb/

The server encountered an internal error or misconfiguration and was unable to complete your request.

What this might mean:

You are trying to access your MyLab and Mastering course before Pearson has finished creating your instructor's course.

Resolution:

If your instructor informs you that the course is set up but you still get the error message when you try to access it, contact Pearson's 24/7 Technical Support at http://247pearsoned.custhelp.com/app/answers/list/kw/+Bb/

My instructor does not see my name listed in the MyLab and Mastering course roster or see my work in the gradebook, but I am enrolled in the course and doing work.

What this might mean:

This might happen if you enrolled in the course directly at the Pearson site and are working in a different course than the one your instructor has linked to his/her Blackboard course.

Resolution:

Talk to your instructor to make sure you are enrolled and are working in the correct course.

An Error Has Occurred

We are sorry, requested course materials have not yet been created: You cannot access this portion of your course until your instructor has logged in at least one time. Please try again later or contact your instructor.

What this might mean:

You have clicked on a MyLab and Mastering link in your course, but the instructor has not yet set up the MyLab and Mastering course.

Resolution:

Your instructor must set up the MyLab and Mastering course. Once your instructor completes the setup, the MyLab and Mastering links in the course will work.

If you have previously been able to access your MyLab and Mastering courses from either the Tools page or a content area, and now these links are not working, you may receive one of several error messages, including "Unable to load page."

What this might mean:

A server may be down, preventing you from connecting.

Resolution:

Try again later to see if the issue has been resolved.

If the problem persists, contact Pearson 24/7 Technical Support to report the problem or ask about any known system outage that may be happening.

An Error Has Occurred

We are sorry. We are unable to connect.
Required message is missing from the URL. Please contact Support and provide
this error message.
Customer Support Code: url3

What this might mean:

You clicked the link to MyLab and Mastering but the session has timed out.

Resolution:

Restart your browser and log back into Blackboard. Then click the MyLab and
Mastering link again.

PEARSON

ALWAYS LEARNING

Samuel E. Wood • Ellen Green Wood • Denise G. Boyd

Mastering the World of Psychology

Custom Edition for KCTCS Somerset

Taken from:
Mastering the World of Psychology, Fifth Edition
by Samuel E. Wood, Ellen Green Wood, and Denise G. Boyd

Pearson Learning Solutions, 501 Boylston Street, Suite 900, Boston, MA 02116
A Pearson Education Company
www.pearsoned.com

Printed in the United States of America

5 6 7 8 9 10   V0ZN 17 16 15 14

000200010271787768

LDP

ISBN 10: 1-269-38374-4
ISBN 13: 978-1-269-38374-5

Brief Contents

Contents

6   Memory   *178*

7   Cognition, Language, and Intelligence   *212*

8   Human Development   *251*

9 Motivation and Emotion 294

10 Health and Stress 328

14 Social Psychology *453*

Preface

Why Do You Need This New Edition?

1. **Enhanced Pedagogical Program.** The SQ3R learning method continues to be the pedagogical foundation of *Mastering the World of Psychology*. In this edition, we have added new section reviews to encourage retrieval practice. We have made the instructions for SQ3R clearer and more concise and the Pearson eText contains an SQ3R study guide for each chapter to assist you in using this pedagogical method for effective studying.

2. **MyPsychLab Video Series.** This new series features over 100 original video clips covering the most recent research, science, and applications across the general psychology curriculum and utilizing the latest in film and animation technology. Each 4–6 minute video clip has automatically graded assessment questions tied to it. As you read, you will see cues that tell you which of these videos to watch to better grasp the concepts in the text or extend your learning beyond it. The information in one of the Chapter 1 videos, *Debunking Myths*, will help you put aside a few misconceptions that most people have about behavior and mental processes. One of the videos for Chapter 6, *Making It Stick*, will tell you how to sharpen your memory skills.

3. **New *Remember It* Feature.** At the end of each major section of each chapter, you will see a feature called *Remember It* that will help you assess how much information you retained while reading the section. Most of the questions in the *Remember Its* are fill-in-the-blank, so they'll challenge your memory and help you get ready to be tested.

4. **New MyPsychLab Writing Assignments.** Writing prompts in MyPsychLab provide instant feedback and give you the opportunity to practice writing while learning important psychological concepts. A collection of conceptual and applied writing prompts corresponding with videos from the MyPsychLab Video Series cover key concepts across the general psychology curriculum. This unique tool will give you instant feedback on both content and mechanics, allowing you to revise and improve your writing before receiving a final grade from your instructor.

5. **New and Expanded Coverage.** There is a wide range of new and expanded topics (including several hundred new research citations) covered in this edition, including, but not limited to, positive psychology (Chapter 1); the prefrontal cortex (Chapter 2); social perception (Chapter 3); "larks" and "owls" (Chapter 4); additive strategy for decision making (Chapter 7 emerging adulthood (Chapter 8); the complexities underlying correlations between socioeconomic status and health (Chapter 10); Maslow's humanistic theory of personality (Chapter 11); and childhood disorders (Chapter 12). Please see the overview of changes and additions to each chapter on page xiii.

As psychology instructors, your backgrounds, experiences, and resources are as varied as those of your students. Each of you approaches the course with a unique set of challenges but with common goals: to provide students with a solid introduction to the diverse field of psychology; to show them how psychology applies to their lives; and to teach them how to think critically. We have designed the fifth edition of *Mastering the World of Psychology* to help you meet these goals.

Changes to the Fifth Edition

As with each edition, we have closely examined and thoroughly updated all aspects of the text's content, organization, and pedagogy. All of our revisions were designed to create an engaging learning tool that gives students the support they need to succeed in the course. Among the improvements made to the fifth edition are the following:

- **Enhanced Pedagogical System:** SQ3R continues to be the pedagogical foundation of *Mastering the World of Psychology*. In the fifth edition, we have enhanced the SQ3R method by adding *Remember It* quizzes following each major section in the text. This helps students to periodically check their understanding of the material and to ensure they have mastered one section before moving on to the next.

- **Critical Thinking Questions:** We have added several writing prompts at the end of each chapter to encourage students to think critically about the material presented in the chapter. In each chapter, at least one of the prompts comes from the MyPsychLab Writing Assignments engine, which allows students to submit their responses for automated grading. This unique tool provides students with instant feedback on both content and mechanics, allowing them to revise and improve their writing before receiving a final grade from the instructor. Instructors are supplied with a numerical grade. In this way, *Mastering the World of Psychology* allows instructors the flexibility to incorporate writing in their course in the way that best suits their needs.

- **New *Try-It* Activities:** Some chapters contain new *Try It* activities, many of which have accompanying video clips.

- **New Video Integration:** References to relevant videos have been added to many of the feature boxes and in the margins throughout the text. These videos can be accessed on MyPsychLab or by clicking on the image in the etext. These videos enhance the material in the text and within the boxes, and allow students to experience and interact with the material in a different way.

- **Engaging, Current Examples:** To ensure that students identify with the material, examples have been updated and/or added throughout the text to both help students understand the material and to apply the material to their everyday lives.

Overview of Changes and Additions to Each Chapter

We have made a number of changes to improve the clarity of the discussions and overall flow of material. A number of new and expanded examples of difficult concepts provide students with additional support for connecting information in the text to real-world settings. We also increased the number of chapter cross-references in the text to heighten students' awareness of interconnections among the major concepts that are taught in introductory psychology. We remain dedicated to citing current research and writing the most up-to-date text possible, while promoting an understanding of the foundation of psychology. Several hundred new research citations appear in the fifth edition to ensure that all presentations reflect current thinking about the science of psychology. Here is a chapter-by-chapter list of the changes we have made in the fifth edition, along with the, MyPsychLab Video Series episodes and features for each chapter:

Chapter 1: Introduction to Psychology

- Streamlined SQ3R instructions
- New key term *positive psychology*
- MyPsychLab Video Series

  - *Debunking Myths*
  - *Making It Stick*
  - *Asking Tough Questions*
  - *Diverse Perspectives*
  - *How to Answer Psychological Questions*
  - *Thinking Critically*
  - *Speed Dating*
  - *Research Ethics*

Chapter 2: Biology and Behavior

- Expanded discussion of the prefrontal cortex
- New figure depicting the prefrontal cortex
- New *Try It* Mirror Tracing
- New key term *prefrontal cortex*
- MyPsychLab Video Series

  - *My Brain Made Me Do It*
  - *How the Brain Works Part 1*
  - *Neurotransmitters*
  - *How the Brain Works Part 2*
  - *The Pre-Frontal Cortex: The Good, the Bad, the Criminal*
  - *The Plastic Brain*
  - *Genetic Mechanisms and Behavioral Genetics*
  - *Epigenetics*
  - *Genes, Evolution, and Human Behavior*
  - *Taking Control of Our Genes*

Chapter 3: Sensation and Perception

- New *Try It* Absolute Threshold
- New figure illustrating amplitude
- New discussion of social perception
- New discussion of cross-modal perception
- New key term *mirror neuron system*
- MyPsychLab Video Series

  - *Taking in the World Around Us*
  - *Can Smells Alter Mood and Behavior?*
  - *In Full Appreciation of the Cookie*
  - *Managing Pain*
  - *The Myth of Multitasking*
  - *Recognizing Faces*
  - *Perceptual Magic in Art*

Chapter 4: Consciousness

- New *Think About It*: Are You a Lark or an Owl?
- New discussion of the contribution of individual differences in patterns of cortisol secretion to chronotypes (larks and owls)
- MyPsychLab Video Series

  - *States of Consciousness*
  - *Rhythms of Consciousness*
  - *Sleep, Memory, and Learning*
  - *Sleep Disorders*
  - *Altered States of Consciousness*
  - *The Uses and Limitations of Hypnosis*

Chapter 5: Learning

- New *Try It* Conditioned Eye Blink
- Expanded discussion of culture and punishment
- MyPsychLab Video Series

  - *What Does It Mean to Learn?*
  - *Classical Conditioning*
  - *Operant Conditioning*
  - *Physical Punishment-You Decide!*
  - *How to Make Healthier Choices*
  - *Learning Aggression*

Chapter 6: Memory

- New *Think About It*: Chunking
- New *Try It* Creating a False Memory
- New discussion of test anxiety as a context effect
- MyPsychLab Video Series

  - *The Woman Who Cannot Forget*
  - *Making It Stick*
  - *When Memory Fails*
  - *Do You Remember When...?*
  - *Police Line-Up*

Chapter 7: Cognition, Language, and Intelligence

- New *Try It* Using the Additive Strategy to Choose an Apartment
- New discussion of costs and benefits of using heuristics
- New key term *intellectual disability*
- MyPsychLab Video Series

  - *I Am, Therefore I Think*
  - *Mental Imagery: In the Mind's Eye*
  - *Making Choices*
  - *Changing Your Mind*
  - *Multilingualism: Speaking Your Mind*
  - *What Is Intelligence?*
  - *Theories of Intelligence*
  - *Intelligence Tests and Success*
  - *Intelligence Testing Then and Now*

- *How Resilient Are You?*
- *Intelligence Tests and Stereotypes*

Chapter 8: Human Development

- New *Think About It*: Emerging Adulthood
- New *Try It*: The Heinz Dilemma
- Gender dysphoria discussed in the context of typical gender development
- New discussion of emerging adulthood
- MyPsychLab Video Series

  - *Different Perspectives on the World*
  - *How Thinking Develops*
  - *Attachment*
  - *Risky Behavior and Brain Development*
  - *Smart Babies by Design*
  - *Parenting Styles and Socialization*
  - *Identity*

Chapter 9: Motivation and Emotion

- MyPsychLab Video Series

  - *Motivation and Emotion*
  - *Theories of Emotion and Motivation*
  - *Detecting Lies*
  - *Affective Forecasting*
  - *Eating Disorders*
  - *Meeting Our Needs*
  - *The Power of Sex*
  - *Sex and Gender Differences*
  - *Cultural Norms and Sexual Behavior*
  - *Sexual Orientation*
  - *Sexual Problems and Dysfunction*
  - *The Dating Game*

Chapter 10: Health and Stress

- New *Try It*: Personal Resilience Assessment
- MyPsychLab Video Series

  - *Health Psychology*
  - *Stress and Your Health*
  - *Health Disparities*
  - *Personality and Health*
  - *Reducing Stress, Improving Health*
  - *The Challenge of Quitting Bad Health Habits*

Chapter 11: Personality Theory and Assessment

- New *Think About It*: What Is Your Personality Like?
- New *Try It*: Personal Self-Esteem Assessment
- New *Try It*: What Is Your Locus of Control?
- Expanded coverage of Maslow's humanistic theory of personality
- MyPsychLab Video Series

  - *What Is Personality?*
  - *Personality Theories*
  - *Twins and Personality*
  - *Measuring Personality*
  - *Popular Personality Assessments*
  - *Psychological Resilience*

Chapter 12: Psychological Disorders

- New discussion of *DSM-5*
- Terminology modified to conform to *DSM-5*
- New section covering childhood disorders, including the pediatric bipolar disorder controversy
- MyPsychLab Video Series

  - *What Does It Mean to Have a Mental Disorder*
  - *Living with a Disorder*
  - *Diagnosing Mental Disorders*

Chapter 13: Therapies

- New research on the effects of nicotine and transcranial magnetic stimulation on symptoms of schizophrenia
- MyPsychLab Video Series

  - *Therapies in Action*
  - *Assessing Treatment Effectiveness*
  - *Cognitive Behavioral Therapy*
  - *Finding a Therapist If You Need One*

Chapter 14: Social Psychology

- New research on the comparative persuasiveness of online and television advertising, cross-cultural differences in attributions, and methodological problems with research on the influence of violent video games on players' behavior
- MyPsychLab Video Series

  - *The Social World*
  - *Under the Influence of Others*
  - *Mental Shortcuts in a Social Context*
  - *Changing Attitudes and Behaviors*
  - *Are Stereotypes and Prejudice Inevitable?*
  - *Attraction*
  - *Persuasion*

Our Commitment to Learning: SQ3R

The text's commitment to learning begins with the learning method called SQ3R. Made up of five steps—Survey, Question, Read, Recite, and Review—this method serves as the foundation for your students' success. Introduced in Chapter 1, the SQ3R method is integrated throughout the text to help students make the connection between psychology and life, while promoting a more efficient way to approach reading, studying, and test taking.

Among the key learning features that promote use of the SQ3R method are the following:

Learning Objectives Each chapter in this text is structured around specific learning objectives. These numbered learning objectives are stated as questions, because research shows that open-ended questions help readers locate critical information, process it deeply, and commit it to memory. The learning objectives appear in each chapter opener, in the margins of their corresponding sections, and again in the end-of-chapter Summary, to help focus students' attention on key information.

> ⊙ [Watch *the Video Episode 5: Big Picture: Taking in the World Around Us in* **MyPsychLab**
>
> **3.1** What are the absolute and difference thresholds?
>
> throughout the chapter. Before we consider perception, we will take a look at the process of sensation. ⊙
>
> **The Absolute and Difference Thresholds**
>
> What is the softest sound you can hear, the dimmest light you can see, the most diluted substance you can taste? Researchers in sensory psychology have performed many experiments over the years to answer these questions. Their research has established

Key Terms Boldfaced key terms are highlighted in the text and defined in the margin on the page on which they first appear. A complete list of key terms, with page references, is supplied at the end of the chapter, and a complete Glossary can be found at the end of the text.

> **absolute threshold** *The minimum amount of sensory stimulation that can be detected 50% of the time.*
>
> measures for the senses known as absolute thresholds. Just as the threshold of a doorway is the dividing point between being outside a room and inside, the **absolute threshold** of a sense marks the difference between not being able to perceive a stimulus and being just barely able to perceive it. Psychologists have arbitrarily defined this absolute threshold as the minimum amount of sensory stimulation that can be detected 50% of the time. The absolute thresholds for vision, hearing, taste, smell, and touch are illustrated in Figure 3.1. You can experience an absolute threshold by doing

Summarize It These comprehensive summary tables help consolidate major concepts, their components, and their relationships to one another, providing students with a unique visual study tool.

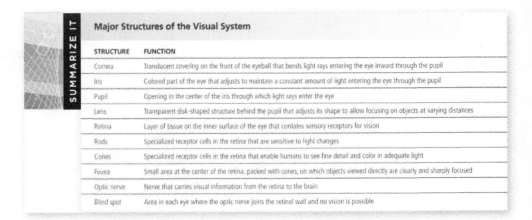

Major Structures of the Visual System

STRUCTURE	FUNCTION
Cornea	Translucent covering on the front of the eyeball that bends light rays entering the eye inward through the pupil
Iris	Colored part of the eye that adjusts to maintain a constant amount of light entering the eye through the pupil
Pupil	Opening in the center of the iris through which light rays enter the eye
Lens	Transparent disk-shaped structure behind the pupil that adjusts its shape to allow focusing on objects at varying distances
Retina	Layer of tissue on the inner surface of the eye that contains sensory receptors for vision
Rods	Specialized receptor cells in the retina that are sensitive to light changes
Cones	Specialized receptor cells in the retina that enable humans to see fine detail and color in adequate light
Fovea	Small area at the center of the retina, packed with cones, on which objects viewed directly are clearly and sharply focused
Optic nerve	Nerve that carries visual information from the retina to the brain
Blind spot	Area in each eye where the optic nerve joins the retinal wall and no vision is possible

Remember It These fill-in-the-blank quizzes appear at the end of every major section in the text allowing students to check their understanding of the material before moving on to the next section in the chapter.

> **REMEMBER IT** *Check your answers and take additional quizzes in MyPsychLab.com.* ✓ [Study *and* Review *on* MyPsychLab
>
> 1. Taking in sensory information from the environment and transmitting it to the brain is called _____
> 2. Interpreting sensory information is called _____.
> 3. The _____ threshold is the point at which you sense a stimulus 50% of the time.
> 4. The _____ threshold is the smallest increase or decrease in a physical stimulus that produces a difference in sensation 50% of the time.
> 5. _____ transmit sensory information from the sense organs to the brain.
> 6. _____ is the process in which sensory receptors grow accustomed to constant, unchanging stimuli over time.

Chapter Summary Organized around the learning objectives, each end-of-chapter Summary provides a comprehensive study tool as well as a quick reference to the chapter's key terms, which are listed alphabetically by section.

CHAPTER 3 SUMMARY

THE PROCESS OF SENSATION (pp. 76–79)

3.1 What are the absolute and difference thresholds? (pp. 76–78)
The absolute threshold is the minimum amount of sensory stimulation that can be detected 50% of the time. The difference threshold is a measure of the smallest increase or decrease in a physical stimulus that can be detected 50% of the time.

Key Terms
sensation, p. 76
perception, p. 76
absolute threshold, p. 76
difference threshold, p. 77
just noticeable difference (JND), p. 77
Weber's law, p. 77

3.2 How does transduction change sensory information? (pp. 78–79)
For each of the senses, the body has sensory receptors that detect and respond to sensory stimuli. Through the process of transduction, the receptors change the sensory stimuli into neural impulses, which are then transmitted to precise locations in the brain.

Key Terms
sensory receptors, p. 78
transduction, p. 78
sensory adaptation, p. 79

VISION (pp. 79–85)

3.3 How does each part of the eye function in vision? (pp. 79–81)
The cornea bends light rays inward through the pupil—the small, dark opening in the eye. The iris dilates and contracts two optic nerves come together, and some of the nerve fibers from each eye cross to the opposite side of the brain. They synapse with neurons in the thalamus, which transmit the neural impulses to the primary visual cortex.

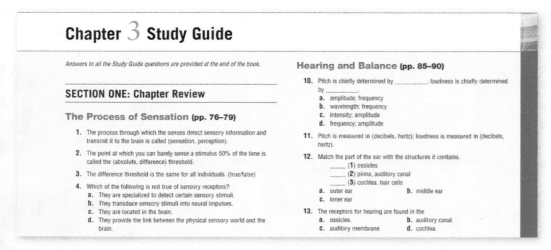

Chapter 3 Study Guide

Answers to all the Study Guide questions are provided at the end of the book.

SECTION ONE: Chapter Review

The Process of Sensation (pp. 76–79)

1. The process through which the senses detect sensory information and transmit it to the brain is called (sensation, perception).

2. The point at which you can barely sense a stimulus 50% of the time is called the (absolute, difference) threshold.

3. The difference threshold is the same for all individuals. (true/false)

4. Which of the following is not true of sensory receptors?
   a. They are specialized to detect certain sensory stimuli.
   b. They transduce sensory stimuli into neural impulses.
   c. They are located in the brain.
   d. They provide the link between the physical sensory world and the brain.

Hearing and Balance (pp. 85–90)

10. Pitch is chiefly determined by _____; loudness is chiefly determined by _____.
    a. amplitude; frequency
    b. wavelength; frequency
    c. intensity; amplitude
    d. frequency; amplitude

11. Pitch is measured in (decibels, hertz); loudness is measured in (decibels, hertz).

12. Match the part of the ear with the structures it contains.
    _____ **(1)** ossicles
    _____ **(2)** pinna, auditory canal
    _____ **(3)** cochlea, hair cells
    a. outer ear   b. middle ear
    c. inner ear

13. The receptors for hearing are found in the
    a. ossicles.   b. auditory canal.
    c. auditory membrane. d. cochlea.

Built-in Study Guide In addition to all of the SQ3R features in the text, each chapter concludes with a Study Guide, featuring multiple-choice, true/false, matching, critical thinking writing prompts, and application essay prompts. Answers to the Study Guide questions are located at the end of the text.

Learning through Application

To gain a full understanding of psychology, it is vital that students apply the principles they learn about in this course to their own life and the lives of others. We, the authors, have designed five features to help students accomplish this goal.

Think About It Each chapter opens with a *Think About It* feature that encourages students to become actively involved with the content right from the beginning of the chapter. These openers will invite students to complete an activity (i.e., a quiz, an experiment) that introduces the chapter content in a fun and an interesting way.

THINK ABOUT IT

Try standing on one foot like the woman in the accompanying illustration. You'll probably have no trouble maintaining your balance for at least 30 seconds. But what will happen if you try to maintain this position with your eyes closed? Try it and find out.

No doubt you found it more difficult to keep your balance with your eyes closed. Your body's system for maintaining balance is a complex one that depends on several types of input. As you just learned, visual input is critical. In fact, visual input is so important that doctors use the one-leg/eyes-closed test to assess neurological health (Chaitow & DeLany, 2002). Because performance on the test normally declines as we get older (due to the aging of the cerebellum that we learned about in Chapter 2), it can also be used to determine whether your brain is aging normally. Studies suggest that, if you're between the ages of 20 and 49, and you can't maintain your balance on one foot with your eyes closed for at least

25 seconds, your brain might be aging more rapidly than those of your peers (Bohannon et al., 1984). But take heart, exercise regimens that emphasize balance, such as the ancient Chinese mediation practice of *Tai Chi*, which consists of slow, deliberate movements, can help to counteract the effects of aging (Fuzhong, Harmer, Fisher, & McAutey, 2004).

Your body's ability to maintain its position is just one of many topics that we'll address as we explore the interactive processes of *sensation* and *perception*.

First, we'll consider the two dominant senses: vision and hearing. Then we'll turn our attention to the other senses: smell, taste, touch, pain, and balance. You will learn how the senses detect sensory information and how this sensory information is actively organized and interpreted by the brain.

Apply It This feature combines scientific research with practical advice to teach students how to improve their study habits or handle challenging situations that may arise in their personal, academic, or professional lives.

APPLY IT   How Dangerous Is It to Talk on a Cell Phone or Text while Driving?

When you read about the research demonstrating inattentional blindness, did it raise your level of concern about the possible dangers of driving while talking or texting on a cell phone? Interestingly, surveys suggest that we are more concerned about other drivers' cell phone use than our own. In one study, researchers found that, although 94% of participants viewed texting while driving as dangerous and 87% support laws prohibiting it, some 35% admitted to having done so themselves (AAA Foundation for Traffic Safety, 2012). In another survey, just 6% of drivers reported that their cell phone use had caused them to get into a potentially dangerous situation on the road. Remarkably, when participants were asked whether another driver's cell phone use had ever put them at risk, 66% said yes (Troglauer, Hels, & Christens, 2006). As much as we would like to believe that cell phones affect other drivers' behavior but not our own, research clearly shows that talking or texting on a cell phone, or engaging in other kinds of attention-demanding tasks, results in potentially dangerous changes in our behind-the-wheel behavior.

Behavioral Effects of Cell Phone Use

Most experiments examining cell phone use while driving take place in laboratories in which participants use driving simulators. Experimental group participants talk, text on, or follow instructions to ignore e-mail alerts and other auditory signals emitted by the cell phone while driving, but those in the control groups do not have a cell phone in the driving environment. Studies of this type show that both cell phone use and ignored signals from cell phones affect drivers' behavior in the following ways (Beede & Kass, 2006; Harrold et al., 2009; Holland & Rathod, 2012; Liu & Lee, 2006):

- Drivers slow down when using the phone.
- Drivers have slower reaction times when engaged in phone conversations or texting.
- Drivers who talk on a cell phone often fail to stay within the boundaries of the lane in which they are driving.
- Cell-phone-using drivers sometimes stop at green lights but drive through red lights and stop signs.
- Drivers who ignore auditory signals from cell phones have more collisions with pedestrians and other vehicles than drivers in phone-free driving environments do.

These effects have been observed just as often in studies using hands-free phones as conventional handheld models (Strayer & Drews, 2004). However, one study suggested that hands-free phone use gave drivers a false sense of safety (Langer, Holzner, Magnet, & Kopp, 2005). Thus, experimental studies show definitively that, on average, cell phone use impairs driving ability.

Compensating for the Effects of Cell Phone Use

Despite the clear findings of these studies, other research suggests that several factors help drivers compensate for the distractions associated with cell phone use (Hunton & Rose, 2005; Pöysti, Rajalin, & Summala, 2005; Shinar, Tractinsky, & Compton, 2005; Sullman, 2012). Here are a few of them:

- Experience with multitasking improves drivers' ability to juggle the demands of cell phone use and driving.
- Reducing other distractions, such as turning off the radio, helps drivers keep their minds on driving while also talking on the phone.
- Some drivers end a cell phone call with "I'll call you back later when I'm not driving," when they realize that the attentional demands of a specific conversation are incompatible with those of driving.

These findings show that drivers are well aware of the potentially risk-enhancing effects of behavior changes caused by distractions. As a result, they actively work to manage the number of demands on their attention while driving.

It's about Attention, Not Cell Phones

You may know from personal experience that several attention-demanding tasks impair driving behaviors just as much as cell phone use does. For example, talking to a passenger or searching for a radio station while driving produces the same kinds of detrimental effects on drivers' behavior as cell phone use (Amado & Ulupinar, 2005; Horberry et al., 2006; Sullman, 2012). Therefore, for drivers, the takeaway message from this chapter's discussion of inattentional blindness is clear: When drivers pay attention to anything that is not relevant to the task of operating a vehicle—be it a cell phone, a radio, or a conversation with a passenger—they limit their ability to focus on driving. Consequently, the goal of anyone who is operating a vehicle ought to be to minimize distractions to as great a degree as possible:

- Texting is more dangerous than talking on a cell phone because you must divert your eyes from the road (Harrold et al., 2009). Therefore, experts recommend that drivers NEVER text while driving.
- If possible, drivers should pull off the road to talk on their cell phones.
- Radio station adjustments should be postponed until drivers are stopped at a red light or stop sign.
- Whenever passengers are distracting them, drivers should politely request that they refrain from talking.

By taking these measures, drivers will reduce their risk of missing important cues such as traffic lights and decrease the likelihood that they will, at best, get a traffic ticket, or, at worst, cause an accident. In addition, laws that restrict or prohibit the use of cell phones by drivers have been passed in several jurisdictions, so following these guidelines may prevent you from getting a ticket.

 ▶)Watch on MyPsychLab

Try It This popular feature provides brief applied experiments, self-assessments, and hands-on activities, which help personalize psychology, making it simple for students to actively relate psychological principles to everyday life. For instance, students can find their absolute threshold for hair movement (Chapter 3) or take a quiz to find their life stress score (Chapter 10).

TRY IT   Absolute Threshold

You will need a partner for this activity. You will be the experimenter, and your partner will be the observer. Ask the observer to close his eyes (no peeking allowed!) and tell you when he feels something. Locate a small hair on the observer's forearm. Using a pencil or similar object with a very small point, and taking care not to touch the observer's skin, slowly move the hair until the observer notices the sensation. Now switch roles so that you can experience the other role. If you have an appropriate measuring device handy, you can repeat the procedure and measure how far the hair must be moved before the observer notices the sensation. The amount of movement required is the absolute threshold for hair movement.

Explain It This feature provides psychological explanations for some common everyday occurrences. For instance, "What does your credit score mean, and how is it used by lenders?" (Chapter 1) and "Why are some individuals drawn to dangerous hobbies like skydiving?" (Chapter 9).

EXPLAIN IT   Why Can't Everyone Hear the "Mosquito" Ring Tone?

Have you ever tested your hearing to find out if you can hear the "Mosquito," a tone with a frequency of about 17,000 Hz? If not, search online for "mosquito ringtone hearing test" and you'll be directed to dozens of websites where you can do so. As the figure to the right suggests, the ability to hear the Mosquito declines with age. However, research suggests that the truth about age differences in sensitivity to the Mosquito is that the ability to hear it is nearly universal in the teens and early 20s but highly variable from the mid-20s on (Lawton, 2001). What accounts for the variability in sensitivity to high-pitched tones among adults?

The ability to hear high-pitched tones declines with age for a variety of reasons. A few conditions that are more common to middle-aged and older adults (e.g., excessive ear wax, chronic fluid in the ear, overgrowth of the bones in the inner ear) than to younger adults explain some of the decline (Mathur & Roland, 2009). However, hearing loss in adulthood often results from lifelong exposure to excessive noise. Noise above 85 decibels or so, if experienced repeatedly for long periods of time, damages the tiny hair cells inside the cochlea (Mathur & Roland, 2009). And the longer the exposure to excessive noise goes on, the more hearing people who are exposed to it lose. For instance, many long-time rock and pop musicians who are now in their middle- and late-adulthood years—Bono, Pete Townshend, Eric Clapton, Ozzy Osbourne, Ted Nugent, Phil Collins, Trent Reznor, to name a few—have much poorer hearing than others their age. Moreover, Townshend has reported that he began to notice his hearing loss when he was still in his 20s. Classical musicians who regularly play in orchestras show similar losses (Laitinen, 2005).

What can you do to increase your chances of maintaining the ability to hear the Mosquito and other high-pitched sounds, which happen to be critical to the ability to understand speech, for as long as possible? If you're a musician, investigate hearing protectors that shield your inner ear from potentially damaging noise but still allow you to hear the sounds you need to in order to play and perform effectively. Even if you're not a musician, you should be aware that regular use of headphones greatly increases your risk of suffering the kind of hearing loss that is common among professional musicians (Britt, 2006). To protect your hearing, adopt a practice that experts call the "60/60 rule": Use headphones no more than a total of 60 minutes each day with the player set on 60% of its maximum volume (Fligor, 2010).

25 khz
Dog whistles

20 khz
Highest pitch children, teens, and young adults can hear

17 khz Mosquito
16 khz
Highest pitch 30- to 60-year-olds can hear

12 khz
Highest pitch adults over 60 can hear

4 khz
Highest note on a piano

MyPsychLab Icons MyPsychLab icons—Watch, Listen, Explore, and Simulate—are integrated throughout the text in the margins—these icons highlight specific MyPsychLab assets that can be found online.

To access MyPsychLab, simply go to *www.mypsychlab.com* and enter your login name and password. First-time users of MyPsychLab can buy access here as well.

know, distinctive odors can serve as memory cues, both pleasant and unpleasant. For instance, the smell of peanut butter may transport you back to your elementary school lunchroom and, in turn, remind you either of the bully who stole your cookies or the best friend who sat next to you every day. ◉

You cannot smell a substance unless some of its molecules vaporize—that is, pass from a solid or liquid into a gaseous state. Heat speeds up the vaporization of mol-

◉ **Watch** the Video *Episode 5: Thinking Like a Psychologist: Can Smells Alter Mood and Behavior?* in **MyPsychLab**

A Complete Teaching and Learning Program

We have created a complete collection of resources for the fifth edition that will help you prepare for class, enhance your course presentations, and assess your students' understanding of the material.

MyPsychLab™

MyPsychLab (www.mypsychlab.com). MyPsychLab is an online homework, tutorial, and assessment program that truly engages students in learning. It helps students better prepare for class, quizzes, and exams—resulting in better performance in the course. It provides educators a dynamic set of tools for gauging individual and class performance. And, MyPsychLab comes from Pearson—your partner in providing the best digital learning experiences.

MyPsychLab for *Mastering the World of Psychology*, Fifth Edition contains the following learning tools and resources:

- **An Interactive eBook** with highlighting and note-taking features and powerful embedded media including over 100 simulations, more than 3,000 video clips (available in closed caption), dozens of podcasts, and an interactive timeline that presents the history of psychology.

- **Customized Study Plans and Assessments** allow students to take a Pre-Test to self-assess how much they already know about the topics in a section of the chapter they're working on. These Pre-Tests pair together with Post-Tests on the website to generate customized study plans and eBook self-assessments.

- **New! MyPsychLab Writing Assignments** give students the opportunity to practice writing while learning important psychological concepts. A collection of conceptual and applied writing prompts corresponding with videos from the MyPsychLab Video Series cover key concepts across the general psychology curriculum. This unique tool provides students with instant feedback on both content and mechanics, allowing them to revise and improve their writing before receiving a final grade from the instructor.

- **APA Learning Goals Assessment Bank:** For instructors interested in assessing their students progress against the APA Psychology Learning Goals and Outcomes, we have provided a separate bank of assessment items keyed specifically to those goals in MyPsychLab.

- **NEW! MyPsychLab Simulations** allow students to participate in online simulations of virtual classic psychology experiments and research-based inventories, helping to reinforce what they are learning in class and in their book.

- **A Gradebook for Instructors** as well as full course management capabilities for instructors teaching online or hybrid courses are included in the instructor version of MyPsychLab.

- **Audio Files of Each Chapter** benefit students who are blind and others who prefer sound-based materials, and conform to ADA guidelines.

- **New! Visual Brain** designed to help students better understand neuroanatomy, physiology, and human behavior.

- **Interactive Mobile-Ready Flash Cards** of the key terms from the text can be used by students to build their own stacks, print the cards, or export their flashcards to their cell phones.

You decide the extent of integration, from independent self-assessment for students to total course management. Students benefit from an easy-to-use site at which they can test themselves on key content, track their progress, and create individually tailored study plans. By transferring faculty members' most time-consuming tasks—content delivery, student assessment, and grading—to automated tools, MyPsychLab allows you to spend more quality time with students.

Instructor's Resource DVD: Bringing all of the fifth edition's instructor resources together in one place, the Instructor's Resource DVD contains the following resources:

- **Hyperlinked Instructor's Manual:** The Instructor's Manual gives you unparalleled access to a huge selection of classroom-proven assets. First-time instructors will appreciate the detailed introduction to teaching the introductory psychology course, with suggestions for preparing for the course, sample syllabi, and current trends and strategies for successful teaching. Each chapter offers activities, exercises, assignments, handouts, and demos for in-class use, as well as guidelines for integrating media resources into the classroom and syllabus. The material is organized in an easy-to-use Chapter Lecture Outline. A unique hyperlinking system allows for easy reviewing of relevant sections and resources. The Instructor's Manual is also available for download from the Instructor's Resource Center at **http://www.pearsonhighered.com/irc.**

- **Test Bank:** Thoroughly revised and updated for the fifth edition, the Test Bank contains over 2,500 multiple-choice, fill-in-the-blank, short-answer, and essay questions, each referencing the relevant page in the text. Rationales for the correct answer in the conceptual and applied multiple-choice questions allow you to see the logic of the questions when reviewing them, making it easier to generate an answer key for your students if desired. Feedback from customers indicates that this unique feature is useful for ensuring quality and quick response to student queries. A two-page Total Assessment Guide chapter overview makes creating tests easier by listing all of the test items in an easy-to-reference grid. The Total Assessment Guide organizes all test items by text section and question type/level of difficulty. All multiple-choice questions are categorized as factual, conceptual, or applied. The Test Bank is also available for download from the Instructor's Resource Center at **http://www.pearsonhighered.com/irc.**

- **Interactive PowerPoint Slides:** Available on the Instructor's Resource DVD, these slides bring the design of *Mastering* right into the classroom, drawing students into the lecture and providing wonderful interactive activities and visuals. A video walk-through is available and provides clear guidelines on using and customizing the slides. The slides are built around the text's learning objectives and offer many links across content areas. Icons integrated throughout the slides indicate interactive exercises, simulations, and activities that can be accessed directly from the slides if instructors want to use these resources in the classroom.

- **Standard Lecture PowerPoint Slides:** These slides, presented in a more traditional format with excerpts of the text material and art work, are also available for download at **http://www. pearsonhighered.com/irc.**

- **Pearson MyTest Computerized Test Bank (www.pearsonmytest. com):** The fifth edition Test Bank comes with Pearson MyTest, a powerful assessment-generation program that helps instructors easily create and print quizzes and exams. You can do this online, allowing flexibility and the ability to efficiently manage assessments at any time. You can easily access existing questions and edit, create, and store questions using the simple drag-and-drop and Word-like controls. Each question comes with information on its level of difficulty and related page number in the text, mapped to the appropriate learning objective. For more information, go to **www.PearsonMyTest.com**.

- **Classroom Response System (CRS) slides:** Classroom Response questions ("clicker" questions) created for *Mastering the World of Psychology,* are intended to be the basis of class discussions as well as lectures. Each student uses a personal remote or "clicker" to send immediate communication to the instructor. The system will gather the individual responses and show the compiled feedback for the class as a whole. Based on these results, you can then tailor the pace of each lecture, further explain difficult concepts if needed, and conduct in-class surveys, polls, and quizzes. Pearson offers exclusive, money-saving rebates with several CRS leading systems.

- **MyPsychLab Video Series (18 half-hour episodes):** Comprehensive, current, and cutting edge, the new MyPsychLab Video Series features over 100 original video clips covering the most recent research, science, and applications across the general psychology curriculum and utilizing the latest in film and animation technology. Each 4–6 minute video clip has automatically graded assessment questions tied to it. Each episode features several brief segments that bring psychology to life:

  - *The Big Picture* introduces the topic of the episode and provides the hook to draw students in.
  - *The Basics* uses the power of video to present foundational topics, especially those that typically trip up students.
  - *Special Topics* dives deeper into high-interest and often cutting-edge topics, and often features research in action.
  - *In the Real World* focuses on applications of psychological research.
  - *What's in It for Me?* These narrated segments emphasize why students should care about the research and how it may have a real impact on their lives.

The Pearson MyPsychLab Video Series is only available to adopters of Pearson psychology textbooks. An Instructor's Guide to the video series is also available to adopters.

Additional Course Management Resources:

- **Online Resource MyPsychLab for BlackBoard/MyPsychLab for WebCT** The customized BlackBoard cartridge and WebCT epack include the complete Test Bank, each chapter's Learning Objectives, Glossary Flashcards, Chapter Summaries, a link to MyPsychLab, and Chapter Exams.

- Ask your Pearson representative about custom offerings for other learning management systems or visit **www.mypsychlab.com** for more information.

Acknowledgments

We are thankful for the support of several people at Pearson Education who helped bring our plans for the fifth edition of *Mastering the World of Psychology* to fruition. On the editorial side, Amber Chow monitored the progress of the text and ensured that the final product is an introductory text that achieves the goal of being thorough while also being timely and accessible. We are grateful for the assistance of our developmental editor, LeeAnn Doherty, whose suggestions and encouragement helped immeasurably in the pursuit of this goal.

Our Reviewers Numerous reviewers were invaluable to the development of this text. Their help provided a solid foundation for creating *Mastering the World of Psychology,* Fifth Edition:

Mary Evans *Pierce College;* Suzanne Weston *Estrella Mountain Community College;* Alissa Minten *Western Technical College;* Dora Falls *Eastfield College;* Rick Piper *Estrella Mountain Community College;* Wanda VanGilder *Antelope Valley College;* Ryan Messatzzia *Wor-Wic Community College;* Staci Simmelink Johnson *Walla Walla Community College;* Shawn Talbot *Kellogg Community College;* Kevin Dooley *San Diego City College;* Cheryl Chopard *Des Moines Area Community College*

We would also like to thank reviewers of the first four editions of *Mastering the World of Psychology* for their encouragement and insights:

Carol Anderson, *Bellevue College;* Bakhtawar Bhadha, *Pasadena City College;* Dr. Ken Callis, *Southeast Missouri State University;* Evelyn N. Doody, *College of Southern Nevada;* Mary Christina Evans, *Pierce College;* Cecilia Erlund, *University of Mary Hardin-Baylor;* Hallie Feil, *Western Nebraska Community College;* Jamie S. Hughes, *New Mexico State University;* Yasmine Kalkstein, *North Hennepin Community College;* Eric Kim, *Lane Community College;* Steve Kittrell, *North Metro Technical College;* Holly Schofield, *Central Carolina Community College;* David Shepard, *South Texas College;* Staci Simmelink-Johnson, *Walla Walla Community College;* Debra M. Yoder, *Mountain View College* Elaine P. Adams, *Houston Community College;* David W. Alfano, *Community College of Rhode Island;* Jill Barton, *Keiser College;* Kenneth Benson, *Hinds Community College;* John Brennecke, *Mount San Antonio College;* Robin Campbell, *Brevard Community College;* Cari Cannon, *Santiago Canyon College;* Dennis Cogan, *Texas Tech University;* Berry J. Daughenbaugh, *Wor-Wic Community College;* Wayne Dixon, *Southeastern Oklahoma State University;* Wendy Domjan, *University of Texas;* Jim Dorman, *St. Charles Community College;* Laura Duvall, *Heartland Community College;* Darlene Earley-Hereford, *Southern Union State Community College;* Hallie Feil, *Western Nebraska Community College;* Joseph Feldman, *Phoenix College;* Colleen L. Gift, *Highland Community College;* Paula Goolkasian, *UNC Charlotte;* Chuck Hallock, *University of Arizona;* Julie Hanauer, *Suffolk Community College;* Brett Heintz, *Delgado Community College;* Carmon Weaver Hicks, *Ivy Tech Community College;* Alan Hughes, *Nazareth College (New York);* Carolyn Kaufman, *Columbus State Community College;* Norman E. Kinney, *Southeast Missouri State University;* Leslee Koritzke, *Los Angeles Trade Technical College;* Leslie Minor-Evans, *Central Oregon Community College;* Paulina Multhaupt, *Macomb Community College;* Enrique Otero, *North Lake College;* Debra Parish, *North Harris Montgomery Community College;* Jeffrey Pedroza, *Santa Anna College;* Ralph Pifer, *Sauk Valley College;* Michelle Pilati, *Rio Hondo College;* Cynthia Reed, *Tarrant County College Northeast;* Vicki Ritts, *St. Louis Community College, Meramec;* Amy Shapiro, *University of Massachusetts, Amherst;* David Shepard, *South Texas College;* Jason Spiegelman, *Community College of Baltimore County;* Robert B. Stennett, *Gainesville State College;* Robert Stickgold, *Harvard University;* Lisa Valentino, *Seminole Community College;* Edie Woods, *Macomb County Community College;* Gayle Abbott, *New Mexico Junior College;* Christan Amundsen, North Lake College; Julie Hanauer, *Suffolk County Community College;* Annette Jankiewicz, *Iowa Western Community College;* Warren Lambert, *Somerset Community College;* Amy Overman, *Elon University;* Sandra Todaro, *Bossier Parish Community College*

And, last, to all the instructors and students who have taken time out of their busy lives to send along feedback about their experiences teaching and studying from *Mastering the World of Psychology,* we are grateful to you. Please feel free to write *drdeniseboyd@sbcglobal.net* with your comments about the text.

List of Features

APPLY IT

More Tips for Effective Studying (Chapter 1)
Should You Consult a Genetic Counselor? (Chapter 2)
How Dangerous Is It to Talk on a Cell Phone or Text while Driving? (Chapter 3)
How to Get a Good Night's Sleep (Chapter 4)
How to Win the Battle against Procrastination (Chapter 5)
Improving Memory (Chapter 6)
How to Build a Powerful Vocabulary (Chapter 7)
Where Are You in the Career Development Process? (Chapter 8)
The Quest for Happiness (Chapter 9)
Interpreting Health Information on the Internet (Chapter 10)
Put Your Best Foot Forward (Chapter 11)
Overcoming the Fear of Public Speaking (Chapter 12)
Is E-therapy Right for You? (Chapter 13)
"Unlearning" Prejudice (Chapter 14)

TRY IT

What Is the Third Variable Problem? (Chapter 1)
Does Random Assignment Really Make Groups Equal? (Chapter 1)
A Balancing Act (Chapter 2)
Mirror Tracing (Chapter 2)
Absolute Threshold (Chapter 3)
Sensory Adaptation (Chapter 3)
A Negative Afterimage (Chapter 3)
Bottom-Up and Top-Down Processing (Chapter 3)
Lucid Dreaming (Chapter 4)
The Relaxation Response (Chapter 4)
Classical Conditioning (Chapter 5)
Using Behavior Modification (Chapter 5)
Creating a False Memory (Chapter 6)
A Penny for Your Thoughts (Chapter 6)
Using the Additive Strategy to Choose an Apartment (Chapter 7)
Water Lily Problem (Chapter 7)
Find Your EQ (Chapter 7)
Conservation of Volume (Chapter 8)
The Heinz Dilemma (Chapter 8)
Stereotypes about Later Adulthood (Chapter 8)
What Is Your *n* Ach? (Chapter 9)
Recognizing Basic Emotions (Chapter 9)
Finding a Life Stress Score (Chapter 10)
How Resilient Are You? (Chapter 10)
AIDS Quiz (Chapter 10)
How High Is Your Self-Esteem? (Chapter 11)
What Is Your Locus of Control? (Chapter 11)
Phobia Names (Chapter 12)
A Possible Hierarchy of Fears (Chapter 13)
Choosing a Life Partner (Chapter 14)

EXPLAIN IT

What Is a Credit Score? (Chapter 1)
Why Are Most People Right-Handed? (Chapter 2)
Why Can't Everyone Hear the "Mosquito" Ring Tone? (Chapter 3)
How Does the Brain Keep Track of Time? (Chapter 4)
How Do the Principles of Learning Explain the Behavior of Smoking Cigarettes? (Chapter 5)
Why Is Cramming an Ineffective Study Method? (Chapter 6)
Why Do People Overestimate the Likelihood of Rare Events? (Chapter 7)
Why Are Peer Groups Important in Adolescence? (Chapter 8)
Why Are Dangerous Hobbies Appealing to Some People? (Chapter 9)
Why Do Pop Quizzes Facilitate Learning? (Chapter 10)
How Personality Theories Answer the Question, "Why Do Some People Fail to Develop a Conscience?" (Chapter 12)
How Do Cultural Beliefs about Ideal Emotional States Lead to Depression? (Chapter 11)
Why Are Smoking Rates So High among People with Schizophrenia? (Chapter 13)
Why Doesn't Groupthink Occur in Every Tightly Knit Group? (Chapter 14)

SUMMARIZE IT

The Goals of Psychology (Chapter 1)
Contemporary Perspectives in Psychology (Chapter 1)
Research Methods in Psychology (Chapter 1)
Major Structures of the Visual System (Chapter 3)
Sleep Disorders (Chapter 4)
Theories of Hypnosis (Chapter 4)
The Effects and Withdrawal Symptoms of Some Psychoactive Drugs (Chapter 4)
Reinforcement Schedules Compared (Chapter 5)
Classical and Operant Conditioning Compared (Chapter 5)
Cognitive Learning (Chapter 5)
Forgetting (Chapter 6)
Approaches to Decision Making (Chapter 7)
Theories of Intelligence (Chapter 7)
Piaget's Stages of Cognitive Development (Chapter 8)
Kohlberg's Stages of Moral Development (Chapter 8)
Erikson's Psychosocial Stages of Development (Chapter 8)
Approaches to Motivation (Chapter 9)
Theories of Emotion (Chapter 9)
Theories of Stress Responses (Chapter 10)
Factors that Promote Resilience (Chapter 10)
Freud's Psychosexual Stages of Development (Chapter 11)
Theories of Personality (Chapter 11)
Three Approaches to Personality Assessment (Chapter 11)
Five Perspectives on Psychological Disorders (Chapter 12)
Drugs Used to Treat Psychological Disorders (Chapter 13)
Summary and Comparison of Therapies (Chapter 13)
Possible Biological Causes of Aggression (Chapter 14)

About the Authors

Samuel E. Wood (deceased) received his doctorate from the University of Florida. He taught at West Virginia University and the University of Missouri–St. Louis and was a member of the doctoral faculty at both universities. From 1984 to 1996, he served as president of the Higher Education Center, a consortium of 14 colleges and universities in the St. Louis area. He was a cofounder of the Higher Education Cable TV channel (HEC-TV) in St. Louis and served as its president and CEO from its founding in 1987 until 1996.

Ellen Green Wood received her doctorate in educational psychology from St. Louis University and was an adjunct professor of psychology at St. Louis Community College at Meramec. She has also taught in the clinical experiences program in education at Washington University and at the University of Missouri–St. Louis. In addition to her teaching, Dr. Wood has developed and taught seminars on critical thinking. She received the Telecourse Pioneer Award from 1982 through 1988 for her contributions to the field of distance learning.

Denise Boyd received her Ed.D. in educational psychology from the University of Houston and has been a psychology instructor in the Houston Community College System since 1988. From 1995 until 1998, she chaired the psychology, sociology, and anthropology department at Houston Community College–Central. She has coauthored five other Pearson Allyn and Bacon texts: With Samuel Wood and Ellen Green Wood, *The World of Psychology* (Seventh Edition); with Helen Bee, *Lifespan Development* (Sixth Edition), *The Developing Child* (Thirteenth Edition), and *The Growing Child* (First Edition); and with Genevieve Stevens, *Current Readings in Lifespan Development*. A licensed psychologist, she has presented a number of papers at professional meetings, reporting research in child, adolescent, and adult development. She has also presented workshops for teachers whose students range from preschool to college.

Together, Sam, Evie, and Denise have several decades of experience teaching introductory psychology to thousands of students of all ages, backgrounds, and abilities. *Mastering the World of Psychology,* Fifth Edition, is the direct result of their teaching experience.

APA Correlation

APA Learning Outcomes	Number	Learning Objective	Book Learning Objectives	Book Features	Videos, Simulations, and Assessments
GOAL 1: Scientific Inquiry and Critical Thinking					
Understand scientific reasoning and problem solving, including effective research methods.					
1.1 Use scientific reasoning to interpret behavior	1.1a	Identify basic biological, psychological, and social components of behavioral explanations (e.g., inferences, observations, operational definitions, interpretations)	2.13, 2.14, 5.5	Chapter 2: Explain It: Why Are Most People Right-Handed?	**Simulations:** Implicit Association Test: Cats and Dogs Hemispheric Specialization Ambiguous Figures Weber's Law Müller-Lyer Illusion
	1.1b	Use psychology concepts to explain personal experiences and recognize the potential for flaws in behavioral explanations based on simplistic, personal theories	3.6, 3.7, 3.8		Learning Digit Span Serial Position Effect Depth of Processing
	1.1c	Use an appropriate level of complexity to interpret behavior and mental processes	1.9	Chapter 3: Try It: A Negative Afterimage	Mental Rotation Selective Attention
	1.1d	Ask relevant questions to gather more information about behavioral claims	4.13, 10.17		Stroop Effect Implicit Association Test: Food
	1.1e	Describe common fallacies in thinking (e.g., confirmation bias, post hoc explanations, implying causation from correlation) that impair accurate conclusions and predictions	1.12, 3.18	Chapter 10: Try It: AIDS Quiz	IPIP Neo Personality Inventory **Video Series** **Basics:** Scientific Research Methods
1.2 Demonstrate psychology information literacy	1.2a	Read and summarize general ideas and conclusions from psychological sources accurately	4.10, 4.11, 7.6, 13.16	Chapter 3: Explain It: Why Can't Everyone Hear the Mosquito Ring Tone	**Thinking Like a Psychologist:** Thinking Critically The Pre-Frontal Cortex: The Good, the Bad, and the Criminal
	1.2b	Describe what kinds of additional information beyond personal experience are acceptable in developing behavioral explanations (i.e., popular press reports versus scientific findings)	3.19, 5.17	Chapter 7: Explain It: Why Do People Overestimate the Likelihood of Rare Events?	Evolutionary Psychology—Why We Do the Things We Do Can Smells Alter Mood and Behavior?
	1.2c	Identify and navigate psychology databases and other legitimate sources of psychology information			The Uses and Limitations of Hypnosis Police Line-Up Babies by Design
	1.2d	Articulate criteria for identifying objective sources of psychology information	9.7		Speaking One's Mind Intelligence Tests and Success
	1.2e	Interpret simple graphs and statistical findings	5.4	Chapter 7: Try It: Using the Additive Strategy to Choose an Apartment	Predicting Future Emotion and Desire Measuring Personality Personality and Health Assessing Treatment Effectiveness

(continued)

(continued)

The APA Guidelines for the Undergraduate Psychology Major					MyPsychLab Content
APA Learning Outcomes	**Number**	**Learning Objective**	**Book Learning Objectives**	**Book Features**	**Videos, Simulations, and Assessments**
1.3 Engage in innovative and integrative thinking and problem solving	1.3a	Recognize and describe well-defined problems	6.7, 6.8	Chapter 2: Try It: A Balancing Act	**In the Real World:** Neurotransmitters Taking Control of Our Genes Pain Management Sleep, Memory, and Learning The Memories We Don't Want Changing Your Mind Eating Disorders Putting Popular Personality Assessments to the Test Sexual Problems and Dysfunction Reducing Stress, Improving Health Cognitive Behavioral Therapy
	1.3b	Apply simple problem-solving strategies to improve efficiency and effectiveness	7.1, 7.2, 7.3		
	1.3c	Describe the consequences of problem-solving attempts		Chapter 2: Try It: Mirror Tracing	
1.4 Interpret, design, and conduct basic psychological research	1.4a	Describe research methods used by psychologists including their respective advantages and disadvantages	1.2, 1.10, 1.11, 7.4, 11.13		**What's in It for Me?:** The Myth of Multitasking Perceptual Magic in Art and Movies Altered States of Consciousness How to Make Healthier Choices Making It Stick Making Choices How Resilient Are You? Meeting Our Needs Psychological Resilience The Challenge of Quitting Bad Health Habits Finding a Therapist If You Need One
	1.4b	Discuss the value of experimental design (i.e., controlled comparisons) in justifying cause-effect relationships	1.13, 1.14	Chapter 1: Try It: Does Random Assignment Really Make Groups Equal?	
	1.4c	Define and explain the purpose of key research concepts that characterize psychological research (e.g., hypothesis, operational definition)	1.8	Chapter 1: Try It: What Is the Third Variable Problem?	
	1.4d	Replicate or design and conduct simple scientific studies (e.g., correlational or two-factor) to confirm a hypothesis based on operational definitions		Chapter 4: Try It: Lucid Dreaming; Chapter 6: Try It: A Penny for Your Thoughts	
	1.4e	Explain why conclusions in psychological projects must be both reliable and valid	11.14, 11.15		
	1.4f	Explain why quantitative analysis is relevant for scientific problem solving		Chapter 7: Try It: Water Lily Problem	
	1.4g	Describe the fundamental principles of research design	7.1		
1.5 Incorporate sociocultural factors in scientific inquiry	1.5a	Relate examples of how a researcher's value system, sociocultural characteristics, and historical context influence the development of scientific inquiry on psychological questions	9.14		
	1.5b	Analyze potential challenges related to sociocultural factors in a given research study	6.9		
	1.5c	Describe how individual and sociocultural differences can influence the applicability/generalizability of research findings	1.15	Chapter 3: Try It: Bottom-Up and Top-Down Processing; Chapter 8: Try It: The Heinz Dilemma	
	1.5d	Identify under what conditions research findings can be appropriately generalized		Chapter 8: Try It: Conservation of Volume	

The APA Guidelines for the Undergraduate Psychology Major					MyPsychLab Content
APA Learning Outcomes	**Number**	**Learning Objective**	**Book Learning Objectives**	**Book Features**	**Videos, Simulations, and Assessments**
GOAL 2: Ethical and Social Responsibility					
Develop ethically and socially responsible behaviors for professional and personal settings.					
2.1 Apply ethical standards to psychological science and practice	2.1a	Describe key regulations in the APA Ethics Code for protection of human or nonhuman research participants	1.16		**Simulations** Participating in a Research Survey **Video Series** **Special Topics:** Ethics and Psychological Research
	2.1b	Identify obvious violations of ethical standards in psychological contexts	14.6	Chapter 6: Try It: Creating a False Memory	
	2.1c	Discuss relevant ethical issues that reflect principles in the APA Code of Ethics	5.3		
	2.1d	Define the role of the institutional review board			
2.2 Promote values that build trust and enhance interpersonal relationships	2.2a	Describe the need for positive personal values (e.g., integrity, benevolence, honesty, respect for human dignity) in building strong relationships with others	9.9	Chapter 8: Explain It: Why Are Peer Groups Important in Adolescence?	**Simulations** Implicit Association Test: Sexuality Implicit Association Test: Prejudice **Video Series** **Thinking Like a Psychologist:** Physical Punishment—You Decide! Sexual Orientation Changing Attitudes and Behaviors
	2.2b	Treat others with civility	9.16, 13.14, 13.15		
	2.2c	Explain how individual differences, social identity, and world view may influence beliefs, values, and interaction with others and vice versa	9.6		**In the Real World:** Speed Dating Resolving Conflict Socialization
	2.2d	Maintain high standards for academic integrity, including honor code requirements			Are Stereotypes and Prejudices Inevitable? How Am I Being Influenced? Learning Aggression
2.3 Adopt values that build community at local, national, and global levels	2.3a	Identify human diversity in its many forms and the interpersonal challenges that often result from the diversity	6.16, 6.17, 7.8, 8.8	Chapter 9: Explain It: Why Are Dangerous Hobbies Appealing to Some People?	**What's in It for Me?:** Identity The Dating Game Attraction Persuasion
	2.3b	Recognize potential for prejudice and discrimination in oneself and others	7.15, 9.12, 12.1, 14.7		
	2.3c	Explain how psychology can promote civic, social, and global outcomes that benefit others	5.12, 5.13, 10.10	Chapter 14: Apply It: Unlearning Prejudice	
	2.3d	Describe psychology-related issues of global concern (e.g., poverty, health, migration, human rights, international conflict, sustainability)	4.15, 5.9, 5.11, 8.18, 8.19, 8.20, 9.11, 10.12, 14.16, 14.17	Chapter 5: Explain It: How Do the Principles of Learning Explain the Behavior of Smoking Cigarettes?	
	2.3e	Articulate psychology's role in developing, designing, and disseminating public policy	7.13, 7.14, 10.9		
	2.3f	Accept opportunity to serve others through civic engagement, including volunteer service	14.14, 14.15		

(continued)

(continued)

The APA Guidelines for the Undergraduate Psychology Major					MyPsychLab Content
APA Learning Outcomes	Number	Learning Objective	Book Learning Objectives	Book Features	Videos, Simulations, and Assessments
GOAL 3: Communication					
Demonstrate competence in written, oral, and interpersonal communication skills and be able to develop and present a scientific argument.					
3.1 Demonstrate effective writing in multiple formats	3.1a	Express ideas in written formats that reflect basic psychological concepts and principles	6.5, 6.6	Think About It, Remember It	**Writing Assignments** Diagnosing Anxiety Designing an Experiment Parts of the Brain on Pizza Night Musical Talent as a Heritable Trait The Gestalt Perspective Effects of Sleep Deprivation in College Operant Conditioning and Weight Loss Memory and Study Strategies Describing Thinking Patterns with Piaget's Theory of Cognitive Development Mental Sets and Studying a Foreign Language Exploring Gardner's Types of Intelligence Describing Theories of Emotion Describing Theories of Personality Comparing Gender Concepts Analyzing Stress Assessing Work Environments and Motivation Discussing Prejudice and Discrimination Considering Schizophrenia Comparing Psychotherapy Approaches
	3.1b	Recognize writing content and format differ based on purpose (e.g., blogs, memos, journal articles) and audience		Think About It, Remember It	
	3.1c	Use generally accepted grammar		Think About It, Remember It	
	3.1d	Describe how writing using APA writing style is different from regular writing or writing in other conventions			
	3.1e	Recognize and develop overall organization (e.g., beginning, development, ending) that fits the purpose			
	3.1f	Interpret quantitative data displayed in statistics, graphs, and tables, including statistical symbols in research reports	7.7	Chapter 1: Explain It: What Is a Credit Score?	
	3.1g	Use expert feedback to revise writing of a single draft			
3.2 Exhibit effective presentation skills in multiple formats	3.2a	Construct plausible oral argument based on a psychological study			
	3.2b	Deliver brief presentations within appropriate constraints (e.g., time limit, appropriate to audience)		Chapter 12: Apply It: Overcoming the Fear of Public Speaking	
	3.2c	Describe effective delivery characteristics of professional oral performance			
	3.2d	Incorporate appropriate visual support			
	3.2e	Pose questions about psychological content	2.1, 2.2, 4.14	Chapter 13: Explain It: Why Are Smoking Rates So High among People with Schizophrenia?	
3.3 Interact Effectively with Others	3.3a	Identify key message elements in communication through careful listening			
	3.3b	Recognize that culture, values, and biases may produce misunderstandings in communication	7.17		
	3.3c	Attend to language and nonverbal cues to interpret meaning	7.16	Chapter 7: Apply It: How to Build a Powerful Vocabulary	
	3.3d	Ask questions to capture additional detail			
	3.3e	Respond appropriately to electronic communications		Chapter 10: Apply It: Interpreting Health Information on the Internet	

The APA Guidelines for the Undergraduate Psychology Major					MyPsychLab Content
APA Learning Outcomes	**Number**	**Learning Objective**	**Book Learning Objectives**	**Book Features**	**Videos, Simulations, and Assessments**

GOAL 4: Professional Development

Apply psychology-specific content and skills, effective self-reflection, project management skills, teamwork skills, and career preparation to support occupational planning and pursuit.

4.1 Apply psychological content and skills to professional work	4.1a	Recognize the value and application of research and problem-solving skills in providing evidence beyond personal opinion to support proposed solutions	14.1		**Video Series** **Surveys:** Which Sense Do You Use? Do You Fly or Fight? What Altered States Have You Experienced?
	4.1b	Identify range of possible factors that influence beliefs and conclusions	14.2, 14.12		Are Dreams Meaningful? What Drugs Have You Used?
	4.1c	Expect to deal with differing opinions and personalities in the college environment	7.12		What Learning Techniques Do You Use?
	4.1d	Describe how psychology's content applies to business, healthcare, educational, and other workplace settings	2.11, 2.12	Chapter 5: Try It: Using Behavior Modification	What Do You Remember? What Has Your Father Done for You? What Is Creativity?
	4.1e	Recognize and describe broad applications of information literacy skills obtained in the psychology major			What Is Intelligence? How to Deal with Your Emotions? What Motivates You?
	4.1f	Describe how ethical principles of psychology have relevance to non-psychology settings		Chapter 11: Explain It: How Personality Theories Answer the Question, "Why Do Some People Fail to Develop a Conscience?"	What Has Shaped Your Personality? How Does Gender Affect You? Will This Survey Stress You Out? Could You Be a Hero? Are You Normal?
4.2 Exhibit self-efficacy and self-regulation	4.2a	Recognize the link between effort and achievement	9.1, 9.2	Chapter 6: Explain It: Why Is Cramming an Ineffective Study Method?	How Do You Take Care of Your Mental Health?
	4.2b	Accurately self-assess performance quality by adhering to external standards (e.g., rubric criteria, teacher expectations)	11.12	Chapter 6: Apply It: Improving Memory; Chapter 10: Explain It: Why Do Pop Quizzes Facilitate Learning?	
	4.2c	Incorporate feedback from educators and mentors to change performance	14.11	Chapter 7: Try It: Find Your EQ	
	4.2d	Describe self-regulation strategies (e.g., reflection, time management)	1.1	Chapter 1: Apply It: More Tips for Effective Studying; Chapter 11: Try It: What Is Your Locus of Control?	
4.3 Refine project management skills	4.3a	Follow instructions, including timely delivery, in response to project criteria			
	4.3b	Identify appropriate resources and constraints that may influence project completion			
	4.3c	Anticipate where potential problems can hinder successful project completion	10.4	Chapter 5: Apply It: How to Win the Battle against Procrastination	
	4.3d	Describe the processes and strategies necessary to develop a project to fulfill its intended purpose		Chapter 9: Try It: What Is Your *n* ACH?	

(continued)

(continued)

The APA Guidelines for the Undergraduate Psychology Major				MyPsychLab Content
APA Learning Outcomes	Number	Learning Objective	Book Learning Objectives	Book Features	Videos, Simulations, and Assessments

APA Learning Outcomes	Number	Learning Objective	Book Learning Objectives	Book Features	Videos, Simulations, and Assessments
4.4 Enhance teamwork capacity	4.4a	Collaborate successfully on small group classroom assignments	14.8		
	4.4b	Recognize the potential for developing stronger solutions through shared problem solving	14.9	Chapter 14: Explain It: Why Doesn't Groupthink Occur in Every Tightly Knit Group?	
	4.4c	Articulate problems that develop when working with teams	6.11		
	4.4d	Assess one's strengths and weaknesses in performance as a project team member	10.2		
	4.4e	Describe strategies used by effective group leaders	10.3		
	4.4f	Describe the importance of working effectively in diverse environments	14.1		
4.5 Develop meaningful professional direction for life after graduation	4.5a	Describe the types of academic experiences and advanced course choices that will best shape career readiness	1.7		
	4.5b	Articulate the skills sets desired by employers who hire people with psychology backgrounds	9.3, 13.13, 14.13	Chapter 8: Apply It: Where Are You in the Career Development Process?	
	4.5c	Recognize the importance of having a mentor	5.16		
	4.5d	Describe how a curriculum vitae or resume is used to document the skills expected by employers		Chapter 11: Apply It: Put Your Best Foot Forward	
	4.5e	Recognize how rapid social change influences behavior and affects one's value in the workplace			

GOAL 5: Knowledge Base in Psychology

Demonstrate fundamental knowledge and comprehension of major concepts, theoretical perspectives, historical trends, and empirical findings to discuss how psychological principles apply to behavioral problems.

APA Learning Outcomes	Number	Learning Objective	Book Learning Objectives	Book Features	Videos, Simulations, and Assessments
5.1 Describe key concepts, principles, and overarching themes in psychology	5.1a	Use basic psychological terminology, concepts, and theories in psychology to explain behavior and mental processes	2.6, 2.7, 3.3, 3.4, 3.5, 3.15, 3.16, 3.17, 5.10, 7.5, 8.6, 8.9, 9.8, 9.10, 9.13, 10.1, 10.15, 11.8, 12.3, 12.4, 12.5, 12.6, 12.13, 12.14, 13.4, 13.5, 14.3		**Video Series** **The Big Picture:** Asking the Tough Questions How to Answer Psychological Questions My Brain Made Me Do It Genes, Evolution, and Human Behavior Taking in the World Around Us States of Consciousness What Does It Mean to Learn? The Woman Who Cannot Forget Different Perspectives on the World I Am, Therefore I Think What Is Intelligence? Motivation and Emotion What Is Personality?
	5.1b	Explain why psychology is a science with the primary objectives of describing, understanding, predicting, and controlling behavior and mental processes	1.3, 2.3, 2.4, 2.5, 3.1, 3.2, 4.1, 4.5, 4.6, 5.2, 6.1, 6.2, 6.3, 6.4, 6.13, 8.11, 8.14, 12.7, 12.8	Chapter 3: Try It: Sensory Adaptation	
	5.1c	Interpret behavior and mental processes at an appropriate level of complexity	3.9, 3.10, 3.11, 12.11, 12.12		
	5.1d	Recognize the power of the context in shaping conclusions about individual behavior	4.7		

The APA Guidelines for the Undergraduate Psychology Major					MyPsychLab Content
APA Learning Outcomes	**Number**	**Learning Objective**	**Book Learning Objectives**	**Book Features**	**Videos, Simulations, and Assessments**
	5.1e	Identify fields other than psychology that address behavioral concerns	6.12, 6.14, 6.15, 8.5, 8.15, 12.2, 12.18, 12.19, 13.11, 13.12		The Power of Sex Health Psychology The Social World What Does It Mean to Have a Mental Disorder?
5.2 Develop a working knowledge of the content domains of psychology	5.2a	Identify key characteristics of major content domains in psychology (e.g., cognition and learning, developmental, biological, and sociocultural)	2.8, 2.9, 2.10, 6.10, 11.10		**Basics:** Diverse Perspectives How the Brain Works Genetic Mechanisms and Behavioral Genetics
	5.2b	Identify principle research methods and types of questions that emerge in specific content domains	4.3, 4.4, 11.6	Chapter 4: Explain It: How Does the Brain Keep Track of Time?	In Full Appreciation of the Cookie Rhythms of Consciousness Classical Conditioning: An Involuntary Response
	5.2c	Recognize major historical events, theoretical perspectives, and figures in psychology and their link to trends in contemporary research	1.4, 1.5, 1.6, 5.1, 5.7, 5.15, 7.9, 7.11, 8.1, 8.2, 8.3, 8.4, 9.4, 10.7, 11.1, 11.2, 11.5, 11.7, 11.11, 13.1, 13.2, 13.3, 13.9, 14.5		Operant Conditioning: Learning from Consequences Do You Remember When...? How Thinking Develops Attachment The Mind Is What the Brain Does Theories of Intelligence
	5.2d	Provide examples of unique contributions of content domain to the understanding of complex behavioral issues	5.8, 8.12, 11.3, 11.4		Theories of Emotion and Motivation Personality Theories
	5.2e	Recognize content domains as having distinctive sociocultural origins and development	4.2, 8.7, 8.10, 11.9	Chapter 12: Try It: Phobia Names	Sex and Gender Differences Stress and Your Health Under the Influence of Others Living with a Disorder
5.3 Describe applications that employ discipline-based problem solving	5.3a	Describe examples of relevant and practical applications of psychological principles to everyday life	5.6, 8.13, 9.5, 10.5, 10.6, 10.8	Chapter 2: Apply It: Should You Consult a Genetic Counselor?; Chapter 4: Apply It: How to Get a Good Night's Sleep; Chapter 4: Try It: The Relaxation Response; Chapter 13: Try It: A Possible Hierarchy of Fears; Chapter 13: Apply It: Is E-Therapy Right for You?; Chapter 14: Try It: Choosing a Life Partner	Therapies in Action **Special Topics:** The Plastic Brain Epigenetics: A Revolutionary Science Recognizing Faces Sleep Disorders Learning to Overcome Phobias When Memory Fails Risky Behavior and Brain Development Mental Imagery: In the Mind's Eye
	5.3b	Summarize psychological factors that can influence the pursuit of a healthy lifestyle	4.8, 4.12, 10.13, 10.14, 10.16, 14.4	Chapter 10: Try It: Finding a Life Stress Score	Intelligence Testing, Then and Now Detecting Lies Twins and Personality
	5.3c	Correctly identify antecedents and consequences of behavior and mental processes	3.12, 3.14, 4.16, 4.17, 4.18, 7.7, 12.9, 12.10, 12.15, 12.16, 12.17, 13.6, 13.7, 13.8, 13.10	Chapter 12: Explain It: How Do Cultural Beliefs about Ideal Emotional States Lead to Depression?	Cultural Norms and Sexual Behavior Health Disparities Mental Shortcuts in a Social Context Diagnosing Mental Disorders
	5.3d	Predict how individual differences influence beliefs, values, and interactions with others, including the potential for prejudicial and discriminatory behavior in oneself and others	3.13, 5.14, 8.16, 8.17, 9.15, 10.11, 14.18, 14.19	Chapter 8: Try It: Stereotypes about Later Adulthood	

Introduction to Psychology

The SQ3R method will help you maximize your learning in five steps:
- *Survey*
- *Question*
- *Read*
- *Recite*
- *Review*

The sticky notes in Chapter 1 will help you master this learning system so that you can use it on your own in the remaining chapters.

⊙⟲ THINK ABOUT IT

Here you are taking your first psychology course and wondering what it's all about. When you focus on the word *psychology*, what ideas spring to mind as you concentrate? Do terms such as *therapy, brain, psychological disorder, emotion,* and *hypnosis* come to mind? Your introductory psychology course will touch on all of these concepts, but it will also help you learn how to deal with pressing practical issues in your everyday life. How can you study more effectively? (You can start answering this one by reading the *Apply It* section on page 4.) How can you know which career is right for you? How can you solve conflicts and maintain satisfying relationships with others? These are the kinds of practical questions that a good understanding of psychology can help you answer?

Let's begin your exploration of psychology with an assessment of how much you already know, or think you know, about the topic:

Indicate whether each statement is true (T) or false (F).

1. Once damaged, brain cells never work again.
2. All people dream during a night of normal sleep.
3. As the number of bystanders at an emergency increases, the time it takes for the victim to get help decreases.
4. Humans do not have a maternal instinct.
5. It's impossible for human beings to hear a watch ticking 20 feet away.
6. Eyewitness testimony is often unreliable.
7. Chimpanzees have been taught to speak.
8. Creativity and high intelligence do not necessarily go together.
9. When it comes to close personal relationships, opposites attract.
10. The majority of teenagers have good relationships with their parents.

You may be surprised to learn that all the odd-numbered items are false, and all the even-numbered items are true. Learning all you can from this text is a good first step toward a better understanding of behavior and mental processes. The text's features will help you learn because they are part of a systematic—that is, a goal-oriented, planned, and effortful—way of studying. Similarly, the procedures that scientists use yield reliable answers to questions about behavior and mental processes because they are part of a systematic approach to what some philosophers deem to be the primary goal of science: to search for truth (Popper, 1972). ⊙

⊙▸**Watch** the Video *Episode 1: Thinking Like a Psychologist: Debunking Myths* in **MyPsychLab**

SQ3R method A study method involving the following five steps: (1) survey, (2) question, (3) read, (4) recite, and (5) review.

1.1 How will the SQ3R method help you master psychology?

Step 1: Survey
- *Read over the learning objectives in the outline at the beginning of the chapter.*
- *Look over the other major elements of the chapter. They include the following:*
  - *Think About It chapter opener*
  - *Key terms*
  - *Summarize It tables*
  - *Try It activities*
  - *Explain It boxes*
  - *Apply It boxes*
- *Skim the Chapter Summary.*
- *Create note-taking outline you'll use as you read the chapter. Your outline will include these elements:*
  - *The titles and main ideas of the chapter's sections*
  - *The learning questions each section answers*
- *Do the Think About It activity at the beginning of the chapter.*

An Introduction to *Mastering the World of Psychology*

A Ugandan expression says, "The hunter in pursuit of an elephant does not stop to throw stones at birds." In other words, to achieve any goal, including succeeding in a psychology course, one must remain focused on it. The study strategies we have incorporated into *Mastering the World of Psychology* can help you stay focused on your goal of successfully completing your course in introductory psychology. Here is how the features of the text can help you.

Studying Psychology: Some Tricks of the Trade

To help you maximize your learning, *Mastering the World of Psychology* includes a set of tried and true study strategies—*Survey, Question, Read, Recite,* and *Review*—that are collectively known as the **SQ3R method** (Robinson, 1970). Here's how to make the most of the SQ3R features that we have included in *Mastering the World of Psychology*:

STEP 1: **Survey.** The goal of the survey step is to get the chapter's "big picture," a mental map of what it's all about. That's the purpose of the list of learning questions at the beginning of each chapter. The questions give you a blueprint to use as you navigate through the chapter and tell you what you will learn in each section. Use the learning questions to create a note-taking outline that you will fill in as you read the chapter. Next, look over the major elements of the chapter. These elements include the chapter-opening activity called *Think About It,* the section headings, *Summarize It* tables, *Try It* activities, *Explain It* boxes, and *Apply It* boxes. You should also survey the learning questions in the margins by each subheading (the same questions that are listed at the beginning of the chapter) and the boldfaced terms that are also in the margins. Next, skim over the *Chapter Summary.* It includes answers for all the learning questions. Next, do the *Think About It* activity at the beginning of the chapter, keeping in mind the mental overview of the chapter that you constructed with the help of the learning questions. Now you're ready to start working your way through the chapter.

STEP 2: **Question.** Do the Question step as you come to each subheading in the chapter. This step has two parts: First, read the learning question in the margin.

For instance, the learning question for this subsection is "How will the SQ3R method help you master psychology?" Next, think of additional questions you have about the topic and add them to the note-taking outline you created notes in the Survey step.

STEP 3: Read. Read the text under each subheading, keeping in mind the learning question and your own questions. Use the *Apply It* boxes, *Try It* activities, *Explain It* boxes, and *Summarize It* tables, if any are present, to help you understand the section.

STEP 4: Recite. When you finish reading each subsection, answer its learning question and your own questions aloud in your own words. Jot your answers, along with brief definitions for the section's key terms, in your outline. When you're finished, look back at the section to see if you've missed anything and modify your notes if necessary. Repeat this process for each subsection and you'll end up with a well-organized set of notes on the entire chapter.

STEP 5a: Review I. To be sure you've understood each major section before you move on to the next one, answer the Remember It questions. You should find many of the answers in your notes. If you don't, you should probably go back and revise them. Next, log on to MyPsychLab and take the section's Quick Review quiz. Research shows that repeated testing is one of the most effective study strategies you can use (Karpicke, Butler, & Roediger, 2009).

STEP 5b: Review II. After you have worked your way through the all the major sections, you need to review the entire chapter to be sure that you're ready to be tested on it. Begin by reading the *Chapter Summary* and comparing it to your notes. Revise your notes if necessary. Next, complete the Study Guide and check your answers against the key in the back of the book. Revisit your notes and restudy the parts of the chapter you scored the lowest on in the Study Guide. Finally, take the chapter Practice Test in the back of the book or log on to MyPsychLab to take the online Chapter Exam. Reread the parts of the chapter that relate to any questions that you miss, and be sure that you understand where you went wrong. At this point, you should be feeling confident about your mastery of the chapter.

Now that you know how to study this text effectively, let's consider in more detail what impact the work of psychologists has on our everyday lives. Before we begin, think about all of the ways in which psychology—and the language of psychology—plays an integral role in our lives.

Is Psychology a Science? ▶

Psychology is defined as the scientific study of behavior and mental processes. If you are like most people, you have made many observations about both and perhaps have developed a few of your own theories to explain them. From television, radio, or the Internet, you probably also have had some exposure to "expert" opinions on behavior and mental processes. In fact, those may be the very sources that led you astray on the quiz at the beginning of the chapter.

Many people believe that a field is a science because of the nature of its body of knowledge. Few people question whether physics, for example, is a true science. But a science isn't a science because of its subject matter. A field of study qualifies as a science if it uses the scientific method to acquire knowledge. The **scientific method** consists of the orderly, systematic procedures that researchers follow as they identify a research problem, design a study to investigate the problem, collect and analyze data, draw conclusions, and communicate their findings. The knowledge gained is dependable because of the method used to obtain it. The scientific method includes the following steps:

■ Step 1: Observe and theorize
■ Step 2: Formulate a hypothesis
■ Step 3: Design a study

Step 2: Question
Use the question step for each subheading in the chapter. It has two parts:
• Read the learning question in the margin.
• Think of additional questions you have about the topic.

Step 3: Read
Read the text under each subheading and be sure you understand it before you go on to the next one. As you read:
• Keep the learning question in mind.
• Keep your own questions in mind.
• Use the Apply It boxes, Try It activities, Explain It boxes, and Summarize It tables, if any are present, to help you understand the subsection.

Step 4: Recite
When you finish reading each section:
• Answer the learning question and your own questions aloud in your own words.
• Add the answers to your outline.
• Look back at the section to see if you've missed anything.
• Modify your outline if necessary. Repeat this process for each subsection and you will end up with a well-organized set of notes on the entire chapter.

1.2 Why do psychologists use the scientific method?

psychology The scientific study of behavior and mental processes.

scientific method The orderly, systematic procedures that researchers follow as they identify a research problem, design a study to investigate the problem, collect and analyze data, draw conclusions, and communicate their findings.

APPLY IT   **More Tips for Effective Studying**

Decades of research on learning and memory have uncovered a number of strategies that you can use, in addition to the SQ3R method, to make your study time more efficient and effective.

- Establish a quiet place, free of distractions, where you do nothing else but study. You can condition yourself to associate this environment with studying, so that entering the room or area will be your cue to begin work.

- Schedule your study time. Research on memory has proven that spaced learning is more effective than massed practice (cramming). Instead of studying for five hours straight, try five study sessions of one hour each.

- To be prepared for each class meeting, set specific goals for yourself each week and for individual study sessions. Your goals should be challenging but not overwhelming. If the task for an individual study session is manageable, it will be easier to sit down and face it. Completing the task you have set for yourself will give you a sense of accomplishment.

- The more active a role you play in the learning process, the more you will remember. Spend some of your study time reciting rather than rereading the material. One effective method is to use index cards as flash cards. Write a key term or study question on the front of each card. On the back, list pertinent information from the text and class lectures. Use these cards to help you prepare for tests.

- *Overlearning* means studying beyond the point at which you can just barely recite the information you are trying to memorize. Review the information

again and again until it is firmly locked in memory. If you are subject to test anxiety, overlearning will help.

- Forgetting takes place most rapidly within the first 24 hours after you study. No matter how much you have studied for a test, always review shortly before you take it. Refreshing your memory will raise your grade.

- Sleeping immediately after you study will help you retain more of what you have learned. If you can't study before you go to sleep, at least review what you studied earlier in the day. This is also a good time to go through your index cards.

- Test, retest, and test again! A great deal of research indicates that testing and retesting yourself over material you have read enhances your ability to recall it when you are tested. For this reason, use all of the self-testing tools we have included in the text as well as those that are available on MyPsychLab.

Once you've mastered these study strategies, use them to improve your comprehension and success in all of your courses.

◉ Watch on **MyPsychLab**

◉ Watch the Video *Episode 6: What's in It for Me? Making It Stick* in **MyPsychLab**

- Step 4: Collect data
- Step 5: Apply results to the hypothesis

We describe each of these steps in detail in the following section and Figure 1.1 on page 5 will help you visualize the process.

STEP **1: Observe and Theorize.** The first step in the scientific method is an interactive one in which a researcher observes some phenomenon and *theorizes,* or develops a hunch, about what might have led to it. For instance, suppose a psychologist observes students playing video games on a big-screen TV in a student lounge and notices that the men tend to get higher scores than the women do. She might speculate that this gender difference results from differences in the amount of time that men and women spend playing video games. In other words, her hunch is that, in general, men get higher scores on video games because they practice more than women do. Such hunches are often derived from a psychological **theory**, a general principle or set of principles proposed to explain how a number of separate facts are related. In our example, the researcher's hunch seems to be based on a theory that emphasizes the role of experience in shaping behavior; that is, her theory proposes that the more experience people have doing something, the better they are at it.

theory A general principle or set of principles proposed to explain how a number of separate facts are related.

STEP **2: Formulate a Hypothesis.** Based on her hunch about the cause of gender differences in video game scores, the researcher next comes up with a **hypothesis**, a specific prediction that can be tested *empirically*—that is, with data. Although the researchers' theory suggests many possible hypotheses, one, in particular, is key

hypothesis A testable prediction about the conditions under which a particular behavior or mental process may occur.

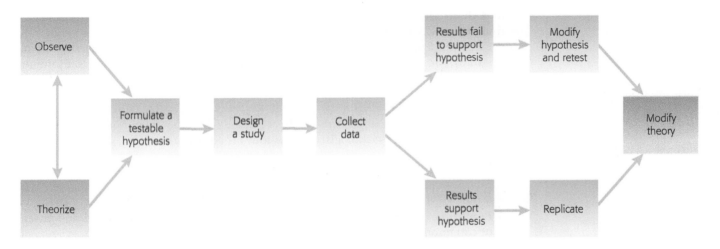

FIGURE 1.1 **The Scientific Method**
These are the steps involved in the scientific method.

to understanding the contribution of practice to video game scores: *If males and females spend equal amounts of time practicing a game, their scores will be equal.*

STEP 3: **Design a Study.** Next, to test the hypothesis about equal practice, the researcher could design a study in which she uses the same procedures to teach male and female students how to play a new video game. Then she allows them 30 minutes to practice it on their own. At the end of the practice session, she tells participants to play the game one more time but to try for the highest score possible.

STEP 4: **Collect Data.** Once the researcher conducts her study, she collects data that are relevant to her hypothesis. First, she calculates an average score for male and female participants. Then she calculates the amount of time that participants actually spent practicing the game. This information could be critical in interpreting the study's results because, even though each participant is allowed 30 minutes to practice, the researcher cannot assume that they will all practice an equal amount of time.

STEP 5: **Apply Results to the Hypothesis.** If the scores for males and females are equivalent, the researcher can conclude that the data support her hypothesis. That is, given the same amount of practice time, males and females will score equally well. Next, the researcher will make other psychologists aware of her findings by presenting them at a professional meeting, such as the annual convention of the American Psychological Association, or by publishing them in a professional journal. Such journals publish the results of studies that have been reviewed by other researchers and found to be methodologically sound, a process called *peer review.*

However, publication is only one facet of the final step of the scientific. The other is a process called **replication** in which the researcher or another psychologist who is intrigued by her findings or wants to challenge them to repeat the study using the same procedures. The purpose of replication is to determine whether the original results were a one-time phenomenon or evidence of a true, underlying psychological principle.

On the other hand, if the researcher finds that males still get higher scores than females, she must concede that the results do not support her hypothesis and she must modify it. However, this is where the researcher's data on actual practice time may come in handy: If the data show that males spent more time engaged in actual practice than the females did, the researcher can assert that the study's outcome supports her

replication The process of repeating a study to verify research findings.

hypothesis after all. Still, she must modify her hypothesis to include a testable assertion about why the men in her study chose to practice more than the women did. If she hypothesizes that the practice difference was caused by the type of game used in the study, for example, in a subsequent study, the researcher would go on to examine how different types of games affect practice time.

1.3 What are the goals of psychology?

The Goals of Psychology

What goals do psychological researchers pursue when they plan and conduct their studies? Briefly put, psychologists pursue four broad goals:

- *Description:* Identifying and classifying behaviors and mental processes as accurately as possible
- *Explanation:* Proposing reasons for behaviors and mental processes
- *Prediction:* Offering predictions (or hypotheses) about how a given condition or set of conditions will affect behaviors and mental processes
- *Influence:* Using the results of research to solve practical problems that involve behavior and mental processes

basic research Research conducted to seek new knowledge and to explore and advance general scientific understanding.

applied research Research conducted specifically to solve practical problems and improve the quality of life.

Two types of research help psychologists accomplish the four goals just described: basic research and applied research. The purpose of **basic research** is to seek new knowledge and to explore and advance general scientific understanding. Basic research explores such topics as the nature of memory, brain function, motivation, and emotional expression. **Applied research** is conducted specifically for the purpose of solving practical problems and improving the quality of life. Applied research focuses on finding methods to improve memory or increase motivation, therapies to treat psychological disorders, ways to decrease stress, and so on. This type of research is primarily concerned with the fourth goal of psychology—influence—because it specifies ways and means of changing behavior.

The scientific method has enabled psychologists to accumulate a vast knowledge base about behavior and mental processes. However, information alone doesn't necessarily advance our understanding of psychological phenomena. As we noted earlier, using knowledge acquired through the scientific method to develop cohesive theories can help us in the quest for understanding. With that point in mind, we'll turn our attention to some early attempts at psychological theory building and the schools of thought and psychological perspectives that arose from the debate stimulated by them.

The *Summarize It* below summarizes the goals of psychology and applies them to the video game hypothesis we discussed earlier.

Step 5a: Review!
To be sure you've understood each major section before you move on to the next one:
- Look over the notes in your outline for each of the section's subheadings.
- Answer the Remember It questions at the end of each section
- Log on to MyPsychLab and take the section's Quick Review quiz.

SUMMARIZE IT

The Goals of Psychology

Watch the Video *Episode 1: The Big Picture: Asking the Tough Questions* in **MyPsychLab**

GOAL	DEFINITION	EXAMPLE
Description	Describe behavior or mental process as accurately as possible.	Calculate average video game scores for males and females.
Explanation	Suggest causes for behavior or mental processes of interest.	Propose that males score higher on video games because they practice more than females do.
Prediction	Specify conditions under which behavior or mental process is likely to occur.	Hypothesize that males and females will obtain equivalent video game scores if they practice the same amount of time.
Influence	Apply the results of a study to change a condition in order to bring about a desired real-world outcome or prevent an undesired real-world outcome.	Use the results of video game practice studies to develop games that can enhance females' achievement in math and science.

1. The orderly, systematic procedures scientists follow in acquiring a body of knowledge comprise the
_____ _____.

2. _____ is the process of repeating a study to determine whether the results were reliable.

3. The four goals of psychology are _____, _____, _____, and
_____.

4. Applied research addresses the _____ goal.

Psychology Then and Now

If you were to trace the development of psychology from the beginning, you would need to start before the earliest pages of recorded history, beyond even the early Greek philosophers, such as Aristotle and Plato. Psychology became distinct from philosophy when researchers began to use the scientific method to study behavior and mental processes. By the 1920s, the field's earliest researchers had laid the foundations of the major schools of thought and psychological perspectives that exist in psychology today. As the field grew and research findings accumulated, specialty areas within the field began to follow distinctive pathways.

Exploring Psychology's Roots ▶

Psychology became a science and an academic discipline in the 19th century when people who wanted to learn more about behavior and mental processes began to use the scientific method. Conventional thought at the time held that such endeavors were the exclusive province of white males. Nevertheless, several researchers overcame gender and ethnic prejudice in the late 19th and early 20th centuries to make notable contributions to the field of psychology.

1.4 What did the early psychologists contribute to the field?

Structuralism and Functionalism. Who were the "founders" of psychology? Historians acknowledge that three German scientists—Ernst Weber, Gustav Fechner, and Hermann von Helmholtz—were the first to systematically study behavior and mental processes. But it is Wilhelm Wundt (1832–1920) who is generally thought of as the "father" of psychology. Wundt's vision for the new discipline included studies of social and cultural influences on human thought (Benjafield, 1996).

Wundt established a psychological laboratory at the University of Leipzig in Germany in 1879, an event considered to mark the birth of psychology as a formal academic discipline. Using a method called *introspection,* Wundt and his associates studied the perception of a variety of visual, tactile, and auditory stimuli, including the rhythm patterns produced by metronomes set at different speeds. (A *metronome* is a mechanical or electronic device that emits ticking sounds that represent musical rhythms such as 2/4 and 4/4 time at varying tempos.) Introspection as a research method involves looking inward to examine one's own conscious experience and then reporting that experience.

Wundt's most famous student, Englishman Edward Bradford Titchener (1867–1927), took the new field to the United States, where he set up a psychological laboratory

▲ Even though these skydivers share the same sensations—the feeling of falling, the rush of air on their faces as they fall, and the sudden lurch of their parachutes opening—their reported introspections of the experience would probably differ.

structuralism The first formal school of thought in psychology, aimed at analyzing the basic elements, or structure, of conscious mental experience.

functionalism An early school of psychology that was concerned with how humans and animals use mental processes in adapting to their environment.

▲ During the 1880s, Christine Ladd-Franklin became one of the first women to complete a doctoral degree in psychology, although Johns Hopkins University refused to officially grant her the degree until the mid-1920s.
Source: Archives of the History of American Psychology—The University of Akron.

at Cornell University. He gave the name **structuralism** to this first formal school of thought in psychology, which aimed at analyzing the basic elements, or the structure, of conscious mental experience. Like Wundt before him, Titchener thought that consciousness could be reduced to its basic elements, just as water (H_2O) can be broken down into its constituent elements—hydrogen (H) and oxygen (O). For Wundt, pure sensations—such as sweetness, coldness, or redness—were the basic elements of consciousness. And these pure sensations, he believed, combined to form perceptions.

The work of both Wundt and Titchener was criticized for its primary method, introspection. Introspection is not objective, even though it involves observation, measurement, and experimentation. When different introspectionists were exposed to the same stimulus, such as the click of a metronome, they frequently reported different experiences. Therefore, structuralism was not in favor for long. Later schools of thought in psychology were established, partly as a reaction against structuralism, which did not survive after the death of its most ardent spokesperson, Titchener. Nevertheless, the structuralists were responsible for establishing psychology as a science through their insistence that psychological processes could be measured and studied using methods similar to those employed by scientists in other fields.

As structuralism began losing its influence in the United States in the early 20th century, a new school of psychology called functionalism was taking shape. **Functionalism** was concerned not with the structure of consciousness but with how mental processes function—that is, how humans and animals use mental processes in adapting to their environment. The influential work of Charles Darwin (1809–1882), especially his ideas about evolution and the continuity of species, was largely responsible for an increasing use of animals in psychological experiments. Even though Darwin, who was British, contributed important seeds of thought that helped give birth to the new school of psychology, functionalism was primarily American in character and spirit.

The famous American psychologist William James (1842–1910) was an advocate of functionalism, even though he did much of his writing before this school of psychology emerged. James's best-known work is his highly regarded and frequently quoted textbook *Principles of Psychology,* published more than a century ago (1890). James taught that mental processes are fluid and have continuity, rather than the rigid, or fixed, structure that the structuralists suggested. James spoke of the "stream of consciousness," which, he said, functions to help humans adapt to their environment.

How did functionalism change psychology? Functionalism broadened the scope of psychology to include the study of behavior as well as mental processes. It also allowed the study of children, animals, and the mentally impaired, groups that could not be studied by the structuralists because they could not be trained to use introspection. Functionalism also focused on an applied, more practical use of psychology by encouraging the study of educational practices, individual differences, and adaptation in the workplace (industrial psychology).

The Changing Face of Psychology. As we noted earlier, during the early days of psychology, most people believed that academic and scientific pursuits were the exclusive province of white males. However, there were a number of women and minority group members who refused to allow convention to stand in the way of their quest for a better understanding of behavior and mental processes. They broke barriers that paved the way for later scholars and, at the same time, made important contributions to the field. Here are a few examples:

■ *Christine Ladd-Franklin (1847–1930):* completed Ph.D. requirements at Johns Hopkins University in the mid-1880s but had to wait 40 years to receive her degree; formulated evolutionary theory of color vision.

■ *Mary Whiton Calkins (1863–1930):* completed Ph.D. requirements at Harvard in 1895, but the university refused to grant doctorate to a woman (Dewsbury, 2000);

established psychology laboratory at Wellesley College; developed methods for studying memory; first female president of the American Psychological Association in 1905.

- *Margaret Floy Washburn (1871–1939):* received a Ph.D. in psychology from Cornell University; taught at Vassar College (Dewsbury, 2000); wrote influential books on animal behavior and mental imagery.
- *Francis Cecil Sumner (1895–1954):* first African American to earn a Ph.D. in psychology; translated more than 3,000 research articles from German, French, and Spanish; chaired psychology department at Howard University; known as the "father" of African American psychology.
- *Albert Sidney Beckham (1897–1964):* established the first psychological laboratory at an African American institution of higher education (Howard University); studied relationship of intelligence to occupational success.
- *Kenneth Clark (1914–2005) and Mamie Phipps Clark (1917–1983):* conducted studies of detrimental effects of racial segregation on African American children's self-esteem that were cited in Supreme Court ruling that declared racial segregation in U.S. schools unconstitutional (Benjamin & Crouse, 2002; Lal, 2002).
- *George Sánchez (1906–1972):* studied cultural and linguistic bias in intelligence testing during the 1930s (Sánchez, 1932, 1934).

Today, more women than men obtain degrees in psychology, and minority group representation is growing (NCES, 2006, 2008). However, there continues to be a gap between the proportion of minorities in the U.S. population and their representation among professional psychologists (APA, 2008). Consequently, the APA and other organizations have established programs to encourage minority enrollment in graduate programs in psychology.

▲ Kenneth (1914–2005) and Mamie (1917–1983) Clark's research examining self-esteem in African American children was cited in the 1954 U.S. Supreme Court decision *Brown v. Board of Education* that led to the desegregation of public schools in the United States.

Schools of Thought in Psychology ▶

1.5 What are the major schools of thought in psychology?

Why don't we hear about structuralism and functionalism today? In the early 20th century, the debate between the two points of view sparked a veritable explosion of theoretical discussion and research examining psychological processes. The foundations of the major schools of thought in the field were established during that period and continue to be influential today.

Behaviorism. Psychologist John B. Watson (1878–1958) looked at the study of psychology as defined by the structuralists and functionalists and disliked virtually everything he saw. In his article "Psychology as the Behaviorist Views It" (1913), Watson proposed a radically new approach to psychology, one that rejected the subjectivity of both structuralism and functionalism. This new school redefined psychology as the "science of behavior." Termed **behaviorism** by Watson, this school of psychology confines itself to the study of behavior because behavior is observable and measurable and, therefore, objective and scientific. Behaviorism also emphasizes that behavior is determined primarily by factors in the environment.

Behaviorism was the most influential school of thought in American psychology until the 1960s. It remains a major force in modern psychology, in large part because of the profound influence of B. F. Skinner (1904–1990). Skinner agreed with Watson that concepts such as mind, consciousness, and feelings are neither objective nor measurable and, therefore, not appropriate subject matter for psychology. Furthermore, Skinner argued that these concepts are not needed to explain behavior. One can explain behavior, he claimed, by analyzing the conditions that are present before a behavior occurs and then analyzing the consequences that follow the behavior.

Skinner's research on operant conditioning emphasized the importance of reinforcement in learning and in shaping and maintaining behavior. He maintained that any behavior that is reinforced (followed by pleasant or rewarding consequences) is

behaviorism The school of psychology that views observable, measurable behavior as the appropriate subject matter for psychology and emphasizes the key role of environment as a determinant of behavior.

more likely to be performed again. Skinner's work has had a powerful influence on modern psychology. You will read more about operant conditioning in Chapter 5.

Psychoanalysis. Sigmund Freud (1856–1939), whose work you will study in Chapter 11, developed a theory of human behavior based largely on case studies of his patients. Freud's theory, **psychoanalysis**, maintains that human mental life is like an iceberg. The smallest, visible part of the iceberg represents the conscious mental experience of the individual. But underwater, hidden from view, floats a vast store of unconscious impulses, wishes, and desires. Freud insisted that individuals do not consciously control their thoughts, feelings, and behavior; these are instead determined by unconscious forces.

The overriding importance that Freud placed on sexual and aggressive impulses caused much controversy both inside and outside the field of psychology. The most notable of Freud's famous students—Carl Jung, Alfred Adler, and Karen Horney—broke away from their mentor and developed their own theories of personality. These three and their followers are often collectively referred to as *neo-Freudians*. Thus, the psychoanalytic approach continues to be influential, albeit in a form that has been modified considerably over the past several decades by the neo-Freudians.

Humanistic Psychology. Humanistic psychologists reject with equal vigor (1) the behaviorist view that behavior is determined by factors in the environment and (2) the view of the psychoanalytic approach stating that human behavior is determined primarily by unconscious forces. **Humanistic psychology** focuses on the uniqueness of human beings and their capacity for choice, growth, and psychological health.

Abraham Maslow and other early humanists, such as Carl Rogers (1902–1987), pointed out that Freud based his theory primarily on data from his disturbed patients. By contrast, the humanists emphasize a much more positive view of human nature. They maintain that people are innately good and that they possess free will. The humanists believe that people are capable of making conscious, rational choices, which can lead to personal growth and psychological health. As you will learn in Chapter 9, Maslow proposed a theory of motivation that consists of a hierarchy of needs. He considered the need for self-actualization (developing to one's fullest potential) to be the highest need on the hierarchy. Rogers developed what he called *client-centered therapy,* an approach in which the client, or patient, directs a discussion focused on his or her own view of a problem rather than on the therapist's analysis. Rogers and other humanists also popularized group therapy (more on humanistic therapies in Chapter 13).

The humanistic perspective continues to be important in research examining human motivation and in the practice of psychotherapy via a relatively new approach known as **positive psychology**. Martin Seligman (2011), the best known proponent of this approach, defines positive psychology as the scientific study of psychological characteristics, such as optimism, that enable individuals and communities to thrive in the face of adversity. He argues that these characteristics help to protect individuals from traumatic experiences that behaviorists and psychoanalysts suggest almost always doom them to emotional maladjustment. You will read more about positive psychology in Chapter 9.

Cognitive Psychology. Cognitive psychology grew and developed partly in response to strict behaviorism, especially in the United States (Robins, Gosling, & Craik, 1999). **Cognitive psychology** sees humans not as passive recipients who are pushed and pulled by environmental forces but as active participants who seek out experiences, who alter and shape those experiences, and who use mental processes to transform information in the course of their own cognitive development. It studies mental processes such as memory, problem solving, reasoning, decision making, perception, language, and other forms of cognition. Historically, modern cognitive psychology is derived from two streams of thought: one that began with a small group of German

---

psychoanalysis (SY-ko-ah-NAL-ih-sis) The term Freud used for both his theory of personality and his therapy for the treatment of psychological disorders; the unconscious is the primary focus of psychoanalytic theory.

humanistic psychology The school of psychology that focuses on the uniqueness of human beings and their capacity for choice, growth, and psychological health.

positive psychology The scientific study of psychological characteristics that enable individuals and communities to thrive in the face of adversity.

cognitive psychology The school of psychology that sees humans as active participants in their environment; studies mental processes such as memory, problem solving, reasoning, decision making, perception, language, and other forms of cognition.

scientists studying human perception in the early 20th century and another that grew up alongside the emerging field of computer science in the second half of the century.

Gestalt psychology made its appearance in Germany in 1912. The Gestalt psychologists, notably Max Wertheimer, Kurt Koffka, and Wolfgang Köhler, emphasized that individuals perceive objects and patterns as whole units and that the perceived whole is more than the sum of its parts. The German word *Gestalt* roughly means "whole, form, or pattern."

To support the Gestalt theory, Wertheimer, the leader of the Gestalt psychologists, performed his famous experiment demonstrating the *phi phenomenon*. In this experiment, two lightbulbs are placed a short distance apart in a dark room. The first light is flashed on and then turned off just as the second light is flashed on. As this pattern of flashing the lights on and off continues, an observer sees what appears to be a single light moving back and forth from one position to another. Here, said the Gestaltists, is proof that people perceive wholes or patterns rather than collections of separate sensations.

When the Nazis came to power in Germany in the 1930s, the Gestalt school disbanded, and its most prominent members immigrated to the United States. Today, the fundamental concept underlying Gestalt psychology—that the mind *interprets* experiences in predictable ways rather than simply reacts to them—is central to cognitive psychologists' ideas about learning, memory, problem solving, and even psychotherapy.

The advent of the computer provided cognitive psychologists with a new way to conceptualize mental structures and processes, known as **information-processing theory**. According to this view, the brain processes information in sequential steps, in much the same way as a computer does serial processing—that is, one step at a time. But as modern technology has changed computers and computer programs, cognitive psychologists have changed their models. For example, many contemporary researchers are examining the human memory system's capacity for *parallel processing*, the management of multiple bits of information at once, a type of information processing that is commonly used in today's computers (Bajic & Rickard, 2009; Sung, 2008).

Over the past 100 years or so, cognitive psychologists have carried out studies that have greatly increased our knowledge of the human memory system and the mental processes involved in problem solving. Moreover, the principles discovered in these experiments have been used to explain and study all kinds of psychological variables—from gender role development to individual differences in intelligence. As a result, cognitive psychology is currently thought by many psychologists to be the most prominent school of psychological thought (Robins et al., 1999). As a result, you will encounter many references to cognitive approaches to a variety of issues in subsequent chapters.

Evolutionary Psychology. Why do you think all babies form attachments to their primary caregivers? This is the kind of question that interests *evolutionary psychologists*. **Evolutionary psychology** focuses on how the human behaviors required for survival have adapted in the face of environmental pressures over the long course of evolution (Archer, 1996). As such, evolutionary psychology draws heavily on Charles Darwin's theory of natural selection. Darwin's theory asserts that individual members of a given species who possess characteristics that help them survive are the most likely to pass on the genes underlying those characteristics to subsequent generations. As a result, traits that support individual survival become universal in the species; that is, every individual member of the species has them. For example, every human being possesses the capacity to acquire language. Natural selection would explain this universality as the result of the survival advantage conferred on humans by having an efficient means of communicating information from one person to another.

Gestalt psychology The school of psychology that emphasizes that individuals perceive objects and patterns as whole units and that the perceived whole is more than the sum of its parts.

information-processing theory An approach to the study of mental structures and processes that uses the computer as a model for human thinking.

evolutionary psychology The school of psychology that studies how human behaviors required for survival have adapted in the face of environmental pressures over the long course of evolution.

▲ Is this person having a bad day? The perceptual processes described by the Gestalt psychologists are observable in everyday life. We often put frustrating events—such as getting up late and then having a flat tire—together to form a "whole" concept, such as "I'm having a bad day."

▲ According to evolutionary psychology, natural selection has provided infants and caregivers with a built-in genetic predisposition to form an emotional attachment to one another because such bonds help infants survive.

biological psychology The school of psychology that looks for links between specific behaviors and equally specific biological processes that often help explain individual differences.

neuroscience An interdisciplinary field that combines the work of psychologists, biologists, biochemists, medical researchers, and others in the study of the structure and function of the nervous system.

sociocultural approach The view that social and cultural factors may be just as powerful as evolutionary and physiological factors in affecting behavior and mental processing and that these factors must be understood when interpreting the behavior of others.

Evolutionary psychology has been called, simply, a combination of evolutionary biology and cognitive psychology (Barker, 2006; Evans & Zarate, 2000). Two widely recognized proponents of evolutionary psychology, Leda Cosmides and John Tooby, hold that this perspective combines the forces of evolutionary biology, anthropology, cognitive psychology, and neuroscience. They explain that an evolutionary perspective can be applied to any topic within the field of psychology (Tooby & Cosmides, 2005). For example, one of the most influential evolutionary psychologists, David Buss, and his colleagues have conducted a number of fascinating studies examining men's and women's patterns of behavior in romantic relationships (Buss, 1999, 2000a, 2000b, 2001, 2008). You'll read more about Buss's work and that of his critics in Chapter 9.

Biological (Physiological) Psychology. Sometimes students are confused about the difference between evolutionary psychology and **biological psychology** (also referred to as *physiological psychology*). After all, many think, isn't evolution "biological" in nature? Yes, it is, but evolutionary psychology provides explanations of how certain biologically based behaviors came to be common in an entire species. Consequently, it focuses on *universals,* traits that exist in every member of a species. For instance, language is a human universal.

By contrast, biological psychologists look for links between specific behaviors and particular biological factors that often help explain *individual differences.* They study the structures of the brain and central nervous system, the functioning of neurons, the delicate balance of neurotransmitters and hormones, and the effects of heredity to look for links between these biological factors and behavior. For example, the number of ear infections children have in the first year of life (a *biological* individual difference) is correlated with learning disabilities in the elementary school years (a *behavioral* individual difference) (Golz et al., 2005).

Many biological psychologists work under the umbrella of an interdisciplinary field known as **neuroscience**. Neuroscience combines the work of psychologists, biologists, biochemists, medical researchers, and others in the study of the structure and function of the nervous system. Important findings in psychology have resulted from this work. For example, researchers have learned that defects in nerve cell membranes interfere with the cells' ability to make use of brain chemicals that help us control body movement (Kurup & Kurup, 2002). These findings shed light on the physiological processes underlying serious neurological disorders such as Parkinson's disease and help pharmacological researchers in their efforts to create more effective medications for these disorders.

The Sociocultural Approach. How do your background and cultural experiences affect your behavior and mental processing? The **sociocultural approach** emphasizes social and cultural influences on human behavior and stresses the importance of understanding those influences when interpreting the behavior of others. For example, several psychologists (e.g., Tweed & Lehman, 2002) have researched philosophical differences between Asian and Western cultures that may help explain cross-national achievement differences. Similarly, researcher Lesley Lambright (2003) explored the cultural characteristics that have helped the Vietnamese survive centuries of warfare. In in-depth interviews with Vietnamese men and women ranging in age from 24 to 68, she learned that Vietnam's multicultural background and the tolerance derived from it, the Vietnamese people's strong family system, and their tendencies toward optimism, patience, and flexibility were instrumental to the resilience of this group. Another factor that emerged from Lambright's study was the tendency of Vietnamese to endorse forgiveness and practicality over vengeful responses to their enemies. A follow-up study that presented Lambright's interview questions in survey form to Vietnamese college students suggested that younger individuals perceive some of these aspects of traditional culture, such as strong family ties, to be changing. Thus, a sociocultural approach to understanding psychological variables such as resilience can shed light both on how culture and cultural changes shape the individual's experiences.

▲ A sociocultural approach helps psychologists explain cross-cultural differences in behavior.

Social and cultural influences on behavior are often studied within the broader context of a *systems perspective*. The primary idea behind the systems approach is that multiple factors work together holistically; that is, their combined, interactive influences on behavior are greater than the sum of the individual factors that make up the system. A good example of the systems approach may be found in a theory proposed by psychologist Gerald Patterson and his colleagues that explains how variables interact to predispose some teenagers to antisocial behavior (Granic & Patterson, 2006). This systems approach argues that poverty (a sociocultural factor), for example, is predictive of juvenile delinquency, but in and of itself, it is insufficient to produce the behavior. As a result, most teens from poor families do not engage in antisocial behavior. However, poverty may function as part of a system of influential variables that includes disengagement from school, association with peers who encourage antisocial behavior, lack of parental supervision, and a host of other variables to increase the risk of antisocial behavior for individual teenagers. At the same time, these variables interact to maintain themselves and, in some cases, to create a multi-generational cycle. For instance, disengagement from school increases the likelihood that teenagers will live in poverty when they reach adulthood. Poverty, in turn, increases the chances that they will have to work long hours, rendering them less able to supervise their own children's behavior, thus putting another generation at risk for antisocial behavior.

Contemporary Psychological Perspectives ▷

The views of modern psychologists are frequently difficult to categorize into traditional schools of thought. Thus, rather than discussing schools of thought, it is often more useful to refer to **psychological perspectives**—general points of view used for explaining people's behavior and thinking, whether normal or abnormal. For example, a psychologist may adopt a behavioral perspective without necessarily agreeing with all of Watson's or Skinner's ideas. What is important is that the psychologist taking such a view will explain behavior in terms of environmental forces.

The major perspectives in psychology today and the kinds of variables each emphasizes in explaining behavior are as follows:

- *Behavioral perspective:* Environmental factors
- *Psychoanalytic perspective:* Emotions, unconscious motivations, early childhood experiences
- *Humanistic perspective:* Subjective experiences, intrinsic motivation to achieve self-actualization
- *Cognitive perspective:* Mental processes
- *Evolutionary perspective:* Inherited traits that enhance adaptability
- *Biological perspective:* Biological structures, processes, heredity
- *Sociocultural perspective:* Social and cultural variables

1.6 What are the seven contemporary psychological perspectives?

psychological perspectives General points of view used for explaining people's behavior and thinking, whether normal or abnormal.

SUMMARIZE IT

Contemporary Perspectives in Psychology

Watch the Video *Episode 1: Basics: Diverse Perspectives* in **MyPsychLab**

PERSPECTIVE	EMPHASIS	EXPLANATION OF A STUDENT'S POOR PERFORMANCE ON EXAMS
Behavioral	The role of environment in shaping and controlling behavior	The student has not been reinforced for getting good grades in the past.
Psychoanalytic	The role of unconscious motivation and early childhood experiences in determining behavior and thought	An unresolved early childhood emotional trauma is distracting the student from his academic work.
Humanistic	The importance of an individual's subjective experience as a key to understanding his or her behavior	Studying for exams does not fit into this student's definition of a meaningful life.
Cognitive	The role of mental processes—perception, thinking, and memory—that underlie behavior	The student does not use effective learning strategies such as the SQ3R method.
Evolutionary	The roles of inherited tendencies that have proven adaptive in humans	The student believes that studying is unimportant because potential mates are more interested in his physical appearance and capacity for social dominance than they are in his grades.
Biological	The role of biological processes and structures, as well as heredity, in explaining behavior	An inappropriate level of emotional arousal (i.e., test anxiety) is preventing this student from performing at an optimal level.
Sociocultural	The roles of social and cultural influences on behavior	The student doesn't want to be perceived as a "nerd," so he studies just enough to avoid failing.

The *Summarize It* lists these perspectives and illustrates how each might explain a student's poor performance on exams.

Psychologists need not limit themselves to just one perspective or approach. Many take an *eclectic position,* choosing a combination of approaches to explain a particular behavior. For example, a psychologist may explain a behavior in terms of both environmental factors and mental processes. A child's unruly behavior in school may be seen as maintained by teacher attention (a behavioral explanation) but as initially caused by an emotional reaction to a family event such as divorce (a psychoanalytic explanation). By adopting multiple perspectives, psychologists are able to devise more complex theories and research studies, resulting in improved treatment strategies. In this way, their theories and studies can more closely mirror the behavior of real people in real situations.

1.7 What specialty areas exist in psychology?

Specialties in Psychology

Stop for a minute and reflect on the definition of psychology: *the study of behavior and mental processes.* Clearly, this definition covers a lot of territory. Thus, it's not surprising that, over the years, psychology has become a highly specialized field. For instance, some psychologists work exclusively with issues related to mental illnesses, such as schizophrenia, that affect a small number of people, while others address questions that concern just about everyone, such as how stress affects health. Likewise, some psychologists focus on research, while others apply the principles of psychology to practical problems. Regardless of specialty area, all psychologists have advanced degrees, typically a Ph.D., in the field. Here is an overview of the major specialty areas in the field today:

- *Clinical psychologists* specialize in the diagnosis and treatment of mental and behavioral disorders, such as anxiety, phobias, and schizophrenia. Some also conduct research in these areas.
- *School psychologists* are clinical psychologists who specialize in the diagnosis and treatment of learning and behavioral problems that interfere with learning.
- *Forensic psychologists* apply their training in clinical psychology to issues involving psychology and law.

- *Counseling psychologists* help people who have adjustment problems (marital, social, or behavioral) that are generally less severe than those handled by clinical psychologists.
- *Physiological psychologists,* also called *biological psychologists* or *neuropsychologists,* study the relationship between physiological processes and behavior.
- *Experimental psychologists* conduct experiments in most areas of psychology—learning, memory, sensation, perception, motivation, emotion, and others.
- *Developmental psychologists* study how people grow, develop, and change throughout the life span.
- *Educational psychologists* specialize in the study of teaching and learning. (*Note:* Do not confuse educational psychology with school psychology. Recall that school psychology is the subfield of clinical psychology that deals with the diagnosis and treatment of learning problems. Educational psychologists study learning in typically developing people. As such, they are trained in theory and research methods but not in the diagnosis and treatment of learning problems.)
- *Social psychologists* investigate how the individual feels, thinks, and behaves in a social setting—in the presence of others.
- *Industrial/organizational (I/O) psychologists* study the relationships between people and their work environments.

At this point, you may be wondering how the psychological perspectives relate to the various specialty areas. Think of it this way. Each perspective is a theoretical point of view that a psychologist in any of the specialty areas can use to explain a behavior or mental process that is relevant to her field of study. For instance, the behavior explained in the *Summarize It* table on page 14, a student's poor performance on exams, falls within the domain of educational psychology. By contrast, a clinical psychologist might use the various perspectives to explain the symptoms of a psychological disorder such as depression. A counseling psychologist might use them to explain how people cope with major life changes such as divorce. An industrial/organizational psychologist would use them to explain individual differences in job satisfaction. In other words, it's possible to apply any of the perspectives within the boundaries of any of the specialty areas. Moreover, regardless of which perspective they adopt or their area of specialization, all psychologists approach questions about behavior and mental processes with a set of intellectual tools that you can acquire with a little practice.

REMEMBER IT *Check your answers and take additional quizzes in MyPsychLab.com.* ✓ Study and Review on MyPsychLab

1. The major criticism of Wundt's and Titchener's research methods was that they were not _____.
2. American psychologist _____ was an advocate of functionalism.
3. Today, more (women than men/men than women) obtain degrees in psychology.
4. The major emphasis of _____ is the study of the unconscious.
5. John Watson was the founder of _____.
6. The _____ school of thought focuses on mental processes such as memory and problem solving.
7. One finding of interest to psychologists who represent the _____ perspective is the fact that attachment is a universal feature of infant-caregiver relations.
8. The _____ perspective emphasizes the role of social and cultural variables in explanations of individual behavior.
9. The _____ _____ argues that multiple perspectives are necessary to comprehensively explain behavior and mental processes.
10. _____ psychologists specialize in the diagnosis and treatment of psychological disorders.

Thinking about Theories and Research

Now that you have read about the various theoretical perspectives in psychology, you probably want to know which of them are "true" and which are "false." However, psychologists don't think about theories in this way. Instead, they evaluate theories in terms of their usefulness. ◉

Likewise, you may wonder whether learning about research methods is of any practical value to people who do not intend to become professional researchers. As you'll see, knowledge about research methods can prove extremely useful in everyday life.

Evaluating Theories

As you learned earlier in this chapter, useful theories help psychologists achieve the prediction goal by generating testable hypotheses. When assessed against this criterion, the theories of behaviorists and cognitive psychologists appear more useful than those of psychoanalysts and humanists. B. F. Skinner's prediction that reinforcement increases behavior, for example, is far more testable than Maslow's claim that self-actualization is the highest of all human needs.

Useful theories also lead to the development of solutions to real-world problems. For instance, research based on the information-processing model has resulted in the development of practical strategies for improving memory. Similarly, even though psychoanalytic and humanistic theories have been criticized for lacking testability, they have produced a number of beneficial psychotherapies.

Hypotheses and practical applications are important, but a theory that possesses *heuristic value* is useful even if it falls short in these two areas. A theory that has heuristic value stimulates debate among psychologists and motivates both proponents and opponents of the theory to pursue research related to it. In other words, a theory that possesses heuristic value makes people think and spurs their curiosity and creativity.

All of the theories discussed so far earn high marks for their heuristic value. In fact, even if a theory has limited empirical support, professors who teach introductory psychology are justified in including it in the course if it has been of heuristic importance in the field. This is why we still teach about the structuralists and functionalists and why we continue to rate Freud's theory as one of the most important in the field. Moreover, such theories usually affect students in the same way that they affect psychologists—that is, learning about them stimulates students' thinking about behavior and mental processes. Thus, introducing these theories helps professors achieve one of their most important instructional goals, that of motivating students to think critically.

Evaluating Research

Another important goal of most professors who teach introductory psychology is to equip students with the intellectual tools needed to evaluate claims based on psychological research. Living in the Information Age, we are bombarded with statistics and claims of all types every day. For instance, not long ago, the news media carried a number of reports warning that working the night shift increases an employee's risk of developing heart problems. These warnings were based, reporters said, on a scientific analysis of 34 studies that involved more than two million workers across a number of countries. The study was published in the prestigious *British Medical Journal* (Vyas et al., 2012) How can a person who is not an expert on the subject in question evaluate claims such as these? ✷

The thinking strategies used by psychologists and other scientists can help us sift through this kind of information. **Critical thinking,** the foundation of the scientific method, is the process of objectively evaluating claims, propositions, and conclusions

---

◉ **Watch** the Video *Episode 2: Big Picture: How to Answer Psychological Questions* in **MyPsychLab**

1.8 How do psychologists evaluate theories?

1.9 How will critical thinking help you evaluate research?

✷ **Explore** the Concept *How to Be a Critical Thinker* on **MyPsychLab**

critical thinking The process of objectively evaluating claims, propositions, and conclusions to determine whether they follow logically from the evidence presented.

to determine whether they follow logically from the evidence presented. When we engage in critical thinking, we exhibit these characteristics:

- *Independent thinking:* When thinking critically, we do not automatically accept and believe what we read or hear.
- *Suspension of judgment:* Critical thinking requires gathering relevant and up-to-date information on all sides of an issue before taking a position.
- *Willingness to modify or abandon prior judgments:* Critical thinking involves evaluating new evidence, even when it contradicts preexisting beliefs.

Applying the first of these three characteristics to the shift work–heart problems study requires recognizing that the validity of any study is not determined by the authority of its source. Prestigious journals—or psychology textbooks for that matter—shouldn't be regarded as sources of fixed, immutable truths. In fact, learning to question accepted "truths" is important to the scientific method itself.

The second and third characteristics of critical thinking, suspension of judgment and willingness to change, may require abandoning some old habits. If you are like most people, you respond to media reports about research on the basis of your own personal experiences, a type of evidence scientists call *anecdotal evidence.* For instance, in response to the media report about shift work and heart problems, a person might say, "I don't agree with that study because my father has worked the late shift for years, and he doesn't have heart problems."

Suspension of judgment requires that you postpone either accepting or rejecting the study's findings until you have accumulated more evidence. It might involve determining what, if any, findings other researchers have reported regarding a possible link between shift work and heart problems. Analysis of other relevant studies can help to create a comprehensive picture of what the entire body of research says about the issue. Ultimately, when enough evidence has been gathered, a critical thinker must be willing to abandon preconceived notions and prior beliefs that conflict with it.

The quality of the evidence is just as important as the quantity. Thus, a critical thinker would evaluate the findings of the shift work–heart problems study by considering the methods used to obtain them. Did the researchers randomly assign employees to experimental and control groups who worked day and night shifts and then assess whether experimental and control employees differed in the frequency of heart problems later? If so, then the study was an experiment, and media claims that shift work leads to heart problems might be justified. Conversely, if the researchers simply compared rates of heart problems in day- and night-shift employees, then claims of a causal relationship between the two variables would not be justified. Instead, the appropriate response would be to look for underlying variables, such as how day- and night-shift workers differ in eating and exercise habits, that might explain the connection. In fact, the research cited in these reports was correlational in nature, so the strong causal claims implied by many media accounts of the study were inappropriate.

Watch the Video *Episode 2: Thinking Like a Psychologist: Thinking Critically* in **MyPsychLab**

REMEMBER IT   *Check your answers and take additional quizzes in MyPsychLab.com.*   **Study** and **Review** on **MyPsychLab**

1. A theory that generates debate among psychologists is said to have _____ value.

2. Useful theories provide researchers with _____ hypotheses.

3. Willingness to change one's prior beliefs is a component of _____ about research.

4. Critical thinking about media reports of research requires some familiarity with _____.

descriptive research methods Research methods that yield descriptions of behavior.

1.10 What are the pros and cons of observational and case studies?

naturalistic observation A descriptive research method in which researchers observe and record behavior in its natural setting, without attempting to influence or control it.

laboratory observation A descriptive research method in which behavior is studied in a laboratory setting.

case study A descriptive research method in which a single individual or a small number of persons are studied in great depth.

👁 Watch the Video *Episode 1: In The Real World: Speed Dating* in **MyPsychLab**

▲ Naturalistic observation plays an important role in studies of animal behavior.

Descriptive Research Methods

The goals of psychological research are often accomplished in stages. In the early stages of research, **descriptive research methods** are usually the most appropriate. Descriptive research methods yield descriptions of behavior and include naturalistic and laboratory observation, the case study, and the survey.

Observational and Case Studies

Have you ever sat in an airport or shopping mall and simply watched what people were doing? Such an activity is quite similar to **naturalistic observation**, a descriptive research method in which researchers observe and record behavior in its natural setting, without attempting to influence or control it. The major advantage of naturalistic observation is the opportunity to study behavior in normal settings, where it occurs more naturally and spontaneously than it does under artificial and contrived laboratory conditions. Sometimes, naturalistic observation is the only feasible way to study behavior—for example, there is no other way to study how people typically react during disasters such as earthquakes and fires.

Naturalistic observation has its limitations, however. Researchers must wait for events to occur; they cannot speed up or slow down the process. And because they have no control over the situation, researchers cannot reach conclusions about cause–effect relationships. Another potential problem with naturalistic observation is *observer bias,* which is a distortion in researchers' observations. Observer bias can result when researchers' expectations about a situation cause them to see what they expect to see or to make incorrect inferences about what they observe. Suppose, for example, that you're a psychologist studying aggression in preschool classrooms. You have decided to count every time a child hits or pushes another child as an aggressive act. Your decision to label this type of physical contact between children as "aggressive" may cause you to notice more such acts and label them as "aggressive" than you would if you were casually watching a group of children play. The effects of observer bias can be reduced substantially when two or more independent observers view the same behavior. If you and another observer independently count, say, 23 aggressive acts in an hour of free play, the findings are considered unbiased. If you see 30 such acts and the other observer records only 15, some kind of bias is at work. In such situations, observers usually clarify the criteria for classifying behavior and repeat the observations. Using video can also help eliminate observer bias because behavior can be reviewed several times prior to making classification decisions.

Another method of studying behavior involves observation that takes place not in its natural setting but in a laboratory. Researchers using **laboratory observation** can exert more control and use more precise equipment to measure responses. Much of what is known about attraction, for example, has been learned through laboratory observation. However, like other research methods, laboratory observation has limitations. For one, laboratory behavior may not accurately reflect real-world behavior. For example, in attraction studies, some of the behavior people display in laboratory simulations of dating may not occur in real-world dating situations. As a result, conclusions based on laboratory findings may not generalize beyond the walls of the laboratory itself. Another disadvantage is that building, staffing, equipping, and maintaining research laboratories can be expensive. 👁

In a **case study**, a single individual or a small number of persons are studied in great depth, usually over an extended period of time. A case study involves the use of observations, interviews, and sometimes psychological testing. Like observational studies, case studies are exploratory in nature. Their purpose is to provide a detailed description of some behavior or disorder. This method is particularly appropriate for studying people who have uncommon psychological or physiological disorders or brain injuries. Many case studies are written about patients being treated for such problems. In some instances, the results of detailed case studies have provided the foundation for psychological theories. In particular, the theory of Sigmund Freud was based primarily on case studies of his patients.

Although the case study has proven useful in advancing knowledge in several areas of psychology, it has certain limitations. Researchers cannot establish the cause of behavior observed in a case study, and observer bias is a potential problem. Moreover, because so few individuals are studied, researchers do not know how applicable, or generalizable, their findings may be to larger groups or to different cultures.

Survey Research ▶

1.11 How do researchers design useful surveys?

Have you ever been questioned about your voting behavior or about the kind of toothpaste you prefer? If you have, chances are that you were a participant in another kind of research study. The **survey** is a descriptive research method in which researchers use interviews and/or questionnaires to gather information about the attitudes, beliefs, experiences, or behaviors of a group of people. The results of carefully conducted surveys have provided valuable information about drug use, sexual behavior, and the incidence of various mental disorders.

survey A descriptive research method in which researchers use interviews and/or questionnaires to gather information about the attitudes, beliefs, experiences, or behaviors of a group of people.

Researchers in psychology rarely conduct studies using all members of a group. For example, researchers interested in studying the sexual behavior of American women do not survey every woman in the United States. (Imagine trying to interview about 140 million people!) Instead of studying the whole **population** (the entire group of interest to researchers, to which they wish to apply their findings), researchers select a sample for study. A **sample** is a part of a population that is studied to reach conclusions about the entire population.

population The entire group of interest to researchers to which they wish to generalize their findings; the group from which a sample is selected.

Perhaps you have seen a carton of ice cream that contains three separate flavors—chocolate, strawberry, and vanilla—packed side by side. To properly sample the carton, you would need a small amount of ice cream containing all three flavors in the same proportions as in the whole carton—a representative sample. A **representative sample** mirrors the population of interest—that is, it includes important subgroups in the same proportions as they are found in that population. A *biased sample,* on the other hand, does not adequately reflect the larger population.

sample A part of a population that is studied to reach conclusions about the entire population.

representative sample A sample that mirrors the population of interest; it includes important subgroups in the same proportions as they are found in that population.

The best method for obtaining a representative sample is to select a *random sample* from a list of all members of the population of interest. Individuals are selected in such a way that every member of the larger population has an equal chance of being included in the sample. Using random samples, polling organizations can accurately represent the views of the American public with responses from as few as 1,000 people (O'Brien, 1996).

It might seem that simply interviewing people with a standard set of questions would be the best way to gather survey data. In reality, the truthfulness of participants' responses can be affected by characteristics of the interviewers, such as their gender, age, race, ethnicity, religion, and social class. Thus, to use interviews effectively, survey researchers must select interviewers who have personal characteristics that are appropriate for the intended respondents.

Questionnaires can be completed more quickly and less expensively than interviews, especially when respondents can fill them out in their homes or online. The Internet offers psychologists a fast and inexpensive way of soliciting participants and collecting questionnaire data, and Internet surveys often generate large numbers of responses (Azar, 2000). For example, an Internet survey posted by researchers who wanted to collect data about suicidal feelings attracted more than 38,000 respondents from all over the world (Mathy, 2002). However, researchers who use Web-based surveys must be cautious about generalizing the results of their studies because respondents represent only the population of Internet users who choose to participate, not the general population or even the entire population of Internet users. Moreover, they must take steps to ensure that a respondent can participate in the study only once (Gosling et al., 2004).

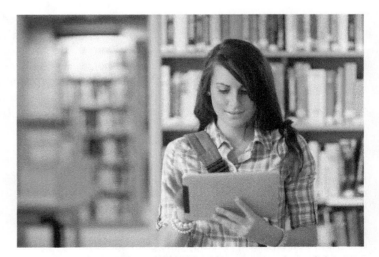

▲ Internet surveys allow psychologists to gather lots of data from large numbers of respondents in a very short period of time. But how representative of the general population are people who respond to Internet surveys? How representative are they of Internet users in general? Questions such as these remain to be answered.

If conducted properly, surveys can provide highly accurate information. They can also track changes in attitudes or behavior over time. For example, Johnston and others (Johnston, O'Malley, Bachman, & Schulenberg, 2010) have tracked drug use among high school students since 1975. However, large-scale surveys can be costly and time consuming. Another important limitation of survey research is that respondents may provide inaccurate information. False information can result from a faulty memory or a desire to please the interviewer. Respondents may try to present themselves in a good light (a phenomenon called the *social desirability response*), or they may even deliberately mislead the interviewer. Finally, when respondents answer questions about sensitive subjects, such as sexual behavior, they are often less candid in face-to-face interviews than in self-administered or computerized questionnaires (Tourangeau, Smith, & Rasinski, 1997).

1.12 What are the strengths and weaknesses of the correlational method?

correlational method A research method used to establish the degree of relationship (correlation) between two characteristics, events, or behaviors.

The Correlational Method

Perhaps the most powerful descriptive method available to psychologists is the **correlational method**, a method used to establish the degree of relationship (correlation) between two characteristics, events, or behaviors. A group is selected for study, and the variables of interest are measured for each participant. For example, one researcher studied the relationship between attainment of a college degree and subsequent income. Another might look for a correlation between the amount of time students devote to studying and their grade point averages.

Correlations are not just important to scientists; they are also common in our everyday thinking. For example, what is the relationship between the price of a new car and the social status you gain from owning it? Isn't it true that as price goes up, status goes up as well? And isn't status one of the variables that many people take into account when buying a new car? As this example illustrates, correlations are part of our everyday lives, and we often use them in decision making.

When scientists study correlations, they apply a statistical formula to data representing two or more variables to obtain a correlation coefficient. A **correlation coefficient** is a numerical value that indicates the strength and direction of the relationship between two variables. A correlation coefficient ranges from +1.00 (a perfect positive correlation) to .00 (no relationship) to −1.00 (a perfect negative correlation). The number in a correlation coefficient indicates the relative strength of the relationship between two variables—the higher the number, the stronger the relationship. Therefore, a correlation of −.85 is stronger than a correlation of +.64.

correlation coefficient A numerical value that indicates the strength and direction of the relationship between two variables; ranges from +1.00 (a perfect positive correlation) to −1.00 (a perfect negative correlation).

The sign of a correlation coefficient (+ or −) indicates whether the two variables vary in the same or opposite directions. A positive correlation indicates that two variables vary in the same direction, like the price of a car and its associated social status. As another example, there is a positive though weak correlation between stress and illness. When stress increases, illness is likely to increase; when stress decreases, illness tends to decrease (see Figure 1.2).

FIGURE 1.2 Positive and Negative Correlations
Here are two graphs showing positive and negative correlations. (a) When positively correlated scores on two variables are graphed, the points fall along a line that rises from left to right. This graph might represent two variables such as amount of time spent studying and grades on an exam. As study time goes up, exam grades go up as well. (b) When negatively correlated scores on two variables are graphed, the points follow a line that declines from left to right. This graph might represent two variables such as amount of time spent watching television and grades on an exam. As TV time goes up, grades go down.

(a) Positive Correlation, +.50

(b) Negative Correlation, −.94

A negative correlation means that an increase in the value of one variable is associated with a decrease in the value of the other variable. For example, as mileage accumulates on a car's odometer, the less reliable the car becomes. And there is a negative correlation between the number of cigarettes people smoke and the number of years they can expect to live. (For more information about correlation coefficients, see the Appendix.)

Does the fact that there is a correlation between two variables indicate that one variable causes the other? No. For instance, when two variables such as stress and illness are correlated, we cannot conclude that stress makes people sick. It might be that illness causes stress, or that a third factor such as poverty or poor general health causes people to be more susceptible to both illness and stress, as shown in Figure 1.3 and illustrated in the *Try It* on page 22.

So, you might be thinking, if a researcher can't draw cause–effect conclusions, why do correlational studies? There are four reasons. First, correlations are quite useful for making predictions. One prediction of this type with which you may be familiar involves the use of a college applicant's high school class rank as a factor in admissions decisions. In general, the positive correlation between high school class rank and success in college means that the higher an applicant's rank in high school, the more likely he or she is to succeed in college. Likewise, as you will learn from the *Explain It* on page 22, several correlations determine whether a particular individual gets a credit card or loan.

Correlational studies are also useful when it is impossible, for ethical reasons, to study variables of interest using more direct methods. Scientists can't ethically ask pregnant women to drink alcohol just so they can find out whether it causes birth defects. The only option available in such cases is the correlational method. Researchers have to ask mothers about their drinking habits and note any association with birth defects in their babies. Knowing the correlation between prenatal alcohol consumption and the incidence of birth defects helps scientists make predictions about what may happen when pregnant women consume alcohol.

Another reason for using the correlational method is that many variables of interest to psychologists cannot be manipulated. Everyone wants to know whether biological sex (whether one is male or female) causes the differences we observe in men's and women's behavior. But we can't assign individuals to become male or female as we might ask them to take a drug or a placebo. Again, the only option is to study the correlations between biological sex and particular variables of interest, such as cognitive functioning and personality.

Finally, correlational studies can often be done fairly quickly. By contrast, as you will learn in the section that follows, *experiments* can be time consuming and complex.

Two variables—stress and illness—are correlated.

Stress	could lead to →	Illness
Illness	could lead to →	Stress
Stress	← The two variables could have mutual effects.	Illness

A third factor could underlie both stress and illness.

| Stress | Poverty | Illness |

FIGURE 1.3 Correlation Does Not Prove Causation
A correlation between two variables does not prove that a cause–effect relationship exists between them. There is a correlation between stress and illness, but that does not mean that stress necessarily causes illness. Both stress and illness may result from another factor, such as poverty or poor general health.

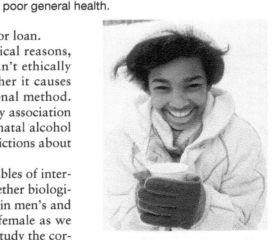

▲ Temperature is correlated with snow-cone sales. As temperature increases, so does the number of snow cones sold. Is this a positive or a negative correlation? What about the corresponding correlation between temperature and coffee sales? Is it positive or negative?

REMEMBER IT   *Check your answers and take additional quizzes in MyPsychLab.com.*   ✓●—Study and Review on MyPsychLab

1. One problem with the _____ is that it often does not generalize to individuals other than the subject of the study.

2. In order to be useful, a survey must be based on a _____ sample.

3. A(n) _____ is a number describing the strength and direction of a relationship between two variables.

4. In positive correlations, two variables move in _____.

5. In negative correlations, two variables move in _____.

6. The closer a correlation coefficient is to +1.0 or −1.0, the _____ the relationship between two variables.

TRY IT

What Is the *Third Variable Problem*?

The *third variable problem* occurs when one variable is associated with another because both are linked to a third, unmeasured variable. See if you can determine the unmeasured variable that underlies these correlations.

1. The more churches a town has, the more bars it has.
2. The more mileage a car has accumulated, the less reliable it is.
3. The larger a child's shoe size, the higher his raw score on an intelligence test (i.e., the number of questions he answers correctly).

Answers:

1. The third variable is population. The larger the town, the more establishments of all kinds there are in it.
2. Many answers are possible, but the best one is that a car's parts wear out as it accumulates mileage. So, the third variable is wear and tear on the car's parts.
3. The third variable is age. The older children are, the more questions they answer correctly on intelligence tests.

EXPLAIN IT

What Is a Credit Score?

Have you seen television commercials or pop-up ads that ask, "What's your credit score?" If so, you probably inferred from the ad itself that credit scores are connected in some way to your financial well-being. That's true, but do you really know what a credit score is? You can use what you've just learned about correlations to get a better understanding of what credit scores are and how they are determined.

A credit score is a numerical summary of an individual's financial history that predicts the likelihood that he or she will have a delinquency in the future. A delinquency is failure to pay back a loan, declaration of bankruptcy, or any instance in which a person makes a payment on a loan or credit card more than 90 days after the original due date. The higher a person's credit score, the lower the likelihood of a future delinquency (Equifax, 2006). Thus, the connection between credit scores and delinquencies is a correlation, one that allows financial institutions to make predictions about the likelihood that an applicant will fulfill her financial obligations. Can you determine the nature (positive or negative) of the correlation between credit scores and delinquency risk? The graph in Figure 1.4 may help you visualize it.

If you compare this graph to the scatterplots in Figure 1.2 on page 20, you will see that the correlation between credit scores and delinquencies is negative. In other words, the higher your score, the lower your chances of a delinquency. Consequently, using credit scores helps lenders minimize the chances that consumers will fail to pay them back.

The credit score itself is based on several correlations. Some of these correlations are positive, and some are negative. See if you can determine which of the three credit score factors below is based on positive correlations and which is derived from negative correlations (see answers following):

- The longer your credit history, the higher your score.
- The more credit cards you have, the lower your score.
- The more reports of late payments there are on your credit report, the lower your score.

If you guessed that a positive correlation is the basis of the first item on the list, and the others are based on negative correlations, you are correct.

Thanks to the association between length of credit history and credit scores, the scores of young adults tend to go up somewhat automatically during the first few years after they get their first loan or credit card. Of course, young consumers don't benefit from this factor unless they also make payments on time, refrain from running up large credit card balances, and resist the temptation to borrow money excessively as they work to build their credit histories. Once young consumers grasp the nature of the correlations that are embodied in credit scores, they can manipulate those correlations in their favor to increase the scores.

Watch on MyPsychLab

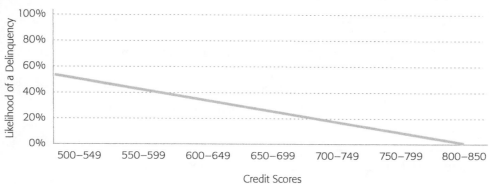

FIGURE 1.4 Predicting Credit Delinquencies

The Experimental Method

What comes to mind when you hear the word *experiment?* Many people use the word to refer to any kind of study. Among psychologists, though, the term *experiment* refers only to one kind of study, the kind in which researchers seek to determine the causes of behavior.

Experiments and Hypothesis Testing ▶

The **experimental method**, or the experiment, is the *only* research method that can be used to identify cause–effect relationships. An experiment is designed to test a **causal hypothesis**, a prediction about a cause–effect relationship between two or more variables. A **variable** is any condition or factor that can be manipulated, controlled, or measured. One variable of interest to you is the grade you will receive in this psychology course. Another variable that probably interests you is the amount of time you will spend studying for this course. Do you suppose that a cause–effect relationship exists between the amount of time students spend studying and the grades they receive? Consider two other variables, alcohol consumption and aggression. Alcohol consumption and aggressive behavior are often observed occurring at the same time. But can we assume that alcohol consumption causes aggressive behavior?

An Example of an Experimental Study. Alan Lang and his colleagues (1975) conducted a classic experiment to determine whether alcohol consumption itself increases aggression or whether the beliefs or expectations about the effects of alcohol cause the aggressive behavior. The participants in the experiment were 96 male college students. Half of the students were given plain tonic to drink; the other half were given a vodka-and-tonic drink in amounts sufficient to raise their blood alcohol level to .10, which is higher than the .08 level that is the legal limit for intoxication in most states. Participants were assigned to four groups:

Group 1: Expected alcohol, received only tonic

Group 2: Expected alcohol, received alcohol mixed with tonic

Group 3: Expected tonic, received alcohol mixed with tonic

Group 4: Expected tonic, received only tonic

After the students had consumed the designated amount, the researchers had an accomplice, who posed as a participant, purposely provoke half the students by belittling their performance on a difficult task. All the students then participated in a learning experiment, in which the same accomplice posed as the learner. The subjects were told to administer an electric shock to the accomplice each time he made a mistake on a decoding task. Each participant was allowed to determine the intensity and duration of the "shock." (Although the students thought they were shocking the accomplice, no shocks were actually delivered.) The researchers measured the aggressiveness of the students in terms of the duration and the intensity of the shocks they chose to deliver.

What were the results of the experiment? As you might imagine, the students who had been provoked gave the accomplice stronger shocks than those who had not been provoked. But the students who drank the alcohol were not necessarily the most aggressive. Regardless of the actual content of their drinks, the participants who thought they were drinking alcohol gave significantly stronger shocks, whether provoked or not, than those who assumed they were drinking only tonic (see Figure 1.5 on page 24). The researchers concluded that it was the *expectation* of drinking alcohol, not the alcohol itself, that caused the students to be more aggressive.

Independent and Dependent Variables. Recall that experiments test hypotheses about cause and effect. Examples of such hypotheses include "Studying causes good grades" and "Taking aspirin causes headaches to go away." Note that each hypothesis

1.13 How do researchers use experiments to test causal hypotheses?

experimental method The only research method that can be used to identify cause–effect relationships between two or more conditions or variables.

causal hypothesis A prediction about a cause–effect relationship between two or more variables.

variable Any condition or factor that can be manipulated, controlled, or measured.

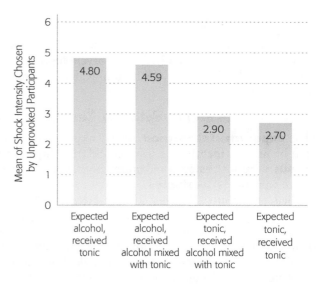

FIGURE 1.5 **The Mean Shock Intensity Chosen by Provoked and Unprovoked Participants**
In the Lang experiment, participants who thought they were drinking alcohol chose to give significantly stronger shocks, whether provoked or not, than those who believed they were drinking only tonic.
Source: Data from Lang et al. (1995)

independent variable In an experiment, a factor or condition that is deliberately manipulated to determine whether it causes any change in another behavior or condition.

involves two variables: One is thought to be the cause (studying, taking aspirin), and the other is thought to be affected by the cause. These two kinds of variables are found in all experiments. An experiment has at least one **independent variable**— a variable that the researcher believes causes a change in some other variable. The researcher deliberately manipulates the independent variable (hypothesized cause) to determine whether it causes any change in another behavior or condition. Sometimes the independent variable is referred to as the *treatment*. The Lang experiment had two independent variables, the alcoholic content of the drink and the expectation of drinking alcohol.

The second type of variable found in all experiments, the one that the hypothesis states is affected by the independent variable, is the **dependent variable**. It is measured at the end of the experiment and is presumed to vary (increase or decrease) as a result of the manipulations of the independent variable(s). Researchers must provide operational definitions of all variables in an experiment—that is, they must specify precisely how the variables will be observed and measured. In the Lang study, the dependent variable—aggression—was operationally defined as the intensity and duration of the "shocks" the participants chose to deliver to the accomplice. ⊙→

dependent variable The factor or condition that is measured at the end of an experiment and is presumed to vary as a result of the manipulations of the independent variable(s).

⊙→ Simulate *Distinguishing Independent and Dependent Variables* on **MyPsychLab**

Experimental and Control Groups. Most experiments are conducted using two or more groups of participants. There must always be at least one **experimental group**—a group of participants who are exposed to the independent variable, or the treatment. The Lang experiment, as noted earlier, used three experimental groups:

experimental group In an experiment, the group that is exposed to an independent variable.

Group 1: Expected alcohol, received only tonic

Group 2: Expected alcohol, received alcohol mixed with tonic

Group 3: Expected tonic, received alcohol mixed with tonic

control group In an experiment, a group similar to the experimental group that is exposed to the same experimental environment but is not given the treatment; used for purposes of comparison.

Most experiments also have a **control group**—a group that is similar to the experimental group and is also measured on the dependent variable at the end of the experiment, for purposes of comparison. The control group is exposed to the same experimental environment as the experimental group but is not given the treatment. The fourth group in the Lang study was exposed to neither of the two independent variables; that is, this group did not expect alcohol and did not receive alcohol. Because this group was similar to the experimental groups and was exposed to the same experimental environment, it served as a control group.

You may be wondering why a control group is necessary. Couldn't an experimenter just expose one group to the independent variable and see if a change occurs? While this approach is sometimes used, it is usually preferable to have a control group because people and their behaviors often change without intervention. Having a control group reveals what kinds of changes happen "naturally" and provides a way of separating the effect of the independent variable from such changes. Suppose you want to find out if a certain medication relieves headaches. You could just find some people with headaches, give them the medication, and then count how many still have headaches an hour later. But some headaches go away without treatment. So if the medication appears to work, it may be only because a number of headaches went away on their own. Having a control group allows you to know whether the medicine relieves headaches in addition to those that disappear without treatment.

Limitations of the Experimental Method ▶

1.14 What are the limitations of the experimental method?

You now know that experiments provide information about cause–effect relationships. But what are their limitations?

Confounding Variables. One of the advantages of the experimental method is that it enables researchers to exercise strict control over the setting. However, the more control they exercise, the more unnatural and contrived the research setting becomes. And the more unnatural the setting becomes, the less applicable findings may be to the real world. However, the most important limitation of the experimental method is that, even when a researcher follows the method's steps scrupulously, **confounding variables**, factors other than the independent variable(s) that are unequal across groups, can prevent her from concluding that the independent variable caused a change in the dependent variable. Three sources of bias are frequently responsible for the presence of confounding variables in an experiment: selection, the placebo effect, and experimenter bias.

confounding variables Factors other than the independent variable(s) that are unequal across groups.

Selection Bias. When participants are assigned to experimental or control groups in such a way that systematic differences among the groups are present at the beginning of the experiment, **selection bias** occurs. If selection bias occurs, then differences at the end of the experiment may not reflect the change in the independent variable but may be due to preexisting differences in the groups. To control for selection bias, researchers must use **random assignment**. This process consists of selecting participants by using a chance procedure (such as drawing the names of participants out of a hat) to guarantee that each participant has an equal probability of being assigned to any of the groups as the *Try It* on page 26 illustrates. Random assignment maximizes the likelihood that the groups will be as similar as possible at the beginning of the experiment. If there were preexisting differences in students' levels of aggressiveness in the Lang experiment, random assignment would have spread those differences across all the groups.

selection bias The assignment of participants to experimental or control groups in such a way that systematic differences among the groups are present at the beginning of the experiment.

random assignment The process of selecting participants for experimental and control groups by using a chance procedure to guarantee that each participant has an equal probability of being assigned to any of the groups; a control for selection bias.

Participant and Experimenter Bias. Can participants' expectations influence an experiment's results? Yes. The **placebo effect** occurs when a participant's response to a treatment is due to his or her expectations about the treatment rather than to the treatment itself. Suppose a drug is prescribed for a patient and the patient reports improvement. The improvement could be a direct result of the drug, or it could be a result of the patient's expectation that the drug will work. Studies have shown that sometimes patients' remarkable improvement can be attributed solely to the power of suggestion—the placebo effect.

In drug experiments, the control group is usually given a **placebo**—an inert or harmless substance such as a sugar pill or an injection of saline solution. To control for the placebo effect, researchers do not let participants know whether they are in

placebo effect The phenomenon that occurs in an experiment when a participant's response to a treatment is due to his or her expectations about the treatment rather than to the treatment itself.

placebo (pluh-SEE-bo) An inert or harmless substance given to the control group in an experiment as a control for the placebo effect.

experimenter bias A phenomenon that occurs when a researcher's preconceived notions or expectations in some way influence participants' behavior and/or the researcher's interpretation of experimental results.

the experimental group (receiving the treatment) or in the control group (receiving the placebo). If participants getting the real drug or treatment show a significantly greater improvement than those receiving the placebo, then the improvement can be attributed to the drug rather than to the participants' expectations about the drug's effects. In the Lang experiment, some students who expected alcohol mixed with tonic were given only tonic. The tonic without alcohol functioned as a placebo, allowing researchers to measure the effect of the expectations alone in producing aggression.

Experimenter bias occurs when researchers' preconceived notions or expectations become a self-fulfilling prophecy and cause the researchers to find what they expect to find. A researcher's expectations can be communicated to participants, perhaps unintentionally, through tone of voice, gestures, or facial expressions. These communications can influence the participants' behavior. Expectations can also influence a researcher's interpretation of the experimental results, even if no influence occurred during the experiment. To control for experimenter bias, researchers must not know which participants are assigned to the experimental and control groups until after the research data are collected and recorded. (Obviously, someone assisting the researcher does know.) When neither the participants nor the researchers know which participants are getting the treatment and which are in the control group, the experiment is using the **double-blind technique**.

double-blind technique A procedure in which neither the participants nor the experimenters know who is in the experimental and control groups until after the data have been gathered; a control for experimenter bias.

Quasi-Experiments. Some treatments cannot ethically be given to human participants because their physical or psychological health would be endangered. For instance, as we noted earlier, it would be unethical to intentionally expose fetuses to alcohol for the purpose of experimentation. For this reason, researchers must conduct **quasi-experiments**, comparisons of groups that have differing degrees of exposure to a variable of interest, to study variables such as the effects of prenatal drug exposure. Quasi-experiments do not provide evidence of causal relationships, but they are the only option available for studying variables such as prenatal alcohol exposure.

quasi-experiments Comparisons of groups that differ in exposure to a variable of interest that cannot be manipulated for ethical or practical reasons.

Quasi-experiments are also useful when it is impractical or impossible to manipulate an independent variable of interest. For instance, when educational researchers compare test scores of children attending different schools, they are conducting quasi-experiments. Likewise, comparisons of groups that differ in gender, age, income, educational attainment, and a host of other variables are quasi-experiments.

cross-cultural research Comparisons of mental processes and behaviors among humans living in different cultures.

Cross-cultural research, comparisons of mental processes and behaviors in different cultures, is also quasi-experimental. As we noted in the discussion of the sociocultural perspective earlier in the chapter, research examining the influence of culture on behavior and mental processes has become increasingly important in recent years. Cross-cultural research is important in evolutionary psychology as well due to its focus on universal phenomena such as infant attachment.

 TRY IT **Does Random Assignment Really Make Groups Equal?**

You will need a set of 100 poker chips with 50 white chips, 25 red chips, and 25 blue chips for this activity. Put all of the chips in an opaque bag or container. Draw one chip out of the container and flip a coin. If heads comes up, assign the chip to the "experimental group." If it's tails, assign the chip to the "control group." Repeat the procedure for all 100 chips. When you are finished, determine the proportion of white, red, and blue chips in each group. The proportions should be very close to 50% white, 25% red, and 25% blue. Repeat the activity imagining that each chip color represents a human characteristic, such as

ethnicity, that a researcher might be interested in. As you will see, by randomly assigning participants to experimental and control conditions, a researcher can construct groups that are equally representative of the population from which they are drawn.

⊙─[**Watch** the Video *Episode 2: Basics: Scientific Research Methods* in **MyPsychLab**

The *Summarize It* summarizes the different types of research we have discussed in this chapter.

SUMMARIZE IT

Research Methods in Psychology

METHOD	DESCRIPTION	ADVANTAGES	LIMITATIONS
Naturalistic and laboratory observation	Observation and recording of behavior in its natural setting or in a laboratory.	Behavior studied in everyday setting is more natural. A laboratory setting allows for precise measurement of variables. Can provide basis for hypotheses to be tested later.	Researcher's expectations can distort observations (observer bias). In a natural setting the researcher has little or no control over conditions. Laboratory observations may not generalize to real-world settings, and they can be expensive.
Case study	In-depth study of one or a few individuals using observation, interview, and/or psychological testing.	Source of information for rare or unusual conditions or events. Can provide basis for hypotheses to be tested later.	May not be generalizable. Does not establish cause of behavior. Subject to misinterpretation by the researcher.
Survey	Interviews and/or questionnaires used to gather information about attitudes, beliefs, experiences, or behaviors of a group of people.	Can provide accurate information about large numbers of people. Can track changes in attitudes and behavior over time.	Responses may be inaccurate. Sample may not be representative. Characteristics of the interviewer may influence responses. Can be costly and time consuming.
Correlational method	Method used to determine the relationship (correlation) between two events, characteristics, or behaviors.	Can assess strength of the relationship between variables and can often be done quickly. Provides basis for prediction.	Does not demonstrate cause and effect.
Experimental method	Random assignment of participants to groups. Manipulation of the independent variable(s) and measurement of the effect on the dependent variable.	Enables identification of cause–effect relationships.	Laboratory setting may inhibit natural behavior of participants. Findings may not be generalizable to the real world. In some cases, experiment is unethical or impossible.

REMEMBER IT   *Check your answers and take additional quizzes in MyPsychLab.com.*   ✓● Study and Review on MyPsychLab

1. The _____ is the only research method that can be used to identify cause–effect relationships between variables.
2. In an experiment, the _____ is manipulated by the researcher, and its effects on the _____ are measured at the end of the study.
3. The _____ group sometimes receives a placebo.
4. Random assignment is used to control for _____ bias.
5. _____ bias is controlled for when researchers do not know which participants are in the experimental and control groups.

Research Participants

You have learned about observer and experimenter bias in research, but were you aware that the findings of a study can be biased by the participants themselves? Furthermore, researchers are bound by ethical guidelines that specify how human participants and animal subjects are to be treated.

1.15 How can participants' characteristics influence a study's usefulness?

Participant-Related Bias in Psychological Research

Do you remember reading earlier about the importance of representative samples in survey research? With other methods, representativeness becomes an issue when psychologists want to generalize the findings of studies to individuals other than the studies' participants. During the 1990s, several psychologists offered critiques of the lack of representativeness of participants in psychological research. These critiques raised awareness of the failure of psychologists to consider the effects of their sample selection procedures on the results of their studies. As a result, the American Psychological Association and other professional organizations began to require that researchers make every effort to ensure that participants are representative of the population to which the study's results will be generalized. These organizations also require that researchers include detailed information about participants' characteristics (i.e., age, ethnicity) in all published research. A few areas of concern are race, gender, and age.

Researcher Sandra Graham (1992) put forward two important criticisms regarding study participants. She pointed out that whites are often overrepresented in psychological studies because the majority of studies with human participants have drawn from the college student population (Graham, 1992), which has a lower proportion of minorities than the population in general. Moreover, college students, including those of minority ethnicity, are a relatively select group in terms of age, socioeconomic class, and educational level. Thus, they are not representative of the general population. This lack of representativeness in a research sample is called **participant-related bias**. Graham (1992) also reported finding a methodological flaw—failure to include socioeconomic status—in much of the research literature comparing white Americans and African Americans. Graham pointed out that African Americans are overrepresented among the economically disadvantaged. She maintained that socioeconomic status should be incorporated into research designs "to disentangle race and social class effects" in studies that compare white and African Americans (634).

participant-related bias A type of bias in which a study's participants are not representative of the population to which results will be generalized.

Gender bias is another type of participant-related bias. For example, Ader and Johnson (1994) found that, when conducting research in which all of the participants are of one sex, researchers typically specify the gender of the sample clearly when it is female but not when the sample is exclusively male. Such a practice, according to Ader and Johnson, reveals a "tendency to consider male participants 'normative,' and results obtained from them generally applicable, whereas female participants are somehow 'different,' and results obtained from them are specific to female participants" (pp. 217–218). On a positive note, however, these researchers report that over the decades, gender bias in the sampling and selection of research subjects has been decreasing.

Ageism is another continuing source of participant-related bias and is especially apparent in the language used in psychological research (Schaie, 1993). For example, the titles of research studies on aging often include words such as *loss, deterioration, decline,* and *dependency.* Moreover, researchers are likely to understate the great diversity among the older adults they study. According to Schaie, "most research on adulthood shows that differences between those in their 60s and those in their 80s are far greater than those between 20- and 60-year-olds" (p. 50). Researchers should guard against using descriptions or reaching conclusions that imply that all members of a given age group are defined by negative characteristics.

1.16 How do researchers protect human participants' and animals' rights?

Protecting Human Participants' and Animals' Rights

In 2002, the American Psychological Association (APA) adopted its most recent set of ethical standards governing research with human participants so as to safeguard their rights while supporting the goals of scientific inquiry. Following are some of the main provisions of the code:

- *Legality:* All research must conform to applicable federal, state, and local laws and regulations. In 2010, the APA amended the code of ethics to clarify this provision. These amendments require psychologists to act in accord with basic human rights even if the laws under which they are practicing or the policies and regulations of the organizations for which they work violate such rights (APA Ethics Committee, 2010).

■ *Institutional approval:* Researchers must obtain approval from all institutions involved in a study. For example, a researcher cannot conduct a study in a school without the school's approval.

■ *Informed consent:* Participants must be informed of the purpose of the study and its potential for harming them.

■ *Deception:* Deception of participants is ethical when it is necessary. However, the code of ethics cautions researchers against using deception if another means can be found to test the study's hypothesis.

■ *Debriefing:* Whenever a researcher deceives participants, including through the use of placebo treatments, he or she must tell participants about the deception as soon as the study is complete.

■ *Clients, patients, students, and subordinates:* When participants are under another's authority (for example, a therapist's client, a patient in a hospital, a student in a psychology class, or an employee), researchers must take steps to ensure that participation in a study, and the information obtained during participation, will not damage the participants in any way. Professors, for example, cannot reduce students' grades if the students refuse to participate in a research study.

■ *Payment for participation:* Participants can be paid, but the code of ethics requires that they be fully informed about what is expected in return for payment.

■ *Publication:* Psychological researchers must report their findings in an appropriate forum, such as a scientific journal, and they must make their data available to others who want to verify their findings.

The APA code of ethics also includes guidelines for using animals in psychological research. Here are a few of the important guidelines:

■ *Legality:* Like research with human participants, animal research must follow all relevant federal, state, and local laws.

■ *Supervision by experienced personnel:* The use of animals must be supervised by people who are trained in their care. These experienced personnel must teach all subordinates, such as research assistants, how to properly handle and feed the animals and to recognize signs of illness or distress.

■ *Minimization of discomfort:* Researchers are ethically bound to minimize any discomfort to research animals. For example, it is unethical to perform surgery on research animals without appropriate anesthesia. And when researchers must terminate the lives of research animals, they must do so in a humane manner.

Even with these safeguards in place, the use of animals in research is controversial. Many animal rights advocates want all animal research stopped immediately. Thus, it is important to address the question of whether animal research is really necessary.

The fact that virtually all of the marvels of modern medicine are at least partially the result of experimentation using animals supports the view that animal research is indeed necessary (Aaltola, 2005). Such research has also increased knowledge in the areas of learning, motivation, stress, memory, and the effects on the unborn of various drugs ingested during pregnancy. Similarly, animal research has helped psychopharmacologists better understand the side effects of drugs that are used to relieve the symptoms of serial mental illnesses such as schizophrenia (Thaaker & Himabindhu, 2009). Thus, animal research is critically important to experiments that involve variables that cannot be ethically manipulated in human beings.

However, the material benefits derived from an action cannot stand alone as an ethical justification for it (Brody, 2012). For this reason, decisions about the use of animals in research must balance the potential benefits of a given study against the pain and suffering that might be inflicted upon its animal subjects. For example, studying potential cures for cancer might justify intentionally making an animal fatally ill. By contrast, a study that goes to this extreme in search of a cure for male pattern baldness might not. Emphasis on achieving this kind of ethical balance in animal research has led to a search for alternative research methods that are reportedly resulting in a decrease in the numbers of animals needed (Garrett, 2012). ◉

◉ [Watch the Video *Episode 2: Special Topics: Ethics and Psychological Research* in **MyPsychLab**

REMEMBER IT   *Check your answers and take additional quizzes in MyPsychLab.com.*   ✓● [Study and **Review** on **MyPsychLab**

1. _____, _____, and _____ have been overrepresented in many kinds of psychological studies.

2. Psychologists are required to debrief participants thoroughly after a study involving _____.

3. By using _____ in research, researchers have learned a great deal about topics such as the effects of drugs ingested during pregnancy.

⚘ Looking Back

In this chapter, you have learned a great deal about psychologists, the methods they use, and a tried-and-true approach to studying textbook chapters, the SQ3R method. To be most effective, a general study method such as SQ3R must be adapted to each individual's learning preferences and study skill level. To implement this goal, think about how personally helpful each of the SQ3R features was as you worked your way through Chapter 1. Use the following table to rate each feature according to this scale: 2 = very useful, 1 = somewhat useful, and 0 = not useful. As you read each chapter, make a conscious effort to follow the SQ3R steps, devoting the most emphasis to those features to which you gave a rating of 1 or 2. Such an approach will enable you to use your study time efficiently and effectively and, we hope, avoid those pre-exam "all-nighters."

LEARNING TOOLS	USEFULNESS		
Think About It	0	1	2
Learning questions	0	1	2
Key terms	0	1	2
Explain It	0	1	2
Apply It	0	1	2
Try It	0	1	2
Summarize It	0	1	2
Remember It	0	1	2
Chapter Summary	0	1	2
Study Guide	0	1	2

Step 5b: Review II
Now you need to review the entire chapter to be sure that you're ready to be tested. Follow these steps:
• Read the Chapter Summary. The notes in your outline should be fairly similar to the learning question answers in the summary.
• Modify your outline if necessary.
• Complete the Study Guide and check your answers against the key in the back of the book. You should be able to find many of the answers in your outline.
• Take the chapter Practice Test in the back of the book or log on to MyPsychLab to take an online version.

CHAPTER 1 SUMMARY

AN INTRODUCTION TO *MASTERING THE WORLD OF PSYCHOLOGY* (pp. 2–7)

1.1 How will the SQ3R method help you master psychology? (pp. 2–3)

The SQ3R method—survey, question, read, recite, and review—provides you with a systematic approach to studying the material. Using this approach to studying will help you manage your time more efficiently and give you a sense of control over your learning and academic performance.

Key Term
SQ3R method, p. 2

1.2 Why do psychologists use the scientific method? (pp. 3–6)

The scientific method consists of the orderly, systematic procedures researchers follow as they identify a research problem, design a study to investigate the problem, collect and analyze data, draw conclusions, and communicate their findings. Psychologists use it because it is the most objective method known for obtaining dependable knowledge.

Key Terms
psychology, p. 3
scientific method, p. 3
theory, p. 4
hypothesis, p. 4
replication, p. 5

1.3 What are the goals of psychology? (pp. 6–7)

The four goals of psychology are to describe, explain, predict, and influence behavior and mental processes. The purpose of basic research is to seek new knowledge and to expand general scientific understanding. Applied research explores the application of psychological principles to practical problems and everyday life.

Key Terms
basic research, p. 6
applied research, p. 6

PSYCHOLOGY THEN AND NOW (pp. 7–15)

1.4 What did the early psychologists contribute to the field? (pp. 7–9)

Wundt launched the study of psychology as a formal academic discipline. One of his students, Titchener, founded the school of thought called structuralism. Functionalism was the first American school of psychology and broadened the scope of the field to include examination of behavior as well as conscious mental processes. Early female and minority psychologists had to overcome significant educational and professional barriers to work in the field. Still, many of these individuals made noteworthy contributions. Today minority group representation is growing, and more women than men obtain degrees in psychology.

Key Terms
structuralism, p. 8
functionalism, p. 8

1.5 What are the major schools of thought in psychology? (pp. 9–13)

Behaviorists emphasize the environment as the key determinant of behavior. Psychoanalytic theorists claim that an individual's thoughts, feelings, and behavior are determined primarily by the unconscious—the part of the mind that one cannot see and cannot control. Humanistic theorists focus on the uniqueness of human beings and their capacity for choice, personal growth, and psychological health. Cognitive psychology focuses on mental processes such as memory, problem solving, reasoning, decision making, language, perception, and other forms of cognition. Evolutionary psychology focuses on how human behaviors necessary for survival have adapted in the face of environmental pressures over the course of evolution. Biological psychologists look for connections between specific behaviors (such as aggression) and particular biological factors (such as hormone levels) to help explain individual differences. Sociocultural psychology emphasizes social and cultural influences on human behavior and stresses the importance of understanding those influences when interpreting the behavior of others.

Key Terms
behaviorism, p. 9
psychoanalysis, p. 10
humanistic psychology, p. 10
positive psychology, p. 10
cognitive psychology, p. 10
Gestalt psychology, p. 11
information-processing theory, p. 11
evolutionary psychology, p. 11
biological psychology, p. 12
neuroscience, p. 12
sociocultural approach, p. 12

1.6 What are the seven contemporary psychological perspectives? (pp. 13–14)

Psychological perspectives are general points of view used for explaining people's behavior and thinking that have arisen from the major schools of thought. The seven contemporary perspectives include behavioral, psychoanalytic, humanistic, cognitive, evolutionary, biological, and sociocultural. In taking an eclectic position, psychologists use a combination of two or more perspectives to explain a particular behavior.

Key Term
psychological perspectives, p. 13

1.7 What specialty areas exist in psychology? (pp. 14–16)

Psychology today is highly specialized. Clinical psychologists are members of one specialty group, a subfield that also includes school and forensic psychologists. Other important specialists in the field are counseling psychologists, physiological psychologists, experimental psychologists, developmental psychologists, educational psychologists, social psychologists, and industrial/organizational (I/O) psychologists.

THINKING ABOUT THEORIES AND RESEARCH (pp. 16–17)

1.8 How do psychologists evaluate theories? (p. 16)

Psychologists evaluate theories in terms of their usefulness rather than whether they are true or false. Useful theories generate testable hypotheses and practical solutions to problems. Theories possessing heuristic value are useful for stimulating debate and research.

1.9 How will critical thinking help you evaluate research? (pp. 16–18)

Critical thinkers are independent, able to suspend judgment, and willing to change prior beliefs. These skills help them evaluate claims about research. Critical thinkers also use knowledge of research methods to evaluate research findings.

Key Term
critical thinking, p. 16

DESCRIPTIVE RESEARCH METHODS (pp. 18–22)

1.10 What are the pros and cons of observational and case studies? (pp. 18–19)

In naturalistic observation, researchers observe and record the behavior of human participants or animal subjects in a natural setting without attempting to influence or control it. In laboratory observation, researchers exert more control and use more precise equipment to measure responses. The case study is appropriate for studying people with rare psychological or physiological disorders or brain injuries. Disadvantages of this method include possible observer bias, an inability to establish the cause of behavior, and lack of generalizability.

Key Terms
descriptive research methods, p. 18
naturalistic observation, p. 18
laboratory observation, p. 18
case study, p. 18

1.11 How do researchers design useful surveys? (pp. 19–20)

To be useful, surveys must involve a sample that is representative of the population to which the results will be applied. Useful surveys also avoid wording questions and in ways that influence respondents' answers and employ interviewers whose characteristics are similar to those of respondents.

Key Terms
survey, p. 19
population, p. 19
sample, p. 19
representative sample, p. 19

1.12 What are the strengths and weaknesses of the correlational method? (pp. 20–23)

When the correlation between two variables is known, information about one variable can be used to predict the other. However, a correlation cannot be used to support the conclusion that either variable causes the other.

Key Terms
correlational method, p. 20
correlation coefficient, p. 20

THE EXPERIMENTAL METHOD (pp. 23–27)

1.13 How do researchers use experiments to test causal hypotheses? (pp. 23–25)

The experimental method is the only research method that can identify cause–effect relationships. In an experiment, an independent variable is a condition or factor manipulated by the researcher to determine its effect on the dependent variable. By comparing experimental and control groups, researchers can judge the effects of the independent variable(s) compared to outcomes that occur naturally or in the presence of a placebo.

Key Terms
experimental method, p. 23
causal hypothesis, p. 23
variable, p. 23
independent variable, p. 24
dependent variable, p. 24
experimental group, p. 24
control group, p. 24

1.14 What are the limitations of the experimental method? (pp. 25–27)

Several types of bias introduce confounding variables that make it difficult to conclude that changes in the independent variable caused changes in the dependent variable. Selection bias occurs when there are systematic differences among the groups before the experiment begins. The placebo effect occurs when a person's expectations influence the outcome of a treatment or an experiment. Experimenter bias occurs when the researcher's expectations affect the outcome of the experiment. In addition, experiments are often conducted in unnatural settings, a factor that limits the applicability of results beyond the experimental setting. When researchers are interested in independent variables that cannot be manipulated for ethical or practical reasons, they often conduct quasi-experiments.

Key Terms
confounding variables, p. 25
selection bias, p. 25
random assignment, p. 25
placebo effect, p. 25
placebo, p. 25
experimenter bias, p. 26
double-blind technique, p. 26
quasi-experiments, p. 26
cross-cultural research, p. 26

RESEARCH PARTICIPANTS (pp. 27–30)

1.15 How can participants' characteristics influence a study's usefulness? (p. 28)

Participant-related bias happens when researchers fail to include underrepresented groups in their samples. Historically, psychological researchers have relied heavily on studies in which the primary participants were college students, a group that includes fewer minorities and people of limited means than the general population does. Similarly, many studies have failed to include women. Ageism is another participant-related issue.

Key Term
participant-related bias, p. 28

1.16 How do researchers protect human participants' and animals' rights? (pp. 28–30)

All research must conform to applicable laws and regulations. Researchers must obtain approval from all institutions involved in the study. Participants must give informed consent, may not be deceived unless necessary, and, if deceived, must be debriefed as soon as possible after they participate. Subordinates' participation in a study may not negatively affect them in any way. Participants may be paid after being fully informed about what is expected in return for payment. Researchers must report their findings in an appropriate forum, and results must be made available to participants.

Chapter 1 Study Guide

Answers to all the Study Guide questions are provided at the end of the book.

SECTION ONE: Chapter Review

An Introduction to *Mastering the World of Psychology* (pp. 2–7)

1. The orderly, systematic procedures scientists follow in acquiring a body of knowledge is the _____ _____.

2. The four goals of psychology are _____, _____, _____, and _____.

3. The purpose of basic research is to seek new knowledge and advance scientific understanding. (true/false)

Psychology Then and Now (pp. 7–15)

4. Classify each of the following people and concepts as being associated with (a) structuralism or (b) functionalism.

   _____ (1) James
   _____ (2) based on Darwin's theory of evolution
   _____ (3) stream of consciousness
   _____ (4) elements of experience
   _____ (5) Titchener
   _____ (6) introspection
   _____ (7) became known in the 19th century

5. Match each of the following individuals with his or her contribution to psychology.
   _____ (1) Francis Cecil Sumner
   _____ (2) Mary Whiton Calkins
   _____ (3) Kenneth Clark
   _____ (4) Christine Ladd-Franklin
   _____ (5) Jorge Sanchez
   a. first female president of APA
   b. published studies on cultural bias in intelligence testing
   c. first African American to receive a PhD in psychology
   d. studied African American children's self-esteem
   e. had to wait 40 years to receive a PhD in psychology after completing the degree requirements

6. Match the major figure with the appropriate school of psychology. Answer(s) may be used more than once.
   _____ (1) Freud
   _____ (2) Skinner
   _____ (3) Maslow
   _____ (4) Wertheimer
   _____ (5) Watson
   _____ (6) Rogers
   a. Gestalt psychology
   b. humanistic psychology
   c. behaviorism
   d. psychoanalysis

7. Match the school of psychology with its major emphasis.
   _____ (1) the scientific study of behavior
   _____ (2) the perception of whole units or patterns
   _____ (3) the unconscious
   _____ (4) the computer as a model for human cognition
   _____ (5) the uniqueness of human beings and their capacity for growth
   _____ (6) the study of mental processes
   a. Gestalt psychology
   b. humanistic psychology
   c. cognitive psychology
   d. behaviorism
   e. information-processing theory
   f. psychoanalysis

8. Match each of the following variables with the psychological approach that is most likely to be interested in it: (a) evolutionary psychology, (b) biological psychology, or (c) sociocultural psychology.
   _____ (1) the effects of drugs and alcohol on reaction time
   _____ (2) the relationship between minority status and self-esteem
   _____ (3) universal behaviors such as infants' attachment to caregivers
   _____ (4) links between hormones and aggression
   _____ (5) gender role beliefs that are consistent across cultures
   _____ (6) gender role beliefs that vary across cultures

9. Match the psychological perspective with its major emphasis.
   _____ (1) the role of biological processes and heredity
   _____ (2) the role of environmental factors
   _____ (3) the role of mental processes
   _____ (4) the role of the unconscious and early childhood experience
   _____ (5) the importance of the individual's own subjective experience
   _____ (6) the role of social and cultural influences
   _____ (7) the role of inherited tendencies that have proved adaptive in humans
   a. psychoanalytic
   b. biological
   c. behavioral
   d. cognitive
   e. humanistic
   f. evolutionary
   g. sociocultural

10. Write "Yes" by the statements below that represent eclecticism in psychology.
   _____ (1) Individual differences in aggression are genetic, but parents and teachers can teach highly aggressive children to be less so.
   _____ (2) Children who are highly aggressive have not received enough punishment for their inappropriate behavior.
   _____ (3) Aggressive children are probably using aggression to release pent-up feelings of frustration.

_____ **(4)** Going through a trauma like parental divorce may lead to increased aggression in children because they are experiencing strong emotions, and their parents are likely to be too distracted by their own problems to discipline children effectively.

11. Adjustment problems are the concern of specialists in (clinical/counseling) psychology.

Thinking about Theories and Research (pp. 16–17)

12. Useful theories
    a. lead to practical solutions to problems.
    b. provide researchers with many testable hypotheses.
    c. stimulate debate and research.
    d. all of the above

13. The three characteristics of critical thinkers are _____, _____, and _____.

14. A television reporter claimed that people should stop eating cabbage because scientists have found that it causes cancer. The first response of a critical thinker to this report would be to
    a. find out if the research was published in a prestigious journal.
    b. determine whether the research was correlational or experimental in nature.
    c. find out how many people participated in the study.
    d. stop eating cabbage.

Descriptive Research Methods (pp. 18–22)

15. Which descriptive research method would be best for studying each topic?
    _____ **(1)** attitudes toward exercise
    _____ **(2)** gender differences in how people position themselves and their belongings in a library
    _____ **(3)** physiological changes that occur during sleep
    _____ **(4)** the physical and emotional effects of a rare brain injury
    a. naturalistic observation
    b. laboratory observation
    c. case study
    d. survey

16. One problem with _____ _____ is that they often do not generalize to cases other than the one that is the subject of the study.

17. When conducting a survey, a researcher can compensate for a sample that is not representative by using a sample that is very large. (true/false)

18. The correlational method is used to demonstrate cause–effect relationships. (true/false)

19. The _____ is a number describing the strength and direction of a relationship between two variables.

20. Which of the following correlation coefficients indicates the strongest relationship?
    a. +.65
    b. −.78
    c. .00
    d. +.25

21. There is a (positive/negative) correlation between the amount of fat people eat and their body weight.

22. A (positive/negative) correlation exists between the temperature and the number of layers of clothing people wear.

23. The main strength of the correlational method is that it can be used to establish cause–effect relationships. (true/false)

The Experimental Method (pp. 23–27)

24. The experimental method is the *only* research method that can be used to identify cause–effect relationships between variables. (true/false)

25. In an experiment, the _____ _____ is manipulated by the researcher, and its effects on the _____ _____ are measured at the end of the study.

26. A researcher investigates the effectiveness of a new antidepressant drug. She randomly assigns depressed patients to two groups. Group 1 is given the drug, and Group 2 is given a placebo. At the end of the experiment, the level of depression of all participants is measured as a score on a test called a depression inventory. Match the elements of this experiment with the appropriate term.
    _____ **(1)** score on depression inventory
    _____ **(2)** the antidepressant drug
    _____ **(3)** Group 1
    _____ **(4)** Group 2
    a. experimental group
    b. control group
    c. independent variable
    d. dependent variable

27. Random assignment is used to control for
    a. experimenter bias.
    b. the placebo effect.
    c. selection bias.
    d. participant bias.

28. The placebo effect occurs when a participant responds according to
    a. the hypothesis.
    b. the actual treatment.
    c. how other participants behave.
    d. his or her expectations.

29. A psychological researcher conducted a study in which the flight skills of female pilots were compared to those of male pilots. This type of study is called a(n) _____.

Research Participants (pp. 27–30)

30. Which of the following groups has *not* been overrepresented as participants in psychological research?
    a. whites
    b. males
    c. females
    d. college students

31. Psychologists are required to debrief participants thoroughly after a research study when the study
    a. violates participants' rights to privacy.
    b. deceives participants about the true purpose of the research.
    c. exposes participants to unreasonable risk or harm.
    d. wastes taxpayers' money on trivial questions.

32. Investigators use animals in psychological research to learn more about humans. (true/false)

SECTION TWO: Who Said This?

Read each statement below and then, in the blank that follows, identify the person mentioned in Chapter 1 who would be most likely to make the statement.

1. I thought that behavior could be explained by analyzing the conditions that were present before it occurs and the consequences it produces. _____

2. I established the first psychological laboratory in Leipzig, Germany. _____

3. I wrote *Principles of Psychology* and advocated functionalism. _____

4. I introduced the term *behaviorism.* _____

5. I proposed a theory of motivation that consists of a hierarchy of needs. _____

6. I was the first African American to earn a PhD in psychology. _____

7. I became the first female president of the American Psychological Association. _____

8. I invented a popular form of psychotherapy called *client-centered therapy.* _____

9. I demonstrated the phi phenomenon. _____

SECTION THREE: Comprehensive Practice Test

1. Which of the following psychological perspectives likened human mental life to an iceberg?
   a. behaviorism
   b. psychoanalysis
   c. humanistic psychology
   d. structuralism

2. _____ is the approach to psychology that arose from the belief that the study of the mind and consciousness was not scientific.
   a. structuralism
   b. behaviorism
   c. humanistic psychology
   d. psychoanalysis

3. The _____ perspective in psychology would explain behavior by referring to the operation of the brain and the central nervous system.
   a. evolutionary
   b. structuralist
   c. behavioral
   d. biological

4. A _____ psychologist specializes in the diagnosis and treatment of mental and behavioral disorders.
   a. social
   b. developmental
   c. clinical
   d. cognitive

5. "The whole is perceived as greater than the sum of its parts" is a statement you would be most likely to hear from a _____ psychologist.
   a. behavioral
   b. clinical
   c. Gestalt
   d. developmental

6. Description, explanation, prediction, and influence of behavior and mental processes are the _____ of psychology.
   a. reasons
   b. goals
   c. perspectives
   d. methods

7. In an experiment, a researcher would use the double-blind approach to control for _____.
   a. experimenter bias
   b. independent bias
   c. selection bias
   d. random bias

8. The disadvantages of survey research include that
   a. respondents may provide inaccurate information.
   b. they can be costly and time consuming.
   c. the "social desirability effect" may cause respondents to give misleading answers.
   d. all of the above

9. A researcher who wants to establish evidence for a cause–effect relationship between variables should use _____.
   a. naturalistic observation
   b. correlation
   c. the experimental method
   d. the survey method

10. Which of the following psychologists is associated with the humanistic perspective?
    a. Maslow
    b. Darwin
    c. Watson
    d. Freud

11. Researchers who are interested in the adaptive significance of behavior are known as _____ psychologists.
    a. cognitive
    b. humanistic
    c. evolutionary
    d. psychoanalytic

12. A social psychologist would be most interested in how individuals behave in isolated settings, such as when they are alone at home. (true/false)

13. Basic research is aimed at solving practical problems and improving the quality of life. (true/false)

14. Watson would suggest that Freud's psychological approach is invalid because of Freud's emphasis on unconscious motivation and other mental events. (true/false)

15. In an experiment, the experimental group is exposed to all aspects of the treatment except the independent variable. (true/false)

16. Structuralism used introspection to study the basic elements of conscious mental experience. (true/false)

17. Most psychologists believe that animal research is of little value in the study of human mental processes and behavior. (true/false)

18. The best way to establish a cause–effect relationship between variables is to use the case study method because that method gives a researcher an in-depth knowledge of the subject matter from spending so much time with just a few participants. (true/false)

19. A researcher is studying the relationship between styles of computer keyboards and typing accuracy. In this case, the dependent variable is the different types of computer keyboards included in the study. (true/false)

20. You would probably expect to find a negative correlation between the number of alcoholic drinks consumed and the number of accidents a participant has while being tested on an experimental driving simulator. (true/false)

SECTION FOUR: Critical Thinking

1. Consider three of the major forces in psychology: behaviorism, psychoanalysis, and humanistic psychology. Which appeals to you most and which least, and why?

2. Suppose you hear on the news that a researcher claims to have "proven" that day care is harmful to infants. How could you use what you've learned in this chapter about research methods to evaluate this statement?

SECTION FIVE: Application Essays

1. Lamont often keeps a game window open when he is doing classwork on his computer so that he can quickly navigate to the game whenever he gets bored. Lately, he has started to wonder whether this is a good idea, as he often finds he has difficulty staying on task. How could he use the steps of the scientific method to determine whether his habit of keeping a game window open while he is doing classwork is responsible for the problems he has with staying on task?

Apply your critical thinking skills with MyPsychLab Writing Assignments

Submit your answer to the following question inside the MyPsychLab Writing Assessment program for immediate feedback.

2. Jake has become very anxious ever since he started taking harder classes in his major. The university's counselor diagnosed him with an anxiety disorder. Compare and contrast how the behavioral, humanistic, and cognitive approaches would view the origins and treatment of Jake's anxiety. Then, describe how psychologists view each of the three approaches today.

3. Imagine you have been asked to create an experimental design to test the hypothesis that talking on a cell phone impairs driving skills. Explain why a control condition would be important to include in testing this hypothesis. How should subjects be assigned to conditions? How can the researchers design the experiment so that the only difference between both conditions is the use of a cell phone?

THINK ABOUT IT

Interpreting others' facial expressions is such a commonplace task that we usually do it without thinking about it. But your eyes can sometimes fool you. See if you can figure out which of the faces below is the happier of the two (Jaynes, 1976).

Which face did you say was the happier one? Your answer probably depended on whether you are right- or left-handed. You see, the brain tends to assign some tasks to the right side of the brain and others to the left. These assignments are correlated to some degree with handedness. For instance, if you are right-handed, you tend to use the right side of the brain to interpret emotions. Since the right side of the brain controls the left side of the body, you would use the left side of people's faces to make inferences about their emotional states (Abbott, Cumming, Fidler, & Lindell, 2012). Consequently, even though the faces

in the drawing are mirror images, right-handed people tend to see the face on the left as the happier one. Left-handers display the opposite pattern. They rely on the left side of the brain to interpret emotions, and because the left side of the brain controls the right side of the body, they usually judge the face on the right to be the happier one.

How the brain divides functions between its left and right halves is just one of many interesting things about the biological foundations of behavior and mental processes that you will read about in this chapter. We will tell you much more about the brain and nervous system, and we will introduce you to the endocrine system. You will also read about genetics. Pay close attention to the information in this chapter because we will refer back to its major concepts in all the chapters that follow. ◉

Discovering the Mysteries of the Nervous System

◉ Watch the Video *Episode 3: Big Picture: My Brain Made Me Do It* in **MyPsychLab**

How do we know what we know about the nervous system? Until quite recently, researchers had few techniques for directly studying it. Scientists relied on case studies of people in whom an injury to a specific part of the system, a *lesion*, had led to specific changes in behavior to identify the functions associated with the various parts of the system. For instance, because severe injuries to the back of the head were observed to result in visual problems, researchers were able to infer that the back of the brain was involved in vision. By the mid-19th century, researchers began making great strides in understanding the nervous system thanks to the availability of more powerful microscopes that enabled them to directly examine the nervous system tissues of deceased humans and animals. Today, scientists continue to use both case studies and microscopic tissue studies to answer questions about the nervous system. But since the early 20th century, researchers have also been able to observe the living brain in action. How do they do this? Through a variety of tools and imaging techniques, researchers are able to observe different parts of the brain and their functions. Exactly what the researcher is trying to study determines which tool or technique works best.

The EEG and the Microelectrode ▶

2.1 What does the electroencephalogram (EEG) reveal about the brain?

In 1924, Austrian psychiatrist Hans Berger invented the electroencephalograph, a machine that records the electrical activity occurring in the brain. This electrical activity, detected by electrodes placed at various points on the scalp and amplified greatly, provides the power to drive a pen across paper, producing a record of brain-wave activity called an **electroencephalogram (EEG).**

A computerized EEG imaging technique shows the different levels of electrical activity occurring every millisecond on the surface of the brain (Gevins et al., 1995). It can show an epileptic seizure in progress and can be used to study neural activity in people with schizophrenia, Alzheimer's disease, sleep disorders, and other neurological problems.

Although the EEG is able to detect electrical activity in different areas of the brain, it cannot reveal what is happening in individual neurons. However, the **microelectrode** inserted directly into the brain can. A microelectrode is a wire so small that it can be inserted near or into a single neuron without damaging it. Microelectrodes can be used to monitor the electrical activity of a single neuron or

electroencephalogram (EEG) (ee-lek-tro-en-SEFF-uh-lo-gram) A record of brain-wave activity made by a machine called the electroencephalograph.

microelectrode A small wire used to monitor the electrical activity of or stimulate activity within a single neuron.

(a)

beta wave

delta wave

▲ The electroencephalograph, or EEG, uses electrodes placed on the scalp to amplify and record electrical activity in the brain, as shown in (a). An EEG typically measures brain waves while the person is awake and asleep, because the characteristics of the brain's electrical activity vary across sleeping and waking states, as shown in (b) and (c).

2.2 How do researchers use imaging techniques to study the nervous system?

CT scan (computerized axial tomography) A brain-scanning technique that uses a rotating, computerized X-ray tube to produce cross-sectional images of the structures of the brain.

MRI (magnetic resonance imaging) A diagnostic scanning technique that produces high-resolution images of the structures of the brain.

PET scan (positron-emission tomography) A brain-imaging technique that reveals activity in various parts of the brain, based on patterns of blood flow, oxygen use, and glucose consumption.

functional MRI (fMRI) A brain-imaging technique that reveals both brain structure and brain activity more precisely and rapidly than PET.

to stimulate activity within it. They are used in *intracranial electroencephalograms* (iEEG) that enable neurologists to pinpoint the precise neuronal origin of seizures in individuals who have epilepsy (Rummel et al., 2013).

Imaging Techniques

Since the early 1970s, a number of techniques that provide scientists and physicians with images of the brain's structures have become available. For example, a person undergoing a **CT scan (computerized axial tomography)** of the brain is placed inside a large, doughnut-shaped structure where an X-ray tube encircles the entire head. The tube rotates in a complete circle, shooting X-rays through the brain as it does so. A series of computerized, cross-sectional images reveal the structures within the brain as well as abnormalities and injuries, including tumors and evidence of old or more recent strokes.

MRI (magnetic resonance imaging), which became widely available in the 1980s, produces clearer and more detailed images without exposing people to potentially dangerous X-rays (Potts, Davidson, & Krishman, 1993). MRI can be used to find abnormalities in the central nervous system and in other systems of the body. Although the CT scan and MRI do a remarkable job of showing what the brain looks like both inside and out, they cannot reveal what the brain is doing. But other technological marvels can.

Several techniques capture images of both brain structures and their functions. The oldest of these techniques, the **PET scan (positron-emission tomography)** has been used since the mid-1970s to identify malfunctions that cause physical and psychological disorders. For example, researchers have found that patterns of glucose metabolism in the brains of individual with autism differs from that of people who do not have this condition (Brasic & Kao, 2011). PET scanning has also been used to study normal brain activity. A PET scan maps the patterns of blood flow, oxygen use, and glucose consumption (glucose is the food of the brain). It can also show the action of drugs and other biochemical substances in the brain and other bodily organs (Farde, 1996).

A technique that became available in the 1990s, **functional MRI (fMRI)**, uses magnetic impulses to create images of brain structures and functions. It has several important advantages over PET: (1) it requires no injections (of radioactive or other material); (2) it can identify locations of activity more precisely than PET can; and (3) it can detect changes that take place in less than a second, compared with about a minute for PET ("Brain Imaging," 1997).

Still other imaging devices are now available. SQUID (superconducting quantum interference device) shows brain activity by measuring the magnetic changes produced by the electric current that neurons discharge when they fire. Another imaging marvel, MEG (magnetoencephalography), also measures such magnetic changes and shows neural activity within the brain as rapidly as it occurs, much faster than PET or fMRI.

A new kind of MRI, diffusion tensor imaging (DTI), enables researchers to examine individual neuron bundles. These new techniques enable researchers and clinicians to identify the exact locations of brain lesions and malfunctions associated with conditions such as epilepsy, strokes, Alzheimer's disease, and multiple sclerosis with greater precision and speed than the older imaging techniques do.

Brain-imaging techniques have helped neuroscientists accumulate an impressive store of knowledge about brain functions such as memory (Logothetis, 2008). Studies using these imaging techniques have also shown that, to varying degrees, the structures and functions of the brain differ in people who have serious psychological disorders from those who do not. In addition, imaging techniques have revealed where and how drugs affect the brain (Gorman, 2007). Some neuroscientists have experimented with combining virtual reality with fMRI to study how the brain responds to situations and environments that would be impossible to observe using conventional imaging techniques (Wiederhold & Wiederhold, 2008). For example, virtual reality therapy is useful for treating phobias such as fear of flying. By using fMRI monitoring in conjunction with virtual reality treatments that simulate real-world situations that trigger phobic responses, researchers can determine how the brain processes such treatments. The information that researchers obtain the fMRI helps them improve the effectiveness of virtual reality interventions. 👁

👁 **Watch** the Video *Brain Building* in **MyPsychLab**

REMEMBER IT   *Check your answers and take additional quizzes in MyPsychLab.com.*   ✓ **Study** and **Review** on **MyPsychLab**

1. The CT scan and MRI are used to produce images of the _____ of the brain.
2. The _____ reveals the electrical activity of the brain by producing a record of brain waves.
3. A _____ scan reveals brain activity and function, rather than the structure of the brain.
4. A newer imaging technique called _____ reveals both brain structure and brain activity.

The Neurons and the Neurotransmitters

Earlier we mentioned that 19th-century researchers used microscopes to study the nervous system tissues of deceased humans and animals. These studies led to the discovery of the specialized cells that conduct impulses through the nervous system, the **neurons**. In the early 20th century, the invention of the microelectrode allowed researchers to study the connections between neurons. These studies revealed the existence of chemicals that are essential to nervous system functioning. These chemicals, the **neurotransmitters**, can facilitate or inhibit the transmission of impulses from one neuron to the next. Working together, neurons and neurotransmitters convey messages within the nervous system and from the nervous system to other parts of the body.

neuron (NEW-ron) A specialized cell that conducts impulses through the nervous system.

neurotransmitters Specialized chemicals that facilitate or inhibit the transmission of impulses from one neuron to the next.

The Structure of the Neuron ▶

All of our thoughts, feelings, and behavior can ultimately be traced to the activity of neurons. Afferent (sensory) neurons relay messages from the sense organs and receptors —eyes, ears, nose, mouth, and skin—to the brain or spinal cord. Efferent (motor) neurons convey signals from the central nervous system to the glands and the muscles, enabling the body to move. Interneurons, thousands of times more numerous than motor or sensory neurons, carry information between neurons in the brain and between neurons in the spinal cord. ✳ 👁

Although no two neurons are exactly alike, nearly all are made up of three important parts: the cell body, the dendrites, and the axon. The **cell body**, or *soma*, contains the nucleus and carries out the metabolic, or life-sustaining, functions of a neuron. Branching out from the cell body are the **dendrites**, which look much like the leafless branches of a tree (*dendrite* comes from the Greek word for "tree"). The dendrites are the primary receivers of signals from other neurons, but the cell body can also receive signals directly.

2.3 What does each part of the neuron do?

✳ **Explore** the **Concept** *The Nerve Impulse and Afferent and Efferent Neurons* in **MyPsychLab**

👁 **Watch** the Video *Episode 3: How the Brain Works: Part 1* in **MyPsychLab**

cell body The part of a neuron that contains the nucleus and carries out the metabolic functions of the neuron.

dendrites (DEN-drytes) In a neuron, the branch-like extensions of the cell body that receive signals from other neurons.

axon (AK-sahn) The slender, tail-like extension of the neuron that transmits signals to the dendrites or cell body of other neurons and to muscles, glands, and other parts of the body.

axon terminal Bulbous end of the axon where signals move from the axon of one neuron to the dendrites or cell body of another.

glial cells (GLEE-ul) Specialized cells in the brain and spinal cord that support neurons, remove waste products such as dead neurons, and perform other manufacturing, nourishing, and cleanup tasks.

The **axon** is the slender, tail-like extension of the neuron that sprouts into many branches, each ending in a bulbous **axon terminal**. Signals move from the axon terminals to the dendrites or cell bodies of other neurons and to muscles, glands, and other parts of the body. In humans, some axons are short—only thousandths of an inch long. Others can be as long as a meter (39.37 inches)—long enough to reach from the brain to the tip of the spinal cord, or from the spinal cord to remote parts of the body. Figure 2.1 shows the structure of a neuron.

Glial cells are specialized cells in the brain and spinal cord that support the neurons. They are smaller than neurons and make up more than one-half the volume of the human brain. Glial cells remove waste products, such as dead neurons, from the brain by engulfing and digesting them, and they handle other manufacturing, nourishing, and cleanup tasks. Glial cells in the spinal cord are also involved in pain sensations that are associated with damaged nerves (Gwak, Kang, Unabia, & Hulsebosch, 2012).

2.4 How do neurons transmit messages through the nervous system?

Communication between Neurons

Remarkably, the billions of neurons that send and receive signals are not physically connected. The axon terminals are separated from the receiving neurons by tiny, fluid-filled

FIGURE 2.1 **The Structure of a Typical Neuron**
A typical neuron has three important parts: (1) a cell body, which carries out the metabolic functions of the neuron; (2) branched fibers called dendrites, which are the primary receivers of the impulses from other neurons; and (3) a slender, tail-like extension called an axon, the transmitting end of the neuron, which sprouts into many branches, each ending in an axon terminal. The photograph shows human neurons greatly magnified.

Cell body
Dendrites
Axon

Dendrites
The branches extending from the cell body, which receive most of the signals from other neurons

Axon
The slender extension that projects from the cell body and transmits signals to the dendrites or cell bodies of other neurons and to muscles, glands, and other parts of the body

Cell body
The metabolic center of the neuron, enclosed by the semipermeable cell membrane

Nodes of Ranvier
The gaps in the myelin sheath

Myelin sheath
The fatty coating on some axons that acts as insulation

Branches
Sprouts from the axon that end in bulbous axon terminals

Synaptic clefts
The gaps between axon terminals and receiving neurons, across which signals are transmitted

Axon terminal
Bulbous end of the axon where signals move from the axon of one neuron to the dendrites or cell body of another

gaps called *synaptic clefts*. The **synapse** is the junction where the axon terminal of a sending (presynaptic) neuron communicates with a receiving (postsynaptic) neuron across the synaptic cleft. It is estimated that one cubic centimeter of the cerebral cortex, the brain's outer covering, contains as a trillion synapses (Drachman, 2005). A single neuron may also form thousands of synapses with other neurons (Drachmann, 2005). If neurons aren't connected, how do they communicate with one another? ✷

A small but measurable electrical impulse is present every time you move or have a thought. As the impulse travels down the axon, the permeability of the cell membrane (its capability of being penetrated or passed through) changes. In other words, the membrane changes in a way that makes it easier for molecules to move through it and into the cell. This process allows ions (electrically charged atoms or molecules) to move into and out of the axon through ion channels in the membrane.

Body fluids contain ions, some with positive electrical charges and others with negative charges. Inside the axon, there are normally more negative than positive ions. When at rest (not firing), the axon membrane carries a negative electrical potential of about −70 millivolts (−70 thousandths of a volt) relative to the fluid outside the cell. This slight negative charge is referred to as the neuron's **resting potential**.

When an impulse reaches a neuron, ion channels begin to open in the cell membrane of the axon at the point closest to the cell body, allowing positive ions to flow into the axon (see Figure 2.2 on p. 44). This inflow of positive ions causes the membrane potential to change abruptly, to a positive value of about +50 millivolts (Pinel, 2000). This sudden reversal of the resting potential, which lasts for about 1 millisecond (1 thousandth of a second), is the **action potential**. Then, the ion channels admitting positive ions close, and other ion channels open, forcing some positive ions out of the axon. As a result, the original negative charge, or resting potential, is restored. The opening and closing of ion channels continues, segment by segment, down the length of the axon, causing the action potential to move along the axon (Cardoso de Mello & Sabbatini, 2000). The action potential operates according to the "all-or-none" law—a neuron either fires completely or does not fire at all. Immediately after a neuron fires, it enters a *refractory period*, during which it cannot fire again for 1 to 2 milliseconds. But even with these short resting periods, neurons can fire hundreds of times per second.

If a neuron only fires or does not fire, how can we tell the difference between a very strong and a very weak stimulus? In other words, what is the neurological distinction between feeling anxious about being disciplined by your boss for being late to work and running for your life to avoid being the victim of a criminal attacker? The answer lies in the number of neurons firing at the same time and their rate of firing. A weak stimulus may cause relatively few neurons to fire, while a strong stimulus may

synapse (SIN-aps) The junction where the axon terminal of a sending neuron communicates with a receiving neuron across the synaptic cleft.

✷⌐Explore the **Concept** *The Synapse* in **MyPsychLab**

resting potential The slight negative electrical potential of the axon membrane of a neuron at rest, about −70 millivolts.

action potential The sudden reversal of the resting potential, which initiates the firing of a neuron.

▶ In 1786, Luigi Galvani discovered that electrical stimulation caused the muscles of dissected animals to move briefly on their own. These findings led proponents of "reanimation" to speculate that a jolt of electricity might bring dead organisms back to life. Such speculations inspired Mary Shelley to write a shocking (at the time) novel about a scientist, Victor Frankenstein, who developed a procedure for reanimating human corpses, *Frankenstein: The Modern Prometheus*, first published in 1818. Although scientists have known for some time that the link between electricity and life is far more complex than the advocates of reanimation imagined, Shelley's powerful message about the moral dilemmas that arise when science enables humankind to grant and withhold the "spark of life" lives on.

FIGURE 2.2 **The Action Potential**
The action potential moves down the
axon to the axon terminals.
Source: Adapted from Lilienfeld, Lynn, Namy, &
Wolf (2009).

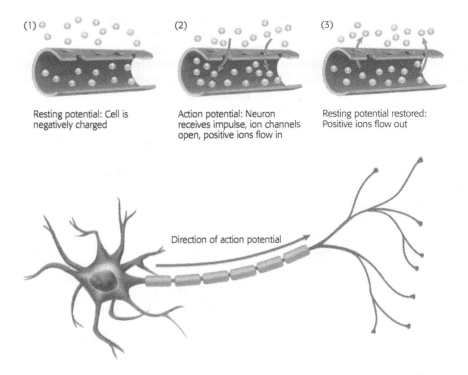

(1) Resting potential: Cell is
negatively charged

(2) Action potential: Neuron
receives impulse, ion channels
open, positive ions flow in

(3) Resting potential restored:
Positive ions flow out

Direction of action potential

▲ This scanning electron micrograph
shows numerous axon terminals (the
orange, button-shaped structures) that
could synapse with the cell body of the
neuron (shown in green).

2.5 How do neurotransmitters work?

myelin sheath (MY-uh-lin) The white, fatty
coating wrapped around some axons that acts
as insulation and enables impulses to travel
much faster.

receptors Protein molecules on the surfaces
of dendrites and cell bodies that have distinctive
shapes and will interact only with specific
neurotransmitters.

trigger thousands of neurons to fire at the same time. Also, a weak stimulus may be signaled by neurons firing very slowly; a stronger stimulus may incite neurons to fire hundreds of times per second.

Impulses travel at speeds from about 1 meter per second to approximately 100 meters per second (about 224 miles per hour). The most important factor in speeding the impulse on its way is the **myelin sheath**—a white, fatty coating wrapped around most axons that acts as insulation. If you look again at Figure 2.1 (p. 42), you will see that the coating has numerous gaps, called *nodes of Ranvier.* The electrical impulse is retriggered or regenerated at each node (or naked gap) on the axon. This regeneration makes the impulse up to 100 times faster than impulses in axons without myelin sheaths. Damage to the myelin sheath causes interruptions in the transmission of neural messages. In fact, the disease multiple sclerosis (MS) involves deterioration of the myelin sheath, resulting in loss of coordination, jerky movements, muscular weakness, and disturbances in speech.

Neurotransmitters

Once a neuron fires, how does it get its message across the synaptic cleft and on to another neuron? Inside the axon terminal are many small, sphere-shaped containers with thin membranes called *synaptic vesicles,* which hold the neurotransmitters. (*Vesicle* comes from a Latin word meaning "little bladder.") When an action potential arrives at the axon terminal, synaptic vesicles move toward the cell membrane, fuse with it, and release their neurotransmitter molecules. This process is shown in Figure 2.3.

Once released, neurotransmitters do not simply flow into the synaptic cleft and stimulate all the adjacent neurons. Each neurotransmitter has a distinctive molecular shape, as do **receptors**, which are protein molecules on the surfaces of dendrites and cell bodies. In other words, each receptor is somewhat like a lock that only certain neurotransmitter keys can unlock. However, the binding of neurotransmitters with receptors is not as fixed and rigid a process as keys fitting locks or jigsaw puzzle pieces interlocking. Receptors on neurons are somewhat flexible; they can expand and contract their enclosed volumes. And neurotransmitters of different types can have similar shapes. Thus, two different neurotransmitters may compete for the same receptor. The

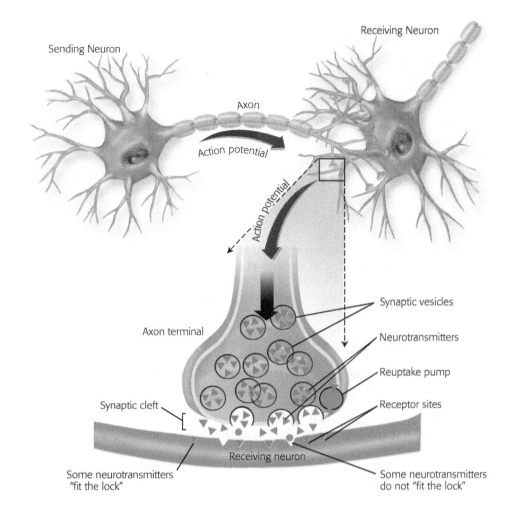

FIGURE 2.3 **Synaptic Transmission**
Sending neurons transmit their messages to receiving neurons by electrochemical action. When a neuron fires, the action potential arrives at the axon terminal and triggers the release of neurotransmitters from the synaptic vesicles. Neurotransmitters flow into the synaptic cleft and move toward the receiving neuron, which has numerous receptors. The receptors will bind only with neurotransmitters whose molecular shapes match their enclosed volumes. Neurotransmitters influence the receiving neuron to fire or not to fire.

receptor will admit only one of the competing neurotransmitters—the one that fits it best. A receptor may receive a certain neurotransmitter sometimes but not receive it in the presence of a better-fitting neurotransmitter.

When neurotransmitters bind with receptors on the dendrites or cell bodies of receiving neurons, their action is either excitatory (influencing the neurons to fire) or inhibitory (influencing them not to fire). Because a single receiving neuron may have synapses with thousands of other neurons at the same time, it will always be subject to both excitatory and inhibitory influences from incoming neurotransmitters. For the neuron to fire, the excitatory influences must exceed the inhibitory influences by a sufficient amount (the threshold). 👁

You may wonder how the synaptic vesicles can continue to pour out neurotransmitters, yet maintain a ready supply so that the neuron can respond to continuing stimulation. First, the cell body of the neuron is always working to manufacture more of the neurotransmitter. Second, unused neurotransmitters in the synaptic cleft may be broken down into components and reclaimed by the axon terminal to be recycled and used again. Third, by an important process called **reuptake**, the neurotransmitter is taken back into the axon terminal, intact and ready for immediate use. This terminates the neurotransmitter's excitatory or inhibitory effect on the receiving neuron.

Researchers have identified more than 100 chemical substances that are manufactured in the brain, spinal cord, glands, and other parts of the body and may

reuptake The process by which neurotransmitters are taken from the synaptic cleft back into the axon terminal for later use, thus terminating their excitatory or inhibitory effect on the receiving neuron.

👁 **Watch** the Video *Episode 3: In the Real Word: Neurotransmitters* in **MyPsychLab**

▲ The neurotransmitter acetylcholine helps you process new information by facilitating neural transmissions involved in learning.

TABLE 2.1 **Major Neurotransmitters and Their Functions**

NEUROTRANSMITTER	FUNCTIONS
Acetylcholine (Ach)	Affects movement, learning, memory, REM sleep
Dopamine (DA)	Affects movement, attention, learning, reinforcement, pleasure
Norepinephrine (NE)	Affects eating, alertness, wakefulness
Epinephrine	Affects metabolism of glucose, energy release during exercise
Serotonin	Affects mood, sleep, appetite, impulsivity, aggression
Glutamate	Active in areas of the brain involved in learning, thought, and emotion
GABA	Facilitates neural inhibition in the central nervous system
Endorphins	Provide relief from pain and feelings of pleasure and well-being

act as neurotransmitters (Purves et al., 2011). Table 2.1 lists the major neurotransmitters. As you look over the table, keep in mind that neurotransmitters can serve different functions in different parts of the body. For example, *acetylcholine* (Ach) exerts excitatory effects on the skeletal muscle fibers, causing them to contract so that the body can move. But it has an inhibitory effect on the muscle fibers in the heart, which keeps the heart from beating too rapidly. Thus, when you run to make it to class on time, acetylcholine helps your leg muscles contract quickly, while simultaneously preventing your heart muscle from pumping so rapidly that you pass out. The differing natures of the receptors on the receiving neurons in the two kinds of muscles cause these opposite effects. Acetylcholine also plays an excitatory role in stimulating the neurons involved in learning new information. So, as you are reading this text, acetylcholine is helping you understand and store the information in your memory.

As you will learn in Chapter 4, drugs influence the nervous system through their action on neurotransmitters. For instance, responses to cocaine involve the neurotransmitters *dopamine* and *glutamate* (Fasano et al., 2009). Moreover, in Chapter 11 you will learn that researchers have discovered links between neurotransmitter functioning and several psychological disorders. For example, researchers suspect that the neurotransmitter *dopamine* plays a role in attention-deficit/hyperactivity disorder (ADHD) (Volkow et al., 2009).

REMEMBER IT

Check your answers and take additional quizzes in MyPsychLab.com. ✓● Study and Review on MyPsychLab

1. The branchlike extensions of neurons that act as the *primary* receivers of signals from other neurons are the _____.

2. _____ support neurons, supplying them with nutrients and carrying away their waste products.

3. The _____ is the junction where the axon of a sending neuron communicates with a receiving neuron.

4. When a neuron fires, neurotransmitters are released from the synaptic vesicles in the _____ into the _____.

5. The _____ potential is the firing of a neuron; the _____ potential is the state in which the cell membrane is relatively impermeable.

6. Receptor sites on the receiving neuron receive only neurotransmitter molecules whose _____ is similar to theirs.

7. The neurotransmitter called _____ keeps the heart from beating too fast.

8. _____ affects eating habits by stimulating the intake of carbohydrates.

9. _____ are neurotransmitters that act as natural painkillers.

The Human Nervous System

Now that you understand how the cells of the nervous system function, you're ready to learn more about how the system is organized. As you can see in Figure 2.4, there are two major divisions in the system. You'll be happy to learn that it's easy to remember the difference between the two. The **peripheral nervous system (PNS)** includes all of the nerves (i.e., bundles of neurons) that are not encased in bone, that is, all of the neural tissue that lies outside your skull and backbone. The function of these tissues is to transmit messages to and from the body and brain. The **central nervous system (CNS)** includes all of the neural tissues inside the skull and backbone. In other words, the CNS is made up of the spinal cord and brain.

The Peripheral Nervous System ▶

What makes your heart pound and palms sweat when you watch a scary movie? Such reactions are the result of signals from the brain's limbic system and other structures that regulate emotions to the peripheral nervous system. The peripheral nervous system (PNS) is made up of all the nerves that connect the central nervous system to the rest of the body. It has two subdivisions: the somatic nervous system and the autonomic nervous system, which is further divided into the sympathetic nervous system and parasympathetic nervous system.

The *somatic nervous system* consists of (1) all the sensory nerves, which transmit information from the sense receptors—eyes, ears, nose, tongue, and skin—to the central nervous system, and (2) all the motor nerves, which relay messages from the central nervous system to all the skeletal muscles of the body. In short, the nerves of the somatic nervous system make it possible for you to sense your environment and to move, and they are primarily under conscious control.

The *autonomic nervous system* operates without any conscious control or awareness on your part. It transmits messages between the central nervous system and the glands, the cardiac (heart) muscle, and the smooth muscles (such as those in the

peripheral nervous system (PNS) (peh-RIF-er-ul) The nerves connecting the central nervous system to the rest of the body.

central nervous system (CNS) The part of the nervous system comprising the brain and the spinal cord.

2.6 What are the structures and functions of the peripheral nervous system?

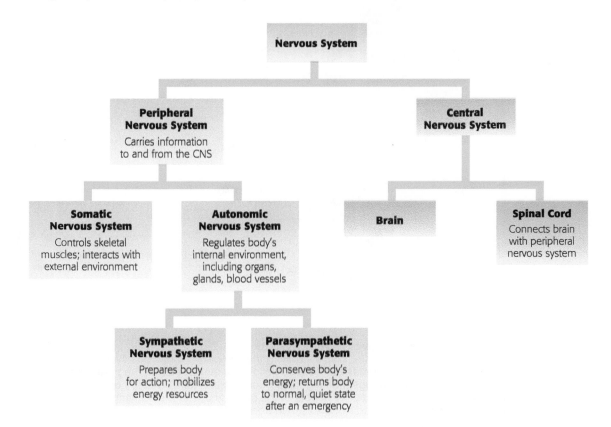

FIGURE 2.4 The Human Nervous System
The nervous system is divided into two parts: the peripheral nervous system and the central nervous system. The diagram shows the relationships among the parts of the nervous system and provides a brief description of the functions of those parts.

✳—⎡Explore the Concept *The Autonomic Nervous System* in **MyPsychLab**

sympathetic nervous system The division of the autonomic nervous system that mobilizes the body's resources during stress and emergencies, preparing the body for action.

parasympathetic nervous system The division of the autonomic nervous system that brings the heightened bodily responses back to normal following an emergency.

large arteries and the gastrointestinal system), which are not normally under voluntary control. This system is further divided into two parts—the sympathetic and the parasympathetic nervous systems. ✳

Any time you are under stress or faced with an emergency, the **sympathetic nervous system** automatically mobilizes the body's resources, preparing you for action. This physiological arousal produced by the sympathetic nervous system was named the *fight-or-flight response* by Walter Cannon (1929, 1935). If an ominous-looking stranger started following you down a dark, deserted street, your sympathetic nervous system would automatically go to work. Your heart would begin to pound, your pulse rate would increase rapidly, your breathing would quicken, your digestive system would nearly shut down, and the blood flow to your skeletal muscles would be enhanced. These reactions would make all of your bodily resources ready to handle the emergency.

Once the emergency is over, the **parasympathetic nervous system** brings these heightened bodily functions back to normal. As a result of its action, your heart stops pounding and slows to normal, your pulse rate and breathing slow down, and your digestive system resumes its normal functioning. As shown in Figure 2.5 the sympathetic

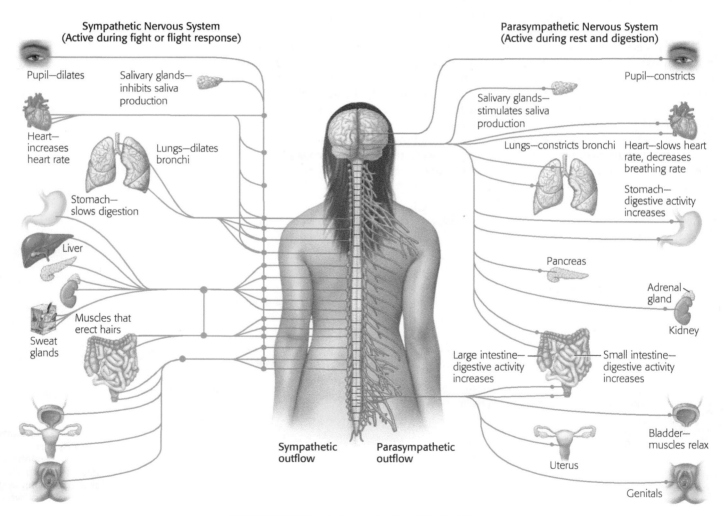

FIGURE 2.5 The Autonomic Nervous System
The autonomic nervous system consists of (1) the sympathetic nervous system, which mobilizes the body's resources during emergencies or stress, and (2) the parasympathetic nervous system, which brings the heightened bodily responses back to normal afterward. This diagram shows the opposite effects of the sympathetic and parasympathetic nervous systems on various parts of the human body.
Source: Lilienfeld, Lynn, Namy, & Woolf (2009).

and parasympathetic branches act as opposing but complementary forces in the autonomic nervous system. Their balanced functioning is essential for health and survival.

The Central Nervous System ▶

As we noted earlier, the central nervous system includes the spinal cord and the brain. The spinal cord is the link between the peripheral nervous system and the brain. As you will see, the brain itself includes several different components, each of which has distinctive functions.

The Spinal Cord. The **spinal cord** can best be thought of as an extension of the brain. A cylinder of neural tissue about the diameter of your little finger, the spinal cord reaches from the base of the brain, through the neck, and down the hollow center of the spinal column. It is protected by bone and also by spinal fluid, which serves as a shock absorber. The spinal cord literally links the body with the brain. It transmits messages between the brain and nerves in other parts of the body. Thus, sensory information can reach the brain, and messages from the brain can be sent to the muscles, the glands, and other parts of the body.

Although the spinal cord and the brain usually function together, the spinal cord can act without help from the brain to protect the body from injury. A simple withdrawal reflex triggered by a painful stimulus—touching a hot iron, for example—involves three types of neurons (see Figure 2.6). Sensory neurons in your fingers detect the painful stimulus and relay this information to interneurons in the spinal cord. These interneurons activate motor neurons that control the muscles in your arm and cause you to jerk your hand away. All this happens within a fraction of a second, without any involvement of your brain. However, the brain quickly becomes aware and involved when the pain signal reaches it. At that point, you might plunge your hand into cold water to relieve the pain.

The Hindbrain. Brain structures are often grouped into the *hindbrain,* the *midbrain,* and the *forebrain,* as shown in Figure 2.7 (p. 50). The structures of the **hindbrain** control heart rate, respiration, blood pressure, and many other vital functions. The part of the hindbrain known as the **brainstem** begins at the site where the spinal cord enlarges as it enters the skull. The brainstem handles functions that are so critical to physical survival that damage to it is life threatening. The **medulla** is the part of the brainstem that controls heartbeat, breathing, blood pressure, coughing, and swallowing. Fortunately, the medulla handles these functions automatically, so you do not have to decide consciously to breathe or remember to keep your heart beating.

Above the medulla and at the top of the brainstem is a bridgelike structure called the **pons** that extends across the top front of the brainstem and connects to both halves of the cerebellum. The pons plays a role in body movement and even exerts an influence on sleep and dreaming.

Extending through the central core of the brainstem into the pons is another important structure, the **reticular formation**, sometimes called the *reticular activating system* (RAS) (refer to Figure 2.7). The reticular formation plays a crucial role in arousal and attention (Gadea et al., 2004). For example, a driver may be listening intently to a radio program when, suddenly, a car cuts in front of her. In response, the reticular formation blocks the sensory information coming from the radio and fixes the driver's attention on the potential danger posed by the other driver's action. Once the traffic pattern returns to normal, the reticular formation allows her to attend to the radio again, while continuing to monitor the traffic situation.

The reticular formation also determines how alert we are. When it slows down, we doze off or go to sleep. But thanks to the reticular formation, important messages get through even when we are asleep. This is why parents may be able to sleep through a thunderstorm but will awaken to the slightest cry of their baby.

The **cerebellum** is critically important to the body's ability to execute smooth, skilled movements (Spencer et al., 2003). It also regulates muscle tone and posture. Furthermore, it has been found to play a role in motor learning (Orban et al., 2009).

2.7 What are the structures and functions of the central nervous system?

spinal cord An extension of the brain, from the base of the brain through the neck and spinal column, that transmits messages between the brain and the peripheral nervous system.

hindbrain A link between the spinal cord and the brain that contains structures that regulate physiological functions, including heart rate, respiration, and blood pressure.

brainstem The structure that begins at the point where the spinal cord enlarges as it enters the brain and handles functions critical to physical survival. It includes the medulla, the reticular formation, and the pons.

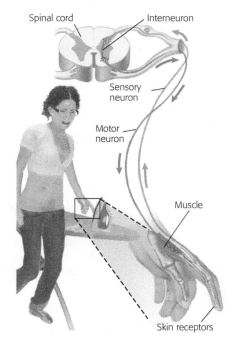

FIGURE 2.6 The Spinal Reflex
The sequence that begins with a sensory stimulus (such as touching something hot) and ends with a behavioral response (withdrawing the hand) involves sensory neurons, interneurons, and motor neurons.
Source: Adapted from Lilienfeld, S., Lynn, S., Namy, L., & Woolf, N. (2009).

medulla (muh-DUL-uh) The part of the brainstem that controls heartbeat, blood pressure, breathing, coughing, and swallowing.

pons The bridgelike structure that connects the medulla and the cerebellum.

reticular formation A structure in the brainstem that plays a crucial role in arousal and attention and that screens sensory messages entering the brain.

cerebellum (sehr-uh-BELL-um) The brain structure that helps the body execute smooth, skilled movements and regulates muscle tone and posture.

FOREBRAIN

Hypothalamus	Cerebrum	Cerebral cortex	Corpus callosum	Limbic system	Thalamus
Controls functions such as hunger, thirst, body temperature; helps control endocrine system; involved in emotion	The thinking part of the brain	Convoluted covering of the cerebral hemispheres that is responsible for higher mental processes	Band of nerve fibers that connects the two sides of the brain	Group of structures involved in emotional expression, memory, and motivation	Relay station between cerebral cortex and lower brain centers

MIDBRAIN

Substantia nigra
Controls unconscious motor actions

Pons	Medulla	Spinal cord	Reticular formation	Cerebellum
Plays role in relaying motor messages between cerebellum and motor cortex; exerts influence on sleep and dreaming	Control center for heartbeat, breathing, blood pressure, swallowing, and coughing	Extension of the brain; controls simple reflexes; connects brain to peripheral nervous system	Arousal system; activates cerebral cortex	Coordinates skilled movement; regulates muscle tone and posture; plays a role in motor learning and probably cognition

HINDBRAIN

FIGURE 2.7 Major Structures of the Human Brain
This drawing shows some of the major structures of the brain with a brief description of the function of each. The brainstem contains the medulla, the reticular formation, and the pons.

midbrain Area that contains structures linking the physiological functions of the hindbrain to the cognitive functions of the forebrain.

It coordinates the series of movements necessary to perform many simple activities —such as walking in a straight line or touching your finger to the tip of your nose— without conscious effort. For people who have damage to their cerebellum or who are temporarily impaired by too much alcohol, such simple acts may be difficult or impossible to perform.

The Midbrain. As shown in Figure 2.7, the **midbrain** lies between the hindbrain and the forebrain. The structures of this brain region act primarily as relay stations through which the basic physiological functions of the hindbrain are linked to the cognitive functions of the forebrain. For example, when you burn your finger, the physical feeling travels through the nerves of your hand and arm, eventually reaching the spinal cord, resulting in the reflexive action of dropping a pot. From there, nerve impulses are sent through the midbrain to the forebrain, where they are interpreted ("Next time, I'll remember to use a potholder!").

The **substantia nigra** is located in the midbrain. This structure is composed of the darkly colored nuclei of nerve cells that control our unconscious motor actions. When you ride a bicycle or walk up stairs without giving your movements any conscious thought, the nuclei of the cells that allow you to do so are found in the substantia nigra. Research suggests that the defects in dopamine-producing neurons in the substantia nigra may explain the inability of people with Parkinson's disease to control their physical movements (Bergman et al., 2010).

The Forebrain. The largest part of the brain is the **forebrain**. This is the part of the brain where cognitive and motor functions are controlled. Two important forebrain structures lie just above the brainstem (see Figure 2.7). The **thalamus**, which has two egg-shaped parts, serves as the relay station for virtually all the information that flows into and out of the forebrain, including sensory information from all the senses except smell. (You'll learn more about the sense of smell in Chapter 3.)

The thalamus, or at least one small part of it, affects our ability to learn new verbal information (Soei, Koch Schwarz, & Daum, 2008). Another function of the thalamus is the regulation of sleep cycles, which is thought to be accomplished in cooperation with the pons and the reticular formation (Saper, Scammell, & Lu, 2005). The majority of people who have had acute brain injury and remain in an unresponsive "vegetative" state have suffered significant damage to the thalamus, to the neural tissue connecting it to parts of the forebrain, or to both (Young, 2009).

The **hypothalamus** lies directly below the thalamus and weighs only about 2 ounces. It regulates hunger, thirst, sexual behavior, and a wide variety of emotional behaviors. The hypothalamus also regulates internal body temperature, starting the process that causes you to perspire when you are too hot and to shiver to conserve body heat when you are too cold. It also houses the biological clock—the mechanism responsible for the timing of the sleep/wakefulness cycle and the daily fluctuation in more than 100 body functions (Wirz-Justice, 2009). Because of the biological clock, once your body gets used to waking up at a certain time, you tend to awaken at that time every day—even if you forget to set your alarm. The physiological changes in the body that accompany strong emotion—sweaty palms, a pounding heart, a hollow feeling in the pit of your stomach—are also initiated by neurons concentrated primarily in the hypothalamus.

The **limbic system**, shown in Figure 2.8 is a group of structures in the brain, including the amygdala and the hippocampus, that are collectively involved in emotional expression, memory, and motivation. The **amygdala** plays an important role in emotion, particularly in response to potentially punishing stimuli (Murty, Labar, & Adcock, 2012). Heavily involved in the learning of fear responses, the amygdala helps form vivid memories of emotional events, which enable humans and other animals to avoid dangerous situations (Roozendaal, et al., 2008).

The **hippocampus** is an important brain structure of the limbic system (see Figure 2.8). If your hippocampal region—the hippocampus and the underlying cortical areas—were destroyed, you would not be able to store any new personal or cognitive information, such as that day's baseball score or the phone number of the person you met at dinner (Wirth et al., 2003). Yet, memories already stored before the hippocampal region was destroyed would

substantia nigra (sub-STAN-sha NI-gra) The structure in the midbrain that controls unconscious motor movements.

forebrain The largest part of the brain where cognitive functions as well as many of the motor functions of the brain are carried out.

thalamus (THAL-uh-mus) The structure, located above the brainstem, that acts as a relay station for information flowing into or out of the forebrain.

hypothalamus (HY-po-THAL-uh-mus) A small but influential brain structure that regulates hunger, thirst, sexual behavior, internal body temperature, other body functions, and a wide variety of emotional behaviors.

limbic system A group of structures in the brain, including the amygdala and hippocampus, that are collectively involved in emotional expression, memory, and motivation.

amygdala (ah-MIG-da-la) A structure in the limbic system that plays an important role in emotion, particularly in response to unpleasant or punishing stimuli.

hippocampus (hip-po-CAM-pus) A structure in the limbic system that plays a central role in the storing of new memories, the response to new or unexpected stimuli, and navigational ability.

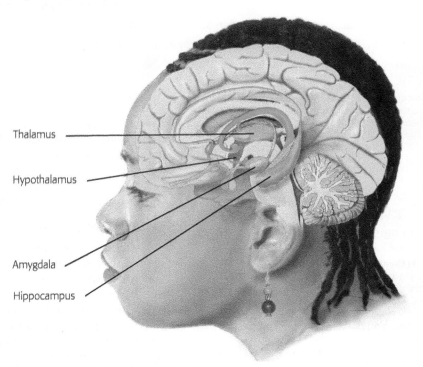

Thalamus

Hypothalamus

Amygdala

Hippocampus

FIGURE 2.8 The Principal Structures in the Limbic System
The amygdala plays an important role in emotion; the hippocampus is essential in the formation of new memories.

remain intact. You will learn more about the central role of the hippocampal region in the formation of memories in Chapter 6.

The hippocampus also plays a role in the brain's internal representation of space in the form of neural "maps" that help us learn our way about in new environments and remember where we have been (Wilson & McNaughton, 1993). A widely cited study of taxi drivers in London revealed that their posterior (rear) hippocampus was significantly larger than that of participants in a control group who did not have extensive experience navigating the city's streets (Maguire et al., 2000). In fact, the more experience a taxi driver had, the larger that part of the hippocampus was. This study shows that the posterior hippocampus is important for navigational ability and that experience strongly influences its functioning.

Finally, the *cerebral cortex* is the forebrain structure that is responsible for the functions we usually associate with the word *brain*. It is the wrinkled, gray covering of the *cerebrum*, or the thinking part of the brain. In the next section, you will read about the cerebrum in more detail.

REMEMBER IT

Check your answers and take additional quizzes in MyPsychLab.com.   ✓— Study and Review on MyPsychLab

1. The _____ and _____ make up the central nervous system.
2. Internal body temperature is regulated by the _____.
3. The _____ is associated with emotions, and the _____ is involved in memory and learning.
4. The _____ serves as a relay station for most sensory information.
5. The _____ consists of the pons, medulla, and reticular formation.
6. Coordinated body movements are controlled by the _____.
7. The _____ nervous system connects the brain and spinal cord to the rest of the body.
8. The _____ nervous system mobilizes the body's resources during times of stress.
9. The _____ nervous system restores the body's functions to normal once a crisis has passed.

cerebrum (seh-REE-brum) The largest structure of the human brain, consisting of the two cerebral hemispheres connected by the corpus callosum and covered by the cerebral cortex.

2.8 What are the components of the cerebrum?

cerebral hemispheres (seh-REE-brul) The right and left halves of the cerebrum, covered by the cerebral cortex and connected by the corpus callosum; they control movement and feeling on the opposing sides of the body.

corpus callosum (KOR-pus kah-LO-sum) The thick band of nerve fibers that connects the two cerebral hemispheres and makes possible the transfer of information and the synchronization of activity between the hemispheres.

cerebral cortex (seh-REE-brul KOR-tex) The gray, convoluted covering of the cerebral hemispheres that is responsible for the higher mental processes of language, memory, and thinking.

A Closer Look at the Thinking Part of the Brain

Researchers have known for more than a century that the majority of the functions that distinguish the human species from others, such as language, reside in the part of the forebrain known as the *cerebrum*. Modern techniques, such as the EEG and the CT and MRI scans, have enabled researchers to localize many important functions, such as planning and logic, to specific parts of the cerebrum. They have also learned a great deal about the communication that goes on between the two sides and four lobes of the cerebrum.

Components of the Cerebrum

If you could peer into your skull and look down on your brain, what you would see would resemble the inside of a huge walnut. Like a walnut, which has two matched halves connected to each other, the **cerebrum** is composed of two **cerebral hemispheres**—a left and a right hemisphere resting side by side (see Figure 2.9). The two hemispheres are physically connected at the bottom by a thick band of nerve fibers called the **corpus callosum**. This connection makes possible the transfer of information and the coordination of activity between the hemispheres. In general, the right cerebral hemisphere controls movement and feeling on the left side of the body; the left hemisphere controls the right side of the body.

The cerebral hemispheres have a thin outer covering about $1/8$ inch thick called the **cerebral cortex**, which is primarily responsible for the higher mental processes of language, memory, and thinking. The presence of the cell bodies of billions of neurons

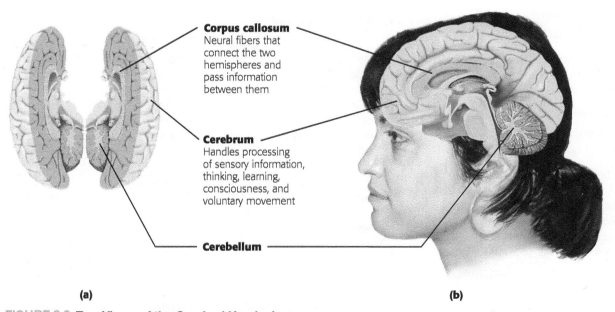

Corpus callosum
Neural fibers that connect the two hemispheres and pass information between them

Cerebrum
Handles processing of sensory information, thinking, learning, consciousness, and voluntary movement

Cerebellum

(a)

(b)

FIGURE 2.9 **Two Views of the Cerebral Hemispheres**
(a) The two hemispheres rest side by side like two matched halves, physically connected by the corpus callosum. (b) An inside view of the right hemisphere.

in the cerebral cortex gives it a grayish appearance. Thus, the cortex is often referred to as *gray matter*. Immediately beneath the cortex are the white myelinated axons (referred to as *white matter*) that connect the neurons of the cortex with those of other brain regions. Research suggests that the amount of gray matter is positively correlated with intelligence in humans (Taki et al., 2012). In other words, the more gray matter you have, the higher your scores on intelligence tests are likely to be.

In humans, the cerebral cortex is very large—if it were spread out flat, it would measure about 2 feet by 3 feet, about the size of a large poster board you might have used for a project in your school days. Because the cortex is roughly three times the size of the cerebrum itself, it does not fit smoothly around the cerebrum. Rather, it is arranged in numerous folds or wrinkles, called *convolutions*. About two-thirds of the cortex is hidden from view in these folds. The cortex of less intelligent animals is much smaller in proportion to total brain size and, therefore, is much less convoluted. The cerebral cortex contains three types of areas: (1) sensory input areas, where vision, hearing, touch, pressure, and temperature register; (2) motor areas, which control voluntary movement; and (3) **association areas**, which house memories and are involved in thought, perception, and language.

Finally, the brain assigns different functions to different regions of the cerebral cortex. The first functional division involves the left and right sides of the cortex. The second involves areas known as the *lobes*—the front (frontal), top (parietal), side (temporal), and back (occipital) of the cortex. As you read about the various neurological divisions of labor in the next two sections, keep in mind that all parts of the brain are in communication with one another at all times. Consequently, everything we do involves the coordination of neural activity in several areas of the brain at once.

association areas Areas of the cerebral cortex that house memories and are involved in thought, perception, and language.

The Cerebral Hemispheres ▶

2.9 What are the specialized functions of the left and right cerebral hemispheres?

We all know that some people are right-handed and others are left-handed. As discussed in the *Explain It* (p. 54), handedness is neurologically based. Consequently, discussions in the media about the differences between "right-brained" and "left-brained" people might seem to make sense. However, there is no scientific basis for the notion that hemisphere dominance varies across individuals in the same way that hand preference

EXPLAIN IT 　　Why Are Most People Right-Handed?

Scientists have searched for an answer to this question for more than a century and have yet to find a definitive answer. In your own thinking about the matter, you have probably concluded that there are three possibilities:

- Handedness is completely determined by genes.
- Handedness is completely determined by learning.
- Handedness is determined by both genes and learning.

If you are drawn to the first hypothesis, consider the finding that only 82% of identical twins, whose genotypes (genetic makeup) are identical, have the same hand preference (Klar, 2003). If handedness were completely determined by genes, then identical twins' phenotypes (actual characteristics) would always be the same for handedness. Therefore, handedness cannot be entirely explained as a function of our genes. Does this mean that handedness is determined by learning? Not necessarily.

The learning hypothesis cannot explain why handedness appears very early in infancy, long before children are exposed to formal instruction that requires them to use one hand or the other (Rönnqvist & Domellöf, 2006). Moreover, the proportions of left-handers and right-handers in the human population have been about the same for thousands of years (Hopkins & Cantalupo, 2004). In fact, these proportions are evident even in the skeletons of humans who died long before writing was invented as well as Neanderthals (Steele & Mays, 1995; Volpato et al., 2012).

The key to understanding the evidence on handedness is to adopt the view that both genes and learning are at work in the development of hand preferences, but not in the way that you might expect. In most of us, right-handedness is completely determined by our genes, but in a few of us handedness, whether left or right, is influenced by learning. Sound confusing? To clarify, here is the most current thinking on the genetics of handedness.

Researchers suspect that right-handedness is determined by a single dominant gene, *R* (Francks et al., 2003). If an individual receives a copy of *R* from one or both parents, then she will be right-handed. The frequency of *R* in the human population is extremely high, scientists believe, because it is tied to the genes that support left-lateralization of language function in the brain.

(Remember, the left side of the brain controls the right side of the body.) It makes sense that motor functions are linked to language, experts claim, because producing language requires activity in both the language centers and motor cortex of the brain. Putting both on the same side of the brain facilitates the rapid development of neural connections between the two without having to go through the slowly developing membrane between the two hemispheres (corpus callosum). But what happens to the relatively small proportion of humans who do not receive a copy of *R* from either parent?

The dominant gene for right-handedness, *R*, is complemented by a recessive gene, *r* (Francks et al., 2007). You might think that the phenotype of an individual who receives a copy of *r* from both parents would include left-handedness, but, in reality, the phenotype that is associated with *rr* is *non-handedness*. In individuals with the *rr* genotype, learning shapes handedness. Because most people are right-handed, and the tools that humans have developed for use in fine motor activities (e.g., scissors) favor righties, there is a considerable amount of cultural pressure on those who lack innate handedness, those with the genotype *rr*, to become right-handed. Nevertheless, some of them do develop left-handedness. Why?

Researchers believe that other genes come into play as well. Specifically, if a person possesses genes that cause language functions to lateralize to her right rather than her left cerebral hemisphere, then she is also likely to be left-handed. Here again, the lateralization of handedness follows the lateralization of language function. To make matters more complicated, in 2007, scientists discovered a gene that pushes us in the direction of left-handedness when we receive it from our fathers. When we get the gene from our mothers, it seems to have no influence on hand dominance (Francks et al., 2007).

Finally, although genetics appears to play a complex, but important, role in the development of hand preferences, the capacity of individuals to adapt to severe injuries to or the loss of the dominant hand demonstrates the adaptability of the brain with regard to motor functions. Thus, as the trait of hand preference illustrates, nature and nurture are often linked in complex ways. Remember this the next time you are involved in a debate with someone about whether a given trait is *either* genetic *or* learned.

---

lateralization The specialization of one of the cerebral hemispheres to handle a particular function.

left hemisphere The hemisphere that controls the right side of the body, coordinates complex movements, and, in most people, handles most of the language functions.

does. In everyone's brain, the right and left hemispheres are in constant contact with one another, thanks to the corpus callosum (shown in Figure 2.9 on p. 53). But research has shown that some **lateralization** of the hemispheres exists; that is, each hemisphere is specialized to handle certain functions. Let's look at the specific functions associated with the left and right hemispheres.

The Left Hemisphere. The **left hemisphere** handles math, logic, analytical thought, and most of the language functions, including speaking, writing, reading, speech comprehension, and comprehension of written information (Hellige, 1990; Long & Baynes, 2002). Many of these functions have specific regions of the left hemisphere devoted to them. For instance, the sounds and meanings associated with spoken language are processed in different areas of the left hemisphere (Poldrack & Wagner, 2004).

The left hemisphere coordinates complex movements by directly controlling the right side of the body and by indirectly controlling the movements of the left side of the body. It accomplishes this by sending orders across the corpus callosum to the right hemisphere so that the proper movements will be coordinated and executed smoothly. (Remember that the cerebellum also plays an important role in helping coordinate complex movements.)

The Right Hemisphere. The **right hemisphere** is generally considered to be the hemisphere more adept at visual–spatial relations. Also, the auditory cortex in the right hemisphere appears to be far better able to process music than the left (Zatorre, Belin, & Penhune, 2002). When you arrange your bedroom furniture or notice that your favorite song is being played on the radio, you are relying primarily on your right hemisphere.

The right hemisphere also augments the left hemisphere's language-processing activities. For example, it produces verbal associations characteristic of creative thought and uses of language (Kounios et al., 2008). Consider this well-known phrase from President John F. Kennedy's inaugural address, a type of expression known as a *parallelism*:

Ask not what your country can do for you, but what you can do for your country.

Writers employ parallelisms because the echoing of the first part of the expression in the second engages the listener's attention. The writer's right hemisphere is the one that judges whether the parallelism succeeds at this goal while simultaneously conveying the speaker's message as accurately as possible. To experience an effect of the specialization of the cerebral hemispheres, try your hand at the *Try It* below.

As you read earlier, the left hemisphere processes the linguistic aspects of speech. However, researchers have found that the processing of natural language involves an interaction between the two halves of the brain in which the right hemisphere carries out a number of critical functions (Berckmoes & Vingerhoets, 2004). One such function is the comprehension of idiomatic expressions, such as "She let the cat out of the bag." The right hemisphere also processes causal links between statements such as "I fell off my bicycle yesterday. My knee is killing me" (Mason & Just, 2004). The right hemisphere also responds to the emotional message conveyed by another's tone of voice (LeDoux, 2000). Reading and interpreting nonverbal behavior, such as gestures and facial expressions, is another right hemisphere task (Hauser, 1993; Kucharska-Pietura & Klimkowski, 2002). For example, the subtle clues that tell us someone is lying (such as excessive blinking or lack of eye contact) are processed in the right hemisphere (Etcoff et al., 2000). Figure 2.10 summarizes the functions associated with the left and right hemispheres.

The Split Brain. A great deal of knowledge about lateralization has been gained from studies involving individuals in whom the corpus callosum is absent or has been surgically modified. Many such individuals have had their corpus callosum severed in a drastic surgical procedure called the **split-brain operation**. Neurosurgeons Joseph

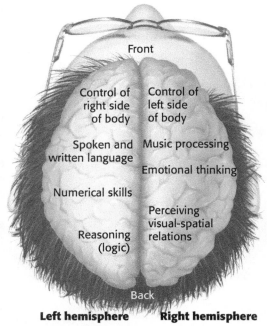

FIGURE 2.10 Lateralized Functions of the Brain
Assigning functions to one hemisphere or the other allows the brain to function more efficiently.
Source: Based on Gazzaniga (1983).

right hemisphere The hemisphere that controls the left side of the body and, in most people, is specialized for visual-spatial perception.

split-brain operation A surgical procedure, performed to treat severe cases of epilepsy, in which the corpus callosum is cut, separating the cerebral hemispheres.

TRY IT   **A Balancing Act**

Get a meter stick or yardstick. Try balancing it vertically on the end of your left index finger, as shown in the drawing. Then try balancing it on your right index finger. Most people are better with their dominant hand—the right hand for right-handers, for example. Is this true for you?

Now try this: Begin reciting the ABCs out loud as fast as you can while balancing the stick with your left hand. Do you have less trouble this time? Why should that be? The right hemisphere controls the act of balancing with the left hand. However, your left hemisphere, though poor at controlling the left hand, still tries to coordinate your balancing efforts.

When you distract the left hemisphere with a steady stream of talk, the right hemisphere can orchestrate more efficient balancing with your left hand without interference.

◉ Watch on **MyPsychLab**

Bogen and Philip Vogel (1963) found that people with severe epilepsy, who had frequent and uncontrollable grand mal seizures, could be helped by surgery that severed their corpus callosum, rendering communication between the two hemispheres impossible. The operation decreases the frequency of seizures in two-thirds of such people and causes minimal loss of cognitive functioning or change in personality (Washington University School of Medicine, 2003).

Watch the Video *Episode 3: Basics: How the Brain Works: Part 2* in **MyPsychLab**

Research with split-brain patients by Roger Sperry (1964) and colleagues Michael Gazzaniga (1970, 1989) and Jerre Levy (1985) expanded knowledge of the unique capabilities of the individual hemispheres. Sperry (1968) found that when the brain was surgically separated, each hemisphere continued to have individual and private experiences, sensations, thoughts, and perceptions. However, most sensory experiences are shared almost simultaneously because each ear and eye has direct sensory connections to both hemispheres.

Sperry's research, for which he won a Nobel Prize in medicine in 1981, revealed some fascinating findings. In Figure 2.11, a split-brain patient sits in front of a screen that

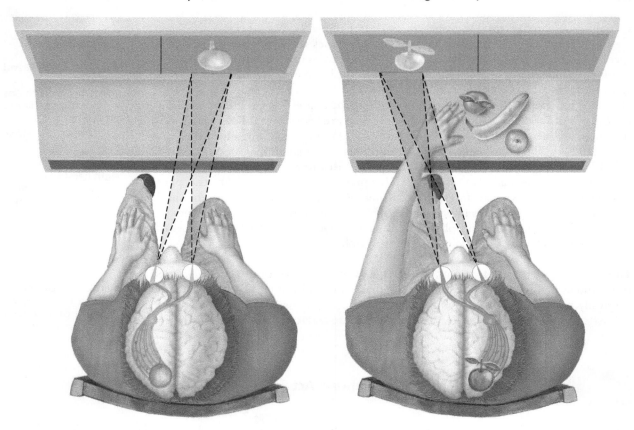

Left Hemisphere   Right Hemisphere

"I see an orange."   "I see nothing."

FIGURE 2.11 **Testing a Split-Brain Person**
Using special equipment, researchers are able to study the independent functioning of the hemispheres in split-brain patients. In this experiment, when a visual image (an orange) is flashed on the right side of the screen, it is transmitted to the left (talking) hemisphere. When asked what he sees, the split-brain patient replies, "I see an orange." When an image (an apple) is flashed on the left side of the screen, it is transmitted only to the right (nonverbal) hemisphere. Because the split-brain patient's left (language) hemisphere did not receive the image, he replies, "I see nothing." But he can pick out the apple by touch if he uses his left hand, proving that the right hemisphere "saw" the apple.
Source: Based on Gazzaniga, M. (1983).

separates the right and left fields of vision. If an orange is flashed to the right field of vision, it will register in the left (verbal) hemisphere. If asked what he saw, the patient will readily reply, "I saw an orange." Suppose that, instead, an apple is flashed to the left visual field and is relayed to the right (nonverbal) hemisphere. The patient will reply, "I saw nothing."

Why could the patient report that he saw the orange but not the apple? Sperry (1964, 1968) maintains that in split-brain patients, only the verbal left hemisphere can report what it sees. In these experiments, the left hemisphere does not see what is flashed to the right hemisphere, and the right hemisphere is unable to report verbally what it has viewed. But did the right hemisphere actually see the apple that was flashed in the left visual field? Yes, because with his left hand (which is controlled by the right hemisphere), the patient can pick out from behind a screen the apple or any other object shown to the right hemisphere. The right hemisphere knows and remembers what it sees just as well as the left, but unlike the left hemisphere, the right cannot name what it has seen. (In these experiments, images must be flashed for no more than 1/10 or 2/10 of a second so that the subjects do not have time to refixate their eyes and send the information to the opposite hemisphere.)

The Four Cerebral Lobes ▶

Each of the cerebral hemispheres has four further divisions. These divisions, or *lobes*, are named for the skull bones to which they are adjacent, the *frontal, parietal, occipital*, and *temporal* bones (see Figure 2.12). Each lobe is responsible for a different set of functions.

The Frontal Lobes: Prefrontal Cortex. Have you ever thought about how many tasks your brain is doing at once when you read a textbook? Your brain is simultaneously translating the letters on the page into words, pulling up the information from memory needed to comprehend them, monitoring how well you understand what you are reading, giving you instructions to go back and reread when needed, and making judgments about what might be on your next exam. All of this activity takes place in your **frontal lobes**, the largest of the brain's lobes (see Figure 2.12 on p. 58). Thanks to the **prefrontal cortex**, the part of the frontal lobes that coordinates multiple functions to serve cognitive goals, a function called *executive processing*, you experience all of these tasks as a unified whole instead of a collection of fragmentary, disconnected activities (Moss et al., 2011). Imaging studies suggest that individuals who have difficulty with cognitive functions such as problem solving display a different, less efficient pattern of prefrontal cortex activation than people who do not have such problems do (Ashkenazi, Rosenberg-Lee, Tenison, & Menon, 2012). 👁

The prefrontal cortex also contributes to personality functioning (DeYoung et al., 2010). People who experience damage to the prefrontal cortex can lose the ability to control impulses, modulate emotions, and anticipate the consequences of their behavior. One of the best known cases involving this type of damage, that of the unfortunate railroad construction worker Phineas Gage, took place on September 13, 1848. Twenty-five-year-old Gage was using dynamite to blast rocks and dirt out of the pathway of the railroad tracks he was helping to lay that would connect the east and west coasts of the United States by rail. Suddenly, an unplanned explosion sent a 3-foot-long, 13-point metal rod under his left cheekbone and out through the top of his skull. Much of the brain tissue in his prefrontal cortex was torn away, and he was rendered unconscious for a few minutes. A few weeks later, Gage appeared to be fully recovered. However, prior to the accident, Gage had been an easygoing fellow. Afterward, he was rude and impulsive. His changed personality cost him his job, and he lived out the rest of his life as a circus sideshow exhibit (adapted from Harlow, 1848).

Frontal Lobes: Motor Cortex. The **motor cortex** is the frontal lobe region that coordinates voluntary body movements. The right motor cortex controls movement on the left side of the body, and the left motor cortex controls movement on the right side of the body. In 1937, Canadian neurosurgeon Wilder Penfield applied electrical

2.10 Which functions are associated with each of the four lobes of the cerebral cortex?

frontal lobes The largest of the brain's lobes, which contain the motor cortex, Broca's area, and the frontal association areas.

prefrontal cortex The part of the frontal lobes directly behind the forehead that controls executive processing, the coordination of multiple brain activities in pursuit of cognitive goals.

👁 **Watch** the Video *Episode 3: Thinking Like a Psychologist: The Pre-Frontal Cortex: The Good, the Bad, and the Criminal* in **MyPsychLab**

motor cortex The strip of tissue at the rear of the frontal lobes that controls voluntary body movement and participates in learning and cognitive events.

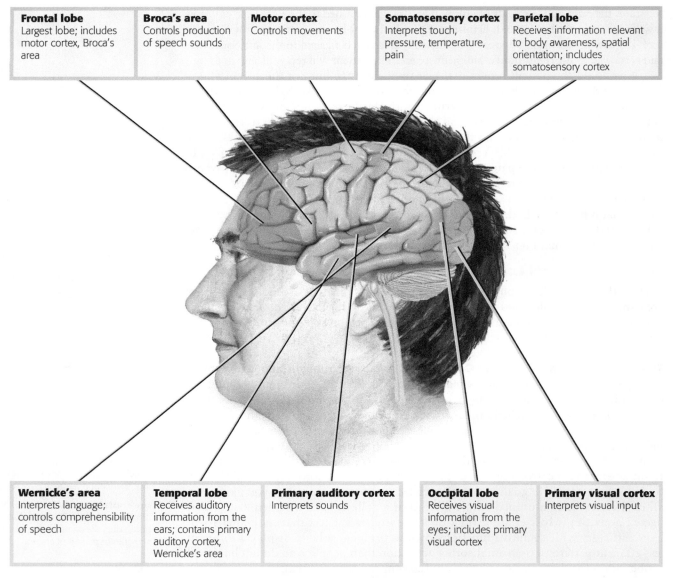

Frontal lobe
Largest lobe; includes motor cortex, Broca's area

Broca's area
Controls production of speech sounds

Motor cortex
Controls movements

Somatosensory cortex
Interprets touch, pressure, temperature, pain

Parietal lobe
Receives information relevant to body awareness, spatial orientation; includes somatosensory cortex

Wernicke's area
Interprets language; controls comprehensibility of speech

Temporal lobe
Receives auditory information from the ears; contains primary auditory cortex, Wernicke's area

Primary auditory cortex
Interprets sounds

Occipital lobe
Receives visual information from the eyes; includes primary visual cortex

Primary visual cortex
Interprets visual input

FIGURE 2.12 The Four Lobes of the Cerebral Cortex
This illustration of the left cerebral hemisphere shows the four lobes: (1) the frontal lobe, including the motor cortex and Broca's area; (2) the parietal lobe, with the somatosensory cortex; (3) the occipital lobe, with the primary visual cortex; and (4) the temporal lobe, with the primary auditory cortex and Wernicke's area.

stimulation to the motor cortex of conscious human patients undergoing neurosurgery. He then mapped the primary motor cortex in humans. The parts of the body that are capable of the most finely coordinated movements, such as the fingers, lips, and tongue, have a larger share of the motor cortex. Movements in the lower parts of the body are controlled primarily by neurons at the top of the motor cortex, whereas movements in the upper body parts (face, lips, and tongue) are controlled mainly by neurons near the bottom of the motor cortex. For example, when you wiggle your right big toe, the movement is produced mainly by the firing of a cluster of brain cells at the top of the left motor cortex.

How accurately and completely does Penfield's map account for the control of body movement? Although it may be useful in a broad sense, more recent research has shown that there is not a precise one-to-one correspondence between specific points on the motor cortex and movement of particular body parts. Motor neurons that control the fingers, for example, play a role in the movement of more than a single finger. In fact, the control of movement of any single finger is handled by a network of neurons that are widely distributed over the entire hand area of the motor cortex (Sanes & Donoghue, 2000).

Frontal Lobes: Broca's Area. In 1861, physician Paul Broca performed autopsies on two patients—one who had been totally without speech and another who could say only four words (Jenkins et al., 1975). Broca found that both individuals had damage in the left hemisphere, slightly in front of the part of the motor cortex that controls movements of the jaw, lips, and tongue. He concluded that the site of left hemisphere damage he identified through the autopsies was the part of the brain responsible for speech production, now called **Broca's area** (refer to Figure 2.12). Broca's area is involved in directing the pattern of muscle movement required to produce speech sounds.

If Broca's area is damaged as a result of head injury or stroke, **Broca's aphasia** may result. **Aphasia** is a general term for a loss or impairment of the ability to use or understand language, resulting from damage to the brain (Kirshner & Jacobs, 2008). Characteristically, patients with Broca's aphasia know what they want to say but can speak very little or not at all. If they are able to speak, their words are produced very slowly, with great effort, and are poorly articulated.

The Parietal Lobes. The **parietal lobes** lie directly behind the frontal lobes, in the top middle portion of the brain (refer back to Figure 2.12). The parietal lobes are involved in the reception and processing of touch stimuli. The front strip of brain tissue in the parietal lobes is the **somatosensory cortex**, the site where touch, pressure, temperature, and pain register in the cerebral cortex (Purves et al., 2011). Thesomatosensory cortex also makes you aware of movement in your body and the positions of your body parts at any given moment.

The two halves of the somatosensory cortex, in the left and right parietal lobes, are wired to opposite sides of the body. Also, cells at the top of the somatosensory cortex govern feeling in the lower extremities of the body. If you drop a brick on your right foot, the topmost brain cells of the left somatosensory cortex will fire and register the pain sensation. (*Note:* This is *not* a *Try It!*) The large somatosensory areas are connected to sensitive body parts such as the tongue, lips, face, and hand, particularly the thumb and index finger.

Other parts of the parietal lobes are responsible for spatial orientation and sense of direction—for example, helping you to retrace your path when you take a wrong turn. The hippocampus cooperates with these parts of the parietal lobes in performing such functions, as the study of London taxi drivers discussed on page 52 indicates (Maguire et al., 2000). Association areas in the parietal lobes also house memories of how objects feel against the human skin, a fact that explains why we can identify objects by touch. People with damage to these areas could hold a computer mouse, a CD, or a baseball in their hand but not be able to identify the object by touch alone.

The Occipital Lobes. Behind the parietal lobes at the rear of the brain lie the **occipital lobes**, which are involved in the reception and interpretation of visual information (refer to Figure 2.12). At the very back of the occipital lobes is the **primary visual cortex**, the site where vision registers in the cortex.

Each eye is connected to the primary visual cortex in both the right and the left occipital lobes. Look straight ahead and draw an imaginary line down the middle of what you see. Everything to the left of the line is referred to as the left visual field and registers in the right visual cortex. Everything to the right of the line is the right visual field and registers in the left visual cortex. A person who sustains damage to

▲ The skull of Phineas Gage is on display at the Warren Anatomical Museum at Harvard University. As you can see, the tamping rod tore through his frontal lobes leaving him with an altered personality.

Broca's area (BRO-kuz) The area in the frontal lobe, usually in the left hemisphere, that controls the production of speech sounds.

Broca's aphasia (BRO-kuz uh-FAY-zyah) An impairment in the physical ability to produce speech sounds or, in extreme cases, an inability to speak at all; caused by damage to Broca's area.

aphasia (uh-FAY-zyah) A loss or impairment of the ability to use or understand language, resulting from damage to the brain.

parietal lobes (puh-RY-uh-tul) The lobes that contain the somatosensory cortex (where touch, pressure, temperature, and pain register) and other areas that are responsible for body awareness and spatial orientation.

somatosensory cortex (so-MAT-oh-SENS-or-ee) The strip of tissue at the front of the parietal lobes where touch, pressure, temperature, and pain register in the cerebral cortex.

occipital lobes (ahk-SIP-uh-tul) The lobes that are involved in the reception and interpretation of visual information; they contain the primary visual cortex.

primary visual cortex The area at the rear of the occipital lobes where vision registers in the cerebral cortex.

▲ Because the left hand of a professional string player like Boyd Tinsley of the Dave Matthews Band must rapidly and accurately execute fine movements and slight pressure variations, it is not surprising that these musicians have an unusually large area of the somatosensory cortex dedicated to the fingers of that hand.

temporal lobes The lobes that are involved in the reception and interpretation of auditory information; they contain the primary auditory cortex, Wernicke's area, and the temporal association areas.

primary auditory cortex The part of each temporal lobe where hearing registers in the cerebral cortex.

Wernicke's area (VUR-nih-keys) The language area in the left temporal lobe involved in comprehending the spoken word and in formulating coherent speech and written language.

Wernicke's aphasia Aphasia that results from damage to Wernicke's area and in which the person's speech is fluent and clearly articulated but does not make sense to listeners.

one half of the primary visual cortex will still have partial vision in both eyes because each eye sends information to both the right and the left occipital lobes.

The association areas in the occipital lobes are involved in the interpretation of visual stimuli. They hold memories of past visual experiences and enable us to recognize what is familiar among the things we see. That's why the face of a friend stands out in a crowd of unfamiliar people. When these areas are damaged, people can lose the ability to identify objects visually, although they will still be able to identify the same objects by touch or through some other sense.

The Temporal Lobes. The **temporal lobes**, located slightly above the ears, are involved in the reception and interpretation of auditory stimuli. The site in the cortex where hearing registers is known as the primary auditory cortex. The **primary auditory cortex** in each temporal lobe receives sound inputs from both ears. Injury to one of these areas results in reduced hearing in both ears, and the destruction of both areas causes total deafness.

Adjacent to the primary auditory cortex in the left temporal lobe is **Wernicke's area**, which is the language area involved in comprehending the spoken word and in formulating coherent written and spoken language (refer to Figure 2.12). When you listen to someone speak, the sound registers first in the primary auditory cortex. The sound is then sent to Wernicke's area, where the speech sounds are unscrambled into meaningful patterns of words.

Wernicke's aphasia is a type of aphasia resulting from damage to Wernicke's area. Although speech is fluent and words are clearly articulated, the actual message does not make sense to listeners (Kirshner & Hoffmann, 2012). The content may be vague or bizarre and may contain inappropriate words, parts of words, or a gibberish of nonexistent words. One Wernicke's patient, when asked how he was feeling, replied, "I think that there's an awful lot of mung, but I think I've a lot of net and tunged in a little wheat duhvayden" (Buckingham & Kertesz, 1974). People with Wernicke's aphasia are not aware that anything is wrong with their speech. Thus, this disorder is difficult to treat.

The remainder of the temporal lobes consists of the association areas that house memories and are involved in the interpretation of auditory stimuli. For example, the association area where your memories of various sounds are stored enables you to recognize the sounds of your favorite band, a computer booting up, your roommate snoring, and so on. There is also a special association area where familiar melodies are stored.

We've covered all of the various parts of the brain and their respective functions unique to all humans, but are all human brains the same? In the next section, we'll look at the ways our brains may or may not be different.

REMEMBER IT *Check your answers and take additional quizzes in MyPsychLab.com.* ✓—Study and Review on MyPsychLab

1. The band of fibers connecting the left and right cerebral hemispheres is the _____.

2. When you listen to a person talk, you most likely process her words in your _____ hemisphere.

3. You process facial expressions in your _____ hemisphere.

4. The split-brain operation is sometimes performed to cure _____.

5. _____ is to speech production as _____ is to speech understanding.

6. The primary auditory cortex is found in the _____ lobe, while the primary visual cortex is located in the _____ lobe.

7. A person with brain damage who has problems regulating emotion most likely has an injury to the _____ lobe.

8. The sense of touch is associated with the _____ lobe.

Age, Gender, and the Brain

How many adults express concern that the moon might be following them? It is likely that you have never heard an adult express such a concern. Nevertheless, it is one of several irrational worries that are frequently expressed by preschoolers. Nowadays, most people have heard something about the link between brain development and such differences in children's and adults' thinking. And it is common to hear people attribute the cognitive deficits displayed by some elderly people to deterioration of their brains. Likewise, interest never seems to wane in the idea that men's and women's brains process information differently. What is the evidence regarding these popular notions about age and gender differences in the brain?

The Ever-Changing Brain ▶

2.11 How does the brain change across the lifespan?

When do you think the brain reaches full maturity? The answer to this question might surprise you. In fact, the brain grows in spurts from conception until well into adulthood (Chamley, Carson, & Sandwell, 2005). In childhood and adolescence, many of these spurts are correlated with major advances in physical and intellectual skills, such as the acquisition of fluency in language that happens around age 4 for most children. Each growth spurt also seems to involve a different brain area. For example, the spurt that begins around age 17 and continues into the early 20s mainly affects the frontal lobes, where the abilities to plan and to control one's emotions are located. Differences between teens and adults in these abilities may be due to this growth spurt. Changes in brain function are influenced by several development processes.

Synapses develop as a result of the growth of both dendrites and axons. This process, known as *synaptogenesis,* occurs in spurts throughout the life span. Each spurt is followed by a period of **pruning**, the process through which the developing brain eliminates unnecessary or redundant synapses. The activity of neurotransmitters within the synapses also varies with age. For example, acetylcholine is less plentiful in the brains of children than in the brains of teens and adults. This difference may help explain age differences in memory and other functions influenced by this excitatory neurotransmitter.

pruning The process through which the developing brain eliminates unnecessary or redundant synapses.

The process of *myelination,* or the development of myelin sheaths around axons, begins prior to birth but continues well into adulthood. For example, the brain's association areas are not fully myelinated until age 12 or so (Tanner, 1990). And the reticular formation, which regulates attention, isn't fully myelinated until the mid-20s (Spreen et al., 1995). Thus, differences in myelination may account for differences between children and adults in processing speed, memory, and other functions.

Some degree of hemispheric specialization is present very early in life. Language processing, for example, occurs primarily in the left hemisphere of the fetal and infant brain, just as it does in the adult brain (Chilosi et al., 2001; de Lacoste et al., 1991). Other functions, such as spatial perception, aren't lateralized until age 8 or so. Consequently, children younger than age 8 exhibit much poorer spatial skills than do older children (Roberts & Bell, 2000). For instance, children younger than 8 have difficulty using maps and distinguishing between statements such as *It's on your left* and *It's on my left.*

The brain's **plasticity**—its capacity to adapt to changes such as brain damage—is maintained throughout life. This plasticity allows synapses to strengthen and reorganize their interconnections when stimulated by experience and practice as the *Try It* on page 62 demonstrates. Plasticity is greatest in young children within whom the hemispheres are not yet completely lateralized. However, researchers have found that the correction of hearing defects in late-middle-aged adults results in changes in all the areas of the brain that are involved in sound perception (Fallon, Irvine, & Shepherd, 2008). Moreover, the brains of these individuals appear to develop responses to sounds in areas in which the brains of people with normal hearing do not. ◉

plasticity The capacity of the brain to adapt to changes such as brain damage.

◉ **Watch** the Video *Special Topics: The Plastic Brain* in **MyPsychLab**

TRY IT   Mirror Tracing

For this activity, you will need a mirror, some way to stand the mirror up, a pencil, and two pieces of lined paper. First, write the word PSYCHOLOGY in block letters two lines high five times working from the top of the paper to the bottom, as shown below:

Next, prop up the mirror at the top of the paper so that it is at a right angle to the paper as shown below:

Now comes the difficult part. Looking only at the images of the paper and your hand in the mirror, trace the letters. If you can't resist looking at your hand as you write, hold the second piece of paper in your other hand so that it blocks your view and forces you to look in the mirror. When you're finished tracing, determine your error rate by counting the number of times your tracings deviate from the letters' lines and curves. Repeat the exercise four more times, recording your error rate for each trial.

If you're like most people, you will find that your error rate declines somewhat from the first to the fifth trial. Why? At first, the task is extremely difficult, because interpretations of visual information that are produced by the visual cortex in the occipital lobes guide the actions of the frontal lobes' motor cortex. In the mirror image, the effects of your movements are the opposite of what years of experience with handwriting have led your visual cortex to expect. As a result, it must acquire a new set of expectations that apply to mirror image movements before it can effectively guide your motor cortex. Each time you practice the task, you are providing your visual cortex with the information it needs to create these new expectations. (Practice makes perfect!) This activity demonstrates that, no matter how much we have practiced a particular skill, some degree of neural plasticity remains.

Despite the retention of some degree of plasticity, the brain is subject to the physical effects of aging. For example, the brain both gains and loses synapses throughout life. At some point in adulthood, however, losses begin to exceed gains (Huttenlocher, 1994). Brain weight begins to decline around age 30 (Raz et al., 2006). Age-related deficits due to the loss of brain weight are common. For example, shrinkage of the cerebellum causes elderly people tend to experience problems with balance, they become less steady on their feet, and their gait is affected.

In addition, as you will learn in Chapter 10, the health of the heart and blood vessels often deteriorates as adults get older. With this deterioration comes an increased risk of **stroke**, an event in the cardiovascular system in which a blood clot or plug of fat blocks an artery and cuts off the blood supply to a particular area of the brain. Strokes cause brain damage that can range from mild to severe. Some survivors have long-term intellectual and physical impairments. However, physical therapy can help most of them recover at least partial motor functions, providing yet another example of the brain's plasticity (Bruno-Petrina, 2009).

stroke An event in the cardiovascular system in which a blood clot or plug of fat blocks an artery and cuts off the blood supply to a particular area of the brain.

Gender Differences in the Brain ▶

⌈ **2.12** How do the brains of
⌊ men and women differ?

Throughout development, the brains of males and females differ to some degree. However, these differences and their possible links to behavior have been most thoroughly researched among adults. One such difference involves gender differences in the distribution of gray and white matter and gray matter. Generally, the more white matter there is in an area of the brain, the more neural communication there is in it. Thus, that the brains of men have a higher proportion of white matter than do the brains of women may be relevant to understanding gender differences in cognitive functioning (Gur et al., 1999). Moreover, men have a lower proportion of white matter in the left brain than in the right brain. In contrast, in women's brains, the proportions of gray matter and white matter in the two hemispheres are equivalent. Such findings have led some neuropsychologists to speculate that gender differences in the distribution of gray and white matter across the two hemispheres may explain men's superior performance on right-hemisphere tasks such as mental rotation of geometric figures. Likewise, women's superior abilities in the domain of emotional perception (more on this in Chapter 9) may be attributable to the fact that they have more gray matter than men do in the right hemisphere where information about emotions is processed (Gur et al., 2002).

Other research has revealed that some tasks stimulate different parts of the brain in men and women. For example, imaging studies have shown that men process navigational information, such as that needed to find the way out of a maze, in the left hippocampus. By contrast, women who are engaged in the same task use the right parietal cortex and the right frontal cortex (Gron et al., 2000). Similarly, studies show that men and women use different areas of the brain when searching for the location of a sound (Lewald, 2004).

What is the meaning of these gender differences in the brain? The short answer is that scientists won't know for certain until a great deal more research is done. Moreover, studies that look for links between these brain differences and actual behavior are needed before any conclusions can be drawn regarding the possible neurological bases for gender differences in behavior.

REMEMBER IT   *Check your answers and take additional quizzes in MyPsychLab.com.*   ✓●⌈Study and Review on MyPsychLab

1. _____ is a gradual process during which connections between neurons develop.
2. The ability of the brain to adapt and change is known as _____.
3. Tasks that require _____ and _____ stimulate different parts of the brain in men and women.

Beyond the Nervous System

The body has two additional systems that influence how we function both physically and psychologically. The glands of the *endocrine system* exert their influences by producing, secreting, and regulating *hormones*. By contrast, in some cases, information encoded in our *genes* affects us from the moment of conception; in others, the influences of the genes appear later in life or depend on input from the environment.

The Endocrine System ▶

⌈ **2.13** What are the functions
of the glands of the endocrine
⌊ system?

Most people think of the reproductive system when they hear the word *hormones*. Or they may associate hormones with particular physical changes, such as those of puberty, pregnancy, or menopause. However, these substances regulate many other physical and psychological functions, and their influence reaches far beyond the reproductive system.

The **endocrine system** is a series of ductless glands, located in various parts of the body, that manufacture and secrete the chemical substances known as **hormones,**

endocrine system (EN-duh-krin) A system of ductless glands in various parts of the body that manufacture hormones and secrete them into the bloodstream, thus affecting cells in other parts of the body.

hormone A chemical substance that is manufactured and released in one part of the body and affects other parts of the body.

which are manufactured and released in one part of the body but have an effect on other parts of the body. Hormones are released into the bloodstream and travel throughout the circulatory system, but each hormone performs its assigned job only when it connects with the body cells that have receptors for it. For instance, in women, the ovaries and adrenal glands produce *progesterone* for which there are receptor sites in the reproductive tissues of women's bodies. Some of the same chemical substances that are neurotransmitters act as hormones as well—norepinephrine and vasopressin, to name two. Figure 2.13 shows the glands in the endocrine system and their locations in the body.

pituitary gland The endocrine gland located in the brain that releases hormones that activate other endocrine glands as well as growth hormone; often called the "master gland."

The **pituitary gland** rests in the brain just below the hypothalamus and is controlled by it (see Figure 2.13). The pituitary is considered to be the "master gland" of the body because it releases the hormones that activate, or turn on, the other glands in the endocrine system—a big job for a tiny structure about the size of a pea. The pituitary also produces the hormone that is responsible for body growth (Howard et al., 1996). Too little of this powerful substance will make a person a dwarf; too much will produce a giant.

pineal gland The endocrine gland that secretes the hormone that controls the sleep/wakefulness cycle.

The **pineal gland** lies deep within the brain. Its function is to produce and regulate the hormone *melatonin*. As you will learn in Chapter 4, this hormone regulates sleep and wakefulness. Deficiencies are associated with jet lag and other disturbances of the sleep/wakefulness cycle.

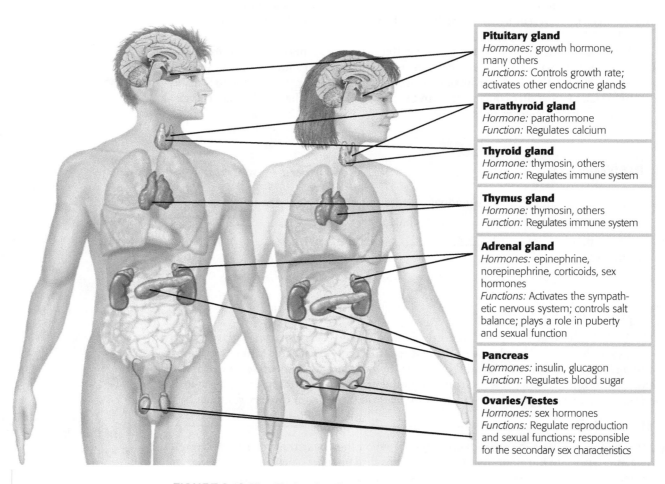

Pituitary gland
Hormones: growth hormone, many others
Functions: Controls growth rate; activates other endocrine glands

Parathyroid gland
Hormone: parathormone
Function: Regulates calcium

Thyroid gland
Hormone: thymosin, others
Function: Regulates immune system

Thymus gland
Hormone: thymosin, others
Function: Regulates immune system

Adrenal gland
Hormones: epinephrine, norepinephrine, corticoids, sex hormones
Functions: Activates the sympathetic nervous system; controls salt balance; plays a role in puberty and sexual function

Pancreas
Hormones: insulin, glucagon
Function: Regulates blood sugar

Ovaries/Testes
Hormones: sex hormones
Functions: Regulate reproduction and sexual functions; responsible for the secondary sex characteristics

FIGURE 2.13 The Endocrine System
The endocrine system is a series of glands that manufacture and secrete hormones. The hormones travel through the circulatory system and have important effects on many bodily functions.

The **thyroid gland** rests in the front, lower part of the neck just below the voice box (larynx). The thyroid produces the important hormone thyroxine, which regulates the rate at which food is metabolized, or transformed into energy. The **parathyroid glands** are attached to the left and right lobes of the thyroid. Parathyroid hormone (PTH) is involved in the absorption of calcium and magnesium from the diet and regulates the levels of these minerals in the bloodstream. Dysfunctions of the parathyroid are also linked to depression and memory loss (Kim & Makdissi, 2009).

The **thymus gland**, as you will learn in Chapter 10, produces hormones such as thymosin that are needed for the production of specialized white blood cells that circulate throughout the body and destroy microorganisms that can cause diseases. When the body is threatened by one of these invaders, the thymus gland signals the body to produce more of these cells. The **pancreas** regulates the body's blood sugar levels by releasing the hormones insulin and glucagon into the bloodstream. In people with diabetes, too little insulin is produced. Without insulin to break down the sugars in food, blood-sugar levels can get dangerously high.

The two **adrenal glands**, which rest just above the kidneys (as shown in Figure 2.13), produce epinephrine and norepinephrine. By activating the sympathetic nervous system, these two hormones play an important role in the fight-or-flight syndrome. A group of adrenal hormones called the corticoids are also involved in the fight-or-flight syndrome. Animal research suggests that these hormones contribute to both the emotion of rage and aggressive behavior by signaling the brain to maintain the fight-or-flight response long after the threat that initiated the response has passed (Kruk et al., 2004).

The adrenals also produce small amounts of sex hormones. However, the **gonads**—the ovaries in females and the testes in males—have the primary responsibility for these hormones (refer to Figure 2.13). Activated by the pituitary gland, the gonads release the sex hormones that make reproduction possible and that are responsible for the secondary sex characteristics—pubic and underarm hair in both sexes, breasts in females, and facial hair and a deepened voice in males. Androgens, the male sex hormones, influence sexual motivation. Estrogen and progesterone, the female sex hormones, help regulate the menstrual cycle. Although both males and females have androgens and estrogens, males have considerably more androgens, and females have considerably more estrogens. (The sex hormones and their effects are discussed in more detail in Chapter 9.)

Genes and Behavioral Genetics ▸

2.14 How does heredity affect physical and psychological traits?

You may have heard of the Human Genome Project, a 13-year enterprise spearheaded by the U.S. Department of Energy and devoted to mapping the entire human genetic code. Remarkably, in April 2003, only 50 years after scientists James Watson and Francis Crick discovered the structure of DNA (of which genes consist), the international team of scientists involved in the project announced that they had achieved their goal (U.S. Department of Energy, 2009). Of course, you received your own genetic code from your parents. But just how do the chemical messages that make up your genes affect your body and your behavior? 👁

The Mechanisms of Heredity. Genes are segments of DNA located on rod-shaped structures called **chromosomes**. The nuclei of normal body cells, with two exceptions, have 23 pairs of chromosomes (46 in all). The two exceptions are the sperm and egg cells, each of which has 23 single chromosomes. At conception, the sperm adds its 23 chromosomes to the 23 of the egg. From this union, a single cell called a *zygote* is formed; it has the full complement of 46 chromosomes (23 pairs), which contain about 20,000 to 25,000 genes (U.S. Department of Energy, 2012). These genes carry all the genetic information needed to make a human being. The Human Genome Project is aimed at identifying the functions of all the genes and their locations on the chromosomes. 👁

Twenty-two of the 23 pairs of chromosomes are matching pairs, called *autosomes,* and each member of these pairs carries genes for particular physical and mental traits.

thyroid gland The endocrine gland that produces thyroxine and regulates metabolism.

parathyroid glands The endocrine glands that produce PTH, a hormone that helps the body absorb minerals from the diet.

thymus gland The endocrine gland that produces hormones that are essential to immune system functioning.

pancreas The endocrine gland responsible for regulating the amount of sugar in the bloodstream.

adrenal glands (ah-DREE-nal) A pair of endocrine glands that release hormones that prepare the body for emergencies and stressful situations and also release corticoids and small amounts of the sex hormones.

gonads The ovaries in females and the testes in males; endocrine glands that produce sex hormones.

👁 Watch the Video *Basics: How the Human Genome Affects You* in **MyPsychLab**

genes The segments of DNA that are located on the chromosomes and are the basic units for the transmission of all hereditary traits.

chromosomes Rod-shaped structures in the nuclei of body cells, which contain all the genes and carry all the genetic information necessary to make a human being.

👁 Watch the Video *Episode 4: Genetic Mechanisms and Behavioral Genetics* in **MyPsychLab**

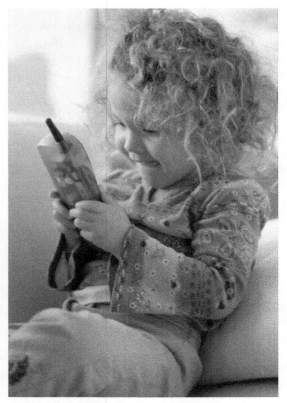

▲ This child's *phenotype* includes curly hair. What can you infer about her *genotype*? How likely is it that neither of her parents has curly hair?

genotype An individual's genetic makeup.

phenotype An individual's actual characteristics.

dominant–recessive pattern A set of inheritance rules in which the presence of a single dominant gene causes a trait to be expressed but two genes must be present for the expression of a recessive trait.

polygenic inheritance A pattern of inheritance in which many genes influence a trait.

◉〔**Watch** the Video *Episode 4: Special Topics: Epigenetics: A Revolutionary Science* in **MyPsychLab**

multifactorial inheritance A pattern of inheritance in which a trait is influenced by both genes and environmental factors.

The chromosomes in the 23rd pair are called *sex chromosomes* because they carry the genes that determine a person's sex. The sex chromosomes of females consist of two X chromosomes (XX); males have an X chromosome and a Y chromosome (XY). The egg cell always contains an X chromosome. Half of a man's sperm cells carry an X chromosome, and half carry a Y. Thus, the sex of an individual depends on which type of chromosome is carried by the sperm that fertilizes the egg. A single gene found only on the Y chromosome causes a fetus to become a male. This gene, which has been labeled Sry, orchestrates the development of the male sex organs (Capel, 2000).

Our individual genetic codes include some genes that are expressed and some that are not expressed. For example, some people carry the gene for a disease but do not have the disorder associated with it. To help distinguish genetic traits that are expressed from those that are not expressed, scientists use the term **genotype** to refer to an individual's genetic makeup and **phenotype** to refer to his or her actual traits. Thus, if a person carries the gene for a disease but does not have it, the disease is part of her genotype but not part of her phenotype. The *Apply It* feature on page 67 outlines some situations in which you might consider genetic counseling. Scientists still do not fully understand all of the factors that govern the expression of genes. However, a few of the rules that determine which aspects of an individual's genotype are expressed in her phenotype have been well established by research.

Many traits are influenced by complementary gene pairs, one from the sperm and the other from the egg. In most cases, these gene pairs follow a set of inheritance rules known as the **dominant–recessive pattern**. The gene for curly hair, for example, is dominant over the gene for straight hair. Thus, a person having one gene for curly hair and one for straight hair will have curly hair, and people with straight hair have two recessive genes.

Several neurological and psychological characteristics are associated with dominant or recessive genes. Hand preference appears to follow the dominant recessive pattern, although in a somewhat complex way, as discussed in the *Explain It* feature on page 54. However, most of the traits of interest to psychologists follow more complex inheritance patterns.

In **polygenic inheritance**, many genes influence a particular characteristic. For example, skin color is determined by several genes. When one parent has dark skin and the other is fair skinned, the child will have skin that is somewhere between the two. Many polygenic characteristics are subject to **multifactorial inheritance**; that is, they are influenced by both genes and environmental factors. For instance, a man's genes may allow him to reach a height of 6 feet, but if he suffers from malnutrition while still growing, his height may not reach its genetic potential. As you'll learn in later chapters, both intelligence (Chapter 7) and personality (Chapter 11) are believed to be polygenic and multifactorial in nature. In addition, many psychological disorders are both polygenic and multifactorial (Leonardo & Hen, 2006; McMahon et al., 2010). ◉

Sex-linked inheritance involves the genes on the X and Y chromosomes. In females, the two X chromosomes function pretty much like the autosomes: If one carries a harmful gene, the other usually has a gene that offsets its effects. In males, however, if the single X chromosome carries a harmful gene, there is no offsetting gene on the Y chromosome because it is very small and carries only the genes needed to create the male body type. Consequently, disorders caused by genes on the X chromosome occur far more often in males than in females. For example, one fairly common sex-linked disorder you will read about in Chapter 3 is *red-green color blindness*. About 5% of men have the disorder, but fewer than 1% of women have it (Mather, 2006). About 1 in every 4,000 males and 1 in every 8,000 females have a far more serious sex-linked disorder called *fragile-X syndrome*, which can cause mental retardation (Jewell & Buehler, 2011).

APPLY IT   Should You Consult a Genetic Counselor?

The purpose of genetic counseling is to estimate individuals' risk of having a child with a genetic disorder or of developing an inherited disorder themselves. If you have relatives who have such disorders, you may have wondered whether you should seek genetic counseling. Such counseling can be helpful to just about anyone, but there are a few situations in which professionals advise that genetic counseling is especially important.

Birth Defects and Inherited Diseases of Childhood
As you may know, prenatal testing can identify many birth defects and genetic disorders before a child is born. However, experts say that screening for such risks should be done prior to conception if any of the following applies to you or your partner (Brundage, 2002):

- You or your partner has previously had a child with a birth defect (e.g., spina bifida) or an inherited disorder (e.g., phenylketonuria).

- There is someone in your or your partner's family who displayed an unexplained developmental delay or disability (i.e., visual or hearing impairment, mental retardation) early in life.

- You or your partner belongs to an ethnic group in which there is a particularly high incidence of a specific inherited disorder (e.g., African Americans: sickle cell disease; European Jews: Tay-Sachs disease; Caucasians: cystic fibrosis; people of Greek, Middle Eastern, or North African descent: thalassemia).

Adult-Onset Genetic Disorders
Genetic counselors suggest that you seriously consider genetic counseling if anyone in your family has ever been diagnosed with one of these adult-onset genetic disorders:

- Huntington disease
- Myotonic muscular dystrophy
- Amyotrophic lateral sclerosis (ALS, Lou Gehrig disease)
- Schizophrenia

Hereditary Cancers
If someone in your family has been diagnosed with cancer, then genetic counseling can be helpful in determining your own risk of developing the disease. According to the Massey Cancer Center at Virginia Commonwealth University (2006), the following types of family histories are especially indicative of a need for genetic counseling:

- A family history of multiple cases of the same or related types of cancers
- One or more relatives with rare cancers
- Cancers occurring at an earlier age of onset than usual (for instance, under the age of 50 years) in at least one member

- Bilateral cancers (two cancers that develop independently in a paired organ, i.e., both kidneys or both breasts)
- One or more family members with two primary cancers (two original tumors that develop in different sites)
- Eastern European Jewish background

Multifactorial Disorders
Many chronic health conditions are attributable to a combination of genetic and lifestyle factors. While there are no genetic tests for these disorders, a genetic counselor can analyze your family history and help you determine your risk of developing one or more of them. A genetic counselor can also advise you as to the degree to which lifestyle changes might enable you to avoid some of the effects of a disorder that you have seen diminish the quality of life of one of your family members. Thus, you may want to seek genetic counseling if anyone in your family has been diagnosed with one or more of these multifactorial disorders:

- Adult-onset diabetes
- Hypertension
- Glaucoma
- Heart disease
- Rheumatoid arthritis
- Disorders of the endocrine system (e.g., hypothyroidism, pancreatitis)
- Autoimmune disorders (e.g., lupus, multiple sclerosis)
- Liver or kidney disease
- Depression
- Parkinson disease
- Alzheimer's disease

Making the Decision
Even if these checklists have led you to the conclusion that you should consult a genetic counselor, you may find it difficult to confront the possibility that you or your child may have to deal with a serious health problem. Such feelings are common among individuals whose family members have one of the conditions previously described. However, researchers have found that people who are uninformed about their personal genetic vulnerability actually tend to overestimate their chances of developing an inherited disorder (Quaid et al., 2001; Tercyak et al., 2001). Thus, genetic counseling will help you formulate a realistic assessment of your own personal risks and will also enable you to develop a plan for coping with them if a genetic disorder is likely to be in your future. ◉

◉—Watch the Video *Episode 4: In the Real World: Taking Control of Our Genes* in **MyPsychLab**

Behavioral Genetics. **Behavioral genetics** is a field of research that investigates the relative effects of heredity and environment—nature and nurture—on behavior (Loehlin, 2009). In twin studies, behavioral geneticists study identical twins (monozygotic twins) and fraternal twins (dizygotic twins) to determine how much they resemble each other on a variety of characteristics (Johnson, Turkheimer,

behavioral genetics A field of research that uses twin studies and adoption studies to investigate the relative effects of heredity and environment on behavior.

Gorresman, & Bouchard, 2009). Identical twins have exactly the same genes because a single sperm of the father fertilizes a single egg of the mother, forming a cell that then splits and forms two human beings—"identical copies." In the case of fraternal twins, two separate sperm cells fertilize two separate eggs that happen to be released at the same time during ovulation. Fraternal twins are no more alike genetically than any two siblings born to the same parents.

Twins who are raised together, whether identical or fraternal, have similar environments. If identical twins raised together are found to be more alike on a certain trait than fraternal twins raised together, then that trait is assumed to be more influenced by heredity. But if the identical and fraternal twin pairs do not differ on the trait, then that trait is assumed to be influenced more by environment. ◉

In adoption studies, behavioral geneticists study children adopted shortly after birth. Researchers compare the children's abilities and personality traits to those of their adoptive parents and those of their biological parents. This strategy allows researchers to disentangle the effects of heredity and environment.

Because heredity and environment work together to influence so many of the variables of interest to psychologists, you'll be reading a great deal more in later chapters about the debate concerning their relative influence.

◉ **Watch** the Video *Episode 4: Big Picture: Genes, Evolution, and Human Behavior* in **MyPsychLab**

REMEMBER IT

Check your answers and take additional quizzes in MyPsychLab.com. ✔ Study and Review on **MyPsychLab**

1. The endocrine glands secrete _____ directly into the _____.

2. The _____ gland acts as a "master gland" that activates the others.

3. Blood sugar levels are regulated by the _____ through the release of _____ and _____.

4. Sex hormones are produced by both the _____ and the _____.

5. The _____ is the gland responsible for maintaining balanced metabolism.

6. A _____ gene will not be expressed if the individual carries only one copy of it.

7. Characteristics that are affected by both genes and environment are said to be _____.

8. _____ is the field of research that investigates the relative effects of heredity and environment on behavior.

◉ Looking Back

One of the many things you learned about the nervous system in this chapter is that adaptability is one of its important features. For instance, as the case of Phineas Gage illustrates, many areas of the adult brain are irrevocably committed to certain functions, leaving us with a more vulnerable but more efficient brain than we had as children. Nevertheless, even in the face of devastating injury, the brain may continue to function. The complementary functions of excitatory and inhibitory neurotransmitters enable our brains to respond appropriately to different kinds of situations. Individuals who have split-brain surgery function quite well in everyday life; only in certain kinds of tasks do they show any effects from the loss of interhemispheric communication. When we need to react to an emergency, our endocrine and peripheral nervous systems collaborate to produce the temporary burst of energy we need. Finally, although a few characteristics and diseases are fully determined by our genes, most of our psychological traits are shaped by both heredity and environment, a theme that will be emphasized repeatedly in the coming chapters.

CHAPTER 2 SUMMARY

DISCOVERING THE MYSTERIES OF THE NERVOUS SYSTEM (pp. 39–41)

2.1 What does the electroencephalogram (EEG) reveal about the brain? (pp. 39–40)

An electroencephalogram (EEG) is a record of brain-wave activity. It can reveal an epileptic seizure and can show patterns of neural activity associated with learning disabilities, schizophrenia, Alzheimer's disease, sleep disorders, and other problems.

Key Terms

electroencephalogram (EEG), p. 39
microelectrode, p. 39

2.2 How do researchers use imaging techniques to study the nervous system? (pp. 40–41)

Both the CT scan and MRI provide detailed images of brain structures. The PET scan reveals patterns of blood flow, oxygen use, and glucose metabolism in the brain. It can

also show the action of drugs in the brain and other organs. PET scan studies show that different brain areas are used to perform different tasks. Functional MRI (fMRI) can provide information about brain function and structure more precisely and more rapidly than a PET scan. Two more recently developed technologies, SQUID and MEG, measure magnetic changes to reveal neural activity within the brain as it occurs.

Key Terms

CT scan (computerized axial tomography), p. 40
MRI (magnetic resonance imagery), p. 40
PET scan (positron-emission tomography), p. 40
functional MRI (fMRI), p. 40

THE NEURONS AND THE NEUROTRANSMITTERS (pp. 41–46)

2.3 What does each part of the neuron do? (pp. 41–42)

The cell body carries out metabolic functions. The dendrites receive messages from cell bodies and other neurons. The axon transmits messages to the dendrites and cell bodies of other neurons and to the muscles, glands, and other parts of the body. Glial cells support neurons' vital functions.

Key Terms

neuron, p. 41
neurotransmitters, p. 41
cell body, p. 41
dendrites, p. 41
axon, p. 42
axon terminal, p. 42
glial cells, p. 42

2.4 How do neurons transmit messages through the nervous system? (pp. 42–44)

The action potential, the primary means by which the brain and body communicate with one another via the nervous system, is the sudden reversal (from a negative to a positive value) of the resting potential on the cell membrane of a

neuron; this reversal initiates the firing of a neuron. A strong stimulus will cause many more neurons to fire and to fire much more rapidly than a weak stimulus will.

Key Terms

synapse, p. 43
resting potential, p. 43
action potential, p. 43
myelin sheath, p. 44

2.5 How do neurotransmitters work? (pp. 44–47)

Neurotransmitters are chemicals released into the synaptic cleft from the axon terminal of the sending neuron. They cross the synaptic cleft and bind to receptors on the receiving neuron, influencing the cell to fire or not to fire. Neurotransmitters work by speeding up, slowing down, or blocking messages between neurons. Drugs affect the nervous system by altering or mimicking neurotransmitters. Some neurotransmitters contribute to psychological disorders.

Key Terms

receptors, p. 44
reuptake, p. 45

THE HUMAN NERVOUS SYSTEM (pp. 47–52)

2.6 What are the structures and functions of the peripheral nervous system? (pp. 47–49)

The peripheral nervous system includes all of the nerves that connect the various parts of the body to the central nervous system. The somatic subdivision governs voluntary control of the body; the autonomic subdivision governs involuntary processes. Within the autonomic subdivision, the sympathetic nervous system mobilizes the body's resources during emergencies or during stress, and the parasympathetic nervous system brings the heightened bodily responses back to normal after an emergency.

Key Terms
peripheral nervous system, p. 47
central nervous system, p. 47
sympathetic nervous system, p. 48
parasympathetic nervous system, p. 48

2.7 What are the structures and functions of the central nervous system? (pp. 49–52)

The spinal cord transmits information from the body to the brain and from the brain to the body. The hindbrain contains the cerebellum, which regulates movement, muscle tone, and posture. The brainstem contains the medulla, which controls vital functions; the reticular formation, which controls arousal and attention; and the pons, which connects the two halves of the cerebellum. The substantia nigra, a structure in the midbrain, controls unconscious motor actions, such as riding a bicycle. The structures of the forebrain include (1) the thalamus, the relay station for information flowing into and out of the brain; (2) the hypothalamus, which regulates hunger, thirst, sexual behavior, internal body temperature, and emotional behaviors; (3) the limbic system, including the amygdala and the hippocampus, which is involved in emotional expression, memory, and motivation. The cerebrum is also part of the forebrain.

Key Terms
spinal cord, p. 49
hindbrain, p. 49
brainstem, p. 49
medulla, p. 49
pons, p. 49
reticular formation, p. 49
cerebellum, p. 49
midbrain, p. 50
substantia nigra, p. 51
forebrain, p. 51
thalamus, p. 51
hypothalamus, p. 51
limbic system, p. 51
amygdala, p. 51
hippocampus, p. 51

A CLOSER LOOK AT THE THINKING PART OF THE BRAIN (pp. 52–60)

2.8 What are the components of the cerebrum? (pp. 52–53)

The cerebral hemispheres are connected by the corpus callosum and covered by the cerebral cortex, which is primarily responsible for higher mental processes such as language, memory, and thinking.

Key Terms
cerebrum, p. 52
cerebral hemispheres, p. 52
corpus callosum, p. 52
cerebral cortex, p. 52
association areas, p. 53

2.9 What are the specialized functions of the left and right cerebral hemispheres? (pp. 53–57)

The left hemisphere controls the right side of the body, coordinates complex movements, and handles most of the language functions, including speaking, writing, reading, and understanding the written and the spoken word. The right hemisphere controls the left side of the body. It is specialized for visual–spatial perception, the interpretation of nonverbal behavior, and the recognition and expression of emotion.

Key Terms
lateralization, p. 54
left hemisphere, p. 54
right hemisphere, p. 55
split-brain operation, p. 55

2.10 Which functions are associated with each of the four lobes of the cerebral cortex? (pp. 57–61)

The frontal lobes contain (1) the motor cortex, which controls voluntary motor activity; (2) Broca's area, which functions in speech production; and (3) the frontal association areas, which are involved in thinking, motivation, planning for the future, impulse control, and emotional responses. The somatosensory cortex, where touch, pressure, temperature, and pain register, is in the parietal lobes. The occipital lobes receive and interpret visual information. The temporal lobes contain (1) the primary auditory cortex, where hearing registers in the cortex; (2) Wernicke's area, which processes the spoken word and formulates coherent speech and written language; and (3) the temporal association areas, which interpret auditory stimuli.

Key Terms
frontal lobes, p. 57
prefrontal cortex, p. 57
motor cortex, p. 57
Broca's area, p. 59

Broca's aphasia, p. 59
aphasia, p. 59
parietal lobes, p. 59
somatosensory cortex, p. 59
occipital lobes, p. 59
primary visual cortex, p. 59
temporal lobes, p. 60
primary auditory cortex, p. 60
Wernicke's area, p. 60
Wernicke's aphasia, p. 60

AGE, GENDER, AND THE BRAIN (pp. 61–63)

2.11 How does the brain change across the lifespan? (pp. 61–62)

The brain grows in spurts, each of which is followed by a period of pruning of unnecessary synapses. The activity of neurotransmitters within the synapses also varies with age. Few neurons are myelinated at birth, but the process of myelination continues into the adult years. Language appears to be lateralized very early in life, but other functions, such as spatial perception, aren't fully lateralized until age 8 or so. Aging eventually leads to a reduction in the number of synapses.

Key Terms
pruning, p. 61
plasticity, p. 61
stroke, p. 62

2.12 How do the brains of men and women differ? (p. 63)

Men's brains have a lower proportion of white matter in the left than in the right brain; women have equal proportions of gray and white matter in the two hemispheres. Some tasks tap different areas in men's brains than they do in the brains of women.

BEYOND THE NERVOUS SYSTEM (pp. 63–68)

2.13 What are the functions of the glands of the endocrine system? (pp. 63–65)

The pituitary gland releases hormones that control other glands in the endocrine system and also releases a growth hormone. The thyroid gland produces thyroxine, which regulates metabolism. The pancreas produces insulin and glucagon and regulates blood sugar levels. The adrenal glands release epinephrine and norepinephrine, which prepare the body for emergencies and stressful situations; these glands also release corticoids and small amounts of the sex hormones. The gonads are the sex glands, which produce the sex hormones and make reproduction possible.

Key Terms
endocrine system, p. 63
hormone, p. 63
pituitary gland, p. 64
pineal gland, p. 64
thyroid gland, p. 65
parathyroid glands, p. 65
thymus gland, p. 65
pancreas, p. 65
adrenal glands, p. 65
gonads, p. 65

2.14 How does heredity affect physical and psychological traits? (pp. 65–68)

Some genetic traits follow the dominant–recessive pattern in which pairs of genes control their manifestation. Others involve multiple genes (polygenic), and still others depend on the combined effects of genes and environmental factors (multifactorial). Behavioral geneticists use twin studies to examine the relative effects of heredity and environment on behavior as well as adoption and family studies. Such studies suggest that both intelligence and personality are polygenic and multifactorial.

Key Terms
genes, p. 65
chromosomes, p. 65
genotype, p. 66
phenotype, p. 66
dominant–recessive pattern, p. 66
polygenic inheritance, p. 66
multifactorial inheritance, p. 66
behavioral genetics, p. 67

Chapter 2 Study Guide

Answers to all the Study Guide questions are provided at the end of the book.

SECTION ONE: Chapter Review

Discovering the Mysteries of the Nervous System (pp. 39–41)

1. A(n) _____ requires that electrodes be placed on a person's scalp, while a(n) _____ requires that microelectrodes be inserted directly into the brain.

2. The CT scan and MRI are used to
   a. show the amount of activity in various parts of the brain.
   b. produce images of the brain's structures.
   c. measure electrical activity in the brain.
   d. observe neural communication at synapses.

3. Which of the following reveals the electrical activity of the brain by producing a record of brain waves?
   a. electroencephalogram
   b. CT scan
   c. PET scan
   d. MRI

4. Which of the following reveals brain structures, but not brain activity?
   a. CT scan
   b. EEG
   c. PET scan
   d. fMRI

5. Which of the following reveals both brain structure and brain activity?
   a. MRI
   b. PET scan
   c. fMRI
   d. CT scan

The Neurons and the Neurotransmitters (pp. 41–46)

6. The branchlike extensions of neurons that act as receivers of signals from other neurons are the
   a. dendrites.
   b. axons.
   c. neurotransmitters.
   d. cell bodies.

7. _____ support neurons, supplying them with nutrients and carrying away their waste products.

8. The junction where the axon of a sending neuron communicates with a receiving neuron is called the
   a. reuptake site.
   b. receptor site.
   c. synapse.
   d. axon terminal.

9. When a neuron fires, neurotransmitters are released from the synaptic vesicles in the _____ terminal into the synaptic cleft.
   a. dendrite
   b. cell body's
   c. receptor
   d. axon

10. The (resting, action) potential is the firing of a neuron that results when the charge within the neuron becomes more positive than the charge outside the cell membrane. The (resting, action) potential is the slight negative charge of the neuron.

11. Receptor sites on the receiving neuron
    a. receive any available neurotransmitter molecules.
    b. receive only neurotransmitter molecules of specific shapes.
    c. can only be influenced by neurotransmitters from a single neuron.
    d. are located only on the dendrites.

12. The neurotransmitter called *acetylcholine* is involved in
    a. memory.
    b. motor function.
    c. rapid eye movement during sleep.
    d. all of the above

13. _____ is a neurotransmitter that may be associated with ADHD.

14. _____ are neurotransmitters that act as natural painkillers.

15. Responses to cocaine involve the neurotransmitters _____ and _____.

16. The _____ nervous system connects the central nervous system to the rest of the body.
    a. central
    b. peripheral
    c. somatic
    d. autonomic

17. The _____ nervous system mobilizes the body's resources during times of stress; the _____ nervous system brings the heightened bodily responses back to normal when the emergency is over.
    a. somatic; autonomic
    b. autonomic; somatic
    c. sympathetic; parasympathetic
    d. parasympathetic; sympathetic

The Human Nervous System (pp. 47–52)

18. Match the brain structure with its description.
    _____ (1) connects the brain with the peripheral nervous system
    _____ (2) controls heart rate, breathing, and blood pressure
    _____ (3) consists of the medulla, the pons, and the reticular formation
    _____ (4) influences attention and arousal
    _____ (5) coordinates complex body movements
    _____ (6) serves as a relay station for sensory information flowing into the brain
    _____ (7) controls unconscious movements
    a. medulla
    b. spinal cord
    c. reticular formation
    d. thalamus
    e. cerebellum
    f. brainstem
    g. substantia nigra

19. The hypothalamus regulates all the following *except*
    a. internal body temperature.
    b. coordinated movement.
    c. hunger and thirst.
    d. sexual behavior.

20. The part of the limbic system primarily involved in the formation of memories is the (amygdala, hippocampus).

21. The _____ is associated with emotions, and the _____ is involved in memory.

A Closer Look at the Thinking Part of the Brain (pp. 52–60)

22. What is the thick band of fibers connecting the two cerebral hemispheres?
   a. cortex
   b. corpus callosum
   c. cerebrum
   d. motor cortex

23. The outer covering of the cerebrum is the
   a. cerebral cortex.
   b. cortex callosum.
   c. myelin sheath.
   d. white matter.

24. Match the lobes with the brain areas they contain.
   _____ (**1**) primary auditory cortex
   _____ (**2**) primary visual cortex
   _____ (**3**) motor cortex
   _____ (**4**) somatosensory cortex
   a. frontal lobes
   b. parietal lobes
   c. occipital lobes
   d. temporal lobes

25. Match the specialized area with the appropriate description of function.
   _____ (**1**) hearing registers
   _____ (**2**) vision registers
   _____ (**3**) touch, pressure, and temperature register
   _____ (**4**) voluntary movement
   _____ (**5**) thinking, motivation, impulse control
   a. primary visual cortex
   b. motor cortex
   c. association areas
   d. auditory cortex
   e. somatosensory cortex

26. Match the hemisphere with the specialized abilities usually associated with it.
   _____ (**1**) visual–spatial skills
   _____ (**2**) speech
   _____ (**3**) recognition and expression of emotion
   _____ (**4**) musical perception
   _____ (**5**) mathematics
   a. right hemisphere
   b. left hemisphere

27. Which of these statements is *not* true of the split-brain operation?
   a. It is used on people with severe epilepsy.
   b. It provides a means of studying the functions of the individual hemispheres.
   c. It causes major changes in intelligence, personality, and behavior.
   d. It makes transfer of information between hemispheres impossible.

Age, Gender, and the Brain (pp. 61–63)

28. Synaptic development (synaptogenesis) involves growth of
   a. dendrites.
   b. axons.
   c. both dendrites and axons.

29. One developmental process that contributes to differences in processing speed between children and adults is _____.

30. Men have a lower proportion of _____ _____ in the left hemisphere than in the right.

31. Navigational tasks stimulate (different, the same) areas of the brain in men and women.

32. As adults get older, brain weight (increases, decreases).

33. As adults get older, the risk of brain damage from _____ increases.

Beyond the Nervous System (pp. 63–68)

34. Match the endocrine gland with the appropriate description.
   _____ (**1**) keeps body's metabolism in balance
   _____ (**2**) acts as a master gland that activates the other glands
   _____ (**3**) regulates the blood sugar
   _____ (**4**) makes reproduction possible
   _____ (**5**) releases hormones that prepare the body for emergencies
   _____ (**6**) regulates sleep
   a. pituitary gland
   b. adrenal glands
   c. gonads
   d. thyroid gland
   e. pancreas
   f. pineal gland

35. A _____ gene will not be expressed unless an individual carries two copies of it.

36. Characteristics that are affected by both genes and environment are said to be
   a. polygenic.
   b. dominant.
   c. recessive.
   d. multifactorial.

37. Researchers use _____ and _____ to examine the effects of heredity and environment.

SECTION TWO: Label the Brain

Identify each of the numbered parts in the brain diagram.

1. _____   5. _____
2. _____   6. _____
3. _____   7. _____
4. _____   8. _____

SECTION THREE: Comprehensive Practice Test

1. Phineas Gage changed from a polite, dependable, well-liked railroad fore-man to a rude and impulsive person who could no longer plan realistically for the future after he suffered serious damage to his
   a. occipital lobe.
   b. frontal lobe.
   c. medulla.
   d. cerebellum.

2. A researcher interested in getting information about the brain's activity based on the amount of oxygen and glucose consumed should use a(n)
   a. MRI.
   b. EEG.
   c. PET scan.
   d. CT scan.

3. Functional MRI (fMRI) reveals both brain structure and brain activity. (true/false)

4. Afferent is to efferent as
   a. sensory is to sensation.
   b. sensation is to perception.
   c. motor is to sensory.
   d. sensory is to motor.

5. _____ plays an important role in regulating mood, sleep, impulsivity, aggression, and appetite.
   a. Dopamine
   b. Norepinephrine
   c. Acetylcholine
   d. Serotonin

6. Neurons can conduct messages faster if they have
   a. an axon with a myelin sheath.
   b. a positive resting potential.
   c. more than one cell body.
   d. fewer dendrites.

7. The electrical charge inside a neuron is about –70 millivolts and is known as the _____ potential.
   a. action
   b. refractory
   c. resting
   d. impulse

8. The main divisions of the nervous system are the _____ and the _____ systems.
   a. somatic; autonomic
   b. central; peripheral
   c. brain; spinal cord
   d. sympathetic; parasympathetic

9. The structure that is located above the brainstem and serves as a relay station for information flowing into or out of the forebrain is the
   a. pituitary gland.
   b. hypothalamus.
   c. thalamus.
   d. hippocampus.

10. The structure that is located in the brainstem and is important for basic life functions such as heartbeat and breathing is the
    a. pons.
    b. medulla.
    c. hypothalamus.
    d. amygdala.

11. The _____ is sometimes referred to as the body's thermostat because it controls temperature, hunger, thirst, and emotional behaviors.
    a. corpus callosum
    b. pituitary gland
    c. cerebellum
    d. hypothalamus

12. The lobe that contains the primary visual cortex is the
    a. parietal lobe.
    b. occipital lobe.
    c. temporal lobe.
    d. frontal lobe.

13. The primary motor cortex is located in the _____ lobe.
    a. frontal
    b. occipital
    c. temporal
    d. oculo-visual

14. The pituitary gland, known as the master gland, is part of the _____ system.
    a. somatic
    b. peripheral nervous
    c. endocrine
    d. central nervous

15. The _____ nervous system controls skeletal muscles and allows the body to interact with the external environment.
    a. autonomic
    b. parasympathetic
    c. sympathetic
    d. somatic

16. Damage to Broca's area will result in a type of aphasia that impairs one's ability to produce speech sounds. (true/false)

17. The prefrontal cortex is involved in all of the following functions *except*
    a. controlling heart beat and respiration
    b. impulse control
    c. personality
    d. coordination of multiple brain functions to accomplish cognitive goals

18. _____ _____ isn't lateralized to the right hemisphere until age 8 or so.

19. Women are more likely than men to process navigational tasks in the _____ _____ _____ and _____ _____ _____.

20. Red-green color blindness is caused by a defective gene on the _____.

SECTION FOUR: Critical Thinking

1. Much of the brain research you have read about in this chapter was carried out using animals. In many studies, it is necessary to euthanize animals to study their brain tissues directly. Many people object to this practice, but others say it is justified because it advances knowledge about the brain. Prepare arguments to support both of the following positions:
   a. The use of animals in brain research projects is ethical and justifiable because of the possible benefits to humankind.
   b. The use of animals in brain research projects is not ethical or justifiable on the grounds of possible benefits to humankind.

SECTION FIVE: Application Essays

1. How would your life change if you had a massive stroke affecting your left hemisphere? How would it change if the stroke damaged your right hemisphere? Which stroke would have the greater effect on the quality of your life, and why?

2. Imagine that your parent has been diagnosed with diabetes, and you are worried about whether the disease is hereditary. What would a genetic counselor be able tell you about your risk of developing it?

Apply your critical thinking skills with **MyPsychLab** Writing Assignments

Submit your answer to the following question inside the MyPsychLab Writing Assessment program for immediate feedback.

Your best friends invite you over for pizza and a friendly game of cards. Describe how each lobe of your cerebral cortex is involved in your evening of eating pizza, socializing, and playing cards.

Sensation and Perception

3

CHAPTER

◎ THINK ABOUT IT

Try standing on one foot like the woman in the accompanying illustration. You'll probably have no trouble maintaining your balance for at least 30 seconds. But what will happen if you try to maintain this position with your eyes closed? Try it and find out.

No doubt you found it more difficult to keep your balance with your eyes closed. Your body's system for maintaining balance is a complex one that depends on several types of input. As you just learned, visual input is critical. In fact, visual input is so important that doctors use the one-leg/eyes-closed test to assess neurological health (Chaitow & DeLany, 2002). Because performance on the test normally declines as we get older (due to the aging of the cerebellum that we learned about in Chapter 2), it can also be used to determine whether your brain is aging normally. Studies suggest that, if you're between the ages of 20 and 49, and you can't maintain your balance on one foot with your eyes closed for at least

25 seconds, your brain might be aging more rapidly than those of your peers (Bohannon et al., 1984). But take heart, exercise regimens that emphasize balance, such as the ancient Chinese mediation practice of *Tai Chi,* which consists of slow, deliberate movements, can help to counteract the effects of aging (Fuzhong, Harmer, Fisher, & McAutey, 2004).

Your body's ability to maintain its position is just one of many topics that we'll address as we explore the interactive processes of *sensation* and *perception.*

First, we'll consider the two dominant senses: vision and hearing. Then we'll turn our attention to the other senses: smell, taste, touch, pain, and balance. You will learn how the senses detect sensory information and how this sensory information is actively organized and interpreted by the brain.

The Process of Sensation

sensation The process through which the senses pick up visual, auditory, and other sensory stimuli and transmit them to the brain.

perception The process by which the brain actively organizes and interprets sensory information.

Sensation is the process through which the senses pick up visual, auditory, and other sensory stimuli and transmit them to the brain. **Perception** is the process by which the brain actively organizes and interprets sensory information. Sensation furnishes the raw material of sensory experience, whereas perception provides the finished product. In a way, sensation and perception are somewhat like cooking. To bake a cake, for example, you have to gather the various ingredients—eggs, flour, baking powder, and so on. This part of the process is analogous to sensation. A process analogous to perception enters the picture when you follow a recipe to combine the ingredients. The recipe's instructions are analogous to the principles of perception that the brain applies to sensations. In cooking, the finished product, which is analogous to a finished perception in the brain, is the cake. Both the cake and the perception result from the application of a set of rules and procedures to an array of raw ingredients.

However, we can only carry this analogy so far. In reality, sensation and perception are not entirely discrete, independent processes. Instead, they are interactive: Sensation provides the data for perception, but perceptual processes influence sensation. Keep this in mind as you read about sensory and perceptual processes throughout the chapter. Before we consider perception, we will take a look at the process of sensation. ◉

◉ Watch the Video *Episode 5: Big Picture: Taking in the World Around Us* in **MyPsychLab**

3.1 What are the absolute and difference thresholds?

The Absolute and Difference Thresholds

What is the softest sound you can hear, the dimmest light you can see, the most diluted substance you can taste? Researchers in sensory psychology have performed many experiments over the years to answer these questions. Their research has established measures for the senses known as absolute thresholds. Just as the threshold of a doorway is the dividing point between being outside a room and inside, the **absolute threshold** of a sense marks the difference between not being able to perceive a stimulus and being just barely able to perceive it. Psychologists have arbitrarily defined this absolute threshold as the minimum amount of sensory stimulation that can be detected 50% of the time. The absolute thresholds for vision, hearing, taste, smell, and touch are illustrated in Figure 3.1. You can experience an absolute threshold by doing the *Try It* on page 78.

absolute threshold The minimum amount of sensory stimulation that can be detected 50% of the time.

If you are listening to music, the very fact that you can hear it means that the absolute threshold has been crossed. But how much must the volume be turned up or down

(a) For vision, a candle flame 30 miles away on a clear night

(b) For hearing, a watch ticking 20 feet away

(c) For taste, 1 teaspoon of sugar dissolved in 2 gallons of water

(d) For smell, a single drop of perfume in a three-room house

(e) For touch, a bee's wing falling a distance of 1 centimeter onto the cheek

FIGURE 3.1 Absolute Thresholds Just as the threshold of a doorway is the dividing point between being outside a room and being inside it, the absolute threshold of a sense marks the difference between not being able to perceive a stimulus and being just barely able to perceive it.

for you to notice a difference? Or, if you are carrying some bags of groceries, how much weight must be added or taken away for you to be able to sense that your load is heavier or lighter? The **difference threshold** is a measure of the smallest increase or decrease in a physical stimulus that is required to produce the **just noticeable difference (JND)**. The JND is the smallest change in sensation that a person is able to detect 50% of the time. If you were holding a 5-pound weight and 1 pound were added, you could easily notice the difference. But if you were holding 100 pounds and 1 additional pound were added, you could not sense the difference. Why not?

More than 150 years ago, researcher Ernst Weber (1795–1878) observed that the JND for all the senses depends on a proportion or percentage of change in a stimulus rather than on a fixed amount of change. This observation became known as **Weber's law**. A weight you are holding must increase or decrease by 1/50, or 2%, for you to notice the difference; in contrast, if you were listening to music, you would notice a difference if a tone became slightly higher or lower in pitch by about only 0.33%. According to Weber's law, the greater the original stimulus, the more it must be increased or decreased for the difference to be noticeable.

As you might suspect, the difference threshold is not the same for all the senses. A very large (1/5, or 20%) difference is necessary for some changes in taste to be detected. Moreover, Weber's law best applies to people with average sensitivities and to sensory stimuli that are neither very strong (loud thunder) nor very weak (a faint whisper). For instance, expert wine tasters would know if a particular vintage was a little too sweet, even if its sweetness varied by only a fraction of the 20% necessary for changes in taste, but an average person wouldn't detect the change. Furthermore, people who have lost one sensory ability often gain greater sensitivity in others. One study found that children with early-onset blindness were more capable of correctly labeling 25 common odors than were sighted children, whereas another found that congenitally deaf students possessed motion-perception abilities superior to those of hearing students (Bavelier et al., 2000). Moreover, students who are deaf appear tend to have sharper visual acuity that those with normal hearing do (Codina et al., 2011). Likewise, people who were born blind or became blind shortly thereafter tend to have better hearing than others (Gougoux et al., 2004).

difference threshold A measure of the smallest increase or decrease in a physical stimulus that is required to produce a difference in sensation that is noticeable 50% of the time.

just noticeable difference (JND) The smallest change in sensation that a person is able to detect 50% of the time.

Weber's law The law stating that the just noticeable difference (JND) for all the senses depends on a proportion or percentage of change in a stimulus rather than on a fixed amount of change.

▲ What is the dimmest light this lifeguard could perceive in the darkness? Researchers in sensory psychology have performed many experiments over the years to answer such questions. Their research has established measures known as absolute thresholds. Just as the threshold of a doorway is the dividing point between being outside a room and being inside it, the absolute threshold of a sense marks the difference between not being able to perceive a stimulus and being just barely able to perceive it.

TRY IT

Absolute Threshold

You will need a partner for this activity. You will be the experimenter, and your partner will be the observer. Ask the observer to close his eyes (no peeking allowed!) and tell you when he feels something. Locate a small hair on the observer's forearm. Using a pencil or similar object with a very small point, and taking care not to touch the observer's skin, slowly move the hair until the observer notices the sensation. Now switch roles so that you can experience the other role. If you have an appropriate measuring device handy, you can repeat the procedure and measure how far the hair must be moved before the observer notices the sensation. The amount of movement required is the absolute threshold for hair movement.

3.2 How does transduction change sensory information?

Transduction and Adaptation

Would you be surprised to learn that our eyes do not actually see and that our ears do not hear? The sense organs provide only the beginning of sensation, which must be completed by the brain. As you learned in Chapter 2, specific clusters of neurons in specialized parts of the brain must be stimulated for us to see, hear, taste, and so on. Yet the brain itself cannot respond directly to light, sound waves, odors, and tastes. How, then, does it get the message? The answer is through the sensory receptors.

The body's sense organs are equipped with highly specialized cells called **sensory receptors** that detect and respond to one type of sensory stimulus—light, sound waves, odors, and so on.

Through a process known as **transduction** the sensory receptors convert the sensory stimulation into neural impulses, the electrochemical language of the brain. The neural impulses are then transmitted to precise locations in the brain, such as the primary visual cortex for vision or the primary auditory cortex for hearing (we'll learn more about these parts of the brain later in the chapter). We experience a sensation only when the appropriate part of the brain is stimulated. The sense receptors provide the essential link between the physical sensory world and the brain.

sensory receptors Highly specialized cells in the sense organs that detect and respond to one type of sensory stimulus—light, sound, or odor, for example—and transduce (convert) the stimuli into neural impulses.

transduction The process through which sensory receptors convert the sensory stimulation into neural impulses.

TRY IT

Sensory Adaptation

Take three large cereal bowls or small mixing bowls. Fill one with very cold water, another with hot water (*not* boiling or scalding), and the third with lukewarm water. Hold your left hand in the cold water and your right hand in the hot water for at least 1 minute. Then quickly plunge both hands into the lukewarm water at the same time.

Why do you experience the illusion that the lukewarm water feels simultaneously warmer and colder than its actual temperature? The answer is adaptation. You perceive the lukewarm water as warm on your cold-adapted left hand and as cold on your warm-adapted right hand. This illustrates that our perceptions of sensory stimuli are relative and are affected by differences between stimuli we are already adapted to and new stimuli.

After a time, the sensory receptors grow accustomed to constant, unchanging levels of stimuli—sights, sounds, or smells—so we notice them less and less, or not at all. For example, smokers become accustomed to the smell of cigarette smoke in their homes and on their clothing. This process is known as **sensory adaptation** (refer back to the *Try It* on p. 78). Even though it reduces our sensory awareness, sensory adaptation enables us to shift our attention to what is most important at any given moment. However, sensory adaptation is not likely to occur in the presence of a very strong stimulus, such as the smell of ammonia, an earsplitting sound, or the taste of rancid food.

sensory adaptation The process in which sensory receptors grow accustomed to constant, unchanging levels of stimuli over time.

REMEMBER IT   *Check your answers and take additional quizzes in MyPsychLab.com.*   ✓●—Study and Review on MyPsychLab

1. Taking in sensory information from the environment and transmitting it to the brain is called _____.
2. Interpreting sensory information is called _____.
3. The _____ threshold is the point at which you sense a stimulus 50% of the time.
4. The _____ threshold is the smallest increase or decrease in a physical stimulus that produces a difference in sensation 50% of the time.
5. _____ transmit sensory information from the sense organs to the brain.
6. _____ is the process in which sensory receptors grow accustomed to constant, unchanging stimuli over time.

Vision

Vision is the most studied of all the senses. One thing vision researchers have known for a long time is that there is a great deal more information in the sensory environment than our eyes can take in. Our eyes can respond only to a band of light waves called the **visible spectrum** (see Figure 3.2). These waves are measured in **wavelengths**, the distance from the peak of one wave to the peak of the next. The shortest light waves we can see appear violet, while the longest visible waves appear red. However, sight is much more than just response to light. Sight involves specialized structures in the eye and specific parts of the brain that receive and process neural impulses from the eye. The ability to sense color and the theories that explain how color sensations are produced are also important parts of sight.

visible spectrum The narrow band of light waves that are visible to the human eye.

wavelength A measure of the distance from the peak of a light wave to the peak of the next.

The Eye ▶

The globe-shaped human eyeball, shown in Figure 3.3 on p. 80, measures about 1 inch in diameter. Curving outward from the eye's surface is the **cornea**—the tough, transparent, protective layer covering the front of the eye. The cornea performs the first step

3.3 How does each part of the eye function in vision?

cornea (KOR-nee-uh) The tough, transparent, protective layer that covers the front of the eye and bends light rays inward through the pupil.

Invisible Long Waves	Visible Light Spectrum	Invisible Short Waves
Infrared rays (beyond red)		Ultraviolet rays (beyond violet)

| 1500 ... 800 | 700 | 600 | 500 | 400 | 300 |

Wavelength (in nanometers)

| AC circuits | Broadcast bands | Radar | Microwaves | IR | | UV | X-rays | Gamma rays | Cosmic rays |

FIGURE 3.2 The Electromagnetic Spectrum
Human eyes can perceive only a very thin band of electromagnetic waves, known as the visible spectrum.

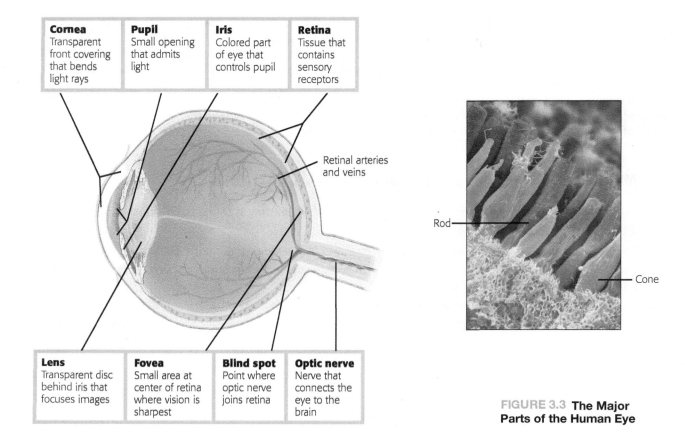

Cornea	**Pupil**	**Iris**	**Retina**
Transparent front covering that bends light rays	Small opening that admits light	Colored part of eye that controls pupil	Tissue that contains sensory receptors

Retinal arteries and veins

Rod

Cone

Lens	**Fovea**	**Blind spot**	**Optic nerve**
Transparent disc behind iris that focuses images	Small area at center of retina where vision is sharpest	Point where optic nerve joins retina	Nerve that connects the eye to the brain

FIGURE 3.3 **The Major Parts of the Human Eye**

lens The transparent disk-shaped structure behind the iris and the pupil that changes shape as it focuses on objects at varying distances.

accommodation The flattening and bulging action of the lens as it focuses images of objects on the retina.

retina The layer of tissue that is located on the inner surface of the eyeball and contains the sensory receptors for vision.

rods The light-sensitive receptor cells in the retina that look like slender cylinders and allow the eye to respond to as few as five photons of light.

Explore the Concept *Normal Vision, Nearsightedness* on MyPsychLab

cones The light-sensitive receptor cells in the retina that enable humans to see color and fine detail in adequate light but do not function in very dim light.

in vision by bending the light rays inward. It directs the light rays through the *pupil,* the small, dark opening in the center of the *iris,* or colored part of the eye. The iris dilates and contracts the pupil to regulate the amount of light entering the eye.

Suspended just behind the iris and the pupil, the **lens** is composed of many thin layers and looks like a transparent disk. The lens performs the task of focusing on viewed objects. It flattens as it focuses on objects at a distance and becomes more spherical, bulging in the center, as it focuses on close objects. This flattening and bulging action of the lens is known as **accommodation**. With age, the lens loses the ability to change its shape to accommodate for near vision, a condition called *presbyopia* ("old eyes"). This is why many people over age 40 must hold a book or newspaper at arm's length or use reading glasses to magnify the print.

The lens focuses the incoming image onto the **retina**—a layer of tissue about the size of a small postage stamp and as thin as onion skin, located on the inner surface of the eyeball and containing the sensory receptors for vision. The image that is projected onto the retina is upside down and reversed from left to right, as illustrated in Figure 3.4.

In some people, the distance through the eyeball (from the lens to the retina) is either too short or too long for proper focusing. Nearsightedness (*myopia*) occurs when the lens focuses images of distant objects in front of, rather than on, the retina. A person with this condition will be able to see near objects clearly, but distant images will be blurred. Farsightedness (*hyperopia*) occurs when the lens focuses images of close objects behind, rather than on, the retina. The individual is able to see far objects clearly, but close objects are blurred. Both conditions are correctable with eyeglasses or contact lenses or by surgical procedures.

At the back of the retina is a layer of light-sensitive receptor cells—the **rods** and the **cones**. Named for their shapes, the rods look like slender cylinders, and the cones appear shorter and more rounded. There are about 120 million rods and 6 million cones in each retina. The cones are the receptor cells that enable us to see color and fine detail in adequate light, but they do not function in very dim light. By contrast, the rods in the human eye are extremely sensitive, allowing the eye to respond to as few as five photons of light (Hecht, Shlaer, & Pirenne, 1942).

A substance called *rhodopsin* present in the rods enables us to adapt to variations in light. Rhodopsin has two components, *opsin* and *retinal* (a chemical similar to vitamin A). In bright light, opsin and retinal break apart, as the process of *light adaptation* takes place. During *dark adaptation,* opsin and retinal bond to one another, re-forming rhodopsin. As you've no doubt experienced, when you move from bright light to total darkness, as when you enter a darkened movie theater, you are momentarily blind until the opsin and retinal recombine. Similarly, when you leave the theater again, you become temporarily blind until the two substances break apart once again.

At the center of the retina is the **fovea**, a small area about the size of the period at the end of this sentence. When you look directly at an object, the image of the object is focused on the center of your fovea. The fovea contains no rods but has about 30,000 cones tightly packed together, providing the clearest and sharpest area of vision in the whole retina. The cones are most densely packed at the center of the fovea; their density decreases sharply just a few degrees beyond the fovea's center and then levels off more gradually to the periphery of the retina.

FIGURE 3.4 **From Retinal Image to Meaningful Information** Because of the way the lens alters light rays in order to produce a clear image, images are upside down on the retina. The brain's visual processing system takes the upside-down retinal image and flips it so it is properly orientated.

Vision and the Brain ▶

As you can see in Figure 3.4, the brain is responsible for converting the upside-down retinal images into meaningful visual information. But the first stages of neural processing actually take place in the retina itself. Before light rays reach the sensory receptors on the rods and cones, they pass through four layers of tissue, each of which contains specialized neurons—*ganglion cells, amacrine cells, bipolar cells*, and *horizontal cells* (see the inset in Figure 3.4). When the light rays reach the sensory receptors (the rods and cones), the receptors transduce, or change, them to neural impulses. The impulses are then transmitted to the bipolar, amacrine, and horizontal cells, which carry them to the ganglion cells. The approximately 1 million axonlike extensions of the ganglion cells are bundled together in a pencil-sized cable that extends through the wall of the retina, leaving the eye and leading to the brain. There are no rods or cones where the cable runs through the retinal wall, so this point is a **blind spot** in each eye.

Beyond the retinal wall of each eye, the cable becomes the **optic nerve**, the nerve that carries visual information from the retinas to the brain (refer back to Figure 3.3). The two optic nerves come together at the *optic chiasm,* a point where some of their nerve fibers cross to the opposite side of the brain. The nerve fibers from the right half of each retina go to the right hemisphere, and those from the left half of each retina go to the left hemisphere. This crossing over is important because it allows visual information from a single eye to be represented in the primary visual cortex of both hemispheres of the brain. Moreover, it plays an important part in the types of depth perception that require information from both eyes (more on this later in the chapter).

3.4 How does visual information get from the retina to the primary visual cortex?

fovea (FO-vee-uh) A small area at the center of the retina that provides the clearest and sharpest vision because it has the largest concentration of cones.

blind spot The point in each retina where there are no rods or cones because the cable of ganglion cells is extending through the retinal wall.

optic nerve The nerve that carries visual information from each retina to both sides of the brain.

primary visual cortex The part of the brain in which visual information is processed.

From the optic chiasm, the optic nerve fibers extend to the thalamus, where they form synapses with neurons that transmit the impulses to the **primary visual cortex**, the part of the brain that is devoted to visual processing. Thanks to researchers David Hubel and Torsten Wiesel (1959, 1979; Hubel, 1963, 1995), who won a Nobel Prize for their work in 1981, we know a great deal about how specialized the neurons of the primary visual cortex are. By inserting tiny microelectrodes into single cells in the visual cortexes of cats, Hubel and Wiesel (1959) were able to determine what was happening in individual cells when the cats were exposed to different kinds of visual stimuli. They discovered that each neuron responded only to specific patterns. Some neurons responded only to lines and angles, while others fired only when the cat saw a vertical or horizontal line. Still others were responsive to nothing but right angles or lines of specific lengths. Neurons of this type are known as **feature detectors**, and they are already coded at birth to make their unique responses. Yet we see whole images, not collections of isolated features, because visual perceptions are complete only when the primary visual cortex transmits the millions of pieces of visual information it receives to other areas in the brain, where they are combined and assembled into whole visual images (Self & Zeki, 2005).

feature detectors Neurons in the brain that respond only to specific visual patterns (for example, to lines or angles).

The major structures of the visual system are summarized in the following *Summarize It*.

SUMMARIZE IT

Major Structures of the Visual System

STRUCTURE	FUNCTION
Cornea	Translucent covering on the front of the eyeball that bends light rays entering the eye inward through the pupil
Iris	Colored part of the eye that adjusts to maintain a constant amount of light entering the eye through the pupil
Pupil	Opening in the center of the iris through which light rays enter the eye
Lens	Transparent disk-shaped structure behind the pupil that adjusts its shape to allow focusing on objects at varying distances
Retina	Layer of tissue on the inner surface of the eye that contains sensory receptors for vision
Rods	Specialized receptor cells in the retina that are sensitive to light changes
Cones	Specialized receptor cells in the retina that enable humans to see fine detail and color in adequate light
Fovea	Small area at the center of the retina, packed with cones, on which objects viewed directly are clearly and sharply focused
Optic nerve	Nerve that carries visual information from the retina to the brain
Blind spot	Area in each eye where the optic nerve joins the retinal wall and no vision is possible

3.5 How does color vision work?

Color Vision

Why does the skin of an apple appear to be red, while its flesh is perceived as an off-white color? What we actually see is reflected light. Some light waves striking an object are absorbed by it; others are reflected from it. So, why does an apple's skin look red?

Sensing Color. If you hold a red apple in bright light, light waves of all the different wavelengths strike the apple, but more of the longer red wavelengths of light are reflected from the apple's skin. The shorter wavelengths are absorbed, so you see only the reflected red. Bite into the apple, and it looks off-white. Why? You see the near-white color because, rather than being absorbed, almost all of the wavelengths of the visible spectrum are reflected from the inside part of the apple. The presence of all visible wavelengths gives the sensation of a near-white color. If an object does indeed reflect 100% of visible wavelengths, it appears to be pure white.

Our everyday visual experience goes far beyond the colors in the rainbow. We can detect thousands of subtle color shadings. What produces these fine color distinctions? Researchers have identified three dimensions of light that combine to provide the rich world of color we experience: The chief dimension is **hue**, which refers to the specific color perceived—red, blue, or yellow, for example. **Saturation** refers to the purity of a color; a color becomes less saturated, or less pure, as other wavelengths of light are mixed with it. **Brightness** refers to the intensity of the light energy that is perceived as a color and corresponds to the amplitude (height) of the color's light wave. Differences in the three dimensions are illustrated in Figure 3.5 below.

Theories of Color Vision. Scientists know that the cones are responsible for color vision, but exactly how do they work to produce color sensations? Two major theories have been offered to explain color vision, and both were formulated before the development of laboratory technology capable of testing them (Stabell & Stabell, 2009). The **trichromatic theory**, first proposed by Thomas Young in 1802, was modified by Hermann von Helmholtz about 50 years later. This theory states that there are three kinds of cones in the retina and that each kind makes a maximal chemical response to one of three colors—blue, green, or red. Research conducted in the 1950s and the 1960s by Nobel Prize winner George Wald (1964; Wald, Brown, & Smith, 1954) supports the trichromatic theory. Wald discovered that even though all cones have basically the same structure, the retina does indeed contain three kinds of cones. Subsequent research demonstrated that each kind of cone is particularly sensitive to one of three colors—blue, green, or red (Roorda & Williams, 1999).

The other major attempt to explain color vision is the **opponent-process theory**, which was first proposed by physiologist Ewald Hering in 1878 and revised in 1957 by researchers Leon Hurvich and Dorthea Jamison. According to the opponent-process theory, three kinds of cells respond by increasing or decreasing their rate of firing when different colors are present. The red/green cells increase their firing rate when red is present and decrease it when green is present. The yellow/blue cells have an increased response to yellow and a decreased response to blue. A third kind of cells increase their response rate for white light and decrease it in the absence of light.

If you look long enough at one color in the opponent-process pair and then look at a white surface, your brain will give you the sensation of the opposite color—a negative **afterimage**, a visual sensation that remains after the stimulus is withdrawn. After you have stared at one color in an opponent-process pair (red/green, yellow/blue, white/black), the cell responding to that color tires and the opponent cell begins to fire, producing the afterimage. Demonstrate this for yourself in the *Try It* on p. 84.

hue The dimension of light that refers to the specific color perceived.

saturation The purity of a color, or the degree to which the light waves producing it are of the same wavelength.

brightness The intensity of light energy perceived as a color; based on amplitude of light wave.

trichromatic theory The theory of color vision suggesting that three types of cones in the retina each make a maximal chemical response to one of three colors—blue, green, or red.

opponent-process theory The theory of color vision suggesting that three kinds of cells respond by increasing or decreasing their rate of firing when different colors are present.

afterimage A visual sensation that remains after a stimulus is withdrawn.

FIGURE 3.5 Hue, Brightness, and Saturation
Manipulations of hue, brightness, and saturation alter the appearance of a photo. (1) natural color; (2) altered hues; (3) altered brightness; (4) altered saturation.

A Negative Afterimage

Stare at the dot in the green, black, and yellow flag for approximately 1 minute. Then shift your gaze to the dot in the blank rectangle. You will see the American flag in its true colors—red, white, and blue, which are the opponent-process opposites of green, black, and yellow.

Which theory of color vision is correct? It turns out that each theory explains a different phase of color processing. It is now generally accepted that the cones perform color processing in a way that is best explained by the trichromatic theory. The cones pass on information about wavelengths of light to the ganglion cells, the site of opponent processes. Color perception appears to involve more than just these two phases. Researchers think that color processing starts at the level of the retina, continues through the bipolar and ganglion cells, and is completed in the color detectors in the visual cortex (Masland, 1996; Sokolov, 2000). However, the trichromatic theory alone does not fully explain color perception because the cones are not distributed evenly across the surface of the retina. New theories that include motoric aspects of vision, such as the nearly invisible movements of the eyes called *saccades,* may turn out to provide researchers with a more comprehensive understanding of color vision (Wittenberg, Bremmer, & Wachter, 2008).

Color Blindness. You may have wondered what it means if someone is "color-blind." Does that person see the world in black and white? No—the term **color blindness** refers to an inability to distinguish certain colors from one another. About 8% of males experience some kind of difficulty in distinguishing colors, most commonly red from green (Mather, 2006). By contrast, fewer than 1% of females suffer from color blindness. (Recall from Chapter 2 that this sex difference is explained by the fact that genes for color vision are carried on the X chromosome.)

Research has shown that color blindness can have degrees; it isn't simply a matter of either-you-have-it-or-you-don't. Why are some of us better able to make fine distinctions between colors, as we must do when sorting black and navy blue socks, for instance? These differences appear to be related to the number of color vision genes individuals have. Researchers have found that, in people with normal color vision, the

color blindness The inability to distinguish certain colors from one another.

▲ On the left a hot air balloon is shown as it would appear to a person with normal color vision; on the right is the same balloon as it would appear to a person with red-green color blindness.

X chromosome may contain as few as two or as many as nine genes for color perception (Neitz & Neitz, 1995). Those who have more of such genes appear to be better able to make very fine distinctions between colors. These genetic differences lead to differences in the way that the various kinds of cones are distributed on an individual's retina (Hofer et al., 2005). Moreover, animal studies suggest that gene therapy aimed at increasing the number of cones in the retinas of individuals with color blindness may cure the condition (Simunovic, 2010).

REMEMBER IT   *Check your answers and take additional quizzes in MyPsychLab.com.*   ✓●─Study and Review on MyPsychLab

1. The _____ _____ includes the light waves that can be sensed by the human eye.

2. Number each part of the eye to show the order in which each part of the visual system receives sensory information (light waves):

_____ **(a)** pupil   _____ **(c)** retina   _____ **(e)** lens

_____ **(b)** visual cortex   _____ **(d)** cornea   _____ **(f)** optic nerve

3. Interpretation of visual information takes place in the _____ in the brain's _____ .

Hearing and Balance

"In space, no one can hear you scream!" Years ago, the frightening science fiction movie *Alien* was advertised this way. Although the movie was fiction, the statement is true. Light can travel through the vast nothingness of space, a vacuum, but sound cannot. In this section, we'll discuss the properties of sound, the different structures that make up the ear, and how they function and affect our balance and movement.

Sound ▶

3.6 What are the physical characteristics of sound?

Sound requires a medium, such as air, water, or a solid object, through which to move. This fact was first demonstrated by Robert Boyle in 1660 when he suspended a ringing pocket watch by a thread inside a specially designed jar. When Boyle pumped all the air out of the jar, he could no longer hear the watch ring. But when he pumped the air back into the jar, he could again hear the watch ringing. What gives sound its unique qualities? The answer is its frequency, amplitude, and timbre, or the physical characteristics of sound (see Figure 3.6).

Frequency is determined by the number of cycles completed by a sound wave in one second. The unit used to measure a wave's frequency, or cycles per second, is known as the hertz (Hz). The *pitch*—how high or low the sound is—is chiefly determined by frequency—the higher the frequency (the more cycles per second), the

frequency The number of cycles completed by a sound wave in one second, determining the pitch of the sound; expressed in the unit called the hertz.

Amplitude

One cycle

FIGURE 3.6 **Sounds Produced by a Tuning Ford**
As the tuning fork vibrates, it alternately compresses and expands molecules of air creating a sound wave.

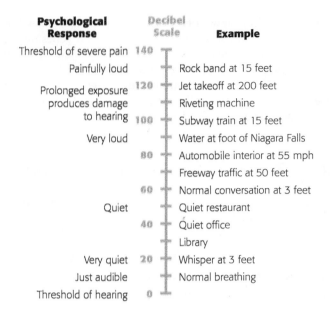

Psychological Response	Decibel Scale	Example
Threshold of severe pain	140	
Painfully loud		Rock band at 15 feet
Prolonged exposure produces damage to hearing	120	Jet takeoff at 200 feet
		Riveting machine
	100	Subway train at 15 feet
Very loud		Water at foot of Niagara Falls
	80	Automobile interior at 55 mph
		Freeway traffic at 50 feet
	60	Normal conversation at 3 feet
Quiet		Quiet restaurant
	40	Quiet office
		Library
Very quiet	20	Whisper at 3 feet
Just audible		Normal breathing
Threshold of hearing	0	

FIGURE 3.7 Decibel Levels of Various Sounds
The loudness of a sound (its amplitude) is measured in decibels. Each increase of 10 decibels makes a sound 10 times louder. A normal conversation at 3 feet measures about 60 decibels, which is 10,000 times louder than a soft whisper of 20 decibels. Any exposure to sounds of 130 decibels or higher puts a person at immediate risk for hearing damage, but levels as low as 90 decibels can cause hearing loss if one is exposed to them over long periods of time.

Explore the **Concept** *Frequency and Amplitude of Sound Waves* on **MyPsychLab**

amplitude The measure of the loudness of a sound; expressed in the unit called the decibel.

decibel (dB) (DES-ih-bel) A unit of measurement for the loudness of sounds.

timbre (TAM-burr) The distinctive quality of a sound that distinguishes it from other sounds of the same pitch and loudness.

higher the sound. The human ear can hear sound frequencies from low bass tones of around 20 Hz up to high-pitched sounds of about 20,000 Hz. However, as discussed in *Explain It* on page 88, adults' ability to hear such high frequencies varies a lot from one individual to another. By contrast, many mammals, such as dogs, cats, bats, and rats, can hear tones much higher in frequency than 20,000 Hz. Amazingly, dolphins can respond to frequencies up to 100,000 Hz.

The loudness of a sound is determined by a measure called **amplitude**. The force or pressure with which air molecules move chiefly determines loudness, which is measured using a unit called the *bel,* named for Alexander Graham Bell. Because the bel is a rather large unit, sound levels are expressed in tenths of a bel, or **decibels (dB)**. The threshold of human hearing is set at 0 dB, which does not mean the absence of sound but rather the softest sound that can be heard in a very quiet setting. Each increase of 10 decibels makes a sound 10 times louder. Figure 3.7 shows comparative decibel levels for a variety of sounds.

Another characteristic of sound is **timbre**, the distinctive quality of a sound that distinguishes it from other sounds of the same pitch and loudness. Have you ever thought about why a given musical note sounds different when played on a piano, a guitar, and a violin, even though all three instruments use vibrating strings to produce sounds? The characteristics of the strings, the technique used to initiate the vibrations, and the way the body of the instrument amplifies the vibrations work together to produce a unique "voice," or timbre, for each instrument. Human voices vary in timbre as well, providing us with a way of recognizing individuals when we can't see their faces. Timbres vary from one instrument to another, and from one voice to another, because most sounds consist of several different frequencies rather than a single pitch. The range of those frequencies gives each musical instrument, and each human voice, its unique sound.

3.7 How does each part of the ear function in hearing?

The Ear and Hearing

Audition is the sensation and process of hearing. The oddly shaped, curved flap of cartilage and skin called the *pinna* is the visible part of the **outer ear** (see Figure 3.8). Inside the ear, the *auditory canal* is about 1 inch long, and its entrance is lined with hairs. At the end of the auditory canal is the *eardrum* (or *tympanic membrane*), a thin, flexible membrane about 1/3 inch in diameter. The eardrum moves in response to the sound waves that travel through the auditory canal and strike it.

The **middle ear** is no larger than an aspirin tablet. Inside its chamber are the *ossicles,* the three smallest bones in the human body. Named for their shapes, the ossicles—the hammer, the anvil, and the stirrup—are connected in that order, linking

audition The sensation and process of hearing.

outer ear The visible part of the ear, consisting of the pinna and the auditory canal.

middle ear The portion of the ear containing the ossicles, which connect the eardrum to the oval window and amplify sound waves.

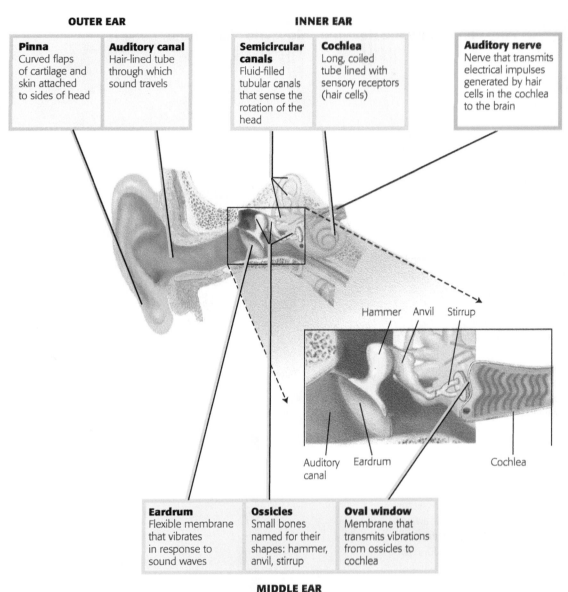

OUTER EAR

Pinna
Curved flaps
of cartilage and
skin attached
to sides of head

Auditory canal
Hair-lined tube
through which
sound travels

INNER EAR

**Semicircular
canals**
Fluid-filled
tubular canals
that sense the
rotation of the
head

Cochlea
Long, coiled
tube lined with
sensory receptors
(hair cells)

Auditory nerve
Nerve that transmits
electrical impulses
generated by hair
cells in the cochlea
to the brain

**FIGURE 3.8 The Anatomy of
the Human Ear**
Sound waves pass through the
auditory canal to the eardrum,
causing it to vibrate and set
in motion the ossicles in the
middle ear. When the stirrup
pushes against the oval window,
it sets up vibrations in the inner
ear. This moves the fluid in the
cochlea back and forth and sets
in motion the hair cells, causing
a message to be sent to the
brain via the auditory nerve.

Hammer   Anvil   Stirrup

Auditory   Eardrum   Cochlea
canal

Eardrum
Flexible membrane
that vibrates
in response to
sound waves

Ossicles
Small bones
named for their
shapes: hammer,
anvil, stirrup

Oval window
Membrane that
transmits vibrations
from ossicles to
cochlea

MIDDLE EAR

the eardrum to the *oval window* (see Figure 3.8). The ossicles amplify sound waves some 22 times (Békésy, 1957). When vibrations of the stirrup cause it to push against the oval window, the vibrations are transmitted to the **inner ear**, which begins at the inner side of the oval window, at the **cochlea**—a fluid-filled, snail-shaped, bony chamber. Vibrations move the fluid in the cochlea back and forth in waves. Inside the cochlea, attached to its thin basilar membrane are about 15,000 sensory receptors called **hair cells**, each with a bundle of tiny hairs protruding from it. The tiny hair bundles are pushed and pulled by the motion of the fluid inside the cochlea. If the tip of a hair bundle is moved only as much as the width of an atom, an electrical impulse is generated, which is transmitted to the brain by way of the auditory nerve.

As you'll see in the *Explain It* on p. 88 damage to the cochlea's hair cells is a major source of hearing loss. Figure 3.9 on p. 89 dramatically illustrates the effects of excessive noise on these delicate cells. About 5% of 12- to 19-year-olds has significant hearing loss compare to less than 1% among young children (Shargorodsky, Curhan, Curhan, & Eavey, 2010). Researchers believe that this age-related increase in hearing loss is due to exposure to noise. In support of this hypothesis, one study found that

inner ear The innermost portion of the ear, containing the cochlea, the vestibular sacs, and the semicircular canals.

cochlea (KOK-lee-uh) The fluid-filled, snail-shaped, bony chamber in the inner ear that contains the basilar membrane and its hair cells (the sound receptors).

hair cells Sensory receptors for hearing that are attached to the basilar membrane in the cochlea.

Why Can't Everyone Hear the "Mosquito" Ring Tone?

Have you ever tested your hearing to find out if you can hear the "Mosquito," a tone with a frequency of about 17,000 Hz? If not, search online for "mosquito ringtone hearing test" and you'll be directed to dozens of websites where you can do so. As the figure to the right suggests, the ability to hear the Mosquito declines with age. However, research suggests that the truth about age differences in sensitivity to the Mosquito is that the ability to hear it is nearly universal in the teens and early 20s but highly variable from the mid-20s on (Lawton, 2001). What accounts for the variability in sensitivity to high-pitched tones among adults?

The ability to hear high-pitched tones declines with age for a variety of reasons. A few conditions that are more common to middle-aged and older adults (e.g., excessive ear wax, chronic fluid in the ear, overgrowth of the bones in the inner ear) than to younger adults explain some of the decline (Mathur & Roland, 2009). However, hearing loss in adulthood often results from lifelong exposure to excessive noise. Noise above 85 decibels or so, if experienced repeatedly for long periods of time, damages the tiny hair cells inside the cochlea (Mathur & Roland, 2009). And the longer the exposure to excessive noise goes on, the more hearing people who are exposed to it lose. For instance, many long-time rock and pop musicians who are now in their middle- and late-adulthood years—Bono, Pete Townshend, Eric Clapton, Ozzy Osbourne, Ted Nugent, Phil Collins, Trent Reznor, to name a few—have much poorer hearing than others their age. Moreover, Townshend has reported that he began to notice his hearing loss when he was still in his 20s. Classical musicians who regularly play in orchestras show similar losses (Laitinen, 2005).

What can you do to increase your chances of maintaining the ability to hear the Mosquito and other high-pitched sounds, which happen to be critical to the ability to understand speech, for as long as possible? If you're a musician, investigate hearing protectors that shield your inner ear from potentially damaging noise but still allow you to hear the sounds you need to in order to play and perform effectively. Even if you're not a musician, you should be aware that regular use of headphones greatly increases your risk of suffering the kind of hearing loss that is common among professional musicians (Britt, 2006). To protect your hearing, adopt a practice that experts call the "60/60 rule": Use headphones no more than a total of 60 minutes each day with the player set on 60% of its maximum volume (Fligor, 2010).

25 khz
Dog whistles

20 khz
Highest pitch
children, teens,
and young adults
can hear

17 khz Mosquito
16 khz
Highest pitch 30-
to 60-year-olds
can hear

12 khz
Highest pitch
adults over 60
can hear

4 khz
Highest note
on a piano

72% of teenaged study participants' hearing declined significantly after attending a rock concert where sound levels averaged 98.5 decibels (Derebery et al., 2012). Such event-related hearing loss may be temporary, but repeatedly exposing hair cells to very loud stimuli can lead to permanent hearing problems. For this reason, experts recommend that concert-goers wear protective ear plugs that allow them to enjoy the music without exposing the ear to the potentially damaging effects of high decibel levels.

We can hear some sounds through *bone conduction*, the vibrations of the bones in the face and skull. When you click your teeth or eat crunchy food, you hear these sounds mainly through bone conduction. And if you have heard a recording of your voice, you may have thought it sounded odd. This is because recordings do not reproduce the sounds you hear through bone conduction when you speak, so you are hearing your voice as it sounds to others.

Having two ears, one on each side of the head, enables you to determine the direction from which sounds are coming. Unless a sound is directly above, below, in front of, or behind you, it reaches one ear very shortly before it reaches the other (Colburn, Shinn-Cunningham, Kidd, & Durlach, 2006). The brain can detect differences as small as 0.0001 second and interpret them, revealing the direction of the sound (Rosenzweig, 1961). The source of a sound may also be determined by the difference in the intensity of the sound reaching each ear, as well as the position of the head when the sound is detected (Colburn, Shinn-Cunningham, Kidd, & Durlach, 2006).

Scientists have proposed two theories to explain hearing. In the 1860s, Hermann von Helmholtz helped develop **place theory**. This theory of hearing holds that each individual pitch a person hears is determined by the particular spot or place along the basilar membrane that vibrates the most. Observing the living basilar membrane, researchers verified that different locations do, indeed, vibrate in response to differently pitched sounds (Ruggero, 1992). Even so, place theory seems to apply only to frequencies higher than 150 Hz.

Another attempt to explain hearing is **frequency theory**. According to this theory, the hair cells vibrate the same number of times per second as the sounds that reach them. Thus, a tone of 500 Hz would stimulate the hair cells to vibrate 500 times per second. However, frequency theory cannot account for frequencies higher than 1,000 Hz because individual neurons linked to the hair cells cannot fire more than about 1,000 times per second. So, even if a receptor vibrated as rapidly as the sound wave associated with a higher tone, the information necessary to perceive the pitch wouldn't be faithfully transmitted to the brain. Consequently, frequency theory seems to be a good explanation of how we hear low-frequency tones (lower than 500 Hz), but place theory better describes the way in which tones with frequencies higher than 1,000 Hz are heard (Matlin & Foley, 1997). Both frequency and location are involved when we hear sounds with frequencies between 500 and 1,000 Hz.

Balance and Movement ▶

No one doubts the importance of the ears and the auditory information they provide to the brain in everyday life, but did you know that structures in the ears also play an important role in your ability to move and to maintain your balance? The **kinesthetic sense** provides information about (1) the position of body parts in relation to each other and (2) the movement of the entire body or its parts. This information is detected by receptors in the joints, ligaments, and muscles. The other senses provide additional information about body position and movement. For example, as you learned at the beginning of the chapter, the kinesthetic sense functions poorly when the brain is deprived of visual information. Still, it does function fairly well, even without visual input. If you tried the balance activity we described, you probably found that your body maintained its balance by prompting you to periodically lower your raised foot and make contact with the floor. Consequently, although you were unable to continuously maintain your balance on one leg, you didn't fall over completely. That's because the kinesthetic sense is capable of compensating for missing sensory information either by using information from the other senses or by prompting us to move in particular ways. As a result, we are usually able to maintain control of our bodies without visual feedback or a studied, conscious effort.

The visual and kinesthetic systems work with the *vestibular sense* to enable you to execute smooth, coordinated movements. The **vestibular sense** detects movement and provides information about the body's orientation in space. The vestibular

Normal inner ear "hair" cells

Damaged inner ear "hair" cells

FIGURE 3.9 Effects of Noise on Cochlear Hair Cells
Source: House Ear Institute (2006).

place theory The theory of hearing that holds that each individual pitch a person hears is determined by the particular location along the basilar membrane of the cochlea that vibrates the most.

frequency theory The theory of hearing that holds that hair cell receptors vibrate the same number of times per second as the sounds that reach them.

3.8 How do the kinesthetic and vestibular senses help us move and stay balanced?

kinesthetic sense The sense providing information about the position and movement of body parts.

vestibular sense (ves-TIB-yu-ler) The sense that provides information about the body's orientation in space.

Semicircular
canals

Cochlea

Vestibular sacs

FIGURE 3.10 **Sensing Balance and Movement**
You sense the rotation of your head in any direction because the movement sends fluid coursing through the tubelike semicircular canals in the inner ear. The moving fluid bends the hair cell receptors, which, in turn, send neural impulses to the brain.

semicircular canals Three fluid-filled tubular canals in the inner ear that sense the rotation of the head.

sense organs are located in the semicircular canals and the *vestibular sacs* in the inner ear. The **semicircular canals** sense the rotation of your head, such as when you are turning your head from side to side or when you are spinning around (see Figure 3.10). Because the canals are filled with fluid, rotating movements of the head in any direction send the fluid coursing through the tubelike semicircular canals. In the canals, the moving fluid bends the hair cells, which act as receptors and send neural impulses to the brain. Because there are three canals, each positioned on a different plane, rotation in a given direction will cause the hair cells in one canal to bend more than the hair cells in the other canals.

The semicircular canals and the vestibular sacs signal only changes in motion or orientation. If you were blindfolded and had no visual or other external cues, you would not be able to sense motion once your speed reached a constant rate. For example, in an airplane, you would feel the takeoff and the landing, as well as any sudden changes in speed. But once the plane leveled off and maintained a fairly constant cruising speed, your vestibular organs would not signal the brain that you are moving, even if you were traveling at a rate of hundreds of miles per hour.

REMEMBER IT *Check your answers and take additional quizzes in MyPsychLab.com.* ✔●[Study and Review on MyPsychLab

1. The human ear can hear frequencies between _____ and _____.

2. Number the parts of the auditory system to show the order in which each structure receives sensory information (sound waves):

   _____ (**a**) auditory canal   _____ (**d**) oval window   _____ (**g**) eardrum

   _____ (**b**) auditory nerve   _____ (**e**) hair cells

   _____ (**c**) auditory cortex   _____ (**f**) ossicles

3. The auditory system's sensory receptors are called _____ and are located in the _____.

4. The _____ sense provides information about the position of body parts in relation to each other.

5. Vestibular sense organs are located in the _____ and the _____ in the inner ear.

Smell, Taste, and Touch

Clearly, our sensory experiences would be extremely limited without vision and hearing, but what about the chemical senses—smell and taste?

3.9 How do smell sensations get from the nose to the brain?

 Smell

olfaction (ol-FAK-shun) The sense of smell.

If you suddenly lost your capacity for **olfaction** (the sense of smell), you might think, "This isn't so bad. I can't smell flowers or food, but, on the other hand, I no longer have to endure the foul odors of life." But your *olfactory system*—the technical name for the organs and brain structures involved in the sense of smell—aids your survival. You smell smoke and can escape before the flames of a fire envelop you. Your nose broadcasts an odor alarm to the brain when certain poisonous gases or noxious fumes are present. Smell, aided by taste, provides your line of defense against putting spoiled food or drink into your body. Olfactory experiences also influence our emotional states, that is, taking advice such as "stop and smell the roses" literally could actually cheer you up when you're feeling down (Gottfried, 2010). And as you probably know, distinctive odors can serve as memory cues, both pleasant and unpleasant. For instance, the smell of peanut butter may transport you back to your elementary school lunchroom and, in turn, remind you either of the bully who stole your cookies or the best friend who sat next to you every day. 👁

You cannot smell a substance unless some of its molecules vaporize—that is, pass from a solid or liquid into a gaseous state. Heat speeds up the vaporization of molecules, which is why food that is cooking has a stronger and more distinct odor than uncooked food. When odor molecules vaporize, they become airborne and make their way up each nostril to the **olfactory epithelium**. The olfactory epithelium consists of two 1-square-inch patches of tissue, one at the top of each nasal cavity; together these patches contain about 10 million olfactory neurons, which are the receptor cells for smell. Each of these neurons contains only one of the 1,000 different types of odor receptors (Olender, Lancet, & Nebert, 2008). Because humans are able to detect some 10,000 odors, each of the 1,000 types of odor receptors must be able to respond to more than one kind of odor molecule. Moreover, some odor molecules trigger more than one type of odor receptor (Axel, 1995). The intensity of a smell stimulus—how strong or weak it is—is apparently determined by the number of olfactory neurons firing at the same time (Freeman, 1991). Figure 3.11 shows a diagram of the human olfactory system.

Have you ever wondered why dogs have a keener sense of smell than humans? Not only do many dogs have a long snout, but, in some breeds, the olfactory epithelium can be as large as the area of a handkerchief and can contain 20 times as many olfactory neurons as in humans (Engen, 1982). It is well known that dogs use scent to recognize not only other members of their species but also the humans with whom they live. Humans have this ability, too. The mothers of newborns can recognize their own babies by smell within hours after birth. But can humans recognize the scents of other species—their own pets, for example? Yes, to a remarkable degree. When presented with blankets permeated with the scents of dogs, some 89% of the dog owners easily identified their own dog by smell (Wells & Hepper, 2000).

Olfactory neurons are different from all other sensory receptors: They both come into direct contact with sensory stimuli and reach directly into the brain. These neurons have a short life span; after functioning for only about 60 days, they die and are replaced by new cells (Bensafi et al., 2004).

The axons of the olfactory neurons relay a smell message directly to the **olfactory bulbs**—two brain structures the size of matchsticks that rest above the nasal cavities (refer to Figure 3.11). Smell sensations then travel to the amygdala, part of the limbic system, and the nearby olfactory cortex. Olfactory messages leave the amygdala and olfactory cortex via two pathways. One of these pathways carries smell sensations to other parts of limbic system for emotional interpretation. The other pathway sends olfactory information to cells in the thalamus that relay it to the orbitofrontal cortex for cognitive interpretation.

The process of sensing odors is the same in every individual, but there are large differences in sensitivity to smells. For example, perfumers and whiskey blenders can distinguish subtle variations in odors that are indistinguishable to the average person. Young people are more sensitive to odors than older people, and nonsmokers are more sensitive than smokers (Boyce & Shone, 2006; Danielides et al., 2009).

olfactory epithelium Two 1-square-inch patches of tissue, one at the top of each nasal cavity, which together contain about 10 million olfactory neurons, the receptors for smell.

👁🗝**Watch** the Video *Episode 5: Thinking Like a Psychologist: Can Smells Alter Mood and Behavior?* in **MyPsychLab**

olfactory bulbs Two matchstick-sized structures above the nasal cavities, where smell sensations first register in the brain.

| **Orbitofrontal cortex** Interprets olfactory information | **Olfactory bulb** Receives information from odor receptor cells | **Thalamus** Relays olfactory information from olfactory bulb to orbitofrontal cortex |

Olfactory bulb

| **Olfactory receptor cells** React to odor molecules | **Olfactory epithelium** Site of olfactory receptor cells |

FIGURE 3.11 The Olfactory System
Odor molecules travel up the nostrils to the olfactory epithelium, which contains the receptor cells for smell. Olfactory receptors are special neurons whose axons form the olfactory nerve. The olfactory nerve relays smell messages to the olfactory bulbs, which pass them on to the amygdala and olfactory cortex. From there, they go to the limbic system, the thalamus, and orbitofrontal cortex.

3.10 How do we detect the primary taste sensations?

gustation The sense of taste.

taste buds Structures along the sides of many of the tongue's papillae that are composed of 60 to 100 receptor cells for taste.

▲ Cultures vary widely in their taste preferences. Curry, for example, is commonly used in Indian foods. Westerners may find it to be too spicy for their tastes when they first try Indian food, but the process of sensory adaptation will occur if they regularly consume such foods.

Taste

You might be surprised to learn that much of the pleasure you attribute to the sense of taste actually arises from smells, when odor molecules are forced up the nasal cavity by the action of the tongue, cheeks, and throat when you chew and swallow. Even without a sense of taste, your sense of smell would provide you with some taste sensations. Still, life without the ability to fully experience the tastes of the foods we love would, no doubt, be less enjoyable.

Psychology textbooks long maintained that **gustation**, the sense of taste, produced four distinct kinds of taste sensations: sweet, sour, salty, and bitter. This is true, but researchers now know that there is a fifth taste sensation in humans (Herness, 2000). This fifth taste sensation, called *umami,* is triggered by the substance glutamate, which, in the form of monosodium glutamate (MSG), is widely used as a flavoring in Asian foods (Matsunami, Montmayeur, & Buck, 2000). Many protein-rich foods, such as meat, milk, aged cheese, and seafood, also contain glutamate.

All five taste sensations can be detected on all locations of the tongue. Indeed, even a person with no tongue could still taste to some extent, thanks to the taste receptors found in the palate, in the mucous lining of the cheeks and lips, and in parts of the throat, including the tonsils. When tastes are mixed, the specialized receptors for each type of flavor are activated and send separate messages to the brain (Sugita & Shiba, 2005). In other words, your brain perceives the two distinctive flavors present in sweet-and-sour sauce quite separately. This analytical quality of the sense of taste prevents your being fooled into eating spoiled or poisoned food when the characteristic taste of either is combined with some kind of pleasant flavor.

If you look at your tongue in a mirror, you will see many small bumps called *papillae* which help to move molecules of food dissolved in saliva across the surface of the tongue. **Taste buds** lie alongside some of these papillae (see Figure 3.12). Each taste bud is composed of 60 to 100 receptor cells. The life span of the taste receptors is very short—only about 10 days—and they are continually being replaced.

Research indicates that individuals vary widely in their capacity for experiencing taste sensations (Yackinous & Guinard, 2002). Nontasters are unable to taste certain sweet and bitter compounds, but they do taste most other substances, albeit with less sensitivity. Supertasters taste these sweet and bitter compounds with far stronger intensity than other people. Researchers are currently investigating links between taste sensitivity, eating behaviors, and health status variables, such as obesity (Tepper, 2008). For example, supertasters who are particularly sensitive to the chemical that gives fruits and vegetables a bitter taste eat less salad than medium tasters and nontasters (Yackinous & Guinard, 2002). Still, supertasters appear no more likely to be

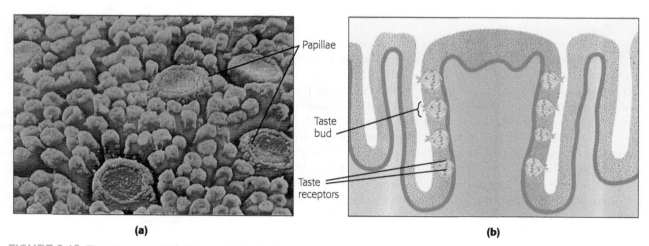

(a)   **(b)**

FIGURE 3.12 **The Tongue's Papillae and Taste Buds**
(a) A photomicrograph of the surface of the tongue shows several papillae. (b) This vertical cross-section through a papilla reveals the location of the taste buds and taste receptors.

overweight than medium tasters or nontasters. In fact, among individuals who report that they never deliberately restrict their diets to try to lose weight, supertasters of the bitter chemical have less body fat than medium tasters or nontasters (Tepper & Ullrich, 2002). So, researchers know that taste sensitivity is linked to food preferences but not how these preferences may be connected to nutritional status.

Touch and Pain ▶

3.11 How does the skin provide pleasant and unpleasant sensations?

Your natural clothing, the skin, is the largest organ of your body. It performs many important biological functions while also providing much of what is known as sensual pleasure. In addition, the skin's unpleasant sensations can alert us that something is wrong in our bodies.

Touch **Tactile** information is conveyed to the brain when an object touches and depresses the skin, stimulating one or more of the several distinct types of receptors found in the nerve endings. These sensitive nerve endings in the skin send the touch message through nerve connections to the spinal cord. The message travels up the spinal cord and through the brainstem and the midbrain, finally reaching the somatosensory cortex. (Recall from Chapter 2 that the somatosensory cortex is the strip of tissue at the front of the parietal lobes where touch, pressure, temperature, and pain register.) Once the somatosensory cortex has been activated, you become aware of where and how hard you have been touched. In the 1890s, one of the most prominent researchers of the tactile sense, Max von Frey, discovered the *two-point threshold*—the measure of how far apart two touch points on the skin must be before they are felt as two separate touches. If you could examine the skin from the outermost to the deepest layer, you would find a variety of nerve endings that differ markedly in appearance. Most or all of these nerve endings appear to respond in some degree to all types of tactile stimulation. The more densely packed with these sensory receptors a part of the body's surface is, the more sensitive it is to tactile stimulation. For instance, the finger tips have more touch receptors than other parts of the body.

tactile Pertaining to the sense of touch.

How important is the sense of touch? Classic research in the mid-1980s demonstrated that premature infants who were massaged for 15 minutes three times a day gained weight 47% faster than other premature infants who received only regular intensive care treatment (Field et al., 1986). The massaged infants were more responsive and were able to leave the hospital about 6 days earlier on average than those who were not massaged. Thus, the sense of touch is not only one of the more pleasant aspects of life, but is also critical to our survival. 👁

👁 **Watch** the Video *Basics: In Full Appreciation of the Cookie* in **MyPsychLab**

Pain Scientists are not certain how pain works, but one major theory that attempts to answer this question is the *gate-control theory* of Ronald Melzack and Patrick Wall (1965, 1983). These researchers contend that an area in the spinal cord can act like a "gate" and either block pain messages or transmit them to the brain. Only so many messages can go through the gate at any one time. You feel pain when pain messages carried by small, slow-conducting nerve fibers reach the gate and cause it to open. Large, fast-conducting nerve fibers carry other sensory messages from the body; these can effectively tie up traffic at the gate so that it will close and keep many of the pain messages from getting through. What is the first thing you do when you stub your toe or pound your finger with a hammer? If you rub or apply gentle pressure to the injury, you are stimulating the large, fast-conducting nerve fibers, which get their message to the spinal gate first and block some of the pain messages from the slower-conducting nerve fibers. Applying ice, heat, or electrical stimulation to the painful area also stimulates the large nerve fibers and closes the spinal gate.

The gate-control theory also accounts for the fact that psychological factors, both cognitive and emotional, can influence the perception of pain. Melzack and Wall (1965, 1983) contend that messages from the brain to the spinal cord can inhibit the transmission of pain messages at the spinal gate, thereby affecting the perception of pain. This phenomenon explains why soldiers injured in battle or athletes injured during games

▲ The skills that women learn in prepared childbirth classes help them cope with the anxieties that accompany the pain of childbirth. However, women who attend such classes are no less likely to request pain-relieving drugs than women who do not.

endorphins (en-DOR-fins) The body's own natural painkillers, which block pain and produce a feeling of well-being.

can be so distracted that they do not experience pain until sometime after the injury. Likewise, distraction can be an effective pain management strategy. In one study, researchers applied a vibrator to one of the children's arms while they were getting an injection in the other. They also instructed the children to watch as the vibrator moved up and down their arms. The study showed that the children who were in the vibrator group experienced little or no pain from the injection.

But what about long-term pain? Not surprisingly, distraction is of little use in managing the ongoing pain of conditions such as *arthritis*, chronic inflammation of the joints. Still, there are psychological techniques that help. Strategies such as relaxation techniques, which you will read about in Chapter 4, provide some relief for the anxiety associated with chronic pain (Singh et al., 2012). However, they do not seem to actually prevent pain sensations.

Intense types of pain seem to be resistant to psychological management as well. For example, many pregnant women attend prepared childbirth classes in which they learn controlled breathing, focused massage, and other strategies for managing labor pains. However, research indicates that women who use them are no less likely to request pharmacological pain relief than are those who do not (Bergström, Kieler, & Waldenström, 2009). Nevertheless, these strategies help women manage the anxieties associated with labor and delivery (Kimber et al., 2008).

Although psychological pain management may not be of much help during childbirth, research suggests that the mind gets a lot of help from the body when it comes to managing the pain of labor and delivery. During the last few weeks of pregnancy, a woman's body is flooded with higher levels of estrogen than she experiences at any other time of life. Estrogen levels determine how sensitive a woman's neurons are to the effects of **endorphins**, the pain-blocking neurotransmitters you learned about in Chapter 2.) Smith et al., 2006. The higher estrogen levels are, the better the neurons are at using endorphins. Moreover, the quantity of endorphins in a woman's system increases dramatically in the last few weeks of pregnancy and rises again when she goes into labor (Abboud et al., 1983; Hughes, Levinson, Rosen, & Shnider, 2002). Even after administration of pain-relieving drugs, the laboring woman's level of endorphins remains much higher than is typical in the nonpregnant state.

Similarly, endorphins are released when you are injured, when you experience stress or extreme pain, and when you laugh, cry, or exercise. Recent findings suggest that the release of endorphins that occurs during acupuncture treatments may be one of the factors involved in individuals who respond favorably to such treatments for conditions such as chronic back pain (Caby´oglu, Ergene, & Tan, 2006).

Some people release endorphins even when they merely *think* they are receiving pain medication but are being given, instead, a placebo in the form of a sugar pill or an injection of saline solution (Zubieta et al., 2005). Imaging studies confirm that placebo administration causes a reduction of activity in the regions of the brain that are associated with pain perception (Price, Finniss, & Benedetti, 2008). Why? Apparently, when patients believe that they have received a drug for pain, that belief stimulates the release of their own natural pain relievers, the endorphins. ◉

◉─Watch the Video *Episode 5: In the Real World: Managing Pain* in **MyPsychLab**

REMEMBER IT   *Check your answers and take additional quizzes in MyPsychLab.com.*   ✓●─Study and Review on **MyPsychLab**

1. Olfaction is the technical term for the sense of _____.
2. Smell sensations are routed to the _____ for emotional interpretation and the _____ for cognitive interpretation.
3. Taste receptors are located on the _____.
4. The part of the brain that is responsible for interpreting tactile information is the _____.
5. _____ in the skin respond to all kinds of tactile stimuli.
6. _____ are the body's own natural painkillers.

Influences on Perception

So far, you have been reading about *sensation,* the process of taking in information from the outside world through the senses. We've discussed vision, hearing, smell, taste, touch, and the spatial orientation senses. However, we have yet to discuss *perception,* the process through which the brain assigns meaning to sensations. For instance, your senses provide you with information about the color, taste, and smell of an apple, as well as the sound that happens when you bite into one. Sensation even provides you with the kinesthetic sense needed to toss an apple to your roommate. By contrast, perception enables you to link these sensations to the knowledge that apples are food, that you either like or dislike them, and that they have a variety of symbolic associations (e.g., "an apple for the teacher").

Perception is influenced by a number of factors. Before we discuss some of the principles that govern perception in all human beings, we will consider three factors that contribute to perceptual processes: attention, prior knowledge, and cross-modal perception.

Attention ▶

3.12 What do we gain and lose when we attend to a stimulus?

In some cases, linking sensations to meanings—the essence of the process of perception—requires very little mental effort. For instance, when reading familiar words, the sensation of seeing the word and the perception of its meaning occur almost simultaneously (Heil Rolke, & Pecchinenda, 2004). Likewise, while we are driving, perceiving that the other objects on the road with us are cars takes very little mental effort because we are so familiar with them. In other words, connecting the sensation of seeing a car with the perception that the object is a car is an *automatic* (noneffortful) mental process. However, more mental effort is required to determine which cars we should watch most closely. When we engage in this kind of mental effort, the process of *attention* is at work. **Attention** is defined as the process of sorting through sensations and selecting some of them for further processing. Without attention, perception of all but the most familiar sensations would be impossible.

attention The process of sorting through sensations and selecting some of them for further processing.

Of course, we cannot pay attention to everything at once. Thus, in a complex perceptual task, such as the everyday experience of driving in traffic, it's important to realize that attention carries certain perceptual costs. Research examining the phenomenon of **inattentional blindness** has helped to illustrate these costs (Bressan & Pizzighello, 2008; Simons & Rensink, 2005). Inattentional blindness occurs when we shift our attention from one object to another and, in the process, fail to notice changes in objects to which we are not directly paying attention (Woodman & Luck, 2003). In many studies of inattentional blindness, experimenters have presented participants with a scene and asked them to attend to a particular element in it. For example, in a classic study, Daniel Simons and colleagues (e.g., Bredemeier & Simons, 2012; Chabris & Simons, 2012) showed participants a videotape of a basketball game in which one team wore white uniforms and the other team wore black uniforms. Participants were instructed to count how many times the ball was passed from one player to another, either on the white team or on the black team. Under such conditions, about one-third of participants typically failed to later recall the appearance on the screen of even extremely incongruent stimuli (for example, a man dressed in a gorilla costume). The inattentional blindness happens even when the incongruous stimulus is present on the screen for a long period of time. Interestingly, too, expertise does not influence inattentional blindness; that is, a person is just as likely to exhibit the phenomenon when observing scenes that depict activities in which she has a great deal of knowledge and experience as she is when observing other types of scenes (Memmert, Simons, & Grimme, 2009). For instance, basketball experts would respond to Simons's basketball video featuring an unexpected gorilla in the same way as non-experts. Simons's research helps us understand why we sometimes exclaim, "Where did that car come from?" when a car we had been ignoring suddenly swerves into our path. Read the *Apply It* feature on p. 96 to learn about the possible dangers of using a cell phone while driving.

inattentional blindness The phenomenon in which we shift our focus from one object to another and, in the process, fail to notice changes in objects to which we are not directly paying attention.

How Dangerous Is It to Talk on a Cell Phone or Text while Driving?

When you read about the research demonstrating inattentional blindness, did it raise your level of concern about the possible dangers of driving while talking or texting on a cell phone? Interestingly, surveys suggest that we are more concerned about other drivers' cell phone use than our own. In one study, researchers found that, although 94% of participants viewed texting while driving as dangerous and 87% support laws prohibiting it, some 35% admitted to having done so themselves (AAA Foundation for Traffic Safety, 2012). In another survey, just 6% of drivers reported that their cell phone use had caused them to get into a potentially dangerous situation on the road. Remarkably, when participants were asked whether another driver's cell phone use had ever put them at risk, 66% said yes (Troglauer, Hels, & Christens, 2006). As much as we would like to believe that cell phones affect other drivers' behavior but not our own, research clearly shows that talking or texting on a cell phone, or engaging in other kinds of attention-demanding tasks, results in potentially dangerous changes in our behind-the-wheel behavior.

Behavioral Effects of Cell Phone Use

Most experiments examining cell phone use while driving take place in laboratories in which participants use driving simulators. Experimental group participants talk, text on, or follow instructions to ignore e-mail alerts and other auditory signals emitted by the cell phone while driving, but those in the control groups do not have a cell phone in the driving environment. Studies of this type show that both cell phone use and ignored signals from cell phones affect drivers' behavior in the following ways (Beede & Kass, 2006; Harrold et al., 2009; Holland & Rathod, 2012; Liu & Lee, 2006):

- Drivers slow down when using the phone.
- Drivers have slower reaction times when engaged in phone conversations or texting.
- Drivers who talk on a cell phone often fail to stay within the boundaries of the lane in which they are driving.
- Cell-phone-using drivers sometimes stop at green lights but drive through red lights and stop signs.
- Drivers who ignore auditory signals from cell phones have more collisions with pedestrians and other vehicles than drivers in phone-free driving environments do.

These effects have been observed just as often in studies using hands-free phones as conventional handheld models (Strayer & Drews, 2004). However, one study suggested that hands-free phone use gave drivers a false sense of safety (Langer, Holzner, Magnet, & Kopp, 2005). Thus, experimental studies show definitively that, on average, cell phone use impairs driving ability.

Compensating for the Effects of Cell Phone Use

Despite the clear findings of these studies, other research suggests that several factors help drivers compensate for the distractions associated with cell phone use (Hunton & Rose, 2005; Pöysti, Rajalin, & Summala, 2005; Shinar, Tractinsky, & Compton, 2005; Sullman, 2012). Here are a few of them:

- Experience with multitasking improves drivers' ability to juggle the demands of cell phone use and driving.
- Reducing other distractions, such as turning off the radio, helps drivers keep their minds on driving while also talking on the phone.
- Some drivers end a cell phone call with "I'll call you back later when I'm not driving," when they realize that the attentional demands of a specific conversation are incompatible with those of driving.

These findings show that drivers are well aware of the potentially risk-enhancing effects of behavior changes caused by distractions. As a result, they actively work to manage the number of demands on their attention while driving.

It's about Attention, Not Cell Phones

You may know from personal experience that several attention-demanding tasks impair driving behaviors just as much as cell phone use does. For example, talking to a passenger or searching for a radio station while driving produces the same kinds of detrimental effects on drivers' behavior as cell phone use (Amado & Ulupinar, 2005; Horberry et al., 2006; Sullman, 2012). Therefore, for drivers, the takeaway message from this chapter's discussion of inattentional blindness is clear. When drivers pay attention to anything that is not relevant to the task of operating a vehicle—be it a cell phone, a radio, or a conversation with a passenger—they limit their ability to focus on driving. Consequently, the goal of anyone who is operating a vehicle ought to be to minimize distractions to as great a degree as possible:

- Texting is more dangerous than talking on a cell phone because you must divert your eyes from the road (Harrold et al., 2009). Therefore, experts recommend that drivers NEVER text while driving.
- If possible, drivers should pull off the road to talk on their cell phones.
- Radio station adjustments should be postponed until drivers are stopped at a red light or stop sign.
- Whenever passengers are distracting them, drivers should politely request that they refrain from talking.

By taking these measures, drivers will reduce their risk of missing important cues such as traffic lights and decrease the likelihood that they will, at best, get a traffic ticket, or, at worst, cause an accident. In addition, laws that restrict or prohibit the use of cell phones by drivers have been passed in several jurisdictions, so following these guidelines may prevent you from getting a ticket.

◉ Watch on MyPsychLab

◉ Watch the Video *Episode 1: What's in It for Me?: The Myth of Multitasking* in **MyPsychLab**

Similar costs arise when we attend to auditory sensations. Suppose you are standing in a crowded room in which a large number of conversations are going on simultaneously. What would happen if someone mentioned your name? Research shows that you would zero in on the conversation that included your name and ignore others. This *cocktail party phenomenon* was documented in classic research by E. C. Cherry (1953). Remember, perception is the process of attaching meaning to sensations—and what is more meaningful to a person than his or her own name? Thus, when you hear your name, you assume that whatever is to follow will be personally meaningful to you. The process of attending to the conversation that included your name, however, would prevent you from adequately perceiving other conversations. Thus, you might fail to pick up on other conversations that might have more meaning for you but are free from obvious attentional cues such as your name.

Although attending to a stimulus is associated with deficits in the ability to attend to other stimuli, attention is clearly not an all-or-nothing process. We can, and often do, process more than one stimulus at a time. Indeed, research shows that we are capable of accurately perceiving some sensations to which we do not pay direct attention. For example, in the same series of classic studies that led to the discovery of the cocktail party phenomenon, E. C. Cherry (1953) discovered that listeners who were presented with different verbal messages in either ear could remember the content of only the message to which the experimenter directed their attention (e.g., "Pay attention to the message in your left ear"). Nevertheless, they were able to remember many things about the unattended message, such as whether it had been delivered by a male or a female.

But what happens when we get conflicting information from two or more senses? How do we know which one to pay attention to? Experiments in which participants are exposed to conflicting visual and auditory information have shown that **cross-modal perception**, a process through which the brain integrates information from more than one sense, depends on the comparative accuracy of the conflicting sensations. For example, you have participated in a cross-modal perception "experiment" if you have ever seen a movie in which the actors' lip movements didn't match their spoken language. Research shows that it is very difficult to understand speech under such conditions (Thomas & Jordan, 2004). In effect, we must block out the visual information to understand what the speakers are saying. The opposite happens when facial expressions and vocal characteristics seem to be conveying different emotional messages. When a person looks angry but speaks in a happy voice, the visual information is typically judged to be more reliable than the auditory input (Vroomen, Driver, & Degelder, 2001).

▲ If you were walking across campus and this fellow rode past you, do you think you would notice him? Research on inattentional blindness suggests that you probably wouldn't if you were talking on a cell phone (Hyman et al., 2009).

cross-modal perception A process whereby the brain integrates information from more than one sense.

Prior Knowledge ▶

3.13 How does prior knowledge influence perception?

Think back to the example of attending to cars on the road while driving. How do we make judgments about which cars require most of our attention? To a great extent, our past driving experiences, or prior knowledge, help us make such decisions. For example, you may pay more attention to a car driven by someone on a cell phone since you know that they're more distracted than other drivers. Prior knowledge is helpful when interpreting the meanings of sensations, but it can lead to perceptual errors as well.

Suppose you were presented with this array of letters and numbers. How would you go about trying to use your prior knowledge to make sense of it?

DP

6 – 4 – 3

If you don't immediately recognize the array, you might begin trying to decipher it by guessing what the letters *DP* stand for, a classic example of **bottom-up processing** or *data-driven* processing. This strategy involves looking for patterns in individual bits of information that can be interpreted using prior knowledge. For example, bottom-up processing might lead you to call up compound nouns (nouns made up of two words) from your memory, such as the band "Drowning Pool" or "Dr. Pepper," that the letters might stand for. Perhaps you would try to decide which

bottom-up processing Information processing in which individual components or bits of data are combined until a complete perception is formed.

of these two possible meanings of "DP" was more feasible based on the information given in "6 – 4 – 3." Ultimately, you would probably give up and declare the array either meaningless or indecipherable.

Suppose we told you that the array has something to do with baseball. Now, if you have some knowledge of the game, you might try to think of baseball terms that could be represented by the letters *DP*. In so doing, you would be using **top-down processing** or *concept-driven* processing. In top-down processing, prior knowledge limits the range of one's guesses by providing a "whole" that can serve as a context for individual bits of information. Thus, given that baseball is the context for the array, neither "Drowning Pool" nor "Dr. Pepper" will fit. Of course, if you know how to score a baseball game, you probably instantly moved into top-down processing mode when you saw the array. No doubt, you recognized the array as representing a double play (DP) in which the short-stop (6) threw the ball to the second baseman (4) who, in turn, threw it to the first baseman (3) to get two runners out.

This example might lead you to think that bottom-up processing seldom leads to accurate perceptions. However, there are some situations in which only bottom-up processing will work. A "find the differences" activity, such as the one in Figure 3.13, provides a good example of a task that can only be accomplished through bottom-up processing. Why? Top-down processing causes you to perceive the scene as a whole and, as a result, to overlook details. To find the differences, you have to look at the items individually, without allowing the picture to contextualize them.

However, as you'll learn from doing the *Try It*, bottom-up and top-down processes are interactive. Technically speaking, decoding tasks like the one in the *Try It* call for bottom-up processing. Thus, you'll probably start out using the key to decode the first couple of letters in each word (bottom-up processing). But after you decode one or two letters in each word, you're likely to develop a hunch about what the word might be. Subsequently, when you look at the key, your hunch will guide your search (top-down processing).

Prior knowledge also contributes to perception by leading us to expect certain perceptions. For example, if you ordered raspberry sherbet and it was colored green, would it still taste like raspberry, or might it taste more like lime? The **perceptual set**—what we expect to perceive—determines, to a large extent, what we actually see, hear, feel, taste, and smell. Such expectations are, of course, based on prior knowledge (that lime sherbet is usually green). Such expectations do seem to influence perception. So, green raspberry sherbet might, indeed, taste a bit like lime.

In a classic study of perceptual set, psychologist David Rosenhan (1973) and some of his colleagues were admitted as patients to various mental hospitals with "diagnoses" of schizophrenia. Once admitted, they acted normal in every way. The purpose? They wondered how long it would take the doctors and the hospital staff to realize that they were not mentally ill. The doctors and the staff members saw what they expected to see and not what actually occurred. They perceived everything the

top-down processing Information processing in which previous experience and conceptual knowledge are applied to recognize the whole of a perception and thus easily identify the simpler elements of that whole.

✳ Explore the Concept *Top Down Processing* on MyPsychLab

perceptual set An expectation of what will be perceived, which can affect what actually is perceived.

FIGURE 3.13 **A Bottom-Up Processing Task**
A bottom-up processing strategy is the best approach to some kind of tasks because top-down processing prevents you from processing the details in the two senses pictured.
Source: Highlights for Children (May, 1995).

TRY IT   **Bottom-Up and Top-Down Processing**

Decode these words:
1. GIVV
2. DRMWLD
3. ELOFMGVVI
4. NZTRX
5. YILMGLHZFIFH

KEY

A = Z	F = U	K = P	P = K	U = F	Z = A
B = Y	G = T	L = O	Q = J	V = E	
C = X	H = S	M = N	R = I	W = D	
D = W	I = R	N = M	S = H	X = C	
E = V	J = Q	O = L	T = G	Y = B	

Answers: 1. TREE; 2. WINDOW; 3. VOLUNTEER; 4. MAGIC; 5. BRONTOSAURUS

pseudo-patients said and did, such as note taking, to be symptoms of their illness. The real patients, however, were not fooled; they were the first to realize that the psychologists were not really mentally ill.

Social Perception ▶

⌐ **3.14** How do we perceive social
⌐ stimuli?

Up to this point, we have been considering how the brain processes information about objects. What happens when the object of an individual's sensory and perceptual processes is another human? Interestingly, the brain perceives social information differently from the way that it interprets other types of input. For example, brain-imaging studies suggest that a specialized neurological system helps us interpret others' behaviors and guide our own. These studies show that both observation and production of motor actions (e.g., grasping a cup) and emotion-related behaviors (e.g., smiling) activate the **mirror neuron system (MNS)** (Iacoboni, 2009). The MNS contributes to our ability to learn physical skills by observing others perform them and to teach such skills by demonstrating them. Similarly, the MNS operates as a filter that helps us "decode" others' emotional behavior and to properly "code" our own expressions according to the rules and symbols of our culture.

mirror neuron system (MNS) A network of cells that the brain uses to interpret and produce motor actions and emotion-related behavior.

As you might guess, when the MNS is decoding others' emotional expressions, the brain's ability to process information about the human face plays a key role. Perception of faces appears to be particularly complex and distinctive from perceptions of other kinds of visual stimuli. Researcher James Haxby and his colleagues suggest that there is a core system of face perception that uses the universal features of the human face (eyes, nose, and mouth) to make judgments about people's identities (Haxby et al., 2001; Pavizi et al., 2012). We move beyond the core system when we engage in verbal and nonverbal communication with others and, in so doing, activate a larger neural network. Other researchers have found equally distinctive neural systems for processing images of human body parts (Downing et al., 2001). ◉

The way we combine information from two sensory modalities—a process known as *cross-modal perception* (refer back to p. 97)—also differs for nonsocial and social stimuli. For example, how would your brain respond to the sight of an approaching train paired with the sound of a departing train? Research indicates that, when judging motion based on conflicting visual and auditory cues, we tend to rely on the auditory input (Meyer & Wuerger, 2001). So, your brain would decide that the train was moving away rather than approaching.

◉—Watch the Video *Episode 5: Special Topics: Recognizing Faces* in **MyPsychLab**

In the case of social perception, the opposite is true. Facial expressions, the visual cues for emotional perceptions, often take priority over the auditory cues associated with a person's speech intonation and volume, as well as the actual words spoken. Thus, a person who exhibits an angry face but speaks in a happy voice will typically be judged to be angry rather than happy (Vroomen et al., 2001). Perhaps this is why one old song suggests that we "put on a happy face."

1. When individuals focus on one of several moving objects in their visual field, they often exhibit _____.

2. _____ processing uses individual bits of information to construct a perception; _____ processing uses previous experience and knowledge to interpret individual bits of information.

3. _____ refers to what people expect to perceive.

4. The _____ is a network of cells in the brain that processes information about our own and others' motor actions and emotional expressions.

5. In social situations in which visual and auditory information are in conflict, individuals tend to rely on _____.

Principles of Perception

Some influences on perception—particularly the application of prior knowledge to perceptual tasks—can lead to wide variations in how a stimulus is perceived. However, researchers have found a few principles that appear to govern perceptions in all human beings.

3.15 What are the Gestalt principles of perceptual organization?

Perceptual Organization and Constancy

Remember the discussion of Gestalt psychology from Chapter 1? The Gestalt psychologists maintained that people cannot understand the perceptual world by breaking down experiences into tiny parts and analyzing them separately. When sensory elements are brought together, something new is formed. That is, the whole is more than just the sum of its parts. The German word **Gestalt** has no exact English equivalent, but it roughly refers to the whole form, pattern, or configuration that a person perceives. The Gestalt psychologists claimed that sensory experience is organized according to certain basic principles of perceptual organization:

Gestalt (geh-SHTALT) A German word that roughly refers to the whole form, pattern, or configuration that a person perceives.

- *Figure–ground.* As we view the world, some object (the figure) often seems to stand out from the background (the ground) as shown in Figure 3.14(a).

- *Similarity.* Objects that have similar characteristics are perceived as a unit. In Figure 3.14(b), dots of a similar color are perceived as belonging together to form horizontal rows on the left and vertical columns on the right.

- *Proximity.* Objects that are close together in space or time are usually perceived as belonging together. Because of their spacing, the lines in Figure 3.14(c) are perceived as four pairs of lines rather than as eight separate lines.

FIGURE 3.14 Gestalt Principles of Perceptual Organization
Gestalt psychologists proposed several principles of perceptual organization, including figure–ground, similarity, proximity, continuity, and closure.

- *Continuity.* We tend to perceive figures or objects as belonging together if they appear to form a continuous pattern such as a line or wave, as in Figure 3.14(d).

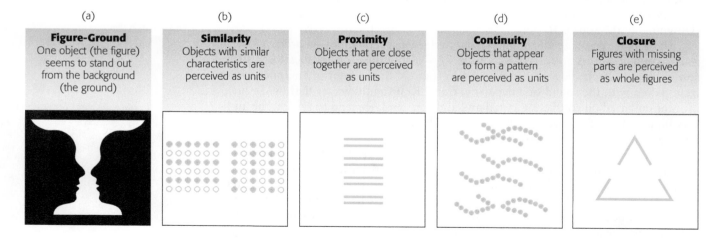

(a)	(b)	(c)	(d)	(e)
Figure-Ground One object (the figure) seems to stand out from the background (the ground)	**Similarity** Objects with similar characteristics are perceived as units	**Proximity** Objects that are close together are perceived as units	**Continuity** Objects that appear to form a pattern are perceived as units	**Closure** Figures with missing parts are perceived as whole figures

FIGURE 3.15 **Shape Constancy**
The door projects very different images on the retina when viewed from different angles. But because of shape constancy, you continue to perceive the door as rectangular.

- *Closure.* We perceive figures with gaps in them to be complete. Even though parts of the figure in Figure 3.14(e) are missing, we use closure and perceive it as a triangle.

When you say good-bye to friends and watch them walk away, the image they cast on your retina grows smaller and smaller until they finally disappear in the distance. So how does your brain know that they are still the same size? Scientists call this phenomenon **perceptual constancy**. Thanks to perceptual constancy, when you watch someone walk away, the information that the retina sends to the brain (the sensation that that person is shrinking in size) does not fool the perceptual system. As objects or people move farther away, you continue to perceive them as being about the same size. This perceptual phenomenon is known as *size constancy*. You do not make a literal interpretation about the size of an object from its retinal image—the image of the object projected onto the retina. If you did, you would believe that objects become larger as they approach and smaller as they move away. ◉➟

The shape or image of an object projected onto the retina changes according to the angle from which it is viewed. But your perceptual ability includes *shape constancy*—the tendency to perceive objects as having a stable or unchanging shape, regardless of changes in the retinal image resulting from differences in viewing angle. In other words, you perceive a door as rectangular and a plate as round from whatever angle you view them (see Figure 3.15).

We normally see objects as maintaining a constant level of brightness, regardless of differences in lighting conditions—a perceptual phenomenon known as *brightness constancy*. Nearly all objects reflect some part of the light that falls on them, and white objects reflect more light than black objects. However, a black asphalt driveway at noon in bright sunlight actually reflects more light than a white shirt does indoors at night in dim lighting. Nevertheless, the driveway still looks black, and the shirt still looks white. Why? We learn to infer the brightness of an object by comparing it with the brightness of all other objects viewed at the same time.

perceptual constancy The phenomenon that allows us to perceive objects as maintaining stable properties, such as size, shape, and brightness, despite differences in distance, viewing angle, and lighting.

◉➟ **Complete** the Simulation *Distinguishing Figure–Ground Relationships on Simulate* in **MyPsychLab**

Depth Perception ▶

Depth perception is the ability to perceive the visual world in three dimensions and to judge distances accurately. We judge how far away objects and other people are. We climb and descend stairs without stumbling and perform numerous other actions requiring depth perception. Depth perception is three dimensional. Yet each eye is able to provide only a two-dimensional view. The images cast on the retina do not contain depth; they are flat, just like a photograph. How, then, do we perceive depth so vividly?

3.16 What do monocular and binocular cues contribute to perception?

depth perception The ability to perceive the visual world in three dimensions and to judge distances accurately.

binocular depth cues Depth cues that depend on both eyes working together.

monocular depth cues (mah-NOK-yu-ler) Depth cues that can be perceived by one eye alone.

Some cues to depth perception depend on both eyes working together. These **binocular depth cues** include convergence and binocular disparity. *Convergence* occurs when the eyes turn inward to focus on nearby objects—the closer the object, the more the two objects appear to come together. Hold the tip of your finger about 12 inches in front of your nose and focus on it. Now, slowly begin moving your finger toward your nose. Your eyes will turn inward so much that they virtually cross when the tip of your finger meets the tip of your nose. Many psychologists believe that the tension of the eye muscles as they converge conveys to the brain information that serves as a cue for depth perception. Fortunately, the eyes are just far enough apart, about 2½ inches or so, to give each eye a slightly different view of the objects being focused on and, consequently, a slightly different retinal image. The difference between the two retinal images, known as *binocular disparity* (or *retinal disparity*), provides an important cue for depth perception (see Figure 3.16). The farther away from the eyes (up to 20 feet or so) the objects being viewed, the less the disparity, or difference, between the two retinal images. The brain integrates the two slightly different retinal images and creates the perception of three dimensions.

Close one eye, and you will see that you can still perceive depth. The visual depth cues perceived with one eye alone are called **monocular depth cues**. The following is a description of seven monocular depth cues, many of which have been used by artists in Western cultures to give the illusion of depth to their paintings:

- *Interposition.* When one object partly blocks your view of another, you perceive the partially blocked object as being farther away.
- *Linear perspective.* Parallel lines that are known to be the same distance apart appear to grow closer together, or converge, as they recede into the distance.
- *Relative size.* Larger objects are perceived as being closer to the viewer and smaller objects as being farther away.
- *Texture gradient.* Objects close to you appear to have sharply defined features, and similar objects that are farther away appear progressively less well defined or fuzzier in texture.
- *Atmospheric perspective* (sometimes called *aerial perspective*). Objects in the distance have a bluish tint and appear more blurred than objects close at hand.
- *Shadow or shading.* When light falls on objects, they cast shadows, which add to the perception of depth.
- *Motion parallax.* When you ride in a moving vehicle and look out the side window, the objects you see outside appear to be moving in the opposite direction and at

FIGURE 3.16 Retinal Disparity and Viewing a Stereogram
Retinal disparity enables most of us to perceive 3-D images in stereograms. Place this picture against the tip of your nose and then very, very slowly move the book straight back from your face. Look at the image without blinking. A 3-D image will suddenly appear.

different speeds; those closest to you appear to be moving faster than those in the distance. Objects very far away, such as the moon and the sun, appear to move in the same direction as the viewer. Photos illustrating each of these cues are shown in Figure 3.17.

Perception of Motion

3.17 How does the brain perceive motion?

Imagine you're sitting in a bus looking through the window at another bus parked parallel to the one in which you are sitting. Suddenly, you sense your bus moving; then, you realize that it is not your bus that moved but the one next to it. In other words, your ability to perceive the motion of objects has been fooled in some way. This example illustrates the complexity of motion perception.

One of the most important contributors to our understanding of motion perception is psychologist James Gibson. Gibson points out that our perceptions of motion appear to be based on fundamental, but frequently changing, assumptions about stability (Gibson, 1994). Our brains seem to search for some stimulus in the environment to serve as the assumed reference point for stability. Once the stable reference point is chosen, all objects that move relative to that reference point are judged to be in motion. For example, in the bus situation, your brain assumes that the other bus is stable, and when the motion sensors linked to your retina detect movement, it concludes that your bus is moving. And when you're driving a car, you sense the car to be in motion relative to the outside environment. But your brain uses the inside of the

Interposition
When one object partially blocks your view of another, you perceive the partially blocked object as being farther away.

Linear Perspective
Parallel lines are the same distance apart but appear to grow closer together, or converge, as they recede into the distance.

Relative Size
Larger objects are perceived as being closer to the viewer, and smaller objects as being farther away.

Texture Gradient
Objects close to you appear to have sharply defined features, and similar objects farther away appear progressively less well defined, or fuzzier in texture.

Atmospheric Perspective
Objects in the distance have a bluish tint and appear more blurred than objects close at hand (sometimes called *aerial perspective*).

Shadow or Shading
When light falls on objects, they cast shadows, which add to the perception of depth.

Motion Parallax
When you ride in a moving train and look out the window, the objects you see outside appear to be moving in the opposite direction and at different speeds; those closest to you appear to be moving faster than those in the distance.

FIGURE 3.17 Monocular Depth Cues

car as the stable point of reference for your own movements. Only your movements in relation to the seat, steering wheel, and so on are sensed as motion by your brain.

The fact that the eyes are never really completely still also contributes to perceptions of motion. For instance, if you stare at a single unmoving light in a dark room for a few seconds, the light will appear to begin moving, a phenomenon called the *autokinetic illusion*. If you look away from the light and then return to watching it, it will again appear to be stable. (Could this phenomenon account for some sightings of "unidentified flying objects"?) Two lights placed close to each other will appear to move together, as if they are linked by an invisible string. What is really happening is that your eyes, not the lights, are moving. Because of the darkness of the room, the brain has no stable visual reference point to use in deciding whether the lights are actually moving (Gibson, 1994). But when the room is lit up, the brain immediately "fixes" the error because it has a stable visible background for the lights.

In one kind of study of false-motion perceptions, several stationary lights in a dark room are flashed on and off in sequence, causing participants to perceive a single light moving from one spot to the next. This type of illusion, called the *phi phenomenon* (sometimes called *stroboscopic motion*), was first discussed by Max Wertheimer (1912), one of the founders of Gestalt psychology. You encounter one of the most common examples of the phi phenomenon whenever you go to the movies. As you probably know, movies are simply a series of still photographs shown in rapid succession.

REMEMBER IT

Check your answers and take additional quizzes in MyPsychLab.com. ✔●─[Study and Review on **MyPsychLab**

1. The hole form, pattern, or configuration that a person perceived is a(n) _____.
2. _____ depth cues depend on both eyes working together.
3. _____ depth cues can be perceived by one eye alone.
4. The apparent motion produced by several lights flashing off and on in sequence is known as the _____.
5. The apparent motion produced by movements of the eyes is known as the _____.

Unusual Perceptual Experiences

Having read about the senses and the factors that influence and govern perception, you are probably convinced by now that sensation and perception enable us to make sense of the world we live in. But what happens when these vital processes are fooled, that is, when they lead us to believe that we see or hear something that really isn't there? Further, is it possible to perceive without sensing?

3.18 What are three puzzling perceptions?

●─[Watch the Video *Episode 5: What's in it for Me?: Perceptual Magic in Art* in **MyPsychLab**

Puzzling Perceptions

Not only can we perceive motion that doesn't exist, but we can also perceive objects that aren't present in a stimulus and misinterpret those that are. ●

When you are faced for the first time with an *ambiguous figure,* you have no experience to call on. Your perceptual system is puzzled and tries to resolve the uncertainty by seeing the ambiguous figure first one way and then another, but not both ways at once. You never get a lasting impression of ambiguous figures because they seem to jump back and forth beyond your control. In some ambiguous figures, two different objects or figures are seen alternately. One such image is shown in Figure 3.18(a). Do you see just a collection of black dots on a white background? If you look closely, you'll see the image of a Dalmatian sniffing the ground. Such examples of object ambiguity offer striking evidence that perceptions are more than the mere sum of sensory parts. It is hard to believe that the same drawing (the same sum of sensory parts) can convey such dramatically different perceptions. ❋

❋─[Explore the **Concept** *Five Well-Known Illusions* on **MyPsychLab**

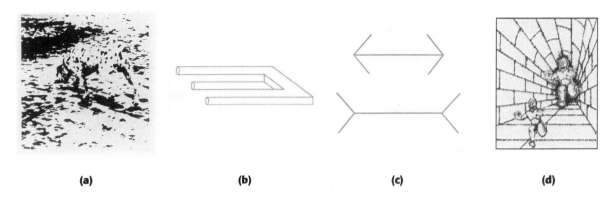

(a)   (b)   (c)   (d)

At first glance, many impossible figures do not seem particularly unusual—at least not until you examine them more closely. Would you invest your money in a company that manufactured the three-pronged device shown in Figure 3.18(b)? Such an object could not be made as pictured because the middle prong appears to be in two different places at the same time. However, this type of impossible figure is more likely to confuse people from Western cultures. Classic research in the 1970s showed that people in some African cultures do not represent three-dimensional visual space in their art, and they do not perceive depth in drawings that contain pictorial depth cues. These people see no ambiguity in drawings similar to the three-pronged trident, and they can draw the figure accurately from memory much more easily than people from Western cultures can (Bloomer, 1976).

An **illusion** is a false perception or a misperception of an actual stimulus in the environment. We can misperceive size, shape, or the relationship of one element to another. We need not pay to see illusions performed by magicians. Illusions occur naturally, and we see them all the time. For example, the moon looks much larger at the horizon than it does overhead. Why? One explanation of the *moon illusion* involves relative size. This idea suggests that the moon looks very large on the horizon because it is viewed in comparison to trees, buildings, and other objects. When viewed overhead, the moon cannot be directly compared with other objects, and it appears smaller.

In Figure 3.14(c), the two lines are the same length, but the diagonals extending outward from both ends of the upper line make it look longer than the lower line, which has diagonals pointing inward, a phenomenon known as the *Müller-Lyer illusion*. The *Ponzo illusion* also plays an interesting trick on our estimation of size. Look at Figure 3.18(d). Contrary to your perceptions, the two "monsters" are the same size. Again, perceptions of size and distance, which we trust and which are normally accurate in informing us about the real world, can be wrong. If you saw two figures like the ones in the illusion running down the hallway of a real building, the one that looks larger would indeed be larger. So the Ponzo illusion is not a natural illusion but a contrived one. In fact, all these illusions are really misapplications of principles that nearly always work properly in normal everyday experience.

Because responses to a number of illusions are universal, many psychologists believe they are inborn. However, British psychologist R. L. Gregory believed that susceptibility to the Müller-Lyer and other such illusions is not innate. Rather, the culture in which people live is responsible to some extent for the illusions they perceive. To test whether susceptibility to the Müller-Lyer and similar illusions is due to experience, Segall and others (1966) tested 1,848 adults and children from 15 different cultures in Africa, the Philippines, and the United States. Included were a group of Zulus from South Africa and a group of Illinois residents. The study revealed that "there were marked differences in illusion susceptibility across the cultural groups included in this study" (Segall, 1994, p. 137). People from all the cultures showed some tendency to perceive the Müller-Lyer illusion, indicating a biological component, but experience

FIGURE 3.18 **Some Puzzling Perceptions**
(a) Do you see random dots or something else? (b) Why couldn't you build a replica of this three-pronged device? (c) Which horizontal line appears to be longer? (d) Which monster is larger?

illusion A false perception or a misperception of an actual stimulus in the environment.

▲ Some visual illusions seem to be culture dependent. For example, Zulus and people from other cultures in which the houses lack straight sides and corners do not perceive the Müller-Lyer illusion.

was clearly a factor. Zulus, who have round houses and see few corners of any kind, are not fooled by this illusion. Illinois residents saw the illusion readily, while the Zulu tribes people tended not to see it.

In another classic cross-cultural study of illusions, Pedersen and Wheeler (1983) studied perceptions of the Müller-Lyer illusion among two groups of Navajos. The group who lived in rectangular houses and had experienced corners, angles, and edges tended to see the illusion. The members of the other group, like the Zulus, tended not to see it because their cultural experience consisted of round houses.

3.19 What do studies of subliminal perception, ESP, and synesthesia show?

Subliminal Perception, Extrasensory Perception, and Synesthesia

Illusions result from misperceptions of sensory input. By contrast, the phenomena you will read about in this section involve perceptions that are entirely independent of sensory input. Thus, they represent perception without sensation, or at least an awareness of sensation.

subliminal perception The capacity to perceive and respond to stimuli that are presented below the threshold of awareness.

Subliminal Perception. For decades, psychologists have studied a similar phenomenon known as **subliminal perception**, the capacity to perceive and respond to stimuli that are presented below the threshold of awareness. Neuroimaging studies show that the brain does, indeed, respond physiologically to subliminally presented stimuli (Hsieh & Colas, 2012; Kouider et al., 2009). Moreover, subliminal information can influence behavior to some degree. For example, when people are subliminally exposed to a picture of one person hitting another, they are more likely to judge a consciously perceived neutral scene, such as two people talking in a restaurant, as involving some kind of aggression (Todorov & Bargh, 2002).

But how strongly does subliminal perception affect behavior? The use of messages presented below the threshold of awareness in advertising, often called *subliminal persuasion,* has been around for decades. However, most research on subliminal perception suggests that, although the phenomenon does exist, it probably cannot produce the kinds of behavior changes claimed by the proponents of its use for advertising purposes (Greenwald, 1992; Hsieh & Colas, 2012).

Similarly, people who want to lose weight sometimes download commercially available MP3s containing subliminal messages, such as "I will eat less," embedded in recordings of music or ocean waves in the hopes that listening to them will help them control their appetite. Recordings of this kind are also marketed to people who want to quit smoking. However, experimental, placebo-controlled studies have found that such subliminal messages have no effect on behavior (Greenwald, 1992; Greenwald et al., 1991; Russell, Rowe, & Smouse, 1991).

extrasensory perception (ESP) Gaining information about objects, events, or another person's thoughts through some means other than the known sensory channels.

Extrasensory Perception. Extrasensory perception (ESP) is defined as gaining information about objects, events, or another person's thoughts through some means other than the known sensory channels. Several different kinds of ESP have been proposed to exist. *Telepathy* means gaining awareness of the thoughts, feelings, or activities of another person without the use of the senses—in other words, reading a person's mind. *Clairvoyance* means gaining information about objects or events without use of the senses, such as knowing the contents of a letter before opening it. *Precognition* refers to an awareness of an event before it occurs. Most of the reported cases of precognition in everyday life have occurred while people were dreaming.

Many studies of ESP employ the *Ganzfeld procedure,* a study design in which two individuals, a "sender" and a "receiver," are placed in separate rooms. The rooms are specially designed to minimize distractions and to facilitate deep concentration. Experimenters provide senders with messages that they are supposed to attempt to transmit to receivers. Some studies using the Ganzfeld technique have suggested that ESP exists and that some people are more capable of sending and receiving extrasensory messages than others (Pérez-Navarro, Lawrence, & Hume, 2009). However, in almost all cases, attempts at replication of these studies have failed (Milton & Wiseman, 2001). Thus, most psychologists remain skeptical about the existence of ESP.

Synesthesia. Synesthesia is the capacity for experiencing unusual sensations along with ordinary ones. For instance, one person with synesthesia who has been examined by researchers sees the color blue simultaneously with the taste of beef, and an orange blob appears in his field of vision when he consumes foods that have been seasoned with ginger (Carpenter, 2001). However, the most common type of synesthesia is one in which individuals sense colors in response to spoken words, or so-called colored hearing (Carpenter, 2001). Neuroimaging studies suggest that colored hearing is not the result of learned associations. These studies show that different brain areas are active in people with synesthesia who associate words with colors than in research participants who have been trained to consciously engage in such associations (Nunn et al., 2002).

Some psychologists speculate that all newborn brains are synesthetic and that the capacity for synesthesia is lost in most people as the various brain areas become more specialized over the years of childhood and adolescence (Spector & Maurer, 2009). However, some drugs produce temporary synesthesia, leading a few scientists to hypothesize that the neural connections that underlie synesthetic experiences are present in everyone (Sinke et al., 2012). Nevertheless, the jury is still out with regard to both the origin and neurological basis of synesthesia (Sinke et al., 2012). A great deal more research needs to be done.

synesthesia The capacity for experiencing unusual sensations along with ordinary ones.

REMEMBER IT   *Check your answers and take additional quizzes in MyPsychLab.com.* ✓●—Study and Review on MyPsychLab

1. Studies of subliminal perception show that the brain (*does/does not*) respond to stimuli that are presented below the threshold of awareness.
2. The Ganzfeld procedure is used to study _____.
3. People with synesthesia (*sense, perceive*) the world differently from others.

Looking Back

We began the chapter by demonstrating to you how our senses work together to enable our bodies to do the tasks we require them to do. We ended this chapter with an examination of some unusual kinds of perceptual experiences. In synesthesia, one kind of perception (e.g., visual) occurs in response to stimuli that normally elicit another kind of perception (e.g., auditory). Subliminal perception occurs in response to stimuli that we are unaware of having sensed. ESP, if it exists, involves perception in the absence of any sensory stimulus. While such phenomena are intriguing, navigating through our everyday sensory environments would be much more difficult without reliable connections among sensory stimuli, the process of sensation, and the process of perception that mark our more typical sensory and perceptual experiences.

CHAPTER 3 SUMMARY

THE PROCESS OF SENSATION (pp. 76–79)

3.1 What are the absolute and difference thresholds? (pp. 76–78)

The absolute threshold is the minimum amount of sensory stimulation that can be detected 50% of the time. The difference threshold is a measure of the smallest increase or decrease in a physical stimulus that can be detected 50% of the time.

Key Terms
sensation, p. 76
perception, p. 76
absolute threshold, p. 76
difference threshold, p. 77
just noticeable difference (JND), p. 77
Weber's law, p. 77

3.2 How does transduction change sensory information? (pp. 78–79)

For each of the senses, the body has sensory receptors that detect and respond to sensory stimuli. Through the process of transduction, the receptors change the sensory stimuli into neural impulses, which are then transmitted to precise locations in the brain.

Key Terms

sensory receptors, p. 78
transduction, p. 78
sensory adaptation, p. 79

VISION (pp. 79–85)

3.3 How does each part of the eye function in vision? (pp. 79–81)

The cornea bends light rays inward through the pupil—the small, dark opening in the eye. The iris dilates and contracts the pupil to regulate the amount of light entering the eye. The lens changes its shape as it focuses images of objects at varying distances on the retina, a thin layer of tissue that contains the sensory receptors for vision. The cones detect color and fine detail; they function best in adequate light. The rods are extremely sensitive and enable vision in dim light.

Key Terms

visible spectrum, p. 79
wavelength, p. 79
cornea, p. 79
lens, p. 80
accommodation, p. 80
retina, p. 80
rods, p. 80
cones, p. 80
fovea, p. 81

3.4 How does visual information get from the retina to the primary visual cortex? (pp. 81–82)

The rods and the cones transduce light waves into neural impulses that pass from the bipolar, amacrine, and horizontal cells to the ganglion cells, whose axons form the optic nerve beyond the retinal wall of each eye. At the optic chiasm, the two optic nerves come together, and some of the nerve fibers from each eye cross to the opposite side of the brain. They synapse with neurons in the thalamus, which transmit the neural impulses to the primary visual cortex.

Key Terms

blind spot, p. 81
optic nerve, p. 81
primary visual cortex, p. 82
feature detectors, p. 82

3.5 How does color vision work? (pp. 82–85)

The perception of color results from the reflection of particular wavelengths of the visual spectrum from the surfaces of objects. For example, an object that appears to be red reflects light of longer wavelengths than one that appears to be blue. Color blindness is the inability to distinguish certain colors from one another, rather than the total absence of color vision. Two major theories that attempt to explain color vision are the trichromatic theory and the opponent-process theory.

Key Terms

hue, p. 83
saturation, p. 83
brightness, p. 83
trichromatic theory, p. 83
opponent-process theory, p. 83
afterimage, p. 83
color blindness, p. 84

HEARING AND BALANCE (pp. 85–90)

3.6 What are the physical characteristics of sound? (pp. 85–86)

The pitch of a sound is determined by the frequency of the sound waves, which is measured in hertz. The loudness of a sound is determined largely by the amplitude of the sound waves, which is measured in decibels.

Key Terms

frequency, p. 85
amplitude, p. 86
decibel (dB), p. 86
timbre, p. 86

3.7 How does each part of the ear function in hearing? (pp. 86–89)

Sound waves enter the pinna, the visible part of the outer ear, and travel to the end of the auditory canal, causing the eardrum to vibrate. This sets in motion the ossicles in the middle ear, which amplify the sound waves. The vibration of the oval window causes activity in the inner ear, setting in motion the fluid in the cochlea. The moving fluid pushes and pulls the hair cells attached to the thin basilar membrane, which transduce the vibrations into neural impulses. The auditory nerve then carries the neural impulses to the brain.

Key Terms
audition, p. 86
outer ear, p. 86
middle ear, p. 86
inner ear, p. 87
cochlea, p. 87
hair cells, p. 87
place theory, p. 89
frequency theory, p. 89

3.8 How do the kinesthetic and vestibular senses help us move and stay balanced? (pp. 89–90)

The kinesthetic sense provides information about the position of body parts in relation to one another and movement of the entire body or its parts. This information is detected by sensory receptors in the joints, ligaments, and muscles. The vestibular sense detects movement and provides information about the body's orientation in space. Sensory receptors in the semicircular canals and the vestibular sacs sense changes in motion and the orientation of the head.

Key Terms
kinesthetic sense, p. 89
vestibular sense, p. 89
semicircular canals, p. 90

SMELL, TASTE, AND TOUCH (pp. 90–94)

3.9 How do smell sensations get from the nose to the brain? (pp. 90–91)

The act of smelling begins when odor molecules reach the smell receptors in the olfactory epithelium, at the top of the nasal cavity. The axons of these receptors relay the smell message to the olfactory bulbs. From there, the smell message travels to the thalamus and the orbitofrontal cortex, which distinguish the odor and relay that information to other parts of the brain.

Key Terms
olfaction, p. 90
olfactory epithelium, p. 91
olfactory bulbs, p. 91

3.10 How do we detect the primary taste sensations? (pp. 92–93)

The primary taste sensations are sweet, salty, sour, bitter, and umami. The receptor cells for taste are found in the taste buds on the tongue and in other parts of the mouth and throat.

Key Terms
gustation, p. 92
taste buds, p. 92

3.11 How does the skin provide pleasant and unpleasant sensations? (pp. 93–94)

Sensitive nerve endings in the skin convey tactile information to the brain when an object touches and depresses the skin. The neural impulses for touch sensations ultimately register in the brain's somatosensory cortex. Pain can be a valuable warning and a protective mechanism, motivating people to tend to an injury, to restrict activity, and to seek medical help. Negative thinking can influence the perception of pain. Some cultures encourage individuals to suppress (or exaggerate) emotional reactions to pain. Endorphins are natural painkillers produced by the body, which block pain and produce a feeling of well-being.

Key Terms
tactile, p. 93
endorphins, p. 94

INFLUENCES ON PERCEPTION (pp. 95–100)

3.12 What do we gain and lose when we attend to a stimulus? (pp. 95–97)

Attention enables the brain to focus on some sensations while screening others out. Unattended stimuli may be missed altogether or incorrectly perceived. Inattentional blindness occurs when we try to keep track of several moving objects at the same time.

Key Terms
attention, p. 95
inattentional blindness, p. 95
cross-modal perception, p. 97

3.13 How does prior knowledge influence perception? (pp. 97–99)

Individuals use bottom-up and top-down processing to apply their prior knowledge to perceptual problems. Expectations based on prior knowledge may predispose people to perceive sensations in a particular way.

Key Terms
bottom-up processing, p. 97
top-down processing, p. 98
perceptual set, p. 98
mirror neuron system (MNS), p. 99

3.14 How do we perceive social stimuli? (pp. 99–100)

Research suggests that the mirror neuron system processes information about others' motor actions and emotional expressions. It is also active when we attempt to mimic these behaviors from models. The brain also possesses a network devoted to face processing. In addition, cross-modal perception of human actions varies from that which we use to perceive objects. When visual and auditory information from a human source is in conflict, we rely on visual cues. The opposite is true for object perception.

PRINCIPLES OF PERCEPTION (pp. 100–104)

3.15 What are the Gestalt principles of perceptual organization? (pp. 100–101)

The Gestalt principles of perceptual organization include figure–ground, similarity, proximity, continuity, and closure. Perceptual constancy is the tendency to perceive objects as maintaining the same size, shape, and brightness, despite changes in lighting conditions or changes in the retinal image that result when an object is viewed from different angles and distances.

Key Terms
Gestalt, p. 100
perceptual constancy, p. 101

3.16 What do monocular and binocular cues contribute to perception? (pp. 101–103)

The binocular depth cues include convergence and binocular disparity, which depend on both eyes working together for depth perception. The monocular depth cues, those that can be perceived by one eye, include interposition, linear perspective, relative size, texture gradient, atmospheric perspective, shadow or shading, and motion parallax.

Key Terms
depth perception, p. 101
binocular depth cues, p. 102
monocular depth cues, p. 102

3.17 How does the brain perceive motion? (pp. 103–104)

The brain perceives real motion by comparing the movement of images across the retina to information derived from the spatial orientation senses. Apparent motion is the result of a psychological response to specific kinds of stimuli, such as flashing lights. The brain may also mistakenly perceive eye movement as object movement.

UNUSUAL PERCEPTUAL EXPERIENCES (pp. 104–107)

3.18 What are three puzzling perceptions? (pp. 104–106)

Three types of puzzling perceptions are ambiguous figures, impossible figures, and illusions.

Key Term
illusion, p. 105

3.19 What do studies of subliminal perception, ESP, and synesthesia show? (pp. 106–107)

Subliminal perception has subtle influences on behavior but appears to be ineffective at persuading people to buy products or to vote in certain ways. Researchers have been unable to replicate the small number of experiments that support the existence of ESP. All humans may be born with the capacity for synesthesia but lose it as sensory and perceptual experiences gradually influence the structure of the brain during the first months of life.

Key Terms
subliminal perception, p. 106
extrasensory perception (ESP), p. 106
synesthesia, p. 107

Chapter 3 Study Guide

Answers to all the Study Guide questions are provided at the end of the book.

SECTION ONE: Chapter Review

The Process of Sensation (pp. 76–79)

1. The process through which the senses detect sensory information and transmit it to the brain is called (sensation, perception).

2. The point at which you can barely sense a stimulus 50% of the time is called the (absolute, difference) threshold.

3. The difference threshold is the same for all individuals. (true/false)

4. Which of the following is not true of sensory receptors?
   a. They are specialized to detect certain sensory stimuli.
   b. They transduce sensory stimuli into neural impulses.
   c. They are located in the brain.
   d. They provide the link between the physical sensory world and the brain.

5. The process by which a sensory stimulus is converted into a neural impulse is called _____.

6. Each morning when Jackie goes to work at a dry cleaner, she smells a strong odor of cleaning fluid. After she is there for a few minutes, she is no longer aware of it. What accounts for this?
   a. signal detection theory
   b. sensory adaptation
   c. transduction
   d. the just noticeable difference

Vision (pp. 79–85)

7. Match each part of the eye with its description.
   _____ (1) the colored part of the eye
   _____ (2) the opening in the iris that dilates and constricts
   _____ (3) the transparent covering of the iris
   _____ (4) the transparent structure that focuses an inverted image on the retina
   _____ (5) the thin layer of tissue at the back of the eye on which the lens projects an inverted image
   a. retina
   b. cornea
   c. pupil
   d. iris
   e. lens

8. The receptor cells in the retina that enable you to see in dim light are the (cones, rods); the cells that enable you to see color and sharp images are (cones, rods).

9. Neural impulses are carried from the retina to the thalamus by the _____ and then relayed to their final destination, the _____.
   a. optic chiasm; primary visual cortex
   b. rods and cones; optic nerve
   c. optic nerve; primary visual cortex
   d. optic nerve; optic chiasm

Hearing and Balance (pp. 85–90)

10. Pitch is chiefly determined by _____; loudness is chiefly determined by _____.
    a. amplitude; frequency
    b. wavelength; frequency
    c. intensity; amplitude
    d. frequency; amplitude

11. Pitch is measured in (decibels, hertz); loudness is measured in (decibels, hertz).

12. Match the part of the ear with the structures it contains.
    _____ (1) ossicles
    _____ (2) pinna, auditory canal
    _____ (3) cochlea, hair cells
    a. outer ear
    b. middle ear
    c. inner ear

13. The receptors for hearing are found in the
    a. ossicles.
    b. auditory canal.
    c. auditory membrane.
    d. cochlea.

14. The two major theories that attempt to explain hearing are
    a. conduction theory and place theory.
    b. hair cell theory and frequency theory.
    c. place theory and frequency theory.
    d. conduction theory and hair cell theory.

15. The (kinesthetic, vestibular) sense provides information about the position of body parts in relation to each other and about movement in those body parts.

16. The receptors for the (kinesthetic, vestibular) sense are located in the semicircular canals and vestibular sacs in the (middle ear, inner ear).

Smell, Taste, and Touch (pp. 90–94)

17. The technical name for the process or sensation of smell is (gustation, olfaction).

18. The olfactory, or smell, receptors are located in the
    a. olfactory tract.
    b. olfactory nerve.
    c. olfactory epithelium.
    d. olfactory bulbs.

19. The five taste sensations are _____, _____, _____, _____, and _____.

20. Each (papilla, taste bud) contains from 60 to 100 receptor cells.

21. Each skin receptor responds only to touch, pressure, warmth, or cold. (true/false)

Influences on Perception (pp. 95–100)

22. When people try to keep track of several moving objects at once, they often exhibit _____ _____ .

23. When people look for a perceptual pattern in individual bits of sensory information, they are using _____ _____ .

24. When a speaker's lips don't match what she is saying, it is difficult to understand what she is saying because speech perception requires

_____ _____.

25. In situations where you have some prior knowledge and experience, you are likely to rely more on (bottom-up, top-down) processing.

26. Perceptual set is most directly related to a person's
a. needs.   b. interests.
c. expectations.   d. emotions.

Principles of Perception (pp. 100–104)

27. Match each Gestalt principle with its example:

_____ (**1**) **** **** **** perceived as three groups of four

_____ (**2**) - - - - > perceived as an arrow

_____ (**3**) ***&&&###@@@ perceived as four groups of three
a. closure   b. similarity
c. proximity

28. Retinal disparity and convergence are two (monocular, binocular) depth cues.

29. Match the appropriate monocular depth cue with each example.

_____ (**1**) one building partly blocking another

_____ (**2**) railroad tracks converging in the distance

_____ (**3**) closer objects appearing to move faster than objects farther away

_____ (**4**) objects farther away looking smaller than near objects
a. motion parallax   b. linear perspective
c. interposition   d. relative size

30. Rob had been staring at a point of light in the night sky when it suddenly appeared to start moving. Rob's experience is an example of the phi phenomenon. (true/false)

Unusual Perceptual Experiences
(pp. 104–107)

31. An illusion is
a. an imaginary sensation.
b. an impossible figure.
c. a misperception of a real stimulus.
d. a figure–ground reversal.

32. Images that are presented below the level of conscious awareness have no effect on subsequent behavior. (true/false)

33. ESP is often studied using the _____ _____.

SECTION TWO: Multiple Choice

1. Perception is the process we use to
a. organize and interpret stimuli.
b. detect stimuli.
c. gather information from the environment.
d. retrieve information from memory.

2. Which part of the nose serves the same function as the retina in the eye and the basilar membrane in the ear?
a. olfactory bulbs   b. olfactory lining
c. olfactory neurons   d. olfactory epithelium

3. The vestibular system is most closely related to
a. audition.   b. olfaction.
c. gustation.   d. kinesthetics.

4. As you look down a sandy beach, the sand seems to become finer as it goes into the distance. This depth cue is called
a. elevation.   b. onvergence.
c. texture gradient.   d. linear perspective.

5. The minimum amount of physical stimulation necessary for a person to experience a sensation 50% of the time is called the
a. figure-to-ground ratio.   b. blind spot.
c. difference threshold.   d. absolute threshold.

6. Which of the following is the correct sequence of structures encountered by light moving toward the retina?
a. lens, cornea, pupil   b. pupil, lens, cornea
c. pupil, cornea, lens   d. cornea, pupil, lens

7. Which theory suggests that color vision can be explained by the existence of three types of cones, which are maximally sensitive to blue, green, or red?
a. opponent-process theory   b. trichromatic theory
c. signal detection theory   d. gate-control theory

8. Ms. Scarpaci complains that the street noise in her apartment is much louder than the noise in her upstairs neighbor's apartment. To test her claim, you use a sound meter to check the noise in each apartment. Your meter registers 50 dB in Ms. Scarpaci's apartment and only 30 dB in her neighbor's. From these readings, how much louder is Ms. Scarpaci's apartment than her neighbor's?
a. 20% louder   b. 10 times louder
c. 100 times louder   d. not enough to be noticeable

9. When you hear a tone of 400 Hz, some of the hair cells in your ear are stimulated, but most others are not. This is the basic idea behind the
a. place theory of hearing.
b. volley principle of hearing.
c. frequency theory of hearing.
d. bone conduction theory of hearing.

10. Smell sensations first register in the brain in the
a. olfactory epithelium.   b. nasal mucosa.
c. olfactory bulbs.   d. olfactory nerve.

11. Nerve endings in the skin send signals to the somatosensory cortex for processing. This area of the brain is found in the
a. frontal lobe.   b. temporal lobe.
c. parietal lobe.   d. occipital lobe.

12. Which of the following sensations would best be explained by the gate-control theory?
a. the pain of a pin prick
b. the smell of dinner cooking
c. the taste of your favorite cookie
d. the sound of paper rustling

13. The receptors for the kinesthetic sense are located in the
a. outer ear.   b. retina.
c. joints, ligaments, and muscles. d. cortex.

14. The depth cue that occurs when your eyes "cross" to see an object that is very near your face is called
    a. convergence.
    b. elevation.
    c. aerial perspective.
    d. binocular disparity.

15. Weber's law applies to
    a. difference thresholds.
    b. absolute thresholds.
    c. transduction thresholds.
    d. retinal thresholds.

16. Gustation is also known as the sense of
    a. taste.
    b. hearing.
    c. smell.
    d. vision.

17. In the Ponzo illusion, two bars of equal length are superimposed over a picture of railroad tracks that recede into the distance and eventually converge at a single point. One reason the bars appear to be of unequal lengths is because the illusion takes advantage of
    a. binocular disparity cues.
    b. linear perspective cues.
    c. apparent motion cues.
    d. depth disparity cues.

18. Perceptual set reflects
    a. bottom-up processing.
    b. top-down processing.
    c. subliminal processing.
    d. extrasensory processing.

19. The process through which the senses detect sensory stimuli and transmit them to the brain is called
    a. consciousness.
    b. perception.
    c. sensation.
    d. reception.

20. If you were listening to music and your friend wanted to know how far he could turn the volume down without your noticing, he would need to know your
    a. sensory threshold for sound.
    b. absolute threshold for sound.
    c. transduction threshold for sound.
    d. difference threshold for sound.

21. Margaret is reaching middle age and is having trouble reading fine print. She did not have this problem when she was younger. Her optometrist has concluded that she has presbyopia, or "old eyes." Given this diagnosis, you know that Margaret's difficulty is due to the aging of her
    a. corneas.
    b. lenses.
    c. retinas.
    d. rods and cones.

22. The trichromatic theory of color is based on the idea that the retina contains three types of
    a. rods.
    b. cones.
    c. bipolar cells.
    d. ganglion cells.

23. Megan watches from the car as her parents drive away from her grandfather's house. Because of _____, Megan knows her grandfather's house remains the same size, even though the image gets smaller as they drive farther away.
    a. the law of good continuation
    b. the law of proximity
    c. size constancy
    d. the Müller-Lyer illusion

24. If you are sitting in a restaurant and hear someone at a nearby table mention your name, research examining the _____ suggests that you are likely to focus your attention on the table where that conversation is occurring.
    a. autokinetic illusion
    b. principle of closure
    c. cocktail party phenomenon
    d. Ponzo illusion

25. _____ is a type of ESP in which people know what is going to happen in the future.
    a. Telepathy
    b. Clairvoyance
    c. Precognition
    d. Sublimation

SECTION THREE: Comprehensive Practice Test

1. The process by which humans detect visual, auditory, and other stimuli is known as
    a. perception.
    b. transduction.
    c. sensation.
    d. threshold.

2. The process of organizing and interpreting the information gathered through vision, hearing, and the other senses is known as
    a. perception.
    b. the absolute threshold.
    c. transduction.
    d. sensory induction.

3. The _____ _____ is the minimum amount of stimulus that can be detected 50% of the time.
    a. difference reaction
    b. absolute reaction
    c. difference threshold
    d. absolute threshold

4. The _____ _____ is a measure of the smallest change in a stimulus required for a person to detect a change in the stimulus 50% of the time.
    a. difference reaction
    b. absolute difference
    c. difference threshold
    d. sensory threshold

5. Sense organs have specialized cells called _____ _____ that detect and respond to particular stimuli.
    a. sensory detectors
    b. sensory receptors
    c. perceptual responders
    d. perceptual receptors

6. When you see, hear, taste, smell, or feel a sensory stimulus, the physical energy that caused the stimulus is changed to neural impulses that are processed in your brain. This process is known as
    a. sensory adaptation.
    b. the absolute threshold.
    c. perceptual organization.
    d. transduction.

7. Joe installed an in-ground pool last spring; although his wife thought he was crazy to do so when it was still cool outside. The first day it seemed a little warm Joe jumped in the new pool, but soon he realized just how cold the water really was. As he continued to "enjoy" the water, it seemed to become less cold and even comfortable. This was probably due to a process called
    a. sensory adaptation.
    b. difference threshold.
    c. sensory threshold.
    d. perceptual adaptation.

8. If someone tells you he loves the color of your eyes, he is actually talking about your
    a. pupils.
    b. corneas.
    c. irises.
    d. retinas.

9. Rods are to cones as _____ is to _____.
    a. dim light; color
    b. color; dim light
    c. bright light; color
    d. color; bright light

10. The blind spot in the back of the eye is where
    a. the rods and cones come together.
    b. the retina converges on the fovea.
    c. the optic nerve leaves the eye.
    d. the blood supply enters the eye.

11. When you read a book, the lenses in your eyes are probably a little more spherical, and when you gaze up at the stars at night, your lenses become flatter. These differences are due to a process known as
    a. retinal disparity.
    b. lens reactivity.
    c. accommodation.
    d. adaptation.

12. LaShonda tells her roommate that we see color because three kinds of cones react to one of three colors—blue, green, or red. LaShonda has been reading about the _____ theory of color vision.
    a. opponent-process
    b. trichromatic
    c. relative disparity
    d. complementary color

13. The number of cycles completed by a sound wave in 1 second is the wave's
    a. decibel level.
    b. timbre.
    c. amplitude.
    d. frequency.

14. The job of the _____, also known as the hammer, the anvil, and the stirrup, is to amplify sound as it moves from the eardrum to the oval window.
    a. ossicles
    b. cochlear bones
    c. hair cells
    d. timbre bones

15. Tomas says that we hear different pitches depending on which spot along the basilar membrane vibrates the most. He is talking about the _____ theory of hearing.
    a. frequency
    b. position
    c. cochlea
    d. place

16. Olfaction refers to
    a. the sense of taste.
    b. the sense of smell.
    c. the ability to detect skin temperature.
    d. the ability to differentiate sounds.

17. All parts of the tongue can detect sweet, sour, salty, and bitter. (true/false)

18. Tactile is used in reference to the sense of
    a. smell.
    b. balance.
    c. taste.
    d. touch.

19. The gate-control theory of pain suggests that slow-conducting nerve fibers carry pain messages and that these messages can be blocked by messages from fast-conducting nerve fibers. (true/false)

20. An athlete's ability to move gracefully on the parallel bars is due to the _____ sense.
    a. tactile
    b. olfactory
    c. kinesthetic
    d. eustachian

21. The vestibular sense provides information that allows you to know that a red door is still red even in a dark room. (true/false)

22. The half-time show at a football game involved a hundred people marching on the field—all in different colored uniforms. Then they took on a formation and suddenly all the red uniforms spelled out the initials of the home team. Gestalt psychologists would suggest that the principle of _____ explains why fans could read the initials.
    a. similarity
    b. continuity
    c. closure
    d. constancy

23. Which of the following is not a Gestalt principle of grouping?
    a. closure
    b. similarity
    c. constancy
    d. proximity

24. If you move your finger closer and closer to your nose and focus on perceiving only one image of the finger even when it is almost touching the nose, your eyes begin to turn inward. This eye movement is known as
    a. disparity.
    b. monocular adjustment.
    c. congruity.
    d. convergence.

25. Cues such as interposition, linear perspective, and relative size are known as _____ depth cues.
    a. binocular
    b. divergent
    c. monocular
    d. bimodal

26. Lines of the same length with diagonals at their ends pointing in or out appear to be of different lengths because of the _____ illusion.
    a. Ponzo
    b. Müller-Lyer
    c. trident
    d. ambiguous

27. Bottom-up processing is to _____ stimuli as top-down processing is to _____ stimuli.
    a. unfamiliar; familiar
    b. visual; auditory
    c. familiar; unfamiliar
    d. perceptual; subliminal

28. In the game "Name That Tune," players try to guess the name of a song after hearing only its first few notes. Succeeding at this game requires
    a. top-down processing.
    b. bottom-up processing.
    c. cross-modal perception.
    d. perceptual set.

29. Most psychologists think that
    a. subliminal advertising is very effective.
    b. some people have a special talent for ESP.
    c. synesthesia is the result of an overactive imagination.
    d. the brain is capable of perceiving stimuli presented below the threshold of awareness.

SECTION FOUR: Critical Thinking

1. Using what you have learned about how noise contributes to hearing loss, prepare a statement indicating what you think should be done to control noise pollution, even to the extent of banning certain noise hazards. Consider the workplace, the home, automobiles and other vehicles, toys, machinery, rock concerts, and so on.

2. Based on your own point of view, choose one of these statements and explain why you agree with it: (1) Research on subliminal perception could be exploited to help people learn to behave in ways that are more beneficial to themselves and to society. For example, subliminal antidrug messages could be embedded in popular television programs. (2) Secretly embedding subliminal messages in entertainment media violates individuals' freedom of choice; therefore, this practice should be illegal.

SECTION FIVE: Application Essays

1. Vision and hearing are generally believed to be the two most highly prized senses. How would your life change if you lost your sight? How would your life change if you lost your hearing? Which sense would you find more traumatic to lose? Why?

2. Explain how the Gestalt principles of figure-ground, similarity, proximity, and closure can help you determine how best to display several framed photographs or pieces of art work on your living room wall.

> **Apply your critical thinking skills with MyPsychLab Writing Assignments**
>
> *Submit your answer to the following question inside the MyPsychLab Writing Assessment program for immediate feedback.*
>
> The Gestalt psychologists maintained that when people perceive sensory elements their tendency is to see things in terms of the entire form or pattern rather than as individual parts. Identify and describe these basic principles of perceptual organization from the Gestalt perspective: figure-ground, similarity, proximity, and closure.

Consciousness

◎⊙ THINK ABOUT IT

Do you wake up early every morning and leap out of bed with enthusiasm, eager to start the day? Or, are you more inclined to fumble for the alarm clock and push the snooze button to get a few more precious minutes of shut-eye? To put it differently, what's your *chronotype* ?If you're among the early-rising go-getters, you are a *lark*, but if you're a habitual snooze-button-pusher, the *owl* chronotype might be a better fit for you. Take this quiz to find out which chronotype best suits you. Give yourself 1, 3, or 5 points for each answers as indicated in the parentheses.

1. On days when I can get up when I choose, I am usually up:
   _____ Before 7:00 a.m. (1)
   _____ Between 7 and 9 a.m. (3)
   _____ After 9 a.m. (5)

2. For me, getting out of bed on school or work days is:
   _____ Fairly easy (1)
   _____ Sometimes difficult (3)
   _____ Always difficult (5)

3. When I get up in the morning, I usually feel:
   _____ Alert/fresh (1)
   _____ It varies (3)
   _____ Sleepy-tired (5)

4. If I could go to bed whenever I chose, it would probably be:
   _____ By 10:30 p.m. (1)
   _____ Between 10:30 p.m. and midnight (3)
   _____ After midnight (5)

5. About an hour or two before going to bed on school days, I usually feel:
   _____ Very tired, sleepy (1)
   _____ Moderately tired (3)
   _____ Not very tired (5)
   Add all your points together: _____

If you scored between 5 and 10, start chirping; you're among the 25% of the population with the lark chronotype. If your total score was between 11 and 19, your chronotype is "intermediate," that is, you're neither a lark nor an owl. You're a true owl if your total score was more than 20 points. That is, you're part of the 25% of the population that keeps 24/7 cable television channels in business.

All kidding aside, lark/owl patterns have important implications for people's lives, because larks and owls differ in how well they perform at various times of the day (Preckel, Lipnevich, Schneider, & Roberts, 2011). For example, larks get higher grades in morning classes, and owls shine in afternoon and evening classes (Guthrie et al., 1995). These differences are probably due to the fact that larks' levels of awareness, or *consciousness*, peak early in the day, while owls are more aware in the afternoon and evening.

What exactly do we mean when we say "consciousness"? It stands to reason that psychologists need a working definition of this concept before they can understand individual differences such as those that distinguish larks from owls. Thus, we begin our exploration of phenomena such as biological rhythms, sleep, meditation, and the brain's response to mind-altering substances with a discussion of states of awareness.

◉ **Watch** the Video *Episode 6: Big Picture: States of Consciousness* in **MyPsychLab**

What Is Consciousness?

What if, in a middle-of-the-night phone call, your mother told you that your grandmother had had a stroke and had been in a coma for a short while, but then had regained consciousness? You would most likely understand your mother to mean that your grandmother was in a state of unawareness of her own and others' activities but then returned to a state of awareness, or wakefulness. One way of understanding the meaning of consciousness is to think of it in contrast to its opposite, unconsciousness. But is that all there is to consciousness—simply being awake? What about when you arrive home from shopping but have no recollection of the drive from the mall to your home? Certainly, you were awake, so the reason you don't remember is *not* that you were unconscious. Thus, **consciousness** is defined as everything of which we are aware at any given time—our thoughts, feelings, sensations, and perceptions of the external environment.

consciousness Everything of which we are aware at any given time-our thoughts, feelings, sensations, and perceptions of the external environment.

4.1 How do psychologists view consciousness?

Changing Views of Consciousness

The early psychologists held widely varying views of the nature of consciousness. William James likened consciousness to a flowing stream (the stream of consciousness) that seems to be under our control at some times but not at others. Sigmund Freud emphasized the notion that unconscious wishes, thoughts, and feelings are hidden from consciousness because they evoke too much anxiety. In contrast to both James and Freud, behaviorist John Watson urged psychologists to abandon the study of consciousness, claiming that it could not be studied scientifically. Because of the strong influence of behaviorism, with its emphasis on observable behavior, psychologists did not study consciousness for several decades (Nelson, 1996).

In recent decades, though, psychological researchers have returned to the study of consciousness, in examining physiological rhythms such as sleep and wakefulness cycles as well as **altered states of consciousness** (changes in awareness produced by sleep, meditation, hypnosis, or drugs). Modern brain-imaging techniques, such as the ones discussed in Chapter 2, have allowed psychologists to accumulate a large body of evidence leading to a better understanding of the neurological basis of consciousness. Consequently, today's psychologists think about consciousness largely in neurobiological terms. In other words, psychologists tend to equate the subjective experience of consciousness with objective observations of what's actually happening in the brain during states such as sleep and hypnosis (Morsella, Krieger, & Bargh, 2010).

altered states of consciousness Change in awareness produced by sleep, meditation, hypnosis, or drugs.

Culture and Altered States of Consciousness ▶

4.2 What is the connection between altered states of consciousness and culture?

Religious and cultural traditions the world over have proposed supernatural explanations for naturally occurring altered states of consciousness. For example, the ancient Greeks believed that a special group of gods and goddesses, the *muses,* were responsible for inducing the trancelike state that artists and musicians often experience in association with their creative activities. In today's world, many people continue to express such culturally based views of altered states.

The belief that an altered state can be a pathway to the supernatural world has led people in many cultures to develop rituals that enable them to intentionally induce altered states of consciousness. For example, in the United States, the use of an illegal drug called *peyote* by members of the Native American Church, sometimes called *peyotism,* is controversial (Feeney, 2007). Some mental health professionals have argued that the religious use of peyote may lead to the development of substance abuse problems among church members. In response to these critics, advocates for the use of peyote in the Native American Church argue that church officials take care to regulate the dosages of the drug that are available for consumption during their rituals. In support of this claim, advocates cite the fact that there has never been a reported case of peyote overdose resulting from a church ceremony (Jones, 2005). The church's official doctrines also condemn substance dependence as a moral failing. As a result, advocates say, dependence is unlikely to develop.

The fact that so many different means of altering consciousness are practiced by members of so many cultures around the world has led some experts to wonder whether "there may be a universal human need to produce and maintain varieties of conscious experiences" (Ward, 1994, p. 60). This may be why some people use drugs to deliberately induce altered states of consciousness.

REMEMBER IT   *Check your answers and take additional quizzes in MyPsychLab.com.*   ✔●─[Study and Review on **MyPsychLab**

1. A synonym for consciousness is _____.
2. Because of the influence of _____, psychologists avoided the study of consciousness for several decades.
3. Today's psychologists focus on the _____ aspects of consciousness.
4. Changes in awareness associated with sleep, meditation, hypnosis, and drugs are called _____.

Circadian Rhythms

Now that we understand what consciousness and altered states of consciousness are, let's take a look at the rhythms that guide the ways in which consciousness naturally ebbs and flows in our daily lives. Do you notice changes in the way you feel throughout the day—fluctuations in your energy level, moods, or efficiency? More than 100 bodily functions and behaviors follow **circadian rhythms**—that is, they fluctuate regularly from a high to a low point over a 24-hour period (Dement, 1974). 👁

circadian rhythms (sur-KAY-dee-un) Within each 24-hour period, the regular fluctuation from high to low points of certain bodily functions and behaviors.

👁─[Watch the Video *Episode 6: Basics: Rhythms of Consciousness* in **MyPsychLab**

EXPLAIN IT   How Does the Brain Keep Track of Time?

Have you ever been in this situation? You stop at a red light and wait patiently for it to change to green. As time goes on, you start to think that the light has been red for an unusually long period of time. You look around at other drivers, wondering if they have the same impression. Finally, you decide that the light is malfunctioning and cautiously proceed through the intersection even though the light is still red. What happened?

An interval timer in your brain functions similarly to the device in your kitchen that you use to remind yourself to take a pizza out of the oven before it burns. The brain's interval timer consists of a network of neurons in the cerebral cortex that fire randomly and independently until something gets their attention (Wright, 2002). When an attention-getting stimulus that has time characteristics (e.g., a traffic light) occurs, the substantia nigra sends out a pulse of dopamine that signals these neurons to fire simultaneously. This simultaneous firing becomes a neurological marker for the beginning of the event. When the event ends, the substantia nigra does the same thing, creating a marker for the end of the event. The brain's timer compares its measurements to time-stamped memories of similar events. This is what happens when you are sitting at a traffic light and have the impression that the light has been red too long.

How accurate is the brain's interval timer? Here's a prime illustration. Your alarm goes off, but you decide to allow yourself to sleep 10 more minutes. Sometimes, you wake up again, look at the clock, and note that you have slept for about 10 minutes, just as you planned. But on other occasions, you wake up to find that you have slept for 2 hours rather than 10 minutes. What accounts for such variations in accuracy?

In such cases, the interval timer is superseded by another of the brain's clocks, the one that governs sleep cycles. When you go back to sleep after a brief period of awakening, your brain begins a new sleep cycle. If your target waking-up time happens to fall within the brief initial phase of the new sleep cycle when you are merely drowsy, you will probably not sleep past it. But if you slip into a deeper sleep phase before the interval timer wakes you up, you are likely to sleep for 90 minutes or so. This happens because, when you enter a deeper phase of sleep, your brain automatically switches off its interval timer. Thus, when you want to get a few extra minutes of shut-eye, turn to your alarm clock, one of the many devices humans have invented to compensate for the inaccuracies of our built-in neurological timers.

Two circadian rhythms of particular importance are the sleep/wakefulness cycle and the daily fluctuation in body temperature. Normal human body temperature ranges from a low of about 97 to 97.5°F between 3:00 and 4:00 a.m. to a high of about 98.6°F between 6:00 and 8:00 p.m. People sleep best when their body temperature is at its lowest, and they are most alert when their body temperature is at its daily high point.

4.3 How do circadian rhythms affect physiological and psychological functions?

suprachiasmatic nucleus (SCN) A pair of tiny structures in the brain's hypothalamus that control the timing of circadian rhythms; the biological clock.

The Influence of Circadian Rhythms

Physiological functions such as blood pressure, heart rate, appetite, secretion of hormones and digestive enzymes, sensory acuity, elimination, and even the body's response to medication all follow circadian rhythms (Hrushesky, 1994; Morofushi et al., 2000). Many psychological functions—including learning efficiency, the ability to perform a wide range of tasks, and even moods—ebb and flow according to these daily rhythms (Boivin et al., 1997; Johnson et al., 1992; Manly et al., 2002). Indeed, the circadian timing system is involved in the 24-hour variation of virtually every physiological and psychological variable researchers have studied (Kunz & Herrmann, 2000).

The biological clock that controls circadian rhythms along with other kinds of timekeeping mechanisms in the brain (see the *Explain It*) is the **suprachiasmatic nucleus (SCN),** located in the brain's hypothalamus (Ruby et al., 2002). However, the ebb and flow of circadian rhythms is not strictly biological. Environmental cues also play a part. The most significant environmental cue is bright light, particularly sunlight. Specialized cells (photoreceptors) in the retina at the back of each eye respond to the amount of light reaching the eye and relay this information via the optic nerve to the SCN (Foster, Hankins, & Peirson, 2007). From dusk until just before dawn, the message from the retina to the SCN is relayed to the pineal gland, causing it to secrete the hormone *melatonin*. During the daylight hours, the pineal gland does not produce melatonin (Kripke et al., 2005). Melatonin induces sleep, perhaps through its ability to keep all of the body's tissues aware of both the time of day and the time of year (Benarroch, 2008).

Alertness also follows a circadian rhythm, one that is quite separate from the sleep/wakefulness cycle (Monk, 1989). For most people, the larks and intermediates you read about at the beginning of the chapter, alertness decreases between 2:00 and 5:00 p.m. and between 2:00 and 7:00 a.m. (Webb, 1995). Owls display the reverse pattern. Their alertness starts to rise at the time when that of most others is declining. Studies indicate that the bodies of larks and intermediates possess their highest levels of the hormone *cortisol*, the biochemical substance that ramps up our bodies' alertness in emergencies (see Chapter 2), before noon (Kudielka et al., 2006). By contrast, cortisol peaks in owls' bodies in the late afternoon. Researchers think that these differences may be genetic, but the findings are mixed, with some studies showing a genetic link and others not (Allebrandt et al., 2010; Osland et al., 2011). Moreover, the percentage of owls among children seems to be far lower than it is among adults, suggesting that learning plays a role in the development of the owl chronotype (Achari, Venu, & Atanu, 2007).

Disruptions in Circadian Rhythms ▶

4.4 How do disruptions in circadian rhythms affect the body and mind?

Suppose you fly from Chicago to London, and the plane lands at 12:00 a.m. Chicago time, about the time you usually go to sleep. At the same time that it is midnight in Chicago, it is 6:00 a.m. in London, almost time to get up. The clocks, the sun, and everything else in London tell you it is early morning, but you still feel as though it is midnight. You are experiencing jet lag.

Chronic jet lag, such as that experienced by many airline pilots and flight attendants, produces memory deficits that may be permanent (Cho, 2001; Cho et al., 2000). You might think that airline employees who regularly fly across time zones would adjust to their schedules. However, research indicates that experienced airline workers are just as likely to suffer from jet lag as passengers on their first intercontinental flight (Ariznavaretta et al., 2002). Melatonin supplements have been found to be helpful for alleviating jet lag in some long-distance travelers (Doghramji, Brainard, & Balaicuis, 2010). However, melatonin is most effective when taken during the day, when natural melatonin levels are low. People who take it at night, just before bedtime, are likely to see little effect because natural melatonin levels are near their peak at that time. Thus, for some people with jet lag, other remedies are preferable. For instance, some travelers benefit from exposure to bright sunlight during the early morning hours, and avoidance of bright lights during the evening may be more effective than melatonin for restoring circadian rhythms (Arendt, 2009).

Similarly, alertness and performance deteriorate if people work during **subjective night**, when their biological clock is telling them to go to sleep (Sack et al., 2007a). During subjective night, energy and efficiency are at their lowest points, reaction time is slowest, productivity is diminished, and industrial accidents are significantly higher. In one study, researchers found that pilots who were flying between midnight and 6:00 a.m. were 50% more likely to make errors (de Mello et al., 2008). Furthermore, shift workers get less sleep overall than nonshift workers (Bonnefond et al., 2006). Some studies show that the deleterious effects of shift work persist for months or even years after shift work ends (Rouch, Wild, Ansiau, & Marquie, 2005).

Moving work schedules forward from days to evenings to nights makes adjustment easier because people find it easier to go to bed later and wake up later than the reverse. And rotating shifts every 3 weeks instead of every week lessens the effect on sleep even more (Karlson, Eck, Ørbæk, & Österberg, 2009). Some researchers are investigating the use of a new wakefulness drug called *modafinil* that helps people remain alert without the side effects of stimulants such as caffeine (Morgenthaler et al., 2007). Others have used a device called a "light mask" to reset shift workers' biological clocks. This mask allows researchers to control the amount of light to which the closed eyelids of research participants are exposed. The findings of light mask studies suggest that exposing participants to bright light during the last 4 hours of sleep is an effective treatment for the kinds of sleep-phase delays experienced by shift workers (Cole et al., 2002). Thus, this device may become important in the treatment of sleep disorders associated with shift work.

subjective night The time during a 24-hour period when the biological clock is telling a person to go to sleep.

▼ Research indicates that frequent flyers, such as this pilot, are just as likely to suffer from jet lag when crossing several time zones as travelers who are on their first intercontinental journey.

1. The two circadian rhythms of particular importance are the sleep-wakefulness cycle and the daily fluctuation in _____.

2. People sleep best when their body temperature is at its _____ point in the 24-hour cycle.

3. The suprachiasmatic nucleus serves as the body's _____.

4. Alertness and performance deteriorate when people work during _____.

5. _____ is a hormone that regulates the sleep-wakefulness cycle.

Sleep

As noted earlier, the sleep/wakefulness cycle is a circadian rhythm. But what actually happens during our periods of sleep? Before the 1950s, there was little understanding of what goes on during the state of consciousness known as sleep. Then, in the 1950s, several universities set up sleep laboratories where people's brain waves, eye movements, chin-muscle tension, heart rate, and respiration rate were monitored through a night of sleep. From analyses of sleep recordings, known as *polysomnograms,* researchers discovered the characteristics of two major types of sleep.

4.5 How do the restorative and circadian theories explain sleep?

Why We Sleep

Are you one of those people who regards sleep as a waste of time—especially when you have a term paper due the next day? (Of course, you wouldn't be facing a sleepless night if you hadn't procrastinated about the paper in the first place!) In fact, consistent sleep habits are probably important to getting good grades. Why?

Two complementary theories have been advanced to explain why we need to sleep. Taken together, they provide us with a useful explanation. One, the **restorative theory of sleep**, holds that being awake produces wear and tear on the body and the brain, while sleep serves the function of restoring body and mind (Gökcebay et al., 1994). Research on the effects of sleep deprivation that you will read about later in this section support the restorative theory. The second explanation, the **circadian theory of sleep**, sometimes called the *evolutionary* or *adaptive theory,* is based on the premise that sleep evolved to keep humans out of harm's way during the dark of night, possibly from becoming prey for some nocturnal predator (Siegel, 2009).

Alexander Borbely (1984; Borbely et al., 1989) explains how a synthesis of the circadian and restorative theories can be used to explain the function of sleep. That people feel sleepy at certain times of day is consistent with the circadian theory and that sleepiness increases the longer a person is awake is consistent with the restorative theory. In other words, the urge to sleep is partly a function of how long a person has been awake and partly a function of the time of day (Sack et al., 2007a).

restorative theory of sleep The theory that the function of sleep is to restore body and mind.

circadian theory of sleep The theory that sleep evolved to keep humans out of harm's way during the night; also known as the evolutionary or adaptive theory.

sleep cycle A period of sleep lasting about 90 minutes and including one or more stages of NREM sleep, followed by REM sleep.

4.6 What types of sleep occur during a typical night of sleep?

How We Sleep

Sleep follows a fairly predictable pattern each night. Each **sleep cycle** lasts about 90 minutes and consists of the stages shown in Figure 4.1. The type of sleep we experience in all four stages is known as **NREM (non-REM) sleep**. It is a type of sleep in which our heart and respiration rates are slow and steady, our movements are minimal, and our blood pressure and brain activity are at their lowest points of the 24-hour period.

As you can see in Figure 4.1, when we are fully awake, beta waves predominate. As we become drowsy, **alpha waves** which are associated with deep relaxation begin

NREM (non-REM) sleep Four sleep stages characterized by slow, regular respiration and heart rate, little body movement, and blood pressure and brain activity that are at their 24-hour low points.

alpha waves The brain wave pattern associated with deep relaxation.

Brain-Wave Patterns

FIGURE 4.1 **Brain-Wave Patterns Associated with Different Stages of Sleep**
By monitoring brain-wave activity on an EEG throughout a night's sleep, researchers have identified the brain-wave patterns associated with different stages of sleep. As sleepers progress through the four NREM stages, the brain-wave pattern changes from faster, smaller waves in Stages 1 and 2 to the slower, larger delta waves in Stages 3 and 4.

to appear. When alpha waves outnumber **beta waves**, which are associated with mental or physical activity, we enter the first of the four NREM sleep stages:

- *Stage 1:* Transition from waking to sleeping; irregular waves with occasional alpha waves

- *Stage 2:* Transition from light to deeper sleep; **sleep spindles** (waves with alternating periods of calm and flashes of intense activity) appear

- *Stage 3:* Deeper sleep; **slow-wave sleep** begins when EEG shows 20% of brain waves are delta waves

- *Stage 4:* Deepest sleep; **Stage 4 sleep** begins when 50% of waves are delta waves

About 40 minutes after we enter Stage 4 sleep, delta waves begin to disappear. When that happens, we transition back through Stage 3 and Stage 2 until we reach Stage 1 sleep again. As we reenter Stage 1, our pathway through the night takes a brief side trip into **REM (rapid eye movement) sleep**. During the REM period, our brains are highly active. Epinephrine is released into the system, causing blood pressure to rise and heart rate and respiration to become faster and less regular. In contrast to this storm of internal activity, there is an external calm during REM sleep. The large muscles of the body—arms, legs, trunk—become paralyzed.

Observe a sleeper during the REM state and you will see her or his eyes darting around under the eyelids. Eugene Azerinsky first discovered these bursts of rapid eye movements in 1952, and William Dement and Nathaniel Kleitman (1957) made the connection between rapid eye movements and dreaming. It is during REM sleep that the most vivid dreams occur. When awakened from REM sleep, most people report that they were dreaming.

Researchers have also found that REM sleep may be critical to the consolidation of memories after learning (Nishida, Pearsall, Buckner, & Walker, 2008; Valeo, 2008). Several experiments have shown that participants' performance on previously acquired motor and verbal tasks improves after a period of normal sleep (Walker & Stickgold, 2006). In one classic study, Karni and others (1994) found that research participants who were learning a new perceptual skill showed an improvement in performance, with no additional practice, 8 to 10 hours later if they had a normal night's sleep or if the researchers disturbed only their NREM sleep. Performance did not improve, however, in those who were deprived of REM sleep. This may be why, when people are deprived of REM sleep, they make up for it by getting an increased amount of REM sleep afterward, a phenomenon called **REM rebound**. 👁

beta waves The brain wave pattern associated with mental activity.

sleep spindles Sleep Stage 2 brain waves that feature short periods of calm interrupted by brief flashes of intense activity.

slow-wave sleep Deep sleep; associated with Stage 3 and Stage 4 sleep.

stage 4 sleep The deepest stage of NREM sleep, characterized by an EEG pattern of more than 50% delta waves.

REM (rapid eye movement) sleep A type of sleep characterized by rapid eye movements, paralysis, fast and irregular heart and respiration rates, increased brain-wave activity, and vivid dreams.

REM rebound The increased amount of REM sleep that occurs after REM deprivation.

👁 **Watch** the Video *Episode 6: In the Real World: Sleep, Memory, and Learning* in **MyPsychLab**

▲ In a sleep laboratory or sleep clinic, researchers attach electrodes to a person's head to monitor brain-wave activity, eye movements, and muscle tension.

After the first REM period of the night ends, a new sleep cycle begins. However, the remaining sleep cycles differ from the first one (refer back to Figure 4.1). Typically, the second cycle includes only Stages 2, 3, and 4, followed by a REM period. The third cycle usually includes Stages 2, 3, and a REM period. Later cycles include only Stage 2 and REM sleep. In addition, with each cycle, the REM period increases in duration, from a few minutes at the end of the first cycle to a half-hour or longer at the end of the fifth cycle. Overall, sleepers average five cycles in a 7- to 8-hour night of sleep, which provides them with a total of 1 to 2 hours of slow-wave sleep and 1 to 2 hours of REM sleep.

4.7 How does age influence sleep patterns?

Variations in Sleep

The amount of sleep people get varies a lot from one person to another. But how much sleep do we need? Many of us have heard that 8 hours of sleep are required for optimal health. Research suggests that this is not true. In a longitudinal study begun in 1982, more than a million Americans were asked about their sleep habits. Twenty years later, people who reported sleeping 6 or fewer hours per night, along with those who slept more than 8, showed somewhat higher death rates than adults who slept about 7 hours each night (Kripke et al., 2002).

As Figure 4.2 demonstrates, sleep varies with age. Infants and young children have the longest sleep time and the highest percentages of REM and slow-wave sleep (Siegel, 2005). However, infants and children also have more erratic sleep patterns than individuals in other age groups (Millman, 2005). By contrast, children from age 6 to puberty are the most consistent sleepers and wakers. They fall asleep easily, sleep soundly for 10 to 11 hours at night, and feel awake and alert during the day. Moreover, they tend to fall asleep and wake up at about the same time every day. By contrast, adolescents' sleep patterns are strongly influenced by their schedules. Factors such as part-time employment and early school start times cause many teenagers to sleep little more than 7 hours on a typical week night (Carskadon et al., 1998). When adolescents are free from such scheduling pressures, however, they tend to sleep even longer than elementary-age children. Thus, some sleep researchers think that insufficient sleep may be at least partly responsible for discipline and learning problems in secondary schools.

As people age, the quality and quantity of their sleep usually decrease. Some researchers hypothesize that the decline is due to a reduction in the need for sleep that is a part of the natural aging process (Klerman & Dijk, 2008). Nevertheless, many older adults view the decline as a threat to their quality of life. Large-scale surveys of older adults in North America, Europe, and Japan suggest that up to two-thirds of them experience daytime sleepiness, nighttime awakenings, and insomnia on a regular basis (Diaper & Hindmarch, 2005).

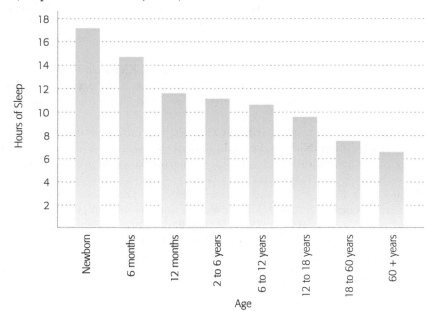

FIGURE 4.2 **Average Hours of Daily Sleep across the Life Span.** The number of hours devoted to sleep in each 24-hour period decreases dramatically across the life span.

Sources: Foley, Ancoli-Israel, Britz, & Walsh, 2004; Iglowstein, Jenni, Molinari, & Largo, 2003; Hansen, Janssen, Schiff, & Zee, 2005; Millman, 2005; Mindell, 1999; Ohayan, Carskadon, Guilleminault, & Vitiello, 2004.

Sleep Deprivation ▶

What is the longest you have ever stayed awake? Most people have missed no more than a few consecutive nights of sleep, perhaps studying for final exams. If you have ever missed two or three nights of sleep, you may remember having had difficulty concentrating, lapses in attention, and general irritability. Research indicates that even the rather small amount of sleep deprivation associated with delaying your bedtime on weekends leads to decreases in cognitive performance (Chee et al., 2008).

How does a lack of sleep affect the brain? The effects of sleep deprivation go beyond simply feeling tired. In fact, research has shown that failing to get enough sleep affects your ability to learn. So, if you stay up all night to study for a test, you may actually be engaging in a somewhat self-defeating behavior. In a ground-breaking study Drummond and others (2000) used brain-imaging techniques to map the patterns of brain activity during a verbal learning task in two groups of participants—those in an experimental group who were deprived of sleep for about 35 hours, and those in a control group who slept normally. In the control group, the prefrontal cortex was highly active, as were the temporal lobes. As expected, on average, these rested participants scored significantly higher on the learning task than did their sleep-deprived counterparts. Surprisingly, however, areas of the prefrontal cortex (coordination of thought processes) were even more active in the sleep-deprived participants than in those who slept normally. Moreover, the temporal lobes (language perception) that were so active in the rested group were almost totally inactive in the sleep-deprived group. The parietal lobes (integration of information from different senses) of the latter group became highly active, however, as if to compensate for their sleep-deprived condition. And, the more active the parietal lobes, the higher a sleep-deprived participant scored on the learning task.

This study, the first to use brain-imaging techniques to examine the effects of sleep deprivation on verbal learning, indicates that the cognitive functions used in such learning are significantly impaired by sleep deprivation. It also shows that there are compensatory mechanisms in the parietal lobes that can reduce this impairment to some degree (Drummond et al., 2000, 2004).

Sleep Disorders ▶

So far, our discussion has centered on a typical night for a typical sleeper. But what about the one-third of people who report sleep problems (Lubit, Bonds, & Lucia, 2009)?

Do you walk or talk in your sleep? If you do, you suffer from one of the **parasomnias**, sleep disturbances in which behaviors and physiological states that normally occur only in the waking state take place during sleep (Schenck & Mahowald, 2000). Sleepwalking, or *somnambulism*, occurs during a partial arousal from Stage 4 sleep in which the sleeper does not come to full consciousness. *Somniloquy*, the technical term for sleeptalking, can occur in any stage. Typically, sleeptalkers mumble nonsensical words and phrases.

Frightening dreams are also parasomnias. *Sleep terrors* happen during Stage 4 sleep and often begin with a piercing scream. The sleeper springs up in a state of panic—eyes open, heart pounding, perspiring, breathing rapidly, and so on. Typically, such sleep terrors resolve quickly, and the individual falls back to sleep. *Nightmares* are more frightening than sleep terrors because they occur during REM sleep and, as a result, are far more vivid. Moreover, sleepers often awaken to full consciousness during a nightmare and remember it in detail. Whereas sleep terrors occur early in the night, nightmares more often occur in the early-morning hours, when REM periods are the longest.

Physicians often begin the process of treating a parasomnia by investigating hidden illnesses and/or psychological factors in the patient's life that may be causing her sleep disturbances (Sharma, 2006). If such an underlying condition is discovered, then the physician treats it directly and assumes that curing it will also relieve the patient's parasomnia symptoms. Sleep-inducing medications, whether over-the-counter or prescription drugs, are regarded as a last resort in the treatment of parasomnias. The reason for medication avoidance is that the potential side effects of sleep medications and the possibility that a patient will become dependent on them outweigh the temporary benefits. Instead, physicians recommend that patients practice the principles of *sleep hygiene* that are outlined in the *Apply It* feature.

[**4.8** What are the effects of sleep deprivation?

▲ Health care professionals who work in hospitals often work long hours including, in some cases, two or more consecutive 24-hour shifts. How do you think these working conditions affect their on-the-job performance?

[**4.9** What are the various sleep disorders?

parasomnias Sleep disturbances in which behaviors and physiological states that normally take place only in the waking state occur while a person is sleeping.

APPLY IT

How to Get a Good Night's Sleep

Hand washing may come to mind when you hear the term *hygiene,* but health care professionals use it as a catch-all term for all kinds of preventive health measures. Thus, *sleep hygiene* refers to practices that reduce your risk of developing sleep problems. The Mayo Clinic (2006b) has compiled a list of tips for practicing sleep hygiene that you will find at *http://mayoclinic.com/health/sleep/ HQ01387.* Here are a few highlights:

- Keep a regular schedule that includes fairly consistent going-to-bed and getting-up times.
- Avoid eating or drinking to excess just before going to bed.
- Limit your intake of nicotine and caffeine throughout the day.
- Get regular exercise.
- Maintain a comfortable temperature and light level in the place where you sleep.
- Do not nap during the day.

- Make your bed as comfortable as possible.
- Establish a going-to-bed routine that relaxes you.
- Do not lie in bed awake for more than 30 minutes. Get up and do something until you feel sleepy enough to go back to bed.
- Don't push yourself to stay awake beyond the point at which you begin to feel sleepy.
- Avoid resorting to sleep medications unless absolutely necessary.

◉—Watch on **MyPsychLab**

◉—Watch the Video *Episode 6: Special Topics: Sleep Disorders* in **MyPsychLab**

dyssomnias Sleep disorders in which the timing, quantity, or quality of sleep is impaired.

narcolepsy An incurable sleep disorder characterized by excessive daytime sleepiness and uncontrollable attacks of REM sleep.

◉—Watch the Video *The Effects of Sleep and Stress on Memory: Jessica Payne* in **MyPsychLab**

sleep apnea A sleep disorder characterized by periods during sleep when breathing stops and the individual must awaken briefly in order to breathe.

In contrast to parasomnias, **dyssomnias** are disorders that involve the timing, quantity, or quality of sleep. For instance, **narcolepsy** is an incurable sleep disorder characterized by excessive daytime sleepiness and uncontrollable attacks of REM sleep, usually lasting 10 to 20 minutes (Bozorg & Benbadis, 2009). People with narcolepsy, who number from 250,000 to 350,000 in the United States alone, tend to be involved in accidents virtually everywhere—while driving, at work, and at home. Narcolepsy is caused by an abnormality in the part of the brain that regulates sleep, and it appears to have a strong genetic component. Some dogs are subject to narcolepsy, and much has been learned about the genetics of this disorder from research on canine subjects (Lamberg, 1996). Although there is no cure for narcolepsy, stimulant medications improve daytime alertness in most patients. ◉

More than 1 million Americans—mostly obese men—suffer from another sleep disorder, **sleep apnea**. Sleep apnea consists of periods during sleep when breathing stops, and the individual must awaken briefly to breathe (Becker & Wallace, 2010). The major symptoms of sleep apnea are excessive daytime sleepiness and extremely loud snoring, often accompanied by snorts, gasps, and choking noises. A person with sleep apnea will drop off to sleep, stop breathing altogether, and then awaken struggling for breath. After gasping several breaths in a semiawakened state, the person falls back to sleep and stops breathing again. People with severe sleep apnea may partially awaken as often as one to two times per minute to gasp for air. Alcohol and sedatives aggravate the condition (Valipour et al., 2007).

Severe sleep apnea can lead to chronic high blood pressure and other types of cardiovascular disease (Somers et al., 2008). Neuroscientists have also found that sleep apnea may cause mild brain damage (Macey et al., 2002). Physicians sometimes treat sleep apnea by surgically modifying the upper airway. When the surgery is effective, sleep apnea sufferers not only sleep better but also exhibit higher levels of

▶ This dog is experiencing a narcoleptic sleep attack. Much has been learned about narcolepsy through research with dogs.

performance on tests of verbal learning and memory (Dahloef et al., 2002). These findings suggest that the interrupted sleep experienced by individuals with this disorder affects cognitive as well as physiological functioning.

Many adults in the United States suffer from **insomnia,** a sleep disorder characterized by difficulty falling or staying asleep, by waking too early, or by sleep that is light, restless, or of poor quality (Passaro, 2009). Any of these symptoms can lead to distress and impairment in daytime functioning (Sateia et al., 2000). Transient (temporary) insomnia, lasting 3 weeks or fewer, can result from jet lag, emotional highs (as when preparing for an upcoming wedding) or lows (losing a loved one or a job), or a brief illness or injury that interferes with sleep (Passaro, 2009). Much more serious is chronic insomnia, which lasts for months or even years and plagues about 10% of the adult population (Passaro, 2009). The percentages are even higher for women, the elderly, and people suffering from psychiatric and medical disorders. Chronic insomnia may begin as a reaction to a psychological or medical problem but persist long after the problem is resolved.

Earlier you read that physicians avoid using sleep medicines to treat parasomnias. The same is true for the dyssomnias, but the life-threatening nature of some of these conditions means that individuals who suffer from them are more likely to be prescribed medications than those who have parasomnias. Narcolepsy sufferers, for example, may be given stimulant drugs to keep them awake during times when it would be dangerous for them to fall asleep, such as when they are driving (Bozorg & Benbadis, 2009). Sleep apnea may also be treated with medications. Electronic devices that awaken sleepers who stop breathing may also be used, and there are surgical treatments for sleep apnea as well (Dahloef et al., 2002). Finally, insomnia may be treated with drugs, but, in most cases, physicians encourage patients to adopt sleep hygiene practices to obtain long-term relief (Passaro, 2009).

The following *Summarize It* lists the various sleep disorders.

insomnia A sleep disorder characterized by difficulty falling or staying asleep, by waking too early, or by sleep that is light, restless, or of poor quality.

SUMMARIZE IT

Sleep Disorders

DISORDER	DESCRIPTION
PARASOMNIAS	
Somnambulism	Sleepwalking; occurs during partial arousal from Stage 4 sleep
Sleep terrors	Frightening dreams that occur during partial arousal from Stage 4 sleep; sleeper springs up in a state of panic, usually shortly after falling asleep
Nightmares	Frightening dreams that occur during REM sleep; likely to be remembered in vivid detail
Somniloquy	Sleeptalking; can occur during any sleep stage
DYSSOMNIAS	
Narcolepsy	Excessive daytime sleepiness; uncontrollable attacks of REM sleep; incurable
Sleep apnea	Periods during sleep when breathing stops; individual must awaken briefly in order to breathe
Insomnia	Difficulty falling or staying asleep, waking too early, and/or sleep that is light, restless, or of poor quality

REMEMBER IT   *Check your answers and take additional quizzes in MyPsychLab.com.*   ✓—Study and Review on MyPsychLab

1. The two main theories that attempt to explain the function of sleep are the _____ and the _____ theories.

2. In _____ sleep, heart rate and respiration are slow and regular.

3. There is intense brain activity and large muscle paralysis during _____ sleep.

4. During _____ sleep, the brain consolidates and organizes memories.

5. _____ and _____ have the highest percentages of REM and slow-wave sleep of any age group.

Dreams

In the previous section, we learned that our most vivid dreams occur during REM sleep, but why do we dream and what do our dreams mean? What does a young woman mean when she says, "I met the guy of my dreams last night?" Or how about a telemarketer who promises you a "dream vacation" in exchange for listening to a sales pitch? Most of the time, we think of dreaming as a pleasant, imaginative experience. But when a fellow student exclaims, "That exam was a nightmare!" he or she means, of course, that the exam was somewhat less than pleasant, like a frightening dream. Good or bad, just exactly what is a dream?

4.10 What have researchers learned about dreams?

REM dream A type of dream occurring almost continuously during each REM period and having a story-like quality; typically more vivid, visual, and emotional than NREM dreams.

NREM dream A type of dream occurring during NREM sleep that is typically less frequent and less memorable than REM dreams are.

The Content of Our Dreams

The vivid dreams people remember and talk about are usually **REM dreams**, the type that occur almost continuously during each REM period. But people also have **NREM dreams**, which occur during NREM sleep, although these are typically less frequent and less memorable than REM dreams (McNamara McLaren & Durso, 2007). REM dreams have a story-like or dreamlike quality and are more visual, vivid, and emotional than NREM dreams (Hobson, 1989). Blind people who lose their sight before age 5 usually do not have visual dreams, although they do have vivid dreams involving the other senses.

Brain-imaging studies suggest that the general perception that events in REM dreams are stranger and more emotion provoking than waking experiences is probably true. The areas of the brain responsible for emotions, as well as the primary visual cortex, are active during REM dreams (Dang-Vu et al., 2007). Similarly, vivid REM dreams are associated with distributions of activity in the forebrain that are very similar to those exhibited by individuals with delusional disorders while they are awake (Schwartz & Maquet, 2002). By contrast, the prefrontal cortex, the more rational part of the brain, is suppressed during REM sleep, suggesting that the bizarre events that happen in REM dreams result from the inability of the brain to structure perceptions logically during that type of sleep. Areas associated with memory are also suppressed during REM sleep, which may explain why REM dreams are difficult to remember.

What is it about REM sleep that predisposes people to bizarre dreams? One hypothesis is based on the finding that different neurotransmitters are dominant in the cortex during wakefulness and during REM sleep (Gottesmann, 2000). When we are awake, powerful inhibiting influences exert control over the functioning of the cortex, keeping us anchored to reality, less subject to impulsive thoughts and acts, and more or less "sane." These inhibiting influences are maintained principally by cortical neurons that are responding to serotonin and norepinephrine. These neurotransmitters are far less plentiful during REM dreaming, when a higher level of dopamine causes other cortical neurons to show intense activity. This uninhibited, dopamine-stimulated activity of the dreaming brain has been likened to a psychotic mental state (Gottesmann, 2000).

lucid dream A dream that an individual is aware of dreaming and whose content the individual is often able to influence while the dream is in progress.

Finally, researchers have devised procedures such as those in the *Try It* on page 127 that sometimes enable people to control their dreams, so you won't be surprised to learn that some people have been taught to deliberately control dream content in order to stop unwanted, recurrent dreams. In **lucid dreams**, people attempt to exert control over a dream while it is in progress. Researchers have compared EEG and brain-imaging data from experimental group participants who have been instructed to engage in procedures like the one in the *Think About It* at the beginning of the chapter to control group participants who sleep naturally. Such studies show that activity in the brains of lucid dreamers differs from that in the brains of control group participants (Dresler et al., 2012). As a result, lucid dreaming has been advocated as an intervention for psychological problems such as depression. However, its effects appear to be inconsistent among individuals with depression (Taitz, 2011). ◉

◉ᐧ**Watch** the Video *Living with a Sleep Disorder-Narcolepsy* in **MyPsychLab**

4.11 How do the various theorists explain dreams?

Interpreting Dreams

Most people believe that dreams, especially those that frighten us or that recur, have hidden meanings (Morewedge & Norton, 2009). Sigmund Freud believed that dreams function to satisfy unconscious sexual and aggressive desires. Because such wishes are

TRY IT   **Lucid Dreaming**

Have you ever awakened in the midst of a dream that was so good that you wished you could continue it? If so, then you might be interested to learn the steps involved in a technique that researchers have devised to study the controllability of dreams. Here are the steps:

1. Relax.
2. Close your eyes and focus on an imaginary spot in your field of vision.

3. Focus on your intention to control your dream.
4. Tell yourself that you're going to dream about whatever you want.
5. Imagine yourself having the dream that you are trying to create.
6. Repeat the steps until you fall asleep. 👁

👁 **Watch** the Video *Lucid Dreaming* in **MyPsychLab**

---

unacceptable to the dreamer, they have to be disguised and therefore appear in dreams in symbolic forms. Freud (1900/1953a) claimed that objects such as sticks, umbrellas, tree trunks, and guns symbolize the male sex organ; objects such as chests, cupboards, and boxes represent the female sex organ. Freud differentiated between the **manifest content** of a dream—the content of the dream as recalled by the dreamer—and the **latent content**—or the underlying meaning of the dream—which he considered more significant.

Beginning in the 1950s, psychologists began to move away from the Freudian interpretation of dreams. For example, Hall (1953) proposed a **cognitive theory of dreaming** in which he suggested that dreaming is simply thinking while asleep. Advocates of Hall's approach argued for a greater focus on the manifest content—the actual dream itself—which is seen as an expression of a broad range of the dreamer's concerns rather than as an expression of sexual impulses (Glucksman & Kramer, 2004).

Well-known sleep researcher J. Allan Hobson (1988) rejects the notion that nature would equip humans with the capability of having dreams that would require a specialist to interpret. Hobson and McCarley (1977) advanced the **activation-synthesis hypothesis of dreaming**. This hypothesis suggests that dreams are simply the brain's attempt to make sense of the random firing of brain cells during REM sleep. Just as people try to make sense of input from the environment during their waking hours, they try to find meaning in the conglomeration of sensations and memories that are generated internally by this random firing of brain cells. Hobson (1989) believes that dreams also have psychological significance, because the meaning a person imposes on the random mental activity reflects that person's experiences, remote memories, associations, drives, and fears.

Finally, advocates of the **evolutionary theory of dreaming** suggest that vivid, emotionally charged REM dreams serve a protective function (Barrett, 2007). Such dreams often involve threatening situations in which we may actually find ourselves. For example, an individual may dream that he is driving at 70 miles per hour on a highway when his car's brakes suddenly go out. According to the evolutionary view, such a dream would provide the dreamer with an opportunity to rehearse strategies that may help him manage a similar threat in real life.

manifest content Freud's term for the content of a dream as recalled by the dreamer.

latent content Freud's term for the underlying meaning of a dream.

cognitive theory of dreaming The view that dreaming is thinking while asleep.

activation-synthesis hypothesis of dreaming The hypothesis that dreams are the brain's attempt to make sense of the random firing of brain cells during REM sleep.

evolutionary theory of dreaming The view that vivid REM dreams enable people to rehearse the skills needed to fend off threats and predators.

◀ If you dream that you are a hobbit living underground in a place known as the Shire, the cognitive theory of dreaming would predict that you had recently watched a movie that included such content. The evolutionary theory would say that the adaptive function of the dream is to help you be ready to defend yourself against your enemies by forming strong social bonds with others in your community.

REMEMBER IT

Check your answers and take additional quizzes in MyPsychLab.com. ✓ Study and Review on **MyPsychLab**

1. The least memorable dreams occur during _____ sleep.
2. Match each theory of dreaming with its explanation.

____ **(1)** Freud's view ____ **(3)** cognitive theory

____ **(2)** activation-synthesis hypothesis ____ **(4)** evolutionary theory

a. Dreaming is the brain's attempt to make sense of the random firing of neurons.

c. Vivid dreams serve a protective function.

b. Dreams satisfy unconscious sexual and aggressive desires.

d. Dreaming is thinking while sleeping.

Meditation and Hypnosis

We all have to sleep. Even if you fight it, your body will eventually force you to sleep. But there are other forms of altered consciousness that we may experience only if we choose to do so. Meditation and hypnosis are two of these.

Meditation

4.12 What are the benefits of meditation?

meditation A group of techniques that involve focusing attention on an object, a word, one's breathing, or one's body movements in an effort to block out all distractions, to enhance well-being, and to achieve an altered state of consciousness.

Watch the Video *Episode 6: What's In It for Me? Altered States of Consciousness* in **MyPsychLab**

Do you know that a mental and physical relaxation technique can actually induce an altered state of consciousness? **Meditation** is a group of techniques that involve focusing attention on an object, a word, one's breathing, or one's body movements in an effort to block out all distractions, to enhance well-being, and to achieve an altered state of consciousness. Some forms of meditation, such as yoga, Zen, and transcendental meditation (TM), have their roots in Eastern religions and are practiced by followers of those religions to attain a higher spiritual state. In the United States, these approaches are often used to increase relaxation, reduce arousal, or expand consciousness (Wolsko et al., 2004). Brain-imaging studies support the conclusion that meditation, in addition to being relaxing, induces an altered state of consciousness (Cahn & Polich, 2006; Newberg et al., 2001). 👁

Studies suggest that meditation can be helpful for a variety of physical and psychological problems, especially those that involve the emotions (Sedlmeier et al., 2012). For example, researchers have found that regular meditation helps individuals, even those who are severely depressed, learn to control their emotions (Butler et al., 2008). In addition, meditation may prove helpful in lowering blood pressure, cholesterol levels, and other measures of cardiovascular health (Seeman, Dubin, & Seeman, 2003). Keep in mind, though, that meditation is not a "quick fix" for either mental or physical health problems. Deriving benefits from meditation requires self-discipline and commitment (Murray, 2002). Use the steps in the *Try It* to learn how to induce a relaxation state that is very similar to that experienced by those who meditate; practice the technique until you become proficient in it. You will then be ready to incorporate it into your daily routine.

TRY IT   The Relaxation Response

Find a quiet place and sit in a comfortable position.

1. Close your eyes.
2. Relax all your muscles deeply. Beginning with your feet and moving slowly upward, relax the muscles in your legs, buttocks, abdomen, chest, shoulders, neck, and finally your face. Allow your whole body to remain in this deeply relaxed state.
3. Now concentrate on your breathing, and breathe in and out through your nose. Each time you breathe out, silently say the word *one* to yourself.
4. Repeat this process for 20 minutes. (You can open your eyes to look at your watch periodically, but don't use an alarm.) When you are finished,

remain seated for a few minutes—first with your eyes closed, then with them open.

👁 Watch on **MyPsychLab**

Neuroimaging studies have suggested that several areas of the brain may be permanently changed by the long-term practice of meditation (Luders et al., 2012; Newberg, 2010). However, these findings are preliminary. Much research remains to be done before neuroscientists will have a complete understanding of how such neurological changes affect meditators' cognitive or emotional functioning.

Hypnosis ▶

Hypnosis may be formally defined as a procedure through which one person, the hypnotist, uses the power of suggestion to induce changes in thoughts, feelings, sensations, perceptions, or behavior in another person, the subject. Interestingly, research shows that some people cannot be hypnotized (Milling et al., 2010). Individual differences in the degree to which people are open to suggestions when they are fully conscious is linked to hypnotizability. Moreover, there are many misconceptions about hypnosis. Have you ever heard of the myths listed in Table 4.1?

Hypnosis has come a long way from the days when it was used mainly by entertainers. It is now recognized as a viable technique to be used in medicine, dentistry, and psychotherapy, especially for pain management (Goodin et al., 2012; Uman, Chambers, McGrath, & Kisley, 2008; Weisberg, 2008). For example, experimental studies have shown that patients who are hypnotized and exposed to suggestions designed to induce relaxation prior to surgery experience less postsurgery pain than do nonhypnotized patients (Montgomery et al., 2002).

According to the **sociocognitive theory of hypnosis**, the behavior of a hypnotized person is a function of that person's expectations about how subjects behave under hypnosis. People are motivated to be good subjects, to follow the suggestions of the hypnotist, and to fulfill the social role of the hypnotized person as they perceive it (Spanos, 1986, 1991, 1994). The *Summarize It* on page 130 lists the theories that explain hypnosis. Does this mean that hypnotized people are merely acting or faking it? No, "most hypnotized persons are neither faking nor merely complying with suggestions" (Kirsch & Lynn, 1995, p. 847). In fact, using the single most effective and reliable indicator of deception in the laboratory—skin conductance, which indicates emotional response by measuring perspiration—Kinnunen and others (1994) found that 89% of supposedly hypnotized people had been truly hypnotized.

hypnosis A procedure through which one person, the hypnotist, uses the power of suggestion to induce changes in thoughts, feelings, sensations, perceptions, or behavior in another person, the subject.

[**4.13** How and why does hypnosis influence the body and mind?

sociocognitive theory of hypnosis A theory suggesting that the behavior of a hypnotized person is a function of that person's expectations about how subjects behave under hypnosis.

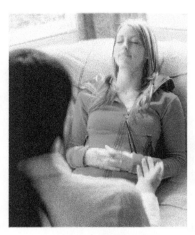

▲ A hypnotized person is in a state of heightened suggestibility. This hypnotherapist may therefore be able to help the woman control chronic or postsurgery pain.

TABLE 4.1 What Do You Know about Hypnosis?

IF YOU THINK	THE REALITY IS
It's all a matter of having a good imagination.	Ability to imagine vividly is unrelated to hypnotizability.
Relaxation is an important feature of hypnosis.	It's not. Hypnosis has been induced during vigorous exercise.
It's mostly just compliance.	Many highly motivated subjects fail to experience hypnosis.
It's a matter of willful faking.	Physiological responses indicate that subjects are not lying.
It is dangerous.	Standard procedures are no more distressing than lectures.
It has something to do with a sleeplike state.	It does not. Hypnotized subjects are fully awake.
Certain personality types are likely to be hypnotizable.	There are no substantial correlates with personality measures.
People who are hypnotized lose control of themselves.	Subjects are capable of saying no or terminating hypnosis.
Hypnosis can enable people to "relive" the past.	Age-regressed adults behave like adults playacting as children.
A person's responsiveness to hypnosis depends on the technique used and who administers it.	Neither is important under laboratory conditions. It is the subject's capacity that is important.
When hypnotized, people can remember more accurately.	Hypnosis may actually muddle the distinction between memory and fantasy and may artificially inflate confidence.
Hypnotized people can be led to do acts that conflict with their values.	Hypnotized subjects fully adhere to their usual moral standards.
People do not remember what happens during hypnosis.	Posthypnotic amnesia does not occur spontaneously.
Hypnosis can enable people to perform otherwise impossible feats of strength, endurance, learning, and sensory acuity.	Performance following hypnotic suggestions for increased muscle strength, learning, and sensory acuity does not exceed what can be accomplished by motivated subjects outside hypnosis.

neodissociation theory of hypnosis
A theory proposing that hypnosis induces a split, or dissociation, between two aspects of the control of consciousness: the planning function and the monitoring function.

theory of dissociated control The theory that hypnosis weakens the control that the executive function exerts over other subsystems of consciousness.

Ernest Hilgard (1986, 1992) has proposed a theory to explain why hypnotized individuals can accomplish very difficult acts, even undergoing surgery without anesthesia. According to his **neodissociation theory of hypnosis**, hypnosis induces a split, or dissociation, between two aspects of the control of consciousness: the planning function and the monitoring function. During hypnosis, it is the planning function that carries out the suggestions of the hypnotist and remains a part of the subject's conscious awareness. The monitoring function monitors or observes everything that happens to the subject, but without his or her conscious awareness. Hilgard called the monitoring function, when separated from conscious awareness, "the hidden observer."

Bowers and his colleagues (Bowers, 1992; Woody & Bowers, 1994) have proposed a view of hypnosis as an authentic altered state of consciousness. Their **theory of dissociated control** maintains that hypnosis does not induce a splitting of different aspects of consciousness, as Hilgard's model suggests. Rather, they believe that hypnosis weakens the control of the executive function over other parts (subsystems) of consciousness, allowing the hypnotist's suggestions to contact and influence those subsystems directly. Bowers further believes that the hypnotized person's responses are automatic and involuntary, like reflexes, and are not controlled by normal cognitive functions (Kirsch & Lynn, 1995). Indeed, some research supports this viewpoint (Bowers & Woody, 1996; Hargadon, Bowers, & Woody, 1995).

Although the majority of hypnosis researchers seem to support the sociocognitive theory, most clinicians, and some influential researchers in the field, apparently believe that hypnosis is a unique altered state of consciousness (Kallio & Revonsuo, 2003). Kihlstrom (2007) has suggested that a more complete picture of hypnosis could emerge from some combination of the sociocognitive and neodissociation theories. But even though researchers still have theoretical differences, hypnosis is being increasingly used in clinical practice and in selected areas of medicine and dentistry. 👁

👁 **Watch** the Video *Episode 6: Thinking Like a Psychologist: The Uses and Limitations of Hypnosis* in **MyPsychLab**

SUMMARIZE IT

Theories of Hypnosis

THEORY	EXPLANATION OF HYPNOSIS
Sociocognitive	Expectations and a desire to be a "good subject" motivate people to respond to the suggestions of a hypnotist.
Neodissociation	The mind's planning function consciously responds to a hypnotist's suggestions while its monitoring function observes these responses unconsciously.
Dissociated control	Subjects respond to a hypnotist's suggestions because hypnosis weakens the influence of the executive control system over other aspects of consciousness.

REMEMBER IT   *Check your answers and take additional quizzes in MyPsychLab.com.*   ✔● Study and Review on MyPsychLab

1. Researchers have found that meditation may be useful in prevention and treatment of _____, _____ and other measures of cardiovascular health.

2. Match each theory of hypnosis with the factor it most emphasizes in explanations of people's behavior under hypnosis.

_____ **(1)** sociocognitive   _____ **(2)** neodissociation   _____ **(3)** dissociated control

   a. weakened executive functions of consciousness

   b. hypnotized's person's expectations

   c. split between the planning and monitoring functions of consciousness

Psychoactive Drugs

The last time you took a pain reliever or an antibiotic, you probably didn't think of yourself as engaging in a mind-altering experience. However, all chemical substances, even the aspirin you take for a headache, affect the brain because they alter the functioning of neurotransmitters (Munzar et al., 2002). As you can probably guess, most such substances have no noticeable effect on your state of consciousness. Some drugs, however, have especially powerful effects on the brain and induce dramatically altered states of consciousness.

A **psychoactive drug** is any substance that alters mood, perception, or thought. When psychoactive drugs, such as antidepressants, are approved for medical use, they are called *controlled substances*. The term *illicit* denotes psychoactive drugs that are illegal. Many *over-the-counter drugs,* such as antihistamines and decongestants, as well as many herbal preparations, are psychoactive. Certain foods, such as chocolate, may also alter our moods (Macht & Mueller, 2007). Note to restaurant servers: Giving customers a piece of chocolate along with their checks increases tips (Strohmetz et al., 2002).

How Drugs Affect the Brain ▶

psychoactive drug Any substance that alters mood, perception, or thought; called a controlled substance if approved for medical use.

4.14 How do drugs affect the brain's neurotransmitter system?

You may recall from Chapter 2 that drugs affect our brains and behavior through their influence on neurotransmitters, the chemicals that regulate communication between neurons. For instance, did you know that all kinds of physical pleasure have the same neurological basis? Whether derived from sex, a psychoactive chemical, or any other source, a subjective sense of physical pleasure is brought about by an increase in the availability of the neurotransmitter dopamine in a part of the brain's limbic system known as the *nucleus accumbens*, often called the brain's "pleasure center" (Panksepp, 2010). Thus, it isn't surprising that researchers have found that a surge of dopamine is involved in the rewarding and motivational effects produced by most psychoactive drugs including alcohol, amphetamines, marijuana, heroin, cocaine, and nicotine (Wise, 2009). Why, then, does the altered state associated with alcohol feel different from that associated with nicotine or marijuana? Because the effect drugs have on the dopamine system is just the beginning of a cascade of effects that involve the brain's entire neurotransmitter system. Each drug influences the whole system differently and is associated with a distinctive altered state of consciousness. Consider a few examples of how different drugs act on neurotransmitters and the associated beneficial effects:

- Opiates such as morphine and heroin mimic the effects of the brain's own endorphins, chemicals that have pain-relieving properties and produce a feeling of well-being. For this reason, opiates are useful in pain management.

- Depressants such as alcohol, barbiturates such as propofol, and benzodiazepines (Valium and Librium, for example) act on GABA receptors to produce a calming, sedating effect. Thus, depressants can play a role in reducing a patient's nervousness prior to undergoing a medical procedure.

- Stimulants such as amphetamines (such as "speed" or "ice") and cocaine mimic the effects of epinephrine, the neurotransmitter that triggers the sympathetic nervous system. The effects of the sympathetic nervous system include suppressed hunger and digestion; this is why "diet pills" typically contain some kind of stimulant, such as caffeine.

As we all know, drugs don't always have solely beneficial effects. Why? Because too much of a good thing, or the wrong combination of good things, can lead to disaster. For example, opiates, when taken regularly, will eventually completely suppress the production of endorphins. As a result, natural pain management systems break down, and the brain becomes dependent on the presence of opiates to function normally. Similarly, if ingestion of too much alcohol, or of a combination of alcohol and other depressants, floods the brain with GABA, consciousness will be lost, and death may follow. Excessive amounts of a stimulant can send heart rates and blood pressure levels zooming; death can even result from the ingestion of a single, large dose.

Substance Abuse and Addiction ▶

substance abuse Continued use of a substance after several episodes in which use of the substance has negatively affected an individual's work, education, and social relationships.

4.15 How do physical and psychological drug dependence differ?

When people intentionally use drugs to induce an altered state of consciousness, they risk developing a *substance abuse* problem. Psychologists usually define **substance abuse** as continued use of a substance after several episodes in which use

Watch the Video *Kathy: Substance Abuse* in **MyPsychLab**

physical drug dependence A compulsive pattern of drug use in which the user develops a drug tolerance coupled with unpleasant withdrawal symptoms when the drug use is discontinued.

drug tolerance A condition in which the user becomes progressively less affected by the drug and must take increasingly larger doses to maintain the same effect or high.

withdrawal symptoms The physical and psychological symptoms that occur when a regularly used drug is discontinued and that terminate when the drug is taken again.

psychological drug dependence A craving or irresistible urge for a drug's pleasurable effects.

▲ Seeing the paraphernalia that are associated with the drug an addict uses can trigger a craving for the drug's psychological effects. Thus, learning to avoid such cues is important in the process of recovery from addiction.

of the substance has negatively affected an individual's work, education, and social relationships (American Psychiatric Association, 2000a). For example, a person who has missed work several times because of alcohol intoxication, but who continues to drink, has a substance abuse problem. ◉

What causes people to progress from substance use to substance abuse? The physical pleasure associated with drug-induced altered states of consciousness is one reason. Genetically based differences in the way people respond physiologically to drugs also contribute to substance abuse (Ehlers et al., 2010; Palmer et al., 2012). For example, some people feel intoxicated after drinking very small amounts of alcohol; others require a much larger "dose" to feel the same effects. People who have to drink more to experience intoxication are more likely to become alcoholics. Genetic researchers are currently searching for the gene or genes that contribute to low response to alcohol (Palmer et al., 2012). Of course, personality and social factors contribute to substance abuse as well. Impulsivity, for instance, is associated with experimentation with drugs (Simons & Carey, 2002). Stress-related variables, such as a history of having been a victim of child abuse or domestic violence, are also associated with substance abuse (Ehlers et al., 2012). Social and cultural factors play important roles in the development of substance abuse problems, too. For instance, associating with peers who use drugs may influence teenagers to begin doing so or may help to maintain substance abuse behavior once it begins (Van Ryzin, Fosco, & Dishion, 2012).

Some people progress from substance abuse to full-blown substance dependence, commonly called *addiction*. **Physical drug dependence** results from the body's natural ability to protect itself against harmful substances by developing a **drug tolerance**. That is, the user becomes progressively less affected by the drug and must take increasingly larger doses to achieve the same effect or high (Koob, 2008). Tolerance occurs because the brain adapts to the presence of the drug by responding less intensely to it. In addition, the liver produces more enzymes to break down the drug. The various bodily processes adjust so that they can continue to function with the drug in the system.

Once drug tolerance is established, a person cannot function normally without the drug. If the drug is taken away, the user begins to suffer withdrawal symptoms. These **withdrawal symptoms**, which are both physical and psychological, are usually the exact opposite of the effects produced by the drug. For example, withdrawal from stimulants leaves a person exhausted and depressed; withdrawal from tranquilizers leaves a person nervous and agitated. Because taking the drug is the only way to escape these unpleasant symptoms, withdrawal supports continued addiction. Moreover, the lasting behavioral and cognitive effects of abused substances on the brain often interfere with attempts to stop using them. Among other effects, researchers have learned that addiction is associated with attention and memory deficits, loss of the ability to accurately sense the passage of time, and declines in the capacity to plan and control behavior (Bates, Laboovie, & Voelbel, 2002; Buhusi & Meck, 2002). Abusers need all of these skills to overcome addiction and rebuild their lives, but regaining them once drug abuse is stopped—if they can be recovered at all—takes time.

Psychological drug dependence is a craving or irresistible urge for the drug's pleasurable effects; it is even more difficult to combat than physical dependence (O'Brien, 1996). Continued use of drugs to which an individual is physically addicted is influenced by the psychological component of the habit. Some drugs that are probably not physically addictive (e.g., marijuana) may nevertheless create psychological dependence.

Learning processes are important in the development and maintenance of psychological dependence. For example, drug-taking cues—the people, places, and things associated with using the drug—can trigger a strong craving for the substance of abuse (Koob, 2008). PET scans of cocaine addicts' brains indicate that such cues arouse a cue-specific neural network, which may explain why it is difficult for addicts to divert their attention from them (Bonson et al., 2002). Furthermore, research with animals indicates that drug-related cues elicit the same responses in the brain as the drugs themselves (Kiyatkin & Wise, 2002). These findings underscore the need for further research aimed at revealing the relationships among the physiological effects of drugs and the social contexts in which drug use occurs (Crombag & Robinson, 2004).

Stimulants ▶

Have you ever advised a friend to "switch to decaf"? This advice comes from a bit of drug knowledge we all share: Caffeine can make us jumpy. **Stimulants** (also called "uppers") speed up activity in the central nervous system, suppress appetite, and can make a person feel more awake, alert, and energetic. Stimulants increase pulse rate, blood pressure, and respiration rate, and they reduce cerebral blood flow. In higher doses, stimulants make people feel nervous, jittery, and restless, and they can cause shaking or trembling and interfere with sleep.

Caffeine. Coffee, tea, cola drinks, chocolate, energy drinks such as Red Bull, and more than 100 prescription and over-the-counter drugs contain caffeine. Caffeine makes people more mentally alert and can help them stay awake (De Bruin et al., 2011). Caffeine may even improve visual acuity by making the retina more sensitive to light (Arushanyan & Shikina, 2004). However, contrary to popular opinion, mixing alcohol with caffeine does not enable a person to party for a longer period of time than she would without the caffeine (Gulick & Gould, 2009). In fact, combining alcohol and caffeine can lead to severe dehydration which, it so happens, is the underlying cause of the constellation of symptoms popularly known as a "hangover." Thus, anyone who wants to avoid a hangover should also avoid mixing caffeine with alcohol. Moreover, caffeine appears to impair drinkers' ability to assess the degree to which they are intoxicated, an effect that leads to poor decision making about driving under the influence of alcohol and other risky behaviors (Ferreira et al., 2006).

When moderate to heavy caffeine users abstain, they suffer withdrawal symptoms such as nervousness, instability, headaches, drowsiness, and decreased alertness. Using EEGs and sonograms, researchers looked at the effects of caffeine withdrawal symptoms on the brain and were able to correlate the symptoms with significant increases in blood pressure and in the velocity of blood flow in all four of the cerebral arteries. The EEGs also showed an increase in slower brain waves, which correlates with decreased alertness and drowsiness (Sigmon et al., 2009).

Nicotine. Like caffeine, nicotine increases alertness, but few people who have tried to quit smoking doubt its addictive power. (The many serious health problems associated with smoking are discussed in Chapter 10.) Many treatment methods advertised as being helpful to smokers who are trying to quit appear to have limited value. For example, Green and Lynn (2000) reviewed the results of 59 studies of hypnosis and smoking and concluded that hypnosis cannot be considered effective in helping smokers break the habit. However, experiments have shown that over-the-counter nicotine patches help about one in five smokers quit and enable many others to cut down on the number of cigarettes they smoke (Ferguson, Gitchell, & Shiffman, 2012).

Amphetamines. Amphetamines increase arousal, relieve fatigue, improve alertness, suppress the appetite, and give a rush of energy. Research suggests that in high doses (100 milligrams or more) amphetamines can cause confused and disorganized behavior, extreme fear and suspiciousness, delusions and hallucinations, aggressiveness and antisocial behavior, even manic behavior and paranoia (Thirthalli & Benegal, 2006). The powerful amphetamine methamphetamine (known as "crank" or "speed") comes in a smokable form ("ice"), which is highly addictive and can be fatal.

Withdrawal from amphetamines leaves a person physically exhausted; he or she will sleep for 10 to 15 hours or more, only to awaken in a stupor, extremely depressed and intensely hungry. Stimulants constrict the tiny capillaries and the small arteries. Over time, high doses can stop blood flow, causing hemorrhaging and leaving parts of

4.16 How do stimulants affect behavior?

stimulants A category of drugs that speed up activity in the central nervous system, suppress appetite, and can cause a person to feel more awake, alert, and energetic; also called "uppers."

▲ Methamphetamine abuse leads to dramatic changes in appearance, because the drug interferes with the body's ability to maintain and repair the skin, hair, and teeth (Wells, 2007).

the brain deprived of oxygen. In fact, victims of fatal overdoses of stimulants usually have multiple hemorrhages in the brain.

Cocaine. Cocaine, a stimulant derived from coca leaves, can be sniffed as a white powder, injected intravenously, or smoked in the form of crack. The effects of snorting cocaine are felt within 2 to 3 minutes, and the high lasts 30 to 45 minutes. The euphoria from cocaine is followed by an equally intense crash, marked by depression, anxiety, agitation, and a powerful craving for more of the drug.

Cocaine stimulates the reward, or "pleasure," pathways in the brain, which use the neurotransmitter dopamine (Wise, 2009). With continued use, these reward systems fail to function normally, and the user becomes incapable of feeling any pleasure except from the drug. The main withdrawal symptoms are psychological—the inability to feel pleasure and the craving for more cocaine.

Cocaine constricts the blood vessels, raises blood pressure, speeds up the heart, and quickens respiration. Over time, or even quickly in high doses, cocaine can cause heart palpitations, an irregular heartbeat, and heart attacks, and high doses can cause strokes in healthy young individuals. Chronic cocaine use can also result in holes in the nasal septum (the ridge of cartilage running down the middle of the nose) and in the palate (the roof of the mouth) (Greenfield & Hennessy, 2008).

Animals become addicted more readily to cocaine than to any other drug, and those who are addicted to multiple substances prefer cocaine when offered a choice of drugs (Manzardo, Stein, & Belluzi, 2002). Given unlimited access to cocaine, animals will lose interest in everything else, including food, water, and sex, and will rapidly and continually self-administer cocaine. They tend to die within 14 days, usually from cardiopulmonary collapse (Gawin, 1991). Cocaine-addicted monkeys will press a lever as many as 12,800 times to get one cocaine injection (Yanagita, 1973).

Crack, or "rock," the most dangerous form of cocaine, can produce a powerful dependency in several weeks. Users who begin with cocaine in powder form are likely to progress to crack, while users who start on crack are more likely to continue using it exclusively. When both powder and crack are used interchangeably, a mutual reinforcement seems to occur, and the user develops a dependence on both forms of cocaine (Shaw et al., 1999).

4.17 How do depressants affect behavior?

depressants A category of drugs that decrease activity in the central nervous system, slow down bodily functions, and reduce sensitivity to outside stimulation; also called "downers."

Depressants

Another class of drugs, the **depressants**, decrease activity in the central nervous system, slow down bodily functions, and reduce sensitivity to outside stimulation. Within this category are the sedative-hypnotics (alcohol, barbiturates, and minor tranquilizers) and the narcotics (opiates). When different depressants are taken together, their sedative effects are additive and, thus, potentially dangerous.

Alcohol. The more alcohol a person consumes, the more the central nervous system is depressed (Knapp, Ciraulo, & Kramzler, 2008). As drinking increases, the symptoms of drunkenness mount—slurred speech, poor coordination, staggering. Impaired depth and motion perception—two good reasons to avoid driving after you have been drinking—are also features of alcohol intoxication (Nawrot et al., 2004; Weschke & Niedeggen, 2012). (We will discuss the health consequences of alcohol abuse in detail in Chapter 10.) Alcohol also decreases the ability to form new memories (Kirchner & Sayette, 2003; Ray & Bates, 2006). That's why an episode of heavy drinking is often followed by a "morning after," during which the drinker is unable to remember the events that occurred while he or she was under the influence of alcohol. Interestingly, alcohol placebos have similar effects on memory function, so a drinker's expectations contribute to alcohol's effects to some extent (Assefi & Garry, 2003). ✳

✳ Explore the Concept *Behavioral Effects Associated With Various Blood Alcohol Levels* in MyPsychLab

Barbiturates. Barbiturates, such as *phenobarbital* and *propofol* (the anesthetic that caused the death of pop star Michael Jackson), depress the central nervous system (Lafferty, 2008). Depending on the dose, a barbiturate can act as an anesthetic, sedative, or a sleeping pill. People who abuse barbiturates become drowsy and confused, their thinking and judgment suffer, and their coordination and reflexes are affected. Barbiturates can kill if taken in overdose. Alcohol and barbiturates, when taken together, are a potentially fatal combination.

Minor Tranquilizers. The popular minor tranquilizers, the *benzodiazepines,* came on the scene in the early 1960s and are sold under the brand names Valium, Librium, Dalmane, and, more recently, Xanax (also used as an antidepressant). Benzodiazepines are prescribed for several medical and psychological disorders (Mantooth, 2010). Abuse of these drugs is associated with both temporary and permanent impairment of memory and other cognitive functions. (A more detailed discussion of tranquilizers can be found in Chapter 13.)

Narcotics. Narcotics are derived from the opium poppy and produce both pain-relieving and calming effects. Opium affects mainly the brain, but it also paralyzes the intestinal muscles, which is why it is used medically to treat diarrhea. If you have ever taken paregoric, you have had a tincture (extract) of opium. Because opium suppresses the cough center, it is used in some cough medicines. Morphine and codeine, natural constituents of opium, may be found in some drugs prescribed for pain relief. Such drugs, including Oxycontin and Vicodin, are addictive and are sold illegally to millions of people in the United States every year (Preda, 2012).

> **narcotics** A class of depressant drugs derived from the opium poppy that produce both pain-relieving and calming effects.

A highly addictive narcotic derived from morphine is heroin. Heroin addicts describe a sudden "rush" of euphoria, followed by drowsiness, inactivity, and impaired concentration. Withdrawal symptoms begin about 6 to 24 hours after use, and the addict becomes physically sick. Nausea, diarrhea, depression, stomach cramps, insomnia, and pain grow worse and worse until they become intolerable—unless the person gets another "fix."

Hallucinogens ▶

> **4.18** How do hallucinogens affect behavior?

The **hallucinogens**, or *psychedelics,* are drugs that can alter and distort perceptions of time and space, alter mood, and produce feelings of unreality. As the name implies, hallucinogens also cause hallucinations, sensations that have no basis in external reality (Parish, Richards, & Cameron, 2011). Rather than producing a relatively predictable effect like most other drugs, hallucinogens usually magnify the mood of the user at the time the drug is taken. Contrary to the belief of some, hallucinogens hamper rather than enhance creative thinking (Bourassa & Vaugeois, 2001).

> **hallucinogens** (hal-LU-sin-o-jenz) A category of drugs that can alter and distort perceptions of time and space, alter mood, produce feelings of unreality, and cause hallucinations; also called *psychedelics.*

Marijuana. *THC* (tetrahydrocannabinol), the ingredient in marijuana that produces the high, remains in the body for 2 to 4 weeks (Cary, 2006). Marijuana impairs attention and coordination and slows reaction time, and these effects make operating complex machinery such as an automobile dangerous, even after the feeling of intoxication has passed. Marijuana can interfere with concentration, logical thinking, formation of new memories, and retrieval of stored memories (Niyuhire et al., 2007; Verdejo-Garcia et al., 2005). Many of the receptors for THC are in the hippocampus, which explains why the drug affects memory (Genen, 2012).

Studies comparing marijuana users who began taking the drug before age 17 with those who started later show that early marijuana use is associated with a somewhat smaller brain volume and a lower percentage of the all-important gray matter in the brain's cortex. Marijuana users who started younger were also shorter and weighed less than users who started when older (Wilson et al., 2000). Longitudinal studies also suggest that marijuana causes the cerebral cortices of users who begin smoking it in adolescence to age more rapidly than those of nonusers (Mata et al., 2010). At the same time, marijuana appears to permanently stunt the development of neurons in the hippocampal regions of the brains of young users, an effect that may lead to memory impairment that persists into adulthood (Rubino et al., 2009). Further, early marijuana use affects the capacity of the prefrontal cortex to respond to danger alerts from the

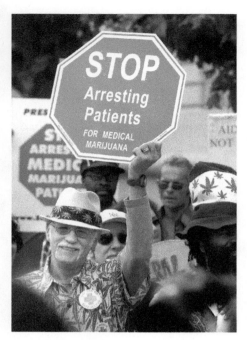

▲ Many Americans believe that the use of marijuana for medical purposes ought to be legal. However, the U.S. Food and Drug Administration insists that there are no legitimate medical uses for smoked marijuana (FDA, 2006). They point out that the active ingredient in marijuana, THC, is available in pill form and can be legally prescribed to patients by any licensed physician in the United States.

amygdala, a factor that may explain correlations between marijuana use and other risky behaviors among adolescents and young adults (Lin et al., 2008). Taken together, these results suggest that marijuana's effects on the developing brain are complex.

Despite marijuana's potential for abuse, some researchers argue that marijuana shows promise as a treatment for certain medical conditions. It has been found effective for treating the eye disease glaucoma, for controlling nausea and vomiting in cancer patients receiving chemotherapy, and for improving appetite and curtailing weight loss in some AIDS patients (Genen, 2012). It may also be helpful in the treatment of spinal cord injuries and other kinds of nerve damage (Wade et al., 2003). In addition, longitudinal studies of long-term users have demonstrated that smoking marijuana is not as harmful to the lungs as cigarette smoking (Pletcher & Vittinghoff, 2012). However, because pills containing the active ingredients in marijuana are already legally available by prescription, many experts contend that it is not necessary to legalize the use of marijuana cigarettes for medical purposes. These experts point out that, in contrast to patients who take THC pills, people who smoke marijuana for medicinal purposes determine the dose of THC they receive by increasing and decreasing how deeply they inhale. As a result, determining the dosage required for symptom relief as well as the amount of the drug that constitutes an overdose use of the drug is very difficult (Genen, 2012). Moreover, the U.S. Food and Drug Administration has stated unequivocally that smoked marijuana has no known medical benefits and should continue to be regarded as a dangerous drug (U.S. Food and Drug Administration, 2006).

LSD (Lysergic Acid Diethylamide). LSD is lysergic acid diethylamide, sometimes referred to simply as "acid." The average LSD "trip" lasts for 10 to 12 hours and usually produces extreme perceptual and emotional changes, including visual hallucinations and feelings of panic (Weaver & Schnoll, 2008). On occasion, bad LSD trips have ended tragically in accidents, death, or suicide. Former LSD users sometimes experience *flashbacks,* brief recurrences of previous trips that occur suddenly and without warning. Some develop a syndrome called *hallucinogen persisting perception disorder (HPPD),* in which the visual cortex becomes highly stimulated whenever the individuals shut their eyes, causing them to experience chronic visual hallucinations whenever they try to sleep (Parish, Richards, & Cameron, 2011).

Designer Drugs. Designer drugs are so called because they are specially formulated to mimic the pleasurable effects of hallucinogenic stimulants such as mescaline without, supposedly, their negative side effects. Ecstasy, or methylene-dioxy-methamphetamine (MDMA), is the best known of the designer drugs. Users of MDMA describe a wonderfully pleasant state of consciousness (Parish, Richards, & Cameron, 2011). However, MDMA is known to impair a variety of cognitive functions, including memory, sustained attention, analytical thinking, and self-control (Weaver & Schnoll, 2008). More specifically, the drug is believed to have devastating effects on the critically important neurotransmitter serotonin (Parish, Richards, & Cameron, 2011). Serotonin, as you learned in Chapter 2, influences cognitive performance (including memory), as well as moods, sleep cycles, and the ability to control impulses. In addition, MDMA causes dehydration, a side effect that can lead to fatal heat exhaustion (Parish, Richards, & Cameron, 2011).

Moreover, MDMA seems to impair the capacity for judging social cues in frequent users. In one study, Ecstasy users were more likely than nonusers to incorrectly classify the actions of others as having aggressive intent (Hoshi et al., 2006). As you will learn in Chapter 14, poor social judgments of this type are thought to be the cognitive basis of some acts of aggression. Thus, by changing the way Ecstasy users think about social cues, the drug may indirectly increase their proclivity for aggressive behavior.

The following *Summarize It* provides a summary of the effects and withdrawal symptoms of the major psychoactive drugs.

SUMMARIZE IT

The Effects and Withdrawal Symptoms of Some Psychoactive Drugs

PSYCHOACTIVE DRUG	EFFECTS	WITHDRAWAL SYMPTOMS
STIMULANTS		
Caffeine	Produces wakefulness and alertness; increases metabolism but slows reaction time	Headache, depression, fatigue
Nicotine (tobacco)	Effects range from alertness to calmness; lowers appetite for carbohydrates; increases pulse rate and other metabolic processes	Irritability, anxiety, restlessness, increased appetite
Amphetamines	Increase metabolism and alertness; elevate mood, cause wakefulness, suppress appetite	Fatigue, increased appetite, depression, long periods of sleep, irritability, anxiety
Cocaine	Brings on euphoric mood, energy boost, feeling of excitement; suppresses appetite	Depression, fatigue, increased appetite, long periods of sleep, irritability
DEPRESSANTS		
Alcohol	First few drinks stimulate and enliven while lowering anxiety and inhibitions; higher doses have a sedative effect, slowing reaction time, impairing motor control and perceptual ability	Tremors, nausea, sweating, depression, weakness, irritability, and in some cases hallucinations
Barbiturates	Promote sleep, have calming and sedative effect, decrease muscular tension, impair coordination and reflexes	Sleeplessness, anxiety; sudden withdrawal can cause seizures, cardiovascular collapse, and death
Tranquilizers (e.g., Valium, Xanax)	Lower anxiety, have calming and sedative effect, decrease muscular tension	Restlessness, anxiety, irritability, muscle tension, difficulty sleeping
Narcotics	Relieve pain; produce paralysis of intestines	Nausea, diarrhea, cramps, insomnia
HALLUCINOGENS		
Marijuana	Generally produces euphoria, relaxation; affects ability to store new memories	Anxiety, difficulty sleeping, decreased appetite, hyperactivity
LSD	Produces excited exhilaration, hallucinations, experiences perceived as insightful and profound	None
MDMA (Ecstasy)	Typically produces euphoria and feelings of understanding others and accepting them; lowers inhibitions; often causes overheating, dehydration, nausea; can cause jaw clenching, eye twitching, and dizziness	Depression, fatigue, and in some cases a "crash," during which the person may be sad, scared, or annoyed

REMEMBER IT

Check your answers and take additional quizzes in MyPsychLab.com. ✓● Study and Review on MyPsychLab

1. All addictive drugs increase the effect of the neurotransmitter _____ in the _____.

2. The impulsivity associated with substance abuse is probably caused by the effects of drugs on the _____.

3. Classify each drug by matching it with the appropriate category.

___ (1) marijuana ___ (3) Ecstasy ___ (5) heroin ___ (7) amphetamine ___ (9) nicotine

___ (2) caffeine ___ (4) STP ___ (6) LSD ___ (8) cocaine ___ (10) alcohol

a. depressant b. stimulant

c. hallucinogen d. designer drug

👀 Looking Back

This chapter began with a look at dreams. Studies of sleep and dreams have been important to researchers' attempts to understand consciousness. The strong tendency across cultural groups to identify ways of altering consciousness suggests that this domain of experience is important in everyday lives as well. As you learned, however, consciousness itself is regulated by circadian rhythms. Waking and sleeping, too, occur in natural cycles. Still, humans sometimes take control of these natural regulatory mechanisms through meditation, hypnosis, and by using psychoactive drugs. As is always the case, more research is needed to help us more fully understand both involuntary and voluntary alterations of consciousness.

CHAPTER 4 SUMMARY

WHAT IS CONSCIOUSNESS? (pp. 116–117)

4.1 How do psychologists view consciousness? (pp. 116–117)

Early psychologists saw consciousness, or awareness, as psychological in nature. Freud distinguished between conscious and unconscious experiences. James emphasized the continuous flow of thought and feeling in consciousness. Today's psychologists view consciousness as a neurobiological phenomenon rather than an exclusively psychological one.

Key Terms
consciousness, p. 116
altered states of consciousness, p. 117

4.2 What is the connection between altered states of consciousness and culture? (pp. 117–118)

Practices in many cultures allow individuals to deliberately induce altered states, often as part of tribal ceremonies or religious rituals.

CIRCADIAN RHYTHMS (pp. 117–120)

4.3 How do circadian rhythms affect physiological and psychological functions? (pp. 118–119)

The suprachiasmatic nucleus (SCN) is the body's biological clock, which regulates circadian rhythms and signals the pineal gland to secrete or suppress secretion of melatonin, a hormone that acts to induce sleep. The amount of melatonin released by the pineal gland depends on the amount of light perceived by specialized photoreceptor cells on the retina.

Key Terms
circadian rhythm, p. 117
suprachiasmatic nucleus (SCN), p. 118

4.4 How do disruptions in circadian rhythms affect the body and mind? (pp. 119–120)

Jet lag and shift work disrupt circadian rhythms, which can lead to sleep difficulties as well as reduced alertness during periods of wakefulness.

Key Term
subjective night, p. 119

SLEEP (pp. 120–125)

4.5 How do the restorative and circadian theories explain sleep? (p. 120)

The restorative theory of sleep claims that being awake causes stress on the body and the brain; repairs are made during sleep. The circadian (evolutionary) theory maintains that circadian rhythms, which evolved to protect humans from predators during the night, dictate periods of sleep and alertness.

Key Terms
restorative theory of sleep, p. 120
circadian theory of sleep, p. 120

4.6 What types of sleep occur during a typical night of sleep? (pp. 120–122)

During a typical night of sleep, a person goes through about five sleep cycles, each lasting about 90 minutes. During NREM sleep, heart rate and respiration are slow and regular, and blood pressure and brain activity are at a 24-hour low point; there is little body movement and no rapid eye movements. During REM sleep, the large muscles of the body are paralyzed, respiration and heart rate are fast and irregular, brain activity increases, and rapid eye movements and vivid dreams occur. REM sleep appears to be essential to the consolidation of memories. The first sleep cycle contains Stages 1, 2, 3, and 4 of NREM sleep as well as a period of REM sleep; the second contains Stages 2, 3, and 4 of NREM sleep and a period of REM sleep. In the third cycle, only Stages 2 and 3 are present, along with a period of REM sleep. In the remaining sleep cycles, the sleeper alternates mainly between Stage 2 and REM sleep, with each sleep cycle having progressively longer periods of REM.

Key Terms
sleep cycle, p. 120
NREM sleep, p. 120
alpha waves, p. 120
beta waves, p. 121
sleep spindles, p. 121
slow-wave sleep, p. 121
stage 4 sleep, p. 121
REM sleep, p. 121
REM rebound, p. 121

4.7 How does age influence sleep patterns? (pp. 122)

Infants and young children have the longest sleep time and largest percentages of REM and slow-wave sleep. Children from age 6 to puberty sleep best. Older adults typically have shorter total sleep time, more awakenings, and substantially less slow-wave sleep.

4.8 What are the effects of sleep deprivation? (p. 123)

Sleep deprivation can lead to lapses in concentration and emotional irritability. Research examining the effects of sleep deprivation on verbal learning have shown that sleep deprivation may lead to suppression of neurological activity in the temporal lobes.

4.9 What are the various sleep disorders? (pp. 123–125)

Parasomnias occur during partial arousal from Stage 4 sleep. In a sleep terror, the sleeper awakens in a panicked state with a racing heart. Episodes last 5 to 15 minutes, and then the person falls back to sleep. Nightmares occur during REM sleep and are usually remembered in vivid detail. Somniloquy (sleeptalking) can occur during any sleep stage and is more common in children than adults. The symptoms of narcolepsy include excessive daytime sleepiness and sudden attacks of REM sleep. Sleep apnea is a sleep disorder in which a sleeper's breathing stops and the person must awaken briefly to breathe. Its symptoms are excessive daytime sleepiness and loud snoring. Insomnia is a sleep disorder characterized by difficulty falling or staying asleep, waking too early, or sleep that is light, restless, or of poor quality.

Key Terms
parasomnias, p. 123
dyssomnia, p. 124
narcolepsy, p. 124
sleep apnea, p. 124
insomnia, p. 125

DREAMS (pp. 126–128)

4.10 What have researchers learned about dreams? (p. 126)

REM dreams have a story-like or dreamlike quality and are more visual, vivid, and emotional than NREM dreams. Common dream themes include falling or being attacked or chased. During REM dreams, areas of the brain responsible for emotions and the primary visual cortex are active, but the neurotransmitters serotonin and norepinephrine are less plentiful. Lucid dreaming is a set of techniques that enables dreamers to exert cognitive control over the content of their dreams.

Key Terms
REM dream, p. 126
NREM dream, p. 126
lucid dream, p. 126

4.11 How do the various theorists explain dreams? (pp. 126–128)

Freud claimed that dreams carry hidden meanings and function to satisfy unconscious sexual and aggressive desires.

He claimed that the manifest content of dreams differs from their latent content. Today, some psychologists support the cognitive theory of dreaming, which claims that dreaming is thinking while asleep; others support the activation-synthesis hypothesis, which claims that dreams are the brain's attempt to make sense of the random firing of brain cells during REM sleep and others support the evolutionary theory of dreaming, which says that vivid REM dreams enable people to rehearse the skills they need to fend off predators.

Key Terms
manifest content, p. 127
latent content, p. 127
cognitive theory of dreaming, p. 127
activation-synthesis hypothesis of dreaming, p. 127
evolutionary theory of dreaming, p. 127

MEDITATION AND HYPNOSIS (pp. 128–130)

4.12 What are the benefits of meditation? (pp. 128–129)

Meditation promotes relaxation, reduces arousal, or expands consciousness. It may also help prevent and treat cardiovascular disease.

Key Term
meditation, p. 128

4.13 How and why does hypnosis influence the body and mind? (pp. 129–130)

Hypnosis is a procedure through which a hypnotist uses the power of suggestion to induce changes in the thoughts, feelings, sensations, perceptions, or behavior of a subject. It has been used most successfully for the control of pain. The three main theories proposed to explain hypnosis are the sociocognitive theory, the neodissociation theory, and the theory of dissociated control.

Key Terms
hypnosis, p. 129
sociocognitive theory of hypnosis, p. 129
neodissociation theory of hypnosis, p. 130
theory of dissociated control, p. 130

PSYCHOACTIVE DRUGS (pp. 130–137)

4.14 How do drugs affect the brain's neurotransmitter system? (p. 131)

Psychoactive drugs increase the availability of dopamine in the nucleus accumbens. Beyond that, each drug has a unique influence on a specific neurotransmitter or group of neurotransmitters.

Key Term
psychoactive drug, p. 131

4.15 How do physical and psychological drug dependence differ? (pp. 131–133)

With physical drug dependence, the user develops a drug tolerance, and so larger and larger doses of the drug are needed to get the same effect or high. Withdrawal symptoms appear when the drug is discontinued and disappear when the drug is taken again. Psychological drug dependence involves an intense craving for the drug's pleasurable effects.

Key Terms
substance abuse, p. 131
physical drug dependence, p. 132
drug tolerance, p. 132
withdrawal symptoms, p. 132
psychological drug dependence, p. 132

4.16 How do stimulants affect behavior? (pp. 133–134)

Stimulants (amphetamines, cocaine, caffeine, and nicotine) speed up activity in the central nervous system, suppress appetite, and make a person feel more awake, alert, and energetic.

Key Term
stimulants, p. 133

4.17 How do depressants affect behavior? (pp. 134–135)

Depressants decrease activity in the central nervous system, slow down bodily functions, and reduce sensitivity to outside stimulation. Depressants include sedative-hypnotics (alcohol, barbiturates, and minor tranquilizers) and narcotics (opiates such as opium, codeine, morphine, and heroin), which have both pain-relieving and calming effects.

Key Terms
depressants, p. 134
narcotics, p. 135

4.18 How do hallucinogens affect behavior? (pp. 135–137)

Hallucinogens—including marijuana, LSD, and MDMA—can alter and distort perceptions of time and space, alter mood, produce feelings of unreality, and cause hallucinations.

Key Term
hallucinogens, p. 135

Chapter 4 Study Guide

Answers to all the Study Guide questions are provided at the end of the book.

SECTION ONE: Chapter Review

What Is Consciousness? (pp. 116–117)

1. Which of the following best defines consciousness?
   - **a.** awareness
   - **b.** wakefulness
   - **c.** receptiveness
   - **d.** rationality

Circadian Rhythms (pp. 117–120)

2. The structure that regulates the body's internal clock is the _____ _____ .

3. People who are suffering from jet lag or the effects of working rotating shifts or night shifts are experiencing
   - **a.** a deficiency in melatonin production.
   - **b.** an excess of melatonin production.
   - **c.** a defect in their suprachiasmatic nucleus.
   - **d.** a disturbance in their circadian rhythms.

4. The performance of shift workers is enhanced during their subjective night. (true/false)

Sleep (pp. 120–125)

5. The circadian theory of sleep is also known as the _____ or _____ theory of sleep.

6. State the type of sleep—NREM or REM—that corresponds to each characteristic.
   - _____ **(1)** paralysis of large muscles
   - _____ **(2)** slow, regular respiration and heart rate
   - _____ **(3)** rapid eye movements
   - _____ **(4)** intense brain activity
   - _____ **(5)** vivid dreams
   - **a.** REM
   - **b.** NREM

7. The average length of a sleep cycle in adults is
   - **a.** 30 minutes.
   - **b.** 60 minutes.
   - **c.** 90 minutes.
   - **d.** 120 minutes.

8. After the first two sleep cycles, most people get equal amounts of deep sleep and REM sleep. (true/false)

9. Which type of sleep seems to aid learning and memory?
   - **a.** Stage 1
   - **b.** Stage 2
   - **c.** Stages 3 and 4
   - **d.** REM sleep

10. Following REM deprivation, there is usually
    - **a.** an absence of REM sleep.
    - **b.** an increase in REM sleep.
    - **c.** a decrease in REM sleep.
    - **d.** no change in the amount of REM sleep.

11. Match the age group with the appropriate description of sleep.
    - _____ **(1)** have most difficulty sleeping
    - _____ **(2)** sleep 10 to 11 hours
    - _____ **(3)** have highest percentage of REM and deep sleep
    - **a.** infants and young children
    - **b.** children aged 6 to puberty
    - **c.** elderly adults

12. Sleepwalking and sleep terrors occur during a partial arousal from
    - **a.** Stage 1 sleep.
    - **b.** Stage 2 sleep.
    - **c.** Stage 4 sleep.
    - **d.** REM sleep.

13. Sleep terrors typically occur in Stage 2 sleep. (true/false)

14. Match each sleep problem with the description or associated symptom.
    - _____ **(1)** uncontrollable sleep attacks during the day
    - _____ **(2)** cessation of breathing during sleep
    - _____ **(3)** difficulty falling or staying asleep
    - _____ **(4)** very frightening REM dream
    - **a.** sleep apnea
    - **b.** nightmare
    - **c.** insomnia
    - **d.** narcolepsy

Dreams (pp. 126–128)

15. Compared to REM dreams, NREM dreams are
    - **a.** more emotional.
    - **b.** more visual.
    - **c.** less storylike.
    - **d.** more vivid.

16. Dreams are difficult to remember because most of them occur during Stage 4 sleep. (true/false)

17. According to researchers,
    - **a.** most dreams are bizarre in nature.
    - **b.** dreams involving bizarre content are more likely to be remembered than other kinds of dreams.
    - **c.** people who have delusional disorders rarely have bizarre dreams.
    - **d.** only children have bizarre dreams.

18. Experts tend to agree on how dreams should be interpreted. (true/false)

Meditation and Hypnosis (pp. 128–130)

19. Which is not a proposed use of meditation?
    - **a.** to promote relaxation
    - **b.** to substitute for anesthesia during surgery
    - **c.** to bring a person to a higher level of spirituality
    - **d.** to alter consciousness

20. Many people who meditate are motivated by a desire to attain a higher spiritual state of consciousness. (true/false)

21. Meditation can help people control their emotions. (true/false)

22. Which of the following statements is true of people under hypnosis?
    a. They will often violate their moral code.
    b. They are much stronger than they are in the normal waking state.
    c. They can be made to experience distortions in their perceptions.
    d. Their memory is more accurate than it is during the normal waking state.

23. For a fairly hypnotizable person, which use of hypnosis would probably be most successful?
    a. for relief from pain
    b. instead of a general anesthetic during surgery
    c. for treating drug addiction
    d. for improving memory

24. The three main theories proposed to explain hypnosis are the _____, _____, and _____ theories.

Psychoactive Drugs (pp. 130–137)

25. Psychoactive drugs create pleasurable sensations in the brain by stimulating the _____ _____ .

26. Which of the following does not necessarily occur with drug tolerance?
    a. The body adjusts to functioning with the drug in the system.
    b. The user needs increasingly larger doses of the drug to achieve the desired effect.
    c. The user becomes progressively less affected by the drug.
    d. The user develops a craving for the pleasurable effects of the drug.

27. During withdrawal from a drug, the user experiences symptoms that are the opposite of the effects produced by the drug. (true/false)

28. Psychological dependence on a drug is more difficult to combat than physical dependence. (true/false)

29. Match the stimulant with the appropriate description.

    _____ (1) used to increase arousal, relieve fatigue, and suppress appetite

    _____ (2) found in coffee

    _____ (3) snorted or injected

    _____ (4) smokable form of cocaine
    a. caffeine   b. amphetamines
    c. crack   d. cocaine

30. Decreased activity in the central nervous system is the chief effect of
    a. stimulants.   b. depressants.
    c. hallucinogens.   d. narcotics.

31. Which of the following is a narcotic?
    a. cocaine   b. heroin
    c. LSD   d. Valium

32. Narcotics have
    a. pain-relieving effects.
    b. stimulating effects.
    c. energizing effects.
    d. perception-altering effects.

33. Which category of drugs alters perception and mood and can cause feelings of unreality?
    a. stimulants   b. depressants
    c. hallucinogens   d. narcotics

34. People who stop smoking marijuana usually experience no withdrawal symptoms. (true/false)

35. Some addictive drugs increase the effect of the neurotransmitter _____ in the nucleus accumbens.
    a. acetylcholine   b. GABA
    c. dopamine   d. serotonin

SECTION TWO: Identify the Drug

Match the description of drug effects with the drug.

    _____ (1) Produces excited exhilaration and hallucinations

    _____ (2) Produces wakefulness and alertness with increased metabolism but slowed reaction time

    _____ (3) Increases metabolism and alertness, elevates mood and wakefulness, and decrease appetite

    _____ (4) Produces euphoria and relaxation but also affects ability to store new memories

    _____ (5) Produces an energy boost and feeling of excitement while suppressing appetite

    _____ (6) Initial doses stimulate and enliven while lowering anxiety, but higher doses have a sedative effect

    _____ (7) Produces euphoria and feelings of social acceptance; stimulates appetite; leads to depression and fatigue
    a. alcohol   b. hallucinogens
    c. marijuana   d. caffeine
    e. cocaine   f. amphetamines
    g. MDMA (Ecstasy)

SECTION THREE: Comprehensive Practice Test

1. The suprachiasmatic nucleus signals the pineal gland to secrete _____ from dusk until dawn.

2. People who work during their _____, when their biological clock is telling them it is time to sleep, can suffer lowered efficiency and productivity.
    a. REM rebound
    b. subjective night
    c. circadian rebound
    d. episodes of narcolepsy

3. Which theory proposes that the purpose of sleep is to allow the body to rest and recover?
    a. restorative theory of sleep
    b. evolutionary theory of sleep
    c. adaptive theory of sleep
    d. circadian theory of sleep

4. REM sleep is the _____ stage of sleep in a typical sleep cycle.
   - **a.** first
   - **b.** second
   - **c.** last
   - **d.** middle

5. Delta waves appear primarily in Stages _____ sleep.
   - **a.** 1 and 2
   - **b.** 2 and 3
   - **c.** 3 and 4
   - **d.** 1 and 4

6. Researchers have found that REM sleep
   - **a.** is increased in the elderly.
   - **b.** is associated with memory consolidation.
   - **c.** occurs only in some sleep cycles.
   - **d.** is rarely associated with dreaming.

7. As we grow older we sleep more than when we were younger; we also sleep more deeply, with more REM sleep. (true/false)

8. Freud believed dreams functioned to satisfy unconscious _____ and _____ urges.
   - **a.** parental; childhood
   - **b.** sexual; superego
   - **c.** aggressive; violent
   - **d.** sexual; aggressive

9. J. Allan Hobson believes dreams are merely the brain's attempt to make sense of the random firing of brain cells. This view is known as the
   - **a.** Hobson dream hypothesis.
   - **b.** somniloquy hypothesis.
   - **c.** activation-synthesis hypothesis.
   - **d.** physiological activation hypothesis.

10. The technical term for sleepwalking is
    - **a.** somniloquy.
    - **b.** mobile insomnia.
    - **c.** narcolepsy.
    - **d.** somnambulism.

11. People who talk in their sleep often mumble nonsensical words and phrases. (true/false)

12. Some people suffer from a sleep disorder known as _____, which causes them to stop breathing and then to wake for a brief time so as to start breathing again.
    - **a.** narcolepsy
    - **b.** sleep apnea
    - **c.** somniloquy
    - **d.** somnambulism

13. The sleep disorder characterized by either difficulty falling asleep or frequently waking is known as
    - **a.** sleep apnea.
    - **b.** insomnia.
    - **c.** somnambulism.
    - **d.** REM rebound.

14. Jack pleaded not guilty to his public indecency charges. He claimed he would never do such a thing if he were in his right mind and that he was the victim of the effects of hypnosis. A psychologist would probably support this claim. (true/false)

15. Personality has little impact on substance abuse. (true/false)

16. LSD, MDMA, and marijuana are classified as
    - **a.** narcotics.
    - **b.** stimulants.
    - **c.** hallucinogens.
    - **d.** depressants.

17. Animals addicted to several drugs prefer _____ when offered a choice of drugs.
    - **a.** marijuana
    - **b.** heroin
    - **c.** cocaine
    - **d.** alcohol

18. Caffeine is a depressant. (true/false)

SECTION FOUR: Critical Thinking

1. Explain the similarities and differences among the four theories of dreaming discussed in the chapter. Choose the theory that you believe best explains dreaming and explain why.

SECTION FIVE: Application Essays

1. Suppose you have been hired by a sleep clinic to formulate a questionnaire for evaluating patients' sleep habits. List 10 questions you would include in your questionnaire. Explain your rationale for each question.

2. Luanne is a full-time student who wants to find a way to keep up her class schedule while working full-time. She decides to work the 11:00 p.m. to 7:00 a.m. shift at a hospital and then attend morning classes. After her classes end at noon, she intends to sleep from 1:00 p.m. until 7:00 p.m., at which time she will get up and study until it is time to leave for work. Based on what you have learned about circadian rhythms in this chapter, what kinds of problems is Luanne likely to encounter in trying to carry out her plan?

> **Apply your critical thinking skills with MyPsychLab Writing Assignments**
>
> *Submit your answer to the following question inside the MyPsychLab Writing Assessment program for immediate feedback.*
>
> Your roommate has been coming back to the dorm at all hours of the night, disrupting your sleep. Explain how the timing of your roommate's interruptions of your sleep might affect your ability to learn and your health.

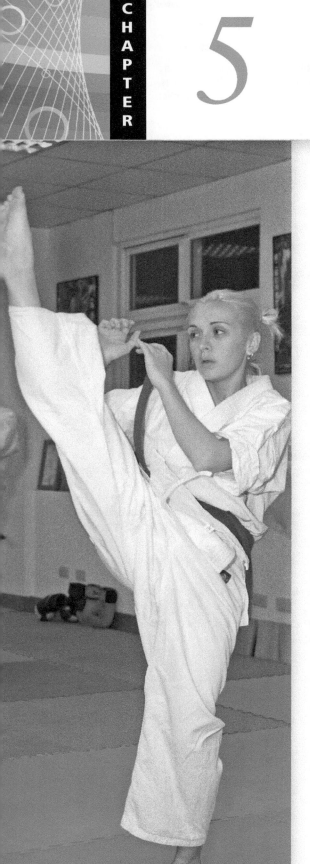

Learning

⊙ THINK ABOUT IT

On an episode of a popular cable television comedy program, the hosts offered $100 to any studio audience member who would eat an entire stick of butter. As you would probably predict, they had no trouble finding a volunteer; we all know that the expectation of some kind of a payoff influences our behavior. But do all rewards influence behavior in the same way? Would the hosts have been successful if they had offered $1 instead of $100? Not likely—the reward would have to be worth completing the task. In addition, what if there was only a 75% chance that the audience member would actually receive the $100 after eating the stick of butter—would this affect his or her willingness to participate?

The predictability of an expected reward does matter, but not in the way that you might think. To find out what we mean, estimate the likelihood that each behavior in the accompanying chart will actually yield its associated payoff. Use a scale of 0 to 10, with 0 = no chance at all and 10 = absolute certainty that the behavior, if executed correctly, will lead to the payoff. For example, how likely is it that you will find a TV program you want to watch when you channel surf? Is there no chance (0)? Some chance (5)? Will you definitely find a program (10)? Make your estimations for this and the other items listed in the chart.

Chances are good that your ratings for some behaviors were higher than for others; for example, the likelihood that you would get money from an ATM was probably rated higher than the likelihood that you would win the lottery.

But now take a moment to think about which of these behaviors you could get so involved in that you continue them for much longer than you originally intended. The chances are good that you don't see yourself repetitively punching in your PIN at an ATM or baking cookies for hours on end, even if these have a high probability of paying off. On the other hand, who hasn't wasted time channel surfing or playing video games? And how many people regularly buy lottery tickets despite having never won any money? In this way, everyday experience confirms an important principle that you will read about in this chapter: Unpredictable rewards usually influence behavioral changes (what psychologists call *learning*) more strongly than predictable rewards do.

Behavior	Potential Payoff	Probability of Payoff
Channel-surfing	Find a program you want to watch	0 ←——————→ 10
Using an ATM	Get cash	0 ←——————→ 10
Playing a video game	Beat opponent or your own past performance	0 ←——————→ 10
Baking cookies according to a recipe	Cookies turn out as expected	0 ←——————→ 10
Buying lottery tickets	Win money	0 ←——————→ 10

Psychologists define **learning** as a relatively permanent change in behavior, knowledge, capability, or attitude that is acquired through experience and cannot be attributed to illness, injury, or maturation. Several parts of this definition warrant further explanation. First, defining learning as a "relatively permanent change" excludes temporary changes that could result from illness, fatigue, or fluctuations in mood. Second, limiting learning to changes that are "acquired through experience" excludes some readily observable changes in behavior that occur as a result of brain injuries or certain diseases. Also, certain observable changes that occur as individuals grow and mature have nothing to do with learning. For example, technically speaking, infants do not *learn* to crawl or walk. Basic motor skills and the maturational plan that governs their development are a part of the genetically programmed behavioral repertoire of every species. By contrast, children do not learn to read without, at a minimum, exposure to printed language. Typically, much more than mere exposure is required. Children must be instructed in the use of strategies that enable them to translate written language into spoken language. In other words, we can classify the acquisition of reading skills as *learning*, because it depends on specific experiences that must be provided by a child's environment. Moreover, barring some kind of brain injury or neurological disorder, once learned, the ability to read is never lost. The first kind of learning we'll consider is classical conditioning. ⊙

Classical Conditioning

Why do sodas that contain artificial sweeteners (so-called diet drinks) make some people hungry? The answer can be found in the principles of **classical conditioning**, a type of learning through which an organism learns to associate one stimulus with another. This kind of learning is sometimes referred to as *Pavlovian conditioning* or *respondent conditioning*. A **stimulus** (the plural is *stimuli*) is any event or object in the environment to which an organism responds. Be patient; at the end of this section, we'll explain why drinking diet sodas might actually cause you to gain weight. As you read about classical conditioning, see if you can figure it out on your own.

learning A relatively permanent change in behavior, knowledge, capability, or attitude that is acquired through experience and cannot be attributed to illness, injury, or maturation.

⊙ **Watch** the Video *Episode 7: Big Picture: What Does It Mean to Learn?* in **MyPsychLab**

classical conditioning A type of learning through which an organism learns to associate one stimulus with another.

stimulus (STIM-yu-lus) Any event or object in the environment to which an organism responds; plural is *stimuli*.

5.1 How does the kind of learning Pavlov discovered happen?

unconditioned response (UR) A response that is elicited by an unconditioned stimulus without prior learning.

unconditioned stimulus (US) A stimulus that elicits a specific unconditioned response without prior learning.

conditioned stimulus (CS) A neutral stimulus that, after repeated pairing with an unconditioned stimulus, becomes associated with it and elicits a conditioned response.

conditioned response (CR) The learned response that comes to be elicited by a conditioned stimulus as a result of its repeated pairing with an unconditioned stimulus.

higher-order conditioning Conditioning that occurs when conditioned stimuli are linked together to form a series of signals.

Pavlov and the Process of Classical Conditioning

Ivan Pavlov (1849–1936) organized and directed research in physiology at the Institute of Experimental Medicine in St. Petersburg, Russia, from 1891 until his death 45 years later. There, he conducted his classic experiments on the physiology of digestion, which won him a Nobel Prize in 1904—the first time a Russian received this honor.

Pavlov's contribution to psychology came about quite by accident. Pavlov, a physician by training and profession, was engaged in research aimed at clarifying the role of saliva in the process of digestion. In pursuit of this goal, he developed a procedure for collecting and measuring the amount of saliva in a dog's mouth (Figure 5.1).

Pavlov's purpose was to collect the saliva that the dogs would secrete naturally in response to food placed inside the mouth. But he noticed that, in many cases, the dogs would begin to salivate even before the food was presented. Pavlov observed drops of saliva collecting in the containers when the dogs heard the footsteps of the laboratory assistants coming to feed them. He observed saliva collecting when the dogs heard their food dishes rattling, saw the attendant who fed them, or spotted their food. How could an involuntary response such as salivation come to be associated with the sights and sounds involved in feeding? Pavlov spent the rest of his life studying this question. The type of learning he studied is known today as classical conditioning.

Pavlov (1927/1960) used tones, bells, buzzers, lights, geometric shapes, electric shocks, and metronomes in his conditioning experiments. In a typical experiment, food powder was placed in the dog's mouth, causing salivation. Because dogs do not need to be conditioned to salivate to food, salivation to food is an unlearned response, or **unconditioned response (UR)**. Any stimulus, such as food, that without prior learning will automatically elicit, or bring forth, an unconditioned response is called an **unconditioned stimulus (US)**.

Following is a list of some common unconditioned reflexes, showing their two components: the unconditioned stimulus and the unconditioned response.

UNCONDITIONED REFLEXES

Unconditioned Stimulus (US)	Unconditioned Response (UR)
food	salivation
loud noise	startle
light in eye	contraction of pupil
puff of air in eye	eyeblink response

Pavlov demonstrated that dogs could be conditioned to salivate to a variety of stimuli never before associated with food, as shown in Figure 5.2. During the conditioning process, the researcher would present a neutral stimulus such as a musical tone shortly before placing food powder in the dog's mouth. The food powder would cause the dog to salivate. Pavlov found that after the tone and the food were paired many times, usually 20 or more, the tone alone would elicit salivation (Pavlov, 1927/1960). Pavlov called the tone the learned stimulus, or **conditioned stimulus (CS)**, and salivation to the tone the learned response, or **conditioned response (CR)**. You can learn first-hand how classical conditioning works by doing the *Try It* on page 148.

Pavlov also discovered that a neutral stimulus could become a conditioned stimulus simply by pairing it with a previously acquired conditioned stimulus, a process called **higher-order conditioning**. Higher-order conditioning is quite common. Think about what happens when you

FIGURE 5.1 The Experimental Apparatus Used in Pavlov's Classical Conditioning Studies
In Pavlov's classical conditioning studies, the dog was restrained in a harness in the cubicle and isolated from all distractions. An experimenter observed the dog through a one-way mirror and, by remote control, presented the dog with food and other conditioning stimuli. A tube carried the saliva from the dog's mouth to a container where it was measured.

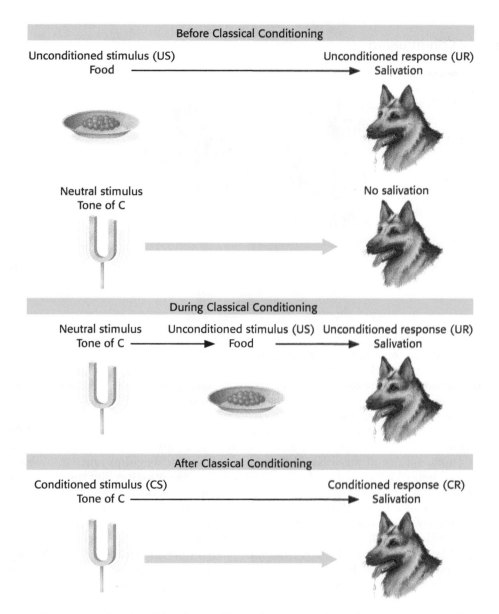

FIGURE 5.2 Classically Conditioning a Salivation Response
A neutral stimulus (a tone) elicits no salivation until it is repeatedly paired with the unconditioned stimulus (food). After many pairings, the neutral stimulus (now called the conditioned stimulus) alone produces salivation. Classical conditioning has occurred.

must have some kind of blood test. Typically, you sit in a chair next to a table on which are arranged materials such as needles, syringes, and such. Next, some kind of constricting device is tied around your arm, and the nurse or technician pats on the surface of your skin until a vein becomes visible. Each step in the sequence tells you that the unavoidable "stick" of the needle and the pain, which is largely the result of reflexive muscle tension, is coming. The stick itself is the unconditioned stimulus, to which you reflexively respond. But all the steps that precede it are conditioned stimuli that cause you to anticipate the pain of the stick itself. And with each successive step, a conditioned response occurs, as your muscles respond to your anxiety by contracting a bit more in anticipation of the stick. Chains of cues such as this are the result of higher-order conditioning.

Changing Conditioned Responses

After conditioning an animal to salivate to a tone, what would happen if you continued to sound the tone but no longer paired it with food? Pavlov found that without the food, salivation to the tone became weaker and weaker and then finally disappeared altogether—a process known as **extinction**. After the response had been extinguished,

extinction In classical conditioning, the weakening and eventual disappearance of the conditioned response as a result of repeated presentation of the conditioned stimulus without the unconditioned stimulus.

Watch the Video *Episode 7: Basics: Classical Conditioning: An Involuntary Response* in **MyPsychLab**

5.2 What causes classically conditioned responses to change?

TRY IT   **Classical Conditioning**

For this activity, you will need a drinking straw and a partner. Try blowing in the straw to aim a puff of air, the unconditioned stimulus (UCS), at your partner's eye to determine just how and where to hold the straw in order to ensure that the puff of air will cause her to blink, the unconditioned response (UCR). Next, precede the puff with a finger snap or another appropriate neutral stimulus. Expose your partner to fifteen pairings of the neutral and unconditioned stimuli. Expose your partner to a second set of fifteen pairings, but, this time, vary presentations of the neutral stimulus such that it sometimes precedes the UCS and sometimes does not. The second set of trials should demonstrate that your partner blinks in response to the neutral stimulus even when it is not followed by the UCS. Thus, the neutral stimulus will have become a conditioned stimulus (CS), and the eye blink a conditioned response (CR).

spontaneous recovery The reappearance of an extinguished response (in a weaker form) when an organism is exposed to the original conditioned stimulus following a rest period.

generalization In classical conditioning, the tendency to make a conditioned response to a stimulus that is similar to the original conditioned stimulus.

Pavlov allowed the dog to rest for 20 minutes and then brought it back to the laboratory. He found that the dog would again salivate to the tone. Pavlov called this recurrence **spontaneous recovery**. But the spontaneously recovered response was weaker and shorter in duration than the original conditioned response. Figure 5.3 shows the processes of extinction and spontaneous recovery.

Assume that you have conditioned a dog to salivate when it hears the tone middle C played on the piano. Would it also salivate if you played B or D? Pavlov found that a tone similar to the original conditioned stimulus would produce the conditioned response (salivation), a phenomenon called **generalization**. But the salivation decreased the farther the tone was from the original conditioned stimulus, until the tone became so different that the dog would not salivate at all (Figure 5.4).

It is easy to see the value of generalization in daily life. For instance, if you get a new clock, you will not have to relearn what to do when the alarm goes off, even if you have never heard it before. Even if the sound of the alarm varies considerably from that of your old clock, you will still recognize it as a sound that is telling you that it's time to wake up and get ready for your early-morning class.

FIGURE 5.3 Extinction of a Classically Conditioned Response
When a classically conditioned stimulus (a tone) was presented in a series of trials without the unconditioned stimulus (food), Pavlov's dogs salivated less and less until there was virtually no salivation. But after a 20-minute rest, one sound of the tone caused the conditioned response to reappear in a weakened form (producing only a small amount of salivation), a phenomenon Pavlov called *spontaneous recovery*.
Source: Data from Pavlov (1927/1960), p. 58.

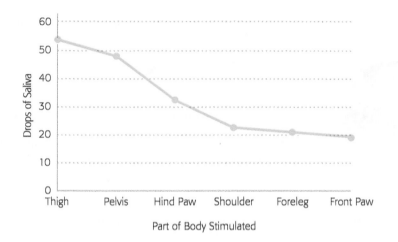

FIGURE 5.4 **Generalization of a Conditioned Response**
Pavlov attached small vibrators to different parts of a dog's body. After conditioning salivation to stimulation of the dog's thigh, he stimulated other parts of the dog's body. Due to generalization, the salivation also occurred when other body parts were stimulated. But the farther away from the thigh the stimulus was applied, the weaker the salivation response.
Source: From Pavlov (1927/1960).

Let's return to the example of a dog being conditioned to a musical tone to trace the process of **discrimination**, the learned ability to distinguish between similar stimuli so that the conditioned response occurs only to the original conditioned stimulus but not to similar stimuli:

discrimination The learned ability to distinguish between similar stimuli so that the conditioned response occurs only to the original conditioned stimulus but not to similar stimuli.

STEP 1: The dog is conditioned to salivate in response to the tone C.

STEP 2: Generalization occurs, and the dog salivates to a range of musical tones above and below C. The dog salivates less and less as the tone moves farther away from C.

STEP 3: The original tone C is repeatedly paired with food. Neighboring tones are also sounded, but they are not followed by food. The dog is being conditioned to discriminate.

Gradually, the salivation response to the neighboring tones (A, B, D, and E) is extinguished, while salivation to the original tone C is strengthened.

Like generalization, discrimination has survival value. Discriminating between the odors of fresh and spoiled milk will spare you an upset stomach. Discriminating between a rattlesnake and a garter snake could save your life.

John Watson and Emotional Conditioning

5.3 What did Watson's "Little Albert" experiment show?

You may recall from Chapter 1 that John B. Watson (1878–1958) claimed that the influence of environmental factors could explain nearly all variations in human behavior. Recall, too, that Watson coined the term *behaviorism* to refer to the school of thought that proposed limiting psychology to the study of overtly observable behavior. To provide empirical evidence that would support his point of view, Watson and his assistant, Rosalie Rayner, conducted a now-famous study in 1919 to prove that fear could be classically conditioned. The subject of the study, known as Little Albert, was a healthy and emotionally stable 11-month-old infant. When tested, he showed no fear except of the loud noise Watson made by striking a hammer against a steel bar near his head.

In the laboratory, Rayner presented Little Albert with a white rat. As Albert reached for the rat, Watson struck the steel bar with a hammer just behind Albert's head. This procedure was repeated, and Albert "jumped violently, fell forward and began to whimper" (Watson & Rayner, 1920, p. 4). A week later, Watson continued the experiment, pairing the rat with the loud noise five more times. Then, at the sight of the white rat alone, Albert began to cry.

When Albert returned to the laboratory five days later, the fear had generalized to a rabbit and, somewhat less, to a dog, a seal coat, Watson's hair, and a Santa Claus mask (see Figure 5.5, p. 150). After 30 days, Albert made his final visit to the laboratory. His fears were still evident, although they were somewhat less intense. Watson concluded that conditioned fears "persist and modify personality throughout life" (Watson & Rayner, 1920, p. 12).

Neutral Stimulus	Unconditioned Stimulus (US)	Unconditioned Response (UR)
White rat ⟶	Loud noise ⟶	Fear reaction

Conditioned Stimulus (CS)		Conditioned Response (CR)
White rat ⟶		Fear reaction

FIGURE 5.5 The Conditioned Fear Response
Little Albert's fear of a white rat was a conditioned response that was generalized to other stimuli, including a rabbit and, to a lesser extent, a Santa Claus mask.
Source: Archives of the History of American Psychology—The University of Akron.

👁 **Watch** the Video *Little Albert* on **MyPsychLab**

5.4 What did Rescorla demonstrate about classical conditioning?

Although Watson had formulated techniques for removing conditioned fears, Albert moved out of the city before they could be tried on him. Because Watson apparently knew that Albert would be moving away before these fear-removal techniques could be applied, he clearly showed a disregard for the child's welfare. The American Psychological Association now has strict ethical standards for the use of human and animal participants in research experiments and would not sanction an experiment such as Watson's. 👁

Some of Watson's ideas for removing fears laid the groundwork for certain behavior therapies used today. For example, three years after his experiment with Little Albert, Watson and a colleague, Mary Cover Jones (1924), worked with 3-year-old Peter, who was afraid of white rabbits. Peter was brought into the laboratory, seated in a high chair, and given candy to eat. A white rabbit in a wire cage was brought into the room but kept far enough away from Peter that it would not upset him. Over the course of 38 therapy sessions, the rabbit was brought closer and closer to Peter, who continued to enjoy his candy. Occasionally, some of Peter's friends were brought in to play with the rabbit at a safe distance from Peter so that he could see firsthand that the rabbit did no harm. Toward the end of Peter's therapy, the rabbit was taken out of the cage and eventually put in Peter's lap. By the final session, Peter had grown fond of the rabbit. As you will learn in Chapter 13, the procedures that Watson and Jones used in the "Little Peter" experiment are similar to those that behavior therapists use today to help clients "unlearn" phobias.

The Cognitive Perspective

Which aspect of the classical conditioning process is most important? Both Pavlov and Watson believed that the critical element in classical conditioning was the repeated pairing of the conditioned stimulus and the unconditioned stimulus, with only a brief interval between the two. Beginning in the late 1960s, though, researchers began to discover exceptions to some of the general principles Pavlov had identified.

Robert Rescorla (1967, 1968, 1988; Rescorla & Wagner, 1972) is largely responsible for changing how psychologists view classical conditioning. Rescorla was able to demonstrate that the critical element in classical conditioning is not the repeated pairing of the conditioned stimulus and the unconditioned stimulus (Rescorla, 2008). Rather, the important factor is whether the conditioned stimulus provides information that enables the organism to reliably *predict* the occurrence of the unconditioned stimulus. In other words, Rescorla was arguing that Pavlov's dogs salivated when they heard the musical tone because the tone was a signal that told them that food was on the way. How was Rescorla able to prove that prediction is the critical element?

Using rats as his subjects, Rescorla used a tone as the conditioned stimulus and a shock as the unconditioned stimulus. For one group of rats, the tone and shock were paired 20 times—the shock always occurred during the tone. The other group of rats also received a shock 20 times while the tone was sounding, but this group also received 20 shocks that were not paired with the tone. If the only critical element in classical conditioning were the number of pairings of the conditioned stimulus and the unconditioned stimulus, both groups of rats should have developed a conditioned fear response to the tone, because both groups experienced exactly the same number of pairings of tone and shock. But this was not the case. Only the first group, for which the tone was a reliable predictor of the shock, developed the conditioned fear response to the tone. The second group showed little evidence of conditioning because the shock was just as likely to occur without the tone as with it. In other words, for this group, the tone provided no additional information about the shock.

Biological Predispositions ▶

Remember that Watson conditioned Little Albert to fear the white rat by pairing the presence of the rat with the loud noise of a hammer striking against a steel bar. Do you think Watson could just as easily have conditioned a fear response to a flower or a piece of ribbon? Probably not. Research has shown that humans are more easily conditioned to fear stimuli, such as snakes, that can have very real negative effects on their well-being (Mineka & Oehlberg, 2008). Moreover, fear of snakes and other potentially threatening animals is just as common in apes and monkeys as in humans, suggesting a **biological predisposition** to develop these fearful responses.

According to Martin Seligman (1972), humans and other animals are prepared to associate only certain stimuli with particular consequences. One example of this preparedness is the tendency to develop **taste aversion**—the intense dislike and/or avoidance of particular foods that have been associated with nausea or discomfort. You may have had some personal experience with this phenomenon if you have ever thrown up after eating spaghetti, chili, or some other food with a very distinctive taste and smell. If so, you know that, for weeks afterward, just the smell of the offending food was sufficient to prompt a wave of nausea. ✳

In a classic study on taste aversion, Garcia and Koelling (1966) exposed rats to a three-way conditioned stimulus: a bright light, a clicking noise, and flavored water. For one group of rats, the unconditioned stimulus was being exposed to either X-rays or lithium chloride, either of which produces nausea and vomiting several hours after exposure; for the other group, the unconditioned stimulus was an electric shock to the feet. The rats that were made ill associated the flavored water with the nausea and avoided it at all times, but they would still drink unflavored water when the bright light and the clicking sound were present. The rats receiving the electric shock continued to prefer the flavored water over unflavored water, but they would not drink at all in the presence of the bright light or the clicking sound. The rats in one group associated nausea only with the flavored water; those in the other group associated electric shock only with the light and the sound.

Garcia and Koelling's research established two exceptions to traditional ideas of classical conditioning. First, the finding that rats formed an association between nausea and flavored water ingested several hours earlier contradicted the principle that the conditioned stimulus must be presented shortly before the unconditioned stimulus. Second, the finding that rats associated electric shock only with noise and light and nausea only with flavored water revealed that animals are apparently biologically predisposed to make certain associations and that associations cannot be readily conditioned between just any two stimuli.

Knowledge about conditioned taste aversion is useful in solving other problems as well. Bernstein and others (1982; Bernstein, 1985) devised a technique to help cancer patients avoid developing aversions to desirable foods. A group of cancer patients were given a novel-tasting, maple-flavored ice cream before chemotherapy. The nausea caused by the treatment resulted in a taste aversion to the ice cream. The researchers found that when an unusual or unfamiliar food becomes the "scapegoat," or target for a taste aversion, other foods in the patient's diet may be protected, and the patient will

5.5 How do biological predispositions affect classical conditioning?

biological predispositions Genetically programmed tendencies to acquire classically conditioned fear responses to potentially life-threatening stimuli.

taste aversion The intense dislike and/or avoidance of a particular food that has been associated with nausea or discomfort.

✳ Explore the Concept *Taste Aversion* on **MyPsychLab**

▲ Chemotherapy treatments can result in a conditioned taste aversion, but providing patients with a "scapegoat" target for the taste aversion can help them maintain a proper diet.

continue to eat them regularly. So, cancer patients should refrain from eating preferred or nutritious foods prior to chemotherapy. Instead, they should be given an unusual-tasting food shortly before treatment. As a result, they are less likely to develop aversions to foods they normally eat and, in turn, are more likely to maintain their body weight during treatment.

Classical Conditioning in Everyday Life

Do you suddenly experience hunger pangs when you smell fresh-baked chocolate chip cookies? Do you cringe in response to the sound of a dental drill? In either case, classical conditioning is the most likely explanation for your behavior. Your stomach rumbles when you smell fresh-baked cookies because smell and taste are so closely linked that food odors, functioning as conditioned stimuli, can actually make you think you are hungry even if you have just finished a large meal. Recall that we began our discussion of classical conditioning by saying that its principles can explain why diet sodas make some people hungry. This can happen because the distinctive flavors of foods can become conditioned stimuli for the digestive processes that typically follow them.

For instance, researchers have found that the pancreas quickly adapts to food cues through the process of classical conditioning (e.g., Stockhorst et al., 2004). Most of the time, the presence of a sweet taste on the tongue (a CS) is a reliable cue indicating that a rise in blood sugar (a UR) will soon occur. As a result, the pancreas "learns" to pump out insulin, the hormone that lowers blood sugar levels, whenever you eat or drink something sweet. A likely consequence of this adaptation is that the pancreas will respond to an artificial sweetener in the same way. Without the presence of real sugar to bring up the blood sugar level, however, the insulin will cause the blood sugar level to drop below normal. Whenever the blood sugar level drops below normal, the body signals the brain to motivate you to eat; in other words, you begin to feel hungry (more on this mechanism in Chapter 10). Over time, of course, the pancreas will probably learn to discriminate between the taste of artificially sweetened beverages and drinks that contain real sugar. The insulin response to artificial sweeteners will then become extinguished, while the link between the taste of sugared beverages and the insulin response will be maintained.

In Chapter 4, we discussed that learning plays an important role in psychological drug addiction. Through classical conditioning, environmental cues associated with drug use become conditioned stimuli and later produce the conditioned responses of drug craving (Epstein, Willner-Reid, & Preston, 2010). The conditioned stimuli associated with drugs become powerful, often irresistible forces that lead individuals to crave the pleasurable effects of those substances (Potenza et al., 2012). Consequently, drug counselors strongly urge recovering addicts to avoid any cues (people, places, and things) associated with their past drug use.

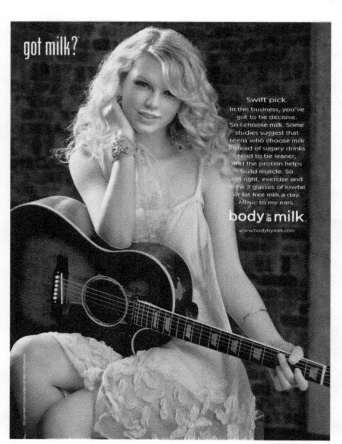

▲ Classical conditioning has proved to be a highly effective tool for advertisers. Here, a neutral product (milk) is paired with an image of an attractive celebrity. Can you identify the UCS, UCR, CS, and CR at work here?

The prevalence of classical conditioning in our everyday lives raises questions about the degree to which laboratory studies may or may not faithfully represent the process of classical conditioning. As noted earlier, laboratory learning typically requires a large number of trial pairings of conditioned and unconditioned stimuli, but many kinds of everyday conditioning (e.g., taste aversion) can happen after just one experience.

This and other differences have led experts in the field to hypothesize that a stimulus that has *ecological relevance* is more likely to function as a conditioned stimulus (Domjan, 2005). In other words, to serve as a conditioned stimulus, a neutral stimulus must have some authentic connection to the unconditioned stimulus in the real-world environment in which the organism lives (i.e., *eco*-is derived from the Greek word *oikos* meaning dwelling place). For example, real links exist among smells, tastes, and digestive processes. Likewise, a dental drill really can cause pain, and drugs do create altered states of consciousness. Compare these everyday conditioned stimuli to the arbitrary ones that Pavlov used—musical tones, buzzers, and the like. Research indicates that ecologically valid conditioned stimuli are acquired much more quickly than arbitrary stimuli and are also more resistant to extinction (Domjan, 2005).

REMEMBER IT   *Check your answers and take additional quizzes in MyPsychLab.com.*   ✓●─[Study and Review on MyPsychLab]

1. In Pavlov's famous experiment, the dog's salivation in response to a musical tone was a(n) _____ response.
2. The weakening of a conditioned response that occurs when a conditioned stimulus is presented without the unconditioned stimulus is called _____.
3. For _____ conditioning to occur, conditioned stimuli are linked together to form a series of signals.
4. Little Albert's fear of the white rat transferred to a rabbit, a dog, a fur coat, and a mask, in a learning process known as _____.
5. According to Rescorla, the most critical element in classical conditioning is _____.
6. Garcia and Koelling's research suggests that classical conditioning is influenced by _____.
7. Classical conditioning can suppress or boost the _____.

Operant Conditioning

Understanding the principles of classical conditioning can provide a great deal of insight into human behavior. But is there more to human learning than simply responding reflexively to stimuli? Think about a ringing telephone, for example. Do you respond to this stimulus because it has been paired with a natural stimulus of some kind or because of a consequence you anticipate when you hear it? The work of two psychologists, Edward L. Thorndike and B. F. Skinner, helps answer this question. ◉

Thorndike, Skinner, and the Consequences of Behavior ▶

Have you ever watched a dog learn how to turn over a trash can, or a cat learn how to open a door? If so, you probably observed the animal fail several times before finding just the right physical technique for accomplishing the goal. Based on his observations of animal behavior, Edward Thorndike (1874–1949) formulated several laws of learning, the most important being the law of effect (Thorndike, 1911/1970). The **law of effect** states that the consequence, or effect, of a response will determine whether the tendency to respond in the same way in the future will be strengthened or weakened. Responses closely followed by satisfying consequences are more likely to be repeated.

In Thorndike's best-known experiments, a hungry cat was placed in a wooden box with slats, which was called a *puzzle box*. The box was designed so that the animal had to manipulate a simple mechanism—pressing a pedal or pulling down a loop—to escape and claim a food reward that lay just outside the box. The cat would first try to squeeze through the slats; when these attempts failed, it would scratch, bite, and claw the inside of the box. In time, the cat would accidentally trip the mechanism, which would open the door. Each time, after winning freedom and claiming the food reward, the cat was returned to the box. After many trials, the cat learned to open the door almost immediately after being placed in the box.

Thorndike's law of effect was the conceptual starting point for B. F. Skinner's work in **operant conditioning**, the process through which consequences increase or decrease the frequency of a behavior. Skinner's research revealed that the process begins with an **operant**, or voluntary behavior, that accidentally brings about some kind of consequence. A consequence that increases the frequency of an operant is known as a **reinforcer**, while one that decreases an operant's frequency is called a **punisher**. We will examine both these processes later in the chapter.

5.7 What did Thorndike and Skinner discover about the consequences of behavior?

law of effect One of Thorndike's laws of learning, which states that the consequence, or effect, of a response will determine whether the tendency to respond in the same way in the future will be strengthened or weakened.

operant conditioning A type of learning in which the consequences of behavior are manipulated so as to increase or decrease the frequency of an existing response or to shape an entirely new response.

operant A voluntary behavior that accidentally brings about a consequence.

reinforcer Anything that follows a response and strengthens it or increases the probability that it will occur.

punisher Anything that follows a response and weakens it or decreases the probability that it will occur.

5.8 How do shaping, generalization, and discriminative stimuli influence operant conditioning?

shaping An operant conditioning technique that consists of gradually molding a desired behavior (response) by reinforcing any movement in the direction of the desired response, thereby gradually guiding the responses toward the ultimate goal.

Skinner box A soundproof chamber with a device for delivering food to an animal subject; used in operant conditioning experiments.

successive approximations A series of gradual steps, each of which is more similar to the final desired response.

extinction In operant conditioning, the weakening and eventual disappearance of the conditioned response as a result of the withholding of reinforcement.

generalization In operant conditioning, the tendency to make the learned response to a stimulus similar to that for which the response was originally reinforced.

▲ B. F. Skinner shapes a rat's bar-pressing behavior in a Skinner box.

The Process of Operant Conditioning

Have you ever attended a show that featured trained animals? Trainers use an operant conditioning technique called **shaping** in which animals learn their tricks in small steps rather than all at once. Moreover, like learning based on classical conditioning, behaviors acquired through operant conditioning can be altered in a variety of ways.

B. F. Skinner first demonstrated that shaping was particularly effective in training animals to exhibit complex behaviors. With shaping, rather than waiting for the desired response to occur and then reinforcing it, a researcher reinforces any movement in the direction of the desired response, thereby gradually guiding the responses toward the ultimate goal.

Skinner designed a soundproof apparatus, commonly called a **Skinner box**, with which he conducted his experiments in operant conditioning. One type of box is equipped with a lever, or bar, that a rat presses to gain a reward of food pellets or water from a dispenser. A record of the animal's bar pressing is registered on a device called a *cumulative recorder,* also invented by Skinner. Through the use of shaping, a rat in a Skinner box is conditioned to press a bar for rewards. It may be rewarded first for simply turning toward the bar. The next reward comes only when the rat moves closer to the bar. Each step closer to the bar is rewarded. Next, the rat must touch the bar to receive a reward; finally, it is rewarded only when it presses the bar.

Shaping—rewarding **successive approximations** of the desired response—has been used effectively to condition complex behaviors in people as well as other animals. Parents may use shaping to help their children develop good table manners, praising them each time they show an improvement. Teachers often use shaping with disruptive children, reinforcing them at first for very short periods of good behavior and then gradually expecting them to work productively for longer and longer periods. Through shaping, circus animals have earned to perform a wide range of amazing feats, and pigeons have learned to bowl and play Ping-Pong.

Of course, the motive of the shaper is very different from that of the person or animal whose behavior is being shaped. The shaper seeks to change another's behavior by controlling its consequences. The motive of the person or animal whose behavior is being shaped is to gain rewards or avoid unwanted consequences.

What happens when reinforcement is no longer available? In operant conditioning, **extinction** occurs when reinforcers are withheld. A rat in a Skinner box will eventually stop pressing a bar when it is no longer rewarded with food pellets.

In humans and other animals, the withholding of reinforcement can lead to frustration or even rage. Consider a child having a temper tantrum. If whining and loud demands do not bring the reinforcer, the child may progress to kicking and screaming. If a vending machine takes your coins but fails to deliver candy or soda, you might shake the machine or even kick it before giving up. When we don't get something we expect, it makes us angry.

The process of *spontaneous recovery,* which we discussed in relation to classical conditioning, also occurs in operant conditioning. A rat whose bar pressing has been extinguished may again press the bar a few times when it is returned to the Skinner box after a period of rest.

Skinner conducted many of his experiments with pigeons placed in a specially designed Skinner box. The box contained small illuminated disks that the pigeons could peck to receive bits of grain from a food tray. Skinner found that **generalization** occurs in operant conditioning, just as in classical conditioning. A pigeon reinforced for pecking at a yellow disk is likely to peck at another disk similar in color. The less similar a disk is to the original color, the lower the rate of pecking will be.

Discrimination in operant conditioning involves learning to distinguish between a stimulus that has been reinforced and other stimuli that may be very similar.

Discrimination develops when the response to the original stimulus is reinforced but responses to similar stimuli are not reinforced. For example, to encourage discrimination, a researcher would reinforce the pigeon for pecking at the yellow disk but not for pecking at the orange or red disk. Pigeons have even been conditioned to discriminate between a cubist-style Picasso painting and a Monet with 90% accuracy ("Psychologists' pigeons…," 1995).

Certain cues come to be associated with reinforcement or punishment. For example, children are more likely to ask their parents for a treat when the parents are smiling than when they are frowning. A stimulus that signals whether a certain response or behavior is likely to be rewarded, ignored, or punished is called a **discriminative stimulus**. If a pigeon's peck at a lighted disk results in a reward but a peck at an unlighted disk does not, the pigeon will soon be pecking exclusively at the lighted disk. The presence or absence of the discriminative stimulus—in this case, the lighted disk—will control whether the pecking takes place.

Why do children sometimes misbehave with a grandparent but not with a parent, or make one teacher's life miserable yet be model students for another? The children may have learned that in the presence of some people (the discriminative stimuli), their misbehavior will almost certainly lead to punishment, but in the presence of certain other people, it may even be rewarded.

Reinforcement ▶

How did you learn the correct sequence of behaviors involved in using an ATM? Simple—a single mistake in the sequence will prevent you from getting your money, so you learn to do it correctly. What about paying bills on time? Doesn't prompt payment allow you to avoid those steep late-payment penalties? In each case, your behavior is reinforced, but in a different way.

Positive and Negative Reinforcement. Reinforcement is a key concept in operant conditioning and may be defined as an increase in behavior that occurs as a result of a consequence. Another way to say this is that reinforcement involves learning or increasing the frequency of a behavior in order to make something happen. Reinforcement can be either positive or negative. These terms are used in their mathematical sense in operant conditioning. Thus, *positive* is equivalent to *added,* and *negative* is equivalent to *subtracted* or *removed.*

Combining two of the concepts you have just learned yields the definition of **positive reinforcement**: an increase in behavior that results from an added consequence. For instance, performing the correct sequence of behaviors at the ATM is the only way to obtain money. Thus, you are careful to get the sequence right (increased behavior) because doing so will cause the machine to dispense the money (added consequence) that you need. Here are a few more examples of positive reinforcement:

- Rat learns to press a lever (increased behavior) to obtain a food pellet (added consequence)
- College student studies more often (increased behavior) after getting an *A* on an exam for which she studied more than usual (added consequence)
- Person buys more lottery tickets (increased behavior) after hitting a $100 jackpot (added consequence)

You may have already predicted the definition of **negative reinforcement** because it follows logically from the definitions of its constituent terms (negative + reinforcement). It simply means an increase in behavior (reinforcement) that is brought about by the subtraction of something that is typically unpleasant. Stated differently, negative reinforcement involves learning or increasing a behavior in order to make something unpleasant go away. For instance, you take cough medicine (learned

5.9 How do positive and negative reinforcement affect behavior?

discriminative stimulus A stimulus that signals whether a certain response or behavior is likely to be rewarded, ignored, or punished.

reinforcement Any event that follows a response and strengthens or increases the probability that the response will be repeated.

positive reinforcement Any pleasant or desirable consequence that follows a response and increases the probability that the response will be repeated.

negative reinforcement The termination of an unpleasant condition after a response, which increases the probability that the response will be repeated.

behavior) to make your coughing go away (removed consequence). Here are a few more examples:

- Rat learns to press a lever (increased behavior) to turn off an annoying stimulus such as a loud buzzer (removed consequence)
- College student studies more often (increased behavior) in order to avoid getting another *F* on an exam (removed consequence)
- Individual calls his mother more often (increased behavior) in order to keep the mother from nagging him (removed consequence)

primary reinforcer A reinforcer that fulfills a basic physical need for survival and does not depend on learning.

secondary reinforcer A reinforcer that is acquired or learned through association with other reinforcers.

Primary and Secondary Reinforcers. Are all reinforcers created equal? Not necessarily. A **primary reinforcer** is one that fulfills a basic physical need for survival and does not depend on learning. Food, water, sleep, and termination of pain are examples of primary reinforcers and sex is a powerful reinforcer that fulfills a basic physical need for survival of the species. Fortunately, learning does not depend solely on primary reinforcers. If that were the case, people would need to be hungry, thirsty, or sex starved before they would respond at all. Much observed human behavior occurs in response to secondary reinforcers. A **secondary reinforcer** is acquired or learned through association with other reinforcers. Some secondary reinforcers (money, for example) can be exchanged at a later time for other reinforcers. Praise, good grades, awards, applause, attention, and signals of approval, such as a smile or a kind word, are all examples of secondary reinforcers.

5.10 What are the four types of schedules of reinforcement?

Schedules of Reinforcement

Think about the difference between an ATM and a slot machine. Under the right conditions, you can get money from either of them. But the ATM gives you a reinforcer every time you use the right procedure (*continuous reinforcement*), while the slot machine does so only intermittently (*partial reinforcement*). These two familiar machines use different **schedules of reinforcement**, or systematic processes for administering reinforcement.

The two basic types of schedules of reinforcement are ratio and interval schedules. Both the ATM and the slot machine use ratio schedules—that is, behavior brings about reinforcement. With interval schedules, a given amount of time must pass before a reinforcer is administered. Workers who get weekly paychecks are reinforced on an interval schedule. Ratio and interval schedules are further subdivided into fixed and variable categories (see Figure 5.6). Each kind of schedule has a different effect on behavior.

On a **fixed-ratio (FR) schedule**, a reinforcer is given after a fixed number of correct, nonreinforced responses. For example, if your favorite coffee bar offers a frequent buyer program in which you get a free cup of coffee for every 10 cups you buy, it is reinforcing you on a fixed ratio schedule. This schedule is a very effective way to maintain a high response rate because the number of reinforcers received depends directly on the response rate. The faster people or animals respond, the more reinforcers they earn and the sooner they earn them. When large ratios are used, people and animals tend to pause after each reinforcement but then return to the high rate of responding.

Intermittent reinforcement is characteristic of a **variable-ratio (VR) schedule** in which a reinforcer is provided after a varying number of nonreinforced responses. For instance, suppose your favorite coffee bar offers you a chance to participate in a drawing each time you purchase a drink. You draw a card out of a jar that contains dozens of cards, 1 in 10 of which says "Get a free coffee next time you visit" and 9 in 10 of which say "Sorry. Try again next time." The coffee bar is using a variable-ratio schedule of reinforcement. This kind of schedule takes longer to produce learning than a fixed-ratio schedule does. However, once learned, behaviors that are acquired through variable reinforcement are highly resistant to

▲ Recall that negative reinforcement involves learning a behavior in order to make something unpleasant go away. For many students, studying with classmates (learned behavior) reduces test anxiety (removed consequence). Thus, for these students, test anxiety is an important source of negative reinforcement, one that encourages them to engage in effective study behaviors.

schedule of reinforcement A systematic process for administering reinforcement.

fixed-ratio (FR) schedule A schedule in which a reinforcer is given after a fixed number of correct, nonreinforced responses.

variable-ratio (VR) schedule A schedule in which a reinforcer is given after a varying number of non-reinforced responses, based on an average ratio.

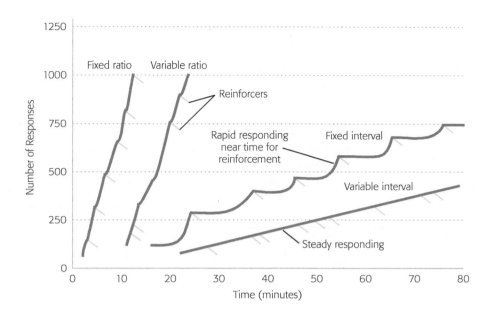

FIGURE 5.6 Four Types of Reinforcement Schedules
Skinner's research revealed distinctive response patterns for four reinforcement schedules (the reinforcers are indicated by the diagonal marks). The ratio schedules, based on the number of responses, yielded a higher response rate than the interval schedules, which are based on the amount of time elapsed between reinforcers.

extinction. This is known as the **partial reinforcement effect**. For instance, how many times have you sat down at your computer to work on a research paper and found yourself still playing solitaire or some other PC game hours later? Many other enjoyable leisure pursuits—hunting, fishing, channel surfing, and even shopping for bargains—involve variable schedules of reinforcement and are often difficult to break away from. In fact, when you set your MP3 player to "shuffle," you are creating a variable ratio schedule in which the songs you like most are serving as unpredictable reinforcers that maintain the behavior of listening to music. Likewise, video games involve the partial reinforcement effect because players don't succeed every time they play. Finally, slot machines and other forms of gambling employ a variable-ratio reinforcement schedule. For some gamblers, the partial reinforcement produces a self-destructive behavior pattern (i.e., *compulsive gambling*, a pattern of behavior in which a person continues to gamble even when doing so seriously damages him financially, academically, professionally, and socially) that requires professional help to overcome.

On a **fixed-interval (FI) schedule**, a specific period of time must pass before a response is reinforced. For example, a teacher who gives weekly exams is reinforcing the behavior of studying on a fixed-interval schedule. Characteristic of the fixed-interval schedule is a pause or a sharp decline in responding immediately after each reinforcement and a rapid acceleration in responding just before the next reinforcer is due (the "scalloping" effect). In other words, with weekly exams, students are likely to slack off for a few days after each exam and study intensely the day before the next test.

Variable-interval schedules eliminate the pause after reinforcement typical of the fixed-interval schedule. On a **variable-interval (VI) schedule**, a reinforcer is given after the first correct response following a varying time of nonreinforced responses. For instance, a teacher who gives pop quizzes at unpredictable intervals is reinforcing studying on a variable-interval schedule. This schedule maintains remarkably stable and uniform rates of responding, but the response rate is typically lower than that for ratio schedules because reinforcement is not tied directly to the number of responses made. Thus, pop quizzes are more likely to influence students to study continuously than weekly exams are. ◉

The *Summarize It* on p. 158 will help you review the characteristics of the four schedules of reinforcement.

▲ Two examples of variable-ratio schedules of reinforcement: Gamblers can't predict when the payoff (reinforcement) will come, so they are highly motivated to keep playing. Likewise, many computer users find themselves in the predicament of knowing they should stop playing solitaire and get to work, but they just can't seem to tear themselves away from the game. Why? The power of variable-ratio reinforcement motivates them to stick with the game until the next win, and the next, and the next. . . .

partial reinforcement effect The typical outcome of a variable ratio of reinforcement in which a slow rate of initial learning is coupled with resistance to extinction.

fixed-interval (FI) schedule A schedule in which a reinforcer is given following the first correct response after a specific period of time has elapsed.

variable-interval (VI) schedule A schedule in which a reinforcer is given after the first correct response that follows a varying time of nonreinforcement, based on an average time.

◉ **Watch** the Video *Episode 7: Basics: Operant Conditioning: Learning From Consequences* in **MyPsychLab**

SUMMARIZE IT

Reinforcement Schedules Compared

SCHEDULE OF REINFORCEMENT	RESPONSE RATE	PATTERN OF RESPONSES	RESISTANCE TO EXTINCTION
RATIO			
Fixed-ratio (FR) schedule	Very high	Steady response with low ratio. Brief pause after each reinforcement with very high ratio.	The higher the ratio, the more resistance to extinction.
Variable-ratio (VR) schedule	Highest response rate	Constant response pattern, no pauses.	Most resistance to extinction.
INTERVAL			
Fixed-interval (FI) schedule	Lowest response rate	Long pause after reinforcement, followed by gradual acceleration.	The longer the interval, the more resistance to extinction.
Variable-interval (VI) schedule	Moderate	Stable, uniform response.	More resistance to extinction than fixed-interval schedule with same average interval.

5.11 How does punishment affect behavior?

punishment The removal of a pleasant stimulus or the application of an unpleasant stimulus, thereby lowering the probability of a response.

positive punishment A decrease in behavior that results from an added consequence.

negative punishment A decrease in behavior that results from a removed consequence.

Punishment

You may be wondering about one of the most common types of consequences, punishment. **Punishment** is the opposite of reinforcement. Thus, it is a decrease in the frequency of a behavior that follows some kind of consequence.

Positive and Negative Punishment. Like reinforcement, punishment can involve either positive (added) or negative (removed) consequences. In **positive punishment** behavior decreases after the addition of a consequence, usually an unpleasant one. For example, a driver avoids taking a particular route (decreased behavior) because it has caused him to become bogged down in traffic jams in the past (added consequence). Here are a few more examples:

- Rat stops pressing a lever (decreased behavior) when doing so causes a loud, annoying buzzing sound (added consequence)
- Student stops staying up late (decreased behavior) after sleeping through an important exam (added consequence)

Students sometimes confuse negative reinforcement and positive punishment because both involve unpleasant stimuli. However, negative reinforcement increases behavior, whereas positive punishment decreases the behavior that it follows. The simplest examples are those that happen in the context of laboratory experiments. In a negative reinforcement experiment, a rat might be put into a cage with an electrical current running through its metal floor, causing an unpleasant sensation on the rat's feet. By pressing a lever, the rat can turn off the current. After some trial and error, the rat stands on his hind legs and uses his front paws to keep the lever in the depressed position, thus eliminating the electric shocks. His lever-pressing behavior has increased (reinforcement) as a result of the removal of the unpleasant shock sensation.

In a positive punishment experiment, the lever would turn on the electricity instead of turning it off. As a result, the rat would learn to not press the lever (a decrease in behavior) because he gets a shock when he does so.

Negative punishment happens when a behavior decreases after the removal of a consequence. The consequence usually involves the loss of something desirable. For example, a driver who speeds less often (decreased behavior) after suffering through a 6-month suspension of his license (removed consequence) has experienced negative punishment. Here are a few more examples:

- Rat stops pressing a lever (decreased behavior) when doing so causes a dish of food to disappear from his cage (removed consequence)
- Teenager stops coming home late (decreased behavior) after parents take away her going-out privileges for two weeks (removed consequence)

Table 5.1 includes definitions and examples for positive reinforcement, negative reinforcement, positive punishment, and negative punishment.

The Disadvantages of Punishment. If punishment can suppress behavior, why do so many people oppose its use? A number of potential problems are associated with the use of punishment:

1. According to Skinner, punishment does not extinguish an undesirable behavior; rather, it suppresses that behavior when the punishing agent is present. But the behavior is apt to continue when the threat of punishment is removed or in settings where punishment is unlikely. If punishment (imprisonment, fines, and so on) reliably extinguished unlawful behavior, there would be fewer repeat offenders in the criminal justice system.

2. Punishment indicates that a behavior is unacceptable but does not help people develop more appropriate behaviors. If punishment is used, it should be administered in conjunction with reinforcement or rewards for appropriate behavior.

3. The person who is severely punished often becomes fearful and feels angry and hostile toward the punisher. These reactions may be accompanied by a desire to retaliate or to avoid or escape from the punisher and the punishing situation. Many runaway teenagers leave home to escape physical abuse. Punishment that involves a loss of privileges is more effective than physical punishment and engenders less fear and hostility (Fasotti, 2003).

4. Punishment frequently leads to aggression. Those who administer physical punishment, such as spanking, may become models of aggressive behavior, by demonstrating aggression as a way of solving problems and discharging anger. Children of abusive, punishing parents are at greater risk than other children of becoming aggressive and abusive themselves (Boutwell, Franklin, Barnes, & Beaver, 2011).

If punishment can cause these problems, what can be done to discourage undesirable behavior? 👁

Watch the Video *Episode 7: Thinking Like a Psychologist: Physical Punishment—You Decide!* in **MyPsychLab**

Alternatives to Punishment. Are there other ways to suppress behavior? Many psychologists believe that removing the rewarding consequences of undesirable behavior is the best way to extinguish a problem behavior. According to this view, parents should extinguish a child's temper tantrums not by punishment but by never giving in to the child's demands during a tantrum. A parent might best extinguish problem behavior that is performed merely to get attention by ignoring it and giving attention

TABLE 5.1 The Effects of Reinforcement and Punishment

REINFORCEMENT (INCREASES OR STRENGTHENS A BEHAVIOR)	PUNISHMENT (DECREASES OR SUPRESSES A BEHAVIOR)
Adding a pleasant stimulus (positive reinforcement)	**Adding an aversive stimulus (positive punishment)**
Presenting food, money, praise, attention, or other rewards.	Delivering a pain-producing or otherwise aversive stimulus, such as a spanking or an electric shock.
Subtracting an aversive stimulus (negative reinforcement)	**Subtracting a pleasant stimulus (negative punishment)**
Removing or terminating some pain-producing or otherwise aversive stimulus, such as an electric shock.	Removing some pleasant stimulus or taking away privileges, such as TV watching, use of automobile.

to more appropriate behavior. Sometimes, simply explaining why a certain behavior is not appropriate is all that is required to extinguish the behavior.

Using positive reinforcement such as praise will make good behavior more rewarding for children. This approach brings with it the attention that children want and need—attention that often comes only when they misbehave.

It is probably unrealistic to believe that punishment will ever become unnecessary. If a young child runs into the street, puts a finger near an electrical outlet, or reaches for a hot pan on the stove, a swift punishment may save the child from a potentially disastrous situation.

Making Punishment More Effective. When punishment is necessary (e.g., to stop destructive behavior), how can we be sure that it will be effective? Research has revealed several factors that influence the effectiveness of punishment: its timing, its intensity, and the consistency of its application (Parke, 1977):

1. Punishment is most effective when it is applied during the misbehavior or as soon afterward as possible. Interrupting the problem behavior is most effective because doing so abruptly halts its rewarding aspects. The longer the delay between the response and the punishment, the less effective the punishment is in suppressing the response (Camp, Raymond, & Church, 1967). When there is a delay, most animals do not make the connection between the misbehavior and the punishment. For example, anyone who has tried to housebreak a puppy knows that it is necessary to catch the animal in the act of soiling the carpet for the punishment to be effective. With humans, however, if the punishment must be delayed, the punisher should remind the perpetrator of the incident and explain why the behavior was inappropriate.

2. Ideally, punishment should be of the minimum severity necessary to suppress the problem behavior. Animal studies reveal that the more intense the punishment, the greater the suppression of the undesirable behavior (Church, 1963). But the intensity of the punishment should match the seriousness of the misdeed. Unnecessarily severe punishment is likely to produce the negative side effects mentioned earlier. The purpose of punishment is not to vent anger but, rather, to modify behavior. Punishment meted out in anger is likely to be more intense than necessary to bring about the desired result. Yet, if the punishment is too mild, it will have no effect. Similarly, gradually increasing the intensity of the punishment is not effective because the perpetrator will gradually adapt, and the unwanted behavior will persist (Azrin & Holz, 1966). At a minimum, if a behavior is to be suppressed, the punishment must be more punishing than the misbehavior is rewarding. In human terms, a $200 ticket is more likely to suppress the urge to speed than a $2 ticket. On the other hand, the perceived injustice associated with receiving a $500 ticket for a minor speeding offense such as driving 50 miles an hour on a 45-mile-per-hour zone might incite defiance.

3. To be effective, punishment must be applied consistently. A parent cannot ignore misbehavior one day and punish the same act the next. And both parents should react to the same misbehavior in the same way. An undesired response will be suppressed more effectively when the probability of punishment is high. Would you be tempted to speed if you saw a police car in your rearview mirror?

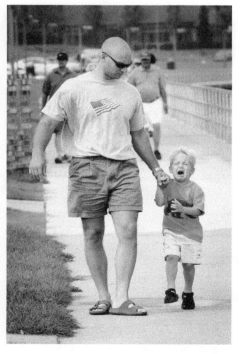

▲ What strategies other than punishment might a parent use to get this child to behave more appropriately?

Culture and Punishment. Do you think stoning is an appropriate punishment for adultery? Probably not, unless you come from a culture in which such punishments are acceptable. Punishment is used in every culture to control and suppress people's behavior. It is administered when important values, rules, regulations, and laws are violated. But not all cultures share the same values or have the same laws regulating behavior. U.S. citizens traveling in other countries need to be aware of how different cultures view and administer punishment. For example, selling drugs is a serious crime just about everywhere. In the United States, it carries mandatory prison time; in some other countries, it is a death penalty offense. Similarly, desecration of religious objects in the United States is offensive to many and may result in social punishment in the form of verbal expressions of disapproval. However, legally speaking, it falls within the boundaries of free expression. By contrast, in some other nations, portraying religious objects in an irreverent way or defacing a written work that is deemed to be sacred can result in imprisonment or even capital punishment. Likewise, people in the U.S. can be jailed for assaulting an intimate partner, while such behavior is not regarded as a legal matter in some other societies.

Escape and Avoidance Learning

5.12 How do escape and avoidance learning occur?

Do you pay bills on time to avoid late fees? Learning to perform a behavior because it prevents or terminates an aversive event is called **escape learning**, and it reflects the power of negative reinforcement. Running away from a punishing situation and taking aspirin to relieve a pounding headache are examples of escape behavior. In these situations, the aversive event has begun, and an attempt is being made to escape it.

Avoidance learning, in contrast, depends on two types of conditioning. Through classical conditioning, an event or condition comes to signal an aversive state. Drinking and driving may be associated with automobile accidents and death. Because of such associations, people may engage in behaviors to avoid the anticipated aversive consequences. Making it a practice to avoid riding in a car with a driver who has been drinking is sensible avoidance behavior.

Much avoidance learning is maladaptive, however, and occurs in response to phobias. Students who have had a bad experience speaking in front of a class may begin to fear any situation that involves speaking before a group. Such students may avoid taking courses that require class presentations or taking leadership roles that necessitate public speaking. Avoiding such situations prevents them from suffering the perceived dreaded consequences. But the avoidance behavior is negatively reinforced and thus strengthened through operant conditioning. It is negatively reinforced because it enables the person to avoid or terminate an undesirable stimulus.

Likewise, procrastination is a maladaptive avoidance behavior that plagues many students. The behavior patterns that contribute to procrastination are negatively reinforced because they enable students to avoid the confusion, anxiety, and boredom they experience while studying. While maladaptive behavior patterns of this sort are difficult to extinguish, they can be overcome. The *Apply It* on page 162 feature contains a number of useful tips for overcoming procrastination.

There is an important exception to the ability of humans and other animals to learn to escape and avoid aversive situations: **Learned helplessness** is a passive resignation to aversive conditions, learned by repeated exposure to aversive events that are inescapable or unavoidable. The initial experiment on learned helplessness was conducted by Overmeier and Seligman (1967). Dogs in the experimental group were strapped into harnesses from which they could not escape and were exposed to electric shocks. Later, these same dogs were placed in a box with two compartments separated by a low barrier. The dogs then experienced a series of trials in which a warning signal was followed by an electric shock administered through the box's floor. However, the floor was electrified only on one side, and the dogs could have escaped the electric shocks simply by jumping the barrier. Surprisingly, the dogs did not do so. Dogs in the control group had not previously experienced the inescapable shock and behaved in an entirely different manner and quickly learned to jump the barrier when the warning signal sounded and thus escaped the shock. Seligman (1975) later reasoned that humans who have suffered painful experiences they could neither avoid nor escape may also experience learned helplessness. For example, children who fail repeatedly in school may stop doing their school work because they believe that it is impossible for them to succeed. Similarly, people who are abused by their intimate partners may adopt the view that they deserve such treatment and submit to their partners' aggressive behavior. As a result, says Seligman, such people become inactive, withdrawn, and depressed (Seligman, 1991).

escape learning Learning to perform a behavior because it prevents or terminates an aversive stimulus.

avoidance learning Learning to avoid events or conditions associated with aversive consequences or phobias.

learned helplessness A passive resignation to aversive conditions that is learned through repeated exposure to inescapable or unavoidable aversive events.

APPLY IT | How to Win the Battle against Procrastination

Have you often thought that you could get better grades if only you had more time? Do you often find yourself studying for an exam or completing a term paper at the last minute? If so, it makes sense for you to learn how to overcome the greatest time waster of all—procrastination. Research indicates that academic procrastination arises partly out of a lack of confidence in one's ability to meet expectations (Levrini & Prevatt, 2012; Wolters, 2003). Other studies suggest that a preference for short-term over long-term gratification is sometimes to blame (Knipe, 2010). In other words, when students procrastinate, they may be choosing the immediate pleasures of activities such as watching television or chatting with friends over the sense of satisfaction that they will experience in the future by meeting academic goals. Once procrastination has become established as a behavior pattern, it often persists for years (Lee, Kelly, & Edwards, 2006). Nevertheless, anyone can overcome procrastination, and gain self-confidence in the process, by using behavior modification techniques. Systematically apply the following suggestions to keep procrastination from interfering with your studying:

- *Identify the environmental cues that habitually interfere with your studying.* Television, computer or video games, and even food can be powerful distractors that consume hours of valuable study time. However, these distractors can be useful positive reinforcers to enjoy after you've finished studying.

- *Schedule your study time and reinforce yourself for adhering to your schedule.* Once you've scheduled it, be just as faithful to your schedule as you would be to a work schedule set by an employer. And be sure to schedule something you enjoy to immediately follow the study time.

- *Get started.* The most difficult part is getting started. Give yourself an extra reward for starting on time and, perhaps, a penalty for starting late.

- *Use visualization.* Much procrastination results from the failure to consider its negative consequences. Visualizing the consequences of not studying, such as trying to get through an exam you haven't adequately prepared for, can be an effective tool for combating procrastination.

- *Beware of jumping to another task when you reach a difficult part of an assignment.* This procrastination tactic gives you the feeling that you are busy and accomplishing something, but it is, nevertheless, an avoidance mechanism.

- *Beware of preparation overkill.* Procrastinators may actually spend hours preparing for a task rather than working on the task itself. For example, they may gather enough library materials to write a book rather than a five-page term paper. This enables them to postpone writing the paper.

- *Keep a record of the reasons you give yourself for postponing studying or completing important assignments.* If a favorite rationalization is "I'll wait until I'm in the mood to do this," count the number of times in a week you are seized with the desire to study. The mood to study typically arrives after you begin, not before.

Don't procrastinate! Begin now! Apply the steps outlined here to gain more control over your behavior and win the battle against procrastination.

5.13 What are some applications of operant conditioning?

Applications of Operant Conditioning

You have probably realized that operant conditioning is an important learning process that we experience almost every day. Operant conditioning can also be used intentionally by one person to change another person's behavior.

Can you train yourself to control your body's responses to stress? For years, scientists believed that internal responses such as heart rate, brain-wave patterns, and blood flow were not subject to operant conditioning. It is now known that when people are given very precise feedback about these internal processes, they can learn, with practice, to exercise control over them. **Biofeedback** is a way of getting information about internal biological states. Biofeedback devices have sensors that monitor slight changes in these internal responses and then amplify and convert them into visual or auditory signals. Thus, people can see or hear evidence of internal physiological processes, and by trying out various strategies (thoughts, feelings, or images), they can learn which ones routinely increase, decrease, or maintain a particular level of activity.

biofeedback The use of sensitive equipment to give people precise feedback about internal physiological processes so that they can learn, with practice, to exercise control over them.

Biofeedback has been used to regulate heart rate and to control migraine and tension headaches, gastrointestinal disorders, asthma, anxiety tension states, epilepsy, sexual dysfunctions, and neuromuscular disorders such as cerebral palsy, spinal cord injuries, and stroke (Gauchet et al., 2012).

Can operant conditioning help you get better grades? Perhaps, if you apply its principles to your study behavior. **Behavior modification** is a method of changing behavior through a systematic program based on the learning principles of classical conditioning, operant conditioning, or observational learning (which we will discuss soon). The majority of behavior modification programs use the principles of operant conditioning. The *Try It* next challenges you to create your own behavior modification plan.

behavior modification A method of changing behavior through a systematic program based on the learning principles of classical conditioning, operant conditioning, or observational learning.

TRY IT   **Using Behavior Modification**

Use conditioning to modify your own behavior.

1. *Identify the target behavior.* It must be both observable and measurable. You might choose, for example, to increase the amount of time you spend studying.
2. *Gather and record baseline data.* Keep a daily record of how much time you spend on the target behavior for about a week. Also note where the behavior takes place and what cues (or temptations) in the environment precede any slacking off from the target behavior.
3. *Plan your behavior modification program.* Formulate a plan and set goals to either decrease or increase the target behavior.
4. *Choose your reinforcers.* Any activity you enjoy more can be used to reinforce any activity you enjoy less. For example, you could reward yourself with a movie after a specified period of studying.
5. *Set the reinforcement conditions and begin recording and reinforcing your progress.* Be careful not to set your reinforcement goals so high that it

becomes nearly impossible to earn a reward. Keep in mind Skinner's concept of shaping through rewarding small steps toward the desired outcome. Be perfectly honest with yourself and claim a reward only when you meet the goals. Chart your progress as you work toward gaining more control over the target behavior.

◉ Watch on **MyPsychLab**

Behavior modification programs have been used to change self-injurious behavior in autistic children and adults. Such programs are highly individualized and are frequently studied in a "one-subject" design, meaning that the study includes only one participant. One such study was designed to address a common problem among adults with autism and their caretakers (Beare et al., 2004). Adults with autism frequently reside in group homes and are employed in modified work settings. However, self-injurious behaviors can disturb these individuals' co-workers and supervisors, interfere with the performance of their duties, and cause them to lose their jobs. In the study, researchers successfully used behavior modification to stop a 41-year-old man with autism from exhibiting such behavior in his workplace, thereby enabling him to keep his job. ◉

Some institutions, such as schools, mental hospitals, and prisons, use a **token economy**—a program that motivates socially desirable behavior by reinforcing it with tokens. The tokens (poker chips or coupons) may later be exchanged for desired items such as candy and privileges such as free time or participation in desired activities. People in the program know in advance exactly what behaviors will be reinforced and how they will be reinforced. Token economies have been used effectively in mental hospitals to encourage patients to attend to grooming, to interact with other patients, and to carry out housekeeping tasks (Swartz et al., 2012). Prisons also sometimes use token economies to encourage prosocial behavior among inmates (Seegert, 2004). Even schoolchildren's behavior can be modified with a well-designed token economy that is based on age-appropriate statements of desired behavior (Reitman et al., 2004). For example, a statement such as "raise your hand and wait for permission from the teacher before you speak" is appropriate for even the youngest elementary school students and can be encouraged through the implementation of a token economy. Although the positive behaviors generally stop when the tokens are discontinued, this does not mean that the programs are not worthwhile. After all, most people who are employed would probably quit their jobs if they were no longer paid.

Many classroom teachers and parents use *time out*—a behavior modification technique in which a child who is misbehaving is removed for a short time from sources of positive reinforcement. (Remember, according to operant conditioning, a behavior that is no longer reinforced will extinguish.)

◉ Watch the Video *Episode 7: What's in It for Me? How to Make Healthier Choices* in **MyPsychLab**

token economy A program that motivates socially desirable behavior by reinforcing it with tokens that can be exchanged for desired items or privileges.

▲ With biofeedback devices, people can see or hear evidence of internal physiological states and learn how to control them through various mental strategies.

Behavior modification is also used successfully in business and industry to increase profits and to modify employee behavior related to health, safety, and job performance (Hickman & Geller, 2003). To keep their premiums low, some companies give annual rebates to employees who do not use up the deductibles in their health insurance plan. To reduce costs associated with automobile accidents and auto theft, insurance companies offer incentives in the form of reduced premiums for installing airbags and burglar alarm systems. To encourage employees to take company-approved college courses, some companies offer tuition reimbursement to employees who complete such courses with acceptable grades. Many companies promote sales by giving salespeople bonuses, trips, and other prizes for increasing sales.

The *Summarize It* table lists the principles of classical and operant conditioning.

SUMMARIZE IT

Classical and Operant Conditioning Compared

CHARACTERISTICS	CLASSICAL CONDITIONING	OPERANT CONDITIONING
Type of association	Between two stimuli	Between a response and its consequence
State of subject	Passive	Active
Focus of attention	On what precedes response	On what follows response
Type of response typically involved	Involuntary or reflexive response	Voluntary response
Bodily response typically involved	Internal responses; emotional and glandular reactions	External responses; muscular and skeletal movement and verbal responses
Range of responses	Relatively simple	Simple to highly complex
Responses learned	Emotional reactions; fears, likes, dislikes	Goal-oriented responses

REMEMBER IT   *Check your answers and take additional quizzes in MyPsychLab.com.*   ✓● Study and Review on MyPsychLab

1. The process of reinforcing successive approximations of a behavior is known as _____.

2. When reinforcers are withheld, _____ of a response occurs.

3. Taking a pain reliever to relieve a headache is an example of _____ reinforcement; studying to get a good grade on a test is an example of _____ reinforcement.

4. Glen and Megan are hired to do laundry. Glen receives $5 for each load of laundry he does; Megan is paid $5 per hour. Glen is paid according to a(n) _____ schedule; Megan is paid according to a(n) _____ schedule.

5. Negative reinforcement _____ behavior, while punishment _____ behavior.

6. Victims of intimate partner abuse who have repeatedly failed to escape or avoid the abuse may eventually passively resign themselves to it, a condition known as _____.

7. The use of sensitive electronic equipment to monitor physiological processes in order to bring them under conscious control is called _____.

8. Applying learning principles to eliminate undesirable behavior and/or encourage desirable behavior is called _____.

Cognitive Learning

By now, you are probably convinced of the effectiveness of both classical and operant conditioning. But can either type of conditioning explain how you learned a complex mental function like reading? Behaviorists such as Skinner and Watson believed that any kind of learning could be explained without reference to internal mental processes. Today, however, a growing number of psychologists stress the role of mental processes. They choose to broaden the study of learning to include such **cognitive processes** as thinking, knowing, problem solving, remembering, and forming mental representations. According to cognitive theorists, understanding these processes is critically important to a more complete, more comprehensive view of learning. We will consider the work of three important researchers in the field of cognitive learning: Wolfgang Köhler, Edward Tolman, and Albert Bandura.

Learning by Insight ▶

Have you ever been worried about a problem, only to have a crystal clear solution suddenly pop into your mind? If so, you experienced an important kind of cognitive learning first described by Wolfgang Köhler (1887–1967). In his book *The Mentality of Apes* (1925), Köhler described experiments he conducted on chimpanzees confined in caged areas. In one experiment, Köhler hung a bunch of bananas inside the caged area but overhead, out of reach of the chimps; boxes and sticks were left around the cage. Köhler observed the chimps' unsuccessful attempts to reach the bananas by jumping up or swinging sticks at them. Eventually, the chimps solved the problem by piling the boxes on top of one another and climbing on the boxes until they could reach the bananas.

Köhler observed that the chimps sometimes appeared to give up in their attempts to get the bananas. However, after an interval, they returned with the solution to the problem, as if it had come to them in a flash of **insight**. They seemed to have suddenly realized the relationship between the sticks or boxes and the bananas. Köhler insisted that insight, rather than trial-and-error learning, accounted for the chimps' successes, because they could easily repeat the solution and transfer this learning to similar problems. In human terms, a solution gained through insight is more easily learned, less likely to be forgotten, and more readily transferred to new problems than a solution learned through rote memorization (Rock & Palmer, 1990). For example, while plodding through a series of similar math problems, many students have an "aha!" experience in which they suddenly "get" the procedure for solving the problems and, as a result, work through the remaining problems more quickly and with fewer errors. Brain-imaging studies indicate that insight learning is associated with a unique pattern of interaction involving several different brain areas (Jing, 2004).

Latent Learning and Cognitive Maps ▶

Like Köhler, Edward Tolman (1886–1959) held views that differed from the prevailing ideas on learning. First, Tolman (1932) believed that learning could take place without reinforcement. Second, he differentiated between learning and performance. He maintained that **latent learning** could occur; that is, learning could occur without apparent reinforcement and not be demonstrated until the organism was motivated to do so. A classic experimental study by Tolman and Honzik (1930) supports this position. ⊚➤

Three groups of rats were placed in a maze daily for 17 days. The first group always received a food reward at the end of the maze. The second group never received a reward, and the third group did not receive a food reward until the 11th day. The first group showed a steady improvement in performance over the 17-day period. The second group showed slight, gradual improvement. The third group, after being rewarded on the 11th day, showed a marked improvement the next day and, from then on, outperformed the rats that had been rewarded daily (see Figure 5.7, p. 166). The rapid improvement of the third group indicated to Tolman that latent learning had occurred—that the rats had actually learned the maze during the first 11 days but were not motivated to display this learning until they were rewarded for it. Tolman concluded that the rats had learned to form a **cognitive map**, a mental representation or picture, of the maze but had not demonstrated their learning until they were reinforced. In later studies, Tolman showed how rats quickly learn to rearrange their established cognitive maps and readily find their way through increasingly complex mazes.

cognitive processes (COG-nih-tiv) Mental processes such as thinking, knowing, problem solving, remembering, and forming mental representations.

> **5.14** How does insight affect learning?

insight The sudden realization of the relationship between elements in a problem situation, which makes the solution apparent.

> **5.15** What did Tolman discover about the necessity of reinforcement?

latent learning Learning that occurs without apparent reinforcement and is not demonstrated until the organism is motivated to do so.

⊚➤ **Simulate** the **Experiment** *Latent Learning* on **MyPsychLab**

cognitive map A mental representation of a spatial arrangement such as a maze.

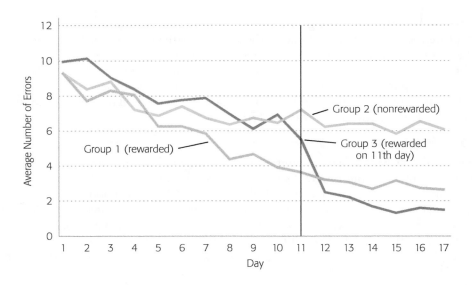

FIGURE 5.7 **Latent Learning**
Rats in Group 1 were rewarded every day for running the maze correctly, while rats in Group 2 were never rewarded. Group 3 rats were rewarded only on the 11th day and thereafter outperformed the rats in Group 1. The rats had "learned" the maze but were not motivated to perform until rewarded, demonstrating that latent learning had occurred.
Source: From Tolman & Honzik (1930).

5.16 How do we learn by observing others?

observational learning (social-cognitive learning) Learning by observing the behavior of others and the consequences of that behavior; learning by imitation.

model The individual who demonstrates a behavior or whose behavior is imitated.

✳ Explore the Concept *Bandura's Study on Observational Learning* on **MyPsychLab**

Observational Learning

Have you ever wondered why you slow down when you see another driver getting a speeding ticket? In all likelihood, no one has ever reinforced you for slowing down under these conditions, so why do you do it? Psychologist Albert Bandura (1986) contends that many behaviors or responses are acquired through observational learning, or *social-cognitive learning*. **Observational learning** results when people observe the behavior of others and note the consequences of that behavior. Thus, you slow down when you see another driver getting a ticket because you assume that person's consequence will also be your consequence. The same process is involved when we see another person get a free soft drink by hitting the side of a vending machine. We assume that if we hit the machine, we will also get a free drink.

A person who demonstrates a behavior or whose behavior is imitated is called a **model**. Parents, movie stars, and sports personalities are often powerful models for children. The effectiveness of a model is related to his or her status, competence, and power. Other important factors are the age, sex, attractiveness, and ethnicity of the model. Moreover, observers' own characteristics influence the degree to which they learn from models. For instance, women who are dissatisfied with their appearance pay more attention to and are more likely to try to emulate physically attractive models than women who are satisfied with the way they look. ✳

Whether learned behavior is actually performed depends largely on whether the observed models are rewarded or punished for their behavior and whether the observer expects to be rewarded for the behavior (Bandura, 1969, 1977). Note, too, that a model doesn't have to be a person. For instance, Bandura would agree that the instructions in Chapter 1 that show you how to use the SQ3R method to study this textbook constitute an important kind of model, as do the diagrams that accompany "ready-to-assemble" furniture.

As you may have learned in math, chemistry, and physics classes, or in other subjects in which teachers use modeling to teach students how to solve problems, simply watching a model does not necessarily result in learning. Bandura proposed that four processes determine whether observational learning will occur:

■ *Attention:* The observer must attend to the model.

■ *Retention:* The observer must store information about the model's behavior in memory.

■ *Reproduction:* The observer must be physically and cognitively capable of performing the behavior to learn it. In other words, no matter how much time you devote to watching Serena Williams play tennis or listening to Beyoncé sing, you won't be able to acquire skills like theirs unless you possess talents that are equal to theirs. Likewise, it is doubtful that a kindergartener will learn geometry from watching her high-school-age sister do her homework.

■ *Reinforcement:* Ultimately, to exhibit a behavior learned through observation, an observer must be motivated to practice and perform the behavior on his own.

Just as there are factors that determine whether an observer will learn from a model, there are varying types of learning that involve models and observers. These different types of learning are called *effects* because they represent the different ways in which models affect the behavior of observers. See whether you can determine which of these effects is involved in the examples of observational learning we have given so far:

■ *Modeling:* The **modeling effect** involves learning a new behavior.

■ *Facilitation:* In the **facilitation effect**, an observer learns a behavior that is similar to that of a model in an unfamiliar situation.

■ *Inhibition:* The tendency of observers to suppress socially unacceptable behaviors for which they see models punished is the **inhibitory effect**.

■ *Disinhibition:* When observers see models get away with or be rewarded for exhibiting socially unacceptable behavior, the **disinhibitory effect** can occur.

Here is how our examples would be classified. The modeling effect is in evidence when you successfully learn how to solve a math problem from a teacher's demonstration. When you watch gifted athletes and artists perform and try to imitate them, you are demonstrating the facilitation effect. Slowing down when you see a fellow motorist getting a speeding ticket is an example of the inhibitory effect. Spending your time at work surfing the Internet because you have seen your co-workers do so without getting caught represents the disinhibitory effect.

The *Summarize It* table reviews the principles of cognitive learning that we have discussed in this section. Now that you have learned about various principles of learning, read the *Explain It* feature on page 168 to see how they explain the behavior of smoking cigarettes.

modeling effect Learning a new behavior from a model through the acquisition of new responses.

facilitation effect Exhibiting a behavior similar to that shown by a model in an unfamiliar situation.

inhibitory effect Suppressing a behavior because a model is punished for displaying the behavior.

disinhibitory effect Displaying a previously suppressed behavior because a model does so without receiving punishment.

SUMMARIZE IT

Cognitive Learning

TYPE OF LEARNING	DESCRIPTIONS	MAJOR CONTRIBUTORS	CLASSIC RESEARCH
Insight	Sudden realization of how to solve a problem	Wolfgang Köhler	Observations of chimpanzees' attempts to retrieve bananas suspended from the tops of their cages
Latent learning	Learning that is hidden until it is reinforced	Edward Tolman	Comparisons of rats that were rewarded for learning to run a maze with others that were allowed to explore it freely but were not rewarded
Observational learning	Learning from watching others	Albert Bandura	Comparisons of children who observed an adult model behaving aggressively with those who did not observe such an aggressive model

Learning from Media ▶

5.17 What has research shown regarding learning from media?

How much of your day is spent in the presence of information that is flowing from some kind of electronic source? Many people nowadays are exposed to such information almost every waking minute. There is even a 24/7 cable television channel just

EXPLAIN IT   **How Do the Principles of Learning Explain the Behavior of Smoking Cigarettes?**

Now that you have studied all of the major principles of learning, you may be able to use them to develop a comprehensive explanation for the health-threatening behavior of smoking cigarettes. It may help to break the behavior of smoking, and that of quitting smoking, into several components: the learning phase, the maintenance phase, and the quitting phase. Before going on, think for a few minutes about how the principles of classical conditioning, operant conditioning, and observational learning contribute to each of these phases. Your analysis may be different from ours, but here's how we see it.

The Learning Phase

Observational learning is critical to the initiation of cigarette smoking. Non-smokers see models whom they believe to be competent and successful—popular peers, movie characters, models in magazine advertisements—smoking cigarettes and think that this behavior helps people make friends or makes them look sophisticated and sexy. Operant conditioning comes into play when the mild brain-stimulating effects of nicotine are experienced by the new smoker as rewarding. At the same time, the aversive antismoking reactions of the lungs gradually subside with increased exposure to cigarette smoke. As a result, a behavior that began in response to social influences is now maintained by physiological factors.

The Maintenance Phase

Once the smoking habit is established, several different learning principles work together to keep it going. For instance, many smokers light up immediately after a meal. As a result of classical conditioning, the physiological feeling of being full becomes associated with the effects of nicotine, and the feeling of fullness becomes a stimulus that triggers a desire for a cigarette. Social settings in which most people are smoking bring observational principles to the fore as smokers feel freer to engage in the habit when others are doing so. In addition, negative reinforcement, an operant learning principle, is at work in the maintenance of smoking behavior. Specifically, smoking a cigarette makes a smoker's craving for nicotine go away.

The Quitting Phase

In the quitting phase, success depends on taking control of the principles of learning. First, those who hope to quit must learn to suppress classically conditioned triggers such as the feeling of fullness after a meal. Likewise, smokers can harness the power of observational learning by avoiding social situations in which many people are likely to be smoking and spending more time in settings in which smoking is prohibited or strongly discouraged. Finally, smokers who want to quit can exploit the fact that the negative reinforcement that occurs as a result of smoking a cigarette (i.e., alleviating craving) operates on a continuous schedule of reinforcement. Recall that behaviors that involve a continuous schedule are more easily learned than those that involve a variable schedule, but they are also more easily extinguished. Thus, smokers who want to quit should be aware that while the first three days or so of denying one's cravings can be quite miserable, the cravings diminish considerably thereafter.

for babies these days ("Round-the-clock baby TV..." 2006). What impact does this constant exposure to media have on how we learn?

Effects of the Multitasking Environment. The various kinds of electronic information media that are common in today's world comprise what some researchers call an *electronic multitasking environment* in which we attempt to manage several different sources of information at once (Rideout, Roberts, & Foehr, 2005). Studies involving college students find that many students work on papers and other assignments in a split-screen format, with one part of the screen devoted to their work and another to a game or a social network site (Jones, 2003; Junco & Cotton, 2012). And many of these students listen to music or exchange text messages with friends at the same time.

Research examining the effects on learning of the multitasking environment is still too preliminary to support definitive conclusions, but the questions being examined are likely to be of great interest to people who spend their days juggling multiple information sources. One such question concerns the degree to which the brain adapts to multiple sources of information by changing its attentional strategies (e.g., Zhang et al., 2005). Another has led researchers to examine the possibility that simultaneous exposure to multiple information sources degrades learning from any one of those sources (e.g., Law, Logie, & Pearson, 2006). Other hypotheses currently being investigated include the possibility that keeping track of multiple streams of information induces anxiety and diminishes academic performance (e.g., Bailey & Konstan, 2006; Junco & Cotton, 2012).

Researchers are also interested in how multitasking influences our cognitive abilities beyond the multitasking environment. Surprisingly, these studies show that the more time people spend multitasking, the less capable they are of managing their thought processes when they are not multitasking (Ophir, Nass, & Wagner, 2009).

▲ In Bandura's observational learning research, children learned to copy aggression by observing adult models act aggressively toward a Bobo doll.

Psychologists say that these results suggest that multitasking reduces our ability to differentiate between relevant and irrelevant information. In other words, multitasking causes us to develop the habit of attending to everything in the environment rather than filtering out information that is unimportant.

Television and Other Entertainment Media. More than four decades ago, Albert Bandura raised concerns regarding the impact of televised violence on children's behavior with a classic series of studies. Bandura suspected that aggression and violence on television programs, including cartoons, tend to increase aggressive behavior in children. His pioneering work has greatly influenced current thinking on these issues. In several classic experiments, Bandura demonstrated how children are influenced by exposure to aggressive models. One study involved three groups of preschoolers. Children in one group individually observed an adult model punching, kicking, and hitting a 5-foot, inflated plastic "Bobo Doll" with a mallet, while uttering aggressive phrases (Bandura et al., 1961, p. 576). Children in the second group observed a nonaggressive model who ignored the Bobo Doll and sat quietly assembling Tinker Toys. The children in the control group were placed in the same setting with no adult present. Later, each child was observed through a one-way mirror. Those children exposed to the aggressive model imitated much of the aggression and also engaged in significantly more nonimitative aggression than did children in either of the other groups. The group that observed the nonaggressive model showed less aggressive behavior than the control group. 👁

A further study compared the degree of aggression in children following exposure to (1) an aggressive model in a live situation, (2) a filmed version of the same situation, or (3) a film depicting an aggressive cartoon character using the same aggressive behaviors in a fantasy-like setting (Bandura et al., 1963). A control group was not exposed to any of the three situations of aggression. The groups exposed to aggressive models used significantly more aggression than the control group. The researchers concluded that "of the three experimental conditions, exposure to humans on film portraying aggression was the most influential in eliciting and shaping aggressive behavior" (p. 7).

👁 **Watch** the Video *Bandura's Bobo Doll Experiment* on **MyPsychLab**

▲ Aggressive behaviors aren't the only kinds of behaviors people can learn from watching television. Rachael Ray became famous by showing millions of viewers how to add creativity to everyday activities such as preparing family meals.

Watch the Video *Episode 7: In the Real World: Learning Aggression* in **MyPsychLab**

Bandura's research sparked interest in studying the effects of violence and aggression portrayed in other entertainment media. For example, researchers have also shown in a variety of ways—including carefully controlled laboratory experiments with children, adolescents, and young adults—that violent video games increase aggressive behavior (Anderson & Carnagey, 2009). Moreover, the effects of media violence are evident whether the violence is presented in music, music videos, advertising, or on the Internet (Villani, 2001). Such research has spawned a confusing array of rating systems that parents may refer to when choosing media for their children. However, researchers have found that the various rating systems do a poor job of communicating the frequency and intensity of violent acts in programs (Linder & Gentile, 2009). Moreover, researchers have found that labeling media as "violent" may enhance children's desire to experience it, especially in boys over age 11 (Bushman & Cantor, 2003).

But, you might argue, if televised violence is followed by appropriate consequences, such as an arrest, it may actually teach children not to engage in aggression. However, experimental research has demonstrated that children do not process information about consequences in the same ways as adults do (Krcmar & Cooke, 2001). Observing consequences for aggressive acts does seem to help preschoolers learn that violence is morally unacceptable. By contrast, school-age children appear to judge the rightness or wrongness of an act of violence on the basis of provocation; that is, they believe that violence demonstrated in the context of retaliation is morally acceptable even if it is punished by an authority figure.

Remarkably, too, longitudinal evidence shows that the effects of childhood exposure to violence persist well into the adult years (Bushman & Huesmann, 2012). Psychologist L. Rowell Huesmann and his colleagues (2003) have found that individuals who watch the greatest number of violent television programs in childhood are the most likely to engage in actual acts of violence as young adults. This study was the first to show that observations of media violence during childhood are linked to real acts of violence in adulthood. Brain-imaging studies suggest that these long-term effects may be the result of patterns of neural activation that underlie emotionally laden behavioral scripts that children learn while watching violent programming (Murray et al., 2006).

But just as children imitate the aggressive behavior they observe on television, they also imitate the prosocial, or helping, behavior they see there. Programs such as *Daniel Tiger's Neighborhood* and *Sesame Street* have been found to have a positive influence on children. And, hopefully, the findings of Huesmann and his colleagues also apply to the positive effects of television.

Electronic Games. In recent years, concerns about media violence have shifted away from television and toward an emphasis on electronic games. This shift has occurred because children and teenagers now spend as much time playing these games as they do watching television (Cummings & Vandewater, 2007). Adults also devote a considerable amount of time to gaming (see Figure 5.8). A number of longitudinal studies have linked video game playing to aggressive behavior (e.g., Willoughby, Adachi, & Good, 2012). Moreover, some research has shown that playing violent games increases feelings of hostility and decreases sensitivity to violent images (Carnagey, Anderson, & Bushman, 2007). However, there is also evidence that playing violent video games neither increases hostility nor decreases sensitivity (Valadez & Ferguson, 2012). Thus, more research is needed before psychologists will have definitive answers as to how violent video games affect players' emotional states.

Some psychologists argue that violent electronic games allow individuals, especially adolescent and young adult males, to express socially unacceptable feelings in a socially acceptable and safe manner (Jansz, 2005). They point out that these games are most often played in groups and are a central shared activity in many young males' peer relationships (Jansz & Martens, 2005). Consequently, learning to channel aggressive impulses into competitive play among friends, even when such play involves simulated violence, may be an essential part of the social development of adolescent males. As such, video game playing may be simply a form of digitally based rough-and-tumble play, a type of interaction that is far more common among males than females.

Like television, video games can be used to teach positive messages and skills (Greitmeyer & Osswald, 2010). For example, researchers at the University of Michigan have found that video games are an effective medium through which to teach teenagers how to drive more safely (University of Michigan Transportation Research Institute [UMTRI], 2003). Furthermore, playing video games appears to enhance women's spatial cognitive skills, a domain in which females typically perform more poorly than males (Spence & Feng, 2010).

The Internet. Educators agree that the Internet holds great promise as a teaching tool (Schofield & Ward, 2006). Still, researchers note that teachers ought not to assume that media-rich, Internet-based instruction is, by default, more effective than conventional approaches (Mayer, 2010). For instance, when text is presented online, embedded video and audio help to maintain students' attention, but such links don't necessarily contribute to learning (Liu, Liao, & Pratt, 2009). Moreover, physical manipulations of the computer itself, such as typing and moving the mouse, distract online readers and hinder their ability to comprehend and remember what they are reading (Mangen, 2008). Several well-designed studies have also shown that conventional classroom lectures and textbooks are just as useful for learning complex material as multimedia presentations are (Mayer, Hegarty, Mayer, & Campbell, 2005). However, the most powerful approach appears to be one that integrates print and digital learning materials (Fiorella & Mayer, 2012).

Research suggests that educators must be especially cautious when using Internet-based instruction with children. For one thing, until they are about 10 years old, children have difficulty recognizing online advertising even though they recognize television advertisements as early as age 5 (Ali, Blades, Oates, & Blumberg, 2009; Kunkel & Castonguay, 2012). As a result, younger children who are using Web-based materials are more likely to be distracted by ads than older children are. Moreover, researcher Teena Willoughby and her colleagues have found that, even among college students, differences in background knowledge contribute significantly to individual differences in learning from online references such as Wikipedia (Willoughby, Anderson, Wood, Mueller, & Ross, 2009). Thus, it is likely such sources would be even less useful for children whose background knowledge is, generally, much less developed than that of adults. Thus, educators who study the phenomenon of online reading suggest that children be allowed time to develop both background knowledge and reading skill from conventional materials before they are introduced to online text (Ali et al., 2009; Mangen, 2008).

FIGURE 5.8 "Gamers" in Four Age Groups
Researchers at the Pew Internet & American Life Project track all kinds of media use among children and adults in the United States. One of their findings is that younger adults are more likely to play video games at least occasionally than those who are older. However, older adults who play are more likely to do so every day than younger adults are.
Source: Data from Lenhart, A., Jones, S., & Macgill, A. (2008).

1. The sudden realization of the relationship between the elements in a problem situation that results in the solution to the problem is called _____ .
2. Learning not demonstrated until the organism is motivated to perform the behavior is called _____ learning.
3. Grant has been afraid of mice for as long as he can remember and his mother has the same paralyzing fear. Grant may have acquired his fear through _____ learning.

Looking Back

At the beginning of this chapter, you learned that the principles of learning can be used to explain why some activities are more engaging than others. As you read through the chapter, you encountered examples of other kinds of everyday experiences that involve classical conditioning, operant conditioning, and cognitive learning. At this point, you may be wondering how the various topics covered in this chapter relate to the mental processes that we commonly associate with academic learning, such as memory and problem solving. The answer is that the principles explained in this chapter represent only a few of the many different kinds of learning that we experience in our daily lives. Other aspects of learning, including memory and problem solving, will be considered in the next two chapters.

CHAPTER 5 SUMMARY

CLASSICAL CONDITIONING (pp. 145–153)

5.1 How does the kind of learning Pavlov discovered happen? (pp. 146–147)

Pavlov's study of a conditioned reflex in dogs led him to discover a model of learning called classical conditioning. In classical conditioning, a neutral stimulus (a tone in Pavlov's experiments) is presented shortly before an unconditioned stimulus (food in Pavlov's experiments), which naturally elicits, or brings forth, an unconditioned response (salivation for Pavlov's dogs). After repeated pairings, the conditioned stimulus alone (the tone) comes to elicit the conditioned response (salivation).

Key Terms
learning, p. 145
classical conditioning, p. 145
stimulus, p. 145
unconditioned response (UR), p. 146
unconditioned stimulus (US), p. 146
conditioned stimulus (CS), p. 146
conditioned response (CR), p. 146
higher-order conditioning, p. 146

5.2 What causes classically conditioned responses to change? (pp. 147–149)

If the conditioned stimulus (tone) is presented repeatedly without the unconditioned stimulus (food), the conditioned response (salivation) eventually disappears, a process called extinction. That response can reappear in a weaker form if the organism is exposed to the conditioned stimulus again after a period of rest, which is a process called spontaneous recovery. Generalization occurs when an organism makes a conditioned response to a stimulus that is similar to the original conditioned stimulus. Discrimination is the ability to distinguish between similar stimuli.

Key Terms
extinction, p. 147
spontaneous recovery, p. 148
generalization, p. 148
discrimination, p. 149

5.3 What did Watson's "Little Albert" experiment show? (pp. 149–150)

Watson showed that fear could be classically conditioned by presenting a white rat to Little Albert along with a loud, frightening noise, thereby conditioning the child to fear the white rat.

5.4 What did Rescorla demonstrate about classical conditioning? (pp. 150–151)

Rescorla found that the critical element in classical conditioning is whether the conditioned stimulus provides information that enables the organism to reliably predict the occurrence of the unconditioned stimulus.

5.5 How do biological predispositions affect classical conditioning? (pp. 151–152)

Garcia and Koelling conducted a study in which rats formed an association between nausea and flavored water ingested several hours earlier. This represented an exception to the principle that the conditioned stimulus must be presented shortly before the unconditioned stimulus. It also revealed that animals appear to be biologically predisposed to make certain associations, meaning associations cannot be conditioned between just any two stimuli.

Key Terms
biological predispositions, p. 151
taste aversion, p. 151

5.6 What are some examples of classical conditioning in everyday life? (pp. 152–153)

Types of responses acquired through classical conditioning include positive and negative emotional responses (including likes, dislikes, fears, and phobias), responses to environmental cues associated with drug use, responses to advertisements, and conditioned immune system responses. Studies of classical conditioning in everyday life indicate that neutral stimuli cannot serve as conditioned stimuli unless they have authentic connections to unconditioned stimuli (ecological relevance).

OPERANT CONDITIONING (pp. 153–164)

5.7 What did Thorndike and Skinner discover about the consequences of behavior? (p. 153)

Thorndike concluded that most learning occurs through trial and error. He claimed that the consequences of a response determine whether the tendency to respond in the same way in the future will be strengthened or weakened (the law of effect). In Skinner's operant conditioning, behaviors change as a result of the consequences they produce. Reinforcement occurs when consequences cause behaviors to increase. Punishment occurs when consequences cause behaviors to decrease.

Key Terms
law of effect, p. 153
operant conditioning, p. 153
operant, p. 153
reinforcer, p. 153
punisher, p. 153

5.8 How do shaping, generalization, and discriminative stimuli influence operant conditioning? (pp. 154–155)

In one kind of operant conditioning, shaping, complex behaviors are learned in small steps. In extinction, behaviors disappear when the consequences they formerly produced are no longer available. A discriminative stimulus is one that through its association with reinforcement signals learners about behaviors that are likely to be reinforced.

Key Terms
shaping, p. 154
Skinner box, p. 154
successive approximations, p. 154
extinction, p. 154
generalization, p. 154
discriminative stimulus, p. 155

5.9 How do positive and negative reinforcement affect behavior? (pp. 155–156)

Both positive (added) and negative (subtracted, removed) reinforcement increase behavior. In positive reinforcement, a behavior occurs more frequently because it produces a desired consequence. In negative reinforcement, a behavior is learned because it makes an undesirable condition or stimulus go away. Primary reinforcers are consequences that satisfy basic needs. Secondary reinforcers are those that have some kind of association with a primary reinforcer.

Key Terms
reinforcement, p. 155
positive reinforcement, p. 155
negative reinforcement, p. 155
primary reinforcer, p. 156
secondary reinforcer, p. 156

5.10 What are the four types of schedules of reinforcement? (pp. 156–158)

The four types of schedules of reinforcement are the fixed-ratio, variable-ratio, fixed-interval, and variable-interval schedules. The variable-ratio schedule provides the highest response rate and the most resistance to extinction. The partial-reinforcement effect is the greater resistance to extinction that occurs when responses are maintained under partial reinforcement, rather than under continuous reinforcement.

Key Terms
schedule of reinforcement, p. 156
fixed-ratio (FR) schedule, p. 156
variable-ratio (VR) schedule, p. 156
partial reinforcement effect, p. 157
fixed-interval (FI) schedule, p. 157
variable-interval (VI) schedule, p. 157

5.11 How does punishment affect behavior? (pp. 158–161)

Punishment happens when either an added (positive) or a removed (negative) consequence leads to a reduction in the frequency of a behavior. Generally, punishment does not help people develop more appropriate behaviors, and it can cause fear, anger, hostility, and aggression in the punished person. Punishment is most effective when it is given immediately after undesirable behavior, when it is consistently applied, and when it is just intense enough to suppress the behavior.

Key Terms
punishment, p. 158
positive punishment, p. 158
negative punishment, p. 158

5.12 How do escape and avoidance learning occur? (pp. 161–162)

Avoidance learning is desirable when it leads to a beneficial response, such as buckling a seat belt to stop the annoying sound of a buzzer. It is maladaptive when it occurs in response to fear. For example, fear of speaking to a group may lead you to skip class on the day your oral report is scheduled.

Key Terms
escape learning, p. 161
avoidance learning, p. 161
learned helplessness, p. 161

5.13 What are some applications of operant conditioning? (pp. 162–165)

Applications of operant conditioning include training animals to provide entertainment or to help physically challenged people, using biofeedback to gain control over internal physiological processes, and using behavior modification techniques to eliminate undesirable behavior and/or encourage desirable behavior in individuals or groups.

Key Terms
biofeedback, p. 162
behavior modification, p. 162
token economy, p. 163

COGNITIVE LEARNING (pp. 164–172)

5.14 How does insight affect learning? (p. 165)

Insight is the sudden realization of the relationship of the elements in a problem situation that makes the solution apparent; this solution is easily learned and transferred to new problems.

Key Terms
cognitive processes, p. 165
insight, p. 165

5.15 What did Tolman discover about the necessity of reinforcement? (pp. 165–166)

Tolman demonstrated that rats could learn to run to the end of a maze just as quickly when allowed to explore it freely as when they were reinforced with food for getting to the end. His hypothesis was that the rats formed a cognitive map of the maze.

Key Terms
latent learning, p. 165
cognitive map, p. 165

5.16 How do we learn by observing others? (pp. 166–167)

Learning by observing the behavior of others (called models) and the consequences of that behavior is known as observational learning. We learn from models when we assume that the consequences they experience will happen to us if we perform their behaviors.

Key Terms
observational learning (social-cognitive learning), p. 166
model, p. 166
modeling effect, p. 167
facilitation effect, p. 167
inhibitory effect, p. 167
disinhibitory effect, p. 167

5.17 What has research shown regarding learning from media? (pp. 167–172)

When the brain receives information from more than one source at a time, learning from one or all of the sources may be compromised. Violence in both television programs and electronic games can induce feelings of hostility and lessen viewers' and players' capacity for empathy. However, games may provide young adult males with socially acceptable outlets for such feelings. Background knowledge and experience with reading print strongly influence how much people learn from reading online text.

Chapter 5 Study Guide

Answers to all the Study Guide questions are provided at the end of the book.

SECTION ONE: Chapter Review

Classical Conditioning (pp. 145–153)

1. Classical conditioning was originally researched most extensively by _____.

2. In Pavlov's classical experiment, the musical tone served as a(n) (conditioned, unconditioned) stimulus.

3. The reappearance of an extinguished conditioned response is called _____.

4. For higher-order conditioning to occur, a neutral stimulus is typically paired repeatedly with an (existing conditioned stimulus, unconditioned stimulus).

5. Five-year-old Jesse was bitten by his neighbor's collie. He won't go near that dog but seems to have no fear of other dogs, even other collies. Which learning process accounts for his behavior?
   a. generalization   **b.** discrimination
   c. extinction   **d.** spontaneous recovery

6. In Watson's experiment with Little Albert, the white rat was the (conditioned, unconditioned) stimulus, and Albert's crying when the hammer struck the steel bar was the (conditioned, unconditioned) response.

7. The purpose of Watson's Little Albert experiment was to provide support for the psychological perspective called _____.
   a. behaviorism   **b.** psychoanalysis
   c. cognitivism   **d.** humanism

8. Researchers hypothesize that _____ contribute to classical conditioning in order to explain why humans and chimpanzees can be more easily conditioned to fear snakes than other types of stimuli.

9. If a person is exposed to a situation in which specific food is eaten just prior to the development of nausea, the person will develop a(n) _____ for that food.

10. Counselors usually advise recovering drug addicts to avoid cues (people, places, and things) that are associated with their past drug use because the environmental cues may serve as conditioned stimuli for drug cravings. (true/false)

Operant Conditioning (pp. 153–164)

11. Who researched trial-and-error learning using cats in puzzle boxes and formulated the law of effect?
    a. Watson   **b.** Thorndike
    c. Skinner   **d.** Pavlov

12. Operant conditioning was researched most extensively by _____.
    a. Watson   **b.** Thorndike
    c. Skinner   **d.** Pavlov

13. Which of the following processes occurs in operant conditioning when reinforcers are withheld?
    a. generalization   **b.** discrimination
    c. spontaneous recovery **d.** extinction

14. Many people take aspirin to relieve painful headaches. Taking aspirin is a behavior that is likely to continue because of the effect of (positive, negative) reinforcement.

15. (Partial, Continuous) reinforcement is most effective in conditioning a new response.

16. Jennifer and Ashley are both employed raking leaves. Jennifer is paid $1 for each bag of leaves she rakes; Ashley is paid $4 per hour. Jennifer is paid according to the _____ schedule; Ashley is paid according to the _____ schedule.
    a. fixed-interval; fixed-ratio   **b.** variable-ratio; fixed-interval
    c. variable-ratio; variable-interval **d.** fixed-ratio; fixed-interval

17. Which schedule of reinforcement yields the highest response rate and the greatest resistance to extinction?
    a. variable-ratio schedule   **b.** fixed-ratio schedule
    c. variable-interval schedule **d.** fixed-interval schedule

18. Danielle's parents have noticed that she has been making her bed every day, and they would like this to continue. Because they understand the partial-reinforcement effect, they will want to reward her every time she makes the bed. (true/false)

19. Punishment is roughly the same as negative reinforcement. (true/false)

20. Depending on the circumstances, avoidance learning can be either adaptive or maladaptive. (true/false)

21. In the classic study done by Overmeir and Seligman, dogs who received multiple electric shocks eventually stopped trying to avoid them, a condition known as _____.

22. Physiological processes such as heart rate and respiration can be brought under conscious control through an operant conditioning procedure called _____.

23. Applying learning principles to eliminate undesirable behavior and/or encourage desirable behavior is called _____ _____.

Cognitive Learning (pp. 164–172)

24. The Latent learning is the sudden realization of the relationship between the elements in a problem situation that results in the solution to the problem. (true/false)

25. Insight is learning that is not demonstrated until one is motivated to perform the behavior. (true/false)

26. Hayley has been afraid of snakes for as long as she can remember, and her mother has the same paralyzing fear. Hayley may have acquired her fear through
    a. learning by insight.   **b.** observational learning.
    c. classical conditioning.   **d.** latent learning.

27. You are unlikely to learn a modeled behavior unless you
    a. repeat the behavior in different settings.
    b. are physically capable of performing the behavior.
    c. have never seen the behavior before.
    d. are personally acquainted with the model.

28. Match each of the effects of modeling with its definition:
    ___ (1) modeling
    ___ (2) facilitation
    ___ (3) inhibitory
    ___ (4) disinhibitory
    a. exhibiting a behavior similar to that of a model
    b. exhibiting a previously learned unacceptable behavior after seeing a model do so
    c. learning a new behavior from a model
    d. suppressing a previously learned unacceptable behavior after seeing a model be punished for it

29. Match the researcher with the subject(s) researched.
    ___ (1) Edward Tolman
    ___ (2) Albert Bandura
    ___ (3) Wolfgang Köhler
    a. observational learning
    b. learning by insight
    c. latent learning

30. _____ was a pioneer in the study of the ways in which observing aggressive behavior on television and in films influences children's behavior.

SECTION TWO: Identify the Concept

In the blank following each statement, list the learning principle(s) illustrated by the statement.

1. Ben continues to play a slot machine even though he never knows when it will pay off. _____

2. Tamake watched a movie about tornadoes and is now afraid of bad storms. _____

3. Joey is crying and asking for a candy bar. His mother gives in because doing so will make him stop crying for now—but Joey will most likely behave this way again. _____

4. Hans got sick eating lasagna and now never eats food containing tomato sauce. _____

5. Helen washed the dinner dishes, and her mother allowed her to watch television for 30 extra minutes that evening. From then on, Helen dutifully washed the dishes after every family meal. _____

6. Natasha's parents are advised to stop paying attention to her crying when it is time for bed and instead ignore it. _____

7. Jorge is paid for his factory job once every two weeks. _____

8. Maria is scolded for running into the road and never does it again. _____

9. Ellen watches her lab partner mix the chemicals and set up the experiment. She then repeats the same procedure and completes her assignment. _____

10. Through associations with such things as food and shelter, pieces of green paper with pictures of past U.S. presidents on them become very powerful reinforcers. _____

11. Although he studied the problem, Jack did not seem to be able to figure out the correct way to reconnect the pipes under the sink. He took a break before he became too frustrated. Later he returned and immediately saw how to do it. _____

12. Morgan often listens to her iPod while chatting with friends online and watching television. _____

SECTION THREE: Comprehensive Practice Test

1. Pavlov is associated with _____ conditioning.
   a. classical
   b. operant
   c. cognitive
   d. Watsonian

2. This theorist believed that the causes of behavior are in the environment and that inner mental events are themselves shaped by environmental forces.
   a. Bandura
   b. Pavlov
   c. Skinner
   d. Tolman

3. Which of the following theorists developed the concepts of latent learning and cognitive mapping?
   a. Pavlov
   b. Köhler
   c. Tolman
   d. Skinner

4. This theorist researched observational learning and the effects of modeling on behavior.
   a. Köhler
   b. Thorndike
   c. Skinner
   d. Bandura

5. Which of the following theorists is associated with research on reinforcement theory?
   a. Pavlov
   b. Skinner
   c. Tolman
   d. Bandura

6. The concept that is associated with cognitive learning is
   a. negative reinforcement.
   b. positive reinforcement.
   c. latent learning.
   d. the discriminative stimulus.

7. Jim has been sober since he completed a treatment program for alcoholics. He was told to stay away from his old drinking places. The danger is that he may start drinking again as a result of the conditioned stimuli in those environments. If he did, it would be a practical example of _____ in classical conditioning.
   a. extinction
   b. spontaneous recovery
   c. stimulus generalization
   d. observational response sets

8. The seductive nature of a slot machine in a gambling casino is based on its _____ schedule of reinforcement.
   a. continuous
   b. fixed-interval
   c. variable-ratio
   d. variable-interval

9. For Little Albert, the conditioned stimulus was _____.
   a. the white rat
   b. a loud noise
   c. Watson
   d. based on negative reinforcement

10. Positive reinforcement increases behavior; negative reinforcement
_____ behavior.
- **a.** decreases
- **b.** has no effect on
- **c.** removes a
- **d.** also increases

11. A good example of a fixed-interval schedule of reinforcement is
_____.
- **a.** factory piecework
- **b.** a child's weekly allowance
- **c.** a slot machine
- **d.** turning on a light switch

12. The nice thing about continuous reinforcement is that it creates a behavior that is very resistant to extinction. (true/false)

13. Taste aversion is a real-world example of
- **a.** operant conditioning.
- **b.** classical conditioning.
- **c.** observational learning.
- **d.** cognitive mapping.

14. In _____ learning, a person or animal learns a response that _____ a negative reinforcer.
- **a.** escape; prevents the occurrence of
- **b.** escape; terminates
- **c.** avoidance; terminates
- **d.** avoidance; initiates

15. Ms. Doe, a new teacher, is having a difficult time with her misbehaving second graders. When the principal enters the room, the children behave like perfect angels. In this case, the principal may be thought of as a(n)
_____.
- **a.** positive reinforcer
- **b.** unconditioned stimulus
- **c.** shaping reinforcer
- **d.** discriminative stimulus

16. According to Tolman, _____ is defined as learning that occurs without apparent reinforcement but is not demonstrated until the organism is sufficiently reinforced to do so.
- **a.** classical conditioning
- **b.** modeling behavior
- **c.** latent learning
- **d.** cognitive mapping

17. Which statement best sums up research on learning from video games?

SECTION FOUR: Critical Thinking

1. Compare and contrast the strengths and limitations of classical conditioning, operant conditioning, and observational learning in explaining how behaviors are acquired and maintained.

2. The use of behavior modification has been a source of controversy among psychologists and others. Prepare arguments supporting each of these positions:
- **a.** Behavior modification should be used in society to shape the behavior of others.
- **b.** Behavior modification should not be used in society to shape the behavior of others.

SECTION FIVE: Application Essay

1. Like most schools, Pine Meadows High School has an awards assembly at the end of each school year during which students receive awards for straight-A report cards and other academic achievements. Mr. Smith, the principal, has always wondered why watching peers receive rewards does not seem to motivate low-achieving students to do better in school. Using what you have learned about the factors that influence the effectiveness of models (status, attractiveness) and the principles of observational learning (attention, retention, reproduction, reinforcement), write a letter to Mr. Smith explaining why poor students may not be motivated by watching good students receive awards.

Apply your critical thinking skills with **MyPsychLab** Writing Assignments

Submit your answer to the following question inside the MyPsychLab Writing Assessment program for immediate feedback.

Imagine you are asked by a roommate to help him devise a weight loss program to increase his chances of making the football team. Create a one month behavior modification program based on the principles of operant conditioning that will get him started towards his goal. Be sure to describe how you will measure your roommate's progress and what schedules of reinforcement will be included in your program.

6 Memory

THINK ABOUT IT

How good is your memory? Are you willing to put it to the test? If so, read the letter clusters below individually at the rate of about one per second and then see if you can repeat them.

N-F   L-C-B   S-U-S   A-D-V   D-F-B   I

How well did you do? Was the task difficult? Probably so, because there are 15 different letters, a number that exceeds most people's capacity for processing information. But don't despair, the letter clusters can be made much easier to remember if we rearrange them like so:

N-F-L   C-B-S   U-S-A   D-V-D   F-B-I

As this activity suggests, the meaningfulness of information and how it is organized influence our ability to remember it. Thus, clearly, the human memory system does not function like a camera. Instead, the system combines new input with previously stored information to create a representation of an event rather than a copy of it. In this chapter, you will read about the fascinating processes that, together, make up human memory.

Watch the Video *Episode 8: Big Picture: The Woman Who Cannot Forget* in **MyPsychLab**

The Structure of Human Memory

How do our minds create memories? Psychologists have been studying memory for more than a century. However, the need to break down the memory process into its individual parts that was necessitated by the invention of modern computers and computer programming has opened the doors to psychologists' understanding of how the human memory system works. Thinking about how computers store information will help you to understand what memory is and how it works. Keep in mind that just like a computer is made up of different parts, our memory is also composed of different structures, some of which are devoted to temporary storage and others of which focus on permanent storage of information. Before considering these structures, though, we need to begin with the definition of memory itself.

What Is Memory?

Most current studies aimed at understanding human memory are conducted within a framework known as **information-processing theory** (Mayer, 2012). This approach makes use of modern computer science and related fields to provide models that help psychologists understand the processes involved in memory. In keeping with the computer analogy, information-processing theorists sometimes apply such terms as *hardware* (e.g., brain structures that are involved in memory) and *software* (e.g., learned memory strategies) to various aspects of the human memory system.

The general principles of the information processing approach to memory include the notion that memory involves three distinct processes. The first process, **encoding**, is the transformation of information into a form that can be stored in memory. The second memory process, **storage**, involves keeping or maintaining information in memory. In order for encoded information to be stored, some physiological change must take place in the brain—a process called *consolidation*. The final process, **retrieval**, occurs when information stored in memory is brought to mind. To remember something, you must perform all three processes—encode the information, store it, and then retrieve it. Thus, **memory** is a cognitive process that includes encoding, storage, and retrieval of information (see Figure 6.1). For example, if you witness a car crash, you are likely to generate a brief "story" of it in your mind, the encoding step. Next, you would store the story in your memory somewhat temporarily by retelling it to yourself and other witnesses. The process of retelling would cause your brain

6.1 How does information-processing theory describe memory?

information-processing theory A framework for studying memory that uses the computer as a model of human cognitive processes.

encoding The process of transforming information into a form that can be stored in memory.

storage The process of keeping or maintaining information in memory.

retrieval The process of bringing to mind information that has been stored in memory.

memory The process of encoding, storage, and retrieval of information.

Encoding		**Storage**		**Retrieval**
Transforming information into a form that can be stored in memory	→	Maintaining information in memory	→	Bringing stored material to mind

FIGURE 6.1 The Processes Required for Remembering
The act of remembering requires successful completion of all three of these processes: encoding, storage, and retrieval.

✳⎡Explore the **Concept** *Encoding, Storage, and Retrieval in Memory* in **MyPsychLab**

6.2 What are the characteristics of sensory memory?

sensory memory The memory system that holds information from the senses for a period ranging from only a fraction of a second to about 2 seconds.

eidetic imagery (eye-DET-ik) The ability to retain the image of a visual stimulus for several minutes after it has been removed from view and to use this retained image to answer questions about the visual stimulus.

6.3 What happens to information in short-term memory?

short-term memory (STM) The component of the memory system that holds about seven (from five to nine) items for less than 30 seconds without rehearsal; also called working memory.

◉⎡Watch the Video *Short-Term Memory* in **MyPsychLab**

to consolidate the story as a permanent memory. Retrieval comes into play when a police officer asks you questions about what you saw. ✳

Information-processing theory is not associated with any one theorist. However, several theorists have been especially influential; two of these influential theorists are Richard Atkinson and Richard Shiffrin. They proposed the model of memory that almost all researchers employ (Atkinson & Shiffrin, 1968; Shiffrin, 1999). Their model characterizes memory as three different, interacting memory systems: sensory memory, short-term memory, and long-term memory. We will examine each of these three memory systems, which are shown in Figure 6.2, in detail.

Sensory Memory

Virtually everything we see, hear, or otherwise sense is held in **sensory memory**, where each piece of information is stored only for the briefest period. As shown in Figure 6.2, sensory memory normally holds visual images for a fraction of a second and sounds for about 2 seconds (Crowder, 1992; Klatzky, 1980).

Exactly how long does visual sensory memory last? Glance at the three rows of letters shown below for a fraction of a second and then close your eyes. How many of the letters can you recall?

```
X   B   D   F
M   P   Z   G
L   C   N   H
```

Most people can correctly recall only four or five of the letters when they are briefly presented. Does this indicate that visual sensory memory can hold only four or five letters at a time? To find out, researcher George Sperling (1960) briefly flashed 12 letters, as shown above, to participants. Immediately upon turning off the display, he sounded a high, medium, or low tone that signaled the participants to report only the top, middle, or bottom row of letters. Before they heard the tone, the participants had no way of knowing which row they would have to report. Yet Sperling found that when the participants could view the rows of letters for $^{15}/_{1000}$ to ½ second, they could report correctly all the items in any one row nearly 100% of the time. But the items faded from sensory memory so quickly that during the time it took to report three or four of them, the other eight or nine had already disappeared. Thus, sensory memory can take in an enormous amount of information, but it can only hold on to it for a very brief period.

A very small proportion of individuals, most of them children, have an exceptional ability to extend the amount of time that an image is present in sensory memory (Haber, 1980). This ability is called **eidetic imagery**, and it is the memory phenomenon that comes closest to the popular notion of a "photographic memory" (Solso, MacLin, & MacLin, 2008). People with eidetic imagery abilities can retain the image of a visual stimulus, such as a picture, for several minutes after it has been removed from view and use this retained image to answer questions about the visual stimulus. However, they generally have no better long-term memory than others, and virtually all children with eidetic imagery lose it before adulthood.

Short-Term Memory

So, you might be thinking, if almost everything flows out of sensory memory, how do we ever remember anything? Fortunately, our ability to pay attention allows us to grab on to some sensory information and send it to the next stage of processing, **short-term memory (STM)**. Whatever you are thinking about right now is in your STM (see Figure 6.2). Short-term memory usually codes information according to sound. For example, the letter *T* is coded as the sound "tee," not as the shape T. The information that is stored in our STM is dependent on several factors. ◉

FIGURE 6.2 Characteristics of and Processes Involved in the Three Memory Systems Proposed by Atkinson and Shiffrin The three memory systems differ in what and how much they hold and for how long they store it.

The diagram shows three memory systems:

Sensory Memory
Temporary storage for sensory information
Capacity: Large
Duration: Visual, fraction of a second; auditory, 2 seconds

Short-Term Memory
Brief storage for information currently being used
Capacity: About 7 items (a range of 5–9)
Duration: Less than 30 seconds without rehearsal

Long-Term Memory
Permanent or relatively permanent storage
Capacity: Virtually unlimited
Duration: From minutes to a lifetime

Sensory Input → Transfer (encoding) → Short-Term Memory → Transfer (encoding) → Long-Term Memory; Rehearsal loop on Short-Term Memory; Retrieval from Long-Term Memory to Short-Term Memory

Capacity Short-term memory has a very limited capacity—about seven (plus or minus two) different items or bits of information at one time. This is just enough for phone numbers and ordinary ZIP codes. (Nine-digit ZIP codes strain the capacity of most people's STM.) When short-term memory is filled to capacity, displacement can occur. In **displacement**, each new incoming item pushes out an existing item, which is then forgotten. Think of what happens when the top of your desk gets too crowded. Things start to "disappear" under other things; some items even fall off the desk. So, you can remember that short-term memory is the limited component of the memory system by associating it with the top of your desk: The desk is limited in size, causing you to lose things when it gets crowded, and the same is true of short-term memory. (See the *Explain It* on p. 182.)

One way to overcome the limitation of seven or so bits of information is to use a memory strategy that George A. Miller (1956), a pioneer in memory research, calls **chunking**—organizing or grouping separate bits of information into larger units, or chunks. A *chunk* is an easily identifiable unit, such as a syllable, a word, an acronym, or a number (Cowan, 1988). For example, nine digits, such as 5 2 9 7 3 1 3 2 5, can be divided into three more easily memorized chunks, 529 73 1325. (Notice that this is the form of Social Security numbers in the United States.) (We'll learn about some other memory strategies in our discussion of working memory.)

Any time you chunk information on the basis of knowledge stored in long-term memory—that is, by associating it with some kind of meaning—you increase the effective capacity of short-term memory (Baddeley, 2009). As a result, chunking is just as useful in remembering large amounts of information as it is in remembering short bits of data such as telephone numbers. For instance, the headings, subheadings, and margin questions in this textbook help you sort information into manageable chunks. Thus, you will remember more of a chapter if you use them as organizers for your notes and as cues to recall information when you are reviewing for an exam.

Duration. As you might have guessed, chunking alone won't do the trick. In fact, items in short-term memory are lost in less than 30 seconds unless you repeat them over and over to yourself. This process is known as **rehearsal**. But rehearsal is easily disrupted. It is so fragile, in fact, that an interruption can cause information to be lost in just a few seconds. In a series of early studies, participants were briefly shown three consonants (such as H, G, and L) and then asked to count backward by threes from a given number (738, 735, 732, and so on) (Peterson & Peterson, 1959). After intervals lasting from 3 to 18 seconds, participants were instructed to stop counting backward and recall the three letters. Following a delay of 9 seconds, the participants could recall an average of only one of the three letters.

displacement The event that occurs when short-term memory is filled to capacity and each new, incoming item pushes out an existing item, which is then forgotten.

chunking A memory strategy that involves grouping or organizing bits of information into larger units, which are easier to remember.

rehearsal The act of purposely repeating information to maintain it in short-term memory.

▲ Suppose the person with whom this driver is talking is giving her directions. As you can see, the driver has no way to write down the directions, and her short-term memory is trying to juggle the tasks of driving and talking on the phone while also trying to understand and remember the directions. If you have ever been in this situation, you probably learned the hard way that your performance on at least one of the tasks suffered because of the limitation of short-term memory.

EXPLAIN IT   **Why Is Cramming an Ineffective Study Method?**

Have you ever found yourself in a situation like this one? It's the night before your psychology exam, and you have not read the three chapters that will be covered on the exam. Seeing no other option, you stay awake all night cramming for the test. Despite your best efforts, when you are faced with the exam the next day, you find yourself able to recall only fragments of information from the three chapters you studied so diligently the night before. Do you think that the characteristics of short-term memory might have something to do with your inability to remember what you were sure you had learned the night before? Think for a moment about how these characteristics come into play when you cram for an exam.

Did the limited capacity of short-term memory come to mind? It should have because cramming, by its nature, overloads the short-term memory. Although cramming strains the memory system in many other ways as well, the primary cause of its ineffectiveness is this tendency to exceed the capacity of STM.

For clarity, let's consider an example. Suppose you are cramming for an exam over this chapter, and you need to learn the characteristics of the STM. You skim the text and predict that what you need to know for the exam boils down to these units of information:

- Capacity limited to 7±2 bits of information
- Information lost through decay, displacement, and interference
- Information lost in 30 seconds if not rehearsed
- Also known as working memory
- Strategies executed in STM
- Chunking can increase its capacity

You might be thinking that, since there are only six items on this list, they easily fit within the seven-unit capacity of the STM. This observation might be valid if rote memorization were sufficient for the purposes of a college-level

exam. But, as you probably know by now, most college exams require more than simple memorization.

Let's look at just how complex this six-item list really is from the perspective of your STM. The first item is fairly straightforward, but take a look at the second one. It is essentially a summary statement that requires you to know what the terms *decay*, *displacement*, and *interference* mean to process it. The definitions of these terms also include multiple bits of information that must be understood in order to be stored in memory before you can use them to understand the summary statement. Thus, this single item includes numerous bits of information. The entire list encompasses several dozen bits of information, all of which must be understood and stored in meaningful networks in your long-term memory in order to be accessible when you take the exam.

Given the limitations of STM, the only way to learn complex material of this kind is to employ a chunking strategy. Building up the underlying knowledge that you must have before you can even begin to chunk the information takes time and effort. Thus, it could take an hour or more just to learn the characteristics of STM. And, remember, your task for the purposes of this example is to learn the entire chapter, not just the characteristics of STM.

Clearly, then, an all-night cram session during which you are tired and anxious as well as engaged in a task that taxes your information-processing system beyond its limits is a poor approach to learning even a single chapter in a college textbook. And how often do you have an exam that covers only one chapter? In most cases, college exams are based on several textbook chapters and, often, extra reading material and lecture notes to boot. That's why sound advice about studying usually begins with an admonition to forestall the need to cram by developing a disciplined and realistic approach to time management.

After 18 seconds, there was practically no recall whatsoever. An 18-second distraction had completely erased the three letters from short-term memory.

Short-Term Memory and Working Memory. Allan Baddeley (2012) has suggested that short-term memory is one component of a broader system of temporary storage structures and processes known as **working memory**. Simply put, working memory is the memory subsystem with which you work on information to understand it, remember it, or use it to solve a problem or to communicate with someone. Baddeley argues that STM is largely speech-based. Consequently, other kinds of information (e.g., visual) that we need to carry out an information-processing task are sent to other components of the working memory system for temporary storage while the STM is engaged in processing verbal information. Research shows that the prefrontal cortex is the site that is activated when we are using our working memories (Schreppel et al., 2008).

So, just what kind of "work" goes on in working memory? One of the most important working memory processes is the application of *memory strategies*, such as chunking. Using a memory strategy involves manipulating information in ways that make it easier to remember. We use some memory strategies almost automatically, but others require more effort. For example, sometimes we repeat information over and over again until we can recall it easily. (Remember learning those multiplication tables in elementary

working memory The memory subsystem that we use when we try to understand information, remember it, or use it to solve a problem or communicate with someone.

school?) This strategy, called **maintenance rehearsal**, works well for remembering telephone numbers and license plate numbers, particularly when the information is needed for only a short time. However, it isn't the best way to remember more complex information, such as the kind you find in a textbook. For this kind of information, the best strategy is **elaborative rehearsal**, which involves relating new information to something you already know. For example, suppose you are taking a French class and have to learn the word *escaliers,* which is equivalent to *stairs* in English. You might remember the meaning of *escaliers* by associating it with the English word *escalator.*

maintenance rehearsal Repeating information over and over again until it is no longer needed; may eventually lead to storage of information in long-term memory.

elaborative rehearsal A memory strategy that involves relating new information to something that is already known.

Levels of Processing in Working Memory. Maintenance and elaborative rehearsal were first described by memory researchers Fergus Craik and Robert Lockhart (1972) in the context of their **levels-of-processing model** of memory (Baddeley, 1998). This model proposed that maintenance rehearsal involves "shallow" processing (encoding based on superficial features of information, such as the sound of a word), whereas elaborative rehearsal involves "deep" processing (encoding based on the meaning of information). Craik and Lockhart hypothesized that deep processing is more likely to lead to long-term retention than is shallow processing. Their hypothesis was tested in classic research by Craik and Tulving (1975). They had participants answer "yes" or "no" to questions asked about words just before the words were flashed to them for $\frac{1}{5}$ of a second. The participants had to process the words in three ways: (1) visually (Is the word in capital letters?); (2) acoustically (Does the word rhyme with another particular word?); and (3) semantically (Does the word make sense when used in a particular sentence?). Thus, this test required shallow processing for the first question, deeper processing for the second question, and still deeper processing for the third question. Later retention tests showed that the deeper the level of processing, the higher the accuracy of memory.

levels-of-processing model The memory model that describes maintenance rehearsal as "shallow" processing and elaborative rehearsal as "deep" processing.

Automaticity. The combined effects of memory strategies and repeated retrieval can lead to the development of **automaticity** for some information. For instance, when you first learned to tell time on an analogical clock, the process of translating the positions of the short and long hands into time-of-day information required a great deal of mental effort. But with practice, you became capable of instantly knowing the time by simply glancing at the clock. When information can be retrieved automatically, working memory space is freed up for other tasks. So, thanks to automaticity, you can look at your clock, realize that you're going to be late for class, and, within microseconds, formulate a plan to get there as quickly as possible.

automaticity The ability to recall information from long-term memory without effort.

Do Some People Have "Super-Memories"? You may have heard stories about people who are capable of seemingly impossible feats of memory, such as memorizing the value of *pi* to thousands of digits. In all such cases research has shown that the people involved used the kinds of strategies you have just read about and those you will see in the *Apply It* on page 184 (Guenther, 2002). Moreover, many people who display exceptional memory abilities have neurological conditions that have both positive and negative effects on memory functioning. For example, Kim Peek, the man who was portrayed by Dustin Hoffman in the movie *Rainman*, was capable of rapidly carrying out complex mental calculations and could memorize hundreds of pages of text. Yet, his developmental disability, *autism*, prevented him from forming long-term memories of the types of interpretive information that people who do not have such disabilities use to understand the world. Thus, Peek could memorize a novel but lacked the knowledge he needed to understand it. Research suggests that having a good memory isn't some kind of mysterious gift that some have and others lack. It results from using effective strategies, a practice that anyone can adopt.

long-term memory (LTM) The memory system with a virtually unlimited capacity that contains vast stores of a person's permanent or relatively permanent memories.

Long-Term Memory ▶

6.4 What are the subsystems of long-term memory?

If information is processed effectively in short-term memory, it makes its way to long-term memory. **Long-term memory (LTM)** is a person's vast storehouse of permanent or relatively permanent memories (refer back to Figure 6.2). There are no known

APPLY IT

Improving Memory

Writing notes, making lists, writing on a calendar, or keeping an appointment book is often more reliable and accurate than trusting to memory (Intons-Peterson & Fournier, 1986). But what if you need information at some unpredictable time, when you do not have external aids handy? Several *mnemonics,* or memory devices, and study strategies have been developed over the years to aid memory.

Mnemonics

Rhymes are a common aid to remembering material that otherwise might be difficult to recall. Perhaps as a child you learned to recite "*i* before *e* except after *c*" when you were trying to spell a word containing that vowel combination.

The *method of loci* is a mnemonic device that can be used when you want to remember a list of items such as a grocery list or when you give a speech or a class report and need to make your points in order without using notes. The word *loci* (pronounced "LOH-sye") is the plural form of *locus,* which means "location" or "place." Select any familiar place—your home, for example—and simply associate the items to be remembered with locations there. Progress in an orderly fashion. For example, visualize the first item or idea you want to remember in its place on the driveway, the second in the garage, the third at the front door, and so on, until you have associated each item you want to remember with a specific location. When you want to recall the items, take an imaginary walk starting at the first place—the first item will pop into your mind. When you think of the second place, the second item will come to mind, and so on.

Another useful mnemonic is to take the first letter of each item to be remembered and form a word, a phrase, or a sentence with those letters. For example, suppose you had to memorize the seven colors of the visible spectrum in their proper order:

  Red
  Orange
  Yellow
  Green
  Blue
  Indigo
  Violet

You could make your task easier by using the first letter of each color to form the name Roy G. Biv. Three chunks are easier to remember than seven different items.

Study Strategies

Mnemonics are helpful for some kinds of information, but much of what you need to learn from textbooks calls for more comprehensive strategies. For example, *organization* is a powerful study strategy. Try to organize items you want to remember in alphabetical order, or according to categories, historical sequence, important people, or in any other way that will make retrieval easier for you.

Overlearning is practicing or studying material beyond the point where it can be repeated once without error. It makes material more resistant to forgetting. So, the next time you study for a test, don't stop studying as soon as you think you know the material. Spend another hour or so going over it, using features of your textbook such as margin questions. You will be surprised at how much more you will remember.

Most students have tried cramming for examinations, a strategy that psychologists call *massed practice.* But, *spaced practice,* a strategy that breaks studying into several brief sessions with rest periods in between, is generally more effective. Long periods of memorizing make material particularly subject to forgetting and often result in fatigue and poor concentration.

Research shows that you will recall more if you increase the amount of *recitation* in your study. For example, it is better to read a page or a few paragraphs and then recite what you remember of what you have read. Then, continue reading, stop and practice reciting again, and so on.

Finally, memory researcher Henry Roediger and his colleagues have demonstrated in countless studies that there is no better strategy for studying textbook material than *repeated testing* (Karpicke, Butler, & Roediger, 2009). Roediger's research shows that repeatedly taking quizzes and looking back at the book to figure out why you missed items is a highly effective approach to creating long-term, accessible memories of the kinds of detailed information that students must master to succeed on exams. That's why, we keep reminding you to complete the Study Guide, take the practice quizzes at the end of each section and in the back of the book, and take the additional quizzes on MyPsychLab. It's a lot of work, but Roediger's studies show that it pays off in better performance on exams.

◉ **Watch** the Video *Episode 8: What's in It for Me? Making It Stick* in **MyPsychLab**

---

limits to the storage capacity of this memory system, and long-term memories can persist for years, some of them for a lifetime. Information in long-term memory is usually stored in terms of its meaning, although visual images, sounds, and odors can be stored there as well.

declarative memory The subsystem within long-term memory that stores facts, information, and personal life events that can be brought to mind verbally or in the form of images and then declared or stated; also called explicit memory.

episodic memory (ep-ih-SOD-ik) The type of declarative memory that records events as they have been subjectively experienced.

Declarative Memory. Some experts believe that there are two main subsystems within long-term memory. The first, **declarative memory** (also called *explicit memory*), stores facts, information, and personal life events that can be brought to mind verbally or in the form of images and then declared or stated. It holds information that we intentionally and consciously recollect. There are two types of declarative memory, episodic memory and semantic memory. **Episodic memory** is the type of declarative memory that records events as they have been subjectively experienced (Wheeler, Stuss, & Tulving, 1997). It is somewhat like a mental diary, a record of the episodes of your life—the people you have known, the places you have seen, and

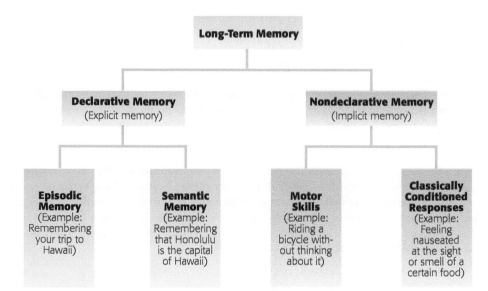

FIGURE 6.3 **Subsystems of Long-Term Memory**
Declarative memory can be divided into two subsystems: episodic memory, which stores memories of personally experienced events, and semantic memory, which stores facts and information. Nondeclarative memory consists of motor skills acquired through repetitive practice and simple classically conditioned responses.

the personal experiences you have had. Using episodic memory, a person might make this statement: "I remember being in Florida on my vacation last spring, lying on the sand, soaking up some rays, and listening to the sound of the waves rushing to the shore." **Semantic memory**, the other type of declarative memory, is memory for general knowledge, or objective facts and information. Semantic memory is involved when a person recalls that Florida is bounded by the Atlantic Ocean on the east and the Gulf of Mexico on the west. It is not necessary to have ever visited Florida to know these facts. Consequently, semantic memory is more like an encyclopedia or a dictionary than a personal diary.

Memory researcher Endel Tulving (1995) points out that the two types of declarative memory do not function independently. For instance, your memory of lying on a beach in Florida (episodic) relies on your understanding of what a beach is (semantic). Likewise, the experience of actually being there (episodic) undoubtedly enhanced your general knowledge of the state (semantic).

Nondeclarative Memory. The second kind of memory, called **nondeclarative memory** (also called *implicit memory*), is the subsystem within long-term memory that stores procedures, motor skills, habits, and simple classically conditioned responses (Squire et al., 1993). Motor skills are acquired through repetitive practice and include such things as eating with a fork, riding a bicycle, or driving a car. Although acquired slowly, once learned, these skills become habit, are quite reliable, and can be carried out with little or no conscious effort. For example, you probably use the keyboard on a computer without consciously being able to name the keys in each row from left to right. Figure 6.3 shows the two subsystems of long-term memory.

semantic memory The type of declarative memory that stores general knowledge, or objective facts and information.

nondeclarative memory The subsystem within long-term memory that stores motor skills, habits, and simple classically conditioned responses; also called implicit memory.

REMEMBER IT

Check your answers and take additional quizzes in MyPsychLab.com.   ✓—Study and Review on MyPsychLab

1. The three processes that comprise memory are _____, _____, and _____.
2. _____ is the ability to retain the image of a visual stimulus in _____ memory for several minutes after it has been removed from view.
3. Information stored in _____ memory must be processed or it will be lost.
4. Declarative memory includes information that can be put into _____ form.
5. Information that you use to ride a bicycle is stored in _____ memory.

A Closer Look at Retrieval

Now that you have an idea of how information flows through the information-processing system, we will turn to a closer examination of the process of extracting information from long-term memory. Wilder Penfield (1969), a Canadian neurosurgeon, proposed an interesting metaphor when he likened memory to a recording, implying that retrieval involves pushing the play button on a mental memory recorder. As you will see, the process is a bit more complex than Penfield's metaphor suggests.

6.5 What are the differences among the recall, recognition, and relearning methods of measuring retrieval?

Measuring Retrieval

As we noted earlier, *retrieval* is the process of bringing information that has been encoded and stored to mind. In general, memory researchers use three types of tasks to measure retrieval. In **recall**, a person must produce required information simply by searching memory. Trying to remember someone's name, the items on a shopping list, or the words of a speech or a poem is a recall task. Which of the following test questions do you think is easier?

What are the three basic memory processes?

Which of the following is *not* one of the three basic memory processes?

a. retrieval **b.** encoding **c.** relearning **d.** storage

Most people think that the second question is easier because it requires only recognition, whereas the first requires recall.

A recall task may be made a little easier if cues are provided to jog memory. A **retrieval cue** is any stimulus or bit of information that aids in retrieving a particular memory. Think about how you might respond to these two test questions:

What are the four basic memory processes?

The four processes involved in memory are e_____, s_____, c_____, and r_____.

Both questions require you to recall information. However, most students would find the second question easier to answer because it includes four retrieval cues.

Recognition is exactly what the name implies. A person simply recognizes something as familiar—a face, a name, a taste, a melody. Multiple-choice, matching, and true/false questions are examples of test items based on recognition. The main difference between recall and recognition is that a recognition task does not require you to supply the information but only to recognize it when you see it. The correct answer is included along with other items in a recognition question.

There is another, more sensitive way to measure memory. With the **relearning method**, retention is expressed as the percentage of time saved when material is relearned relative to the time required to learn the material originally. Suppose it took you 40 minutes to memorize a list of words, and one month later you were tested on those words, using recall or recognition. If you could not recall or recognize a single word, would this mean that you had absolutely no memory of anything on the list? Or could it mean that the recall and recognition tasks were not sensitive enough to measure what little information you may have stored? How could a researcher measure such a remnant of former learning? Using the relearning method, a researcher could time how long it would take you to relearn the list of words. If it took 20 minutes to relearn the list, this would represent a 50% savings over the original learning time of 40 minutes. The percentage of time saved—the *savings score*—reflects how much material remains in long-term memory.

College students demonstrate the relearning method each semester when they study for comprehensive final exams. Relearning material for a final exam takes less time than it took to learn the material originally.

▲ Are you better at remembering faces than names? Have you ever wondered why? It's because the task involves recognition rather than recall. You must recall the name but merely recognize the face.

recall A memory task in which a person must produce required information by searching memory.

retrieval cue Any stimulus or bit of information that aids in retrieving particular information from long-term memory.

recognition A memory task in which a person must simply identify material as familiar or as having been encountered before.

relearning method A measure of memory in which retention is expressed as the percentage of time saved when material is relearned compared with the time required to learn the material originally.

6.6 How do the serial position, context, and state-dependent memory effects influence retrieval?

Influences on Retrieval

As you have probably learned from everyday experience, retrieval sometimes happens effectively and efficiently, but there are also times when retrieval is more elusive. Studies show that a number of factors influence the process.

The Serial Position Effect. What would happen if you were introduced to a dozen people at a party? You would most likely recall the names of the first few people you met and the last one or two, but forget many of the names in the middle. The reason is the **serial position effect**—the finding that, for information learned in a sequence, recall is better for items at the beginning and the end than for items in the middle of the sequence.

Information at the beginning of a sequence is subject to the **primacy effect**—the tendency to recall the first items in a sequence more readily than the middle items. Such information is likely to be recalled because it already has been placed in long-term memory. Information at the end of a sequence is subject to the **recency effect**—the tendency to recall the last items in a sequence more readily than those in the middle. This information has an even higher probability of being recalled because it is still in short-term memory. The poorer recall of information in the middle of a sequence occurs because that information is no longer in short-term memory and has not yet been placed in long-term memory. The serial position effect lends strong support to the notion of separate systems for short-term and long-term memory (Postman & Phillips, 1965). ✳

The Context Effect. Have you ever stood in your living room and thought of something you needed from your bedroom, only to forget what it was when you got there? Did the item come to mind again when you returned to the living room? Tulving and Thompson (1973) suggested that many elements of the physical setting in which a person learns information are encoded along with the information and become part of the memory, a process called the **context effect**. If part or all of the original context is reinstated, it may serve as a retrieval cue. That is why returning to the living room elicits the memory of the object you intended to get from the bedroom. In fact, just visualizing yourself in the living room might do the trick (Smith, Glenberg, & Bjork, 1978). (*Hint:* Next time you're taking a test and having difficulty recalling something, try visualizing yourself in the room where you studied.)

Godden and Baddeley (1975) conducted one of the early studies of context and memory with members of a university diving club. Participants memorized a list of words when they were either 10 feet underwater or on land. They were later tested for recall of the words in the same or a different environment. Words learned underwater were best recalled underwater, and words learned on land were best recalled on land. In fact, when the divers learned and recalled the words in the same context, their scores were 47% higher than when the two contexts were different (see Figure 6.4).

Odors can also supply powerful and enduring retrieval cues for memory. In one study, researchers introduced vanilla scent into a room in which participants were learning a memory-for-location task, that is, a task in which experimenters asked them remember locations of objects that were placed in a variety of places around the room (Schwab & Wolf, 2009). When the experimenters tested participants on the task the next day, those who were tested in a vanilla-scented room outperformed those who were tested in an unscented setting.

serial position effect The finding that, for information learned in a sequence, recall is better for the beginning and ending items than for the middle items in the sequence.

primacy effect The tendency to recall the first items in a sequence more readily than the middle items.

recency effect The tendency to recall the last items in a sequence more readily than those in the middle.

✳ Explore the **Concept** *Retrieval of Long-Term Memories* on **MyPsychLab**

context effect The tendency to encode elements of the physical setting in which information is learned along with memory of the information itself.

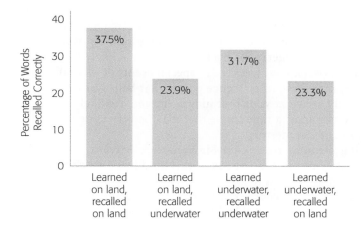

FIGURE 6.4 **The Context Effect**

state-dependent memory effect The tendency to recall information better if one is in the same pharmacological or psychological state as when the information was encoded.

The State-Dependent Memory Effect. The emotional state that a person was in when she formed a memory affects her ability to recall it. Psychologists call this the **state-dependent memory effect**. The effect appears to be greater for episodic than for semantic memories (Eysenck & Keane, 2010). It is also stronger when positive emotions are involved. However, animal studies suggest that anxiety is one negative emotion for which state-dependent memory effects are pronounced (Packard, 2009).

Research with human participants has also revealed an association between anxiety and the state-dependent memory effect. For example, when researchers exposed college students to spiders and/or snakes while they were learning lists of words (presumably an anxiety-inducing experience!), the students recalled more words when the creatures were also present during tests of recall (Lang et al., 2001).

REMEMBER IT   *Check your answers and take additional quizzes in MyPsychLab.com.*   ✓—Study and **Review** on **MyPsychLab**

1. One way in which a researcher using the _____ method to study memory for stories would be to ask participants to read a brief story and then retell it to her.
2. If you attempted to recall a series of events but could only remember the first and last one, you would be experiencing the _____.
3. The _____ happens when individuals acquire information while in an altered state of consciousness or when experiencing a particular emotion.

Remembering as Reconstruction

Memory researcher Henry Roediger (1980) has pointed out that the Atkinson–Shiffrin model and others like it seem to suggest that getting information out of memory requires little more than opening the door to a mental closet and pulling out a needed item. However, quite often, the process of remembering more closely resembles creating a multicolored, multitextured work of art than searching a mental closet (Loftus & Loftus, 1980). Thus, in addition to retrieval, the act of remembering often includes a creative element.

6.7 What does "Memory is reconstructive" mean?

The Process of Reconstruction

reconstruction An account of an event that has been pieced together from a few highlights.

In some cases, the act of bringing stored information to mind involves piecing together a plausible representation of an object or event based on fragmentary information, a process called **reconstruction** (Loftus & Loftus, 1980). For example, suppose you were asked to recall the last time you saw your best friend. Because it's unlikely that you encoded the date of your last meeting along with your memory of it, you can't truly "retrieve" an answer to the question. So, you would have to use reconstructive memory. You would probably begin with the current day and think backwards. If you saw your friend within the last few days, you should be able to recall the time frame—yesterday, a couple of days ago, last week—fairly quickly. If the interval has been longer, your backward search is likely to be marked by different kinds of days (weekdays, weekends), special events (a football game), or holidays (Thanksgiving) that serve as reference points that help you narrow the time frame. When you finally arrive at your best judgment, you are likely to say something like "a couple of weeks ago," a time frame that may be very close to or very far from the actual date of your last meeting.

schemas Frameworks of knowledge and assumptions that we have about people, objects, and events.

Pioneering memory researcher Sir Frederick Bartlett (1886–1969) suggested that reconstructive memory processes of this kind employ **schemas**, frameworks of knowledge, and assumptions that we have about people, objects, and events. Schemas are helpful to memory because they provide us with meaningful ways of chunking individual bits of information, thereby increasing the efficiency of working memory.

Schema-based processing is evident when we process complex types of information. For instance, suppose you read the headline, "Dog Saves Boy from Drowning." What facts would you expect to be included in the story? You might expect to read about where the incident took place; perhaps it happened at a beach or in a neighborhood swimming pool. But you would be unlikely to expect to read about a canine rescue that occurred in a bathtub. Why?—because schemas are based on situational averages. Drownings occur most often in bodies of water in which people swim. Thus, the schema evoked by the headline would cause you to picture the incident taking place in the setting that would be most likely.

Once invoked, schemas focus our attention on the essential elements in new information and increase the chances that we will store them in long-term memory. At the same time, schema-based processing causes us to ignore unimportant details. Thus, in the "Dog Saves Boy…" story, the fact that the incident happened in a lake rather than a swimming pool would be an essential element, but the name of the lake would not be. Consequently, you would probably remember that the episode took place in a lake but fail to remember its name. If, while recounting the story at a later time, you were asked about the name of the lake, you would reconstruct your memory of it by considering plausible alternatives, a process that is somewhat like entering terms in an Internet search engine such as Google. The possible names that you generated would be based on your knowledge of lakes or on some feature of the name that you recall from the story. For example, you might remember that the name was the name of a tree along with the word "forest." As a result, you would search your memory by trying out combinations such as "oak forest" or "pine forest" that make sense as names for lakes. That is, you would accept "oak forest" as plausible and reject "palm forest" as implausible because palm trees are associated with oceans rather than lakes. The name you finally settle on, if any, as a result of using these reconstructive strategies may or may not be accurate, but it will be plausible.

As you can see, using schemas to reconstruct memories can lead to inaccuracies (See the *Try It* on p. 190). Bartlett (1932) studied the distorting effects of reconstruction by giving participants stories to read and asking them to reproduce the stories after varying amounts of time. Accurate reports were rare. Participants made the stories shorter and substituted familiar objects for the unusual ones that the stories described. These errors increased over time, and participants were unable to distinguish between the parts of their reproduced stories that they actually remembered from those that they had created.

Source, Flashbulb, and Autobiographical Memories ▶

6.8 What have researchers learned about source, flashbulb, and autobiographical memories?

You might be thinking that reconstructive memory processes should be avoided because of their potential for distorting our recollections. Perhaps we should make an effort to commit every detail of our experiences to memory. Following this practice might enable us to reduce the chances of generating inaccurate memories, but we would lose a great deal of efficiency in the process. Thus, reconstructive memory processes are common in everyday life. Moreover, there are some types of memories, such as *source memories*, *flashbulb memories*, and *autobiographical memories*, that are best understood as a function of reconstructive processes.

Source Memory. A **source memory** is a recollection of the circumstances in which you formed a memory. Most of our memories do not include source information. For example, you know that Paris is the capital of France, but you probably have no idea exactly when or how you acquired the information. Thus, when we need to know the source of a memory, we usually must reconstruct it (Johnson, Hashtroudi, & Lindsay, 1993). For instance, suppose you see a new brand of shampoo on a store shelf, recognize it as one you have heard of, but are unable to remember how you learned about it. If you are really curious about the source, you could use your "ways-of-learning-about-products" schemas to search your memory for the most plausible source. You would probably consider television commercials, pop-up ads, and so on.

source memory A recollection of the circumstances in which you formed a memory.

TRY IT   Creating a False Memory

Perhaps you have heard that people sometimes suddenly "remember" an event that happened long ago only to find out that the event never actually happened. Such "false" memories make us wonder about the accuracy of human memory—just how easy is it to create such a memory? Read all these words aloud at a rate of about one word per second. Then close your book and write down all the words you can remember.

bed	dream	nap	rest
wake	yawn	awake	snooze
snore	tired	doze	slumber

Now check your list. Did you "remember" the word *sleep*? Many people do, even though it is not one of the words on the list (Deese, 1959). As you can see, creating a false memory really isn't all that difficult, and it is something that can happen to anyone.

source monitoring Intentionally keeping track of the sources of incoming information.

flashbulb memories Memories for shocking, emotion-provoking events that include information about the source from which the information was acquired.

▲ Eyewitnesses to the aftermath of the terrorist attacks on the World Trade Center almost certainly formed flashbulb memories of the horrific events they witnessed. Do you remember where you were and what you were doing when you heard the news on September 11, 2001?

And, as is true of all schema-based processing, the source you come up with might not be accurate.

In order to encode source information along with a memory, you must engage in **source monitoring**, the practice of intentionally keeping track of the sources of incoming information. Source monitoring is particularly important when you are working on a research paper. This is so because the memory system tends to focus on the meaning of information rather than its source, especially when forming semantic memories. Thus, when you read a passage of text in an article or other reference and store it in your semantic memory for future use, reconstructive memory processes may lead you to mistakenly believe that you thought of it yourself when you are writing your paper (a phenomenon called *cryptomnesia*). As a result, you may, at best, omit a needed citation, or, at worst, unknowingly commit plagiarism (Carroll & Perfect, 2002). Fortunately, research shows that, when we consciously practice source monitoring, we can protect our memories from distortions of this kind.

Flashbulb Memories.   Do you remember how you learned about the terrorist attacks of September 11, 2001? Memories for shocking, emotion-provoking events that include information about the source from which the information was acquired are called **flashbulb memories**. This term reflects early researchers' hypothesis (e.g., Brown & Kulik, 1977) that the shocking nature of such events works somewhat like a camera flash that freezes a moment in time. They believed that flashbulb memories were photographic, highly detailed, and resistant to change. However, since the early 1990s, psychologists have thought of flashbulb memory as a subcategory of source memory. Studies showing that the inclusion of source information is the primary characteristic that distinguishes flashbulb from other types of memories were responsible for this shift (Brewer, 1992).

Research has also shown that flashbulb memories are reconstructive in nature (Curci, 2009). That is, we don't pull up a mental snapshot when we recall them. Instead, we rebuild flashbulb memories piece by piece. Moreover, some of the pieces do not come from our own memories of the traumatic event but are derived from the memories of other people that we acquire through casual conversation and later misidentify as our own (Hirst & Echterhoff, 2012). As a result, like other kinds of reconstructed recollections, flashbulb memories change over time. Results such as those of researcher William Hirst and his colleagues illustrate this pattern of findings (Hirst et al., 2009). Hirst and his team questioned participants about their memories of September 11 a few days after the event, 1 year later, and 3 years later. At all three points, the researchers asked flashbulb/source memory questions, such as "How did you hear about the attacks?" along with event memory questions, such as "How many planes were involved?" They found that over the 3-year period, participants forgot source and event details at about the same rate. Nevertheless, participants expressed far more confidence in their flashbulb memories than they did in their event memories. Research findings on the unshakable faith that participants have in the accuracy of their flashbulb memories are so consistent that most researchers now agree that a high degree of confidence (justified or not) in their accuracy is a defining feature of flashbulb memories (Talarico & Rubin, 2009).

Autobiographical Memories. Autobiographical memories are recollections that a person includes in an account of his or her own life (Kelley & Jacoby, 2012). They are reconstructive in nature and include factual, emotional, and interpretive information. For example, an autobiographical memory of your first day at college would include facts such as which classes you attended, images such as the classroom where you heard your psychology professor's first lecture of the term, and emotions such as the anxiety you felt about finding your way around campus. Your interpretation of the day might be reflected in the content of an e-mail you sent to your best friend that evening in which you summarized the events of the day and your feelings of relief that your first day was over. As a result, the text of the e-mail is likely to be linked to your other memories of the day in your long-term memory and become the outline for the "first-day-of-college-story" that you retell every time the topic comes up in conversation. Years later, you might pass on the same story to your children when they go to college. (Failure to engage in source monitoring would probably cause you to forget that the story began as an e-mail to a friend, by the way.)

Interestingly, research has shown that autobiographical memories are particularly subject to **positive bias**, the tendency for pleasant autobiographical memories to be more easily recalled than unpleasant ones and memories of unpleasant events to become more emotionally positive over time (Rubin, Boals, & Klein, 2010; Wood & Conway, 2006). In one study of positive bias that examined college students' memories of their high school grades, nearly all of the participants remembered their As accurately, but only 29% remembered their Ds (Bahrick, Hall, & Berger, 1996). Researchers speculate that positive bias results when our current need for emotional well-being serves as a schema that we use to reconstruct unpleasant memories (Kennedy, Mather, & Carstensen, 2004). In other words, if maintaining our current mental health requires recasting a memory of an unpleasant or traumatic event in a more positive light, our memories seem to be willing to sacrifice a bit of accuracy in the interest of our emotional well-being.

Influences on Reconstructive Memory ▶

You learned earlier that some features of information, such as the headlines of news stories, influence reconstructive memory processes by invoking schemas. Like other information we acquire through experience, schemas are stored in long-term memory. Thus, research on schema-based processing shows that prior knowledge contributes to reconstructive memory processes. Two important sources of prior knowledge are *expertise* and *culture*.

Expertise. If you possess an extensive amount of relevant background knowledge, or **expertise**, for a reconstructive memory task, your performance on the task will exceed that of others who are less knowledgeable. In classic research, Chase and Simon (1973) presented chess champions and volunteers who had little or no experience with the game with several arrays of pieces on chess boards. Some of the arrays were plausible within the rules of the game, but others were random. After participants viewed each array for a few seconds, the researchers removed the pieces from the board and asked the participants to reproduce the configuration they had just seen. Chase and Simon found that the champions were much better than the non-champions at reproducing the plausible configurations both immediately and after a brief delay. That is, the experts introduced fewer reconstructive distortions into

autobiographical memories Recollections that a person includes in an account of the events of his or her own life.

positive bias The tendency for pleasant autobiographical memories to be more easily recalled than unpleasant ones and memories of unpleasant events to become more emotionally positive over time.

6.9 How do expertise and culture influence reconstructive memory?

expertise An extensive amount of background knowledge that is relevant to a reconstructive memory task.

the reproduction task than the nonexperts did. By contrast, there were no group differences with regard to the random arrangements. Chase and Simon concluded that the expertise the chess champions had acquired over many years of playing the game enabled them to integrate the individual pieces into meaningful chunks, rendering their reconstructive memories for the arrays more efficient and more accurate than those of the nonchampions.

Researchers have examined the impact of expertise on reconstructive memory in knowledge domains ranging from baseball to waiting tables. The results of all of these studies are consistent with the classic findings of Chase and Simon. That is, people who know a lot about baseball can reconstruct the events of a baseball game more accurately than nonexperts can (Ricks & Wiley, 2009). Similarly, professional restaurant servers can faithfully reconstruct complicated food orders from memory, while nonservers perform poorly on the task (Bekinschtein, Cardozo, & Manes, 2008). Researchers attribute the effects of expertise on reconstructive memory to increased efficiency in working memory (Ricks & Wiley, 2009). Thus, having a lot of relevant knowledge for a reconstructive memory task enables you to take in more information, encode it more efficiently, and apply it more accurately than you can to tasks for which you do not possess much relevant knowledge.

Culture. The effects of expertise are evident in research examining cultural influences on reconstructive memory as well. In one classic study, Sir Frederick Bartlett (1932) described the amazing ability of the Swazi people of Africa to remember the slight differences in individual characteristics of their cows. One Swazi herdsman, Bartlett claimed, could remember details of every cow he had tended the year before. Such a feat is less surprising when you consider that the key component of traditional Swazi culture is the herds of cattle the people tend and depend on for their living. Do the Swazi people have super memory powers? Bartlett asked young Swazi men and young European men to recall a message consisting of 25 words. In this case, the Swazi had no better recall ability than the Europeans.

The effects of cultural schemas on reconstructive memory are also evident in studies showing that people more easily remember stories set in their own cultures than those set in others, just as they more easily recognize photographs of people of their own ethnic group than they do those of others (Corenblum & Meissner, 2006). In one of the first of these studies, researchers told women in the United States and Aboriginal women in Australia a story about a sick child (Steffensen & Calker, 1982). Participants were randomly assigned to groups for which story outcomes were varied. In one version, the girl got well after being treated by a physician. In the other, a traditional native healer was called in to help the girl. Aboriginal participants better recalled the story with the native healer, while the American women were more accurate in their recall of the story in which a physician treated the girl. Most likely, these results reflect the influence of culturally based schemas. Aboriginal participants' schemas led them to expect a story about a sick child to include a native healer, and the story that fit with these expectations was easier for them to understand and remember. Just the opposite was true for the Western participants.

In addition, cultural values prompt oral historians to engage in source monitoring as they recount important information, thereby protecting information that must be passed on verbatim (i.e., word-for-word) from the potentially distorting effects of reconstructive memory. Source monitoring provides such protection by enabling oral historians to distinguish the original material they learned from older group members from their own interpretive thoughts about the material and from ideas proposed by others.

For example, among many tribal peoples in Africa, the history of the tribe is preserved orally by specialists, who must be able to encode, store, and retrieve huge

▲ In many traditional cultures, elders are oral historians, remembering and passing on the details of tribal traditions and myths as well as genealogical data.

volumes of historical data (D'Azevedo, 1982). Elders of the Iatmul people of New Guinea are also said to have committed to memory the lines of descent for the various clans of their people, stretching back for many generations (Bateson, 1982). The unerring memory of the elders for the kinship patterns of their people is used to resolve disputed property claims (Mistry & Rogoff, 1994).

Barbara Rogoff, an expert in cultural psychology, maintains that such phenomenal memory feats are best explained and understood in their cultural context (Rogoff & Mistry, 1985). The tribal elders perform their impressive memory feats because the information is an integral and critically important part of the culture in which they live. Most likely, their ability to remember nonmeaningful information would be no better than your own.

REMEMBER IT   *Check your answers and take additional quizzes in MyPsychLab.com.* ✔●—Study and Review on MyPsychLab

1. When a person uses _____ to process information, both encoding and retrieval can be affected.
2. Remembering how you learned a particular piece of information is known as _____ memory.
3. _____ memories are vivid memories of where and when an individual learned of a particularly dramatic event.
4. _____ memories are subject to positive bias.
5. Oral historians who have memorized hundreds of years of a culture's history possess memory abilities that are superior to those of individuals who do not serve in these roles. (true/false)

Forgetting

As you have seen, both retrieval and reconstruction are associated with memory failure to some degree. **Forgetting**, the inability to bring to mind information that was previously remembered, represents another kind of memory failure. Pioneering researcher Hermann Ebbinghaus (1850–1909) studied forgetting extensively. Since Ebbinghaus's time, memory researchers have proposed a number of different explanations of forgetting.

forgetting The inability to bring to mind information that was previously remembered.

Ebbinghaus and the Curve of Forgetting ▶

6.10 What did Ebbinghaus discover about forgetting?

Hermann Ebbinghaus (1850–1909) conducted the first experimental studies on learning and memory. He performed his studies on memory using 2,300 nonsense syllables as his material and himself as the only participant (1885/1964). He carried out all his experiments at about the same time of day in the same surroundings, eliminating all possible distractions. Ebbinghaus memorized lists of nonsense syllables (strings of letters such as LEJ and XIZ) by repeating them over and over at a constant rate of 2.5 syllables per second, marking time with a metronome or a ticking watch. He repeated a list until he could recall it twice without error, a measure he called *mastery.*

Ebbinghaus recorded the amount of time or the number of trials it took to memorize his lists to mastery. Then, after different periods of time had passed and forgetting had occurred, he recorded the amount of time or number of trials needed to relearn the same list to mastery (remember the relearning method that we discussed earlier?). Ebbinghaus compared the time or number of trials required for relearning with that for original learning and then computed the percentage of time saved. This savings score represented the percentage of the original learning that remained in memory.

Ebbinghaus learned and relearned more than 1,200 lists of nonsense syllables to discover how rapidly forgetting occurs. Figure 6.5 on p. 194 shows his famous **curve of forgetting**, which consists of savings scores at various time intervals after the original learning. The curve of forgetting shows that the largest amount of forgetting occurs very quickly, after which forgetting tapers off. Of the information

curve of forgetting The pattern of forgetting discovered by Ebbinghaus, which shows that forgetting tapers off after a period of rapid information loss that immediately follows learning.

FIGURE 6.5 **Ebbinghaus's Curve of Forgetting**
After memorizing lists of nonsense syllables similar to those at left, Ebbinghaus measured his retention after varying intervals of time using the relearning method. Forgetting was most rapid at first, as shown by his retention of only 58% after 20 minutes and 44% after 1 hour. Then, the rate of forgetting tapered off, with a retention of 34% after 1 day, 25% after 6 days, and 21% after 31 days.

Source: Data from Ebbinghaus (1885/1964, 1913).

Ebbinghaus retained after a day or two, very little more would be forgotten even a month later. But, remember, this curve of forgetting applies to nonsense syllables. Meaningful material is usually forgotten more slowly, as is material that has been carefully encoded, deeply processed, and frequently rehearsed.

What Ebbinghaus learned about the rate of forgetting is relevant for everyone. Do you, like most students, cram before a big exam? If so, don't assume that everything you memorize on Monday can be held intact until Tuesday. So much forgetting occurs within the first 24 hours that it is wise to spend at least some time reviewing the material on the day of the test. The less meaningful the material is to you, the more you will forget and the more necessary a review is. Recall from Chapter 4 that the quantity and quality of sleep you get between studying and taking the test also influences how much you will remember.

6.11 **Why do we forget?**

Why Do We Forget?

Why do we fail to remember, even when we put forth a lot of effort aimed at remembering? Psychologists have proposed several explanations. Studies examining these proposals have led researchers to conclude that there are several different causes for forgetting.

encoding failure A cause of forgetting that occurs when information was never put into long-term memory.

Encoding Failure. The inability to remember is sometimes a result of **encoding failure**—the information was never put into long-term memory in the first place. Of the many things we encounter every day, it is surprising how little we actually encode. Can you recall accurately, or even recognize, something you have seen thousands of times before? Read the *Try It* on the next page to find out.

In your lifetime, you have seen thousands of pennies, but unless you are a coin collector, you probably have not encoded the details of a penny's appearance. If you did poorly on the *Try It,* you have plenty of company. After studying a large group of participants, Nickerson and Adams (1979) reported that few people could reproduce a penny from recall. In fact, only a handful of participants could even recognize an accurate drawing of a penny when it was presented along with incorrect drawings. (The correct penny is the one labeled A in the *Try It.*)

decay theory The oldest theory of forgetting, which holds that memories, if not used, fade with time and ultimately disappear altogether.

Decay. **Decay theory**, which is probably the oldest theory of forgetting, assumes that memories, if not used, fade with time and ultimately disappear entirely. The word *decay* implies a physiological change in the neurons that recorded the experience. According to this theory, the neuronal record may decay or fade within seconds, days, or even much longer periods of time. While decay, or the fading of memories, is probably a cause of forgetting in sensory and short-term memory, there does not appear to be a gradual, inevitable decay of long-term memories. In one study, Harry

TRY IT   **A Penny for Your Thoughts**

On a sheet of paper, draw a sketch of a U.S. penny from memory using recall. In your drawing, show the direction in which President Lincoln's image is facing and the location of the date and include all the words on the heads side of the penny. Or try the easier recognition task and see if you can recognize the real penny in the drawings. (From Nickerson & Adams, 1979.)

Tip: The next time someone you know claims to have "photographic" memory, use this _Try It_ to put him or her to the test.

A   B

Bahrick and others (1975) found that after 35 years, participants could recognize 90% of their high school classmates' names and photographs, the same percentage as for recent graduates.

Interference. A major cause of forgetting that affects people every day is **interference**, when information stored either before or after a given memory can hinder the ability to remember it. For example, a well-known experiment in psychology called the _Stroop test_ requires research participants to memorize color words that are shown in colored type (see Figure 6.6). As you might guess, remembering the word _red_ is much easier when it is written in red than when it is written in yellow. The colors of the words interfere with retrieval of their meanings because the colors prime, or prompt, participants to retrieve the names of the colors rather than the meanings of the words. ◉▶

Whenever you try to recall any given memory, two types of interference can hinder the effort. Information or associations stored either _before_ or _after_ a given memory can interfere with the ability to remember it (see Figure 6.7). Also, the more similar the interfering associations are to the information a person is trying to recall, the more difficult it is to recall the information (Underwood, 1964).

Proactive interference occurs when information or experiences already stored in long-term memory hinder the ability to remember newer information (Underwood, 1957). For example, Laura's romance with her new boyfriend, Todd, got off to a bad start when she accidentally called him "Dave," her former boyfriend's name. One explanation for proactive interference is the competition between old and new responses (Bower, Thompson-Schill, & Tulving, 1994).

Retroactive interference happens when new learning interferes with the ability to remember previously learned information. The more similar the new material is to that learned earlier, the more interference there is. For example, when you take a psychology class, it may interfere with your ability to remember what you learned

interference A cause of forgetting that occurs because information or associations stored either before or after a given memory hinder the ability to remember it.

◉▶ **Simulate** _The Stroop Effect_ on **MyPsychLab**

RED   RED

GREEN   GREEN

BLUE   BLUE

FIGURE 6.6 The Stroop Test
Which list of words do you think would be easier to remember?

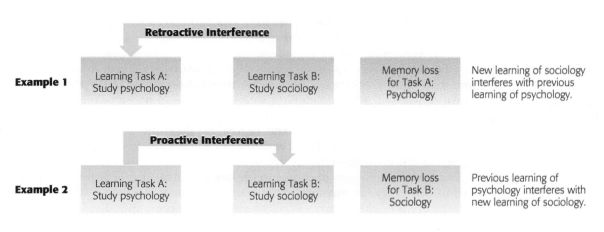

Retroactive Interference

| Example 1 | Learning Task A: Study psychology | Learning Task B: Study sociology | Memory loss for Task A: Psychology | New learning of sociology interferes with previous learning of psychology. |

Proactive Interference

| Example 2 | Learning Task A: Study psychology | Learning Task B: Study sociology | Memory loss for Task B: Sociology | Previous learning of psychology interferes with new learning of sociology. |

FIGURE 6.7
Retroactive and Proactive Interference
As shown in Example 1, retroactive interference occurs when new learning hinders the ability to recall information learned previously. As shown in Example 2, proactive interference occurs when prior learning hinders new learning.

in your sociology class, especially with regard to theories (e.g., psychoanalysis) that are shared by the two disciplines but applied and interpreted differently. However, research shows that the effects of retroactive interference are often temporary (Lustig, Konkel, & Jacoby, 2004). In fact, after some time has passed, the old information may be better remembered than the information that was learned more recently. As a consequence, what a student learned in a previous sociology course may appear to fade when she encounters similar information presented in a somewhat different light in a psychology course. In the long run, however, her sociology knowledge may outlast what she learned in psychology.

Consolidation Failure. *Consolidation* is the physiological process by which encoded information is stored in memory. **Consolidation failure** can result from anything that disrupts the consolidation process, typically an event that causes a person to lose consciousness—a car accident, a blow to the head, an epileptic seizure, or an electroconvulsive shock treatment given for severe depression. Moreover, as you learned in Chapter 4, REM sleep is critical to memory consolidation (Walker & Stickgold, 2006). As a result, when you don't get enough REM sleep, the information you acquired during the day may be lost due to consolidation failure (Fogel, Smith, & Beninger, 2010).

consolidation failure Any disruption in the consolidation process that prevents a long-term memory from forming.

Motivated Forgetting. We have discussed ways to avoid forgetting, but there are occasions when people may want to avoid remembering—times when they want to forget. Victims of rape or physical abuse, war veterans, and survivors of airplane crashes or earthquakes all have had terrifying experiences that may haunt them for years. These victims are certainly motivated to forget their traumatic experiences, but even people who have not experienced any trauma use **motivated forgetting** to protect themselves from experiences that are painful, frightening, or otherwise unpleasant. With one form of motivated forgetting, *suppression,* a person makes a conscious, active attempt to put a painful, disturbing, anxiety- or guilt-provoking memory out of mind, but the person is still aware that the painful event occurred. With another type of motivated forgetting, *repression,* unpleasant memories are literally removed from consciousness, and the person is no longer aware that the unpleasant event ever occurred (Freud, 1922).

motivated forgetting Forgetting through suppression or repression in an effort to protect oneself from material that is painful, frightening, or otherwise unpleasant.

Prospective Forgetting. Prospective forgetting is not remembering to carry out some intended action (e.g., forgetting to go to your dentist appointment). People are most likely to forget to do the things they view as unimportant, unpleasant, or burdensome. They are less likely to forget things that are pleasurable or important to them (Winograd, 1988). However, as you probably know, prospective forgetting isn't always motivated by a desire to avoid something. Have you ever arrived home and suddenly remembered that you had intended to go to the bank to deposit your paycheck? If so, then you have personally experienced prospective forgetting.

prospective forgetting Not remembering to carry out some intended action.

Retrieval Failure. How many times have you had this experience? While taking a test, you can't remember the answer to a question that you are sure you know. Often, people are certain they know something but are not able to retrieve the information when they need it. This type of forgetting is called **retrieval failure**. A common experience with retrieval failure is known as the **tip-of-the-tongue (TOT) phenomenon** (Brown & McNeil, 1966). You have surely experienced trying to recall a name, a word, or some other bit of information, knowing that you knew it but are not able to come up with it. You were on the verge of recalling the word or name, perhaps aware of the number of syllables and the beginning or ending letter. It was on the tip of your tongue, but it just wouldn't quite come out.

retrieval failure Not remembering something one is certain of knowing.

tip-of-the-tongue (TOT) phenomenon The experience of knowing that a particular piece of information has been learned but being unable to retrieve it.

The tip-of-the-tongue phenomenon is one of the most thoroughly researched of all of our everyday memory experiences (Gollan & Brown, 2006). A similar experience, *tip-of-the-fingers (TOF) phenomenon,* occurs in individuals who use sign language to communicate. In both speakers and signers, proper names are the subject of this kind of retrieval failure more often than other kinds of words (Thompson, Emmorey, & Gollan, 2005). Regardless of the object of a TOT event, research suggests that the best strategy for overcoming this kind of retrieval failure is to divert your attention from it for a brief period and return to your retrieval efforts at a later time (Choi & Smith, 2005). This finding provides support for one frequently heard test-taking tip: Skip items for which answers do not immediately come to mind and return to them after you have answered all of the questions that you are sure you know the answers to.

SUMMARIZE IT

Forgetting

TYPE OF FORGETTING	DESCRIPTION	EXAMPLE
Encoding failure	Information was never stored in memory	Failing to remember details of everyday objective such as coins
Decay	Unused information fades over time	Information in sensory memory disappears if not moved on to short-term memory
Interference	One piece of information displaces another	A person recalls her old phone number when she intends to recall her new one
Consolidation failure	Disruption of consolidation prevents information from being stored in long-term memory	A blow to the head causes a person to forget everything that happened in the minutes immediately preceding the blow
Motivated forgetting	Loss of information that is emotionally unpleasant	A soldier forgets about witnessing the combat-related death of his best friend
Prospective forgetting	Forgetting to carry out an intended action	A student forgets to transfer his laundry from the washer to the dryer until he discovers the washer full of wet clothes the next day
Retrieval failure	Forgetting something you are sure that you know	Remembering the answer to a test question after you turn in the exam

REMEMBER IT

Check your answers and take additional quizzes in MyPsychLab.com.   ✓● Study and Review on **MyPsychLab**

1. _____ invented the nonsense syllable, conceived the relearning method for retention, and plotted the curve of forgetting.

2. _____ explains why the word *red* is easier to remember when it is written in red rather than in another color.

3. _____ theory assumes that memories, if not used, fade with time and ultimately disappear altogether.

Biology and Memory

Obviously, a person's vast store of memories must exist physically somewhere in the brain. Neuronal processes are also involved in the storage of information in the brain. Trauma and disorders that affect brain structures, neuronal health, or both can seriously impair memory function.

6.12 What brain structures are associated with memory?

hippocampal region A part of the limbic system, which includes the hippocampus itself and the underlying cortical areas, involved in the formation of semantic memories.

◉⊣**Watch** the Video *Episode 8: Special Topics: When Memory Fails* in **MyPsychLab**

6.13 Why is long-term potentiation important?

The Hippocampus and Hippocampal Region

Researchers continue to identify specific locations in the brain that mediate functions and processes in memory (Rissman & Wagner, 2012). One important source of information comes from people who have experienced memory loss resulting from damage to specific brain areas. One especially significant case is that of H. M., a man who suffered from such severe epilepsy that, out of desperation, he agreed to a radical surgical procedure. The surgeon removed the part of the brain believed to be causing H. M.'s seizures—the middle portions of both temporal lobes just above the ears, containing the amygdala and the **hippocampal region**, which includes the hippocampus itself and the underlying cortical areas (look back at Figure 2.8 on page 51). It was 1953, and H. M. was 27 years old.

After his surgery, H. M. remained intelligent and psychologically stable, and his seizures were drastically reduced. But unfortunately, the tissue cut from H. M.'s brain housed more than the site of his seizures. It also contained his ability to use working memory to store new information in long-term memory. Although the capacity of his short-term memory remained the same and he remembered life events that were stored before the operation, H. M. was unable to remember a single event that occurred after the surgery. And when H. M. passed away in 2008 at the age of 82, as far as his conscious long-term memory was concerned, it was still 1953 and he was still 27 years old.

Surgery affected only H. M.'s declarative, long-term memory—his ability to store facts, personal experiences, names, faces, telephone numbers, and the like. But researchers were surprised to discover that he could still form nondeclarative memories; that is, he could still acquire skills through repetitive practice, although he could not remember having done so. For example, after the surgery, H. M. learned to play tennis and improve his game, but he had no memory of ever having played (Milner, 1966, 1970; Milner et al., 1968). ◉

Most research supports the hypothesis that the hippocampus is especially important in forming episodic memories (Redish & Ekstrom, 2013). Semantic memory, however, depends not only on the hippocampus but also on the other parts of the hippocampal region (Wolk & Budson, 2010). Once stored, memories can be retrieved without the involvement of the hippocampus (Gluck & Myers, 1997; McClelland, McNaughton, & O'Reilly, 1995). Consequently, many researchers argue that the neurological networks that store episodic and semantic memories are entirely separate (e.g., Tulving, 2002). But the degree to which the brain processes associated with episodic and semantic memories can be clearly distinguished is being questioned by some neuroscientists. Research involving older adults who suffer from semantic dementia due to frontal lobe damage shows that many of them suffer from deficiencies in episodic memory (Nestor et al., 2002). Moreover, other studies show that damage to the temporal and occipital lobes can affect episodic memory (Wheeler & McMillan, 2001).

An interesting series of studies (Maguire, Nannery, & Spiers, 2006; Maguire et al., 2000), which were described briefly in Chapter 2, suggest that the hippocampus may serve special functions in addition to those already known. A part of the hippocampus evidently specializes in navigational skills by helping to create intricate neural spatial maps. Using magnetic resonance imaging (MRI) scans, researchers found that the rear (posterior) region of the hippocampus of London taxi drivers was significantly larger than that of participants in a matched control group whose living did not depend on navigational skills (see Figure 6.8). In addition, the more time spent as a taxi driver, the greater the size of this part of the hippocampus.

Neuronal Changes and Memory

Some researchers are exploring memory at deeper levels than the structures of the brain. Some look at the actions of single neurons; others study collections of neurons and their synapses and the neurotransmitters whose chemical action begins the process of recording and storing a memory (Carriba et al., 2012). The first close look at how memory works in single neurons was provided by Eric Kandel and his colleagues, who traced the effects of learning and memory in the sea snail *Aplysia* (Dale & Kandel, 1990). Using tiny

(a)   **(b)**

FIGURE 6.8 **MRI Scans Showing the Larger Size of the Posterior Hippocampus in the Brain of an Experienced Taxi Driver**
The posterior (rear) hippocampus of an experienced London taxi driver, shown in red in the MRI scan on the left, is significantly larger than the posterior hippocampus of a research participant who was not a taxi driver, shown in red in the scan on the right.
Source: Adapted from Maguire et al. (2000).

electrodes implanted in several single neurons in this snail, the researchers mapped the neural circuits that are formed and maintained as the animal learns and remembers. They also discovered the different types of protein synthesis that facilitate short-term and long-term memory (Sweatt & Kandel, 1989). Kandel won a Nobel Prize in 2000 for his work.

The studies of learning and memory in *Aplysia* reflect only simple classical conditioning, which is a type of nondeclarative memory. Other researchers studying mammals report that physical changes occur in the neurons and synapses in brain regions involved in declarative memory (Lee & Kesner, 2002).

As far back as the 1940s, Canadian psychologist Donald O. Hebb (1949) argued that learning and memory must involve the enhancement of transmission at the synapses between neurons. The most widely studied model for learning and memory at the level of the neurons meets the requirements of the mechanism Hebb described (Fischbach, 1992). **Long-term potentiation (LTP)** is an increase in the efficiency of neural transmission at the synapses that lasts for hours or longer (De Roo et al., 2008). (*Potentiate* means "to make potent, or to strengthen.") Long-term potentiation does not take place unless both the sending neurons and the receiving neurons are activated at the same time by intense stimulation. Also, the receiving neuron must be depolarized (ready to fire) when the stimulation occurs, or LTP will not happen. LTP is common in the hippocampal region, which, as you have learned, is essential in the formation of declarative memories (Eichenbaum & Otto, 1993). When a disruption in this process occurs, a long-term memory usually does not form.

If the changes in synapses produced by LTP are the same changes that take place during learning, then blocking or preventing LTP should interfere with learning. And it does. When Davis and others (1992) gave rats a drug that blocks certain receptors in doses large enough to interfere with a maze-running task, they discovered that LTP in the rats' hippocampi was also disrupted. In contrast, Riedel (1996) found that LTP was enhanced and the rats' memory improved when a drug that excites those same receptors was administered shortly after maze training. 👁

long-term potentiation (LTP) An increase in the efficiency of neural transmission at the synapses that lasts for hours or longer.

Hormones and Memory ▶

👁 **Watch** the Video *Episode 8: Basics: Do You Remember When...?* in **MyPsychLab**

6.14 How do hormones influence memory?

The strongest and most lasting memories are usually those fueled by emotion. Research by McGaugh and Cahill (2009) suggested that there may be two pathways for forming memories—one for ordinary information and another for memories that are fired by emotion. When a person is emotionally aroused, the adrenal glands release the hormones epinephrine (adrenalin) and norepinephrine (noradrenaline) into the bloodstream. Long known to be involved in the "fight-or-flight response," which we learned about in Chapter 2, these hormones enable humans to survive, and they also imprint powerful and enduring memories of the circumstances surrounding threatening situations. Such emotionally laden memories activate the amygdala (known to play a central role in emotion) and other parts of the memory system. This widespread activation in the brain may be the most important factor in explaining the intensity of flashbulb memories.

Other hormones may have important effects on memory. Excessive levels of the stress hormone *cortisol,* for example, have been shown to interfere with memory in patients who have diseases of the adrenal glands, the site of cortisol production (Jelicic & Bonke, 2001). Furthermore, people whose bodies react to experimenter-induced stressors, such as forced public speaking, by releasing higher than average levels of cortisol perform less well on memory tests than those whose bodies release lower than average levels in the same situations (Al'absi et al., 2002). By contrast, moderate levels of cortisol seem to enhance memory when researchers ask study participants to recall academic information they studied several days earlier (Hupbach & Fieman, 2012). Consequently, test-takers in college classes who feel somewhat stressed about an exam may be better able to remember material from textbooks and lectures than those who are not anxious about it.

Estrogen, the female sex hormone, appears to improve working memory efficiency (Epperson et al., 2012). This hormone, along with others produced by the ovaries, also plays some role in the development and maintenance of synapses in areas of the brain known to be associated with memory (e.g., the hippocampus). This finding caused researchers to hypothesize that hormone replacement therapy might prevent or reverse the effects of Alzheimer's disease (Dohanich, 2003). However, research shows that post-menopausal women who take a combination of synthetic estrogen and progesterone, the two hormones that regulate the menstrual cycle, may actually increase their risk of developing the disease (Espeland et al., 2009). Some researchers have explained these seemingly contradictory findings by claiming that the timing of estrogen replacement is the most critical factor in its effect on memory function (Marriott & Wenk, 2004). Most researchers agree, however, that much more research is needed to ascertain the definitive role of hormone treatment in the prevention and treatment of age-related memory loss.

6.15 What kinds of memory loss occur in amnesia and dementia?

Memory Loss

Everyone has lapses of memory at one time or another, but for individuals such as H. M., whose story you read at the beginning of this section, memory loss is an enduring feature of their everyday lives. Such cases result from some kind of physical or psychological trauma or disease process in the brain. There are two broad categories that involve this kind of memory loss, *amnesia* and *dementia.*

Amnesia. Amnesia is a general term that can signify either a partial or total loss of memory. Unlike the memory disorders that are experienced by some older adults that you will read about in a moment, amnesia can be experienced at any age. In some cases, such as that of H. M., amnesia takes the form of an inability to store new information. This kind of amnesia is known as **anterograde amnesia**.

Some individuals with amnesia can form new memories, but they cannot remember the past, a disorder known as **retrograde amnesia**. Retrograde amnesia typically involves episodic rather than semantic memories, however, so people who have it usually have a clear understanding of the world around them. What they often lack is knowledge of themselves and/or the events surrounding the development of their memory loss. The character that is known by the name "Jason Bourne" in the popular books and films *The Bourne Identity, The Bourne Supremacy, The Bourne Ultimatum,* and the rest, has this kind of amnesia.

Most cases of amnesia are far less dramatic than those that are common in novels and movies. For example, it is not unusual for a person to have both retrograde and anterograde amnesia with regard to the events that immediately preceded and followed a serious car crash or other traumatic event. In such cases, researchers believe that the fear and panic induced by the trauma interfered with the process of long-term potentiation such that the victim actually did not store any memories of the "forgotten" events. Paradoxically, the biochemical processes associated with these memory deficits also enhance the victims' memories of other aspects of the event such as visual images in which the size of a train or bus that hit their car is far out of proportion to other objects in the environment (Strange, Hurlemann, & Dolan, 2003). Thus, emotion may be better thought of as a source of memory distortion rather than of true amnesia.

amnesia A partial or complete loss of memory due to loss of consciousness, brain damage, or some psychological cause.

anterograde amnesia The inability to form long-term memories of events occurring after a brain injury or brain surgery, although memories formed before the trauma are usually intact and short-term memory is unaffected.

retrograde amnesia (RET-ro-grade) A loss of memory for experiences that occurred shortly before a loss of consciousness.

In some cases, debilitating anterograde and retrograde amnesia occur in the same individual. H. M. had retrograde amnesia with respect to the two years or so immediately prior to his surgery. However, this aspect of his condition, though it was distressing to him at times, proved to be far less consequential to his daily life than his anterograde amnesia. By contrast, in another well-known case of memory loss, that of British musician Clive Wearing, a combination of anterograde and retrograde amnesia has left him psychologically suspended entirely in the present. Because of a severe infection that destroyed the hippocampal regions in both sides of his brain many years ago, Wearing is able neither to form new memories nor to retrieve information that was stored in his long-term memory prior to his illness. Well-practiced skills such as self-care, language, and the ability to read and play music have been preserved in Wearing's brain. However, he is often at a loss to recall his family members' names and has no awareness of the fact that he was once a professional musician. If asked, he will adamantly insist that he has never played a single note of music in his life though he continues to play on a regular basis.

Dementia. The lost sense of connection to one's own past that has been so dramatically demonstrated in the life of Clive Wearing is a prominent feature of the **dementias**, a collection of neurological disorders in which degenerative processes in the brain diminish people's ability to remember and process information. Dementia can result from such conditions as cerebral arteriosclerosis (hardening of the arteries in the brain), chronic alcoholism, and irreversible damage by a series of small strokes. Dementia is most common among older adults—it occurs in about 14% in individuals over the age of 70. However, the prevalence of the disorder increases dramatically as people age. Only 5% of those between the ages of 71 and 79 have dementia compared with 37% of those over age 90 (Plassman et al., 2007). However, diseases such as HIV/AIDS can cause dementia to develop in a younger person as well.

Individuals with dementia lose touch with both their episodic and semantic memories. Most have difficulty forming new memories as well. Repeatedly asking the same questions or expressing confusion about location and time are behaviors that are exhibited by many individuals with dementia. Many become completely incapable of carrying out daily activities such as cooking, financial transactions, and self-care routines such as dressing themselves.

About 50–60% of all cases of dementia result from Alzheimer's disease. In **Alzheimer's disease**, there is a progressive deterioration of intellect and personality that results from widespread degeneration of brain cells. At first, victims show a gradual impairment in memory and reasoning and in efficiency in carrying out everyday tasks (Salmon & Bondi, 2009). Many have difficulty finding their way around in familiar locations. As the disorder progresses, people with Alzheimer's disease become confused and irritable, tend to wander away from home, and become increasingly unable to take care of themselves. Eventually, their speech becomes unintelligible, and they become unable to control bladder and bowel functions. If they live long enough, they reach a stage where they do not respond when spoken to and no longer recognize even spouse or children.

Age and a family history of Alzheimer's disease are two risk factors that have been consistently associated with the disorder (Farrer & Cupples, 1994; Payami et al., 1994; Williams, 2003). Can Alzheimer's disease be delayed? According to brain reserve theory, a high IQ coupled with lifelong intellectual activity may delay or lessen Alzheimer's symptoms in those who are at risk for the disease (Fratiglioni & Wang, 2007). Unfortunately, though, research aimed at finding ways to prevent or cure the disease has yielded little in the way of positive findings. Vitamins, anti-inflammatory drugs, and the female hormone estrogen have all been ruled out as potential cures or preventives for Alzheimer's disease. However, experimental studies of *deep brain stimulation*, a treatment in which a device implanted in the brain delivers electrical impulses to the parts of the brain that are critical to memory, have yielded encouraging results (Fontaine et al., 2013).

▲ British musician Clive Wearing suffers from a combination of anterograde and retrograde amnesia that prevents him from forming new memories and from retrieving old ones. However, memories that he stored prior to his illness remain intact. As a result, he is able to perform pieces that he learned earlier in life as proficiently as he ever did.

dementia A state of mental deterioration characterized by impaired memory and intellect and by altered personality and behavior.

Alzheimer's disease (ALZ-hye-mer's) An incurable form of dementia characterized by progressive deterioration of intellect and personality, resulting from widespread degeneration of brain cells.

1. The _____ is especially important in forming episodic memories.
2. When _____ is disrupted, long-term memories are not formed.
3. Memories that elicit the "fight-or-flight response" activate the _____ glands.
4. A person who receives a blow to the head resulting in unconsciousness who has difficulty recalling the events just prior to and during the injury has _____ amnesia.
5. Alzheimer's disease is one type of a group of disorders known as the _____.

Memory in Legal and Therapeutic Settings

In most cases, memory failure is an annoyance. But there are times when it has profound consequences. For example, you have probably heard news reports about people being convicted of crimes on the basis of eyewitness testimony who are later exonerated by DNA evidence. Likewise, the news media from time to time carry reports of cases in which adults "recover" decades-old memories of childhood abuse. As you'll see, research on remembering, forgetting, and the biology of memory can help us understand both eyewitness testimony and the controversy surrounding "recovered" memories.

6.16 What factors influence the reliability of eyewitness testimony?

Eyewitness Testimony

The U.S. Department of Justice issued the first set of national guidelines for the collection of eyewitness evidence in the United States in 1999 (Wells et al., 2000). Research attesting to the inaccuracy of such testimony and the number of wrongful convictions that occur because of its poor reliability rendered these guidelines necessary (Laney & Loftus, 2009). According to one of the leading researchers in this area, Elizabeth Loftus, studies on the reconstructive nature of human memory suggest that eyewitness testimony is highly subject to error and that it should always be viewed with caution (Loftus, 1979).

Why is the reliability of eyewitness testimony in question? One reason is biological. Witnessing a crime causes physiological stress, and, as you learned earlier, stress hormones disrupt memory functioning (Wolf, 2009). Yet, it is also true that fear can enhance memory. The combined effects of stress and fear on eyewitnesses causes them to remember the central, most frightening details of the event, but to fail to encode less emotion-provoking details (Burke, Heuer, & Reisberg, 1992; Christianson, 1992). As a result, eyewitnesses typically experience memory gaps (Yovell, Bannett, & Shalev, 2003). These gaps may involve just the sort of information investigators need, such as license plate numbers, addresses, the clothing worn by the perpetrator, and so on.

As you might suspect, when eyewitnesses experience memory gaps, reconstructive processes come to the fore to fill in the missing information. Consequently, distortions and even false memories sometimes replace such gaps. Predictably, the longer the delay between witnessing an event and being questioned about it, the more likely a witness is to include reconstructions rather than true memories in her descriptions of the perpetrator and the crime itself (Pansky, 2012).

Moreover, misleading information that is inadvertently supplied to an eyewitness during the process of an investigator's interview can result in erroneous recollections of the actual event, a phenomenon known as the **misinformation effect** (Laney & Loftus, 2009). Interestingly, the misinformation effect appears to be stronger for emotionally negative events, such as witnessing a crime, than it is for emotionally positive events, such as being a guest at a party (Porter et al., 2010).

An example will help you see how the misinformation effect works. Suppose you are walking across campus one day, thinking about an upcoming exam, and a man suddenly accosts you and steals your backpack. Because of the stress involved in

misinformation effect Erroneous recollections of witnessed events that result from information learned after the fact.

being a crime victim, your hippocampus records only a vague recollection of what the man looked like. Your memory includes his height, weight, and ethnicity, but lacks a definitive image of his face. When you talk to a campus police officer, she shows you a photo of a man who is suspected of committing several such crimes and says, "Is this the man who stole your backpack?" The photo and question set into motion the process of retroactive interference (new information displaces old information) in which the photo and its verbal label "man who stole your backpack" fill in the gaps in your own incomplete memory of the man's appearance (Chan, Thomas, & Bulevich, 2009). Remember, too, that source monitoring isn't something we normally do, so you are likely to forget that you have replaced your own memory with information suggested by the photo and the officer's question. As a result, you may mentally superimpose the photo over your own incomplete memory of the perpetrator's face and believe that it is what you actually saw during the event. Furthermore, over the course of the investigation and in chatting with friends, you are likely to repeat your story several times. Your story may include a verbal description of the perpetrator based on the misinformation that is now part of your memory of the event. Research shows that, after eyewitnesses have repeatedly recalled information, whether accurate or inaccurate, they become more confident of the information's accuracy (Shaw, 1996). That is, by "practicing" your distorted memory through repetition, you will become even more convinced of its accuracy and resistant to the suggestion that you may have identified the wrong person.

Furthermore, the confidence eyewitnesses have in their testimony is not necessarily an indication of its accuracy (Laney & Loftus, 2009). In fact, eyewitnesses who perceive themselves to be more objective have more confidence in their testimony, regardless of its accuracy, and are more likely to include incorrect information in their verbal descriptions (Geiselman et al., 2000). When witnesses make incorrect identifications with great certainty, they can be highly persuasive to judges and jurors alike.

Fortunately, eyewitness mistakes can be minimized. For instance, training interviewers to use questioning strategies that minimize the effects of reconstructed memory, such as asking witnesses to recall the details of an event before questioning them, can prevent the misinformation effect (LaPaglia & Chan, 2012; U.S. Department of Justice, 1999). Such interviewing strategies usually involve asking open-ended questions that prompt the eyewitness to tell his or her own story of the event prior to being asked specific questions. Moreover, investigators typically separate witnesses so that their stories are as free from the distorting effects of others' recollections as possible.

Similarly, if eyewitnesses view photographs of a suspect before viewing the lineup, eyewitnesses may mistakenly identify that suspect in the lineup because the person looks familiar. Research suggests that it is better to have an eyewitness first describe the perpetrator and then search for photos matching that description than to have the eyewitness start by looking through photos and making judgments as to their similarity to the perpetrator (Pryke, Lindsay, & Pozzulo, 2000). In addition, asking witnesses to assign a confidence rating (i.e., 90% sure, 80% sure, etc.) to each subject in a line-up is more likely to lead to correct identification of a perpetrator than asking witnesses to make a yes/no decision about each one (Brewer, Weber, Wootton, & Lindsay, 2012).

The composition of the lineup is also important. Other subjects in a lineup must resemble the suspect in age, body build, and certainly race. Even then, if the lineup does not contain the guilty party, eyewitnesses may identify the person who most closely resembles the perpetrator (Gonzalez, Ellsworth, & Pembroke, 1993). Eyewitnesses are less likely to make errors if a sequential lineup is used—that is, if the members of the lineup are viewed one after the other, rather than simultaneously (Loftus, 1993). Some police officers and researchers prefer a "showup," in which the witness sees only one suspect at a time and indicates whether or not that person is the perpetrator. There are fewer misidentifications with a showup but also more failures to make a positive identification (Wells, 1993). 👁

Watch the Video *Episode 8: Thinking Like a Psychologist: Police Line-Up* in **MyPsychLab**

▲ When people recall an event, such as a car accident, they are actually reconstructing it from memory by piecing together bits of information that may or may not be totally accurate.

6.17 What is the "repressed memory controversy"?

repression A psychological process in which traumatic memories are buried in the unconscious.

The Repressed Memory Controversy

Memory distortions, as well as "memories" that turn out to be entirely false, have been the subject of debate in regard to the claims made by some therapists about their clients' recoveries of memories of child abuse (Haaken & Reavey, 2010). These therapists, like Freud and other psychoanalysts before them, believe that a process called **repression**, a form of motivated forgetting, can cause traumatic memories to be so deeply buried in an individual's unconscious mind that he or she has lost all awareness of them. In 1988, Ellen Bass and Laura Davis published a best-selling book called *The Courage to Heal*. It became the "bible" for sex abuse victims and the leading "textbook" for some therapists who specialized in treating them. Bass and Davis not only sought to help survivors who remember having suffered sexual abuse but also reached out to other people who had no memory of any sexual abuse and tried to help them determine whether they might have been abused. They suggested that "if you are unable to remember any specific instances ... but still have a feeling that something abusive happened to you, it probably did" (p. 21). They offered a definite conclusion: "If you think you were abused and your life shows the symptoms, then you were" (p. 22). And they freed potential victims of sexual abuse from the responsibility of establishing any proof: "You are not responsible for proving that you were abused" (p. 37).

However, many psychologists are skeptical about such "recovered" memories, claiming that they are actually false memories created by the suggestions of therapists. Critics charge that recovered memories of sexual abuse are suspect because of the techniques therapists usually use to uncover them—namely, hypnosis and guided imagery. As you have learned (in Chapter 4), hypnosis does not improve the accuracy of memory, only the confidence that what one remembers is accurate. And a therapist using guided imagery might tell a patient something similar to what Wendy Maltz (1991) advocates in her book:

> Spend time imagining that you were sexually abused, without worrying about accuracy, proving anything, or having your ideas make sense.... Ask yourself ... these questions: What time of day is it? Where are you? Indoors or outdoors? What kind of things are happening? (p. 50)

Can merely imagining experiences in this way lead people to believe that those experiences had actually happened to them? Yes, according to some studies. The research of eyewitness testimony expert Elizabeth Loftus on the misinformation effect has been instrumental in helping psychologists and the public understand how these techniques lead to both false and distorted memories. Many research participants who are instructed to imagine that a fictitious event happened do, in fact, develop a false memory of that imagined event (Laney & Loftus, 2009; Mazzoni & Memon, 2003).

False childhood memories can also be experimentally induced. In one classic study of false memory, Garry and Loftus (1994) were able to implant a false memory of being lost in a shopping mall at 5 years of age in 25% of participants aged 18 to 53, after verification of the fictitious experience by a relative. Repeated exposure to suggestions of false memories can create those memories (Zaragoza & Mitchell, 1996). Further, researchers have found that adults who claim to have recovered memories of childhood abuse or of abduction by extraterrestrials are more vulnerable to experimentally induced false memories than are adults who do not report such recovered memories (McNally, 2003). So, individual differences in suggestibility may play a role in the recovery of memories.

Critics are especially skeptical of recovered memories of events that occurred in the first few years of life, in part because the hippocampus, vital in the formation of episodic memories, is not fully developed then and neither are the areas of the cortex where memories are stored (Squire, Knowlton, & Musen, 1993). Furthermore, young children, who are still limited in language ability, do not store semantic memories in categories that are accessible to them later in life. The relative inability of older children and adults to recall events from the first few years of life is referred to as **infantile amnesia**.

infantile amnesia The relative inability of older children and adults to recall events from the first few years of life.

In light of these developmental limitations, is it possible that some individuals cannot recall incidents of childhood sexual abuse? Widom and Morris (1997) found that 64% of a group of women who had been sexually abused as children reported no memory of the abuse in a 2-hour interview 20 years later. Following up on women who had documented histories of sexual victimization, Williams (1994) found that 38% of them did not report remembering the sexual abuse some 17 years later. Memories of abuse were better when the victimization took place between the ages of 7 and 17 than when it occurred in the first 6 years of life. Keep in mind, however, that it is possible that some of these women may have remembered the abuse but, for whatever reason, chose not to admit it. There is also some indication that individuals who are traumatized develop an attentional style that involves distracting themselves from potentially unpleasant stimuli (DePrince & Freyd, 2004; Goodman, Quas, & Ogle, 2010). It is this attentional style, some researchers argue, that prevents such individuals from forming memories of abuse that can be easily recalled.

The American Psychological Association (1994), the American Psychiatric Association (1993a), and the American Medical Association (1994) have issued status reports on memories of childhood abuse. The position of all three groups is that current evidence supports both the possibility that repressed memories exist and the likelihood that false memories can be constructed in response to suggestions of abuse. Moreover, individuals who hold false memories are often thoroughly convinced that they are accurate because of the details such memories contain and the strong emotions associated with them (Dodson, Koutstaal, & Schacter, 2000; Gonsalves et al., 2004; Henkel et al., 2000; Loftus, 2004; Loftus & Bernstein, 2005; McNally et al., 2004). Neuroimaging studies suggest that engaging in visually vivid mental replays of false memories may serve to strengthen them even further (Lindsay et al., 2004). Still, as you learned earlier in this section, being confident that a memory is accurate does not mean that it is such. Experts also point out that individuals who report recovered memories often have symptoms of *dissociation*, the tendency to mentally detach oneself from reality. In fact, one study found that participants who reported recovered memories were more likely to have had episodes of dissociation in the past that to have actually experienced the kind of traumatic events that proponents of repressed memories argue trigger them (Chiu et al., 2012). For these reasons, many experts recommend that recovered memories of abuse should be verified independently before they are accepted as facts.

REMEMBER IT   *Check your answers and take additional quizzes in MyPsychLab.com.*   ✓●─[Study and Review on MyPsychLab

1. Eyewitness testimony can be influenced by the _____ effect.
2. The _____ controversy has arisen from research showing that some "recovered" memories are actually false memories induced by therapists.

👓 Looking Back

Sometimes psychologists learn more about a mental process from situations in which it goes wrong than they do from those in which it functions as expected. This is especially true of human memory. For instance, by breaking down the inaccurate memories of eyewitnesses and people who claim to have recovered long-lost memories, psychologists have developed a good understanding of how reconstruction, despite its drawbacks, contributes to the efficiency of memory. Moreover, cases in which a physical trauma or condition has caused massive memory failure, such as those of H. M. and Clive Wearing, have helped neuroscientists better understand the biology of memory. And the scientist who initiated the scientific study of memory, Hermann Ebbinghaus, learned a lot about remembering by studying forgetting. You can take a cue from the history of the study of memory the next time you experience a memory failure of your own. Use what you have learned in this chapter to figure out exactly where your effort to remember went awry. Your analysis should equip you with the knowledge you need to avoid similar failures in the future.

CHAPTER 6 SUMMARY

THE STRUCTURE OF HUMAN MEMORY (pp. 179–185)

6.1 How does information-processing theory describe memory? (pp. 179–180)

The information-processing approach uses the computer as an analogy to describe human cognition. It conceptualizes memory as involving the processes of encoding, storage, and retrieval. The model proposes that information flows through a three-part system—sensory memory, short-term memory, and long-term memory.

Key Terms
information-processing theory, p. 179
encoding, p. 179
storage, p. 179
retrieval, p. 179
memory, p. 179

6.2 What are the characteristics of sensory memory? (p. 180)

Sensory memory holds information coming in through the senses for up to 2 seconds, just long enough for the nervous system to begin to process it.

Key Terms
sensory memory, p. 180
eidetic imagery, p. 180

6.3 What happens to information in short-term memory? (pp. 180–183)

Short-term (working) memory holds about seven (plus or minus two) unrelated items of information for less than 30 seconds without rehearsal. Short-term memory also acts as a mental workspace for carrying out any mental activity.

Key Terms
short-term memory, p. 180
displacement, p. 181
chunking, p. 181
rehearsal, p. 181
working memory, p. 182
maintenance rehearsal, p. 183
elaborative rehearsal, p. 183
levels-of-processing model, p. 183
automaticity, p. 183

6.4 What are the subsystems of long-term memory? (pp. 183–185)

The subsystems of long-term memory are (1) declarative memory, which holds facts and information (semantic memory) along with personal life experiences (episodic memory); and (2) nondeclarative memory, which consists of motor skills, conditioned behaviors, and other types of memories that are difficult or impossible to put into verbal form.

Key Terms
long-term memory, p. 183
declarative memory, p. 184
episodic memory, p. 184
semantic memory, p. 185
nondeclarative memory, p. 185

A CLOSER LOOK AT RETRIEVAL (pp. 186–188)

6.5 What are the differences among the recall, recognition, and relearning methods of measuring retrieval? (p. 186)

Three methods of measuring retention of information in memory are (1) recall, where information must be supplied with few or no retrieval cues; (2) recognition, where information must simply be recognized as having been encountered before; and (3) the relearning method, which measures retention in terms of time saved when relearning material compared with the time required to learn it originally.

Key Terms
recall, p. 186
retrieval cue, p. 186
recognition, p. 186
relearning method, p. 186

6.6 How do the serial position, context, and state-dependent memory effects influence retrieval? (pp. 186–188)

The serial position effect is the tendency, when recalling a list of items, to remember the items at the beginning of the list (primacy effect) and the items at the end of the list (recency effect) better than items in the middle. People tend to recall material more easily if they are in the same physical location during recall as during the original learning. The state-dependent memory effect is the tendency to recall information better if one is in the same pharmacological or psychological state as when the information was learned.

Key Terms
serial position effect, p. 187
primacy effect, p. 187

REMEMBERING AS RECONSTRUCTION (pp. 188–193)

6.7 What does "Memory is reconstructive" mean? (pp. 188–189)

People reconstruct memories, piecing them together using schemas to organize fragments of information, a process that has both advantages and disadvantages. Information that fits with preexisting schemas can be efficiently remembered, but schemas can also introduce distortions into memory. Sir Frederick Bartlett's research demonstrated how reconstructive processing changes memory over time.

Key Terms

6.8 What have researchers learned about source, flashbulb, and autobiographical memories? (pp. 189–191)

Most memories do not include source information, so memories for sources must be reconstructed. Source monitoring results in encoding of source memories. Flashbulb memories are different from others in that they always include source information, although the source information is subject to reconstruction changes over time. Autobiographical memories are reconstructed memories that include factual, emotional, and interpretive elements. They are subject to positive bias.

Key Terms

6.9 How do expertise and culture influence reconstructive memory? (pp. 191–193)

People with extensive background knowledge (expertise) introduce fewer distortions into reconstructive memory tasks than nonexperts do. Culturally based schemas influence reconstructive memory in the same way that expertise does. In addition, cultural schemas that emphasize the valued status of information such as oral histories encourage source monitoring that protects the information from the distorting effects of reconstruction.

Key Term

FORGETTING (pp. 193–197)

6.10 What did Ebbinghaus discover about forgetting? (pp. 193–194)

In conducting the first experimental studies of learning and memory, Ebbinghaus invented the nonsense syllable, used the relearning method as a test of memory, and plotted the curve of forgetting. He discovered that the largest amount of forgetting occurs very quickly and then tapers off.

Key Terms

6.11 Why do we forget? (pp. 194–197)

Encoding failure happens when an item is perceived as having been forgotten but, in fact, was never stored in memory. Decay theory, the oldest theory of forgetting, assumes that information that has not been retrieved from memory for a long time may fade and ultimately disappear entirely. Interference occurs when information or associations stored either before or after a given memory hinder the ability to remember it. Consolidation failure results from a loss of consciousness as new memories are being encoded. Sometimes, we forget because we don't want to remember something, a process called motivated forgetting. Other times, an item is stored in memory, but we are unable to retrieve it (retrieval failure).

Key Terms

BIOLOGY AND MEMORY (pp. 197–202)

6.12 What brain structures are associated with memory? (p. 198)

The hippocampus itself is involved primarily in the formation of episodic memories; the rest of the hippocampal region is involved in forming semantic memories.

Key Term
hippocampal region, p. 198

6.13 Why is long-term potentiation important? (pp. 198–199)

Long-term potentiation (LTP) is a long-lasting increase in the efficiency of neural transmission at the synapses. LTP is important because it may be the basis for learning and memory at the level of the neurons.

Key Term
long-term potentiation (LTP), p. 199

6.14 How do hormones influence memory? (pp. 199–200)

Memories of threatening situations tend to be more powerful and enduring than ordinary memories because of the hormones associated with the strong emotions aroused in such situations.

6.15 What kinds of memory loss occur in amnesia and dementia? (pp. 200–202)

Trauma and disease in the brain can cause anterograde amnesia (inability to learn new information) and/or retrograde amnesia (inability to remember a specific period of time in the past). Patients with Alzheimer's disease and other types of dementia forget the names of people and objects they have known all their lives as well as how to do everyday tasks such as managing money.

Key Terms
amnesia, p. 200
anterograde amnesia, p. 200
retrograde amnesia, p. 200
dementia, p. 201
Alzheimer's disease, p. 201

MEMORY IN LEGAL AND THERAPEUTIC SETTINGS (pp. 202–205)

6.16 What factors influence the reliability of eyewitness testimony? (pp. 202–203)

Stress hormones may disrupt witnesses' memories, leading to gaps that eventually are filled in through reconstructive memory processes. Interviewers' questions can introduce information that witnesses believe is a part of their own memory of the event. The reliability of eyewitness testimony is reduced when witnesses view a photograph of the suspect before viewing the lineup, when members of a lineup don't sufficiently resemble each other; when members of a lineup are viewed at the same time rather than one by one, and when the perpetrator's race is different from that of the eyewitness.

Key Term
misinformation effect, p. 202

6.17 What is the "repressed memory controversy"? (pp. 204–205)

Critics argue that therapists using hypnosis and guided imagery to help their patients recover repressed memories of childhood sexual abuse are actually implanting false memories in those patients. They are especially critical of claims of recovered memories in the first 3 years of life, because the hippocampus isn't well developed enough to store long-term memories. Therapists who use these techniques believe that a number of psychological problems can be treated successfully by helping patients recover repressed memories of sexual abuse.

Key Terms
repression, p. 204
infantile amnesia, p. 204

Chapter 6 Study Guide

Answers to all the Study Guide questions are provided at the end of the book.

SECTION ONE: Chapter Review

The Structure of Human Memory
(pp. 179–185)

1. Transforming information into a form that can be stored in memory is called _____; bringing to mind the material that has been stored is called _____.
   - **a.** encoding; decoding
   - **b.** consolidation; retrieval
   - **c.** consolidation; decoding
   - **d.** encoding; retrieval

2. Match the memory system with the best description of its capacity and the duration of time it holds information.
   _____ **(1)** sensory memory
   _____ **(2)** short-term memory
   _____ **(3)** long-term memory
   - **a.** virtually unlimited capacity; long duration
   - **b.** large capacity; short duration
   - **c.** very limited capacity; short duration

3. Match each example with the appropriate memory system:
   _____ **(1)** semantic memory
   _____ **(2)** episodic memory
   _____ **(3)** nondeclarative memory
   - **a.** movements involved in playing tennis
   - **b.** names of the presidents of the United States
   - **c.** what you did during spring break last year

4. In which subsystem of long-term memory are responses that make up motor skills stored?
   - **a.** episodic memory
   - **b.** semantic memory
   - **c.** nondeclarative memory
   - **d.** declarative memory

A Closer Look at Retrieval (pp. 186–188)

5. Which of the following methods can detect learning when other methods cannot?
   - **a.** recall
   - **b.** recognition
   - **c.** relearning
   - **d.** retrieval

6. Match the example with the corresponding method of measuring retention:
   _____ **(1)** identifying a suspect in a lineup
   _____ **(2)** answering a fill-in-the-blank question on a test
   _____ **(3)** having to study less for a comprehensive final exam than for all of the previous exams put together
   _____ **(4)** answering multiple-choice questions in this Study Guide
   _____ **(5)** reciting one's lines in a play
   - **a.** recognition
   - **b.** relearning
   - **c.** recall

7. When children learn the alphabet, they often learn "*A, B, C, D*" and "*W, X, Y, Z*" before learning the letters in between. This is due to the
   - **a.** primacy effect.
   - **b.** recency effect.
   - **c.** serial position effect.
   - **d.** state-dependent memory effect.

8. Recall is best when it takes place in the same context in which information was learned. (true/false)

9. Scores on recognition tests (either multiple-choice or true/false) will be higher if testing and learning take place in the same physical environment. (true/false)

10. Which best explains why information learned when one is feeling anxious is best recalled when experiencing feelings of anxiety?
    - **a.** consistency effect
    - **b.** state-dependent memory effect
    - **c.** context-dependent effect
    - **d.** consolidation failure

Remembering as Reconstruction
(pp. 188–193)

11. Which of the following is *not* true of schemas?
    - **a.** Schemas are the integrated frameworks of knowledge and assumptions a person has about people, objects, and events.
    - **b.** Schemas affect the way a person encodes information.
    - **c.** Schemas affect the way a person retrieves information.
    - **d.** When a person uses schemas, memories are always accurate.

12. In order to prevent plagiarism, it is important to practice _____ _____ while you are doing research for a research paper.

13. When you remember where you were and what you were doing when you received a shocking piece of news, you are experiencing
    - **a.** flashbulb memory.
    - **b.** sensory memory.
    - **c.** semantic imagery.
    - **d.** interference.

14. Expertise influences reconstructive memory by making _____ function more efficiently.
    - **a.** sensory memory
    - **b.** working memory
    - **c.** semantic memory
    - **d.** source memory

15. Cultural values protect some information from the distorting effects of reconstructive memory. (true/false)

16. In general, reconstructed memories of unpleasant events become more (positive/negative) over time.

Forgetting (pp. 193–197)

17. Who plotted the curve of forgetting?
    - **a.** George Sperling
    - **b.** E. Burtt
    - **c.** Frederick Bartlett
    - **d.** Hermann Ebbinghaus

18. The curve of forgetting shows that memory loss
    - **a.** occurs most rapidly at first and then levels off to a slow decline.
    - **b.** begins to occur about 3–4 hours after learning.
    - **c.** occurs at a fairly steady rate over a month's time.
    - **d.** occurs slowly at first and increases steadily over a month's time.

19. Match the example with the appropriate cause of forgetting.

_____ (**1**) encoding failure
_____ (**2**) consolidation failure
_____ (**3**) retrieval failure
_____ (**4**) repression
_____ (**5**) interference

a. failing to remember the answer on a test until after you turn in the test
b. forgetting a humiliating childhood experience
c. not being able to describe the back of a dollar bill
d. calling a friend by someone else's name
e. waking up in the hospital and not remembering you had an automobile accident

20. Retroactive interference is most likely to occur when prior knowledge and new information are
a. very different.   **b.** recently learned.
c. learned from the same source.   **d.** similar.

21. Most psychologists accept decay theory as a good explanation for the loss of information from long-term memory. (true/false)

22. According to the text, a major cause of forgetting is interference. (true/false)

Biology and Memory (pp. 197–202)

23. H. M. retained his ability to add to his nondeclarative memory. (true/false)

24. The hippocampus itself is involved primarily in the formation of _____ memories; the entire hippocampal region is involved primarily in the formation of _____ memories.

25. What is the term for the long-lasting increase in the efficiency of neural transmission at the synapses that may be the basis for learning and memory at the level of the neurons?
a. long-term potentiation   **b.** synaptic facilitation
c. synaptic potentiation   **d.** presynaptic potentiation

26. Memories of circumstances surrounding threatening situations that elicit the "fight-or-flight response" tend to be more powerful and enduring than ordinary memories. (true/false)

Memory in Legal and Therapeutic Settings (pp. 202–205)

27. When eyewitnesses incorporate details from an interviewer's questions into their memories of an event, they are demonstrating
a. source monitoring.   **b.** the content effect.
c. the misinformation effect.   **d.** event monitoring.

28. There are fewer errors in eyewitness testimony if
a. eyewitnesses are identifying a person of their own race.
b. eyewitnesses view suspects' photos prior to a lineup.
c. a weapon has been used in the crime.
d. questions are phrased to provide retrieval cues for the eyewitness.

29. Experts agree that there is no such thing as a recovered memory. (true/false)

SECTION TWO: Complete the Diagrams

Fill in the blanks in each diagram with the missing words.

SECTION THREE: Comprehensive Practice Test

1. The first step in the memory process is known as _____, when information is transformed into a form that can be stored in short-term memory.
   - **a.** retrieval
   - **b.** storage
   - **c.** encoding
   - **d.** rehearsal

2. The process in which information is stored in permanent memory involves a change in the brain's physiology. This change is known as
   - **a.** consolidation.
   - **b.** transformation.
   - **c.** hippocampal transformation.
   - **d.** recalcitration.

3. You are at a party and meet someone you are really interested in. You get that person's phone number but have no way to write it down, so you use the process of _____ to get it into memory.
   - **a.** encoding
   - **b.** latent retrieval
   - **c.** rehearsal
   - **d.** recalcitration

4. The kind of memory that has a large capacity but a very short duration is _____ memory.
   - **a.** short-term
   - **b.** sensory
   - **c.** long-term
   - **d.** temporary

5. Alice's ability to remember all the actions required to ride her motorcycle is due to her repetitive practice, to the point where riding it is almost reflexive. Any set of skills acquired this way is part of _____ memory.

6. Implicit memory is to explicit memory as _____ are to _____.
   - **a.** motor skills; facts and information
   - **b.** episodic memories; semantic memories
   - **c.** semantic memories; episodic memories
   - **d.** facts and information; motor skills

7. Cristina and her friends were talking about some great times they had in high school. Recounting those stories as if they had happened yesterday, the friends were relying on _____ memory.
   - **a.** semantic
   - **b.** implicit
   - **c.** personal
   - **d.** episodic

8. You use _____ memory when you answer questions such as "What is the capital of California?"
   - **a.** episodic
   - **b.** semantic
   - **c.** geographic
   - **d.** flashbulb

9. An example of good recall is doing well on an essay test. (true/false)

10. An example of good recognition ability is doing well on a fill-in-the-blank test. (true/false)

11. Freud did extensive research on memory. He used nonsense syllables to determine forgetting curves. (true/false)

12. When she was 16 years old, Sarah was severely injured in a car accident and was unconscious for 14 days. She can remember nothing immediately preceding the accident. This is known as _____ amnesia.
    - **a.** trauma
    - **b.** retroactive
    - **c.** proactive
    - **d.** retrograde

13. With retroactive interference, _____ information interferes with _____ information.
    - **a.** new; old
    - **b.** old; new
    - **c.** unpleasant; pleasant
    - **d.** factual; emotional

14. Using _____, a person removes an unpleasant memory from consciousness.
    - **a.** regression
    - **b.** traumatic amnesia
    - **c.** repression
    - **d.** degeneration

15. Psychologists doubt the validity of people's recovered memories of having been abused in infancy because the hippocampal region of the infant brain is not sufficiently developed to form such memories. (true/false)

16. It appears that the _____ is important in the formation of episodic memory.
    - **a.** hippocampus
    - **b.** cerebellum
    - **c.** amygdala
    - **d.** temporal lobe

17. Pablo's vivid memory of the day Princess Diana was killed is known as a _____ memory.
    - **a.** histrionic
    - **b.** flashbulb
    - **c.** semantic
    - **d.** retroactive

18. Eyewitnesses are more likely to identify the wrong person if the person is of a different race. (true/false)

19. Autobiographical memories are highly resistant to reconstructive distortions. (true/false)

20. Flashbulb memories are a subcategory of _____ memory.
    - **a.** nondeclarative
    - **b.** sensory
    - **c.** photographic
    - **d.** source

SECTION FOUR: Critical Thinking

1. Some studies cited in this chapter involved only one or a few participants.
   - **a.** Select two of these studies and discuss the possible problems in drawing conclusions based on results from so few participants.
   - **b.** Suggest several possible explanations for the findings other than those proposed by the researchers.

2. Summarize the arguments presented in the final section of the chapter in favor and against the hypothesis that recovered memories are reports of actual events. Take a position on one side or the other and explain the reasoning behind your choice.

SECTION FIVE: Application Essays

1. Typically, students who are pursuing bachelor's degrees must take general education courses in the domains of English composition and rhetoric, social science, mathematics, natural science, and humanities. What does the discussion of the influence of schemas and expertise on reconstructive memory suggest about students' perceptions of the relative difficulty of courses in these five domains?

Apply your critical thinking skills with MyPsychLab Writing Assignments

Submit your answer to the following question inside the MyPsychLab Writing Assessment program for immediate feedback.

You are reading your textbook and studying for an upcoming exam in psychology. Identify and describe each step in the process required for remembering information from your textbook in order to do well on the exam. Discuss a strategy for improving memory and provide an example of how it could help you on the exam.

CHAPTER 7

Cognition, Language, and Intelligence

⊚ THINK ABOUT IT

On a scale of 1 to 100, with 1 = not very important and 100 = very important, how vital is each of the following to your long-term happiness?

Being involved in a stable romantic relationship
Having enough money to live comfortably
Achieving professional goals

Now look at these three issues from a different perspective. Imagine your life 10 years from now and assume that you are 100% happy, or perfectly, totally happy at that point. How much would each of these three factors contribute to your sense that you were totally happy? Make a proportional estimate of the contribution of each factor such that they add up to 100%:

_____ % Romance +
_____ % Money +
_____ % Professional goals =
100__ % Happiness

Did you notice that the emphasis you placed on each factor changed when you thought about balancing them rather than when you thought about them individually? That's because our thinking is distorted by a process called , or the , when we think about one factor in isolation from others that affect a decision (Tversky & Kahneman, 1974). As a result, we often overestimate the importance of the factor we happen to be thinking about at the moment. In fact, focusing on a single factor, such as a desire for money, can actually make us quite miserable because it causes us to emphasize what we lack rather than what we have (Kahneman et al., 2006).

We address distortions such as anchoring, and how the information-processing system manages and compensates for them in the opening section of this chapter. In it, we introduce you to the universal intellectual tools that we use to make sense of the world—reasoning, imagery, and concepts—and discuss how we put these tools to work to make decisions, solve problems, and develop technological devices that mirror our own thought processes. Next, we turn to another vital cognitive tool: language. Finally, we end with a discussion of intelligence, creativity, and other aspects of cognitive functioning that vary from one person to another.

⊙ **Watch** the Video *Episode 10: Big Picture: I Am, Therefore I Think* in **MyPsychLab**

Cognition

All of us have an idea of what thinking is. We say, "I think it's going to rain" (a prediction) and "I think this is the right answer" (a decision). But, our everyday use of the word *think* obscures the fact that thinking actually involves a number of coordinated subprocesses. Psychologists use the term **cognition** to refer collectively to these processes, which include acquiring, storing, retrieving, and using information. You have already learned about some of them (sensation, perception, and memory) in earlier chapters. Now, we turn our attention to some of the other cognitive processes.

cognition The mental processes that are involved in acquiring, storing, retrieving, and using information and that include sensation, perception, imagery, concept formation, reasoning, decision making, problem solving, and language.

Imagery and Concepts ▶

Can you imagine hearing a recording of your favorite song or someone calling your name? In doing such a thing, you take advantage of your own ability to use mental **imagery**—that is, to represent or picture a sensory experience.

According to psychologist Stephen Kosslyn and his colleagues (Kosslyn, Thompson, & Ganis, 2009), we mentally construct our images of objects one part at a time. Stored memories of how the parts of an object look are retrieved and assembled in working memory to form a complete image. Such images can correspond directly to the real world or they can be creative. In the *Apply It* box in Chapter 6, you read about several mnemonic devices that rely on imagery. Such images can be extremely helpful to memory. For example, to remember that the independent variable is the one in an experiment that is manipulated by the experimenter, you might imagine a puppeteer with a large "I" on his forehead manipulating a marionette.

Images can also be helpful in learning or maintaining motor skills. Brain-imaging studies show that, in general, the same brain areas are activated whether a person is performing a given task or mentally rehearsing the same task using imagery (Fourkas, Bonavolonta, Avenanti & Aglioti, 2008). Thus, it isn't surprising that professionals whose work involves repetitive physical actions, such as musicians and athletes, use imaging effectively. One remarkable demonstration of the power of imagery may be found in the case of professional pianist Liu Chi Kung, who was imprisoned for 7 years during China's Cultural Revolution (1960s–1970s). He mentally rehearsed all the pieces he knew every day and was able to play them all immediately following his release (Garfield, 1986). ⊙

⌈ **7.1** How do imagery
⌊ and concepts help us think?

imagery The representation in the mind of a sensory experience—visual, auditory, gustatory, motor, olfactory, or tactile.

⊙ **Watch** the Video *Episode 10: Special Topics: Mental Imagery: In the Mind's Eye* in **MyPsychLab**

▲ Many professional athletes use visualization to improve performance.

concept A mental category used to represent a class or group of objects, people, organizations, events, situations, or relations that share common characteristics or attributes.

formal concept A concept that is clearly defined by a set of rules, a formal definition, or a classification system.

natural concept A concept acquired not from a definition but through everyday perceptions and experiences.

prototype An example that embodies the most common and typical features of a concept.

exemplars The individual instances, or examples, of a concept that are stored in memory from personal experience.

The ability to form concepts is another important aid to thinking. A **concept** is a mental category used to represent a class or group of objects, people, organizations, events, situations, or relations that share common characteristics or attributes. *Furniture, tree, student, college,* and *wedding* are all examples of concepts. As fundamental units of thought, concepts are useful tools that help us to organize our perceptions of the world and to think and communicate with speed and efficiency.

Thanks to our ability to use concepts, we are not forced to consider and describe everything in great detail before we make an identification. If you see a hairy, brown-and-white, four-legged animal with its mouth open, tongue hanging out, and tail wagging, you recognize it immediately as a representative of the concept *dog. Dog* is a concept that stands for a class of animals that share similar characteristics or attributes, even though they may differ in significant ways. Great Danes, dachshunds, collies, Chihuahuas, and other breeds—you recognize all these varied creatures as fitting into the concept *dog.* Moreover, the concepts we form do not exist in isolation, but rather in hierarchies. For example, dogs represent one subset of the concept *animal;* at a higher level, animals are a subset of the concept *living things.* Thus, concept formation has a certain logic to it.

Psychologists identify two basic types of concepts: formal concepts and natural concepts. A **formal concept** is one that is clearly defined by a set of rules, a formal definition, or a classification system. For example, the notion that *a triangle has three sides* is a formal concept as is the idea that *a square has four equal sides.* Most of the concepts we form and use are **natural concepts**, acquired not from definitions but through everyday perceptions and experiences. A leading cognition researcher, Eleanor Rosch, and her colleagues studied concept formation in its natural setting and concluded that in real life, natural concepts (such as *fruit, vegetable,* and *bird*) are not clear-cut and systematic (Gabora, Rosch, & Aerts, 2008; Rosch, 1973, 1978).

Many formal concepts are acquired in school. For example, we learn that an equilateral triangle is one in which all three sides are the same size. We acquire many natural concepts through experiences with examples, or positive instances of the concept. When children are young, parents may point out examples of a car—the family car, the neighbor's car, cars on the street, and pictures of cars in books. But, if a child points to some other type of moving vehicle and says "car," the parent will say, "No, that's a truck," or "This is a bus." *Truck* and *bus* are negative instances, or nonexamples, of the concept *car.* After experience with positive and negative instances of the concept, a child begins to grasp some of the properties of a car that distinguish it from other wheeled vehicles.

How do we use concepts in our everyday thinking? One view suggests that, in using natural concepts, we are likely to picture a **prototype** of the concept—an example that embodies its most common and typical features. Your *bird* prototype is more likely to be a robin or a sparrow than either a penguin or a turkey: Those birds can fly, while penguins and turkeys can't. Nevertheless, both penguins and turkeys are birds. So, not all examples of a natural concept fit it equally well. This is why natural concepts often seem less clear-cut than formal ones. Nevertheless, the prototype most closely fits a given natural concept, and other examples of the concept most often share more attributes with that prototype than with the prototype of any other concept.

A more recent theory of concept formation suggests that concepts are represented by their **exemplars**—individual instances, or examples, of a concept that are stored in memory from personal experience (Estes, 1994). So, if you work with penguins or turkeys every day, your exemplar of *bird* might indeed be a penguin or a turkey. By contrast, most people encounter robins or sparrows far more often than penguins or turkeys (except the roasted variety!). Thus, for the majority of people, robins or sparrows are exemplars of the *bird* concept.

As noted earlier, the concepts we form do not exist in isolation, but rather in hierarchies, or nested categories. Thus, concept formation has a certain orderliness about it, just as the process of *decision making* does—or, at least, sometimes does.

◀ A prototype is an example that embodies the most typical features of a concept. Which of the animals shown here best fits your prototype for the concept of *bird*?

Decision Making ▶

7.2 How do we make decisions?

Do you recall the last time you made an important decision? Would you describe the process you used to make the decision as a logical one? Psychologists define **decision making** as the process of considering alternatives and choosing among them. Some psychologists and other scientists with an interest in decision making—particularly economists—maintain that humans make decisions by systematically examining all possible alternatives and then choosing the one that will be most beneficial to them (Loewenstein, Rick, & Cohen, 2008).

The belief that decision making always proceeds in this fashion was challenged by psychologist Herbert Simon in 1956, when he introduced the notion of *bounded rationality* into the discussion. Bounded rationality simply means that boundaries, or limitations, around the decision-making process prevent it from being entirely logical. One important limitation is the size of working memory. We can think about only so much at any given time. Moreover, many decisions require us to predict how they will affect a future outcome. That is, in the grappling with an important decision, we ask ourselves questions such as "Five years from now, will I regret having done this or be glad that I did it?" Psychologists have identified several strategies that we use to deal with the cognitive limitations and personal uncertainties associated with decision making.

Additive Strategy. Suppose you wanted to rent an apartment starting next semester. How would you go about deciding among different apartments? You could use the **additive strategy**, a decision making approach in which each alternative is rated on each of the important factors affecting the decision and the alternative with the highest overall rating is chosen. The *Try It* on page 216 can help you get a feel for how the additive strategy works.

The additive strategy is useful, but it doesn't take into account the fact that some factors are more important than others. Instead, it assumes that high ratings on one factor compensate for low ratings on another. While this might work well for some decisions, we need a different strategy if we want to explicitly address factor priorities.

Elimination by Aspects. In one of the most important early studies of decision making along these lines, psychologist Amos Tversky (1972) suggested that we deal with the limitations on decision making by using a strategy he called **elimination by aspects**. With this approach, the factors on which the alternatives are to be evaluated are ordered from most important to least important. Any alternative that does not satisfy the most important factor is automatically eliminated. The process of elimination continues as each factor is considered in order. The alternative that survives is the one chosen. For example, if the most important factor for your apartment search was that you could afford a

decision making The process of considering alternatives and choosing among them.

additive strategy a decision making approach in which each alternative is rated on each of the important factors affecting the decision and the alternative with the highest overall rating is chosen

elimination by aspects A decision-making approach in which alternatives are evaluated against criteria that have been ranked according to importance.

Using the Additive Strategy to Choose an Apartment

To use the additive strategy to choose an apartment, you would first decide on a target rent (the amount you would like to pay) and then list the other important factors in choosing an apartment in a table like the one below. Next, you would select a rating scale, such as −5 to +5, and rate each of the apartments you were considering. Try your hand at applying the rating scale to apartments A, B, and C, using your own real-world priorities as a guide. Which apartment would you choose?

A. 15% below target rent; one block from campus; high-crime area but near police station; no amenities

B. Rent equal to target; 3 miles from campus but on a bus route; low-crime area; pool

C. Rent 20% above target; two blocks from campus; high-rise with security guard and electronic card-keys; pool, fitness center, game room, social activities director

Factor	A	B	C
Target rent			
Convenience			
Safety			
Amenities			
Total			

Watch the Video *Episode 10: What's in It for Me? Making Choices* in **MyPsychLab**

maximum rent of $800 per month, then you would automatically eliminate all the apartments that rented for more than that. If the second most important factor was availability of parking, you would then look at the list of apartments that cost $800 or less per month and weed out those without appropriate parking. You would then continue with your third most important factor and so on, until you had trimmed the list down.

Heuristics. Of course, decision making is often less systematic than Tversky's model suggests. For instance, have you ever decided to leave home a bit earlier than necessary so as to allow time for a possible traffic jam? Such decisions are often based on a **heuristic**—a rule of thumb that is derived from experience. Psychologists argue that we use heuristics to speed up the decision making process although we usually have some degree of awareness of the shortcomings of heuristics-based decisions (Brighton & Gigerenzer, 2012). That is, we know that rapidly formed judgments often ignore important information, but our cognitive systems often favor speed in the speed-versus-accuracy trade-off, especially when we are making decisions about relatively unimportant matters.

One heuristic that has been studied a great deal is the **availability heuristic**, a rule stating that the perceived probability of an event corresponds to the ease with which the event comes to mind. Thus, a decision to leave home early to avoid a possible traffic jam may result from having been stuck in one recently. The availability heuristic can cause us to overestimate probabilities in our daily lives as well (see the *Explain It*). Another type of heuristic is the **representativeness heuristic**, a decision strategy based on how closely a new situation resembles a familiar one. For instance, a decision about whether to go out with someone you have just met may be based on how much the person resembles someone else you know.

The **recognition heuristic**, a strategy in which the decision-making process terminates as soon as a factor that moves one toward a decision has been recognized, has also been the subject of much research. Suppose you are voting and the only information you have is the list of names vying for a particular office on the ballot. If you recognize one of the candidates' names as being that of a woman, and you have a predisposition toward seeing more women elected to public office, the recognition heuristic may cause you to decide to vote for the female candidate. Be aware, however, that researchers have found that decision makers rely on recognition heuristics only when they lack relevant information (Newell, 2011; Newell, Lagnado, & Shanks, 2007). Thus, with regard to voting, the more information people gather before an election, the less likely they are to vote for someone simply because the candidate's

heuristic (yur-RIS-tik) A rule of thumb that is derived from experience and used in decision making and problem solving, even though there is no guarantee of its accuracy or usefulness.

availability heuristic A cognitive rule of thumb that says that the perceived probability of an event or the importance assigned to it is based on its availability in memory.

representativeness heuristic A thinking strategy based on how closely a new object or situation is judged to resemble or match an existing prototype of that object or situation.

recognition heuristic A strategy in which decision making stops as soon as a factor that moves one toward a decision has been recognized.

EXPLAIN IT

Why Do People Overestimate the Likelihood of Rare Events?

When was the last time you read a news story about someone who bought a lottery ticket and didn't win? By its nature, the news focuses on the unusual, so the good fortune of lottery winners is trumpeted by the news media, while the more typical outcome of buying a lottery ticket is ignored. How does such news affect our ability to estimate probabilities in our everyday lives? Think about how heuristics may be involved in such effects before reading on.

If you are like most people who have favorable attitudes toward playing the lottery, you probably don't think about the results of your personal experiences with gambling when you are deciding whether to buy a lottery ticket. Instead, you think about the story you read on the Internet about a college student who won $30 million on a $1 lottery ticket. You should recognize this thought process as an instance of the availability heuristic.

Research suggests that focusing on the possible benefits associated with buying a lottery ticket can lead you to overestimate your chances of winning (Griffiths, 2003). Such irrationality isn't limited to just buying the ticket; this kind of thinking extends to people's number-picking strategies as well. For example, surveys show that 21% of regular ticket buyers believe their chances of winning the lottery are better if they choose the same numbers every time they play, while in reality, the odds are always the same (BBC World Service, 2007). Faulty thinking of this kind may reflect our inability to grasp very large numbers (Griffiths, 2003). Moreover, brain-imaging studies suggest that we tend to rely on our emotions when our minds have difficulty interpreting and integrating all of the facts that are relevant to a decision (De Martino et al., 2006). The fact that most people don't think of wasting a single dollar as all that important, especially as compared to the possibility of winning millions in return, contributes to the decision as well (Camerer, 2005). Thus, with the thought "Wouldn't it be great if I won the lottery?" firmly ensconced in our minds, we plunk down a dollar for a lottery ticket.

Wasting money on a lottery ticket is hardly a life-and-death matter. By contrast, the availability heuristic sometimes leads to tragic outcomes. For example, immediately after the terrorist attacks of September 11, 2001, researchers hypothesized that the number of deaths due to traffic accidents in the United States would increase dramatically in the ensuing weeks (Gigerenzer, 2004). They believed that memories of the attacks would serve as availability heuristics that would cause people to choose to travel by car rather than by plane. These decisions, hypothesized researchers, would reflect people's tendency to rely on the availability heuristic rather than on knowledge that their chances of being the target of a terrorist attack were far less than those of getting into an automobile accident. To test the hypothesis, researchers compared police records of fatal car crashes during September, October, and November of 2001 to the same months in 1996 through 2000. They found that there were substantially more such accidents in the months immediately after September 11, 2001, than during the same period in the 5 previous years.

To avoid making poor decisions, we need to be aware of the availability heuristic and be on guard against it. Sometimes this requires a conscious effort to shift our attention from the most cognitively available outcome of a decision to its actual statistical likelihood. So, if you would like to avoid spending your hard-earned money on lottery tickets, use imagery to develop a mental picture of yourself tossing yet another losing ticket into the trash and get into the habit of substituting it for the media images of winners that spring to mind when you think about buying a ticket.

Holly
YOUR COMMUNICATIONS

⊙ Watch on **MyPsychLab**

---

name is associated with one gender or the other, is suggestive of a particular ethnic group, or happens to be the one that the voter last heard in a radio ad or saw on a billboard before heading to the polls.

Framing. Whether we use heuristics or more time-consuming strategies, we should be aware that the manner in which information is presented can affect the decision-making process. For example, **framing** refers to the way information is presented so as to emphasize either a potential gain or a potential loss as the outcome. To study the effects of framing on decision making, Kahneman and Tversky (1984) presented the following options to a group of participants. Which program would you choose?

> *The United States is preparing for the outbreak of a dangerous disease, which is expected to kill 600 people. There have been designed two alternative programs to combat the disease. If program A is adopted, 200 people will be saved. If program B is adopted, there is a one-third probability that all 600 will be saved and a two-thirds probability that no people will be saved.*

The researchers found that 72% of the participants selected the "sure thing" of program A over the "risky gamble" of program B. Now consider the options as they were reframed:

> *If program C is adopted, 400 people will die. If program D is adopted, there is a one-third probability that nobody will die and a two-thirds probability that all 600 people will die.*

framing The way information is presented so as to emphasize either a potential gain or a potential loss as the outcome.

▲ How do you decide which fast-food restaurant to patronize when you want a quick bite to eat? Chances are you use a representativeness heuristic, a prototype that guides your expectations about how long it will take to get your food and what it will taste like. Fast-food chains use the same ingredients and food preparation methods at every location in order to maintain patrons' representativeness heuristics as guides for their future fast-food buying decisions.

intuition Rapidly formed judgments based on "gut feelings" or "instincts."

anchoring Overestimation of the importance of a factor by focusing on it to the exclusion of other relevant factors.

Which program did you choose? Of research participants given this version of the problem, 78% chose program D. A careful reading will reveal that program D has exactly the same consequences as program B in the earlier version. How can this result be explained? The first version of the problem was framed to focus attention on the number of lives that could be saved. When people are primarily motivated to achieve gains (save lives), they are more likely to choose a safe option over a risky one, as 72% of the participants did. The second version was framed to focus attention on the 400 lives that would be lost. When trying to avoid losses, people appear much more willing to choose a risky option, as 78% of the participants were.

Intuition. How often have you heard someone advise another to "go with your gut feelings"? Psychologists use the term **intuition** to refer to rapidly formed judgments based on "gut feeling" or "instincts." Despite our faith in intuition, it's important to understand that it is strongly influenced by emotion. Thus, at times, intuition can interfere with logical reasoning. Researchers have found this to be the case even when people are asked to make judgments about emotionally neutral issues, such as whether a given string of words constitutes a grammatically correct statement (Topolinski & Strack, 2009). Including emotion-provoking words in such strings (e.g., fight, death) influences study participants' accuracy in judging their grammaticality.

Intuition can also lead us to base important decisions on the degree to which one of the available options offers us some kind of gain. For example, what if you had to make an on-the-spot decision about whether you would rather purchase an $18,000 car and receive a $1,000 rebate or buy a $17,000 car? Information-processing researchers argue that, in the face of such decisions, intuitive judgments are generated by a mental representation of the gist of a body of information rather than by its factual details (Reyna, 2004). The gist of a car dealer's advertisement for a $1,000 rebate on an $18,000 automobile is "you'll save money if you buy it here," not "$18,000 − $1,000 = $17,000; therefore, it doesn't matter where you buy the car." Furthermore, researchers have found that intuition can lead to errors in reasoning about decisions that carry far greater risks than those associated with buying a car. One study found that intuitive thought processes caused physicians to overestimate the degree to which condoms reduce the risk of sexually transmitted diseases (Adam & Reyna, 2005). Study participants' assessments of the comparative risks of sexual behavior with and without condoms tended to ignore infections that have modes of transmission other than sexual intercourse (e.g., chlamydia).

Anchoring. At the beginning of the chapter, we introduced you to the concept of **anchoring**, the notion that focusing on a single factor magnifies the importance of that factor relative to others that are relevant to a decision. In one series of studies, British psychologist Neil Stewart examined how anchoring on the minimum payment required on a credit card bill influences decisions about repayment (Stewart, 2009). First, researchers conducted a survey in which participants answered questions about their most recent credit card bill. Respondents reported their balances, minimum payments required on their accounts, and actual payments. The researchers found that the smaller the required minimum payments were the smaller participants' actual payments were. Moreover, there was no correlation between account balances and actual payments. In other words, survey participants anchored their payment decisions on the size of the minimum payment rather than on the size of the balance.

In a follow-up laboratory experiment, Stewart presented participants with credit card bills on which the full balance was about $900. Half of the bills included a minimum payment, while half did not. Participants were asked to think about how big a payment they would be able to afford if the bill were theirs and then to tell the researchers how much they would probably pay on the bill. On average, participants who were given bills without minimum payments reported that they would pay nearly twice as much as those whose bills included minimum payments. Extrapolating from these results, Stewart predicted that banks and other financial institutions double the amount of interest they make off the average credit card balance (about $4,000) by requiring small minimum payments without warning consumers of the effects of such payments on interest charges. Stewart suggests that the effects of anchoring might be lessened if credit card bills included tables showing the effects of various payment amounts on interest charges. Such research contributed to the passage of the Credit Card Accountability, Responsibility, and Disclosure Act in 2009. The law requires credit card companies to warn consumers that paying minimum payments increases the amount of interest they will ultimately pay. In addition, companies must tell consumers how long it will take to pay off their balances if they make only minimum payments. 👁

The *Summarize It* recaps the various approaches to decision making.

SUMMARIZE IT

Approaches to Decision Making

👁 **Watch** the Video *Episode 10: In the Real World: Changing Your Mind* in **MyPsychLab**

APPROACH	DESCRIPTION
Elimination by aspects	Factors on which alternatives are to be evaluated are ordered from most to least important; any alternatives that do not satisfy the most important factor are eliminated; elimination of alternatives then continues factor by factor until one choice remains.
Availability heuristic	Information that comes easily to mind determines the decision that is made, often because of a recent experience.
Representativeness heuristic	The decision is based on how closely an object or situation resembles or matches an existing prototype.
Recognition heuristic	A rapid decision based on recognition of one of the alternatives.
Framing	Potential gains and losses associated with alternatives are emphasized and influence the decision.
Intuition	Decisions are motivated by "gut feelings" that may be influenced by perceptions of gains.
Anchoring	Decisions are influenced by focusing on a single factor, thereby overestimating its importance.

Problem Solving ▶

7.3 How do the basic approaches and obstacles to problem solving differ?

The process of decision making shares many features with **problem solving**, the thoughts and actions required to achieve a desired goal. Notably, heuristics are just as important in problem solving as they are in decision making.

Heuristics and Algorithms in Problem Solving. The **analogy heuristic** involves comparing a problem to others you have encountered in the past. The idea is that if a particular strategy worked with similar problems in the past, it will be effective for solving a new one.

Another heuristic that is effective for solving some problems is **working backward**, sometimes called the *backward search*. This approach starts with the solution, a known condition, and works back through the problem. Once the backward search has revealed the steps to be taken and their order, the problem can be solved. Try working backward to solve the water lily problem in the *Try It* on page 220.

Another popular heuristic strategy is **means–end analysis**, in which the current position is compared with a desired goal, and a series of steps are formulated and then taken to close the gap between the two (Sweller & Levine, 1982). Many problems are large and complex and must be broken down into smaller steps or subproblems before a solution can be reached. If your professor assigns a term paper, for example, you

problem solving Thoughts and actions required to achieve a desired goal that is not readily attainable.

analogy heuristic A rule of thumb that applies a solution that solved a problem in the past to a current problem that shares many features with the past problem.

working backward A heuristic strategy in which a person discovers the steps needed to solve a problem by defining the desired goal and working backward to the current condition; also called *backward search*.

means–end analysis A heuristic strategy in which the current position is compared with the desired goal and a series of steps are formulated and taken to close the gap between them.

TRY IT   **Water Lily Problem**

Water lilies double the area they cover every 24 hours. At the beginning of the summer there is one water lily on a pond. It takes 60 days for the pond to become covered with water lilies. On what day is the pond half covered? (From Fixx, 1978)

Answer: The most important fact is that the lilies double in number every 24 hours. If the pond is to be completely covered on the 60th day, it has to be half covered on the 59th day.

⊙ Watch on **MyPsychLab**

Source: Fixx (1978).

probably do not simply sit down and write it. You must first determine how you will approach the topic, research the topic, make an outline, and then write the sections over a period of time. At last, you will be ready to assemble the complete term paper, write several drafts, and put the finished product in final form before handing it in and receiving your *A*.

When you adopt a heuristic strategy, it may or may not lead to a correct solution. By contrast, an **algorithm** is a problem-solving strategy that always leads to a correct solution if it is applied appropriately. For example, the formula you learned in school for finding the area of a rectangle (width × length) is an algorithm. We'll talk more about algorithms when we look at artificial intelligence on the next page.

algorithm A systematic, step-by-step procedure, such as a mathematical formula, that guarantees a solution to a problem of a certain type if applied appropriately and executed properly.

functional fixedness The failure to use familiar objects in novel ways to solve problems because of a tendency to view objects only in terms of their customary functions.

mental set The tendency to apply a familiar strategy to the solution of a problem without carefully considering the special requirements of that problem.

Obstacles to Problem Solving. In some cases, we are hampered in our efforts to solve problems in daily life because of **functional fixedness**—the failure to use familiar objects in novel ways to solve problems. We tend to see objects only in terms of their customary functions. Just think of all the items you use daily—tools, utensils, and other equipment—that help you perform certain functions. Often, the normal functions of such objects become fixed in your thinking so that you do not consider using them in new and creative ways (McCaffrey, 2012).

Suppose you wanted a cup of coffee, but the glass pot for your coffeemaker was broken. If you suffered from functional fixedness, you might come to the conclusion that there was nothing you could do to solve your problem at that moment. But, rather than thinking about the object or utensil that you don't have, think about the function that it needs to perform. What you need is something to catch the coffee, not necessarily the specific type of glass pot that came with the coffeemaker. Could you catch the coffee in a bowl or cooking utensil, or even in coffee mugs?

Another impediment to problem solving is **mental set**, the tendency to continue to use the same old method even though another approach might be better. Perhaps you hit on a way to solve a problem once in the past and continue to use the same technique in similar situations, even though it is not highly effective or efficient. People are much more susceptible to mental set when they overlook or are distracted from the true meaning of a problem of a problem. For instance, a mental set is imposed on our thinking when we are asked a brain-teaser question such as *"What occurs twice and February, once in March and April, but never in May?"* The

▲ Many of us are hampered in our efforts to solve problems in daily life because of functional fixedness—the failure to use familiar objects in novel ways to solve problems.

question creates a mental set that prompts us to search for events that occur in each of these months. When we hear the answer, "*the letter* r," we realize that the appropriate framework of meaning for the question was something quite different from what we assumed it to be.

Why do people tend to hang on to ineffective problem-solving strategies? The cognitive process that underlies both functional fixedness and mental set is **confirmation bias**, the tendency to selectively pay attention to information that confirms preexisting beliefs and ignore data that contradict them. For example, when faced with an operating system "crash," most computer users know that the first line of defense is to reboot. Every time rebooting solves the problem, confirmation bias in favor of rebooting as a solution for computer problems becomes stronger. As a result, when a problem arises that proves resistant to rebooting, most of us try rebooting a few more times before we confront the reality that rebooting isn't going to solve the problem. Confirmation bias (i.e., "it worked last time") is responsible for the fact that multiple reboots are required before the belief that rebooting will solve any computer problem gives way and we look for a different approach.

Artificial Intelligence ▶

In the previous section you read that mathematical formulas are algorithms, or problem-solving strategies that always lead to a correct solution. Another kind of algorithm tests all possible solutions and then executes the one that works best. In most situations, the limits of human working memory render this kind of algorithm difficult, if not impossible, to employ. By contrast, computers are capable of completing such an algorithm and doing so in a matter of seconds. This particular feature of computer "thinking" has been well illustrated by **artificial intelligence** programs that have been designed to match the skills of human experts in games such as chess. You may have heard of the series of chess matches that pitted renowned player Garry Kasparov against IBM computers named "Deep Blue" and "Deep Junior." The best Kasparov has been able to do is to play the computers to a draw.

If a computer can beat a human at chess, does it mean that computers process information in exactly the same way as the human brain does? Not necessarily. However, computer scientists hope to design artificial intelligence that accomplishes that goal. Programs designed to mimic human brain functioning are called **artificial neural networks (ANNs)**. Such networks have proved very useful in computer programs designed to carry out highly specific functions within a limited domain, known as **expert systems**. One of the first expert systems was MYCIN, a program used by physicians to diagnose blood diseases and meningitis. Such systems combined with the information-disseminating power of the Internet enable researchers on the cutting edge of medical innovation to rapidly make new diagnosis and treatment strategies available to health professionals even in the remotest parts of the world (Bennani, Bennani, & Boumalif, 2012). It's important to note here that expert systems do not make decisions for practitioners. Instead, they serve as "assistants" to humans. For example, medical diagnosis programs are most often used to confirm doctors' hypotheses or to generate possible diagnoses that have not occurred to them (Brunetti et al., 2002). Remember, too, that any expert system relies on the accumulated knowledge of human experts. Thus, it is impossible for computers to totally replace human professionals.

Moreover, many cognitive tasks that humans find relatively easy to perform are actually quite difficult to teach a computer to do. Many aspects of language processing, for instance, are extremely difficult for computers to manage (Kwong, 2013). For example, what kind of scene comes to mind when you hear the word *majestic*? Perhaps you see a range of snow-capped mountains. Computer scientists are currently working to develop programs that can enable computers to retrieve images on the basis of such vague, abstract cues (Araujo, 2009). As you will see in the next section, human language, although we use it effortlessly most of the time, is an extremely complex phenomenon.

confirmation bias Selective attention to information that confirms preexisting beliefs about the best way to solve a problem.

7.4 How have computer scientists applied research on artificial intelligence?

artificial intelligence The programming of computer systems to simulate human thinking in solving problems and in making judgments and decisions.

artificial neural networks (ANNs) Computer systems that are intended to mimic human cognitive functioning.

expert systems Computer programs designed to carry out highly specific functions within a limited domain.

▲ World champion Garry Kasparov contemplates a move against Deep Blue, an IBM computer that exhibited artificial intelligence in the area of top-level chess play.

1. Imagining an action stimulates the same brain areas that are active when actually engaging in the action. (true/false)
2. A(n) _____ is the most typical example of a concept.
3. Heuristics have both desirable and undesirable effects on decision making. (true/false)
4. A(n) _____ is a problem-solving strategy that guarantees a correct answer.
5. Computer systems intended to mimic the functioning of the human brain are called _____.

Language

language A means of communicating thoughts and feelings using a system of socially shared but arbitrary symbols (sounds, signs, or written symbols) arranged according to rules of grammar.

Language is a means of communicating thoughts and feelings using a system of socially shared but arbitrary symbols (sounds, signs, or written symbols) arranged according to rules of grammar. Language expands our ability to think because it allows us to consider abstract concepts—such as justice—that are not represented by physical objects. Further, thanks to language, we can share our knowledge and thoughts with one another in an extremely efficient way. Thus, whether spoken, written, or signed, language is our most important cognitive tool. In Chapter 8, we will discuss how language is acquired by infants. Here, we explore the components and the structure of this amazing form of human communication.

7.5 What are the components language?

psycholinguistics The study of how language is acquired, produced, and used and how the sounds and symbols of language are translated into meaning.

The Structure of Language

You use language all the time, but have you ever thought about breaking it down into its components? That is precisely what *psycholinguists* do. **Psycholinguistics** is the study of how language is acquired, produced, and used and how the sounds and symbols of language are translated into meaning. Psycholinguists use specific terms for each of the five basic components of language.

phonemes The smallest units of sound in a spoken language.

The smallest units of sound in a spoken language—such as *b* or *s* in English—are known as **phonemes**. Three phonemes together form the sound of the word *cat*: *c* (which sounds like *k*), *a*, and *t*. Combinations of letters that form particular sounds are also phonemes, such as the *th* in *the* and the *ch* in *child*. The same phoneme may be represented by different letters in different words; this occurs with the *a* in *stay* and the *ei* in *sleigh*. And the same letter can serve as different phonemes. The letter *a*, for example, is sounded as four different phonemes in *day, cap, watch,* and *law*.

morphemes The smallest units of meaning in a language.

Morphemes are the smallest units of meaning in a language. A few single phonemes serve as morphemes, such as the article *a* and the personal pronoun *I*. The ending *-s* gives a plural meaning to a word and is thus a morpheme in English. Many words in English are single morphemes—*book, word, learn, reason,* and so on. In addition to root words, morphemes may be prefixes (such as *re-* in *relearn*) or suffixes (such as *-ed* to show past tense, as in *learned*). The single morpheme *reason* becomes a dual morpheme in *reasonable*. The morpheme *book* (singular) becomes two morphemes in *books* (plural).

syntax The aspect of grammar that specifies the rules for arranging and combining words to form phrases and sentences.

Syntax is the aspect of grammar that specifies the rules for arranging and combining words to form phrases and sentences. The rules of word order, or syntax, differ from one language to another. For example, an important rule of syntax in English is that adjectives usually come before nouns. So English speakers refer to the residence of the U.S. president as "the White House." In Spanish, in contrast, the noun usually comes before the adjective, and Spanish speakers say "*la Casa Blanca,*" or "the House White."

semantics The meaning or the study of meaning derived from morphemes, words, and sentences.

Semantics refers to the meaning derived from morphemes, words, and sentences. The same word can have different meanings depending on how it is used in sentences: "I don't mind." "Mind your manners." "He has lost his mind." Or consider another example: "Loving to read, the young girl read three books last week." Here, the word *read* is pronounced two different ways and, in one case, is the past tense.

Finally, **pragmatics** is the term psycholinguists use to refer to aspects of language such as *intonation,* the rising and falling patterns that are used to express meaning. For example, think about how you would say the single word *cookie* to express each of the following meanings: "Do you want a cookie?" or "What a delicious looking cookie!" or "That's a cookie." The subtle differences reflect your knowledge of the pragmatic rules of English; for example, questions end with a rising intonation, while statements end with a falling intonation. Pragmatic rules also come into play when you speak in one way to your friend and another to your professor. That is, the social rules associated with language use are also included in pragmatics. Likewise, the differences between expressions such as "break a leg" (i.e., "good luck" for people in a theatrical production) and "when pigs fly" (i.e., referring to an outcome that is extremely unlikely) and their literal counterparts lie within the domain of pragmatics.

▲ Gestural languages, such as American Sign Language, include all of the same elements of spoken language. The "phonemes" of sign language are (1) hand shape, (2) location, (3) palm orientation, (4) movements, and (5) holds. Thus, any sign can be analyzed in terms of these elements just as spoken words can be broken down into their constituent sounds. For example, the sign for "cat" shown above includes more phonemes than its spoken equivalent, which, has only three (k/a/t).

pragmatics The patterns of intonation and social roles associated with a language.

Animal Language ▶

7.6 What is the evidence concerning animal communication?

Ask people what capability most reliably sets humans apart from all other animal species, and most will answer "language," and for good reason. As far as scientists know, humans are the only species to have developed this rich, varied, and complex system of communication. Moreover, linguists assert that human language includes several key elements and that all known animal communication systems lack one or more of them (Hockett, 1959). Linguists differ to some degree as to just what the unique features of human language are (Anderson & Patrick, 2006). However, here are a few key elements that most agree on:

- *Duality of patterning:* Phonemes are combined in rule-governed patterns to create words; words are combined in rule-governed patterns to create sentences.
- *Productivity:* A finite number of sounds is used to produce an infinite number of unique utterances.
- *Arbitrariness:* There is no meaningful link between an object, event, or thought and the way it is expressed phonologically.
- *Interchangeability:* Any sound that can be heard can be reproduced.
- *Specialization:* Language sounds are used only for communication.
- *Displacement:* Utterances can be about objects and events that are not present.
- *Cultural transmission:* A social environment is required for language learning; it does not develop on its own.
- *Prevarication:* Language can express ideas that are untrue.
- *Reflexiveness:* Language can describe itself.

Despite their limitations, however, it is clear that animals communicate with one another. Moreover, researchers have taught several different kinds of animals to communicate with humans.

| Give | Take | Apple | Banana | Sarah | Mary |

FIGURE 7.1 Sarah's Symbols
A chimpanzee named Sarah learned to communicate using plastic chips of various shapes, sizes, and colors to represent words in an artificial language developed by her trainer, David Premack.
Source: Premack, D. (1971). Language in chimpanzees? Science, 172, 808–822. Reprinted by permission from AAAS.

As early as 1933 and 1951, researchers attempted to teach chimpanzees to speak by raising the chimps in their homes. These experiments failed because the vocal tract in chimpanzees and the other apes is not adapted to human speech, so researchers turned to sign language. Psychologists Allen and Beatrix Gardner (1969) took in a 1-year-old chimp named Washoe and taught her sign language. Washoe learned signs for objects and certain commands, such as *flower, give me, come, open,* and *more.* By the end of her fifth year, she had mastered about 160 signs (Fleming, 1974).

Psychologist David Premack (1971) taught another chimp, Sarah, to use an artificial language he developed. Its symbols consisted of magnetized chips of various shapes, sizes, and colors, as shown in Figure 7.1. Premack used operant conditioning techniques to teach Sarah to select the magnetic chip representing a fruit and place it on a magnetic language board. The trainer would then reward Sarah with the fruit she had requested. Sarah mastered the concepts of similarities and differences, and eventually she could signal whether two objects were the same or different with nearly perfect accuracy (Premack & Premack, 1983).

At the Yerkes Primate Research Center at Emory University, a chimp named Lana participated in a computer-controlled language training program. She learned to press keys imprinted with geometric symbols that represented words in an artificial language called Yerkish. Researcher Sue Savage-Rumbaugh and a colleague (1986; Rumbaugh, 1977) varied the location, color, and brightness of the keys, so Lana had to learn which symbols to use no matter where they were located. One day, her trainer Tim had an orange that she wanted. Lana had available symbols for many fruits—apple, banana, and so on—but none for an orange. Yet there was a symbol for the color orange. So Lana improvised and signaled, "Tim give apple which is orange." Researcher Herbert Terrace (1979, 1981) and his co-workers taught sign language to a chimp they called Nim Chimpsky (after the famed linguist Noam Chomsky) and reported Nim's progress from the age of 2 weeks to 4 years. Nim learned 125 symbols, which is respectable, but does not amount to language, according to Terrace (1985, 1986). Terrace believed that chimps like Nim and Washoe were simply imitating their trainers and making responses to get reinforcers, according to the laws of operant conditioning, not the laws of language. Finally, Terrace suggested that the studies with primates were probably influenced by experimenter bias; trainers might unconsciously tend to interpret the behavior of the chimps as more indicative of progress toward developing language than it really was. However, Terrace had not heard of Kanzi when he expressed his skepticism.

As impressive as the feats of Washoe, Sarah, and the rest of these talented primates were, the linguistic skills that were acquired by a bonobo chimp named Kanzi eclipsed them all. During the mid-1980s, researchers had taught Kanzi's mother to press symbols representing words. Her progress was not remarkable; but her infant son Kanzi, who stood by and observed her during training, was learning rapidly (thanks to observational learning, discussed in Chapter 5). When Kanzi had a chance at the symbol board, his performance quickly surpassed that of his mother and of every other chimp the researchers had tested.

Kanzi demonstrated an advanced understanding (for chimps) of spoken English and could respond correctly even to new commands, such as "Throw your ball to the river," or "Go to the refrigerator and get out a tomato" (Savage-Rumbaugh, 1990; Savage-Rumbaugh et al., 1992). By the time Kanzi was 6 years old, a team of researchers who

▲ From their studies of communication among chimps and other animals, researchers have gained useful insights into the nature of language. The bonobo chimp Kanzi became skilled at using a special symbol board to communicate.

worked with him had recorded more than 13,000 "utterances" and reported that Kanzi could communicate using some 200 different geometric symbols (Gibbons, 1991). Kanzi could press symbols to ask someone to play chase with him and even ask two others to play chase while he watched. And if Kanzi signaled someone to "chase" and "hide," he was insistent that his first command, "chase," be done first (Gibbons, 1991). Kanzi was not merely responding to nearby trainers whose actions or gestures he might have copied. He responded just as well when requests were made over earphones so that no one else in the room could signal to him purposely or inadvertently.

Most animal species studied by language researchers are limited to motor responses, such as sign language, gestures, using magnetic symbols, or pressing keys on symbol boards. But, these limitations do not extend to some bird species such as parrots, which are capable of making human-like speech sounds. One remarkable case is Alex, an African gray parrot whose remarkable abilities were discovered by a college student, Irene Pepperberg, who purchased the bird from a pet store in 1977. Eventually Pepperberg pursued a research career in *comparative psychology*, the sub-field that studies animal behavior and cognition, in which Alex was the primary subject of her experiments. Pepperberg found that Alex not only could mimic human speech but also seemed to do so intelligently. Able to recognize and name various colors, objects, and shapes, Alex answered questions about them in English. When asked "Which object is green?" Alex easily named the green object (Pepperberg, 1991, 1994b), and he can count as well. When asked such questions as "How many red blocks?" Alex answered correctly about 80% of the time (Pepperberg, 1994a). Studies even suggest that Alex may have been able to add (Pepperberg, 2006). Pepperberg's success in teaching such skills to Alex led to studies with other gray parrots suggesting that the species in more intelligent than was previously understood.

Research with sea mammals such as whales and dolphins has established that they apparently use complicated systems of grunts, whistles, clicks, and other sounds to communicate within their species (Quick & Janik, 2008; Schulz, Whitehead, Gero, & Rendell, 2008). Researchers at the University of Hawaii have trained dolphins to respond to fairly complex commands requiring an understanding of directional and relational concepts. Dolphins can learn to pick out an object and put it on the right or left of a basket, for example, and comprehend such commands as "in the basket" and "under the basket" (Chollar, 1989).

Despite the impressive effects of training on a variety of species' capacity for communication, there are important differences between animal and human communication (Terrace, 2011). One key difference is that humans use language extensively to generate novel utterances. Except in rare instances, animals that have been trained to communicate with symbols do not use them to create new expressions. Their communications are limited to the menu of symbol–object associations on which they have been trained. Another important difference is that human language includes many symbols that have multiple meanings, and humans have little difficulty knowing which meaning a symbol represents in a given expression based on the linguistic and situational context in which the symbol is used. By contrast, animals seem to be incapable of associating a given symbol with more than one object. Although there is a continuing debate on the degree to which animal communication constitutes real language, the consensus seems to be that animals are capable of more sophisticated communication strategies than was once believed but lack the capacity for true language (Terrace, 2011).

Language and Thinking ▶

7.7 How does language influence thinking?

If language is unique to humans, then does it drive human thinking? Does the fact that you speak English mean that you reason, think, and perceive your world differently than does someone who speaks Spanish, or Chinese, or Swahili? According to one hypothesis presented about 50 years ago, it does. Benjamin Whorf (1956) put forth his **linguistic relativity hypothesis**, suggesting that the language a person speaks largely determines the nature of that person's thoughts (Tohidian, 2009). According to this hypothesis, people's worldview is constructed primarily by the words in their language. As proof, Whorf offered his classic example. The languages used by the Inuit people

linguistic relativity hypothesis The notion that the language a person speaks largely determines the nature of that person's thoughts.

have a number of different words for snow—"*apikak,* first snow falling; *aniv,* snow spread out; *pukak,* snow for drinking water"—while the English-speaking world has but one word, *snow* (Restak, 1988, p. 222). Whorf claimed that such a rich and varied selection of words for various snow types and conditions enabled the Inuit to think differently about snow than do people whose languages lack such a range of words.

Eleanor Rosch (1973) tested whether people whose language contains many names for colors would be better at thinking about and discriminating among colors than people whose language has only a few color names. Her participants were English-speaking Americans and the Dani, members of a remote tribe in New Guinea whose language has only two names for colors—*mili* for dark, cool colors and *mola* for bright, warm colors. Rosch showed members of both groups single-color chips of 11 colors—black, white, red, yellow, green, blue, brown, purple, pink, orange, and gray—for 5 seconds each. Then, after 30 seconds, she had the participants select the 11 colors they had viewed from an assortment of 40 color chips. Did the Americans outperform the Dani participants for whom brown, black, purple, and blue are all *mili,* or dark? No. Rosch found no significant differences between the Dani and the Americans in discriminating, remembering, or thinking about those 11 basic colors. Rosch's study did not support the linguistic relativity hypothesis.

Clearly, however, it would be a mistake to go too far in the opposite direction and assume that language has no influence on how people think. Thought both influences and is influenced by language, and language appears to reflect cultural differences more than it determines them (Pinker, 1994; Rosch, 1987).

Learning a Second Language

Do you speak more than one language? Most native-born Americans speak only English. But, in many other countries around the world, the majority of citizens speak two or even more languages (Snow, 1993). In European countries, most students learn English in addition to the languages of the countries bordering their own. Dutch is the native language of the Netherlands, but all Dutch schoolchildren learn German, French, and English. College-bound German students also typically study three languages (Haag & Stern, 2003). What about the effect of learning two languages on the process of language development itself? (You'll learn more about this process in Chapter 8).

Research suggests that there are both advantages and disadvantages to learning two languages early in life. One of the pluses is that, among preschool and school-age children, **bilingualism**, fluency in at least two languages, is associated with better *executive control* skills on language tasks (Morales, Calvo, & Bialystok, 2013). Executive control skills enable bilingual children to suppress impulsive responses to verbal tasks and, as a result, think more carefully about them. Thus, executive control skills are important in learning to read and write. On the downside, even in adulthood, bilingualism is sometimes associated with decreased efficiency in memory tasks involving words (Craik & Bialystok, 2010). However, bilinguals appear to develop compensatory strategies that allow them to make up these inefficiencies. Consequently, they often perform such tasks as accurately as monolinguals, though they may respond more slowly. Many people would argue, however, that the advantages associated with fluency in two languages are worth giving up a bit of cognitive efficiency. ◉

So, you may ask, what about people who did not have the good fortune to grow up bilingual? Is it still possible to become fluent in a second language after reaching adulthood? Researchers have found that there is no age at which it is impossible to acquire a new language. Although it is true that those who begin earlier reach higher levels of proficiency, age is not the only determining factor. Kenji Hakuta and his colleagues (2003) used census data to examine relationships among English proficiency, age at entry into the United States, and educational attainment for Chinese- and Spanish-speaking immigrants. The results of their study are shown in Figure 7.2. As you can see, even when immigrants entered the United States in middle and late adulthood, their ability to learn English was predicted

7.8 How does bilingualism affect thinking and language development?

bilingualism Fluency in at least two languages.

◉ **Watch** the Video *Bilingual Education* in **MyPsychLab**

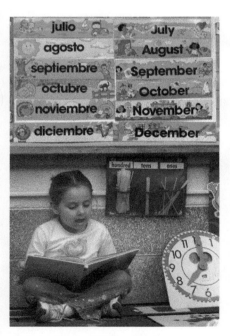

▲ Learning in a bilingual classroom provides distinct advantages in adolescence and adulthood. Spanish and English are the languages spoken by the majority of bilinguals in the United States.

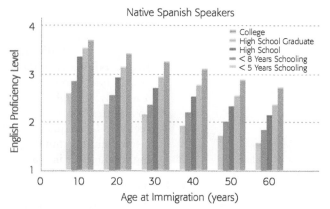

by their educational backgrounds. And other studies have shown that the more you know about your first language—its spelling rules, grammatical structure, and vocabulary—the easier it will be for you to learn another language (Sparks, Patton, & Ganschow, 2012).

It may be that children attain second-language fluency more easily than adults simply because they practice more. Older individuals may rely more on passive strategies such as listening to others' conversations or watching television to pick up a new language. Research has shown that passive listening can help us learn new vocabulary, but it is of no help in learning grammar (Van Lommel, Laenen, & d'Ydewalle, 2006). In fact, listening to others speak actually appears to cause us to forget the grammatical knowledge that we already have. This may happen because natural conversation includes fragmentary expressions rather than complete sentences. For example, a friend might say to you, "How long did you study for the psychology exam?" In reply, you would probably say "about three hours" rather than "I studied about three hours for the psychology exam." Thus, when you take a foreign language class, some of the required exercises may seem silly. (How often does anyone say something like "Here is my aunt's big yellow pencil" or "There is Lucy's beautiful blue hat" in real life?) Yet, they are essential to your acquisition of the language's grammar.

There is one clear advantage to learning two languages earlier in life, however. People who are younger when they learn a new language are far more likely to be able to speak it with an appropriate accent (McDonald, 1997). One reason for this difference between early and late language learners may have to do with slight variations in neural processing in Broca's area, the area of the brain that controls speech production. Research by Kim and others (1997) suggests that bilinguals who learned a second language early (younger than age 10 or 11) rely on the same patch of tissue in Broca's area for both of the languages they speak. In those who learned a second language at an older age, two different sections of Broca's area are active while they are performing language tasks—one section for the first language and another for the second language. Yet, the two sections are very close, only 1/3 inch apart. 👁

FIGURE 7.2 **English Proficiency in Chinese- and Spanish-Speaking Immigrants to the United States** These research results, based on census data involving more than 2 million individuals, suggest that it is never too late to learn a second language. *Source:* Hakuta et al. (2003).

👁 **Watch** the Video *Episode 10: Thinking Like a Psychologist: Multilingualism: Speaking One's Mind* in **MyPsychLab**

REMEMBER IT   *Check your answers and take additional quizzes in MyPsychLab.com.*   ✓● **S**tudy and **Review** on **MyPsychLab**

1. Intonation is one feature of the component of language called _____.
2. Chimpanzees can communicate with humans using symbols or _____.
3. According to the _____, thinking can be limited by language.
4. Children are more likely than adults to learn to speak a new language with a(n) _____.

Intelligence

Have you ever stopped to think what you really mean when you say someone is "intelligent"? Individual differences in language ability influence such judgments. In general, we view individuals with large vocabularies as "smarter" than others, and vocabulary knowledge is an important component of most formal test of intelligence. Typically, though, when we describe another person as "intelligent," we are referring to abilities beyond those in the domain of language. We usually mean that the person seems to learn quickly and can solve problems that appear to mystify others. Spending a few minutes thinking about intelligence in this way will help you realize that defining intelligence in ways that can be measured is quite a challenge. ◉

The Nature of Intelligence

A task force of experts from the American Psychological Association (APA) defined **intelligence** as possessing several basic facets: an individual's "ability to understand complex ideas, ... to adapt effectively to the environment, ... to learn from experience, to engage in various forms of reasoning, and to overcome obstacles by taking thought" (Neisser et al., 1996, p. 77). As you will see, however, there's more to intelligence than this simple definition suggests.

The APA's definition of intelligence includes several factors, such as the ability to understand complex ideas and the capacity for adapting to the environment. But, are these manifestations of a single entity or truly separate abilities? This question has fascinated psychologists for more than a century.

English psychologist Charles Spearman (1863–1945) observed that people who are bright in one area are usually bright in other areas as well. In other words, they tend to be generally intelligent. Spearman (1927) came to believe that intelligence is composed of a general ability that underlies all intellectual functions. Spearman concluded that intelligence tests tap this **g factor**, or general intelligence, and a number of s factors, or specific intellectual abilities. Spearman's influence can be seen in those intelligence tests, such as the Stanford–Binet, that yield one IQ score to indicate the level of general intelligence. Over the decades since Spearman first published his work, many studies have supported his hypotheses about the existence of the g factor and that it strongly influences how we acquire information from the world around us (Kaufman, 2011).

Another early researcher in testing, Louis L. Thurstone (1938), rejected Spearman's notion of general intellectual ability, or g factor. After analyzing the scores of many participants on some 56 separate ability tests, Thurstone identified seven **primary mental abilities**: verbal comprehension, numerical ability, spatial relations, perceptual speed, word fluency, memory, and reasoning. He maintained that all intellectual activities involve one or more of these primary mental abilities. Thurstone and his wife, Thelma G. Thurstone, developed their Primary Mental Abilities Tests to measure these seven abilities. Thurstone believed that a single IQ score obscured more than it revealed. He suggested that a profile showing relative strengths and weaknesses on the seven primary mental abilities would provide a more accurate picture of a person's intelligence.

Harvard psychologist Howard Gardner (Gardner & Hatch, 1989; Gardner, 2011) also denies the existence of a g factor. Instead, he proposes a **theory of multiple intelligences** that includes eight independent forms of intelligence, or *frames of mind,* as illustrated in Figure 7.3. The eight frames of mind are linguistic, logical-mathematical, spatial, bodily-kinesthetic, musical, interpersonal, intrapersonal, and naturalistic. Furthermore, Gardner continues to refine his model. In recent years, he has proposed that a ninth type of intelligence, one that he calls *existential intelligence,* deals with the spiritual realm and enables us to contemplate the meaning of life (Halama & Strízenec, 2004). ✳

Gardner (1983) first developed his theory by studying individuals with different types of brain damage that affect some forms of intelligence but leave others intact. He also studied reports of people with *savant syndrome,* who show a combination of intellectual disability and unusual talent or ability. (You'll read more about this

---

◉ ⌐**Watch** the Video *Episode 11: Big Picture: What Is Intelligence?* in **MyPsychLab**

7.9 How do the theories of Spearman, Thurstone, Gardner, and Sternberg differ?

intelligence An individual's ability to understand complex ideas, to adapt effectively to the environment, to learn from experience, to engage in various forms of reasoning, and to overcome obstacles through mental effort.

g factor Spearman's term for a general intellectual ability that underlies all mental operations to some degree.

primary mental abilities According to Thurstone, seven relatively distinct capabilities that singly or in combination are involved in all intellectual activities.

theory of multiple intelligences Howard Gardner's proposal that there are several independent forms of intelligence.

✳⌐**Explore** the **Concept** *Gardner's Multiple Intelligences* on **MyPsychLab**

Linguistic Intelligence
The ability to use language both as an aid to thinking and in communication
Example: Reading or writing a blog

Logical-Mathematical Intelligence
The ability to think logically and to solve mathematical problems
Example: Developing a budget

Spatial Intelligence
The ability to use images that represent spatial relations
Example: imagining whether a new sofa will fit in your living room

Bodily-Kinesthetic Intelligence
The ability to learn and execute physical movements
Example: Taking a spin class

Musical Intelligence
Sensitivity to and understanding of pitch, rhythm, and other aspects of music
Example: Learning to play an instrument

Interpersonal Intelligence
The ability to communicate and engage in effective social relationships with others
Example: Being a trustworthy friend and pleasant companion

Intrapersonal Intelligence
The ability to understand oneself
Example: Knowing what is important to you in life

Naturalistic Intelligence
The ability to identify patterns in nature and to determine how individual objects or beings fit into them
Example: Embracing and enjoying the challenges of winter camping

phenomenon later in this chapter.) Finally, Gardner considered how various abilities and skills have been valued differently in other cultures and periods of history.

Perhaps, the most controversial aspect of Gardner's theory is his view that all forms of intelligence are of equal importance. In fact, different cultures assign varying degrees of importance to the types of intelligence. For example, linguistic and logical mathematical intelligences are valued most in the United States and other Western cultures; bodily-kinesthetic intelligence is more highly prized in cultures that depend on hunting for survival.

Psychologist Robert Sternberg (2000) is also critical of heavy reliance on Spearman's *g* factor for measuring intelligence. But, Sternberg is not merely a critic; he has developed his own theory of intelligence. Sternberg (1985a; 1986a) has formulated a **triarchic theory of intelligence**, which proposes that there are three types of intelligence (see Figure 7.4 on p. 230). The first type, *componential intelligence,* refers to the mental abilities most closely related to success on conventional IQ and achievement tests. He claims that traditional IQ tests measure only componential, or analytical, intelligence. ☀

The second type, *experiential intelligence,* is reflected in creative thinking and problem solving. People with high experiential intelligence are able to solve novel problems and deal with unusual and unexpected challenges. Another aspect of experiential intelligence is finding creative ways to perform common daily tasks more efficiently and effectively.

The third type, *contextual intelligence,* or practical intelligence, might be equated with common sense or "street smarts." People with high contextual intelligence are survivors, who capitalize on their strengths and compensate for their weaknesses. They either adapt well to their environment, change the environment so that they can succeed, or, if necessary, find a new environment.

Sternberg and others (1995) argue that IQ-test performance and real-world success are based on two different types of knowledge: *formal academic knowledge,* or the knowledge we acquire in school, and *tacit knowledge.* Unlike formal academic knowledge, tacit knowledge is action oriented and is acquired without direct help from others. For instance, knowing how close to stand to a person you have just met is tacit knowledge that is acquired from the culture in which one is raised. According

FIGURE 7.3 Gardner's Eight Frames of Mind
Source: Campbell, Linda C.; Campbell, Bruce; Dickinson, Dee, Teaching and Learning Through Multiple Intelligences, 3rd Ed., © 2004. Reprinted and Electronically reproduced by permission of Pearson Education, Inc., Upper Saddle River, New Jersey.

triarchic theory of intelligence Sternberg's theory that there are three types of intelligence: componential (analytical), experiential (creative), and contextual (practical).

☀ Explore the Concept *Sternberg's Triarchic Theory of Intelligence* on **MyPsychLab**

Componential Intelligence
Mental abilities most
closely related to success on
traditional IQ and achievement tests

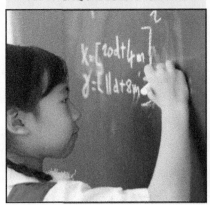

Experiential Intelligence
Creative thinking
and problem solving

Contextual Intelligence
Practical intelligence
or "street smarts"

FIGURE 7.4 Sternberg's Triarchic Theory of Intelligence
According to Sternberg, there are three types of intelligence: componential, experiential, and contextual.

to Sternberg, tacit knowledge is more important to successful real-world performance. Research supports Sternberg's contention that the two forms of knowledge are different (Grigorenko et al., 2004; Taub et al., 2001). However, investigators have found that measures of formal academic knowledge, such as traditional IQ tests, better predict real-world success than do Sternberg's tests of practical intelligence. Sternberg and those who agree with him contend that imperfections in the tests themselves are responsible for such results. Thus, in recent years, Sternberg and his colleagues have focused on developing a reliable and valid intelligence test that measures each of the three hypothesized types of intelligence (Chart, Grigorenko & Sternberg, 2008).

Sternberg's ideas have become popular among educators. Several studies have shown that teaching methods designed to tap into all three types of intelligence can be effective with students who are low achievers (Jarvin et al., 2008). In such instruction, teachers emphasize the practical relevance of formal academic knowledge and help students apply it to real-world problems. 👁

The *Summarize It* recaps the various theories of intelligence.

SUMMARIZE IT

Theories of Intelligence

👁 **Watch** the Video *Episode 10: Basics: Theories of Intelligence* in **MyPsychLab**

THEORY	DESCRIPTION
Spearman's *g* factor	Intelligence consists of a single factor known as *g*, which represents a general intellectual ability.
Thurstone's primary mental abilities	Intelligence has seven separate components: verbal comprehension, numerical ability, spatial relations, perceptual speed, word fluency, memory, and reasoning.
Gardner's frames of mind	There are eight independent forms of intelligence: linguistic, logical-mathematical, spatial, bodily-kinesthetic, musical, interpersonal, intrapersonal, and naturalistic.
Sternberg's triarchic theory	There are three types of intelligence: componential, experiential, and contextual.

7.10 What are the characteristics of good cognitive ability tests?

Measuring Cognitive Abilities

To better understand how psychologists measure intelligence, it may be helpful to you to gain some insight into the various kinds of tests of cognitive ability. Scores on these tests, as you might suspect, tend to overlap somewhat. That is, if an individual does well on one kind, he or she usually gets good scores on the others as well. However, research has also demonstrated that the three kinds of tests you will read about measure distinctive aspects of cognition.

When you were in elementary school, you probably took an **achievement test** every year or two. These tests tap knowledge and skills that a person has acquired through experiences such as formal education up to the point at which the test is taken. *Norm-referenced* achievement tests compare individual students' scores to the average score of all students at their grade level. *Criterion-referenced* achievement tests compare the performance of an individual or group against a predetermined standard. For example, a goal that states "all children in the fourth grade will be able to multiply two-digit numbers with 70% accuracy" is such a standard.

Aptitude tests are norm-referenced tests that are designed to predict a person's probable achievement or performance in a particular setting or in reference to a specific task at some future time. For example, many colleges include scores on aptitude tests such as the SAT and the American College Testing Program (ACT) in the criteria they use to make admissions decisions. These tests are useful because they predict variations in indicators of college success, such as freshman GPAs and degree attainment (Schmitt et al., 2009). Another familiar aptitude test is the Armed Services Vocational Aptitude Battery (ASVAB) that is given to individuals who have applied to serve in the armed forces of the United States. Test scores on the ASVAB help military officials place inductees into the educational programs in which they are most likely to be successful. Similarly, when a company administers tests of mechanical ability to applicants who are seeking positions in which such ability is important, they use aptitude tests specifically designed for that purpose.

An **intelligence test** is a measure of general intellectual ability. An individual's score is determined by how his responses compare to others of his or her age. Thus, intelligence tests are norm-referenced. They attempt to measure all of the aspects of intelligence that are included in the definition of intelligence that you learned a few pages back. Let's look at what distinguishes a good test from a not-so-good test.

All psychological tests, including all the various types of tests that measure cognitive ability, are judged according to the same criteria. First, they must provide consistent results. What if your watch gains 6 minutes one day and loses 3 or 4 minutes the next day? It would not be reliable. You want a watch you can rely on to give the correct time day after day. Like a watch, an intelligence test must have **reliability**; the test must consistently yield nearly the same score when the same person is tested and then retested on the same test or an alternative form of the test. The higher the correlation between the two scores, the more reliable the test.

Tests can be highly reliable but worthless if they are not valid. **Validity** is the ability or power of a test to measure what it is intended to measure. For example, a thermometer is a valid instrument for measuring temperature; a bathroom scale is valid for measuring weight. But, no matter how reliable your bathroom scale is, it will not take your temperature. It is valid only for weighing. Likewise, to be valid, IQ scores must measure individual's performance in domains that should be related to intelligence. For example, most people would agree that intelligence is one of several important factors that are associated with academic success. Therefore, IQ scores must predict academic success in order to be considered valid. Thus, test publishers typically cite correlations between IQ scores and achievement test scores as evidence of a given intelligence test's validity. 👁

Once a test is proven to be valid and reliable, the next requirement is norm-referenced **standardization**. There must be standard procedures for administering and scoring the test. Exactly the same directions must be given, either written or oral, and the same amount of time must be allowed for every test taker. But, even more important, standardization means establishing **norms**, age-based averages, by which all scores are interpreted. A test is standardized by administering it to a large sample of people who are representative of those who will be taking the test in the future. The group's scores are analyzed, and then the average score, standard deviation, percentile rankings, and other measures are computed. (These statistics are explained in detail in Appendix A.) These comparative scores become the norms used as the standard against which all other scores on that test are measured.

---

achievement test A measure of what a person has learned up to a certain point in his or her life.

aptitude test A test that predicts future performance in a particular setting or on a specific task.

intelligence test A test of individual differences in general intellectual ability.

reliability The ability of a test to yield nearly the same score when the same people are tested and then retested on the same test or an alternative form of the test.

validity The ability of a test to measure what it is intended to measure.

👁 **Watch** the Video *Episode 11: Thinking Like a Psychologist: Intelligence Tests and Success* in **MyPsychLab**

standardization Establishing norms for comparing the scores of people who will take a test in the future; administering tests using a prescribed procedure.

norms Age-based averages.

Reliability, validity, and standardization are especially important with regard to intelligence tests because the kinds of decisions that are sometimes based on intelligence test scores can have grave consequences. For instance, a few years ago the U.S. Supreme Court ruled that it is unconstitutional to execute individuals who have *intellectual disabilities,* a condition that will be explained in greater detail shortly. Thus, a psychologist who is charged with the responsibility of administering an intelligence test to a person who will or will not be subject to the death penalty at least partly on the basis of his or her intelligence test score must ensure that the test given is reliable and valid and has been properly standardized. Likewise, children's scores on these tests are often used to place them in special school programs that, in a very real sense, change the course of their lives for years to come. In fact, such a goal was the impetus for the development of the first standardized intelligence test (we'll talk more about this in the next section).

One criticism that continues to plague advocates of IQ testing is the suggestion that minority children and those for whom English is a second language are at a disadvantage when they are assessed on conventional tests because their cultural backgrounds differ from that assumed by the tests' authors. In response, attempts have been made to develop a **culture-fair intelligence test** designed to minimize cultural bias. The questions do not penalize individuals whose cultural experience or language differs from that of the mainstream or dominant culture. See Figure 7.5 for an example of the type of test item found on a culture-fair test. Research shows that such tests are moderately correlated with other measures of intellectual ability, such as the SAT (Frey & Detterman, 2004). Likewise, high-IQ minority children are more likely to be identified as gifted when culture-fair tests are used than when school officials use conventional IQ tests to screen students for inclusion in programs for the gifted (Shaunessy, Karnes, & Cobb, 2004). However, Robert Sternberg (2012) has pointed out that true "culture-fairness" is an impossible goal, because IQ tests must correlate with culturally valued outcomes, such as academic achievement, in order to be valid. As a result, elements of such outcomes must be included in the tests. Thus, according to Sternberg, cultural bias can be reduced but never completely eliminated.

culture-fair intelligence test An intelligence test that uses questions that will not penalize those whose culture differs from the mainstream or dominant culture.

Intelligence Testing: Past and Present

The first successful effort to measure intelligence resulted not from a theoretical approach but as a practical means of solving a problem. In 1903, the French government formed a special commission to look for a way of assessing the intellectual potential of individual schoolchildren. The commission's goal was to find a way to identify children who might need additional instructional support. One of the commission members, Alfred Binet (1857–1911), with the help of his colleague, psychiatrist Theodore Simon, developed a variety of tests that eventually became the first intelligence test, the *Binet–Simon Intelligence Scale,* first published in 1905.

The Binet–Simon Scale used a type of score called *mental age.* A child's mental age was based on the number of items she or he got right as compared with the average number right for children of various ages. In other words, if a child's score equaled the average for 8-year-olds, the child was assigned a mental age of 8, regardless of her or his chronological age (age in years). To determine whether children were bright, average, or had an intellectual disability, Binet compared the children's mental and

7.11 What did Binet, Terman, and Weschler contribute to the study of intelligence?

FIGURE 7.5 **An Example of an Item on a Culture-Fair Test**
This culture-fair test item does not penalize test takers whose language or cultural experiences differ from those of the urban middle or upper classes. Test takers select, from the six samples on the right, the patch that completes the pattern. Patch number 3 is the correct answer.
Source: Adapted from the Raven Standard Progressive Matrices Test.

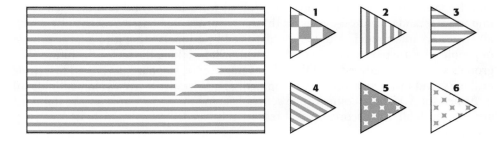

chronological ages. A child who was mentally 2 years ahead of his or her chronological age was considered bright; one who was 2 years behind was classified as having an intellectual disability. But, there was a flaw in Binet's scoring system. A 4-year-old with a mental age of 2 is farther behind her peers than a 12-year-old with a mental age of 10. How could a similar degree of intellectual disability at different ages be expressed?

German psychologist William Stern (1914) provided an answer. In 1912, he devised a simple formula for calculating an index of intelligence—*the intelligence quotient.* But, it was American psychologist Lewis M. Terman, a professor at Stanford University, who perfected this new way of scoring intelligence tests. In 1916, Terman published a thorough revision of the Binet–Simon scale, consisting of items adapted for use with American children. Terman also established new norms, based on the scores of large numbers of children. Within 3 years, 4 million American children had taken Terman's revision, known as the *Stanford–Binet Intelligence Scale.* It was the first test to make use of Stern's concept of the **intelligence quotient (IQ)**. (Terman also introduced the abbreviation *IQ.*) Terman's formula for calculating an IQ score was

$$\frac{\text{Mental age}}{\text{Chronological age}} \times 100 = \text{IQ}$$

For example,

$$\frac{14}{10} \times 100 = 140 \text{ (superior IQ)}$$

The highly regarded Stanford–Binet is an individually administered IQ test for those aged 2 to 23. Stanford–Binet scores correlate well with achievement test scores (Laurent, Swerdik, & Ryburn, 1992). Although intelligence testing became increasingly popular in the United States in the 1920s and 1930s after the Stanford–Binet was published, but it quickly became obvious that it was not useful for testing adults. The original IQ formula could not be applied to adults because at a certain age people achieve maturity in intelligence. According to the original IQ formula, a 40-year-old with the same IQ test score as the average 20-year-old would be diagnosed with an intellectual disability, with an IQ of only 50. Obviously, something was wrong with the formula when applied to populations of all ages.

To address this problem, psychologist David Wechsler developed the first individual intelligence test for individuals over the age of 16 (Wechsler, 1939). Rather than being based on mental and chronological ages, scores on the *Wechsler Adult Intelligence Scale (WAIS)* were based on how much an individual deviated from the average score for adults. Wechsler's new IQ score was so well received that he subsequently published similarly scored tests for children *(Wechsler Intelligence Scale for Children, WISC)* and preschoolers *(Wechsler Preschool and Primary Scale of Intelligence, WPPSI).*

Both Terman's and Wechsler's tests continue to be among the most frequently used of all psychological tests. Psychologists have revised each of them several times. The Stanford–Binet is now known as the SB-V, meaning the fifth revision of the original scale. The current editions of Wechsler's scales are the WAIS-III, WISC-IV, and the WPPSI-III. These scales have changed somewhat since their introduction and now yield several types of scores, a feature of modern intelligence tests that is perhaps best exemplified by the WISC-IV.

When psychologists who work in schools need to find out why a particular child is exhibiting learning problems, they most often turn to the WISC-IV for guidance in determining the child's intellectual strengths and weaknesses. The scale consists of 15 separate subtests. Five of these tests, those that make up the *verbal comprehension index,* measure verbal skills such as vocabulary. The remaining 10 tests demand nonverbal types of thinking, such as arranging pictures to tell a story and repeating digits back to an examiner. The nonverbal tests are divided among the *perceptual reasoning index, processing speed index,* and *working memory index.* Each of these indexes measures a different kind of nonverbal intelligence and generates its own IQ score. The WISC-IV

intelligence quotient (IQ) An index of intelligence, originally derived by dividing mental age by chronological age and then multiplying by 100, but now derived by comparing an individual's score with the scores of others of the same age.

▲ Working with psychiatrist Theodore Simon to develop a test for evaluating children's intelligence, Alfred Binet (shown here) began testing Parisian students in 1904.

also provides a comprehensive *full-scale IQ* score that takes all four types of tests into account. Many psychologists find comparisons of the different kinds of IQ scores generated by the WISC-IV to be helpful in gaining insight into a child's learning difficulties.

Individual intelligence tests such as the Stanford–Binet and the Wechsler scales must be given to one person at a time by a psychologist or educational diagnostician. For testing large numbers of people in a short period of time (often necessary due to budget limitations), group intelligence tests are the answer. Group intelligence tests, such as the *California Test of Mental Maturity,* the *Cognitive Abilities Test,* and the *Otis–Lennon Mental Ability Test,* are widely used. ◉►

The Range of Intelligence

You may have heard the term *bell curve* and wondered just exactly what it is. When large populations are measured on intelligence or physical characteristics such as height and weight, the frequencies of the various scores or measurements usually conform to a *bell-shaped* distribution known as the *normal curve*—hence the term *bell curve*. The majority of the scores cluster around the mean (average). The more scores deviate from the mean (that is, the farther away from it they fall), either above or below, the fewer there are. And the normal curve is perfectly symmetrical; that is, there are just as many cases above as below the mean. The average IQ test score for all people in the same age group is arbitrarily assigned an IQ score of 100. On the Wechsler intelligence tests, approximately 50% of the scores are in the average range, between 90 and 110. About 68% of the scores fall between 85 and 115, and about 95% fall between 70 and 130. Some 2% of the scores are above 130, which is considered superior, and about 2% fall below 70, in the range of intellectual disability (see Figure 7.6). ◉►

But, what does it mean to have a "superior" IQ? In 1921, to try to answer this question, Lewis Terman (1925) launched a longitudinal study, now a classic, in which 1,528 gifted students were selected and measured at different ages throughout their lives. Tested on the Stanford–Binet, the participants—857 males and 671 females—had unusually high IQs, ranging from 135 to 200, with an average of 151. Terman's early findings put an end to the myth that mentally superior people are more likely to be physically inferior. In fact, Terman's gifted participants excelled in almost all the abilities he studied—intellectual, physical, emotional, moral, and social. Terman also exploded many other myths about the mentally gifted (Terman & Oden, 1947). For example, you may have heard the saying that there is a thin line between genius and madness. Actually, Terman's gifted group enjoyed better

◉ **Watch** the Video *Episode 11: Special Topics: Intelligence Testing, Then and Now* in **MyPsychLab**

7.12 How do people at both ends of the IQ score continuum differ from those in the middle?

◉► **Simulate** *The Normal Curve* on **MyPsychLab**

FIGURE 7.6 The Normal Curve
When a large number of test scores are compiled, they are typically distributed in a normal (bell-shaped) curve. On the Wechsler scales, the average, or mean, IQ score is set at 100. As the figure shows, about 68% of the scores fall between 15 IQ points (1 standard deviation) above and below 100 (from 85 to 115), and about 95.5% of the scores fall between 30 points (2 standard deviations) above and below 100 (from 70 to 130).

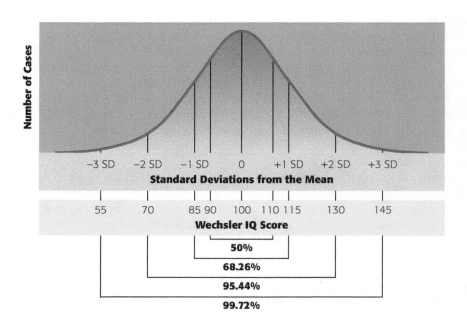

mental health than the general population. Terman's participants also earned more academic degrees, achieved higher occupational status and higher salaries, were better adjusted both personally and socially, and were healthier than their less mentally gifted peers. However, most women at that time did not pursue careers outside of the home, so the findings related to occupational success applied primarily to the men. The Terman study continues today, with the surviving participants in their 80s or 90s. In a report on Terman's study, Shneidman (1989) states its basic findings—that "an unusual mind, a vigorous body, and a relatively well-adjusted personality are not at all incompatible" (p. 687).

At the opposite end of the continuum from Terman's sample are the 2% of the U.S. population whose IQ scores are in the range of **intellectual disability**, formerly known as *mental retardation*. These individuals have IQ scores below 70 and have problems carrying out the everyday activities that are easily managed by others of the same age (Sattler, 2008). There are many causes of intellectual disability, including brain injuries, chromosomal abnormalities such as Down syndrome, chemical deficiencies, and hazards present during fetal development. Also, studies continue to document the enduring mental deficits produced by early exposure to lead (CDC, 2008). The degrees of intellectual disability range from mild to profound (American Psychiatric Association, 2000a). Individuals with IQs ranging from 55 to 70 have mild intellectual disability. Those whose scores fall between 40 and 54 have a moderate degree of intellectual disability, and those whose IQs are between 25 and 39 have severe intellectual disability. An IQ score lower than 25 is required for an individual to be diagnosed with profound intellectual disability. Individuals with mild intellectual disability are able to acquire academic skills such as reading up to about a sixth-grade level and may be able to become economically self-supporting. The academic skills of those with moderate intellectual disability are usually limited to the first- or second-grade level; these individuals can learn self-care skills and often function well in sheltered work environments. People with severe levels of intellectual disability typically are unable to acquire academic skills but can communicate verbally and learn self-care skills such as brushing their teeth. At the profound level of intellectual disability, individuals usually learn only rudimentary motor skills and limited self-help skills such as feeding themselves.

Before the late 1960s, children with intellectual disability in the United States were educated almost exclusively in special schools. Since then, there has been a movement toward **inclusion**—or educating such students in classes with other students. Inclusion, also called *mainstreaming,* may involve placing these students in classes with students without disabilities for part or all of the day. Resources spent on educational programs for students with intellectual disability are proving to be sound investments. Such programs rely heavily on behavior modification techniques and are making it possible for some individuals with intellectual disability to become employed. Everyone benefits—the individual, his or her family, and society as a whole. 👁

intellectual disability A condition in which an individual has scores below 70 on a standardized intelligence test and displays adaptive functioning significantly below that of others of the same age.

inclusion Educating students with intellectual disabilities by placing them in classes with students who do not have disabilities for part or all of the day; also called *mainstreaming.*

👁 **Watch** the Video *Mainstreaming Children with Special Needs* in **MyPsychLab**

REMEMBER IT

Check your answers and take additional quizzes in MyPsychLab.com.   ✓ **Study** and **Review** on **MyPsychLab**

1. _____ proposed that intelligence is strongly influenced by a single factor known as *g*.

2. A test that gives consistent results has _____, whereas one that measures what it claims to measure has _____ .

3. _____ developed the first widely used standardized test of intellectual ability.

4. On Wechsler intelligence tests, IQ scores are based on _____ .

5. The research of _____ challenged the view that individuals with high IQs are physically inferior to others.

6. People are considered to have an intellectual disability if they are clearly deficient in adaptive functioning and their IQ is below _____ .

Explaining Differences in Intelligence

We use several words to refer to people we believe to be intellectually superior—bright, clever, intelligent, smart, and so on. Likewise, we have just as many to describe our peers who seem to possess less intelligence than others. In fact, the presence of these terms in our vocabularies demonstrates that a wide range of differences in intellectual functioning are readily apparent in our everyday interactions with other people. What accounts for these differences?

7.13 What is the evidence for each side of the nature–nurture debate?

Nature, Nurture, and IQ

In many cases, biological factors, such as the presence of an extra chromosome, are to blame for intellectual disability. But, what about normal variations in intelligence? To what degree do they result from biological, or genetic, influences? This question arises out of perhaps the most vocal area of disagreement concerning intelligence, the **nature–nurture debate**, the debate over whether intelligence is primarily the result of heredity or environment. Englishman Sir Francis Galton (1874) initiated this debate, which has raged for more than 100 years, and coined the term. After studying a number of prominent families in England, Galton concluded that intelligence was inherited. Hereditarians agree with Galton, claiming that intelligence is largely inherited—the result of nature. Environmentalists, in contrast, insist that it is influenced primarily by one's environment—the result of nurture. Most psychologists now agree that both nature and nurture contribute to intelligence, but they continue to debate the proportions contributed by each.

nature–nurture debate The debate over whether intelligence and other traits are primarily the result of heredity or environment.

Heritability. As you learned in Chapter 2, *behavioral genetics* is the study of the relative influence of genetics and environment on human behavior and mental processes. Behavioral geneticists sometimes express the results of their studies in terms of **heritability**, an index of the degree to which a characteristic is estimated to be influenced by heredity. Figure 7.7 shows estimates of the proportional contributions of genetic and environmental factors to intelligence. Some research using the adoption study method, comparing children to both their adoptive and biological parents, also supports the assertion that genes strongly influence IQ scores.

heritability An index of the degree to which a characteristic is estimated to be influenced by heredity.

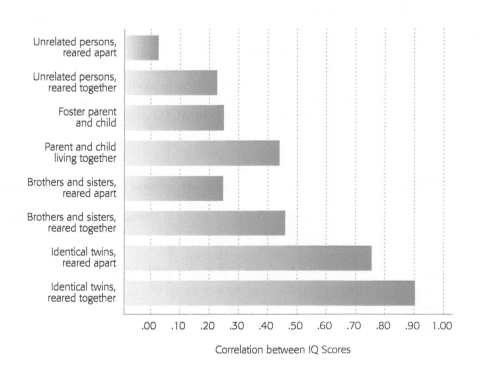

FIGURE 7.7 Correlations between the IQ Scores of Persons with Various Relationships
The more closely related two individuals are, the more similar their IQ scores tend to be. Thus, there is a strong genetic contribution to intelligence.
Source: Based on data from Bouchard & McGue (1981); Erlenmeyer-Kimling & Jarvik (1963).

Minnesota is the site of the most extensive U.S. study of identical and fraternal twins. Since the early 1980s, the Minnesota Center for Twin and Adoption Research has been recruiting fraternal and identical twins to participate in research projects examining genetic and environmental influences on a variety of psychological variables, including intelligence. In 1997, the center's first director, Thomas Bouchard, summarized all of the studies of intelligence that had been done at the center up to that point. Bouchard reported that, taken together, the studies yielded heritability estimates of .60 to .70. (A heritability of 1.00 would mean that all of the variation in intelligence is due to genes.) The center's more recent studies have produced similar estimates (e.g., Johnson et al., 2007).

Other twin studies suggest that the Minnesota researchers may have overestimated the heritability of intelligence. For example, British researchers associated with another large-scale study of twins, the Twins Early Development Study, found estimates of heritability ranging from .34 to .42 in a group of twins they tested at 7, 9, and 10 years of age (Kovas, Haworth, Dale, & Plomin, 2007). Similar heritability estimates were found by researchers in another longitudinal twin study, the Western Reserve Reading Project in Ohio, in which twins were tested at 6, 7, and 8 years of age (Hart, Petrill, Thompson, & Plomin, 2009).

Adoption and Early Intervention. Several studies indicate that IQ test scores are not fixed but can be modified with an enriched environment. Several decades ago, Sandra Scarr and Richard Weinberg (1976) studied 140 African American and interracial children who had been adopted by highly educated, upper-middle-class white American families; 99 of the children had been adopted in the first year of life. The adoptees were fully exposed to middle-class cultural experiences and vocabulary, the "culture of the tests and the school" (p. 737). How did the children perform on IQ and achievement tests? The average IQ score of the 130 adoptees was 106.3. Their achievement test scores were slightly above the national average, not below. On the average, the earlier the children were adopted, the higher their IQs. The mean IQ score of the 99 early adoptees was 110.4, about 10 IQ points above the average for white Americans. Similarly, studies in France show that IQ scores and achievement are substantially higher when children from lower-class environments are adopted by middle- and upper-middle-class families (Duyme, 1988; Schiff & Lewontin, 1986).

In addition to these encouraging adoption studies, research examining the effects of early childhood interventions on the IQ scores of children from poor families clearly indicates that early educational experiences can affect intellectual development even into the adult years (Campbell et al., 2012; Ramey, Ramey, & Lanzi, 2007; Reynolds & Temple, 2008). Some of the best known of these interventions have been carried out by developmental psychologist Craig Ramey. Unlike many studies of early interventions, Ramey's research involves true experiments—so it is clear that the outcomes are caused by the interventions.

In one of Ramey's programs (Campbell & Ramey, 1994), 6- to 12-month-old infants of low-IQ, low-income mothers were randomly assigned to either an intensive 40-hour-per-week day-care program that continued throughout the preschool years or a control group that received only medical care and nutritional supplements. When the children reached school age, half in each group (again based on random assignment) were enrolled in a special after-school program that helped their families learn how to support school learning with educational activities at home. Ramey followed the progress of children in all four groups through age 12, giving them IQ tests at various ages. Figure 7.8 on p. 238 shows that those who participated in the infant and preschool program as well as those who participated in the combined preschool/school-age program scored higher on IQ tests than peers who received either no intervention or only the school-age intervention. Perhaps more important, during the elementary school years, about 40% of the control group participants had IQ scores classified as borderline or as having an intellectual disability (scores

7.14 How do theorists explain ethnic group differences in IQ scores?

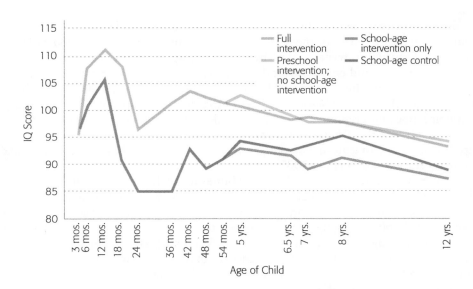

FIGURE 7.8 Ramey's Infant Intervention
In the Ramey study, children were randomly assigned in infancy to an experimental group with special day care (the "full intervention" group) or to a control group. From kindergarten through third grade, half of each group received supplementary family support, and the other half did not. The difference in IQ between the intervention and control groups remained statistically significant even at age 12.

Source: Campbell, F., & Ramey, C. (1994). Effects of achievement: A follow-up study of children from low-income families. *Child Development, 65,* 684–698. Figure 1, p. 690.

below 85), compared with only 12.8% of those who were in the infant program. More recent research shows that the cognitive advantage enjoyed by the infant intervention groups has persisted into adulthood (Campbell et al., 2012). Ramey's work clearly shows that the environment has great potential to influence IQ scores. Does education have similar effects on adults' IQ scores? The *Apply It* discussion addresses this question.

Historical evidence also suggests that environmental factors have a strong influence on IQ scores. Americans and similarly advantaged populations all over the world have gained about 3 IQ points per decade since 1940. James Flynn (1987, 1999; Dickens & Flynn, 2001; Must, te Njienhuis, Must, & van Vianen, 2009; Nisbett et al., 2012) analyzed 73 studies involving some 7,500 participants ranging in age from 12 to 48 and found that "every Binet and Wechsler [standardization group] from 1932 to 1978 has performed better than its predecessor" (Flynn, 1987, p. 225). Studies in developing countries, such as Kenya and the Sudan, have shown that IQ gains can happen over much shorter periods of time when the standard of living improves drastically (Daley et al., 2003; Khaleefa, Abdelwahid, Abdulradi, & Lynn, 2008). This consistent improvement in IQ scores over time is known as the *Flynn effect.*

It should not be surprising that enriched environments alter traits that are highly heritable. Consider the fact that American and British adolescents are 6 inches taller on average than their counterparts a century and a half ago (Tanner, 1990). Height has the same heritability (.90) today as it did in the mid-19th century. So, this tremendous average gain in height of 6 inches is entirely attributable to environmental influences: better health, better nutrition, and so on. The highest heritability estimates for intelligence are far lower than those for height. It seems clear, then, that environmental influences have the power to affect intelligence and achievement. For example, poverty affects nutrition, and research clearly shows that malnutrition, especially early in life, can harm intellectual development (Grigorenko, 2003).

Race and IQ

The nature–nurture debate has also been important in the discussion of race differences in intelligence test scores. Historically, most studies have shown that blacks score, on average, about 15 points lower than whites on standardized IQ tests in the United States (e.g., Loehlin, Lindzey, & Spuhler, 1975; Rushton & Jensen, 2005). Other studies have shown similar differences for blacks and whites in other nations (e.g., Rushton & Jensen, 2003). But why?

How to Build a Powerful Vocabulary

Researchers have often found that vocabulary tests are strongly correlated with IQ scores (Lichtenberger & Kaufman, 2012). These correlations provide one of the best arguments in favor of the view that learning is at least as important to the development of intelligence as any ability with which we are born. Clearly, too, of all the cognitive skills we possess, none is more important for clarity of thinking and academic success than vocabulary. Thus, you may be able to make yourself smarter, in a practical sense, by improving your vocabulary. How can you accomplish this goal? The best way is to realize that almost all words belong to larger networks of meaning and to understand that your mind is already geared toward organizing information in terms of meaning. Thus, with a little effort, you can greatly increase your vocabulary by supporting the kind of learning your brain is already inclined to do. Here are a few techniques for following this advice.

Learn to Think Analytically about Words You Already Know and Relate New Words to Them

What do the words *antiseptic* and *septic tank* have in common? You use an *antiseptic* to prevent bacterial infection of a wound; a *septic tank* is used for removing harmful bacteria from water containing human waste. A logical conclusion would be that *septic* has something to do with bacteria. Knowing this, what do you think a doctor means when she says that a patient is suffering from *sepsis*? By linking *sepsis* to *septic tank* and *antiseptic*, you can guess that she is referring to some kind of bacterial infection.

Be Aware of Word Connections That May Be Hidden by Spelling Differences

You may know that both *Caesar* and *Czar* refer to some kind of ruler or leader. But, you may not know that they are exactly the same word spoken and spelled somewhat differently in Ancient Rome (*Caesar*) and in Russia (*Czar*). Now, if you learn in a history class about *Kaiser Wilhelm* who led Germany during World War I, thinking analytically about his title may help you realize that it is exactly the same word as *Caesar* and *Czar* but with a German spelling. Here's another example: Can you guess something about the location and climate of the nation of *Ecuador* by relating its name to a word that differs only slightly in spelling?

Use Your Knowledge of Word Parts to Actively Seek Out New Words

Don't learn new words one at a time. Instead, be on the lookout for "word families"—root words and prefixes and suffixes. Here is one important root word, *spect*. You've seen it in many words. *Spect* means "look," "look at," "watch," "see." And *spect* appears in dozens of different words, such as *inspect*. What do you do when you *inspect* something? You *look* closely at it. Once you are equipped with this knowledge, other *spect* words may start to come to mind along with an entirely new way of thinking about their meanings: *spectacular, spectator, spectacle, spectacles, perspective, prospect, respect, disrespect, retrospect, suspect,* and so on. The word *circumspect* may be new to you. Look it up in a dictionary and think about how the literal meaning of the word ("look around") relates to the way this word is frequently used. And, when you read Chapter 1, might it have been easier to understand and remember the meaning of Wundt's research method, *introspection,* if you had thought about the *spect* part of the word? Probably so.

A strong vocabulary based on root words, prefixes, and suffixes will yield the word power that will profit you in many ways.

Watch the Video *Episode 11: What's in It for Me? How Resilient Are You?* in **MyPsychLab**

In 1969, psychologist Arthur Jensen published an article in which he attributed the IQ gap to genetic differences between the races. Further, he claimed that the genetic influence on intelligence is so strong that the environment cannot make a significant difference. Jensen even went so far as to claim that blacks and whites possess qualitatively different kinds of intelligence.

Beliefs such as those expressed by Jensen run counter to the results of the studies carried out by Craig Ramey and others that you read about earlier in this chapter. Such studies suggest that racial differences are more likely to result from poverty and lack of access to educational opportunities than from genetics. Moreover, a new testing technique called *dynamic assessment* supports the environmental explanation (Murphy, 2011). In dynamic assessment, examinees are taught the goal and format of each IQ subtest before they are actually tested. The rationale behind the technique is the assumption that children from middle-class backgrounds have more experience with testing procedures and better understand that the goal of testing is to demonstrate competency (Haywood & Lidz, 2007). However, some experts argue that dynamic assessment has more potential as a tool for identifying effective teaching strategies for individual students than as a replacement for intelligence tests (Elliott, 2003; Jeltova et al., 2007). Thus, more research is needed before psychologists will be able to make definitive statements about the validity of dynamic assessment for intelligence testing.

In recent years, psychologists have begun to investigate another variable called *stereotype threat* that may help explain racial differences in IQ scores. The stereotype threat theory was first proposed by psychologist Claude Steele

(Steele & Aronson, 1995). According to Steele, when minority individuals hear discussions of group differences in IQ scores, they may assume that their own intellectual ability is inferior to that of individuals in the majority group. Therefore, when faced with an IQ test, they "disengage," to avoid the threat of being stereotyped as having limited intellectual ability. This disengagement becomes a self-fulfilling prophecy: It causes individuals to obtain low scores, thereby appearing to validate the stereotype. Research has shown that programs designed to help people talk about and overcome the degree to which they sense stereotype threat when they take cognitive ability tests helps them achieve higher scores (Abrams et al., 2008; Alter et al., 2010). Other psychologists have pointed out that, although studies have shown that stereotype threat does exist, it explains only a fraction of test score and achievement differences across racial groups (Sackett & Ryan, 2012). ◉

◉ Watch the Video *Episode 11: In the Real World: Intelligence Tests and Stereotypes* in **MyPsychLab**

Before leaving the topic of race and IQ, stop and consider why the debates spawned by findings showing that one group has a higher average IQ than another group have stirred so much emotional intensity. One reason might be that in Western societies such as the United States intellectual ability is highly valued. Studies show that Asians place little value on intellectual ability even though they tend to get higher scores on cognitive ability tests than whites or other groups (Li, 2003; Lynn, 2006). Instead, Asians emphasize hard work and perseverance as the routes to academic and other kinds of life success (Stevenson, 1992). By contrast, by the time Americans reach the age of 11 or 12, a large majority believe that achievement results more from ability than from effort (Altermatt & Pomerantz, 2003; Heyman, Gee, & Giles, 2003). Psychologists suggest that this belief leads American students to fail to appreciate the importance of effort to academic achievement, even for people who are high in ability. It may also help explain research such as that of two researchers who compared the achievement test scores of Australian school children of Asian descent to those of English/Irish ancestry (Dandy & Nettelbeck, 2002). Their findings showed that Asian Australian students scored higher than their English/Irish peers on achievement tests even when they were matched on IQ (Dandy & Nettelbeck, 2002). These results suggest that, on a practical level, teachers and parents should probably be more concerned about helping each student work to achieve his or her full intellectual potential than about the student's IQ score.

7.15 How do the cognitive abilities of males and females differ?

Gender Differences in Cognitive Abilities

Psychologist Janet Shibley Hyde has studied gender differences for more than three decades. She points out that although there are a few physical characteristics on which males and females differ to a large degree (e.g., arm strength), the few gender gaps that exist for cognitive variables are quite small (Hyde, 2005). Thus, it is important not to exaggerate these differences to such a degree that they cause us to develop gender stereotypes. As you read through the discussion of gender differences, keep your antistereotyping guard up.

▲ Women perform better than men on tasks that require fine motor coordination, such as engineering a circuit board. Men perform better than women on tasks that require target-directed motor skills, such as shooting darts.

There are some types of problems on which each gender tends to excel. But, you need to keep two important points in mind: First, in general, the differences within each gender are greater than the differences between the genders. Second, even though gender differences in cognitive abilities have been generally small on average, there tends to be more variation in such abilities among males than among females (that is, the range of test scores is typically greater for males). Table 7.1 shows some of the variables for which researchers have found zero or near-zero differences across genders.

Girls as young as 18 months of age have been found to have, on average, larger vocabularies than boys of the same age, a difference that persists throughout childhood (Wallentin, 2009). In one frequently cited large-scale study, Hedges and Nowell (1995) analyzed the results of the National Assessment of Educational Progress (NAEP), which has tested a nationally representative sample of 70,000 to 100,000 9-, 13-, and 17-year-olds annually in reading comprehension, writing, math, and science. The researchers compared the achievements of the 17-year-olds from 1971 through 1992 and reported that females outperformed males in reading and writing, while males did better in science and math.

Interestingly, however, girls get higher grades than boys do in all subjects (Duckworth & Seligman, 2006; Kenney-Benson et al., 2006). Researchers often attribute this finding to girls' approach to schoolwork. They have discovered that girls are more likely to take an effortful approach to their work and, as a result, they develop more effective learning strategies than boys do (Kenney-Benson et al., 2006). Studies have also shown that girls, on average, also tend to be more self-disciplined than boys (Duckworth & Seligman, 2006; Else-Quest et al., 2006).

As noted above, analyses of NAEP data show that boys display higher levels of achievement in mathematics than girls. More recent studies show the same pattern (Liu & Wilson, 2009). Some data suggest that hormonal factors explain this difference (Josephs et al., 2003). Other findings indicate that differences in brain structure and function are responsible. For example, some researchers attribute the finding that gender differences

TABLE 7.1 Meta-Analyses of Gender Differences

VARIABLES WITH ZERO OR NEAR-ZERO GENDER DIFFERENCES	
Math concepts	Self-disclosure
Math problem solving	Impulsiveness
Reading comprehension	Outgoingness
Vocabulary	Life satisfaction
Verbal reasoning	Happiness
Abstract reasoning	Self-esteem
VARIABLES WITH MODERATE TO LARGE DIFFERENCES FAVORING MALES	
Mechanical reasoning	Computer self-efficacy
Mental rotation	Assertiveness
Science achievement	Helping when watched
Intrusive interruptions	Physical aggression
Tolerance of academic cheating	Verbal aggression
VARIABLES WITH MODERATE TO LARGE DIFFERENCES FAVORING FEMALES	
Spelling	Smiling
Perceptual speed	Indirect aggression
Language ability	Trust
Speech production	Agreeableness

Source: Hyde (2005).

favoring males first appear or greatly increase during adolescence to the fact that males' brains develop more slowly than those of females do (Ellison & Nelson, 2009). However, most researchers agree that social influences are probably more important.

One possible social factor influencing the difference in math achievement is that parents often expect boys to do better than girls in math (Tiedemann, 2000). Could parental expectations become a self-fulfilling prophecy, leading girls to lack confidence in their math ability and to decide not to pursue advanced math courses? Yes, says sex difference researcher Jacqueline Eccles. Eccles's longitudinal research has shown that parents' beliefs about their children's talents at age 6 predict those children's beliefs about their own abilities at age 17 (Fredricks & Eccles, 2002). However, Eccles's research has also revealed that the gender gap in beliefs about math ability is somewhat smaller among today's high school students than it was in the past, suggesting that educators' efforts to increase girls' interest and success in mathematics have been effective.

Another way in which parents influence boys' and girls' ideas about math competence is their tendency to see academically successful girls as "hard workers" and academically successful boys as "talented" (Ratty et al., 2002). Thus, parents' beliefs may help explain why teenage girls who obtain top scores on standardized mathematics tests typically explain their scores as resulting from effort, while their male peers believe that their scores are due to superior natural mathematical talent (Rebs & Park, 2001). Thus, even girls with extraordinary levels of mathematical achievement may see themselves as lacking in ability. Perhaps, it isn't surprising that mathematically gifted girls are far less likely than similarly gifted boys to choose math-oriented careers (Park, Lubinski, & Benbow, 2012; Perez-Felkner, McDonald, & Schneider, 2012).

Researchers have found that, in general, males tend to perform somewhat better than females on some, but not all, tasks that measure spatial abilities (Casey, 2013). What explains this difference? Some research has shown that spatial abilities appear to be enhanced by prenatal exposure to high levels of androgens (Berenbaum, Korman, & Leveroni, 1995). Further, high blood levels of testosterone in men are associated with good performance on spatial tasks such as route learning (Choi & Silverman, 2002). However, these findings do not minimize the role of social experiences and expectations in shaping children's abilities and interests. Women also outperform men on some kinds of spatial tasks.

REMEMBER IT   *Check your answers and take additional quizzes in MyPsychLab.com.* ✓●─[Study and Review on MyPsychLab

1. Twin studies suggest that variation in IQ scores is strongly influenced by _____.
2. Adoption studies suggest that IQ scores are influenced by _____.
3. The _____ refers to the historical change in average IQ scores that has accompanied improved standards of living.
4. Cross-cultural studies show that Asians are more likely than Americans to attribute success to innate ability. (true/false)
5. Varying levels of prenatal exposure of the brain to _____ have been proposed as an explanation for gender differences spatial abilities.

Beyond Intelligence

Perhaps the most important contribution of Gardner, Sternberg, and others who have suggested multicomponent models of intelligence is their emphasis on the notion that there are many aspects of cognitive functioning that are not captured by standardized tests of intelligence. Such tests cannot measure how well we relate to others, for example. Nor can they assess our ability to use our imaginations to escape the limitations of present reality.

Emotional Intelligence ▶

7.16 What are the components of emotional intelligence?

Whether one is male or female, the understanding we possess about our own and others' emotions influences how we think about ourselves and manage our interactions with others. **Emotional intelligence** is the ability to apply knowledge about emotions to everyday life (Salovey & Pizarro, 2003). Two leading researchers in the field, Peter Salovey and David Pizarro, argue that emotional intelligence is just as important to many important outcome variables, including how we fare in our chosen careers, as the kind of intelligence that is measured by IQ tests. Research supports this view, showing that emotional intelligence is unrelated to IQ scores (Mayer, Caruso, Panter, & Salovey, 2012). At the same time, emotional intelligence is correlated with both academic and social success (DiFabio & Palazzeschi, 2009).

emotional intelligence The ability to apply knowledge about emotions to everyday life.

Emotional intelligence includes two sets of components. The first, known as the *personal* aspects of emotional intelligence, includes awareness and management of our own emotions. People who are able to monitor their feelings as they arise are less likely to be ruled by them. However, managing emotions does not mean suppressing them; nor does it mean giving free rein to every feeling. Instead, effective management of emotions involves expressing them appropriately. Emotion management also involves engaging in activities that cheer us up, soothe our hurts, or reassure us when we feel anxious.

The *interpersonal* aspects of emotional intelligence make up the second set of components. *Empathy,* or sensitivity to others' feelings, is one such component. One key indicator of empathy is the ability to read others' nonverbal behavior—the gestures, vocal inflections, tones of voice, and facial expressions of others. Another of the interpersonal components is the capacity to manage relationships. However, it is related to both the personal aspects of emotional intelligence and to empathy. In other words, to effectively manage the emotional give-and-take involved in social relationships, we have to be able to manage our own feelings and be sensitive to those of others.

In a recent study, men were found to process emotions, especially positive ones, predominantly in the left hemisphere of the brain, whereas women were found to use both cerebral hemispheres more equally for processing emotions (Coney & Fitzgerald, 2000). This finding could account for some of the emotional difference between the genders. You can find your own *emotional quotient*, or *EQ*, by completing the *Try It.* on p. 244

Creativity ▶

7.17 How does creativity differ from other forms of cognition?

Have you ever known a person who was intellectually bright but lacked creativity? **Creativity** can be thought of as the ability to produce original, appropriate, and valuable ideas and/or solutions to problems. Research indicates that there is only a weak to moderate correlation between creativity and IQ (Lubart, 2003). Remember the mentally gifted individuals studied by Lewis Terman? Not one of them has produced a highly creative work (Terman & Oden, 1959). No Nobel laureates, no Pulitzer prizes. Geniuses, yes; creative geniuses, no. Thus, high intelligence does not necessarily mean high creativity.

creativity The ability to produce original, appropriate, and valuable ideas and/or solutions to problems.

Cartoonists often illustrate creative thinking as a flash of insight, a light bulb that suddenly turns on in the mind. But, research studies indicate that useful and genuine creativity rarely appears in the form of sudden flashes (Haberlandt, 1997). For the most part, creative ideas that come to conscious awareness have been incubating for some time. There are basically four stages in the creative problem-solving process (Goleman, Kaufman, & Ray, 1992):

1. **Preparation**—searching for information that may help solve the problem
2. **Incubation**—letting the problem "sit" while the relevant information is digested, often below the level of awareness
3. **Illumination**—being suddenly struck by the right solution
4. **Translation**—transforming the insight into useful action

What is unique about creative thought? According to psychologist J. P. Guilford (1967), who studied creativity for several decades, creative thinkers are highly

Emotional intelligence may be just as important to success in your chosen career as your actual job skills. Take this short test to assess your EQ by checking one response for each item.

1. I'm always aware of even subtle feelings as I have them.
_____ Always _____ Usually _____ Sometimes
_____ Rarely _____ Never

2. I can delay gratification in pursuit of my goals instead of getting carried away by impulse.
_____ Always _____ Usually _____ Sometimes
_____ Rarely _____ Never

3. Instead of giving up in the face of setbacks or disappointments, I stay hopeful and optimistic.
_____ Always _____ Usually _____ Sometimes
_____ Rarely _____ Never

4. My keen sense of others' feelings makes me compassionate about their plight.
_____ Always _____ Usually _____ Sometimes
_____ Rarely _____ Never

5. I can sense the pulse of a group or relationship and state unspoken feelings.
_____ Always _____ Usually _____ Sometimes
_____ Rarely _____ Never

6. I can soothe or contain distressing feelings, so that they don't keep me from doing things I need to do.
_____ Always _____ Usually _____ Sometimes
_____ Rarely _____ Never

Score your responses as follows: Always = 4 points; Usually = 3 points; Sometimes = 2 points; Rarely = 1 point; Never = 0 points. The closer your total number of points is to 24, the higher your EQ probably is.

divergent thinking The ability to produce multiple ideas, answers, or solutions to a problem for which there is no agreed-on solution.

proficient at divergent thinking. **Divergent thinking** is the ability to produce multiple ideas, answers, or solutions to a problem for which there is no agreed-on solution (Guilford, 1967). More broadly, divergent thinking is novel, or original, and involves the synthesis of an unusual association of ideas; it is flexible, switching quickly and smoothly from one stream of thought or set of ideas to another; and it requires fluency, or the ability to formulate an abundance of ideas (Benedek, Könen, & Neubauer, 2012; Csikszentmihalyi, 1996). For example, divergent thinking would help policymakers come up with new answers to questions such as "What is the most efficient way of distributing surplus agricultural products grown in developed nations to hungry people in the developing world?" In contrast to divergent thinking, Guilford defined *convergent thinking* as the type of mental activity measured by IQ and achievement tests; it consists of solving precisely defined, logical problems for which there is a known correct answer. For instance, convergent thinking would be required to answer a question such as "How much surplus food is grown in each of the world's developed nations?"

However, divergent and convergent thinking are not always separate phenomena. Both are required for most cognitive tasks. For example, to be creative, a person must develop divergent thinking, but convergent thinking is required to discriminate between good and bad ideas (Csikszentmihalyi, 1996). Similarly, solving precisely defined problems can involve divergent thinking, as one tries to think of possible solutions.

Researchers are identifying the different brain areas involved in convergent and divergent thinking. In general, convergent thinking is characterized by greater activity in the left frontal cortex, while divergent thinking is marked by higher levels of activity in the right frontal cortex (Razoumnikova, 2000). Other studies show that processes involved in convergent thinking, such as searching for patterns in events, are carried out in the left hemisphere (Wolford, Miller, & Gazzaniga, 2000). Studies by Carlsson and others (2000) that measured regional cerebral blood flow (rCBF) revealed striking differences in frontal lobe activity between participants who were engaged in highly creative thinking and those who were not. Figure 7.9(a) shows the frontal lobe activity during highly creative thinking. There is activity in both hemispheres but a significantly greater amount in the right frontal cortex. In contrast, Figure 7.9(b) shows that during periods when no creative thinking is occurring, the left frontal lobe is highly active, and there is very little activity in the right hemisphere.

How might individual differences in creativity be measured? Tests designed to measure creativity emphasize original approaches to arriving at solutions for

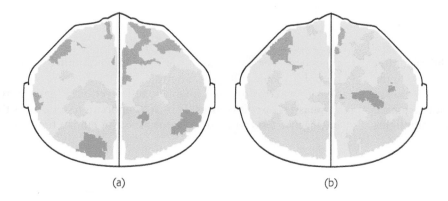

FIGURE 7.9 Maps of Regional Cerebral Blood Flow (rCBF)
(a) Highly creative thinking is associated with activity in both hemispheres, but with significantly higher levels in the right hemisphere (red indicates activity).
(b) During thinking that is not creative, activity is largely restricted to the left hemisphere.
Source: Adapted from Carlsson et al. (2000).

(a)   (b)

open-ended problems or to producing artistic works (Piffer, 2012). One creativity test, the Unusual Uses Test, asks respondents to name as many uses as possible for an ordinary object (such as a brick). Another measure of creativity is the Consequences Test, which asks test takers to list as many consequences as they can that would be likely to follow some basic change in the world (such as the force of gravity being reduced by 50%). Researchers Mednick and Mednick (1967), who reasoned that the essence of creativity consists of the creative thinker's ability to fit together ideas that to the noncreative thinker might appear remote or unrelated, created the Remote Associates Test (RAT). Items on the RAT ask test-takers to propose a single-word link for three seemingly unrelated objects or ideas. For example, what word would you propose as a link for the words *gold*, *tender*, and *attorney*? The best answer might be *bar*. What about *office*, *fence*, and *modern*. A plausible answer is *post*.

Psychologists studying exceptionally creative individuals (e.g., Bloom, 1985) have learned that they share a number of characteristics that distinguish them from less creative individuals. For one, they have a great deal of expertise in a specific area that has been built up over years of disciplined study and practice. Creative individuals are also open to new experiences and ideas, even those that may seem quite odd to others; moreover, they seem to be inherently curious and inquisitive (Sternberg, 1985a). Creative people also tend to be independent thinkers who are less influenced by the opinions of others than their less creative counterparts are. Perhaps because of their independence, creative individuals are more likely to be motivated by the anticipation, excitement, and enjoyment of their work than by a desire to please others. Finally, creative endeavor requires hard work and persistence in the face of failure. For instance, Albert Einstein published 248 papers on his theory of relativity before it was finished, and Mozart, when he died at age 35, had created 609 musical compositions (Haberlandt, 1997).

REMEMBER IT   *Check your answers and take additional quizzes in MyPsychLab.com.* ✓—Study and Review on MyPsychLab

1. Identify the category in which each component of emotional intelligence belongs.
   a. personal
   b. interpersonal
   _____**(1)** empathy
   _____**(2)** awareness of one's own emotions
   _____**(3)** self-motivation
   _____**(4)** ability to handle relationships

2. Divergent thinking is associated with activity in the _____ of the brain.

⊙° Looking Back

We began this chapter by introducing you to anchoring, after which you learned about the cognitive strategies we use to think, make decisions, and solve problems. Next, we discussed human language and animal communication. Thinking about cognition and language, a vast body of knowledge and skills, highlights the narrowness of some of the ways in which intelligence has been measured in the past. That is, all humans possess a remarkable set of cognitive and linguistic tools, yet intelligence testing emphasizes our differences. Thus, it's important to remember that intelligence tests measure only one aspect of human functioning.

CHAPTER 7 SUMMARY

COGNITION (pp. 213–222)

7.1 How do imagery and concepts help us think? (pp. 213–215)

Imagery is helpful for learning new skills and for practicing those we already know. It can also help us store and retrieve information. Concepts are categories that allow us to quickly comprehend information. Rules and definitions determine formal concepts, whereas natural concepts arise out of everyday experiences. We also match information with prototypes, or examples, that include most or all of the features associated with the concepts they represent. Exemplars are examples of concepts with which we have the most familiarity.

Key Terms
cognition, p. 213
imagery, p. 213
concept, p. 214
formal concept, p. 214
natural concept, p. 214
prototype, p. 214
exemplars, p. 214

7.2 How do we make decisions? (pp. 215–219)

Systematic processes involve considering all possible options prior to making a decision. Sometimes we use priorities to eliminate some of these options to speed up the decision-making process. By contrast, heuristics, or "rules of thumb," allow us to make decisions quickly, with little effort. Framing causes us to weigh a decision's gains and losses, and intuition relies on "gut feelings." Anchoring on one piece of information rather than considering all of the factors that are relevant to a decision may cause distortions in thinking.

Key Terms
decision making, p. 215
additive strategy, p. 215
elimination by aspects, p. 215
heuristic, p. 216
availability heuristic, p. 216
representativeness heuristic, p. 216
recognition heuristic, p. 216

framing, p. 217
intuition, p. 218
anchoring, p. 218

7.3 How do the basic approaches and obstacles to problem solving differ? (pp. 219–221)

Analogy, working backward, and means–end analysis are problem solving heuristics that may or may not lead to a correct solution. Analogy heuristics apply proven solutions to new problems. Working backward discovers the steps to solving a problem by first defining the solution. In means–end analysis, the current state is compared to the desired state, and a series of steps are proposed to close the gap between the two. An algorithm is a strategy that always yields a correct solution. Obstacles to problem solving include functional fixedness, the inability to see new uses for familiar objects, and mental set, using a previously successful problem-solving strategy without determining whether it is appropriate for a new problem.

Key Terms
problem solving, p. 219
analogy heuristic, p. 219
working backward, p. 219
means–end analysis, p. 219
algorithm, p. 220
functional fixedness, p. 220
mental set, p. 220
confirmation bias, p. 221

7.4 How have computer scientists applied research on artificial intelligence? (pp. 221–222)

Artificial neural networks (ANNs) are used to simulate human thinking. They process information like human experts and learn from experience. ANNs are the basis for expert systems, computer programs that do the work of human decision makers.

Key Terms
artificial intelligence, p. 221
artificial neural networks (ANNs), p. 221
expert systems, p. 221

LANGUAGE (pp. 222–227)

7.5 What are the components of language? (pp. 222–223)

The components of language are (1) phonemes, (2) morphemes, (3) syntax, (4) semantics, and (5) pragmatics. Phonemes are the basic units of sound, and morphemes are the basic units of meaning. Syntax includes all of a language's rules for combining words into phrases and sentences. Semantics includes the rules for combining units of meaning such as morphemes, words, and sentences. Pragmatics includes the social and nonverbal aspects of language.

Key Terms
language, p. 222
psycholinguistics, p. 222
phonemes, p. 222
morphemes, p. 222
syntax, p. 222
semantics, p. 222
pragmatics, p. 223

7.6 What is the evidence concerning animal communication? (pp. 223–225)

Chimpanzees can learn to use sign language to communicate. Birds that can vocalize have been taught to use words to communicate. For the most part, research indicates that animals string symbols together rather than create true sentences.

7.7 How does language influence thinking? (pp. 225–226)

In general, thinking has a greater influence on language than language has on thinking. Whorf's linguistic relativity hypothesis has not been supported by research.

Key Term
linguistic relativity hypothesis, p. 225

7.8 How does bilingualism affect thinking and language development? (pp. 226–227)

People who learn a second language when they are younger than age 10 or 11 usually speak it without an accent. However, adolescents and adults know more about their own languages, and they can use this knowledge when they are learning a second one.

Key Term
bilingualism, p. 226

INTELLIGENCE (pp. 228–235)

7.9 How do the theories of Spearman, Thurstone, Gardner, and Sternberg differ? (pp. 228–230)

Spearman believed that intelligence is composed of a general ability factor (*g*) and a number of specific abilities (*s*). Thurstone proposed seven primary mental abilities. Gardner claims that there are eight kinds of intelligence, and Sternberg's triarchic theory proposed that three types exist.

Key Terms
intelligence, p. 228
g factor, p. 228
primary mental abilities, p. 228
theory of multiple intelligences, p. 228
triarchic theory of intelligence, p. 229

7.10 What are the characteristics of good cognitive ability tests? (pp. 230–232)

Achievement tests measure learning, while an aptitude test predicts future performance on a specific task. Intelligence tests measure general intellectual ability. Reliable tests yield consistent results. Tests are valid if they predict appropriate outcome variables. Standardization is necessary so that individuals' scores can be compared. Cultural bias threatens the validity of a test, so test makers must reduce it as much as possible.

Key Terms
achievement test, p. 231
aptitude test, p. 231
intelligence test, p. 231
reliability, p. 231
validity, p. 231
standardization, p. 231
norms, p. 231
culture-fair intelligence test, p. 232

7.11 What did Binet, Terman, and Wechsler contribute to the study of intelligence? (pp. 232–234)

Binet developed the first standardized intelligence test. Terman adapted Binet's test for use in the United States and adopted Stern's "intelligence quotient" or "IQ" as the scoring system for the new test. Wechsler developed tests for children and adults. Scores in Wechsler's tests are based on deviation from age-based averages.

Key Term
intelligence quotient (IQ), p. 233

7.12 How do people at both ends of the IQ score continuum differ from those in the middle? (pp. 234–235)

Graphing the frequencies of a large number of IQ scores produces a symmetrical curve (the normal curve) shaped like a bell. Half of scores fall above and half below the mean. Terman's longitudinal study revealed that, in general, gifted individuals enjoy better physical and mental health and are more successful than members of the general population. To be classified as having an intellectual disability, an individual must have an IQ score below 70 and show a severe deficiency in everyday adaptive functioning.

Key Terms
intellectual disability, p. 235
inclusion, p. 235

EXPLAINING DIFFERENCES IN INTELLIGENCE (pp. 236–242)

7.13 What is the evidence for each side of the nature–nurture debate? (pp. 236–238)

The nature–nurture debate concerns the relative contributions of heredity and environment to variations in IQ test scores. Studies involving identical twins are important to this debate because twins have exactly the same genes. If identical twins raised together are found to be more alike on a certain trait than are fraternal twins raised together, then that trait is assumed to be more influenced by heredity. Adoption studies have also shown that infants from disadvantaged environments adopted into middle-class families have higher IQs than infants who remain in disadvantaged homes. Early educational experiences may also raise IQ scores. Also, IQ scores have been steadily rising over the past 70 years, presumably because of changes in standards of living.

Key Terms
nature–nurture debate, p. 236
heritability, p. 236

7.14 How do theorists explain ethnic group differences in IQ scores? (pp. 238–241)

Some researchers claim that racial differences result from genetics. Others argue that poverty, lack of educational opportunities, familiarity with testing situations, and stereotype threat explain these differences. Theorists also argue that individuals in some groups experience stereotype threat when they take tests, a factor that depresses their scores. Differences in cultural beliefs about the source and importance of intellectual ability may also contribute to group differences.

7.15 How do the cognitive abilities of males and females differ? (pp. 241–242)

Females outperform males in reading and writing. Males seem to do better in science, math, and some spatial tasks. In general, females get higher grades and are more self-disciplined. Parents may influence gender differences in math performance by characterizing high performance in girls as resulting from effort and in boys as resulting from innate ability.

BEYOND INTELLIGENCE (pp. 242–245)

7.16 What are the components of emotional intelligence? (p. 243)

The components of emotional intelligence include awareness of one's own emotions, an ability to manage those emotions, self-motivation, empathy, and the ability to handle relationships.

Key Term
emotional intelligence, p. 243

7.17 How does creativity differ from other forms of cognition? (pp. 243–245)

Guilford suggests that creativity involves divergent thinking. Tests used to measure creativity include the Unusual Uses Tests, the Consequences Test, and the Remote Associates Test.

Key Terms
creativity, p. 243
divergent thinking, p. 244

Chapter 7 Study Guide

Answers to all the Study Guide questions are provided at the end of the book.

SECTION ONE: Chapter Review

Cognition (pp. 213–222)

1. When we create a mental picture to remember something, we are using
   a. an exemplar.
   b. conceptualization.
   c. imagery.
   d. a prototype.

2. A mental category that represents a class or group of items that share common characteristics or attributes is called a(n)
   a. image.
   b. concept.
   c. positive instance.
   d. prototype.

3. A prototype is the most _____ example of a concept.
   a. abstract
   b. unusual
   c. recent
   d. typical

4. _____ refers to the way information is presented so as to focus on a potential gain or loss.

5. Which of the following is guaranteed, if properly applied, to result in the correct answer to a problem?
   a. an algorithm
   b. a heuristic
   c. trial and error
   d. applying prior knowledge

6. Working backward and means–end analysis are examples of
   a. algorithms.
   b. heuristics.
   c. mental sets.
   d. functional fixedness.

7. John uses a wastebasket to keep a door from closing. In solving his problem, he was not hindered by
   a. a heuristic.
   b. an algorithm.
   c. functional fixedness.
   d. mental set.

8. One characteristic of good problem solvers is mental set. (true/false)

9. Artificial intelligence systems surpass the problem-solving ability of experts in a number of fields. (true/false)

Language (pp. 222–227)

10. Match the component of language with the appropriate description.
    _____ (1) the smallest units of meaning
    _____ (2) the meaning derived from phonemes, morphemes, and sentences
    _____ (3) grammatical rules for arranging and combining words to form phrases and sentences
    _____ (4) the smallest units of sound in a spoken language
    _____ (5) intonation patterns
    a. pragmatics
    b. syntax
    c. morphemes
    d. semantics
    e. phonemes

11. Communication in trained chimpanzees approaches human language in form and complexity. (true/false)

12. The linguistic relativity hypothesis is not supported by research. (true/false)

13. In general, thought influences language more than language influences thought. (true/false)

Intelligence (pp. 228–235)

14. Match the theorist with the theory of intelligence.
    _____ (1) seven primary abilities
    _____ (2) multiple intelligences
    _____ (3) the *g* factor
    a. Spearman
    b. Thurstone
    c. Gardner

15. The first successful effort to measure intelligence was made by
    a. Binet and Simon.
    b. Spearman.
    c. Wechsler.
    d. Terman.

16. According to Terman's formula, what is the IQ of a child with a mental age of 12 and a chronological age of 8?
    a. 75
    b. 150
    c. 125
    d. 100

17. In which range will the scores of the largest percentage of people taking an IQ test fall?
    a. 85 to 115
    b. 85 to 100
    c. 100 to 130
    d. 70 to 85

Explaining Differences in Intelligence (pp. 236–242)

18. Twin studies suggest that environment is stronger than heredity as a factor in shaping IQ differences. (true/false)

19. In general, differences in cognitive abilities are greater within each gender than between the genders. (true/false)

20. For each cognitive ability, indicate whether males or females, in general, tend to score higher on tests of that ability.
    _____ (1) writing
    _____ (2) science
    _____ (3) spatial ability
    _____ (4) reading comprehension
    _____ (5) mathematics
    a. males
    b. females

Beyond Intelligence (pp. 242–245)

21. The ability to produce multiple ideas or answers to a problem is known as
    a. convergent thinking.
    b. practical intelligence.
    c. divergent thinking.
    d. creativity.

22. People with high IQ scores are typically highly creative. (true/false)

23. The stages in the creative problem-solving process occur in the following sequence:
- **a.** illumination, incubation, preparation, translation
- **b.** incubation, illumination, preparation, translation
- **c.** preparation, incubation, illumination, translation
- **d.** translation, preparation, incubation, illumination

SECTION TWO: Important Concepts and Psychologists

On the line opposite each term, write the name of the theorist or researcher who is most closely associated with it.

1. bounded rationality _____

2. elimination by aspects _____

3. linguistic relativity hypothesis _____

4. *g* factor _____

5. triarchic theory of intelligence _____

6. Stanford–Binet Intelligence Scale _____

7. WAIS _____

8. nature–nurture debate _____

9. stereotype threat _____

10. multiple intelligences _____

SECTION THREE: Comprehensive Practice Test

1. Thinking about one factor in isolation from others that affect a decision is called
- **a.** cognition.
- **b.** elimination by aspects.
- **c.** anchoring.
- **d.** prioritizing.

2. *Dog, car, honesty,* and *trees* are all examples of
- **a.** images.
- **b.** concepts.
- **c.** verbal images.
- **d.** typographs.

3. A gun would be identified by many people as a _____ of the concept *weapon.*

4. Formal concepts are often learned in school. (true/false)

5. A good example of a formal concept is
- **a.** the periodic table of the elements.
- **b.** social display rules.
- **c.** ethical guidelines.
- **d.** established table manners.

6. Students who learn systematic, step-by-step procedures to solve their statistics problems are learning
- **a.** algorithms.
- **b.** trial and error.
- **c.** elimination by aspects.
- **d.** means–end analysis.

7. An artificial neural network is a computer system that is designed to mimic
- **a.** artificial intelligence.
- **b.** animal intelligence.
- **c.** human heuristics.
- **d.** human cognition.

8. _____ are the smallest units of sound in a spoken language.
- **a.** Phonemes
- **b.** Semantics
- **c.** Morphemes
- **d.** Consonants

9. It is obvious that other animals have no real language or communication abilities at all. Any apparent display of such abilities has been shown to be simply a matter of operant conditioning. (true/false)

10. Research suggests that language has no influence on thinking. (true/false)

11. Thurstone believed that the single IQ score method of measuring and describing intelligence was the most effective manner of measuring intelligence. (true/false)

12. Sternberg's experiential intelligence includes
- **a.** the ability to learn from past events.
- **b.** the ability to manipulate people's opinions.
- **c.** creative problem solving.
- **d.** basic academic skills.

13. Mike has just taken a test that is designed to predict future achievement or performance. Mike took a(n)
- **a.** aptitude test.
- **b.** projective test.
- **c.** intelligence test.
- **d.** creativity test.

14. About what percentage of IQ test scores fall between −1 and +1 standard deviation from the mean of 100 on a normal curve?
- **a.** 34%
- **b.** 68%
- **c.** 50%
- **d.** 13%

15. Culture-fair intelligence tests use nonverbal stimuli. (true/false)

16. Intelligence is not fixed at birth; rather, evidence suggests that improved environmental factors can increase IQ scores. (true/false)

17. Although intelligence may be necessary for creativity, it is not sufficient. (true/false)

SECTION FOUR: Critical Thinking

1. Compare and contrast the approaches to decision making discussed in this chapter. Be sure to include information about the pros and cons of each one. For each strategy, give an example of an everyday decision for which it would be helpful.

2. Prepare an argument supporting each of the following positions:
- **a.** Intelligence tests should be used in the schools.
- **b.** Intelligence tests should not be used in the schools.

SECTION FIVE: Application Essays

1. Maria's method of studying worked effectively throughout high school until she took her first foreign language course. In this course, her grades were much lower than usual. How might mental set have played a role in Maria's academic problem?

Apply your critical thinking skills with MyPsychLab Writing Assignments

Submit your answer to the following question inside the MyPsychLab Writing Assessment program for immediate feedback.

Provide real-world examples for the following types of intelligences as theorized by Gardner: verbal/linguistic, body-kinesthetic (movement), and logical/mathematical. Explain why each example represents one of the types of intelligence. Present some of the arguments critics have offered against Gardner's research.

Human Development 8

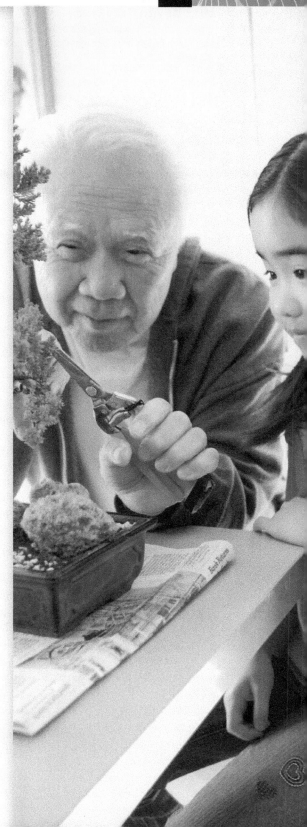

THINK ABOUT IT

What would you say has been the most challenging period of your life so far? One period that many people find especially challenging is the transition from adolescence to adulthood, a phase that psychologists call *emerging adulthood* and which includes the years from 18 to the mid-20s. To get a feel for how psychologists organize research examining this period of life, use these questions to think about your own experiences with emerging adulthood:

- In what ways are the friendship maintenance strategies you used in high school different from those that are required in emerging adulthood?
- How well did your high school study strategies transfer to college-level work?
- In what ways are the strategies you used in high school to initiate and maintain intimate relationships different from those that are required in emerging adulthood?
- When you're ready to look for an internship or post-graduation job, how useful will the techniques you used to get a part-time job in high school be to you?

Research suggests that emerging adulthood is a difficult phase of life because it requires us to adapt previously learned skills and acquire new ones within a fairly short period of time. For example, in answering the first two questions, those that deal with academic and friendship skills, most people see a good deal of overlap between the demands of adolescence and emerging adulthood (Roisman et al., 2004). Consequently, emerging adults need only fine-tune them. By contrast, intimate relationships become far more challenging as we enter emerging adulthood, perhaps because we view them as more important and as having life-long implications. Clearly, too, the demands of finding employment in emerging adulthood are more complex than they are in adolescence. For these reasons, most emerging adults find these two domains of experience to be fraught with an unsettling mix of anxiety and excitement. However, the reward for surmounting the challenges they pose is the attainment of full-fledged, independent adult status.

◉ **Watch** the Video *Episode 9: What's in It for Me? Identity* in **MyPsychLab**

Thankfully, as the complexity of life's demands grows, so does our capacity for handling it. In fact, the whole sweep of human development can be thought of as a series of challenges that prompt us to develop new capacities and hone previously acquired ones. Just when we think we have everything handled, the world hands us a new set of challenges, and we rise to the occasion. As you will see in this chapter, this is as true at every point in the lifespan, as it is in emerging adulthood.

developmental psychology The study of how humans grow, develop, and change throughout the life span.

We begin this chapter with a discussion of several theories that have strongly influenced the field of **developmental psychology**, the scientific study of how humans grow, develop, and change throughout the life span. Then, we will consider the challenges and milestones associated with each of the major phases of development. Note that when we discuss changes in the *physical domain*, we are referring to changes that take place in the body. The *cognitive domain* includes changes in thinking, memory, and so on. The *psychosocial domain* includes changes in how we relate to others and understand the social world. It's important to remember that changes in all of these domains occur simultaneously and affect each other. For example, as toddlers become more mobile and develop language skills, they interact with their peers more. As you're reading this chapter, keep in mind that none of these developments occur in isolation from other developments.

Theories of Development

You may not realize it, but you have already learned about several theories of development. The learning theories you studied in Chapter 5, for instance, can explain many age-related changes as resulting from conditioned stimuli, reinforcement, punishment, observational learning, and the like. Learning theories favor the nurture side of the nature–nurture debate you read about in earlier chapters.

All developmental theories take a position in the nature–nurture debate. Most also address the question of whether development is continuous or occurs in stages. The learning theories assume that development happens in a continuous fashion as the result of environmental influences. Stage theories, by contrast, assert that development occurs in phases—or "leaps" to put it metaphorically—that are distinct from one another. We will begin our discussion of developmental theories with perhaps the most influential of all stage theories, that of Swiss developmentalist Jean Piaget.

Piaget's Theory of Cognitive Development ▶

Thanks to the work of Swiss psychologist Jean Piaget (PEE-ah-ZHAY) (1896–1980), psychologists have gained insights into the cognitive processes of children. In the following sections, we'll learn about his theory of cognitive development and the four stages of cognitive development that he discovered.

How Development Happens. According to Piaget, cognitive development begins with a few basic **schemes**—plans of action to be used in similar circumstances. For instance, once you've experienced the series of actions involved in using a fast-food restaurant's drive-through service, you can construct a drive-through scheme and apply it to any such restaurant. Each time you use this scheme at a different restaurant, there will be a few differences from your experience at other places, but the basic plan of action you follow will be the same. The point is that you don't have to start from scratch every time you go to a new fast-food restaurant; experience has provided you with a general plan of action—a scheme—to follow.

The essence of cognitive development, for Piaget, is the refinement of schemes. For example, an infant who has had experience playing with rubber balls has constructed a scheme that she uses whenever she encounters a ball-like object. The scheme leads her to expect anything resembling a ball to bounce. Consequently, when she is presented with a plum, her ball scheme (her mental plan of action to be applied to ball-like objects) leads her to throw the plum to the floor, expecting it to bounce. Piaget used the term **assimilation** to refer to the mental process by which we incorporate new objects, events, experiences, and information into existing schemes.

When the infant sees that the plum doesn't bounce, her ball scheme changes (although she may try bouncing plums a few more times just to be sure!). This change of scheme will result in a better intellectual adaptation to the real world because the revised scheme includes the knowledge that some ball-like objects bounce but others do not. Piaget used the term **accommodation** for the mental process of modifying existing schemes and creating new ones to incorporate new objects, events, experiences, and information.

According to Piaget (1963, 1964; Piaget & Inhelder, 1969), changes in schemes underlie four stages of cognitive development, each of which reflects a qualitatively different way of reasoning and understanding the world. The stages occur in a fixed sequence in which the accomplishments of one stage provide the foundation for the next stage. Although children throughout the world seem to progress through the stages in the same order, they show individual differences in the rate at which they pass through them. And each child's rate is influenced by her or his level of maturation and experiences, such as going to school. The transition from one stage to another is gradual, not abrupt, and children often show aspects of two stages while going through these transitions. Let's take a closer look at Piaget's four stages of cognitive development.

The Sensorimotor Stage. In Piaget's first stage, the *sensorimotor stage* (age birth to 2 years), infants gain an understanding of the world through their senses and their motor activities (actions or body movements). An infant's behavior, which is mostly reflexive at birth, becomes increasingly complex and gradually evolves into intelligent behavior. At this stage, thought is confined to objects that are present and events that are directly perceived.

The major achievement of the sensorimotor period is the development of **object permanence**—the realization that objects (including people) continue to exist, even when they are out of sight. For example, if an infant is playing with a ball that rolls under a piece of furniture where it can't be seen, he won't look for it unless he has developed object permanence. This concept develops gradually and is complete when the child is able to represent objects mentally in their absence. The attainment of this ability marks the end of the sensorimotor period.

The Preoperational Stage. According to Piaget, children move into the *preoperational stage* of cognitive development when they begin to exhibit signs of the **symbolic function**—the understanding that one thing can stand for another. Children act on the world in ways

8.1 How does Piaget's theory explain cognitive development?

schemes Plans of action, based on previous experiences, to be used in similar circumstances.

assimilation The process by which new objects, events, experiences, or information is incorporated into existing schemes.

accommodation The process by which existing schemes are modified and new schemes are created to incorporate new objects, events, experiences, or information.

object permanence The realization that objects continue to exist, even when they can no longer be perceived.

symbolic function The understanding that one thing—an object, a word, a drawing—can stand for another.

that help them develop symbolic schemes throughout this stage, which is typical of children between the ages of 2 and 7 years. Two ways in which children display the symbolic function are through the use of words to represent objects and through *pretend play,* such as imagining that a block is a car or a doll is a real baby. As children practice using symbols, they become increasingly able to represent objects and events mentally with words and images.

During the preoperational stage, children exhibit a tendency Piaget called *egocentrism:* They believe that everyone sees what they see, thinks as they think, and feels as they feel. As a result, their thinking is often illogical. In addition, their thinking about objects is dominated by appearances. For example, a 3-year-old may believe that a cookie is ruined when it breaks. Adults' attempts to convince her otherwise usually fail because adult thinking is based on the assumption that the identity of an object does not change when its appearance changes, a concept that is not yet understood by children in this stage.

conservation The concept that a given quantity of matter remains the same despite being rearranged or changed in appearance, as long as nothing is added or taken away.

reversibility The realization that any change in the shape, position, or order of matter can be reversed mentally.

The Concrete Operations Stage. In the third stage, the *concrete operations stage* (age 7 to 11 or 12 years), new schemes allow children to understand that a given quantity of matter remains the same despite rearrangement or change in its appearance, as long as nothing is added or taken away—a concept Piaget called **conservation**. Conservation develops because new schemes enable children in this stage to understand the concept of **reversibility**—the understanding that any change in the shape, position, or order of matter can be reversed mentally. As a result, they can think about a broken cookie before and after it broke, realizing that the change in appearance did not change the substance that makes up the cookie. You can see how younger and older children differ in their reasoning about such problems by doing the *Try It.*

TRY IT **Conservation of Volume***

Show a preschooler two glasses of the same size and then fill them with the same amount of juice. After the child agrees they are the same, pour the juice from one glass into a taller, narrower glass and place that glass beside the other original one. Now ask the child if the two glasses have the same amount of juice or if one glass has more than the other. Children at this stage will insist that the taller, narrower glass has more juice, although they will quickly agree that you neither added juice nor took any away.

Now, repeat the procedure with a school-age child. The older child will be able to explain that even though there appears to be more liquid in the taller glass, pouring liquid into a different container doesn't change its quantity.

*Be sure to get permission from the child's parents before you do this *Try It.*

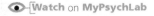

Watch on MyPsychLab

The concepts of conservation of number, substance (liquid or mass), length, area, weight, and volume are not all acquired at once. They come in a certain sequence and usually at specific ages (see Figure 8.1). Moreover, children in the concrete operations stage are unable to apply logic to hypothetical situations. For instance, they find it difficult to think logically about careers they might pursue as adults. They also have difficulty with problems that involve systematically coordinating several variables. For example, they usually cannot solve reasoning problems like these: If Mary is taller than Bill, and Bill is taller than Harry, is Harry shorter than Mary? or, How many different two-letter, three-letter, and four-letter combinations of the letters *A, B, C,* and *D* are possible? This kind of reasoning isn't possible until children enter the next stage.

The Formal Operations Stage. The *formal operations stage* (age 11 or 12 years and beyond) is Piaget's fourth and final stage of cognitive development. At this stage, preadolescents and adolescents can apply logical thought to abstract, verbal, and hypothetical situations and to problems in the past, present, or future—a capacity Piaget called **hypothetico-deductive thinking**. Teenagers can comprehend abstract subjects, such as philosophy and politics, and they become interested in the world of ideas as they begin to formulate their own theories. However, not all people attain full formal operational thinking (Keller, 2011).

Formal operational thinking enables adolescents to think of what might be. Thus, they begin to conceive of "perfect" solutions to the world's and their own problems. For example, a teen whose parents are divorced may idealize her noncustodial parent and believe that her life would be wonderful if only she could live with that parent. Piaget used the term **naive idealism** to refer to this kind of thinking.

Psychologist David Elkind (1967, 1974) claims that the early teenage years are marked by another kind of unrealistic thought, *adolescent egocentrism,* which takes two forms, the imaginary audience and the personal fable. The **imaginary audience** consists of admirers and critics that adolescents conjure up and that exist only in their imagination. In their minds, they are always on stage. Teens may spend hours in front of the mirror trying to please this audience. Teenagers also have an exaggerated sense of personal uniqueness and indestructibility that Elkind calls the **personal fable**. Many believe they are somehow indestructible and protected from the misfortunes that befall others, such as unwanted pregnancies or drug overdoses (Alberts, Elkind, Ginsberg, 2007). The *Summarize It* provides a recap of Piaget's four stages.◉

Cross-Cultural Research. Cross-cultural studies have affirmed the universality of the types of reasoning and the sequence of stages formulated by Piaget. But, cross-cultural research has also revealed differences in the rates of cognitive development in various domains. Whereas the children Piaget observed began to acquire the concept of conservation between ages 5 and 7, Australian Aboriginal children show this change between the ages of 10 and 13 (Dasen, 1994). Yet, the Aboriginal children function at the concrete operations level earlier on spatial tasks than on quantification (counting) tasks, while the reverse is true for Western children. This difference makes sense in light of the high value Aborigines place on spatial skills and the low premium they place on quantification. In the Australian desert, moving from place to place, hunting, gathering, and searching for water, Aborigines have few possessions and rarely count things. Their language has words for numbers up to five, and their word for "many" applies to anything above five.

Another important cultural variable that contributes to cognitive development is formal education. Developmental psychologists know that children who live in cultures in which they have access to formal education progress more rapidly through Piaget's stages than peers whose societies do not require them to attend school or do not provide them with educational opportunities (Mishra, 1997). Moreover, formal operational thinking is so strongly correlated with formal education that some psychologists have suggested that it may be more a product of specific learning experiences than of a universal developmental process, as Piaget hypothesized (Keller, 2011).

hypothetico-deductive thinking The ability to base logical reasoning on a hypothetical premise.

naive idealism A type of thought in which adolescents construct ideal solutions for problems.

imaginary audience A belief of adolescents that they are or will be the focus of attention in social situations and that others will be as critical or approving as they are of themselves.

personal fable An exaggerated sense of personal uniqueness and indestructibility, which may be the basis for adolescent risk taking.

◉ Watch the Video *Episode 9: Basics: How Thinking Develops* in **MyPsychLab**

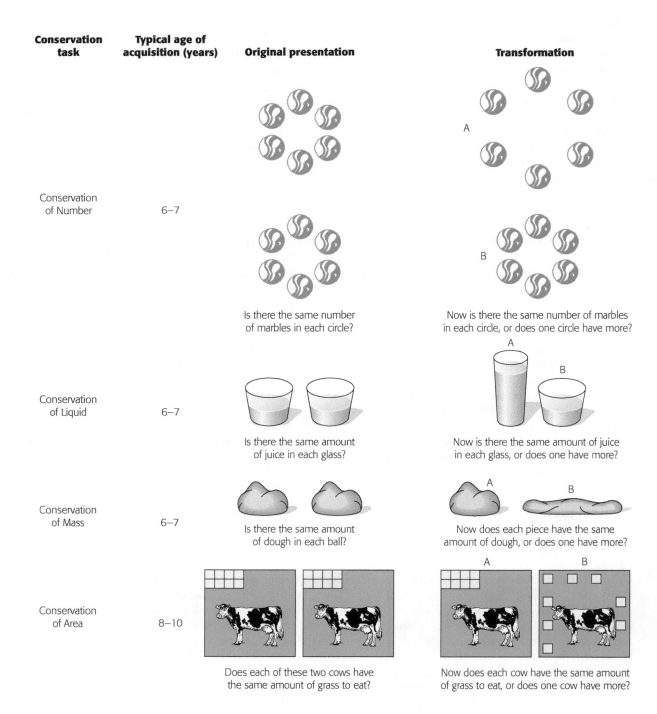

Conservation task	Typical age of acquisition (years)	Original presentation	Transformation
Conservation of Number	6–7	Is there the same number of marbles in each circle?	Now is there the same number of marbles in each circle, or does one circle have more?
Conservation of Liquid	6–7	Is there the same amount of juice in each glass?	Now is there the same amount of juice in each glass, or does one have more?
Conservation of Mass	6–7	Is there the same amount of dough in each ball?	Now does each piece have the same amount of dough, or does one have more?
Conservation of Area	8–10	Does each of these two cows have the same amount of grass to eat?	Now does each cow have the same amount of grass to eat, or does one cow have more?

FIGURE 8.1 **Piaget's Conservation Tasks**
Piaget's research involved several kinds of conservation tasks. He classified children's thinking as concrete operational with respect to a particular task if they could correctly solve the problem and provide a concrete operational reason for their answer. For example, if a child said, "The two circles of marbles are the same because you didn't add any or take any away when you moved them," the response was judged to be concrete operational. Conversely, if a child said, "The two circles are the same, but I don't know why," the response was not classified as concrete operational.
Source: Bee & Boyd, *The Developing Child,* 11e.

Piaget's Stages of Cognitive Development

STAGE		DESCRIPTION
Sensorimotor (0 to 2 years)		Infants experience the world through their senses, actions, and body movements. At the end of this stage, toddlers develop the concept of object permanence and can mentally represent objects in their absence.
Preoperational (2 to 7 years)		Children are able to represent objects and events mentally with words and images. They can engage in imaginary play (pretend), using one object to represent another. Their thinking is egocentric; that is, they fail to consider the perspective of others.
Concrete operational (7 to 11 or 12 years)		Children at this stage become able to think logically in concrete situations. They acquire the concepts of conservation and reversibility, can order objects in a series, and can classify them according to multiple dimensions.
Formal operational (11 or 12 years and beyond)		At this stage, adolescents learn to think logically in abstract situations, learn to test hypotheses systematically, and become interested in the world of ideas. Not all people attain full formal operational thinking.

Alternatives to Piaget's theory ▶

8.2 How do the neo-Piagetians and Vygotsky explain cognitive development?

Although Piaget's genius and his monumental contribution to scientists' knowledge of mental development are rarely disputed, his methods and some of his findings and conclusions have been criticized (Beins, 2012). It now seems clear that children are more advanced cognitively and adults are less competent cognitively than Piaget concluded (Flavell, 1985, 1992; Mandler, 1990; Siegler, 1991). Nevertheless, decades of research, much of which was aimed at challenging Piaget's original findings, strongly suggest that cognitive development follows the sequence that Piaget's stages describe (Morra, Gobbo, Marini, & Sheese, 2008). However, a number of important questions about the process of age-related cognitive change remain, and other theories have proposed answers to them.

The Neo-Piagetian Approach. Some developmentalists, called neo-Piagetians, explain age-based differences in performance on the problems Piaget used in his studies as a function of changes in children's use of their working memories (Morra et al., 2008).

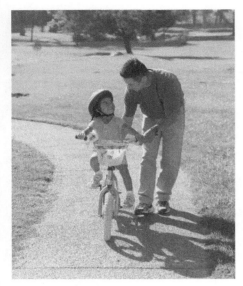

▲ This father teaching his daughter to ride a bike is using Vygotsky's technique called *scaffolding*. A parent or teacher provides direct and continuous instruction at the beginning of the learning process and then gradually withdraws from active teaching as the child becomes more proficient at the new task or skill. How might scaffolding help a child acquire cognitive skills such as reading?

zone of proximal development A range of cognitive tasks that a child cannot yet do but can learn to do through the guidance of an older child or adult.

scaffolding A type of instruction in which an adult adjusts the amount of guidance provided to match a child's present level of ability.

Research has shown, for instance, that the younger children are, the more slowly they process information (Kail, 2007). Because they process information more slowly, they are more likely to fail to store information in long-term memory before new information comes along and pushes the old information out of working memory. (Recall the interference explanation of forgetting from Chapter 6.) Think about how this might affect children's responses to the conservation of number task shown in Figure 8.1 (refer back to p. 256). If the neo-Piagetians are correct, then children younger than age 6 or 7 will likely forget what the original presentation of marbles looked like when they are shown the transformation. As a result, they cannot mentally compare the original and transformed arrays. By contrast, older children, with their faster rates of information processing and more efficient working memories, can keep both presentations in mind as well as the process that was used to make the transformation. Thus, the older children can come up with a correct solution because they are better able to integrate all of the relevant information in working memory.

Vygotsky's Sociocultural Approach. The Russian developmentalist Lev Vygotsky (1896–1934) claimed that Piaget's theory of cognitive development placed too much emphasis on forces within the child. Vygotsky hypothesized that much of cognitive development results from the child's internalization of information that is acquired socially, primarily through the medium of language.

For instance, have you ever noticed children talking to themselves as they assemble a puzzle or paint a picture? Vygotsky asserted that this and other spontaneous language behaviors exhibited by children are important to the process of cognitive development. Vygotsky maintained that human infants come equipped with basic skills such as perception, the ability to pay attention, and certain capacities of memory not unlike those of many other animal species (Vygotsky, 1936/1986). During the first two years of life, these skills grow and develop naturally through direct experiences and interactions with the child's sociocultural world. As children develop the ability to represent ideas, activities, and so on through speech, they are often observed "talking to themselves." Vygotsky believed that talking to oneself—*private speech*—is a key component in cognitive development. Through private speech, children can specify the components of a problem and verbalize steps in a process to help them work through a puzzling activity or situation. As young children develop greater competence, private speech fades into barely audible mumbling and muttering, and finally becomes simply thinking.

Vygotsky saw a strong connection among social experience, speech, and cognitive development. He also maintained that a child's readiness to learn resides within a **zone of proximal development** (*proximal* means "potential"). This zone, according to Vygotsky, is a range of cognitive tasks that the child cannot yet perform alone but can learn to perform with the instruction and guidance of a parent, teacher, or more advanced peer. This kind of help, in which a teacher or parent adjusts the quality and degree of instruction and guidance to fit the child's present level of ability or performance, is often referred to as **scaffolding**. In scaffolding, direct instruction is given, at first, for unfamiliar tasks (Maccoby, 1992). But, as the child shows increasing competence, the teacher or parent gradually withdraws from direct and active teaching, and the child may continue toward independent mastery of the task. For example, when a child is learning to read, parents and teachers often read along with her and provide hints (i.e., scaffolding) that help her figure out unfamiliar words. As the child's reading skills improve, fewer and fewer hints are required, and she eventually gets to the point where she can read independently. Of course, hints are of no help to a child who hasn't yet acquired some basic information about letters and the sounds they represent. In other words, when a child has become capable of reading simple words on her own, she has entered a zone of proximal development for reading in which hints, or scaffolding, will enable her to read much more text than she would be able to on her own. Vygotsky hypothesized that scaffolding episodes that are perfectly tailored to children's zones of proximal development occur frequently within the context of parent–child relationships and are essential to children's cognitive development.

Kohlberg's Theory of Moral Development ▸

8.3 How does Kohlberg's theory explain moral reasoning?

Lawrence Kohlberg (1927–1987) proposed a stage theory of moral reasoning that has been extremely influential in the study of moral development. Long before Kohlberg's work began, both Vygotsky and Piaget applied their theories to moral development. Vygotsky (1926/1992) asserted that culture, by means of language and religious instruction, molds individuals to conform to its standards of acceptable behavior. Piaget did not deny the role that culture plays in moral development. However, he hypothesized that children's levels of cognitive development interact with society's efforts to instill moral values in them such that moral reasoning develops in stages that parallel those of cognitive development (Piaget, 1927/1965). In the following sections, we'll take a closer look at Kohlberg's theory and the stages he proposed.

Measuring Moral Reasoning. Kohlberg studied changes in moral reasoning across the life span by presenting study participants with moral dilemmas like the story in the *Try It* below. After participants listened to these stories, Kohlberg asked them open-ended questions such as "What do you think Heinz should do?" After participants offered their opinions, Kohlberg would ask for their reasons. By analyzing participants' responses to such questions, Kohlberg found that he could classify moral reasoning into three levels, each of which has two stages.

Levels and Stages. At Kohlberg's first level of moral development, the **preconventional level**, moral reasoning is governed by the physical consequences of behavior rather than one's own internalized standards of right and wrong. An act is judged good or bad based on its physical consequences. In Stage 1, "right" is whatever avoids punishment; in Stage 2, "right" is whatever is rewarded, benefits the individual, or results in a favor being returned. "You scratch my back and I'll scratch yours" is the type of thinking common at this stage. Children usually function at the preconventional level through age 10.

At Kohlberg's second level of moral development, the **conventional level**, the individual has internalized the standards of others and judges right and wrong in terms of those standards. At Stage 3, sometimes called the *good boy–nice girl orientation,* moral judgments focus on social approval. Morally acceptable actions are those of which one's social group approves. Actions that one's group disapproves of are immoral. For example, a person might view drinking alcohol as immoral because her religious group condemns it. In order to maintain solidarity with the group, she must adopt the view that drinking alcohol is morally wrong. Another person might view smoking marijuana as morally acceptable because all of his friends hold that view. Again, to maintain social bonds, the individual adopts the moral standards of the group.

preconventional level Kohlberg's lowest level of moral development, in which moral reasoning is based on the physical consequences of an act; "right" is whatever avoids punishment or gains a reward.

conventional level Kohlberg's second level of moral development, in which right and wrong are based on the internalized standards of others; "right" is whatever helps or is approved of by others, or whatever is consistent with the laws of society.

TRY IT   **The Heinz Dilemma**

Kohlberg studied moral development by presenting research participants with moral dilemmas such as this one.

In Europe, a woman was near death from a special kind of cancer. There was one drug the doctors thought might save her. It was a form of radium that a druggist in the same town had recently discovered. The drug was expensive to make, and the druggist was charging ten times what it cost him. He paid $200 for the radium and charged $2,000 for a small dose of the drug. The sick woman's husband, Heinz, went to everyone he knew to borrow the money, but he could only get together $1,000, which was half of what the drug cost. He told the druggist that his wife was dying and asked him to sell it cheaper or let him pay later. But the druggist said, "No, I discovered the drug, and I am going to make money from it." So Heinz got desperate and broke into the man's store to steal the drug for his wife. (Colby et al., 1983, p. 77)

If Heinz had asked for your advice before he broke into the store, would you have agreed with his decision? Why or why not?

At Stage 4, the orientation moves beyond the social group and shifts to the maintenance of the larger social order in which the group is imbedded and obedience to authority. However, Stage 4 is not about blind obedience to authority. Instead, it is based on the realization that rules are necessary and that, to some degree, individuals' and sub-groups' needs and desires must be subjugated to those of the larger group in order to avoid an "every man for himself" type of world. Themes of duty and responsibility are central to Stage 4 reasoning, as is the notion that, when challenges to authority are necessary, they must be carried out in morally acceptable ways. For example, suppose you received a speeding ticket but had evidence that you were not speeding. Stage 4 reasoning would whole-heartedly endorse your right to challenge the police officer's authority by taking your case to court. If you lost, however, Stage 4 reasoning would urge you to accept the court's verdict and would see merit in exhibiting respect for a process that does not always yield a just outcome but serves to maintain social order.

postconventional level Kohlberg's highest of moral development, in which moral reasoning involves weighing moral alternatives; "right" is whatever furthers basic human rights.

Kohlberg's highest level of moral development is the **postconventional level**, which requires the ability to think at Piaget's stage of formal operations. At this level, people do not simply internalize the standards of others. Instead, they weigh moral alternatives, realizing that the law may sometimes conflict with basic human rights. At Stage 5, the person believes that laws are formulated to protect both society and the individual and should be changed if they fail to do so. Thus, whereas Stage 4 reasoning focuses on the need to maintain order, Stage 5 reasoning argues that it is morally unacceptable to favor order over individual rights. For example, discriminatory laws that prohibited African Americans from attending certain schools or using public facilities restricted to Whites satisfied the Stage 4 criterion of order, but they violated the Stage 5 focus on basic human rights. Consequently, Stage 5 reasoning was at the heart of the civil rights movement of the 1950s and 1960s. Likewise, Stage 5 reasoning was the basis of the U.S. Declaration of Independence, a document that asserted that the American colonists were justified in declaring themselves no longer subject to British rule because their rights had been violated.

At Stage 6, ethical decisions are based on universal ethical principles, which emphasize respect for human life, justice, equality, and dignity for all people. People who reason morally at Stage 6 believe that they must follow such principles even if it results in a violation of the law.

Ages, Stages, and Culture. The *Summarize It* describes Kohlberg's six stages of moral development. Kohlberg claimed that people progress through these stages one at a time in a fixed order, without skipping any stage. If movement occurs, it is to the next higher stage. Moreover, each level is associated with a prerequisite stage of cognitive development. Conventional moral reasoning is based on concrete operational thought, and postconventional reasoning is impossible until an individual has attained Piaget's formal operational stage. However, researchers have found that moral reasons lags behind cognitive development to a greater degree than Kohlberg originally hypothesized (Smith, 1978). Thus, conventional moral reasoning is more strongly linked to formal operations than to concrete operations. Similarly, postconventional reasoning is rarely seen before adulthood.

The gap between cognitive and moral development demonstrates that cognitive development alone is insufficient to produce advances in moral reasoning. In addition to the prerequisite level of cognitive development, individuals' environments must provide them with ample opportunities to apply their reasoning skills to moral issues. Direct teaching of moral principles also supports movement from one stage to the next, especially when parents and teachers explicitly explain such principles to children and teenagers and help them relate the principles to issues in their own lives (Narvaez, 2002; Weinstock, Assor, & Broide, 2009). Consequently, moral development tends to lag behind cognitive development, as suggested by Figure 8.2. Notice that conventional moral reasoning does not

Kohlberg's Stages of Moral Development

LEVEL	STAGE
Level I: Preconventional Level Moral reasoning is governed by the physical consequences of behavior; an act is good or bad depending on its physical consequences—whether it is punished or rewarded.	**Stage 1** The stage in which behavior that avoids punishment is right. Children obey out of fear of punishment. **Stage 2** The stage of self-interest. What is right is what benefits the individual or gains a favor in return. "You scratch my back and I'll scratch yours."
Level II: Conventional Level The child internalizes the standards of others and judges right and wrong according to those standards.	**Stage 3** The morality of mutual relationships. The "good boy–nice girl" orientation. Child acts to please and help others. **Stage 4** The morality of the social system and conscience. Orientation toward authority. Morality is doing one's duty, respecting authority, and maintaining the social order.
Level III: Postconventional Level Moral conduct is under internal control; this is the highest level and the mark of true morality.	**Stage 5** The morality of contract; respect for individual rights and laws that are democratically agreed on. Rational valuing of the wishes of the majority and the general welfare. Belief that society is best served if citizens obey the law. **Stage 6** The highest stage of the highest social level. The morality of universal ethical principles. The person acts according to internal standards independent of legal restrictions or opinions of others.

predominate until after age 12, even though most children attain the required level of cognitive development (i.e., concrete operations) at age 6 or 7. Similarly, postconventional thought does not appear until adulthood, many years after most individuals have shown the first signs of formal operational thinking. Notice, too, that postconventional reasoning is the exception rather than the rule even among adults in their 30s. These findings suggest that moral development is a lifelong process.

There is a great deal of evidence that Kohlberg's stages of moral reasoning occur in all cultures. In a classic review of 45 studies of Kohlberg's theory conducted in 27 countries, Snarey (1985) found support for the universality of Stages 1 through 4 and for the invariant sequence of these stages in all groups studied. Although extremely rare, Stage 5 was found in almost all samples from urban or middle-class populations and was absent in all of the tribal or village folk societies studied. A more recent review by Snarey and others of a large number of studies across more than 20 countries supports the conclusions of Snarey's earlier work (Gibbs, Basinger, Grime, & Snarey, 2007). By contrast, Stage 6 is exceedingly rare. Almost all examples of Stage 6 reasoning cited by Kohlberg and other researchers are historical. Still, reasoning at this level does not appear to be tied to any particular culture.

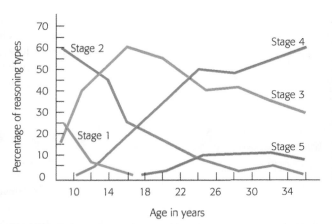

FIGURE 8.2 Longitudinal Study of Moral Development These findings are from Colby and Kohlberg's long-term longitudinal study of a group of boys who were asked about Kohlberg's moral dilemmas every few years from age 10 through early adulthood. Note that postconventional, or principled, reasoning was quite uncommon, even in adulthood.

Source: Colby, A., Kohlberg, L., Gibbs, J., & Lieberman, M. (1983). A longitudinal study of moral judgment. *Monographs of the Society for Research in Child Development, 48,* pp. 1–124.

Challenges to Kohlberg's View. One controversy concerning Kohlberg's theory involves the possibility of gender bias. Kohlberg indicated that the majority of women remain at Stage 3, while most men attain Stage 4. Do men typically attain a higher level of moral reasoning than women? Carol Gilligan (1982) asserts that Kohlberg's theory is sex biased. Not only did Kohlberg fail to include females in his original research, Gilligan points out, but he also limited morality to abstract reasoning about moral dilemmas. And, at his highest level, Stage 6, Kohlberg emphasized justice and equality but not mercy, compassion, love, or concern for others. Gilligan suggests that females, more than males, tend to view moral behavior in terms of compassion, caring, and concern for others. Thus, she agrees that the content of moral reasoning differs between the sexes, but she contends that males and females do not differ in the complexity of their moral reasoning.

Some evidence suggests that females do tend to emphasize care and compassion in resolving moral dilemmas, while males tend to stress justice or at least to give it equal standing with caring (Garmon et al., 1996; Wark & Krebs, 1996). Although Kohlberg's theory does emphasize rights and justice over concern for others, researchers, nevertheless, have found that females score as high as males in moral reasoning (Walker, 1989). For this reason, Gilligan and others who have carried out research inspired by her approach have come to think of the caring and justice ethics as different dimensions of moral reasoning that contribute to both males' and females' thinking about issues of right and wrong (Jorgensen, 2006).

Finally, some critics point out that moral reasoning and moral behavior are not one and the same. Kohlberg readily acknowledged that people can be capable of making mature moral judgments yet fail to live morally (Kohlberg, 1968). Yet, researchers have found group differences in moral reasoning when groups that are extremely different in moral behavior are compared. For example, researchers have found that teenagers who are less able than their peers to look at situations from others' perspectives are more likely to engage in criminal behavior (Marshall, Marshall, & Serran, 2009). However, critics justifiably point out that such findings tell us little about how variations in moral development contribute to everyday decisions about moral behavior, such as office workers' decisions about whether to break their employers' rules about surfing the Internet on the job. Learning theorists suggest that decisions of this kind are influenced by the rewards associated with rule violation, the likelihood and consequences of getting caught, and the behavior of others (i.e., "everybody does it") rather than by abstract moral reasoning (Bandura 1977, 1989). In support of this view, psychologists Dennis Krebs and Kathy Denton have found that people exhibit lower levels of reasoning in response to real-life dilemmas than they do when formulating judgments about the hypothetical scenarios used in Kohlberg's research (Krebs & Denton, 2005). Regardless of whether we agree with Kohlberg's theory, most of us would agree that moral reasoning and moral behavior are critically important aspects of human development. Moral individuals make moral societies.

8.4 How does Erikson's theory explain psychosocial development?

Erikson's Theory of Psychosocial Development

Piaget's, Vygotsky's, and Kohlberg's theories deal with the intellectual aspects of development. Moral reasoning, of course, involves reasoning about the social world, but it doesn't address the process through which individuals come to feel a part of the families, neighborhoods, and cultures in which they live. By contrast, the theories of the psychoanalysts, first mentioned in Chapter 1, focus on precisely this domain of development. We will discuss the developmental theory of the founder of psychoanalysis, Sigmund Freud, in Chapter 11. But, the theory of one of the psychoanalysts who came after Freud, Erik Erikson (1902–1994), is best discussed in the context of life-span development, because Erikson (1980) proposed the only major theory of development to include the entire life span. According to Erikson, individuals progress through eight **psychosocial stages**, each of which is defined by a conflict involving the individual's relationship with the social environment, which must be resolved satisfactorily for healthy development to occur (Erikson, 1980).

psychosocial stages Erikson's eight developmental stages for the entire life span; each is defined by a conflict that must be resolved satisfactorily for healthy personality development to occur.

According to Erikson's view, the foundations of adult personality are laid in four childhood stages. During the first stage, *basic trust versus basic mistrust,* infants (birth to 1 year) develop a sense of trust or mistrust depending on the degree and regularity of care, love, and affection they receive from the mother or primary caregiver. Erikson (1980) considered "basic trust as the cornerstone of a healthy personality" (p. 58). During the second stage, *autonomy versus shame and doubt,* children aged 1 to 3 begin to express their independence (often by saying "No!") and develop their physical and mental abilities. In the third stage, *initiative versus guilt,* 3- to 6-year-old children go beyond merely expressing their autonomy and begin to develop initiative. During the fourth stage, *industry versus inferiority,* school-aged children (age 6 years to puberty) begin to enjoy and take pride in making things and doing things.

Erikson's later stages begin with puberty, but they are not as strongly tied to chronological age as those that occur during childhood. Instead, the adolescent and adult stages represent important themes of adult life. These themes occur in a fixed sequence, Erikson claimed, because the resolution of each depends on how well prior stages were resolved.

The first of these stages is *identity versus role confusion,* during which adolescents experience a phenomenon Erikson called the *identity crisis.* During the identity crisis, teens must develop an idea of how they will fit into the adult world. A healthy identity, Erikson claimed, is essential to the next stage, *intimacy versus isolation,* which begins around age 18. During this stage, young adults must find a life partner or come to a healthy acceptance of living in a single state. The next major theme of adult life, *generativity versus stagnation,* is at its peak during the years of middle age. Generativity, according to Erikson, is the desire to guide the next generation, through parenting, teaching, or mentoring. If a middle-aged person does not engage with the next generation, she becomes stagnant. Finally, in later years, adults experience *ego integrity versus despair.* The goal of this stage is an acceptance of one's life in preparation for facing death. Lack of self-acceptance leads to despair and hopelessness. The *Summarize It* on p. 264 outlines Erikson's psychosocial stages.

Most research on Erikson's theory has focused on trust in infants, identity formation in adolescents, and generativity in middle-aged adults. Specific predictions derived from Erikson's descriptions of these three stages have received mixed research support. On the positive side, there is a great deal of evidence that a relationship with a trusted caregiver in infancy is critical to later development.

In contrast, most research examining the development of identity has shown that the process does begin in adolescence, but it is not complete until well into the early adult years (Marcia, 2002; Waterman, 1985). Many college students, for example, have not yet settled on a major or future career when they begin taking classes, and they use experiences in their first few semesters to make these important decisions. One reason for the apparent delay may be that advances in logical reasoning, such as those associated with Piaget's formal operational stage, are strongly related to identity formation (Klaczynski, Fauth, & Swanger, 1998). Formal operational thinking evolves slowly across the adolescent years. Consequently, people may not have the cognitive ability to engage in the kind of thinking necessary for the development of identity until the early adult years. With regard to generativity, in studies of young, midlife, and older women, researchers have found that generativity increases in middle age as Erikson's theory predicts (Warburton, McLaughlin, & Pinsker, 2006; Zucker, Ostrove, & Stewart, 2002). However, it does not decline in old age. So, generativity may be more a characteristic of middle than of early adulthood, as Erikson predicted, but it appears to continue to be important in old age.

Now that you have had an introduction to developmental theories, we will turn our attention to the major milestones of each phase of development. *Prenatal development* refers to the period prior to birth. The first 2 years constitute the period of *infancy.* The period from 2 to 6 years of age is *early childhood,* and *middle childhood* is the period from age 6 to puberty. *Adolescence* begins at puberty and ends when an individual is considered to be an adult in his or her culture. Finally, the adult years are typically divided into phases of *early adulthood* (18 to 40 or 45), *middle adulthood* (40 or 45 to 65), and *late adulthood* (65 and older).

SUMMARIZE IT

Erikson's Psychosocial Stages of Development

STAGE	AGES	DESCRIPTION
Trust vs. mistrust	Birth to 1 year	Infants learn to trust or mistrust depending on the degree and regularity of care, love, and affection provided by parents or caregivers.
Autonomy vs. shame and doubt	1 to 3 years	Children learn to express their will and independence, to exercise some control, and to make choices. If not, they experience shame and doubt.
Initiative vs. guilt	3 to 6 years	Children begin to initiate activities, to plan and undertake tasks, and to enjoy developing motor and other abilities. If not allowed to initiate or if made to feel stupid and considered a nuisance, they may develop a sense of guilt.
Industry vs. inferiority	6 years to puberty	Children develop industriousness and feel pride in accomplishing tasks, making things, and doing things. If not encouraged or if rebuffed by parents and teachers, they may develop a sense of inferiority.
Identity vs. role confusion	Adolescence	Adolescents must make the transition from childhood to adulthood, establish an identity, develop a sense of self, and consider a future occupational identity. Otherwise, role confusion can result.
Intimacy vs. isolation	Young adulthood	Young adults must develop intimacy—the ability to share with, care for, and commit themselves to another person. Avoiding intimacy brings a sense of isolation and loneliness.
Generativity vs. stagnation	Middle adulthood	Middle-aged people must find some way of contributing to the development of the next generation. Failing this, they may become self-absorbed and emotionally impoverished and reach a point of stagnation.
Ego integrity vs. despair	Late adulthood	Individuals review their lives, and if they are satisfied and feel a sense of accomplishment, they will experience ego integrity. If dissatisfied, they may sink into despair.

REMEMBER IT

Check your answers and take additional quizzes in MyPsychLab.com. ✓—Study and Review on MyPsychLab

1. Piaget's theory claims that all people pass through the same cognitive-developmental stages in the same order. (true/false)
2. According to Piaget, _____ are plans of action that are used in similar circumstances.
3. Kohlberg's research examined changes in _____ across the lifespan by presenting participants with _____ and probing the reasoning behind their answers.
4. According to Erikson, satisfactory resolution of the conflict associated with each stage of his psychosocial stages is required for healthy development in future stages. (true/false)
5. Most research on Erikson's theory has focused on his concepts of _____ and _____.

Prenatal Development and Infancy

What is the phase of life during which change takes place at the most rapid rate? You might be surprised to learn that it is during the first 8 weeks after the first of life's developmental milestones, *conception*, the joining of a sperm and an egg. But the changes that occur in the first 2 years after birth also happen very quickly, as you will soon learn.

8.5 What happens in each stage of prenatal development?

From Conception to Birth

Many people divide the 9 months of pregnancy into *trimesters*, three periods of 3 months' duration. However, the division of pregnancy into trimesters is arbitrary and has nothing to do with prenatal development. In fact, the final stage of **prenatal development**, or development from conception to birth, begins before the first trimester ends.

prenatal development Development from conception to birth.

The Stages of Prenatal Development. Conception, of course, marks the beginning of prenatal development and typically takes place in one of the fallopian tubes. Over the next 2 weeks, the **zygote**, the cell that results from the union of a sperm and an ovum, travels to the uterus and attaches itself to the uterine wall. This stage is known as the *period of the zygote* or the *germinal stage.* At the end of this stage, the zygote is only the size of the period at the end of this sentence. The second stage is the *period of the embryo,* when the major systems, organs, and structures of the body develop. Lasting from week 3 through week 8, this period ends when the first bone cells form. Only 1 inch long and weighing 1/7 of an ounce, the **embryo** already resembles a human being, with limbs, fingers, toes, and many internal organs that have begun to function. The final stage of prenatal development, called the *period of the fetus,* lasts from the end of the second month until birth. The **fetus** undergoes rapid growth and further development of the structures, organs, and systems of the body. Table 8.1 describes the characteristics of each stage of prenatal development.

During the last several weeks of prenatal development, the fetus is capable of responding to stimuli from the outside world, particularly sounds. Further, newborns remember the stimuli to which they were exposed prior to birth (Granier-Deferre et al., 2011). In a classic study of prenatal learning, DeCasper and Spence (1986) had 16 pregnant women read *The Cat in the Hat* to their developing fetuses twice a day during the final 6 weeks of pregnancy. A few days after birth, the infants could adjust their sucking on specially designed, pressure-sensitive nipples to hear their mother reading either *The Cat in the Hat* or *The King, the Mice, and the Cheese,* a story they had never heard before. By their sucking behavior, the infants showed a definite preference for the familiar story.

Negative Influences on Prenatal Development. As wondrous as the process of prenatal development is, ample evidence indicates that the developing embryo and the fetus are vulnerable to a number of potentially harmful factors. One is lack of prenatal care, and another is maternal health. The babies of women who have chronic conditions such as diabetes may experience retardation or acceleration of fetal growth (Moore, 2012). And when the mother has a viral disease such as *rubella, chicken pox,* or *HIV,* she may deliver an infant with physical and behavioral abnormalities (Gowen, 2011).

Teratogens are substances that can have a negative impact on prenatal development, causing birth defects and other problems. A teratogen's impact depends on both its intensity and the time during prenatal development when it is present. Teratogens generally have their most devastating consequences during the period of the embryo. During this time, there are **critical periods** when certain body structures develop. If drugs or other harmful substances interfere with development during a critical period, the body structure will not form properly, nor will it develop later (Draper, 2011). (Note that there are critical periods throughout development. You'll read about another one in the section on language development later in this chapter.)

zygote Cell that results from the union of a sperm and an ovum.

embryo The developing human organism during the period (week 3 through week 8) when the major systems, organs, and structures of the body develop.

fetus The developing human organism during the period (week 9 until birth) when rapid growth and further development of the structures, organs, and systems of the body occur.

teratogens Harmful agents in the prenatal environment, which can have a negative impact on prenatal development or even cause birth defects.

critical period A period so important to development that a harmful environmental influence at that time can keep a bodily structure from developing normally or can impair later intellectual or social development.

TABLE 8.1 Stages of Prenatal Development

STAGE	TIME AFTER CONCEPTION	MAJOR ACTIVITIES OF THE STAGE
Period of the zygote	1 to 2 weeks	Zygote attaches to the uterine lining. At 2 weeks, zygote is the size of the period at the end of this sentence.
Period of the embryo	3 to 8 weeks	Major systems, organs, and structures of the body develop. Period ends when first bone cells appear. At 8 weeks, embryo is about 1 inch long and weighs 1/7 of an ounce.
Period of the fetus	9 weeks to birth (38 weeks)	Rapid growth and further development of the body structures, organs, and systems.

▲ These photos show the fertilization of an egg by a sperm (left), an embryo at 7 weeks (center), and a fetus at 22 weeks (right).

fetal alcohol syndrome A condition, caused by maternal alcohol intake during pregnancy, in which the baby is born with mental retardation, with a small head and facial, organ, and behavioral abnormalities.

 Watch the Video *Effects of Prenatal Smoking on Children's Development* in **MyPsychLab**

The use of heroin, cocaine, and crack during pregnancy has been linked to miscarriage, prematurity, low birth weight, breathing difficulties, physical defects, and fetal death. Alcohol also crosses the placental barrier, and alcohol levels in the fetus almost match the levels in the mother's blood (Vaux, 2012). Women who drink heavily during pregnancy risk having babies with **fetal alcohol syndrome**. Babies with this syndrome have mental retardation and abnormally small heads with wide-set eyes and a short nose. They also have behavioral problems such as hyperactivity (Julien, 1995). Some children prenatally exposed to alcohol have *fetal alcohol effects*—they show some of the characteristics of fetal alcohol syndrome but in less severe form (Vaux, 2012). Thus, public health officials recommend that women abstain from drinking alcohol altogether during pregnancy (Vaux, 2012).

Smoking decreases the amount of oxygen and increases the amount of carbon monoxide crossing the placental barrier. The embryo or fetus is exposed to nicotine and several thousand other chemicals as well. Smoking while pregnant increases the probability that the baby will be premature or of low birth weight (Jain, 2012). Further, because researchers disagree as to whether heavy caffeine consumption has an adverse effect on the fetus, the wisest course of action is to restrict caffeine consumption to less than 300 milligrams (3 cups) daily. ◉

Birth. In Chapter 3 you learned that, near the end of pregnancy, the woman's body begins to prepare for the physical discomfort of birth by increasing the levels of *endorphins*, the body's natural painkillers, in her system. At the same time, her levels of *oxytocin*, the hormone that stimulates the uterus to contract during labor, rise as the uterine tissues become more sensitive to its effects (Smith & Brennan, 2009). Interestingly, too, oxytocin seems to influence the woman's emotions in ways that help to prepare her psychologically for both the anxieties of labor and the process of bonding with the infant after birth (Neumann, 2008).

At some point, physiological factors within the woman's body, along with biochemical signals from the fetus and placenta, trigger the beginning of labor, a three-stage process. In Stage 1, the uterus contracts, and the cervix flattens out and gradually increases in diameter to about 10 centimeters. The fetus makes its way through the vagina and into the world in Stage 2. Finally, in Stage 3, the woman's uterus expels the placenta.

Immediately after birth, health care professionals assess the health of the **neonate** (newborn baby). Her weight and *gestational age*, the length of the mother's pregnancy, are key factors. **Low-birth-weight babies** are those weighing less than 5.5 pounds. Infants of this weight born at or before the 37th week are considered **preterm infants**. The smaller and more premature the baby, the greater the risk of problems ranging from subtle learning and behavior problems to severe intellectual and physical disabilities (Furdon, 2012). While neonates are dependent upon their caregivers for their basic needs, they do come into this world equipped with some innate abilities.

neonate A newborn infant up to 1 month old.

low-birth-weight baby A baby weighing less than 5.5 pounds.

preterm infant An infant born before the 37th week and weighing less than 5.5 pounds; a premature infant.

Perceptual and Motor Development ▶

Neonates come equipped with an impressive range of **reflexes**—built-in responses to certain stimuli that are needed to ensure survival in their new world. Sucking, swallowing, coughing, and blinking are some necessary behaviors that newborns can perform right away. Newborns will move an arm, a leg, or other body part away from a painful stimulus and will try to remove a blanket or cloth placed over the face. Stroke a baby on the cheek and you will trigger the rooting reflex—the baby opens his or her mouth and actively searches for a nipple. Moreover, all five senses are working at birth, although a number of refinements are still to come.

The newborn already has preferences for certain odors, tastes, sounds, and visual configurations. Hearing is much better developed than vision in the neonate (Busnel, Granier-Deferre, & Lecanuet, 1992). A newborn is able to turn his or her head in the direction of a sound and shows a general preference for female voices. Newborns are able to discriminate among and show preferences for certain odors and tastes (Bartoshuk & Beauchamp, 1994; Leon, 1992). They favor sweet tastes and are able to differentiate between salty, bitter, and sour solutions. Newborns are also sensitive to pain (Porter, Porges, & Marshall, 1988) and are particularly responsive to touch, reacting positively to stroking and fondling (Field, 2002).

Robert Fantz (1961) made a major breakthrough when he realized that a baby's interest in an object can be gauged by the length of time it fixates on it. Fantz demonstrated that infants prefer the image of a human face to other images, such as a black-and-white abstract pattern. Fantz's study and others have shown that newborns have clear preferences and powers of discrimination—and even memory recognition and learning ability.

At birth, an infant's vision is about 20/600, and it typically does not reach 20/20 until the child is about 2 years old (Courage & Adams, 1990; Held, 1993). Newborns focus best on objects about 9 inches away, and they can follow a slowly moving object. Infants from 22 to 93 hours old already indicate a preference for their own mother's face over that of an unfamiliar female (Field et al., 1984). Although newborns prefer colored stimuli to gray ones, they can't distinguish all of the colors adults normally can until they are about 4 months old (Franklin, Pilling, & Davies, 2005).

One famous experiment was devised to study depth perception in infants. Gibson and Walk (1960) designed an apparatus called the **visual cliff**, which is "a board laid across a sheet of heavy glass, with a patterned material directly beneath the glass on one side and several feet below it on the other" (p. 65). This arrangement made it appear that there was a sudden drop-off, or "visual cliff," on one side. Most babies aged 6 to 14 months could be coaxed by their mothers to crawl to the shallow side, but only three would crawl onto the deep side. Gibson and Walk concluded that most babies "can discriminate depth as soon as they can crawl" (p. 64). ☛

8.6 How do infants' abilities change over the first 18 months of life?

reflexes Built-in responses to certain stimuli that neonates need to ensure survival in their new world.

visual cliff An apparatus used to test depth perception in infants.

☛-[Simulate *The Visual Cliff* on **MyPsychLab**

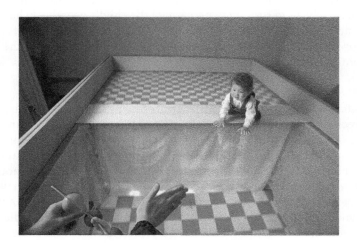

◀ When placed on the visual cliff, most infants older than 6 months will not crawl out over the deep side, indicating that they can perceive depth.

maturation Changes that occur according to one's genetically determined biological timetable of development.

Like perceptual skills, an infant's motor skills become increasingly sophisticated over the first 18 months. The rapid changes in motor skills babies undergo arise primarily because of maturation. **Maturation** occurs naturally according to the infant's own genetically determined biological timetable of development. Many motor milestones, such as sitting, standing, and walking (shown in Figure 8.3), depend on the growth and development of the central nervous system.

Still, experience does have some influence on the development of motor skills. For instance, the rate at which milestones are achieved is slowed when an infant is subjected to extremely unfavorable environmental conditions, such as severe malnutrition or maternal or sensory deprivation. Further, classic cross-cultural research revealed that in some African cultures in Uganda and Kenya, mothers use special motor-training techniques that enable their infants to attain some of the major motor milestones earlier than most infants in the United States (Kilbride & Kilbride, 1975; Super, 1981). But speeding up the attainment of motor skills has no lasting impact on development. Babies will walk, talk, and be toilet trained according to their own developmental schedules.

8.7 How does temperament affect infants' behavior?

temperament A person's behavioral style or characteristic way of responding to the environment.

Temperament

Is each baby born with an individual behavior style or characteristic way of responding to the environment—a particular **temperament**? The New York Longitudinal Study was undertaken in 1956 to investigate temperament and its effect on development. Thomas, Chess, and Birch (1970) studied 2- to 3-month-old infants and followed them into adolescence and adulthood using observation, interviews with parents and teachers, and psychological tests. Three general types of temperament emerged from the study.

"Easy" children—40% of the group studied—had generally pleasant moods, were adaptable, approached new situations and people positively, and established regular sleeping, eating, and elimination patterns. "Difficult" children—10% of the group— had generally unpleasant moods, reacted negatively to new situations and people, were intense in their emotional reactions, and showed irregularity of bodily functions. "Slow-to-warm-up" children—15% of the group—tended to withdraw, were slow to adapt, and were "somewhat negative in mood." The remaining 35% of the children studied were too inconsistent to categorize. ◉

Watch the Video *Temperament* in **MyPsychLab**

Research suggests that variations in infant temperament are strongly influenced by heredity and are somewhat predictive of personality differences later in life (e.g., Saudino, 2012). Thus, most developmentalists who study temperament contend that personality is molded by the continuous interaction of temperament and environment, although the environment can intensify, diminish, or modify these inborn behavioral tendencies. Adjustment in children seems to rest in part on the fit between individual temperament and the accommodation of family and environment to behavioral style. A difficult child may stimulate hostility and resentment in parents and others, which, in turn, may perpetuate the child's negative behavior. On the other hand, an easy child usually elicits a positive response from parents and others, which reinforces the child's behavior and increases the likelihood that the behavioral style will continue.

8.8 What are the causes, characteristics, and consequences of infant–caregiver attachment?

attachment The strong affectionate bond a child forms with the mother or primary caregiver.

Attachment

Almost all infants form a strong **attachment** to their mothers or primary caregivers. But what precisely is the glue that binds caregiver (usually the mother) and infant?

A series of classic studies conducted by Harry Harlow on attachment in rhesus monkeys was critical to developmentalists' understanding of infant–caregiver attachment. Harlow constructed two surrogate (artificial) monkey "mothers." One was a plain wire-mesh cylinder with a blocky wooden head; the other was a wire-mesh cylinder that was padded, covered with soft terry cloth, and fitted with a somewhat more monkey-like head. A baby bottle could be attached to either surrogate mother for feeding. Newborn monkeys were placed in individual cages where they

Lifts head up
2 months

Rolls over
3 months

Sits propped up
3 months

FIGURE 8.3 **The Progression of Motor Development**
Most infants develop motor skills in the sequence shown in the figure. The ages indicated are only averages, so normal, healthy infants may develop any of these milestones a few months earlier or several months later than the average.
Source: Frankenburg et al. (1992).

Sits without support
6 months

Stands holding on
7 months

Walks holding on
9 months

Stands momentarily
10 months

Stands alone
11 months

Walks alone
12 months

Walks backwards
14 months

Walks up steps
17 months

Kicks ball forward
18 months

had equal access to a cloth surrogate and a wire surrogate. The source of their nourishment (cloth or wire surrogate) was unimportant. "The infants developed a strong attachment to the cloth mothers and little or none to the wire mothers" (Harlow & Harlow, 1962, p. 141). Harlow found that it was *contact comfort*—the comfort supplied by bodily contact—rather than nourishment that formed the basis of the infant monkey's attachment to its mother. If the cloth mother was not present when unfamiliar objects were placed in the cage, the monkey would huddle in the corner, clutching its head, rocking, sucking its thumb or toes, and crying in distress. But, when the cloth mother was present, it would first cling to her and then explore and play with the unfamiliar objects.

▲ Harlow found that infant monkeys developed a strong attachment to a cloth-covered surrogate mother and little or no attachment to a wire surrogate mother—even when the wire mother provided nourishment.

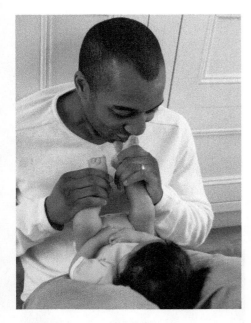

▲ Fathers tend to engage in more physical play with their children than mothers. However, many fathers today share basic child-care responsibilities, such as feeding and diaper changing, with mothers.

👁 Watch the Video *Episode 9: Basics: Attachment* in **MyPsychLab**

Numerous studies have shown that the attachment process is similar in human infants (Posada et al., 2002). The mother holds, strokes, and talks to the baby and responds to the baby's needs, and the baby gazes at and listens to the mother and even moves in synchrony with her voice (Condon & Sander, 1974; Lester, Hoffman, & Brazelton, 1985). Once the attachment has formed, infants show **separation anxiety**—fear and distress when the parent leaves them. Occurring from about 8 months to 24 months, separation anxiety peaks between 12 and 18 months of age (Fox & Bell, 1990). At about 6 or 7 months of age, infants develop a fear of strangers called **stranger anxiety**, which increases in intensity until the first birthday and then declines in the second year (Marks, 1987). Stranger anxiety is greater in an unfamiliar setting, when the parent is not close at hand, and when a stranger abruptly approaches or touches the child.

There are important differences in the quality of attachment. In a classic study of mother–child attachment, Mary Ainsworth (1973, 1979) observed mother–child interactions in the home during the infants' first year and then again at age 12 months in a laboratory. Based on infants' reactions to their mothers after brief periods of separation, Ainsworth and others (1978; Main & Solomon, 1990) identified four patterns of attachment.

The first pattern is *secure attachment* (observed in about 65% of American infants). Although usually distressed when separated from their mother, securely attached infants eagerly seek to reestablish the connection and then show an interest in play. They use the mother as a safe base of operation from which to explore and are typically more responsive, obedient, cooperative, and content than other infants. In addition, secure attachment seems to protect infants from the potentially adverse effects of risk factors such as poverty (Belsky & Fearon, 2002). Further, preschoolers who were securely attached as infants display more advanced social skills, such as the ability to maintain friendships, than peers who were not securely attached to their caregivers (McElwain & Volling, 2004).

Infants with a pattern called *avoidant attachment* (approximately 20% of American infants) are usually not responsive to their mother when she is present and not troubled when she leaves. When the parent returns, the infant may actively avoid contact with her or, at least, not be quick to greet her. In short, these infants do not act much more attached to the parent than to a stranger.

Prior to a period of separation, infants who show *resistant attachment* (10 to 15% of American infants) seek and prefer close contact with their mother. Yet, in contrast to securely attached infants, they do not tend to branch out and explore. And when the mother returns to the room after a period of separation, the resistant infant displays anger and may push the mother away or hit her. When picked up, the infant is hard to comfort and may continue crying.

The pattern of *disorganized/disoriented attachment* (seen in 5 to 10% of American infants) is the most puzzling and apparently the least secure pattern. When reunited with the mother, the infant with this pattern of attachment exhibits contradictory and disoriented responses. Rather than looking at the mother while being held, the child may purposely look away or approach the mother with an expressionless or depressed demeanor. Also characteristic are a dazed and vacant facial expression and a peculiar, frozen posture after being calmed by the mother. 👁

Although mother–child, rather than father–child, attachment relationships have been the traditional focus of research, fathers can be as responsive and competent as mothers (Roberts & Moseley, 1996), and their attachments can be just as strong. Indeed, father–child interactions have many enduring positive influences on children (Stein, Milburn, Zane, & Rotheram-Borus, 2009; Verissimo et al., 2011). Children who experience regular interaction with their fathers tend to have higher IQs and to do better in social situations and at coping with frustration than children lacking such interaction. They also persist longer in solving problems and are less impulsive and less likely to become violent. Positive father–son relationships are also associated with higher-quality parenting behavior by sons when they have children of their own (Shears, Robinson, & Emde, 2002).

Interactions with fathers may be important for development because mothers and fathers interact differently with infants and children. Fathers engage in more exciting and arousing physical play with children (Paquette, 2004). Mothers are more likely to protect their children from overstimulation and potential injury. By contrast, fathers allow infants to crawl farther away, up to twice as far as mothers usually allow. And fathers remain farther away as the infant explores novel stimuli and situations. Ideally, of course, children need both kinds of influences.

REMEMBER IT   *Check your answers and take additional quizzes in MyPsychLab.com.*   ✓●─ Study and **Review** on **MyPsychLab**

1. Because many body structures are at critical periods of development during this time, a teratogen is most likely to cause defects during the _____ stage.

2. _____ follows an infant's own genetically determined timetable of development.

3. Newborns have 20/20 vision. (true/false)

4. Children who have pleasant moods and positive attitudes toward new situations and people have _____ temperaments.

5. Infants who are attached to caregivers show _____ when their caregivers leave them.

Early and Middle Childhood

Think about how remarkable it is that, at birth, an infant's only means of communication is crying, but by age 11 or so, the average child has a vocabulary of more than 60,000 words (Anglin, 1995). Mastery of language, both spoken and written, is just one of several important developmental processes that happen in early (ages 2 to 6) and middle (ages 6 to puberty) childhood.

Language Development ▶

During their first few months, infants communicate distress or displeasure through crying. But then they begin rapidly to acquire language. Language development depends on both physical maturation, especially of the brain, and linguistic input from the environment. If children do not have access to human language during the first 2 years of life, their ability to acquire language and other cognitive skills is permanently impaired (Baird, 2010). Thus, these years are a critical period (remember our discussion of critical periods on page 265) for language development. ◉

Phases of Language Development. During the second or third month, infants begin *cooing*—repeatedly uttering vowel sounds such as "ah" and "oo." At about 4 to 6 months, infants begin **babbling**. They utter *phonemes*—the basic speech sounds of any language, which form words when combined. During the first part of the babbling stage, infants babble all the basic speech sounds that occur in all the languages of the world. Language up to this point seems to be biologically determined, because all babies throughout the world, even deaf children, vocalize this same range of speech sounds.

At about 8 months, babies begin to focus attention on those speech sounds (phonemes) common to the language spoken around them and on the rhythm and intonation of that language. And by 1 year, the babbling stage gives way to the one-word stage. The first words usually represent objects that move or those that infants can act on or interact with. From 13 to 18 months of age, children markedly increase their vocabulary (Woodward, Markham, & Fitzsimmons, 1994), and 2-year-olds know about 270 words (Brown, 1973).

Initially a child's understanding of words differs from that of an adult. When they lack the correct word, children may act on the basis of shared features and apply a word to a broader range of objects than is appropriate. This is known as **overextension**.

8.9 What are the phases of language development, and how do various theorists explain them?

◉─ **Watch** the Video *Episode 9: Thinking Like a Psychologist: Smart Babies by Design* in **MyPsychLab**

babbling Vocalization of the basic speech sounds (phonemes), which begins between 4 and 6 months.

overextension The act of using a word, on the basis of some shared feature, to apply to a broader range of objects than is appropriate.

underextension Restricting the use of a word to only a few, rather than to all, members of a class of objects.

For example, any man may be called "dada" and any four-legged animal, "doggie." **Underextension** occurs, too; this is when children fail to apply a word to other members of the class. The family's poodle is a "doggie," but the German shepherd next door is not.

Between 18 and 20 months of age, when their vocabulary is about 50 words, children begin to put nouns, verbs, and adjectives together in two-word phrases and sentences. At this stage, children depend to a great extent on gesture, tone, and context to convey their meaning (Slobin, 1972). Depending on intonation, their sentences may indicate questions, statements, or possession. Children adhere to a rigid word order. You might hear "mama drink," "drink milk," or "mama milk," but not "drink mama," "milk drink," or "milk mama."

telegraphic speech Short sentences that follow a strict word order and contain only essential content words.

Between 2 and 3 years of age, children begin to use short sentences, which may contain three or more words. Labeled **telegraphic speech** by Roger Brown (1973), these short sentences follow a rigid word order and contain only essential content words, leaving out all plurals, possessives, conjunctions, articles, and prepositions. Telegraphic speech reflects the child's understanding of *syntax*—the rules governing how words are ordered in a sentence. When a third word is added to a sentence, it usually fills in the word missing from the two-word sentence (for example, "mama drink milk"). After using telegraphic speech for a time, children gradually begin to add modifiers to make their sentences more precise.

overregularization The act of inappropriately applying the grammatical rules for forming plurals and past tenses to irregular nouns and verbs.

Children pick up grammatical rules intuitively and apply them rigidly. **Overregularization** is the kind of error that results when a grammatical rule is misapplied to a word that has an irregular plural or past tense (Marcus, 1996). Thus, children who have correctly used the words "went," "came," and "did" incorrectly apply the rule for past tenses and begin to say "goed," "comed," and "doed." What the parents see as a regression in speech actually means that the child has acquired a grammatical rule. ◉

◉ Watch the Video *Learning Language* in **MyPsychLab**

Theories of Language Development. Developmentalists who adopt the *learning perspective* have long maintained that language is acquired in the same way as other behaviors—as a result of learning through reinforcement and imitation. B. F. Skinner (1957) asserted that parents selectively criticize incorrect speech and reinforce correct speech through praise, approval, and attention. Thus, the child's utterances are progressively shaped in the direction of grammatically correct speech. Others argue that children acquire vocabulary and sentence construction mainly through imitation (Bandura, 1977). However, imitation cannot account for patterns of speech such as telegraphic speech or for systematic errors such as overregularization. Moreover, parents seem to reinforce children more for the content of the utterance than for the correctness of the grammar (Brown, Cazden, & Bellugi, 1968).

Noam Chomsky (1957) strongly opposes learning theorists' explanations of language development. He argues that the brain contains a *language acquisition device (LAD),* which enables children to acquire language and discover the rules of grammar easily and naturally, an approach known as the *nativist perspective* (Chomsky, 1968). His research and that of others has shown that language develops in stages that occur in a fixed order and appear at about the same times in most normal children (MacWhinney, 2011). Thus, it appears that biological maturation underlies language development in much the same way as it underlies physical and motor development.

The nativist perspective is better able than learning perspective to account for the fact that children throughout the world go through the same basic stages in language development. It also accounts for the similar errors all children make when they are first learning to form plurals, past tenses, and negatives. As you read earlier, these errors involve overregularization and, consequently, cannot be acquired through imitation and reinforcement. No parent speaking naturally says "Yesterday we wented to the store." By contrast, the normal speech of toddlers and preschoolers includes many such expressions. Nativists argue that these errors reflect the capacity of the young child's mind for extracting rules from natural language and applying them to their own speech.

Nevertheless, some environmental factors do contribute to language development. For example, babies whose parents are responsive to their babbling vocalize more than infants whose parents are not responsive to them (Whitehurst et al., 1989). Moreover, parents can facilitate language acquisition by adjusting their speech to their infant's level of development. Parents often use *motherese*—highly simplified speech with shorter phrases and sentences and simpler vocabulary, which is uttered slowly, at a high pitch, and with exaggerated intonation and much repetition (Fernald, 1993; R. Jones, 2003). Mothers who are deaf communicate with their infants in a similar way, signing more slowly and with exaggerated hand and arm movements and frequent repetition (Masataka, 1996). Thus, most researchers endorse an *interactionist* approach to explaining language development that acknowledges the crucial role of infants' apparently inborn capacity for acquiring language but also recognizes that environmental influences contribute to language development as well (MacWhinney, 2005).

Literacy. Throughout the industrialized world, children must master written as well as spoken language. As you might expect, many aspects of the development of spoken language are critical to the process of learning to read. *Phonological awareness,* or sensitivity to the sound patterns of a language and how they are represented as letters, is particularly important. Children who can correctly answer questions such as "What would bat be if you took away the [b]?" by the age of 4 or so learn to read more rapidly than their peers who cannot (Pearson & Cervetti, 2013). Moreover, children who have good phonological awareness skills in their first language learn to read more easily even when reading instruction is conducted in a second language (Mumtaz & Humphreys, 2002; Quiroga et al., 2002).

Children seem to learn phonological awareness skills through word play. Among English-speaking children, learning nursery rhymes facilitates the development of these skills (Layton et al., 1996). Japanese parents foster phonological awareness in their children by playing a game with them called *shiritori,* in which one person says a word and another must supply a word that begins with its ending sound (Serpell & Hatano, 1997). Activities in which parents and children work together to read or write a story also foster the development of phonological awareness (Aram & Levitt, 2002). Developments in language lead to greater socialization in children. Let's take a look at the social developments that occur in early and middle childhood.

Socialization ▶

The process of learning socially acceptable behaviors, attitudes, and values is called **socialization**. Although parents have the major role in their children's socialization, peers affect the process as well. 👁

Parenting Styles. The methods parents use to control children's behavior also contribute to socialization. Diane Baumrind (1971, 1980, 1991) studied the continuum of parental control and identified three parenting styles: authoritarian, authoritative, and permissive. Each style appears to have distinctive effects on children's behavior.

Authoritarian parents make the rules, expect unquestioned obedience from their children, punish misbehavior (often physically), and value obedience to authority. Rather than giving a rationale for a rule, authoritarian parents consider "because I said so" a sufficient reason for obedience. Parents using this parenting style tend to be uncommunicative, unresponsive, and somewhat distant, and Baumrind (1967) found preschool children disciplined in this manner to be withdrawn, anxious, and unhappy. The authoritarian style has been associated with low intellectual performance and lack of social skills, especially in boys (Maccoby & Martin, 1983). However, research suggests that there are some circumstances in which authoritarian parenting is beneficial to children's development. For instance, children of authoritarian parents who live in impoverished neighborhoods display more favorable developmental outcomes than their peers whose parents are more permissive (Steinberg, Blatt-Eisengart, & Cauffman, 2006).

Authoritative parents set high but realistic and reasonable standards, enforce limits, and at the same time encourage open communication and independence. They are willing to discuss rules and supply rationales for them. Knowing why the rules are

▲ Mothers who are deaf use sign language to communicate with their young children, but they do so in *motherese,* signing slowly and with frequent repetitions.

8.10 What do parenting styles and peer relationships contribute to socialization?

👁 Watch the Video *Episode 9: In the Real World: Parenting Styles and Socialization* in **MyPsychLab**

socialization The process of learning socially acceptable behaviors, attitudes, and values.

authoritarian parents Parents who make arbitrary rules, expect unquestioned obedience from their children, punish transgressions, and value obedience to authority.

authoritative parents Parents who set high but realistic standards, reason with the child, enforce limits, and encourage open communication and independence.

necessary makes it easier for children to internalize them and to follow them, whether in the presence of their parents or not. Authoritative parents are generally warm, nurturant, supportive, and responsive, and they show respect for their children and their opinions. Their children are more mature, happy, self-reliant, self-controlled, assertive, socially competent, and responsible than their peers. The authoritative parenting style is associated with higher academic performance, independence, higher self-esteem, and internalized moral standards in middle childhood and adolescence (Lamborn et al., 1991; Steinberg, Elman, & Mounts, 1989).

permissive parents Parents who make few rules or demands and allow children to make their own decisions and control their own behavior.

Permissive parents make few rules or demands and usually do not enforce those that are made. They allow children to make their own decisions and control their own behavior. Parents in the sub-category *permissive-indulgent* are warm and supportive. They may believe that permissiveness is a way of expressing affection for their children or of maintaining children's affection for them. Children raised in this manner are the most immature, impulsive, and dependent, and they seem to be the least self-controlled and self-reliant (Steinberg et al., 2006).

Permissive parents in the *permissive-neglectful* sub-category lack warmth. They allow children to do as they please because they are not interested in them or in supporting their development (Maccoby & Martin, 1983). This parenting style is associated with drinking problems, promiscuous sex, delinquent behavior, and poor academic performance in adolescents.

The positive effects of authoritative parenting have been found across all ethnic groups in the United States (Querido, Warner, & Eyberg, 2002; Sorkhabi & Mandara, 2013; Steinberg & Dornbusch, 1991). The one exception is among first-generation Asian immigrants, where the authoritarian style is more strongly associated with academic achievement (Chao, 2001). Developmental psychologist Ruth Chao suggests that this finding may be explained by the traditional idea in Asian culture that making a child obey is an act of affection (Chao & Aque, 2009). Moreover, strict parenting tends to be tempered by emotional warmth in Asian families, so children probably get the idea that their parents expect unquestioning obedience because they love them. However, research also shows that the longer first-generation immigrants have lived in the United States, the more the pattern of association between authoritative parenting and social competence resembles that found in other groups (Kim & Chung, 2003).

Peer Relationships. Friendships begin to develop by the age of 3 or 4, and relationships with peers become increasingly important. These early relationships are usually based on shared activities; two children think of themselves as friends while they are playing together. During the elementary school years, friendships tend to be based on mutual trust (Dunn, Cutting, & Fisher, 2002). By middle childhood, membership in a peer group is central to a child's happiness. Peer groups are usually composed of children of the same race, sex, and social class (Schofield & Francis, 1982). The peer group serves a socializing function by providing models of behavior, dress, and language. Peer groups provide objective measures against which children can evaluate their own traits. They are also a continuing source of both reinforcement for appropriate behavior and punishment for deviant behavior. In fact, peer rejection often results in excessive aggression (Wood, Cowan, & Baker, 2002). Research indicates that children who are rejected by their peers are at greater risk of developing bullying behavior than peers who are socially accepted (Smith et al., 2012).

8.11 How do theorists explain gender role development?

Gender Role Development

Traditionally, males have been expected to be independent and competitive; females have been expected to be warm and nurturant. Psychologists use the term **gender roles** to refer to such expectations. Children display play behavior that is consistent with gender roles fairly early in life, by age 2 or so. Psychologists differ in how they explain gender role development. (Note that *gender role* is not the same thing as *sexual orientation*, a topic that you will read about in Chapter 9.)

gender roles Cultural expectations about the behavior appropriate for each gender.

According to the biological view, genes and prenatal sex hormones have an important influence on gender role development. In a review of studies on the effects of prenatal androgens (male sex hormones), Collaer and Hines (1995) found that these hormones have a reasonably strong influence on children's play behavior. Girls exposed to prenatal androgens, usually as a result of sharing the womb with a male twin, are more likely than girls not exposed to these hormones to prefer to play with toys favored by boys, such as trucks, cars, and fire engines (Berenbaum & Snyder, 1995). Prenatal androgens are also known to affect brain development and functioning in humans and many other animal species (Beyenburg et al., 2000).

Of course, biological influences on gender role development don't operate in an environmental vacuum. For example, from infancy on, most of the presents children receive are gender consistent: Girls are given dolls and tea sets, while boys get trucks and sports equipment. And while a girl may feel complimented if someone calls her a "tomboy," almost every boy considers it an insult to be called a "sissy" (Doyle & Paludi, 1995).

As you might expect, for *social learning theorists* environmental influences are considered more important than biological forces in explaining gender role development (Mischel, 1966). These theorists point out that children are usually reinforced for imitating behaviors considered appropriate for their gender. When behaviors are not appropriate (a boy puts on lipstick, or a girl pretends to shave her face), children are quickly informed, often in a reprimanding tone, that boys or girls do not do that. However, there is little evidence that parents reinforce gender role–appropriate behavior in girls and boys often enough to account for the early age at which children begin to show gender-typed behavior (Fagot, 1995). Thus, imitation and reinforcement probably play some part in gender role development, but they do not provide a full explanation of this phenomenon.

Cognitive developmental theory, proposed by Lawrence Kohlberg (1966; Kohlberg & Ullian, 1974), suggests that an understanding of gender is a prerequisite to gender role development. According to Kohlberg, children go through a series of stages in acquiring the concept of gender. Between ages 2 and 3, children acquire *gender identity*—their sense of being a male or a female. Between ages 4 and 5, children acquire the concept of *gender stability*—awareness that boys are boys and girls are girls for a lifetime. Finally, between ages 6 and 8, children understand *gender constancy*—that gender does not change regardless of the activities people engage in or the clothes they wear. Moreover, according to Kohlberg, when children realize their gender is permanent, they are motivated to seek out same-sex models and learn to act in ways considered appropriate for their gender.

Cross-cultural studies reveal that Kohlberg's stages of gender identity, gender stability, and gender constancy occur in the same order in cultures as different as those in Samoa, Kenya, Nepal, and Belize (Munroe, Shimmin, & Munroe, 1984). Moreover, research shows that children's knowledge of gender stereotypes and the value that they attach to being male or female increase as they progress through the gender stability and constancy stages (Ruble et al., 2007). However, this theory fails to explain why many gender-appropriate behaviors and preferences are observed in children as young as age 2 or 3, long before gender constancy is acquired (Bussey & Bandura, 1999; Jacklin, 1989; Martin & Little, 1990).

Gender-schema theory, proposed by Sandra Bem (1981), provides a more complete explanation of gender role development. Like social learning theory, gender-schema theory suggests that young children are motivated to pay attention to and behave in a way consistent with gender-based standards and stereotypes of the culture. Like cognitive developmental theory, gender-schema theory stresses that children begin to use gender as a way to organize and process information (Bussey & Bandura, 1999; Martin & Ruble, 2002). But, gender-schema theory holds that this process occurs earlier, when gender identity rather than gender constancy is attained, and children exhibit strong preferences for sex-appropriate toys and clothing and favor same-sex peers over those of the other sex (Powlishta, 1995). To a large extent, children's self-concepts and self-esteem depend on the match between their abilities and behaviors and the cultural definition of what is desirable for their gender. Consequently, the desire to maintain self-esteem, according to gender-schema theory, motivates children to align their behavior with culturally defined gender roles.

▲ Theorists differ in their explanations for gender differences in play preferences. Learning theorists emphasize the effects of models. Cognitive developmental theorists propose that gender role development is a consequence of general cognitive development. Gender-schema theories use the information-processing approach to explain these differences. What do you think?

Adolescence

adolescence The developmental stage that begins at puberty and encompasses the period from the end of childhood to the beginning of adulthood.

The concept of **adolescence**—a period of transition from childhood to adulthood—did not exist until psychologist G. Stanley Hall first wrote about it in his book by that name in 1904. He portrayed this stage in life as one of "storm and stress," the inevitable result of biological changes occurring during the period.

8.12 How does puberty influence adolescents' bodies, self-concepts, and behavior?

Puberty and Sexual Behavior

puberty A period of rapid physical growth and change that culminates in sexual maturity.

Adolescence begins with the onset of **puberty**—a period of rapid physical growth and change that culminates in sexual maturity. Although the average onset of puberty is age 10 for girls and age 12 for boys, the normal range extends from age 7 to age 14 for girls and from 9 to 16 for boys (Tanner, 1990). Puberty begins with a surge in hormone production followed by a marked acceleration in growth known as the *adolescent growth spurt*. On average, the growth spurt occurs from age 10 to 13 in girls and about 2 years later in boys, from age 12 to 15 (Tanner, 1990). Girls attain their full height between ages 16 and 17 and boys between ages 18 and 20 (Tanner, 1990).

secondary sex characteristics Those physical characteristics that are not directly involved in reproduction but distinguish the mature male from the mature female.

During puberty, the reproductive organs in both sexes mature and **secondary sex characteristics** appear—those physical characteristics not directly involved in reproduction that distinguish the mature male from the mature female. In girls, the breasts develop, and the hips round; in boys, the voice deepens, and facial and chest hair appears; and in both sexes, there is growth of pubic and underarm (axillary) hair. The major landmark of puberty for males is the first ejaculation, which occurs, on average, at age 13 (Jorgensen & Keiding, 1991). For females, it is **menarche**—the onset of menstruation—which occurs, on average, between the ages of 12 and 13, although from 9 to 16 is considered the normal range (Blake & Davis, 2011).

menarche (men-AR-kee) The onset of menstruation.

The timing of puberty can have important psychological consequences, coming as it does at a time when a sense of security is gained from being like other members of the peer group. Many studies show that early-maturing boys, taller and stronger than their classmates, have an advantage in sports and are likely to have a positive body image; to feel confident, secure, independent, and happy; and to be more successful academically (Susman & Dorn, 2009). However, early-maturing boys may also be more hostile and aggressive than later-maturing peers (Arim & Shapka, 2008). In addition, earlier-than-average puberty is correlated with affiliation with deviant peers and substance abuse (Westling, Andrews, Hampton, & Peterson, 2008).

Early-maturing girls, who may tower over their peers, feel more self-conscious about their developing bodies and their size. Consequently, they are more likely than late-maturing girls to develop eating disorders (Kaltiala-Heino et al., 2001). In addition to having earlier sexual experiences and more unwanted pregnancies than late-maturing girls, early-maturing girls are more likely to be exposed to alcohol and drug use (Caspi et al., 1993; Cavanaugh, 2004). Late-maturing girls often experience considerable stress when they fail to develop physically along with their peers, but they are likely to be taller and slimmer than their early-maturing age mates.

Puberty brings with it the awakening of sexual desire. As Figure 8.4 indicates, the incidence of sexual activity among teenagers in the United States increases

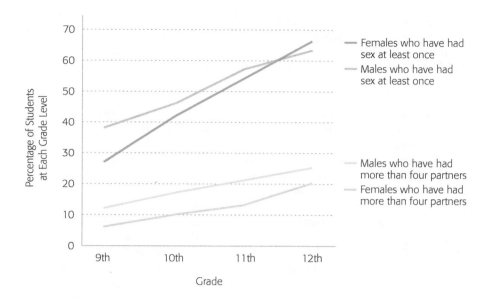

FIGURE 8.4 **Incidence of Sexual Activity in U.S. High School Students**
This graph shows that the proportions of sexually active boys and girls increase dramatically from grade 9 to 12.
Source: Data from Eaton, 2012.

dramatically across grades 9 to 12 (Eaton et al., 2012). One particularly alarming statistic is the proportion of teens who have had multiple sex partners before leaving high school, because the more partners an individual has (whether teen or adult), the more likely he or she is to contract a sexually transmitted disease.

In addition, the rate of teenage pregnancy is higher in the United States than in any other developed country. For example, there are about 34 births per year for every 1,000 teenage girls in the United States, while the rate is less than 7 per 1,000 in Japan, Korea, Switzerland, the Netherlands, and Sweden (Hamilton & Ventura, 2012; Kmietowicz, 2002). It's important to keep in mind, though, that most teen pregnancies occur after the age of 16 and that the incidence of teen pregnancy has actually declined in the United States since the 1960s. What has increased is the number of births to *unmarried* adolescent mothers. In the 1960s, about 80% of teen mothers were married, compared with only 20% today (Martin et al., 2003).

Teens who tend to be less experienced sexually attend religious services frequently and live with both biological parents, who are neither too permissive nor too strict in their discipline and rules (Blinn-Pike et al., 2004; Miller et al., 1998; White & DeBlassie, 1992). Early intercourse is also less prevalent among adolescents whose academic achievement is above average and who are involved in sports (Brooks-Gunn & Furstenberg, 1989; Savage & Holcomb, 1999).

Social Relationships ▶

Most adolescents have good relationships with their parents (Morris, Cui, & Steinberg, 2013). In fact, research shows that good relationships with parents are important to the development of self-esteem in adolescents (Wilkinson, 2004). Moreover, of the three parenting styles discussed earlier in the chapter—authoritative, authoritarian, and permissive—the authoritative style appears to be most effective and the permissive least effective for adolescents (Baumrind, 1991; Sorkhabi & Mandara, 2013; Steinberg et al., 1994). In a classic study of about 2,300 adolescents, those with permissive parents were more likely to use alcohol and drugs and to have conduct problems and less likely to be interested in academic success than were those with authoritative or authoritarian parents (Lamborn et al., 1991). The authoritarian style was related to more psychological distress and less self-reliance and self-confidence in adolescents.

Even adolescents who have good relationships with their parents usually feel the need to separate from them to some degree. As a result, friends become a vital source of emotional support and approval for most of them. Interactions with peers are critical while young people are forming their identities. Adolescents can try out different

8.13 What do parents and peers contribute to teens' development?

roles and observe the reactions of their friends to their behavior and their appearance. The peer group provides teenagers with a standard of comparison for evaluating their personal assets, as well as a vehicle for developing social skills (Berndt, 1992). Read the *Explain It* feature to learn more about the importance of peer groups.

8.14 What are the characteristics of emerging adulthood?

Emerging Adulthood

Physically speaking, the body is fully mature by age 18. There are varied legal definitions of adulthood—voting age, drinking age, and the like. But what are the psychological and social criteria that distinguish an adolescent from an adult? In search of an answer to this question, developmental psychologist Jeffrey Arnett has proposed that the educational, social, and economic demands of modern culture have given rise to a new developmental period he calls **emerging adulthood**, the period from the late teens to the early 20s when individuals experiment with options prior to taking on adult roles (Arnett, 2011). Arnett's studies and those of other researchers indicate that, at least in the United States, young people do not tend to think of themselves as having fully attained adulthood until the age of 25 or so (Galambos, Turner, & Tilton-Weaver, 2005).

emerging adulthood The period from the late teens to early 20s when individuals explore options prior to committing to adult roles.

Neuroimaging studies have provided some support for the notion that emerging adulthood is a unique period of life. These studies suggest that the parts of the brain that underlie rational decision making, impulse control, and self-regulation mature during these years (Crone et al., 2006; Gogtay et al., 2004). As a result, during

---

EXPLAIN IT   **Why Are Peer Groups Important in Adolescence?**

Several years ago, residents of an upscale suburb of Houston, Texas, were shocked when they learned that a group of teenaged girls from their community, armed with handguns, had been responsible for a string of convenience store holdups. When arrested, the girls characterized the robberies as "entertainment" and revealed that they had named their group the "Queens of Armed Robbery." Why would teenagers who, at least in a material sense, had everything they could want or need turn to armed robbery for amusement? Think for a moment about how the features of Erikson's identity versus role confusion stage might be used to explain some teenagers' attraction to gangs.

In traditional societies, teenagers are initiated into adult roles through formal rites of passage at around the same time that they go through puberty. Afterward, boys either enter adult occupations or became apprentices. Girls marry or devote themselves to acquiring domestic skills in preparation for marriage. Teenagers who live in such societies rarely experience doubts about what their adult roles will be and how to transition into them. By contrast, there are no longer any formal rites of passage in the industrialized world, and teenagers are expected to develop their own pathways to adulthood. Moreover, society provides them with no formal role of their own; they are too old for some activities but too young for others. As a result, the state that Erikson called "role confusion," together with all of its associated anxieties, is a daily experience for most teenagers.

Erikson thought that peer groups help teenagers cope with the stress of role confusion by providing them with a temporary resolution, a temporary identity, if you will (Erikson, 1968). To facilitate this temporary identity, group members dress similarly, listen to the same bands, go places together, share criticisms of other groups, and develop standards for what constitutes an acceptable plan for the future. Some of these groups have informal names, such as "jocks" or "nerds" or "preps."

For most teens, group membership serves a constructive purpose by providing them with an escape from the anxieties that go along with being in limbo between childhood and adulthood. But for others, the drive to gain an identity through group membership leads to a self-destructive pathway, one that will interfere with their transition into the adult world. Teen groups whose bonds are maintained through substance abuse represent one example of this kind of group. Likewise, when adolescents forge their bonds with others through criminal activities, they risk not only their present status and comfort but also their future adult roles. This message was driven home to several members of the "Queens of Armed Robbery" who, at age 17, were considered adults under Texas criminal law. The crime spree they referred to as "entertainment" netted them several years in prison. Thus, the temporary reprieve from role confusion that these girls enjoyed ultimately undermined their journey to adulthood.

Of course, the experiences of the "Queens of Armed Robbery" seem somewhat benign when compared to those of teens who, for the same psychosocial reasons, get caught up in violent gangs that endanger not only their pathway to adulthood but their very lives. Erikson suggested that in contrast to other kinds of teenaged groups, society responds to criminally oriented youth gangs by viewing their members collectively rather than as individuals, thereby confirming members' use of the gang as a means of avoiding role confusion (Erikson & Erikson, 1957). To forestall an individual teenager's making a lifelong commitment to a criminal identity, he argued, society should develop policies that allow officials to deal with gang activity at the level of the individual gang member. Thus, Erikson would endorse policies in which school administrators, judges, and other authorities are given a certain degree of latitude in deciding how individual youthful offenders should be dealt with.

Watch on **MyPsychLab**

adolescence and early on in emerging adulthood i, individuals make poorer decisions about matters such as risky behaviors (e.g., unprotected sex) than they do when these brain areas reach full maturity in the early to mid-20s. ◉

The neurological changes of the emerging adult period combine with cultural demands to shape the psychosocial features of this period of development. Researcher Glenn Roisman and his colleagues have hypothesized that emerging adults must address developmental tasks in five domains: academic, friendship, conduct, work, and romantic (Roisman et al., 2004). Roisman's research suggests that skills within the first three of these domains transfer easily from adolescence to adulthood. By contrast, emerging adults must approach the work and romantic domains differently than they did as adolescents. Certainly, many teenagers have jobs and are involved in romances. However, the cultural expectations associated with emerging adulthood require them to commit to a career path that will enable them to achieve full economic independence from their families. Likewise, emerging adults must make decisions about the place of long-term romantic relationships in their present and future lives as well as participate in such relationships. As predicted by his hypothesis, Roisman's findings and those of other researchers suggest that emerging adults experience more adjustment difficulties related to these two domains than they do in the academic, friendship, and conduct domains (Korobov & Thorne, 2006).

◉ **Watch** the Video *Episode 9: Special Topics: Risky Behavior and Brain Development* in **MyPsychLab**

REMEMBER IT

Check your answers and take additional quizzes in MyPsychLab.com. ✓●―[Study and **Review** on **MyPsychLab**

1. _____ sex characteristics are physical characteristics that are directly involved in reproduction.
2. _____ are a vital source of support and approval for most adolescents.
3. Research indicates that the part of the brain that controls _____, _____, and _____ matures during emerging adulthood.

Early and Middle Adulthood

As noted earlier, the long period of 50 or more years known as adulthood is generally divided into three parts: young or early adulthood (ages 20 to 40 or 45), middle adulthood (ages 40 or 45 to 65), and late adulthood (after age 65 or 70). These ages are only approximate because there are no biological or psychological events that neatly define the beginning or ending of a period. Obviously, some things change; but, in many ways, adults remain much the same as they were in their earlier years. The most obvious changes are usually physical ones. ◉

◉ **Watch** the Video *Episode 9: Big Picture: Different Perspectives* in **MyPsychLab**

Physical and Cognitive Changes ▶

8.15 How do the body and mind change in early and middle adulthood?

Most people enjoy good general health and vitality in their 20s and 30s, but the first of these decades is the period of top physical condition, when physical strength, reaction time, reproductive capacity, and fine motor skills all peak. After age 30, there is a slight decline in these physical capacities, which is barely perceptible to most people other than professional athletes. Middle-aged people often complain about a loss of physical vigor and endurance. But such losses have to do less with aging than with exercise, diet, and health habits (Boul, 2003). One unavoidable change in the mid- to late 40s, though, is **presbyopia**, a condition in which the lenses of the eyes no longer accommodate adequately for near vision, and reading glasses or bifocals are required for reading.

The major biological event for women during middle age is **menopause**—the cessation of menstruation, which usually occurs between ages 45 and 55 and signifies the end of reproductive capacity. The most common symptom associated with menopause and the sharp decrease in the level of estrogen is *hot flashes*—sudden feelings of being uncomfortably hot. Some women also experience symptoms such as anxiety, irritability, and/or mood swings.

presbyopia (prez-bee-O-pee-uh) A condition, occurring in the mid- to late 40s, in which the lenses of the eyes no longer accommodate adequately for near vision, and reading glasses or bifocals are required for reading.

menopause The cessation of menstruation, occurring between ages 45 and 55 and signifying the end of reproductive capacity.

Although men do not have a physical event equivalent to menopause, they do experience a gradual decline in testosterone from age 20 until about age 60. During late middle age, many men also experience a reduction in the functioning of the prostate gland that affects the production of semen. Usually coupled with these reductions in testosterone and semen production is a reduction in the sex drive. Still, in contrast to women, men are capable of fathering a child throughout their lives. However, the DNA carried by their sperm show increasing amounts of fragmentation as they get older (Wyrobek, 2006). Scientists have not yet determined if or how damage of this kind is linked to either male fertility or to pregnancy outcomes.

Changes in intellectual functioning also occur across the early and middle adulthood years. However, they're a bit more complicated than you might think. For example, young adults outperform middle-aged and older adults on tests requiring speed or rote memory. But on tests measuring general information, vocabulary, reasoning ability, and social judgment, older participants usually do better than younger ones because of their greater experience and education (Salthouse, 2004). Adults actually continue to gain knowledge and skills over the years, particularly when they lead intellectually challenging lives.

Schaie and his colleagues (Gerstorf et al., 2011; Schaie, 2005) analyzed data from the Seattle Longitudinal Study, which assessed the intellectual abilities of some 5,000 participants. Many of the participants were tested six times over the course of 50 years. Schaie found that in five areas—verbal meaning, spatial orientation, inductive reasoning, numerical reasoning, and word fluency—participants showed modest gains from young adulthood to the mid-40s. Decline did not occur, on average, until after age 60, and even then the decline was modest until the 80s. Half of the participants, even at age 81, showed no decline compared to their earlier performance. The study also revealed several gender differences: Females performed better on tests of verbal meaning and reasoning; males tended to do better on tests of numerical reasoning and spatial orientation. The only ability found to show a continuous decline from the mid-20s to the 80s was perceptual speed.

To better understand changes in intellectual functioning in adulthood, researchers often distinguish between two types of intelligence (Horn, 1982): **Crystallized intelligence**—one's verbal ability and accumulated knowledge—tends to increase over the life span. **Fluid intelligence**—abstract reasoning and mental flexibility—peaks in the early 20s and declines slowly as people age.

crystallized intelligence Aspects of intelligence involving verbal ability and accumulated knowledge, which tend to increase over the life span.

fluid intelligence Aspects of intelligence involving abstract reasoning and mental flexibility, which peak in the early 20s and decline slowly as people age.

8.16 What are the themes of social development in early and middle adulthood?

Social Development

In days gone by, the primary social tasks of adulthood were marriage and starting a family. While it remains true that the majority of adults marry and have children, there is now a great deal of variability in the ages at which they do so. In 1960, the median age at first marriage was 20 for females and 23 for males; today, the median age is 26 for females and 28 for males (U.S. Census Bureau, 2010).

Living Arrangements. Government surveys indicate that households in the United States are now about evenly divided between those that are headed by a married couple and living arrangements that involve other kinds of relationships (Lofquist et al., 2012). Most non-married-couple households are headed by single adults. Despite stereotypes that they are unhappy or searching for a life partner, most single adults say that they are satisfied with their status and do not seek to change it (Davies, 2003).

One important reason for the increase in age at which adults marry is the popularity of cohabitation. In the United States, nearly 7% of all households are headed by a cohabiting opposite-sex couple (Lofquist et al., 2012). An additional 1% of households are headed by a cohabiting same-sex couple. Some studies suggest that if they marry, couples who cohabit are more prone to divorce than those who don't live together prior to marriage. However, these findings may be somewhat misleading in that they often do not take into account the firmness of couples' intention to marry. More careful studies show that couples who undertake a cohabiting relationship with a clear understanding by both partners that the arrangement is a prelude to marriage differ little in relationship satisfaction or stability from those who do not cohabit before marriage (Kline et al., 2004; Teachman, 2003).

As is true for heterosexuals, gay and lesbian committed couples report greater satisfaction with their sex lives than do singles (Home & Biss, 2005). Moreover, same-sex couples argue about the same things as heterosexuals do and report higher levels of satisfaction when partners are equally committed to the relationship (Baucom et al., 2010; Solomon, Rothblum, & Balsam, 2004). Thus, Erikson's view that the status of one's intimate partnerships is an important facet of adult life appears to hold true regardless of sexual orientation.

Marriage and Divorce. Despite the rising age at first marriage and the diversity of living arrangements among today's adults, it is nevertheless true that the vast majority of adults marry at some time during their lives. Research suggests that more than 80% of adults will marry at least once in their lives (Whitehead & Popenoe, 2005). In addition to its economic benefits, marriage is associated with numerous physical and mental health benefits (e.g., lower rates of depression) for both men and women (Bierman, Fazio, & Milkie, 2006; Umberson et al., 2006). Research indicates that these effects arise from spouses' intentional efforts to influence each other's health-related behaviors (Reczek & Umberson, 2012). For instance, spouses encourage (or "nag") each other to exercise, eat healthy foods, maintain optimistic attitudes, and the like.

Some studies suggest that an unhappy, stress-filled marriage may actually be detrimental to the health of one or both spouses (Umberson et al., 2006). Thus, conflict within a marriage sometimes leads to divorce. However, conflict is only one of several factors that are associated with divorce. Overall, the marriages most likely to fail are those between teenagers, nonreligious couples in which the bride was pregnant before marriage, and marriages of people whose parents divorced (Popenoe & Whitehead, 2000).

Divorce often radically alters the course of an adult's life, especially for a woman. For one thing, women who have children often experience a reduced standard of living after divorce. For another, both women and men must often find new networks of friends and often new places to live.

Parenthood. As with the increased age at which people get married, a growing number of couples are delaying parenthood until their 30s. But whenever a person becomes a parent, the adjustment is one of the most challenging—and rewarding—in life. One of the challenges is that both mothers and fathers are more likely to exhibit behaviors that are stereotypically associated with their respective gender roles after becoming parents than they were beforehand (Katz-Wise, Priess, & Hyde, 2010). For example, mothers may increase their focus on domestic chores, while men may devote more energy to career advancement. However, this pattern may reflect gender differences in the availability of leave time from work or other practical factors rather than the preferences of either mothers or fathers. Moreover, research suggests that the quality of a couple's relationship before parenthood predicts how satisfied they are with their relationship after a child is born. For example, low levels of conflict before childbirth predispose couples to maintain high levels of relationship satisfaction during the transition to parenthood (Kluwer & Johnson, 2007).

Careers. Issues involving work and careers constitute an important theme of adult life. As discussed in the *Apply It* on p. 282, psychologists' studies of career development have focused on both personality variables and the stages involved in pursuing a career. Personality and stages aside, how we feel about our work situations, our level of *job satisfaction,* predicts not only how happy and productive we are on the job but also how positively we feel about other aspects of our lives. For example, workers' job satisfaction is strongly related to how satisfied they are with their romantic relationships (Sonnentag, 2003). Thus, these two important themes of adult life are intertwined. The more satisfied a person is with one, the better he or she is likely to feel about the other.

▲ The challenges associated with juggling the demands of family and career are familiar to most working parents.

APPLY IT

Where Are You in the Career Development Process?

Have you ever wondered what type of work you are best suited for? If so, you may want to begin your quest for an answer by looking at two models of career development, the process of choosing and adjusting to a particular career. Recommendations about what you might do to enhance your search for the ideal career can be derived from both. Ultimately, though, the degree to which you are satisfied with your career may depend on how you integrate your work into your life as a whole.

Holland's Personality Types

The work of John Holland has been very influential in shaping psychologists' ideas about personality and career. Holland proposes six basic personality types: realistic, investigative, artistic, social, enterprising, and conventional. His research shows that each of the six types is associated with work preferences. (The types and their associated work preferences are summarized in Table 8.2.) As Holland's theory predicts, people whose personality matches their job are also more likely to be satisfied with their work. Thus, a personality assessment may help you make an appropriate occupational choice and give you confidence about the decision (Francis-Smyth & Smith, 1997).

Super's Career Development Stages

Psychologist Donald Super proposed that career development happens in stages that begin in infancy (Super, 1971, 1986). First comes the growth stage (from birth to 14 years), in which you learn about your abilities and interests. Next is the exploratory stage, roughly between the ages of 15 and 24. According to Super, there's a lot of trial and error in this stage, so job changes happen frequently. Next is the establishment stage (also called the stabilization stage), from 25 to 45. This stage begins with learning how things work in your career, the culture of your organization, and progression through the early steps of the career ladder. Sometimes, additional formal training is required during this stage. Setting goals is also important in this stage. You must decide how far you want to go and how you intend to get there. Mentoring by an experienced co-worker often helps you negotiate this stage successfully. Once an individual has become well established in a career, she or he enters the maintenance phase (age 45 through retirement), in which the goal is to protect and maintain the gains made in earlier years. Of course, in today's rapidly changing economy, people are often required to change careers. Thus, an individual may reenter the exploratory stage at any time. As with most stage theories, the ages associated with Super's stages of career development are less important than the sequence of the stages.

TABLE 8.2 **Holland's Personality Types and Work Preferences**

TYPE	PERSONALITY TRAITS	WORK PREFERENCES
Realistic	Aggressive, masculine, physically strong, often with low verbal or interpersonal skills	Mechanical activities and tool use; often chooses a job such as mechanic, electrician, or surveyor
Investigative	Oriented toward thinking (particularly abstract thinking), organizing, and planning; low in social skills	Ambiguous, challenging tasks; often a scientist or engineer
Artistic	Asocial	Unstructured, highly individual activity; often an artist
Social	Extraverted; people-oriented, sociable, and needing attention; avoids intellectual activity and dislikes highly ordered activity	Working with people in service jobs like nursing and education
Enterprising	Highly verbal and dominating; enjoys organizing and directing others; persuasive and a strong leader	Often chooses a career in sales
Conventional	Prefers structured activities and subordinate roles; likes clear guidelines; accurate and precise	May choose an occupation such as bookkeeping or filing

Source: Holland (1973, 1992).

●─Watch on **MyPsychLab**

Other aspects of adults' lives are interconnected with their careers as well. For example, child-rearing issues are often central in the lives of working women. In the 1960s, only 18% of mothers with children were employed. Today, 64% of mothers of children younger than age 6 and about 76% of the mothers of school-age children work outside the home (Bureau of Labor Statistics, 2012). Further, the idea that a career is an important component of a satisfying life is now shared by men and women alike.

The Myths of Middle Age. You may have heard that parents experience an *empty nest syndrome* when their grown children leave home. Contrary to this popular stereotype, parents often appreciate the opportunity to reexamine their identity that is afforded by their children's departure from home (Noriko, 2004). Moreover, analyses show that the presence of an empty nest has little or no relationship to the appearance of mental disorders such as depression at midlife (Schmidt et al., 2004). Thus, the concept of an empty nest syndrome seems to have little basis in reality.

Similarly, the term *midlife crisis* has been used to describe the angst middle-aged people feel over their lost youth. Research refutes the idea that middle-aged people go through such a crisis, however. More often, individuals between the ages of 40 and 60 are more likely to experience what psychologist David Almeida and his colleagues call *stressor overload* than either younger or older adults (Clay, 2003; Friedman et al., 2012). This condition arises when middle-aged people must balance the demands of mentoring teenaged and young adult children with those associated with caring for aging parents, managing their own careers, finding time for intimate relationships, and looking ahead to retirement. Surprisingly, though, Almeida has found that successful management of these challenges enhances middle-aged adults' sense of competence (Serido, Almeida, & Wethington, 2004).

REMEMBER IT   *Check your answers and take additional quizzes in MyPsychLab.com.*   ✓●─[Study and Review on MyPsychLab

1. From the 20s to the 40s, intellectual performance tends to _____.
2. While attending college, young adults form _____ that serve as the primary source of social support.
3. Marriage is associated with advantages in _____ and _____.

Later Adulthood

In the early years of the 20th century, life expectancy in the United States was only 49 years. By the century's end, the expected life span of someone born in the United States was about 76 years. According to the most recent census, people older than age 65 constitute about 13% of the U.S. population; by 2030, that percentage will rise to 20% (FIFARS, 2012). A sizable number of these elders are likely to be older than age 100. What are your perceptions of life after 65? The statistics in the *Try It* on p. 284 might surprise you.

Physical and Cognitive Changes ▶ ──────────────────

It was long assumed that the number of neurons in the brain declined sharply in later adulthood, but this assumption appears to be false (Gallagher & Rapp, 1997). Research has shown that the shrinking volume of the aging cortex is due more to breakdown of the myelin that covers the axons in the white matter than to loss of the neurons that make up the gray matter, a process that begins in the early 30s (Bartzokis et al., 2004; Peters et al., 1994; Wickelgren, 1996). As you learned in Chapter 2, the myelin sheath facilitates the rapid conduction of neural impulses. The breakdown of myelin thus explains one of the most predictable characteristics of aging—the **general slowing** of behavior—a process in which the reductions in the speed of neural transmission lead to a slowing of physical and mental functions (Birren & Fisher, 1995). With degeneration of the myelin, the brain takes longer to process information, and reaction time is slower.

With advancing age, the elderly typically become more farsighted, have increasingly impaired night vision, and experience hearing loss in the higher frequencies (Long & Crambert, 1990; Slawinski, Hartel, & Kline, 1993). Joints become stiffer, and bones lose calcium and become more brittle, increasing the risk of fractures from falls.

About 80% of Americans older than age 65 have one or more chronic conditions. The most common of these ailments is hypertension (high blood pressure), a condition that afflicts 57% of women and 54% of men older than age 65 (FIFARS, 2012). Arthritis, an inflammatory condition that causes stiffness in the joints, is next, with

8.17 How do the body and mind change in the later adult years?

general slowing A process in which the reductions in the speed of neural transmission lead to a slowing of physical and mental functions.

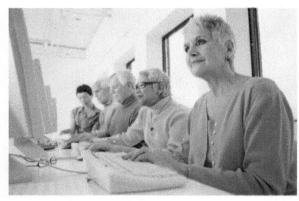

▲ Older adults take more time to learn new skills, but, once learned, they apply new skills as accurately as those who are younger.

prevalence rates of 56% among females and 45% among males. However, these two conditions can be controlled with medication, and many older adults who have them manage quite well.

Research suggests that physical exercise improves the physical fitness levels of older adults (Small, 2005). In one study, 100 frail nursing-home residents, average age 87, exercised their thigh and hip muscles vigorously on exercise machines for 45 minutes three times a week. At the end of 10 weeks, participants had increased their stair-climbing power by 28.4% and their walking speed by 12%, and four of them were able to exchange their walkers for canes (Fiatarone et al., 1994). For many of us, remaining fit and vigorous as we age lies within our power.

General slowing also helps to explain the finding you read about earlier regarding age differences in performance on cognitive tests that require speed. However, intellectual decline in late adulthood is not inevitable. Older adults who keep mentally and physically active tend to retain their mental skills as long as their health is good (Langdon & Corbett, 2012). They do well on tests of vocabulary, comprehension, and general information, and their ability to solve practical problems is generally higher than that of young adults. In laboratory memory tasks, older people do as well or almost as well as younger people on recognition tasks (Hultsch & Dixon, 1990) and on recall of information in their areas of expertise (Charness, 1989). And they are just as capable as younger adults at learning new cognitive strategies (Saczynski, Willis, & Schaie, 2002). Other factors that are positively correlated with good cognitive functioning in the elderly include a higher education level, a complex work environment, a long marriage to an intelligent spouse, and a higher income (Schaie, 2005; Van der Elst et al., 2006).

8.18 What adjustment challenges do older adults face?

Social Adjustment

As noted earlier, most elderly adults are both physically and cognitively healthy. Yet old age involves many losses. Adjusting to these losses is one of the challenges of getting older. Fortunately, most older adults are able to cope effectively. For instance, in the United States, 63% of 65- to 69-year-olds and 85% of those over 70 have retired from paid employment (FIFARS, 2012). Despite stereotypes, most of them are happy to leave work and do not experience a great deal of stress in adjusting to retirement. Generally, the people who are most reluctant to retire are those who are better educated, hold high-status jobs with a good income, find fulfillment in their work, and are in good physical health (von Bonsdorff et al., 2010).

Another common event that may affect life satisfaction for older adults is the loss of a spouse. For most people, losing a spouse is the most stressful event in a lifetime. Disruption of sleep patterns is among the many physical effects associated with this loss (Steeves, 2002). These physical effects take their toll on the bereaved elderly and lead to tiredness and anxiety. In addition, both widows and widowers are at a greater risk for health problems due to suppressed immune function (Khanfer, Lord, & Philliips, 2011).

Loss of a spouse often brings with it another challenge for the 40% of women and 13% of older men who experience it (FIFARS, 2012): They must decide whether to alter their living arrangements. In the United States, older Americans of all ethnic groups have a strong preference for remaining independent as long as possible (FIFARS, 2004; Martinez, 2002). As a result, only 18% of elderly women and 6% of older men live with their relatives (FIFARS, 2012). The living arrangements of elders in European countries are similar to those in the United States (Hellstrom & Hallberg, 2004; Osborn et al., 2003). Predictably, maintaining the ability to live alone is an important factor in elders' life satisfaction in these societies (Osborn et al., 2003).

In other countries, the situation is just the opposite. For instance, in Mexico, 90% of elderly widows live with relatives, usually their adult children (Varley & Blasco, 2003). Multigenerational households are commonplace in other Latin American countries as well (De Vos, 1990). Living with relatives is also more common among the elderly in Asian countries than in the United States or Europe (Sung, 1992). Similarly, in the United States, non-White elders are nearly three times as likely to live with relatives as White older adults are (FIFARS, 2012). Among Whites, just 13% of older adults live with family, compare to 33%, 35%, and 39% of African American, Asian, and Hispanic elders, respectively. Consequently, elders from ethnic groups in which it is considered normative for older adults to live with their adult children who live alone in societies may experience lower levels of life satisfaction than their peers who live with family (Yeh & Lo, 2004).

Successful Aging ▶

As you have learned, for older adults to maintain a sense of life satisfaction, they must be able to adjust to both physical and social changes. Knowing this, you shouldn't be surprised to learn that a majority of older adults rate their health as good (see Figure 8.5 on p. 286), even though 91% of them have at least one chronic ailment (Anderson, 2012; FIFARS, 2012). One reason for this seeming contradiction is that the tendency toward having a generally optimistic outlook on life increases as people get older (Charles, Mather, & Carstengen, 2003). Further, most older adults have learned to think of their lives in relative terms. That is, most believe that others are worse off than they are (Heckhausen & Brim, 1997). In other words, older adults grade their health "on a curve," so to speak.

An optimistic outlook is one of the key components of **successful aging**, the term researchers use to describe maintaining one's physical health, mental abilities, social competence, and overall satisfaction with life as one gets older (Rowe & Kahn, 1998). Successful aging has been the focus of much aging-related research in recent years. As defined by authors John Rowe and Robert Kahn (1998), successful aging has three components: good physical health, retention of cognitive abilities, and continuing engagement in social and productive activities.

Much of what happens to us as we age, of course, is somewhat beyond our control. However, successful aging also includes behaviors aimed at warding off age-related declines, such as eating a healthy diet and remaining mentally and socially active, and adaptive responses to the challenges that inevitably accompany aging. For instance, after a stroke, some older adults work diligently to recover lost abilities, while others despair and put little effort into the rehabilitation regimens prescribed for them by doctors and therapists (Ushikubo, 1998). Not surprisingly, individuals who are willing to do the work required for optimal recovery of functioning gain the most from rehabilitation. The kind of attitude that motivates an individual to try to get better after a devastating event such as a stroke represents the spirit of Rowe and Kahn's successful aging concept.

Death and Dying ▶

One of the developmental tasks for every elderly person is to accept the inevitability of death and to prepare for it. At no time, however, does this task become more critical than when an individual—no matter what age—faces a terminal illness. Elisabeth

8.19 What are the components of successful aging?

successful aging Maintaining one's physical health, mental abilities, social competence, and overall satisfaction with life as one gets older.

8.20 How do people respond to approaching death and bereavement?

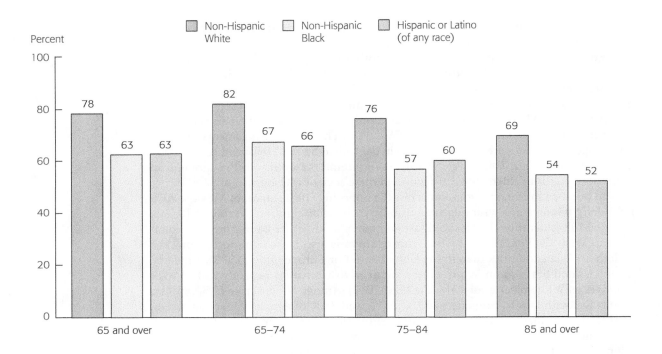

Percent

Non-Hispanic White · Non-Hispanic Black · Hispanic or Latino (of any race)

65 and over: 78, 63, 63
65–74: 82, 67, 66
75–84: 76, 57, 60
85 and over: 69, 54, 52

FIGURE 8.5 Percentage of People Age 65 and Older Who Reported Having Good to Excellent Health, by Age Group and Race and Hispanic Origin, 2008–2010

Source: FIFARS (2012).

Kübler-Ross (1969) interviewed some 200 terminally ill people and found they shared common reactions to their impending death. In her book *On Death and Dying,* she identifies five stages people go through in coming to terms with death.

In the first stage, *denial,* most patients react to the diagnosis of their terminal illness with shock and disbelief (surely, the doctors must be wrong). The second stage, *anger,* is marked by feelings of anger, resentment, and envy of those who are young and healthy. In the third stage, *bargaining,* the person attempts to postpone death in return for a promise of "good behavior." An individual may offer God some special service or a promise to live a certain kind of life in exchange for an opportunity to attend a child's wedding or a grandchild's graduation. The fourth stage, *depression,* brings a great sense of loss and may take two forms—depression over past losses and depression over impending losses. Given enough time, patients may reach the final stage, *acceptance,* in which they stop struggling against death and contemplate its coming without fear or despair. Kübler-Ross claims that the family also goes through stages similar to those experienced by the patient.

Critics deny the universality of Kübler-Ross's proposed stages and their invariant sequence (Konigsburg, 2011). Each person is unique. The reactions of all the terminally ill cannot be expected to conform to some rigid sequence of stages.

Similarly, there are cross-cultural differences in how individuals deal with death (Westerhof et al., 2001). For individuals in Western societies, maintenance of individual autonomy over the dying process is of great importance. Moreover, people often view death as an enemy that must be battled at all costs. By contrast, Native American cultures see death as part of nature's cycle and, as such, it is not to be feared or fought (DeSpelder & Strickland, 1983). In Mexican culture, people's deaths are seen as reflections of their lives. As a result, their behavior during the dying process is assumed to reveal much about what kind of people they were. Furthermore, in Mexican culture, death is discussed frequently and is even celebrated on the Day of the Dead (DeSpelder & Strickland, 1983). Thus, Kübler-Ross's stages of denial, anger, bargaining, and so on, may not exist in such cultures.

Death comes too soon for most people, but not soon enough for others. Some who are terminally ill and subject to intractable pain would welcome an end to their suffering. Should dying patients be left with no choice but to suffer to the end? Today most medical ethicists distinguish between two forms of euthanasia (also known as "mercy killing"). *Passive euthanasia* occurs when a person (typically, a physician) hastens death by not using life support systems or medication that would prolong a patient's life or by withdrawing life support or other treatment that may be keeping a patient alive. *Active euthanasia* (also called "assisted suicide") occurs when a physician or other individual (at a patient's request) hastens a patient's death by active means, such as by administering a fatal dose of a drug.

Active euthanasia is the focus of an ongoing debate. The state of Oregon legalized physician-assisted suicide in 1997. Most patients who request death cite as their reasons loss of control over bodily functions, loss of autonomy, and inability to take part in activities that make life enjoyable (Sullivan, Hedberg, & Fleming, 2000). However, when Oregon physicians provide such patients with prescriptions for lethal doses of drugs, the patients often do not fill the prescriptions, illustrating that the desire to live is a powerful motivator even among people who wish to escape from pain and suffering (Quill, 2007).

A rapidly growing alternative to hospitals and nursing homes is *hospice care*. Hospices are agencies that care for the needs of the dying more humanely and affordably than hospitals can and that use special facilities or, in some cases, the patient's own home. A hospice follows a set of guidelines that make it more attuned to the patient's personal needs and preferences than a hospital or nursing home typically can be.

Finally, many of us have experienced the *grieving process*—the period of bereavement that follows the death of a loved one and sometimes lingers long after the person has gone. Contrary to what many believe, research (Bonanno et al., 1995) has shown that bereaved individuals who suffer the most intense grief initially, who weep inconsolably and feel the deepest pain, do not get through their bereavement more quickly than others. And other research (Folkman et al., 1996) has found that the grieving process for male caregivers whose partners have died of AIDS is very similar to that experienced by spouses.

Death and dying are not pleasant subjects, but remember that life itself is a terminal condition, and each day of life should be treasured like a precious gift.

REMEMBER IT

Check your answers and take additional quizzes in MyPsychLab.com. ✓— Study and Review on MyPsychLab

1. General slowing results from the breakdown of _____ in the nervous system as adults age.
2. A(n) _____ outlook is a key factor in successful aging.
3. _____ identified five stages that people go through in coming to terms with death.
4. _____ is an alternative to hospitals and nursing homes for people who are terminally ill.

Looking Back

Our discussion of death and dying has brought us to the end of the human life span. As you have seen, gains and losses occur in every phase of development. The accumulated experience available to the elderly is punctuated by losses in physical and psychological speed for most and more serious declines for others. In middle adulthood, many people occupy important social roles at the same time that their reproductive capacity is diminishing. For young adults, the joys of youth are left behind as the responsibilities of adulthood are assumed. In similar fashion, adolescents look back wistfully at the time they spent playing during their childhood years as they use their newly acquired mental and physical abilities to make important decisions about their lives. School-age children think more logically than when they were younger, but, at the same time, they have forever left behind the pleasures associated with a day spent pretending to be a superhero, for example. The capacity to use one's own behavior as a symbolic representation of something else is the most important ability gained in the preschool years, but it comes with the loss of caregivers' tolerance of dependency. Finally, the infant trades the warm safety of the womb for the opportunity to take in all the sights and sounds of the outside world and to embark on a journey of unknown length but of certain destination.

CHAPTER 8 SUMMARY

THEORIES OF DEVELOPMENT (pp. 252–264)

8.1 How does Piaget's theory explain cognitive development? (pp. 253–257)

Piaget proposed that humans construct schemes, or general action plans, on the basis of experiences. Schemes change through assimilation and accommodation until they work effectively in the real world. During the sensorimotor stage (ages birth to 2 years), infants act on the world through their senses and motor activities and develop object permanence. Children at the preoperational stage (ages 2 to 6 years) are increasingly able to use symbols, but they exhibit egocentrism. When working real-world problems, children at the concrete operations stage (ages 6 to 11 or 12 years) are able to apply logical operations to problems that can be tested in the real world. At the formal operations stage (ages 11 or 12 years and beyond), adolescents can apply logic to abstract problems and hypothetical situations. Piaget may have underestimated the abilities of children and overestimated those of adults, but research supports the sequence of cognitive development that he proposed.

Key Terms
developmental psychology, p. 252
schemes, p. 253
assimilation, p. 253
accommodation, p. 253
object permanence, p. 253
symbolic function, p. 253
conservation, p. 254
reversibility, p. 254
hypothetico-deductive thinking, p. 255
naive idealism, p. 255
imaginary audience, p. 255
personal fable, p. 255

8.2 How do the neo-Piagetians and Vygotsky explain cognitive development? (pp. 257–259)

Neo-Piagetians explain cognitive development as a function of working memory development. Vygotsky argued that private speech helps children verbalize problem-solving steps. In scaffolding, a teacher or parent adjusts the quality and degree of instruction to fit the child's present level of ability. It allows a child to gradually perform a task independently within her zone of proximal development.

Key Terms
zone of proximal development, p. 258
scaffolding, p. 258

8.3 How does Kohlberg's theory explain moral reasoning? (pp. 259–262)

At the preconventional level, moral reasoning is governed by the physical consequences of an act. At the conventional level, judgments of right and wrong are based on the internalized standards of others. Postconventional moral reasoning involves weighing moral alternatives and realizing that laws may conflict with basic human rights.

Key Terms
preconventional level, p. 259
conventional level, p. 259
postconventional level, p. 260

8.4 How does Erikson's theory explain psychosocial development? (pp. 262–264)

Erikson proposed that individuals progress through eight psychosocial stages that span the entire period from birth to death. Each stage is defined by a conflict involving the individual's relationship with the social environment. A positive resolution of each conflict makes it more likely that an individual will be successful in later stages.

Key Term
psychosocial stages, p. 262

PRENATAL DEVELOPMENT AND INFANCY (pp. 264–271)

8.5 What happens in each stage of prenatal development? (pp. 264–266)

In the germinal stage, from conception to 2 weeks, the egg is fertilized, and the zygote attaches itself to the uterine wall. During the embryonic stage, from week 3 through week 8, all of the major systems, organs, and structures form. In the fetal stage, from week 9 until birth, the fetus experiences rapid growth and body systems, structures, and organs continue their development. Fetuses can hear and remember sounds that they hear repeatedly. Negative influences on prenatal development include drugs, environmental hazards, poor maternal nutrition, and maternal illness. Exposure is most harmful in the period of the embryo during critical periods of development for the various body structures. Physiological signals from the woman's body, the fetus, and the placenta trigger labor, a three-stage process.

Low-birth-weight and preterm infants are at risk for poor developmental outcomes.

Key Terms

prenatal development, p. 264
zygote, p. 265
embryo, p. 265
fetus, p. 265
teratogens, p. 265
critical period, p. 265
fetal alcohol syndrome, p. 266
neonate, p. 266
low-birth-weight baby, p. 266
preterm infant, p. 266

8.6 How do infants' abilities change over the first 18 months of life? (pp. 267–268)

Neonates are born with reflexes that help them survive, and all of their senses are functional at birth. As maturation proceeds, controlled motor skills, such as grasping and walking, develop. Experience can retard or accelerate motor development, but the sequence of motor milestones is universal.

Key Terms

reflexes, p. 267
visual cliff, p. 267
maturation, p. 268

8.7 How does temperament affect infants' behavior? (p. 268)

Temperament refers to an individual's behavioral style or characteristic way of responding to the environment. The three temperament types identified by Thomas, Chess, and Birch are easy, difficult, and slow-to-warm-up. Current research indicates that dimensions of temperament include activity level, sociability, inhibition, negative emotionality, and effortful control.

Key Term

temperament, p. 268

8.8 What are the causes, characteristics, and consequences of infant–caregiver attachment? (pp. 268–271)

Harlow found that the basis of attachment in infant monkeys is contact comfort. According to Bowlby, the infant has usually developed a strong attachment to the mother at age 6 to 8 months. Ainsworth identified four attachment patterns in infants: secure, avoidant, resistant, and disorganized/disoriented. Fathers' patterns of interaction with children differ from those of mothers. Thus, mothers and fathers exert unique influences on children's development, and, ideally, children need both influences. Children who interact regularly with their fathers tend to have higher IQs, do better in social situations, and manage frustration better than children lacking such interaction.

Key Terms

attachment, p. 268
separation anxiety, p. 270
stranger anxiety, p. 270

EARLY AND MIDDLE CHILDHOOD (pp. 271–276)

8.9 What are the phases of language development, and how do various theorists explain them? (pp. 271–273)

Babbling begins at age 6 months, followed by single words sometime during the second year, two-word sentences at ages 18 to 20 months, and telegraphic speech between 2 and 3 years of age, and then the acquisition of grammatical rules. Learning theory suggests that language is acquired through imitation and reinforcement. The nativist position is that language ability is largely innate, because it is acquired in stages that occur in a fixed order at the same ages in most children throughout the world.

Key Terms

babbling, p. 271
overextension, p. 271
underextension, p. 272
telegraphic speech, p. 272
overregularlization, p. 272

8.10 What do parenting styles and peer relationships contribute to socialization? (pp. 273–274)

The three parenting styles identified by Baumrind are authoritarian, authoritative, and permissive. Research suggests that the authoritative style is the most effective and is associated with psychosocial competence in children. Children with authoritarian parents are typically the most anxious and the least socially competent. Permissive parenting is least effective and is often associated with adolescent behavior problems. Friendships begin by age 3 or 4 based on shared activities. Later friendships are based on mutual trust. Peer groups provide children with social models and objective measures against which children can evaluate their own traits and behavior.

Key Terms

socialization, p. 273
authoritarian parents, p. 273
authoritative parents, p. 273
permissive parents, p. 274

8.11 How do theorists explain gender role development? (pp. 274–276)

Learning theorists explained gender roles as the result of reinforcement and modeling. Cognitive-developmental theorists emphasized the stages of gender identity, gender stability, and gender constancy. Gender schema theorists apply the principles of information-processing theory to gender role development. They assert that a child's self-labeling as a boy or a girl initiates gender schema development. While the gender schema is being constructed, children think rigidly about gender roles but become more flexible once they have a better understanding of them.

Key Term
gender roles, p. 274

ADOLESCENCE (pp. 276–279)

8.12 How does puberty influence adolescents' bodies, self-concepts, and behavior? (pp. 276–277)

Puberty begins the adolescent growth spurt, followed by development of the primary and secondary sex characteristics. Early maturation provides enhanced status for boys but is also associated with aggressiveness and substance abuse. Early-maturing girls are often self-conscious and dissatisfied with their bodies. They are also more likely to be exposed prematurely to alcohol and drug use and to have early sexual experiences and unwanted pregnancies. Religious values, family structure, academic achievement, and involvement in sports are correlated with later age at first intercourse.

Key Terms
adolescence, p. 276
puberty, p. 276
secondary sex characteristics, p. 276
menarche, p. 276

8.13 What do parents and peers contribute to teens' development? (pp. 277–278)

Authoritative parenting is most effective and is associated with psychosocial competence in all racial and ethnic groups. Adolescents with authoritarian parents are typically the most psychologically distressed and the least self-reliant and self-confident. Permissive parenting is least effective and is often associated with adolescent drug use and behavior problems. The adolescent peer group (usually composed of teens with similar interests) provides a vehicle for developing social skills and a standard of comparison against which teens' attributes can be evaluated.

8.14 What are the characteristics of emerging adulthood? (pp. 278–279)

The parts of the brain that are involved in decision making and self-control mature between the late teens and early 20s. Emerging adults use skills they acquired earlier in life to accomplish developmental tasks in the academic, conduct, and friendship domains. New skills are required for tasks in the work and romantic domains.

Key Term
emerging adulthood, p. 278

EARLY AND MIDDLE ADULTHOOD (pp. 279–283)

8.15 How do the body and mind change in early and middle adulthood? (pp. 279–280)

Physical skills begin to decline around age 30. Physical changes associated with middle age are a loss of physical vigor and endurance, a need for reading glasses, and the end of reproductive capacity (menopause) in women and a decline in testosterone levels in men. Although younger people tend to do better on mental tasks requiring speed or rote memory, the intellectual performance of adults shows modest gains until the mid-40s. A modest decline occurs from the 60s to the 80s. Crystallized intelligence tends to increase over the life span; fluid intelligence peaks in the early 20s and declines slowly as people age.

Key Terms
presbyopia, p. 279
menopause, p. 279
crystallized intelligence, p. 280
fluid intelligence, p. 280

8.16 What are the themes of social development in early and middle adulthood? (pp. 280–283)

Establishment of an intimate partnership and career development are the social themes of early and middle adulthood. Most adults marry and have children, but they do so at later ages today than in the past. Couples exhibit more gender stereotypical behavior after becoming parents. Relationship satisfaction among new parents depends on factors that were present in the relationship before childbirth. Careers are important to life satisfaction, and many men and women occupy decision-making roles in middle adulthood. Research does not support the popular notions of empty nest syndrome and a midlife crisis. However, middle-aged adults often experience stressor overload as they mentor teen and young adult children while also caring for aging parents.

LATER ADULTHOOD (pp. 283–287)

8.17 How do the body and mind change in the later adult years? (pp. 283–284)

Physical changes associated with later adulthood include a general slowing of behavior, a decline in sensory capacity and in heart, lung, kidney, and muscle function, and an increase in chronic conditions such as arthritis, heart problems, and high blood pressure. Although older adults perform cognitive tasks more slowly, if they keep mentally and physically active, they can usually maintain their mental skills as long as their health holds out.

Key Term
general slowing, p. 283

8.18 What adjustment challenges do older adults face? (pp. 284–285)

Older adults typically retire from work. Many lose a spouse and may alter their living arrangements. In Western societies, most elders prefer to live on their own. In other parts of the world, it is more common for elders to live with family members.

8.19 What are the components of successful aging? (p. 285)

Successful aging includes good physical health, retention of cognitive abilities, and continuing engagement in social and productive activities.

Key Term
successful aging, p. 285

8.20 How do people respond to approaching death and bereavement? (pp. 285–287)

Kübler-Ross suggested five stages of dying: denial, anger, bargaining, depression, and acceptance. Contrary to what many believe, people who openly exhibit signs of intense grieving do not necessarily get through the grief process more quickly than others.

Chapter 8 Study Guide

Answers to all the Study Guide questions are provided at the end of the book.

SECTION ONE: Chapter Review

Theories of Development (pp. 252–264)

1. Match each of Piaget's stages with the relevant concept.
   _____ (1) abstract thought
   _____ (2) conservation, reversibility
   _____ (3) object permanence
   _____ (4) egocentrism, centration
   a. sensorimotor stage
   b. preoperational stage
   c. concrete operations stage
   d. formal operations stage

2. The teenager's personal fable includes all of the following *except*
   a. a sense of personal uniqueness.
   b. a belief that he or she is indestructible and protected from misfortunes.
   c. a belief that no one has ever felt so deeply before.
   d. a feeling that he or she is always on stage.

3. Match Kohlberg's level of moral reasoning with the rationale for engaging in a behavior.
   _____ (1) to avoid punishment or gain a reward
   _____ (2) to ensure that human rights are protected
   _____ (3) to gain approval or follow the law
   a. conventional
   b. preconventional
   c. postconventional

4. Match each description of behavior with the appropriate psychosocial stage.
   _____ (1) reflects on life's accomplishments to achieve a sense of satisfaction
   _____ (2) needs consistent attention to physical, social, and emotional needs
   _____ (3) initiates play and motor activities, asks questions
   _____ (4) strives for sense of independence
   _____ (5) is concerned with influencing future generations
   _____ (6) undertakes projects, makes things
   _____ (7) searches for a life partner
   _____ (8) seeks to answer the question "Who am I?"
   a. trust vs. mistrust
   b. autonomy vs. shame and doubt
   c. initiative vs. guilt
   d. industry vs. inferiority
   e. identity vs. role confusion
   f. intimacy vs. isolation
   g. generativity vs. stagnation
   h. ego integrity vs. despair

Prenatal Development and Infancy (pp. 264–271)

5. Match the stage of prenatal development with its description.
   _____ (1) first two weeks of life
   _____ (2) rapid growth and further development of body structures and systems
   _____ (3) formation of major systems, organs, and structures
   a. period of the fetus
   b. period of the embryo
   c. period of the zygote

6. Which of the following statements about infant sensory development is *not* true?

    a. Vision, hearing, taste, and smell are all fully developed at birth.

    b. Vision, hearing, taste, and smell are all functional at birth.

    c. Infants can show preferences in what they want to look at, hear, and smell shortly after birth.

    d. Hearing is better developed at birth than vision.

7. The primary factor influencing the attainment of the major motor milestones is

    a. experience.   **b.** maturation.

    c. learning.   **d.** habituation.

8. Which statement best describes Thomas, Chess, and Birch's thinking about temperament?

    a. Temperament develops gradually as a result of parental handling and personality.

    b. Temperament is inborn and is not influenced by the environment.

    c. Temperament is inborn but can be modified by the family and the environment.

    d. Temperament is set at birth and is unchangeable.

9. Ainsworth found that most infants had secure attachment. (true/false)

Early and Middle Childhood (pp. 271–276)

10. Match the linguistic stage with the example.

    _____ **(1)** "ba-ba-ba"

    _____ **(2)** "He eated the cookies"

    _____ **(3)** "Mama see ball"

    _____ **(4)** "oo," "ah"

    _____ **(5)** "kitty," meaning a lion

    a. telegraphic speech   **b.** overregularization

    c. babbling   **d.** overextension

    e. cooing

11. Learning theory is better able than the nativist position to account for how language development can be encouraged. (true/false)

12. Match the parenting style with the approach to discipline.

    _____ **(1)** expecting unquestioned obedience

    _____ **(2)** setting high standards, giving rationale for rules

    _____ **(3)** setting few rules or limits

    a. permissive   **b.** authoritative

    c. authoritarian

13. The peer group usually has a negative influence on social development. (true/false)

14. Which theory of gender role development does *not* require that children understand the concept of gender?

    a. Kohlberg's theory   **b.** social learning theory

    c. gender-schema theory

Adolescence (pp. 276–279)

15. The period of emerging adulthood begins at puberty. (true/false)

16. The secondary sex characteristics

    a. are not directly involved in reproduction.

    b. appear at the same time in all adolescents.

    c. distinguish mature males from mature females.

    d. include the testes and ovaries.

17. Most teenagers have good relationships with their parents. (true/false).

Early and Middle Adulthood (pp. 279–283)

18. During which decade do people reach their peak physically?

    a. teens   **b.** 30s

    c. 20s   **d.** 40s

19. (Crystallized/Fluid) intelligence increases with age.

Later Adulthood (pp. 283–287)

20. Which of the following statements is true of adults older than age 65?

    a. They are considerably less satisfied with life than young adults are.

    b. Most retirees are happy to be retired.

    c. Most are unhealthy.

    d. They perform newly learned skills less accurately than younger adults do.

21. Compared to older adults who are mentally and physically active, younger adults do better on

    a. tests requiring speed.   **b.** comprehension tests.

    c. general information tests.   **d.** practical problem solving.

22. Which of the following is *not* a component of successful aging?

    a. high income   **b.** engagement in productive activities

    c. good health   **d.** engagement in social activities

23. According to Kübler-Ross, the first stage experienced by terminally ill patients in coming to terms with death is _____; the last stage is _____.

    a. anger; depression   **b.** denial; depression

    c. bargaining; acceptance   **d.** denial; acceptance

SECTION TWO: Important Concepts and Psychologists

On the line opposite each name, list the major concept or theory associated with that name.

Name	Major Concept or Theory
1. Piaget	_____
2. Erikson	_____
3. Thomas, Chess, and Birch	_____
4. Ainsworth	_____
5. Chomsky	_____
6. Kohlberg	_____
7. Kübler-Ross	_____
8. Bem	_____

SECTION THREE: Comprehensive Practice Test

1. The period of time from conception to birth is called the period of _____ development.

    a. neonatal   **b.** prenatal

    c. post-zygotic   **d.** post-fertilization

2. The second stage of prenatal development is known as the period of

    a. germination.   **b.** the embryo.

    c. the fetus.   **d.** the zygote.

3. Researchers have found that resolution of Erikson's stage of intimacy versus isolation typically occurs in adulthood rather than in adolescence. One reason for this finding is that identity development is correlated with
   a. work experience.
   b. cognitive development.
   c. physical maturation.
   d. finding a life partner.

4. A baby is considered preterm if she or he is born
   a. some place other than a hospital.
   b. prior to the parents paying the doctor's bill.
   c. before the 45th week of pregnancy.
   d. before the 37th week of pregnancy.

5. Jorge is just a few days old. He can see, but not as well as he will later. If he is a typical baby, he probably has _____ vision.
   a. 20/40
   b. 20/600
   c. 40/20
   d. 10/40

6. Maturation is
   a. genetically determined biological changes that follow a timetable of development.
   b. behavioral changes based on the child's interaction with the environment.
   c. behavioral changes that take place when the child enters high school.
   d. applicable only to physiology and not to cognition or psychomotor development.

7. Cindy says that her new baby's responses to things that happen in the environment are generally happy and positive. Cindy is talking about her baby's
   a. response system.
   b. temperament.
   c. latent personality.
   d. infant personification.

8. Assimilation is a process used with _____
   a. new schemes.
   b. existing schemes.
   c. positive responses.
   d. negative responses.

9. The nativist position on speech development is that language ability is basically innate. (true/false)

10. Which of the following is *not* an example of a secondary sex characteristic?
    a. development of breasts in females
    b. differentiation of internal reproductive organs
    c. deepening of the voice in males
    d. rounding of the hips in females

11. Piaget's final stage of cognitive development is known as the _____ stage.
    a. concrete operations
    b. cognitive integrity
    c. generativity
    d. formal operations

12. A child in Kohlberg's _____ level of moral reasoning is governed by the physical consequences of behavior rather than by internalized ideas of right and wrong.
    a. postconventional
    b. conventional
    c. preconventional
    d. preadolescent

13. A person must be at Piaget's stage of formal operations to attain Kohlberg's _____ level of moral reasoning.
    a. conventional
    b. formal conventional
    c. postconventional
    d. ego integrity

14. Evidence suggests that females tend to stress care and compassion in resolving moral dilemmas, whereas males tend to stress _____ (or to give it and caring equal weight).
    a. romance
    b. aggression
    c. justice
    d. morality

15. The children of teenage mothers tend to display academic and/or behavioral difficulties. (true/false)

16. The most obvious changes as an individual gets older are usually
    a. cognitive.
    b. physical.
    c. social.
    d. sexual.

17. Holland's approach to career development focuses on
    a. stages.
    b. gender differences.
    c. personality traits.
    d. conflicts between work and family roles.

18. The results of current research seem to indicate that older adults are _____ younger adults.
    a. less happy and satisfied with life than
    b. as satisfied with life as
    c. as dissatisfied with life as
    d. less satisfied but more secure than

19. For the majority of those who stop working, retirement is not as stressful as popularly believed. (true/false)

20. For most people, which of the following is the most stressful event faced in their lifetime?
    a. retirement
    b. losing a spouse
    c. children leaving home
    d. restricted physical ability due to age

SECTION FOUR: Critical Thinking

1. Evaluate Erikson's stages of psychosocial development, explaining what aspects of his theory seem most convincing. Support your answer.

SECTION FIVE: Application Essays

1. Using Baumrind's categories, classify the parenting style your mother and/or father used in rearing you.
   a. Cite examples of techniques they used that support your classification.
   b. Do you agree with Baumrind's conclusions about the effects of that parenting style on children? Why or why not?
   c. Think back to your junior high school and high school years. To what degree did early or late maturation seem to affect how boys and girls were treated by their peers, their parents, or their teachers? Did early or late maturation affect their adjustment? Explain your answer.

2. Blaine has an ongoing dispute with his 13-year-old son, Duke. The boy argues that he is smart enough to pass his classes without doing homework, so he sees no reason to do it. Blaine asserts that, as a 13-year-old, Duke has a responsibility to conform to his parents' expectation that he pursue the highest grades he can get. Failing to do homework lowers his grade and is, therefore, immoral. How would you explain to Blaine that his conflict with his son is rooted in the difference between Stage 2 and Stage 4 moral reasoning (Kohlberg).

> **Apply your critical thinking skills with MyPsychLab Writing Assignments**
>
> *Submit your answer to the following question inside the MyPsychLab Writing Assessment program for immediate feedback.*
>
> Using specific examples, differentiate between the thinking patterns of a 3-year-old preschooler and a 9-year-old student, according to Piaget's theory of cognitive development.

Motivation and Emotion

THINK ABOUT IT

How would you feel if you found out that your romantic partner was flirting with someone else? Would you be angry? Jealous? Evolutionary psychologists study the ways in which we form, maintain, and think about romantic relationships, or our *mating strategies*, as they would put it. To get an idea about the kinds of research they do, think about your own views on relationships as you respond to the following quiz.

1. For each of the following situations, check the most accurate response.
   a. You are in a serious, committed, romantic relationship and you find your partner flirting with someone else. How jealous would you feel?

   _____ Not jealous at all   _____ Slightly jealous
   _____ Moderately jealous   _____ Quite jealous
   _____ Extremely jealous

   b. If you were flirting with someone else, how jealous would your partner be?

   _____ Not jealous at all   _____ Slightly jealous
   _____ Moderately jealous   _____ Quite jealous
   _____ Extremely jealous

2. Indicate which of the following two situations would make you angrier and/or hurt you more.
   a. You are in a serious, committed, romantic relationship, and you learn that your partner recently became involved in an emotional relationship with another person. There is no sex involved, not even kissing, but your partner spends a lot of time with the other person, seems quite attached, and talks about the person frequently.

   b. You are in a serious, committed, romantic relationship, and you learn that your partner recently had sex with another person, but there are no emotional ties at all and no commitment to the other person. Which situation would be more psychologically distressing to you?
   a. Emotional infidelity   b. Sexual infidelity

3. Are you male or female? _____
   (The reason for this last question will become obvious as you continue reading the text.)

Psychologist David Buss is one of the best-known evolutionary psychologists. His research shows that, across many cultures, men and women have about the same capacity for jealousy (Buss et al., 1990). However, they differ in what it is that makes them jealous. For men, sexual infidelity is more important than emotional infidelity. For women, emotional infidelity—such as finding out that their partner is still talking to and sharing confidences with a former lover—is more likely to cause feelings of jealousy than sexual infidelity would. Interestingly, too, these conclusions are based on two different kinds of evidence. The first set of findings comes from studies that use questions such as the ones you just answered (e.g., Buss et al., 1990; Buss et al., 1992). Another derives from research that measures men's and women's physiological stress levels when they are thinking about infidelity (e.g., Buss et al., 1992). Men show higher stress levels when they think about sexual infidelity, but women's levels are higher when they think about emotional infidelity.

Later in the chapter, we'll explore the explanations that evolutionary pychologists and their critics have offered for the findings reported by Buss and other researchers. Before we get there, though, we'll begin our exploration of motivation and emotion with a discussion of just what motivation is.

Explaining Motivation

What do you mean when you say that someone is "motivated"? Do you think of a person who is eagerly pursuing an important goal? If so, then you've hit on one important aspect of *motivation*. You will soon learn that psychologists define the term more broadly than we do in everyday communication, and they include a number of factors that cause us to pursue goals of which we are usually unaware. ◉

Watch the Video *Episode 12: Big Picture: Motivation and Emotion* in **MyPsychLab**

Foundations of Motivation ▶

The first step in the scientific study of any phenomenon is to establish a workable definition of it. For psychologists, **motivation** is a very broad term that encompasses all the processes that initiate, direct, and sustain behavior. As such, it takes in a lot of mental and behavioral territory. To make the task of studying motivation more manageable, we will break the topic down into its constituent parts and categorize motivations into several types.

9.1 How do psychologists define and classify motivation?

motivation All the processes that initiate, direct, and sustain behavior.

The Components of Motivation. Generally, psychologists consider motivation to have three components: activation, persistence, and intensity. To understand each, think about the role of motivation in studying for an exam. In the *activation* phase, you take the first steps required to achieve your goal of being prepared for the exam. You find out what will be covered on the exam; locate the appropriate material in your textbook, notes, and other resources; and develop a study plan. *Persistence* is the faithful and continued effort put forth in working toward a goal. In other words, this phase of motivation requires that you put your plan into action and stick to it even in the face of distractions and obstacles. *Intensity* refers to the focused energy and attention applied in order to achieve the goal. When you study, do you get caught up in your interest in the subject matter or in the emotional roller coaster that comes from thinking about the alternate possibilities of success and failure? Either way, it's the intensity component of motivation that's at work.

In addition to breaking motivation into its component parts, researchers can further their understanding of motivation by working from a precise definition of the term *motive,* a concept that is narrower than the full scope of motivation itself. A **motive** is a need or desire that energizes and directs behavior toward a goal. The motives that might compel a student to study for an exam are many. The student might derive self-esteem from getting good grades, or she might desire to escape from the anxiety that comes from a failing grade. Either motive would push her in the direction of moving through the motivational steps outlined above. Thus, two people could exhibit exactly the same behavior on the basis of very different motives.

motive Need or desire that energizes and directs behavior toward a goal.

primary drives States of tension or arousal that arise from a biological need and are unlearned.

social motives Motives (such as the needs for affiliation and achievement) that are acquired through experience and interaction with others.

work motivation The conditions and processes responsible for the arousal, direction, magnitude, and maintenance of effort of workers on the job.

achievement motivation Factors that move people to seek success in academic settings.

intrinsic motivation The desire to behave in a certain way because it is enjoyable or satisfying in and of itself.

incentive An external stimulus that motivates behavior (for example, money or fame).

extrinsic motivation The desire to behave in a certain way in order to gain some external reward or to avoid some undesirable consequence.

Primary Drives and Social Motives. Most people would agree that, at times, physiological needs demand our full attention. The **primary drives** direct our behavior toward the fulfillment of these needs. Primary drives are unlearned and include thirst, hunger, and sex. Later in the chapter, you'll learn more about thirst, hunger, and sexual motivation.

In contrast to primary drives, **social motives** are learned through experience and interaction with others. This group of motives includes those that influence our behavior in social settings such as workplaces and schools. One of the social motives is **work motivation**, the conditions and processes responsible for the arousal, direction, magnitude, and maintenance of effort of workers on the job. Another is **achievement motivation**, a social motive that includes the factors that move people to seek success in academic settings.

Intrinsic and Extrinsic Motivation. Motives can arise from something inside yourself, such as when you keep studying because you find the subject matter interesting. Such activities are pursued as ends in themselves, simply because they are enjoyable, not because any external reward is attached. This type of motivation is known as **intrinsic motivation**.

Other motives originate from outside, as when some external stimulus, or **incentive**, pulls or entices you to act. When the desire to get a good grade—or to avoid a bad grade—causes you to study, the grade is serving as this kind of external incentive. When we act so as to gain some external reward or to avoid some undesirable consequence, we are pulled by **extrinsic motivation**.

In Chapter 5, we learned that according to B. F. Skinner, a reinforcer is a consequence that increases the frequency of a behavior. Once the link between a behavior and a reinforcer has been established, the expectation of receiving the reinforcer again serves as an incentive to perform the behavior. For example, the prospect of getting a generous tip serves as an incentive for restaurant servers to serve their customers promptly and courteously.

▲ Which is the more powerful motivator in a game of poker, the gratification that comes from devising a successful strategy (intrinsic motivation) or the money you get when you win (extrinsic motivation)? As is true of many activities, poker is an engaging hobby (or profession, depending on your skill level) that involves both intrinsic and extrinsic motivators.

In real life, the motives for many activities are both intrinsic and extrinsic. You may love your job, but you would probably be motivated to leave if your salary, an important extrinsic motivator, were taken away. Although grades are extrinsic motivators, outstanding grades—especially when earned on a particularly difficult assignment or exam—usually bring with them a sense of pride in a job well done (an intrinsic motivator). Table 9.1 gives examples of intrinsic and extrinsic motivation.

TABLE 9.1 **Intrinsic and Extrinsic Motivation**

	DESCRIPTION	EXAMPLES
Intrinsic motivation	An activity is pursued as an end in itself because it is enjoyable and rewarding.	A person anonymously donates a large sum of money to a university to fund scholarships for deserving students.
		A child reads several books each week because reading is fun.
Extrinsic motivation	An activity is pursued to gain an external reward or to avoid an undesirable consequence.	A person agrees to donate a large sum of money to a university for the construction of a building, provided it will bear the family name.
		A child reads two books each week to avoid losing TV privileges.

Biological Approaches to Motivation ▶

Perhaps you have heard the term *instinct* used to explain why spiders spin webs or birds fly south in the winter. An *instinct* is a fixed behavior pattern that is characteristic of every member of a species and is assumed to be genetically programmed. Thus, instincts represent one kind of biological motivation. Psychologists generally agree that no true instincts motivate human behavior. However, most also agree that biological forces underlie some human behaviors.

One biological approach to motivation, **drive-reduction theory**, was popularized by Clark Hull (1943). According to Hull, all living organisms have certain biological needs that must be met if they are to survive. A need gives rise to an internal state of tension called a **drive**, and the person or organism is motivated to reduce it. For example, when you are deprived of food or go too long without water, your biological need causes a state of tension—in this case, the hunger or thirst drive. You become motivated to seek food or water to reduce the drive and satisfy your biological need.

Drive-reduction theory is derived largely from the biological concept of **homeostasis**—the tendency of the body to maintain a balanced, internal state to ensure physical survival. Body temperature, blood sugar level, water balance, blood oxygen level—in short, everything required for physical existence—must be maintained in a state of equilibrium, or balance. When such a state is disturbed, a drive is created to restore the balance, as shown in Figure 9.1.

9.2 How do drive-reduction and arousal theory explain motivation?

drive-reduction theory A theory of motivation suggesting that biological needs create internal states of tension or arousal—called drives—which organisms are motivated to reduce.

drive An internal state of tension or arousal that is brought about by an underlying need and that an organism is motivated to reduce.

homeostasis The natural tendency of the body to maintain a balanced internal state in order to ensure physical survival.

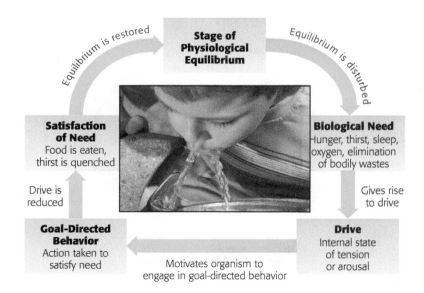

Stage of Physiological Equilibrium

Equilibrium is restored   *Equilibrium is disturbed*

Satisfaction of Need
Food is eaten, thirst is quenched

Drive is reduced

Goal-Directed Behavior
Action taken to satisfy need

Biological Need
Hunger, thirst, sleep, oxygen, elimination of bodily wastes

Gives rise to drive

Drive
Internal state of tension or arousal

Motivates organism to engage in goal-directed behavior

FIGURE 9.1 **Drive-Reduction Theory**
Drive-reduction theory is based on the biological concept of homeostasis—the natural tendency of a living organism to maintain a state of internal balance, or equilibrium. When the equilibrium becomes disturbed (by a biological need such as thirst), a drive (internal state of arousal) emerges. Then the organism is motivated to take action to satisfy the need, thus reducing the drive and restoring equilibrium.

arousal A state of alertness and mental and physical activation.

arousal theory A theory of motivation suggesting that people are motivated to maintain an optimal level of alertness and physical and mental activation.

stimulus motives Motives that cause humans and other animals to increase stimulation when the level of arousal is too low (examples are curiosity and the motive to explore).

Yerkes–Dodson law The principle that performance on tasks is best when the arousal level is appropriate to the difficulty of the task: higher arousal for simple tasks, moderate arousal for tasks of moderate difficulty, and lower arousal for complex tasks.

Drive-reduction theory assumes that humans are always motivated to reduce tension. Other theorists argue just the opposite, that humans are sometimes motivated to increase tension. These theorists use the term **arousal** to refer to a person's state of alertness and mental and physical activation. Arousal levels can range from no arousal (when a person is comatose), to moderate arousal (when pursuing normal day-to-day activities), to high arousal (when excited and highly stimulated). **Arousal theory** states that people are motivated to maintain the level of arousal that each individual considers to be optimal. If arousal is less than the optimal level, we do something to stimulate it; if arousal exceeds the optimal level, we seek to reduce the stimulation (see the *Explain It*).

When arousal is too low, **stimulus motives**—such as curiosity and the motives to explore, to manipulate objects, and to play—cause humans and other animals to increase stimulation. Think about sitting in an airport or at a bus stop or any other place where people are waiting. How many people do you see playing games on their cellphones or laptops? Waiting is boring; in other words, it provides no sources of arousal. Thus, people turn to electronic games to raise their level of arousal.

There is often a close link between arousal and performance. According to the **Yerkes–Dodson law**, performance on tasks is best when the person's arousal level is appropriate to the difficulty of the task. Performance on simple tasks is better when arousal is relatively high. Tasks of moderate difficulty are best accomplished when arousal is moderate; complex or difficult tasks, when arousal is lower (see Figure 9.2 below). But performance suffers when arousal level is either too high or too low for the task. For instance, how often have you heard great athletes who "choke" in critical situations compared to those who "come through" under pressure? Perhaps high-pressure situations push the athletes who choke past the optimal point of arousal but have just the opposite effect on the reliable athletes.

The relationship between arousal and performance is most often explained in terms of attention. Low arousal allows the mind to wander, so performance declines for tasks that require concentration, such as taking a test. By contrast, high arousal interferes with concentration by taking up all the available space in working memory. The ideal level of arousal for test taking, then, is an amount that is sufficient to keep the mind from wandering but not so great as to interfere with the memory demands of taking the test. Critics of this theory have argued that arousal is merely one of many variables that influence attention (Hanoch & Vitouch, 2004; Landers, 2007). Moreover, they point out that the Yerkes–Dodson law is based primarily on animal research (Hancock & Ganey, 2003). For these reasons, they caution against generalizing arousal theory to complex human behaviors such as test performance without taking into account other factors that influence how humans allocate attention.

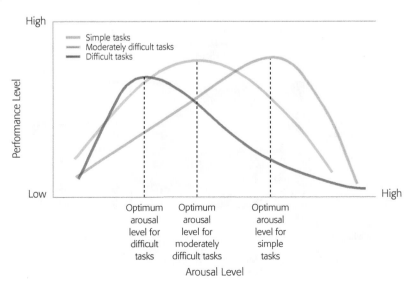

FIGURE 9.2 The Yerkes–Dodson Law The optimal level of arousal varies according to the difficulty of the task. Arousal levels should be relatively high for simple tasks, moderate for moderately difficult tasks, and lower for difficult tasks.

EXPLAIN IT   Why Are Dangerous Hobbies Appealing to Some People?

Suppose you had unlimited funds and unlimited time to pursue the hobby of your dreams. Would you choose skydiving, or would you prefer to spend your time developing an organic garden? Think for a minute about how drive-reduction and arousal theory might be used to explain your choice of a hobby.

Recall that drive-reduction theory proposes that we are motivated to reduce tension. But what is more tension inducing than jumping out of an airplane? Yet some people seem to crave such thrills. By the same token, what could be more calming than patiently working a plot of land until you succeed in getting it to produce the fruits and vegetables that you are trying to grow? Devoted gardeners would probably agree with this observation, but those who prefer skydiving would, no doubt, be bored to tears if they were forced to spend their time tending a garden. Consequently, drive-reduction theory cannot explain why people vary in their choices of leisure activities.

By contrast, arousal theorists would argue that hobby choices reflect individuals' standing with regard to *sensation seeking,* a variable that reflects our tendency to seek stimulation when our levels of arousal are low. Psychological researchers have found that differences in sensation seeking are correlated with activity choices. Thus, if you think you would prefer skydiving to gardening, you might be high in sensation seeking. If gardening is more appealing to you, then you are probably low in sensation seeking. If you are unsure as to where you might fall on a measure of sensation seeking, here are a few questions that can help you decide.

Circle the choice A or B that better describes your feelings:

1. A. I am invigorated by a brisk, cold day.

   B. I can't wait to get indoors on a cold day.

2. A. I get bored seeing the same old faces.

   B. I like the comfortable familiarity of everyday friends.

3. A. I sometimes like to do things that are a little frightening.

   B. A sensible person avoids activities that are dangerous.

4. A. The most important goal of life is to live it to the fullest and experience as much as possible.

   B. The most important goal of life is to find peace and happiness.

5. A. I would like to try parachute jumping.

   B. I would never want to try jumping out of a plane, with or without a parachute.

6. A. I enter cold water gradually, giving myself time to get used to it.

   B. I like to dive or jump right into the ocean or a cold pool.

7. A. A good painting should shock or jolt the senses.

B. A good painting should give one a feeling of peace and security.

8. A. People who ride motorcycles must have some kind of unconscious need to hurt themselves.

   B. I would like to drive or ride a motorcycle.

Count one point for each of the following items that you have circled: 1A, 2A, 3A, 4A, 5A, 6B, 7A, 8B. Add up your total and compare it with the norms: 0–1, Very low; 2–3, Low; 4–5, Average; 6–7, High; 8, Very high.

If your score is low, you may want to start saving now for a set of sturdy gardening tools. Be aware, however, that a low level of sensation seeking may also help you avoid the potentially health-threatening behaviors of substance abuse and even crossing busy streets against "Don't Walk" signals (Rosenbloom, 2006; Sterling et al., 2013). Thus, it may seem that high sensation-seekers have more fun, but they are also more vulnerable to risks that involve high levels of arousal.

⊙ Watch on **MyPsychLab**

Behavioral and Social-Cognitive Approaches to Motivation ▶

[**9.3** How do behavioral and social-cognitive theories explain work and achievement motivation?

The biological approaches that you have read about so far are helpful for understanding motivation on a physiological level, but they don't help us answer questions about the more complex social motives. To better understand motivation in work and school settings, we have to consider behavioral and social-cognitive approaches. You should remember from Chapter 5 that behavioral theories emphasize learning from consequences and social-cognitive theories focus on how people think about models, consequences, and other factors that influence their decisions about behavior.

industrial/organizational (I/O) psychologists
Psychologists who apply their knowledge in the workplace and are especially interested in work motivation and job performance.

goal setting An approach to work motivation that involves establishing specific, difficult goals rather than simply telling people to do their best in the absence of assigned goals.

expectancy theory An approach that explains work motivation in terms of workers' beliefs about the effectiveness and value of the effort they put forth on the job.

need for achievement (*n* Ach) The need to accomplish something difficult and to perform at a high standard of excellence.

Work Motivation. What motivates workers to perform well on the job? Psychologists who apply their knowledge in the workplace are known as **industrial/organizational (I/O) psychologists**. I/O psychologists design behavior modification plans that use reinforcers such as supervisor praise, bonuses, and extra time off to motivate employees to improve job performance. They may also use a strategy called **goal setting** in which supervisors provide employees with specific goals, such as providing salespeople with goals that are defined in dollar amounts or numbers of units sold, which leads to higher levels of performance than simply telling people to do their best (Seitjs & Latham, 2012). An organization can enhance employees' commitment to goals by (1) having them participate in the goal setting, (2) making goals specific, attractive, difficult, and attainable, (3) providing feedback on performance, and (4) rewarding the employees for attaining the goals (Katzell & Thompson, 1990).

Several social-cognitive theories have been applied to research on work motivation. According to one of these—**expectancy theory**—motivation to engage in a given activity is determined by (1) *expectancy,* a person's belief that more effort will result in improved performance; (2) *instrumentality,* the person's belief that doing a job well will be noticed and rewarded; and (3) *valence,* the degree to which a person values the rewards that are offered. Several studies have supported expectancy theory by showing that employees work harder when they believe that more effort will improve their performance, when they think that a good performance will be acknowledged and rewarded, and when they value the rewards that are offered (Diefendorff & Chandler, 2011).

Achievement Motivation. In early research, social-cognitive theorist Henry Murray (1938) developed the *Thematic Apperception Test (TAT)*, which consists of a series of pictures of ambiguous situations. (You will learn more about this test in Chapter 11.) The person taking the test is asked to create a story about each picture—to describe what is going on in the picture, what the person or persons pictured are thinking about, what they may be feeling, and what is likely to be the outcome of the situation. The stories are presumed to reveal the test taker's needs and the strength of those needs. One of the motives identified by Murray was the **need for achievement** (abbreviated *n* Ach), or the motive to accomplish something difficult and to maintain a high standard of performance. The need for achievement, rather than being satisfied with accomplishment, seems to grow as it is fed. Researchers David McClelland and John Atkinson have conducted many studies of the *n* Ach (McClelland, 1958, 1961, 1985; McClelland et al., 1953). People with a high *n* Ach pursue goals that are challenging yet attainable through hard work, ability, determination, and persistence. Goals that are too easy, those anyone can reach, offer no challenge and hold no interest because success would not be rewarding (McClelland, 1985). Impossibly high goals and high risks are not pursued because they offer little chance of success and are considered a waste of time. The goals of those with high *n* Ach are self-determined and linked to perceived abilities; thus, these goals tend to be realistic (Roberts, Treasure, & Conroy, 2007). For example, a player with high school basketball play with a high *n* Ach is likely to do an honest assessment of his skills and pursue scholarship offers from colleges whose teams play at the level that is most appropriate for his abilities.

By contrast, a high school basketball player with low *n* Ach who desires to play at the college level may adopt a goal that says "If I don't get a scholarship offer from a top-tier college, I won't play at all." This is because, according to researchers, people with low *n* Ach are not willing to take chances when it comes to testing their own skills and abilities. They are motivated more by their fear of failure than by their hope and expectation of success. This is why they set either impossibly high goals or ridiculously low ones, which anyone can attain (Geen, 1984). After all, who can fault a person for failing to reach a goal that is impossible for almost anyone? Complete the *Try It,* which describes a game that is said to reveal a high or low need for achievement.

Which peg in the ring toss game described in the *Try It* do you think people low in achievement motivation try for? If you guessed peg 1 or 2, or peg 5 or 6, you are right. People low in *n* Ach are likely to stand right over peg 1 so that they can't possibly fail. Or they may toss the rings at peg 6, hoping that they might be lucky. If

What Is Your *n* ACH?

Imagine yourself involved in a ring-toss game. You have three rings to toss at any of the six pegs pictured here. You will be paid a few pennies each time you are able to ring a peg.

Which peg would you try to ring with your three tosses—peg 1 or 2 nearest you, peg 3 or 4 at a moderate distance, or peg 5 or 6 at the far end of the row?

they fail, no one can blame them for not attaining a nearly impossible goal. A chance to win a few cents is certainly no incentive for people with a high *n* Ach, so they tend to toss their rings at peg 3 or 4, an intermediate distance that offers some challenge.

Another social-cognitive theory known as **goal orientation theory** provides a somewhat different view of achievement motivation. According to this perspective, achievement motivation varies according to which of four goal orientations an individual adopts (Wolters, 2004). Here's how each of the orientations might affect a college student. Students with a *mastery/approach* orientation will study and engage in other behaviors (e.g., attend class) so as to increase their knowledge and overcome challenges. Those who have a *mastery/avoidance* orientation will exhibit whatever behaviors are necessary to avoid failing to learn (a different outcome than a failing grade, by the way). Students with a *performance/avoidance* orientation will measure their performance against that of other students and are motivated to work to the point where they are at least equal to their peers. Finally, those who have a *performance/approach* orientation try to surpass the performance of their peers in an attempt to enhance their own sense of self-worth. (Table 9.2 summarizes the four goal orientations. Stop for a minute and think about which orientation best describes your own.) Research indicates that the performance/approach orientation is more strongly associated with high grades than any of the others (Anderman & Patrick, 2012).

goal orientation theory The view that achievement motivation depends on which of four goal orientations (mastery/approach, mastery/avoidance, performance/avoidance, performance/approach) an individual adopts.

TABLE 9.2 Goal Orientations

Mastery/Approach
Working to attain something of self-determined intrinsic value (e.g., knowledge).

Mastery/Avoidance
Working to avoid an outcome that threatens self-worth (e.g., being unable to learn something new).

Performance/Avoidance
Limiting efforts in order to avoid surpassing the performance of others (e.g., getting mediocre grades to fit in with a peer group).

Performance/Approach
Doing just enough work to ensure that one's performance will be superior to that of others (e.g., working for an A in a difficult class to feel superior to others in a class or being satisfied with a D because most other students are failing).

Note: Mastery involves working toward a personally meaningful goal. *Performance* involves working toward a goal defined by social comparison. *Approach* means that the goal helps the individual move toward something that is desirable. *Avoidance* means that the goal helps the individual move away from something that is undesirable.

9.4 What are Maslow's views on motivation?

self-actualization The pursuit of self-defined goals for personal fulfillment and growth.

✳ Explore the Concept *Maslow's Hierarchy of Needs* on **MyPsychLab**

◉ Watch the Video *Episode 12: What's in It for Me? Meeting Our Needs* in **MyPsychLab**

Maslow's Hierarchy of Needs

Another view of motivation, associated with the humanistic personality theory of Abraham Maslow, suggests that physiological motivations are the foundation for so-called higher-level motives (Maslow, 1970). He proposed that motivation is the process through which humans seek to meet their needs. Human needs, Maslow claimed, are hierarchical in nature, with our need for food and shelter at the bottom and our need for self-actualization at the top. **Self-actualization** is the pursuit of self-defined goals for personal fulfillment and growth. For example, a successful businessman who retires early to devote his time to charitable work is pursuing self-actualization goals. Thus, as Figure 9.3 suggests, in Maslow's view, it is impossible for an individual to attain self-actualization without first meeting his or her needs at the lower levels of the hierarchy. ✳

One implication of Maslow's theory is that we must work through our lower needs to experience the fulfillment that comes from pursuing personal growth for its own sake. However, the hierarchy also implies that humans are motivated by their lowest unmet need. If we ask, for example, why a student in school is failing to achieve one of Maslow's esteem needs, it is possible that the student has an unmet lower need. He or she may be hungry (physiological need), feel threatened in the school environment (safety need), or be concerned about peer rejection (belongingness need). Consequently, Maslow's theory has helped educators understand that providing students with adequate nutrition, ensuring their safety while at school, and supporting their social development may be as critical to achievement as curriculum materials and teaching strategies are.

Despite the practical implications of Maslow's theory, critics have often charged that self-actualization is an elusive concept. Maslow agreed to some extent and, in an effort to better illustrate the phenomenon, he studied people he believed were using their talents and abilities to their fullest. He studied some historical figures, such as Abraham Lincoln and Thomas Jefferson, and some individuals who made significant contributions during his or her own lifetime, including Albert Einstein, Eleanor Roosevelt, and Albert Schweitzer. Maslow found these self-actualizers to be accurate in perceiving reality—able to judge honestly and to spot quickly the fake and the dishonest. Most of them believed that they had a mission to accomplish or need to devote their life to some larger good. Finally, the hallmark of self-actualizers is frequently occurring *peak experiences*—experiences of deep meaning, insight, and harmony within and with the universe. ◉

FIGURE 9.3 Maslow's Hierarchy of Needs
According to humanistic psychologist Abraham Maslow, "higher" motives, such as the need for love, go unheeded when "lower" motives, such as the need for safety, are not met.

Need for Self-Actualization
Need to realize one's fullest potential

Esteem Needs
Needs to achieve, to gain competence, to gain respect and recognition from others

Belonging and Love Needs
Need to love and be loved; need to affiliate with others and be accepted

Safety Needs
Need for safety and security

Physiological Needs
Need to satisfy the basic biological needs for food, water, oxygen, sleep, and elimination of bodily wastes

The *Summarize It* recaps the theoretical approaches to motivation we have discussed in this section.

SUMMARIZE IT

Approaches to Motivation

APPROACH	DESCRIPTION	EXAMPLE
Drive-reduction theory	Behavior results from the need to reduce an internal state of tension or arousal.	Eating to reduce hunger
Arousal theory	Behavior results from the need to maintain an optimal level of arousal.	Climbing a mountain for excitement; listening to classical music for relaxation
Goal setting	Behavior results from establishing specific, difficult goals.	Reducing employees' absences by inviting them to participate in establishing the criteria for an attendance bonus
Expectancy theory	Behavior results from expectancy, instrumentality, and valence.	Employees working harder because they believe that their efforts will be effective and will be noticed by supervisors, and the employees value supervisors' approval
Need for achievement (*n* Ach)	Behavior results from the need to accomplish something difficult and to perform at a high level of excellence.	A medical school graduate choosing a specialty that requires a 6-year residency because he wants to challenge himself to attain the highest, most difficult goal possible
Goal orientation theory	Behavior depends on which of four goal orientations a person adopts (see Table 9.2 on page 301).	A student adopting the performance/approach orientation feeling satisfied with getting a C on an exam when he learns that all of the other students received Ds and Fs
Maslow's hierarchy of needs	Lower needs must be met before higher needs motivate behavior.	Schoolchildren not being able to focus on achievement if they are hungry or don't feel safe

REMEMBER IT

Check your answers and take additional quizzes in MyPsychLab.com.   ✓● Study and Review in MyPsychLab

1. Reading for pleasure is an example of _____ motivation.
2. Drive-reduction theory asserts that the desire to maintain _____ motivates human behavior.
3. The _____ law explains the relationship between arousal and performance.
4. Individuals who have a high need for achievement set goals that are of _____ difficulty.
5. In Maslow's view, after a people's physical and safety needs are satisfied, they seek fulfillment of _____, _____, and _____ needs.
6. _____ psychologists study the factors the influence work motivation.

Hunger

Earlier we told you that primary drives are unlearned motives that serve to satisfy biological needs. For instance, thirst is a basic biological drive. The motivation to drink is largely governed by physiological variables, such as the amount of salt in the body's cells. But what about hunger? In this section we'll look at the motivations related to hunger, body weight, and eating disorders.

Internal and External Cues ▶

Like thirst, hunger is influenced by physiological processes. For instance, you may recall reading in Chapter 4 that eating stimulates the brain's pleasure system. Thus, one of the reasons that we eat is because it is pleasurable. However, some researchers speculate that, as is true for some drugs, something can go awry in the brain's pleasure system such that food loses its capacity for inducing pleasure and, instead, becomes

9.5 How do internal and external cues influence eating?

lateral hypothalamus (LH) The part of the hypothalamus that acts as a feeding center to incite eating.

ventromedial hypothalamus (VMH) The part of the hypothalamus that acts as a satiety (fullness) center to inhibit eating.

✸ Explore the **Concept** *The Effects of the Hypothalamus on Eating Behavior* on **MyPsychLab**

the object of compulsive behavior (Berridge, 2009). As a result, a person becomes driven to eat or to avoid eating without regard to hunger, the pleasure associated with eating, or the consequences of compulsive consumption or avoidance of food.

Excessive food avoidance or consumption may also be caused by dysfunctions in the brain's feeding/satiety (fullness) system. As researchers discovered long ago, the **lateral hypothalamus (LH)** acts as a *feeding center* to incite eating. Stimulating the feeding center causes animals to eat even when they are full (Delgado & Anand, 1953). And when the feeding center is destroyed, animals initially refuse to eat (Anand & Brobeck, 1951). The **ventromedial hypothalamus (VMH)** apparently acts as a *satiety center* that inhibits eating (Hernandez & Hoebel, 1989). If the VMH is surgically removed, animals soon eat their way to gross obesity (Hetherington & Ranson, 1940; Parkinson & Weingarten, 1990). Moreover, some of the substances secreted by the gastrointestinal tract during digestion, such as the hormone cholecystokinin (CCK), act as satiety signals (Geary, 2004). ✸

More recent studies have suggested that referring to the LH as the brain's hunger center and the VMH as its satiety center fails to convey the subtle ways in which the neurons in these organs influence eating and body weight (King, 2006; Pinel, 2007). For one thing, animals eventually recover from LH damage and resume eating (Teitelbaum, 1957). Similarly, the effects of VMH damage are not permanent. A rat whose VMH is damaged will eventually stop overeating. In addition, damage to the VMH renders laboratory rats less willing to work (i.e., press a lever) in order to get food and more particular about what kinds of foods they are willing to eat. Thus, on balance, it's difficult to see how damage to the VMH alone might lead to obesity. Therefore, although the hypothalamus clearly plays a role in eating behavior, researchers have yet to determine precisely how its role is shaped by both its own neurons and biochemical signals from other components of the body's hunger management system.

Changes in blood sugar level and the hormones that regulate it also contribute to sensations of hunger. Blood levels of the sugar called *glucose* are monitored by nutrient detectors in the liver that send this information to the brain (Friedman, Tordoff, & Ramirez, 1986). Hunger is stimulated when the brain receives the message that blood levels of glucose are low. Similarly, insulin, a hormone produced by the pancreas, chemically converts glucose into energy that is usable by the cells. Elevations in insulin cause an increase in hunger, in food intake, and in a desire for sweets (Rodin et al., 1985). In fact, chronic oversecretion of insulin stimulates hunger and often leads to obesity.

As you may have learned from everyday experience, hunger can also be stimulated by external cues and the pleasure we associate with some foods (Harrold et al., 2012). For example, what happens when you smell a steak sizzling on the grill or chocolate chip cookies baking in the oven? For many, the hands of the clock alone, signaling mealtime, are enough to prompt a quest for food. Table 9.3 summarizes the factors that stimulate and inhibit eating.

TABLE 9.3   Biological and Environmental Factors That Inhibit and Stimulate Eating

	BIOLOGICAL	ENVIRONMENTAL
Factors that inhibit eating	Activity in ventromedial hypothalamus Raised blood glucose levels Distended (full) stomach CCK (hormone that acts as satiety signal) Sensory-specific satiety	Unappetizing smell, taste, or appearance of food Acquired taste aversions Learned eating habits Desire to be thin Reaction to stress, unpleasant emotional state
Factors that stimulate eating	Activity in lateral hypothalamus Low blood levels of glucose Increase in insulin Stomach contractions Empty stomach	Appetizing smell, taste, or appearance of food Acquired food preferences Being around others who are eating Foods high in fat and sugar Learned eating habits Reaction to boredom, stress, unpleasant emotional state

Explaining Variations in Body Weight ▶

Health care professionals classify individuals' body weights using a measure of weight relative to height called the **body mass index (BMI)**. A BMI that is less than 18.5 is considered underweight, while one in excess of 25 is classified as overweight. To calculate your BMI, use this formula or search online for a BMI calculator.

BMI = [Weight in pounds ÷ (height in inches × height in inches)] × 703

Why are there variations in human body weight? Heredity is one reason (Hamdy, 2012). One important review of studies that included more than 100,000 participants found that 74% of identical twin pairs had similar body weights. Only 32% of fraternal twins, however, had comparable body weights. The researchers reported an estimated heritability for body weight between 0.50 and 0.90 (refer back to Chapter 7 if you need a refresher on heritability). (Barsh, Farooqi, & O'Rahilly, 2000). More than 40 genes appear to be related to body weight regulation (Barsh et al., 2000).

But what exactly do people inherit that affects body weight? Researchers Friedman and colleagues identified the hormone *leptin,* which affects the hypothalamus and may be an element in the regulation of body weight (Smucny et al., 2012). Leptin is produced by the body's fat tissues. Decreases in body fat cause lower levels of leptin in the body. Lower levels of leptin stimulate food intake because the body "thinks" that it may be in danger of starvation. When leptin levels increase sufficiently people begin to lose weight due to the appetite-suppressing effects of rising levels of leptin. In one study, obese mice injected with leptin lost 30% of their body weight within 2 weeks (Halaas et al., 1995). However, the bodies of humans who are obese appear to develop a tolerance for the effects of leptin. Consequently, researchers are currently searching for a way to counteract this tolerance in hopes of developing a leptin-based anti-obesity drug (Ozcan et al., 2009).

The rate at which the body burns calories to produce energy is called the **metabolic rate**, and it is also influenced by genes. Further, *set point theory* suggests that each person is genetically programmed to carry a certain amount of body weight (Keesey, 1978). **Set point**—the weight the body maintains when one is trying neither to gain nor to lose weight—is affected by the number of fat cells in the body and by metabolic rate, both of which are influenced by the genes (Gurin, 1989).

Researchers think that fat cells send biochemical messages indicating how much energy is stored in them to the hypothalamus (Hallschmid et al., 2004). Presumably, the genes influence what the hypothalamus "believes" to be the appropriate amount of energy to store. One of the most important current lines of research in this area aims to identify these biochemical messages and influence them in ways that will lower the set points of obese individuals (Hallschmid et al., 2004).

Obesity and Weight Loss ▶

Variations in body weight have emerged as an important public health topic in recent years because of the link between excessive weight and health problems, such as heart disease and arthritis (Hamdy, 2012). As you can see in Figure 9.4, the prevalence of both

9.6 What factors contribute to individual differences in body weight?

body mass index (BMI) A measure of weight relative to height.

metabolic rate (meh-tuh-BALL-ik) The rate at which the body burns calories to produce energy.

set point The weight the body normally maintains when one is trying neither to gain nor to lose weight.

9.7 What does research suggest about obesity and dieting?

FIGURE 9.4 **Age-Adjusted* Prevalence of Overweight and Obese among U.S. Adults, Age 20–74 Years**
*Age-adjusted by the direct method to the year 2000 U.S. Bureau of the Census estimates using the age groups 20–39, 40–59, and 60–74 years.
Source: National Center for Health Statistics (2012).

obesity BMI over 30.

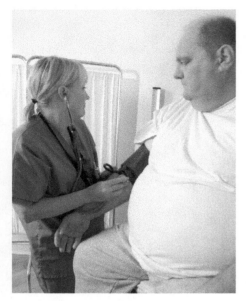

▲ Surgical techniques that limit the amount of food that an individual's digestive system can take in at one time (e.g., gastric bypass) are a last resort for some individuals who are obese. Most patients lose weight after the surgery, but they must adopt a healthy diet and increase their physical activity to maintain a healthy body weight.

overweight (BMI between 25 and 29.9) and **obesity** (BMI over 30) has risen dramatically over the past three decades. More than one-third of adults in the United States are obese.

Most individuals who are obese require the help of a physician to attain a healthy weight. For one thing, many suffer from other health problems, such as diabetes, that are linked to their weight problems in complex ways. Thus, any weight-loss program they undertake must be managed in such a way that does not aggravate other conditions. Children who are obese also require medical assistance to lose weight because caloric restriction diets can interfere with their growth (Krebs & Primak, 2011).

For unknown reasons, some people who suffer from obesity appear to be unable to reverse the trend of continual weight gain. For these individuals, *bariatric surgery*, procedures in which the capacity of the stomach is modified to reduce the amount of food that the person can consume, may be the only alternative (Saber, 2012). Candidates for bariatric surgery must have a BMI in excess of 40. Individuals with BMIs ranging from 35 to 39 may be considered for the surgery if they have a weight-related health problem, such as diabetes or high blood pressure. Among more than 80% of patients, the bariatric surgical technique known as *gastric bypass* results in both weight reduction below the obesity threshold and improvements in weight-related health conditions (Schauer et al., 2000). However, physicians stress that any person who undergoes the surgery must be willing to commit to postoperative lifestyle changes, including following a healthy diet and exercise regimen (Saber, 2012). These changes are needed because, even with reduced stomach capacity, it is quite possible to return to an obese state after a period of postoperative weight loss. Moreover, bariatric surgery is associated with risks, such as the possibility of postoperative infection. In general, the heavier the patient is, the greater the risk of postsurgical complications (Livingston et al., 2002).

For individuals who are not obese, the principles of successful dieting are fairly simple. There is no need to spend your hard-earned money on special foods, food supplements, or the latest celebrity or fad diet. In fact, the Mayo Clinic in Rochester, Minnesota, is one of many health care institutions that have posted everything you need to know about weight loss on the Internet (Mayo Clinic, 2010). Table 9.4

TABLE 9.4 **Six Weight-Loss Strategies from the Mayo Clinic**

Be determined to stick with it.
Approach weight loss as an effortful task, one in which you are likely to have some setbacks. Be determined to persist toward your weight-loss goal.

Get support.
Share your goals with people whom you know will support and encourage you. If possible, participate in an informal weight-loss support group, or suggest to a friend who also wants to lose weight that the two of you become "accountability partners."

Aim for attainable objectives.
Do some research to determine your body type and a target weight that is appropriate for you. A realistic time frame is important as well. Permanent weight loss is best achieved over a long, rather than a short, period of time with a reasonable diet and exercise program that you can stick to.

Change your eating habits.
Making permanent changes in your everyday diet is the best way to insure that the pounds you shed during dieting won't reappear as soon as you return to your normal eating patterns. The Mayo Clinic states, too, that extreme calorie restriction—less than 1,200 calories per day for women and 1,400 for men—is detrimental to your health.

Exercise.
There is simply no way around the fact that increased activity is vital to the success of any weight-loss plan. Find a physical activity that you enjoy, or do something that you enjoy (e.g., listening to music) while engaging in a calorie-burning activity, to motivate yourself to exercise.

Focus on long-term changes.
Devise your entire plan, eating, exercise, and all, with the idea in mind that you are designing a lifelong strategy for weight maintenance.

Source: Mayo Clinic (2010).

summarizes the strategies the clinic recommends for achieving and maintaining a healthy weight.

The complexities of the processes involved in appetite regulation and energy metabolism explain why diets often do not work (Campbell & Dhand, 2000). To be effective, any weight-loss program must help people decrease energy intake (eat less), increase energy expenditure (exercise more), or both (Bray & Tartaglia, 2000). Unfortunately, most people who are trying to lose weight focus only on cutting calories.

Eating Disorders ▶

Eating disorders are a category of mental disorders in which eating and dieting behaviors go far beyond the everyday extremes of overeating and dieting many people experience. One eating disorder, **anorexia nervosa**, is characterized by an overwhelming, irrational fear of gaining weight or becoming fat, compulsive dieting to the point of self-starvation, and excessive weight loss. Some people with anorexia lose as much as 20 to 25% of their original body weight. The disorder typically begins in adolescence, and most of those afflicted are females. About 1 to 4% of females are diagnosed this disorder (American Psychiatric Association, 2006a). The greater prevalence of eating disorders among females appears to be a general phenomenon rather than a culturally specific one. In a large sample of Norwegian adults, for example, women were twice as likely as men to have an eating disorder (Augestad, 2000). ◉

There are important differences between dieting (even obsessive dieting) and anorexia nervosa. For one, among people with anorexia, perceptions of body size are grossly distorted (Castellini et al., 2013). No matter how emaciated they become, they continue to perceive themselves as fat. Researchers have learned that such unrealistic perceptions may result from a general tendency toward distorted thinking (Tchanturia et al., 2001). Moreover, most individuals with anorexia—as many as 88% in some studies—are diagnosed with another kind of psychiatric disorder, such as depression, along with their eating disorder (Swanson et al., 2011). These findings suggest that, for some individuals with anorexia, the eating disorder may be only one component of a larger psychiatric problem.

Frequently, people with anorexia not only starve themselves but also exercise relentlessly in an effort to accelerate the weight loss. Further, they don't necessarily avoid food or the ritual of eating. Indeed, most people with anorexia are fascinated with food and the process of preparing it (Faunce, 2002). Many become skilled in giving the appearance of eating while not actually swallowing food. To accomplish this, some of them habitually chew and spit out their food, often with such dexterity that others with whom they eat don't notice (Kovacs, Mahon, & Palmer, 2002).

Among young females with anorexia, progressive and significant weight loss eventually results in amenorrhea (cessation of menstruation). Some may also develop low blood pressure, impaired heart function, dehydration, electrolyte disturbances, and sterility (American Psychiatric Association, 2006a), as well as decreases in the gray matter volume in the brain (Mainz et al., 2012). Moreover, prolonged self-starvation induces changes in the lining of the stomach that can make it extremely difficult for people with anorexia to recover normal functioning of the digestive system even after they have begun eating normally (Ogawa et al., 2004). Unfortunately, as many as 6% of those suffering from anorexia nervosa eventually die of starvation or complications from organ damage (Arcelus, Mitchell, Wales, & Nielsen, 2011).

It is difficult to pinpoint the cause of this disorder. Most individuals who are diagnosed with anorexia are well behaved and academically successful (Vitousek & Manke, 1994). Psychological risk factors for eating disorders include being overly concerned about physical appearance, worrying about perceived attractiveness, and feeling social pressure in favor of thinness (Whisenhunt et al., 2000). Some investigators

9.8 What are the characteristics of eating disorders?

anorexia nervosa An eating disorder characterized by an overwhelming, irrational fear of gaining weight or becoming fat, compulsive dieting to the point of self-starvation, and excessive weight loss.

◉ **Watch** the Video *Speaking Out: Natasha: Living with Anorexia Nervosa* in **MyPsychLab**

▲ Victoria Beckham is one of many young women who have struggled with anorexia. Individuals with anorexia usually have a distorted body image that causes them to believe they are overweight when they are actually dangerously underweight.

believe that young women who refuse to eat are attempting to control a portion of their lives, which they may feel unable to control in other respects.

Anorexia is very difficult to treat. Most people with anorexia are steadfast in their refusal to eat, while insisting that nothing is wrong with them. The main thrust of treatment, therefore, is to get the individual to gain weight. The patient may be admitted to a hospital, fed a controlled diet, and given rewards for small weight gains and increases in food intake. The treatment usually includes some type of psychotherapy and/or a self-help group. Some studies show that antidepressant drugs may help in the treatment of anorexia (Barbarich et al., 2004). Others suggest that protein-rich supplements help individuals with anorexia regain their normal appetites (Latner & Wilson, 2004). Multidimensional treatment programs—that is, those that combine medication, nutritional therapy, and psychotherapy—may prove to be the most successful approach (Godart et al., 2012).

bulimia nervosa An eating disorder characterized by repeated and uncontrolled (and often secretive) episodes of binge eating.

As many as 50% of those with anorexia also develop **bulimia nervosa**, a chronic disorder characterized by repeated and uncontrolled (and often secretive) episodes of binge eating (American Psychiatric Association, 2006a). And individuals who do not have anorexia can develop bulimia alone. Many people with bulimia come from families in which family members make frequent negative comments about others' physical appearances (Crowther et al., 2002).

An episode of binge eating has two main features: (1) the consumption of much larger amounts of food than most people would eat during the same period of time and (2) a feeling that one cannot stop eating or control the amount eaten. Binges—which generally involve foods that are rich in carbohydrates, such as cookies, cake, and candy—are frequently followed by purging. Purging consists of self-induced vomiting and/or the use of large quantities of laxatives and diuretics. People with bulimia may also engage in excessive dieting and exercise. Athletes are especially susceptible to this disorder.

Bulimia nervosa can cause a number of physical problems. The stomach acid in vomit eats away at the teeth and may cause them to rot, and the delicate balance of body chemistry is destroyed by excessive use of laxatives and diuretics. People with bulimia may have a chronic sore throat as well as a variety of other symptoms, including dehydration, swelling of the salivary glands, kidney damage, and hair loss. The disorder also has a strong emotional component; the person with bulimia is aware that the eating pattern is abnormal and feels unable to control it. Depression, guilt, and shame accompany both binging and purging. Some evidence suggests that decreased function of the neurotransmitters serotonin and dopamine appears to contribute to this disorder (Avena & Bocarsly, 2012).

Bulimia nervosa tends to appear in the late teens and affects 1 to 2% of women (Osterhout, 2011). Like those with anorexia, people with bulimia have high rates of other psychiatric disorders (Milos et al., 2002). Further, perhaps as many as one-third of them have engaged in other kinds of self-injurious behavior, such as cutting themselves intentionally (Paul et al., 2002).

About 10 to 15% of all people with bulimia are males, and homosexuality or bisexuality seems to increase males' risk for bulimia (Carlat, Camargo, & Herzog, 1997). In addition, researchers are finding more evidence of a cultural component to bulimia. Westernized attitudes in Turkey, for example, are clashing with the country's traditional values and, according to researchers, creating an increase in cases of bulimia (Elal et al., 2000). Apparently, some Turkish citizens are succumbing to Western media pressure to have an ultrathin body.

Bulimia, like anorexia, is difficult to treat. Some behavior modification programs have helped extinguish bulimic behavior (Traverso et al., 2000), and cognitive-behavioral therapy has been used successfully to help those with bulimia modify their eating habits and their abnormal attitudes about body shape and weight (Wilson & Sysko, 2006). Certain antidepressant drugs have been found to reduce the frequency of binge eating and purging in some individuals with bulimia. ◉

◉—[**Watch** the Video *Episode 12: In the Real World: Eating Disorders* in **MyPsychLab**

1. A low level of _____ in the bloodstream is one of several hunger signals.

2. The _____ is a measure of weight relative to height.

3. People with eating disorders typically have distorted perceptions of their _____.

Sexual Motivation

Alfred Kinsey and his coauthors' *Sexual Behavior in the Human Male* (1948) and *Sexual Behavior in the Human Female* (1953) shattered many widely held beliefs about sexuality. Though his work has been called into question by many other researchers on both theoretical and methodological grounds, most admit that the topic of sexuality is discussed more openly now than was true before Kinsey's landmark research findings became known. We will begin our consideration of this important motivational domain with a discussion of cultural and gender differences in sexual attitudes and behavior. ●

●─[Watch the Video *Episode 14: Big Picture: The Power of Sex* in **MyPsychLab**

Sexual Attitudes and Behavior ▶───────────

9.9 How do sexual attitudes and behavior vary across cultures and genders?

You probably won't be surprised to learn that a large majority of adults all over the world are sexually active. As you can see in Table 9.5 on p. 310, the average frequency of sexual intercourse varies considerably from one culture to another (Durex Sexual Wellbeing Survey, 2008). Surveys suggest that the percentage of adults who engage in intercourse at least once a week varies from a low of 34% in Japan to a high of 87% in Greece. Of course, individuals vary considerably around these averages. Some people have sex several times each day; while others never have sex at all. Perhaps the reasons behind relatively high rates of sexual activity are simple: People enjoy sex, and attitudes have changed such that they feel free to do so. But what explains the low rate of sexual activity in Japan? Japanese officials, concerned about their country's plummeting birth rate and growing number of elderly, blame long work days, the high cost of raising children, and the increasing number of women who choose to focus on their careers rather than to become mothers (Reuters, 2006). Of course, these trends are found throughout the industrialized world, so they cannot explain why Japanese sexual activity rates are lower than those of other nations. ●

●─[Watch the Video *Episode 14: Special Topics: Cultural Norms and Sexual Behavior* in **MyPsychLab**

As you learned in Chapter 8, sexual activity continues throughout the life span. In one very large survey involving people aged 40 to 80 in 13 different countries, researchers found that 83% of men and 66% of women had engaged in intercourse at least once in the last year (Gingell et al., 2003). One reason why intercourse frequency was lower among women was that many of the elderly women in the study were widows who lacked access to a partner. Nevertheless, men and women of all ages differ with regard to sexual attitudes and behavior, even when both have equal access to a partner.

On average, men are more interested in sex and think about it more often than women do (Peplau, 2003). And they are more likely than women to be interested in purely physical sex and to have more permissive attitudes toward sex (Thompson & O'Sullivan, 2012; Dantzker & Eisenman, 2003). Nevertheless, the gender gap has narrowed considerably since the mid-20th century. Psychologists Brooke Wells and Jean Twenge analyzed the results of attitude surveys from 1958 to 1987 (Wells & Twenge, 2005). They found that among young women (ages 12 to 27), approval rates for premarital sex rose dramatically, from 30% in the early years of their study to 91% in 1987. Behavior, too, had changed. Twenge's analysis showed that

TABLE 9.5 Selected Findings from the Durex Global Sex Survey

COUNTRY	PERCENTAGE OF ADULTS WHO HAVE SEX AT LEAST ONCE A WEEK	PERCENTAGE WHO ARE SATISFIED WITH THEIR SEX LIVES
Greece	87%	51%
Brazil	82%	42%
Russia	80%	42%
China	78%	42%
Italy	76%	36%
South Africa	71%	50%
Germany	68%	38%
Canada	59%	48%
United Kingdom	55%	40%
United States	53%	48%
Nigeria	53%	67%
Japan	34%	15%

Source: Durex Global Sex Survey (2008).

about 13% of teenaged girls admitted to being sexually active during the 1950s. By the 1990s, the proportion had increased to 47%. Thus, even though recent surveys show that there are still gender differences in both sexual attitudes and behavior, the historical perspective helps us see that, over time, this gender gap has narrowed considerably. However, critics of such studies say that what has really changed is people's willingness to talk about their sexual experiences rather than their actual attitudes and behavior (Dobson & Baird, 2006).

Why do these gender differences exist? Evolutionary psychologists often explain these differences as resulting from the influence of evolution on men's and women's mating behaviors. Many use the term **parental investment** to denote the amount of time and effort men or women must devote to parenthood. According to parental investment theory, women and men have adopted mating strategies that correspond to their respective investments in parenting (Shackelford et al., 2012). Men are assumed to be interested in making only a short-term biological investment in parenting, so they typically seek women who are young, healthy (physical attractiveness is taken as a sign of good health), and well suited for child bearing. Because parenting requires a greater investment from women (9 months of pregnancy and a long period of dependency), they tend to prefer men who are somewhat older, more stable and with sufficient resources, generous, emotionally attached, and strong enough to provide protection for the family. These and related gender differences are apparently not culture-specific, since they have been found in 37 different countries (Buss, 1994). ◉

As you learned in Chapter 1, and as the *Think About It* activity at the beginning of this chapter illustrated, Buss's research also shows that men are mostly concerned about sexual fidelity, presumably because they want to be certain that any children conceived are their own. Women, by contrast, are most interested in emotional fidelity, or the idea that they should be able to count on a man to be fully committed to a psychological and social partnership with them. Other researchers have replicated these findings in more recent work (Sagarin et al., 2013). Moreover, Buss and his colleagues have replicated them in both elderly (average age = 67) and young adult (average age = 20) samples (Shackelford et al., 2004).

parental investment A term used by evolutionary psychologists to denote the amount of time and effort men or women must devote to parenthood.

◉ **Watch** the Video *Episode 14: What's in It for Me? The Dating Game* in **MyPsychLab**

As evolutionary theory would predict, women appear to have the strongest desire for sex around the time of ovulation when they are most likely to conceive a child (Durante et al., 2012). Similarly, studies conducted by Viennese researcher Karl Grammar (cited in Holden, 1996) indicate that increases in men's testosterone levels are linked to the *pheromones,* odor-producing hormones, that are found in women's vaginal secretions at the time of ovulation. Thus, it is likely that men are the most rapidly aroused in the presence of female partners who are ovulating. 👁

Other researchers question whether women's reported mate preferences and concerns about emotional fidelity are thoroughly biological in nature. Researchers Wood and Eagly (2012) cite research demonstrating that gender differences in mate preferences are significantly smaller when economic and social conditions for males and females are more equal, as they are becoming in developed countries in the 21st century. In other words, when women are economically dependent on men, the mating "rules" described by evolutionary psychologists may apply; however, gender differences in mate preferences decline as women gain independence. Researchers have found that, under conditions of equality, physical attractiveness in a mate is just as important to women as to men, and a woman's earning capacity and intellectual abilities are more highly valued by men (Zentner & Mitura, 2012).

Eagly and Wood may be right. Research indicates that, in societies with egalitarian attitudes about gender roles, marital status and income are correlated. Longitudinal, prospective research has shown that the higher a woman's economic status, the more likely she is to get married (Ono, 2003). Moreover, the sexual/emotional fidelity distinction appears to be larger among older women than among college students, so younger cohorts of women may be developing beliefs about fidelity that are more similar to those held by men (Shackelford et al., 2004). Today's men may be looking for more in their mates than just good looks and child-bearing potential, and today's women may be more concerned about sexual fidelity than their mothers and grandmothers were.

Sexual Desire and Arousal ▶

Dr. William Masters and Dr. Virginia Johnson conducted the first laboratory investigations of the human sexual response in 1954. They monitored their volunteer participants, who engaged in sex while connected to electronic sensing devices. Masters and Johnson (1966) concluded that both males and females experience a **sexual response cycle** with four phases.

The *excitement phase* is the beginning of the sexual response. Visual cues, such as watching a partner undress, are more likely to initiate the excitement phase in men than in women. Tender, loving touches coupled with verbal expressions of love arouse women more readily than visual stimulation. And men can become aroused almost instantly, while arousal for women is often a more gradual, building process. For both partners, muscular tension increases, heart rate quickens, and blood pressure rises. As additional blood is pumped into the genitals, the male's penis becomes erect, and the female feels a swelling of the clitoris. Vaginal lubrication occurs as the inner two-thirds of the vagina expands and the inner lips of the vagina enlarge. In women especially, the nipples harden and stand erect.

After the excitement phase, the individual enters the *plateau phase,* when excitement continues to mount. Blood pressure and muscle tension increase still more, and breathing becomes heavy and more rapid. The man's testes swell, and drops of liquid, which can contain live sperm cells, may drip from the penis. The outer part of the woman's vagina swells as the increased blood further engorges the area. The clitoris withdraws under the clitoral hood (its skin covering), and the breasts become engorged with blood. Excitement builds steadily during the plateau phase.

The *orgasm,* the shortest of the phases, is the highest point of sexual pleasure, marked by a sudden discharge of accumulated sexual tension. Involuntary muscle contractions may seize the entire body during orgasm, and the genitals contract rhythmically. Orgasm is a two-stage experience for the male. First is his awareness that ejaculation is

👁 **Watch** the Video *Evolution and Sex: Michael Bailey* in **MyPsychLab**

9.10 What are the phases of the human sexual response cycle?

sexual response cycle The four phases—excitement, plateau, orgasm, and resolution—that make up the human sexual response in both males and females, according to Masters and Johnson.

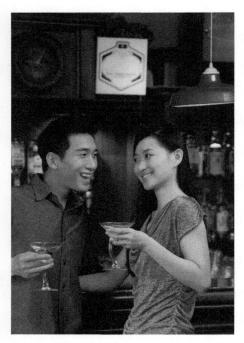

▲ Psychological factors play an important role in sexual attraction and arousal. Such factors include preferences and attitudes we learn from our culture.

9.11 What does research show regarding sexual orientation?

◉ Watch the Video *Episode 14: Thinking Like a Psychologist: Sexual Orientation* in **MyPsychLab**

sexual orientation The direction of one's sexual interest—toward members of the opposite sex (heterosexuality), toward one's own sex (homosexuality), or toward both sexes (bisexuality).

near and that he can do nothing to stop it; second is the ejaculation itself, when semen is released from the penis in forceful spurts. The experience of orgasm in women builds in much the same way as for men. Marked by powerful, rhythmic contractions, the female's orgasm usually lasts longer than that of the male. About 40 to 50% of women regularly experience orgasm during intercourse (Wilcox & Hager, 1980).

The orgasm gives way to the *resolution phase,* a tapering-off period, when the body returns to its unaroused state. Men experience a *refractory period* in the resolution phase, during which they cannot have another orgasm. The refractory period may last from only a few minutes for some men to as long as several hours for others. Women do not have a refractory period and may, if restimulated, experience another orgasm right away.

The sexual response cycle is strongly influenced by hormones. The sex glands manufacture hormones—*estrogen* and *progesterone* in the ovaries and *androgens* in the testes. The adrenal glands in both sexes also produce small amounts of these hormones. Females have considerably more estrogen and progesterone than males do, so these are known as the female sex hormones. Males have considerably more androgens, the male sex hormones.

Testosterone, the most important androgen, influences the development and maintenance of male sex characteristics, as well as sexual motivation. Males must have a sufficient level of testosterone to maintain sexual interest and have an erection. Females, too, need small amounts of testosterone in the bloodstream to maintain sexual interest and responsiveness (Andersen & Cyranowski, 1995). Deficiencies in sexual interest and activity can sometimes be reversed in both men and women with the use of testosterone patches or ointments (Meyer, 1997). However, researchers point out that many hormones work in concert with testosterone to regulate the sexual response cycle and warn against the assumption that pharmacological manipulation of testosterone alone is adequate to solve problems with sexual functioning (Halaris, 2003). You will learn more about the topic of sexual dysfunctions in Chapter 12.

Psychological factors play a large role in sexual arousal. Part of the psychological nature of sexual behavior stems from preferences and practices that people learn from their culture. And cultural norms about sexual behavior vary widely, covering everything from the age at which initiation of sexual behavior is proper to the partners, conditions, settings, positions, and specific sexual acts that are considered acceptable.

Sexual fantasies also influence sexual arousal. Both men and women are likely to fantasize during intercourse. Most sexual fantasies involve conventional imagery about one's current or past partner or an imaginary lover. There are consistent gender differences in fantasies (Schmitt et al., 2012). Men's fantasies generally involve more specific visual imagery, and women's fantasies have more emotional and romantic content.

Sexual Orientation

Now we turn our attention to **sexual orientation**—the direction of an individual's sexual preference, erotic feelings, and sexual activity. In heterosexuals, the human sexual response is oriented toward members of the opposite sex; in homosexuals, toward those of the same sex; and in bisexuals, toward members of both sexes. ◉

Prevalence. Estimating the prevalence of homosexuality is difficult. One problem is that, as you learned in Chapter 1, people sometimes give inaccurate information in response to researchers' questions about personal matters. But the biggest obstacle involves the definition of homosexuality itself. Is a person classified as homosexual if he or she has ever been attracted to someone of the same sex? What if they have had only one sexual experience with someone of the same sex? And if researchers limit the definition of homosexuality to those whose current sexual activity is restricted to partners of the same sex, will they underestimate the prevalence of homosexuality? These questions demonstrate two things. First, that sexual orientation is not a matter of strict categories. Sexual expression can be thought of as a continuum of experience, from, for instance, zero interest and participation in same-sex relations to exclusive interest and participation in same-sex relations. Second, when we are trying to make sense of survey data on homosexual behavior, we must find out how the researchers defined homosexuality, what specific questions they asked, and how they analyzed the data.

Because of the complexities involved in defining sexual orientation combined with people's reluctance to share information about the intimate details of their lives, reliable studies of the prevalence of homosexuality are few and far between. That's why researchers continue to look to studies that were done decades ago, and to compare more recent data to them, in order to determine patterns in the prevalence of homosexuality rather than specific percentages. For instance, Kinsey and his associates (1948, 1953) estimated that 4% of the male participants had nothing but homosexual relations throughout life, and 2 to 3% of the female participants had been in mostly or exclusively lesbian relationships. Interestingly, a recent survey of more than 120,000 adults in the United States found rates of homosexual orientation that were similar to Kinsey's. Some 3.4% of respondents reported that they identified with a gay, lesbian, bisexual, or transgender sexual orientation (Gates & Newport, 2012). By contrast, a survey of more than 20,000 adults conducted by the Centers for Disease Control found that 1.8% of men identified as gay and 1.2% of women as lesbian. An additional 1.2% of men and 3.9% of women reported that they were bisexual (CDC, 2012).

Causes. Ample evidence exists to support the hypothesis that some kind of genetic predisposition increases the likelihood of a homosexual orientation in both men and women (Dawood, Bailey, Martin, & Kim, 2009). Twin studies show that 50 to 60% of the identical twins of gay men are also gay, and slightly less than 50% of the identical twins of lesbian women are also lesbians (Bailey & Pillard, 1991; Bailey et al., 1993; Whitam, Diamond, & Martin, 1993). However, researchers have yet to identify a specific set of genes that accounts for homosexual orientation or the molecular mechanism through which genes may influence sexual orientation (Dawood et al., 2009).

In the last few years, researchers have examined the relationship between prenatal hormones and sexual orientation (Balthazart, 2012). Many of these studies have focused on associations between these hormones and inconsistencies between the left and right sides of the body. One such difference involves the ratio of the second and fourth fingers on the left and right hands (Grimbos et al., 2010). It has long been known that fluctuations of androgen levels in the prenatal environment can produce these inconsistencies. Thus, researchers reason that if prenatal androgens contribute to sexual orientation, then such physical inconsistencies should occur more frequently in homosexuals than in heterosexuals. Studies have shown that this is indeed the case (Grimbos et al., 2010).

Neuroscientist Simon LeVay (1991) reported that an area in the hypothalamus governing sexual behavior is about twice as large in heterosexual men as in homosexual men. Critics were quick to point out that all of the gay men included in LeVay's sample died of AIDS. Many researchers questioned whether the brain differences LeVay observed might have resulted from AIDS rather than being associated with sexual orientation (Byne, 1993). However, more recent animal studies have also suggested a link between the hypothalamus and sexual orientation. Among domestic species of sheep, about 10% of males (i.e., rams) exhibit homosexual behavior. Researchers have found that, like LeVay's subjects, male-oriented rams have a smaller hypothalamus than those who prefer exclusively female partners do (Roselli et al., 2004).

Consequently, many psychologists suggest that sexual orientation should be studied as a complex interaction of nature and nurture, using theoretical models similar to those used by developmental psychologists to explain other phenomena (Dawood, Bailey, & Martin, 2009). For instance, developmentalists often study the ways in which family characteristics contribute to the development of children's traits and behavior. In one early study that examined homosexuality from this perspective, Bell, Weinberg, and Hammersmith (1981) conducted extensive face-to-face interviews with 979 homosexual participants (293 women, 686 men) and 477 heterosexual controls. The researchers found no single condition of family life that in and of itself appeared to be a factor in either homosexual or heterosexual development.

9.12 How have attitudes toward homosexuality changed in recent decades?

Social Attitudes toward Gays and Lesbians

No discussion of sexual orientation would be complete without consideration of the social challenges that have been faced by gays and lesbians and society's increasing tolerance of homosexual relationships. For instance, the American Psychiatric Association considered homosexuality a disorder until 1973 but now views it as such only if the individual considers it a problem. Thanks to such changes, more gay men and lesbians are "coming out," preferring to acknowledge and express their sexual orientation. Nevertheless, attitudes toward homosexuality vary widely across cultures. In numerous jurisdictions in North American and Europe, same-sex couples can marry. At the opposite end of the spectrum, individuals who are caught engaging in homosexual behavior are subject to the death penalty in nations such as Saudi Arabia, Iran, Sudan, and Mauritania.

Homophobia is an intense, irrational hostility toward or fear of homosexuals that can lead to discrimination against gays and lesbians or even motivate acts of violence against them. Fortunately, the negative views of homosexuality held by most people stop short of full-blown homophobia. Generally, men are more likely to express such views. For instance, in one survey, 54% of women believed that homosexuality is morally acceptable, while only 45% of men approved of same-sex relationships (Pew Research Center, 2006).

Importantly, though, most people are opposed to discrimination based on sexual orientation. (Moreover, such discrimination is illegal.) Surveys show that more than three-quarters of Americans believe that homosexuality should not be a factor in hiring public school teachers (Herek, 2002). Similarly, an overwhelming majority of Americans, including those who are strongly opposed to homosexual behavior, adamantly support the rights of homosexuals to speak out and to try to influence public policy. Thus, objections to homosexuality appear to be focused on the behavior itself and not on those who exhibit it.

▲ Social attitudes toward homosexuality vary widely around the world. In the United States, court rulings and legislation in several states have paved the way for same-sex couples to marry.

homophobia An intense, irrational hostility toward or fear of homosexuals.

REMEMBER IT

Check your answers and take additional quizzes in MyPsychLab.com. ✓●─Study and Review in MyPsychLab

1. _____ tend to have more permissive attitudes toward premarital sex than _____ do.
2. _____ theory is an evolutionary explanation of gender differences in mating strategies.
3. The human sexual response cycle was first described by _____ and _____.
4. Surveys suggest that homosexuality is more common in _____ than in _____.

Emotion

emotion A state involving physiological arousal, a cognitive appraisal of the situation that produced the state, and an outward behavior expressing the state.

Much of our motivation to act is fueled by emotional states. In fact, the root of the word *emotion* means "to move," indicating the close relationship between motivation and emotion. Psychologists define **emotion** as a state involving physiological arousal, a cognitive appraisal of the stimulus that brought about the state, and an outward behavior expressing the state. But what, precisely, are emotions?

9.13 What theories have been proposed to explain emotion?

Theories of Emotion

Typically, psychologists have studied emotion in terms of three components: physical, cognitive, and behavioral (Frijda, 2012). The three components appear to be interdependent. For instance, in one study, participants who were better at detecting heartbeat variations (the physical component) rated their subjective experiences of emotion (the cognitive component) as being more intense than did participants who were less able to detect physical changes (Wilken et al., 2000). However, neither the physical nor the cognitive components completely determine how emotion is expressed (the behavioral component). Moreover, there is a long-standing debate among psychologists about which component comes first in the overall experience of emotion.

American psychologist William James (1884) argued that an event causes physiological arousal and a physical response, after which the individual perceives the physical response as an emotion. At about the same time James proposed his theory, a Danish physiologist and psychologist, Carl Lange, independently formulated nearly the same theory. The **James–Lange theory** of emotion (Lange & James, 1922) suggests that different patterns of arousal in the autonomic nervous system produce the different emotions people feel, and that the physiological arousal appears before the emotion is perceived (see Figure 9.5).

Another early theory of emotion that challenged the James–Lange theory was proposed by Walter Cannon (1927), who did pioneering work on the fight-or-flight response and the concept of homeostasis. Cannon claimed that the bodily changes caused by the various emotions are not sufficiently distinct to allow people to distinguish one emotion from another. Cannon's original theory was later expanded by physiologist Philip Bard (1934). The **Cannon–Bard theory** suggests that the following chain of events occurs when a person feels an emotion: Emotion-provoking stimuli are received by the senses and are then relayed simultaneously to the cerebral cortex, which provides the conscious mental experience of the emotion, and to the sympathetic nervous system, which produces the physiological state of arousal. In other words, the feeling of an emotion (fear, for example) occurs at about the same time as the experience of physiological arousal (a pounding heart). One does not cause the other. Consequently, a proponent of the Canon–Bard theory would argue that Figure 9.5 should consist of two cells instead of three. The first would show the growling dog, and the second would show both the physical and the cognitive response of the frightened person.

Stanley Schachter believed that the early theories of emotion left out a critical component—the subjective interpretation of why a state of arousal has occurred. Schachter and Singer (1962) proposed the *two-factor theory*. According to the **Schachter–Singer theory**, two things must happen for a person to feel an emotion: (1) The person must first experience physiological arousal and (2) there must then

James–Lange theory The theory that emotional feelings result when an individual becomes aware of a physiological response to an emotion-provoking stimulus (for example, feeling fear because of trembling).

Cannon–Bard theory The theory that an emotion-provoking stimulus is transmitted simultaneously to the cerebral cortex, providing the conscious mental experience of the emotion, and to the sympathetic nervous system, causing the physiological arousal.

Schachter–Singer theory A two-factor theory stating that for an emotion to occur, there must be (1) physiological arousal and (2) a cognitive interpretation or explanation of the arousal, allowing it to be labeled as a specific emotion.

| Stimulus situation | → | Physiological arousal, action | → | Experience of emotion based on interpretation of arousal and action |

A dog growls at you. → Your heart pounds; you run. → "My heart is racing and I'm running. I must be afraid."

FIGURE 9.5 The James–Lange Theory of Emotion
The James–Lange theory of emotion is the exact opposite of what subjective experience tells us. If a dog growls at you, the James–Lange interpretation is that the dog growls, your heart begins to pound, and only after perceiving that your heart is pounding do you conclude that you must be afraid.

be a cognitive interpretation, or explanation, of the physiological arousal so that the person can label it as a specific emotion. Thus, Schachter concluded, a true emotion can occur only if a person is physically aroused and can find some reason for it. When people are in a state of physiological arousal but do not know why they are aroused, they tend to label the state as an emotion that is appropriate to their situation at the time. For example, a person who feels anxious but doesn't know why might identify the feeling as the same one she felt just before a dentist began performing a root canal procedure on one of her molars. Because she labeled the feeling she experienced in the root canal situation as "anxiety," she will apply the same label to what she is currently feeling.

The theory of emotion that most heavily emphasizes the cognitive aspect has been proposed by Richard Lazarus (1991a, 1991b, 1995). According to the **Lazarus theory**, a cognitive appraisal is the first step in an emotional response; all other aspects of an emotion, including physiological arousal, depend on the cognitive appraisal. This theory is most compatible with the subjective experience of an emotion's sequence of events—the sequence that William James reversed long ago. Faced with a stimulus—an event—a person first appraises it. This cognitive appraisal determines whether the person will have an emotional response and, if so, what type of response. The physiological arousal and all other aspects of the emotion flow from the appraisal. In short, Lazarus contends that emotions are provoked when cognitive appraisals of events or circumstances are positive or negative—but not neutral.

Critics of the Lazarus theory point out that some emotional reactions are instantaneous—occurring too rapidly to pass through a cognitive appraisal (Zajonc, 1980, 1984). Lazarus (1984, 1991a) responds that some mental processing occurs without conscious awareness. And there must be some form of cognitive realization, however brief, or else a person would not know what he or she is responding to or what emotion to feel—fear, happiness, embarrassment, and so on. Further, researchers have found that reappraisal, or changing one's thinking about an emotional stimulus, is related to a reduction in physiological response (Gross, 2002).

The *Summarize It* below recaps the four major theories of emotion: James–Lange, Cannon–Bard, Schachter–Singer, and Lazarus. You might be wondering which is correct. If so, think back to the advice we gave you in Chapter 1 regarding the tendency to think of theories as "true" or "false." We advised you to think of theories as supported or not supported by evidence rather than as "true" or "false." In the case of theories of emotion, there is evidence supporting all of them, the result being that a comprehensive explanation of emotion includes elements of all four theories. Moreover, to truly understand emotion, we have to take into account recent research examining their neurological foundations.

Lazarus theory The theory that a cognitive appraisal is the first step in an emotional response and all other aspects of an emotion, including physiological arousal, depend on it.

SUMMARIZE IT

Theories of Emotion

THEORY	VIEW	EXAMPLE
James–Lange theory	An event causes physiological arousal. You experience an emotion only *after* you interpret the physical response.	You are walking home late at night and hear footsteps behind you. Your heart pounds and you begin to tremble. You interpret these physical responses as fear.
Cannon–Bard theory	An event causes a physiological *and* an emotional response simultaneously. One does not cause the other.	You are walking home late at night and hear footsteps behind you. Your heart pounds, you begin to tremble, and you feel afraid.
Schachter–Singer theory (two-factor theory)	An event causes physiological arousal. You must then be able to identify a reason for the arousal to label the emotion.	You are walking home late at night and hear footsteps behind you. Your heart pounds and you begin to tremble. You know that walking alone at night can be dangerous, so you feel afraid.
Lazarus theory	An event occurs, a cognitive appraisal is made, and then the emotion and physiological arousal follow.	You are walking home late at night and hear footsteps behind you. You think it could be a mugger. So you feel afraid, your heart starts to pound, and you begin to tremble.

Emotion and the Brain ▶

Researchers have used many of the techniques you learned about in Chapter 2—EEG, MRI, fMRI, PET scans, and so on—to study the neurological foundations of emotion, a field called **affective neuroscience** (Dalgleish, Dunn, & Mobbs, 2009). One thing that they have learned is that each emotion has a distinctive response system within the brain as Figure 9.6 suggest (Dalgleish, 2004). In addition, researchers have identified several brain structures that play key roles in our emotional experiences.

You should recall from Chapter 2 that the amygdala is part of the limbic system and is closely associated with fear (LeDoux, 2000). Information comes to the amygdala directly from all five of the senses and is acted on immediately, without initial involvement of the primary "thinking" area of the brain, the cortex. But, as with reflex actions, the cortex does become involved as soon as it "catches up" with the amygdala (LeDoux, 2000). Once it does so, the cortex tempers the amygdala's fear response with its interpretation of the fear-provoking situation. The ability of the cortex to control the amygdala's fear, often through revision of fear-inducing memories, is also vital to our ability to overcome previously learned fears (LeDoux & Droyère, 2011). Thus, when people manage to conquer, say, the fear associated with taking an important exam, they can thank their cortex's ability to regulate the amygdala.

When the emotion of fear first materializes, much of the brain's processing is nonconscious. The person becomes conscious of it later, because the cortex monitors the physiological signals that accompany emotion, such as changes in heart rate. The cortex uses these signals to relate our current circumstances to emotion-provoking experiences that are stored in memory (Dalgleish, 2004). This monitoring function of the cortex contributes to our ability to use stored information about the meaning of our emotions to make decisions in situations in which logic and information are insufficient (Damasio, 1995). Consequently, people who have sustained damage to the parts of the cortex that perform the monitoring function have difficulty making such decisions. For example, researchers have found that such people have a very limited ability to develop effective strategies for playing games that require *intuition*, which you should remember from Chapter 7 is often described as a "hunch" or "gut feeling" (e.g., Clark et al., 2008). An example will help you see how this works. Suppose you are playing a video game in which you have to make split-second, yes/no decisions about choices that are offered to a character that you are controlling, such as deciding whether the character should turn left or right, go through a door, or jump to a new level. The pace of the game does not allow for a logical analysis of all of the possible consequences that

9.14 What have affective neuroscientists learned about emotion and the brain?

affective neuroscience The study of the neurological foundations of emotion.

FIGURE 9.6 Neuroimaging of Emotions
Neuroimaging studies reveal that emotions trigger patterns of brain activity that are different from those that are associated with other types of experiences.

SADNESS

ANGER

HAPPINESS

FEAR

may follow these actions. As a result, you must rely on intuition to make choices for the character (Kuo et al., 2009). The emotion-monitoring system in your cortex guides these decisions based on information stored in your memory about past choices and the emotions they elicited. It does the same when everyday life confronts us with situations in which we must make decisions quickly as well, such as when you notice dark clouds and must make a quick, yes/no decision about taking an umbrella with you to class.

Of course, there are times when decision-making processes must ignore emotion to be effective, as is the case when we must resist the lure of an immediate reward in order to achieve a long-term goal. In such cases, affective neuroscientists say that the *anterior cingulate cortex (ACC)*, the front part of a band that surrounds the corpus callosum, works with the cortex to suppress the emotional cues that are associated with the immediate reward (Tullett et al., 2013). As a result, we are able to focus our attention on the long-term goal and act thoughtfully rather than impulsively. Thus, it isn't surprising that researchers have found links between delayed maturity of the ACC and serious behavior problems among preadolescent boys (De Brito et al., 2009). Similarly, animal studies show that damage to the ACC disrupts animals' social relationships (Rudebeck et al., 2007). This finding makes sense when you consider how important the inhibition of impulses is to social relationships. For instance, most people agree that you will be better off in the long run if you refrain from telling off your boss every time you are angry with her. Thanks to your ACC, you can resist the pull of fantasies about how good you think you will feel in the short run if you tell her off in favor of the long-term goal of keeping your job.

9.15 How do males and females differ with regard to emotion?

Gender Differences in Emotion

Do females and males differ significantly in the way they experience their emotions? According to the evolutionary perspective, your answer to the following question is likely to be gender specific: What emotion would you feel first if you were betrayed or harshly criticized by another person? When asked to respond to this question, male research participants in a classic study were more likely to report that they would feel angry; female participants were more likely to say that they would feel hurt, sad, or disappointed (Brody, 1985). Of course, both males and females express anger, but typically not in the same ways. Women are just as likely as men to express anger in private (at home) but much less likely than men to express it publicly, especially in the workplace (Cupach & Canary, 1995; Sloan, 2012). The reason that women may fail to show anger in public is that in general, women are expected to suppress negative emotions and express positive ones (Simpson & Stroh, 2004). The pattern of expectations is just the opposite for men.

Researchers have also found evidence of sex differences in the intensity of emotional response that may have a biological basis. In one interesting study along these lines, researchers measured levels of *cortisol,* a stress hormone that increases with emotional arousal, in husbands and wives after discussions of positive and negative events in their relationships (Kiecolt-Glaser, 2000). The researchers found that women's cortisol levels increased after discussions of negative events, while men's levels remained constant. This finding suggests that women may be more physiologically sensitive to negative emotions than men are.

▲ Do you think that gender differences in experiencing emotions affect the ways in which men and women argue? If so, how?

9.16 How do humans express and influence emotion?

The Expression of Emotion

Expressing emotion comes as naturally to humans as breathing. Two leading researchers on emotion, Paul Ekman (1993) and Carroll Izard (1992), insist that there are a limited number of basic emotions. **Basic emotions** are unlearned and universal; that is, they are found in all cultures, are reflected in the same facial expressions, and emerge in children according to their own biological timetable of development. Fear, anger, disgust, surprise, joy or happiness, and sadness or distress are usually considered basic emotions. Izard (1992, 1993) suggests that there are distinct neural circuits that underlie each of the basic emotions, and Levenson and others (1990) point to specific autonomic nervous system activity associated with the basic emotions.

basic emotions Emotions that are unlearned and universal, that are reflected in the same facial expressions across cultures, and that emerge in children according to their biological timetable of development; fear, anger, disgust, surprise, happiness, and sadness are usually considered basic emotions.

TRY IT

Recognizing Basic Emotions

Look carefully at the six photographs. Which basic emotion is portrayed in each?
Match the number of the photograph with the basic emotion it conveys.

a. happiness	b. sadness	c. fear	d. anger	e. surprise	f. disgust
1. _____	2. _____	3. _____	4. _____	5. _____	6. _____

ANSWERS: 1. d   2. c   3. f   4. e   5. a   6. b

Watch on **mypsychlab**

In studying the range of emotion, Ekman (1993) has suggested considering emotions as comprising families. The anger family would range from annoyed to irritated, angry, livid, and, finally, enraged. Furthermore, the anger family, if it exists, also includes various forms in which the emotion is expressed, according to Ekman (1993). Resentment, for example, is a form of anger "in which there is a sense of grievance" (p. 386). Just as there are many words in the English language to describe the variations in the range of any emotion, Ekman and Friesen claim that subtle distinctions in the facial expression of a single emotion convey its intensity (Ekman, 1993).

Charles Darwin (1872/1965) maintained that most emotions and the facial expressions that convey them are genetically inherited and characteristic of the entire human species. If Darwin was right, then everyone should label the expressions in the *Try It* the same way. Do your labels agree with those of others? To test his belief, Darwin asked missionaries and people of different cultures around the world to record the facial expressions that accompany the basic emotions. Based on those data, he concluded that facial expressions were similar across cultures. Modern researchers agree that Darwin was right.

Other researchers have found evidence for universality as well as for cultural variations. Scherer and Wallbott (1994) found very extensive overlap in the patterns of emotional experiences reported across cultures in 37 different countries on five continents. They also found important cultural differences in the ways emotions are elicited and regulated and in how they are shared socially. Recent research suggests that Asians pay more attention to indicators of emotion, such as tone of voice, than Westerners do (Ishii, 2011).

Moreover, each culture appears to have an "accent" for facial expressions (Marsh, Elfenbein, & Ambady, 2007). This accent is a pattern of minute muscle movements that are used by most members of a culture when they exhibit a particular facial expression. In other words, there is a Japanese way to make a happy face, an American way to make a happy face that is somewhat different, and a German way of making a happy face that differs from both. In fact, these differences are enough to influence perceptions

display rules Cultural rules that dictate how emotions should generally be expressed and when and where their expression is appropriate.

facial-feedback hypothesis The idea that the muscular movements involved in certain facial expressions produce the corresponding emotions (for example, smiling makes one feel happy).

positive psychology The view that psychologists should study and promote the development of human strengths such as optimism.

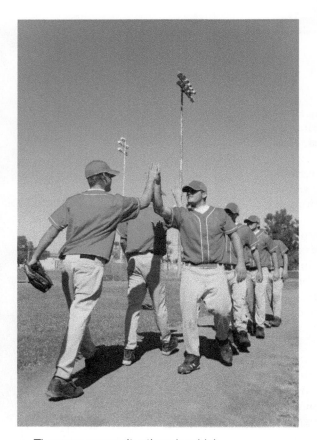

▲ There are many situations in which people must disguise their emotions to comply with the display rules of their culture, which dictate when and how feelings should be expressed. For example, these soccer players—both winners and losers—are expected to be good sports, even if it means hiding their true feelings.

of emotion even when individuals come from very similar cultural backgrounds. In one classic study, researchers found that white Americans more quickly identified the facial expressions of other white Americans than did white Europeans (Izard, 1971).

Each culture has very different **display rules**—cultural rules that dictate how emotions should generally be expressed and where and when their expression is appropriate (Ekman, 1993; Ekman & Friesen, 1975; Scherer & Wallbott, 1994). Often a society's display rules require people to give evidence of certain emotions that they may not actually feel or to disguise their true feelings. For example, Americans are expected to look sad at funerals, to hide disappointment at not winning, and to refrain from making facial expressions of disgust when served food that tastes bad. Display rules in Japanese culture dictate that negative emotions must be disguised when other people are present (Ekman, 1972; Triandis, 1994). In East Africa, young males from traditional Masai society are expected to appear stern and stony-faced and to "produce long, unbroken stares" (Keating, 1994).

There are variations in display rules across groups within the same culture as well. For instance, researchers have found that, in most work settings, supervisors expect the workers they manage to express more positive than negative emotions (Diefendorff & Richard, 2003). Similarly, researchers have learned that, in the United States, teens conform to unspoken display rules acquired from peers that discourage public displays of emotion. The resulting subdued emotional expressions can cause them to appear to be aloof, uncaring, and even rude to parents and other adults (Salisch, 2001). Psychologists speculate that conformity to these peer-based display rules may be the basis of much miscommunication between teens and their parents and teachers.

Could controlling one's facial expressions be a means of controlling the emotions themselves? The idea that the muscular movements involved in certain facial expressions produce the corresponding emotion is called the **facial-feedback hypothesis** (Strack, Martin, & Stepper, 1988). Some evidence supports this notion. In classic research, Ekman and colleagues (1983) demonstrated that physiological measures of emotion such as heart rate and muscle tension changed in response to changes in research participants' facial expressions. More recently, researchers have found that people's facial expressions are more likely to change the intensity of the emotion they are really feeling as well as to enable them to change from one state to another (Soussignan, 2002; Lewis, 2012). Thus, if you are angry and you adopt an angry expression, you will feel angrier. Moreover, neutralizing your facial expression may be the first step toward gaining control when your emotions are heading in a direction that you think may be more harmful than helpful.

If we can control our emotions, is it a good idea to do so? You may have heard that "venting" anger can make you feel better. However, there is no evidence to support this view, and, in fact, venting may actually make you feel worse (Lohr et al., 2007). Moreover, it can lead to aggressive behavior. Thus, research suggests that learning to regulate and manage anger is a better option than venting.

As you learned in Chapter 1, one of today's most influential clinical psychologists, Martin Seligman, has enthusiastically endorsed the idea that people can and should exert control over their emotions to maintain positive emotional states (e.g., happiness) and avoid negative ones (e.g., anger) (Seligman, 2011). Moreover, he has argued that the field of psychology can help people do so by devoting as much time and energy to studying human strengths such as *optimism*, a positive outlook on life, as we do to studying weaknesses such as psychological disorders, an approach called **positive psychology** (Seligman & Csikszentmihalyi, 2000). Positive psychologists such as Barbara Fredrickson (2009) suggest that positive emotions enable us to focus on applying and modifying the coping strategies that have worked well for us in the past to new challenges. By contrast, negative feelings direct our attention to our problems. The *Apply It* provides you with important tips for maintaining a positive outlook.

APPLY IT   **The Quest for Happiness**

Happiness is closely related to life satisfaction—people who feel happy also tend to believe that their lives are satisfying. Of course, there are factors in everyone's life that can't be changed, and some of them can result in unhappiness. However, people can use certain strategies to exercise greater control over the way they respond emotionally to their life situations.

Remove Your Rose-Colored Glasses

Having a generally positive outlook on life is an important factor in maintaining a sense of well-being. However, do you know what it means to "see the world through rose-colored glasses"? The expression derives from a French metaphor, *voire la vie en rose* ("to see life in pink"), which means to see things more favorably than they really are. Psychologist Daniel Gilbert has studied the connection between decision making and happiness (Gilbert, 2006). He points out that we are often disappointed when we make decisions based on what we believe will make us happy. For example, the belief that a new house will make us happy motivates us to save money, spend time searching for a house, and go through the stressful experience of moving. But within a very short time, we discover that the new house did not bring us the bliss we expected. Gilbert says that we do the same thing in relationships. In pursuit of happiness, we date, marry, have affairs, divorce, have children, reconcile with estranged relatives, cut off communication with troublesome relatives, join clubs to find new friends, and on and on, only to find that we revert to our original emotional state after all is said and done.

Count Your Blessings

Perhaps we can avoid the hope–disappointment cycle Gilbert describes by learning to be more appreciative of what we already have. Psychologist Martin Seligman (2011) has used a number of exercises geared toward increasing people's sense of well-being by getting them to focus on the positive aspects of their experiences. One such exercise is "Three Good Things." Seligman instructs participants in his studies to keep a journal in which they record three positive things that happen each day. They have found that participants report feeling happier after having kept the "three good things" journal for only a week. Furthermore, those who continue the practice after their participation in the study has ended report enduring effects.

Keep Busy

You will also feel happier if you get so caught up in an activity that you become oblivious to your surroundings. Psychologists refer to this state as *flow*. To be in flow is to be unself consciously absorbed (Csikszentmihalyi et al., 2005). People who are caught up in some activity that engages their skills—whether it is work, play, or simply driving a car—report more positive feelings.

You may not be able to control every aspect of your life situation, but you do have some control over how you respond to it. 👁

👁 **Watch** the Video *Episode 12: Thinking Like a Psychologist: Affective Forecasting* in **MyPsychLab**

REMEMBER IT

Check your answers and take additional quizzes in MyPsychLab.com.   ✔ **Study** and **Review** in **MyPsychLab**

1. Emotion involves _____, _____, and _____ components.
2. The _____ theory suggests that the feeling of an emotion and the physiological response to an emotional situation occur at about the same time.
3. The _____ theory suggests that the physiological arousal and the emotion flow from a cognitive appraisal of an emotion-provoking event.
4. When fear strikes, the (amygdala/cortex) is activated before the (amygdala/cortex).
5. Because of cultural _____, people sometimes express emotions they do not really feel.

Looking Back

Now that you have finished reading about motivation and emotion, you can probably see how individual differences in optimism contribute to the various topics that were discussed in this chapter. With regard to work motivation, for example, a person who is optimistic may be more strongly motivated to take on new challenges and thereby gain access to opportunities than more pessimistic employees are. Likewise, in romantic relationships, it seems that a basic belief in one's ability to bring about good outcomes, another way of thinking optimistically, would be likely to motivate a person to tolerate the risk of rejection that goes along with approaching a potential romantic party. As a result, optimistic people may have more opportunities to explore relationships than those who are pessimistic. Thus, if you find yourself tending toward the pessimistic side of the optimism–pessimism continuum, it might be worth your while to consult a counselor who is an adherent of positive psychology and who knows how to help you develop a more positive outlook on life.

CHAPTER 9 SUMMARY

EXPLAINING MOTIVATION (pp. 295–303)

9.1 How do psychologists define and classify motivation? (pp. 295–297)

Activation is the component of motivation in which an individual takes the first steps toward a goal. Persistence is the component of motivation that enables a person to continue to work toward the goal even when he or she encounters obstacles. The intensity component of motivation refers to the energy and attention a person must employ to reach a goal. Primary drives are unlearned biological motives, such as thirst and hunger. Social motives are learned from experience and interactions with others. With intrinsic motivation, an act is performed because it is satisfying or pleasurable. With extrinsic motivation, an act is performed to gain a reward or avert an undesirable consequence.

Key Terms
motivation, p. 295
motives, p. 296
primary drives, p. 296
social motives, p. 296
work motivation, p. 296
achievement motivation, p. 296
intrinsic motivation, p. 296
incentive, p. 296
extrinsic motivation, p. 296

9.2 How do drive-reduction and arousal theory explain motivation? (pp. 297–299)

Drive-reduction theory suggests that a biological need creates an unpleasant state of emotional arousal that compels the organism to engage in behavior that will reduce the arousal level. Arousal theory suggests that the aim of motivation is to maintain an optimal level of arousal.

Key Terms
drive-reduction theory, p. 297

drive, p. 297
homeostasis, p. 297
arousal, p. 298
arousal theory, p. 298
stimulus motives, p. 298
Yerkes–Dodson law, p. 298

9.3 How do behavioral and social-cognitive theories explain work and achievement motivation? (pp. 299–301)

Behavioral techniques such as reinforcement and goal setting are used by industrial-organizational psychologists to enhance workers' motivation. Expectancy theory is a social-cognitive theory that focuses on workers' beliefs about the effectiveness and value of their efforts. Two other social-cognitive theories, need for achievement theory and goal orientation theory, help to explain achievement motivation.

Key Terms
industrial/organizational (I/O) psychologists, p. 300
goal setting, p. 300
expectancy theory, p. 300
need for achievement (n Ach), p. 300
goal orientation theory, p. 301

9.4 What are Maslow's views on motivation? (pp. 302–303)

According to Maslow, higher needs cannot be addressed until lower needs are met. Lower needs include both physiological needs (e.g., for food) and the need for safety. Once these are satisfied, behavior can be motivated by higher needs, such as the needs for belonging, esteem, and self-actualization.

Key Term
self-actualization, p. 302

HUNGER (pp. 303–309)

9.5 How do internal and external cues influence eating behavior? (pp. 303–304)

The brain's pleasure system influences eating behavior. The lateral hypothalamus (LH) signals us to eat when we are hungry, and the ventromedial hypothalamus (VMH) motivates us to stop eating when we are full. Other internal hunger signals are low blood glucose levels and high insulin levels. Some satiety signals are high blood glucose levels and the presence in

the blood of other satiety substances (such as CCK) that are secreted by the gastrointestinal tract during digestion. External hunger cues, such as the taste, smell, and appearance of food; eating with other people; and the time of day can cause people to eat more food than they actually need.

Key Terms
lateral hypothalamus (LH), p. 304
ventromedial hypothalamus (VMH), p. 304

9.6 What factors contribute to individual differences in body weight? (p. 305)

Variations in body weight are influenced by genes, hormones, metabolic rate, activity level, number of fat cells, and eating habits. Fat-cell theory claims that individuals who are overweight have more fat cells in their bodies. Set point theory suggests that an internal homeostatic system functions to maintain body weight by adjusting appetite and metabolic rate.

Key Terms

body mass index (BMI), p. 305
metabolic rate, p. 305
set point, p. 305

9.7 What does research suggest about obesity and dieting? (pp. 305–307)

Some people who are obese cannot lose weight and must undergo gastric bypass surgery to attain a healthy body weight. Weight-loss programs for such individuals and those for children must be carefully supervised by health professionals. To be effective, a weight-loss strategy must include calorie reduction and exercise.

Key Term

obesity, p. 306

9.8 What are the characteristics of eating disorders? (pp. 307–309)

The symptoms of anorexia nervosa are an overwhelming, irrational fear of being fat, compulsive dieting to the point of self-starvation, and excessive weight loss. It damages the heart and other organs and can be fatal. The symptoms of bulimia nervosa are repeated and uncontrolled episodes of binge eating, usually followed by purging. Intentional vomiting can cause dental and digestive problems for people who have bulimia nervosa. Both anorexia and nervosa are more common in females than in males, are difficult to treat, and often occur along with other psychiatric disorders.

Key Terms

anorexia nervosa, p. 307
bulimia nervosa, p. 308

SEXUAL MOTIVATION (pp. 309–314)

9.9 How do sexual attitudes and behavior vary across cultures and genders? (pp. 309–311)

Men are more likely than women to think of sex in purely physical terms and to have more permissive attitudes toward sex. The frequency of sexual activity varies across cultures. During ovulation women have the strongest desire for sex, and men are likely to be most rapidly aroused by ovulating female partners. Evolutionary psychologists say that differences in parental investment explain gender differences in attitudes and behavior, but others argue that social factors are responsible.

Key Term

parental investment, p. 310

9.10 What are the phases of the human sexual response cycle? (pp. 311–312)

The sexual response cycle consists of four phases: the excitement phase, the plateau phase, orgasm, and the resolution phase. Hormones influence the cycle in both men and women.

Key Term

sexual response cycle, p. 311

9.11 What does research show regarding sexual orientation? (pp. 312–313)

Two general patterns in the prevalence of homosexuality are that males are more likely to identify with an exclusive homosexual orientation than women are, and same-sex attraction is more common than homosexual behavior. The biological factors suggested as possible causes of a gay or lesbian sexual orientation are (1) androgens; (2) structural differences in an area of the hypothalamus of gay men; and (3) genetic factors.

Key Term

sexual orientation, p. 312

9.12 How have attitudes toward homosexuality changed in recent decades? (p. 314)

Prior to 1973, homosexuality was considered to be a disorder by mental health professionals. Today most people are opposed to discrimination based on homosexuality. Homosexual relationships are similar to those involving heterosexuals. Gay men are more tolerant of sexual infidelity than heterosexual and lesbian couples. Like heterosexual women, lesbians place more emphasis on mutual emotional support than they do on sexual intimacy.

Key Term

homophobia, p. 314

EMOTION (pp. 314–321)

9.13 What theories have been proposed to explain emotion? (pp. 314–316)

The three components of emotions are the physiological arousal that accompanies the emotion, the cognitive appraisal of the stimulus or situation, and the outward behavioral expression of the emotion. According to the James–Lange theory of emotion, environmental stimuli produce a physiological response, and then awareness of this response causes the emotion to be experienced. The Cannon–Bard theory suggests that emotion-provoking stimuli received by the senses are relayed simultaneously to the cerebral cortex, providing the mental experience of the emotion, and to the sympathetic nervous system, producing physiological arousal. The Schachter–Singer theory states that for an emotion to occur, (1) there must be physiological arousal, and (2) the person must perceive some reason for the arousal in order to label the emotion. According to the Lazarus theory, an emotion-provoking stimulus triggers a cognitive appraisal, which is followed by the emotion and the physiological arousal.

Key Terms
emotion, p. 314
James–Lange theory, p. 315
Cannon–Bard theory, p. 315
Schachter–Singer theory, p. 315
Lazarus theory, p. 316

9.14 What have affective neuroscientists learned about emotion and the brain? (pp. 317–318)

Affective neuroscientists have identified associations between emotions and different areas of the brain, and most believe a distinct neurological system underlies each emotion. The amygdala contributes to fear-based learning. The cortex monitors physiological cues associated with emotion and relates them to past experiences to help us make decisions. The anterior cingulate cortex suppresses emotional cues to help us control impulsivity.

Key Term
affective neuroscience, p. 317

9.15 How do males and females differ with regard to emotion? (p. 318)

Men and women appear to manage emotions differently. Women are more likely to feel hurt or disappointed after a betrayal or harsh criticism from another person, while men are more likely to feel angry. Men and women also differ in their likeliness to express anger publicly.

9.16 How do humans express and influence emotion? (pp. 318–321)

The basic emotions (happiness, sadness, disgust, and so on) are those that are unlearned and universal and that emerge in children according to their biological timetable of development. Studies also show that there is variation across cultures in the ways emotions are elicited and regulated and how they are shared socially. The customs of an individual's culture determine when, where, and under what circumstances various emotions are exhibited. Children learn these rules as they mature so that, as adults, they will be able to suppress and exhibit emotions in accordance with the rules of their cultures. Violating a culture's display rules can cause a person's behavior to be interpreted as rude or offensive. The facial-feedback hypothesis suggests that the muscular movements involved in certain facial expressions trigger corresponding emotions (for example, smiling triggers happiness). Positive psychologists study the impact of positive emotional states on other aspects of functioning.

Key Terms
basic emotions, p. 318
display rules, p. 320
facial-feedback hypothesis, p. 320
positive psychology, p. 320

Chapter 9 Study Guide

Answers to all the Study Guide questions are provided at the end of the book.

SECTION ONE: Chapter Review

Explaining Motivation (pp. 295–303)

1. Motives move us toward goals. (true/false)

2. When you engage in an activity to gain a reward or to avoid an unpleasant consequence, your motivation is (intrinsic, extrinsic). The desire to behave a certain way because it is enjoyable and satisfying in and of itself is (intrinsic, extrinsic) motivation.

3. Drive-reduction theory states that people are motivated to
   a. reduce tension created by biological drives.
   b. seek emotional highs such as the feelings you have on a roller coaster.
   c. obey genetically programmed instincts.
   d. maintain appropriate levels of arousal.

4. According to arousal theory, people seek _____ arousal.
   a. minimized
   b. increased
   c. decreased
   d. optimal

5. According to Maslow's hierarchy of needs, which needs must be satisfied before a person will try to satisfy the belonging and love needs?
   a. safety and self-actualization needs
   b. self-actualization needs and esteem needs
   c. physiological and safety needs
   d. physiological and esteem needs

6. Murray used the Thematic Apperception Test (TAT) to study the need for achievement. (true/false)

7. Individuals who have a _____ goal orientation are motivated by a desire to outperform others.

8. Industrial/organizational psychologists use reinforcement and goal setting to increase
   a. achievement motivation.
   b. mastery motivation.
   c. performance motivation.
   d. work motivation.

9. According to _____ theory, an employee's belief that increased effort will lead to improved performance is an important element of work motivation.

Hunger (pp. 303–309)

10. The lateral hypothalamus (LH) acts as a (feeding, satiety) center; the ventromedial hypothalamus (VMH) acts as a (feeding, satiety) center.

11. All of the following are hunger signals *except*
    a. activity of the lateral hypothalamus.
    b. low levels of glucose in the blood.
    c. the hormone CCK.
    d. a high insulin level.

12. The smell of food
    a. has little effect on hunger.
    b. can substitute for food itself when you are dieting.
    c. may make you feel hungry even when you are not.
    d. motivates you to eat only when you are very hungry.

13. Which factor is most responsible for how fast your body burns calories to produce energy?
    a. calories consumed
    b. fat cells
    c. eating habits
    d. metabolic rate

14. According to set point theory, the body works to (increase, decrease, maintain) body weight.

15. Which of the following might indicate a tendency for obesity to be inherited?
    a. metabolic rate
    b. set point
    c. hormones
    d. all of the above

16. Adopted children are more likely to be very thin or obese if their (biological, adoptive) parents are very thin or obese.

17. To be effective, a weight loss program should
    a. focus more on calorie reduction than on exercise.
    b. include specially prepared "diet" foods.
    c. include both calorie reduction and increased exercise.
    d. exclude all high-fat foods.

18. Self-starvation is the defining symptom of _____; binge eating followed by purging is the main symptom of _____.

Sexual Motivation (pp. 309–314)

19. Who conducted the first major surveys of sexual attitudes and behaviors of American males and females?
    a. Alfred Kinsey
    b. Masters and Johnson
    c. George Gallup
    d. Laumann and others

20. Which of the following statements about the human sexual response is *false*?
    a. It consists of four phases.
    b. It occurs in sexual intercourse and can occur in other types of sexual activity.
    c. It is very different in males and females.
    d. It was researched by Masters and Johnson.

21. Androgens, estrogen, and progesterone are present in both males and females. (true/false)

22. Testosterone plays a role in maintaining sexual interest in males and females. (true/false)

23. The direction of one's sexual interest—toward members of the opposite sex or members of one's own sex—is termed one's
    a. sexual role.
    b. sexual orientation.
    c. sexual desire.
    d. sexual motive.

24. Statistics suggest that homosexuality is more common in males than in females. (true/false)

25. Which of the following did Bell, Weinberg, and Hammersmith's study reveal about the childhood experiences of their gay and lesbian participants?

  a. Abuse was more common in their families than in those of heterosexuals.

  b. No single characteristic of family life distinguished their families from those of heterosexuals.

  c. Most were raised in single-parent homes.

  d. Most were from middle-class backgrounds.

26. Evolutionary theory suggests that gender differences in sexual behavior are caused by gender differences in

  a. hormones.

  b. parental investment.

  c. cultural roles.

  d. ideas about the importance of physical attractiveness.

Emotion (pp. 314–321)

27. According to the text, emotions have all of the following *except* a _____ component.

  a. physical   **b.** cognitive

  c. sensory   **d.** behavioral

28. Which theory of emotion holds that you feel a true emotion only when you become physically aroused and can identify some cause for the arousal?

  a. Schachter–Singer theory   **b.** James–Lange theory

  c. Cannon–Bard theory   **d.** Lazarus theory

29. Which theory of emotion suggests that you would feel fearful because you were trembling?

  a. Schachter–Singer theory   **b.** James–Lange theory

  c. Cannon–Bard theory   **d.** Lazarus theory

30. Which theory suggests that the feeling of emotion and the physiological response to an emotional situation occur at about the same time?

  a. Schachter–Singer theory   **b.** James–Lange theory

  c. Cannon–Bard theory   **d.** Lazarus theory

31. Which theory suggests that the physiological arousal and the emotion flow from a cognitive appraisal of an emotion-provoking event?

  a. Schachter–Singer theory   **b.** James–Lange theory

  c. Cannon–Bard theory   **d.** Lazarus theory

32. Which of the following is *not* true of the basic emotions?

  a. They are reflected in distinctive facial expressions.

  b. They are found in all cultures.

  c. There are several hundred known to date.

  d. They are unlearned.

33. All of the following are true of display rules *except* that they

  a. are the same in all cultures.

  b. dictate when and where emotions should be expressed.

  c. dictate what emotions should not be expressed.

  d. often cause people to display emotions they do not feel.

34. The idea that making a happy, sad, or angry face can actually trigger the psychological response and feeling associated with the emotion is called the

  a. emotion production theory.   **b.** emotion and control theory.

  c. facial-feedback hypothesis.   **d.** facial expression theory.

SECTION TWO: Important Concepts and Psychologists

On the line opposite each name, list the major concept or theory discussed in this chapter.

Name	Major Concept or Theory
1. Hull	_____
2. Maslow	_____
3. Murray	_____
4. James and Lange	_____
5. Cannon and Bard	_____
6. Lazarus	_____
7. Salovey and Pizarro	_____

SECTION THREE: Comprehensive Practice Test

1. If James is responding to an incentive, he is responding to an _____ stimulus.

  a. extrinsic   **b.** internal

  c. explicit   **d.** intrinsic

2. Courtney reads books on research and statistics because these subjects fascinate her; she really enjoys learning about new approaches to research and the results of major research projects. Courtney is being driven by _____ motivation.

  a. intrinsic   **b.** intellectual

  c. academic   **d.** extrinsic

3. Keisha studies chemistry every night because she wants to excel in this field; she believes she will make a great deal of money as a chemist. Keisha is being driven mainly by _____ motivation.

  a. career   **b.** intrinsic

  c. extrinsic   **d.** academic

4. A _____ is a state of tension or arousal brought about by an underlying need, which motivates one to engage in behavior that will satisfy the need and reduce the tension.

  a. drive   **b.** balance stimulus

  c. tension stimulus   **d.** homeostatic condition

5. Angel's behavior sometimes scares his friends. He drives his motorcycle fast, he loves bungee jumping, and he can't wait for his first parachute jump. These interests could be explained by the _____ theory of motivation.

  a. instinct   **b.** risky shift

  c. arousal   **d.** homeostasis

6. According to Maslow, the need for love and affiliation is satisfied _____ basic biological needs and the need for safety.

  a. instead of   **b.** before

  c. at the same time as   **d.** after

7. Cody realizes that the goals he has set for himself are going to take too much time and effort, so he decides to compromise and go for what he considers less difficult but more rational goals. Cody has a high *n* Ach. (true/false)

8. When you are hungry, you experience the effects of the _____ hypothalamus; when you have eaten and feel full, you experience the effects of the _____ hypothalamus.
- **a.** proximal; distal
- **b.** distal; proximal
- **c.** ventromedial; lateral
- **d.** lateral; ventromedial

9. Murray developed the Thematic Apperception Test as a way to measure
- **a.** anger.
- **b.** personal perceptions of success.
- **c.** social needs.
- **d.** extrinsic motivation.

10. Which of the following theories asserts that, when presented with an emotion-producing stimulus, we feel the physiological effects and the subjective experience of emotion at about the same time?
- **a.** James–Lange
- **b.** Lazarus
- **c.** Cannon–Bard
- **d.** Schachter–Singer

11. Researchers agree that all humans experience basic emotions. (true/false)

12. Trina smiled and thanked her friend for a birthday gift that she really did not like. Trina has learned the _____ of her culture.
- **a.** social rules
- **b.** interpersonal rules
- **c.** display rules
- **d.** expressive rules

13. The facial-feedback hypothesis states that the muscular movements that cause facial expressions trigger the corresponding emotions. (true/false)

14. The orgasm is the shortest phase in the sexual response cycle. (true/false)

15. Boys who display early effeminate behavior usually are homosexual in adulthood. (true/false)

16. Which of the following is the most accurate description of sexual orientation?
- **a.** Homosexuality is inherited.
- **b.** Homosexuality is determined by prenatal hormones.
- **c.** Homosexuality results from alterations in brain structures.
- **d.** Homosexuality is associated with both biological and environmental causal factors.

17. Homophobia is
- **a.** a type of sexual orientation.
- **b.** an irrational fear of homosexuals.
- **c.** the belief that homosexuals should not be discriminated against in employment.
- **d.** found more often in women than in men.

18. The study of the neurological foundations of emotion is called _____ neuroscience.
- **a.** affective
- **b.** emotional
- **c.** motivational
- **d.** limbic

SECTION FOUR: Critical Thinking

1. In your view, which theory or combination of theories best explains motivation: drive-reduction theory, arousal theory, or Maslow's hierarchy of needs? Which theory do you find least convincing? Support your answers.

2. In your view, which is the better explanation of gender differences in sexual attitudes and behavior: parental investment theory or the social factors proposed by Wood and Eagly?

SECTION FIVE: Application Essays

1. Which level of Maslow's hierarchy provides the strongest motivation for your behavior in general? Give specific examples to support your answer.

Apply your critical thinking skills with **MyPsychLab** Writing Assignments

Submit your answer to the following question inside the MyPsychLab Writing Assessment program for immediate feedback.

Imagine you are walking alone late at night and hear footsteps behind you. Think about your emotional reaction to this situation. Consider the major theories of emotion: James–Lange, Cannon–Bard, and Schacter–Singer. From the perspective of these major theories of emotion, describe how each would predict the sequence of events that would occur as you experience a reaction to this situation.

10 Health and Stress

THINK ABOUT IT

What kinds of things make you feel "stressed out"? If you are like most students, one of the things that irritates you is the feeling that you don't have enough time. In fact, having too much to do and not enough time to do it is one of the topics addressed by the "Hassles Scale," a test that measures people's stress levels (Kanner et al., 1981). The questions on the test came from a survey of college students taken in 1981. The researchers presented students with a list of potentially irritating things and asked them to identify the items that were currently causing stress for them. The following graph shows the things that the researchers asked about and the percentage of students that identified each one as a current cause of stress. How many of them are sources of stress in your own life?

Thinking about the sources of stress listed in the table may make you more aware of just how stressful your own life is at the moment. This chapter will acquaint you with some strategies for managing stress. It will also introduce you to theories and research that will help you understand more about what stresses us, how we respond to stress, and how stress affects our health.

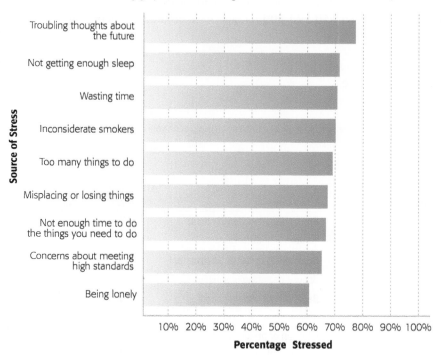

Sources of Stress

Psychologists define **stress** as the physiological and psychological response to a condition that threatens or challenges an individual and requires some form of adaptation or adjustment. A **stressor** is a stimulus or an event that is capable of producing a stress response. Everyone would probably agree that major events such as changing jobs, starting a new intimate relationship, breaking up with an intimate partner, graduating from college, and so on, are stressful. Notice, too, that stressors can be either positive or negative life events. Change is the critical factor, not whether an event is perceived as desirable or undesirable. But do major life events cause us more stress than the everyday stressors that we asked you reflect on in the *Think About It* activity above? As you might guess, there's evidence to support both points of view.

The Life Events Approach ▶

One way of describing, measuring, and explaining stress is the **life events approach**, the view that a person's state of well-being can be threatened by major life changes. This approach includes events that most people experience at one time or another, such as beginning and ending romantic relationships. It also includes both positive and negative events that most of us never or rarely experience first-hand, such as winning the lottery, combat, and natural disasters.

stress The physiological and psychological response to a condition that threatens or challenges a person and requires some form of adaptation or adjustment.

stressor Any stimulus or event capable of producing physical or emotional stress.

⌈ **10.1** How does the life events
⌊ approach describe stress?

life events approach The view that a person's state of well-being can be threatened by major life changes.

Social Readjustment Rating Scale (SRRS) Holmes and Rahe's measure of stress, which ranks 43 life events from most to least stressful and assigns a point value to each.

The Social Readjustment Rating Scale. The classic studies of researchers Thomas Holmes and Richard Rahe are representative of this approach. Holmes and Rahe (1967) developed the **Social Readjustment Rating Scale (SRRS)** to measure stress by ranking different life events from most to least stressful and assigning a point value to each event. Life events that produce the greatest life changes and require the greatest adaptation are considered the most stressful, regardless of whether the events are positive or negative. The 43 life events on the scale range from death of a spouse (assigned 100 stress points) to minor law violations, such as getting a traffic ticket (11 points). Find your life stress score by completing the *Try It* below.

Holmes and Rahe claim that there is a connection between the degree of life stress and major health problems. People who score 300 or more on the SRRS, the researchers say, run about an 80% risk of suffering a major health problem within the next 2 years. Those who score between 150 and 300 have a 50% chance of becoming ill within

TRY IT   Finding a Life Stress Score

To assess your level of life changes, check all of the events that have happened to you in the past year. Add up the points to derive your life stress score. (Based on Holmes & Masuda, 1974.)

Rank	Life Event	Life Change Unit Value	Your Points		Rank	Life Event	Life Change Unit Value	Your Points
1	Death of spouse	100	_____		23	Son or daughter leaving home	29	_____
2	Divorce	73	_____		24	Trouble with in-laws	29	_____
3	Marital separation	65	_____		25	Outstanding personal achievement	28	_____
4	Jail term	63	_____		26	Spouse beginning or stopping work	26	_____
5	Death of close family member	63	_____		27	Beginning or ending school	26	_____
6	Personal injury or illness	53	_____		28	Change in living conditions	25	_____
7	Marriage	50	_____		29	Revision of personal habits	24	_____
8	Getting fired at work	47	_____		30	Trouble with boss	23	_____
9	Marital reconciliation	45	_____		31	Change in work hours or conditions	20	_____
10	Retirement	45	_____		32	Change in residence	20	_____
11	Change in health of family member	44	_____		33	Change in schools	20	_____
12	Pregnancy	40	_____		34	Change in recreation	19	_____
13	Sex difficulties	39	_____		35	Change in church activities	19	_____
14	Gain of new family member	39	_____		36	Change in social activities	18	_____
15	Business readjustment	39	_____		37	Taking out loan for lesser purchase (e.g., car or TV)	17	_____
16	Change in financial state	38	_____		38	Change in sleeping habits	16	_____
17	Death of close friend	37	_____		39	Change in number of family get-togethers	15	_____
18	Change to different line of work	36	_____		40	Change in eating habits	15	_____
19	Change in number of arguments with spouse	35	_____		41	Vacation	13	_____
20	Taking out loan for major purchase (e.g., home)	31	_____		42	Christmas	12	_____
21	Foreclosure of mortgage or loan	30	_____		43	Minor violation of the law	11	_____
22	Change in responsibilities at work	29	_____			**Life stress score:**		_____

a 2-year period (Rahe et al., 1964). More recent research has shown that the weights given to life events by Holmes and Rahe continue to be appropriate for adults in North America and that SRRS scores are correlated with a variety of health indicators (Blasco-Fontecilla et al., 2012; Dohrenwend, 2006; Thorsteinsson & Braun, 2009).

One of the main shortcomings of the SRRS is that it assigns a point value to each life change without taking into account how an individual copes with that stressor. One study found that SRRS scores did reliably predict disease progression in multiple sclerosis patients (Mohr et al., 2002). But the patients who used more effective coping strategies displayed less disease progression than did those who experienced similar stressors but coped poorly with them.

Catastrophic Events. Catastrophic events such as war, terrorist attacks, earthquakes, hurricanes, plane crashes, and the like are stressful both for those who experience them directly and for people who learn of them via news media. Most people are able to manage the stress associated with such catastrophes. However, for some, these events lead to **posttraumatic stress disorder (PTSD)**, a prolonged and severe stress reaction to a catastrophic event or to severe, chronic stress, such as that experienced by soldiers engaged in combat (North & Surris, 2012).

Studies show that the effects of such traumatic events can linger for years, particularly for those who have some kind of personal connection to them. For example, surveys of New York City residents indicate that some were continuing to suffer from symptoms of PTSD up to 6 years after the terrorist attacks of 2001 (Brackbill et al., 2009). Moreover, PTSD sometimes does not appear until many years after an event has been experienced, and in some cases, it is triggered by the anniversary of a traumatic event. For example, mental health professionals in the United States reported that the number of World War II veterans seeking treatment from the Veterans Administration for war-related symptoms of PTSD increased substantially in the years that followed the fiftieth anniversary of the war's end in 1945 (Johnston, 2000). Researchers hypothesize that age-related changes in the brain lessened some older veterans' ability to manage the emotions that were associated with traumatic combat experiences, an effect that was particularly marked in veterans who also suffered from dementia. ◉

People with PTSD often have flashbacks, nightmares, or intrusive memories that make them feel as though they are actually re-experiencing the traumatic event. Many survivors of war or catastrophic events experience *survivor guilt,* one factor in a cluster of variables known as *moral injury,* because they lived while others died (Litz et al., 2009). Some feel that perhaps they could have done more to save others; moral injuries experienced by others include deep feelings of regret over having taken another person's life. Extreme combat-related guilt is a risk factor for suicide and other mental health issues (Hendin & Haas, 1991; Stein et al., 2012). There is also an association between PTSD and substance abuse (Najavits, Highley, Dolan, & Fee, 2012). Individuals with PTSD also experience cognitive difficulties, such as poor concentration (Vasterling et al., 2002).

Everyday Stressors ▶

Which is more stressful—major life events or those little problems and frustrations that seem to crop up every day? Richard Lazarus believes that everyday stressors, which he calls **hassles**, cause more stress than major life events do (Lazarus & DeLongis, 1983). Daily hassles include irritating, frustrating experiences such as standing in line, being stuck in traffic, being put on hold when you are trying to resolve an issue over the phone, and so on. Relationships are another frequent source of hassles, such as happens when another person misunderstands us or when co-workers or customers are hard to get along with. Likewise, environmental conditions such as traffic noise and pollution are among the daily hassles reported by city dwellers (Moser & Robin, 2006).

▲ Even positive life events, such as getting married, can cause stress.

posttraumatic stress disorder (PTSD) A prolonged and severe stress reaction to a catastrophic event or to severe, chronic stress.

◉ **Watch** the Video *9/11 Post Traumatic Stress Disorder* in **MyPsychLab**

10.2 What do hassles, uplifts, and choices contribute to stress?

hassles Irritating demands that occur daily and may cause more stress than major life changes do.

To illustrate the usefulness of Lazarus's approach, Kanner and others (1981) developed the Hassles Scale that you learned about in the *Think About It* activity at the beginning of the chapter to assess various categories of hassles. Unlike the Holmes and Rahe scale, the Hassles Scale takes into account the fact that items may or may not represent stressors to individuals and that the amount of stress produced by an item varies from person to person. People completing the scale indicate the items that have been a hassle for them and rate those items for severity on a 3-point scale.

DeLongis, Folkman, & Lazarus (1988) studied 75 American couples over a 6-month period and found that daily stress (as measured on the Hassles Scale) related significantly to present and future "health problems such as flu, sore throat, headaches, and backaches" (p. 486). Research also indicates that minor hassles that accompany stressful major life events, such as those measured by the SRRS, are better predictors of a person's level of psychological distress than the major events themselves (Pillow, Zautra, & Sandlar, 1996).

uplifts The positive experiences in life, which may neutralize the effects of many hassles.

According to Lazarus, **uplifts**, or positive experiences in life such as getting a better grade on an assignment than you expected, may neutralize the effects of many hassles. Lazarus and his colleagues also constructed an Uplifts Scale. As with the Hassles Scale, people completing this scale make a cognitive appraisal of what they consider to be an uplift. Research has demonstrated links among hassles, uplifts, and a personal sense of well-being. It appears that a hectic daily schedule increases hassles, decreases uplifts, and diminishes their subjective sense of how well they feel (Erlandsson & Eklund, 2003).

Hassles and uplifts aren't the only sources of everyday stress that we experience. Making choices is stressful as well. Some decisions cause us stress by forcing us to choose between equally desirable alternatives. Such dilemmas are known as **approach-approach conflicts**. Some approach-approach conflicts are minor, such as deciding which movie to see. Others can have major consequences, such as the conflict between building a promising career or interrupting that career to raise a child. In an **avoidance-avoidance conflict**, a person must choose between two undesirable alternatives. For example, you may want to avoid studying for an exam, but at the same time you want to avoid failing the test. An **approach-avoidance conflict** involves a single choice that has both desirable and undesirable features. The person facing this type of conflict is simultaneously drawn to and repelled by a choice—for example, wanting to take a wonderful vacation but having to empty a savings account to do so.

approach-approach conflict A conflict arising from having to choose between equally desirable alternatives.

avoidance-avoidance conflict A conflict arising from having to choose between undesirable alternatives.

approach-avoidance conflict A conflict arising when the same choice has both desirable and undesirable features.

10.3 What variables contribute to workers' comfort zone?

Stress in the Workplace

Have you ever had a boss who was difficult to work with? If so, then you are well acquainted with the phenomenon of work-related stress, an experience that varies somewhat from both the life events and everyday stressors approaches you just read about. Work-related stress is unique in that it has more to do with the characteristics of the setting in which a person is functioning than with specific life events or the cumulative effects of everyday stressors.

Albrecht (1979) suggested that if people are to function effectively and find satisfaction on the job, the following nine variables must fall within their comfort zone (see also Figure 10.1):

- *Workload.* Too much or too little to do can cause people to feel anxious, frustrated, and unrewarded.
- *Clarity of job description and evaluation criteria.* Anxiety arises from confusion about job responsibilities and performance criteria or from a job description that is too rigidly defined to leave room for individual initiative.
- *Physical variables.* Temperature, noise, humidity, pollution, amount of workspace, and the physical positions (standing or sitting) required to carry out job duties should fall within a person's comfort zone.
- *Job status.* People with very low-paying, low-status jobs may feel psychological discomfort; those with celebrity status often cannot handle the stress that fame brings.

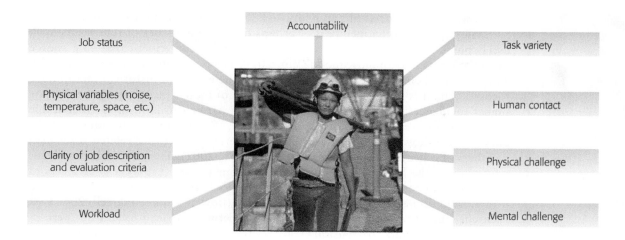

Job status

Physical variables (noise, temperature, space, etc.)

Clarity of job description and evaluation criteria

Workload

Accountability

Task variety

Human contact

Physical challenge

Mental challenge

FIGURE 10.1 Variables in Work Stress For a person to function effectively and find satisfaction on the job, these nine variables should fall within the person's comfort zone. *Source:* Albrecht (1979).

- *Accountability.* Accountability overload occurs when people have responsibility for the physical or psychological well-being of others but only a limited degree of control (air-traffic controllers, emergency room nurses and doctors); accountability underload occurs when workers perceive their jobs as meaningless.

- *Task variety.* To function well, people need a comfortable amount of variety and stimulation.

- *Human contact.* Some workers have virtually no human contact on the job (forest-fire lookouts); others have almost continuous contact with others (welfare and employment office workers). People vary greatly in how much interaction they enjoy or even tolerate.

- *Physical challenge.* Jobs range from being physically demanding (construction work, professional sports) to requiring little to no physical activity. Some jobs (firefighting, police work) involve physical risk.

- *Mental challenge.* Jobs that tax people beyond their mental capability, as well as those that require too little mental challenge, can be frustrating.

Workplace stress can be especially problematic for women because they experience sex discrimination and sexual harassment in the workplace more frequently than men do. Likewise, many women report that they find the difficulties associated with combining work and family roles to be especially stressful (Pedersen & Minotte, 2012). These added stressors have been shown to increase the negative effects of occupational stress on the health and well-being of working women (Buchanan & Fitzgerald, 2008).

Job stress can have a variety of consequences. Perhaps the most frequently cited is reduced effectiveness on the job. But job stress can also lead to absenteeism, tardiness, accidents, substance abuse, and lower morale (Wilhelm et al., 2004). Chronic stress can also lead to work-related **burnout** (Freudenberger & Richelson, 1981). People with burnout lack energy, feel emotionally drained, and are pessimistic about the possibility of changing their situations. People who feel that their work is unappreciated are more subject to burnout than others. For example, one survey suggested that nearly half of the social workers in the United Kingdom suffer from burnout, and the sense of being unappreciated was the best predictor of the condition (Evans et al., 2006). Likewise, nurses who care for patients in vegetative states exhibit higher rates of emotional exhaustion and burnout than other types of health care professionals do (Gosseries et al., 2012).

▲ Air-traffic controllers have an extremely high-stress job. The on-the-job stress they experience increases the risk of coronary disease and stroke.

burnout Lack of energy, exhaustion, and pessimism that results from chronic stress.

Social Sources of Stress ▶

10.4 What are some social sources of stress?

Like work-related stress, social stress is largely a function of the characteristics of the overall context in which a person faces the challenges of life. For example, members of ethnic minority groups are exposed to stressors that rarely affect the lives of those in the so-called dominant group. Likewise, aspects of economic status, such as poverty and unemployment, are also characterized by unique sources of stress.

▲ A strong sense of ethnic identity helps African Americans cope with the stress that may arise from living with racism.

socioeconomic status A collective term for the economic, occupational, and educational factors that influence an individual's relative position in society.

Racism. Some theorists have proposed that a phenomenon called *historical racism*—experienced by members of groups that have a history of repression, such as Hispanic Americans, Native Americans, and African Americans—is a source of social stress (Alamilla, Kim, & Lam, 2010; Belcourt-Dittloff & Stewart, 2000; Troxel et al., 2003). Researchers interested in the effects of historical racism have focused primarily on African Americans. Many of these researchers claim that the higher incidence of high blood pressure among African Americans is attributable to stress associated with historical racism (Gee, Walsemann, & Brondolo, 2012). Surveys have shown that African Americans experience more race-related stress than members of other minority groups do (Utsey et al., 2002). Those African Americans who express the highest levels of concern about racism display higher levels of cardiovascular reactivity to experimentally induced stressors, such as sudden loud noises, than do peers who express less concern (Bowen-Reid & Harrell, 2002). At least one study has demonstrated a correlation between African Americans' perceptions of racism and hypertension (Din-Dzietham et al., 2004). Researchers found that African Americans who reported the highest levels of race-related stressors in their workplaces were more likely to have high blood pressure than workers who reported fewer such stressors.

African Americans are also more likely than members of other minority groups to have a strong sense of ethnic identity, a factor that helps moderate the effects of racial stress (Tovar-Murray et al., 2012). But some studies show that personal characteristics, such as hostility, may increase the effects of racial stress (Fang & Myers, 2001; Raeikkoenen, Matthews, & Saloman, 2003). So, the relationship between historical racism and cardiovascular health is probably fairly complex and varies considerably across individuals.

Socioeconomic Status. The term **socioeconomic status** is often used to refer to differences in income levels, but it includes much more than just financial resources. Occupation and education are also important components of socioeconomic status, as is the more subjective variable of social status. These variables interact to influence the status that is assigned to an individual, and these interactions can vary differently from one setting to another. For example, in some neighborhoods, police officers have low status even though they may have more education and higher incomes than the people who live in the communities they serve. In other neighborhoods, police officers have high status despite having less education and lower incomes than many members of the community. Thus, socioeconomic status is a fairly complex variable.

Despite these complexities, large-scale studies of health and other variables of interest often rely on data such as income and educational level to sort people into socioeconomic status categories. When this technique is used, as you can probably predict, people who are low in socioeconomic status are usually found to more frequently have stress-related health conditions such as colds and the flu. In addition, health risk factors such as high levels of LDL cholesterol (the bad cholesterol associated with heart disease) are typically more common among them (Goodman et al., 2005).

Closer scrutiny of the variables associated with socioeconomic status reveals other factors that help us interpret links between socioeconomic status and health. For example, one frequent finding is that people of lower socioeconomic status have higher levels of stress hormones than people of higher status (Cohen, Doyle, & Baum, 2006). Looking further into this relationship, researchers have identified several behavioral and social factors among such people that help to explain the relationship between status and stress hormones. These factors included higher rates of smoking, more limited social networks, and less regular patterns of eating as compared to people at higher levels of socioeconomic status. This is not to say that these factors apply to everyone who has a low income, but they are found more frequently among those who are economically disadvantaged. Their presence affects the averages of health variables among low-income groups, thus creating correlations between socioeconomic status and these variables.

Unemployment. You probably won't be surprised to learn that, as the unemployment rate rises, so do the number of Interest searches with key terms such as "stress" and "distress" (Ayers et al., 2012). This is probably because unemployment, or the fear of unemployment, is another aspect of socioeconomic status that is related to stress and health. People who are forced out of their jobs experience heightened risks of stress-related illnesses in the months that follow (Isaksson et al., 2004). These effects are found among people of low, middle, and high socioeconomic status, by the way. This consistency is the result of the financial strain that accompanies the loss of income and the uncertainty about the future that is part of the experience of looking for a new job. These aspects of unemployment are stressful no matter how much money people made in their former jobs. However, unemployment is also stressful because it diminishes people's sense of control over what happens to them.

Acculturative Stress. You can probably guess that adjusting to life in a new culture can be extremely stressful, a phenomenon that researchers call *acculturative stress* (Berry, Kim, Minde, & Mok, 1987). Some theorists suggest that immigrants who develop an *integration orientation*, the belief that they will be able to fit into the social structure of the new culture while retaining links to their home cultures, are well equipped to manage the stresses that go along with transitioning from one culture to another (Motti-Stafanidi et al., 2012). Research shows that immigrants with an integration orientation are more satisfied with their lives than those who adopt a different way of thinking about the immigration experience, such as turning completely away from their culture of origin (Peeters & Oerlemans, 2009). Thus, cultural psychologists suggest that schools and other institutions encourage immigrants to maintain ties to their cultures of origin as they acquire the skills they need to fit in to their new surroundings.

REMEMBER IT   *Check your answers and take additional quizzes in MyPsychLab.com.*   ✓● [Study and Review on MyPsychLab

1. According to Holmes and Rahe, health may be adversely affected if a person experiences many stressful _____ in a short period.
2. According to Lazarus, _____ typically cause more stress than major life events do.
3. Rich cannot decide whether to spend spring break at the beach or in the mountains. This is an example of an _____ conflict.
4. The belief that one has _____ over a situation can moderate the effects of stress.
5. The nine variables proposed by Albrecht to account for most job-related stress are _____, _____, _____, _____, _____, _____, _____, _____, and _____.
6. _____ is a prolonged and severe stress reaction that can result from experiencing a catastrophic event.
7. Some researchers have found links between _____ and high blood pressure in African Americans.
8. Socioeconomic status includes _____, _____, and _____.

The Health-Stress Connection

There's no doubt that stress affects the quality of our lives, but can it actually threaten our health? The answer to this question depends at least partially on how we define health. It also depends on a careful analysis of the physiological and psychological effects of stress, and the factors that protect us against it, on the body and mind.

The Biopsychosocial Model of Health and Illness ▶

For centuries researchers focused on an explanatory model that defined health as the absence of disease. This approach, known as the **biomedical model**, explains illness exclusively in terms of biological factors. Consequently, it focuses on illness more than

biomedical model A perspective that explains illness solely in terms of biological factors.

10.5 How does the biopyschosocial model approach health and illness?

it does on health. In some cases, the biomedical model works quite well. For example, streptococcus bacteria cause many infections of the respiratory system. Thus, when a person who has one of these ailments takes an antibiotic drug that kills streptococcus, she usually experiences a speedy and complete recovery. But why doesn't everyone who is exposed to streptococcus get sick?

Individual differences in people's responses to *pathogens* (microorganisms that cause illness) such as streptococcus suggest that there's more to health than the biomedical model suggests. Thus, researchers and practitioners have turned to the **biopsychosocial model**—an approach that includes psychological and social factors in addition to physical causes of disease—in their search for more comprehensive explanations of health than the biomedical model can provide. As you can see in Figure 10.2, these explanations often include psychological factors. Moreover, the biopsychosocial model seeks answers to questions about what keeps us healthy as well as what makes us sick.

Interest in the contributions of psychological factors to health and illness among psychologists has led to the development of the specialized field of **health psychology**. Health psychologists use principles of psychology to prevent illness and to help restore people who are ill to health. Furthermore, for health psychologists, the concept of health extends beyond the simple absence of disease. It includes all aspects of well-being in the physical, psychological, and social domains (Brannon & Feist, 2010). Consequently, the scope of health psychology is quite broad. One important goal of health psychology is to find ways to improve communication between health care professionals and the people they serve. Another is to identify the psychological, behavioral, and social factors that contribute to conditions such as chronic pain, asthma, heart disease, diabetes, cancer, and so on. Health psychologists also design strategies for helping people make behavioral changes that can enhance people's health. 👁

Health psychologists have found that stress contributes to individual differences in each of these areas. For example, some patients find communicating with health professionals about their condition to be highly stressful (Cruess et al., 2010). Researchers hypothesize that stress distracts such patients from the information that care providers are attempting to convey to them. As a result, these patients are less

biopsychosocial model A perspective that focuses on health as well as illness and holds that both are determined by a combination of biological, psychological, and social factors.

health psychology The subfield within psychology that is concerned with the psychological factors that contribute to health, illness, and recovery.

👁 Watch the Video *Episode 15: Big Picture: Health Psychology* in **MyPsychLab**

FIGURE 10.2 **The Biopsychosocial Model of Health and Illness**
According to the biopsychosocial model, the combined effects of risk and protective factors determine both health and illness. Risk factors move the system toward illness, while protective factors moderate the effects of risk factors and increase the chances that a state of health will be maintained.

likely to follow instructions about medication and other aspects of their treatment than those for whom communication with providers is less stressful. Thus, patients' responses to providers' instructions may improve if they learn how to manage their stress responses more effectively.

Another important finding in health psychology is that providing people with training in stress management can improve their health in more direct ways. For example, some people who have chronic pain conditions learn to manage their discomfort more effectively if their treatment includes training in stress management techniques such as meditation (Rosenzweig et al., 2010). Likewise, such training is critical to helping people who have a low tolerance for stress make health-related behavior changes such as giving up smoking (Libby et al., 2012). But what is it about stress that influences health?

The Physiology of the Health-Stress Connection ▶

10.6 How does the fight-or-flight response affect health?

You should recall from Chapter 2 that the sympathetic nervous system responds to threats (stressors) by preparing the body to resist or escape. It does so by increasing heart rate, blood pressure, and respiration rate while at the same time shutting down unnecessary functions, such as those of the digestive system. This set of reactions is called the **fight-or-flight response** because it enables us to fight the stressor or flee from it. When the stressor is no longer present, the parasympathetic nervous system reverses the fight-or-flight response, and the body returns to normal. But when stressors are present for long periods, and the person's efforts to adjust to them fail, the body's tendency to keep the fight-or-flight response going can threaten our health.

fight-or-flight response A response to stress in which the sympathetic nervous system and the endocrine glands prepare the body to fight or flee.

Maintaining the fight-or-flight response over an extended period influences health in two ways. First, research suggests that the biochemicals associated with the fight-or-flight response directly affect how the body functions. For example, when we are exposed to stressors, our bodies pump out large amounts of a substance called *neuropeptide Y (NPY)* (Hirsch & Zukowska, 2012). NPY helps us adapt to stress by reducing anxiety (Bowers, Choi, & Ressler, 2012). However, it also constricts the blood vessels that serve the heart and brain. As a result, the vessels become more vulnerable to blockages, an important cause of heart attacks and strokes (Hirsch & Zukowska, 2012).

Second, the fight-or-flight response indirectly affects health by suppressing the body's immune system. Composed of an army of highly specialized cells and organs, the immune system works to identify and search out and destroy bacteria, viruses, fungi, parasites, and any other foreign matter that may enter the body. The key components of the immune system are white blood cells known as **lymphocytes**, which include B cells and T cells. *B cells* are so named because they are produced in the bone marrow. *T cells* derive their name from the thymus gland, where they are produced. All cells foreign to the body, such as bacteria, viruses, and so on, are known as *antigens*. B cells produce proteins called *antibodies,* which are highly effective in destroying antigens that live in the bloodstream and in the fluid surrounding body tissues (Paul, 1993). For defeating harmful foreign invaders that have taken up residence inside the body's cells, however, T cells are critically important. Thus, the fight-or-flight response on its own is not detrimental to health. Instead, its influence on health operates through its indirect effects on the cells that protect the body from stressors.

lymphocytes The white blood cells—including B cells and T cells—that are the key components of the immune system.

Psychoneuroimmunology is a field of study in which psychologists, biologists, and medical researchers combine their expertise to learn the effects of psychological factors—stress, emotions, thinking, and behavior—on the immune system through the mechanism of the fight-or-flight response (Fleshner & Laudenslager, 2004; Robles, Glaser, & Kiecolt-Glaser, 2005). Their studies show that periods of high stress are correlated with increased inflammation in many kinds of tissue as well as symptoms of many infectious diseases, including oral and genital herpes, mononucleosis, colds, and flu (Cohen et al., 2012; Gouin et al., 2012). Stress may also decrease the effectiveness of certain kinds of vaccines (Miller et al., 2004; Moynihan et al., 2004).

psychoneuroimmunology (sye-ko-NEW-ro-IM-you-NOLL-oh-gee) A field in which psychologists, biologists, and medical researchers combine their expertise to study the effects of psychological factors on the immune system.

Stress has the power to suppress the immune system long after the stressful experience is over. An experimental group of medical students who were enduring the stress of major exams was compared with a control group of medical students who were on vacation from classes and exams. When tested for the presence of disease-fighting antibodies, participants in the exam group, but not those in the control group, had a significant reduction in their antibody count because of the stress. The lowered antibody count was still present 14 days after the exams were over. At that point, the students were not even aware that they were still stressed and reported feeling no stress (Deinzer et al., 2000).

In addition to academic pressures, poor marital relationships and sleep deprivation have been linked to lowered immune response (Kiecolt-Glaser et al., 1987; Maier & Laudenslager, 1985). Likewise, for several months after the death of a spouse, the widow or widower suffers weakened immune system function and is at a higher risk of mortality. Severe bereavement weakens the immune system, increasing a person's chance of suffering from a long list of physical and mental ailments for as long as 2 years following a partner's death (Khanfer, Lord, & Phillips, 2011). 👁

◉ Watch the Video *Episode 15: Basics: Stress and Your Health* in **MyPsychLab**

Theories of Stress Response

As you have seen, prolonged stress threatens health. However, the body doesn't simply surrender to the stressors. Instead, it calls upon a variety of resources to defend itself against the stressors' potentially damaging effects. Theories of stress response explain how the body does so. One important theory focuses on the body's physiological response, and another emphasizes psychological responses to stress.

10.7 How do theorists explain physiological and psychological responses to stress?

The General Adaptation Syndrome. Hans Selye (1907–1982), the researcher most prominently associated with the effects of stress on health, established the field of stress research. At the heart of Selye's concept of stress is the **general adaptation syndrome (GAS)**, the predictable sequence of reactions that organisms show in response to stressors. It consists of three stages: the alarm stage, the resistance stage, and the exhaustion stage (Selye, 1956; see Figure 10.3).

The first stage of the body's response to a stressor is the **alarm stage**, in which the adrenal cortex releases hormones called *glucocorticoids* that increase heart rate, blood pressure, and blood sugar levels, supplying a burst of energy that helps the person deal with the stressful situation, that is, the fight-or-flight syndrome (Pennisi, 1997). Next, the organism enters the **resistance stage**, during which the adrenal cortex continues to release glucocorticoids to help the body resist stressors. The length of the resistance stage depends both on the intensity of the stressor and on the body's power to adapt. If the organism finally fails in its efforts to resist, it reaches the **exhaustion stage**, at which point all the stores of deep energy are depleted, and disintegration and death follow.

general adaptation syndrome (GAS) The predictable sequence of reactions (alarm, resistance, and exhaustion stages) that organisms show in response to stressors.

alarm stage The first stage of the general adaptation syndrome, in which the person experiences a burst of energy that aids in dealing with the stressful situation.

resistance stage The second stage of the general adaptation syndrome, when there are intense physiological efforts to either resist or adapt to the stressor.

exhaustion stage The third stage of the general adaptation syndrome, which occurs if the organism fails in its efforts to resist the stressor.

FIGURE 10.3 The General Adaptation Syndrome
The three stages in Selye's general adaptation syndrome are (1) the alarm stage, during which there is emotional arousal and the defensive forces of the body are mobilized for fight or flight; (2) the resistance stage, in which intense physiological efforts are exerted to resist or adapt to the stressor; and (3) the exhaustion stage, when the organism fails in its efforts to resist the stressor.
Source: Selye (1956).

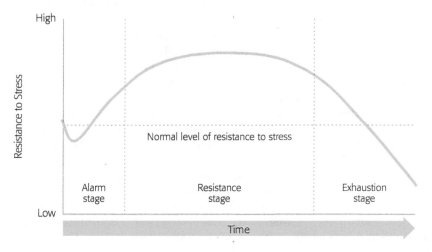

Selye found that the most harmful effects of stress are due to the prolonged secretion of glucocorticoids, which can lead to permanent increases in blood pressure, suppression of the immune system, weakening of muscles, and even damage to the hippocampus (Stein-Behrens et al., 1994). Thanks to Selye, the connection between extreme, prolonged stress and certain diseases is now widely accepted by medical experts.

Lazarus's Cognitive Theory of Stress. Is it the stressor itself that upsets us, or the way we think about it? You should remember Richard Lazarus's cognitive approach to emotion from Chapter 9 in which he argues that our intellectual interpretations of emotions determine how we respond to them. Similarly, Lazarus (1966; Lazarus & Folkman, 1984) contends that it is not the stressor that causes stress but rather a person's perception of it. According to Lazarus, when people are confronted with a potentially stressful event, they engage in a cognitive process that involves a primary and a secondary appraisal. A **primary appraisal** is an evaluation of the meaning and significance of the situation—whether its effect on one's well-being is positive, irrelevant, or negative. An event appraised as stressful could involve (1) harm or loss—that is, damage that has already occurred; (2) threat, or the potential for harm or loss; or (3) challenge—that is, the opportunity to grow or to gain. An appraisal of threat, harm, or loss can occur in relation to anything important to you—a friendship, a part of your body, your property, your finances, your self-esteem. When people appraise a situation as involving threat, harm, or loss, they experience negative emotions, such as anxiety, fear, anger, and resentment (Folkman, 1984). An appraisal that sees a challenge, on the other hand, is usually accompanied by positive emotions such as excitement, hopefulness, and eagerness.

During **secondary appraisal**, if people judge the situation to be within their control, they make an evaluation of available resources—physical (health, energy, stamina), social (support network), psychological (skills, morale, self-esteem), material (money, tools, equipment), and time. Then, they consider the options and decide how to deal with the stressor. The level of stress they feel is largely a function of whether their resources are adequate to cope with the threat, and how severely those resources will be taxed in the process. Figure 10.4 summarizes the Lazarus and Folkman psychological model of stress. Research supports their claim that the physiological,

primary appraisal A cognitive evaluation of a potentially stressful event to determine whether its effect is positive, irrelevant, or negative.

secondary appraisal A cognitive evaluation of available resources and options prior to deciding how to deal with a stressor.

Potentially Stressful Event

↓

Primary Appraisal
Person evaluates event as positive, neutral, or negative.
Negative appraisal can involve:
- **Harm or loss** (damage has already occurred)
- **Threat** (the potential for harm or loss)
- **Challenge** (the opportunity to grow or gain)

↓

Secondary Appraisal
If the situation is judged to be within the person's control:
1. Person evaluates coping resources (physical, social, psychological, material) to determine if they are adequate to deal with stressor.
2. Person considers options in dealing with stressor.

↓

Stress Response
- **Physiological:** Autonomic arousal, fluctuations in hormones
- **Emotional:** Anxiety, fear, grief, resentment, excitement
- **Behavioral:** Coping behaviors (including problem-focused and emotion-focused coping strategies)

FIGURE 10.4 Lazarus and Folkman's Psychological Model of Stress
Lazarus and Folkman emphasize the importance of a person's perceptions and appraisal of stressors. The stress response depends on the outcome of the primary and secondary appraisals, whether the person's coping resources are adequate to cope with the threat, and how severely the resources are taxed in the process.
Source: Folkman (1984).

emotional, and behavioral reactions to stressors depend partly on whether the stressors are appraised as challenging or threatening. The *Summarize It* below recaps the theories of stress response we have discussed.

SUMMARIZE IT

Theories of Stress Responses

THEORY	DESCRIPTION
Selye's general adaptation syndrome (GAS)	Three stages: alarm, resistance, and exhaustion
Lazarus's cognitive theory	Primary appraisal (evaluation of stressor), followed by secondary appraisal (evaluation of resources and options)

10.8 What factors promote resilience in the face of stress?

risk/resilience model A perspective that proposes that risk and protective factors interact to produce or protect us from illness.

coping Efforts through action and thought to deal with demands that are perceived as taxing or overwhelming.

problem-focused coping A direct response aimed at reducing, modifying, or eliminating a source of stress.

emotion-focused coping A response involving reappraisal of a stressor to reduce its emotional impact.

✳─ Explore the **Concept** *Coping Strategies and Their Effects* on **MyPsychLab**

proactive coping Active measures taken in advance of a potentially stressful situation in order to prevent its occurrence or to minimize its consequences.

Risk and Resilience

Fortunately, stressors and our responses to them aren't the only factors that determine how our bodies respond to stress. A helpful way to understand how stress and other factors interact to influence our health is to think about stress in terms of a **risk/resilience model**. This perspective proposes that risk and protective factors interact to produce or protect us from illness. Risk factors such as exposure to pathogens, hereditary predispositions for certain illnesses, and stress increase the chances of getting sick. Protective factors counteract the effects of risk factors and enable us to "bounce back" from their effects, that is, to exhibit *resilience* (Almeida, 2005). Researchers have identified several factors that promote resilience in the face of stress.

Coping Strategies. If you're like most people, the stresses you have experienced have helped you develop some coping strategies. **Coping** refers to a person's efforts through action and thought to deal with demands perceived as taxing or overwhelming. **Problem-focused coping** is direct; it consists of reducing, modifying, or eliminating the source of stress itself. If you are getting a poor grade in history and appraise this as a threat, you may study harder, talk over your problem with your professor, form a study group with other class members, get a tutor, or drop the course (see the *Explain It*).

Emotion-focused coping involves reappraising a stressor to reduce its emotional impact. Research has shown that emotion-focused coping can be a very effective way of managing stress (Austenfeld & Stanton, 2004). If you lose your job, you may decide that it isn't a major tragedy and instead view it as a challenge, an opportunity to find a better job with a higher salary. Despite what you may have heard, ignoring a stressor—one form of emotion-focused coping—can be an effective way of managing stress. Researchers studied 116 people who had experienced heart attacks (Ginzburg, Soloman, & Bleich, 2002). All of the participants reported being worried about suffering another attack. However, those who tried to ignore their worries were less likely to exhibit anxiety-related symptoms such as nightmares and flashbacks. Other emotion-focused strategies, though, such as keeping a journal in which you write about things you feel grateful for, may be even more effective (Flinchbaugh et al., 2012).

A combination of problem-focused and emotion-focused coping is probably the best stress-management strategy (Folkman & Lazarus, 1980). For example, a heart patient may ignore her anxiety (emotion-focused coping) while conscientiously adopting recommended lifestyle changes such as increasing exercise (problem-focused coping). Moreover, people who respond to stressors with emotion- or problem-focused coping, or a combination of the two, tend to be healthier than those whose behavioral responses to stress include eating more or less, drugs, alcohol, or social withdrawal (Wang et al., 2009). ✳

Some stressful situations can be anticipated in advance, allowing people to use a strategy called **proactive coping**, which consists of efforts or actions taken in advance of a potentially stressful situation to prevent its occurrence or to minimize

Why Do Pop Quizzes Facilitate Learning?

What happens when your professor walks into class and announces in a seemingly gleeful tone, "Good morning, class. We're going to start today with a pop quiz"? On hearing these words, you think back to your decision to watch a poker tournament on television instead of reading your assigned chapter, and your heart rate increases dramatically. This is a sure sign that your sympathetic nervous system has triggered the fight-or-flight response, and you are in the throes of a stressful experience. But you suppress the urge you feel to run from the room by resolving never to be caught off guard again in this particular class. The next time you are tempted to while away an evening in front of the television, you force yourself to study instead. How do the various types of coping come into play in this series of events?

As you have learned, emotion-focused coping is the strategy we use when we are faced with a stressor about which we can do little. Being faced with a pop quiz for which you are unprepared is just such a situation. To counter the fight-or-flight response, you modify your thinking about the situation in an effort to indirectly quell the tumultuous emotions you are experiencing. That's why your resolution to be better prepared next time around makes you feel better.

Problem-focused coping addresses the actual stressor and attempts to modify it. Obviously, resolving to be better prepared won't get the job done. You have to actually follow through on your goal. If you do, then you are engaging in problem-focused coping. In so doing, you are exerting some degree of control over the future appearance of this particular stressor. Recall from our discussion of controllability earlier in the chapter that we cope more effectively with stressors over which we believe we have control.

What do these coping strategies have to do with learning? To find out, we have to examine what might happen the next time your professor announces a pop quiz, assuming that you have kept your resolution to prepare for class. If you have read the assigned material, your emotional response to the quiz announcement is likely to be less intense than it was when you were unprepared. However, it is unlikely that you will perform well on the quiz unless you have actually learned the material. In other words, pop quizzes give prepared students feedback about the effectiveness of their study strategies. Presumably, if you took the time to prepare, but you are disappointed by your quiz grade, you will take steps to not only prepare for class but also to be certain that you are effectively processing what you read. This, of course, is exactly what professors are trying to get you to do when they employ pop quizzes as an instructional strategy. And research suggests that, whether professors count pop quizzes as regular grades or use them for extra credit, they are effective both for motivating students to prepare for class and for helping them learn (Ruscio, 2001; Thorne, 2000).

its consequences (Greenglass & Fiksenbaum, 2009). Proactive copers anticipate and then prepare for upcoming stressful events and situations. For example, one certain stressor associated with attending college is that college bookstores are very busy at the beginning of the semester. To cope with this stress proactively, that is, to avoid the stress associated with standing in line with a heavy stack of books, you may order some of your books online or go to the bookstore well in advance of the start of the semester. Parents proactively cope, too, when they take along their children's favorite snacks and toys in anticipation of the children becoming hungry and restless at a relative's home or a doctor's office. Research suggests that proactive coping diminishes the anxieties that are associated with everyday stressors such as these (Sheikhiani & Nair, 2012). Moreover, trauma survivors who learn to cope proactively with PTSD symptoms are less likely to develop other types of emotional problems (Vernon, 2012; Wagner & Martin, 2012).

Optimism. People who are generally optimistic tend to cope more effectively with stress, which in turn may reduce their risk of illness (Low, Bower, Moskowitz, & Epel, 2011). An important characteristic shared by optimists is that they generally expect good outcomes. Such positive expectations help make them more stress-resistant than pessimists, who tend to expect bad outcomes. Similarly, individuals who are optimistic seem to be able to find positives even in the darkest of circumstances (Rini et al., 2004). An especially lethal form of pessimism is hopelessness. A longitudinal study of a large number of Finnish men revealed that participants who reported feeling moderate to high hopelessness died from all causes at two to three times the rates of those reporting low or no hopelessness (Everson et al., 1996).

Hardiness. A cluster of characteristics called **hardiness** moderate the effects of stress on health (Maddi, 2013). The term was coined by psychologist Suzanne Kobasa who grouped the characteristics into three major factors, *commitment*, *control*, and *challenge* (1979; Kobasa, Maddi, & Kahn, 1982). In a classic study of male executives with high levels of stress, Kobasa and her colleagues found that "hardy" individuals feel a strong

hardiness A combination of three psychological qualities—commitment, control, and challenge—shared by people who can handle high levels of stress and remain healthy.

sense of commitment to both their work and their personal life. They see themselves not as victims of whatever life brings but as people who have control over consequences and outcomes. They act to solve their own problems, and they welcome challenges in life, viewing them not as threats but as opportunities for growth and improvement.

Researchers have identified important links between hardiness and health. For example, in one study, researchers found that adults with high levels of hardiness adjusted more effectively to the stressors associated with recovering from a sports-related injury than low-hardiness peers did (Wadey et al., 2012a). As a result, high-hardiness participants responded more positively to the demands of the injury recovery process. In a follow-up study, the researchers found that the critical difference between the two groups was that high-hardiness participants used more effective emotion-focused and problem-focused coping strategies than their low-hardiness counterparts did (Wadey et al., 2012b). These strategies appeared to have been developed by high-hardness participants through successful navigation of previous stress-inducing experiences. Thus, the challenge component of hardiness seems to be important to high-hardiness individuals' capacity for learning from stressful experiences and applying what they have learned to subsequent problems. In addition, these findings illustrate that protective factors are interrelated, that is, hardiness helps us develop effective coping strategies, and effective coping strategies enhance hardiness.

Religious and Social Involvement. Another personal factor that contributes to resilience is religious involvement (Gall & Guirgis-Younger, 2013). For example, a meta-analysis of 42 separate studies combined data on some 126,000 individuals and revealed that religious involvement is positively associated with measures of physical health and lower rates of cancer, heart disease, and stroke (McCullough et al., 2000). Why is religious involvement linked to health? Researchers are currently examining a number of hypotheses (Gall & Guirgis-Younger, 2013). One proposal is that attendance at religious services is linked to healthy habits and positive emotions (Koenig & Vaillant, 2009). For example, people who attend church regularly are less likely to smoke and to drink alcohol to excess than other adults. In addition, they are more likely to tell researchers that they are content with their lives than nonattenders are.

Researchers also note that religious involvement may contribute to health because it provides people with a variety of opportunities for social involvement. In support of this conclusion, health psychologists cite research showing that other forms of social involvement, such as serving as a volunteer at a community agency, promote health. In one study, researchers gave volunteers nasal drops containing a cold virus. Within the next few days, symptoms of the viral infection rose sharply in some of the 151 women and 125 men who participated in the study, but less so or not at all in others. Participants with a rich social life in the form of frequent interactions with others—spouses, children, parents, co-workers, friends, and volunteer and religious groups—seemed to enjoy a powerful shield of protection against the virus infection. This pattern of protection held across age and racial groups, for both sexes, at all educational levels, and at every season of the year (Ader, 2000; Cohen et al., 1997).

Social Support. Religious and social involvement may also provide people with a stronger form of social support than is available to others (Graham & Roemer, 2012). **Social support** is support provided, usually in time of need, by a spouse, other family members, friends, neighbors, colleagues, support groups, or others. It can involve tangible aid such as food or money, information, and advice, as well as emotional support. It can also be viewed as the feeling of being loved, valued, and cared for by those toward whom we feel a similar obligation.

Social support appears to have positive effects on the body's immune system as well as on the cardiovascular and endocrine systems (Kiecolt-Glaser, Gouin, & Hantsoo, 2010). Social support may help encourage health-promoting behaviors and reduce the impact of stress so that people are less likely to resort to unhealthy methods of

social support Tangible and/or emotional support provided in time of need by family members, friends, and others; the feeling of being loved, valued, and cared for by those toward whom we feel a similar obligation.

coping, such as smoking or drinking. Further, social support has been shown to reduce depression and enhance self-esteem in individuals who suffer from chronic illnesses, such as kidney disease (Symister & Friend, 2003).

It's important to note here that researchers distinguish between *perceived support*, the degree to which a person believes help is available when needed, and *received support*, the actual help a person receives from others (Newman & Roberts, 2013). Interestingly, many have found that perceived support is more important than received support (Reinhardt et al., 2006). Other research has shown that high levels of perceived social support are associated with lower levels of depression (Sheets & Mohr, 2009). Such perceived support may be more a function of individual personality than of the actual availability of family and friends who can offer help. One longitudinal study found that college-aged participants who had sociable, outgoing personalities were more likely to report having high levels of perceived social support later in adulthood (Von Dras & Siegler, 1997). These results underscore the importance of psychological variables in health.

▲ A strong social support network can help a person recover faster from an illness.

Perceived Control. Further evidence for the notion that how we perceive a stress-inducing situation may be just as important as the objective features of it comes from research showing that resilience is influenced by *perceived control*, the degree to which we feel a sense of control over our lives (Rodin & Salovey, 1989). In one classic study, Langer and Rodin (1976) studied the effects of perceived control on nursing-home residents. Residents in one group were given some measure of control over their lives, such as choices in arranging their rooms and in the times they could see movies. They showed improved health and well-being and had a lower death rate than another group who were not given such control. Within 18 months, 30% of the residents given no choices had died, compared with only 15% of those who had been given some control over their lives. Perceived control is important for cancer patients, too. Some researchers suggest that a sense of control over their daily physical symptoms and emotional reactions may be even more important for cancer patients than control over the course of the disease itself (Thompson et al., 1993).

Several studies suggest that we are less subject to stress when we have the power to do something about it, whether we exercise that power or not (John, 2004). Glass and Singer (1972) subjected two groups of participants to the same loud noise. Participants in one group were told that they could, if necessary, terminate the noise by pressing a switch. These participants suffered less stress, even though they never did exercise the control they were given. Friedland and others (1992) suggest that when people experience a loss of control because of a stressor, they are motivated to try to reestablish control in the stressful situation. Failing this, they often attempt to increase their sense of control in other areas of their lives. For instance, a person in the midst of an inescapable stressful situation over which she has little control, such as loss of a job, might initiate a goal-oriented exercise regime. Implementing the regime and tracking progress towards its goals helps her regain a sense of control over her life in the face of an uncontrollable stressor.

TRY IT   How Resilient Are You?

To what extent are the factors that increase resilience present in your own life? Assign a score of 1 to 10 to each factor.

1. I use emotion-focused and problem-focused coping strategies effectively. _____
2. I usually maintain an optimistic outlook. _____
3. My efforts to manage stress include the three components of hardiness—commitment, control, and challenge. _____
4. I am active in a religious or social organization. _____

5. I have access to a supportive network of friends and relatives. _____
6. I view myself as having a great deal of control over what happens to me. _____

Are there any ways that you could increase the factors that you rates 5 or less? If so, take a moment to jot them down. If not, think about how you can use the other resilience factors to offset their effects.

◉ **Watch** the Video *Episode 15: In the Real World: Reducing Stress, Improving Health* in **MyPsychLab**

SUMMARIZE IT

Factors That Promote Resilience

FACTOR	DESCRIPTION
Coping	Problem-focused coping, directed toward stress; emotion-focused coping, directed toward the emotional response to the stressor; proactive coping, actions taken to prevent future stress
Optimism	Positive expectations for the future
Hardiness	Commitment to work and personal life; sense of control over outcomes; view stressors as challenges
Religious faith	Healthy habits, positive emotions, social involvement
Social support	Tangible, emotional support provided by family, friends, other; perceived support may be more important than actual support
Perceived control	Belief that one has some degree of control over stressors

REMEMBER IT

Check your answers and take additional quizzes in MyPsychLab.com. ✔●─Study and Review on MyPsychLab

1. The _____ model of health and illness includes physical, psychological, and social variables.

2. The fight or flight syndrome can impair the body's _____ system.

3. Match each stage of the GAS with its description.

   a. depletion of all stores of deep energy   ____ **(1)** alarm stage

   b. intense physiological efforts to adapt to the stressor   ____ **(2)** resistance stage

   c. emotional arousal and preparation for fight or flight   ____ **(3)** exhaustion stage

4. During _____ appraisal, a person determines whether an event is positive, negative, or neutral.

5. _____ coping involves adjusting one's emotions to deal with a stressor, while _____ coping involves modifying or eliminating a particular stressor.

6. Hardiness includes _____, _____, and _____.

Health and Illness

As we noted earlier, health psychologists apply the biopsychosocial model to better understand the prevention and treatment of specific illnesses. For example, they have studied two life-threatening illnesses, heart disease and cancer, extensively. In addition, the biopsychosocial model has helped health psychologists explain gender and ethnic group differences in health and illness.

10.9 How do lifestyle, heredity, and personality influence coronary heart disease?

Coronary Heart Disease

To survive, the heart muscle requires a steady, sufficient supply of oxygen and nutrients carried by the blood. Coronary heart disease is caused by the narrowing or the blockage of the coronary arteries, the arteries that supply blood to the heart muscle. As you learned earlier, stress-related biochemicals play an important role in this process. Although coronary heart disease remains the leading cause of death in the United States, responsible for 25% of all deaths, deaths due to this cause have declined 50% during the past 40 years (Heron, 2012).

A health problem of modern times, coronary heart disease is largely attributable to lifestyle and is therefore an important field of study for health psychologists. A *sedentary lifestyle*—one that includes a job at which one spends most of the time sitting and less than 20 minutes of exercise three times per week—is the primary modifiable risk factor contributing to death from coronary heart disease (Pereira, Ki, & Power, 2012). Other modifiable risk factors are high serum cholesterol level, cigarette smoking, and obesity. ✹

Though not modifiable, another important risk factor is family history. The association between family history and coronary heart disease is both genetic and behavioral. For instance, individuals whose parents have high blood pressure, but who have not yet developed the disorder themselves, exhibit the same kinds of emotional reactivity and poor coping strategies as their parents (Frazer, Larkin, & Goodie, 2002).

Personality type is also associated with an individual's risk of heart disease. After extensive research, cardiologists Meyer Friedman and Ray Rosenman (1974) concluded that there are two types of personality: Type A, associated with a high rate of coronary heart disease, and Type B, commonly found in persons unlikely to develop heart disease.

People with the **Type A behavior pattern** have a strong sense of time urgency. Most try to achieve as much as possible in as little time as is feasible. In contrast, people with the **Type B behavior pattern** are relaxed and easygoing and are not driven by a sense of time urgency. They are not impatient or hostile and are able to relax without guilt. They play for fun and relaxation rather than to exhibit superiority over others. Yet, a Type B individual may be as bright and ambitious as a Type A person, and more successful as well.

In addition to time urgency, some people with Type A personality are also excessively competitive, hostile, and easily angered. Research indicates that these facets of Type A personality are largely responsible for its association with heart disease (Williams, 1987). These associations have been found across cultures and in both men and women (Mohan, 2006; Olson et al., 2005). As a result, contemporary research on personality and heart disease focuses more specifically on the relationship between hostility and heart disease than on the more general Type A behavior pattern (Allan, 2011).

Careful studies of the association between hostility and heart disease have shown that it may be part of a larger complex of variables that includes other forms of emotional distress (Kubzansky et al., 2006; Olson et al., 2005). When anger and hostility are considered as single variables, both prove to be predictive of coronary heart disease. However, when other distress variables, such as anxiety and cynicism, are added to them, statistical analyses suggest that it is the whole cluster of negative emotions that best predicts heart disease rather than any one of the variables alone.

The finding that negative emotions collectively predict coronary disease better than any one of the variables alone has led some researchers to propose a new classification, **Type D behavior pattern** ("D" for distress; Denollet, 1997). People with this profile exhibit a chronic pattern of emotional distress combined with a tendency to suppress negative emotions. Many studies have revealed a link between Type D behavior pattern and heart disease (Grande, Romppel, & Barth, 2012) For example, in one study of men who were enrolled in a rehabilitative therapy program after having had a heart attack, those with the Type D profile were found to have four times the risk of death as other patients in the program (Sher, 2004). However, more research is needed before the correlation between Type D personality and heart disease will be fully understood. Critics of this line of research point out that it is based on small samples and that personality is not as strong a predictor of heart disease as factors such as heredity, diet, and exercise (de Voogd, Sanderman, & Coyne, 2012).

The relationship between personality and heart disease may be rooted in the contribution of personality to health behaviors and social support. For example, individuals who, like those with Type D personality, tend to have a negative view of life, are less likely to abstain from tobacco after completing a smoking cessation program (Hooten et al., 2005). Furthermore, researchers have found that Type D personality in the partners of patients who have coronary heart disease impairs these partners' ability to be supportive (Pedersen, van Domburg, & Theuns, 2004). As you can see, the ramifications of personality for heart disease may turn out to be quite complex. ◉

✹⌐ **Explore** the **Concept** *Heart Disease* on **MyPsychLab**

Type A behavior pattern A behavior pattern marked by a sense of time urgency, impatience, excessive competitiveness, hostility, and anger; considered a risk factor in coronary heart disease.

Type B behavior pattern A behavior pattern marked by a relaxed, easygoing approach to life, without the time urgency, impatience, and hostility of the Type A pattern.

Type D behavior pattern People who exhibit chronic emotional distress combined with a tendency to suppress negative emotions.

◉⌐ **Watch** the Video *Episode 15: Thinking Like a Psychologist: Personality and Health* in **MyPsychLab**

▲ Hostility, such as road rage, is a key component of the Type A behavior pattern.

10.10 How do psychological factors influence cancer patients' quality of life?

Cancer

Cancer is the second leading cause of death in the United States, accounting for 23% of all deaths (Heron, 2012). Cancer strikes frequently in the adult population, and about 30% of Americans will develop cancer at some time in their lives. The young are not spared the scourge of cancer, for it takes the lives of more children aged 3 to 14 than any other disease.

Cancer, a collection of diseases rather than a single illness, can invade cells in any part of a living organism—humans, other animals, and even plants. Normal cells in all parts of the body divide, but fortunately they have built-in instructions about when to stop dividing. Unlike normal cells, cancer cells do not stop dividing. And, unless caught in time and destroyed, they continue to grow and spread, eventually killing the organism. Health psychologists point out that an unhealthy diet, smoking, excessive alcohol consumption, promiscuous sexual behavior, or becoming sexually active in the early teens (especially for females) are all behaviors that increase the risk of cancer. Moreover, while there is no solid evidence that stress causes cancer, it does influence how people with the disease respond to and cope with treatment (Garssen, 2004; Pedersen et al., 2009).

▲ This group of cancer patients is involved in art therapy, which is believed to lower the stress level associated with having a serious illness.

The 1.5 million people in the United States who are diagnosed with cancer each year have the difficult task of adjusting to a potentially life-threatening disease and the chronic stressors associated with it (American Cancer Society, 2009). Thus, researchers claim that cancer patients need more than medical treatment. Their therapy should include help with psychological and behavioral factors that can influence their quality of life. Carver and others (1993) found that 3 and 6 months after surgery, breast cancer patients who maintained an optimistic outlook, accepted the reality of their situation, and maintained a sense of humor experienced less distress. Patients who engaged in denial—refusal to accept the reality of their situation—and had thoughts of giving up experienced much higher levels of distress. Dunkel-Schetter and others (1992) found that the most effective elements of a strategy for coping with cancer were social support (such as through self-help groups), a focus on the positive, and distraction. Avoidant coping strategies, such as fantasizing, denial, and social withdrawal, were associated with more emotional distress.

10.11 How do males and females differ with regard to health?

Gender and Health

Until quite recently, nearly all medical research involved only male participants (Matthews et al., 1997). Consequently, little was known about how women's health differs from that of men. One area where the failure to study women's health care needs has been particularly evident is in research examining mortality risk following open-heart surgery. Women are more likely to die after such surgery than are men. To date, studies have shown that the gender gap in surgical survival narrows with age, but researchers are still investigating why women's postsurgical mortality rate is higher than men's (Vaccarino et al., 2002). One important reason for the disparity is that women are more likely than men to have an additional chronic disease, such as diabetes, that impairs their ability to recover from surgery (Kim et al., 2007). Another is that women have higher rates of postsurgical infection and stroke than men do (Rogers et al., 2006). Higher rates of blood transfusion among female patients may be responsible for the gender gap in postoperative infections (Rogers et al., 2007). Both men and women who receive transfusions during or after heart surgery have higher infection rates than nontransfused patients do, but women are about 50% more likely than men to require transfusions during or after surgery.

In general, however, men have higher death rates from most causes than women do, although women tend to be less healthy. These seemingly contradictory findings have puzzled researchers for decades (Rieker, Bird, & Lang, 2011). The finding that women are 50% more likely than men are to seek medical care explains some of this difference (NCHS, 2012). However, differences in care seeking fall short of fully explaining gender differences in illness and death.

Ethnic Group Differences in Health ▶

10.12 How do researchers explain ethnic group differences in health?

Like gender, ethnic categories are associated with different patterns of health outcomes. Remember as you read that the methods used to collect health statistics often obscure important variations among subgroups of the five major groups whose health is tracked by government agencies—White Americans, African Americans, Hispanic Americans, Asian Americans and Pacific Islanders, and Native Americans. That is, we may tend to focus on differences in group averages, overlooking the fact that there is a great deal of variation within each group. Consequently, we must be careful to avoid overgeneralizing cross-group differences to the point where they become stereotypes that cast some groups as healthier than others. Here are a few highlights from the many findings in this area.

Group Differences in Health. African Americans have higher rates of many chronic conditions such as high blood pressure and diabetes than do White Americans (National Center for Health Statistics, 2012). African Americans are 40% more likely than White Americans to die of heart disease and 30% more likely to die of cancer. Even when African and White Americans of the same age suffer from similar illnesses, the mortality rate of African Americans is higher (NCHS, 2010). And the rate of AIDS is more than three times higher among African Americans than among White Americans (CDC, 2012a).

Hypertension is more prevalent among Hispanic Americans than among non-Hispanic White Americans. However, heart problems are less prevalent (NCHS, 2012). Rates of diabetes are also dramatically higher among Hispanic Americans than for other groups (NCHS, 2012).

In general, Asian Americans are less likely than adults of other ethnicities to be diagnosed with chronic disorders such as diabetes and high blood pressure. This general trend is true for cancer as well. Nevertheless, it is cancer, rather than heart disease, that is the leading cause of death among Asian Americans. This is because they are far more likely to be diagnosed with stomach and liver cancer, two especially lethal forms of the disease, than members of other groups (Howlader et al., 2012). This disparity is thought to have an infectious source. Rates of infection with various strains of viruses that cause *hepatitis* (liver inflammation) and contribute to the development of liver cancer and *helicobacter pylori*, a bacterium linked to stomach cancer, are far higher among Asian Americans and among residents of most Asian countries than is true for other groups. Consequently, researchers are examining factors such as the characteristics of strains of hepatitis B and helicobacter pylori that more commonly infect Asians than other groups, cultural practices that may increase Asians' exposure to these pathogens, and inherited susceptibilities to their effects (Al-Mahtab, 2010; Fock & Ang, 2010).

Among Native Americans, diabetes rates are higher than they are among Whites (NCHS, 2012). Rates of alcohol abuse are higher among Native Americans as well, leading to high rates of liver disease. Deaths from liver disease are far more frequent among Native Americans than in other groups (NCHS, 2012).

Explaining Group Differences. How can such differences be explained? As you learned earlier, historical racism is one possible explanatory factor. Another is socioeconomic status. About one-fifth of African Americans, Native Americans, and Hispanic Americans live in poverty (U.S. Census Bureau, 2012). Thus, we might conclude that variables related to poverty—nutritional status, access to health care, and education, for example—explain racial differences in health. However, more detailed studies of socioeconomic factors suggest that variations in poverty rates alone cannot explain group differences in health. For example, about 70% of poor White

Americans and African Americans have health insurance, while only about one-third of Hispanic Americans do (NCHS, 2012). Nevertheless, on many measures, poor African Americans, on average, are less healthy than either poor Whites or Hispanics. For instance, low-income African American children are nearly twice as likely as White or Hispanic poor children to have asthma (NCHS, 2012). By contrast, poor White children are more likely than their African American or Hispanic peers to be diagnosed with neurpsychological disorders such as *attention deficit hyperactivity disorder*. With regard to obesity, poverty increases the risk of obesity among Whites, Asians, and African American women, but it decreases the risk among Hispanic Americans and African American men (Boykin et al., 2011). Thus, as these findings illustrate, group differences in socioeconomic factors do not fully account for group differences in health, so what other variables might contribute to them? ◉

◉ **Watch** the Video *Episode 15: Special Topics: Health Disparities* in **MyPsychLab**

Bioethics professor Pilar Ossorio and sociologist Troy Duster suggest that the phenomenon of *racial patterning* underlies such differences (Ossorio & Duster, 2005). Racial patterning is the tendency of groups of people to maintain their collective identities through shared behavior patterns (e.g., diet, leisure activities, multigenerational living arrangements). Moreover, groups tend to share certain aspects of living conditions that may have health consequences as well (e.g., the concentration of Hispanic Americans in the desert regions of the southwestern United States). As a result of these patterns, risk and protective factors occur at different rates in different groups.

REMEMBER IT   *Check your answers and take additional quizzes in MyPsychLab.com.*   ✓ Study and Review on **MyPsychLab**

1. _____ is largely responsible for the link between Type A personality and heart disease.
2. _____ and _____ factors can influence the quality of life of cancer patients.
3. In general, women are (healthier/less healthy) than men, and men are (more/less) likely to die from most diseases.
4. A phenomenon called _____ has been proposed to explain group differences in health.

Lifestyle and Health

Thanks to the proliferation of computers all over the world and to the availability of the Internet, people who live in the industrialized nations of the world have something very important in common with those who live in the remotest regions of the developing world: a penchant for turning to the Internet for information about health (see the *Apply It;* Borzekowski, Fobil, & Asante, 2006; Cohen & Stussman, 2010). If you have searched the Net for health information, you know that any health-related search term will turn up dozens of Web sites that remind you of what you probably already know: For most of us, health enemy number one is our own habits—lack of exercise, too little sleep, alcohol or drug abuse, an unhealthy diet, and overeating. What can make someone change an unhealthy lifestyle? Perhaps vanity is the key. Health psychologists have found that people are more likely to adopt healthy behaviors if they believe behavioral change will make them look better or appear more youthful than if they simply receive information about the health benefits of the suggested change (Mahler et al., 2003). Still, there are some health-threatening behaviors that carry such grave risks that everyone ought to take them seriously. We'll discuss several of them here including alcohol abuse, sexually transmitted diseases, and the most dangerous unhealthy behavior of all, smoking. We'll also learn about the importance of diet and exercise and the role of alternative medicine in maintaining health and treating disease.

10.13 How does smoking affect health?

Smoking and Health

Smoking remains the foremost cause of preventable diseases and deaths in the United States. About 22% of men and 18% of women in the United States smoke cigarettes (NCHS, 2012). Still, the message that smoking is detrimental to health appears to

APPLY IT

Interpreting Health Information on the Internet

How reliable is the information available on the Internet? Studies of health-related Web sites have found that the quality of information varies widely from one site to another, and many contain incomplete or inaccurate information (Eysenbach et al., 2002; North et al., 2012). Nevertheless physicians' organizations acknowledge the potential value of the Internet in helping people learn about and manage their own health. To this end, the National Library of Medicine has published an online tutorial to help consumers evaluate health information on the Internet (National Library of Medicine, 2012). The tutorial includes several points to keep in mind when surfing the Web for health information and advice:

- *Remember that there are no rules governing what is published on the Internet.* Unlike scientific journal articles, which are usually written and reviewed by experts in the field, Internet articles can be posted by anyone, without review of any kind. Without expert knowledge, it is extremely difficult to tell whether the information and advice these articles contain are valid.

- *Consider the source.* Generally, Web sites sponsored by medical schools, government agencies, and public health organizations are reliable. Others, especially those promoting a health-related product, should be considered suspect.

- *Get a second opinion.* Ask your health care provider about Internet-based information or read what's available from several different sources on the topic.

- *Examine references.* Sites that refer to credible sources (e.g., books, other Web sites) that you can find on the Internet or in a library or bookstore are probably more reliable than sites that offer no references to support their advice.

- *How current is the information?* Health-related information changes frequently. Be certain that you are reading the most current findings and recommendations.

- *Is it too good to be true?* As in all areas of life, if something sounds too good to be true (e.g., a vitamin that cures cancer), it probably is. Try to find experimental, placebo-controlled studies that support any claims.

Using these guidelines, you can become a better consumer of Internet-based health information.

Watch on **MyPsychLab**

---

have taken root because the prevalence of smoking among American adults has declined dramatically since the 1960s when more than half of American adults were smokers and one-quarter were former smokers (American Lung Association, 2010). Moreover, smoking has come to be viewed as a socially unacceptable behavior now than in the past (Chassin et al., 2003). But there are wide variations in smoking habits according to gender and ethnic group. The highest rates of smoking are found among Native American men (25%) and women (21%), while the lowest rates are reported for Asian American men (15%) and women (6%) (NCHS, 2012).

Smoking increases the risk for heart disease, lung cancer, other smoking-related cancers, and emphysema. It is now known that smoking suppresses the action of T cells in the lungs, increasing susceptibility to respiratory tract infections and tumors (McCue et al., 2000). Other negative consequences from smoking include the widespread incidence of chronic bronchitis and other respiratory problems; the deaths and injuries from fires caused by smoking; and the low birth weight and retarded fetal development in babies born to smoking mothers. And millions of nonsmokers engage in *passive smoking* by breathing smoke-filled air—with proven ill effects. Research indicates that nonsmokers who are regularly exposed to *second-hand smoke* have twice the risk of heart attack of those who are not exposed (National Center for Chronic Disease Prevention and Health Promotion, 2006). Likewise, second-hand smoke increases children's risk of a variety of lung disorders, including asthma, bronchitis, and pneumonia (CDC, 2012b). ◉

There are many ways to quit smoking, but overall success rates for these methods, or for smoking cessation in general, can be somewhat misleading. There are many variables that affect success rates other than the desire to quit and the cessation method that a person chooses. Thus, if a study shows that only 20% of smokers using nicotine replacement, such as patches or chewing gum, succeed, reasons other than the purely physical aspects of nicotine addiction may be to blame (Rose, 2006).

The circumstances in smokers' lives may affect the outcome of their attempts to quit smoking. In one study involving more than 600 college students, researchers found that those who perceived that their lives were not very stressful had more success than

◉ Watch the Video *Smoking Damage* in **MyPsychLab**

other participants who felt more stress (Norman et al., 2006). Participants' overall success rate over the 18-month-long study was only 18%, but the low-perceived-stress group achieved a success rate of 52%. By contrast, only 13% of participants who perceived their lives to be highly stressful managed to quit in 18 months. The implication of these findings for others who want to quit smoking is that the often-heard recommendation that they choose a "quit date" is probably good advice. Planning a quit date to coincide with times of reduced stress, such as immediately after final exams, might be better than trying to quit at times of great stress.

10.14 What are some health risks of alcohol abuse?

Alcohol Abuse

Do you use alcohol regularly? Many Americans do. Recall from Chapter 4 that *substance abuse* is defined as continued use of a substance that interferes with a person's major life roles at home, in school, at work, or elsewhere and contributes to legal difficulties or any psychological problems (Dryden-Edwards, 2013). Alcohol is perhaps the most frequently abused substance of all, and the health costs of alcohol abuse are staggering—in fatalities, medical bills, lost work, and family problems.

When consumed to excess, alcohol can damage virtually every organ in the body, but it is especially harmful to the liver. Moreover, even a person who has never previously had a drink in his or her life can die from ingesting too much alcohol over a short period (see Table 10.1). One Norwegian longitudinal study involving more than 40,000 male participants found that the rate of death prior to age 60 was significantly higher among alcoholics than nonalcoholics (Rossow & Amundsen, 1997). Alcoholics are about three times as likely to die in automobile accidents or of heart disease as nonalcoholics, and they have twice the rate of deaths from cancer.

Damage to the brains of alcoholics has been found by researchers using MRI scans (van Eijk et al., 2013). CT scans also show brain shrinkage in a high percentage of alcoholics, even in those who are young and in those who show normal cognitive functioning (Lishman, 1990). Moreover, heavy drinking can cause cognitive impairment that

---

TABLE 10.1 Alcohol Poisoning

How much alcohol does it take to cause alcohol poisoning?
- This varies according to weight and tolerance for alcohol.
- Eight to ten drinks in one hour is sufficient to induce alcohol poisoning in anyone.

Are there any quick ways to sober up?
- No. There is no way to speed up elimination of alcohol from the body.
- Coffee, cold showers, walking it off, and sleeping it off don't work.

What are the signs of alcohol poisoning?
- Confusion, stupor, coma, or person can't be roused
- No response to pinching the skin
- Vomiting while asleep
- Seizures
- Slow breathing (fewer than 8 breaths per minute)
- Irregular breathing (10 seconds or more between breaths)
- Low body temperature, bluish skin, paleness

What should I do if I think someone has alcohol poisoning?
- Call 911.
- Stay with the person.
- Keep the person from choking on vomit.
- Tell paramedics how much and what type of alcohol the person drank.

Source: National Highway and Traffic Safety Administration (2007).

continues for several months after the drinking stops (Sullivan et al., 2002). The only good news in recent studies is that some of the effects of alcohol on the brain seem to be partially reversible with prolonged abstinence. In fact, the brains of those who abuse alcohol begin to recover within a few days of stopping drinking (van Eijk et al., 2013).

Since the late 1950s, the American Medical Association has maintained that alcoholism is a disease and that once an alcoholic, always an alcoholic. According to this view, even a small amount of alcohol can cause an irresistible craving for more, leading alcoholics to lose control of their drinking (Jellinek, 1960). Thus, total abstinence is seen as the only acceptable and effective method of treatment. Alcoholics Anonymous (AA) also endorses both the disease concept and the total abstinence approach to treatment. And there is a drug that may make abstinence somewhat easier. Researchers report that the drug acamprosate helps prevent relapse in recovering alcoholics (Rösner et al., 2010).

Some studies suggest a genetic influence on alcoholism and lend support to the disease model. For example, the late neuroscientist Henri Begleiter (1935–2006) and his colleagues have accumulated a large body of evidence suggesting that the brains of alcoholics respond differently to visual and auditory stimuli than those of nonalcoholics (Hada et al., 2000, 2001; Prabhu et al., 2001). Further, many relatives of alcoholics, even children and adults who have never consumed any alcohol in their lives, display the same types of response patterns (Rangaswamy et al., 2007). The relatives of alcoholics who do display these patterns are more likely to become alcoholics themselves or to suffer from other types of addictions (Anokhin et al., 2000; Beirut et al., 1998). Consequently, Begleiter suggested that the brain-imaging techniques he used in his research may someday be used to determine which relatives of alcoholics are genetically predisposed to addiction (Porjesz et al., 1998).

Sexually Transmitted Diseases ▶

What is the most common infectious disease in the United States? You might be surprised to learn that it is *chlamydia,* a sexually transmitted disease (CDC, 2012c). **Sexually transmitted diseases (STDs)** are infections spread primarily through sexual contact. The incidence of many STDs has increased dramatically over the past 30 years or so. This trend can be partly explained by more permissive attitudes toward sex and increased sexual activity among young people, some of whom have had several sexual partners by the time they graduate from high school (look back at Figure 8.5 on page 286). Another factor is the greater use of nonbarrier methods of contraception, such as the birth control pill, which do not prevent the spread of STDs. Barrier methods, such as condoms and vaginal spermicide, provide some protection against STDs.

Chlamydia is one of many **bacterial STDs**, diseases that can be cured by antibiotics. It can be transmitted through many kinds of physical contact involving the genitals as well as actual intercourse (CDC, 2012c). Women are about three times as likely as men to suffer from chlamydia. The prevalence of another bacterial STD, *gonorrhea,* declined considerably from 1975 to 2009. Unfortunately, the prevalence of gonorrhea is once again on the rise public health officials are concerned about this uptick in gonorrhea cases, because the strains that exist today are far more resistant to antibiotics than those that existed decades ago (CDC, 2012c). One of the long-term effects of both chlamydia and gonorrhea is *pelvic inflammatory disease,* an infection of the female reproductive tract that can cause infertility.

Another bacterial STD is *syphilis,* which can lead to serious mental disorders and death if it is not treated in the early stages of infection. At one time, syphilis had been almost completely eradicated. However, in 2008, about 46,000 cases were reported to the Centers for Disease Control and Prevention (CDC, 2009a). Most of these cases involved homosexual males who live in urban areas (CDC, 2009a). Subsequently, educating such men about the dangers of syphilis and measures that may be taken to prevent its transmission became a major focus of public health officials. Thankfully, syphilis rates declined dramatically thereafter, with only 13,970 new cases reported to the CDC in 2011 (CDC, 2012c).

10.15 What is the difference between bacterial and viral STDs?

sexually transmitted diseases (STDs) Infections that are spread primarily through intimate sexual contact.

bacterial STDs Sexually transmitted diseases that are caused by bacteria and can be treated with antibiotics.

viral STDs Sexually transmitted diseases that are caused by viruses and are considered to be incurable.

Unlike STDs caused by bacteria, **viral STDs** cannot be treated with antibiotics and are considered to be incurable. One such disease is *genital herpes,* a disease that can be acquired through either intercourse or oral sex. The Centers for Disease Control and Prevention reports that 16% of the adult population in the United States is infected with herpes (CDC, 2012d). Outbreaks of the disease, which include the development of painful blisters on the genitals, occur periodically in most people who carry the virus.

A more serious viral STD is *genital warts* caused by infection with *human papillomavirus (HPV).* The primary symptom of the disease, the presence of growths on the genitals, is not its most serious effect, however. HPV is strongly associated with cervical cancer (CDC, 2012e). Studies indicate that, in the United States, 50% of sexually active men and women are infected with HPV at some time in their lives (CDC 2012e).

The Food and Drug Administration approved a vaccine that officials believe will protect both men and women against four types of HPV (CDC, 2012e). However, researchers do not yet know how long the vaccine's protective effects will last. Moreover, officials point out that there are other forms of HPV against which the vaccine offers no protection. For these reasons, public health officials state that those who get the vaccine should continue to be vigilant about safe sex practices and routine medical screening.

acquired immune deficiency syndrome (AIDS) A devastating and incurable illness that is caused by infection with the human immunodeficiency virus (HIV) and progressively weakens the body's immune system, leaving the person vulnerable to opportunistic infections that usually cause death.

human immunodeficiency virus (HIV) The virus that causes AIDS.

The most feared STD is **acquired immune deficiency syndrome (AIDS),** caused by infection with the **human immunodeficiency virus (HIV).** The virus attacks the immune system until it is essentially nonfunctional. Although the first case was diagnosed in this country in 1981, there is still no cure for AIDS. Test your knowledge about AIDS in the *Try It* (p. 354).

The long search for effective treatments for HIV, chronicled in Figure 10.5, has produced two major victories. First, the discovery that drugs such as AZT can prevent the transmission of HIV from a pregnant woman to her fetus has saved thousands of lives. During the 1990s, nearly 2,000 infants were diagnosed with HIV each year. Thanks to widespread prenatal HIV screening and to the availability of these preventive drugs, fewer than 100 infants were diagnosed with HIV in 2009 (CDC, 2012f).

Second, the advent of *antiretroviral drugs* has probably prevented millions of deaths from AIDS by interfering with HIV's ability to invade healthy cells, the process through which HIV destroys its victims' immune systems. At present, the United Nations, aided by the World Bank, governments throughout the industrialized world, corporations, charitable foundations, and celebrity spokespersons, such as U2 singer Bono, is working to provide the funding needed to supply antiretroviral drugs to developing regions in which HIV-infection rates are particularly high, such as sub-Saharan Africa (Global Fund to Fight AIDS, Tuberculosis, and Malaria, 2005; Merson, 2006). Preliminary results suggest that these efforts have been quite effective. The number of new cases of HIV/AIDS in developing regions has leveled off and may even be declining (UNAIDS, 2011). These programs have also reduced rates of mother-to-child transmission of the disease as well as HIV-related infant deaths in these parts of the world (Violari et al., 2008).

Researchers believe that HIV is transmitted primarily through the exchange of blood, semen, or vaginal secretions during sexual contact or when IV (intravenous) drug users share contaminated needles or syringes. In the United States, about 11% of those with AIDS are IV drug users, but homosexual men represent the largest number of HIV carriers and AIDS cases (CDC, 2012f). Anal intercourse is more dangerous than coitus because rectal tissue often tears during penetration, allowing HIV ready entry into the bloodstream. However, it is a mistake to view AIDS as a disease confined to gay men; about one-quarter of those diagnosed with AIDS are women. Figure 10.6 (p. 354) illustrates the rates of infection in the United States in 2010 for four different modes of transmission: (1) male/male sexual relations; (2) male/female sexual relations; (3) intravenous drug use; and (4) male/male sexual relations combined with intravenous drug use (CDC, 2012a).

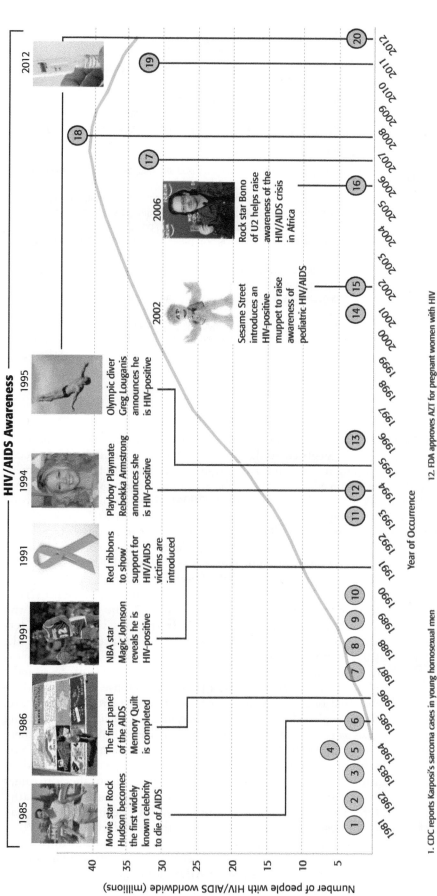

HIV/AIDS Awareness

Number of people with HIV/AIDS worldwide (millions)

Year of Occurrence

1985	Movie star Rock Hudson becomes the first widely known celebrity to die of AIDS
1986	The first panel of the AIDS Memory Quilt is completed
1991	NBA star Magic Johnson reveals he is HIV-positive
1991	Red ribbons to show support for HIV/AIDS victims are introduced
1994	Playboy Playmate Rebekka Armstrong announces she is HIV-positive
1995	Olympic diver Greg Louganis announces he is HIV-positive
2002	Sesame Street introduces an HIV-positive muppet to raise awareness of pediatric HIV/AIDS
2006	Rock star Bono of U2 helps raise awareness of the HIV/AIDS crisis in Africa

1. CDC reports Karposi's sarcoma cases in young homosexual men
2. CDC names and defines Acquired Immune Deficiency Syndrome (AIDS)
3. Officials warn public about infection risk associated with blood transfusions
4. Researchers identify HIV as cause of AIDS
5. Officials issue advisories about infection risk associated with IV-drug use
6. Blood banks begin screening supplies for HIV
7. FDA approves experimental drugs for AIDS
8. CDC mails brochure about HIV/AIDS to every home in the United States
9. Government changes policies to speed up drug approval process
10. FDA approves AZT treatment for children with HIV
11. Government launches large-scale studies on women with HIV/AIDS
12. FDA approves AZT for pregnant women with HIV
13. HIV/AIDS cases decline for the first time since 1982 in the U.S.
14. Lower-cost generic drugs for HIV/AIDS become available
15. FDA approves first finger-prick test for HIV
16. FDA approves triple-drug therapy
17. Experts recommend circumcision to reduce risk of HIV transmission
18. Number of HIV-positive adults receiving antiretroviral drugs in poor countries has increased sevenfold since 2004.
19. Increased awareness of HIV and availability of antiretroviral drugs causes worldwide rates of new HIV infections to fall 21% and AIDS-related deaths to decline 15% since 2001.
20. Over-the-counter HIV tests become available to consumers in the United States and many other regions of the world.

FIGURE 10.5 Milestones from the History of HIV/AIDS
Source: Kaiser Family Foundation (2012); UNAIDS (2011).

TRY IT

AIDS Quiz

Answer *true* or *false* for each statement.

1. AIDS is a single disease. (true/false)
2. AIDS symptoms vary widely from country to country and even from risk group to risk group. (true/false)
3. Those at greatest risk for getting AIDS are people who have sex without using condoms, drug users who share needles, and infants born to AIDS-infected mothers. (true/false)
4. AIDS is one of the most highly contagious diseases. (true/false)
5. One way to avoid contracting AIDS is to use an oil-based lubricant with a condom. (true/false)

● Watch on **MyPsychLab**

Answers:

1. *False:* AIDS is not a single disease. Rather, a severely impaired immune system leaves a person with AIDS highly susceptible to a whole host of infections and diseases.
2. *True:* In the United States and Europe, AIDS sufferers may develop Kaposi's sarcoma (a rare form of skin cancer), pneumonia, and tuberculosis. In Africa, people with AIDS usually waste away with fever, diarrhea, and symptoms caused by tuberculosis.
3. *True:* Those groups are at greatest risk. Screening of blood donors and testing of donated blood have greatly reduced the risk of contracting AIDS through blood transfusions. Today, women make up the fastest-growing group of infected people worldwide, as AIDS spreads among heterosexuals, especially in Africa.
4. *False:* AIDS is not among the most highly infectious diseases. You cannot get AIDS from kissing, shaking hands, or using objects handled by people who have AIDS.
5. *False:* Do not use oil-based lubricants, which can eat through condoms. Latex condoms with an effective spermicide are safer. Learn the sexual history of any potential partner, including HIV test results. Don't have sex with prostitutes.

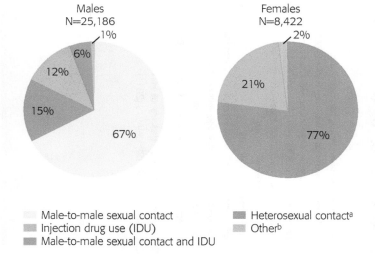

Males
N=25,186
1%
6%
12%
15%
67%

Females
N=8,422
2%
21%
77%

☐ Male-to-male sexual contact
■ Injection drug use (IDU)
■ Male-to-male sexual contact and IDU
■ Heterosexual contact[a]
☐ Other[b]

FIGURE 10.6 **How HIV Is Transmitted in AIDS Cases in the United States**
Source: Centers for Disease Control (CDC) (2012a). HIV surveillance - Epidemiology of HIV infection (through 2010). Retrieved January 7, 2013 from http://www.cdc.gov/hiv/topics/surveillance/resources/slides/general/index.htm

Researchers have recently discovered that circumcision substantially reduces the risk of HIV transmission (Siegfried et al., 2009). In response, public health officials in many of the developing nations that have large populations of HIV-positive men, such as Uganda, have begun educating the public about the procedure along with other ways of reducing risk of infection (Cassell et al., 2006). Screening and treatment for other STDs are vital to the prevention of HIV (CDC, 2009a) as well. Research has shown that the presence of another STD in an HIV-infected person causes him or her to have higher levels of the communicable form of the virus in his or her bodily fluids. Anyone who has sex with such a person is, therefore, at a greatly increased risk of becoming infected with HIV.

What are the psychological effects on people who struggle to cope with this fearsome disease? The reaction to the news that one is HIV-positive is frequently shock, bewilderment, confusion, or disbelief (Bargiel-Matusiewicz et al., 2005). Another common reaction is anger—at past or present sexual partners, family members, health care professionals, or society in general. Often, a person's response includes guilt, a sense that one is being punished for homosexuality or drug abuse. Other people exhibit denial, ignoring medical advice and continuing to act as if nothing has changed in their lives. Then, of course, there is fear—of death; of mental and physical deterioration; of rejection by friends, family, and co-workers; of sexual rejection; of abandonment. Experiencing emotional swings ranging from shock to anger to guilt to fear can lead to serious clinical depression and apathy (Tate et al., 2003). Once apathy sets in, HIV-positive patients may become less likely to comply with treatment (Dilorio et al., 2009).

Once AIDS develops, a sequence of events that devastates the brains of 40% of its victims is set in motion (Thompson et al., 2005). The cortex of an AIDS victim gradually thins as the disease gains ground in its attack on the person's immune system.

Motor and language impairments often result from slow deterioration of the areas of the cortex that are involved in these functions. Cortical thinning causes some AIDS patients to develop *AIDS-related dementia,* a disorder that is similar to Alzheimer's disease. Researchers say that some people who are HIV-positive but who have not developed full-blown AIDS show cortical thinning to some extent as well. Thus, studies are currently underway to determine the best way to approach this effect of the virus.

To cope psychologically, AIDS patients, those infected with HIV, and their loved ones need education and information about the disease. They can be helped by psychotherapy, self-help groups, and medications such as antidepressants and anti-anxiety drugs. Self-help groups and group therapy may serve as an extended family for some patients.

Diet and Exercise ▶

10.16 How do diet and exercise affect health?

In Chapter 9, you learned about obesity as it relates to the primary motive of hunger and read that a BMI in excess of 30 is considered obese. Obesity increases a person's chances of developing several chronic diseases (CDC, 2006e). These conditions include high blood pressure, type 2 diabetes, gallbladder disease, arthritis, and respiratory disorders. In addition, people who are obese are more likely to develop coronary heart disease and to have elevated levels of LDL cholesterol (the bad cholesterol that is associated with heart disease).

Health problems may also develop in people whose diets have insufficient amounts of particular nutrients (CDC, 2006e). For example, a diet that is deficient in iron leads to *anemia,* a condition that impairs the blood's ability to deliver oxygen to the body's organs. Likewise, a diet that lacks sufficient calcium may cause degeneration of the bones. And pregnant women whose diets lack folic acid are more likely to deliver infants with spinal defects.

People who regularly consume fast foods are at risk for both obesity and specific nutritional deficiencies. Thus, nutrition experts recommend that such food be eaten infrequently or not at all. To help consumers achieve this goal, experts have also developed several strategies for improving overall diet quality. One simple approach is the "5-a-day" plan in which people are advised to try to eat at least five servings of fruits and vegetables every day. Another involves reading the labels of processed foods and avoiding those that are high in saturated fats, trans fats, and sodium, all of which are associated with high levels of LDL cholesterol. Labels can also guide people to foods that are high in monosaturated fats, a type of fat that may increase levels of HDL cholesterol (the good cholesterol).

aerobic exercise (ah-RO-bik) Exercise that uses the large muscle groups in continuous, repetitive action and increases oxygen intake and breathing and heart rates.

Studies show that regular exercise also pays rich dividends in the form of physical and mental fitness. However, many people still express reluctance to exercise. About half of Americans do not engage in any kind of physical activity on a regular basis (CDC, 2012b). Some simply prefer not to be physically active; others blame such factors as the cost of joining a health club or even the unpredictability of the weather for their lack of physical activity (Salmon et al., 2003). Such individuals are missing out on one of the simplest and most effective ways of enhancing one's health.

Aerobic exercise (such as running, swimming, brisk walking, bicycling, rowing, and jumping rope) is exercise that uses the large muscle groups in continuous, repetitive action and increases oxygen intake and breathing and heart rates. To improve cardiovascular fitness and endurance and to lessen the risk of heart attack, an individual should perform aerobic exercise regularly—five times a week for 20 to 30 minutes (CDC, 2006b). Individuals who engage in more than 3 hours of aerobic activity each week are more successful at losing excess weight and keeping it off than are those who exercise less (Votruba, Horvitz, & Schoeller, 2000).

▲ Regular aerobic exercise improves cardiovascular fitness in people of all ages.

In case you are not yet convinced, consider the following benefits of exercise (Mayo Clinic, 2009):

- Improves mood
- Combats chronic diseases such as high blood pressure, diabetes, and osteoporosis
- Helps manage weight
- Boosts energy level
- Promotes better sleep
- Improves sexual intimacy
- Enhances enjoyment of life

Exercise also appears to moderate the effects of aging on the body. Strength training, for example, has been found to reduce *sarcopenia,* an age-related process in which the muscles deteriorate (CDC, 2006b). Such training appears to prevent the loss of bone mass, or *osteoporosis,* as well. Moreover, physical exercise helps seniors with balance, coordination, and stamina.

10.17 What are the benefits and risks associated with alternative medicine?

Alternative Medicine

Americans spend billions of dollars each year on unconventional treatments—herbs, massage, self-help groups, megavitamins, folk remedies, and homeopathy—for a variety of illnesses and conditions. In one such survey, the National Science Foundation (NSF, 2002) found that 88% of Americans believe that there are valid ways of preventing and curing illnesses that are not recognized by the medical profession. Thus, it isn't surprising that more than half of adults and children in the United States take at least one vitamin pill each day for the purpose of preventing or treating some kind of health condition (Consumer Reports, 2012). In addition, 38% of adults and 12% of children use some kind of nonmedical therapy to treat a current medical condition (Barnes, Bloom, & Nahin, 2008). Figure 10.7 shows the most popular therapies. The "other" category in the figure includes treatments such as acupuncture, biofeedback, guided imagery, progressive relaxation, hypnosis, Pilates, traditional healers, and a host of other alternative therapies.

alternative medicine Any treatment or therapy that has not been scientifically demonstrated to be effective.

The National Science Foundation (2002) defines **alternative medicine** as any treatment or therapy that has not been scientifically demonstrated to be effective. Even a simple practice such as taking vitamins sometimes falls into this category. For instance, if you take Vitamin C to protect yourself against the common cold, you are using alternative medicine because Vitamin C has not been scientifically proven to prevent colds.

Most people who use alternative treatments do not inform their physicians about them. Health professionals cite this tendency toward secrecy as a major risk factor in the use of alternative medicine (Yale–New Haven Hospital, 2003). They point out that many therapies, especially those that involve food supplements, have pharmacological effects that can interfere with treatments prescribed by physicians. Consequently, individuals who use alternative treatments should tell their physicians about them. While doctors may be skeptical about the utility of the alternative treatments, they need to have this information about their patients to practice conventional medicine effectively. Therefore, medical educators urge physicians to openly and respectfully discuss patients' beliefs about alternative medicine with them before initiating standard forms of treatment (George, 2012).

Although it is true that some alternative therapies may be helpful in both preventing and treating illness, most health professionals agree that lifestyle changes bring greater health benefits than do any methods of alternative medicine. Unfortunately, many people resist making lifestyle changes because they see them as taking too long to be effective or being too difficult to carry out. However, Table 10.2 shows that the benefits of various lifestyle changes, some of which are fairly easy to achieve, can be well worth the effort.

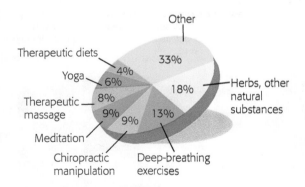

FIGURE 10.7 Alternative Therapies
In the United States, 38% of adults and 12% of children use one or more alternative treatments to treat or prevent disease. The "other" category includes acupuncture, biofeedback, guided imagery, progressive relaxation, hypnosis, Pilates, traditional healers, and a host of other treatments.
Source: Barnes et al. (2007).

TABLE 10.2 **Benefits of Lifestyle Changes**

LIFESTYLE CHANGE	BENEFITS
If overweight, lose just 10 pounds.	34% reduction in triglyceride levels; 16% decrease in total cholesterol; 18% increase in HDL ("good" cholesterol); significant reduction in blood pressure; decreased risk of diabetes, sleep apnea, and osteoarthritis (Still, 2001).
Add 20 to 30 grams of fiber to your diet each day.	Improved bowel function; reduced risk of colon cancer and other digestive system diseases; decrease in total cholesterol; reduced blood pressure; improved insulin function in both diabetics and nondiabetics (HCF, 2003).
Engage in moderate physical activity every day (e.g., walk up and down stairs for 15 minutes; spend 30 minutes washing a car).	Reduced feelings of anxiety and sadness; increased bone density; reduced risk of diabetes, heart disease, high blood pressure, and many other life-shortening diseases (CDC, 1999).
Stop smoking at any age, after any number of years of smoking.	*Immediate:* improved circulation; reduced blood level of carbon monoxide; stabilization of pulse rate and blood pressure; improved sense of smell and taste; improved lung function and endurance; reduced risk of lung infections such as pneumonia and bronchitis. *Long-term:* reduced risk of lung cancer (declines substantially with each year of abstinence); decreased risk of other smoking-related illnesses such as emphysema and heart disease; decreased risk of cancer recurrence in those who have been treated for some form of cancer (National Cancer Institute, 2000).
Get recommended annual or 5-year screenings beginning at these ages	*Women:* (21) Chlamydia, cervical cancer screenings if sexually active; (35), cholesterol test; (50) mammogram, colorectal exam; (65) vision, hearing tests *Men:* (30) EKG, cholesterol test; (40) PSA test for prostate cancer; (50) colorectal exam; (65) vision, hearing tests

▲ Many individuals turn to alternative treatments such as acupuncture to improve their health and fight disease.

👁 Watch the Video *Episode 15: What's in It for Me? The Challenge of Quitting Bad Health Habits* in **MyPsychLab**

REMEMBER IT   *Check your answers and take additional quizzes in MyPsychLab.com.*   ✓ Study and Review in **MyPsychLab**

1. The greatest threat to Americans' health and longevity is a(n) _____.

2. _____ is the leading preventable cause of disease and death.

3. A single episode of excessive alcohol intake can damage health. (true/false)

4. If left untreated, _____, a bacterial STD, can be fatal.

5. A vaccine is available to prevent _____.

6. Cardiovascular fitness and endurance can be improved through _____.

7. _____ may be a more effective way of enhancing health than turning to alternative medicine.

🔭 Looking Back

In the section of this chapter that discussed stress, you learned that exerting control over controllable stressors can help you cope. The same is true of health. And, although the list of lifestyle changes in Table 10.2 may be intimidating, you need not make *all* of them to improve your chances of a healthy future. You might consider starting with just one. Even if you never make another change, you are likely to live longer and be healthier than you would have otherwise been.

CHAPTER 10 SUMMARY

SOURCES OF STRESS (pp. 329–335)

10.1 How does the life events approach describe stress? (pp. 329–331)

The life events approach focuses on individuals' responses to the stresses associated with major life changes. The SRRS assesses stress in terms of major life events, positive or negative, that necessitate change and adaptation. Holmes and Rahe found a relationship between degree of life stress (as measured on the scale) and major health problems. Research on responses to catastrophic events shows that people respond differently to such stressors. Some people develop posttraumatic stress disorder (PTSD), a prolonged, severe stress reaction, often characterized by flashbacks, nightmares, or intrusive memories of the traumatic event.

Key Terms
stress, p. 329
stressor, p. 329
life events approach, p. 329
Social Readjustment Rating Scale (SRRS), p. 330
posttraumatic stress disorder (PTSD), p. 331

10.2 What do hassles, uplifts, and choices contribute to stress? (pp. 331–332)

Some theorists argue that everyday stressors are more important than major life events. According to Lazarus, daily hassles typically cause more stress than major life changes. Positive experiences in life—or uplifts—can neutralize the effects of many of the hassles, however. Choices are another important source of stress in everyday life. In an approach-approach conflict, a person must decide between equally desirable alternatives. In an avoidance-avoidance conflict, the choice is between two undesirable alternatives. In an approach-avoidance conflict, a person is both drawn to and repelled by a single choice.

Key Terms
hassles, p. 331
uplifts, p. 332
approach-approach conflict, p. 332
avoidance-avoidance conflict, p. 332
approach-avoidance conflict, p. 332

10.3 What variables contribute to workers' comfort zone? (pp. 332–333)

Nine variables influence a worker's comfort zone. They include workload, clarity of job description and evaluation criteria, physical variables, job status, accountability, task variety, human contact, physical challenge, and mental challenge. Discrimination and harassment contribute to work-related stress. Job stress affects employees' effectiveness, absenteeism, tardiness, accidents, substance abuse, and morale. Chronic work stress can lead to burnout.

Key Term
burnout, p. 333

10.4 What are some social sources of stress? (pp. 333–335)

People of low socioeconomic status have more stress-related health problems than those of higher status. Stressors associated with low SES include lifestyle factors such as smoking as well as higher levels of stress hormones. Perceived status may predict health outcomes better than objective status. Unemployment is another status variable that is related to health. People who lose their jobs suffer more stress-related illnesses in the months following job loss than peers who are still employed.

Key Term
socioeconomic status, p. 334

THE HEALTH-STRESS CONNECTION (pp. 335–344)

10.5 How does the biopsychosocial model approach health and illness? (pp. 335–337)

The biomedical model focuses on illness rather than on health and explains illness in terms of biological factors. The biopsychosocial model focuses on health as well as on illness and holds that both are determined by a combination of biological, psychological, and social factors. Health psychologists use the biopsychosocial model to understand and influence the contributions of psychological factors to communication between health care professionals and patients, pain management, the influence of psychological and behavioral factors on specific diseases, gender and group differences in health, and health-related lifestyle behaviors. They have found that stress plays a role in all of these domains.

Key Terms
biomedical model, p. 335
biopsychosocial model, p. 336
health psychology, p. 336

10.6 How does the fight-or-flight response affect health? (pp. 337–338)

When a stressor occurs, the sympathetic nervous system prepares the body to oppose it or flee from it (the fight-or-flight response). Prolonged stress causes the body to try to maintain the fight-or-flight response over a long period. The biochemicals associated with the fight-or-flight response can make the body more vulnerable to illness through their direct actions on tissues. The fight-or-flight response also influences health indirectly because it suppresses the immune system.

Key Terms
fight-or-flight response, p. 337
lymphocytes, p. 337
psychoneuroimmunology, p. 337

10.7 How do theorists explain physiological and psychological responses to stress? (pp. 338–340)

The general adaptation syndrome (GAS) proposed by Selye is the predictable sequence of reactions that organisms show in response to stressors. It consists of the alarm stage, the resistance stage, and the exhaustion stage. Lazarus maintains that when confronted with a potentially stressful event, a person engages in a cognitive appraisal process consisting of (1) a primary appraisal, to evaluate the relevance of the situation to one's well-being (whether it will be positive, irrelevant, or negative), and (2) a secondary appraisal, to evaluate one's resources and determine how to cope with the stressor.

Key Terms
general adaptation syndrome (GAS), p. 338
alarm stage, p. 338
resistance stage, p. 338
exhaustion stage, p. 338
primary appraisal, p. 339
secondary appraisal, p. 339

10.8 What factors promote resilience in the face of stress? (pp. 340–344)

Coping strategies help us overcome stress. Problem-focused coping is a direct response aimed at reducing, modifying, or eliminating the source of stress; emotion-focused coping involves reappraising a stressor in order to reduce its emotional impact. Other factors that promote resilience include optimism, hardiness, social involvement, social support, and perceived control.

Key Terms
risk/resilience model, p. 340
coping, p. 340
problem-focused coping, p. 340
emotion-focused coping, p. 340
proactive coping, p. 340
hardiness, p. 341
social support, p. 342

HEALTH AND ILLNESS (pp. 344–348)

10.9 How do lifestyle, heredity, and personality influence coronary heart disease? (pp. 344–345)

The Type A behavior pattern, often cited as a risk factor for coronary heart disease, is characterized by a sense of time urgency, impatience, excessive competitive drive, hostility, and easily aroused anger. The Type B behavior pattern is characterized by a relaxed, easygoing approach to life, without the time urgency, impatience, and hostility of the Type A pattern. People with the Type D behavior pattern experience high levels of negative emotions that they usually suppress.

Key Terms
Type A behavior pattern, p. 345
Type B behavior pattern, p. 345
Type D behavior pattern, p. 345

10.10 How do psychological factors influence cancer patients' quality of life? (pp. 346–346)

Research does not support the idea that stress causes cancer. However, stress associated with cancer treatment affects how the immune system responds to treatment. In addition, variables such as optimism contribute to cancer patients' resistance to stress. Therapy can help patients maintain a positive emotional state and cope more effectively with the pain they experience.

10.11 How do males and females differ with regard to health? (pp. 346–347)

Women are more likely than men to die following heart surgery. Generally, though, men are more likely than women to die from most diseases, but women are generally less healthy. When men and women have the same diseases, men are often more seriously ill. Researchers suspect these patterns may be caused by the unique physiology of each gender.

10.12 How do researchers explain ethnic group differences in health? (pp. 347–348)

Some researchers believe that African Americans have greater levels of high blood pressure than members of other groups because of stress due to historical racism. African Americans who express high levels of concern about racism display larger cardiovascular responses to experimentally induced stressors than do their peers who express lower levels of concern. Racial patterning produces correlations between race and health through its influence on group differences in risk and protective factors.

LIFESTYLE AND HEALTH (pp. 348–357)

10.13 How does smoking affect health? (pp. 348–350)

Smoking is considered the most dangerous health-related behavior because it is directly related to over 400,000 deaths each year, including deaths from heart disease, lung cancer, and respiratory diseases.

10.14 What are some health risks of alcohol abuse? (pp. 350–351)

Alcohol abuse damages virtually every organ in the body, including the liver, heart, and brain. Alcoholics are three times as likely to die in motor vehicle accidents as nonalcoholics.

10.15 What is the difference between bacterial and viral STDs? (pp. 351–355)

The major sexually transmitted diseases caused by bacteria are chlamydia, gonorrhea, and syphilis. All can be cured with antibiotics. However, chlamydia and gonorrhea pose a particular threat to women because, unlike men, women with these infections typically have no symptoms or very mild symptoms, making prompt diagnosis and treatment less likely. If the infection spreads, it may result in infertility. Viral STDs include the human papilloma virus (HPV), genital herpes, and HIV/AIDS. Viral infections presently are not curable, but a vaccine is available to protect women against some strains of HPV. HIV gradually renders the immune system nonfunctional. Psychotherapy, self-help groups, and antidepressant medication can be helpful to those coping with HIV/AIDS.

Key Terms

sexually transmitted diseases (STDs), p. 351
bacterial STDs, p. 351
viral STDs, p. 352
acquired immune deficiency syndrome (AIDS), p. 352
human immunodeficiency virus (HIV), p. 352

10.16 How do diet and exercise affect health? (pp. 355–356)

Obesity is related to many chronic health conditions. Nutrient deficiencies also cause problems. Fast-food consumers are at risk for both obesity and dietary deficiencies. Guidelines based on the latest research are available to help people improve the quality of their diets. Regular aerobic exercise reduces the risk of cardiovascular disease, increases muscular strength, makes bones denser and stronger, and helps one maintain a desirable weight.

Key Term

aerobic exercise, p. 355

10.17 What are the benefits and risks associated with alternative medicine? (pp. 356–357)

Alternative medicine, or the use of any treatment that has not been proven scientifically to be effective, may be helpful in both preventing and treating illness in some instances. However, many patients increase their risk of poor outcomes by not telling their physicians about their use of alternative treatments. And some people delay seeking necessary conventional medical treatment because they believe that alternative approaches will work.

Key Term

alternative medicine, p. 356

Chapter 10 Study Guide

Answers to all the Study Guide questions are provided at the end of the book.

SECTION ONE: Chapter Review

Sources of Stress (pp. 329–335)

1. On the Social Readjustment Rating Scale, only negative life changes are considered stressful. (true/false)

2. The Social Readjustment Rating Scale takes account of the individual's perceptions of the stressfulness of the life change in assigning stress points. (true/false)

3. Posttraumatic stress disorder is a prolonged and severe stress reaction that results when a number of common sources of stress occur simultaneously. (true/false)

4. According to Lazarus, hassles typically account for more life stress than major life changes. (true/false)

5. Lazarus's approach to measuring hassles and uplifts considers individual perceptions of stressful events. (true/false)

6. Travis cannot decide whether to go out or stay home and study for his test. What kind of conflict does he have?
   a. approach-approach
   b. avoidance-avoidance
   c. approach-avoidance
   d. ambivalence-ambivalence

7. Sources of workplace stress for women include
   a. being quickly promoted to management positions.
   b. on-the-job injuries.
   c. balancing family and work demands.
   d. conflicts with co-workers.

8. The group that has received the most attention from researchers interested in the association between stress and racism is
   a. Native Americans.
   b. Hispanic Americans.
   c. Asian Americans.
   d. African Americans.

The Stress-Health Connection (pp. 335–344)

9. The biomedical model focuses on _____; the biopsychosocial model focuses on _____.
   a. illness; illness
   b. health and illness; illness
   c. illness; health and illness
   d. health and illness; health and illness

10. Lowered immune response has been associated with
   a. stress.
   b. depression.
   c. stress and depression.
   d. neither stress nor depression.

11. The stage of the general adaptation syndrome marked by intense physiological efforts to adapt to the stressor is the (alarm, resistance) stage.

12. Susceptibility to illness increases during the (alarm, exhaustion) stage of the general adaptation syndrome.

13. Selye focused on the (psychological, physiological) aspects of stress; Lazarus focused on the (psychological, physiological) aspects of stress.

14. During secondary appraisal, a person
   a. evaluates his or her coping resources and considers options for dealing with the stressor.
   b. determines whether an event is positive, neutral, or negative.
   c. determines whether an event involves loss, threat, or challenge.
   d. determines whether an event causes physiological or psychological stress.

15. Coping aimed at reducing, modifying, or eliminating a source of stress is called (emotion-focused, problem-focused) coping; that aimed at reducing an emotional reaction to stress is called (emotion-focused, problem-focused) coping.

16. People typically use a combination of problem-focused and emotion-focused coping when dealing with a stressful situation. (true/false)

17. Some research suggests that optimists are more stress-resistant than pessimists. (true/false)

18. Which of the following is not a dimension of psychological hardiness?
   a. a feeling that adverse circumstances can be controlled and changed
   b. a sense of commitment and deep involvement in personal goals
   c. a tendency to look on change as a challenge rather than a threat
   d. close, supportive relationships with family and friends

19. Social support tends to reduce stress but is unrelated to health outcomes. (true/false)

Health and Illness (pp. 344–348)

20. Most research has pursued the connection between the Type A behavior pattern and
   a. cancer.
   b. coronary heart disease.
   c. stroke.
   d. ulcers.

21. Recent research suggests that the most toxic component of the Type A behavior pattern is
   a. hostility.
   b. impatience.
   c. a sense of time urgency.
   d. perfectionism.

22. Stress causes cancer. (true/false)

23. Which statement about gender differences in health is false?
   a. Women are more likely than men to die within a year of having heart surgery.
   b. Men seek medical care more often than women.
   c. Fatal diseases progress more quickly in men than in women.
   d. Smoking-related diseases afflict male and female smokers about equally.

24. Which ethnic group has the highest rate of death from liver disease?
   a. Whites
   b. African Americans
   c. Hispanic Americans
   d. Native Americans

Lifestyle and Health (pp. 348–357)

25. Which is the most important factor leading to disease and death?
   a. unhealthy lifestyle
   b. a poor health care system
   c. environmental hazards
   d. genetic disorders

26. Which health-compromising behavior is responsible for the most deaths?
   a. overeating
   b. smoking
   c. lack of exercise
   d. excessive alcohol use

27. (Alcohol, Smoking) damages virtually every organ in the body.

28. Viral STDs are those that can be effectively treated with antibiotics. (true/false)

29. HIV eventually causes a breakdown in the _____ system.
   a. circulatory
   b. vascular
   c. immune
   d. respiratory

30. The incidence of AIDS in the United States is highest among
   a. IV drug users.
   b. hemophiliacs.
   c. homosexuals.
   d. heterosexuals.

31. To improve cardiovascular fitness, aerobic exercise should be done
   a. 15 minutes daily.
   b. 1 hour daily.
   c. 20 to 30 minutes five times a week.
   d. 20 to 30 minutes three or four times a week.

32. Alternative health treatments have proven to be just as effective as traditional approaches to illness. (true/false)

SECTION TWO: The Biopsychosocial Model of Health and Illness

List at least two forces for each of the following:

1. Biological forces favoring health and wellness _____

_____

2. Biological forces working against health and wellness _____

_____

3. Psychological forces favoring health and wellness _____

_____

4. Psychological forces working against health and wellness _____

   _____

5. Social forces favoring health and wellness _____

   _____

6. Social forces working against health and wellness _____

   _____

SECTION THREE: Comprehensive Practice Test

1. Stress consists of the threats and problems we encounter in life. (true/false)

2. Hans Selye developed the
   a. diathesis stress model.
   b. general adaptation syndrome model.
   c. cognitive stress model.
   d. conversion reaction model.

3. The fight-or-flight response is seen in the _____ stage of the general adaptation syndrome.
   a. alarm
   b. exhaustion
   c. resistance
   d. arousal

4. Lack of exercise, poor diet, and disease and injury are considered to be _____ forces that work against health and wellness.
   a. environmental
   b. psychological
   c. biological
   d. social

5. Charlotte has been looking for new bedroom furniture and has found two styles that she really likes. She is trying to decide which one she will purchase. Charlotte is experiencing an _____ conflict.
   a. approach-approach
   b. approach-avoidance
   c. avoidance-avoidance
   d. avoidance-approach

6. Perceived control over a situation can have an important beneficial influence on how a stressor affects you even if you do not exercise that control. (true/false)

7. Posttraumatic stress disorder leaves some people more vulnerable to future mental health problems. (true/false)

8. Which of the following is not a variable in work stress?
   a. workload
   b. clarity of job description
   c. perceived equity of pay for work
   d. task variety

9. Research indicates that African Americans who are highly concerned about _____ are more sensitive to stressors than their peers who are less concerned.

10. Religious faith can help people cope with negative life events. (true/false)

11. Lazarus's term for the positive experiences that can serve to cancel out the effects of day-to-day hassles is
    a. stress assets.
    b. coping mechanisms.
    c. uplifts.
    d. appraisals.

12. Type B behavior patterns seem to be more correlated with heart disease than do Type A behavior patterns. (true/false)

13. B cells produce antibodies that are effective in destroying antigens that live _____ the body cells; T cells are important in the destruction of antigens that live _____ the body cells.
    a. outside; inside
    b. inside; outside

14. AIDS is caused by HIV, often called the AIDS virus. (true/false)

15. HIV weakens the immune system by attacking T cells. (true/false)

SECTION FOUR: Critical Thinking

1. In your view, which is more effective for evaluating stress: the Social Readjustment Rating Scale or the Hassle Scale? Explain the advantages and disadvantages of each.

2. Prepare two arguments: one supporting the position that alcoholism is a genetically inherited disease, and the other supporting the position that alcoholism is not a medical disease but results from learning.

SECTION FIVE: Application Essays

1. Choose several stress-producing incidents from your life and explain what problem-focused and emotion-focused coping strategies you used. From the knowledge you have gained in this chapter, list other coping strategies that might have been more effective.

Apply your critical thinking skills with MyPsychLab Writing Assignments

Submit your answer to the following question inside the MyPsychLab Writing Assessment program for immediate feedback.

Imagine a friend has just lost his job which helped him cover tuition costs. Apply Lazarus and Folkman's cognitive theory of stress and describe his potential reactions to this job loss. In your answer, be sure to describe the following: Stressful Event, Primary Appraisal, Secondary Appraisal, and Stress Response.

Personality Theory and Assessment

◎ THINK ABOUT IT

What is your personality like? One way of answering this question is to use words that personality psychologists call *descriptors*. To get a feel for the kinds of descriptors that psychologists use to describe individual differences in personality, think about which adjectives in the list to the right best describe you. Which characterize your mother? Your father?

decisive	outgoing	generous	industrious
funny	inhibited	sloppy	deceptive
intelligent	religious	laid-back	cooperative
disorganized	arrogant	rebellious	reckless
shy	loyal	calm	sad
fearful	competitive	good-natured	honest
jealous	liberal	nervous	happy
controlled	friendly	serious	selfish
responsible	compulsive	humble	organized
rigid	quick	lazy	quiet

◉ **Watch** the Video *Episode 13: Big Picture: What Is Personality?* in **MyPsychLab**

personality A person's characteristic patterns of behaving, thinking, and feeling.

conscious (KON-shus) The thoughts, feelings, sensations, or memories of which a person is aware at any given moment.

11.1 What concepts did Freud propose to explain personality?

preconscious The thoughts, feelings, and memories that a person is not consciously aware of at the moment but that may be easily brought to consciousness.

unconscious (un-KON-shus) For Freud, the primary motivating force of human behavior, containing repressed memories as well as instincts, wishes, and desires that have never been conscious.

▶ Sigmund Freud (1856–1939), with his daughter Anna (1895-1982) who became a prominent proponent of psychoanalytic theory after her father's death. She was best known for her application of Freud's theory and therapeutic techniques to children's and adolescents' emotional problems.

The use of descriptors to study, explain, and assess **personality**—a person's characteristic patterns of behaving, thinking, and feeling—belongs to a particular perspective on personality that you will learn about later in the chapter, the *trait approach*. The trait approach suggests that we exhibit consistent characteristics—responsibility, honesty, recklessness, sense of humor, and so on—across situations and that these characteristics make up our personalities. However, there several other ways to approach personality that have made important contributions to the scientific study of personality, as you will soon learn.

Psychoanalytic Theories

You learned about one important theory of personality in Chapter 1: psychoanalysis. You may recall that the term *psychoanalysis* refers not only to Freud's approach to therapy but also to the influential personality theory he proposed. The central idea of psychoanalytic theory is that unconscious forces shape human thought and behavior.

Freud's Theory of Personality

Freud proposed that there are three levels of awareness in consciousness: the conscious, the preconscious, and the unconscious. The **conscious** consists of whatever we are aware of at any given moment—thoughts, feelings, sensations, or memories. The **preconscious** is somewhat like long-term memory: It contains all the memories, feelings, experiences, and perceptions that we are not consciously thinking about at the moment but that may be easily brought to consciousness.

The most important of the three levels is the **unconscious**, which Freud believed to be the primary motivating force of human behavior. The unconscious holds memories that once were conscious but were so unpleasant or anxiety provoking that they were repressed (involuntarily removed from consciousness). For instance, a situation in which a person was severely embarrassed might be "forgotten" by relegating to the unconscious. The unconscious also contains all of the instincts (sexual and aggressive), wishes, and desires that have never been allowed into consciousness. Freud traced the roots of psychological disorders to these impulses and repressed memories and proposed a three-part model of personality to explain how the unconscious, preconscious, and conscious minds interact.

The Id, Ego, and Superego. Freud also proposed three systems of personality. Figure 11.1 shows these three systems and how they relate to his conscious, preconscious, and unconscious levels of awareness. These systems do not exist physically; they are only concepts, or ways of looking at personality.

The **id** is the only part of the personality that is present at birth, and it is often compared to a newborn infant who never grows up. It is inherited, primitive, inaccessible, and completely unconscious. The id contains (1) the life instincts, which are the sexual instincts and the biological urges, such as hunger and thirst and (2) the death instinct, which accounts for aggressive and destructive impulses (Freud, 1933/1965). Operating according to the *pleasure principle,* the id tries to seek pleasure, avoid pain, and gain immediate gratification of its wishes. The id is the source of the *libido,* the psychic energy that fuels the entire personality; yet, the id can only fantasize and demand.

The **ego** is the logical, rational, and realistic part of the personality. The ego evolves from the id and draws its energy from the id. One of the ego's functions is to satisfy the id's urges. But the ego, which is mostly conscious, acts according to the *reality principle.* It considers the constraints of the real world in determining appropriate times, places, and objects for gratification of the id's wishes. The ego's focus is highly practical. It operates on what it deems to be possible rather than ideal outcomes. As a result, sometimes compromises must be made—such as settling for a fast-food hamburger instead of steak or lobster.

When a child is age 5 or 6, the **superego,** the moral component of the personality, is formed. The superego has two parts: (1) The *conscience* consists of all the behaviors for which the child has been punished and about which he or she feels guilty and (2) the *ego ideal* comprises the behaviors for which the child has been praised and rewarded and about which he or she feels pride and satisfaction. At first, the superego reflects only the parents' expectations of what is good and right, but it expands over time to incorporate teachings from the broader social world. In its quest for moral perfection, the superego sets guidelines that define and limit the ego's flexibility. A harsher judge than any external authority, including one's parents, the superego judges not only behavior, but also thoughts, feelings, and wishes. ✴

Defense Mechanisms. All would be well if the id, the ego, and the superego had compatible aims. But the id's demands for pleasure are often in direct conflict with the superego's desire for moral perfection. At times the ego needs some way to defend itself against the anxiety created by the excessive demands of the id and the harsh judgments of the superego. When it cannot solve problems directly, the ego may use a **defense mechanism,** a technique used to defend against anxiety and to maintain self-esteem. All people use defense mechanisms to some degree, but research supports Freud's view that the overuse of defense mechanisms can adversely affect mental health and interfere with psychotherapy (LaFarge, 2012; Watson, 2002). Table 11.1 lists and defines the various defense mechanisms along with examples of each one.

According to Freud, *repression* is the most frequently used defense mechanism. (Look back at Chapter 6.) It involves removing painful or threatening memories, thoughts, or perceptions from consciousness and keeping them in the unconscious. It may also prevent unconscious sexual and aggressive impulses from breaking into consciousness. Several studies have shown that people do, indeed, try to repress unpleasant thoughts, such as you might experience when you "forget" that you have an important exam coming up (Koehler, Tiede, & Thoens, 2002). Freud believed that repressed thoughts lurk in the unconscious and can cause psychological disorders in adults. He thought that the way to cure such disorders was to bring the repressed material back to consciousness, and this was the basis for his system of therapy—psychoanalysis.

Conscious mind
(current state of awareness)

Preconscious
(outside awareness but accessible)

Unconscious mind
(outside awareness and inaccessible)

FIGURE 11.1 Freud's Conception of Personality
According to Freud, personality, which may be conceptualized as a giant iceberg, is composed of three structures: the id, the ego, and the superego. The id, completely unconscious, is wholly submerged, floating beneath the surface. The ego is largely conscious and visible, but partly unconscious. The superego also operates at both the conscious and unconscious levels.

id (ID) The unconscious system of the personality, which contains the life and death instincts and operates on the pleasure principle; source of the libido.

ego (EE-go) In Freud's theory, the logical, rational, largely conscious system of personality, which operates according to the reality principle.

superego (sue-per-EE-go) The moral system of the personality, which consists of the conscience and the ego ideal.

✴ Explore the Concept *The Id, Ego, and Super Ego* on MyPsychLab

defense mechanism A means used by the ego to defend against anxiety and to maintain self-esteem.

TABLE 11.1 Freud's Defense Mechanisms

DEFENSE MECHANISM	DESCRIPTION	EXAMPLE
Repression	Involuntarily removing an unpleasant memory, thought, or perception from consciousness or barring disturbing sexual and aggressive impulses from consciousness	Jill forgets a traumatic incident from childhood.
Projection	Attributing one's own undesirable traits, thoughts, behavior, or impulses to another	A very lonely divorced woman accuses all men of having only one thing on their minds.
Denial	Refusing to acknowledge consciously the existence of danger or a threatening situation	Amy fails to take a tornado warning seriously and is severely injured.
Rationalization	Supplying a logical, rational, or socially acceptable reason rather than the real reason for an action or event	Fred tells his friend that he didn't get the job because he didn't have connections.
Regression	Reverting to a behavior that might have reduced anxiety at an earlier stage of development	Susan bursts into tears whenever she is criticized.
Reaction formation	Expressing exaggerated ideas and emotions that are the opposite of disturbing, unconscious impulses and desires	A former purchaser of pornography, Bob is now a tireless crusader against it.
Displacement	Substituting a less threatening object or person for the original object of a sexual or aggressive impulse	After being spanked by his father, Bill hits his baby brother.
Sublimation	Rechanneling sexual and aggressive energy into pursuits or accomplishments that society considers acceptable or even admirable	Tim goes to a gym to work out when he feels hostile and frustrated.

11.2 What is the role of the psychosexual stages in Freud's theory?

psychosexual stages A series of stages through which the sexual instinct develops; each stage is defined by an erogenous zone around which conflict arises.

fixation Arrested development at a psychosexual stage occurring because of excessive gratification or frustration at that stage.

Oedipus or Elektra complex (ED-uh-pus) Occurring in the phallic stage, a conflict in which the child is sexually attracted to the opposite-sex parent and feels hostility toward the same-sex parent (Oedipus for males; Elektra for females).

▲ Freud believed that a fixation at the anal stage, resulting from harsh parental pressure, could lead to an anal retentive personality—characterized by excessive stubbornness, rigidity, and neatness.

The Psychosexual Stages of Development

The sex instinct, Freud said, is the most important factor influencing personality. It is present at birth and then develops through a series of **psychosexual stages**. Each stage centers on a particular part of the body that provides pleasurable sensations (an *erogenous zone*) and around which a conflict arises (Freud, 1905/1953b, 1920/1963b). If the conflict is not readily resolved, the child may develop a **fixation**. This means that a portion of the libido (psychic energy) remains invested at that particular stage, leaving less energy to meet the challenges of future stages. Overindulgence at any stage may leave a person psychologically unwilling to move on to the next stage, whereas too little gratification may leave the person trying to make up for unmet needs. Freud believed that certain personality characteristics develop as a result of difficulty at one or another of the stages. The *Summarize It* describes Freud's psychosexual stages.

One of the most controversial features of Freud's theory is the central theme of the phallic stage, the **Oedipus complex**. Freud named the complex after the central character in the ancient Greek tragedy *Oedipus Rex* by Sophocles, in which the ill-fated king discovers that he has unknowingly married his mother. When it is used in reference to females, the complex is called the **Elektra complex** after a similar play in which a woman is the main character. These two plays were quite popular in Europe during the later years of the 19th century, and Freud thought that their popularity was due to the fact that their theme, love for one's opposite-sex parent, represented a universal conflict that all human beings must resolve early on in their development (Freud, 1900/1953a).

Working from this assumption of universality, Freud claimed that, during the phallic stage, boys seek their mother's attention and behavior in a hostile way towards their fathers. The boy usually resolves the Oedipus complex by identifying with his father and repressing his sexual feelings for his mother. With identification, the child takes on his father's behaviors, mannerisms, and superego standards; in this way, the superego develops (Freud, 1930/1962).

Freud proposed an equally controversial developmental process for girls (the Elektra complex) in the phallic stage. When they discover they have no penis, girls in this stage develop "penis envy," and they turn to their father because he has the desired organ (Freud, 1933/1965). They feel sexual desires for him and develop jealousy and rivalry toward their mother. But eventually girls, too, experience anxiety as a result of

SUMMARIZE IT

Freud's Psychosexual Stages of Development

STAGE		PART OF THE BODY	CONFLICTS/ EXPERIENCES	ADULT TRAITS ASSOCIATED WITH PROBLEMS AT THIS STAGE
Oral (birth to 1 year)		Mouth	Weaning Oral gratification from sucking, eating, biting	Optimism, gullibility, dependency, pessimism, passivity, hostility, sarcasm, aggression
Anal (1 to 3 years)		Anus	Toilet training Gratification from expelling and withholding feces	Excessive cleanliness, orderliness, stinginess, messiness, rebelliousness, destructiveness
Phallic (3 to 5 or 6 years)		Genitals	Oedipal conflict Sexual curiosity Masturbation	Flirtatiousness, vanity, promiscuity, pride, chastity
Latency (5 or 6 years to puberty)		None	Period of sexual calm Interest in school, hobbies, same-sex friends	None
Genital (from puberty on)		Genitals	Revival of sexual interests Establishment of mature sexual relationships	Sexual dysfunctions

their hostile feelings. They repress their sexual feelings toward the father and identify with the mother, leading to the formation of their superego (Freud, 1930/1962).

According to Freud, failure to resolve these conflicts can have serious consequences for both boys and girls. Tremendous guilt and anxiety may be carried over into adulthood and cause sexual problems, great difficulty relating to members of the opposite sex, or homosexuality. ✳

✳ **Explore** the **Concept** *Freud's Five Psychosexual Stages of Personality Development* on **MyPsychLab**

11.3 How do modern psychologists evaluate Freud's ideas?

Evaluating Freud's Contribution

Do you believe that a person can be motivated by impulses of which he or she is unaware? Or that someone's current problems are the result of a long-forgotten childhood trauma or emotional conflict? If so, then you are a living example of the lasting influence of Freud's psychoanalytic theory on Western culture. Psychologists disagree as to whether Freudian ideas have benefited or harmed society. Critics such as E. Fuller Torrey argue that the infusion of psychoanalytic concepts into Western culture has led to an overemphasis on sexual pleasure (Torrey, 1992). Freud's supporters argue that the popularization of his theory has made people more aware of the importance of sexuality in their lives and of the significance of early childhood experiences to later development. Supporters often claim, too, that critics mischaracterize Freud's ideas both in the popular media and in academic circles (Knafo, 2009).

What about the scientific status of Freud's theory? Some have pointed out that Freud's work on defense mechanisms foreshadowed theories such as those of Lazarus in which cognitive appraisals are thought to shape emotional experiences (Knafo, 2009). In addition, some aspects of psychoanalytic theory, such as Freud's emphasis on family dynamics, continue to be important in explanations of psychological disorders such as depression (e.g., Clark, 2009). Moreover, today's *psychodynamic* therapies are direct descendants of Freud's techniques (Borden, 2009). (You will read about these and other therapies in detail in Chapter 13.)

However, in Chapter 4 you learned that neurological approaches to dreaming have overtaken Freud's notions regarding symbolism in dreams. Likewise, in Chapter 6 you learned that, generally, people do not repress traumatic memories as Freud claimed. These challenges to psychoanalytic theory have arisen largely because of psychoanalysts' failure to test the psychoanalytic theory's major concepts in correlational and experimental research. Psychoanalysts rely almost exclusively on the case study method, which you may remember from Chapter 1 is a method that is open to subjective misinterpretation by researchers (Grünbaum, 2006). Moreover, a few observers claim that the unquestioning acceptance of Freud's theory by many therapists in the early decades of the 20th century went against Freud's own view of psychoanalysis as a scientific theory that ought to be tested like any other.

When tests of Freud's hypotheses are available, the results show a mixed pattern. For instance, his suggestion that *catharsis,* the release of pent-up emotions, is good for one's psychological health has been refuted by studies showing that expressing negative emotions such as anger actually intensifies such feelings (Farber, Khurgin-Bott, & Feldman, 2009). In contrast, his assertion that childhood trauma leads to the development of psychological disorders in adulthood has received partial support. One study found that more than 70% of women who had been sexually victimized in childhood were diagnosed with some kind of psychological disorder in adulthood (Katerndahl, Burge, & Kellogg, 2005). At the same time, though, studies show that individual differences among victims better predict adult outcomes than the experience of victimization itself (Eisold, 2005). Thus, many victims of sexual abuse display a greater degree of resilience—the capacity to overcome potentially damaging early experiences—than psychoanalytic theory might predict.

11.4 How do the views of the neo-Freudians differ from those of Freud?

The Neo-Freudians

Is it possible to construct a theory of personality that builds on the strengths of Freud's approach and avoids its weaknesses? Several personality theorists, referred to as *neo-Freudians,* have attempted to do so. You read about the theory of one of the most prominent neo-Freudians, Erik Erikson, in Chapter 8. Like Erikson, most neo-Freudians started their careers as followers of Freud but began to disagree on certain basic principles of psychoanalytic theory.

One of the most important neo-Freudians, Carl Jung (1875–1961), did not consider the sexual instinct to be the main factor in personality, nor did he believe that the personality is almost completely formed in early childhood. For Jung (1933), middle age was an even more important period for personality development. Jung conceived of the personality as consisting of three parts: the ego, the personal unconscious, and the collective unconscious, as shown in Figure 11.2. He saw the ego as the conscious component of personality, which carries out normal daily activities. Like Freud, he believed the ego to be secondary in importance to the unconscious.

The **personal unconscious** develops as a result of one's own experience and is therefore unique to each person. It contains all the experiences, thoughts, and perceptions accessible to the conscious, as well as repressed memories, wishes, and impulses. The **collective unconscious**, the most inaccessible layer of the unconscious, contains the universal experiences of humankind such as what daily life was like when humans lived in caves. This is how Jung accounted for the similarity of certain myths, dreams, symbols, and religious beliefs in cultures widely separated by distance and time. Moreover, the collective unconscious contains what he called **archetypes**, inherited tendencies to respond to universal human situations in particular ways. Jung would say that the tendencies of people to believe in a god, a devil, evil spirits, and heroes all result from inherited archetypes that reflect the shared experience of humankind.

Another neo-Freudian, Alfred Adler (1870–1937), emphasized the unity of the personality rather than the separate warring components of id, ego, and superego. Adler (1927, 1956) also maintained that the drive to overcome feelings of inferiority acquired in childhood motivates most of our behavior. He claimed that people develop a "style of life" at an early age—a unique way in which the child and later the adult will go about the struggle to achieve superiority (Adler, 1956). Sometimes inferiority feelings are so strong that they prevent personal development, a condition Adler called the *inferiority complex* (Dreikurs, 1953). Because Adler's theory stresses the uniqueness of each individual's struggle to achieve superiority and refers to the "creative self," a conscious, self-aware component of an individual's personality, it is known as *individual psychology*.

The work of neo-Freudian Karen Horney (1885–1952) (pronounced *horn-eye*) centered on two main themes: the *neurotic personality* (Horney, 1937, 1945, 1950) and *feminine psychology* (Horney, 1967). She defined the neurotic personality as one that includes the need for constant affirmation combined with hostility and manipulativeness toward others. Feminine psychology, Horney proposed, involved a focus on the cultural and social forces that shape women's personalities. Horney flatly rejected Freud's psychosexual stages and the concepts of the Oedipus complex and penis envy. Furthermore, Horney did not accept Freud's division of personality into id, ego, and superego. She also believed that Freud overemphasized the role of the sexual instinct

personal unconscious In Jung's theory, the layer of the unconscious that contains all of the thoughts, perceptions, and experiences accessible to the conscious, as well as repressed memories, wishes, and impulses.

collective unconscious In Jung's theory, the most inaccessible layer of the unconscious, which contains the universal experiences of humankind.

archetype (AR-ka-type) Existing in the collective unconscious, an inherited tendency to respond to universal human situations in particular ways.

▲ Carl Gustav Jung (1875–1961) disagreed with Freud's emphasis on sexual motivation as the driving force behind personality development.

FIGURE 11.2 Jung's Conception of Personality
Like Freud, Jung saw three components in personality. The ego and the personal unconscious are unique to each individual. The collective unconscious accounts for the similarity of myths and beliefs in diverse cultures.

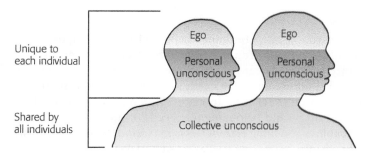

Structure	Characteristics
Ego	The conscious component of personality; carries out normal daily activities.
Personal unconscious	The component containing all the individual's memories, thoughts, and feelings that are accessible to consciousness, and all repressed memories, wishes, and impulses; similar to a combination of Freud's preconscious and unconscious.
Collective unconscious	The most inaccessible layer of the unconscious, shared by all people; contains the universal experiences of humankind, as well as the archetypes.

Labels in figure: Unique to each individual; Shared by all individuals; Ego; Personal unconscious; Collective unconscious and neglected cultural and environmental influences on personality. While she did stress the importance of early childhood experiences, Horney (1939) believed that personality could continue to develop and change throughout life.

As Horney's feminine psychology evolved, her forceful arguments against Freud's notion that a woman's desire to have a child and to have a man is nothing more than a conversion of the unfulfilled wish for a penis became its centerpiece. Horney (1945) believed that many of women's psychological difficulties arise from failure to live up to an idealized version of themselves. To be psychologically healthy, she claimed, women—and men, for that matter—must learn to overcome irrational beliefs about the need for perfection. Horney's influence may be seen in modern cognitive-behavioral therapies, which we will explore in Chapter 13. In addition, although she died before the rise of feminism, her ideas were key elements in many of the psychosocial theories of gender that began to appear in the 1960s.

REMEMBER IT

Check your answers and take additional quizzes in MyPsychLab.com. ✔️—Study and Review on **MyPsychLab**

1. _____ is both a theory of personality and a therapy for the treatment of psychological disorders.
2. Freud considered the _____ to be the primary motivating force of human behavior.
3. You just found a gold watch in a darkened movie theater. Your _____ would urge you to turn it in to the lost-and-found.
4. The part of the personality that Freud believed determines how to satisfy biological urges is the _____.
5. In Jung's theory, the collective unconscious—stored memories of all humankind—is (inherited/learned).
6. _____ believed that the basic human drive is to overcome and compensate for feelings of inferiority.
7. _____ believed that Freud was wrong about the concept of penis envy.

Humanistic Theories

In *humanistic psychology*, people are assumed to have a natural tendency toward growth and the realization of their fullest potential. Thus, humanistic personality theories are more optimistic than Freud's psychoanalytic theory. However, like Freud's theory, these perspectives are often criticized as being difficult to test scientifically.

11.5 How do humanistic theorists explain personality?

Two Humanistic Theories

For humanistic psychologist Abraham Maslow (1908–1970), motivational factors are at the root of personality. You may remember from Chapter 9 that Maslow constructed a hierarchy of needs, ranging from physiological needs at the bottom upward to safety needs, belonging and love needs, esteem needs, and finally to the highest need—self-actualization (refer back to Figure 9.3 on page 302). Maslow argued that the physiological safety, and belongingness needs of individuals must be met before they will be capable of pursuing *esteem needs* and *self-actualization*, clusters of aspirations that, in his theory, form the foundation of personality development.

esteem needs Motives that drive people to pursue goals such as academic achievement and success in a career.

Esteem needs include academic, social, and professional achievements. Examples, respectively, are college graduation, establishment of long-term intimate relationships, and career entry. According to Maslow, individuals whose physiological, safety, and belongingness needs are unfulfilled will be hampered in their efforts to work toward such goals. Research involving children provides support for Maslow's theory. Children whose families and schools support their physiological, safety, and belongingness needs exhibit higher levels of academic achievement than peers who lack such support (Noltemeyer et al., 2012). However, in adulthood, esteem needs may actually come to be more important than lower needs (Majerscik, 2005). This is because it is difficult, if not impossible, to fulfill esteem needs without taking risks that involve some degree of threat to lower needs. For example, young adults risk experiencing deficits in the realms of physiological, safety, and belongingness needs when they leave home and venture out on their own. In fact, it is their esteem needs that drive them to reach beyond the safety and security of their life-long support systems. Thus, Maslow's theory of personality is more complex than a simple progression from lower to higher needs. Instead, it is about how the interconnections among the various need states work together to enhance an individual's psychosocial growth.

After people fulfill their esteem needs, they can progress to **self-actualization**, the developmental level at which each individual seeks to fulfill his or her fullest potential. According to Maslow, the personality of a self-actualizing individual is continually changing, growing, and improving as the person strives to become all that he or she can be (Bauer et al., 2011). In his research, Maslow found that most self-actualizers believe they have a mission to accomplish and express the need to devote their life to some larger good. For example, studies of successful business leaders have found that many of them view themselves as fulfilling needs at all levels of Maslow's hierarchy through their businesses (Stoll & Ha-Brookshire, 2012). Consider the example of Microsoft founder Bill Gates, who, in 2008, left the company he guided to stellar success to lend his fortune and talents to a number of causes to which he feels personally drawn.

Not everyone reaches Maslow's self-actualization level. So, why do some people reach it while others do not? One explanation can be found in the personality theory of humanistic psychologist Carl Rogers (1902–1987). According to Rogers, the answer lies in our upbringing. Some parents set up **conditions of worth**, or conditions on which their positive regard hinges. Conditions of worth force children to live and act according to someone else's values rather than their own. In their efforts to gain positive regard, children deny their true selves by inhibiting some of their behavior, denying or distorting some of their perceptions, and closing off parts of their experience. In so doing, they experience stress and anxiety, and their whole self-structure may be threatened. Moreover, Rogers says, these patterns carry over into adulthood and cause adults to habitually use others' approval as the standard by which they judge their values and actions. As a result, they are incapable of pursuing the kinds of self-defined goals that are the hallmark of self-actualization.

For Rogers, a major goal of psychotherapy is to enable people to open themselves up to experiences and begin to live according to their own values rather than living by the values of others in an attempt to gain positive regard. He called his therapy *person-centered therapy*, preferring not to use the term *patient* (Rogers's therapy will be discussed further in Chapter 13). Rogers believed that the therapist must give the client **unconditional positive regard**—that is, unqualified caring and nonjudgmental acceptance, no matter what the client says, does, has done, or is thinking of doing. Unconditional positive regard is designed to reduce threat, eliminate conditions of worth, and bring the person back in tune with his or her true self. If successful, the therapy helps the client become what Rogers called a *fully functioning person*, one who is functioning at an optimal level and living fully and spontaneously according to his or her own inner value system.

Although humanists have been criticized for being unscientific and for seeing, hearing, and finding no evil within the human psyche, they have inspired the study of positive personality qualities, including altruism, cooperation, love, acceptance of others, and especially self-esteem. Most of us do not form a global idea about our own self-worth on the basis of a single area of competence. Instead, we view ourselves in terms of strengths and weaknesses.

Self-Esteem ▶

No doubt you have heard discussions of the importance of **self-esteem**, a person's sense of self-worth, to mental health. Complete the *Try It* on p. 372 below to estimate your current level of self-esteem.

self-actualization Developing to one's fullest potential.

conditions of worth Conditions on which the positive regard of others rests.

unconditional positive regard Unqualified caring and nonjudgmental acceptance of another.

11.6 What have psychologists learned about self-esteem?

self-esteem A person's sense of self-worth.

TRY IT   How High Is Your Self-Esteem?

For each statement that follows, choose the option that best reflects your feelings:

a. strongly agree   **b.** agree   **c.** neutral
d. disagree   **e.** strongly disagree

_____ **1.** I feel confident in most social situations.

_____ **2.** I believe I have something worthwhile to offer in life.

_____ **3.** I feel that others respect my opinion.

_____ **4.** I compare favorably with most people I know.

_____ **5.** I feel that, on the whole, other people like me.

_____ **6.** I deserve the love and respect of others.

Compute your score as follows: a = 4 points, b = 3, c = 2, d = 1, e = 0. A total score of 20–24 points indicates that you have excellent self-esteem; 15–19 means good, 10–14 is fair, and below 10 indicates that you could work on this quality.

How does self-esteem develop? One source of variations in self-esteem arises from comparisons of actual to desired traits. For example, a tone-deaf person who desires to be an accomplished musician might suffer from low self-esteem. However, most of us do not form a global idea about our own self-worth on the basis of a single area of competence. Instead, we view ourselves in terms of strengths and weaknesses. When our strengths lie in areas that we value and believe to be important, we have high self-esteem. Conversely, even outstanding achievements in areas we consider to be of little value may not affect our self-esteem. So, a person who is a great plumber, but who believes that being a good plumber isn't very important, is likely to have low self-esteem. At the same time, a person who feels incompetent because he has to pay a plumber a handsome sum to fix a leaking faucet might be in awe of the plumber's skill.

Developmental psychologists have found that self-esteem is fairly stable from childhood through the late adult years (Robins & Trzesniewski, 2005). So, the self-worth beliefs we adopt in childhood can affect us for a lifetime. Children and adolescents form ideas about their competencies in various domains—academics, sports, fine arts—that become increasingly stable across the elementary and secondary school years (Harter, 2012). And by age 7, most children have a sense of global self-esteem as well. These judgments come from both actual experiences and information provided by others. Thus, to develop high self-esteem, children need to experience success in domains they view as important and to be encouraged by parents, teachers, and peers to value themselves.

REMEMBER IT

Check your answers and take additional quizzes in MyPsychLab.com.   ✓●—Study and Review on MyPsychLab

1. _____ maintained that human beings have a natural tendency toward self-actualization.
2. _____ believed that individuals require unconditional positive regard to become fully functioning persons.
3. Self-esteem results from the comparison of _____ to _____ characteristics.

Trait Theories

trait A personal characteristic that is stable across situations and is used to describe or explain personality.

Traits are personal qualities or characteristics that make it possible for us to face a wide variety of situational demands and deal with unforeseen circumstances (De Raad & Kokkonen, 2000). For example, persistence is a trait that helps us overcome adversity. *Trait theories* are attempts to explain personality and differences among people in terms of personal characteristics that are stable across situations.

11.7 What ideas did the early trait theorists propose?

Early Trait Theories

One of the early trait theorists, Gordon Allport (1897–1967), claimed that each person inherits a unique set of raw materials for given traits, which are then shaped by experiences (Allport & Odbert, 1936). A *cardinal trait* is a major theme of a person's life. Almost all of the person's behavior seems to flow from it (Allport, 1961). It is so strong a part of a person's personality that he or she may become identified with or known for that trait. For example, what comes to mind when you hear the name *Einstein?* Most likely, you associate this name with intellectual genius; in fact, it is sometimes used as a synonym for genius. Thus, for Albert Einstein, genius is a cardinal trait. Likewise, Abraham Lincoln is known as "Honest Abe," because of his reputation for moral integrity. By contrast, *central traits* are general characteristics that a person would include in a description of himself or another person. Thus, in Allport's terms, the descriptors in the *Think About It* activity at the beginning of the chapter would be classified as central traits. ◉

◉ **Watch** the Video *Gordon Allport Discusses Personality Traits* in **MyPsychLab**

Another important trait theorist, Raymond Cattell, referred to observable qualities of personality as *surface traits* (Cattell, 1950) Using observations and questionnaires, Cattell studied thousands of people and found certain clusters of surface traits that appeared together time after time. He thought these were evidence of deeper, more general, underlying personality factors, which he called *source traits*. People differ in the degree to which they possess each source trait. For example, Cattell claimed that intelligence is a source trait: Everyone has it, but the amount possessed varies from person to person.

Cattell found 23 source traits in normal individuals, 16 of which he studied in great detail. Cattell's Sixteen Personality Factor Questionnaire, commonly called the 16PF, yields a personality profile (Cattell, 1950; Cattell, Eber, & Testsuoka, 1977). This test continues to be widely used in research and for personality assessment in career counseling, schools, and employment settings (Cattell & Mead, 2008; Morey, 2013). Results from the 16PF are usually plotted on a graph such as that shown in Figure 11.3.

Building on Cattell's notion of personality factors, the late British psychologist Hans Eysenck (1916–1997) proposed a three-factor model that is sometimes called the

Left Meaning	Standard Ten Score (STEN) |Average| 1 2 3 4 5 6 7 8 9 10	Right Meaning
Reserved, Impersonal, Distant		Warm, Outgoing, Attentive to Others
Concrete		Abstract
Reactive, Emotionally Changeable		Emotionally Stable, Adaptive, Mature
Deferential, Cooperative, Avoids Conflict		Dominant, Forceful, Assertive
Serious, Restrained, Careful		Lively, Animated, Spontaneous
Expedient, Nonconforming		Rule-Conscious, Dutiful
Shy, Threat-Sensitive, Timid		Socially Bold, Venturesome, Thick-Skinned
Utilitarian, Objective, Unsentimental		Sensitive, Aesthetic, Sentimental
Trusting, Unsuspecting, Accepting		Vigilant, Suspicious, Skeptical, Wary
Grounded, Practical, Solution-Oriented		Abstracted, Imaginative, Idea-Oriented
Forthright, Genuine, Artless		Private, Discreet, Nondisclosing
Self-Assured, Unworried, Complacent		Apprehensive, Self-Doubting, Worried
Traditional, Attached to Familiar		Open to Change, Experimenting
Group-Oriented, Affiliative		Self-Reliant, Solitary, Individualistic
Tolerates Disorder, Unexacting, Flexible		Perfectionistic, Organized, Self-Disciplined
Relaxed, Placid, Patient		Tense, High Energy, Impatient, Driven

FIGURE 11.3 The 16PF Personality Profile
The solid line represents the 16PF profile for a man named "Eric" (Cattell, Cattell & Cattell, 2003). The broken line is the average 16PF profile for business executives.
Source: Cattell, R., & Schuerger, J. (2003). Essentials of 16PF assessment. New York: John Wiley & Sons.

PEN model, see Figure 11.4 (Eysenck, 1990). The first of the dimensions, *psychoticism*, is a continuum that represents an individual's link to reality. At one extreme are "psychotics," those who live in a world of hallucinations and delusions. At the other end are people whose thought processes are so rigidly tied to the material world that they lack creativity. The second dimension, *extraversion*, ranges from people who are outgoing to those who are shy. The third, *neuroticism*, describes emotional stability, with highly stable people at one end and anxious, irritable people at the other.

Eysenck proposed that all three of the PEN dimensions are rooted in neurological functioning. As a result, his theory has served as a useful framework for neurological studies of personality. For example, researchers have found a link between dopamine activity in the brain and extraversion (Munafó et al., 2008). Studies using electroencephalography (EEG) have shown that neuroticism is correlated with a distinctive pattern of brain-wave activity (Knyazev, 2009). In addition, Eysenck developed a series of personality tests that are still widely used by researchers and clinicians today (Morey, 2013).

11.8 How does the five-factor model describe personality?

five-factor model A model that describes personality using five broad dimensions, each of which is composed of a constellation of personality traits.

Explore the Concept *The Five-Factor Model* on **MyPsychLab**

The Five-Factor Model

The most important trait approach today is the **five-factor model**, the view that personality consists of five broad dimensions, each of which is composed of a cluster of personality traits (McCrae, 2011). The assertion that five factors are needed to account for personality, as opposed to Eysenck's three factors, dates back to the early 1960s (e.g., Norman, 1963). However, over the past three decades, the model has become most closely associated with the research of Robert McCrae and Paul Costa (Costa & McCrae, 1985). Another important five-factor model, known as the *Big Five*, proposed by psychologist Lewis Goldberg, varies somewhat from that of McCrae and Costa in its approach to measuring the factors (Goldberg, 1993). However, research based on both models supports the hypothesis that personality can be usefully described in terms of five factors (McCrae, 2011). You will notice that the names of these factors can be easily remembered by using the acronym OCEAN.

Openness. Are you eager to try new things and consider new ideas? If so, then you might get a high score on a test that measures openness. This dimension contrasts individuals who seek out varied experiences and who are imaginative, intellectually curious, and broad minded with those whose interests are narrower.

Openness may also be an important factor in adapting to new situations. In one 4-year study, researchers found that college students who scored high on this factor as freshmen adjusted to college life more easily than peers who scored lower (Harms, Roberts, & Winter, 2006). Apparently, students who were higher in openness were better able to adapt their own personality characteristics to the demands of the college environment than their low-scoring peers.

Conscientiousness. Do you always fold your laundry before putting it away? Individuals who score high on measures of conscientiousness pay more attention to such details than those who get lower scores. They are often viewed as reliable by others. By contrast, those at the lower end of this dimension may be perceived

FIGURE 11.4 **Trait Structure of Extraversion in Eyesenck's Three-Factor Model of Personality** Eysenck's research focused on three major traits. A trait such as extraversion encompasses several other traits, as illustrated here. Based on Eysenck's research focused on three major traits.

as lazy and undependable, but they also tend to be more spontaneous than people who get higher scores on this dimension.

Research suggests that the components of conscientiousness include order, self-control, and industriousness (Jackson et al., 2009). Thus, it isn't surprising that conscientiousness is correlated with measures of health. Longitudinal studies, for example, suggest that, compared to peers who obtained low scores on measures of conscientiousness, children who were high in conscientiousness as elementary school students were less likely to be smokers or to be obese in middle adulthood (Hampson et al., 2006). Likewise, conscientiousness shows long-term links to the tendency to maintain health-protective factors, such as avoiding obesity, during middle adulthood (Sutin et al., 2011).

Conscientiousness also predicts both academic performance from elementary school through college (Corker et al., 2012). Among elementary school students, those who are highest in conscientiousness tend to be the highest achievers later in high school (Shiner, 2000). Likewise, across the years of undergraduate and graduate school, assessments of conscientiousness during students' first year predict their standing at the end of their programs of study (Chamorro-Premuzic & Furnham, 2003).

Extraversion. If you have a free evening, would you rather go to a party or stay home and read a book or watch a movie? Individuals who are high in extraversion prefer being around people. Chances are that anyone who is known as "the life of the party" is an extravert. Those at the opposite end of the continuum, introverts, may feel most comfortable when they are on their own.

Researchers have found that extraversion is strongly linked to a number of important job-related variables. These variables include subjective feelings of happiness at work, satisfaction with one's job, and engagement with co-workers (Bono, Davies, & Rasch, 2012). Moreover, extraverts may have an easier time getting a job than their more introverted peers (Tay, Ang, & Dyne, 2006). Researchers have found that extraverts receive more job offers after being interviewed than do introverts. However, extraverts also may be more likely than introverts to engage in risky behaviors, such as unprotected sex (Miller et al., 2004).

Agreeableness. Do people describe you as easygoing? Individuals who are high in agreeableness are often characterized in this way. This dimension is composed of a collection of traits that range from compassion to antagonism toward others. A person who is low in agreeableness would not be viewed as easygoing. Instead, this individual would be described as unfriendly, argumentative, cold, and perhaps vindictive.

Like conscientiousness, agreeableness is predictive of health outcomes, especially those that have to do with emotional well-being. Individuals who are high in agreeableness establish more effective relationships with psychotherapists, the result of which is that they seem to benefit more from therapy than those with low levels of agreeableness (Hirsh et al., 2012). As you might guess, this trait is also related to employees' ability to function well in work teams (Stewart, Fulmer, & Barrick, 2005). However, people who are high in agreeableness also seem to be more likely to succumb to peer influence with regard to decisions about risky behavior, such as binge drinking (van Schoor, Bott, & Engels, 2008).

Neuroticism. If you see an 8-ounce glass that contains 4 ounces of water, is it half empty or half full? People who are high in neuroticism tend to be pessimistic and always see the negative aspects of situations—the "half-empty" interpretation of life. At the same time, they are prone to emotional instability because of their tendency to overreact to the kinds of daily annoyances that most people take in stride. For example, an individual who is high in neuroticism might be very demonstrative about his or her frustration while standing in a slow-moving line at the campus bookstore. When such behaviors are exhibited by neurotic characters in television shows (e.g., Sheldon Cooper in *The Big Bang Theory*), they are often perceived as humorous by audiences and regarded sympathetically by other characters. However, in real life, individuals who are high in neuroticism have difficulty maintaining social relationships and are at higher risk than others for a variety of psychological disorders (Korten et al., 2012; Shiner & Masten, 2012).

Predictably, individuals who get high scores on measures of neuroticism receive low ratings on cooperativeness from their co-workers (Stewart et al., 2005). There is also evidence that high neuroticism impedes learning (Robinson & Tamir, 2005). It appears that the worrisome thoughts that result from neuroticism distract individuals with this characteristic from information that they are trying to learn, thereby interfering with the transfer of information from short- to long-term memory.

Gender Differences in the Five Factors. As you read through the discussions of the various traits, you may have speculated about whether males and females differ with regard to them. In general, researchers have found that women score higher than men do on measures of conscientiousness, agreeableness, and neuroticism, while men tend to score more highly on the trait of openness to experience (Soto, Oliver, Gosling, & Potter, 2011). Both hormonal and social factors have been proposed as explanations for these differences. Importantly, though, gender differences across the five factors are small. Moreover, as is true of most variables that are not directly linked to the anatomical differences between males and females, the range of individual differences within each gender is far greater than the differences across genders (Hyde, 2005).

11.9 What does research say about the effects of heredity and environment on personality traits?

Nature, Nurture, and Personality Traits

Critics of the five-factor model point out that, while it may describe personality well, it does not explain individual differences. In response, McCrae and Costa (2003) have proposed a behavioral genetic theory known as the *five-factor theory of personality*. The theory asserts that heredity is largely responsible for individual differences in the Big Five, although environmental factors, such as parenting and culture, also influence them. McCrae and Costa cite twin and adoption studies in support of their theory.

In one classic twin study, Rushton and colleagues (1986) found that nurturance, empathy, and assertiveness are substantially influenced by heredity. Even altruism and aggressiveness, traits we might expect to be strongly influenced by parental upbringing, are actually more heavily influenced by heredity. A meta-analysis by Miles and Carey (1997) revealed that the heritability of aggressiveness may be as high as .50. (Recall from Chapter 7 that *heritability* is an estimate of the percentage of variation in a trait that is due to genes. So, a heritability estimate of .50 means that 50% of the variation in aggressiveness is due to heredity.)

A number of longitudinal studies indicate that heredity makes substantial contributions to individual differences in the Big Five personality dimensions, as shown in Figure 11.5 (South et al., 2013). These studies suggest that genes exert more

FIGURE 11.5 Estimated Influence of Heredity and Environment on the Big Five Personality Dimensions
The Minnesota study of twins reared apart yielded an average heritability estimate of .41 (41%) for the Big Five personality factors; the Loehlin twin studies, a heritability estimate of .42 (42%). Both studies found the influence of the shared environment to be only about .07 (7%). The remaining percentage represents a combination of nonshared environmental influences and measurement error.
Source: Bouchard, T. (1994). Genes, environment, and personality. *Science, 264,* 1700–1701. Reprinted by permission of AAAS.

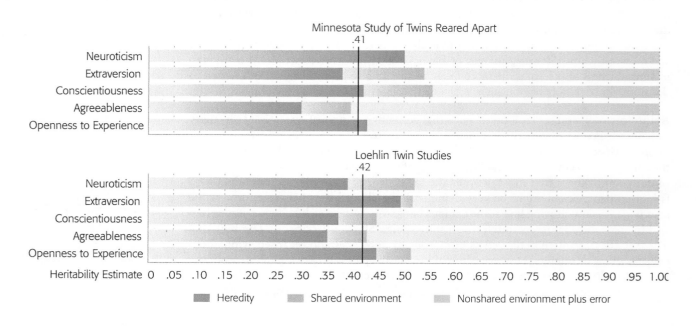

influence on extraversion and neuroticism than on the other dimensions of the Big Five (Krueger & Johnson, 2004). Thus, genetically based similarities in personality, rather than modeling, may be responsible for the ways in which our adult lives relate to those of our parents.

Adoption studies have also shown that heredity strongly influences personality. Loehlin and others (1987) assessed the personalities of 17-year-olds who had been adopted at birth. When the adopted children were compared to other children in the family, the researchers found that the shared family environment had virtually no influence on their personalities. In another study, Loehlin and colleagues (1990) measured change in personality of adoptees over a 10-year period and found that children's personalities tended to become more like those of their biological parents over time. The prevailing thinking among behavioral geneticists, then, is that the shared environment plays a negligible role in the formation of personality (Loehlin et al., 1988).

Clearly, heredity influences personality. However, it is equally clear that personality is not determined by genes in the same way that physical traits such as eye color and blood type are. Instead, according to many psychologists, genes *constrain* the ways in which environments affect personality traits (Kagan, 2003). For example, a child who has a genetic tendency toward shyness may be encouraged by parents to be more sociable. As a result, he will be more outgoing than he would have been without such encouragement but will still be less sociable than a child who is genetically predisposed to be more sociable. 👁

👁⟶⌐**Watch** the Video *Episode 13: Special Topics: Twins and Personality* in **MyPsychLab**

Personality and Culture ▶

⌐ **11.10** How do personality traits
⌐ vary across cultures?

Most advocates of the five-factor theory assert that the factors are universal, but does research support this claim? Evidence for the universality of the five factors comes from research in which psychologists have successfully measured them in countries the world over (McCrae, 2011). However, research also suggests that culture influences personality in ways that may not be captured by the five-factor model. In classic research, Hofstede (1980, 1983) analyzed questionnaire responses measuring the work-related values of more than 100,000 IBM employees in 53 countries around the world. Factor analysis revealed four separate dimensions related to culture and personality, of which one, the **individualism/collectivism dimension**, is of particular interest here. In individualist cultures, such as the United States, Canada, and most European countries, more emphasis is placed on individual achievement than on group achievement. High-achieving individuals are accorded honor and prestige in individualist cultures. People in collectivist cultures, on the other hand, tend to be more interdependent and define themselves and their personal interests in terms of their group membership. Asians, for example, have highly collectivist cultures, and collectivism is compatible with Confucianism, an ethical and philosophical system that is found in many Asian cultures. In fact, according to the Confucian values, the individual finds his or her identity in interrelatedness, as a part of the larger group. Moreover, this interrelatedness is an important ingredient of happiness for Asians (Kitayama & Markus, 2000).

individualism/collectivism dimension A measure of a culture's emphasis on either individual achievement or social relationships.

It is important to note that some psychologists warn against overemphasizing cultural differences in personality. For example, Constantine Sedikides and his colleagues have argued that the goal of all individuals, regardless of cultural context, is to enhance self-esteem (Sedikides, Gaertner, & Toguchi, 2003; Gaertner, Sedikides, & Chang, 2008). That is, even in collectivist cultures, the process of conforming to one's culture is motivated by an individualistic concern, the desire for self-esteem. Moreover, the development of an individual identity that is distinct from that of others in one's culture is a goal that is highly valued and actively pursued by people in all cultures (Becker et al., 2012). Consequently, at least to some degree, an individualist orientation is universal. Furthermore, while members of different cultures display varying commitments to an individualistic philosophy, autonomy—a sense of personal control over one's life—predicts well-being in all cultures (Ryan, Kim, & Kaplan, 2003).

▲ For these native Alaskans, participating in the traditional blanket toss ceremony is one manifestation of their culture's values related to community and cooperation.

1. According to Gordon Allport, _____ traits are those that would be included in a general description of oneself or another person.

2. According to Raymond Cattell, _____ traits are clusters of _____ traits.

3. _____ claimed that psychologists can best understand personality by assessing people on three major dimensions: psychoticism, extraversion, and neuroticism.

4. Robert McCrae and Paul Costa are proponents of the _____ of personality.

5. People in collectivist cultures tend to be more _____ than people in individualist cultures.

Social-Cognitive Theories

As useful as the five-factor model is, it still does not provide psychologists with a complete explanation of individual differences in personality. For instance, why are even the most extraverted individuals among us sometimes quiet and withdrawn? How do people who are disorganized—that is, who are low in conscientiousness—manage to complete tasks that require attention to detail, such as college research papers? Researchers who examine the influence of learning on personality have provided psychologists with some clues as to how these questions might be answered. For the most part, their hypotheses come from **social-cognitive theory**, the view that personality is a collection of learned behaviors that have been acquired through interactions with others.

social-cognitive theory The view that personality can be defined as a collection of learned behaviors acquired through social interactions.

11.11 How do Mischel and Bandura address the situation–trait debate?

situation–trait debate A discussion among theorists about the relative influence of traits and situations on personality.

The Situation–Trait Debate

Social-cognitive theorist Walter Mischel has been among the most vocal critics of the five-factor model and of trait theories in general (Mischel, 1968, 2004). Mischel initiated the **situation–trait debate**, an ongoing discussion among psychologists about the relative importance of factors within the situation and factors within the person in accounting for behavior (Rowe, 1987). For instance, you probably wouldn't steal money from a store, but what if you see a stranger unknowingly drop a $5 bill? Mischel and those who agree with him say that characteristics of the two situations dictate your behavior, not a trait such as honesty. Stealing from a store might require devising and carrying out a complicated plan, and it would carry a heavy penalty if you were caught, so you opt for honesty. Picking up a $5 bill is easy and may only result in embarrassment if you get caught, so you may do it. Mischel (1973, 1977) later modified his original position and admitted that behavior is influenced by both the person and the situation. Mischel views a trait as a conditional probability that a particular action will occur in response to a particular situation (Wright & Mischel, 1987).

The weight of evidence supports the view that there are internal traits that strongly influence behavior across situations (Costa & McCrae, 2009). Still, situational variables do affect personality traits. Consequently, social-cognitive theorist Albert Bandura, whose research on observational learning you learned about in Chapter 5, has proposed a comprehensive theory of personality that takes both traits and situations into account (1977, 1986). Moreover, Bandura's model incorporates cognitive variables such as the limited capacity of short-term memory into the mix.

▲ Research on personality suggests that some traits, such as agreeableness, actually increase as we get older.

Because the model includes so many variables and provides a systematic explanation of how these variables interact, it has generated a great deal of research and has helped psychologists better understand both consistencies and inconsistencies in personality.

FIGURE 11.6 Bandura's Reciprocal Determinism
Bandura takes a social-cognitive view of personality. He suggests that three components—the external environment, individual behaviors, and cognitive factors, such as beliefs, expectancies, and personal dispositions—are all influenced by each other and play reciprocal roles in determining personality.

Bandura has proposed that internal, environmental, and behavioral variables interact to influence personality. He calls this interaction **reciprocal determinism**, a term that conveys his view that mutual influences contribute to variations across all three types of variables (see Figure 11.6). Internal variables, or *person* variables as they are usually called, include traits such as the five factors, information-processing variables such as short-term memory strategies, individual differences in intelligence, stages of cognitive and social development, learned expectancies about how the environment will respond to behaviors, and physiological factors such as neurological functioning. Environmental variables include social sources of information, the various kinds of consequences that are elicited by our behaviors, and the characteristics of specific situations. Behavioral variables are our actual behaviors.

reciprocal determinism Bandura's concept of a mutual influential relationship among behavior, cognitive factors, and environment.

Self-Efficacy and Locus of Control ▶

[11.12 What do self-efficacy and locus of control contribute to personality? **]**

One of the cognitive factors that Bandura (1997a, 1997b) considers especially important is **self-efficacy**, the perception people have of their ability to perform competently whatever they attempt. Cross-cultural researchers examining self-efficacy in 25 countries found it to be an important individual difference in all of them (Scholz et al., 2002). According to Bandura, people high in self-efficacy approach new situations confidently, set high goals, and persist in their efforts because they believe success is likely. People low in self-efficacy, on the other hand, expect failure; consequently, they avoid challenges and typically give up on tasks they find difficult. Bandura's research has shown that people with high self-efficacy are less likely to experience depression than those with low self-efficacy (Bandura, 1997b).

self-efficacy The perception a person has of his or her ability to perform competently whatever is attempted.

Similarly, Julian Rotter proposed that a cognitive factor known as **locus of control** has effects on personality. Some people see themselves as primarily in control of their behavior and its consequences. This perception Rotter (1966, 1971, 1990) defines as an *internal locus of control*. Other people perceive that whatever happens

locus of control Rotter's concept of a cognitive factor that explains how people account for what happens in their lives—either seeing themselves as primarily in control of their behavior and its consequences (internal locus of control) or perceiving what happens to them to be in the hands of fate, luck, or chance (external locus of control).

TRY IT   **What Is Your Locus of Control?**

1. Heredity determines most of a person's personality.
2. Chance has a lot to do with being successful.
3. Whatever plans you make, something will always interfere.
4. Being at the right place at the right time is essential for getting what you want in life.
5. Intelligence is a given, and it cannot be improved.
6. If I successfully accomplish a task, it's because it was an easy one.
7. You cannot change your destiny.
8. School success is mostly a result of one's socioeconomic background.
9. People are lonely because they are not given the chance to meet new people.

10. Setting goals for yourself is of little use because nobody knows what might happen in the future to interfere with them.

Give yourself 1 point for each "agree" and 0 points for each "disagree." To translate the scoring instructions in the activity into Rotter's terms: 0–4 = internal locus of control, and 7–10 = external locus of control. Scores of 5 and 6 suggest that your views are consistent with the internal view for some outcomes but are more akin to the external end of the continuum for others.

👁‑**Watch** the Video *Episode 13: What's in It for Me? Psychological Resilience* in **MyPsychLab**

▲ Individuals who are high in self-efficacy pursue challenging goals and persist until they reach them.

to them is in the hands of fate, luck, or chance. These individuals exhibit an *external locus of control* and may claim that it does not matter what they do because "whatever will be, will be." Rotter contends that people with an external locus of control are less likely to change their behavior as a result of reinforcement, because they do not see reinforcers as being tied to their own actions. Students who have an external locus of control are less likely to be academically successful than those with an internal locus of control because their belief that effort and outcomes are only minimally related undermines the effectiveness of their study strategies (Kesici, Sahin, & Akturk, 2009). Similarly, construction workers who have an internal locus of control are more likely than their external-locus co-workers to take the time to implement safety procedures before beginning a dangerous project (Kuo & Tsaur, 2004). External locus of control is also associated with lower levels of life satisfaction (Kirkcaldy, Shephard, & Furnham, 2002). Where is your locus of control? The *Try It* on page 379 will tell you.

At this point, you may be feeling overwhelmed by all the information on personality you have encountered in this chapter. To help you better understand what you have learned, the *Explain It* below applies each of the theories to the problem of explaining why some individuals never develop a conscience. In addition, the *Summarize It* recaps the theories of personality.

EXPLAIN IT   How Personality Theories Answer the Question, "Why Do Some People Fail to Develop a Conscience?"

You may recall that Pinocchio's six-legged friend, Jiminy Cricket, advised him when he left home to always let his conscience be his guide. This is sound advice for the vast majority of people, but about 1% of human beings appear to lack a conscience, a condition known as *psychopathy* (Hare, 1998). How do personality theories explain the absence of a conscience? Before reading on, consider for a moment how Freud and the other theorists you have learned about so far in this chapter would answer this question.

Recall that Freud claimed that the superego develops in the context of child–parent relationships. According to his view, then, any disruption of these relationships could potentially disrupt the process of conscience development. A humanistic theorist would counter that a conscience is unlikely to develop in a child whose parents failed to provide him or her with unconditional positive regard, while a social-cognitive perspective would lead to a hypothesis that emphasizes parental discipline and modeling. Surprisingly, though, while all of these theories touch upon important and influential factors in a child's upbringing, none of them can fully explain why some adults appear to be completely without a conscience and, as a result, lack the capacity to feel guilty when they harm others (Aksan & Kochaska, 2005).

In our quest to explain the failure to develop a conscience, trait theory may turn out to be the most helpful. For many years, researcher Paul Frick of the University of New Orleans and his colleagues have been studying *callous-unemotional (CU) traits* in children (Thornton et al., 2013; Frick et al., 2003). Children who possess these traits lack empathy and the capacity to feel guilt. Frick and others have identified CU traits in children as young as 4 years of age (Dadds et al., 2005). Moreover, longitudinal studies have shown that these children are at greater risk of engaging in behaviors that are hurtful to others than their peers who lack CU traits.

As is true for the traits that are associated with the five-factor model of personality, twin studies suggest that CU traits are inherited rather than the product of environmental influence (Larsson, Andershed, & Lichtenstein, 2006; Viding et al., 2005). Furthermore, individuals who lack a conscience are far more likely than others to suffer from psychological disorders (Assadi et al., 2006). Taken together, these findings suggest that the failure to develop a conscience might be best explained by a genetic vulnerability model in which an inherited risk can either be enhanced or mitigated by factors in a child's environment.

Do such findings mean that some human beings are simply destined to grow up without a conscience? Not necessarily, because studies have identified therapies that can help some of these children modify their CU traits. And if therapies can help them, then it might be possible to identify parenting strategies that could prevent these traits from condemning a child to an adult life that is sure to be fraught with social difficulties at best and incarceration at worst. The key is to recognize that, to be effective, both therapeutic approaches and parenting strategies must be adapted in light of the emotional limitations of children with CU traits. Paul Frick and his research team are committed to finding out exactly what those adaptations are.

⏵ Watch the Video *Episode 13: Basics: Personality Theories* in **MyPsychLab**

SUMMARIZE IT

Theories of Personality

THEORY	MAIN IDEAS
PSYCHOANALYTIC THEORIES	
Freud's Psychosexual Theory	Unconscious forces shape personality; three components of personality are id, ego, superego; defense mechanisms protect self-esteem; personality stages are characterized by a focus on different areas of the body.
Neo-Freudians	Jung distinguished between personal and collective unconscious; Adler emphasized the inferiority complex and striving for superiority; Horney focused on neurotic personality and feminine psychology.
HUMANISTIC THEORIES	
Maslow's and Rogers's Theories	Maslow emphasized self-actualization; Rogers believed that unconditional positive regard helped individuals attain potential.
Self-Esteem	Humanistic theory promotes research on self-esteem, which is somewhat stable across the life span; there is global and domain-focused self-esteem.
TRAIT THEORIES	
Early Theories	Allport proposed cardinal and central traits; Cattell developed the 16PF personality test to measure source traits; Eysenck's three-factor model includes psychoticism, extraversion, and neuroticism.
Five-Factor Model	The five-factor model (Big Five) includes openness, conscientiousness, extraversion, agreeableness, neuroticism (OCEAN); traits are influenced by heredity and environment; they are generally stable from childhood through adulthood and predict important outcomes.
SOCIAL-COGNITIVE THEORIES	
Situation–Trait Debate	Trait theorists argue that traits influence behavior more than situations; social-cognitive theorists argue that situations matter more than traits.
Reciprocal Determinism	Bandura claims that personal/cognitive factors (traits, thinking), the environment (reinforcement), and behavior interact to shape personality.
Self-Efficacy/Locus of Control	Two cognitive factors that influence personality are self-efficacy (Bandura) and locus of control (Rotter).

REMEMBER IT

Check your answers and take additional quizzes in MyPsychLab.com. ✓●─Study and Review on MyPsychLab

1. Walter Mischel proposed that personality traits vary across _____, giving rise to an ongoing discussion among personality psychologists known as the _____.
2. In Bandura's _____ model, personality is shaped by interactions among personal/cognitive, behavioral, and environmental factors.
3. A person who believes that he or she can be successful at a task has high _____.
4. People who believe that luck determines what happens to them have an _____ locus of control, while those who believe their own efforts are more important than luck have an _____ locus of control.

Personality Assessment

Have you ever taken a personality test? You may have as part of a job application and screening process. Personality assessment is commonly used in business and industry to aid in hiring decisions. Various ways of measuring personality are used by clinical psychologists, psychiatrists, and counselors in the diagnosis of patients and in the assessment of progress in therapy.

Observation, Interviews, and Rating Scales ▶

Psychologists use observation in personality assessment in a variety of settings—hospitals, clinics, schools, and workplaces. Behaviorists, in particular, prefer observation to other methods of personality assessment. Using an observational technique

11.13 How do psychologists use observations, interviews, and rating scales?

known as *behavioral assessment,* psychologists can count and record the frequency of particular behaviors. This method is often used in behavior modification programs in settings such as psychiatric hospitals, where psychologists may chart the progress of people with psychological disorders toward reducing aggressive acts or other undesirable behaviors. However, behavioral assessment is time consuming, and behavior may be misinterpreted. Probably the most serious limitation is that the very presence of the observer can alter the behavior being observed.

Clinical psychologists and psychiatrists use interviews to help in the diagnosis and treatment of people with psychological disorders. Counselors use interviews to screen applicants for admission to college or other special programs, and employers use them to evaluate job applicants and employees for job promotions. Interviewers consider not only a person's answers to questions but the person's tone of voice, speech, mannerisms, gestures, and general appearance also. Interviewers often use a *structured interview,* in which the content of the questions and even the manner in which they are asked are carefully planned ahead of time. The interviewer tries not to deviate in any way from the structured format so that more reliable comparisons can be made between different subjects. As you probably know from experience, interviews are also an integral part of any job search, and the *Apply It* includes numerous tips for using the interview process to your advantage.

Examiners sometimes use *rating scales* to record data from interviews or observations. Such scales are useful because they provide a standardized format, including a list of traits or behaviors to evaluate. A rating scale helps to focus the rater's attention on all the relevant traits to be considered so that none is overlooked or weighed too heavily. The major limitation of these scales is that the ratings are often subjective. A related problem is the *halo effect*—the tendency of raters to be excessively influenced in their overall evaluation of a person by one or a few favorable or unfavorable traits. Often, traits or attributes that are not even on the rating scale, such as physical attractiveness or similarity to the rater, heavily influence a rater's perception of an individual. To overcome these limitations, it is often necessary to have individuals rated by more than one interviewer.

11.14 What do the MMPI-2, the CPI, and the MBTI reveal about personality?

inventory A paper-and-pencil test with questions about a person's thoughts, feelings, and behaviors, which measures several dimensions of personality and can be scored according to a standard procedure.

Minnesota Multiphasic Personality Inventory (MMPI) The most extensively researched and widely used personality test, which is used to screen for and diagnose psychiatric problems and disorders; revised as MMPI-2.

Personality Inventories

As useful as observations, interviews, and rating scales are, another method of measuring personality offers greater objectivity. This method is the **inventory**, a paper-and-pencil test with select-response questions (i.e., true/false, multiple-choice) about an individual's thoughts, feelings, and behaviors, which measures several dimensions of personality and can be scored according to a standard procedure. Psychologists favoring the trait approach prefer the inventory because it reveals where people fall on various dimensions of personality, and it yields a personality profile.

The most widely used personality inventory is the **Minnesota Multiphasic Personality Inventory (MMPI)** or its revision, the MMPI-2. Developed in the late 1930s and early 1940s by researchers J. Charnley McKinley and Starke Hathaway, the MMPI was originally intended to identify tendencies toward various types of psychiatric disorders. The researchers administered more than 1,000 questions about attitudes, feelings, and specific symptoms to groups of people at the University of Minnesota hospital who had been clearly diagnosed with various specific disorders and to a control group of individuals who had no diagnosed disorders. They retained the 550 items that differentiated the specific groups of people with psychological disorders from the group of participants without disorders.

The MMPI-2 was published in 1989 (Butcher et al., 1989). Most of the original test items were retained, but new items were added to more adequately cover areas such as alcoholism, drug abuse, suicidal tendencies, eating disorders, and the Type A behavior pattern. New norms were established to reflect national census data and achieve a better geographical, racial, and cultural balance (Ben-Porath & Butcher, 1989).

APPLY IT

Put Your Best Foot Forward

Did you ever think of a job interview as a personality assessment? You should, because that's precisely what it is. The interviewer isn't measuring your personality as a psychologist would. Instead, he or she is assessing whether you fit the organization's needs and whether you can fit in with the others who work there. Here are a few tips for successful interviewing.

Impression Management
Think of the interview as an opportunity to make a particular impression on a potential employer. However, you should refrain from exaggerating your qualifications or experience. Surveys suggest that 90% of job candidates do so (Levashina & Campion, 2007). Thus, most experienced interviewers are skilled at recognizing such exaggerations and tend to look unfavorably upon interviewees who use them (Paulhus et al., 2003).

Educate Yourself
Learn as much as you can about the business or industry you want to work in and about the particular firm to which you are applying. Study the qualifications for the job you are seeking, both required and preferred, if they're available, and get a good idea of how your qualifications match up.

Prepare an Effective Resume
Even if the job you're applying for doesn't require a resume, it's a good idea to prepare one and take it—along with some extra copies—with you to the interview. A good resume is a quick source of information for the interviewer, who needs to know about your entire work history to create questions based on it. Most colleges and universities have career centers that provide advice on résumé preparation and related services.

Practice
Practice answering interview questions with a friend. Many college career centers have lists of frequently asked interview questions, and you should always create your own list of questions that you think the interviewer might ask. Try to avoid saying negative things about yourself. Remember, too, that consistent eye contact will show the interviewer that you have confidence.

Dress Professionally
When you are interviewing for a job, your clothing, visible adornments on your body (e.g., tattoos, jewelry), how well groomed you are, and even the way you smell can be forms of communication. Your appearance should communicate to the interviewer that you understand the environment in which you hope to be working. Keep in mind, too, that your appearance influences your own self-confidence. Researchers have found that the more formal interviewees' clothing is, the more positive are the remarks they make about themselves during the interview (Hannover & Kuehnen, 2002). Furthermore, studies suggest that professional attire more strongly influences an interviewer's perception of a job candidate than any other variable (Ruetzler et al., 2012).

Be Punctual
Do you feel frustrated when others keep you waiting? Interviewers respond emotionally to tardiness, just as you do. Consequently, it's best to arrive early. And if you are unavoidably delayed, call and reschedule.

Greet the Interviewer Appropriately
Your greeting plays an important role in the interview process as well. In the United States, it's best to look your interviewer directly in the eyes, shake hands firmly, pronounce her or his name correctly, and have good posture.

Follow Up
After the interview, it's a good idea to send a thank you note. If you met with more than one interviewer, send a note to each of them, mentioning some specific aspect of the discussion that you found interesting. This will indicate that you were fully engaged in the conversation, listening intently, and interested in the interviewer's knowledge about the open position and the organization. The note should also express your appreciation for the interviewer's time and your interest in the position.

Watch on **MyPsychLab**

Table 11.2 on p. 384 shows the 10 clinical scales of the MMPI-2. Following are examples of items on the test, which are to be answered "true" or "false."

I wish I were not bothered by thoughts about sex.

When I get bored, I like to stir up some excitement.

In walking I am very careful to step over sidewalk cracks.

If people had not had it in for me, I would have been much more successful.

A high score on any of the scales does not necessarily mean that a person has a problem or a psychiatric symptom. Rather, the psychologist looks at the individual's MMPI profile—the pattern of scores on all the scales—and then compares it to the profiles of normal individuals and those with various psychiatric disorders.

But what if someone lies on the test to appear mentally healthy or to try to "fake" a psychological disorder? The MMPI-2 includes questions that help psychologists assess test takers' truthfulness. Collectively, these questions comprise the

TABLE 11.2 The Clinical Scales of the MMPI-2

SCALE NAME	INTERPRETATION
1. Hypochondriasis (Hs)	High scorers exhibit an exaggerated concern about their physical health.
2. Depression (D)	High scorers are usually depressed, despondent, and distressed.
3. Hysteria (Hy)	High scorers complain often about physical symptoms that have no apparent organic cause.
4. Psychopathic deviate (Pd)	High scorers show a disregard for social and moral standards.
5. Masculinity/femininity (Mf)	High scorers show "traditional" masculine or feminine attitudes and values.
6. Paranoia (Pa)	High scorers demonstrate extreme suspiciousness and feelings of persecution.
7. Psychasthenia (Pt)	High scorers tend to be highly anxious, rigid, tense, and worrying.
8. Schizophrenia (Sc)	High scorers tend to be socially withdrawn and to engage in bizarre and unusual thinking.
9. Hypomania (Ma)	High scorers are usually emotional, excitable, energetic, and impulsive.
10. Social introversion (S)	High scorers tend to be modest, self-effacing, and shy.

validity scales of the MMPI-2. One variable that the validity scales measure is *social desirability,* or the degree to which a test taker desires to appear to conform to society's concept of a "good" person. For instance, a test taker who is influenced by social desirability is likely to claim to have never told a lie. In addition, validity scales control for people who are faking a psychiatric illness, as in the case of someone hoping to be judged not guilty of a crime by reason of insanity. They also help psychologists identify individuals who are trying to appear healthier than they actually are, perhaps in order to be released from a psychiatric hospital. Thus, an individual's scores on the clinical scales of the MMPI-2 are always interpreted in light of his or her scores on the validity scales.

The MMPI-2 is reliable, easy to administer and score, and inexpensive to use. It is useful in the screening, diagnosis, and clinical description of abnormal behavior, but it does not reveal normal personality differences very well. A special form of the test, the MMPI-A, was developed for adolescents in 1992. The MMPI-A includes some items that are especially relevant to adolescents, such as those referring to eating disorders, substance abuse, and problems with school and family. There have been more than 115 recognized translations of the MMPI-2, and it is used in more than 65 countries (Butcher & Graham, 1989).

California Personality Inventory (CPI) A highly regarded personality test developed especially for typical individuals aged 13 and older.

An important limitation of the MMPI-2, though, is that it was designed specifically to assess psychopathology. By contrast, the **California Personality Inventory (CPI)** is a highly regarded personality test developed especially for typical individuals aged 13 and older. Similar to the MMPI, the CPI even has many of the same questions, but it does not include any questions designed to reveal psychiatric illness (Gough, 1987). The CPI is particularly useful in predicting school achievement in high school and beyond, leadership and executive success, and the effectiveness of police, military personnel, and student teachers (Gregory, 1996; Miller, Watkins, & Webb, 2009; Weiss & Weiss, 2011).

Myers-Briggs Type Indicator (MBTI) A personality inventory useful for measuring individual differences; based on Jung's theory of personality.

The **Myers-Briggs Type Indicator (MBTI)** is another personality inventory that is useful for measuring individual differences. This test is based on Jung's personality theory. The MBTI is scored on four separate bipolar dimensions:

Extraversion (E)	⟷	Introversion (I)
Sensing (S)	⟷	Intuition (N)
Thinking (T)	⟷	Feeling (F)
Judging (J)	⟷	Perceptive (P)

A person can score anywhere along a continuum for each of the four bipolar dimensions, and these individual scores are usually summarized according to a system of personality types. Sixteen types of personality profiles can be derived from the possible combinations of the four bipolar dimensions. For example, a person whose scores were more toward the Extraversion, Intuition, Feeling, and Perceptive ends of the four dimensions would be labeled an ENFP personality type, which is described as follows:

> Relates more readily to the outer world of people and things than to the inner world of ideas (E); prefers to search for new possibilities over working with known facts and conventional ways of doing things (N); makes decisions and solves problems on the basis of personal values and feelings rather than relying on logical thinking and analysis (F); and prefers a flexible, spontaneous life to a planned and orderly existence (P). (Gregory, 1996)

The MBTI is widely used in business and educational settings (Wilde, 2011). Critics point to the absence of rigorous, controlled validity studies of the inventory (Pittenger, 2005). However, many studies have shown that the MBTI personality types are associated with career choices and job satisfaction. For example, physicians who choose different specialties (e.g., pediatrics, surgery) tend to have different MBTI types (Stilwell et al., 2000). Consequently, the MBTI continues to enjoy popularity among career counselors. 👁

Projective Tests ▶

Responses on interviews and questionnaires are conscious responses and, for this reason, are less useful to therapists who wish to probe the unconscious. Such therapists may choose a completely different technique called a projective test. A **projective test** is a personality test consisting of inkblots, drawings of ambiguous human situations, or incomplete sentences for which there are no correct or incorrect responses. People respond by projecting their inner thoughts, feelings, fears, or conflicts onto the test materials.

One of the oldest and most popular projective tests is the **Rorschach Inkblot Method** developed by Swiss psychiatrist Hermann Rorschach (ROR-shok) in 1921. It consists of 10 inkblots, which the test-taker is asked to describe (see Figure 11.7). Rorschach experimented with thousands of inkblots on different groups of people and found that 10 of the inkblots could be used to discriminate among different diagnostic groups, such as people with bipolar disorder, schizophrenia, and other serious disorders. These 10 inkblots—5 black and white, and 5 with color—were standardized and are still widely used.

The Rorschach can be used to describe personality, make differential diagnoses, plan and evaluate treatment, identify defense mechanisms and predict behavior (Ganellen, 1996; Erdberg, 2012; Weiner, 1997, 2004). Thus, although it was first developed nearly a century ago, it continues to be one of the most frequently used measures of personality (Choca, 2013). The test taker is shown the 10 inkblots and asked to tell everything that he or she thinks about what each inkblot looks like or resembles. The examiner writes down the test taker's responses and then goes through the cards again, asking questions to clarify what the test taker has reported. In scoring the Rorschach, the examiner considers whether the test taker has used the whole inkblot in the description or only parts of it. The test taker is asked whether the shape of the inkblot, its color, or something else prompted the response. The examiner also considers whether the test taker sees movement, human figures or parts, animal figures or parts, or other objects in the inkblots.

Until the 1990s, the main problem with the Rorschach was that the results were too dependent on the interpretation and judgment of the examiner. In response to such criticisms, Exner (1993) developed the Comprehensive System, a more reliable procedure for scoring the Rorschach. It provides some normative data so that the responses of a person taking the test can be compared to those of others with known personality

👁 Watch the Video *Episode 13: In the Real World: Popular Personality Assessments* in **MyPsychLab**

11.15 How do projective tests provide insight into personality?

projective test A personality test in which people respond to inkblots, drawings of ambiguous human situations, or incomplete sentences by projecting their inner thoughts, feelings, fears, or conflicts onto the test materials.

Rorschach Inkblot Method (ROR-shok) A projective test composed of 10 inkblots that the test taker is asked to describe; used to assess personality, make differential diagnoses, plan and evaluate treatment, and predict behavior.

FIGURE 11.7 An Inkblot Similar to One Used for the Rorschach Inkblot Method

▶ The Thematic Apperception Test requires test takers to make inferences about drawings that can be interpreted in a variety of ways. The drawings typically include human figures in different kinds of settings. To get a feeling for the projective technique, make up a story to explain what the two people in this photo are discussing.

Thematic Apperception Test (TAT) A projective test consisting of drawings of ambiguous human situations, which the test taker describes; thought to reveal inner feelings, conflicts, and motives, which are projected onto the test materials.

◉ Watch the Video *Episode 13: Thinking Like a Psychologist: Measuring Personality* in **MyPsychLab**

characteristics. Using this system, some researchers have found high agreement among different raters interpreting the same responses (interrater agreement) (McDowell & Acklin, 1996). Others believe that more research is necessary before it can be concluded that the Comprehensive System yields reliable and valid results (Wood, Nezworski, & Stejskal, 1996).

Another projective test is the **Thematic Apperception Test (TAT)** developed by Henry Murray and his colleagues in 1935 (Morgan & Murray, 1935; Murray, 1938). You may remember from Chapter 9 that researchers have used the TAT to study the need for achievement, but it is also useful for assessing other aspects of personality. The TAT consists of one blank card and 19 other cards showing vague or ambiguous black-and-white drawings of human figures in various situations. If you were taking the TAT, this is what you would be told:

This is a test of your creative imagination. I shall show you a picture, and I want you to make up a plot or story for which it might be used as an illustration. What is the relation of the individuals in the picture? What has happened to them? What are their present thoughts and feelings? What will be the outcome? (Morgan & Murray, 1962, p. 532)

The TAT is time consuming and difficult to administer and score. Although it has been used extensively in research, it suffers from the same weaknesses as other projective techniques: (1) it relies heavily on the interpretation skills of the examiner and (2) it may reflect too strongly a person's temporary motivational and emotional states and not indicate more permanent aspects of personality. The *Summarize It* recaps the three approaches to personality assessment discussed in this chapter. ◉

SUMMARIZE IT

Three Approaches to Personality Assessment

METHOD	EXAMPLES	DESCRIPTION
Observation and rating	Observation	Performance (behavior) is observed in a specific situation, and personality is assessed based on the observation.
	Interviews	In interviews, the responses to questions are taken to reveal personality characteristics.
	Rating scales	Rating scales are used to score or rate test takers on the basis of traits, behaviors, or results of interviews.
		Assessment is subjective, and accuracy depends largely on the ability and experience of the evaluator.
Inventories	Minnesota Multiphasic Personality Inventory-2 (MMPI-2)	Test takers reveal their beliefs, feelings, behavior, and/or opinions on paper-and-pencil tests.
	California Personality Inventory (CPI)	Scoring procedures are standardized, and responses of test takers are compared to group norms.
	Myers-Briggs Type Indicator (MBTI)	Used for measuring individual differences; based on Jung's theory of personality.
Projective tests	Rorschach Inkblot Method Thematic Apperception Test (TAT)	Test takers respond to ambiguous test materials and presumably reveal elements of their own personalities by what they report they see in inkblots and by themes they write about scenes showing possible conflict.

REMEMBER IT

Check your answers and take additional quizzes in MyPsychLab.com. ✓ Study and Review on MyPsychLab

1. In _____, psychologists ask a standard set of questions to assess an individual's personality.

2. The _____ was originally designed to measure individuals' tendencies towards psychiatric problems.

3. _____ tests are design to elicit information about unconscious personality processes.

Looking Back

The development of reliable and valid measures of personality has been a boon to psychologists' attempts to define and explain individual differences in this important domain. Comprehensive theories of personality have been useful to these attempts as well. To review, psychoanalytic theories emphasize unconscious forces, while humanistic approaches focus on individuals' attempts to better themselves and find acceptance. Trait theories describe personality in terms of individual differences across a number of universal dimensions. Social-cognitive theories assert that personality traits are influenced by learning and that their manifestation is often dependent on situational factors. Each of these perspectives has been used to explain how and why variations in mental health develop. Keep them in mind as you read the upcoming chapter about psychological disorders.

CHAPTER 11 SUMMARY

PSYCHOANALYTIC THEORIES (pp. 364–370)

11.1 What concepts did Freud propose to explain personality? (pp. 364–366)

The three levels of awareness in consciousness are the conscious, the preconscious, and the unconscious. The conscious mind includes everything we are thinking about at any given moment. The preconscious includes thoughts and feelings we can easily bring to mind. The unconscious contains thoughts and feelings that are difficult to call up because they have been repressed. The id is the primitive, unconscious part of the personality, which contains the instincts and operates on the pleasure principle. The ego is the rational, largely conscious system, which operates according to the reality principle. The superego is the moral system of the personality, consisting of the conscience and the ego ideal. A defense mechanism is a means used by the ego to defend against anxiety and to maintain self-esteem.

Key Terms
personality, p. 364
conscious, p. 364
preconscious, p. 364
unconscious, p. 364
id, p. 365
ego, p. 365
superego, p. 365
defense mechanism, p. 365

11.2 What is the role of the psychosexual stages in Freud's theory? (pp. 366–368)

Freud asserted that the sexual instinct is present at birth and develops through a series of psychosexual stages, providing the driving force for all feelings and behaviors. The stages are the oral stage, anal stage, phallic stage (followed by the latency period), and genital stage. One of the most controversial features of Freud's stage theory is the Oedipus complex, a conflict that arises during the phallic stage in which the child is sexually attracted to the opposite-sex parent and feels hostility toward the same-sex parent.

Key Terms
psychosexual stages, p. 366
fixation, p. 366
Oedipus or Elektra complex, p. 366

11.3 How do modern psychologists evaluate Freud's ideas? (pp. 368–368)

Freud is credited with calling attention to the unconscious, the importance of early childhood experiences, and the role of defense mechanisms. However, his theory is often criticized because it defies scientific testing.

11.4 How do the views of the neo-Freudians differ from those of Freud? (pp. 368–370)

Jung's model of personality includes three parts: the ego, the personal unconscious, and the collective unconscious. Adler claimed that the predominant force of the personality is not sexual in nature but rather the drive to overcome and compensate for feelings of weakness and inferiority and to strive for superiority or significance. Horney took issue with Freud's sexist view of women and added the feminine dimension to the world of psychology.

Key Terms
personal unconscious, p. 369
collective unconscious, p. 369
archetype, p. 369

HUMANISTIC THEORIES (pp. 370–372)

11.5 How do humanistic theorists explain personality? (pp. 370–371)

According to Maslow, the goal of personality development is to reach a level where most behavior is motivated by self-actualization, the drive to attain one's fullest potential. According to Rogers, individuals often do not become fully functioning persons because in childhood they did not receive unconditional positive regard from their parents. To gain positive regard, they had to meet their parents' conditions of worth.

Key Terms
esteem needs, p. 370
self-actualization, p. 371
conditions of worth, p. 371
unconditional positive regard, p. 371

11.6 What have psychologists learned about self-esteem? (pp. 371–372)

The sense of self-esteem is influenced by comparisons of one's real self to one's desired self. Most people's self-esteem is based on what they perceive to be their strengths and weaknesses rather than on a single desired accomplishment or trait. By age 7, most children have a global sense of self-esteem and continue developing beliefs about their competencies in specific domains (e.g., sports) for several years.

Key Term
self-esteem, p. 371

TRAIT THEORIES (pp. 372–378)

11.7 What ideas did the early trait theorists propose? (pp. 372–374)

Allport defined a cardinal trait as a personal quality that pervades a person's personality to the point where he or she may become identified with that trait. A central trait is the type you might mention when writing a letter of recommendation. Cattell used the term surface traits to refer to observable qualities of personality. Source traits, which underlie the surface traits, are possessed in varying amounts by people. Eysenck considered the three most important dimensions of personality to be psychoticism, extraversion, and neuroticism.

Key Term
traits, p. 372

11.8 How does the five-factor model describe personality? (pp. 374–376)

According to the five-factor model, personality is influenced by five dimensions. The Big Five are neuroticism, extraversion, conscientiousness, agreeableness, and openness to experience.

Key Term
five-factor model, p. 374

11.9 What does research say about the effects of heredity and environment on personality traits? (pp. 376–377)

Both twin and adoption studies have shown that heredity strongly influences personality. However, some traits change over time, suggesting that the environment also contributes to personality traits.

11.10 How do personality traits vary across cultures? (pp. 377–378)

The cultural dimension known as individualism/collectivism is associated with personality. Individualist cultures encourage people to view themselves as separate from others and to value independence and assertiveness. Collectivist cultures emphasize social connectedness among people and encourage individuals to define themselves in terms of their social relationships.

Key Term
individualism/collectivism dimension, p. 377

SOCIAL-COGNITIVE THEORIES (pp. 378–381)

11.11 How do Mischel and Bandura address the situation–trait debate? (pp. 378–379)

Mischel initiated the situation-trait debate to show how situations influence the manifestation of personality traits. He views a trait as a conditional probability that an action will occur in response to a specific situation. Bandura's reciprocal determinism model explains how traits and situations interact. The external environment (situation), behavior (partly due to traits), and cognitive factors (partly due to traits) are the three components of reciprocal determinism, each influencing and being influenced by the others.

Key Terms
social-cognitive theory, p. 378
situation-trait debate, p. 378
reciprocal determinism, p. 379

11.12 What do self-efficacy and locus of control contribute to personality? (pp. 379–381)

Self-efficacy gives people the confidence they need to accomplish goals. An internal locus of control helps them do so as well. An external locus of control may lead to procrastination.

Key Terms
self-efficacy, p. 379
locus of control, p. 379

PERSONALITY ASSESSMENT (pp. 381–387)

11.13 How do psychologists use observations, interviews, and rating scales? (pp. 381–382)

During observations, psychologists count behaviors that may be representative of an individual's personality. They use structured interviews to compare the responses of one interviewee to those of others given under similar circumstances. Rating scales are used to quantify behaviors that occur during observations or interviews.

11.14 What do the MMPI-2, the CPI, and the MBTI reveal about personality? (pp. 382–385)

An inventory is a paper-and-pencil test with questions about a person's thoughts, feelings, and behaviors, which measures several dimensions of personality and can be scored according to a standard procedure. The MMPI-2 is designed to screen and diagnose psychiatric problems, and the CPI is designed to assess the normal personality. The MBTI uses examinees' scores to group them into sixteen categories that represent combinations of four dimensions: extraversion/introversion, sensing/intuition, thinking/feeling, judging/perceptive.

Key Terms
inventory, p. 382
Minnesota Multiphasic Personality Inventory (MMPI), p. 382
California Personality Inventory (CPI), p. 384
Myers-Briggs Type Indicator (MBTI), p. 384

11.15 How do projective tests provide insight into personality? (pp. 385–387)

In a projective test, people respond to inkblots or drawings of ambiguous human situations or by projecting their inner thoughts, feelings, fears, or conflicts onto the test materials. Examples are the Rorschach Inkblot Method and the Thematic Apperception Test (TAT).

Key Terms
projective test, p. 385
Rorschach Inkblot Method, p. 385
Thematic Apperception Test (TAT), p. 386

Chapter 11 Study Guide

Answers to all the Study Guide questions are provided at the end of the book.

SECTION ONE: Chapter Review

Psychoanalytic Theories (pp. 364–370)

1. Psychoanalysis is both a theory of personality and a therapy for the treatment of psychological disorders. (true/false)

2. Freud considered the (conscious, unconscious) to be the primary motivating force of human behavior.

3. The part of the personality that would make you want to eat, drink, and be merry is your
   a. id.　　**b.** ego.　　**c.** superego.

4. You just found a gold watch in a darkened movie theater. Which part of your personality would urge you to turn it in to the lost and found?
   a. id　　**b.** ego　　**c.** superego

5. The part of the personality that determines appropriate ways to satisfy biological urges is the
   a. id.　　**b.** ego.　　**c.** superego.

6. Defense mechanisms are used only by psychologically unhealthy individuals. (true/false)

7. Repression is used to avoid unpleasant thoughts. (true/false)

8. According to Freud, the sex instinct arises at (birth, puberty).

9. Which of the following lists presents Freud's stages in the order in which they occur?
   a. latency, anal, oral, genital, phallic
   b. genital, anal, latency, oral, phallic
   c. oral, phallic, anal, genital, latency
   d. oral, anal, phallic, latency, genital

10. Rich's excessive concern with cleanliness and order could indicate a fixation at the _____ stage.
   a. oral　　　　　**c.** phallic
   b. anal　　　　　**d.** genital

11. When a young boy develops sexual feelings toward his mother and hostility toward his father, he is said to have a conflict called the _____ _____; a girl who develops similar feelings towards her father is experiencing the _____ _____.

12. According to Freud, which of the following represents a primary source of influence on personality?
a. heredity
b. life experiences after beginning school
c. the relative strengths of the id, ego, and superego
d. the problems experienced during adolescence

13. In Jung's theory, the inherited part of the personality that stores the experiences of humankind is the (collective, personal) unconscious.

14. Which personality theorist believed that the basic human drive is to overcome and compensate for inferiority and strive for superiority and significance?
a. Sigmund Freud   **c.** Alfred Adler
b. Carl Jung   **d.** Karen Horney

15. On which of the following did Horney focus?
a. psychoanalysis   **c.** feminine psychology
b. trait theory   **d.** humanistic psychology

Humanistic Theories (pp. 370–372)

16. Humanistic psychologists would *not* say that
a. human nature is innately good.
b. human beings have a natural tendency toward self-actualization.
c. human beings have free will.
d. researchers should focus primarily on observable behavior.

17. Which psychologist identified characteristics that he believed self-actualized persons share?
a. Carl Rogers   **c.** Abraham Maslow
b. Gordon Allport   **d.** Hans Eysenck

18. Which psychologist believed that individuals often do not become fully functioning persons because, in childhood, they fail to receive unconditional positive regard from their parents?
a. Carl Rogers   **c.** Abraham Maslow
b. Gordon Allport   **d.** Hans Eysenck

19. Self-esteem includes assessments of competence in different domains such as academics and sports. (true/false)

Trait Theories (pp. 372–378)

20. According to Allport, the kind of trait that is a defining characteristic of one's personality is a _____ trait.
a. common   **c.** secondary
b. source   **d.** cardinal

21. According to Cattell, the differences between people are explained by the number of source traits they possess. (true/false)

22. Eysenck claimed that psychologists can best understand personality by assessing people on three major dimensions, _____, _____, and _____?
a. extraversion, neuroticism, psychoticism
b. psychoticism, extraversion, introversion
c. neuroticism, extraversion, introversion
d. extraversion, neuroticism, introversion

23. This chapter suggests that, according to a growing consensus among trait theorists, there are _____ major dimensions of personality.
a. 3   **c.** 7
b. 5   **d.** 16

24. Behavioral geneticists have found that the shared family environment has a (strong, negligible) effect on personality development.

25. Children adopted at birth are more similar in personality to their adoptive parents than to their biological parents. (true/false)

Social-Cognitive Theories (pp. 378–381)

26. The situation-trait debate was initiated by
a. Albert Bandura.   **c.** Robert McCrae.
b. Walter Mischel.   **d.** Julian Rotter.

27. Bandura's concept of reciprocal determinism refers to the mutual effects of
a. a person's behavior, personality, and thinking.
b. a person's feelings, attitudes, and thoughts.
c. a person's behavior, personal/cognitive factors, and the environment.
d. classical and operant conditioning and observational learning.

28. Which statement is *not* true of people low in self-efficacy?
a. They persist in their efforts.
b. They lack confidence.
c. They expect failure.
d. They avoid challenge.

29. Who proposed the concept of locus of control?
a. B. F. Skinner   **c.** Hans Eysenck
b. Albert Bandura   **d.** Julian Rotter

Personality Assessment (pp. 381–387)

30. Match each personality test with its description.
_____ (**1**) MMPI-2
_____ (**2**) Rorschach
_____ (**3**) TAT
_____ (**4**) CPI
_____ (**5**) MBTI
a. inventory used to diagnose psychopathology
b. inventory used to assess typical personality
c. projective test using inkblots
d. projective test using drawings of ambiguous human situations
e. inventory used to assess personality types

31. Clay has an unconscious resentment toward his father. Which test might best detect this?
a. MMPI-2   **c.** MBTI
b. CPI   **d.** TAT

32. Which of the following items might appear on the validity scale of the MMPI-2?
a. What is happening in the picture?
b. Hand is to glove as foot is to _____.
c. My mother was a good person.
d. What is your favorite food?

SECTION TWO: Complete the Table

Approach	Key Theorist(s)	Major Assumption about Behavior
1. Psychoanalytic	_____	_____
2. Humanistic	_____	_____
3. Trait	_____	_____
4. Social-cognitive	_____	_____

SECTION THREE: Comprehensive Practice Test

1. A person's unique pattern of behaving, thinking, and feeling is his or her
   a. motivation.
   c. personality.
   b. emotion.
   d. cognition.

2. Freud's theory of personality and his therapy for the treatment of psychological disorders are both known as
   a. behaviorism.
   c. psychoanalysis.
   b. psychosocialism.
   d. humanism.

3. Of Freud's three conceptual systems of personality, the _____ is mainly in the conscious, the _____ is split between the conscious and the unconscious, and the _____ is completely unconscious.
   a. id; ego; superego
   c. superego; ego; id
   b. ego; superego; id
   d. ego; id; superego

4. The libido is Freud's name for the psychic or sexual energy that comes from the superego and provides the energy for the entire personality. (true/false)

5. Ava is 13 months old, and whatever she can pick up is likely to go into her mouth. Ava is in Freud's _____ stage of psychosexual development.
   a. anal
   c. phallic
   b. oral
   d. genital

6. Clint is 5 years old, and he thinks his mother is as beautiful as a princess; he would rather spend time with her than with his father. Clint is in Freud's _____ stage of psychosexual development.
   a. anal
   c. phallic
   b. oral
   d. genital

7. A central theme in Adler's theory is the individual's quest for feelings of
   a. superiority.
   b. the collective unconscious.
   c. adequacy.
   d. ego integrity.

8. According to Horney, maladjustment is often caused by
   a. guilt related to failing to live up to an ideal self.
   b. observation of maladjusted role models.
   c. inherited traits.
   d. repressed memories.

9. Allport and Cattell were proponents of the _____ theory of personality.
   a. stage
   c. biological
   b. trait
   d. humanistic

10. Which of the following Big Five personality factors has been found to be a requirement for creative accomplishment?
    a. extraversion
    c. neuroticism
    b. conscientiousness
    d. openness to experience

11. Bandura's theory includes the concept of _____, the belief a person has regarding his or her ability to perform competently whatever is attempted.
    a. reciprocal determinism
    c. extraversion
    b. self-efficacy
    d. conditions of worth

12. Trey believes that what happens to him is based on fate, luck, or chance, and his philosophy of life is "whatever will be, will be." Rotter would say that Trey has a(n) _____ locus of control.
    a. internal
    c. external
    b. explicit
    d. regressed

13. Rogers's theory included the concept of conditions of worth—the idea that our parents teach us important values in life and that we as individuals will be motivated to seek out those values. (true/false)

14. The MMPI-2 is a good example of a projective personality test. (true/false)

15. The California Psychological Inventory was developed to evaluate the personalities of
    a. the mentally ill.
    c. typical people.
    b. males.
    d. females.

16. You are shown a black-and-white drawing of people and asked to tell a story about it. You are probably responding to
    a. the Rorschach Inkblot Method.
    b. the CPI.
    c. the Myers-Briggs Type Indicator.
    d. the TAT.

SECTION FOUR: Critical Thinking

1. How do you think the Big Five dimensions of personality affect your behavior

2. Most social scientists say that American culture is individualist. What aspects of culture in the United States exemplify individualism? Are there some features of American culture that are collectivist in nature? If so, what are they?

SECTION FIVE: Application Essays

1. In what situations do you exhibit personality traits that are different from those you usually demonstrate? For instance, if you are outgoing most of the time, in what situations do you find yourself feeling and exhibiting shyness?

Apply your critical thinking skills with **MyPsychLab** Writing Assignments

Submit your answer to the following question inside the MyPsychLab Writing Assessment program for immediate feedback.

Describe the four major theories of personality (psychodynamic, trait or five-factor model, humanistic, and social-cognitive) and identify advantages and disadvantages of each theory.

Psychological Disorders

Have you ever worried about what might happen in the future? Who hasn't? Being concerned about what lays ahead, a state that psychologists call *anxiety*, is an experience shared by all humans. But sometimes anxiety becomes so frequent or so intense that it interferes with or even takes over a person's life. If you are wondering whether you or someone close to you has reached that point, thinking about the following descriptions may help you decide. Read each one and place a check mark beside each description that sounds like you or someone about whom you are concerned.

_____1. You are always worried about things, even when there are no signs of trouble. You have frequent aches and pains that can't be traced to physical illness or injury. You tire easily, and yet you have trouble sleeping. Your body is constantly tense.

_____2. You have stopped leaving home because that seems to be the only way you can avoid situations in which, out of the blue, your heart starts pounding. You feel dizzy. You can't breathe. You feel like you are about to die.

_____3. Every day, you fear you will do something embarrassing. You've stopped going to parties because you're afraid to meet new people. When other people look at you, you break out in a sweat and shake uncontrollably. You stay home from work because you're terrified of being called on in a staff meeting.

Later in the chapter, you will learn about the conditions that correspond to these descriptions. The first represents *generalized anxiety disorder* and the second describes *panic disorder*. The third description refers to *social anxiety disorder*. In recent years, psychologists have learned a great deal about psychological disorders like these, including what causes them and how to help people who have them. This chapter addresses these findings. But first let's ask the obvious question: What is abnormal?

◉▸**Watch** the Video *Episode 17: Big Picture: What Does It Mean to Have a Mental Disorder?* in **MyPsychLab**

Defining Psychological Disorders

Psychological disorders are mental processes and/or behavior patterns that cause emotional distress and/or substantial impairment in functioning. You have already learned about several psychological disorders in earlier chapters (see Table 12.1). In this chapter, your will learn about many more. We begin our examination of them with a basic question that we haven't considered up until now: What is abnormal?

What Is Abnormal Behavior? ▸

Human behavior lies along a continuum, from well-adjusted to *maladaptive,* a term that refers to behavior that is poorly suited to a particular situation or function. For example, developing the habit of waiting until the night before an exam to study for it is *maladaptive.* Of course, many students do just this. Thus, clearly, not all maladaptive behavior is abnormal. To be abnormal, a behavior must be maladaptive *and* consistent with other criteria. These criteria help mental health professionals and researchers determine just where along the continuum behavior becomes abnormal. You can think of these criteria as answers to a few critical questions:

• To *what degree is the person's behavior maladaptive?* Some experts believe that the best way to differentiate between normal and abnormal behavior is to consider to

psychological disorders Mental processes and/or behavior patterns that cause emotional distress and/or substantial impairment in functioning.

⌈ **12.1** What criteria do
  psychologists use to classify
⌊ behavior as abnormal?

TABLE 12.1 **Psychological Disorders Discussed in Other Chapters**	
CHAPTER	**DISORDERS**
4	Circadian Rhythm Sleep-Wake Disorders
	Sleep-Wake Disorders
	Breathing-Related Sleep Disorders
	Parasomnias
	Substance Related and Addictive Disorders
6	Alzheimer's Disease
7	Intellectual Disability
8	Gender Dysphoria
9	Eating Disorders
10	Posttraumatic Stress Disorder (PTSD)

▲ Abnormal behavior is defined by each culture. For example, homelessness is considered abnormal in some cultures and completely normal in others.

what extent it impairs an individual's functioning. Washing your hands before you eat is adaptive. Washing them when you handle dirty objects is also adaptive, even if you do so somewhat more often than others. By contrast, washing your hands 100 times a day out of an irrational fear of contamination is both maladaptive and abnormal. Why? Because a person who washes his hands 100 times a day can scarcely do anything else.

• *Is the behavior considered strange within the person's own culture?* What is considered abnormal in one culture is not necessarily considered so in another. For instance, in some cultures, it is normal for women to appear in public bare breasted, but it would be abnormal for a female executive in an industrialized culture to go to work that way.

• *Is the behavior unusual among people who are the same age as the person?* Many behaviors that are considered normal at one age are not considered so in other periods of life. A 2-year-old who physically throws himself onto the floor in the midst of a tantrum would not be considered abnormal, while an adult who does so would be thought of as behaving abnormally. Similarly, a 10-year-old who has temper tantrums that are similar to those of a 2-year-old might be considered abnormal as well.

• *Does the behavior cause distress to the person?* When people experience considerable emotional distress without any life experience that warrants it, they may be diagnosed as having a psychological disorder. Some people may be sad and depressed, and some anxious; others may be agitated or excited; and still others may be frightened, or even terrified, by delusions and hallucinations.

• *Is the person a danger to self or others?* Another consideration is whether people pose any danger to themselves or others. To be committed to a psychiatric hospital, a person must be judged both mentally ill and a danger to self or others.

• *Is the person legally responsible for his or her acts?* Often, the term *insanity* is used to label those who behave abnormally, but mental health professionals do not use this term. It is a legal term used by the courts to declare people not legally responsible for their acts. You should remember from Chapter 1 that *forensic psychologists* are clinical psychologists who specialize in the legal aspects of psychology. They sometimes testify in cases in which a defendant claims to have been insane at the time he or she committed a crime.

Classifying and Tracking Psychological Disorders ▶

In 1952, the American Psychiatric Association published a manual providing a diagnostic system for describing and classifying psychological disorders. Over the years, the manual has been revised several times. The most recent edition, the *Diagnostic and Statistical Manual of Mental Disorder*, 5th Edition, commonly known as the **DSM-5** appeared in 2013. Some of the major guidelines that the mental health professionals who prepared the *DSM-5* used to determine whether proposed changes to *DSM-IV* diagnoses were acceptable are shown in Table 12.2.

The *DSM-5* contains descriptions of hundreds of specific psychological disorders and lists criteria that must be met in order to make a particular diagnosis. Further, the manual organizes these disorders into categories based on similar symptoms. For example, the disorders you read about in the *Think About It* activity at the beginning of the chapter belong to the category called *anxiety disorders*. Irrational fears are the distinguishing feature of disorders in this category, but these fears are manifested differently in each of the individual disorders within the category. The manual is used by researchers, therapists, mental health workers, and most insurance companies. This common language enables professionals to speak the same language when diagnosing, treating, researching, and conversing about a variety of psychological disorders (Clark, Watson, & Reynolds, 1995).

Widespread use of the *DSM* manuals by mental health professionals has enabled public health officials to keep track of the frequency with which the various categories and individual disorders are diagnosed, just as they do for physical ailments. Their findings indicate that psychological disorders are more common than many physical ailments. For instance, each year in the United States, less than 1% of adults, about 1.6 million people, are newly diagnosed with cancer, and 4% are currently living with a cancer diagnosis (U. S. Cancer Statistics Working Group, 2013). By contrast, 26%, or more than 44 million adults, are diagnosed with a mental disorder of some kind (Reeves et al., 2011).

Another way of thinking about the frequency of a disorder is to examine how likely an individual is to be diagnosed with it in his or her lifetime. The lifetime prevalence rate of cancer in the United States is about 38% for women and 44% for men; in other words, about 38% of American women and 44% of American men will be diagnosed with cancer sometime in their lives (American Cancer Society, 2012). Again, mental disorders are more common, with a lifetime prevalence rate of nearly 50% for both women and men (Reeves et al., 2011). Lifetime rates of a few disorders are shown in Figure 12.1 on p. 396. Clearly, mental disorders represent a significant

⌈ 12.2 How do clinicians use the
⌊ DSM-5?

DSM-5, 2013 *The Diagnostic and Statistical Manual of Mental Disorders*, 5th Edition; a manual published by the American Psychiatric Association, which describes the criteria used to classify and diagnose mental disorders.

TABLE 12.2 **Guidelines for the Fifth Edition of the *Diagnostic and Statistical Manual of Mental Disorders***

A CHANGE MUST...	EXAMPLE
Be beneficial to individuals with psychiatric disorders	Modified criteria for a diagnosis enable individuals to gain access to mental health services that were not available to them under *DSM-IV* criteria.
Be useful to mental health professionals	A new diagnosis helps clinicians determine appropriate treatments for individuals whose difficulties were not adequately addressed in *DSM-IV*.
Be supported by research	The age at which a pattern of symptoms must have appeared in order for a diagnosis to be made is changed on the basis of research done since the publication of the *DSM-IV*.
Maintain or improve the reliability and validity of *DSM-IV* diagnoses	A change helps mental health professionals distinguish a diagnosis from others, resulting in greater consistency in the application of the diagnosis across clinicians.
A CHANGE MUST NOT...	**EXAMPLE**
Harm individuals with psychiatric disorders	Modified criteria cause individuals to lose access to mental health services that were available to them under *DSM-IV* criteria.
Increase the likelihood that clinicians will mistakenly characterize normal behavior as abnormal	Religious behaviors are mischaracterized as symptoms of a psychiatric disorder because of a change in the criteria for a diagnosis.

Source: Kendler et al., 2009.

FIGURE 12.1 **Lifetime Prevalence of Psychological Disorders**
The percentages of people in the United States who suffer from various psychological disorders during their lifetime are based on the findings of the National Comorbidity Survey.
Source: Data from Bhugra (2005) & Freeman et al. (2010).

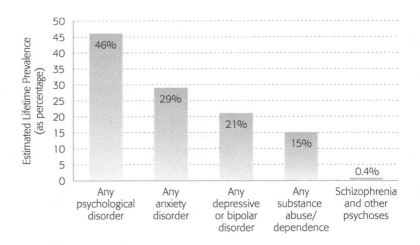

◉┤**Watch** the Video *Episode 17: Basics: Living with a Disorder* in **MyPsychLab**

12.3 What are the five perspectives that psychologists use to explain psychological disorders?

challenge for many individuals and of lost productivity for society. Thus, research aimed at identifying their causes and treatments is just as important as research examining the causes and treatments of physical diseases. ◉

Explaining Psychological Disorders

What causes psychological disorders, and how can they be treated? Psychologists employ five theoretical perspectives to answer these questions. Each perspective has its place in the description, analysis, and treatment of psychological disorders.

The *biological perspective* views abnormal behavior as arising from a physical cause, such as genetic inheritance, biochemical abnormalities or imbalances, structural abnormalities within the brain, and/or infection. Thus, its adherents favor biological treatments, such as drug therapy.

The *biopsychosocial perspective* agrees that physical (biological) causes are of central importance but also recognizes the influence of psychological and social factors in the study, identification, and treatment of psychological disorders. Consequently, biopsychosocial psychologists often advocate treatment strategies that include both drugs and psychotherapy.

Originally proposed by Freud, the *psychodynamic perspective* maintains that psychological disorders stem from early childhood experiences and unresolved, unconscious conflicts, usually of a sexual or aggressive nature. The cause assumed by the psychodynamic approach also suggests the cure—psychoanalysis, which Freud developed to uncover and resolve such unconscious conflicts.

According to the *learning perspective,* psychological disorders are thought to be learned and sustained in the same way as any other behavior. According to this view, people who exhibit abnormal behavior either are victims of faulty learning or have failed to learn appropriate patterns of thinking and acting. Behavior therapists use the learning principles of classical and operant conditioning to eliminate distressing behavior and to establish new, more appropriate behavior in its place.

The *cognitive perspective* suggests that faulty thinking or distorted perceptions can contribute to some types of psychological disorders. Treatment based on this perspective is aimed at changing thinking, which presumably will lead to a change in behavior. Moreover, the cognitive perspective offers advice that may prevent psychological disorders. For example, one step toward healthy thinking is to recognize and avoid five cognitive traps: (1) setting unrealistic standards for yourself ("If I can't get into Harvard, I won't go to college at all."); (2) negative "what if" thinking ("What if I lose my job?"); (3) turning a single negative event, such as a poor grade, into a catastrophe ("I'll never pass this course."); (4) judging anything short of perfection to be a failure ("The cake turned out a bit lopsided, so I threw it out and baked another one."); and (5) demanding perfection in yourself and others ("I broke up with him, because he refused to call me at least once a day."). If your happiness depends on any of these conditions, you are setting the stage for disappointment or even depression.

The *Summarize It* feature lists the main ideas and treatment approaches for each of the theoretical perspectives. You should remember from Chapter 1 that many psychologists favor an eclectic approach rather than a rigid commitment to a single perspective. Thus, mental health professionals often adopt the perspective and treatment method that they believe will be most helpful in each individual case.

SUMMARIZE IT

Five Perspectives on Psychological Disorders

PERSPECTIVE	CAUSES OF PSYCHOLOGICAL DISORDERS	TREATMENT
Biological perspective	A psychological disorder is a symptom of an underlying physical disorder caused by a structural or biochemical abnormality in the brain, by genetic inheritance, or by infection.	Diagnose and treat like any other physical disorder. Drugs, electroconvulsive therapy, or psychosurgery
Biopsychosocial perspective	Psychological disorders result from a combination of biological, psychological, and social causes.	Employ eclectic treatments that include both drugs and psychotherapy
Psychodynamic perspective	Psychological disorders stem from early childhood experiences and unresolved, unconscious sexual or aggressive conflicts.	Bring disturbing repressed material to consciousness and help patient work through unconscious conflicts. Psychoanalysis
Learning perspective	Abnormal thoughts, feelings, and behaviors are learned and sustained like any other behaviors, or there is a failure to learn appropriate behaviors.	Use classical and operant conditioning and modeling to extinguish abnormal behavior and to increase adaptive behavior. Behavior therapy Behavior modification
Cognitive perspective	Faulty thinking or distorted perceptions can cause psychological disorders.	Change faulty, irrational, and/or negative thinking. Beck's cognitive therapy Rational-emotive therapy

REMEMBER IT

Check your answers and take additional quizzes in MyPsychLab.com.   ✓ Study and Review in MyPsychLab

1. To be defined as abnormal, a person's behavior must be considered strange in the _____ in which it occurs.
2. The _____ lists criteria for diagnosing psychological disorders.
3. Nearly _____ of people in the United States will have a psychological disorder at some time in their lives.
4. The _____ perspective explains abnormal behavior as resulting interactions among biological, psychological, and social factors.

Anxiety Disorders

What would you do if your lifelong dream of being a professional entertainer came true? No doubt you would be overjoyed, but what if a severe case of stage fright robbed you of that joy and prevented you from taking advantage of many of the opportunities to perform that came your way? Surprisingly, this is precisely what has happened to many highly talented and successful performers. For example, stage fright prevented Barbara Streisand from performing before live audiences for 27 years. Similarly, actress Scarlett Johansson made her stage debut as a confident 8-year-old child actress. But by

anxiety disorders Psychological disorders characterized by frequent fearful thoughts about what might happen in the future.

the time she reached her teens, Johansson had developed such a severe case of stage fright that she feared she would never be able to perform before a live audience again. Despite her successful film career, Johansson turned down numerous offers to appear on the stage before finally overcoming her fears in early 2010 to play the leading role in a Broadway play. However it isn't always the prospect of facing a live audience that leads to paralyzing stage fright. Film star Hugh Grant reports that he often freezes up in front of the cameras, leading to embarrassment and filming delays.

Stage fright is one manifestation of a fearful state of mind that psychologists call *anxiety*. When anxiety is so severe that it interferes with a person's educational or occupational functioning, it can develop into a serious psychological disorder. **Anxiety disorders** are the most common category of mental disorders affecting about 18% of adults in the United States (NIMH, 2013).

12.4 What are the characteristics of panic attacks, agoraphobia, and panic disorder?

panic attack An episode of overwhelming anxiety, fear, or terror.

agoraphobia (AG-or-uh-FO-bee-ah) An intense fear of being in a situation from which escape is not possible or in which help would not be available if one experienced overwhelming anxiety or a panic attack.

Panic Attacks, Agoraphobia, and Panic Disorder

Feeling anxious is an extremely common experience. However, anxious feelings, even when they occur for unknown reasons and seem to be irrational, are not psychological disorders in and of themselves. As the *Think About It* activity at the beginning of the chapter illustrated, anxious feelings must be of an extreme and severe nature to be considered abnormal. There are two types of anxious feelings of this type for which people often seek professional help, *panic attacks* and *agoraphobia,* both of which are features of *panic disorder.*

Panic Attacks. A **panic attack** is a sudden feeling of fear in which the heart pounds, the body shakes, and the person has a choking sensation. Panicky feelings that have known cues, such as the feeling a person might get while driving through an intersection where she once had a traffic accident, are more often viewed as the result of learning rather than as signs of a disorder. By contrast, uncued attacks are more likely to be symptomatic of a psychological disorder.

Uncued attacks appear to be brought about by a dysfunction in the autonomic nervous system's fight-or-flight system in which the brain misperceives a normal change in bodily functioning to be a danger signal (National Alliance for Mental Illness, 2003). For example, a person's heart rate normally increases after consuming a beverage that contains caffeine. For unknown reasons, in individuals who have panic attacks, this normal change may be perceived as a danger signal by the brain, thereby causing the sympathetic nervous system to put the body's autonomic systems on alert. Next, the person's higher cognitive functions spring into action—"I'm having a heart attack! I'm going to die!"—thus amplifying the sensation of danger. These cognitive interpretations prolong the attack by short-circuiting the parasympathetic system's efforts to counteract the sympathetic system's influence on physiological functions. Thus, clinicians often treat panic attacks by teaching people how to control their cognitive responses to the sensations that accompany these attacks (Teachman, Marker, & Smith-Janik, 2008).

Agoraphobia. A person with **agoraphobia** has an intense fear of being in a situation from which immediate escape is not possible or in which help would not be available if she or he should become overwhelmed by anxiety or experience. In some cases, a person's entire life is planned around avoiding feared situations such as busy streets, crowded stores, restaurants, and/or public transportation. Many will not leave home unless accompanied by a friend or family members, and, in severe cases, not even then.

Although agoraphobia can occur without panic attacks, it often begins during the early adult years with repeated panic attacks (American Psychiatric Association, 2000a). The intense fear of having another attack causes the person to avoid any place or situation where previous attacks have occurred. Thus, when agoraphobia begins to interfere so dramatically with a person's everyday life, clinicians often find that it is one of many debilitating symptoms that a person is experiencing as a result of having developed an anxiety disorder.

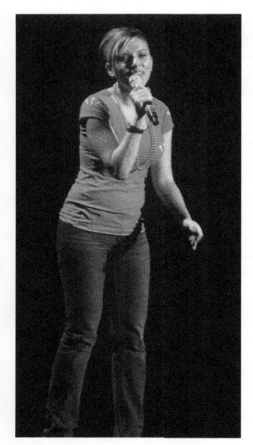

▲ Stage fright led actress Scarlett Johansson to refuse several offers to appear on the Broadway stage until early 2010.

Panic Disorder. People who have recurring panic attacks may be diagnosed with **panic disorder**. People with panic disorder must cope with both repeated attacks and anxiety about the occurrence and consequences of further attacks. This anxiety can lead people to develop agoraphobia, as noted earlier. The presence of agoraphobia complicates clinicians' efforts to help people who have panic disorder because confronting situations in which panic attacks are likely to occur is part of the process of learning to live with this persistent disorder. Obviously, clinicians have a much harder time getting people with agoraphobia to take on this challenging aspect of their treatment. For this reason, panic disorder with agoraphobia is among the most debilitating of all psychological disorders. However, most individuals with this disorder respond to a combination of medication and psychotherapy (Lamplugh et al., 2008).

panic disorder An anxiety disorder in which a person experiences recurring, unpredictable episodes of overwhelming anxiety, fear, or terror.

Watch the Video *Panic Disorder* on **MyPsychLab**

Explaining Panic Disorder. You should remember from Chapter 5 that negative reinforcement increases behaviors that enable us to avoid something unpleasant. Each time a person with panic disorder behaves in a way that prevents or interrupts a panic attack, their behavior is reinforced because it enables them to escape from the unpleasant sensations that are associated with anxiety (e.g., rapidly beating heart, rapid breathing, feelings of doom and impending death). Over time, the frequency of avoidance behaviors increases to the point that the person leaves home only when absolutely necessary and is prone to suddenly returning home in the midst of even the most essential excursions (e.g., doctor's appointments) if a panic attack happens. As a result, a cycle of anxiety, avoidance, and escape becomes established and gains dominance over the life of the person who has panic disorder.

In order to break this cycle, most therapists encourage people with panic disorder to confront situations in which they may experience a panic attack. When people with panic disorder follow this recommendation, they learn that the anxiety they experience when a panic attack occurs will eventually subside on its own (Lamplugh et al., 2008). Thus, relief from anxiety becomes a reinforcer for confronting anxiety-provoking situations rather than for avoiding them.

Generalized Anxiety Disorder, Social Anxiety Disorder (Social Phobia), and Specific Phobia

12.5 How do generalized anxiety disorder, social phobia and specific phobia differ?

At the beginning of this section, you read about several entertainers' battles with stage fright, a manifestation of *social anxiety disorder*, one of the conditions you will read about in this section. Like them, millions of people struggle with and overcome such disorders.

Generalized Anxiety Disorder. **Generalized anxiety disorder (GAD)** is the diagnosis given to people who experience chronic, excessive worry for a prolonged period of time. These people expect the worst; their worrying is either unfounded or greatly exaggerated and, thus, difficult to control. Their excessive anxiety may cause them to feel tense, tired, and irritable and to have difficulty concentrating and sleeping. Other symptoms may include trembling, palpitations, sweating, dizziness, nausea, diarrhea, or frequent urination. This disorder affects twice as many women as men and leads to considerable distress and impairment (Brawman-Mintzer & Lydiard, 1996, 1997; Kranzler, 1996).

generalized anxiety disorder (GAD) An anxiety disorder in which people experience chronic, excessive worry for 6 months or more.

Social Anxiety Disorder (Social Phobia). People who have **social anxiety disorder (social phobia)** are intensely afraid of any social or performance situation in which they might embarrass or humiliate themselves in front of others—by shaking, blushing, sweating, or in some other way appearing clumsy, foolish, or incompetent. Social anxiety disorder may take the specific form of *performance anxiety,* commonly called "stage fright." For example, about one-third of people with social anxiety disorder fear speaking in public (Kessler, Stein, & Berglund, 1998). If you are one of the millions who are afraid of public speaking, see the *Apply It* on p. 400 for advice on overcoming your fear.

Social anxiety disorder can be a disabling disorder (Yates, 2008). In its extreme form, it can seriously affect people's performance at work, preventing them from advancing in their careers or pursuing an education and severely restricting their social

social anxiety disorder (social phobia) An irrational fear and avoidance of any social or performance situation in which one might embarrass or humiliate oneself in front of others by appearing clumsy, foolish, or incompetent.

APPLY IT

Overcoming the Fear of Public Speaking

Do you break out in a cold sweat and start trembling when you have to speak in public? If so, cheer up; you're in good company: Fear of public speaking is the number one fear reported by American adults in surveys. More people fear public speaking than flying, sickness, or even bankruptcy (Dwyer & Davidson, 2012).

What Causes It?

Fear of public speaking is a form of performance anxiety, a common type of social anxiety disorder. Much of the fear of public speaking stems from fear of being embarrassed or of being judged negatively by others. Some people cope with this fear by trying to avoid situations in which they may be required to speak in public. A more practical approach is to examine the incorrect beliefs that can cause the fear of public speaking and then take specific steps to overcome it. Here are some incorrect beliefs associated with public speaking (Orman, 1996):

- To succeed, a speaker has to perform perfectly. (Not true; no audience expects perfection.)

- A good speaker presents as many facts and details about the subject as possible. (Not true; all you need is two or three main points.)

- If some members of the audience aren't paying attention, the speaker needs to do something about it. (Not true; you can't please everyone, and it's a waste of time to try to do so.)

What Can You Do?

Some of the steps you can take to manage fear of public speaking deal with how you present yourself to your audience; others focus on what's going on inside you. Here are some of the many suggestions offered by experts at Toastmasters International (2013), an organization devoted to helping people improve their public speaking skills:

- *Know your material well.* Practice aloud and revise your speech, if necessary.
- *Visualize your speech.* Imagine yourself giving your speech in a confident, clear manner.
- *Relax.* Reduce your tension by doing deep breathing or relaxation exercises.
- *Be familiar with the place where you will speak.* Arrive early and practice using the microphone and any other equipment you plan to use.
- *Connect with the audience.* Greet some members of the audience as they arrive; then, when you give your speech, speak to the audience as though they were a group of your friends.
- *Project confidence through your posture.* Stand or sit in a self-assured manner, smile, and make eye contact with the audience.
- *Focus on your message, not on yourself.* Turn your attention away from your nervousness and focus on the purpose of your speech, which is to transmit information to your audience.
- *Remember that the audience doesn't expect you to be perfect.* Don't apologize for any problems you think you have with your speech. Just be yourself.

By applying these few simple tips, you can overcome nervousness and speak confidently on any topic—even on the spur of the moment.

Sean Dumm

 ▶ Watch on MyPsychLab

---

lives (Bruch, Fallon, & Heimberg, 2003; Stein & Kean, 2000; Yates, 2008). Those with social anxiety disorder sometimes turn to alcohol and tranquilizers to lessen their anxiety in social situations.

phobia (FO-bee-ah) A persistent, irrational fear of some specific object, situation, or activity that poses little or no real danger.

specific phobia A marked fear of a specific object or situation; a general label for any phobia other than agoraphobia and social phobia.

Specific Phobia. A **phobia** is a persistent, irrational fear of some specific object, situation, or activity that poses no real danger (or whose danger is blown out of proportion). Most people realize that their phobias are irrational, but they nevertheless feel compelled to avoid the feared situations or objects. A **specific phobia** is a marked fear of a specific object or situation. This general label is applied to any phobia other than agoraphobia and social phobia. Faced with the object or situation they fear, people who have a specific phobia experience intense anxiety, even to the point of shaking or screaming. The categories of specific phobias, in order of frequency of occurrence, are (1) situational phobias (fear of elevators, airplanes, enclosed places, heights, tunnels, or bridges); (2) fear of the natural environment (fear of storms or water); (3) animal phobias (fear of dogs, snakes, insects, or mice); and (4) blood-injection-injury phobia (fear of seeing blood or an injury or of receiving an injection) (Fredrikson et al., 1996). Two types of situational phobias—*claustrophobia* (fear of closed spaces) and *acrophobia* (fear of heights)—are the specific phobias treated most often by therapists (see the *Try It*, p. 401).

Explaining Generalized Anxiety Disorder, Social Anxiety Disorder, and Specific Phobia. Psychologist Timothy Brown (2007) has argued convincingly that GAD and social anxiety disorder are manifestations of the Big Five personality trait of neuroticism. You should remember from Chapter 11 that people who are high in neuroticism

TRY IT — Phobia Names

You may know that the Greek word *phobia* means "fear." Thus, phobias are named by creating a compound word that includes the Greek or Latin word for the feared object with *-phobia*. For example, *agoraphobia* literally means "fear of the marketplace" (*agora* = marketplace) and, by usage, has come to mean a fear of open spaces or of being anywhere other than one's home. Likewise, *claustrophobia* combines the Latin word *claustrum*, which means "prison," with *-phobia* to denote a fear of enclosed places. Think about the following phobias and see whether you can match them with their definitions.

_____ **(1)** ablutobphobia
_____ **(2)** glossophobia
_____ **(3)** gynephobia
_____ **(4)** lactophobia
_____ **(5)** haptephobia
_____ **(6)** hemophobia
_____ **(7)** xenophobia
_____ **(8)** erythrophobia

a. fear of the color red
b. fear of public speaking
c. fear of washing or bathing
d. fear of strangers
e. fear of women
f. fear of blood
g. fear of being touched
h. fear of milk

ANSWERS: (1) c, (2) b, (3) e, (4) h, (5) g, (6) f, (7) d, (8) a

have a negative outlook on life and tend to be emotionally unstable. That is, they tend to react to stressors in the same way that other people do, but their reactions are more intense and extreme. For example, everyone gets anxious when they have an important exam coming up. But people who are high in neuroticism may worry about the exam so much that they can't sleep or eat, and they may irritate those around them by constantly talking about how stressed they are over the exam. Brown's research suggests that these reactions can develop into generalized anxiety disorder and/or social anxiety disorder (as well as depression, which you'll read about later in the chapter). Moreover, he has found that people with these disorders who are high in neuroticism benefit less from treatment than those who are low in the trait.

Neuroticism is also a risk factor for the development of specific phobias (Bienvenu et al., 2007). However, classical conditioning, which you will recall involves associations between neutral stimuli and fear-provoking situations or objects, is important as well. To cite a simple example: A dog barks menacingly at 3-year-old Bobby (fear-provoking situation); Bobby associates all dogs (neutral stimulus) with the experience. As a result, he cries and runs away every time he sees a dog. Consequently, principles of learning are often used to treat specific phobias. A therapist may use classical conditioning principles to teach people with phobias to associate pleasant emotions with feared objects or situations. For example, a child who fears dogs might be given ice cream while in a room where a dog is present. Behavior modification, in which people with phobias are reinforced for exposing themselves to fearful stimuli, may also be useful. Observation of models who do not exhibit fear in response to the object or situation of which a person with a phobia is afraid has also been an effective treatment technique.

Obsessive-Compulsive Disorder ▶

12.6 What are the symptoms of obsessive-compulsive disorder?

What would your life be like if every time you left your home you were so fearful of having left your door unlocked that you had to go back and check it again and again? **Obsessive-compulsive disorder (OCD)** is an anxiety disorder in which a person has recurrent obsessions or compulsions, or both.

obsessive-compulsive disorder (OCD) An anxiety disorder in which a person has recurrent obsessions and/or compulsions.

Obsessions and Compulsions. Obsessions are persistent, involuntary thoughts, images, or impulses that invade consciousness and cause a person great distress. People with obsessions might worry about contamination by germs or about whether they performed a certain act, such as turning off the stove or locking the door (Greenberg, 2009). Other types of obsessions center on aggression, religion, sex, or treasured objects. For example, individuals with *hoarding disorder* cannot discard unwanted items because doing so makes them feel unbearably anxious. Many people with this condition buy or collect objects they do not need because failing to do so triggers painful bouts of anxiety.

obsession A persistent, involuntary thought, image, or impulse that invades consciousness and causes great distress.

compulsion A persistent, irresistible, and irrational urge to perform an act or ritual repeatedly.

▲ Like this woman, many people with obsessive-compulsive disorder take great pains to avoid contamination from germs and dirt.

People with hoarding disorder acquire and keep things they do not need as a result of inner experiences that psychologists call **compulsions**: persistent, irresistible, irrational urges to perform an act or ritual repeatedly. The individual knows such acts are senseless but cannot resist performing them without experiencing an intolerable buildup of anxiety—which can be relieved only by yielding to the compulsion. Many of us have engaged in compulsive behavior like stepping over cracks on the sidewalk, counting stairsteps, or performing little rituals from time to time. The behavior becomes a psychological problem only if the person cannot resist performing it, if it is very time consuming, and if it interferes with the person's normal activities and relationships with others. Importantly, people with hoarding disorder exhibit these behaviors to such a degree that their occupational, social, and academic functioning is seriously impaired. Moreover, the physical conditions in which many such individuals live often put their health at risk.

In contrast to the compulsions of people with hoarding disorder, many people with obsessive-compulsive disorder experience irresistible urges that involve cleaning and washing behaviors, counting, checking, touching objects, and excessive organizing. Most realize that their behavior is not normal, but they simply cannot help themselves, as shown in the following example.

> Mike, a 32-year-old patient, performed checking rituals that were preceded by a fear of harming other people. When driving, he had to stop the car often and return to check whether he had run over people, particularly babies. Before flushing the toilet, he had to check to be sure that a live insect had not fallen into the toilet, because he did not want to be responsible for killing a living thing. At home he repeatedly checked to see that the doors, stoves, lights, and windows were shut or turned off. . . . Mike performed these and many other checking rituals for an average of 4 hours a day. (Kozak, Foa, & McCarthy, 1988, p. 88)

Explaining Obsessive-Compulsive Disorder. An important feature of OCD is that individuals with the disorder fear or are attracted to the same kinds of objects that others are, in the case of hoarding disorder, or disgusted by things that everyone would prefer not to be exposed to, in the case of cleaning compulsions. Likewise, their compulsions are typically exaggerated forms of behaviors that most people exhibit from time to time. In other words, most of us worry that we will regret throwing something away. Likewise, most people prefer to be clean and experience some degree of concern about exposure to pathogens. Thus, the problem in OCD is that normal aversions are taken to extremes (Deacon & Olatunji, 2007). Experimental studies in which people with and without OCD are exposed to the same kinds of potentially disgusting and anxiety-inducing stimuli have demonstrated this to be true (Olatunji et al., 2007).

But where does the tendency of individuals with OCD toward extreme responses come from? Studies have shown that early autoimmune system diseases, early strep infections, and changes in the brain caused by infection may predispose a person to develop OCD (Swedo & Grant, 2004). Several twin and family studies suggest that a genetic factor is involved in the development of OCD as well (Hur, 2009; Kirvan et al., 2006). Genes affecting serotonin functioning are suspected of causing OCD in some people, many of whom are helped by antidepressant drugs that increase serotonin levels in the brain (Ravindran et al., 2009).

REMEMBER IT   *Check your answers and take additional quizzes in MyPsychLab.com.*   ✔—Study and Review in MyPsychLab

1. Agoraphobia may occur with or without _____.
2. Fear of public speaking is a(n) _____ phobia, while fear of heights is a(n) _____ phobia.
3. Some therapists use _____ to help people with phobias learn to associate pleasant stimuli with feared objects.
4. Biological factors such as autoimmune diseases contribute to the development of _____.

Depressive and Bipolar Disorders

Actor and comedian Jim Carrey is known for his exaggerated humorous facial expressions and slapstick humor, so few people would guess that he has struggled with periods of profound sadness at various points during his successful show business career. A sense of sadness that is severe enough to interfere with a person's work is one of several **depressive disorders**, a group of psychological disorders that are characterized by extreme and unwarranted feelings of sadness. By contrast, **bipolar disorders** involve rapid and profound shifts in mood from deep sadness to extreme elation. Of course, everyone experiences ups and downs, but true depressive and bipolar disorders involve emotional experiences that are characterized by the criteria for abnormality you read about at the beginning of the chapter. In other words, people with these disorders have symptoms that are severe enough to interfere with their normal functioning.

Major Depressive Disorder ▶

People with **major depressive disorder** feel an overwhelming sadness, despair, and hopelessness, and they usually lose their ability to experience pleasure. They may have changes in appetite, weight, or sleep patterns; loss of energy; and difficulty in thinking or concentrating. Key symptoms of major depressive disorder are psychomotor disturbances (Bhalla, Moraille-Bhalla, & Aronson, 2010). For example, body movements, reaction time, and speech may be so slowed that some depressed people seem to be doing everything in slow motion. Others experience the opposite extreme and are constantly moving and fidgeting, wringing their hands, and pacing. The more deeply a person descends into depression over an extended period, the more she or he withdraws from social activities (Judd et al., 2000).

According to the American Psychiatric Association (2000a), one year after their initial diagnosis of major depressive disorder, 40% of people diagnosed with depression are without symptoms; 40% still have the disorder; and 20% are depressed, but not enough to warrant a diagnosis of major depression. For many, recovery is aided by antidepressant drugs. However, some studies show that psychotherapy can be just as effective (Hollon, Thase, & Markowitz, 2002). Some people have only one major depressive episode, but nearly 50% will have a recurrence (Halverson, 2012). Risk of recurrence is greatest for females and for individuals with an onset of depression before age 15 (Halverson, 2012). Recurrences may be frequent or infrequent, and for 20% of people with depression, the episodes are chronic, lasting one year or longer. Thus, finding a way to prevent recurrences is important in depression research. Most researchers suggest that medication, psychotherapy, social support, and even physical exercise may all play some role in the prevention of recurrent episodes of depression (Halverson, 2012).

Bipolar Disorders ▶

As we noted at the beginning of this section, *bipolar disorders* are conditions in which individuals exhibit emotional highs and lows that are extreme in nature. Most individuals with these disorders experience relatively normal periods in between. The "highs" of the bipolar disorders are called **manic episodes** and are marked by excessive euphoria, inflated self-esteem, wild optimism, and hyperactivity. People who exhibit manic episodes that lead to self-destructive behavior that is out of touch with reality are diagnosed with *bipolar I disorder*, such as a man who withdraws all of his money from the bank and flies off to a foreign country to invest in a real estate development he read about on the Internet because he is certain that doing so will make him a billionaire. Quite often, such individuals must be hospitalized during manic episodes to protect them and others from the disastrous consequences of their poor judgment. Those whose manic episodes are milder and do not lead to dysfunctional behavior of this kind are diagnosed with *bipolar II disorder*.

Bipolar disorders are much less common than depressive disorders, affecting about 2.6% of the U.S. population in any given year, and the lifetime prevalence rates are about the same for males and females (NIMH, 2013). Bipolar disorders tend to

depressive disorders Disorders characterized by extreme and unwarranted disturbances in emotion or mood.

bipolar disorder A mood disorder in which manic episodes alternate with periods of depression, usually with relatively normal periods in between.

⌐ 12.7 What are the characteristics
⌊ of major depressive disorder?

major depressive disorder A mood disorder marked by feelings of great sadness, despair, and hopelessness as well as the loss of the ability to experience pleasure.

⌐ 12.8 What kinds of mood
changes do people with bipolar
⌊ disorder experience?

manic episode (MAN-ik) A period of excessive euphoria, inflated self-esteem, wild optimism, and hyperactivity, often accompanied by delusions of grandeur and by hostility if activity is blocked.

appear in late adolescence or early adulthood. About 90% of those with the disorder have recurrences, and about 50% experience another episode within a year of recovering from a previous one. The good news is that 70 to 80% of people with a bipolar disorder return to a state of emotional stability (American Psychiatric Association, 2000a), even though mild cognitive deficits, such as difficulty with planning, persist in many with bipolar I disorder following a manic episode (Chowdhury, Ferrier, & Compson, 2003). Still, in many cases, individuals with bipolar I disorder can manage their symptoms, and thereby live a normal life, with the help of drugs such as lithium and divalproex. Moreover, psychotherapy can help them cope with the stress of facing life with a potentially disabling mental illness (Hollon et al., 2002).

By contrast, bipolar II disorder tends to be chronic and more resistant to treatment than bipolar I disorder (Federman, 2012; Judd et al., 2003). This may be so because individuals with bipolar II disorder manic episodes are far less debilitating than those of people with bipolar I. As a result, individuals with the disorder may find it difficult to accept that they have a problem that requires treatment (Federman, 2012). Moreover, in bipolar II disorder, periods of depressed mood are more frequent than episodes of hypomania are. As a result, bipolar II is often misdiagnosed as major depressive disorder, making it less likely that those who have it will receive appropriate treatment (Judd et al., 2003). ◉

◉─Watch the Video *Bipolar Disorder* on **MyPsychLab**

12.9 What are some risk factors for mood disorders?

Explaining Depressive and Bipolar Disorders

Many factors contribute to the development of depressive and bipolar disorders. Biological factors appear to be central. However, an individual's life circumstances are important as well, along with cultural factors and gender roles.

Neurological Correlates of Mood Disorders. PET scans and MRI studies have revealed abnormal patterns of brain activity in people with depressive and bipolar disorders (Drevets, Price, & Furey, 2008; Victor et al., 2012). Drevets and others (1997) located a brain area that may trigger both the sadness of major depression and the mania of bipolar disorder. A small, thimble-size patch of brain tissue in the lower prefrontal cortex (about 2 to 3 inches behind the bridge of the nose) is a striking 40 to 50% smaller in people with major depression. Earlier research established that this area of the brain plays a key role in the control of emotions.

Moreover, the personality trait called *neuroticism* (see Chapter 11) is associated with both depression and abnormalities in the brain's serotonin levels (Fanous et al., 2002; Lesch, 2003). Research has shown that abnormal levels of serotonin are strongly linked to depression and to suicidal thoughts (Oquendo et al., 2003; Roiser et al., 2012). Thus, individuals who are at the neurotic end of the Big Five personality dimension of neuroticism may be predisposed to develop depression and to have suicidal thoughts.

Researchers have also found that the production, transport, and reuptake patterns for dopamine, GABA, and norepinephrine in people with depressive and bipolar disorders differ from those in other individuals (Kaladindi & McGuffin, 2003). Neurotransmitter abnormalities may reflect genetic variations, thus helping to explain the significant heritability rates for mood disorders.

Heredity. Evidence for a genetic basis for bipolar disorder is also strong. In one twin study, researchers found that 50% of the identical twins of people with bipolar disorder had also been diagnosed with a depressive or bipolar disorder, compared to only 7% of fraternal twins (Kalidindi & McGuffin, 2003). Mounting evidence indicates that the genetic and neurological bases of bipolar disorder are different from those of major depressive disorder (Molnar et al., 2003). These findings may explain why biological relatives of people with bipolar disorder are at increased risk of developing a number of mental disorders, while relatives of those with major depressive disorder display an increased risk only for that disorder (Kaladindi & McGuffin, 2003).

Stressors. Life stresses are also associated with depression. The vast majority of first episodes of depression strike after major life stress (Brown, Harris, & Hepworth, 1994; Frank et al., 1994; Tennant, 2002). A classic longitudinal study of Harvard graduates that continued for over 40 years found that negative life events as well as family history played significant roles in the development of mood disorders (Cui & Vaillant, 1996). This seems particularly true of women, who are more likely to have experienced a severe negative life event just prior to the onset of depression (Welsh, 2009). Yet, recurrences of depression, at least in people who are biologically predisposed, often occur without significant life stress (Monroe & Reid, 2009).

Culture. How is it possible to study depressive and bipolar disorders—or any mental disorder, for that matter—across cultures, since cultural context must be taken into consideration when defining abnormality? Indeed, it is extremely difficult to construct surveys or other instruments for measuring mental disorders that are valid in a variety of cultures (Girolamo & Bassi, 2003). Nevertheless, a few researchers have managed to produce a limited, but informative, body of data about cross-cultural differences in depressive and bipolar disorders (Girolamo & Bassi, 2003). According to surveys conducted by the World Health Organization, the lifetime risk for developing depression varies greatly around the world (Kessler et al., 2007; see Figure 12.2). Some researchers explain these differences as the result of cross-cultural differences in ideal emotional states (Tsai, Knutson, & Fung, 2006). The experience of depression in individuals who live in non-Asian cultures appears to be influenced by those cultures' ideas about how people *ought* to feel, a phenomenon that psychologist Daniel Gilbert (2006) claims to be an important factor in individual differences in happiness (see the *Explain It* feature, p. 406).

Gender. In most countries, the rate of depression for females is about twice that for males (World Health Organization, 2010). Before boys reach puberty, they are more likely than girls to be depressed, but a dramatic reversal of the gender-related depression rates takes place in adolescence (Cyranowski et al., 2000). Not only are women more likely than men to have depression, but they are also more likely to be affected by negative consequences as a result. For example, early-onset major depressive disorder adversely affects the educational attainment and earning power of women, but not men (Berndt et al., 2000). The National Task Force on Women and Depression suggests that the higher rate of depression in women is largely due to social and cultural factors. In fulfilling her many roles—mother, wife, lover, friend, daughter, neighbor—a woman is likely to put the needs of others ahead of her own (Schmitt, Fuchs, & Kirch, 2008).

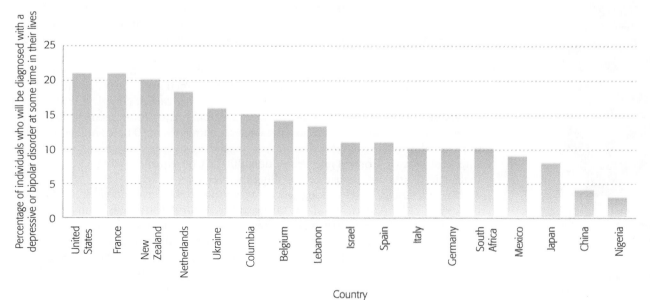

FIGURE 12.2 As you can see, rates of depressive and bipolar disorders vary widely across nations. *Source:* Kessler et al., 2007.

EXPLAIN IT

How Do Cultural Beliefs about Ideal Emotional States Lead to Depression?

Cross-cultural researchers' assert that cultural differences in beliefs about how people *ought* to feel might lead to cultural differences in depression rates. Think about how a thought pattern in which people measure their own emotional state against a cultural ideal might contribute to depression. For example, did you notice in Figure 12.2 that depression rates are much lower in Asian, African, and Latin American countries than they are in others? Some researchers attribute this finding to the belief of people in some cultures that they should be happy most of the time (Uchida, Norasakkunkit, & Kitayama, 2004). As a result, people in such cultures have difficulty coping with the unpleasant emotional states that are a part of everyday life and are at increased risk of depression. Moreover, say these researchers, people in these cultures devote their energies to pursuing achievements that they believe will ensure their future happiness. By contrast, researchers hypothesize that people in cultures with low rates of depressive disorders, such as Nigeria and China, focus more on maintaining a balance between positive and negative emotional states (Uchida et al., 2004). This belief leads people in these cultures to focus more energy on maintaining social connections that provide them with support in times of emotional distress than they do to the pursuit of happiness.

In his book *Stumbling on Happiness* psychologist Daniel Gilbert (2006) offered evidence in support of the view that people in Western cultures often base their life goals on beliefs about how they can attain lasting happiness. He points out that individuals in these societies are often disappointed when they make decisions based on overly optimistic predictions about what will make them happy (Gilbert, 2006). For example, soap operas, movies, and even ads for Valentine's Day cards and treats lead people to believe that their lives will be perfect if they find the right romantic partner. In search of that partner, many people date, marry, have affairs, divorce, date again, marry again, and so on. Why? Because the emotional perfection that they think will come to them as a result of each change in status never materializes. As a result, they perpetually predict that the next relationship will be the perfect one.

The other side of the unrealistic expectation coin is the overestimation of the emotional impact of an imagined loss (Kermer et al., 2006). Just as some people move from partner to partner in search of the perfect one, others stay in unsatisfactory relationships because they fear the emotional trauma that they expect to experience as a result of being alone. This kind of thought pattern leads people to avoid taking risks. As a result, they feel perpetually unhappy both because of the features of the relationships in which they choose to remain and because they are plagued by thoughts about the good outcomes that they might have experienced if they had the courage to take a risk. Here again, people's belief in the necessity of maintaining an ideal emotional state, as defined by Western culture, is the fundamental error in thinking that they are making, in Gilbert's view.

12.10 What are some of the risk factors for suicide?

Suicide and Race, Gender, and Age

Some people with depression commit the ultimate act of desperation—suicide. Depressive and bipolar disorders, as well as schizophrenia and substance abuse, are major risk factors for suicide in all age groups (NIMH, 2013). Suicide risk also increases when people are exposed to particularly troubling life stressors, such as the violent death of a spouse (Ajdacic-Gross et al., 2008). There is also evidence that suicidal behavior runs in families (Brent et al., 1996, 2002). Even among people who have severe disorders, such as bipolar disorder, those with a family history of suicide attempts are far more likely to kill themselves than are those without such history (Tsai et al., 2002).

About 32,000 suicides are reported annually in the United States. Figure 12.3 shows the differences in U.S. suicide rates according to race, gender, and age (NIMH, 2013). As you can see, White Americans are more likely than individuals in other ethnic groups to commit suicide. You will also note in Figure 12.3 that suicide rates are far lower for women than for men. However, studies show that women are four times more likely than men to attempt suicide (Anderson, 2002). The higher rate of completed suicides in males is due to the methods men and women use. Emergency room records show that the rate of firearms use by suicide attempters and completers is 10 times higher in males than in females, while the rates of poisoning and drug overdose are higher in females (Centers for Disease Control and Prevention, 2002). Consequently, a higher proportion of male suicide attempters succeed in killing themselves.

Although suicide rates among teens and young adults have increased in the past few decades, older Americans are at far greater risk for suicide than younger people. White males aged 85 and older have the highest recorded suicide rate, with more than 51 suicides for every 100,000 people in that age group, about five times the average national suicide rate of 12 per 100,000 (National Center for Health Statistics, 2006a; NIMH, 2013). Poor general health, serious illness, loneliness (often due to the death of a spouse), and decline in social and economic status are conditions that may push many older Americans, especially those aged 75 and older, to commit suicide.

▲ Evidence suggests that suicidal behavior tends to run in families. Les Franklin founded the Shaka Franklin Foundation for Youth, a suicide prevention organization, in memory of his son Shaka, who had killed himself. Ten years later, Franklin's other son, Jamon, also committed suicide.

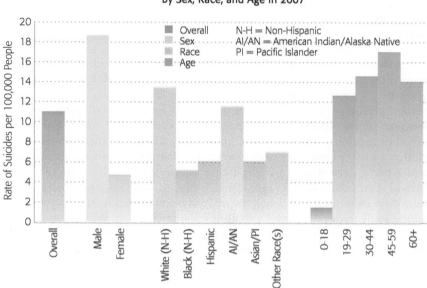

Rate of Suicides in the U.S.
by Sex, Race, and Age in 2007

FIGURE 12.3 **Differences in Suicide Rates According to Race, Gender, and Age**
The general conclusion from these data is that males are more likely to commit suicide than females and that White Americans are more likely to do so than are individuals in other groups.
Source: National Institute of Mental Health (2013).

About 90% of individuals who commit suicide leave clues (NIMH, 2009). They may communicate verbally: "You won't be seeing me again." They may provide behavioral clues, such as giving away their most valued possessions; withdrawing from friends, family, and associates; taking unnecessary risks; showing personality changes; acting and looking depressed; and losing interest in favorite activities. These warning signs should always be taken seriously. If you suspect you are dealing with a suicidal person, the best thing you can do is to encourage the person to get professional help. There are 24-hour suicide hotlines all over the country, and crisis intervention services are available on most college campuses. A call might save a life.

REMEMBER IT   *Check your answers and take additional quizzes in MyPsychLab.com.*   ✓•⌐Study and Review in MyPsychLab

1. Alternating periods of depression and _____ are the hallmark of bipolar disorder.
2. Some episodes of depression follow exposure to major _____.
3. For ethnic groups in the United States, suicide is most frequent among _____.

Schizophrenia

After high school, Tracy Moore enrolled in Musictech College in Minneapolis to pursue her goal of becoming a professional singer (Roberts, 2006). Soon Moore started hearing voices and became convinced that aliens were trying to take over her body, a condition referred to as **psychosis** among psychologists. Doctors determined that she had **schizophrenia**, a serious psychological disorder in which a person loses contact with reality. Medication relieved Moore's symptoms well enough that she was able to audition for the 2003 edition of *American Idol*. Today, Moore continues to sing, but she devotes most of her time to raising public awareness of schizophrenia and the remarkable capacity for resilience that is displayed by many who are afflicted with the disease.

Symptoms of Schizophrenia ▶

The *positive symptoms* of schizophrenia are the abnormal behaviors that are present in people with the disorder. (By the way, *positive* means "added" not "good.") One of the clearest positive symptoms of schizophrenia is the presence of **hallucinations**,

psychosis (sy-CO-sis) A condition characterized by loss of contact with reality.

schizophrenia (SKIT-soh-FREE-nee-ah) A severe psychological disorder characterized by loss of contact with reality, hallucinations, delusions, inappropriate or flat affect, some disturbance in thinking, social withdrawal, and/or other bizarre behavior.

⌐ **12.11** What are the positive and negative symptoms of schizophrenia?

hallucination An imaginary sensation.

▲ Tracy Moore's plans to become a professional singer were cut short by symptoms of schizophrenia when she was a college student. Still, once her doctors found an effective medication for her symptoms, she was able to fulfill her dream of auditioning for *American Idol.*

delusion A false belief, not generally shared by others in the culture.

delusion of grandeur A false belief that one is a famous person or a powerful or important person who has some great knowledge, ability, or authority.

delusion of persecution A false belief that some person or agency is trying in some way to harm one.

or imaginary sensations. People with schizophrenia may see, hear, feel, taste, or smell strange things in the absence of any stimulus in the environment, but hearing voices is the most common type of hallucination. People with schizophrenia also may experience exceedingly frightening and painful bodily sensations and feel that they are being beaten, burned, or sexually violated.

Having **delusions**, or false beliefs not generally shared by others in the culture, is another positive symptom of schizophrenia. Those who have **delusion of grandeur** may believe they are a famous person (the president or Moses, for example) or a powerful or important person who possesses some great knowledge, ability, or authority. Those with **delusion of persecution** have the false notion that some person or agency is trying to harass, cheat, spy on, conspire against, injure, kill, or in some other way harm them.

Another positive symptom is the loosening of associations, or *derailment,* that is evident when a person with schizophrenia does not follow one line of thought to completion but, on the basis of vague connections, shifts from one subject to another in conversation or writing. *Grossly disorganized behavior,* another positive symptom, can include such things as child-like silliness, inappropriate sexual behavior (masturbating in public), disheveled appearance, and peculiar dress. There may also be unpredictable agitation, including shouting and swearing, and unusual or inappropriate motor behavior, including strange gestures, facial expressions, or postures. People with schizophrenia may also display *inappropriate affect;* that is, their facial expressions, tone of voice, and gestures may not reflect the emotion that would be expected under the circumstances. A person might cry when watching a TV comedy and laugh when watching a news story about a fatal automobile accident.

A *negative symptom* of schizophrenia is a loss of or deficiency in thoughts and behaviors that are characteristic of normal functioning. Negative symptoms include social withdrawal, apathy, loss of motivation, lack of goal-directed activity, very limited speech, slowed movements, poor hygiene and grooming, poor problem-solving abilities, and a distorted sense of time (Davalos, Kisley, & Ross, 2002; Hatashita-Wong et al., 2002; Skrabalo, 2000). Many also have difficulty forming new memories and using memory strategies (Matthews & Barch, 2004; Peters et al., 2013). Some with schizophrenia have another negative symptom called *flat affect,* showing practically no emotional response at all, even though they often report feeling the emotion. These patients may speak in a monotone, have blank and emotionless facial expressions, and act and move more like robots than humans.

Not all people with schizophrenia have negative symptoms. Those who do seem to have the poorest outcomes (Guse et al., 2013). Negative symptoms are predictors of impaired overall social and vocational functioning. People who have negative symptoms tend to withdraw from normal social contacts and retreat into their own world. They have difficulty relating to people, and often their functioning is too impaired for them to hold a job or even to care for themselves.

12.12 What factors increase the risk of developing schizophrenia? ⊢ ⊣ **Explaining Schizophrenia**

Despite more than 100 years of research, the cause of schizophrenia remains a mystery. According to leading schizophrenia researcher Elaine Walker and her colleagues (2004), a key assumption underlying recent work on the puzzle of schizophrenia is that there is no single cause. Risk factors interact in complex ways such that an individual might have all of the relevant risk factors but never develop the disorder. Walker's model is shown in Figure 12.4 and includes several components. Walker and her team summarize these components as follows.

Constitutional Vulnerability. *Constitutional vulnerability* refers to the aspects of an individual's congenital (at birth) risk of developing schizophrenia that are attributable to factors within the person. One such factor is gender; that is, males are more likely to develop schizophrenia than females are. Moreover, scientists have known for some time that heredity contributes to schizophrenia (Cannon et al., 1998; Gottesman, 1991; Kendler & Diehl, 1993; Owen & O'Donovan, 2003). Figure 12.5 shows how

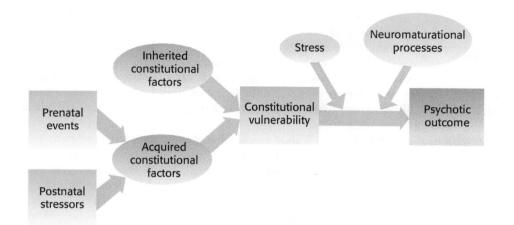

FIGURE 12.4 How Risk Factors Lead to Schizophrenia
This diagram shows how many researchers today view the risk factors for schizophrenia. The central concept is "constitutional vulnerability." Prenatal and postnatal factors derived from both heredity and environmental factors cause some people to be born with a greater sensitivity to stress than others. Stress and neuromaturational processes interact with constitutional vulnerability to produce the symptoms of schizophrenia.
Source: Walker et al. (2004).

the chance of developing schizophrenia varies with the degree of relationship to a person with schizophrenia. However, researchers do not yet know exactly what it is that vulnerable individuals inherit. It is possible that the genes that contribute to schizophrenia affect the structure of the developing fetal brain. On the other hand, they may shape later developmental processes or influence the actions of neurotransmitters such as dopamine in an individual's brain throughout life. Genes are also known to play a role in how well or how poorly individuals with schizophrenia respond to treatment with antipsychotic drugs (Yasui-Furukori et al., 2006).

Some aspects of constitutional vulnerability are acquired as a result of prenatal and/or postnatal experiences. These experiences include, for example, fetal exposure to maternal stress hormones and to substances such as alcohol and drugs that the mother ingests. They also include nutrients that the fetus receives from the mother as well as viruses and bacteria that cross the placenta. Postnatal stressors include birth trauma and other threats to the infant's health that occur during or immediately after birth.

Researchers have also examined the contribution of microorganisms to constitutional vulnerability. For example, schizophrenia is linked to the influenza virus (Perron et al., 2008). Recent studies suggest that the influenza virus activates a group of viruses called *HERV-W* that is dormant in all humans. The HERV-W viruses then trigger an inflammatory process in the brain that leads to schizophrenia. A number of investigations also suggest that the risk of schizophrenia is elevated in people with *cytomegalovirus*, a type of herpes virus, and *toxoplasmosis*, a condition caused by parasites in cat feces (Yolken & Torrey, 2008).

Stress. Walker and her colleagues point out that there is no evidence suggesting that individuals who develop schizophrenia experience more stress than others. Instead, researchers believe that the constitutional factors described previously cause some individuals to be

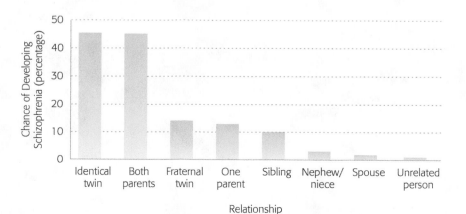

FIGURE 12.5 Genetic Similarity and Probability of Developing Schizophrenia
Research strongly indicates a genetic factor associated with schizophrenia. Identical twins have identical genes, and if one twin develops schizophrenia, the other twin has a 46% chance of also developing it. In fraternal twins, the chance is only 14%. A person with one schizophrenic parent has a 13% chance of developing schizophrenia, but a 46% chance if both parents are schizophrenic.
Source: Data from Nicol & Gottesman (1983).

more vulnerable to stress than others (Walker, Mittal, & Tessner, 2008). Thus, stress plays a role in the development of schizophrenia, but only among those who have the relevant constitutional vulnerability. Researchers hypothesize that the constitutional vulnerabilities of individuals who develop schizophrenia include some kind of neurological sensitivity to the biochemical changes that go along with being under stress. To use a crude analogy to illustrate this idea, stress hormones appear to flip switches in the brains of individuals who are constitutionally vulnerable to schizophrenia that they do not flip in the brains of others.

Neuromaturational Processes. Walker reports that many studies have shown that the brains of individuals with schizophrenia differ both structurally and functionally from those of people who do not have the disorder (Gee et al., 2012). For example, levels of neural activity in the frontal lobes tend to be lower in the brains of people with schizophrenia than they are in others (Glantz & Lewis, 2000; Kim et al., 2000). You may recall reading about the case of Phineas Gage in Chapter 2, the man whose personality changed drastically when his frontal lobes were damaged by an iron rod that shot through his skull. People with schizophrenia exhibit similar changes in their personalities. In addition, many individuals with schizophrenia have defects in the neural circuitry of the cerebral cortex and the limbic system, the parts of the brain that control thinking and feeling (Rasetti, et al., 2009). Further, on average, people with schizophrenia display slower than normal communication between the left and right hemispheres of the brain (Florio et al., 2002).

Because schizophrenia is most often diagnosed in the late teens and early twenties, the theoretical model in Figure 12.4 assumes that the neurological correlates of schizophrenia are somehow linked to the neuromaturational processes that normally occur during late adolescence. Once schizophrenia sets in, the progressive neurological deterioration that is part of the disorder itself also induces changes in the brain. These changes include decreases in gray matter (see Figure 12.6) and in overall brain size, along with deterioration of the cerebral cortex and the hippocampus. Thus, early diagnosis of the disorder plays a critical role in the prevention of schizophrenia-related brain damage (Dell'Osso et al., 2013).

According to Walker and her colleagues (2004), studies of the brains of individuals with schizophrenia after death have shown that the disease is associated with damage to the neurons themselves. Most such damage is found in the parts of the neurons that make up the brain's neurotransmitter system that you learned about in Chapter 2. Some researchers suggest that this damage leads to impaired communication between the emotional and intellectual parts of the brain. Others contend that the damaged neurons ineffectively govern the overall coordination of the brain's various functional subsystems.

FIGURE 12.6 Destruction of Gray Matter in the Brains of Adolescents Diagnosed with Schizophrenia
This figure dramatically depicts the devastating effects of schizophrenia on gray matter in the brains of people with the disorder. The images on the first line of this figure show the average gray matter deficits in the brains of 15 adolescents who ranged from 12 to 15 years of age who had just been diagnosed with schizophrenia. Those on the second line represent the amount of gray matter they had lost to the disease 5 years later.

Source: Thompson, P., Vidal, C., Giedd, J., Gochman, P., Blumenthal, J., Nicolson, R., Toga, A., & Rapoport, J. (2001). Mapping adolescent brain change reveals dynamic wave of accelerated gray matter loss in very early-onset schizophrenia. Proceedings of the National Academy of Sciences, 98, 11650-11655.

Early and *Late* Gray Matter Deficits in Schizophrenia

EARLIEST DEFICIT

5 YEARS LATER (SAME SUBJECTS)

Average Deficit
0%
-5%
-10%
-15%
-20%

Thompson et al., 2001

With regard to neurotransmitters themselves, Walker states that many studies suggest that dopamine plays an important role in schizophrenia, primarily because medications that are known to act on dopamine are usually helpful in the treatment of psychoses (Müller et al., 2006). However, the nature of the brain's neurotransmitter system is such that it is unlikely that deficiencies, excesses, or malfunctions that involve a single neurotransmitter can fully account for the complex features of schizophrenia. It is more likely, says Walker, that many other neurotransmitters, notably glutamate and GABA, also participate in the neurological processes that underlie the symptoms of schizophrenia.

REMEMBER IT

Check your answers and take additional quizzes in MyPsychLab.com.   ✔●┌Study and Review on MyPsychLab

1. Unusual experiences and behaviors, such as hallucinations and inappropriate sexual behavior, are _____ symptoms of schizophrenia.

2. The absence of a typical behavior, such as making eye contact with others, is a(n) _____ symptom of schizophrenia.

3. Researchers agree that there is no single cause of schizophrenia. (true/false)

Somatic Symptom, Dissociative, Gender, and Personality Disorders

In August 2005, a homeless man who could not remember who he was or how he had gotten to their city pleaded with Chicago police to help him determine his identity. He believed that his name was Jay Tower, but he knew nothing more about himself. The police helped the desperate man send his fingerprints to the FBI, but these efforts were to no avail. Months later, one of the residents who lived in the same homeless shelter as Tower recognized him in a picture that was shown on television program about missing persons in February, 2006. The report claimed that the man in the picture was Ray Power, a New York attorney who had disappeared on August 1, 2005. Apparently, Power was experiencing a form of amnesia known as *dissociative amnesia,* one of several disorders you will read about in this section.

Somatic Symptom Disorders ▶

Have you heard the word *psychosomatic* applied to a symptom or illness? Laypersons usually use this term to refer to physical disorders of psychological origin. The *DSM-5* uses the term *somatic symptom disorder* to refer to such conditions. The **somatic symptom disorders** involve physical symptoms that are due to psychological causes rather than any known medical condition. Although their symptoms are psychological in origin, patients are sincerely convinced that they spring from real physical disorders. People with somatic symptom disorders are not consciously faking illness to avoid work or other activities.

Some individuals with a somatic symptom disorder are overly concerned about their health and fear that their bodily symptoms are a sign of some serious disease. For example, such a person might interpret a simple case of indigestion as indicative of stomach cancer. Some may "doctor shop," going from one physician to another, seeking confirmation of their worst fears.

A person is diagnosed with a **conversion disorder** when there is a loss of motor or sensory functioning in some part of the body, which is not due to a physical cause but which solves a problem (Powsner & Dufel, 2009). For instance, debilitating headaches that are triggered by driving a car might provide a person who has a driving-related phobia with a socially acceptable reason for avoiding driving. A person may become blind, deaf, or unable to speak or may develop a paralysis in some part of the body. Many of Freud's patients would be diagnosed with conversion disorder today, and he believed that they unconsciously developed a physical disability to help resolve an unconscious sexual or aggressive conflict.

somatic symptom disorders Disorders in which physical symptoms are present that are due to psychological causes rather than any known medical condition.

conversion disorder A somatoform disorder in which a person suffers a loss of motor or sensory functioning in some part of the body; the loss has no physical cause but solves some psychological problem.

┌ **12.13** What are somatic
└ symptom disorders?

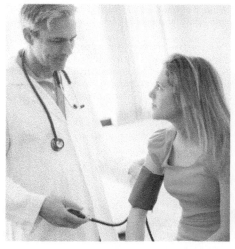

▲ A person who continually complains of various symptoms and seeks medical treatment for them, even though doctors can discover nothing wrong, may be have a somatic symptom disorder.

Research suggests that somatic symptom disorders result from the same kinds of neurological deficits that give rise to anxiety disorders (Bryant & Das, 2012). Experts point out that it is often difficult to distinguish them from diagnoses such as generalized anxiety disorder. Moreover, drugs that are effective for OCD and depression are often effective for somatic symptom disorders as well, another finding that supports the hypothesis that these disorders share a common origin.

Similarly, there is some degree of overlap with conversion disorder and the anxiety disorders (Bryant & Das, 2012). Psychologists think that a conversion disorder can act as an unconscious defense against any intolerable anxiety situation that the person cannot otherwise escape. For example, a soldier who desperately fears going into battle might escape the anxiety by developing a paralysis or some other physically disabling symptom. One reason for this hypothesis is that those with conversion disorder exhibit a calm and cool indifference to their symptoms, called "la belle indifference." Furthermore, many seem to enjoy the attention, sympathy, and concern their disability brings them.

12.14 How do dissociative disorders affect behavior?

Dissociative Disorders

Imagine how disconcerting it would be if you were unable to recognize your own leg. In his book *A Leg to Stand On,* neurologist Oliver Sacks (1984) described the case of a hospitalized man who could not feel or even recognize his own leg. This patient insisted that the leg wasn't even connected to his body, and his attempts to throw the leg out of his bed resulted in numerous falls. This unfortunate man was experiencing a profound disintegration of his physical and psychological self. Mental health professionals refer to this process as *dissociation*—the loss of one's ability to integrate all the components of self into a coherent representation of one's identity. In this case, the patient's dissociation was the result of an underlying physical illness. In many other instances, dissociation has a psychological rather than a physical cause.

In response to unbearable stress, some people develop a **dissociative disorder**, in which they lose the ability to consciously integrate their identities. Their consciousness becomes dissociated from their identity or their memories of important personal events, or both. For example, **dissociative amnesia** is a complete or partial loss of the ability to recall personal information or identify past experiences that cannot be attributed to ordinary forgetfulness or substance use. It is often caused by a traumatic experience—a psychological blow, so to speak—or a situation that creates unbearable anxiety, causing the person to escape by "forgetting."

Even more puzzling is the sub-type of dissociative amnesia called **dissociative fugue**, the disorder that afflicted Ray Power, whose story you read at the beginning of this section. In a fugue state, people not only forget their identity but, like Power, they also travel away from home. Some take on a new identity that is usually more outgoing and uninhibited than their former identity. The fugue state may last for hours, days, or even months. The fugue is usually a reaction to some severe psychological stress, such as a natural disaster, a serious family quarrel, a deep personal rejection, or military service in wartime. Fortunately for most people, recovery from dissociative fugue is rapid, although they may have no memory of the initial stressor that brought on the fugue state. When people recover from the fugue, they often have no memory of events that occurred during the episode.

In **dissociative identity disorder (DID)**, two or more distinct, unique personalities exist in the same individual, and there is severe memory disruption concerning personal information about the other personalities. The change from one personality to another often occurs suddenly and usually during stress. A common complaint is of "lost time"—periods for which a given personality has no memory because he or she was not in control of the body.

Many people with DID have early histories of severe physical and/or sexual abuse (Bremner & Vermetten, 2007). As a result, researchers and clinicians have long assumed that early trauma plays a critical role in the development of DID, an approach that is consistent with the psychoanalytic perspective. However, the connection between abuse and DID is not an absolute one (Brenner, 2009). That is, abuse does not lead to DID in every case, or even in most cases. Likewise, many cases of DID occur in individuals

dissociative disorder A disorder in which, under unbearable stress, consciousness becomes dissociated from a person's identity or her or his memories of important personal events, or both.

dissociative amnesia A dissociative disorder in which there is a complete or partial loss of the ability to recall personal information or identify past experiences.

dissociative fugue (FEWG) A dissociative disorder in which one has a complete loss of memory of one's entire identity, travels away from home, and may assume a new identity.

dissociative identity disorder (DID) A dissociative disorder in which two or more distinct, unique personalities occur in the same person, and there is severe memory disruption concerning personal information about the other personalities.

who do not have histories of abuse. Thus, other theories of the disorder have emerged. For example, research suggesting that individuals with sleep problems experience dissociative symptoms has led to a number of studies suggesting that disruptions of the sleep–wake cycle you read about in Chapter 4 are responsible for many cases of DID (van der Kloet et al., 2012). Another theory holds that DID has social and cognitive origins (Lynn et al., 2012). Advocates for this approach argue that people with DID develop the pattern of behaviors associated with the disorder in response to subtle suggestions made by therapists and/or to media depictions of DID. Theories aside, dissociative identity disorder can be treated successfully with psychodynamic, cognitive, and sleep-normalization therapies (Brand et al., 2012; van der Kloet et al., 2012).

Sexual Dysfunctions ▶

Most psychologists define **sexual dysfunctions** as persistent, recurrent, and distressing problems involving sexual desire, sexual arousal, or the pleasure associated with sex or orgasm (see Chapter 9). Drug treatments for sexual dysfunctions have been successful for both men and women. For men, the drug *sildenafil citrate (Viagra)* has been proven effective in restoring erectile function.

Another important aspect of treatment concerns the link between depression and sexual dysfunction in both men and women (Seidman, 2002). Depression is both a cause and an effect of sexual dysfunctions. Consequently, researchers advise health professionals to question people who complain of sexual difficulties about factors that may indicate the presence of depression. However, antidepressant drugs often increase the incidence of sexual difficulties (Lahon et al., 2011). Thus, experts advocate combined biochemical and psychological interventions that address both mood and sexual functioning for people with depression (Montejo et al., 2001).

Paraphilic disorders are conditions in which a person experiences recurrent sexual urges, fantasies, or behaviors involving children, other nonconsenting persons, nonhuman objects, or the suffering or humiliation of the individual or his or her partner. To be diagnosed as having a paraphilic disorder, the person must experience considerable psychological distress or an impairment in functioning in an important area of his or her life.

Personality Disorders ▶

Do you know someone who is impossible to get along with and who always blames others for his or her problems? Such a person may have a **personality disorder**—a long-standing, inflexible, maladaptive pattern of behaving and relating to others, which usually begins early in childhood or adolescence. About 9% of North Americans have one or more personality disorders (NIMH, 2013). People who have other disorders, especially depressive or bipolar disorders, are often diagnosed with personality disorders as well (Kopp et al., 2009; Valtonen et al., 2009). In most cases, the causes of personality disorders have yet to be identified.

People with personality disorders are extremely difficult to get along with and often blame others for their problems. As a result, most have unstable work and social histories. Because medications have not proved to be very useful in the treatment of personality disorders, treatment options are few. After all, to seek and benefit from therapy, a person must realize that he or she has a problem and be somewhat cooperative with the therapist.

As you can see in Table 12.3 on p. 414, several types of personality disorders exist. The three most common are *obsessive-compulsive personality disorder*, *narcissistic personality disorder*, and *borderline personality disorder* (Sansone & Sansone, 2011). Individuals with obsessive-compulsive personality disorder may become severely distressed if their normal routines are disrupted. People with narcissistic personality disorder demand attention and admiration from others and often exhibit overly dramatic responses to the everyday ups and downs of social relationships. Individuals with borderline personality disorder experience intense fears of abandonment and are especially prone to suicidal thoughts and to self-mutilation (Joiner et al., 2009). Many have histories of childhood abuse and experience intense fears of abandonment in adult relationships (Allen, 2008).

12.15 What are the characteristics of the various sexual disorders?

sexual dysfunctions Persistent, recurrent, and distressing problems involving sexual desire, arousal, or the pleasure associated with sex or orgasm.

paraphilic disorders Sexual disorders in which recurrent sexual urges, fantasies, or behavior involve nonhuman objects, children, other nonconsenting persons, or the suffering or humiliation of the individual or his or her partner.

12.16 What are the similarities and differences among the various personality disorders?

personality disorder A long-standing, inflexible, maladaptive pattern of behaving and relating to others, which usually begins in early childhood or adolescence.

TABLE 12.3 **Types of Personality Disorders**

PERSONALITY DISORDER	SYMPTOMS
Paranoid	Individual is highly suspicious, untrusting, guarded, hypersensitive, easily slighted, and lacking in emotion; holds grudges.
Schizoid	Individual isolates self from others; appears unable to form emotional attachments; behavior may resemble that of autistic children.
Schizotypal	Individual dresses in extremely unusual ways; lacks social skills; may have odd ideas resembling the delusions of schizophrenia.
Narcissistic	Individual has exaggerated sense of self-importance and entitlement; is self-centered, arrogant, demanding, exploitive, and envious; craves admiration and attention; lacks empathy.
Histrionic	Individual seeks attention and approval; is overly dramatic, self-centered, shallow, demanding, manipulative, easily bored, and suggestible; craves excitement; often, is attractive and sexually seductive.
Borderline	Individual is unstable in mood, behavior, self-image, and social relationships; has intense fear of abandonment; exhibits impulsive and reckless behavior and inappropriate anger; makes suicidal gestures and performs self-mutilating acts.
Antisocial	Individual disregards rights and feelings of others; is manipulative, impulsive, selfish, aggressive, irresponsible, reckless, and willing to break the law, lie, cheat, and exploit others for personal gain, without remorse; fails to hold jobs.
Obsessive-compulsive	Individual is concerned with doing things the "right" way and is generally a perfectionist; relationships are emotionally shallow.
Avoidant	Individual fears criticism and rejection; avoids social situations in order to prevent being judged by others.
Dependent	Person overly dependent on others for advice and approval; may cling to lovers and friends, fearing abandonment.

Studies of the prevalence of individual personality disorders show no consistent pattern as to which of the several disorders is most or least common (Sansone & Sansone, 2011). Moreover, prevalence rates for the various disorders have changed a great deal over the past few decades and vary widely from one culture to another (Sansone & Sansone, 2011). By contrast, the overall prevalence rate of the personality disorder category varies little around the average of 10%. These findings suggest that rates of the individual disorders depend largely on therapists varying interpretations of diagnostic criteria as well as cultural perceptions of behavior. Nevertheless, as a category of disorders, clinicians appear to agree that this group of disorders is distinctive from other types of mental problems and has identifiable patterns, such as inflexibility, that run through all of the individual disorders.

Personality disorders are especially resistant to treatment (Bienenfeld, 2013). They do not respond to treatment with medications, and many people with these disorders lack the insight into their own problems that is required to benefit from psychotherapy. Despite the apparently grim prognosis associated with personality disorders, research indicates that their features change over time. In one longitudinal study involving individuals who were diagnosed with personality disorders in adolescence, researchers found that, on average, these diagnoses were fairly stable over a 10-year period (Durbin & Klein, 2006). However, many individuals in the study no longer met the diagnostic criteria for personality disorders at the 10-year follow-up. Of course, these individuals may have been incorrectly diagnosed in the first place. However, the study also identified declines in specific features of these disorders, such as the high prevalence of neuroticism among individuals with personality disorders. Such trends support the view that, in some individuals, the psychological and behavioral factors that lead to a personality disorder diagnosis may be resolved to some degree or become less severe over time.

Because the characteristics involved in personality disorders closely resemble normal variations in personality, it is especially important when thinking about them to remember the criteria for abnormality discussed at the beginning of this chapter. So, if a friend suspects a neighbor of poisoning his cat, and you think this is an unreasonable suspicion, don't jump to the conclusion that your friend has paranoid personality disorder. This tendency toward suspiciousness is likely to be simply a personality trait of your friend.

REMEMBER IT   *Check your answers and take additional quizzes in MyPsychLab.com.*   ✔●┤Study and Review on MyPsychLab

1. _____ disorders involve physical symptoms that have psychological causes.
2. A person with _____ has two or more distinct personalities.
3. Match each personality disorder with its symptom.
    _____ (1) antisocial   _____ (2) paranoid   _____ (3) schizoid   _____ (4) borderline
    a. extreme suspiciousness   b. social isolation   c. intense fear of abandonment   d. cruelty to others

Childhood Disorders

You may have heard of Dr. Temple Grandin of Colorado State University. Dr. Grandin is known not only for her ground-breaking research on animal behavior but also for being "the most accomplished and well-known person with autism in the world" according to the CSU website. The story of Grandin's struggles with *autism spectrum disorder*, one of the disorders you will read about in this section, was told in her autobiography, *Thinking in Pictures: My Life with Autism*. When Grandin was 2, doctors described her as hopelessly brain-damaged and advised her mother to put her in an institution. Today, Dr. Grandin credits her achievements to her mother's refusal to heed the doctors' advice and her determination to find the best teachers and schools possible for her daughter.

Public health officials estimate that about 14% of children in the United States are living with a psychological disorder of some kind (National Institute of Mental Health [NIMH], 2013). Some of these children have been diagnosed with one of the disorders you have already read about. For example, the criteria for anxiety disorders, for example, are the same regardless of whether a case involves a child or an adult. However, there are also a few disorders that are unique to children or are first diagnosed in childhood. You learned about one such disorder in Chapter 7, intellectual disability. In this section, you will learn about three additional childhood disorders, *disruptive mood dysregulation disorder*, *autism spectrum disorder*, and *attention-deficit/hyperactivity disorder (ADHD)*.

▲ Temple Grandin, Ph.D., a professor of animal science at Colorado State University, was diagnosed with autism spectrum disorder at an early age. She attributes her success at overcoming the disorder to her mother's relentless efforts to teach her how to communicate with others.

Disruptive Mood Dysregulation Disorder ▶

Most children have temper tantrums at one time or another. However, some children exhibit severe tantrums and degrees of irritability that bring them to the attention of mental health professionals. Such children display fits of rage that are so frequent and intense that their ability to function in academic and social settings is seriously impaired (Stingaris, 2011; Wozniak et al., 2005). Because of variations in the disorders with which these children have been diagnosed, it is difficult to determine how many children exhibit such behavior. However, the authors of the *DSM-5* have sought to remedy this problem.

The Pediatric Bipolar Disorder Controversy. In the past, some professionals recommended that highly irritable children who exhibited episodes of destructive rage be diagnosed with *pediatric bipolar disorder (PBD)*. They argued that such children's fits of rage were equivalent to mania in adults. Critics of the PBD diagnosis argued that, while true bipolar disorders are stable over the lifespan, longitudinal studies show that children who are diagnosed with PBD rarely grow into adults who fit the criteria for either bipolar I or bipolar II disorder (Harris, 2005). In addition, some critics of PBD argued that the diagnosis caused many children to be unnecessarily treated with psychiatric drugs (Raven & Parry, 2012).

In response to concerns expressed by both sides in the BPD debate, the authors of the *DSM-5* created a new diagnosis, **disruptive mood dysregulation disorder (DMDD)**. Children with DMDD are highly irritable and have outbursts of temper

12.17 What kinds of problem behaviors do children with disruptive mood dysregulation disorder exhibit?

disruptive mood dysregulation disorders (DMDD) a disorder in which children are highly irritable and have frequent outbursts of temper that interfere with social and academic functioning.

three or more times a week that are inappropriate for the situations in which they occur to the extent that the tantrums interfere with their academic and social functioning. Such children may exhibit aggressive and destructive behavior in the midst of their tantrums. Preliminary studies suggest that the new diagnosis will reduce the number of children who are inappropriately diagnosed with bipolar disorder (Margulies et al., 2012). As a result, the number of children taking psychiatric drugs for the symptoms of extreme irritability and rage may also decline.

Describing, Explaining, and Treating Disruptive Mood Dysregulation Disorder. Children with DMDD are behind their peers in the development of emotion management strategies. For example, after a few minutes of anger and disappointment over a denied request, most children turn their attention to something else. By contrast, children with DMDD are likely to become so enraged that they are unable to distract themselves. Moreover, they are highly resistant to adults' efforts to calm them down and to draw their attention away from the rage-inducing stimulus. Because these episodes typically occur three or more times each week, the emotional ups and downs of children with DMDD often become the central focus of family and classroom life, leaving parents and teachers feeling powerless (West & Weinstein, 2012).

Some researchers assert that DMDD has genetic roots. The finding that many children with DMDD displayed difficult temperaments in infancy supports the genetic hypothesis (West, Schenkel, & Pavuluri, 2008). Studies showing that a child whose sibling has been diagnosed with DMDD has an elevated risk of receiving the diagnosis as well provide additional support (Papolos et al., 2009). Slower-than-average rates of growth in the parts of the brain that regulate emotions among children with DMDD may be the mechanism through which hereditary factors produce the symptoms of DMDD (Bitter et al., 2011). However, research demonstrating the effectiveness of behavior modification in treating the symptoms of DMDD suggests that learning may also be a contributing factor (West & Weinstein, 2012).

12.18 How does autism spectrum disorder affect children's development?

Autism Spectrum Disorder

The distinguishing feature of **autism spectrum disorder (ASD)** is a life-long inability to establish and maintain social relationships. Individuals with ASD have a limited understanding of the reciprocal, or "give-and-take," aspects of social relationships. In the United States, just over 1% of all children have some kind of ASD (Baio, 2012). The rates are similar in European countries (Lauritsen, Pedersen, & Mortensen, 2004).

autism spectrum disorder (ASD) a disorder in which a child lacks the ability to establish and maintain social relationships.

Variations in Social Functioning. Children with ASD whose functional capacities place them at the low end of the spectrum have limited or nonexistent language skills, lack the ability to engage in reciprocal social relationships, and have a severely limited range of interests. Most also have intellectual disabilities, and are easily distracted, slow to respond to external stimuli, and highly impulsive (Calhoun & Dickerson Mayes, 2005).

Many children with ASD are capable of some degree of verbal communication and have mild degrees of cognitive impairment. However, most such children never fully develop the ability to look at situations from other people's perspectives (Hughes, 2008). As a result, they typically fail to understand how their statements are perceived by listeners and are incapable of engaging in normal conversations. In addition, some utter repetitive phrases, often in robot-like fashion, that are inappropriate for the situation in which they occur.

The highest-functioning individuals with ASD, those who were diagnosed with *Asperger's Syndrome* under the *DSM-IV-TR* guidelines, have age-appropriate language and cognitive skills and often obtain high scores on IQ tests. However, they usually do not develop the capacity to understand others' thoughts, feelings, and motivations. As preschoolers, such children are often described as "late bloomers." Upon entering school, though, many begin to exhibit the unusual behaviors that most people associate with ASD. For example, they may become intensely focused on memorizing things that have little meaning to them, such as airline flight schedules. They may also engage in obsessive-compulsive behaviors, such as counting and recounting the number of squares on a checkered tablecloth. By school age, their inability to form friendships like those of other children their age is also quite apparent. As a result, most higher-functioning children with ASD are diagnosed in the early elementary school years.

Explaining and Treating Autism Spectrum Disorder. Autism spectrum disorder was once thought to be the result of poor parenting. However, it is now well established that this disorder is one of neurological origin (Kagan & Herschkowitz, 2005). Consequently, ASD is one of several disorders that are included in the *DSM-5* category of **neurodevelopmental disorders,** disorders with neurological causes that are diagnosed in childhood or adolescence. Nevertheless, there is no single brain anomaly or dysfunction that is associated with ASD. In a few cases, there are specific genetic defects that are known to lead to atypical neurological development and, in turn, to cause children to develop ASD. For instance, *fragile X syndrome*, which you may recall reading about in Chapter 2, can cause ASD. Importantly, too, there is no evidence to support the view that vaccines, or the preservatives they contain, increase a child's risk of developing autism spectrum disorder or any other type of neurodevelopmental disorder (Orenstein et al., 2013). Thus, for the most part, the cause of ASD remains a mystery (Kagan & Herschkowitz, 2005).

There is no cure for ASD. However, there are a few effective treatments that lessen the impact of them on children's lives, such as intensive social skills training and behavior modification for self-injurious behavior. Such treatments are most successful when they are initiated prior to a child's third birthday (Cohen, Amerine-Dickens, & Smith, 2006; Konstantareas, 2006; Luiselli & Hurley, 2005). But children who have ASD vary widely in how well they respond to these treatments. The key to success, say experts, is that treatments have to be individually tailored to each child's unique needs (Autism Society of America, 2006).

Attention-Deficit/Hyperactivity Disorder ▸

You have probably heard of **attention-deficit/hyperactivity disorder (ADHD),** a neurodevelopmental disorder that causes children to have difficulty attending to and completing tasks. Worldwide, experts estimate that 3 to 7% of children have ADHD (NIMH, 2001). Some studies indicate that the prevalence of ADHD is as high as 9% in the United States (NIMH, 2013).

Laboratory tests of attention often show that children diagnosed with ADHD do not differ from nondiagnosed children (Lawrence et al., 2004). Nevertheless, children with ADHD differ from peers with regard to their capacity to sustain attention when engaged in real-world tasks that are boring and repetitive. They also seem to be less able than other children of the same age to control impulses. For these reasons, children with ADHD may function well in home settings in which they have the freedom to move from one engaging activity to another. By contrast, when these children enter school, their inattentive, impulsive, and highly active behaviors stand out. Consequently, the diagnosis is most often made during the early school years.

Explaining and Treating ADHD. Twin and family studies show that ADHD is influenced by heredity (Polderman et al., 2009; Thapar, O'Donovan, & Owen, 2005). In addition, children who are born to women who smoke or use drugs while pregnant are at higher risk for the disorder than children who were not prenatally exposed to these substances. However, high IQ and intrinsic motivation are important protective factors for children who are at risk of developing ADHD (Chang & Burns, 2005). For these reasons, most experts believe that ADHD results from a complex interaction of risk and protective factors.

Attention-deficit/hyperactivity disorder is often successfully treated with amphetamines such as methylphenidate. In fact, more than half of the school children in the United States who are diagnosed with ADHD, just over 2 million children, take these

12.19 What are the features of attention-deficit/hyperactivity disorder?

attention-deficit/hyperactivity disorder (ADHD) a disorder characterized by inattention and difficulty completing tasks.

drugs (Bloom & Cohen, 2007). Placebo-controlled studies have consistently shown that the drugs have positive effects on the behavior of 70 to 90% of the children who take them (Ridderinkhof et al., 2005). However, training programs in which teachers and parents learn strategies for managing the behavior of children with ADHD are also effective at reducing these children's symptoms (Carr, 2009).

ADHD in Adulthood. A growing number of adults are being diagnosed with ADHD, a factor that led the authors of the *DSM-5* to expand the diagnostic criteria for the disorder to include adults (Friedman, Sadhu, & Jellnick 2012). Surveys show that about 4.4% of adults in the United States have the disorder (Kessler et al., 2006). However, the results of experimental studies regarding drug treatments for adult ADHD are mixed. Some studies suggest that the drugs that are effective for treating ADHD in children are equally so for adults (Adler et al., 2009). Others, by contrast, show that adults with ADHD are almost as likely to respond favorably to the placebos used in these studies as they are to respond favorably to authentic ADHD drugs (Carpentier et al., 2005). Consequently, more research is needed before researchers will know for certain whether drugs are the best treatment for ADHD in adults.

REMEMBER IT

Check your answers and take additional quizzes in MyPsychLab.com. ✓● ⌐Study and **Review** on **MyPsychLab**

1. Children with _____ exhibit extreme temper tantrums.
2. Individuals with _____ have limited ability to engage in social interactions.
3. Protective factors found in most high-functioning children with autism spectrum disorder include _____ and _____.
4. The main symptom of ADHD is _____.

⚙ Looking Back

In this chapter, you may have found similarities between your own behavior and the patterns associated with one or more psychological disorders. This phenomenon, known as *intern's syndrome,* is common among students of introductory psychology. You need only look at the discussion of the criteria used by mental health professionals to define abnormality at the beginning of the chapter to determine that unless your behavior is interfering with some important domain of functioning—school, work, relationships, and so on—it is probably not indicative of a psychological disorder. If you or someone close to you does have such a disorder, take heart from the many stories of resilience that we included and be aware that there are thousands more like these. There are many people who not only survive the experience of having a disorder or loving someone who does but also manage to grow stronger through the process.

CHAPTER 12 SUMMARY

DEFINING PSYCHOLOGICAL DISORDERS (pp. 393–397)

12.1 **What criteria do psychologists use to classify behavior as abnormal? (pp. 393–394)**

Behavior might be considered abnormal if it differs radically from what is considered normal in the person's own culture, if it leads to personal distress or impaired functioning, or if it results in the person's being a danger to self and/or others.

Key Term
psychological disorders, p. 393

12.2 How do clinicians use the DSM-5? (pp. 395–396)

Clinicians use the *DSM-5* to classify and keep track of psychological disorders. It includes diagnostic criteria for about 300 psychological disorders. They are organized into several major categories. Tracking studies show that psychological disorders are more prevalent than physical diseases. Nearly half of people are diagnosed with some kind of psychological disorder during their lifetimes. The two most prevalent categories are anxiety and mood disorders.

Key Term
DSM-5, p. 395

12.3 What are the five perspectives that psychologists use to explain psychological disorders? (pp. 396–397)

Five theoretical perspectives on the causes of psychological disorders are the biological perspective, the biopsychosocial perspective, the psychodynamic perspective, the learning perspective, and the cognitive perspective. The biological perspective emphasizes genetics and other physiological factors. The biopsychosocial focuses on interactions among biological, psychological, and social factors. Learning theorists explain psychological disorders as the result of experiences, while the cognitive perspective focuses on faulty thinking. The psychodynamic perspective is based on Freud's psychoanalytic theory and emphasizes unconscious processes.

ANXIETY DISORDERS (pp. 397–402)

12.4 What are the characteristics of panic attacks, agoraphobia, and panic disorder? (pp. 398–399)

People who have panic attacks respond to ordinary changes in the body as though they were life threatening. The symptoms of panic attacks include intense fear, rapidly beating heart, and other signs of physiological distress. Repeated panic attacks can lead to agoraphobia, the fear of being in places from which escape is difficult. Panic disorder occurs when panic attacks are so frequent that they interfere with a person's social, occupational, and/or academic functioning.

Key Terms
anxiety disorders, p. 398
panic attack, p. 398
agoraphobia, p. 398
panic disorder, p. 399

12.5 How do generalized anxiety disorder, social anxiety disorder, and specific phobia differ? (pp. 399–401)

Generalized anxiety disorder (GAD) involves chronic, excessive worry. Social anxiety disorder (social phobia) arises out of the fear of embarrassment, whereas specific phobias represent irrational fear responses to objects or situations. The Big

Five personality traits contribute to the development of GAD and phobias. People who are high in the trait of neuroticism are more likely to develop them.

Key Terms
generalized anxiety disorder, p. 399
social anxiety disorder (social phobia), p. 399
phobia, p. 400
specific phobia, p. 400

12.6 What are the symptoms of obsessive-compulsive disorder? (pp. 401–402)

Obsessive-compulsive disorder is characterized by recurrent obsessions (persistent, involuntary thoughts, images, or impulses that cause great distress) and/or compulsions (persistent, irresistible, irrational urges to perform an act or ritual repeatedly). Early infections and a tendency to exhibit exaggerated responses to stimuli that are universally undesirable contribute to the development of obsessive-compulsive disorder.

Key Terms
obsessive-compulsive disorder (OCD), p. 401
obsession, p. 401
compulsion, p. 402

DEPRESSIVE AND BIPOLAR DISORDERS (pp. 403–407)

12.7 What are the characteristics of major depressive disorder? (pp. 403–403)

Major depressive disorder is characterized by feelings of great sadness, despair, and hopelessness, as well as a loss of the ability to feel pleasure. Other symptoms include psychomotor disturbance and, possibly, psychotic depression.

Key Terms
depressive disorders, p. 403
bipolar disorders, p. 403
major depressive disorder, p. 403

12.8 What kinds of mood changes do people with bipolar disorders experience? (pp. 403–404)

Bipolar disorder is a mood disorder in which a person has manic episodes (periods of wild optimism, inflated self-esteem, excessive euphoria, and hyperactivity) that alternate with periods of major depression.

Key Term

manic episode, p. 403

12.9 What are some risk factors for depressive and bipolar disorders? (pp. 404–406)

Risk factors for depressive and bipolar disorders include (1) a genetic predisposition; (2) disturbances in the brain's serotonin levels; (3) abnormal patterns in the neurotransmitters dopamine, GABA, and norepinephrine; (4) the personality trait of neuroticism; and (5) major life stress.

12.10 What are some of the risk factors for suicide? (pp. 406–407)

Depression, depressive and bipolar disorders, schizophrenia, and substance abuse are major risk factors for suicide. Other risk factors include particularly troubling life stressors and a genetic tendency to suicidal behavior. Elderly White males commit suicide more often than members of other race or age groups, perhaps because of poor health or loneliness. Research shows that women are more likely to attempt suicide, but men are more likely to be successful.

SCHIZOPHRENIA (pp. 407–411)

12.11 What are the positive and negative symptoms of schizophrenia? (pp. 407–408)

The positive symptoms of people with schizophrenia are abnormal behaviors and characteristics, including hallucinations, delusions, derailment, grossly disorganized behavior, and inappropriate affect. The negative symptoms of schizophrenia represent loss of or deficiencies in thoughts and behavior that are characteristic of normal functioning. They include social withdrawal, apathy, loss of motivation, lack of goal-directed activity, very limited speech, slowed movements, flat affect, poor problem-solving abilities, a distorted sense of time, and poor hygiene and grooming.

Key Terms

psychosis, p. 407
schizophrenia, p. 407

hallucination, p. 407
delusion, p. 408
delusion of grandeur, p. 408
delusion of persecution, p. 408

12.12 What factors increase the risk of developing schizophrenia? (pp. 408–411)

Theorists propose that schizophrenia arises from an interaction of constitutional vulnerability and external factors. Constitutional vulnerability includes heredity and prenatal risks, such as exposure to teratogens. Stress is an important external factor. Neuromaturational development is also believed to contribute to the finding that schizophrenia usually appears in the late adolescent or early adult years.

SOMATIC SYMPTOM, DISSOCIATIVE, SEXUAL, AND PERSONALITY DISORDERS (pp. 411–415)

12.13 What are somatic symptom disorders? (pp. 411–412)

Somatic symptom disorders involve physical symptoms that cannot be identified as any of the known medical conditions. Some people with somatic symptom disorders have a persistent fear that bodily symptoms are the sign of some serious disease, and conversion disorder involves a loss of motor or sensory functioning in some part of the body, which has no physical cause but does solve a psychological problem.

Key Terms

somatic symptom disorders, p. 411
conversion disorder, p. 411

12.14 How do dissociative disorders affect behavior? (pp. 412–413)

Dissociative disorders cause people to lose the ability to consciously integrate their identities in some important way. People with dissociative amnesia have a complete or partial loss of the ability to recall personal information or identify past experiences. In dissociative fugue, people forget their entire identity, travel away from home, and may assume a new identity somewhere else. In dissociative identity disorder, two or more distinct, unique personalities exist in the same person, and there is severe memory disruption concerning personal information about the other personalities.

Key Terms

dissociative disorder, p. 412
dissociative amnesia, p. 412
dissociative fugue, p. 412
dissociative identity disorder (DID), p. 412

12.15 What are the characteristics of the various sexual dysfunctions? (p. 413)

A sexual dysfunction is a problem with sexual desire, sexual arousal, or the pleasure associated with sex or orgasm. Paraphilias are disorders in which people have recurrent sexual urges, fantasies, and behaviors that involve children, other nonconsenting persons, nonhuman objects, or the suffering and humiliation of the individual or his/her partner.

Key Terms

sexual dysfunctions, p. 413
paraphilic disorders, p. 413

12.16 What are the similarities and differences among the various personality disorders? (pp. 413–415)

People with personality disorders have long-standing, inflexible, maladaptive patterns of behavior that cause problems in their social relationships and at work.

Key Term

personality disorder, p. 413

CHILDHOOD DISORDERS (pp. 415–418)

12.17 What kinds of problem behaviors do children with disruptive mood dysregulation disorder exhibit? (pp. 415– 416)

Children with DMDD are irritable and exhibit episodes of destructive rage. They resist adults' efforts to calm them down and are behind their peers in the development of emotion-management strategies. The disorder is related to difficult temperament in infancy. Behavior modification can reduce symptoms.

Key Term

disruptive mood dysregulation disorder (DMDD), p. 415

12.18 How does autism spectrum disorder affect children's development? (pp. 416–417)

ASD is a neurodevelopmental disorder that interferes with the development of communication skills and cause children to be unable to engage in normal social relationships. Low-functioning children with ASD do not have normal language

and usually have intellectual disabilities. High-functioning children have normal or high levels of intelligence and language but lack social communication skills.

Key Terms

autism spectrum disorder (ASD), p. 416
neurodevelopmental disorders, p. 417

12.19 What are the features of attention-deficit/hyperactivity disorder? (pp. 417–418)

ADHD is a neurodevelopmental disorder that includes restlessness and attentional problems. It is most likely to be diagnosed when children enter school. The effectiveness of medications for ADHD together with the ineffectiveness of behavioral interventions suggests that this disorder has a physiological basis.

Key Term

attention-deficit/hyperactivity disorder(ADHD), p. 417

Chapter 12 Study Guide

Answers to all the Study Guide questions are provided at the end of the book.

SECTION ONE: Chapter Review

Defining Psychological Disorders (pp. 393–397)

1. It is relatively easy to differentiate normal behavior from abnormal behavior. (true/false)

2. The *DSM-5* is a manual that is published by the American Psychiatric Association and is used to

    a. diagnose psychological disorders.
    b. explain the causes of psychological disorders.
    c. outline the treatments for various psychological disorders.
    d. assess the effectiveness of treatment programs.

3. Match the perspective with its suggested cause of abnormal behavior.
    _____ **(1)** faulty learning
    _____ **(2)** unconscious, unresolved conflicts
    _____ **(3)** genetic inheritance or biochemical or structural abnormalities in the brain
    _____ **(4)** faulty thinking
    a. psychodynamic   **b.** biological
    c. learning   **d.** cognitive

Anxiety Disorders (pp. 397–402)

4. Anxiety disorders are the least common of all psychological disorders. (true/false)

5. Psychologists often use principles of learning to treat specific phobias. (true/false)

6. Obsessive-compulsive disorder appears to be caused primarily by psychological rather than biological factors. (true/false)

7. Match the anxiety disorder with the example.
   _____ (1) Lana refuses to eat in front of others for fear her hand will shake.
   _____ (2) Ronin is excessively anxious about his health and his job, even though there is no concrete reason to be.
   _____ (3) Kyla has been housebound for four years.
   _____ (4) Jackson gets hysterical when a dog approaches him.
   _____ (5) Lauren has incapacitating attacks of anxiety that come on her suddenly.
   _____ (6) Michael repeatedly checks his doors, windows, and appliances before he goes to bed.
   a. panic disorder
   b. agoraphobia
   c. specific phobia
   d. generalized anxiety disorder
   e. social anxiety disorder (social phobia)
   f. obsessive-compulsive disorder

Depressive and Bipolar Disorders (pp. 403–407)

8. Monteil has periods in which he is so depressed that he becomes suicidal. At other times he is wildly euphoric. He would probably receive the diagnosis of
   a. antisocial personality disorder.
   b. dissociative fugue.
   c. bipolar disorder.
   d. major depressive disorder.

9. Match the type of factor with the proposed cause of depression.
   _____ (1) negative thoughts about oneself, the world, and one's future
   _____ (2) hereditary predisposition or biochemical imbalance
   _____ (3) negative life events
   a. stress
   b. cognitive factor
   c. biological factor

10. Drugs are seldom used in the treatment of depressive and bipolar disorders. (true/false)

11. The suicide rate is lower for
    a. males than for females.
    b. African American males than for White males.
    c. the elderly than for teenagers.
    d. people who have psychological disorders than for those who do not.

Schizophrenia (pp. 407–411)

12. Match the symptom of schizophrenia with the example.
    _____ (1) Brendon believes he is Moses.
    _____ (2) Dina thinks her family is spreading rumors about her.
    _____ (3) Avi hears voices cursing him.
    _____ (4) Dean laughs at tragedies and cries when he hears a joke.
    a. delusions of grandeur
    b. hallucinations
    c. inappropriate affect
    d. delusions of persecution

13. There is substantial research evidence that all of the following have roles as causes of schizophrenia *except*
    a. genetic factors.
    b. stress in people predisposed to the disorder.
    c. abnormal dopamine activity.
    d. unhealthy family interaction patterns.

Somatic Symptom, Dissociative, Sexual, and Personality Disorders (pp. 411–415)

14. Somatic symptom disorders have physiological rather than psychological causes. (true/false)

15. Dissociative disorders are often associated with trauma. (true/false)

16. Match the psychological disorder with the example.
    _____ (1) Jan is convinced he has some serious disease, although his doctors can find nothing physically wrong.
    _____ (2) Lonnie is found far away from his home town, calling himself by another name and having no memory of his past.
    _____ (3) Natalia suddenly loses her sight, but doctors can find no physical reason for the problem.
    _____ (4) Colane has no memory of being in the boat with other family members the day her older brother drowned.
    _____ (5) Cassandra has no memory for blocks of time in her life and often finds clothing in her closet that she cannot remember buying.
    a. dissociative identity disorder
    b. dissociative fugue
    c. dissociative amnesia
    d. somatic symptom disorder
    e. conversion disorder

17. (Sexual dysfunctions, Paraphilias) are disorders in which sexual urges, fantasies, and behaviors involve children, other nonconsenting partners, or objects.

18. Which statement is true of personality disorders?
    a. Personality disorders usually begin in adulthood.
    b. Persons with these disorders usually realize that they have a problem.
    c. Personality disorders typically cause problems in social relationships and at work.
    d. Persons with these disorders typically seek professional help.

19. Bruce lies, cheats, and exploits others without feeling guilty. His behavior best fits the diagnosis of _____ personality disorder.
    a. avoidant
    b. histrionic
    c. antisocial
    d. narcissistic

Childhood Disorders (pp. 415–418)

20. The new diagnosis of disrupted mood dysregulation disorder (DMDD) may reduce the rates of children who are inappropriately diagnosed with
    a. ADHD.
    b. pediatric bipolar disorder.
    c. generalized anxiety disorder.
    d. somatic symptom disorder.

21. A child who has difficulty forming and maintain relationships, fails to develop language skills, and becomes attached to objects may be diagnosed with
    a. major depressive disorder.
    b. ADHD.
    c. DMDD.
    d. autism spectrum disorder.

22. Autism spectrum disorder and attention-deficit/hyperactivity disorder are
    a. depressive disorders.
    b. neurodevelopmental disorders.
    c. anxiety disorders.
    d. personality disorders.

SECTION TWO: Identifying the Disorder

Name the disorder characterized by each set of symptoms.

Symptoms   **Disorder**

1. Markedly diminished interest or pleasure in all or most activities, combined with psychomotor disturbances, fatigue, insomnia, feelings of worthlessness, and recurrent thoughts of death

2. Grossly disorganized behavior combined with inappropriate affect, disturbed speech and loose associations, and delusions of grandeur—for example, a belief that one is working for a secret government agency and is being followed by foreign spies

3. Intense mood swings, ranging from euphoric and hyperactive highs marked by delusions of grandeur to extreme depression

4. Intense fear of being in a situation from which immediate escape is not possible or help is not available in the case of panic

5. Complete loss of the ability to recall personal information or past experiences, with no physical explanation for the problem

6. A pattern of unstable and intense interpersonal relationships combined with impulsivity, inappropriate and intense anger, a poor self-image, and recurrent thoughts of suicide

7. Problems involving sexual desire, sexual arousal, or the pleasure associated with sex or orgasm

8. Spending excessive amounts of time engaged in daily rituals such as counting and cleaning, accompanied by obsessions

9. Explosive and destructive fits of rage exhibited by a child

SECTION THREE: Comprehensive Practice Test

1. Which perspective sees abnormal behavior as a symptom of an underlying physical disorder?
   a. cognitive
   b. psychodynamic
   c. biological
   d. behavioral

2. Which perspective sees abnormal behavior as the result of faulty and negative thinking?
   a. psychodynamic
   b. cognitive
   c. behavioral
   d. biological

3. Which perspective sees abnormal behavior as the result of early childhood experiences and unconscious sexual and aggressive conflicts?
   a. cognitive
   b. biological
   c. humanistic
   d. psychodynamic

4. Which perspective sees psychological disorders as resulting from both physical and psychological causes?
   a. cognitive
   b. biopsychosocial
   c. biological
   d. behavioral

5. Psychosis is a loss of contact with reality. (true/false)

6. Panic disorder, specific phobia, and obsessive-compulsive disorder are all examples of _____ disorders.
   a. neurotic
   b. anxiety
   c. personality
   d. somatic symptom

7. Dawn is convinced that she has a disease and goes from one doctor to another searching for a diagnosis; however, every doctor she consults says there is nothing physically wrong with her. Dawn is suffering from
   a. somatic symptom disorder.
   b. dissociative identity disorder.
   c. a conversion disorder.
   d. body dysmorphic disorder.

8. Dissociative amnesia, characterized by loss of memory of one's identity, is generally brought on by physical trauma. (true/false)

9. A common early experience of people with dissociative identity disorder is
   a. drug use by their mother while pregnant.
   b. measles or mumps when young.
   c. parental divorce.
   d. early physical and/or sexual abuse.

10. Hallucinations, delusions, and disorganized thinking and speech are _____ symptoms of schizophrenia.
    a. negative
    b. positive
    c. dissociative
    d. obsessive

11. Thao's belief that he is a secret agent for the devil is a good example of a delusion. (true/false)

12. A patient who sits completely still for hours as if he were in a stupor and sometimes experiences periods of great agitation and excitement is suffering from _____ schizophrenia.
    a. disorganized
    b. undifferentiated
    c. paranoid
    d. catatonic

13. Which of these is a symptom of autistic spectrum disorder?
    a. periods of deep despair
    b. hallucinations
    c. inability to understand others' thoughts and feelings
    d. fear of public speaking

14. Major depressive disorder is diagnosed more often in women than in men. (true/false)

15. _____ is characterized by periods of inflated self-esteem, wild optimism, and hyperactivity known as manic episodes.
    a. Schizophrenia
    b. Major depressive disorder
    c. Borderline personality disorder
    d. Bipolar disorder

16. The risk of suicide is especially high in individuals who have
    a. schizophrenia.   b. paraphilias.
    c. depression.   d. specific phobia.

17. Psychological disorders are more common than some physical diseases. (true/false)

18. Depressive and bipolar disorders seems to be the result of
    a. biological factors only.
    b. both biological and environmental factors.
    c. environmental factors only.
    d. poor parenting in early childhood.

SECTION FOUR: Critical Thinking

1. Some psychological disorders are more common in women (depression, agoraphobia, and simple phobia), and some are more common in men (antisocial personality disorder and substance abuse). Give some possible reasons for such gender differences in the prevalence of these disorders. Support your answer.

2. There is continuing controversy over whether specific psychological disorders are chiefly biological in origin (nature) or result primarily from learning and experience (nurture). Select any two disorders from this chapter, and prepare arguments for both the nature and nurture positions for both disorders.

SECTION FIVE: Application Essays

1. Use the Internet or go to a bookstore to do a survey of the types of disorders that are addressed in self-help books. In your essay, summarize the results of your survey and, using the information in this chapter, explain why such books are more common for some disorders than for others.

2. Formulate a specific plan that will help you recognize and avoid the five cognitive traps that contribute to unhealthy thinking. You might enlist the help of a friend to monitor your negative statements.

Apply your critical thinking skills with MyPsychLab Writing Assignments

Submit your answer to the following question inside the MyPsychLab Writing Assessment program for immediate feedback.

Why do most researchers consider schizophrenia a brain disorder? What evidence suggests that schizophrenia could begin in the womb?

Therapies 13

THINK ABOUT IT

Do you believe that you have to get good grades to be a "good person"? Or perhaps you believe that no matter what you do you are destined to get mediocre or even failing grades. Either way, unrealistic expectations for success or failure may be causing you some unpleasant feelings or perhaps even setting you up for a case of depression. A brief exercise can help you determine the extent to which such thinking may be compromising your mental health. First, identify an unrealistic expectation that you have for your own behavior or for some future outcome. Perhaps you think you can't be happy until you find "Mr. Right" or "Ms. Right." Or you may think it is impossible to achieve your ideal body image. Once you've identified the expectation, read and answer the following questions about it:

- Where does this belief come from? Can you identify the time in your life when it began?

- Why do you think this belief is true? What evidence can you think of that "proves" your belief?

- Can you think of any evidence to suggest that this belief is false? What evidence contradicts your belief? Do you know anyone who does not cling to this belief?

- How does holding this belief affect your life, both negatively and positively?

- How would your life be different if you stopped holding this belief? What would you do differently?

You have just completed an "assignment" that a *cognitive behavioral therapist* might give you to help you gain insight into and better control over thoughts that trigger feelings and behavior that you would like to change. But before we give you the details about cognitive behavior therapy, we will introduce you to a few other types of *psychotherapy*. The practice of psychotherapy has grown and changed enormously since its beginnings more than 100 years ago, when Freud and his colleagues began using it. Drug therapies and other physically based approaches to treatment are also far more important today than they were in Freud's time. 👁

👁 **Watch** the Video *Episode 17: Basics: Therapies in Action* in **MyPsychLab**

psychotherapy Any type of approach that uses psychological rather than biological means to treat psychological disorders.

insight therapies Approaches to psychotherapy based on the notion that psychological well-being depends on self-understanding.

13.1 What are the basic techniques of psychodynamic therapies?

psychodynamic therapies Psychotherapies that attempt to uncover repressed childhood experiences that are thought to explain a patient's current difficulties.

psychoanalysis (SY-ko-uh-NAL-ul-sis) The first psychodynamic therapy, which was developed by Freud and uses free association, dream analysis, and transference.

free association A psychoanalytic technique used to explore the unconscious by having patients reveal whatever thoughts, feelings, or images come to mind.

transference An emotional reaction that occurs during psychoanalysis, in which the patient displays feelings and attitudes toward the analyst that were present in another significant relationship.

Insight Therapies

Do you recall a form of learning called *insight* that you read about in Chapter 5? Insight is a form of learning that is the foundation of several approaches to **psychotherapy**, treatments that use psychological rather than biological means to treat emotional and behavioral disorders. These approaches, fittingly enough, are collectively referred to as **insight therapies** because their assumption is that psychological well-being depends on self-understanding—the understanding of one's own thoughts, emotions, motives, behavior, and coping mechanisms.

Psychodynamic Therapies

Psychodynamic therapies attempt to uncover repressed childhood experiences that are thought to explain a client's current difficulties. The techniques associated with the first such therapy—Freud's **psychoanalysis**—are still used by some psychodynamic therapists today (Josephs & Weinberger, 2013). One such technique is **free association**, in which the client is asked to reveal whatever thoughts, feelings, or images come to mind, no matter how trivial, embarrassing, or terrible they might seem. The analyst then pieces together the free-flowing associations, explains their meanings, and helps clients gain insight into the thoughts and behaviors that are troubling them. Some individuals may avoid revealing certain painful or embarrassing thoughts while engaging in free association, a phenomenon Freud called *resistance*. Resistance may take the form of halting speech during free association, "forgetting" appointments with the analyst, or arriving late.

Dream analysis is another technique used by psychoanalysts. Freud believed that areas of emotional concern repressed in waking life are sometimes expressed in symbolic form in dreams. He claimed that patient behavior may have a symbolic quality as well. At some point during psychoanalysis, Freud said, the patient reacts to the analyst with the same feelings that were present in another significant relationship—usually with the mother or father. This reaction of the patient is called **transference**. Freud believed that encouraging patients to achieve transference was an essential part of psychotherapy. He claimed that transference allows the patient to relive troubling experiences from the past with the analyst as a parent substitute, thereby resolving any hidden conflicts.

Object relations therapists represent a somewhat different take on classical psychoanalysis. From their perspective, the main goal of the personality is to forge functional links between the self (the subject) and others in the environment (the objects). The techniques that object relations therapists use are based on the notion that the emotional features of our early relationships become blueprints for future relationships. Thus, if our early relationships involve passive acceptance of another's abusive behavior, then we will follow that pattern in our adult relationships. When faced with clients who are involved in potentially damaging relationships, an object relations therapist would attempt to get them to identify the early relationships they are attempting to act out in the context of their current relationships. In addition, an object relations therapist would help the client change the maladaptive behavior patterns that arise when he or she uses current relationships to act out conflicts that originated in earlier relationships (Martinez, 2006).

Many therapists today practice brief psychodynamic therapy, in which the therapist and client decide on the issues to explore at the outset rather than waiting for them to emerge in the course of treatment (Messer, Sanderson, & Gurman, 2013). The therapist assumes a more active role and places more emphasis on the present than in traditional psychoanalysis. Brief psychodynamic therapy may require only one or two visits per week for as few as 12 to 20 weeks. In a meta-analysis of 46 well-controlled studies, Town and his colleagues (2012) found evidence suggesting that brief psychodynamic therapy is effective. Other studies have also shown that brief psychodynamic therapy is comparable to other forms of psychotherapy in terms of successful outcomes (Crits-Christoph et al., 2008). Brief psychodynamic psychotherapy appears to be most effective with clients who do not have multiple psychological disorders, who lack significant social relationship problems, and who believe that the therapy will be effective (Crits-Christoph et al., 2004).

Interpersonal therapy (IPT) is a brief psychodynamic therapy that has been found to be very effective in the treatment of depression and bipolar disorder and social anxiety disorder (Blatt et al., 2009; Bohn et al., 2012; Swartz et al., 2009). It can be carried out with individual clients or with groups (Mufson et al., 2004). IPT is designed specifically to help clients understand and cope with four types of interpersonal problems commonly associated with major depression (Brakemeier & Frase, 2012). These problems include the following:

1. *Unusual or severe responses to the death of a loved one.* The therapist and client discuss the client's relationship with the deceased person and feelings (such as guilt) that may be associated with the death.

2. *Interpersonal role disputes.* The therapist helps the client to understand others' points of view and to explore options for bringing about change.

3. *Difficulty in adjusting to role transitions, such as divorce, career change, and retirement.* Clients are helped to see the change not as a threat but as a challenge that they can master and an opportunity for growth.

4. *Deficits in interpersonal skills.* Through role-playing and analysis of the client's communication style, the therapist tries to help the client develop the interpersonal skills necessary to initiate and sustain relationships.

Interpersonal therapy is relatively brief, consisting of 12 to 16 weekly sessions. A large study conducted by the National Institute of Mental Health found IPT to be an effective treatment even for severe depression and to have a low dropout rate (Elkin et al., 1989, 1995). Research also indicates that clients who recover from major depression can enjoy a longer period without relapse when they continue with monthly sessions of IPT (Frank et al., 1991).

Humanistic Therapies ▶

Humanistic therapies assume that people have the ability and freedom to lead rational lives and make rational choices. One of the innovations that was introduced into the field by humanistic therapists was the use of the word *client* rather than the word *patient* to refer to individuals who are receiving psychotherapeutic services. Humanistic therapists believe that *patient* conjures up images of an individual with a disease who needs to be healed by a professional who has skills that they lack. By contrast, the word *client* fits better with the humanistic notion that the goal of psychotherapy is to help individuals learn how to better facilitate their own personal growth.

▲ Freud required his patients to lie down for free association sessions because he found that they were better able to engage in uncensored streams of thought than when they sat. This photo depicts the actual couch he used, which is on display in London's Freud Museum, the residence in which he lived and psychoanalyzed patients in from 1939 until this death.

interpersonal therapy (IPT) A brief psychotherapy designed to help people with depression better understand and cope with problems relating to their interpersonal relationships.

13.2 What is the goal of the therapist in person-centered therapy?

humanistic therapies Psychotherapies that assume that people have the ability and freedom to lead rational lives and make rational choices.

▲ Carl Rogers (at upper right) facilitates discussion in a therapy group.

person-centered therapy A nondirective, humanistic therapy developed by Carl Rogers, in which the therapist creates an accepting climate and shows empathy, freeing clients to be themselves and releasing their natural tendency toward self-actualization.

nondirective therapy Any type of psychotherapy in which the therapist allows the direction of the therapy sessions to be controlled by the client; an example is person-centered therapy.

13.3 What is the major emphasis of Gestalt therapy?

Gestalt therapy A therapy that was originated by Fritz Perls and that emphasizes the importance of clients' fully experiencing, in the present moment, their feelings, thoughts, and actions and then taking responsibility for them.

directive therapy Any type of psychotherapy in which the therapist takes an active role in determining the course of therapy sessions and provides answers and suggestions to the client; an example is Gestalt therapy.

One of the founders of the humanistic approach, Carl Rogers (1951), developed **person-centered therapy**, also called *client-centered therapy*. His approach is one of the most frequently used humanistic therapies. According to this view, people are innately good and, if allowed to develop naturally, will grow toward *self-actualization*— the realization of their inner potential. The humanistic perspective suggests that psychological disorders result when a person's natural tendency toward self-actualization is blocked either by oneself or by others. In the 1940s and 1950s, person-centered therapy gained a strong following among psychologists who were dissatisfied with the results of psychodynamic therapies and continues to be popular today.

The person-centered therapist attempts to create an accepting climate, based on *unconditional positive regard* (explained in Chapter 11) for the client. The therapist also empathizes with the client's concerns and emotions. To convey empathetic understanding to the client, Rogers claimed that the therapist must adopt an attitude of *congruence* or *genuineness,* that is, a willingness to communicate with the client on a person-to-person basis rather than as an authority figure who will pass judgment on and give advice to the client. When the client speaks, the therapist responds by restating or reflecting back her or his ideas and feelings, a strategy known as *active listening.* Using these techniques, the therapist allows the client to control the direction of the therapy sessions. Rogers rejected all forms of therapy that cast the therapist in the role of expert and clients in the role of patients who expect the therapist to prescribe something that "cures" their problem. Thus, person-centered therapy is called a **nondirective therapy**.

Gestalt Therapy

Gestalt therapy, developed by Fritz Perls (1969), emphasizes the importance of clients' fully experiencing, in the present moment, their feelings, thoughts, and actions and then taking responsibility for them. The goal of Gestalt therapy is to help clients achieve a more integrated self and become more authentic and self-accepting. In addition, they learn to assume personal responsibility for their behavior rather than blaming society, past experiences, parents, or others.

Gestalt therapy is a **directive therapy**, one in which the therapist takes an active role in determining the course of therapy sessions and provides answers and suggestions to the client. The well-known phrase "getting in touch with your feelings" is a major objective of Gestalt therapy. Perls suggested that those of us who are in need of therapy carry around a heavy load of unfinished business, which may be in the form of resentment toward or conflicts with parents, siblings, lovers, employers, or others. If not resolved, these conflicts are carried forward into our present relationships. One method for dealing with unfinished business is the "empty chair" technique (Paivio & Greenberg, 1995). The client sits facing an empty chair and imagines, for example, that a wife, husband, father, or mother sits there. The client proceeds to tell the chair what he or she truly feels about that person. Then, the client moves to the empty chair and role-plays what the imagined person's response would be to what was said. The "telephone technique" is a variation on this approach in which clients engage in imaginary phone conversations with people with whom they have unfinished business (Weikel, 2011).

REMEMBER IT   *Check your answers and take additional quizzes in MyPsychLab.com.*   ✓● Study and Review on MyPsychLab

1. In psychoanalysis, various techniques are used to explore the client's _____.
2. Attempting to uncover childhood experiences that may explain a patient's current problems is the goal of _____ therapies.
3. It is likely that a person with depression who has had a severe reaction to the death of a loved one (would/would not) benefit from interpersonal therapy (IPT).
4. According to Rogers, therapists should provide clients with an accepting climate based on _____.
5. Gestalt therapy emphasizes a client's past experiences. (true/false)

Relationship Therapies

Insight therapies focus on the self, which is not always the most appropriate approach to a psychological problem. **Relationship therapies**, such as family and couple therapy, look at both the individual's internal struggles and at his or her interpersonal relationships. Some deliberately create new relationships for people that can support them in their efforts to address their problems, such as in group therapy.

Family Therapy and Couple Therapy ▶

Some therapists specialize in treating troubled families. In **family therapy**, parents and children enter therapy as a group. The therapist pays attention to the dynamics of the family unit—how family members communicate, how they act toward one another, and how they view one another (Dattilio, 2010). The goal of the therapist is to help family members reach agreement on certain changes that will help heal the wounds of the family unit, improve communication patterns, and create more understanding and harmony within the group (Doherty & McDaniel, 2010).

Couple therapy can take place at any phase of an intimate relationship and may focus either on behavior change or on partners' emotional responses to each other or on both aspects of an intimate relationship. For example, premarital sessions can help future spouses prepare for their life together. Couples who are considering divorce also often consult with a couple therapist for help in effecting a reconciliation or moderating the effects of a divorce on their children. Experimental studies indicate that couple therapy is effective at raising partners' levels of relationship satisfaction (Baucom, Epstein, & Sullivan, 2012).

In addition to raising levels of satisfaction, couple therapy and family therapy appear to have positive effects in treating a number of disorders such as major depressive disorder (Whisman et al., 2012). Couple therapy can also be helpful in the treatment of sexual dysfunctions (Gehring, 2003). And when it accompanies medication, family therapy can be beneficial in the treatment of schizophrenia and can reduce relapse rates (Snyder et al., 2006).

Group Therapy ▶

Group therapy is a form of therapy in which several clients (usually 7 to 10) meet regularly with one or more therapists to resolve personal problems. Besides being less expensive than individual therapy, group therapy gives the individual a sense of belonging and opportunities to express feelings, to get feedback from other members, and to give and receive help and emotional support (Piper & Ogrodniczuk, 2013). Learning that others also share their problems helps people feel less alone and ashamed. A meta-analysis of studies comparing prisoners who participated in group therapy to those who did not found that group participation was helpful for a variety of problems, including anxiety, depression, and low self-esteem (Morgan & Flora, 2002).

A variant of group therapy is the *self-help group* or *mutual help group* (Lembke & Humphreys, 2012). Approximately 12 million people in the United States participate in roughly 500,000 self-help groups, most of which focus on a single problem, such as substance abuse or depression. Self-help groups usually are not led by professional therapists. They are simply groups of people who share a common problem and meet to give and receive support.

One of the oldest and best-known self-help groups is Alcoholics Anonymous (AA), which claims 1.5 million members worldwide. Studies show that participation in AA and other such programs reduces substance abuse and dependency. The key to AA's effectiveness is that it provides people with substance abuse problems with a social support network consisting of non-substance-using peers (Kelly, Stout, & Slaymaker, 2013). Other self-help groups patterned after Alcoholics Anonymous have been formed to help individuals overcome many other addictive behaviors, from overeating (Overeaters Anonymous) to gambling (Gamblers Anonymous) (Lembke & Humphreys, 2012).

relationship therapies Therapies that attempt to improve clients' interpersonal relationships or create new relationships to support clients' efforts to address psychological problems.

13.4 What are the goals of family and couple therapy?

▲ Couples therapy is effective for helping partners resolve relationship issues. It can also help individuals learn how to better support partners with psychological disorders.

13.5 What are some advantages of group therapy?

family therapy Therapy involving an entire family, with the goal of helping family members reach agreement on changes that will help heal the family unit, improve communication problems, and create more understanding and harmony within the group.

couple therapy Therapy involving intimate partners in which behavior change or partners' emotional responses to each other or both are the focus of treatment.

group therapy A form of therapy in which several clients (usually 7 to 10) meet regularly with one or more therapists to resolve personal problems.

▲ Self-help groups such as Alcoholics Anonymous provide many individuals with the support they need to overcome self-destructive behaviors such as substance abuse.

1. _____ therapy focuses on behavior change or on partners' emotional responses to each other.

2. In family therapy, the therapist pays attention to the _____ of the family unit.

3. Match each description with the appropriate type(s) of therapy.

____ **(1)** provides members with a sense of belonging

____ **(2)** effective for supporting individuals recovering from alcoholism

____ **(3)** led by professional therapists

a. group therapy   **b.** self-help groups   **c.** both group therapy and self-help groups

Behavior Therapies

behavior therapy A treatment approach that is based on the idea that abnormal behavior is learned and that applies the principles of operant conditioning, classical conditioning, and/or observational learning to eliminate inappropriate or maladaptive behaviors and replace them with more adaptive responses.

behavior modification An approach to therapy that uses learning principles to eliminate inappropriate or maladaptive behaviors and replace them with more adaptive responses.

Sometimes individuals seek help from a mental health professional because they want to rid themselves of a troublesome habit, or they want to develop a better way to respond to specific situations in their lives. In such cases, psychotherapists may employ a behavioral approach.

A **behavior therapy** is a treatment approach consistent with the learning perspective on psychological disorders—that abnormal behavior is learned. Instead of viewing maladaptive behavior as a symptom of some underlying disorder, the behavior therapist sees the behavior itself as the disorder. If a person comes to a behavior therapist with a fear of flying, that fear of flying is seen as the problem. Behavior therapies use learning principles to eliminate inappropriate or maladaptive behaviors and replace them with more adaptive responses—an approach referred to as **behavior modification**. The goal is to change the troublesome behavior, not to change the individual's personality structure or to search for the origin of the problem behavior.

13.6 How do behavior therapists modify clients' problematic behavior?

token economy A behavior modification technique that rewards appropriate behavior with tokens that can be exchanged later for desired goods and/or privileges.

Behavior Modification Techniques Based on Operant Conditioning

Behavior modification techniques based on operant conditioning seek to control the consequences of behavior. Extinction of an undesirable behavior is accomplished by terminating or withholding the reinforcement that is maintaining that behavior (Lerman & Iwata, 1996). For example, a therapist may hypothesize that a child whines to get attention and advises parents to ignore the whining in order to extinguish it. Behavior therapists also seek to reinforce desirable behavior to increase its frequency. Institutional settings such as hospitals, prisons, and school classrooms are well suited to behavior modification techniques because they provide a restricted environment where the consequences of behavior can be strictly controlled.

Some institutions use a **token economy** that rewards appropriate behavior with tokens such as poker chips, play money, gold stars, or the like. These tokens can later be exchanged for desired goods (candy, gum, cigarettes) and/or privileges (weekend passes, free time, participation in desirable activities). Sometimes, individuals are fined a certain number of tokens for undesirable behavior. Mental hospitals have successfully used token economies with patients for decades to improve their self-care skills (Kopelowicz, Liberman, & Zarate, 2007). Similar interventions have been helpful in motivating clients at substance abuse clinics to remain abstinent and can even reduce symptoms of schizophrenia in some individuals (Petry et al., 2004; Swartz et al., 2012).

Behavior therapy can be effective in modifying some behaviors of seriously disturbed people. Although these techniques do not cure schizophrenia, autism, or intellectual disabilities, they can increase the frequency of desirable behaviors and decrease the frequency of undesirable behaviors. For example, some children with autism spectrum disorders (ASDs) display self-injurious behaviors, such as head-banging and skin-picking. Research suggests that behavior modification can reduce

▲ A time out is effective because it prevents a child from receiving reinforcers for undesirable behaviors. The child learns that once the behavior is under control, he or she will again have access to reinforcers. Similar behavioral techniques, such as token economies, are useful with adults in mental hospitals and other institutions.

self-injurious behavior of this kind (Furniss et al., 2011). In such a program, a child who exhibits self-injurious behavior might be rewarded with a treat for every 5-minute period during which he exhibits no such behavior. As a result, the family members of children with ASDs are better able to accept and care for them.

Another effective method used to eliminate undesirable behavior, especially in children and adolescents, is **time out** (Warzak et al., 2012). Children are told in advance that if they engage in certain undesirable behaviors, they will be removed from the situation and will have to pass a period of time (usually no more than 15 minutes) in a place containing no reinforcers (no television, books, toys, friends, and so on). Theoretically, the undesirable behavior will stop if it is no longer followed by attention or any other positive reinforcers.

Behavior modification techniques can also be used by people who want to break bad habits such as smoking and overeating or to develop good habits such as a regular exercise regime. If you want to modify any of your behaviors, devise a reward system for desirable behaviors, and remember the principles of shaping. Reward gradual changes in the direction of your ultimate goal. If you are trying to develop better eating habits, don't try to change a lifetime of bad habits all at once. Begin with a small step, such as substituting frozen yogurt for ice cream. Set realistic weekly goals that you are likely to be able to achieve.

Behavior Therapies Based on Other Learning Theories ▶

time out A behavior modification technique used to eliminate undesirable behavior, especially in children and adolescents, by withdrawing all reinforcers for a period of time.

13.7 What behavior therapies are based on classical conditioning and social-cognitive theory?

Behavior therapies based on classical conditioning can be used to rid people of fears and other undesirable behaviors. These therapies employ different means of exposing patients to feared objects or situations or to triggers that elicit undesirable behaviors such as substance abuse. Recent research also suggests that exposing individuals to such stimuli via *virtual reality* can be a useful addition to the standard ways in which such therapies are implemented (Hirsch, 2012; Safir, Wallach, & Bar-Zvi, 2012). Therapies of this type include systematic desensitization, flooding, exposure and response prevention, and aversion therapy.

Systematic Desensitization. One of the pioneers in the application of classical conditioning techniques to therapy, psychiatrist Joseph Wolpe (1958, 1973), reasoned that if he could get people to relax and stay relaxed while they thought about a feared object, person, place, or situation, they could conquer their fear. In Wolpe's therapy, known as **systematic desensitization**, clients are trained in deep muscle relaxation. Then, they confront a hierarchy of fears—a graduated series of anxiety-producing situations—either *in vivo* (in real life) or in their imagination, until they can remain relaxed even in the presence of the most feared situation. The technique can be used for everything from fear of animals to claustrophobia, social phobia, and other situational fears. Try creating such a hierarchy in the *Try It* on p. 432.

Many experiments, demonstrations, and case reports confirm that systematic desensitization is a highly successful treatment for eliminating fears and phobias in a relatively short time (Kolivas, Riordan, & Gross, 2008; Zinbarg & Griffith, 2008). It has proved effective for specific problems, such as test anxiety, stage fright, and anxiety related to sexual disorders.

systematic desensitization A behavior therapy that is based on classical conditioning and used to treat fears by training clients in deep muscle relaxation and then having them confront a graduated series of anxiety-producing situations (real or imagined) until they can remain relaxed while confronting even the most feared situation.

Flooding. Flooding is a behavior therapy used in the treatment of phobias. It involves exposing clients to the feared object or event (or asking them to imagine it vividly) for an extended period, until their anxiety decreases. The person is exposed to the fear all at once, not gradually as in systematic desensitization. An individual with a fear of heights, for example, might have to go onto the roof of a tall building and remain there until the fear subsided.

Flooding sessions typically last from 30 minutes to 2 hours and should not be terminated until clients are markedly less afraid than they were at the beginning of the session. Additional sessions are required until the fear response is extinguished or reduced to an acceptable level. It is rare for a client to need more than six treatment sessions (Marshall & Segal, 1988). *In vivo* flooding, the real-life experience,

flooding A behavior therapy based on classical conditioning and used to treat phobias by exposing clients to the feared object or event (or asking them to imagine it vividly) for an extended period, until their anxiety decreases.

▲ Flooding can be a useful treatment for phobias, such as fear of flying.

TRY IT   A Possible Hierarchy of Fears

Use what you have learned about systematic desensitization to create a step-by-step approach to help someone overcome a fear of taking tests. The person's hierarchy of fears begins with reading in the syllabus that a test will be given and culminates in actually taking the test. Fill in successive steps, according to a possible hierarchy of fears, that will lead to the final step. One set of possible steps is given below.

Taking the test in class

6. _____

5. _____

4. _____

3. _____

2. _____

1. _____

Reading in the syllabus that a test will be given on a certain day

SUGGESTED ANSWERS:

(1) Preparing for each class session by reading the assigned material and/or completing any homework assignments. (2) Attending each class session and taking notes on the material the test will cover. (3) Reviewing the new notes after each class period. (4) Reviewing all class materials beginning one week before the test. (5) Reciting key information from memory the day before the test. (6) Arriving early to take the test, having gotten a good night's sleep.

works faster and is more effective than simply imagining the feared object. That is, in order for flooding to be effective, the fear-inducing stimulus must sufficiently intense to bring about a physiologically based fear response (Siegmund et al., 2011). Thus, a person who fears flying would benefit more from taking an actual plane trip than from just thinking about one, because an actual flight is far more likely than an imagined one to provoke his body's fear response.

exposure and response prevention A behavior therapy that exposes patients with obsessive-compulsive disorder to stimuli that trigger obsessions and compulsive rituals, while patients resist performing the compulsive rituals for progressively longer periods of time.

Exposure and response prevention. Exposure and response prevention has been successful in treating a variety of fears as well as obsessive-compulsive disorder (Alpers, 2010; Baer, 1996; Foa, 1995; Rhéaume & Ladouceur, 2000). The first component of this technique involves *exposure*—exposing clients to objects or situations they have been avoiding because they trigger obsessions and compulsive rituals. The second component is *response prevention,* in which clients agree to resist performing their compulsive rituals for progressively longer periods of time.

Initially, the therapist identifies the thoughts, objects, or situations that trigger the compulsive ritual. For example, touching a doorknob, a piece of unwashed fruit, or a garbage bin might send people with a fear of contamination to the nearest bathroom to wash their hands. Clients are gradually exposed to stimuli that they find more and more distasteful and anxiety provoking. They must agree not to perform the normal ritual (hand washing, bathing, or the like) for a specified period of time after each exposure. A typical treatment course—about 10 sessions over a period of 3 to 7 weeks—can bring about considerable improvement in 60 to 70% of patients (Jenike, 1990). And clients treated with exposure and response prevention are less likely to relapse after treatment than those treated with drugs alone (Greist, 1992). Exposure and response prevention has also proved useful in the treatment of posttraumatic stress disorder (Gallagher & Resick, 2012).

Aversion Therapy. Aversion therapy is used to stop a harmful or socially undesirable behavior by pairing it with a painful, sickening, or otherwise aversive stimulus. Electric shock, emetics (which cause nausea and vomiting), or other unpleasant stimuli are paired with the undesirable behavior time after time until a strong negative association is formed and the person comes to avoid that behavior. Treatment continues until the bad behavior loses its appeal and becomes associated with pain or discomfort. Aversion therapy is controversial because it involves the intentional infliction of harm on a client.

Alcoholics are sometimes given a nausea-producing substance such as Antabuse, which reacts violently with alcohol and causes a person to retch and vomit until the stomach is empty (Abraham, Knudsen, & Roman, 2011). But for most problems, aversion therapy need not be so intense as to make a person physically ill. A controlled comparison of treatments for chronic nail biting revealed that mild aversion therapy—painting a bitter-tasting substance on the fingernails—yielded significant improvement (Allen, 1996).

Therapies derived from Albert Bandura's work on observational learning are based on the belief that people can overcome fears and acquire social skills through modeling. The most effective type of therapy based on observational learning theory is called **participant modeling** (Bandura, 1977; Bandura, Adams, & Beyer, 1977; Bandura, Jeffery, & Gajdos, 1975). In this therapy, not only does the model demonstrate the appropriate response in graduated steps, but the client also attempts to imitate the model step by step while the therapist gives encouragement and support. Most specific phobias can be extinguished in only 3 or 4 hours of client participation in modeling therapy. For instance, participant modeling could be used to help someone overcome a fear of dogs. A session would begin with the client watching others petting and playing with a dog. As the client becomes more comfortable, he or she would be encouraged to join in. Alternatively, a client would be shown a video of people playing with a dog and then would be encouraged to play with a live dog.

aversion therapy A behavior therapy in which an aversive stimulus is paired with a harmful or socially undesirable behavior until the behavior becomes associated with pain or discomfort.

participant modeling A behavior therapy in which an appropriate response to a feared stimulus is modeled in graduated steps and the client attempts to imitate the model step by step, encouraged and supported by the therapist.

REMEMBER IT   *Check your answers and take additional quizzes in MyPsychLab.com.*   ✓ Study and Review on MyPsychLab

1. Behavior therapies are based on the principles of _____ theory.

2. _____ is a treatment for people with panic disorder.

3. Match each therapy with the appropriate description.

_____ **(1)** flooding   _____ **(2)** aversion therapy

_____ **(3)** systematic desensitization   _____ **(4)** participant modeling

a. practicing deep muscle relaxation during gradual exposure to a feared object

b. associating a painful or sickening stimuli with undesirable behavior

c. being exposed directly to a feared object until the fear response is reduced or eliminated

d. imitating a model who is responding appropriately in a feared situation

Cognitive Behavior Therapies

In the *Think about It* activity at the beginning of the chapter, we introduced you to a type of psychotherapy that focuses on people's beliefs and ways of thinking about their problems. **Cognitive behavior therapies (CBTs)** assume that maladaptive behavior results from irrational thoughts, beliefs, and ideas, which the therapist tries to change (Craighead et al., 2013). This approach to therapy has been shown to be effective for treating a wide variety of problems, including eating disorders (Dalle Grave et al., 2013), anxiety disorders (Kellett et al., 2004), psychological drug dependence (Babor, 2004), and depression (Totterdell & Kellett, 2008). The two best known types of CBT are Albert Ellis's *rational emotive behavior therapy (REBT)* and Aaron Beck's *cognitive therapy (CT)*. ◉

Rational Emotive Behavior Therapy

The late clinical psychologist Albert Ellis (1913–2007) developed **rational emotive behavior therapy (REBT)** in the 1950s (Ellis, 1961, 1977, 1993). Ellis claimed to have developed the technique as a way of addressing his own problems with incapacitating anxiety (Ellis, 2004a). This type of therapy is based on Ellis's *ABC theory*. The *A* refers to the activating event, the *B* to the person's belief about the event, and the *C* to the emotional consequence that follows. Ellis claims that it is not the event itself that causes the emotional consequence but rather the person's belief about the event. In other words, *A* does not cause *C*; *B* causes *C*. If the belief is irrational, then the emotional consequence can be extreme distress, as illustrated in Figure 13.1.

Rational emotive behavior therapy is a directive form of psychotherapy designed to challenge clients' irrational beliefs about themselves and others. Most clients in REBT see a therapist individually, once a week, for 5 to 50 sessions.

---

cognitive behavior therapies (CBTs)
Therapies that assume maladaptive behavior can result from irrational thoughts, beliefs, and ideas.

◉ Watch the Video *Episode 17: In the Real World: Cognitive Behavioral Therapy* in **MyPsychLab**

13.8 What is the aim of rational emotive behavior therapy?

rational emotive behavior therapy (REBT)
A directive form of psychotherapy, developed by Albert Ellis and designed to challenge clients' irrational beliefs about themselves and others.

Harry's view: Sally's refusal caused his upset. *A* caused *C*.

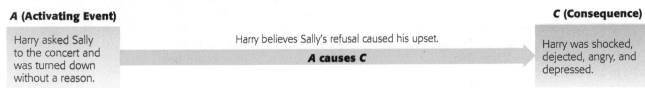

Ellis's view: Harry's belief about the event caused his upset. *B* caused *C*.

FIGURE 13.1 The ABCs of Rational Emotive Behavior Therapy (REBT)
Rational emotive behavior therapy teaches clients that it is not the activating event *(A)* that causes the upsetting consequences *(C)*. Rather, it is the client's beliefs *(B)* about the activating event. According to Albert Ellis, irrational beliefs cause emotional distress. Rational emotive behavior therapists help clients identify their irrational beliefs and replace them with rational ones.

In Ellis's view, clients do not benefit from warm, supportive therapeutic approaches that help them feel better but do not address the irrational thoughts that underlie their problems (Ellis, 2004b). Instead, he argues, as clients begin to replace irrational beliefs with rational ones, their emotional reactions become more appropriate, less distressing, and more likely to lead to constructive behavior. For example, a client might tell a therapist that he is feeling anxious and depressed because of his supervisor's unreasonable demands. Using Ellis's REBT model, the therapist would help the client distinguish between the supervisor's demands and the client's emotional reactions to them. The goal would be to help the client understand that his reactions to his supervisor's demands are the source of his anxiety and depression, not the demands themselves. Ultimately, the rational emotive behavior therapist would lead the client to the conclusion that while he may not be able to control his supervisor's demands, he is capable of controlling his emotional reactions to them. Once the client changes his thinking about the problem, the rational emotive behavior therapist helps him learn behavioral strategies, such as relaxation techniques, that can help him control his emotional reactions. Studies show that REBT is effective for helping college students reduce procrastination (McCown, Blake, & Keiser, 2012).

Beck's Cognitive Therapy ▶

13.9 How does Beck's cognitive therapy approach psychotherapy?

Psychiatrist Aaron T. Beck (1976) claims that much of the misery endured by a person with depression and anxiety can be traced to *automatic thoughts*—unreasonable but unquestioned ideas that rule the person's life ("To be happy, I must be liked by everyone"). These individuals notice only negative, unpleasant things and jump to upsetting conclusions. According to Beck, people who have negative, self-defeating thoughts such as these interpret past, present, and future experiences through the distorted mental filters that such thoughts create.

The goal of **Beck's cognitive therapy (CT)** is to help clients overcome the impact of *cognitive errors* (i.e., errors in thinking) such as those listed in Table 13.1 on p. 436 on their emotions and behavior. This approach is designed to deal with such thoughts as they occur and replace them with more objective thoughts. After identifying and challenging the client's irrational thoughts, the therapist sets up a plan and guides the client so that her or his personal experience can provide actual evidence in the real world to refute the false beliefs. Clients are given homework assignments (see Figure 13.2), such as keeping track of automatic thoughts and the feelings evoked by them and then substituting more rational thoughts.

Beck's cognitive therapy (CT) A therapy designed by Aaron Beck to help clients stop their cognitive errors as they occur and replace them with more objective thoughts.

Cognitive therapy is brief, usually lasting only 10 to 20 sessions (Beck, 1976). This therapy has been researched extensively and is reported to be successful in the treatment of individuals with mild to moderate depression (Craighead et al., 2013). There is some evidence that people who have received cognitive therapy are less likely to relapse than those who have been treated with antidepressant drugs (Hallon, Stewart, & Struck, 2006).

5-3-1

FIGURE 13.2 Cognitive Therapy Homework
Cognitive-behavioral therapist often assign "homework" exercises that help clients gain control of the thoughts that influence the behaviors they wish to change. For instance, a cognitive therapist who is helping a student overcome procrastination might prompt her to practice imagining the consequences of alternative courses of action whenever she is tempted to put off studying in favor of a fun activity such as going to the beach.

TABLE 13.1 Cognitive Errors

ERROR	EXAMPLE
All-or-nothing thinking	"If I don't get into an Ivy League school, I might as well not go to college at all."
Catastrophizing (fortune-telling)	"If I don't find a partner by the time I get out of college, I'll have to spend the rest of my life alone."
Discounting the positive	"I only passed that exam because I got lucky."
Emotional reasoning	"Even though he hasn't called me, my heart tells me that we're meant to be together."
Labeling	"She's too stuck-up to go out with a loser like me."
Magnification or minimization	"Since I missed class today, it won't matter that I have As on the exams. The professor will fail me because she can see how irresponsible I really am."
Mental filter	"I can't go on any interviews because I still haven't found the right shoes to go with my black suit."
Mind reading	"Since I said 'call me any time,' he probably thinks I'm desperate."
Overgeneralization	"I didn't do well in that interview. I'm just not a 'people person' I guess."
Personalization	"The professor seemed to be in a hurry to get out of the classroom. She must have thought my question was really dumb."
Inappropriate use of "should" and "must" statements	"A 'good' daughter should call her mother every day and report everything that she has done in the last 24 hours."
Tunnel vision	"This is my worst semester ever. I don't see how I'll survive it. I'll probably wreck my GPA."

Source: Beck (1995). Based on pp. 118–120 in *Cognitive Therapies: Basics and Beyond* by J. Beck, Copyright © 1995 by The Guilford Press. Reprinted by permission of Guilford Publications, Inc.

Cognitive therapy has also been shown to be effective for treating panic disorder (Clark & Beck, 2010). By teaching clients to change the catastrophic interpretations of their symptoms, cognitive therapy helps prevent the symptoms from escalating into panic. Studies have shown that after 3 months of cognitive therapy, about 90% of individuals with panic disorder are panic free.

REMEMBER IT   *Check your answers and take additional quizzes in MyPsychLab.com.* ✓●—Study and Review on MyPsychLab

1. Cognitive behavior therapists help clients deal with problem behaviors by encouraging them to change their

   _____.

2. _____ therapists challenge clients' irrational beliefs.

3. The goal of Beck's cognitive therapy is to help clients replace _____ with more _____ thoughts.

Biomedical Therapies

Do you know someone who takes or has taken a drug prescribed by a physician or psychiatrist as a means of overcoming a psychological problem? Chances are good that you do because millions of people the world over are now taking various medications for just such reasons. Treatment with drugs is a cornerstone of the biological approach to therapy. Predictably, professionals who favor the biological perspective—the view that psychological disorders are symptoms of underlying physical problems—usually favor a **biomedical therapy**. The three main biological therapies are drug therapy, electroconvulsive therapy (ECT), and psychosurgery.

Drug Therapy ▶

The most frequently used biological treatment is drug therapy. The drugs that mental health professionals prescribe for people with psychological disorders fit the definition of *psychoactive drugs* that you read about in Chapter 4. That is, they are drugs that alter moods, perceptions, and thoughts through their action on the brain's neurotransmitters. In fact, as we point out in the *Explain It*, on p. 438 some researchers believe that people with psychological disorders turn to *self-medication* when they find that a psychoactive substance such as nicotine relieves their symptoms. As a result, substance use and abuse often coexist with psychological disorders. ✳

Breakthroughs in drug therapy lowered the mental hospital patient population in the United States from about 560,000 in 1955, when the drugs were introduced, to about 100,000 by 1990 (see Figure 13.3); this figure continued to drop throughout the 1990s. Furthermore, the average stay of patients who do require hospitalization is now usually a matter of days.

Antipsychotics. Antipsychotic drugs known as *neuroleptics* are prescribed primarily for schizophrenia. You may have heard of these drugs by their brand names—Thorazine, Stelazine, Compazine, and Mellaril. Their purpose is to control hallucinations, delusions, disorganized speech, and disorganized behavior (Newton, 2012). The neuroleptics work primarily by inhibiting the activity of the neurotransmitter dopamine. About 50% of patients have a good response to the standard antipsychotics (Bobes et al., 2003). But many patients, particularly those with an early onset of schizophrenia, are not helped by them (Meltzer et al., 1997), and others show only slight or modest improvement in symptoms. The long-term use of typical antipsychotic drugs carries a high risk of a severe side effect, *tardive dyskinesia*—almost continual twitching and jerking movements of the face and tongue, and squirming movements of the hands and trunk (Brasic, 2012).

Newer antipsychotic drugs called *atypical neuroleptics* (clozapine, risperidone, olanzipine) can treat not only the positive symptoms of schizophrenia (e.g., hallucinations) but also the negative symptoms (e.g., lack of affect), leading to marked improvement in patients' quality of life (Gerstein, 2011). Atypical neuroleptics target both dopamine and serotonin receptors (Kawanishi, Tachikawa, & Suzuki, 2000). About 10% of patients who take clozapine find the results so dramatic that they almost feel as though they have been reborn. Clozapine produces fewer side effects

biomedical therapy A therapy (drug therapy, electroconvulsive therapy, or psychosurgery) that is based on the assumption that psychological disorders are symptoms of underlying physical problems.

13.10 What are the advantages and disadvantages of using drugs to treat psychological disorders?

✳ Explore the Concept *Drugs Commonly Used to Treat Psychiatric Disorders* on MyPsychLab

antipsychotic drugs Drugs used to control severe psychotic symptoms, such as delusions, hallucinations, disorganized speech, and disorganized behavior, by inhibiting dopamine activity; also known as neuroleptics.

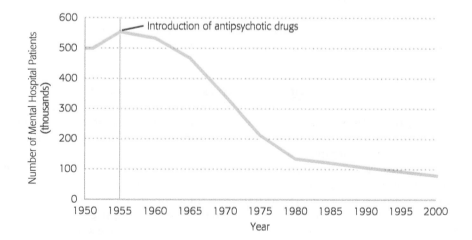

FIGURE 13.3 Decrease in Patient Populations in State and County Mental Hospitals (1950–2000) State and county mental hospital patient populations peaked at approximately 560,000 in 1955, the same year that antipsychotic drugs were introduced. These drugs, coupled with the federal government's efforts to reduce involuntary hospitalization of people with psychological disorders, resulted in a dramatic decrease in the patient population to fewer than 100,000 in 2000. *Source*: Data from Mandersheid & Henderson (2001).

EXPLAIN IT   Why Are Smoking Rates So High among People with Schizophrenia?

Studies show that 58–88% of individuals with schizophrenia smoke cigarettes (Moss et al., 2009). Is it possible then that, prior to being formally diagnosed, many individuals with schizophrenia accidentally happen on an effective biomedical treatment for their disorder when they take up the habit of smoking cigarettes? Among psychological researchers, this idea is known as the *self-medication hypothesis*. Animal research supports this hypothesis. For example, when researchers alter the brains of mice in ways that impair the ability to produce dopamine, the mice behave in agitated, disorganized ways, behavioral patterns that bear some similarity to those of individuals with schizophrenia. Experimental studies have found that such behavior decreases or disappears altogether when nicotine is administered to the mice (Uchiumi et al., 2013).

According to the self-medication hypothesis, the stimulant properties of nicotine help people with schizophrenia deal with the attention, thinking, and memory deficits that often go along with the disease. Studies show that nicotine increases activity in the parts of the brain that carry out these functions in people with schizophrenia (Moss et al., 2009; Yip et al., 2009). It may also protect individuals with schizophrenia from some of the more unpleasant side effects that are associated with antipsychotic drugs (George & Vessicchio, 2001). Advocates of the self-medication hypothesis also point out that, in general, smokers with schizophrenia smoke more heavily than smokers who do not have the disease, and smoking rates have remained constant among them while the rates of tobacco use in the general population have declined (Kelly & McCreadie, 2000).

Critics of the self-medication hypothesis argue that smoking rates are high among individuals with schizophrenia because smoking increases vulnerability to the disorder (Kelly & McCreadie, 2000). Recall from Chapter 12 that researchers believe that schizophrenia arises from a complex interaction of genetic, developmental, and environmental factors. Nicotine dependence, some researchers say, may be one of several factors that contribute to a series of biochemical changes that produce the symptoms of schizophrenia. Evidence in favor of this view comes from studies showing that most smokers with schizophrenia started smoking long before they had their first symptoms (Smith et al., 2009; Zhang et al., 2013). As a result, they could not have initiated the habit as the result of a search for symptom relief.

The verdict on the self-medication hypothesis has yet to be decided. One thing is certain, though. As you would probably predict, cigarette smoking has a deleterious effect on the physical health of individuals with schizophrenia just as it does on the rest of us. Death rates from smoking-related diseases such as lung cancer and the prevalence of chronic conditions such as emphysema that are associated with smoking are far higher among individuals with schizophrenia than in the general population (Schizophrenia.com, 2006). Thus, whatever their differences with regard to the self-medication hypothesis, most researchers and clinicians agree that giving up smoking is just as important for them as for people who do not have a serious psychological disorder. Furthermore, smokers with schizophrenia are just as likely to want to quit smoking as smokers who do not have the disease.

Despite an equivalent desire to quit, individuals with schizophrenia have a more difficult time overcoming nicotine addiction than other people do. For one thing, antipsychotic drugs appear to intensify the unpleasant feelings that are associated with nicotine withdrawal. For another, nicotine moderates the effects of antipsychotic drugs such that an effort to quit smoking often leaves an individual with schizophrenia reeling from the effects of a dosage level of an antipsychotic drug that is too high (George & Vessicchio, 2001). Therefore, clinicians who have studied smoking cessation in individuals with schizophrenia strongly discourage them from quitting "cold turkey." Nicotine replacement, these experts say, is needed to ensure that an individual with schizophrenia remains stable throughout the withdrawal period as well as to increase the person's success. Above all, failing to urge individuals with schizophrenia to quit smoking because they may be getting symptom relief from nicotine is a subtle form of discrimination against them.

than standard neuroleptics, and patients taking it are less likely to develop tardive dyskinesia (Soares-Weiser & Fernandez, 2007). It may also be more effective at suicide prevention than other antipsychotic drugs (Meltzer et al., 2003). However, the levels of various liver enzymes and other substances in patients who take the drug must be monitored regularly (Erdogan et al., 2004).

antidepressant drugs Drugs that act as mood elevators for people with severe depression and are also prescribed to treat some anxiety disorders.

Antidepressants. Antidepressant drugs act as mood elevators for people with depression (Halverson, 2012). About 65 to 75% of people who take antidepressants find themselves significantly improved, and 40 to 50% of those are essentially completely recovered (Frazer, 1997). It is important to note, though, that most antidepressant research involves people with severe depression—those who are most likely to show a significant change after treatment (Zimmerman, Posternak, & Chelminski, 2002). Thus, these studies may not apply to individuals with milder cases of depression. Moreover, research has shown that antidepressants are most effective when combined with psychotherapy (Khan et al., 2012).

The first-generation antidepressants are known as the *tricyclics* (amitriptyline, imipramine) (Nutt, 2000). The tricyclics work against depression by blocking the reuptake of norepinephrine and serotonin into the axon terminals, thus enhancing the action of these neurotransmitters in the synapses. In general, tricyclics are highly effective at reducing the symptoms of depression, but they can have some unpleasant side effects, including sedation, dizziness, nervousness, fatigue, dry mouth, forgetfulness, and weight gain (Nelson, 2009). Progressive weight gain (an average of more than 20 pounds) is the main reason people stop taking tricyclics, in spite of the relief these drugs provide from distressing psychological symptoms.

The second-generation antidepressants, the *selective serotonin reuptake inhibitors (SSRIs)*, block the reuptake of the neurotransmitter serotonin, increasing its availability at the synapses in the brain (Dayan & Huys, 2008). SSRIs (fluoxetine, clomipramine) have fewer side effects (Nelson, 1997). SSRIs have been found to be promising in treating many disorders. Currently, the U.S. Food and Drug Administration (FDA) lists depression, obsessive-compulsive disorder, bulimia nervosa, and panic disorder as the conditions for which it approves the use of most SSRIs (FDA, 2006). It's also important to note that, in 2004, the FDA recommended that people younger than 18 be closely monitored during the first few weeks of SSRI treatment because of some studies showing that the drugs increase the risk of suicide among children and teens (FDA, 2004). However, in the years that followed the FDA's recommendation, some researchers have argued that there is insufficient evidence to conclude that SSRIs increase suicide risk in youths (Dudley, Goldney, & Hadzi-Pavolic, 2010).

Reports indicating that SSRIs, especially fluoxetine (Prozac), increase the risk of suicide in adults have not been substantiated (Ham, 2003; Warshaw & Keller, 1996). However, SSRIs can cause sexual dysfunction, although normal sexual functioning returns when the drug is discontinued. Studies suggest that a newer group of antidepressants, the *serotonin-norepinephrine reuptake inhibitors (SNRIs)*, appears to be more effective than the SSRIs and to produce fewer side effects (Ravindran & Ravindran, 2009).

Another line of treatment for depression is the use of *monoamine oxidase (MAO) inhibitors* (sold under the names Marplan, Nardil, and Parnate). By blocking the action of an enzyme that breaks down norepinephrine and serotonin in the synapses, MAO inhibitors increase the availability of these neurotransmitters. MAO inhibitors are usually prescribed for people with depression who do not respond to other antidepressants (Tobin, 2007). However, MAO inhibitors have many of the same unpleasant side effects as tricyclic antidepressants, and people taking MAO inhibitors must avoid certain foods or run the risk of stroke.

Lithium and Anticonvulsant Drugs. **Lithium,** a naturally occurring salt, is considered a wonder drug for 40 to 50% of people who have bipolar disorder (Thase & Kupfer, 1996). It is said to begin to quiet the manic state within 5 to 10 days and reduces the risk of suicide in people with bipolar disorder (Soreff, 2012). A proper maintenance dose of lithium reduces depressive episodes as well as manic ones. Studies show that the clinical effectiveness of lithium for treating depression and bipolar disorder is unmatched (Ross, Baldessarini, & Tondo, 2000). But 40 to 60% of those who take a maintenance dose will experience a recurrence (Thase & Kupfer, 1996). Also, monitoring the level of lithium in the patient's blood every 2 to 6 months is necessary to guard against lithium poisoning and permanent damage to the nervous system (Soreff, 2012).

lithium A drug used to treat bipolar disorder, which at proper maintenance dosage reduces both manic and depressive episodes.

Recent research suggests that *anticonvulsant drugs,* such as Depakote (divalproex), may be just as effective for managing bipolar symptoms as lithium, with fewer side effects (Soreff, 2012). Moreover, many people with bipolar disorder, especially those whose manic states include symptoms of psychosis, benefit from taking antipsychotic drugs along with the anticonvulsants (Bowden et al., 2004; Vieta, 2003).

Antianxiety Drugs. The family of minor tranquilizers called *benzodiazepines* includes, among others, the well-known drugs sold as Valium and Librium and the newer high-potency drug Xanax (pronounced "ZAN-ax"). Used primarily to treat anxiety, benzodiazepines are prescribed more often than any other class of psychoactive drugs (Cloos & Ferreira, 2009). They have been found to be effective in treating panic disorder (Davidson, 1997; Noyes et al., 1996) and generalized anxiety disorder (Lydiard, Brawman-Mintzer, & Ballenger, 1996).

SUMMARIZE IT

Drugs Used to Treat Psychological Disorders

TYPE OF DRUG	BRAND NAMES	SYMPTOMS TREATED
Neuroleptics	Compazine, Mellaril, Stelazine, Thorazine	Hallucinations, delusions
Atypical neuroleptics	Clozaril, Olanzapine, Risperdal	Hallucinations, delusions Negative symptoms of schizophrenia
Tricyclics	Elavil, Tofranil	Depressed mood/Anxiety
SSRIs	Celexa, Paxil, Prozac, Zoloft	Depressed mood/Anxiety
SNRIs	Effexor, Pristiq, Remeron	Depressed mood/Anxiety
MAOIs	Ensam, Nardil, Parnate, Marplan	Depressed mood/Anxiety
Lithium	Eskalith, Lithobid	Mania
Anticonvulsants	Depakote, Depacon, Depakene	Mania
Benzodiazepines	Librium, Valium, Xanax	Anxiety

Xanax, the largest-selling psychiatric drug (Famighetti, 1997), appears to be particularly effective in relieving anxiety and depression. There is a downside to Xanax. Many people, once they no longer experience panic attacks, find themselves unable to discontinue the drug because they experience moderate to intense withdrawal symptoms, including intense anxiety (Cloos & Ferreira, 2009). The *Summarize It* lists the various drugs that are used to treat the symptoms of psychological disorders.

Disadvantages of Drug Therapy. Beyond the drugs' unpleasant or dangerous side effects, another disadvantage in using drug therapy is the difficulty in establishing the proper dosages. Also, it's important to note that drugs do not cure psychological disorders. Thus, people who take them usually experience a relapse if they stop taking the drugs when their symptoms lift. Maintenance doses of antidepressants following a major depressive episode reduce the probability of recurrence (Boulenger, Loft, & Ferea, 2012). Maintenance doses are usually required with anxiety disorders as well, or symptoms are likely to return (Hallon et al., 2006). Further, some studies suggest that the trend away from involuntary hospitalization brought about by the availability of antipsychotic and other psychiatric drugs has led to an increase in homelessness among people who have chronic mental illnesses such as schizophrenia (Carson et al., 2000). Unfortunately, after being discharged from mental hospitals because they have shown favorable responses to antipsychotic drugs, many people with schizophrenia do not get adequate follow-up care. As a result, some stop taking their medications, relapse into psychotic states, and are unable to support themselves. Finally and perhaps most importantly, critics of drug therapy point out that it often prevents people with psychological disorders from being advised of other forms of therapy that may reduce or eliminate the need for psychiatric drugs (Calton & Spandler, 2009).

13.11 What is electroconvulsive therapy (ECT) used for?

Electroconvulsive Therapy

Antidepressant drugs are relatively slow acting. A person with severe depression needs at least 2 to 6 weeks to obtain relief, and 30% of these patients don't respond at all. This situation can be too risky for people who are at risk for suicide (Keitner & Boschini, 2009). **Electroconvulsive therapy (ECT)**, a biological therapy in which an electric current is passed through the right hemisphere of the brain, is sometimes used in such cases. ECT has a bad reputation because it was misused and overused in the 1940s and 1950s. Nevertheless, when used appropriately and as a last resort when all other treatments have failed, ECT is a highly effective treatment for major depression (Mayur, Byth, & Harris, 2012).

electroconvulsive therapy (ECT) A biological therapy in which an electric current is passed through the right hemisphere of the brain; usually reserved for patients with severe depression who are suicidal.

For many years, ECT was performed by passing an electric current through both cerebral hemispheres, a procedure known as *bilateral ECT.* Today, electric current is administered to the right hemisphere only, and the procedure is called *unilateral ECT.* Research suggests that unilateral ECT is as effective as the more intense bilateral form while producing milder cognitive effects (Sackeim et al., 2000). Also, a patient undergoing ECT today is given anesthesia, controlled oxygenation, and a muscle relaxant.

Experts think that ECT changes the biochemical balance in the brain, resulting in a lifting of depression. When ECT is effective, cerebral blood flow in the prefrontal cortex is reduced, and delta waves (usually associated with slow-wave sleep) appear (Sackeim et al., 1996). However, ECT is also associated with autobiographical memory loss that can persist for months after treatment (Verwijk, 2012).

Toward the end of the 20th century, a new brain stimulation therapy known as *rapid transcranial magnetic stimulation (rTMS)* was developed. This magnetic therapy is not invasive in any way. Performed on people who are not sedated, it causes no seizures, leads to no memory loss, and has no known side effects. Its therapeutic value is similar to that of ECT, and it is much more acceptable to the public (Greenberg, 2012; Higgins & George, 2009). Moreover, it has shown promise as a treatment for the negative symptoms of schizophrenia (Guse et al., 2013). This finding is important because, as you learned in Chapter 12, people with negative symptoms of schizophrenia are less likely to respond to other forms of therapy than those who have only positive symptoms.

▲ In electroconvulsive therapy, a mild electric current is passed through the right hemisphere of the brain for 1 to 2 seconds, causing a brief seizure.

Psychosurgery ▶

An even more drastic procedure than ECT is **psychosurgery**—brain surgery performed to alleviate serious psychological disorders, such as severe depression, severe anxiety, or obsessions, or to provide relief from unbearable chronic pain. The first experimental brain surgery for human patients, the *lobotomy,* was developed by Portuguese neurologist Egas Moniz in 1935 to treat severe phobias, anxiety, and obsessions. Surgeons performing a lobotomy would sever the neural connections between the frontal lobes and the deeper brain centers involved in emotion. But no brain tissue was removed. At first, the procedure was considered a tremendous contribution, and Moniz won the Nobel Prize in medicine in 1949. Eventually, however, it became apparent that this treatment left patients in a severely deteriorated condition. You may recall, for example, the case of H. M. that we discussed in Chapter 6. As a result of an operation of this kind, H. M. lost the ability to form new memories. Devastating aftereffects of the lobotomy and similar operations led to their discontinuation.

Modern psychosurgery procedures result in less intellectual impairment because, rather than using conventional surgery, surgeons deliver electric currents through electrodes to destroy a much smaller, more localized area of brain tissue. In one procedure, called a *cingulotomy,* electrodes are used to destroy the *cingulum,* a small bundle of nerves connecting the cortex to the emotional centers of the brain. Several procedures, including cingulotomy, have been helpful for some extreme cases of obsessive-compulsive disorder (Greenberg, 2012). But the results of psychosurgery are still not predictable, and the consequences—whether positive or negative—are irreversible. For these reasons, the treatment is considered experimental and absolutely a last resort (Glannon, 2006).

13.12 For what problems is psychosurgery used?

psychosurgery Brain surgery performed to alleviate serious psychological disorders or unbearable chronic pain.

REMEMBER IT

Check your answers and take additional quizzes in MyPsychLab.com.   ✓•⎯Study and Review in MyPsychLab

1. The most commonly used biomedical therapy is _____.

2. The availability of antipsychotic drugs led to a decline in _____ among individuals with psychiatric disorders.

3. More prescriptions are written for _____ drugs than for any of the other types of psychiatric medications.

4. Electroconvulsive therapy may reduce the risk of _____ in people with major depressive disorder.

5. Cingulotomy may be helpful in the treatment of extreme cases of _____ disorder.

Practical Issues in Psychotherapy

If you decided that you were ready to enter into a long-term relationship with a romantic partner, would you open the telephone directory and select a name at random? Of course not. Admittedly, establishing a relationship with a therapist isn't quite as momentous as selecting a life partner. But, in both situations, it is wise to arm yourself with relevant information. Becoming familiar with the various professionals who offer therapeutic services is an important step toward that goal. Likewise, you should consider how comfortable you feel with a therapist whose gender or cultural background is different from your own. Finally, you would probably want to know which type of therapy is most effective.

13.13 What are the similarities and differences among the various types of therapists?

Choosing a Therapist

Perhaps you are one of the thousands of people who have considered turning to the Internet for therapy. If so, then you will find the tips in the *Apply It* to be very helpful. Regardless of the mode through which therapy occurs—online, by telephone, or in person—choosing a therapist with the type of training best suited to your problem can be crucial to how helpful the therapy turns out to be. Table 13.2 lists the various types of mental health professionals. One important difference among professionals, about which many people are confused, is that a **psychologist** has an advanced degree, usually at the doctoral level, in psychology, while a **psychiatrist** is a medical doctor. Historically, drug therapy has been available only from psychiatrists. At present, however, there is a movement that is gaining momentum in the United States to allow psychologists with special training in psychopharmacology to prescribe drugs. Only the U.S. military and a few states have authorized prescribing privileges for psychologists so far.

Regardless of their training or theoretical orientation, all therapists are bound by ethical standards established by professional organizations and, in most cases, codified in state laws. Each profession (e.g., psychologists, social workers) has its own ethical standards, but certain features are common to all of them and are exemplified by the ethics code of the American Psychological Association (2002). All of the ethical standards in the APA code are governed by the principle that therapists must

psychologist A mental health professional who possesses a doctoral degree in psychology.

psychiatrist A mental health professional who is a medical doctor.

TABLE 13.2 Mental Health Professionals

PROFESSIONAL TITLE	TRAINING	SERVICES PROVIDED
Psychiatrist	Medical degree (M.D. or O.D.); residency in psychiatry	Psychotherapy; drug therapy; hospitalization for serious psychological disorders
Psychoanalyst	M.D., Ph.D., or Psy.D.; additional training in psychoanalysis	Psychodynamic therapy
Clinical psychologist	Ph.D. or Psy.D.; internship in clinical psychology	Diagnosis and treatment of psychological disorders; can prescribe drugs in some settings after additional training; psychological testing
Counseling psychologist	Ph.D. or Ed.D.; internship in counseling psychology	Assessment and therapy for normal problems of life (e.g., divorce); psychological testing
School psychologist	Ph.D., Ed.D., or master's degree; internship in school psychology	Assessment and treatment of school problems in children and adolescents; psychological testing
Clinical or psychiatric social worker (M.S.W.)	Master's degree; internship in psychiatric social work	Diagnosis and treatment of psychological disorders; identification of supportive community services
Licensed professional counselor (L.P.C.)	Master's degree; internship in counseling	Assessment and therapy for normal problems of life; some psychological testing
Licensed marriage and family therapist (L.M.F.T.)	Master's degree; internship in couple therapy and family therapy	Assessment and therapy for relationship problems
Licensed chemical dependency counselor (L.C.D.C.)	Educational requirements vary from one state to another	Treatment and education for substance abuse problems

APPLY IT

Is E-therapy Right for You?

If you were trying to overcome a substance abuse problem or needed help getting through a period of bereavement, would you turn to an online support group? Some studies suggest that therapy delivered via the Internet can be effective (Sucala et al., 2012). But people aren't waiting for scientific studies that demonstrate the effectiveness of these innovative treatments. Thousands have already turned to *e-therapy*—ongoing online interaction with a trained therapist (Warmerdam et al., 2010). This form of therapy typically involves the exchange of e-mail messages over a period of hours or days but can also include video conferencing and telephone sessions (Day & Schneider, 2002). In addition, some therapists see clients in virtual environments that are similar to the popular online environment *Second Life*. In these virtual environments, therapists and clients manipulate *avatars* (graphic online identities) and settings to interact with each other and to create situations in which clients can practice the coping skills that they learn in either face-to-face or e-therapy (Cho et al., 2008; Gaggioli & Riva, 2007).

Advantages of E-therapy

E-therapy enables clients to be much less inhibited than they might be in a face-to-face situation. It is also less expensive than traditional therapy (Roan, 2000). Another advantage is that the therapist and the client do not have to be in the same place at the same time (Bessell, 2012). A therapist can also keep accurate records of communications with clients and can answer their questions at times of day when telephone calls are inconvenient, thus making his or her therapy practice more efficient (Andrews & Erskine, 2003). E-therapy can be an especially helpful alternative to psychotherapy for people with any of several characteristics (Bessell, 2012):

- They are often away from home or have full schedules.
- They cannot afford traditional therapy.
- They live in rural areas and do not have access to mental health care.
- They have disabilities.
- They are too timid or embarrassed to make an appointment with a therapist.
- They are good at expressing their thoughts and feelings in writing.

Disadvantages of E-therapy

Because of the anonymity of Internet interactions, it is easy for imposters to pose as therapists. So far, there is no system for regulating or licensing e-therapists. In addition, e-therapy poses some potential ethical problems, such as the possibility of breaches of confidentiality (Lee, 2010). But like all reputable therapists, the best e-therapists do everything they can to protect clients' privacy and

confidentiality—except when it is necessary to protect them or someone else from immediate harm (Ainsworth, 2000). Perhaps the most serious drawback of e-therapy is the fact that the therapist cannot see the client and therefore cannot use visual and auditory cues to determine when the person is becoming anxious or upset. This reduces the effectiveness of treatment (Roan, 2000).

Another important limitation of e-therapy is that it is not appropriate for diagnosing and treating serious psychological disorders, such as schizophrenia or bipolar disorder (Manhal-Baugus, 2001). In addition, e-therapy is not appropriate for someone who is in the midst of a serious crisis. There are better ways to get immediate help, such as suicide hotlines.

Finding an E-therapist

If you wish to locate an e-therapist, the best place to start is *www.metanoia.org*. This site lists online therapists whose credentials have been checked by Mental Health Net. It provides information about the location of the therapist, the services offered, the payment method, and so forth (Roan, 2000).

When choosing a therapist, be sure to do the following (Ainsworth, 2000):

- Make sure the person's credentials have been verified by a third party.
- Get real-world contact information.
- Verify that you'll receive a personal reply to your messages.
- Find out in advance how much the therapist charges.

If you decide to contact an e-therapist, bear this in mind: While e-therapy may be a good way to get started, if you have persistent problems, it would be wise in the long run to obtain traditional psychotherapy (Roan, 2000).

take reasonable steps to ensure the well-being and rights of their client and to avoid causing them any kind of immediate or long-term harm. One important standard that serves these goals is *informed consent*. Therapists must inform clients of the cost and expected duration of therapy prior to beginning any intervention. Moreover, clients must be informed of the legal limits of confidentiality. For example, if a client reveals that she or he has committed a crime, in most cases the therapist is obligated to report the confession to the appropriate authorities. In addition, some insurance companies require that therapists' notes be available for review without regard to clients' confidentiality.

The nature of the therapeutic relationship is also governed by ethical standards. Therapists are forbidden to engage in any kind of intimate relationship with a client or with anyone close to the client. They are also prohibited from providing therapeutic services to former intimate partners. When ending a therapeutic relationship, a therapist must counsel a client about the reason for terminating therapy and provide him or her with alternatives.

With regard to testing, therapists are ethically obligated to use tests that are reliable and valid. Moreover, they must have appropriate training for administering, scoring, and evaluating each test they use. They are also required to explain the purpose of testing to clients and to provide them with test results in a timely and confidential manner. ◉

Watch the Video *Episode 17: What's in It for Me? Finding a Therapist If You Need One* in **MyPsychLab**

13.14 What are the characteristics of culturally sensitive therapy?

culturally sensitive therapy An approach to therapy in which knowledge of clients' cultural backgrounds guides the choice of therapeutic interventions.

Culturally Sensitive Therapy

Among most psychotherapists, there is a growing awareness of the need to consider cultural variables in diagnosing and treating psychological disorders (Field, 2009; Thakker, 2013). In fact, the American Psychological Association published guidelines to help psychologists be more sensitive to cultural issues (American Psychological Association, 2003b). According to Kleinman and Cohen (1997), people experience psychological disorders within a cultural context that may dramatically affect the meaning of symptoms, outcomes, and responses to therapy. And cultural differences between therapist and client may undermine the *therapeutic alliance,* the bond between therapist and client that is known to be a factor in the effectiveness of psychotherapy (Blatt et al., 1996). Thus, many experts advocate an approach called **culturally sensitive therapy** in which knowledge of clients' cultural backgrounds guides the choice of therapeutic interventions and informs the way in which therapists implement a particular therapeutic approach (Frew & Spiegler, 2013; Kumpfer et al., 2002). For example, a psychodynamic therapist would approach discussion of family issues with a client whose cultural background frowns on disrespecting one's elders in a less direct way than she would with a client from a different background.

Culturally sensitive therapists recognize that language differences between therapists and clients can pose problems (Santiago-Rivera & Altarriba, 2002). For example, a client who speaks both Spanish and English but is more fluent in Spanish may exhibit hesitations, backtracking, and delayed responses to questions when being interviewed in English. As a result, the therapist may erroneously conclude that this client is experiencing the kind of disordered thinking that is often displayed by people with schizophrenia (Martinez, 1986). Such language differences may also affect clients' results on standardized tests used by clinicians. In one frequently cited study, researchers found that when a group of Puerto Rican clients took the Thematic Apperception Test (TAT) in English, their pauses and their choices of words were incorrectly interpreted as indications of psychological problems (Suarez, 1983). Thus, culturally sensitive therapists become familiar with clients' general fluency in the language in which they will be assessed prior to interviewing and testing them.

When working with recent immigrants to the United States, culturally sensitive therapists take into account the impact of the immigration experience on clients' thoughts and emotions (Polanco-Roman & Miranda, 2013). Some researchers who have studied the responses of recent Asian immigrants to psychotherapy recommend that, prior to initiating diagnosis and treatment, therapists encourage clients who are immigrants to talk about the feelings of sadness they have experienced as a result of leaving their native culture, as well as their anxieties about adapting to life in a new society. Using this strategy, therapists may be able to separate depression and anxiety related to the immigration experience from true psychopathology.

Some advocates of culturally sensitive therapy point out that cultural practices can be used as models for therapeutic interventions. Traditional Native American *healing circles,* for example, are being used by many mental health practitioners who serve Native Americans (Garrett, Garrett, & Brotherton, 2001). Members of a healing circle are committed to promoting the physical, mental, emotional, and spiritual well-being of one another. Healing circle participants typically engage in member-led activities such as discussion, meditation, and prayer. However, some more structured healing circles include a recognized Native American healer who leads the group in traditional healing ceremonies.

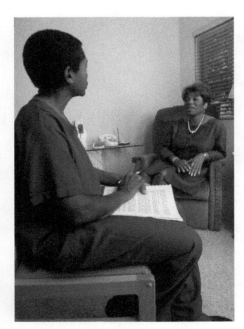

▲ When therapist and client have the same racial or ethnic background, they are more likely to share cultural values and communication styles, which can facilitate the therapeutic process.

Culturally sensitive therapists also attempt to address group differences that can affect the results of therapy. For example, many studies have found that African Americans with mental disorders are less likely than White Americans with the same diagnoses to follow their doctor's or therapist's instruction about taking medications (Fleck et al., 2002; Hazlett-Stevens et al., 2002). A culturally sensitive approach to this problem might be based on a therapist's understanding of the importance of kinship networks and community relationships in African American culture. A therapist might increase an African American client's compliance level by having the client participate in a support group with other African Americans who have similar diagnoses and are taking the same medications (Muller, 2002). In addition, compared to members of other groups, African Americans are more likely to benefit from psychotherapy when the therapist is also African American (Cabral & Smith, 2011).

Gender-Sensitive Therapy ▶

Many psychotherapists also note the need for **gender-sensitive therapy**, a therapeutic approach that takes into the account the effects of gender on both the therapist's and the client's behavior (Gehart & Lyle, 2001). To implement gender-sensitive therapy, therapists must examine their own gender-based prejudices. They may assume men to be more analytical and women to be more emotional, for example. These stereotypical beliefs may be based on a therapist's socialization background or knowledge of research findings on gender differences.

Advocates of gender-sensitive therapy point out that knowledge of real differences between the sexes is important to the practice of gender-sensitive therapy. For instance, because of men's gender role socialization, interventions focused on emotional expression may be less effective for them than for women (Danfort, Olle, & Wester, 2012). Moreover, men may view seeking therapy as a sign of weakness or as a threat to their sense of masculinity (Addis & Mahalik, 2003). As a result, researchers advise therapists to try to avoid creating defensiveness in their male clients (Greer, 2005). Nevertheless, therapists must guard against using research findings as a basis for stereotyping either male or female clients. They have to keep in mind that there is more variation within each gender than across genders, and thus each man or women must be considered as an individual.

Some therapists who are motivated by a sincere desire to be sensitive to gender issues may place too much emphasis on gender issues and misinterpret clients' problems (Addis & Mahalik, 2003). For example, in one study, researchers found that therapists expect people who are working in nontraditional fields—female engineers and male nurses, for instance—to have more psychological problems (Rubinstein, 2001). As a result, therapists may assume that such clients' difficulties arise from gender role conflicts, when, in reality, their problems have completely different origins.

Evaluating the Therapies ▶

If you look over the summaries of the various therapeutic approaches in the *Summarize It* (p. 446), you will notice that they share many similarities. For example, several therapies help clients reflect on their own thoughts and/or emotions. Analyses of therapy sessions representing different perspectives suggest that therapists use a core set of techniques no matter which perspective they adopt; at the same time, each therapeutic approach has elements that distinguish it from others (Crits-Cristoph et al., 2008; de Groot, Verheul, & Trijsburg, 2008). ✳

But to what degree do the various therapies differ in effectiveness? In a classic study of therapeutic effectiveness, Smith and his colleagues (1980) analyzed the results of 475 studies, which involved 25,000 clients. Their findings revealed that psychotherapy was better than no treatment, but that no one type of psychotherapy was more effective than another. A subsequent reanalysis of the same data by Hans Eysenck (1994), however, showed a slight advantage for behavior therapies over other types. A study by Hollon and others (2002) found that cognitive and interpersonal therapies had an advantage over psychodynamic approaches for clients with depression.

13.15 Why is gender-sensitive therapy important?

gender-sensitive therapy An approach to therapy that takes into account the effects of gender on both the therapist's and the client's behavior.

13.16 What does research suggest about the effectiveness of psychotherapy?

✳ **Explore** the **Concept** *Closer Look Simulation: Therapies* on **MyPsychLab**

SUMMARIZE IT

Summary and Comparison of the Therapies

TYPE OF THERAPY	PERCEIVED CAUSE OF DISORDER	GOALS OF THERAPY	METHODS USED	PRIMARY DISORDERS OR SYMPTOMS TREATED
INSIGHT THERAPIES				
Psychoanalysis	Unconscious sexual and aggressive urges or conflicts; fixations; weak ego; objectrelations; life stress	Help patient bring disturbing, repressed material to consciousness and work through unconscious conflicts; strengthen ego functions	Psychoanalyst analyzes and interprets dreams, free associations, resistance, and transference, and past relationships.	General feelings of unhappiness; unresolved problems from childhood
Person-centered therapy	Blocking of normal tendency toward self-actualization; incongruence between real and desired self; overdependence on positive regard of others	Increase self-acceptance and self-understanding; help client become more inner-directed; increase congruence between real and desired self; enhance personal growth	Therapist shows empathy, unconditional positive regard, and genuineness, and reflects client's expressed feelings back to client.	General feelings of unhappiness; interpersonal problems
Gestalt therapy	Difficulties are caused by blaming society, past experiences, parents, or others	Help clients achieve a more integrated self and become more self-accepting	Directive therapy; the "empty chair" technique; role-play	Depression
RELATIONSHIP THERAPIES				
Family therapy and couples therapy	Problems caused by faulty communication patterns, unreasonable role expectations, drug and/or alcohol abuse, and so on	Create more understanding and harmony within the relationships; improve communication patterns; heal wounds of family unit	Therapist sees clients individually or several family members at a time and explores such things as communication patterns, power struggles, and unreasonable demands and expectations.	Family problems such as marriage or relationship problems, troubled or troublesome teenagers, abusive relationships, drug or alcohol problems, schizophrenia family member
Group therapy	None	Give clients sense of belonging, opportunity to express feelings, opportunity to give and receive feedback from others with similar problems	7 to 10 clients meet regularly with one or more therapists to resolve personal problems	Anxiety, depression, low self-esteem
BEHAVIOR THERAPIES				
Behavior therapy	Learning of maladaptive behaviors or failure to learn appropriate behaviors	Extinguish maladaptive behaviors and replace with more adaptive ones; help client acquire needed social skills	Therapist uses methods based on classical and operant conditioning and modeling, which include systematic desensitization, flooding, exposure and response prevention, and aversion therapy.	Fears, phobias, panic disorder, obsessive-compulsive disorder, bad habits
COGNITIVE THERAPIES				
Cognitive therapy	Irrational and negative assumptions and ideas about self and others	Change faulty, irrational, and/or negative thinking	Therapist helps client identify irrational and negative thinking and substitute rational thinking.	Depression, anxiety, panic disorder, general feelings of unhappiness
BIOMEDICAL THERAPIES				
Biomedical therapy	Underlying physical disorder caused by structural or biochemical abnormality in the brain; genetic inheritance	Eliminate or control biological cause of abnormal behavior; restore balance of neurotransmitters	Physician prescribes drugs such as antipsychotics, antidepressants, lithium, or tranquilizers; uses ECT or psychosurgery.	Schizophrenia, depression, bipolar disorder, anxiety disorders

Moreover, socioeconomic status and other personal variables interact with clients' problems, and these interactions influence therapeutic outcomes (Falconnier, 2009). For example, a technique that has proven to be effective for people with adequate means may not be so for people who are struggling financially. Thus, the most important determinant of the effectiveness of any therapeutic technique is its appropriateness for a given client's problems and the circumstances of his or her life (Crits-Christoph et al., 2008).

But how do the clients themselves rate the therapies? To answer this question, Consumer Reports (1995) conducted the largest survey ever done on client attitudes toward psychotherapy. Martin Seligman (1995, 1996), a consultant for the study, summarized its findings:

- Overall, clients believed that they benefited substantially from psychotherapy.

- Patients seemed equally satisfied with their therapy, whether it was provided by a psychologist, a psychiatrist, or a social worker.

- Clients who were in therapy for more than 6 months did considerably better than the rest; generally, the longer patients stayed in therapy, the more they improved.

- Patients who took a drug such as Prozac or Xanax believed it helped them, but overall, psychotherapy alone seemed to work about as well as psychotherapy plus drugs. 👁

👁 **Watch** the Video *Episode 17: Thinking Like a Psychologist: Assessing Treatment Effectiveness* in **MyPsychLab**

REMEMBER IT

Check your answers and take additional quizzes in MyPsychLab.com.   ✔ **Study** and **Review** in **MyPsychLab**

1. The main difference between a psychologist and a psychiatrist is that the latter has a _____ degree.
2. _____ variables can influence the results of standardized tests used by psychologists.
3. _____ may involve incorporation of cultural practices into therapeutic interventions.
4. Gender-sensitive therapy requires that therapists examine their own _____.
5. Match each problem or disorder with the therapy that is used most often to treat it.

   ____ **(1)** debilitating fears   ____ **(2)** schizophrenia

   ____ **(3)** general unhappiness, interpersonal problems   ____ **(4)** bipolar disorder

   a. behavior therapy   **b.** insight therapy   **c.** drug therapy

---

👓 Looking Back

Now that you have read about the various therapies and a few important aspects of the therapeutic relationship, what sort of therapist do you think you would look for if you needed one? Remember that a psychodynamic therapist will probably engage you in an exploration of past relationships, while a humanistic therapist will try to facilitate your search for self-actualization. A family or couple therapist might be the best professional to consult if you would like to change the interaction patterns that have developed between you and the significant people in your life. A behavior therapist can help you modify a troublesome behavior pattern, and a cognitive therapist will do the same for any maladaptive thought patterns that you have. Recall, too, that any of these techniques can be used by any of the professionals listed in Table 13.2. In fact, most therapists are skilled in the use of more than one approach, although most have preferences. Finally, before entering into a therapeutic relationship think about how cultural and gender issues may affect the course of your therapy. As you can see, the information you have acquired from studying this chapter has helped you become a savvier consumer of psychotherapeutic services should a need for such services ever arise in your life.

CHAPTER 13 SUMMARY

INSIGHT THERAPIES (pp. 426–428)

13.1 What are the basic techniques of psychodynamic therapies? (pp. 426–427)

The techniques associated with psychoanalysis are free association, dream analysis, object relations, and transference. They are used to uncover the repressed memories, impulses, and conflicts presumed to be the cause of the patient's problems. Interpersonal therapy (IPT) is designed to help people with depression cope with unusual or severe responses to the death of a loved one, interpersonal role disputes, difficulty in adjusting to role transitions, and deficits in interpersonal skills.

Key Terms
psychotherapy, p. 426
insight therapies, p. 426
psychodynamic therapies, p. 426
psychoanalysis, p. 426
free association, p. 426
transference, p. 426
interpersonal therapy (IPT), p. 427

13.2 What is the goal of the therapist in person-centered therapy? (pp. 427–428)

Person-centered therapy is a nondirective therapy in which the therapist provides empathy and a climate of unconditional positive regard. The goal is to allow the client to determine the direction of the therapy sessions and to move toward self-actualization.

Key Terms
humanistic therapies, p. 427
person-centered therapy, p. 428
nondirective therapy, p. 428

13.3 What is the major emphasis of Gestalt therapy? (p. 428)

Gestalt therapy emphasizes the importance of clients' fully experiencing, in the present moment, their feelings, thoughts, and actions and taking personal responsibility for their behavior.

Key Terms
Gestalt therapy, p. 428
directive therapy, p. 428

RELATIONSHIP THERAPIES (pp. 429–430)

13.4 What are the goals of family and couple therapy? (p. 429)

In couple therapy, therapists help intimate partners change their behavior and their emotional responses to each other in order to improve their relationships. The goals of family therapy include helping family members improve communication patterns and create more interpersonal understanding and harmony.

Key Terms
relationship therapies, p. 429
family therapy, p. 429
couple therapy, p. 429

13.5 What are some advantages of group therapy? (pp. 429–430)

Group therapy is less expensive than individual therapy, and it gives people opportunities to express their feelings, get feedback from other group members, and give and receive help and emotional support.

Key Term
group therapy, p. 429

BEHAVIOR THERAPIES (pp. 430–433)

13.6 How do behavior therapists modify clients' problematic behavior? (pp. 430–431)

Behavior therapists use operant conditioning techniques such as the use of reinforcement to shape or increase the frequency of desirable behaviors (token economies) and the withholding of reinforcement to eliminate undesirable behaviors (time out).

Key Terms
behavior therapy, p. 430
behavior modification, p. 430
token economy, p. 430
time out, p. 431

13.7 What behavior therapies are based on classical conditioning and social-cognitive theory? (pp. 431–433)

Behavior therapies based on classical conditioning are systematic desensitization, flooding, exposure and response prevention, and aversion therapy. In participant modeling, an appropriate response to a feared stimulus is modeled in graduated steps, and the client is asked to imitate each step with the encouragement and support of the therapist.

Key Terms

systematic desensitization, p. 431
flooding, p. 431
exposure and response prevention, p. 432
aversion therapy, p. 433
participant modeling, p. 433

COGNITIVE BEHAVIOR THERAPIES (pp. 434–436)

13.8 What is the aim of rational emotive behavior therapy? (pp. 434–435)

Rational emotive behavior therapy is a directive form of therapy designed to challenge and modify a client's irrational beliefs, which are believed to be the cause of personal distress.

Key Terms

cognitive behavior therapies (CPTs), p. 434
rational emotive behavior therapy (REBT), p. 434

13.9 How does Beck's cognitive therapy approach psychotherapy (pp. 435–436)

Beck's cognitive therapy helps people overcome depression and panic disorder by pointing out the irrational thoughts causing them misery and by helping them learn other, more realistic ways of looking at themselves and their experiences.

Key Term

Beck's cognitive therapy (CT), p. 435

BIOMEDICAL THERAPIES (pp. 436–441)

13.10 What are the advantages and disadvantages of using drugs to treat psychological disorders? (pp. 437–440)

The use of drug therapy has reduced the number of patients in mental hospitals. Antipsychotic drugs control the major symptoms of schizophrenia by inhibiting the activity of dopamine. Antidepressants are helpful in the treatment of severe depression and certain anxiety disorders. Lithium and anticonvulsant drugs can control symptoms of manic episodes and can even out the mood swings in bipolar disorder. Antianxiety drugs are used primarily to treat anxiety. Some problems with the use of drugs are unpleasant or dangerous side effects and the fact that relapse is likely if the drug therapy is discontinued. Also, the movement away from hospitalization has led to an increase in the number of homeless people with mental disorders.

Key Terms

biomedical therapy, p. 437
antipsychotic drugs, p. 437
antidepressant drugs, p. 438
lithium, p. 439

13.11 What is electroconvulsive therapy (ECT) used for? (pp. 440–441)

The unilateral form of ECT is used to treat people with severe depression, especially those who are in imminent danger of committing suicide.

Key Term

electroconvulsive therapy (ECT), p. 440

13.12 For what problems is psychosurgery used? (p. 441)

Psychosurgery is brain surgery performed to relieve some severe, persistent, and debilitating psychological disorders or unbearable chronic pain. A highly controversial technique, psychosurgery is considered experimental and a last resort.

Key Term

psychosurgery, p. 441

PRACTICAL ISSUES IN PSYCHOTHERAPY (pp. 442–447)

13.13 What are the similarities and differences among the various types of therapists? (pp. 442–444)

Therapists vary according to their training and the techniques that they use. Psychiatrists have medical degrees, whereas psychologists have doctoral degrees in psychology. Regardless of training, all psychotherapists must adhere to ethical standards regarding informed consent, confidentiality, the nature of the therapeutic relationship, and termination of therapy.

Key Terms
psychologist, p. 442
psychiatrist, p. 442

13.14 What are the characteristics of culturally sensitive therapy? (pp. 444–445)

This approach to therapy helps mental health professionals be more aware of cultural variables that may influence clients' responses to the therapy and the therapist as well as therapists' responses to clients. Clients' cultural backgrounds and practices may be useful in guiding the choice of therapeutic interventions.

Key Term
culturally sensitive, p. 444

13.15 Why is gender-sensitive therapy important? (p. 445)

Gender sensitivity helps therapists realize how their own gender biases may affect the therapeutic techniques that they choose and their assessments of clients' progress.

Key Term
gender-sensitive therapy, p. 445

13.16 What does research suggest about the effectiveness of psychotherapy? (pp. 445–447)

Although no one therapeutic approach has proved generally superior overall, specific therapies have proven to be most effective for treating particular disorders. For example, cognitive and interpersonal therapies are preferred for people with depression.

Chapter 13 Study Guide

Answers to all the Study Guide questions are provided at the end of the book.

SECTION ONE: Chapter Review

Insight Therapies (pp. 426–428)

1. In psychoanalysis, the technique whereby a client reveals every thought, idea, or image that comes to mind is called _____: the client's attempt to avoid revealing certain thoughts is called _____.
   a. transference; resistance
   b. free association; transference
   c. revelation; transference
   d. free association; resistance

2. (Person-centered, Gestalt) therapy is the directive therapy that emphasizes the importance of the client's fully experiencing, in the present moment, his or her thoughts, feelings, and actions.

3. (Person-centered, Gestalt) therapy is the nondirective therapy developed by Carl Rogers in which the therapist creates a warm, accepting climate so that the client's natural tendency toward positive change can be released.

4. (Psychodynamic, Humanistic) therapy presumes that the causes of the client's problems are repressed childhood experiences.

5. Which person with depression would be *least* likely to be helped by interpersonal therapy (IPT)?
   a. Tyrone, who is unable to accept the death of his wife
   b. Beth, who has been depressed since she was forced to retire
   c. Jen, who was sexually abused by her father
   d. Tony, who feels isolated and alone because he has difficulty making friends

Relationship Therapies (pp. 429–430)

6. Which of the following is *not* true of group therapy?
   a. It allows people to get feedback from other members.
   b. It allows individuals to receive help and support from other members.
   c. It is conducted by untrained therapists.
   d. It is less expensive than individual therapy.

7. Self-help groups are generally ineffective because they are not led by professionals. (true/false)

Behavior Therapies (pp. 430–433)

8. Techniques based on (classical, operant) conditioning are used to change behavior by reinforcing desirable behavior and removing reinforcers for undesirable behavior.

9. Behavior therapies based on classical conditioning are used mainly to
   a. shape new, more appropriate behaviors.
   b. rid people of fears and undesirable behaviors or habits.
   c. promote development of social skills.
   d. demonstrate appropriate behaviors.

10. Exposure and response prevention is a treatment for people with
    a. panic disorder.
    b. phobias.
    c. generalized anxiety disorder.
    d. obsessive-compulsive disorder.

11. To help Serena overcome her fear of dogs, Dr. Jones shows her watch a group of children playing with puppies and encourages her to gradually join in. Dr. Jones is using a therapeutic technique called _____.

Cognitive Behavior Therapies (pp. 434–436)

12. Cognitive behavior therapists believe that, for the most part, emotional disorders
  a. have physical causes.
  b. result from unconscious conflict and motives.
  c. result from faulty and irrational thinking.
  d. result from environmental stimuli.

13. Rational emotive behavior therapy is a nondirective therapy that requires a warm, accepting therapist. (true/false)

14. The goal of Beck's cognitive therapy is best described as helping people
  a. develop effective coping strategies.
  b. replace cognitive errors with more objective thoughts.
  c. develop an external locus of control.
  d. develop realistic goals and aspirations.

15. Beck's cognitive therapy has proved very successful in the treatment of
  a. depression.   **b.** insomnia.
  c. anxiety disorders.   **d.** several psychological disorders

Biomedical Therapies (pp. 436–441)

16. For the most part, advocates of biological therapies assume that psychological disorders have a physical cause. (true/false)

17. Match the disorder with the drug most often used for its treatment.
  _____ **(1)** panic disorder
  _____ **(2)** schizophrenia
  _____ **(3)** bipolar disorder
  _____ **(4)** depression
  _____ **(5)** obsessive-compulsive disorder
  a. lithium   **b.** antipsychotics   **c.** antidepressants

18. Medication that relieves the symptoms of schizophrenia is thought to work by blocking the action of
  a. serotonin.   **b.** dopamine.
  c. norepinephrine.   **d.** epinephrine.

19. Which of the following is *not* true of drug therapy for psychological disorders?
  a. Some clients must take more than one psychiatric drug to relieve their symptoms.
  b. Drugs sometimes have unpleasant side effects.
  c. Clients often relapse if they stop taking the drugs.
  d. Drugs are usually not very effective.

20. For which disorder is ECT typically used?
  a. severe depression   **b.** schizophrenia
  c. anxiety disorders   **d.** panic disorder

21. The major side effect of ECT is tardive dyskinesia. (true/false)

22. Psychosurgery techniques are now so precise that the exact effects of the surgery can be predicted in advance. (true/false)

Practical Issues in Psychotherapy (pp. 442–447)

23. One must have a medical degree to become a
  a. clinical psychologist.
  b. sociologist.
  c. psychiatrist.
  d. clinical psychologist, psychiatrist, or psychoanalyst.

24. The responses and outcomes of clients in therapy (are, are not) influenced by cultural factors.

25. What is true regarding the effectiveness of therapies?
  a. All are equally effective for any disorder.
  b. Specific therapies have proved effective in treating particular disorders.
  c. Insight therapies are consistently best.
  d. Therapy is no more effective than no treatment for emotional and behavioral disorders.

26. Match the problem with the most appropriate therapy.
  _____ **(1)** fears, bad habits
  _____ **(2)** schizophrenia
  _____ **(3)** general unhappiness, interpersonal problems
  _____ **(4)** severe depression
  a. behavior therapy   **b.** insight therapy   **c.** drug therapy

SECTION TWO: Identify the Therapy

Indicate which type of therapy each sentence is describing:
(a) psychoanalytic, (b) behavioral, (c) humanistic, (d) cognitive behavior, (e) Gestalt, (f) interpersonal, or (g) biomedical.

_____ **1.** This directive therapy has as an important objective "getting in touch with your feelings"; clients are encouraged to fully experience the present moment.

_____ **2.** This approach emphasizes early childhood experience and the conflicts one encounters in different stages of development; important concepts include free association and transference.

_____ **3.** Practitioners of this approach believe that faulty and irrational thinking results in emotional distress; a popular application of this approach is rational emotive behavior therapy.

_____ **4.** This therapy is considered a brief psychotherapy and is used in cases of depression due to problems such as the death of a loved one or deficits in interpersonal skills.

_____ **5.** This approach is based on the principles of learning theory and includes treatment strategies that use operant conditioning, classical conditioning, and observational learning.

_____ **6.** This approach sees psychological problems as symptoms of underlying physical disorders and uses medical treatments such as drug therapy and electroconvulsive therapy.

_____ **7.** This approach views people as having free choice; clients are encouraged to seek personal growth and fulfill their potential.

SECTION THREE: Comprehensive Practice Test

1. Your therapist asks you to reveal whatever thoughts, feelings, or images come to mind, no matter how trivial, embarrassing, or terrible they might seem. Your therapist is using a technique known as
  a. analysis of resistance.   **b.** psychodrama.
  c. free association.   **d.** stimulus satiation.

2. Which of the following is *not* considered an insight therapy?
  a. psychoanalysis
  b. Gestalt therapy
  c. rational emotive behavior therapy
  d. person-centered therapy

3. Which of the following is important in humanistic therapy?
   a. challenging irrational beliefs
   b. dream analysis
   c. empathy
   d. behavior modification

4. Person-centered therapy is most effective when the therapist proposes valuable solutions and offers solid advice while directing the therapeutic process. (true/false)

5. In this directive form of therapy, the therapist helps clients to experience their feelings as deeply and genuinely as possible, and then to admit responsibility for them.
   a. behavioral modification
   b. psychodynamic therapy
   c. rational emotive behavior therapy
   d. Gestalt therapy

6. Which type of therapy seems to offer the most effective setting for treating adolescent drug abuse?
   a. family therapy   b. Gestalt therapy
   c. person-centered therapy d. behavioral therapy

7. This therapy involves the application of principles of classical and operant conditioning.
   a. Gestalt therapy   b. behavior modification
   c. psychoanalysis   d. humanistic therapy

8. A therapist treating you for fear of heights takes you to the top floor of a tall building and asks you to look out the window toward the ground until she can see that your fear is significantly diminished. What technique is she using?
   a. flooding   b. psychodrama
   c. systematic desensitization d. stimulus satiation

9. Which therapy emphasizes acceptance and unconditional positive regard?
   a. person-centered therapy
   b. cognitive behavior therapy
   c. rational emotive behavior therapy
   d. psychoanalysis

10. A technique based on Albert Bandura's observational learning theory is
    a. flooding.   b. participant modeling.
    c. systematic desensitization. d. implosive therapy.

11. A type of therapy that is used to treat phobias and employs relaxation training techniques is called
    a. cognitive behavior therapy. b. systematic desensitization.
    c. psychoanalysis.   d. client-centered therapy.

12. Which insight therapy was developed by Fritz Perls?
    a. Gestalt therapy
    b. rational emotive behavior therapy
    c. client-centered therapy
    d. psychoanalysis

13. This type of biological therapy helps reduce symptoms of severe depression by producing a seizure in the patient.
    a. psychosurgery   b. lobotomy
    c. electroconvulsive therapy d. chemotherapy

14. This biological therapy uses an electrical current to destroy a localized section of brain cells.
    a. cingulotomy   b. prefrontal lobotomy
    c. electroconvulsive therapy d. chemotherapy

15. This group of drugs includes tricyclics, MAO inhibitors, and SSRIs.
    a. antimania drugs   b. antidepressant drugs
    c. antianxiety drugs   d. antipsychotic drugs

16. This group of drugs is used to treat symptoms that include hallucinations and delusions.
    a. antimania drugs   b. antidepressant drugs
    c. antianxiety drugs   d. antipsychotic drugs

17. The most severe side effect of typical antipsychotic drugs is
    a. cramps.   b. muscle spasms.
    c. tardive dyskinesia.   d. mania.

18. In a major review of 475 studies, researchers concluded that people who received therapy were better off than those who did not. (true/false)

19. The main problem with interpersonal therapy is the fact that it is so time consuming. (true/false)

20. The *B* in Albert Ellis's *ABC* theory of rational emotive behavior therapy stands for *behavior*. (true/false)

SECTION FOUR: Critical Thinking

1. What are the major strengths and weaknesses of the following approaches to therapy: psychoanalysis, person-centered therapy, behavior therapy, cognitive behavior therapy, and drug therapy?

2. From what you have learned in this chapter, prepare a strong argument to support each of these positions:
   a. Psychotherapy is generally superior to drug therapy in the treatment of psychological disorders.
   b. Drug therapy is generally superior to psychotherapy in the treatment of psychological disorders.

SECTION FIVE: Application Essays

1. In selecting a therapist for yourself or advising a friend or family member, what are some important questions you would ask a therapist in an effort to determine whether he or she would be a good choice?

2. Use the definitions and examples in Table 13.1 to devise a 3-day cognitive behavioral plan for yourself. First, use the information in the table to create a cognitive error. Use the checklist to assess how often you commit such errors in one day. The following day, repeat the procedure but make an effort to correct each cognitive error you detect in your thoughts with a more objective one using the checklist to note your progress. The third day, track your cognitive errors again, noting how often your mind generates an objective counter-thought without your trying to produce one. Summarize the results of your plan and describe the degree to which it changed the way you respond to negative thoughts.

Apply your critical thinking skills with **MyPsychLab** Writing Assignments

Submit your answer to the following question inside the MyPsychLab Writing Assessment program for immediate feedback.

Compare and contrast the following forms of psychotherapy: cognitive, humanistic, and behavioral. Identify the focus of each approach as well as areas of agreement and difference.

Social Psychology

14

THINK ABOUT IT

Imagine that you have just been in an auto accident with the man in this photo. He hit your car from behind, so there is no doubt that he was legally at fault. However, you don't know exactly what it was that caused him to crash into your car. Based strictly on the photo, estimate the likelihood that each of the factors in the following table contributed to the accident.

Did the man's appearance influence your responses? All of us tend to be influenced by the first information we receive about a person. In face-to-face interactions, the first thing we learn about anyone is what they look like. Thus, we often use a person's appearance to form hypotheses about characteristics such as their personalities and moral values.

The nature of the statements in the table may have influenced your responses as well. Notice that items 1, 4, and 6 refer to characteristics of the man, whereas items 2, 3, and 5 refer to the situation. If you tended to see the accident as the product of the man's characteristics rather than those of the situation, then you may have committed a common error in thinking that causes us to see another person's mistakes as a function of personality and our own as caused by situational factors that are beyond our control.

	LIKELIHOOD								
Contributing Factor	**NOT LIKELY**								**VERY LIKELY**
1. He was intoxicated.	1	2	3	4	5	6	7	9	10
2. His sunglasses were fogged up.	1	2	3	4	5	6	7	9	10
3. He was talking on a cell phone.	1	2	3	4	5	6	7	9	10
4. He is an angry person who takes out his frustrations on other drivers.	1	2	3	4	5	6	7	9	10
5. He was distracted by the erratic behavior of another driver.	1	2	3	4	5	6	7	9	10
6. He is an irresponsible person who has little concern for the rights of others.	1	2	3	4	5	6	7	9	10

social psychology The subfield that attempts to explain how the actual, imagined, or implied presence of others influences the thoughts, feelings, and behavior of individuals.

Explore the **Concept** *Closer Look Simulation: Social Psychology* on **MyPsychLab**

Watch the Video *Episode 16: Big Picture: The Social World* in **MyPsychLab**

First impressions and the ways in which we think about the causes of our own and others' behavior are just two of the topics of interest in **social psychology**, the subfield that attempts to explain how the actual, imagined, or implied presence of others influences our thoughts, feelings, and behaviors. The range of topics that are of interest to social psychologists is quite broad. It includes the process of making judgments about others, attraction, conformity, obedience, compliance, group influence, attitudes, and the factors that motivate us to help or harm others (Society for Personality and Social Psychology, 2006).

Social Cognition

social cognition The process of attending to, interpreting, and remembering information about ourselves and others.

When we form judgments of others, we use all of the many cognitive processes that we learned about in earlier chapters—perception (Chapter 3), memory (Chapter 6), and thinking (Chapter 7)—to process information about the social world just as we do when we process information about the physical world. **Social cognition** is the process of attending to, interpreting, and remembering information about ourselves and others. One area of interest in the study of social cognition addresses how we form impressions of others and manage their impressions of us. Another involves *attribution*, the process of making inferences about the causes of human behavior.

14.1 How do we form opinions of others and manage their opinions of us?

Impression Formation and Management

impression formation The mental process of developing opinions about other people.

Impression formation is the mental process of developing judgments about other people. When we meet people for the first time, we begin forming impressions about them right away, and, of course, they are busily forming impressions of us. Naturally, we notice the obvious attributes first—gender, race, age, dress, and physical attractiveness or unattractiveness (Shaw & Steers, 2001). Such attributes, combined with people's verbal and nonverbal behavior, play a part in establishing first impressions.

A number of studies reveal that an overall impression of another person is influenced more by the first information that is received about that person than by information that comes later (Luchins, 1957). For example, psychologist Stephanie Buchert and her colleagues have found that professors' scores on students' end-of-semester evaluations did not differ from those they were given by students just two weeks into the term (Buchert, Laws, Apperson, & Bregman, 2008; Laws, Apperson, Buchert, & Bregman, 2010). This phenomenon is called the **primacy effect**. Once an impression is formed, it provides the framework through which we interpret later information (Gawronski et al., 2002). Any information that is consistent with the first impression is likely to be accepted, thus strengthening the impression. Information that does not fit with the earlier information is more likely to be disregarded. For example, if you get the impression on the first day of class that your professor is going to be tough, then a hard test that most of the class fails will support and strengthen that impression. However, if your professor curves those scores, you're likely to disregard that information and keep your original impression. Remember, any time you list your personal traits or qualities, always list your most positive qualities first. It pays to put your best foot forward—first. ◉

Most of us realize that first impressions are important, and so we intentionally take steps to influence them, through a process called **impression management**. For example, in the United States, a firm handshake and eye contact are associated with positive first impressions; thus, it is common practice to engage in these behaviors when first meeting others (Chaplin et al., 2000). Impression management is most important to us when we meet people who are in a position to provide us with something that we need or desire, such as a job. Accordingly, social psychologists advise interviewers to use interviewing techniques that lessen the impact of job candidates' impression management strategies (Barrick, Shaffer, & DeGrassi, 2009). One such technique is to use a standard set of questions for all interviewees.

Impression management also comes to the fore when we believe that another person has formed an inaccurate judgment of us. To see how this works, suppose that a student wants a professor to give her some extra time to complete a research paper. She probably knows from experience that such requests are most likely to succeed if the professor perceives her to be a good student. If her actions have led the professor to believe otherwise, the student is likely to adopt an impression management strategy that will change the professor's view. For instance, she might include an explanation of the obstacles in her life that have prevented her from being as good a student as she would like along with her request for an extension on the research paper deadline.

Another reason that we strive to ensure that others' impressions of us are accurate is that we are most comfortable in the presence of people whose impressions of us match our own (Goffman, 1959; Swann & Bosson, 2008; Seih et al., 2013). Thus, achieving agreement between others' opinions of us and our own self-concepts plays a key role in the development of social relationships. For instance, if a person thinks of himself as an expert on computers, he is likely to make acquaintances aware of his interest and skill in that area by making comments about computers and recounting anecdotes about the many times he has helped friends fix their computers. Moreover, researchers have found that online identities play an important role in impression management for young adults these days (Mazur & Kozarian, 2010). Thus, if being a "computer guy" is an important part of the person's self-concept, he might post photos of himself working on computers, links to Web sites that discuss computer issues, or blog entries about fixing common computer problems on his social networking site.

Interestingly, impression management also influences how we view ourselves. The feedback that we receive from others through our efforts at impression management helps us affirm and review our own self-concepts (Swann, 2012). Consequently, a student who tries to explain to a professor why she appears to be a poor student

primacy effect The tendency for an overall impression of another to be influenced more by the first information that is received about that person than by information that comes later.

◉ |**Watch** the Video *Episode 16: Special Topics: Mental Shortcuts in a Social Context* in **MyPsychLab**

impression management The intentional steps we take to influence others' opinions of us.

attribution An assignment of a cause to explain one's own or another person's behavior.

situational attribution Attributing a behavior to some external cause or factor operating within the situation; an external attribution.

dispositional attribution Attributing a behavior to some internal cause, such as a personal trait, motive, or attitude; an internal attribution.

self-serving bias The tendency to attribute one's successes to dispositional causes and one's failures to situational causes.

actor-observer effect The tendency to attribute one's own behavior primarily to situational factors and the behavior of others primarily to dispositional factors.

fundamental attribution error The tendency to give more attention to dispositional factors than is appropriate for a situation.

might end up with a more realistic perception of herself. And if a "computer guy" disappoints a friend by being unable to fix the friend's computer problem, his view of the importance of his computer skills to his self-concept might change.

Attribution

Why do people do the things they do? To answer this question, we make an **attribution**—that is, we assign or attribute causes to explain the behavior of others or of ourselves. One kind of attribution is called a **situational attribution** (an external attribution), in which we attribute a person's behavior to some external cause or factor operating within the situation. After failing an exam, you might say, "The test was unfair" or "The professor didn't give us enough time." Or you might make a **dispositional attribution** (an internal attribution) and attribute the behavior to some internal cause, such as a personal trait, motive, or attitude. For example, you might attribute a poor grade to lack of ability or to a poor memory. To some degree, attributions are influenced by informal psychological theories we develop through our observations of and interactions with people (Burton & Plaks, 2013). One such theory might be that children's behavior is primarily a function of parental discipline. A person who holds this theory is likely to attribute a child's misbehavior to poor parenting—a situational attribution. A person who does not hold this view is more likely to attribute misbehavior to the child's own personality or character—a dispositional attribution. Nevertheless, several other factors influence whether we make situational or dispositional attributions.

The attributions that people make for their own behavior tend to differ from those that they make for others. When making judgments about themselves, people tend to attribute their successes to dispositional variables and their failures to situational factors, a tendency known as the **self-serving bias** (Heider, 1958). For instance, a student exhibiting the self-serving bias would attribute a good exam grade to the effort she invested in preparing for the test (dispositional) and a poor exam grade to the confusing nature of the test questions (situational). Some psychologists suggest that the self-serving bias results from our need to protect our self-concepts and helps us manage unpleasant emotions such as disappointment (Heider, 1958). Studies show that people with psychological disorders such as depression exhibit the self-serving bias to a lesser degree than people who do not have such disorders (e.g., Green et al., 2013; Mezulis, Abramson, Hyde, & Hankin, 2004).

When people make judgments about others, they tend to exhibit the **actor-observer effect**, the general tendency to attribute others' behavior to dispositional factors more than we do to our own behavior (Jones & Nisbett, 1971). The term *actor-observer* implies that we make one kind of attribution when we are *actors* and another when we are *observers*. In the actor role, we pay more attention to situational variables, and in the observer role, we focus more on dispositions. Therefore, in a situation such as an auto accident, like the scenario in the *Think About It* activity at the beginning of the chapter, we are likely to attribute the other driver's actions to dispositional variables such as personality and substance abuse and our own behavior to situational variables such as the traffic conditions that existed at the time of the crash. However, research suggests that the amount of information that a person has about his own and others' behavior influences the actor-observer effect (Malle, 2006). That is, a driver may judge her contribution to an accident as resulting from traffic conditions because she is familiar with her own past record of safe driving. Likewise, knowledge of traffic conditions may prevent her from making a dispositional attribution for the other driver's actions until she has more information about the driver's dispositions.

People sometimes exhibit another attributional bias that involves rendering dispositional judgments regarding others' behavior. The **fundamental attribution error** is the tendency to give more attention to dispositional factors than is appropriate for a situation (Ross, 1977). For example, many people unthinkingly assume that a person who is overweight compulsively overeats (Sikorski et al., 2012). In other words, they attribute the person's weight to lack of self-control, a dispositional factor, even though they have no knowledge of the situational factors that may have contributed to the person's weight problem. For example, the person may have a medical condition that makes it difficult for him to control his weight. Similarly, many people automatically attribute homeless people's condition to dispositional factors such as irresponsibility, mental illness, or substance abuse.

Social psychologists suggest that people are most likely to fall prey to the fundamental attribution error when they confront situations with which they have little or no personal experience. For instance, we all make self-serving excuses for our mistakes. Have you ever heard a classmate say something like, "I didn't study for my psychology test because I got the date mixed up with my biology exam"? If so, it is unlikely that you subjected your classmate to a lecture on personal responsibility because you empathize with her plight and can understand how such a slip-up might have happened. By contrast, when people who have been convicted of crimes offer explanations of the factors that led them to violate the law, many people view the excuse making as a cause of the criminal behavior (Maruna & Mann, 2006). Instead of helping the convicted person focus on the changes he needs to make in the present in order to have a better future (i.e., factors that are part of his current situation), relatives and acquaintances make statements such as, "He'll never get his life together until he stops making excuses for what he did and takes responsibility for it." While it might be true that the convicted person is evading responsibility, these statements reflect the fundamental attribution error because they involve an inappropriate emphasis on his disposition as the cause of his behavior and, therefore, a major obstacle to his future success. In reality, his future success is likely to be far more dependent on situational factors such as the degree to which he takes advantage of opportunities for furthering his education than on a change in his disposition.

Culture apparently contributes to attributional biases as well. In a series of studies, researchers compared Koreans' and Americans' situational and dispositional attributions for both desirable and undesirable behaviors (Choi et al., 2003). They found that Koreans, on average, made more situational attributions than Americans did, no matter what kind of behavior participants were asked to explain. The reason for the difference, according to the researchers, was that the Koreans took into account more information than the Americans did before making attributions.

Researchers who analyzed Chinese and American Olympic gold medalists' attributions arrived at a somewhat different conclusion (Hua & Tan, 2012). They found that Chinese athletes tended to attribute their success to situational factors such as coaching, opportunities to train, and parental support. By contrast, American medalists were more likely to attribute their success to dispositional factors such as self-discipline, personal goals, and motivation. The authors suggested that these differences were consistent with Chinese and American cultural norms regarding the relationship of the individual to society rather than the result of variations in cognitive processing.

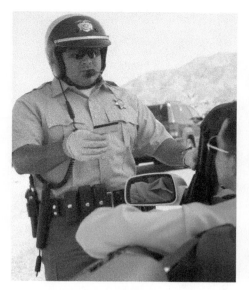

▲ Which of these statements do you think best explains this situation? (A) The driver doesn't respect the traffic laws. (B) This driver was probably in a hurry to get to work or school. You should recognize that (A) is a dispositional attribution and (B) is a situational attribution. You probably also concluded that you don't have enough information to choose between the two options. Yet, in real life, we are quick to blame others' errors on dispositions (fundamental attribution error) and our own on situations (the actor-observer effect).

REMEMBER IT   *Check your answers and take additional quizzes in MyPsychLab.com.*   ✓• Study and Review on MyPsychLab

1. Because of the _____, people pay closer attention to early information they receive about a person than to later information.

2. The tendency to attribute one's own behavior to situational factors and the behavior of others to dispositional factors is called the _____.

3. Attributing a person's good grades to her teacher's competence is a _____ attribution.

Attraction

Think for a moment about your friends. What makes you like, or even fall in love with, one person and ignore or react negatively to someone else? In this section, we'll look at the factors that influence why we're attracted to another person and learn about different kinds of love.

14.3 What factors contribute to attraction?

proximity Physical or geographic closeness; a major influence on attraction.

mere-exposure effect The tendency to feel more positively toward a stimulus as a result of repeated exposure to it.

Factors Influencing Attraction

Several factors influence attraction. One is **proximity**, or physical or geographic closeness. Obviously, it is much easier to make friends with people who are close at hand. One reason proximity matters is the **mere-exposure effect**, the tendency to feel more positively toward a stimulus as a result of repeated exposure to it. People, food, songs, and clothing styles become more acceptable the more we are exposed to them. Advertisers rely on the positive effects of repeated exposure to increase people's liking for products and even for political candidates.

Our own moods and emotions, whether positive or negative, can influence how much we are attracted to people we meet. We may develop positive or negative feelings toward others simply because they are present when very good or very bad things happen to us. Further, we tend to like the people who also like us—or who we *believe* like us—a phenomenon called *reciprocity* or *reciprocal liking*.

Beginning in elementary school and continuing through life, people are also more likely to pick friends of the same age, gender, race, and socioeconomic class. We tend to choose friends and lovers who have similar views on most things that are important to us. Similar interests and attitudes toward leisure-time activities make it more likely that time spent together is rewarding.

Perhaps no other factor influences attraction more than physical attractiveness. People of all ages have a strong tendency to prefer physically attractive people (Langlois et al., 2000). Even 6-month-old infants, when given the chance to look at a photograph of an attractive or an unattractive woman, man, or infant, will spend more time looking at the attractive face (Ramsey et al., 2004). Contextual factors such as people's clothing and even the types of cars they drive influence others' perceptions of their attractiveness (Elliot et al., 2013; Guéguene & Lamy, 2012). But physical appearance matters as well.

halo effect The tendency to assume that a person has generally positive or negative traits as a result of observing one major positive or negative trait.

Symmetrical faces and bodies are seen as more attractive and sexually appealing (Green et al., 2008). In a classic review of 11 meta-analyses of cross-cultural studies of attractiveness, Langlois and others (2000) found that males and females across many cultures have similar ideas about the physical attractiveness of members of the opposite sex. When native Asian, Hispanic American, and White American male students rated photographs of Asian, Hispanic, African American, and White females on attractiveness, Cunningham and others (1995) reported a very high mean correlation (.93) among the groups in attractiveness ratings. When African American and White American men rated photos of African American women, their agreement on facial features was also very high—a correlation of .94. Evolutionary psychologists suggest that this cross-cultural similarity exists because of a tendency, shaped by natural selection, to look for indicators of health in potential mates (Fink & Penton-Voak, 2002).

Why does physical attractiveness matter? When people have one trait that we either admire or dislike very much, we often assume that they have other positive or negative traits—a phenomenon known as the **halo effect** (Nisbett & Wilson, 1977). Dion, Berschied, and Walster (1972) found that people generally attribute additional favorable qualities to those who are attractive. Attractive people are seen as more exciting, personable, interesting, and socially desirable than unattractive people. As a result, job interviewers are more likely to recommend highly attractive people, especially for positions that involve face-to-face contact with a firm's customers (Tsai, Huang, & Yu, 2012). Similarly, when asked to rate pictures of women with regard to the likelihood of career success, research participants give higher ratings to those who are thin than to those who are overweight or obese (Wade & DiMaria, 2003).

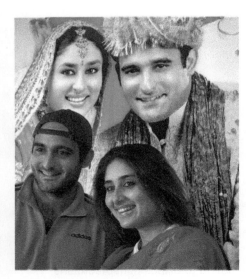

▲ Cross-cultural research suggests that "Bollywood" (Hindi) star Akshay Khanna (left) would be perceived as attractive by people in all cultures.

Does this mean that unattractive people don't have a chance? Fortunately not. Eagly and her colleagues (1991) suggest that the impact of physical attractiveness is strongest in the perception of strangers. But once we get to know people, other qualities assume more importance. In fact, as we come to like people, they begin to look more attractive to us, while people with undesirable personal qualities begin to look less attractive. 👁

Intimate Relationships ▶

Most of the factors that influence attraction in general, such as physical attractiveness, also influence romantic attraction. But what about love? As you will learn, the kind of love that intimate partners experience influences their relationship throughout its duration.

Romantic Attraction. You probably have heard that opposites attract, but is this really true? The **matching hypothesis** suggests that we are likely to end up with a partner similar to ourselves in physical attractiveness and other assets (Berscheid et al., 1971; Burriss et al., 2011; Feingold, 1988; Walster & Walster, 1969). Furthermore, couples mismatched in attractiveness are more likely to end the relationship (Cash & Janda, 1984). It has been suggested that we estimate our social assets and realistically expect to attract someone with approximately equal assets. Fear of rejection prevents many people from pursuing those who are much more attractive than they are. Nevertheless, once a relationship is formed, both men and women develop the ability to screen out the attractiveness of alternative partners (Maner, Gailliot, & Miller, 2009). Thus, while continuing to be attentive to a partner's attractiveness is important to maintaining a romantic relationship, ignoring the attractiveness of other potential partners may be just as important to relationship stability and longevity.

Most research indicates that similarity in needs is mainly what attracts (Buss, 1984; Phillips et al., 1988). Similarities in personality, physical traits, intellectual ability, education, religion, ethnicity, socioeconomic status, and attitudes are also related to partner choice (Escorio & Martin-Buro, 2012; Luo & Klohnen, 2005; O'Leary & Smith, 1991). And similarities in needs and in personality appear to be related to marital success as well as to marital choice (O'Leary & Smith, 1991; Rammstedt et al., 2013). Similarities wear well. If you were to select a life partner, what qualities would attract you? Complete the *Try It* to evaluate your own preferences.

👁 Watch the Video *Explore Attractiveness* in **MyPsychLab**

14.4 What factors contribute to the formation and maintenance of intimate relationships?

matching hypothesis The notion that people tend to have lovers or spouses who are similar to themselves in physical attractiveness and other assets.

▲ You are more likely to be attracted to someone who is similar to you than to someone who is your opposite.

TRY IT — Choosing a Life Partner

Choosing a Life Partner

In your choice of a life partner, which qualities are most and least important to you? Rank these 18 qualities of a potential life partner from most important (1) to least important (18) to you.

_____ Ambition and industriousness

_____ Chastity (no previous sexual intercourse)

_____ Desire for home and children

_____ Education and intelligence

_____ Emotional stability and maturity

_____ Favorable social status or rating

_____ Good cooking and housekeeping skills

_____ Similar political background

_____ Similar religious background

_____ Good health

_____ Good looks

_____ Similar education

_____ Pleasing disposition

_____ Refinement/neatness

_____ Sociability

_____ Good financial prospects

_____ Dependable character

_____ Mutual attraction/love

👁 Watch the Video *Episode 16: What's In It for Me? Attraction and Persuasion* in **MyPsychLab**

Compare your rankings from the *Try It* to those of men and women from 33 countries and 5 major islands around the world. Generally, men and women across those cultures rate these four qualities as most important in life partner selection: (1) mutual attraction/love, (2) dependable character, (3) emotional stability and maturity, and (4) pleasing disposition (Buss et al., 1990). Aside from these first four choices, however, women and men differ somewhat in the attributes they prefer. According to the findings of evolutionary psychologist David Buss (1994), men tend to look for physical attractiveness, while women prefer men who appear to have economic resources and social status. These preferences, he claims, have been adaptive in human evolutionary history. To a male, beauty and youth suggest health and fertility—the best opportunity to send his genes into the next generation. To a female, resources and social status provide security for her and her children (Buss & Shackelford, 2008). As was noted in Chapter 9, social role theorists maintain that gender differences in mate preferences are influenced by economic and social forces as well as evolutionary forces (Wood & Eagly, 2007).

Sternberg's Triangular Theory of Love. In Western culture, affection is an important part of most relationships, including friendships, and being "in love" is the most important factor in the formation of long-term romantic relationships. But what is love? Robert Sternberg (1986b, 1987), whose triarchic theory of intelligence was discussed in Chapter 7, has also proposed a **triangular theory of love**. Its three components are intimacy, passion, and commitment. Sternberg explains intimacy as the emotions associated with the relationship that foster a sense of connection in both partners. Passion refers to those drives in a loving relationship that involve sexual intimacy. The commitment component consists of (1) a short-term aspect, the decision that one loves another person, and (2) a long-term aspect, a commitment to maintaining that love over time.

Sternberg proposes that these three components, singly and in various combinations, produce seven different kinds of love (see Figure 14.1).

1. *Liking* includes only one of the love components—intimacy. In this case, liking is not used in a trivial sense. Sternberg says that this intimate liking characterizes true friendships, in which a person feels a bond, a warmth, and a closeness with another but not intense passion or long-term commitment.

2. *Infatuated love* consists solely of passion and is often what is felt as "love at first sight." But without the intimacy and the commitment components of love, infatuated love may disappear suddenly.

3. *Empty love* consists of the commitment component without intimacy or passion. Sometimes, a stronger love deteriorates into empty love, in which the commitment remains, but the intimacy and passion have died. In cultures in which arranged marriages are common, relationships often begin as empty love.

triangular theory of love Sternberg's theory that three components—intimacy, passion, and commitment—singly and in various combinations produce seven different kinds of love.

FIGURE 14.1 Sternberg's Triangular Theory of Love
Sternberg identifies three components of love—passion, intimacy, and commitment—and shows how the three, singly and in various combinations, produce seven different kinds of love. Consummate love, the most complete form of love, has all three components.
Source: Sternberg (1986b).

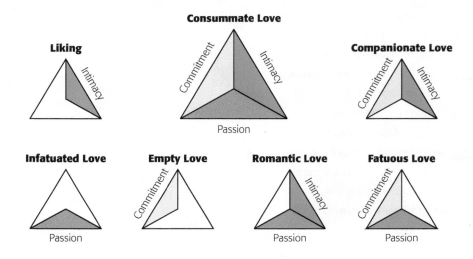

4. *Romantic love* is a combination of intimacy and passion. Romantic lovers are bonded emotionally (as in liking) and physically through passionate arousal.

5. *Fatuous love* has the passion and the commitment components but not the intimacy component. This type of love can be exemplified by a whirlwind courtship and marriage in which a commitment is motivated largely by passion, without the stabilizing influence of intimacy.

6. *Companionate love* consists of intimacy and commitment. This type of love is often found in marriages in which the passion has gone out of the relationship, but a deep affection and commitment remain.

7. *Consummate love* is the only type of love that includes all three components—intimacy, passion, and commitment. **Consummate love** is the most complete form of love, and it represents the ideal love relationship for which many people strive but which apparently few achieve. Sternberg cautions that maintaining a consummate love may be even harder than achieving it. He stresses the importance of translating the components of love into action. "Without expression," he warns, "even the greatest of loves can die" (1987, p. 341).

consummate love According to Sternberg's theory, the most complete form of love, consisting of all three components—intimacy, passion, and commitment.

REMEMBER IT   *Check your answers and take additional quizzes in MyPsychLab.com.*   ✓—[Study and **Review** on **MyPsychLab**

1. The tendency to attribute other positive qualities to people who are physically attractive is called the _____.

2. People are usually drawn to others who are _____ themselves.

3. The four attributes that men and women across cultures view as most important in a prospective mate are _____.

4. The type of love that is often called "love at first sight" is _____.

Conformity, Obedience, and Compliance

Do you think of yourself as independently minded? Most people do. In Western cultures in particular, individuality and independent thinking are highly valued. But what happened to your independent mindedness the last time that someone talked you into doing something that you really didn't want to do? As you have probably learned through experience, we are all subject to social influences in one way or another. Here, we'll look at three types of social influence: conformity, obedience, and compliance.

Conformity ▶

Conformity is changing or adopting a behavior or an attitude in an effort to be consistent with the social norms of a group or the expectations of other people. **Social norms** are the standards of behavior and the attitudes that are expected of members of a particular group. Some conformity is necessary if we are to have a society at all. We cannot drive on the other side of the road anytime we please. And we conform to other people's expectations to have their esteem or approval, their friendship or love, or even their company (Christensen et al., 2004).

The best-known experiment on conformity was conducted by Solomon Asch (1955), who designed the simple test shown in Figure 14.2 on p. 462. Eight male participants were seated around a large table and were asked, one by one, to tell the experimenter which of the three lines matched the standard line. But only one of the eight was an actual participant; the others were confederates assisting the experimenter. A researcher often must use one or more *confederates*—people who pose as participants in a psychology experiment but who are actually assisting the researcher.

⌈ **14.5** What did Asch find in his
⌊ classic experiment on conformity?

conformity Changing or adopting a behavior or an attitude in an effort to be consistent with the social norms of a group or the expectations of other people.

social norms The attitudes and standards of behavior expected of members of a particular group.

Standard Line

1   2   3

FIGURE 14.2 Asch's Classic Study of Conformity
If you were one of eight participants in the Asch experiment who were asked to pick the line (1, 2, or 3) that matched the standard line shown above them, which line would you choose? If the other participants all chose line 3, would you conform and answer line 3?
Source: Based on Asch (1955).

14.6 What did Milgram's classic study reveal about obedience?

Watch the Video *Episode 16: Basics: Under the Influence of Others* in **MyPsychLab**

obedience Behaving in accordance with the rules and commands of those in authority.

There were 18 trials—18 different lines to be matched. During 12 of these trials, the confederates all gave the same wrong answer, which of course puzzled the naive participant. A *naive subject* is a person who has agreed to participate in an experiment but is not aware that deception is being used to conceal its real purpose. Remarkably, Asch found that 5% of the subjects conformed to the incorrect, unanimous majority all of the time, 70% conformed some of the time, but 25% remained completely independent and were never swayed by the group.

Varying the experiment with groups of various sizes, Asch found that the tendency to go along with the majority opinion remained in full force even when there was a unanimous majority of only three confederates. Surprisingly, unanimous majorities of 15 confederates produced no higher conformity rate than did those of three. Asch also discovered that if just one other person voices a dissenting opinion, the tendency to conform is not as strong. When just one confederate in the group disagreed with the incorrect majority, the naive subjects' errors dropped drastically, from 32% to 10.4%.

Other research on conformity and the Big Five personality dimensions (refer to Chapter 11) reveals that people who are low in neuroticism but high in agreeableness and conscientiousness are more likely to conform than those who score oppositely on those dimensions (DeYoung, Peterson, & Higgins, 2002). Moreover, individuals who do not believe in free will are more likely to conform than those who do (Alquist, Ainsworth, & Baumeister, 2013). Even so, those who hold minority opinions on an issue have more influence in changing a majority view if they present a well-organized, clearly stated argument and if they are especially consistent in advocating their views (Wood et al., 1994).

Obedience

Can you imagine a world in which each person always did exactly what he or she wanted, without regard for rules or respect for authority? We would stop at red lights only when we felt like it or weren't in a hurry. Someone might decide that he liked your car better than his own and take it. Or worse, someone might kill you because of an interest in your intimate partner.

Clearly, **obedience**—behaving in accordance with the rules and commands of those in authority—helps to ensure that society survives and functions smoothly. However, unquestioned obedience can cause humans to commit unbelievably horrible

▲ In this scene from Asch's experiment on conformity, all but one of the "subjects" were really confederates of the experimenter. They deliberately chose the wrong line to try to influence the naive subject (second from right) to go along with the majority.

acts. One of the darkest chapters in human history arose from the obedience of officials in Nazi Germany who carried out Adolf Hitler's orders to exterminate Jews and other "undesirables." 👁

Intrigued by questions about what drove the guards in Nazi death camps to obey their superiors, social psychologist Stanley Milgram conducted one of the most startling experiments in the history of psychology in the early 1960s. He placed an advertisement in various newspapers in the New Haven, Connecticut, area that read, "Wanted: Volunteers to serve as subjects in a study of memory and learning at Yale University." Many people responded to the ad, and 40 male participants between the ages of 20 and 50 were selected. Yet, instead of a memory experiment, a staged drama was planned. The cast of characters was as follows:

- The Experimenter: A 31-year-old high school biology teacher, dressed in a gray laboratory coat, who assumed a stern and serious manner
- The Learner: A middle-aged man (an actor and accomplice of the experimenter)
- The Teacher: One of the volunteers

The experimenter led the teacher and the learner into one room, where the learner was strapped into an electric chair apparatus. The teacher was delivered a sample shock of 45 volts, supposedly for the purpose of testing the equipment and showing the teacher what the learner would feel. Next, the script called for the learner to complain of a heart condition and say that he hoped the electric shocks would not be too painful. The experimenter admitted that the stronger shocks would hurt but hastened to add, "Although the shocks can be extremely painful, they cause no permanent tissue damage" (Milgram, 1963, p. 373).

Then the experimenter took the teacher to an adjoining room and seated him in front of an instrument panel with 30 lever switches arranged horizontally across the front. The first switch on the left, he was told, delivered only 15 volts, but each successive switch was 15 volts stronger than the previous one, up to the last switch, which carried 450 volts. The switches on the instrument panel were labeled with designations ranging from "Slight Shock" to "Danger: Severe Shock" to "XXX." The experimenter instructed the teacher to read a list of word pairs to the learner and then test his memory. When the learner made the right choice, the teacher was supposed to go on to the next pair. If the learner missed a question, the teacher was told to flip a switch and shock him, moving one switch to the right—delivering 15 additional volts—each time the learner missed a question.

The learner performed well at first but then began missing about three out of every four questions. The teacher began flipping the switches. When he hesitated, the experimenter urged him to continue. If he still hesitated, the experimenter said, "The experiment requires that you continue," or more strongly, "You have no other choice, you must go on" (Milgram, 1963, p. 374). At the 20th switch, 300 volts, the script required the learner to pound on the wall and scream, "Let me out of here, let me out, my heart's bothering me, let me out!" (Meyer, 1972, p. 461). From this point on, the learner answered no more questions. If the teacher expressed concern or a desire to discontinue the experiment, the experimenter answered, "Whether the learner likes it or not, you must go on" (Milgram, 1963, p. 374). At the flip of the next switch—315 volts—the teacher heard only groans from the learner. Again, if the teacher expressed reluctance to go on, the experimenter said, "You have no other choice, you must go on" (Milgram, 1963, p. 374). If the teacher insisted on stopping at this point, the experimenter allowed him to do so.

How many of the 40 participants in the Milgram study do you think obeyed the experimenter to the end—450 volts? Surprisingly not a single participant stopped before the 20th switch, at supposedly 300 volts, when the learner began pounding the wall (see Figure 14.3 on p. 464). Amazingly, 26 participants—65% of the sample—obeyed the experimenter to the bitter end and only withdrew when they reached the maximum voltage level. But this experiment took a terrible toll on

👁 **Watch** the Video *Obedience* in **MyPsychLab**

▲ In Stanley Milgram's experiments on obedience, "teachers" were led to believe that they could deliver electric shocks to "learners" who were hooked to devices such as the one shown here. Courtesy of Alexandra Milgram. Copyright 1968 by Stanley Milgram. Copyright renewed 1993 by Alexandra Milgram. From the film OBEDIENCE, distributed by Penn State Media Sales.

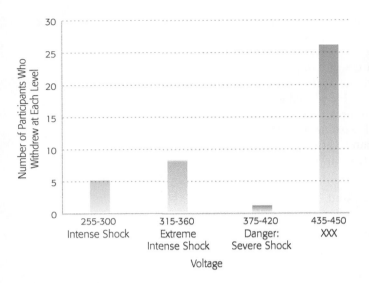

FIGURE 14.3 Milgram's Obedience Experiment
Sixty-five percent of the "teachers" in Milgram's study believed that they were delivering the maximum shock possible to the "learner."
Source: Milgram (1963).

14.7 What techniques do people use to gain compliance from others?

compliance Acting in accordance with the direct requests of other people.

foot-in-the-door technique A strategy designed to gain a favorable response to a small request at first, with the intent of making the person more likely to agree later to a larger request.

door-in-the-face technique A strategy in which someone makes a large, unreasonable request with the expectation that the person will refuse but will then be more likely to respond favorably to a smaller request later.

the participants. They bit their lips, groaned, and stuttered, all of which Milgram took to mean that indicated that they were quite uncomfortable (Milgram, 1963). Moreover, in an effort to avoid administering further shocks, some teachers begged the learners to respond correctly. Curiously, too, some participants began to laugh as the experiment progressed and the "learner" exhibited increasing degrees of distress. In a few, the laughter developed into seizures. Milgram suggested that participants' psychological distress resulted from a conflict between a desire to avoid harming others and a need to conform to the demands of those who hold legitimate authority.

Milgram's follow-up studies tested the limits of obedience. In one such study Milgram (1965) varied the procedures of the original experiment: Each trial involved three teachers, two of whom were confederates and the other, a naive participant. One confederate was instructed to refuse to continue after 150 volts, and the other confederate after 210 volts. In this situation, 36 out of 40 naive participants (90%) defied the experimenter before the maximum shock could be given, compared with only 14 out of 40 participants in the original experiment (Milgram, 1965). In Milgram's experiment, as in Asch's conformity study, the presence of another person who refused to go along gave many of the participants the courage to defy authority.

Many psychologists criticized Milgram's studies because of the distress that his methods caused to participants and the critical role that deception played in the experiment (King, Viney, & Woody, 2009). In fact, criticism of Milgram's methods was instrumental in the development of ethical standards for researchers that eventually prohibited studies such as his. Limitations on deception are a key component of these standards. Nevertheless, deception has continued to be an important element of social psychological research.

Compliance

How often do you do what others want you to do? There are many times when people act in accordance with the direct requests of others. This type of action is called **compliance**. One strategy people use to gain the compliance of others, the **foot-in-the-door technique**, is designed to gain a favorable response to a small request first. The intent is to make the person more likely to agree later to a larger request (the result desired from the beginning). For example, your roommate might ask you to throw a few extra items in the washer for her when you're doing a load of laundry in the hope that you will include her laundry with yours on a regular basis in the future.

In a classic study of the foot-in-the-door technique, a researcher claiming to represent a consumers' group called a number of homes and asked whether the people answering the phone would mind responding to a few questions about the soap products they used. Then, a few days later, the same person called those who had agreed to the first request and asked if he could send five or six of his assistants to conduct an inventory of the products in their home. The researcher told the people that the inventory would take about 2 hours and that the inventory team would have to search all drawers, cabinets, and closets in the house. Nearly 53% of those asked preliminary questions agreed to the larger request, compared to 22% of a control group who were contacted only once with the larger request (Freedman & Fraser, 1966).

How would you respond to a friend who asked to borrow 50 dollars? Suppose that you told your friend that you couldn't afford to loan him the money, and he reduced his request to 20 dollars. If you agree, your compliance was gained through a strategy called the **door-in-the-face technique**, a technique in which a large, unreasonable request is made first. The expectation is that the person will refuse but will then be more likely to respond favorably to a smaller request later (the result desired from the beginning). In a classic study of the door-in-the-face technique, college students were approached on campus. They were asked to agree to serve without pay as counselors to juvenile delinquents for 2 hours each week for a minimum of 2 years. As you would imagine, not a single person agreed (Cialdini et al., 1975). Then, the experimenters presented a much smaller request, asking if the students would agree to take a group of juveniles on a 2-hour trip to the zoo. Half the students agreed, a fairly high compliance rate. The researchers used another group of college students as controls, asking them to respond only to the smaller request, for the zoo trip. Only 17% agreed when the smaller request was presented alone.

Another method used to gain compliance is the **low-ball technique**. A very attractive initial offer is made to get people to commit themselves to an action, and then the terms are made less favorable. For example, suppose you receive a coupon for a free dinner at an expensive restaurant, and when you go the restaurant you learn that you have to listen to a 1-hour sales pitch for a financial services company before you can order your dinner. You have just been subjected to the low-ball technique.

In a classic study of this technique, college students were asked to enroll in an experimental course for which they would receive credit. After the students had agreed to participate, they were informed that the class would meet at 7:00 a.m. Control group participants were told about the class meeting time when first asked to enroll. More than 50% of the low-balled group agreed to participate, but only 25% of control participants did so (Cialdini et al., 1978).

low-ball technique A strategy in which someone makes a very attractive initial offer to get a person to commit to an action and then makes the terms less favorable.

REMEMBER IT   *Check your answers and take additional quizzes in MyPsychLab.com.*   ✓●─Study and Review on MyPsychLab

1. Solomon Asch's classic experiment is the best known study of _____.
2. How many of the participants in Milgram's original obedience experiment stopped administering shocks to the "learner" as soon as he appeared to be in pain?
3. The _____ technique is designed to gain a favorable response to a small request before making a larger request.
4. When members of a group are more concerned with preserving group solidarity than with evaluating all possible alternatives in making a decision, _____ occurs.

Group Influence

Have you ever seen a movie in which you really weren't interested or gone to the beach when you would have preferred to stay home because your friends wanted to? Being part of a group often means giving up a bit of individuality, but the reward is the support and camaraderie of the group. Clearly, we behave differently in a variety of ways when we are part of a group, small or large. What happens when the group of which we are a part is made up of strangers? Do such groups influence our behavior as well? We'll answer these and other questions about group influences in this section.

social facilitation Any positive or negative effect on performance that can be attributed to the presence of others, either as an audience or as coactors.

audience effects The impact of passive spectators on performance.

Social Facilitation and Social Loafing ▶

In certain cases, individual performance can be either helped or hindered by the mere physical presence of others. The term **social facilitation** refers to any effect on performance, whether positive or negative, that can be attributed to the presence of others. Research on this phenomenon has focused on two types of effects: (1) **audience effects**, the impact of passive spectators on performance, and (2) **coaction effects**, the impact on performance caused by the presence of other people engaged in the same task.

⌈ **14.8** How do social facilitation and social loafing affect
⌊ performance?

coaction effects The impact on performance of the presence of other people engaged in the same task.

FIGURE 14.4 **Social Facilitation:**

FIGURE 14.4 Social Facilitation: Performing in the Presence of Others
The presence of others (either as an audience or as coactors engaged in the same task) may have opposite effects, either helping or hindering an individual's performance. Why? First, the presence of others heightens arousal. Second, heightened arousal leads to better performance on tasks the individual is good at and worse performance on tasks that are difficult for him or her.
Source: Based on Zajonc & Sales (1966).

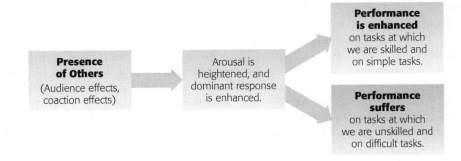

Presence of Others (Audience effects, coaction effects) → Arousal is heightened, and dominant response is enhanced. →

Performance is enhanced on tasks at which we are skilled and on simple tasks.

Performance suffers on tasks at which we are unskilled and on difficult tasks.

social loafing The tendency to put forth less effort when working with others on a common task than when working alone.

In one of the first studies in social psychology, Norman Triplett (1898) looked at coaction effects. He had observed in official records that bicycle racers pedaled faster when they were pedaling against other racers than when they were racing against the clock. Was this pattern of performance peculiar to competitive bicycling? Or was it part of a more general phenomenon whereby people would work faster and harder in the presence of others than when performing alone? Triplett set up a study in which he told 40 children to wind fishing reels as quickly as possible under one of two conditions: (1) alone or (2) in the presence of other children performing the same task. He found that children worked faster when other reel turners were present. But later studies on social facilitation found that in the presence of others people's performance improves on easy tasks but suffers on difficult tasks (Michaels et al., 1982). See Figure 14.4.

Have you ever been assigned by a teacher or professor to work in a group and, at the end of the project, felt that you had carried more than your fair share of the workload? Such feelings are not uncommon. Researcher Bibb Latané used the term **social loafing** to refer to people's tendency to put forth less effort when working with others on a common task than they do when they are working alone (Latané, Williams, & Harkins, 1979). Social loafing occurs in situations where no one person's contribution to the group can be identified and individuals are neither praised for a good performance nor blamed for a poor one (Mefoh & Nwanosike, 2012). However, individuals who display high levels of the Big Five trait conscientiousness or have a strong work ethic are less likely to engage in social loafing than their peers (Ferrari & Pychyl, 2012; Smrt & Karau, 2011).

Similarly, achievement motivation (see Chapter 9) influences social loafing (Hart et al., 2004). Researchers tested participants with regard to their levels of achievement motivation and then assigned them to pairs. Each pair was asked to generate as many uses for a knife that they could think of. The amount of effort exhibited by participants who were low in achievement motivation depended on their partner's effort. When paired with partners who worked hard, individuals with low achievement motivation contributed little; that is, they engaged in social loafing. They did the opposite, however, when paired with others who didn't work. By contrast, participants who were high in achievement motivation worked hard at the task no matter what their partner's level of participation was.

Some 80 experimental studies have been conducted on social loafing in diverse cultures, including those of Taiwan, Japan, Thailand, India, China, and the United States. Social loafing on a variety of tasks was evident to some degree in all of the cultures studied. But it appears to be more common in individualistic Western cultures, such as the United States (Hong, Wyer, & Fong, 2008; Karau & Williams, 1993).

▲ Studying in a group could lead to social loafing through a diffusion of responsibility effect.

Group Decision Making ▶

It is commonly believed that groups tend to make more moderate decisions than individuals. However, research shows that group discussion often causes members of a group to shift to a more extreme position after participating in a discussion in which other group members strongly express agreement with them, a phenomenon known as **group polarization** (Kerr & Tindale, 2004). An example will help you see how this finding applies to everyday discussions of issues about which some people have very strong opinions. Suppose you haven't fully decided whether you support or oppose the death penalty but lean toward favoring it. Research on group polarization suggests that discussing the issue with people who strongly support the death penalty will make you more likely to end up supporting it yourself. By contrast, if you are undecided but lean toward opposing the death penalty, discussing it with people who strongly oppose it will make you more likely to make a firm commitment to opposing the death penalty yourself.

In classic research, Myers and Bishop (1970) found that, as a result of group polarization, group discussions of racial issues can either increase or decrease prejudice, depending on the average "leanings" of the group at the beginning of the discussion. However, studies also show that lower degrees of polarization are exhibited in groups in which two sides of an issue are presented in a balanced manner (Kuhn & Lao, 1996). Moreover, when a group includes two or more factions, or subgroups, that are strongly committed to opposing views, compromise rather than polarization is the most likely outcome.

Groupthink is the term that social psychologist Irving Janis (1982, 2007) applied to the kind of decision making that is sometimes seen in tightly knit groups. For instance, you may have heard news stories about college fraternity parties at which members and guests dress in costumes that are deeply offensive to some ethnic groups. Social psychologists would say that groupthink plays a role in the decision-making process that leads to such parties. That is, when members are planning such a party, most of them get caught up in the idea and think it will be great fun. Members who realize that the party is inappropriate and will offend others keep their doubts to themselves in order to maintain relationships with others in the group, that is, so that they won't be seen as spoiling others' fun.

When tightly knit groups of this kind are more concerned with preserving group solidarity and uniformity than with objectively evaluating all possible alternatives in decision making, individual members may hesitate to voice any dissent. Those individuals who turn against the group may face retaliation for their actions (see the *Explain It* feature on page 468.) The group may also discredit opposing views from outsiders and begin to believe it is incapable of making mistakes.

To guard against groupthink, Janis (1982) suggests that it is necessary to encourage open discussion of alternative views and the expression of any objections and doubts. He further recommends that outside experts sit in and challenge the views of the group. At least one group member should take the role of devil's advocate whenever a policy alternative is evaluated. To avoid groupthink in workplace situations, managers should withhold their own opinions when problem-solving and decision-making strategies are being considered (Bazan, 1998).

There are some situations in which group decision making appears to be better than that of individuals. In one study, college students' attitudes toward risky behaviors such as driving under the influence of alcohol were measured after the students participated in experimental conditions in which they (1) drank alcohol alone, (2) drank alcohol in a group, (3) drank a placebo they believed to be alcohol alone, or (4) drank a placebo they believed to be alcohol in a group (Abrams et al., 2006). Students who drank alcohol alone were more likely than either those who drank in groups (both alcohol and placebo) or those who drank a placebo alone to exhibit a willingness to engage in risky behaviors. The study's authors concluded that drinking in a small group may afford drinkers some protection against making poor decisions about risky behaviors.

group polarization A group member's adoption of a more extreme position about an issue than she or he originally held after participating in a discussion in which other group members strongly express agreement with her or him.

groupthink The tendency for members of a tightly knit group to be more concerned with preserving group solidarity and uniformity than with objectively evaluating all alternatives in decision making.

EXPLAIN IT — Why Doesn't Groupthink Occur in Every Tightly Knit Group?

Suppose that a group of girlfriends who are sophomores in high school promise each other that they will always be friends. To be sure that they stick together, the girls take a solemn oath that they will all attend the same college. Is this an example of groupthink? To determine whether these girls have succumbed to groupthink, predict what will happen if one member of the group changes her mind and goes to a different school. Do you think the other girls will retaliate against her?

You probably predicted that the other girls would be disappointed but would not retaliate in any serious way against the nonconforming member of their group. Groupthink typically occurs only in groups that are characterized by very high levels of interpersonal pressure, or even coercion, to conform to the group. Furthermore, groupthink is likely to be found in groups that have authoritarian leaders who remind members of the need for loyalty. Once groupthink is established, individuals are expected to give greater weight to group loyalty than to their own moral values or those of the larger society. Any member who fails to do so is likely to be punished by the group. Consequently, retaliation against members who turn against the group is another feature of groupthink. There are many real-world examples of individuals who have experienced groupthink-induced retaliation that you can learn more about by searching the Internet:

- *Joe Darby: reported abuse of inmates by his fellow guards at Abu Ghraib prison in Iraq*

- *Jeffrey Wigand: exposed the efforts of the tobacco company for which he worked to increase the addictive power of cigarettes and to hide research findings about smoking and lung disease*
- *Frank Serpico: exposed a number of his colleagues on the New York City police force who were accepting bribes from criminals*
- *John Dean: member of President Nixon's staff who revealed the role that White House staffers and the president himself played in the complex scandal known as "Watergate"*

Researching a few of these cases will help you gain insight into how groupthink develops and how it affects group members. You will also learn a great deal about courage. Each of these individuals regretted hurting the friends he or she left behind and feared retaliation. Moreover, each has experienced varying degrees of retaliation. However, these individuals do not regret the actions they took because they know that doing the right thing is more important than group loyalty.

Watch on MyPsychLab

14.10 How do social roles influence individual behavior?

social roles Socially defined behaviors considered appropriate for individuals occupying certain positions within a given group.

deindividuation A social psychological process in which individuals lose their sense of personal identity as a result of identification with a group.

social identity A social psychological process in which individuals join with others to construct a group identity to insulate themselves from stressors.

Social Roles

Social roles are socially defined behaviors that are considered appropriate for individuals occupying certain positions within a given group. These roles can shape our behavior, sometimes quickly and dramatically. Consider a classic experiment (the Stanford Prison Experiment) in which psychologist Philip Zimbardo (1972) simulated a prison experience. College student volunteers were randomly assigned to be either guards or prisoners. The guards, wearing uniforms and carrying small clubs, strictly enforced harsh rules. The prisoners were stripped naked, searched, and deloused. Then, they were given prison uniforms, assigned numbers, and locked away in small, bare cells. The guards quickly adapted to their new role, some even to the point of becoming heartless and sadistic. One guard remembered forcing prisoners to clean toilets with their bare hands. And the prisoners began to act debased and subservient. The role playing became all too real—so much so that the experiment had to be ended in only 6 days.

Zimbardo invoked social psychologist Leon Festinger's concept of **deindividuation** to explain the study's outcome (Festinger, Pepitone, & Newcomb, 1952; Zimbardo, 1969). Deindividuation occurs when individuals lose their sense of personal identity as a result of identification with a group. Many social psychologists think that deindividuation explains phenomena such as looting, in which being part of a large group causes people to violate norms that they would obey if they were alone.

British psychologists Alexander Haslam and Stephen Reicher (2008) have challenged the deindividuation hypothesis, however. They argue that the outcome of the Stanford Prison Experiment was shaped by **social identity**, or the tendency to join with others to construct a group identity that insulates individual members against a stressor (Haslam et al., 2009; Haslam & Reicher, 2012). Thus, they say that the participants in the Stanford Prison Experiment were strongly influenced by the stressors that were associated with the instructions they were given by Zimbardo in his role as the "Superintendent" of the prison (Haslam & Reicher, 2006). Zimbardo instructed the guards to do whatever was necessary, including inflicting harm on them if needed, to convince the prisoners that they were powerless.

In their own similar experiment, the BBC Prison Study, Reicher and Haslam did not align themselves with either the guards or the prisoners (Haslam & Reicher, 2004; www.bbcprisonstudy.org). The guards were given control of the prisoners' physical environment, their schedule, and so on, but the researchers did not give either group instructions as to how to treat the other. Under these conditions, the guards did not behave abusively toward the prisoners. When asked to explain why they had treated the prisoners humanely, the guards explained that when they were faced with opportunities to treat prisoners abusively, imagining how authority figures in their own lives, such as their parents, would judge their actions motivated them to treat the prisoners well.

The prisoners in the BBC study also behaved differently than those in the Stanford study. Several days into the study, the researchers introduced a new prisoner into the group who had a background in union negotiations. As a result of ideas that were introduced to them by the new member of their group, the prisoners' beliefs about their status in relation to the guards changed. Moreover, the new prisoner taught them how to use collective bargaining strategies to persuade the guards to comply with their demands. As a result, the study's surprising result was that the guards felt themselves to be the more bullied of the two groups and reported experiencing more stress.

The findings of the BBC Prison Study call into question a role-based explanation for the results of the Stanford Prison Experiment. They also show that the degree to which deindividuation occurs when individuals take on social roles may depend on the kind of leadership that the group receives. Moreover, identification with a group may be adaptive in some situations, as it was when the prisoners learned to be good collective bargainers.

Another important point to be made about social roles is that they can have positive effects on behavior. In classic research examining adolescents with learning disabilities, Palinscar and Brown (1984) reported that students' learning behaviors were powerfully affected by their being assigned to play either the "teacher" or the "student" role in group study sessions. Participants summarized reading assignments more effectively, and as a result learned more from them, when functioning as a teacher than when functioning as a student.

▲ Zimbardo's experiment simulated the prison environment by randomly assigning participants to the social roles of prison guards or inmates. The social roles influenced the participants' behavior: The prisoners began acting like real prisoners, and the prison guards like real prison guards.

◉—Watch the Video *Stanford Prison Experiment* in **MyPsychLab**

REMEMBER IT *Check your answers and take additional quizzes in MyPsychLab.com.* ✓•—Study and Review on **MyPsychLab**

1. _____ leads to improved performance on easy tasks and poorer performance on more difficult tasks.
2. Social loafing is most likely to occur when _____ cannot be identified.
3. According to Zimbardo, the process of _____ influenced the behavior of participants in the Stanford Prison Experiment.

Attitudes and Attitude Change

We use the word *attitude* frequently in everyday speech. We say that someone has a "bad attitude," for instance. But what is an attitude? What happens when attitudes contradict one another, or when attitudes and behaviors are inconsistent? Have you ever tried to convince another person to agree with your opinions or to do something you wanted them to do? In this section, we'll learn about attitudes, cognitive dissonance, and persuasion.

Attitudes ▶

Essentially, **attitudes** are relatively stable evaluations of persons, objects, situations, or issues, along a continuum ranging from positive to negative (Bohner & Dickel, 2011). Most attitudes have three components: (1) a cognitive component, consisting of thoughts and beliefs about the attitudinal object; (2) an emotional component, made up of feelings toward the attitudinal object; and (3) a behavioral component,

14.11 What are the three components of an attitude?

attitude A relatively stable evaluation of a person, object, situation, or issue, along a continuum ranging from positive to negative.

FIGURE 14.5 The Three Components of an Attitude
An attitude is a relatively stable evaluation of a person, object, situation, or issue. Most of our attitudes have (1) a cognitive component, (2) an emotional component, and (3) a behavioral component.

composed of predispositions concerning actions toward the object (see Figure 14.5). Attitudes enable us to appraise people, objects, and situations, and provide structure and consistency in the social environment.

Some attitudes are acquired through firsthand experiences with people, objects, situations, and issues. Others are acquired when children hear parents, family, friends, and teachers express positive or negative attitudes toward certain issues or people. The mass media, including advertising, influence people's attitudes and reap billions of dollars annually for their efforts. As you might expect, however, the attitudes that people form through their own direct experience are stronger than those they acquire vicariously and are also more resistant to change (Nieto-Hernandez et al., 2008). Once formed, however, attitudes tend to strengthen when we associate with others who share them (Mercier & Landemore, 2012).

Lively discussions of controversial topics, even when those discussions take place only with others who agree with us, may improve our ability to think analytically about our attitudes. Researchers Joseph Lao and Deanna Kuhn (2002) asked college students to engage in a series of six discussions of a controversial topic with another student. Participants were assigned to three experimental conditions. In one arm of the study, all of the discussions involved a partner who agreed with them. In another, all of the partners disagreed. In the third condition, three discussion partners agreed and three disagreed with the participant. Six weeks later, Lao and Kuhn found that participants who had discussed the topic either with those who agreed with them or with an equal number of agreers and disagreers showed the greatest improvement in critical thinking about the topic. They inferred from these findings that discussing a controversial issue with people who disagree with you is helpful only if it is balanced by discussions with others who share your views. Despite ageist stereotypes, many studies have found that older adults are more likely to change their attitudes than are middle-aged adults (Visser & Krosnick, 1998).

We often hear that attitude change is the key to behavior change. However, a number of studies have shown that attitudes predict behavior only about 10% of the time (Wicker, 1969). People, for example, may express strong attitudes in favor of protecting the environment and conserving natural resources, yet not recycle or join a carpool (Knussen & Yule, 2008). However, attitudes are better predictors of behavior if they are strongly held, are readily accessible in memory, and are associated with pleasant emotional states (Bassili, 1995; Bissing-Olson et al., 2013; Fazio & Williams, 1986; Kraus, 1995). ◉

◉ Watch the Video *Episode 16: Thinking Like a Psychologist: Changing Attitudes and Behaviors* in **MyPsychLab**

14.12 What factors influence cognitive dissonance?

cognitive dissonance The unpleasant state that can occur when people become aware of inconsistencies between their attitudes or between their attitudes and their behavior.

Cognitive Dissonance

According to psychologist Leon Festinger (1957), if people discover that some of their attitudes are in conflict or that their attitudes are not consistent with their behavior, they are likely to experience an unpleasant state called **cognitive dissonance**. Psychologists believe that cognitive dissonance results from a desire to maintain self-esteem (Jordan et al., 2012; Stone, 2003). People usually try to reduce the dissonance by changing the behavior or the attitude or by somehow explaining

FIGURE 14.6 Methods of Reducing Cognitive Dissonance
Cognitive dissonance can occur when people become aware of inconsistencies in their attitudes or between their attitudes and their behavior. People try to reduce dissonance by (1) changing their behavior, (2) changing their attitude, (3) explaining away the inconsistency, or (4) reducing its importance. Here are examples of how a smoker might use these methods to reduce the cognitive dissonance created by his or her habit.

away the inconsistency or minimizing its importance (Crano & Prislin, 2006; Matz & Wood, 2005). By changing the attitude, individuals retain their self-esteem and reduce the discomfort caused by dissonance (Elliot & Devine, 1994).

Smoking creates a perfect situation for cognitive dissonance. Faced with a mountain of evidence linking smoking to a number of diseases, what are smokers to do? The healthiest, but perhaps not the easiest, way to reduce cognitive dissonance is to change the behavior—quit smoking. Another way is to change the attitude, to convince oneself that smoking is not as dangerous as it is said to be. Smokers may also tell themselves that they will stop smoking long before any permanent damage is done, or that medical science is advancing so rapidly that a cure for cancer or emphysema is just around the corner. Figure 14.6 illustrates the methods a smoker may use to reduce cognitive dissonance.

In classic research, Festinger and Carlsmith (1959) placed research participants alone in a room to play a boring game. On completing the game, participants were instructed to tell the next participants that the game was fun. Participants were randomly assigned to two experimental groups. One group was paid $1 for following instructions, while the other was paid $20. Festinger and Carlsmith assumed that the conflict between participants' self-esteem and their lying behavior would cause cognitive dissonance. How could participants resolve this dissonance and get rid of the threat to self-esteem caused by lying? Just as Festinger and Carlsmith had hypothesized, participants who were paid $1 resolved the conflict by convincing themselves that the game really had been fun—a change in attitude. By contrast, participants who were paid $20 resolved the conflict by justifying their actions on the basis of having been paid a fairly large sum of money relative to the amount of effort it had required to lie to the next participant. Consequently, they did not view the lie as a threat to their self-esteem.

Persuasion ▶

Persuasion is a deliberate attempt to influence the attitudes and/or the behavior of another person. Attempts at persuasion are pervasive parts of work experience, social experience, and even family life. Researchers have identified four elements of persuasion: (1) the source of the communication (who is doing the persuading), (2) the audience (who is being persuaded), (3) the message (what is being said), and (4) the medium (the means by which the message is transmitted).

Some factors that make the source (the communicator) more persuasive are credibility, attractiveness, and likability (Klucharev, Smidts, & Fernandez, 2008). A credible communicator is one who has expertise (knowledge of the topic at hand) and trustworthiness (truthfulness and integrity). Other characteristics of the source—including physical attractiveness, celebrity status, and similarity to the audience—also contribute to our responses to the sources of persuasive messages.

Audience characteristics influence responses to persuasion as well. Evidence suggests that a one-sided message is usually most persuasive if the audience is not well informed on the issue, is not highly intelligent, or already agrees with the point of view.

14.13 What are the elements of persuasion?

persuasion A deliberate attempt to influence the attitudes and/or behavior of another person.

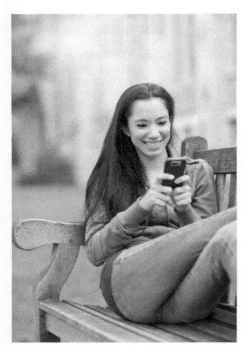

▲ "Likes" and "tweets" about new products, movies, and even candidates for elective office spread rapidly among friends and family members via mobile phone networks. Such messages are the lifeblood of viral marketing strategies.

A two-sided message (where both sides of an issue are mentioned) works best when the audience is well informed on the issue, is fairly intelligent, or is initially opposed to the point of view. A two-sided appeal will usually sway more people than will a one-sided appeal (Hovland, Lumsdaine, & Sheffield, 1949; McGuire, 1985). And people tend to scrutinize arguments that are contrary to their existing beliefs more carefully and exert more effort refuting them; they are also more likely to judge such arguments as being weaker than those that support their beliefs (Edwards & Smith, 1996).

A message can be well reasoned, logical, and unemotional ("just the facts"); it can be strictly emotional ("make their hair stand on end"); or it can be a combination of the two. Arousing fear seems to be an effective method for persuading people to quit smoking, get regular chest X-rays, wear seat belts, get flu vaccine shots, and get screening tests for cancer (Dillard & Anderson, 2004; Umeh, 2012). Appeals based on fear are most effective when the presentation outlines definite actions the audience can take to avoid the feared outcomes (Buller et al., 2000; Stephenson & Witte, 1998). However, nutritional messages are more effective when framed in terms of the benefits of dietary change rather than the harmful effects of a poor diet (van Assema et al., 2002).

The role that the medium plays in persuasion has gained a larger share of researchers' attention in recent years as people have increasingly turned to the Internet for information rather than to television, radio, and print media. Surprisingly, though, experimental studies show that television continues to be the most effective medium through which to communicate a persuasive message (Dijkstra, Buijtels, & van Raaij, 2005). Surveys of marketing researchers suggest that the effectiveness of online video advertisements may soon surpass that of television ads (BrightRoll, Inc., 2012). The reason for this emerging trend is that advertisers can target consumers more precisely and do so at a much lower cost than is the case for television advertising.

Viral marketing strategies have also challenged the dominance of television advertising in recent years. Such strategies employ online videos, Internet pop-up ads, text messages, instant messages, social networking sites, blogs, microblogs, podcasts, mass e-mails, and targeted e-mails that recipients are encouraged to forward to friends to publicize a message more quickly than traditional mass media such as television can disseminate it. Not surprisingly, research shows that product sales go up when marketers augment traditional approaches such as television advertising with viral strategies (Dhar & Chang, 2009). But what makes a message "go viral" in the first place? Research suggests that the emotional qualities of a message, especially one that is presented in an online video, are the determining factors (Berger & Milkman, 2012). Messages that inspire intense feelings of awe or anger are most likely to spread through a social network. Interestingly, too, emotion-provoking content is more important to the viral potential of an online video than its production quality.

REMEMBER IT

Check your answers and take additional quizzes in MyPsychLab.com. ✓ Study and Review on MyPsychLab

1. The three components of an attitude are _____, _____, and _____.
2. Changing an attitude can reduce cognitive _____.
3. The four elements of persuasion are _____, _____, _____, _____.

Prosocial Behavior

prosocial behavior Behavior that benefits others, such as helping, cooperation, and sympathy.

Psychologists define **prosocial behavior** as any behavior that benefits others, such as helping, cooperation, and sympathy. Examples of prosocial behavior abound in everyday life: A customer at a convenience store check-out counter turns up a few cents short, and the next person in line hands him the money. A parent pushing a stroller has difficulty negotiating her way through a heavy shopping mall door, and a customer on the way out of the mall holds the door open for her. And when large-scale tragedies strike, people demonstrate remarkable levels of generosity through donations of money, blood, and supplies. But what does it mean when people ignore others in need? For example, in early 2003, several people were caught on video doing nothing as a man who had just been shot lay dying in a gas station driveway (CNN.com, 2003). One person even stared at the victim for a few minutes and then calmly returned to the task of filling a can with kerosene. What causes such extreme variations in helping behavior?

Reasons for Helping

There are many kinds of prosocial behavior and such impulses arise early in life. Researchers agree that young children respond sympathetically to companions in distress, usually before their second birthday (Hoffman, 2007). The term **altruism** is usually reserved for behavior that is aimed at helping others, requires some self-sacrifice, and is not performed for personal gain. Batson (2010) believes that we help out of *empathy*—the ability to take the perspective of others and to put ourselves in their place.

Commitment is another factor influencing altruism. We are more likely to behave in an altruistic fashion in the context of relationships to which we are deeply committed (Powell & Van Vugt, 2003). The influence of commitment is strongest when the cost of an altruistic act is high. For instance, you would probably be more likely to volunteer to donate a kidney, let's say, to a family member than to a stranger.

The degree to which society values altruism is another variable that can influence individual decisions about altruistic behavior. Cultures vary in their norms for helping others—that is, their *social responsibility norms.* According to Miller and others (1990), people in the United States tend to feel an obligation to help family members, friends, and even strangers in life-threatening circumstances, but only family members in moderately serious situations. In contrast, in India the social responsibility norm extends to strangers whose needs are only moderately serious or even minor.

Whatever the motive for altruism, people who regularly engage in behavior that helps others reap significant benefits (Poulin & Cohen Silver, 2008). One interesting benefit is that, the more people help, the more altruistic they become. In other words, behaving altruistically generates or enhances an individual's altruistic attitudes. Along with this attitude change comes an increased appreciation for life. Thus, the costs of altruistic behavior are balanced by its benefits, both for those who are helped and for the helpers themselves.

The Bystander Effect

A variety of social circumstances contribute to the decision to help another person. One example is the **bystander effect**: As the number of bystanders at an emergency increases, the probability that the victim will receive help from them decreases, and the help, if given, is likely to be delayed.

In now-classic research, Darley and Latané (1968a) placed a series of research participants alone in a small room and told them that they would be participating in a discussion group by means of an intercom system. Some participants were told that they would be communicating with only one other participant; some believed that two other participants would be involved, and some were told that five other people would participate. There really were no other participants in the study—only the prerecorded voices of confederates assisting the experimenter. Shortly after the discussion began, the voice of one confederate was heard over the intercom calling for help, indicating that he was having an epileptic seizure. Of the participants who believed that they alone were hearing the victim, 85% went for help before the end of the seizure. When participants believed that one other person heard the seizure, 62% sought help. But when they believed that four other people were aware of the emergency, only 31% tried to get help before the end of the seizure. Figure 14.7 on p. 474 shows how the number of bystanders affects both the number of people who try to help and the speed of response.

Darley and Latané (1968a) suggest that, when bystanders are present in an emergency, they generally feel that the responsibility for helping is shared by the group, a phenomenon known as **diffusion of responsibility**. Consequently, each

14.14 What motivates people to help others?

altruism Behavior that is aimed at helping another, requires some self-sacrifice, and is not performed for personal gain.

▲ Altruistic acts, such as helping build houses for low-income families, may be motivated by social responsibility norms.

14.15 How do psychologists explain the bystander effect?

bystander effect A social factor that affects prosocial behavior: As the number of bystanders at an emergency increases, the probability that the victim will receive help decreases, and the help, if given, is likely to be delayed.

diffusion of responsibility The feeling among bystanders at an emergency that the responsibility for helping is shared by the group, making each person feel less compelled to act than if he or she alone bore the total responsibility.

FIGURE 14.7 The Bystander Effect
In their intercom experiment, Darley and Latané showed that the more people a participant believed were present during an emergency, the longer it took the participant to respond and help a person in distress.
Source: Data from Darley & Latané (1968a).

▲ Why do people ignore someone who is unconscious on the sidewalk? Diffusion of responsibility is one possible explanation.

✳[Explore the Concept *Bystander Intervention* on MyPsychLab

person feels less compelled to act than if she or he were alone and felt the total responsibility; each bystander thinks, "Somebody else must be doing something." Another reason for the bystander effect is the influence of other bystanders who appear calm. When others seem calm, we may conclude that nothing is really wrong and that no intervention is necessary (Darley & Latané, 1968b).

Ironically, with regard to catastrophes, such as terrorist attacks and natural disasters, the bystander effect is greatly reduced. In fact, people are likely to put forth extraordinary effort to help others in such situations. We noted how much money people donated to Hurricane Katrina victims within the first few days after the storm made landfall. But this phenomenon is also seen in the countless individual acts of altruism that occur in the context of such events. Often, too, people who can't help directly witness the events via the media and contribute money to the families of victims within hours of these tragedies. Research on public responses to large-scale disasters predicts such responses (Iredale & Van Vugt, 2012). ✳

REMEMBER IT   *Check your answers and take additional quizzes in MyPsychLab.com.* ✓●[Study and Review on MyPsychLab

1. _____ involves making a sacrifice to help another person without expectation of reward.
2. Research on the _____ shows that people are less likely to help a person who is in distress if a group rather than an individual witnesses the event that caused the distress.

Aggression

One of the enduring themes of research in social psychology for many years has been the study of aggression. **Aggression** is the intentional infliction of physical or psychological harm on others. Aggression has many forms and takes place in a variety of locations—at home, at work, and even among drivers on the road. Being the target of an aggressive act is an all-too-common experience. But why does one person intentionally harm another?

aggression The intentional infliction of physical or psychological harm on others.

14.16 What biological factors influence aggression?

Biological Factors in Aggression

Sigmund Freud believed that humans have an aggressive instinct that can be turned inward as self-destruction or outward as aggression or violence toward others. While rejecting this view, many psychologists do concede that biological factors are involved. A meta-analysis of 24 twin and adoption studies of several personality measures of aggression revealed a heritability estimate of about .50 for aggression (Miles & Carey, 1997). Twin and adoption studies have also revealed a genetic link for criminal behavior (Baker et al., 2007). Cloninger and others (1982) found that adoptees with a criminal biological parent were four times as likely as members of the general population to commit crimes, while adoptees with a criminal adoptive parent were at twice the risk of committing a crime. But adoptees with both a criminal biological and a criminal adoptive parent were 14 times as likely to commit crimes, indicating the power of the combined influences of nature and nurture. Thus, many researchers believe that genes that predispose individuals to aggressive behavior may cause them to be more sensitive to models of aggressiveness in the environment (Rowe, 2003).

One biological factor that seems very closely related to aggression is a low arousal level of the autonomic nervous system (Caramaschi de Boer & Koolhaas, 2008; Gower & Crick, 2011). Low arousal level (low heart rate and lower reactivity) has been linked to antisocial and violent behavior (Herpetz, et al., 2007). People with a low arousal level tend to seek stimulation and excitement and often exhibit fearlessness, even in the face of danger.

Men are more physically aggressive than women (Hyde, 2005), and a correlation between high testosterone levels and aggressive behavior has been found in males (Montoya et al., 2012). However, testosterone and aggression are most strongly correlated in individuals who display the types of low levels of arousal that we discussed earlier (Popma et al., 2007). Moreover, the connection between testosterone and aggression has a social component. Adolescent males with both high testosterone levels and a tendency to take risks that can lead to aggression, such as insulting someone without provocation, prefer to associate with peers who have similar hormonal and behavioral profiles (Vermeersch et al., 2008). Researchers speculate that a cycle of risky behavior and aggression maintains high levels of testosterone secretion among such males. Furthermore, violent behavior has been associated with low levels of the neurotransmitter serotonin (Montoya et al., 2012). Alcohol and aggression are frequent partners. A meta-analysis of 30 experimental studies indicated that alcohol is related to aggression (Foran & O'Leary, 2008). The use of alcohol and other drugs that affect the brain's frontal lobes may lead to aggressive behavior in humans and other animals by disrupting normal executive functions (Lyvers, 2000). Law enforcement officials estimate that perpetrators who are under the influence of alcohol or drugs commit about 40% of all violent crimes (National Council on Alcoholism and Drug Dependence, 2013).

The *Summarize It* below summarizes the possible biological causes of aggression.

▲ Alcohol impairs the brain's ability to process information, a condition that often leads to poor decisions. For this reason, alcohol is frequently involved in acts of aggression.

Other Influences on Aggression ▶

Beyond biological factors, what other variables contribute to aggression? The **frustration-aggression hypothesis** suggests that frustration usually produces aggression (Dollard et al., 1939; Miller, 1941). If a traffic jam caused you to be late for an appointment and you were frustrated, would you lean on your horn, shout obscenities out of your window, or just sit patiently and wait? Frustration doesn't always cause aggression, but it is especially likely to do so if it is intense and seems to be unjustified (Doob & Sears, 1939; Pastore, 1950). Berkowitz (1988) points out that even if frustration is justified and not aimed specifically at an individual, it can cause aggression if it arouses negative emotions.

14.17 What other factors contribute to aggression?

frustration-aggression hypothesis The hypothesis that frustration usually produces aggression.

SUMMARIZE IT

Possible Biological Causes of Aggression

CAUSE	EVIDENCE
Heredity	If one identical twin is aggressive, there is a 50% chance that the other twin is aggressive as well. Adopted children's aggressive tendencies are more like those of their biological parents than their adopted parents.
Low arousal level	People with low levels of arousal seek stimulation and excitement to increase arousal.
High testosterone level	High levels of testosterone have been found to be correlated with some forms of aggression, such as intimate partner abuse, in both men and women.
Neurological disorders	Brain tumors and other neurological diseases have been linked to aggressive behavior.
Alcohol abuse	People who are intoxicated commit the majority of murders and most other violent crimes.

scapegoating Displacing aggression onto members of minority groups or other innocent targets not responsible for the frustrating situation.

personal space An area surrounding each person, much like an invisible bubble, that the person considers part of himself or herself and uses to regulate the level of intimacy with others.

crowding The subjective judgment that there are too many people in a confined space.

14.18 How does social learning theory explain aggression?

Aggression in response to frustration is not always focused on the actual cause of the frustration. If the preferred target is too threatening or not available, the aggression may be displaced. For example, children who are angry with their parents may take out their frustration on a younger sibling. Sometimes, members of minority groups or other innocent targets who are not responsible for a frustrating situation become targets of displaced aggression, a practice known as **scapegoating** (Koltz, 1983).

People often become aggressive when they are in pain (Berkowitz, 1983) or are exposed to loud noise or foul odors (Rotton et al., 1979). Extreme heat has also been linked to aggression in several studies (Anderson & Anderson, 1996; Rotton & Cohn, 2000). Social exclusion can also lead to aggressive behavior (van Beest et al., 2012). These and other studies lend support to the *cognitive-neoassociationistic model* proposed by Berkowitz (1990). He suggested that anger and aggression result from aversive events and from unpleasant emotional states, such as sadness, grief, and depression. The cognitive component of Berkowitz's model occurs when the angered person appraises the aversive situation and makes attributions about the motives of the people involved. As a result of the cognitive appraisal, the initial reaction of anger can be intensified, reduced, or suppressed. This process makes the person either more or less likely to act on his or her aggressive tendency.

Personal space is an area surrounding each individual, much like an invisible bubble, that the person considers part of himself or herself and uses to regulate the closeness of interactions with others. Personal space serves to protect privacy and to regulate the level of intimacy with others. The size of personal space varies according to the person or persons with whom an individual is interacting and the nature of the interaction. When personal space is reduced, aggression can result.

Crowding—the subjective judgment that there are too many people in a confined space—has been linked to aggression. Researchers have studied the correlation between crowding and aggression in such diverse populations as male heads of households in India, college students and prison inmates in the United States, and nightclub-goers in London (Evans & Lepore, 1993; Graham et al., 2012; Paulus, Cos, & McCain, 1988). In all of these studies, researchers found that fights occur more often in crowded than in noncrowded settings.

Finally, researchers Roy and Judy Eidelson have identified several beliefs that may lead members of a group of people to act aggressively toward outsiders (Eidelson & Eidelson, 2003). One such belief is a group's conviction that its members are superior to others, together with a sense of "chosenness" for a particular task. The view that one's own group has a legitimate grievance against outsiders can also spark aggression. Group members who believe themselves to be vulnerable may justify aggression as a form of defense. Similarly, those who are convinced that promises made by outsiders to respect the rights of group members cannot be trusted may act aggressively. Finally, group members who believe that aggression is the only strategy available to them for addressing grievances or protecting themselves may resort to violence. Group leaders play an important role in either encouraging or discouraging these beliefs among group members. For example, positive leadership may be able to prevent intergroup aggression.

The Social Learning Theory of Aggression

The *social learning theory of aggression* holds that people learn to behave aggressively by observing aggressive models and by having their aggressive responses reinforced (Bandura, 1973). It is well known that aggression levels are higher in groups and subcultures that condone violent behavior and accord high status to aggressive members. A leading advocate of the social learning theory of aggression, Albert Bandura (1976), claims that aggressive models in the subculture, the family, and the media all play a part in increasing the level of aggression in society.

You may recall from Chapter 5 that Bandura performed the famous "Bobo doll" experiment in which children punched and kicked an inflatable clown after observing video of adults doing so. Consequently, Bandura's own research suggests that there is some truth to his assertion that aggressive behavior is strongly influenced by models.

Abused children certainly experience aggression and see it modeled day after day. Moreover, having been abused as a child clearly increases the risk that a person will grow up to abuse his or her own children (Burton, 2003). Nevertheless, on the basis of original research and an analysis of 60 other studies, Oliver (1993) concludes that only one-third of people who are abused go on to become abusers, one-third do not, and the final one-third may become abusers if their lives are highly stressful. However, a more recent review found no consistent pattern across studies of the parenting behaviors of individuals who were abused in childhood (Thornberry et al., 2012). Consequently, there is currently no consensus among psychologists regarding the notion that children who are abused grow up to be abusive to their own children.

The research evidence overwhelmingly supports a relationship between TV violence and viewer aggression (Coyne et al., 2004; Eron, 1987; Huesmann et al., 2003). And the negative effects of TV violence are even worse for individuals who are, by nature, highly aggressive (Bushman, 1995). Researchers have also found a correlation between playing violent video games and aggression (Anderson & Dill, 2000; Carnagey & Anderson, 2004). Moreover, aggressiveness increases as more time is spent playing such games (Colwell & Payne, 2000). However, researchers in the Netherlands found that boys who choose aggressive video games tend to be more aggressive, less intelligent, and less prosocial in their behavior (Weigman & van Schie, 1998). Moreover, critics of video game research point out that many studies are methodologically flawed and exaggerate the negative effects of video games (Ferguson & Kilburn, 2010). These critics point out that longitudinal studies show that playing violent video games does not lead to negative developmental outcomes such as hostility and aggression (Ferguson et al., 2012). So, the correlation between aggression and video games may be due to the tendency of aggressive individuals to prefer entertainment media that feature aggression.

REMEMBER IT   *Check your answers and take additional quizzes in MyPsychLab.com.* ✓●—Study and Review on MyPsychLab

1. Aggression is associated with high levels of the male hormone _____.
2. The kind of aggression that might occur after a person has been stuck in a traffic jam for several hours is best explained by the _____ hypothesis.
3. The _____ theory of aggression claims that aggressive behavior is learned from models.

Prejudice and Discrimination

Do you know the difference between *prejudice* and *discrimination*? **Prejudice** consists of attitudes (usually negative) toward others based on their gender, religion, race, or membership in a particular group. Prejudice involves beliefs and emotions (not actions) that can escalate into hatred. **Discrimination** consists of behavior—actions (usually negative) toward others based on their gender, religion, race, or membership in a particular group. Many Americans have experienced prejudice and discrimination—minority racial groups (racism), women (sexism), the elderly (ageism), people with disabilities, homosexuals, religious groups, and others. What are the roots of prejudice and discrimination?

prejudice Attitudes (usually negative) toward others based on their gender, religion, race, or membership in a particular group.

discrimination Behavior (usually negative) directed toward others based on their gender, religion, race, or membership in a particular group.

The Roots of Prejudice and Discrimination ▶

Social psychologists have proposed several theories to explain the psychological bases for prejudice and discrimination. Moreover, a number of studies have provided insight into their origins.

One of the oldest explanations as to how prejudice arose cites competition among various social groups that must struggle against each other for scarce resources—good jobs, homes, schools, and so on. Commonly called the **realistic conflict theory**, this view suggests that as competition increases, so do prejudice, discrimination, and hatred among the competing groups. Some historical evidence supports the realistic

14.19 What factors contribute to the development of prejudice and discrimination?

realistic conflict theory The view that as competition increases among social groups for scarce resources, so do prejudice, discrimination, and hatred.

▲ Can you perceive differences among the children shown here? Research shows that people typically perceive more variability among members of groups to which they belong and more similarity among members of groups with which they are unfamiliar.

in-group A social group with a strong sense of togetherness, from which others are excluded.

out-group A social group made up of individuals specifically identified by the in-group as not belonging.

conflict theory. Prejudice and hatred were high between the American settlers and the Native Americans, who struggled over land during the westward expansion. The multitudes of Irish and German immigrants who came to the United States in the 1830s and 1840s felt the sting of prejudice and hatred from other Americans who were facing economic scarcity. But prejudice and discrimination are attitudes and actions too complex to be explained solely by economic conflict and competition.

Prejudice can also spring from the distinct social categories into which people divide the world, employing an "us-versus-them" mentality (Turner et al., 1987). An **in-group** is a social group with a strong sense of togetherness, from which others are excluded. Members of college fraternities and sororities often exhibit strong in-group feelings. The **out-group** consists of individuals specifically identified by the in-group as not belonging. For instance, students in your high school, like many others, may have organized themselves into in-groups such as "geeks" and "jocks." If you were a "geek," then you considered anyone who belonged to the "jocks' to be a member of an out-group. Likewise, a "jock" would have considered you to be such. Us-versus-them thinking of this kind can lead to excessive competition, hostility, prejudice, discrimination, and even war.

A famous study by Sherif and Sherif (1967) shows how in-group/out-group conflict can escalate into prejudice and hostility rather quickly, even between groups that are very much alike. The researchers set up their experiment at the Robber's Cave summer camp. Their subjects were 22 bright, well-adjusted, 11- and 12-year-old White middle-class boys from Oklahoma City. Divided into two groups and housed in separate cabins, the boys were kept apart for all their daily activities and games. During the first week, in-group solidarity, friendship, and cooperation developed within each of the groups. One group called itself the "Rattlers"; the other group took the name "Eagles."

During the second week of the study, competitive events were purposely scheduled so that the goals of one group could be achieved "only at the expense of the other group" (Sherif, 1958, p. 353). The groups were happy to battle each other, and intergroup conflict quickly emerged. Name-calling began, fights broke out, and accusations were hurled back and forth. During the third week of the experiment, the researchers tried to put an end to the hostility and to turn rivalry into cooperation. They simply brought the groups together for pleasant activities, such as eating meals and watching movies. However, these situations evolved into opportunities for competing groups to verbally and physically attack each other rather than to cooperate (Sherif, 1956). Finally, experimenters manufactured a series of crises that could be resolved only if all the boys combined their efforts and resources and cooperated. The water supply, sabotaged by the experimenters, could be restored only if all the boys worked together. After a week of several activities requiring cooperation, cutthroat competition gave way to cooperative exchanges. Friendships developed between groups, and before the end of the experiment, peace was declared. Working together toward shared goals had turned hostility into friendship.

According to *social-cognitive theory*, people learn attitudes of prejudice and hatred the same way they learn other attitudes, through modeling and reinforcement. If children hear their parents, teachers, peers, and others openly express prejudices toward different racial, ethnic, or cultural groups, they may be quick to learn such attitudes. And if parents, peers, and others reward children with smiles and approval for parroting their own prejudices (operant conditioning), children may learn these prejudices even more quickly. Classical conditioning also plays a role. A person who is prejudiced is likely to experience negative emotional states in the presence of members of the groups against which he is prejudiced. As a result, members of these groups become conditioned stimuli that elicit negative emotional responses in the prejudiced person (Conger et al., 2012). To avoid these responses, the prejudiced person avoids contact with them.

Earlier in the chapter we told you that *social cognition* refers to the ways in which people typically process social information. The very processes we use to simplify, categorize, and order the social world are the same processes that distort our views of it.

So, prejudice may arise not only from heated negative emotions and hatred toward other social groups, but also from cooler cognitive processes that govern how we think and process social information (Kunda & Oleson, 1995).

One way people simplify, categorize, and order the world is by using stereotypes. **Stereotypes** are widely shared beliefs about the characteristic traits, attitudes, and behaviors of members of various social groups (racial, ethnic, or religious), including the assumption that "they" are usually all alike. Once a stereotype is in place, people tend to pay more attention to information that confirms their beliefs than to information that challenges them (Wigboldus, Dijksterhuis, & Van Knippenberg, 2003).

Stereotyping allows people to make quick, automatic (thoughtless) judgments about others and apply their mental resources to other activities (Verhaegen, Aikman, & Van Gulick, 2011). However, individuals who are prejudiced do not necessarily apply stereotypes equally to all members of a given group. For one thing, people are less likely to apply stereotypes to others with whom they have personal relationships than they are to strangers (Turner et al., 2008). And even when stereotypes are applied to strangers, they can be moderated, or amplified, by other relevant information. For example, Cheryl Kaiser and Jennifer Pratt-Hyatt (2009) asked White college students to rate the "likeability" of several fictitious peers on the basis of personality test results. Along with the test results, the researchers provided participants with information about the fictitious peers' ethnicity and their responses to questions such as "The racial/ethnic group I belong to is an important reflection of who I am." Kaiser and Pratt-Hyatt found that participants were most likely to report having negative first impressions of fictitious African American and Latino peers if the peers attached high levels of importance to racial/ethnic identity.

Some research has revealed that people tend to perceive more diversity or more variability within the groups to which they belong (in-groups), but they see more similarity among members of other groups (out-groups) (Ostrom, Carpenter, & Sedikides, 1993). For example, White Americans see more diversity among themselves but more sameness within groups of African Americans or Asian Americans. Such patterns have been found in children as young as 3 years of age (Tuminello & Davidson, 2011).

The tendency to be less sensitive to variations among members of other groups may arise from a general tendency to look at people and situations from the perspective of one's own racial or cultural group. This tendency is often called **ethnocentrism**. In work settings, ethnocentrism may prevent us from realizing that co-workers from different backgrounds sometimes perceive the same incidents quite differently. For example, researchers have found that African Americans are more likely than Whites to perceive negative encounters between supervisors and subordinates of different races as being racial in nature (J. Johnson et al., 2003). To complicate matters further, members of each group believe that such opinions are either right or wrong. Because of ethnocentrism, Whites will insist that their view is the correct one; African Americans will take the same position about their view. To address this problem, many organizations provide workers with training geared toward helping them understand that such differences do not involve one view that is right and another that is wrong. Instead, each perspective is deserving of respect by the other.

Is Prejudice Decreasing? ▶

Few people will readily admit to being prejudiced. Gordon Allport (1954), a pioneer in research on prejudice, said, "Defeated intellectually, prejudice lingers emotionally" (p. 328). Even those who are sincerely intellectually opposed to prejudice may still harbor some prejudiced feelings (Devine, 1989). However, most people feel guilty when they catch themselves having prejudiced thoughts or engaging in discriminatory behavior (Amodio, Devine, & Harmon-Jones, 2007).

Is there any evidence that prejudice is decreasing in U.S. society? One positive indicator was the election of Barack Obama to the presidency in 2008 and his reelection in 2012. Not only was President Obama the first African American to be elected to the

stereotypes Widely shared beliefs about the characteristic traits, attitudes, and behaviors of members of various social groups (racial, ethnic, or religious), including the assumption that the members of such groups are usually all alike.

ethnocentrism The tendency to look at situations from one's own racial or cultural perspective.

14.20 What evidence suggests that prejudice and discrimination are decreasing?

nation's highest office, but most people in the United States, especially African Americans, perceived his election to be an enormous step forward in race relations (Rasmusenreports.com, 2009). Moreover, Gallup polls have revealed that White Americans became more racially tolerant over the final decades of the 20th century (Gallup & Hugick, 1990). When White Americans were asked in 1990 whether they would move if African Americans were to move next door to them, 93% said no, compared with 65% in 1965. Additional encouragement comes from surveys showing that both White and African Americans overwhelmingly agree that conditions have improved for minorities in the United States over the past several decades (Public Agenda Online, 2002). However, there are still marked differences of opinion among ethnic groups as to whether racism continues to be a problem in the United States. About 44% of African Americans believe racial discrimination is a significant factor in education, employment, and housing, while just 22% of White Americans agree (ABC News/*Washington Post*, 2009). Moreover, studies show that people continue to cite fear of rejection as the reason they don't engage in more social contact with others of different races (Shelton & Richeson, 2005).

Recall, too, that attitudes do not always predict behavior. In one study, researchers asked participants to judge whether a fictitious woman was qualified to be the president of a parent–teacher organization (Lott & Saxon, 2002). Participants were provided with information about the woman's occupation and education. In addition, they were told, based on random assignment, that the woman was Hispanic, Anglo-Saxon, or Jewish in ethnic origin. The experimenters found that participants who believed the woman to be Hispanic were more likely to say that she was not qualified for the position than those who thought her to be Anglo-Saxon or Jewish. Such studies suggest that racial stereotyping is still evident in the United States. But there are many things we can do to combat prejudice and discrimination as discussed in the *Apply It*.

APPLY IT   "Unlearning" Prejudice

Today's college population is more diverse than ever before. In the United States, members of minority groups are attending college in higher numbers. And people from cultures all over the world come to the United States to further their educations. Consequently, for many young people, campus life represents a unique opportunity to interact with others of different racial, ethnic, or cultural groups. How can students make the most of this opportunity to "unlearn" the prejudices they may bring with them to college?

Intergroup Contact
As you learned from the Robber's Cave experiment (Sherif & Sherif, 1967), intergroup contact can sometimes lead to increased stereotyping. Under the right conditions, though, intergroup contact can reduce prejudice. College can provide a context in which students from diverse backgrounds study together, endure the same trials (midterms and finals), develop a shared sense of school spirit, join clubs in which members from different backgrounds share common goals, and so on. Thus, under the right conditions, intergroup contact can reduce prejudice (Page-Gould, Mendoza-Denton, & Tropp, 2008).

The Jigsaw Technique
Methods such as the *jigsaw technique,* a strategy that works well in college classrooms and as a game in less formal interactions, represent a more direct approach. Each participant in a jigsaw group is given a small amount of information and asked to teach it to other participants. The group must use all the individual pieces of information to solve a problem. This approach increases interaction among participants and helps them develop empathy for members of other ethnic and racial groups (Aronson, 1988; Aronson et al., 1978; Singh, 1991;

Walker & Crogan, 1998). A side benefit is that it is an effective way of learning a new solution to a problem.

Diversity Education
Many colleges offer students and faculty opportunities to participate in seminars and workshops designed to combat racism. In such settings, participants learn about racial and cultural perspectives that may differ from their own (Haldeman, 2012). They also learn to identify behaviors that may be construed as racist by others, even when that may not be what they intend. Researchers have found that such programs help to reduce automatic stereotyping among participants (Hill & Augoustinos, 2001; Rudman, Ashmore, & Gary, 2001).

Open Discussions of Prejudice and Discrimination
Perhaps the greatest potential of the college campus for reducing prejudice and discrimination lies in the nature of its intellectual climate. Traditionally, college classes, as well as club meetings, gatherings at restaurants, all-night study sessions in coffee shops, and late-night debates in dorm rooms, often feature lively discussions of a variety of topics. And when we hear others speak passionately about racism, sexism, and other types of injustice, we are likely to adopt more tolerant attitudes ourselves.

So, the next time you hear someone make a statement you feel is racist or sexist or prejudiced in any way, speak up! You never know how influential your voice might be.

Watch the Video *Episode 16: In the Real World: Are Stereotypes and Prejudice Inevitable?* in **MyPsychLab**

1. Members of an in-group usually dislike people in a(n) _____.
2. The social-cognitive theory suggests that prejudice develops and is maintained through _____ and _____.
3. White Americans and members of other groups (agree/disagree) about the extent to which prejudice and discrimination continue to be problems in the United States.

Looking Back

At the beginning of the chapter, you learned that people sometimes do a poor job of forming judgments about others and themselves. Likewise, at the end of the chapter, you learned about the roots of racial prejudice and discrimination. Much of the work of social psychologists seeks to explain and find remedies for human failings such as these. For example, Milgram's brilliant experiment began as an effort to comprehend what appeared to be an incomprehensible event, the Holocaust. His work and that of other social psychologists demonstrate that psychology is a field with a great deal of relevance to the real world, whether that world consists of momentous historical events or the more ordinary happenings of everyday life.

CHAPTER 14 SUMMARY

SOCIAL COGNITION (pp. 454–457)

14.1 How do we form opinions of others and manage their opinions of us? (pp. 454–456)

First impressions shape our opinions of others because we attend more carefully to the first information we receive about another person; and, once formed, an impression acts as a framework through which later information is interpreted. Through impression management, we influence others' opinions of us when they have the ability to provide us with something we want or need and when we believe that their opinions of us are inaccurate.

Key Terms
social psychology, p. 454
social cognition, p. 454
impression formation, p. 454
primacy effect, p. 455
impression management, p. 455

14.2 How do we explain our own and others' behavior? (pp. 456–457)

An attribution is an opinion about another person that is based on an inference about the causes of their behavior. In making a situational attribution, people attribute the cause of the behavior to some factor operating within the situation. With a dispositional attribution, the inferred cause is internal, such as some personal trait, motive, or attitude. People tend to attribute their own shortcomings primarily to situational factors and those of others primarily to dispositional factors, a tendency known as the actor-observer effect.

Key Terms
attribution, p. 456
situational attribution, p. 456
dispositional attribution, p. 456
self-serving bias, p. 456
actor-observer effect, p. 456
fundamental attribution error, p. 456

ATTRACTION (pp. 458–461)

14.3 What factors contribute to attraction? (pp. 458–459)

Proximity contributes to attraction because it is easier to develop relationships with people close at hand. Proximity also increases the likelihood that there will be repeated contacts, and there is a tendency to feel more positively toward a stimulus as a result of repeated exposure to it (the mere-exposure effect). Our moods and emotions influence how much we are attracted to those we meet. We also tend to like people who like us (reciprocity). Other factors that contribute to attraction are similarities in age, gender, race, and socioeconomic class and similar views and interests. Physical attractiveness is a major factor in attraction for people of all ages. People attribute positive qualities to those who are physically attractive, a phenomenon called the halo effect.

Key Terms
proximity, p. 458
mere-exposure effect, p. 458
halo effect, p. 458

14.4 What factors contribute to the formation and maintenance of intimate relationships? (pp. 459–461)

Psychologists have proposed the matching hypothesis to explain the finding that people are often select intimate

partners who are similar to themselves. Others argue that individuals choose partners whose characteristics complement their own. Evolutionary psychologists argue that men and women are attracted to one another on the basis of what each can contribute to the creation and support of a family. Sternberg's triangular theory of love describes different types of intimate relationships, and the changes that happen in relationships over time, in terms of three interactive components: intimacy, passion, and commitment.

Key Terms
matching hypothesis, p. 459
triangular theory of love, p. 460
consummate love, p. 461

CONFORMITY, OBEDIENCE, AND COMPLIANCE (pp. 461–465)

14.5 What did Asch find in his classic experiment on conformity? (pp. 461–462)

In Asch's classic study on conformity, 5% of the participants went along with the incorrect, unanimous majority all the time; 70% went along some of the time; and 25% remained completely independent.

Key Terms
conformity, p. 461
social norms, p. 461

14.6 What did Milgram's classic study reveal about obedience? (pp. 462–464)

Participants were almost as likely to obey experimenters when the study was repeated at a shabby office building rather than at Yale University. However, when participants were paired with confederates who refused to obey the experimenter, they were less likely to obey.

Key Term
obedience, p. 462

14.7 What techniques do people use to gain compliance from others? (pp. 464–465)

One technique that can lead to compliance is the foot-in-the-door technique, in which a person gains compliance with a small request with the intent of making another agree to a larger request later. In the door-in-the-face technique, someone makes a large request with the expectation that another will refuse but be open to a smaller request later. A person who makes an attractive initial offer to gain compliance from another before making the offer less attractive is using the low-ball technique.

Key Terms
compliance, p. 464
foot-in-the-door technique, p. 464
door-in-the-face technique, p. 464
low-ball technique, p. 465

GROUP INFLUENCE (pp. 465–469)

14.8 How do social facilitation and social loafing affect performance? (pp. 465–466)

When others are present, either as an audience or as co-actors, people's performance on easy tasks is usually improved through social facilitation. However, performance on difficult tasks is usually impaired. Social loafing is people's tendency to put forth less effort when they are working with others on a common task than when working alone. It is less likely to occur when individual output can be monitored or when people have a personal stake in the outcome.

Key Terms
social facilitation, p. 465
audience effects, p. 465
coaction effects, p. 465
social loafing, p. 466

14.9 How do groups influence individual decision making? (pp. 467–468)

Group polarization occurs when, after a discussion, a group's decision shifts to a more extreme position in whatever direction the members were leaning initially. Groupthink happens when a group's desire to maintain solidarity outweighs other considerations, a process that often leads to poor decisions.

Key Terms
group polarization, p. 467
groupthink, p. 467

14.10 How do social roles influence individual behavior? (pp. 468–469)

Individual behavior can be guided by the expectations associated with certain social roles. The effects of such roles can be either negative or positive.

Key Terms
social roles, p. 468
deindividuation, p. 468
social identity, p. 468

ATTITUDES AND ATTITUDE CHANGE (pp. 469–472)

14.11 What are the three components of an attitude? (pp. 469–470)

An attitude usually has a cognitive, an emotional, and a behavioral component.

Key Term
attitude, p. 469

14.12 What factors influence cognitive dissonance? (pp. 470–471)

Cognitive dissonance is an unpleasant state that can occur when people become aware of inconsistencies among their attitudes or between their attitudes and their behavior. People can reduce cognitive dissonance by changing the behavior or the attitude, by denying responsibility, or by explaining away the inconsistency or minimizing its importance.

Key Term
cognitive dissonance, p. 470

14.13 What are the elements of persuasion? (pp. 471–472)

The four elements of persuasion are the source of the communication, the audience, the message, and the medium.

Key Term
persuasion, p. 471

PROSOCIAL BEHAVIOR (pp. 472–474)

14.14 What motivates people to help others? (p. 473)

Some prosocial behavior is motivated by altruism. In other cases, cultural norms influence helping behavior. We are more likely to help those in need if we are in a committed relationship with them or we perceive them to be similar to us.

Key Terms
prosocial behavior, p. 472
altruism, p. 473

14.15 How do psychologists explain the bystander effect? (pp. 473–474)

The bystander effect is a social factor that affects prosocial behavior: As the number of bystanders at an emergency increases, the probability that the victim will receive help decreases, and the help, if given, is likely to be delayed. The bystander effect may be due in part to diffusion of responsibility or the influence of other bystanders who seem calm.

Key Terms
bystander effect, p. 473
diffusion of responsibility, p. 473

AGGRESSION (pp. 474–477)

14.16 What biological factors influence aggression? (pp. 474–475)

Biological factors thought to be related to aggression are a genetic link in criminal behavior, low arousal level, high testosterone level, low level of serotonin, brain damage or certain brain disorders, and alcohol abuse.

Key Term
aggression, p. 474

14.17 What other factors contribute to aggression? (pp. 475–476)

The frustration-aggression hypothesis holds that frustration produces aggression and that this aggression may be directed at the person, causing the frustration or displaced onto another target, as in scapegoating. Aggression has been associated with such aversive conditions as pain, heat, loud noise, and foul odors and with unpleasant emotional states, such as sadness, grief, and depression. Invasions of privacy and crowding may also contribute to aggression. Finally, belief in the superiority of one's own group may lead to aggression toward outsiders.

Key Terms
frustration-aggression hypothesis, p. 475
scapegoating, p. 476
personal space, p. 476
crowding, p. 476

14.18 How does social learning theory explain aggression? (pp. 476–477)

According to social learning theory, people acquire aggressive responses by observing aggressive models in the family, the subculture, and the media, and by having aggressive responses reinforced.

PREJUDICE AND DISCRIMINATION (pp. 477–481)

14.19 What factors contribute to the development of prejudice and discrimination? (pp. 477–479)

Prejudice consists of attitudes (usually negative) toward others based on their gender, religion, race, or membership in a particular group. Discrimination consists of actions (usually negative) against others based on the same factors. Prejudice can arise out of competition for scarce resources or from people's tendency to divide the world into distinct social categories—in-groups and out-groups. According to social-cognitive theory, prejudice is learned in the same way that other attitudes are—through modeling and reinforcement.

Key Terms
prejudice, p. 477
discrimination, p. 477

realistic conflict theory, p. 477
in-group, p. 478
out-group, p. 478
stereotypes, p. 479
ethnocentrism, p. 479

14.20 What evidence suggests that prejudice and discrimination are decreasing? (pp. 479–481)

Many Americans believe that the election of the first African American president in 2008 was a sign that prejudice and discrimination have declined significantly. From the 1960s to the 1980s, White Americans became less likely to object to living in racially mixed neighborhoods. But ethnic groups still have varying views of the degree to which prejudice and discrimination continue to be problematic in the United States.

Chapter 14 Study Guide

Answers to all the Study Guide questions are provided at the end of the book.

SECTION ONE: Chapter Review

Social Cognition (pp. 454–457)

1. Which of the following statements about first impressions is *false*?
   a. People usually pay closer attention to early information they receive about a person than to later information.
   b. Early information forms a framework through which later information is interpreted.
   c. First impressions often serve as self-fulfilling prophecies.
   d. The importance of first impressions is greatly overrated.

2. People tend to make _____ attributions to explain their own behavior and _____ attributions to explain the behavior of others.
   a. situational; situational
   b. situational; dispositional
   c. dispositional; situational
   d. dispositional; dispositional

3. Attributing Mike's poor grade to his lack of ability is a dispositional attribution. (true/false)

Attraction (pp. 458–461)

4. Match each term with a description.
   _____ (1) Brian sees Kelly at the library often and begins to like her.
   _____ (2) Lori assumes that because Michael is handsome, he must be popular and sociable.
   _____ (3) Kate and Kurt are dating and are both very attractive.
   a. matching hypothesis   b. halo effect   c. mere-exposure effect

5. Physical attractiveness is a very important factor in initial attraction. (true/false)

6. People are usually drawn to those who are more opposite than similar to themselves. (true/false)

7. Sternberg refers to commitment with passion but without intimacy as
a. empty love.
b. liking.
c. fatuous love.
d. companionate love.

Conformity, Obedience, and Compliance (pp. 461–465)

8. What percentage of subjects in the Asch study never conformed to the majority's unanimous incorrect response?
a. 70%
b. 33%
c. 25%
d. 5%

9. What percentage of the subjects in Milgram's original obedience experiment administered what they thought was the maximum 450-volt shock?
a. 85%
b. 65%
c. 45%
d. 25%

10. Match the technique for gaining compliance with the appropriate example.

_____ **(1)** Meghan agrees to sign a letter supporting an increase in taxes for road construction. Later she agrees to make 100 phone calls urging people to vote for the measure.

_____ **(2)** Jude refuses a phone request for a $24 donation to send four needy children to the circus but does agree to give $6.

_____ **(3)** Lexie agrees to babysit for her next-door neighbors' two girls and then is informed that their three nephews will be there, too.
a. door-in-the-face technique
b. low-ball technique
c. foot-in-the-door technique

Group Influence (pp. 465–469)

11. Which of the following statements regarding the effects of social facilitation (the presence of other people) is true?
a. Performance improves on all tasks.
b. Performance worsens on all tasks.
c. Performance improves on easy tasks and worsens on difficult tasks.
d. Performance improves on difficult tasks and worsens on easy tasks.

12. What occurs when members of a very cohesive group are more concerned with preserving group solidarity than with evaluating all possible alternatives in making a decision?
a. groupthink
b. group polarization
c. social facilitation
d. social loafing

13. Social roles cannot cause an individual to behave in ways that conflict with his/her own moral standards. (true/false)

Attitudes and Attitude Change (pp. 469–472)

14. Which of the following is *not* one of the three components of an attitude?
a. cognitive component
b. emotional component
c. physiological component
d. behavioral component

15. All of the following are ways to reduce cognitive dissonance *except*
a. changing an attitude.
b. changing a behavior.
c. explaining away the inconsistency.
d. strengthening the attitude and behavior.

16. People who have made a great sacrifice to join a group usually decrease their liking for the group. (true/false)

17. Credibility relates most directly to the communicator's
a. attractiveness.
b. expertise and trustworthiness.
c. likability.
d. personality.

18. With a well-informed audience, two-sided messages are more persuasive than one-sided messages. (true/false)

19. High-fear appeals are more effective than low-fear appeals if they provide definite actions that people can take to avoid dreaded outcomes. (true/false)

Prosocial Behavior (pp. 472–474)

20. The bystander effect is influenced by all of the following *except*
a. the number of bystanders.
b. the personalities of bystanders.
c. whether the bystanders appear calm.
d. whether the situation is ambiguous.

21. Altruism is one form of prosocial behavior. (true/false)

22. As the number of bystanders at an emergency increases, the probability that the victim will receive help decreases. (true/false)

23. In an ambiguous situation, a good way to determine if an emergency exists is to look at the reactions of other bystanders. (true/false)

Aggression (pp. 474–477)

24. Social psychologists generally believe that aggression stems from an aggressive instinct. (true/false)

25. Pain, extreme heat, loud noise, and foul odors have all been associated with an increase in aggressive responses. (true/false)

26. According to the frustration-aggression hypothesis, frustration _____ leads to aggression.
a. usually
b. occasionally
c. rarely
d. never

27. Which of the following statements is *not* true of personal space?
a. It functions to protect privacy and regulate intimacy.
b. How much personal space a person requires is affected by culture, race, gender, and personality.
c. The size of a person's personal space is fixed.
d. Invasions of personal space are usually perceived as unpleasant.

28. The social learning theory of aggression emphasizes all of the following *except* that
a. aggressive responses are learned from the family, the subculture, and the media.
b. aggressive acts are learned through modeling.
c. most aggression results from frustration.
d. when aggression responses are reinforced, they are more likely to continue.

29. Research tends to support the notion that a person can drain off aggressive energy by watching others behave aggressively in sports or on television. (true/false)

30. Research suggests that media violence is probably related to increased aggression. (true/false)

Prejudice and Discrimination (pp. 477–481)

31. Match the example with the term.

_____ **(1)** Carlotta hired a woman to be her assistant because she doesn't like working with men.

_____ **(2)** Darlene thinks that all Asian students are good at math.

_____ **(3)** Bill canceled a blind date with Ellen when he heard that she was overweight.

a. stereotypic thinking
b. discrimination
c. prejudice

32. Social learning theory asserts that prejudice develops and is maintained through

a. competition.
b. us-versus-them thinking.
c. modeling and reinforcement.
d. genetic inheritance.

33. African Americans no longer believe that racism is a major problem in U.S. society. (true/false)

34. Ethnocentrism is the tendency to look at others from the perspective of one's own racial or cultural group. (true/false)

SECTION TWO: Match Terms with Definitions

_____ **(1)** effect of one major positive or negative trait

_____ **(2)** as more viewers gather at the scene of an emergency, a victim's chances of help are reduced

_____ **(3)** geographic closeness

_____ **(4)** the blocking of an impulse

_____ **(5)** attitudes and standards of a group

_____ **(6)** relatively stable evaluation of a person, object, situation, or issue

_____ **(7)** impact of passive spectators on performance

_____ **(8)** the tendency of individuals to go along with the group even if they disagree

_____ **(9)** widely shared beliefs about traits of members of certain groups

_____ **(10)** the fact that one's overall impression is influenced by a first impression

_____ **(11)** displacing aggression onto innocent people

_____ **(12)** making a large request in the hope of gaining compliance with a subsequent small request

_____ **(13)** the intentional infliction of harm on another

a. frustration
b. proximity
c. aggression
d. scapegoating
e. bystander effect
f. halo effect
g. door-in-the-face technique
h. social norms
i. attitude
j. groupthink
k. stereotypes
l. audience effect
m. primacy effect

SECTION THREE: Comprehensive Practice Test

1. Dispositional attribution is to _____ as situational attribution is to _____.

a. external factors; internal factors
b. others; self
c. self; others
d. internal factors; external factors

2. Crystal attributed Asher's poor oral presentation to his basic lack of motivation to be a good student and to be prepared for class. Assuming Crystal was wrong and Asher's poor performance was due to some other external factor, Crystal was making an error called the self-serving bias. (true/false)

3. Crystal's own oral presentation was also poor. She explained that the students in the front row were goofing off and distracting her. Crystal was excusing her performance with the

a. primary attribution error.
b. fundamental self-bias error.
c. self-serving bias.
d. error of external factors.

4. The concept of proximity relates to

a. attribution.   **b.** attraction.
c. aggression.   **d.** prejudice.

5. In the past few decades people have become less influenced by physical attractiveness and more influenced by internal factors such as personality. (true/false)

6. Jesse's mother reminded him to check his tie and comb his hair prior to meeting the interviewer at his college admissions interview. Jesse's mother was probably concerned about the _____ effect.

a. attenuation   **b.** Soloman
c. Harvard   **d.** halo

7. The old adage "birds of a feather flock together" summarizes the concept of _____, one of the factors that influence attraction.

a. attribution   **b.** social influence
c. similarity   **d.** proximity

8. Research reveals that low autonomic nervous system arousal levels seem to be related to aggressive behavior. (true/false)

9. Messages about smoking are most effective if framed (positively/negatively), while those about dietary change are best if framed (positively/negatively).

10. The terms stereotype and prejudice are actually different words for the same thing. (true/false)

11. A negative attitude toward a person based on gender, religion, race, or membership in a certain group is known as

a. discrimination.   **b.** prejudice.
c. a stereotype.   **d.** social dissonance.

12. Strategies such as changing a behavior, changing an attitude, explaining away an inconsistency, or minimizing the importance of an inconsistency are all used to reduce

a. cognitive distortion bias.   **b.** relative attribution frustration.
c. cognitive dissonance.   **d.** inconsistency anxiety.

13. _____ are the attitudes and standards of behavior expected of members of a particular group.

a. Values   **b.** Social rules
c. Social norms   **d.** Social postures

14. Those who hold a minority opinion have more influence on a majority group if
    a. the opinion is stated vaguely so its departure from the majority opinion is disguised.
    b. the opinion is clearly stated and well organized.
    c. the opinion is stated as a question.
    d. the opinion is stated with qualifications that complement the majority opinion.

15. One strategy to induce compliance to a request is known as the _____ technique. In this strategy, the person making the request secures a favorable response to a small request with the aim of making the person more likely to agree to a larger request later.
    a. door-in-the-face
    b. low-ball
    c. foot-in-the-door
    d. risky shift

16. A good example of the door-in-the-face technique is to ask $10,000 for your used car, hoping that the buyer, who is likely to refuse to pay that much, will then be willing to agree to pay $8,000, the price you wanted in the first place. (true/false)

17. Social loafing refers to
    a. the tendency to avoid social contact and interpersonal relationships.
    b. the tendency to exert less effort when working with others on a common task.
    c. the tendency to be less productive when working alone than with others.
    d. the tendency to see others' work as more externally motivated than one's own.

18. A common finding on audience effects is that when we are being watched, we tend to do better on easy tasks and on more difficult tasks at which we are more proficient. (true/false)

19. Which of the following is not listed as a component of an attitude?
    a. social component
    b. behavioral component
    c. cognitive component
    d. emotional component

SECTION FOUR: Critical Thinking

1. Prepare a convincing argument supporting each of these positions:
   a. The Milgram study should have been conducted because it provided vitally important information about the troubling human tendency to inflict pain and suffering on others in obedience to authority figures.
   b. Despite the value of the knowledge the Milgram study provided, it should never have been conducted because it subjected research participants to tremendous stress.

2. Prepare a convincing argument supporting each of these positions:
   a. Aggression results largely from biological factors (nature).
   b. Aggression is primarily learned (nurture).

SECTION FIVE: Application Essays

1. Review the factors influencing impression formation and attraction discussed in this chapter. Prepare a dual list of behaviors indicating what you should and should not do if you wish to make a better impression on other people and to increase their liking for you.

Apply your critical thinking skills with MyPsychLab Writing Assignments

Submit your answer to the following question inside the MyPsychLab Writing Assessment program for immediate feedback.

Discuss the factors that contribute to prejudice and discrimination and identify some techniques for reducing the development of prejudice and discrimination.

Appendix: Statistical Methods

operational definition Way of assigning numerical values to a variable that cannot be observed directly, (e.g., test, survey).

data Bits of numerical information that are derived from operational definitions.

statistics Mathematical techniques that are used to analyze data.

descriptive statistics Statistics used to organize, summarize, and describe data.

frequency distribution An arrangement showing the numbers of scores that fall within equal-sized intervals.

histogram A bar graph that depicts the number of scores within each class interval in a frequency distribution.

If you want to know how tall a person is, all you have to do is get hold of a tape measure. But if you want to know whether someone is an extravert or how well he or she solves problems or how large his or her vocabulary is, you have to use a tool that is indispensable to psychological researchers, an **operational definition**. An operational definition is a way of assigning numerical values to a variable that cannot be observed directly. Tests are one type of operational definition, as are survey results. The bits of numerical information that researchers get from these operational definitions are known as **data**. The mathematical techniques that are used to analyze data are collectively called **statistics**. Psychologists and other scientists use statistics to organize, describe, and draw conclusions about the quantitative results of their studies. We will explore the two basic types of statistics that psychologists use—descriptive statistics and inferential statistics.

Descriptive Statistics

Descriptive statistics are statistics used to organize, summarize, and describe data. Simply put, descriptive methods are sophisticated ways of counting things and describing the results of the counting process. For instance, you might count your money and describe it in terms of the total sum, the number of bills of various denominations, and the number of coins you have. You could even make a graph of the number of $1 bills, $5 bills, quarters, dimes, and so on that you have. You might count your money each day for a week and then say something like, "I had a daily average of $22.43 this week. On Monday I had nearly $50, but by Friday, I was down to just $5." All of these actions—counting your money, categorizing your bills and coins, and graphing the results, averaging your money for a week, and describing how your money varied from the beginning to the end of the week—yield descriptive statistics. Researchers use similar strategies to describe the data they gather in experiments and other kinds of studies. Typically, they display the data itself in tables and graphs. To gain more insight into the data, researchers also calculate descriptive statistics that include measures of central tendency, measures of variability, and correlation coefficients. Quite often psychologists and others apply these methods to the results of tests like those you learned about in Chapters 7 and 11 as well as to the kinds of tests that are used in classrooms.

Describing Data with Tables and Graphs

Visual representations of data, such as graphs and tables, allow researchers to see data in an organized fashion. For example, a researcher tested 100 students for recall of 20 new vocabulary words 24 hours after they had memorized the list. The researcher organized the scores in a **frequency distribution**—an arrangement showing the number of times each score occurred. In other words, the frequency distribution shows how many students obtained each score. To organize the 100 test scores, the researcher decided to group the scores into 2-point intervals. Next, the researcher tallied the frequency (number of scores) within each 2-point interval. Table A.1 presents the resulting frequency distribution.

The researcher then made a **histogram**, a bar graph that depicts the number of scores within each interval in the frequency distribution. The intervals are plotted along the horizontal axis, and the frequency of scores in each interval is plotted along the vertical axis. Figure A.1 shows the histogram for the 100 test scores.

TABLE A.1 *Frequency Distribution of 100 Vocabulary Test Scores*

INTERVAL	TALLY OF SCORES IN EACH INTERVAL	NUMBER OF SCORES IN EACH INTERVAL (FREQUENCY)
1–2	I	1
3–4	II	2
5–6	HHT I	6
7–8	HHT HHT HHT III	18
9–10	HHT HHT HHT HHT III	23
11–12	HHT HHT HHT HHT III	23
13–14	HHT HHT HHT II	17
15–16	HHT III	8
17–18	I	1
19–20	I	1

frequency polygon A line graph that depicts the frequency, or number, of scores within each class interval in a frequency distribution.

Another common method of representing frequency data is the **frequency polygon**. As in a histogram, the intervals are plotted along the horizontal axis, and the frequencies are plotted along the vertical axis. However, in a frequency polygon, each interval is represented by a graph point that is placed at the middle (midpoint) of the interval so that its vertical distance above the horizontal axis shows the frequency of that interval. Lines are drawn to connect the points, as shown in Figure A.2. The histogram and the frequency polygon are simply two different ways of presenting data.

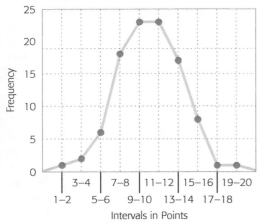

FIGURE A.2 A Frequency Polygon
Vocabulary test scores from the frequency distribution in Table A.1 are plotted here in the form of a frequency polygon. Intervals of 2 points each appear on the horizontal axis. Frequencies of the scores in each class interval are plotted on the vertical axis.

FIGURE A.1 A Frequency Histogram
Vocabulary test scores from the frequency distribution in Table A.1 are plotted here in the form of a histogram. Intervals of 2 points each appear on the horizontal axis. Frequencies of the scores in each interval are plotted on the vertical axis.

Measures of Central Tendency

A **measure of central tendency** is a measure or score that describes the center, or middle, of a distribution of scores. The most widely used and most familiar measure of central tendency is the **mean**, the arithmetic average of a group of scores. The mean is computed by adding all the single scores and dividing the sum by the number of scores.

For instance, consider the case of Carl. Carl sometimes studies and does well in his classes, but he occasionally procrastinates and fails a test. Table A.2 shows how Carl performed on the seven tests in his psychology class last semester. Carl computes his mean score by adding up all his test scores and dividing the sum by the number of tests. Carl's mean, or average, score is 80.

The mean is an important and widely used statistical measure of central tendency, but it can be misleading when a group of scores contains one or several extreme scores. Table A.3 lists the annual incomes of 10 people in rank order. When an income of $1 million is averaged with several more modest incomes, the mean does not provide a true picture of the group. Therefore, when one or a few individuals score far above or below the middle range of a group, a different measure of central tendency should be used. The **median** is the middle score or value when a group of scores are arranged from highest to lowest. When there is an odd number of scores, the score in the middle is the median. When there is an even number of scores, the median is the average of the two middle scores. For the 10 incomes arranged from highest to lowest in Table A.3, the median is $27,000, which is the average of the middle incomes, $28,000 and $26,000. The $27,000 median income is a truer reflection of the comparative income of the group than is the $124,700 mean.

Another measure of central tendency is the **mode**. The mode is easy to find because it is the score that occurs most frequently in a group of scores. The mode of the annual-income group in Table A.3 is $22,000.

measure of central tendency A measure or score that describes the center, or middle, of a distribution of scores (example: mean, median, or mode).

mean The arithmetic average of a group of scores; calculated by adding all the single scores and dividing the sum by the number of scores.

TABLE A.2 *Carl's Psychology Test Scores*

Test 1	98
Test 2	74
Test 3	86
Test 4	92
Test 5	56
Test 6	68
Test 7	86
Sum:	560

Mean: 560 ÷ 7 = 80

median The middle score or value when a group of scores are arranged from highest to lowest.

mode The score that occurs most frequently in a group of scores.

TABLE A.3 *Annual Income for Ten People*

SUBJECT	ANNUAL INCOME
1	$1,000,000
2	$50,000
3	$43,000
4	$30,000
5	$28,000
6	$26,000
7	$22,000
8	$22,000
9	$16,000
10	$10,000
Sum:	$1,247,000

$28,000 and $26,000 → $27,000 = Median

$22,000 and $22,000 → Mode

Mean: $1,247,000 ÷ 10 = $124,700

Median: $27,000

Mode: $22,000

Measures of Variability

variability How much the scores in a distribution spread out, away from the mean.

In addition to a measure of central tendency, researchers need a measure of the **variability** of a set of scores—how much the scores spread out, away from the mean. Both groups in Table A.4 have a mean and a median of 80. However, the scores in Group II cluster tightly around the mean, while the scores in Group I vary widely from the mean.

range The difference between the highest score and the lowest score in a distribution of scores.

The simplest measure of variability is the **range**—the difference between the highest and lowest scores in a distribution of scores. Table A.4 reveals that Group I has a range of 47, indicating high variability, while Group II has a range of only 7, showing low variability. Unfortunately, the range reveals only the difference between the lowest score and the highest score; it tells nothing about the scores in between.

standard deviation A descriptive statistic reflecting the average amount that scores in a distribution deviate, or vary, from their mean.

The **standard deviation** is a descriptive statistic reflecting the average amount that scores in a distribution deviate, or vary, from their mean. The larger the standard deviation, the greater the variability in a distribution of scores. Refer to Table A.4 and note the standard deviations for the two distributions of test scores. In Group I, the relatively large standard deviation of 18.1 reflects the wide variability in that distribution. By contrast, the small standard deviation of 2.14 in Group II indicates that the variability is low, and you can see that the scores cluster tightly around the mean.

TABLE A.4 *Comparison of Range and Standard Deviation for Two Small Groups of Scores Having Identical Means and Medians*

GROUP I		GROUP II	
TEST	**SCORE**	**TEST**	**SCORE**
1	99	1	83
2	99	2	82
3	98	3	81
4	80 Median	4	80 Median
5	72	5	79
6	60	6	79
7	52	7	76
Sum:	560	Sum:	560
Mean: 560 ÷ 7 = 80		Mean: 560 ÷ 7 = 80	
Median: 80		Median: 80	
Range: 99 − 52 = 47		Range: 83 − 76 = 7	
Standard deviation: 18.1		Standard deviation: 2.14	

The Normal Curve

normal curve A symmetrical, bell-shaped frequency distribution that represents how scores are normally distributed in a population; most scores fall near the mean, and fewer and fewer scores occur in the extremes either above or below the mean.

In Chapter 7 we introduced you to the **normal curve**, as shown in Figure A.3. Psychologists and other scientists often use descriptive statistics in connection with an important type of frequency distribution. If a large number of people are measured on any of a wide variety of traits (such as height or IQ score), the great majority of values will cluster in the middle, with fewer and fewer individuals measuring extremely low or high on these variables. Note that slightly more than 68% of the scores in a normal distribution fall within 1 standard deviation of the mean (34.13% within 1 standard deviation above the mean, and 34.13% within 1 standard deviation below the mean). Almost 95.5% of the scores in a normal distribution lie between 2 standard deviations above and below the mean. The vast majority of scores in a normal distribution—99.72%—fall between 3 standard deviations above and below the mean.

FIGURE A.3 The Normal Curve
The normal curve is a symmetrical, bell-shaped curve that represents how scores are normally distributed in a population. Slightly more than 68% of the scores in a normal distribution fall within 1 standard deviation above and below the mean. Almost 95.5% of the scores lie between 2 standard deviations above and below the mean, and about 99.75% fall between 3 standard deviations above and below the mean.

Using the properties of the normal curve and knowing the mean and the standard deviation of a normal distribution, we can find where any score stands (how high or low) in relation to all the other scores in the distribution. For example, on the Wechsler intelligence scales, the mean IQ is 100 and the standard deviation is 15. Thus, 99.72% of the population has an IQ score within 3 standard deviations above and below the mean, ranging from an IQ of 55 to an IQ of 145.

The Correlation Coefficient

As you learned in Chapter 1, a **correlation coefficient** is a number that indicates the degree and direction of relationship between two variables. Correlation coefficients can range from +1.00 (a perfect positive correlation) to .00 (no correlation) to −1.00 (a perfect negative correlation), as illustrated in Figure A.4. A **positive correlation** indicates that two variables vary in the same direction. An increase in one variable is associated with an increase in the other variable, or a decrease in one variable is associated with a decrease in the other. There is a positive correlation between the number of hours college students spend studying and their grades. The more hours they study, the higher their grades are likely to be. A **negative correlation** means that an increase in one variable is associated with a decrease in the other variable. There may be a negative correlation between the number of hours students spend watching television and studying. The more hours they spend watching TV, the fewer hours they may spend studying, and vice versa.

correlation coefficient A numerical value indicating the strength and direction of relationship between two variables, which ranges from +1.00 (a perfect positive correlation) to −1.00 (a perfect negative correlation).

positive correlation A relationship between two variables in which both vary in the same direction.

negative correlation A relationship between two variables in which an increase in one variable is associated with a decrease in the other variable.

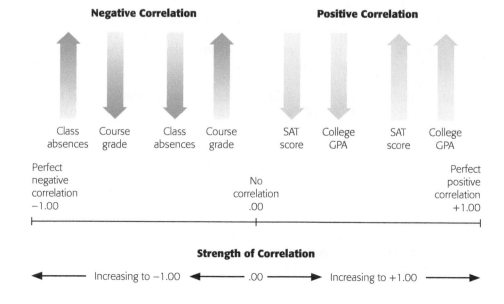

FIGURE A.4 Understanding Correlation Coefficients
Correlation coefficients can range from −1.00 (a perfect negative correlation) through .00 (no correlation) to +1.00 (a perfect positive correlation). As the arrows indicate, a negative correlation exists when an increase in one variable is associated with a decrease in the other variable, and vice versa. A positive correlation exists when both variables tend to either increase or decrease together.

TABLE A.5 *High School and College GPAs for 11 Students*

STUDENT	HIGH SCHOOL GPA (VARIABLE X)	COLLEGE GPA (VARIABLE Y)
1	2.0	1.8
2	2.2	2.5
3	2.3	2.5
4	2.5	3.1
5	2.8	3.2
6	3.0	2.2
7	3.0	2.8
8	3.2	3.3
9	3.3	2.9
10	3.5	3.2
11	3.8	3.5

The sign (+ or –) in a correlation coefficient merely tells whether the two variables vary in the same or opposite directions. (If no sign appears, the correlation is assumed to be positive.) The number in a correlation coefficient indicates the relative strength of the relationship between the two variables—the higher the number, the stronger the relationship. For example, a correlation of –.70 is higher than a correlation of +.56; a correlation of –.85 is just as strong as one of +.85. A correlation of .00 indicates that no relationship exists between the variables. IQ and shoe size are examples of two variables that are not correlated.

Table A.5 shows the measurements of two variables—high school GPA and college GPA for 11 college students. Looking at the data, we can see that 6 of the 11 students had a higher GPA in high school, while 5 of the students had a higher GPA in college. A clearer picture of the actual relationship is shown by the *scatterplot* in Figure A.5. High school GPA (variable X) is plotted on the horizontal axis, and college GPA (variable Y) is plotted on the vertical axis.

One dot is plotted for each of the 11 students at the point where high school GPA, variable X, and college GPA, variable Y, intersect. For example, the first student is represented by a dot at the point where her high school GPA of 2.0 on the horizontal (x) axis and college GPA of 1.8 on the vertical (y) axis intersect. The scatterplot in Figure A.5 reveals a relatively high correlation between high school and college GPAs because the dots cluster near the diagonal line. It also shows that the correlation is positive, because the dots run diagonally upward from left to right. The correlation coefficient for the high school and college GPAs of these 11 students is .71. If the correlation were perfect (1.00), all the dots would fall exactly on the diagonal line.

A scatterplot shows whether a correlation is low, moderate, or high and whether it is positive or negative. Scatterplots that run diagonally up from left to right reveal positive correlations. Scatterplots that run diagonally down from left to right indicate negative correlations. The closer the dots are to the diagonal line, the higher the correlation. The scatterplots in Figure A.6 depict a variety of correlations. It is important to remember that correlation does not demonstrate cause and effect. Even a perfect correlation (+1.00 or –1.00) does not mean that one variable causes or is caused by the other. Correlation shows only that two variables are related.

Not all relationships between variables are positive or negative. The relationships between some variables are said to be *curvilinear*. A curvilinear relationship exists

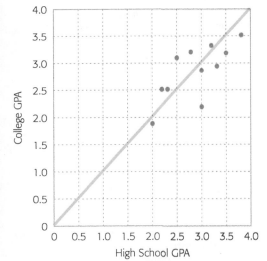

FIGURE A.5 A Scatterplot
A scatterplot reveals a relatively high positive correlation between the high school and college GPAs of the 11 students listed in Table A.5. One dot is plotted for each of the 11 students at the point where high school GPA (plotted on the horizontal axis) and college GPA (plotted on the vertical axis) intersect.

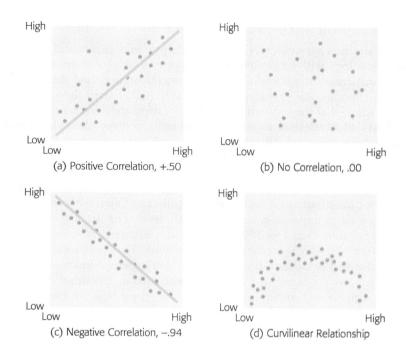

(a) Positive Correlation, +.50

(b) No Correlation, .00

(c) Negative Correlation, −.94

(d) Curvilinear Relationship

FIGURE A.6 A Variety of Scatterplots
A scatterplot moving diagonally up from left to right, as in (a), indicates a positive correlation. A scatterplot moving diagonally down from left to right, as in (c), indicates a negative correlation. The more closely the dots cluster around a diagonal line, the higher the correlation. Scatterplot (b) indicates no correlation. Scatterplot (d) shows a curvilinear relationship that is positive up to a point and then becomes negative. Age and strength of handgrip have a curvilinear relationship: Handgrip increases in strength up to about age 40 and then decreases with continued aging.

when two variables correlate positively (or negatively) up to a certain point and then change direction. For example, there is a positive correlation between physical strength and age up to about 40 or 45 years of age. As age increases from childhood to middle age, so does the strength of handgrip pressure. But beyond middle adulthood, the relationship becomes negative, and increasing age is associated with decreasing handgrip strength. Figure A.6(d) shows a scatterplot of this curvilinear relationship.

Inferential Statistics

As you have learned, descriptive statistics are about counting, tabulating, and using numbers in other ways to communicate information about data. By contrast, **inferential statistics** is based on probabilities. For instance, you know that the probability of getting a "head" when you flip a coin is 1 in 2, or 50%. Knowing that, you *infer* that if you could flip a coin an infinite number of times, heads would turn up half the time. In so doing, you are practicing inferential statistics.

When researchers use inferential statistics, they do so in order to determine how well their findings represent the probabilities that exist outside the confines of the research setting. For example, if the participants in a study obtain a certain average on a test, the psychologist doing the research wants to know how well that average corresponds to the mean that would be obtained if she could test everyone in the group of interest. As such, inferential statistics allow researchers (1) to make inferences about the characteristics of the larger population from their observations and measurements of a sample and (2) to derive estimates of how much faith or confidence can be placed in those inferences. In statistical theory, a **population** is the entire group that is of interest to researchers—the group to which they wish to apply their findings. For example, a population could be all the registered voters in the United States. Usually, researchers cannot directly measure and study the entire population of interest. Consequently, they make inferences about a population from a relatively small **sample** selected from that population. For researchers to draw conclusions about the larger population, the sample must be representative—that is, its characteristics must mirror those of the larger population. (See Chapter 1 for more information about representative samples.)

inferential statistics Statistical procedures that allow researchers to make inferences about the characteristics of the larger population from observations and measurements of a sample and to derive estimates of how much confidence can be placed in those inferences.

population The entire group of interest to researchers and to which they wish to generalize their findings; the group from which a sample is selected.

sample The portion of any population that is selected for study and from which generalizations are made about the entire population.

Statistical Significance

Suppose 200 students are randomly assigned either to an experimental group that will be taught psychology with innovative materials or to a control group that will receive traditional instruction. At the end of the semester, researchers find that the mean test scores of the experimental group are considerably higher than those of the control group. To conclude that the instructional methods caused the difference, the researchers must use **tests of statistical significance** to estimate how often the experimental results could have occurred by chance alone. The estimates derived from tests of statistical significance are stated as probabilities. A probability of .05 means that the experimental results would be expected to occur by chance no more than 5 times out of 100. The .05 level of significance is usually required as a minimum for researchers to conclude that their findings are statistically significant. Often the level of significance reached is even more impressive, such as the .01 level. The .01 level means that the probability is no more than 1 in 100 that the results occurred by chance.

The inferences researchers make are not absolute. They are based on probability, and there is always a possibility, however small, that experimental results could occur by chance. Thus, as we noted in Chapter 1, **replication**, repetition of a study with different participants and preferably a different investigator, is required to determine whether a given result is reliable.

tests of statistical significance Statistical tests that estimate the probability that a particular research result could have occurred by chance.

replication the process of repeating a study with different participants and preferably a different investigator to verify research findings.

Answers to Study Guide Questions

Chapter 1

Section One: Chapter Review   1. scientific method; 2. describe, explain, predict, influence; 3. true; 4. (1) b, (2) b, (3) b, (4) a, (5) a, (6) a, (7) a, b; 5. (1) c, (2) a, (3) d, (4) e, (5) b; 6. (1) d, (2) c, (3) b, (4) a, (5) c, (6) b; 7. (1) d, (2) a, (3) f, (4) e, (5) b, (6) c; 8. (1) b, (2) c, (3) a, (4) b, (5) a, (6) c; 9. (1) b, (2) c, (3) d, (4) a, (5) e, (6) g, (7) f; 10. (1) Yes, (2) No, (3) No, (4) Yes; 11. counseling; 12. d; 13. independent thinking, suspension of judgment, willingness to modify or abandon prior judgments; 14. b; 15. (1) d, (2) a, (3) b, (4) c; 16. case studies; 17. false; 18. false; 19. correlation coefficient; 20. b; 21. positive; 22. negative; 23. false; 24. true; 25. independent variable, dependent variable; 26. (1) d, (2) c, (3) a, (4) b; 27. c; 28. d; 29. quasi-experiment; 30. c; 31. true

Section Two: Who Said This?   1. Skinner; 2. Wundt; 3. James; 4. Watson; 5. Maslow; 6. Sumner; 7. Calkins; 8. Rogers; 9. Wertheimer

Section Three: Comprehensive Practice Test   1. b; 2. b; 3. d; 4. c; 5. c; 6. b; 7. a; 8. d; 9. c; 10. a; 11. c; 12. false; 13. false; 14. true; 15. false; 16. true; 17. false; 18. false; 19. false; 20. false

Chapter 2

Section One: Chapter Review   1. (1) electroencephalogram (EEG); intracranial electroencephalogram (iEEG) (2) c, (3) a; 2. b; 3. a; 4. a; 5. c; 6. a; 7. Glial cells; 8. c; 9. d; 10. action; 11. b; 12. d; 13. dopamine; 14. endorphins; 15. dopamine, glutamate; 16. b; 17. c; 18. (1) b, (2) a, (3) f, (4) c, (5) e, (6) d, (7) g; 19. b; 20. hippocampus; 21. amygdala, hippocampus; 22. b; 23. a; 24. (1) d, (2) c, (3) a, (4) b; 25. (1) d, (2) a, (3) e, (4) b, (5) c; 26. (1) a, (2) b, (3) a, (4) a, (5) b; 27. c; 28. c; 29. myelination; 30. white matter; 31. different; 32. decreases; 33. strokes; 34. (1) d, (2) a, (3) e, (4) c, (5) b, (6) f; 35. recessive; 36. d; 37. twin studies, adoption studies

Section Two: Label the Brain   1. frontal lobe; 2. motor cortex; 3. parietal lobe; 4. occipital lobe; 5. cerebellum; 6. pons; 7. medulla; 8. corpus callosum

Section Three: Comprehensive Practice Test   1. b; 2. c; 3. true; 4. d; 5. d; 6. a; 7. c; 8. b; 9. c; 10. b; 11. d; 12. b; 13. a; 14. c; 15. d; 16. true; 17. a; 18. spatial perception; 19. right parietal cortex; right frontal cortex; 20. X chromosome

Chapter 3

Section One: Chapter Review   1. sensation; 2. absolute; 3. false; 4. c; 5. transduction; 6. b; 7. (1) d (2) c (3) b (4) e (5) a; 8. rods, cones; 9. c; 10. d; 11. hertz, decibels; 12. (1) b (2) a (3) c; 13. d; 14. c; 15. kinesthetic; 16. vestibular, inner ear; 17. olfaction; 18. c; 19. sweet, sour, salty, bitter, umami; 20. taste bud; 21. false; 22. inattentional blindness; 23. bottom-up processing; 24. cross-modal perception; 25. top-down; 26. c; 27. (1) c (2) a (3) b; 28. binocular; 29. (1) c (2) b (3) a (4) d; 30. false; 31. c; 32. false; 33. Ganzfeld procedure

Section Two: Multiple Choice   1. a; 2. d; 3. d; 4. c; 5. d; 6. d; 7. b; 8. c; 9. a; 10. c; 11. c; 12. a; 13. c; 14. a; 15. a; 16. a; 17. b; 18. b; 19. c; 20. d; 21. b; 22. b; 23. c; 24. c; 25. c

Section Three: Comprehensive Practice Test   1. c; 2. a; 3. d; 4. c; 5. b; 6. d; 7. a; 8. c; 9. a; 10. c; 11. c; 12. b; 13. d; 14. a; 15. d; 16. b; 17. true; 18. d; 19. true; 20. c; 21. false; 22. a; 23. c; 24. d; 25. c; 26. b; 27. a; 28. b; 29. d

Chapter 4

Section One: Chapter Review   1. a; 2. suprachiasmatic nucleus; 3. d; 4. false; 5. evolutionary, adaptive; 6. (1) a (2) b (3) a (4) a (5) a; 7. c;

8. false; 9. d; 10. b; 11. (1) c (2) b (3) a; 12. c; 13. false; 14. (1) d (2) a (3) c (4) b; 15. c; 16. false; 17. b; 18. false; 19. b; 20. true; 21. true; 22. c; 23. a; 24. sociocognitive, neodissociation, dissociated control; 25. nucleus accumbens; 26. d; 27. true; 28. true; 29. (1) b (2) a (3) d (4) c; 30. b; 31. b; 32. a; 33. c; 34. false; 35. c;

Section Two: Identify the Drug   (1). b (2). d (3). f (4). c (5). e (6). a (7). g

Section Three: Comprehensive Practice Test   1. melatonin; 2. b; 3. a; 4. c; 5. c; 6. b; 7. false; 8. d; 9. c; 10. d; 11. true; 12. b; 13. b; 14. false; 15. false; 16. c; 17. c; 18. false

Chapter 5

Section One: Chapter Review   1. Pavlov; 2. conditioned; 3. spontaneous recovery; 4. existing conditioned stimulus; 5. b; 6. conditioned, unconditioned; 7. a; 8. biological predispositions; 9. taste aversion; 10. true; 11. b; 12. c; 13. d; 14. negative; 15. continuous; 16. d; 17. a; 18. false; 19. false; 20. true; 21. learned helplessness; 22. biofeedback; 23. behavior modification; 24. false; 25. false d; 26. b; 27. b; 28. (1) c (2) a (3) d (4) b; 29. (1) c (2) a (3) b; 30. Bandura

Section Two: Identify the Concept   1. variable-ratio schedule of reinforcement; 2. classical conditioning of emotions; 3. positive reinforcement for Joey; negative reinforcement for his mother; 4. generalization; 5. positive reinforcement; 6. extinction; 7. fixed-interval reinforcement schedule; 8. positive punishment; 9. observational learning, modeling effect; 10. secondary reinforcer; 11. insight; 12. electronic multitasking environment

Section Three: Comprehensive Practice Test   1. a; 2. c; 3. c; 4. d; 5. b; 6. c; 7. b; 8. c; 9. b; 10. d; 11. b; 12. false; 13. b; 14. b; 15. d; 16. c; 17. a

Chapter 6

Section One: Chapter Review   1. d; 2. (1) b (2) c (3) a; 3. (1) b (2) c (3) a; 4. c; 5. c; 6. (1) a (2) c (3) b (4) a (5) c; 7. c; 8. true; 9. true; 10. b; 11. d; 12. source monitoring; 13. a; 14. b; 15. true; 16. positive; 17. d; 18. a; 19. (1) c (2) e (3) a (4) b (5) d; 20. d; 21. false; 22. true; 23. true; 24. episodic, semantic; 25. a; 26. true; 27. c; 28. a; 29. false

Section Two: Complete the Diagrams   1. large; 2. visual, fraction of a second; auditory, 2 seconds; 3. about 7 items; 4. less than 30 seconds; 5. unlimited; 6. from minutes to a lifetime; 7. declarative; 8. episodic; 9. motor; 10. classically

Section Three: Comprehensive Practice Test   1. c; 2. a; 3. c; 4. b; 5. nondeclarative; 6. a; 7. d; 8. b; 9. true; 10. false; 11. false; 12. d; 13. a; 14. c; 15. true; 16. a; 17. b; 18. true; 19. false; 20. d

Chapter 7

Section One: Chapter Review   1. c; 2. b; 3. d; 4. Framing; 5. a; 6. b; 7. c; 8. false; 9. false; 10. (1) c (2) d (3) b (4) e (5) a; 11. false; 12. true; 13. true; 14. (1) b (2) c (3) a; 15. a; 16. b; 17. a; 18. false; 19. true; 20. (1) b (2) a (3) a (4) b (5) a; 21. c; 22. false; 23. c

Section Two: Important Concepts and Psychologists   1. Simon; 2. Tversky; 3. Whorf; 4. Spearman; 5. Sternberg; 6. Terman; 7. Wechsler; 8. Galton; 9. Steele; 10. Gardner

Section Three: Comprehensive Practice Test   1. c; 2. b; 3. prototype; 4. true; 5. a; 6. a; 7. d; 8. a; 9. false; 10. false; 11. false; 12. c; 13. a; 14. b; 15. true; 16. true; 17. true

Chapter 8

Section One: Chapter Review 1. (1) d; (2) c; (3) a; (4) b 2. d; 3. (1) b (2) c (3) b; 4. (1) d; (2) a; (3) c; (4) b; (5) c; (6) d; (7) b; (8) a; 5. (1) c (2) a (3) b; 6. a; 7. b; 8. c; 9. true; 10. (1) c (2) b (3) a (4) e (5) d; 11. false; 12. (1) c (2) b (3) a; 13. false; 14. b; 15. false; 16. a; 17. true; 18. c; 19. Crystallized; 20. b; 21. a; 22. a; 23. d

Section Two: Important Concepts and Psychologists 1. cognitive development; 2. psychosocial development; 3. temperament; 4. attachment; 5. nativist view of language development; 6. moral reasoning; gender role development; 7. death and dying; 8. gender-schema theory

Section Three: Comprehensive Practice Test 1. b; 2. b; 3. d; 4. d; 5. b; 6. a; 7. b; 8. b; 9. true; 10. b; 11. d; 12. c; 13. c; 14. c; 15. true; 16. b; 17. c; 18. b; 19. true; 20. b

Chapter 9

Section One: Chapter Review 1. true; 2. extrinsic; 3. a; 4. d; 5. c; 6. true; 7. performance; 8. d; 9. expectancy; 10. feeding, satiety; 11. c; 12. c; 13. d; 14. maintain; 15. d; 16. biological; 17. c; 18. anorexia, bulimia; 19. a; 20. c; 21. true; 22. true; 23. b; 24. true; 25. b; 26. b; 27. c; 28. a; 29. b; 30. c; 31. d; 32. c; 33. a; 34. c

Section Two: Important Concepts and Psychologists 1. drive-reduction theory; 2. hierarchy of needs; 3. need for achievement; 4. event creates physical arousal which is identified as an emotion; 5. event creates physical arousal plus emotion; 6. cognitive appraisal of a stimulus results in emotion; 7. facial-feedback hypothesis

Section Three: Comprehensive Practice Test 1. a; 2. a; 3. c; 4. a; 5. c; 6. d; 7. true; 8. d; 9. c; 10. c; 11. true; 12. c; 13. true; 14. true; 15. false; 16. d; 17. b; 18. a

Chapter 10

Section One: Chapter Review 1. false; 2. false; 3. false; 4. true; 5. true; 6. c; 7. c; 8. d; 9. c; 10. c; 11. resistance; 12. exhaustion; 13. physiological, psychological; 14. a; 15. problem-focused, emotion-focused; 16. true; 17. true; 18. d; 19. false; 20. b; 21. a; 22. false; 23. b; 24. d; 25. a; 26. b; 27. Alcohol; 28. false; 29. c; 30. c; 31. c; 32. false

Section Two: The Biopsychosocial Model of Health and Illness 1. genetics, relaxation, healthy lifestyle; 2. lack of exercise, poor diet, disease and injury, toxic chemicals, pollution; 3. stress management skills, giving and receiving love, optimism; 4. depression, pessimism, worry, anxiety, poor coping skills, stress; 5. social responsibility, social policy, social groups; 6. loneliness, poverty, exploitation, violence

Section Three: Comprehensive Practice Test 1. true; 2. b; 3. a; 4. b; 5. a; 6. true; 7. true; 8. c; 9. racism; 10. true; 11. c; 12. false; 13. a; 14. true; 15. true

Chapter 11

Section One: Chapter Review 1. true; 2. unconscious; 3. a; 4. c; 5. b; 6. false; 7. true; 8. birth; 9. d; 10. b; 11. Oedipus complex; Electra complex 12. c; 13. collective; 14. c; 15. c; 16. d; 17. c; 18. a; 19. true; 20. d; 21. true; 22. a; 23. b; 24. negligible; 25. false; 26. b; 27. c; 28. a; 29. d; 30. (1) a (2) c (3) d (4) b (5) e; 31. d; 32. c

Section Two: Complete the Table 1. Freud; behavior arises mostly from unconscious conflict between pleasure-seeking id and moral-perfectionistic superego, with ego as mediator; 2. Maslow, Rogers; behavior springs from the person's motivation to become self-actualized or fully functioning and reflects the person's unique perception of reality and conscious choices; 3. Allport, Cattell, Eysenck, McCrae, Costa; behavior springs from personality traits that are influenced by both heredity and environment.; 4. Mischel, Bandura, Rotter; behavior results from an interaction between internal cognitive factors and environmental factors

Section Three: Comprehensive Practice Test 1. c; 2. c; 3. b; 4. true; 5. b; 6. c; 7. a; 8. a; 9. b; 10. d; 11. b; 12. c; 13. true; 14. false; 15. c; 16. d

Chapter 12

Section One: Chapter Review 1. false; 2. a; 3. (1) c (2) a (3) b (4) d; 4. false; 5. true; 6. false; 7. (1) e (2) d (3) b (4) c (5) a (6) f; 8. c; 9. (1) b (2) c (3) a; 10. false; 11. b; 12. (1) a (2) d (3) b (4) c; 13. d; 14. false; 15. true; 16. (1) d (2) b (3) e (4) c (5) a; 17. paraphilias; 18. c; 19. c; 20. b; 21. d; 22. b

Section Two: Identifying the Disorder 1. major depressive disorder; 2. schizophrenia; 3. bipolar disorder; 4. social phobia; 5. dissociative amnesia; 6. borderline personality disorder; 7. sexual dysfunctions; 8. obsessive-compulsive disorder

Section Three: Comprehensive Practice Test 1. c; 2. b; 3. d; 4. b; 5. true; 6. b; 7. a; 8. false; 9. d; 10. b; 11. true; 12. d; 13. c; 14. true; 15. d; 16. c; 17. true; 18. b

Chapter 13

Section One: Chapter Review 1. d; 2. Gestalt; 3. Person-centered; 4. Psychodynamic; 5. c; 6. c; 7. false; 8. operant; 9. b; 10. d; 11. participant modeling; 13. false; 14. b; 15. d; 16. true; 17. (1) c (2) b (3) a (4) c (5) c; 18. b; 19. d; 20. a; 21. false; 22. false; 23. c; 24. are; 25. b; 26. (1) a (2) c (3) b (4) c

Section Two: Identify the Therapy 1. e; 2. a; 3. d; 4. f; 5. b; 6. g; 7. c

Section Three: Comprehensive Practice Test 1. c; 2. c; 3. c; 4. false; 5. d; 6. a; 7. b; 8. a; 9. a; 10. b; 11. b; 12. a; 13. c; 14. a; 15. b; 16. d; 17. c; 18. true; 19. false; 20. false

Chapter 14

Section One: Chapter Review 1. d; 2. b; 3. true; 4. (1) c (2) b (3) a; 5. true; 6. false; 7. c; 8. c; 9. b; 10. (1) c (2) a (3) b; 11. c; 12. a; 13. false; 14. c; 15. d; 16. true; 17. b; 18. true; 19. true; 20. b; 21. true; 22. true; 23. false; 24. false; 25. true; 26. b; 27. c; 28. c; 29. false; 30. true; 31. (1) b (2) a (3) c; 32. c; 33. false; 34. true

Section Two: Match Terms with Definitions 1. f; 2. e; 3. b; 4. a; 5. h; 6. i; 7. l; 8. j; 9. k; 10. m; 11. d; 12. g; 13. c

Section Three: Comprehensive Practice Test 1. d; 2. false; 3. c; 4. b; 5. false; 6. d; 7. c; 8. true; 9. negatively, positively; 10. false; 11. b; 12. c; 13. c; 14. b; 15. c; 16. true; 17. b; 18. true; 19. a

Glossary

absolute threshold   The minimum amount of sensory stimulation that can be detected 50% of the time.

accommodation   The flattening and bulging action of the lens as it focuses images of objects on the retina.

accommodation   The process by which existing schemes are modified and new schemes are created to incorporate new objects, events, experiences, or information.

achievement motivation   Factors that move people to seek success in academic settings.

achievement test   A measure of what a person has learned up to a certain point in his or her life.

acquired immune deficiency syndrome (AIDS)   A devastating and incurable illness that is caused by infection with the human immunodeficiency virus (HIV) and progressively weakens the body's immune system, leaving the person vulnerable to opportunistic infections that usually cause death.

action potential   The sudden reversal of the resting potential, which initiates the firing of a neuron.

activation-synthesis hypothesis of dreaming   The hypothesis that dreams are the brain's attempt to make sense of the random firing of brain cells during REM sleep.

actor-observer effect   The tendency to attribute one's own behavior primarily to situational factors and the behavior of others primarily to dispositional factors.

additive strategy   a decision making approach in which each alternative is rated on each of the important factors affecting the decision and the alternative with the highest overall rating is chosen

adolescence   The developmental stage that begins at puberty and encompasses the period from the end of childhood to the beginning of adulthood.

adrenal glands   (ah-DREE-nal) A pair of endocrine glands that release hormones that prepare the body for emergencies and stressful situations and also release corticoids and small amounts of the sex hormones.

aerobic exercise   (ah-RO-bik) Exercise that uses the large muscle groups in continuous, repetitive action and increases oxygen intake and breathing and heart rates.

affective neuroscience   The study of the neurological foundations of emotion.

afterimage   A visual sensation that remains after a stimulus is withdrawn.

aggression   The intentional infliction of physical or psychological harm on others.

agoraphobia   (AG-or-uh-FO-bee-ah) An intense fear of being in a situation from which escape is not possible or in which help would not be available if one experienced overwhelming anxiety or a panic attack.

alarm stage   The first stage of the general adaptation syndrome, in which the person experiences a burst of energy that aids in dealing with the stressful situation.

algorithm   A systematic, step-by-step procedure, such as a mathematical formula, that guarantees a solution to a problem of a certain type if applied appropriately and executed properly.

alpha waves   The brain wave pattern associated with deep relaxation.

altered states of consciousness   Change in awareness produced by sleep, meditation, hypnosis, or drugs.

alternative medicine   Any treatment or therapy that has not been scientifically demonstrated to be effective.

altruism   Behavior that is aimed at helping another, requires some self-sacrifice, and is not performed for personal gain.

Alzheimer's disease   (ALZ-hye-mer's) An incurable form of dementia characterized by progressive deterioration of intellect and personality, resulting from widespread degeneration of brain cells.

amnesia   A partial or complete loss of memory due to loss of consciousness, brain damage, or some psychological cause.

amplitude   The measure of the loudness of a sound; expressed in the unit called the decibel.

amygdala   (ah-MIG-da-la) A structure in the limbic system that plays an important role in emotion, particularly in response to unpleasant or punishing stimuli.

analogy heuristic   A rule of thumb that applies a solution that solved a problem in the past to a current problem that shares many features with the past problem.

anchoring   Overestimation of the importance of a factor by focusing on it to the exclusion of other relevant factors.

anorexia nervosa   An eating disorder characterized by an overwhelming, irrational fear of gaining weight or becoming fat, compulsive dieting to the point of self-starvation, and excessive weight loss.

anterograde amnesia   The inability to form long-term memories of events occurring after a brain injury or brain surgery, although memories formed before the trauma are usually intact and short-term memory is unaffected.

antidepressant drugs   Drugs that act as mood elevators for people with severe depression and are also prescribed to treat some anxiety disorders.

antipsychotic drugs   Drugs used to control severe psychotic symptoms, such as delusions, hallucinations, disorganized speech, and disorganized behavior, by inhibiting dopamine activity; also known as neuroleptics.

anxiety disorders   Psychological disorders characterized by frequent fearful thoughts about what might happen in the future.

aphasia   (uh-FAY-zyah) A loss or impairment of the ability to use or understand language, resulting from damage to the brain.

applied research   Research conducted specifically to solve practical problems and improve the quality of life.

approach-approach conflict   A conflict arising from having to choose between equally desirable alternatives.

approach-avoidance conflict   A conflict arising when the same choice has both desirable and undesirable features.

aptitude test   A test that predicts future performance in a particular setting or on a specific task.

archetype   (AR-ka-type) Existing in the collective unconscious, an inherited tendency to respond to universal human situations in particular ways.

arousal   A state of alertness and mental and physical activation.

arousal theory   A theory of motivation suggesting that people are motivated to maintain an optimal level of alertness and physical and mental activation.

artificial intelligence   The programming of computer systems to simulate human thinking in solving problems and in making judgments and decisions.

artificial neural networks (ANNs)   Computer systems that are intended to mimic human cognitive functioning.

assimilation   The process by which new objects, events, experiences, or information is incorporated into existing schemes.

association areas   Areas of the cerebral cortex that house memories and are involved in thought, perception, and language.

attachment   The strong affectionate bond a child forms with the mother or primary caregiver.

attention   The process of sorting through sensations and selecting some of them for further processing.

attention-deficit/hyperactivity disorder (ADHD)   a disorder characterized by inattention and difficulty completing tasks.

attitude   A relatively stable evaluation of a person, object, situation, or issue, along a continuum ranging from positive to negative.

attribution   An assignment of a cause to explain one's own or another person's behavior.

audience effects   The impact of passive spectators on performance.

audition   The sensation and process of hearing.

authoritarian parents   Parents who make arbitrary rules, expect unquestioned obedience from their children, punish transgressions, and value obedience to authority.

authoritative parents   Parents who set high but realistic standards, reason with the child, enforce limits, and encourage open communication and independence.

autism spectrum disorder (ASD)   A disorder in which a child lacks the ability to establish and maintain social relationships.

autobiographical memories   Recollections that a person includes in an account of the events of his or her own life.

automaticity   The ability to recall information from long-term memory without effort.

availability heuristic   A cognitive rule of thumb that says that the perceived probability of an event or the importance assigned to it is based on its availability in memory.

aversion therapy   A behavior therapy in which an aversive stimulus is paired with a harmful or socially undesirable behavior until the behavior becomes associated with pain or discomfort.

avoidance learning   Learning to avoid events or conditions associated with aversive consequences or phobias.

avoidance-avoidance conflict   A conflict arising from having to choose between undesirable alternatives.

axon   (AK-sahn) The slender, tail-like extension of the neuron that transmits signals to the dendrites or cell body of other neurons and to muscles, glands, and other parts of the body.

axon terminal   Bulbous end of the axon where signals move from the axon of one neuron to the dendrites or cell body of another.

babbling   Vocalization of the basic speech sounds (phonemes), which begins between 4 and 6 months.

bacterial STDs   Sexually transmitted diseases that are caused by bacteria and can be treated with antibiotics.

basic emotions   Emotions that are unlearned and universal, that are reflected in the same facial expressions across cultures, and that emerge in children according to their biological timetable of development; fear, anger, disgust, surprise, happiness, and sadness are usually considered basic emotions.

basic research   Research conducted to seek new knowledge and to explore and advance general scientific understanding.

Beck's cognitive therapy (CT)   A therapy designed by Aaron Beck to help clients stop their cognitive errors as they occur and replace them with more objective thoughts.

behavior modification   A method of changing behavior through a systematic program based on the learning principles of classical conditioning, operant conditioning, or observational learning.

behavior modification   An approach to therapy that uses learning principles to eliminate inappropriate or maladaptive behaviors and replace them with more adaptive responses.

behavior therapy   A treatment approach that is based on the idea that abnormal behavior is learned and that applies the principles of operant conditioning, classical conditioning, and/or observational learning to eliminate inappropriate or maladaptive behaviors and replace them with more adaptive responses.

behavioral genetics   A field of research that uses twin studies and adoption studies to investigate the relative effects of heredity and environment on behavior.

behaviorism   The school of psychology that views observable, measurable behavior as the appropriate subject matter for psychology and emphasizes the key role of environment as a determinant of behavior.

beta waves   The brain wave pattern associated with mental activity.

bilingualism   Fluency in at least two languages.

binocular depth cues   Depth cues that depend on both eyes working together.

biofeedback   The use of sensitive equipment to give people precise feedback about internal physiological processes so that they can learn, with practice, to exercise control over them.

biological predispositions   Genetically programmed tendencies to acquire classically conditioned fear responses to potentially life-threatening stimuli.

biological psychology   The school of psychology that looks for links between specific behaviors and equally specific biological processes that often help explain individual differences.

biomedical model   A perspective that explains illness solely in terms of biological factors.

biomedical therapy   A therapy (drug therapy, electroconvulsive therapy, or psychosurgery) that is based on the assumption that psychological disorders are symptoms of underlying physical problems.

biopsychosocial model A perspective that focuses on health as well as illness and holds that both are determined by a combination of biological, psychological, and social factors.

bipolar disorder A mood disorder in which manic episodes alternate with periods of depression, usually with relatively normal periods in between.

blind spot The point in each retina where there are no rods or cones because the cable of ganglion cells is extending through the retinal wall.

body mass index (BMI) A measure of weight relative to height.

bottom-up processing Information processing in which individual components or bits of data are combined until a complete perception is formed.

brainstem The structure that begins at the point where the spinal cord enlarges as it enters the brain and handles functions critical to physical survival. It includes the medulla, the reticular formation, and the pons.

brightness The intensity of light energy perceived as a color; based on amplitude of light wave.

Broca's aphasia (BRO-kuz uh-FAY-zyah) An impairment in the physical ability to produce speech sounds or, in extreme cases, an inability to speak at all; caused by damage to Broca's area.

Broca's area (BRO-kuz) The area in the frontal lobe, usually in the left hemisphere, that controls the production of speech sounds.

bulimia nervosa An eating disorder characterized by repeated and uncontrolled (and often secretive) episodes of binge eating.

burnout Lack of energy, exhaustion, and pessimism that results from chronic stress.

bystander effect A social factor that affects prosocial behavior: As the number of bystanders at an emergency increases, the probability that the victim will receive help decreases, and the help, if given, is likely to be delayed.

California Personality Inventory (CPI) A highly regarded personality test developed especially for typical individuals aged 13 and older.

Cannon–Bard theory The theory that an emotion-provoking stimulus is transmitted simultaneously to the cerebral cortex, providing the conscious mental experience of the emotion, and to the sympathetic nervous system, causing the physiological arousal.

case study A descriptive research method in which a single individual or a small number of persons are studied in great depth.

causal hypothesis A prediction about a cause–effect relationship between two or more variables.

cell body The part of a neuron that contains the nucleus and carries out the metabolic functions of the neuron.

central nervous system (CNS) The part of the nervous system comprising the brain and the spinal cord.

cerebellum (sehr-uh-BELL-um) The brain structure that helps the body execute smooth, skilled movements and regulates muscle tone and posture.

cerebral cortex (seh-REE-brul KOR-tex) The gray, convoluted covering of the cerebral hemispheres that is responsible for the higher mental processes of language, memory, and thinking.

cerebral hemispheres (seh-REE-brul) The right and left halves of the cerebrum, covered by the cerebral cortex and connected by the corpus callosum; they control movement and feeling on the opposing sides of the body.

cerebrum (seh-REE-brum) The largest structure of the human brain, consisting of the two cerebral hemispheres connected by the corpus callosum and covered by the cerebral cortex.

chromosomes Rod-shaped structures in the nuclei of body cells, which contain all the genes and carry all the genetic information necessary to make a human being.

chunking A memory strategy that involves grouping or organizing bits of information into larger units, which are easier to remember.

circadian rhythms (sur-KAY-dee-un) Within each 24-hour period, the regular fluctuation from high to low points of certain bodily functions and behaviors.

circadian theory of sleep The theory that sleep evolved to keep humans out of harm's way during the night; also known as the evolutionary or adaptive theory.

classical conditioning A type of learning through which an organism learns to associate one stimulus with another.

coaction effects The impact on performance of the presence of other people engaged in the same task.

cochlea (KOK-lee-uh) The fluid-filled, snail-shaped, bony chamber in the inner ear that contains the basilar membrane and its hair cells (the sound receptors).

cognition The mental processes that are involved in acquiring, storing, retrieving, and using information and that include sensation, perception, imagery, concept formation, reasoning, decision making, problem solving, and language.

cognitive behavior therapies (CBTs) Therapies that assume maladaptive behavior can result from irrational thoughts, beliefs, and ideas.

cognitive dissonance The unpleasant state that can occur when people become aware of inconsistencies between their attitudes or between their attitudes and their behavior.

cognitive map A mental representation of a spatial arrangement such as a maze.

cognitive processes (COG-nih-tiv) Mental processes such as thinking, knowing, problem solving, remembering, and forming mental representations.

cognitive psychology The school of psychology that sees humans as active participants in their environment; studies mental processes such as memory, problem solving, reasoning, decision making, perception, language, and other forms of cognition.

cognitive theory of dreaming The view that dreaming is thinking while asleep.

collective unconscious In Jung's theory, the most inaccessible layer of the unconscious, which contains the universal experiences of humankind.

color blindness The inability to distinguish certain colors from one another.

compliance Acting in accordance with the direct requests of other people.

compulsion A persistent, irresistible, and irrational urge to perform an act or ritual repeatedly.

concept A mental category used to represent a class or group of objects, people, organizations, events, situations, or relations that share common characteristics or attributes.

conditioned response (CR)   The learned response that comes to be elicited by a conditioned stimulus as a result of its repeated pairing with an unconditioned stimulus.

conditioned stimulus (CS)   A neutral stimulus that, after repeated pairing with an unconditioned stimulus, becomes associated with it and elicits a conditioned response.

conditions of worth   Conditions on which the positive regard of others rests.

cones   The light-sensitive receptor cells in the retina that enable humans to see color and fine detail in adequate light but do not function in very dim light.

confirmation bias   Selective attention to information that confirms preexisting beliefs about the best way to solve a problem.

conformity   Changing or adopting a behavior or an attitude in an effort to be consistent with the social norms of a group or the expectations of other people.

confounding variables   Factors other than the independent variable(s) that are unequal across groups.

conscious   (KON-shus) The thoughts, feelings, sensations, or memories of which a person is aware at any given moment.

consciousness   Everything of which we are aware at any given time-our thoughts, feelings, sensations, and perceptions of the external environment.

conservation   The concept that a given quantity of matter remains the same despite being rearranged or changed in appearance, as long as nothing is added or taken away.

consolidation failure   Any disruption in the consolidation process that prevents a long-term memory from forming.

consummate love   According to Sternberg's theory, the most complete form of love, consisting of all three components—intimacy, passion, and commitment.

context effect   The tendency to encode elements of the physical setting in which information is learned along with memory of the information itself.

control group   In an experiment, a group similar to the experimental group that is exposed to the same experimental environment but is not given the treatment; used for purposes of comparison.

conventional level   Kohlberg's second level of moral development, in which right and wrong are based on the internalized standards of others; "right" is whatever helps or is approved of by others, or whatever is consistent with the laws of society.

conversion disorder   A somatoform disorder in which a person suffers a loss of motor or sensory functioning in some part of the body; the loss has no physical cause but solves some psychological problem.

coping   Efforts through action and thought to deal with demands that are perceived as taxing or overwhelming.

cornea   (KOR-nee-uh) The tough, transparent, protective layer that covers the front of the eye and bends light rays inward through the pupil.

corpus callosum   (KOR-pus kah-LO-sum) The thick band of nerve fibers that connects the two cerebral hemispheres and makes possible the transfer of information and the synchronization of activity between the hemispheres.

correlation coefficient   A numerical value that indicates the strength and direction of the relationship between two variables; ranges from +1.00 (a perfect positive correlation) to −1.00 (a perfect negative correlation).

correlational method   A research method used to establish the degree of relationship (correlation) between two characteristics, events, or behaviors.

couple therapy   Therapy involving intimate partners in which behavior change or partners' emotional responses to each other or both are the focus of treatment.

creativity   The ability to produce original, appropriate, and valuable ideas and/or solutions to problems.

critical period   A period so important to development that a harmful environmental influence at that time can keep a bodily structure from developing normally or can impair later intellectual or social development.

critical thinking   The process of objectively evaluating claims, propositions, and conclusions to determine whether they follow logically from the evidence presented.

cross-cultural research   Comparisons of mental processes and behaviors among humans living in different cultures.

cross-modal perception   A process whereby the brain integrates information from more than one sense.

crowding   The subjective judgment that there are too many people in a confined space.

crystallized intelligence   Aspects of intelligence involving verbal ability and accumulated knowledge, which tend to increase over the life span.

CT scan (computerized axial tomography)   A brain-scanning technique that uses a rotating, computerized X-ray tube to produce cross-sectional images of the structures of the brain.

culturally sensitive therapy   An approach to therapy in which knowledge of clients' cultural backgrounds guides the choice of therapeutic interventions.

culture-fair intelligence test   An intelligence test that uses questions that will not penalize those whose culture differs from the mainstream or dominant culture.

curve of forgetting   The pattern of forgetting discovered by Ebbinghaus, which shows that forgetting tapers off after a period of rapid information loss that immediately follows learning.

decay theory   The oldest theory of forgetting, which holds that memories, if not used, fade with time and ultimately disappear altogether.

decibel (dB)   (DES-ih-bel) A unit of measurement for the loudness of sounds.

decision making   The process of considering alternatives and choosing among them.

declarative memory   The subsystem within long-term memory that stores facts, information, and personal life events that can be brought to mind verbally or in the form of images and then declared or stated; also called explicit memory.

defense mechanism   A means used by the ego to defend against anxiety and to maintain self-esteem.

deindividuation   A social psychological process in which individuals lose their sense of personal identity as a result of identification with a group.

delusion   A false belief, not generally shared by others in the culture.

delusion of grandeur   A false belief that one is a famous person or a powerful or important person who has some great knowledge, ability, or authority.

delusion of persecution   A false belief that some person or agency is trying in some way to harm one.

dementia   A state of mental deterioration characterized by impaired memory and intellect and by altered personality and behavior.

dendrites   (DEN-drytes) In a neuron, the branch-like extensions of the cell body that receive signals from other neurons.

dependent variable   The factor or condition that is measured at the end of an experiment and is presumed to vary as a result of the manipulations of the independent variable(s).

depressants   A category of drugs that decrease activity in the central nervous system, slow down bodily functions, and reduce sensitivity to outside stimulation; also called "downers."

depressive disorders   Disorders characterized by extreme and unwarranted disturbances in emotion or mood.

depth perception   The ability to perceive the visual world in three dimensions and to judge distances accurately.

descriptive research methods   Research methods that yield descriptions of behavior.

developmental psychology   The study of how humans grow, develop, and change throughout the life span.

difference threshold   A measure of the smallest increase or decrease in a physical stimulus that is required to produce a difference in sensation that is noticeable 50% of the time.

diffusion of responsibility   The feeling among bystanders at an emergency that the responsibility for helping is shared by the group, making each person feel less compelled to act than if he or she alone bore the total responsibility.

directive therapy   Any type of psychotherapy in which the therapist takes an active role in determining the course of therapy sessions and provides answers and suggestions to the client; an example is Gestalt therapy.

discrimination   Behavior (usually negative) directed toward others based on their gender, religion, race, or membership in a particular group.

discrimination   The learned ability to distinguish between similar stimuli so that the conditioned response occurs only to the original conditioned stimulus but not to similar stimuli.

discriminative stimulus   A stimulus that signals whether a certain response or behavior is likely to be rewarded, ignored, or punished.

disinhibitory effect   Displaying a previously suppressed behavior because a model does so without receiving punishment.

displacement   The event that occurs when short-term memory is filled to capacity and each new, incoming item pushes out an existing item, which is then forgotten.

display rules   Cultural rules that dictate how emotions should generally be expressed and when and where their expression is appropriate.

dispositional attribution   Attributing a behavior to some internal cause, such as a personal trait, motive, or attitude; an internal attribution.

disruptive mood dysregulation disorders (DMDD)   a disorder in which children are highly irritable and have frequent outbursts of temper that interfere with social and academic functioning.

dissociative amnesia   A dissociative disorder in which there is a complete or partial loss of the ability to recall personal information or identify past experiences.

dissociative disorder   A disorder in which, under unbearable stress, consciousness becomes dissociated from a person's identity or her or his memories of important personal events, or both.

dissociative fugue   (FEWG) A dissociative disorder in which one has a complete loss of memory of one's entire identity, travels away from home, and may assume a new identity.

dissociative identity disorder (DID)   A dissociative disorder in which two or more distinct, unique personalities occur in the same person, and there is severe memory disruption concerning personal information about the other personalities.

divergent thinking   The ability to produce multiple ideas, answers, or solutions to a problem for which there is no agreed-on solution.

dominant–recessive pattern   A set of inheritance rules in which the presence of a single dominant gene causes a trait to be expressed but two genes must be present for the expression of a recessive trait.

door-in-the-face technique   A strategy in which someone makes a large, unreasonable request with the expectation that the person will refuse but will then be more likely to respond favorably to a smaller request later.

double-blind technique   A procedure in which neither the participants nor the experimenters know who is in the experimental and control groups until after the data have been gathered; a control for experimenter bias.

drive   An internal state of tension or arousal that is brought about by an underlying need and that an organism is motivated to reduce.

drive-reduction theory   A theory of motivation suggesting that biological needs create internal states of tension or arousal—called drives—which organisms are motivated to reduce.

drug tolerance   A condition in which the user becomes progressively less affected by the drug and must take increasingly larger doses to maintain the same effect or high.

DSM-5, 2013   *The Diagnostic and Statistical Manual of Mental Disorders,* 5th Edition; a manual published by the American Psychiatric Association, which describes the criteria used to classify and diagnose mental disorders.

dyssomnias   Sleep disorders in which the timing, quantity, or quality of sleep is impaired.

ego   (EE-go) In Freud's theory, the logical, rational, largely conscious system of personality, which operates according to the reality principle.

eidetic imagery   (eye-DET-ik) The ability to retain the image of a visual stimulus for several minutes after it has been removed from view and to use this retained image to answer questions about the visual stimulus.

elaborative rehearsal   A memory strategy that involves relating new information to something that is already known.

electroconvulsive therapy (ECT)   A biological therapy in which an electric current is passed through the right hemisphere of the brain; usually reserved for patients with severe depression who are suicidal.

electroencephalogram (EEG)   (ee-lek-tro-en-SEFF-uh-lo-gram) A record of brain-wave activity made by a machine called the electroencephalograph.

elimination by aspects   A decision-making approach in which alternatives are evaluated against criteria that have been ranked according to importance.

embryo   The developing human organism during the period (week 3 through week 8) when the major systems, organs, and structures of the body develop.

emerging adulthood   The period from the late teens to early 20s when individuals explore options prior to committing to adult roles.

emotion   A state involving physiological arousal, a cognitive appraisal of the situation that produced the state, and an outward behavior expressing the state.

emotional intelligence   The ability to apply knowledge about emotions to everyday life.

emotion-focused coping   A response involving reappraisal of a stressor to reduce its emotional impact.

encoding   The process of transforming information into a form that can be stored in memory.

encoding failure   A cause of forgetting that occurs when information was never put into long-term memory.

endocrine system   (EN-duh-krin) A system of ductless glands in various parts of the body that manufacture hormones and secrete them into the bloodstream, thus affecting cells in other parts of the body.

endorphins   (en-DOR-fins) The body's own natural painkillers, which block pain and produce a feeling of well-being.

episodic memory   (ep-ih-SOD-ik) The type of declarative memory that records events as they have been subjectively experienced.

escape learning   Learning to perform a behavior because it prevents or terminates an aversive stimulus.

esteem needs   Motives that drive people to pursue goals such as academic achievement and success in a career.

ethnocentrism   The tendency to look at situations from one's own racial or cultural perspective.

evolutionary psychology   The school of psychology that studies how human behaviors required for survival have adapted in the face of environmental pressures over the long course of evolution.

evolutionary theory of dreaming   The view that vivid REM dreams enable people to rehearse the skills needed to fend off threats and predators.

exemplars   The individual instances, or examples, of a concept that are stored in memory from personal experience.

exhaustion stage   The third stage of the general adaptation syndrome, which occurs if the organism fails in its efforts to resist the stressor.

expectancy theory   An approach that explains work motivation in terms of workers' beliefs about the effectiveness and value of the effort they put forth on the job.

experimental group   In an experiment, the group that is exposed to an independent variable.

experimental method   The only research method that can be used to identify cause–effect relationships between two or more conditions or variables.

experimenter bias   A phenomenon that occurs when a researcher's preconceived notions or expectations in some way influence participants' behavior and/or the researcher's interpretation of experimental results.

expert systems   Computer programs designed to carry out highly specific functions within a limited domain.

expertise   An extensive amount of background knowledge that is relevant to a reconstructive memory task.

exposure and response prevention   A behavior therapy that exposes patients with obsessive-compulsive disorder to stimuli that trigger obsessions and compulsive rituals, while patients resist performing the compulsive rituals for progressively longer periods of time.

extinction   In classical conditioning, the weakening and eventual disappearance of the conditioned response as a result of repeated presentation of the conditioned stimulus without the unconditioned stimulus.

extinction   In operant conditioning, the weakening and eventual disappearance of the conditioned response as a result of the withholding of reinforcement.

extrasensory perception (ESP)   Gaining information about objects, events, or another person's thoughts through some means other than the known sensory channels.

extrinsic motivation   The desire to behave in a certain way to gain some external reward or to avoid some undesirable consequence.

facial-feedback hypothesis   The idea that the muscular movements involved in certain facial expressions produce the corresponding emotions (for example, smiling makes one feel happy).

facilitation effect   Exhibiting a behavior similar to that shown by a model in an unfamiliar situation.

family therapy   Therapy involving an entire family, with the goal of helping family members reach agreement on changes that will help heal the family unit, improve communication problems, and create more understanding and harmony within the group.

feature detectors   Neurons in the brain that respond only to specific visual patterns (for example, to lines or angles).

fetal alcohol syndrome   A condition, caused by maternal alcohol intake during pregnancy, in which the baby is born with mental retardation, with a small head and facial, organ, and behavioral abnormalities.

fetus   The developing human organism during the period (week 9 until birth) when rapid growth and further development of the structures, organs, and systems of the body occur.

fight-or-flight response   A response to stress in which the sympathetic nervous system and the endocrine glands prepare the body to fight or flee.

five-factor model   A model that describes personality using five broad dimensions, each of which is composed of a constellation of personality traits.

fixation   Arrested development at a psychosexual stage occurring because of excessive gratification or frustration at that stage.

fixed-interval (FI) schedule   A schedule in which a reinforcer is given following the first correct response after a specific period of time has elapsed.

fixed-ratio (FR) schedule   A schedule in which a reinforcer is given after a fixed number of correct, nonreinforced responses.

flashbulb memories   Memories for shocking, emotion-provoking events that include information about the source from which the information was acquired.

flooding   A behavior therapy based on classical conditioning and used to treat phobias by exposing clients to the feared object or event (or asking them to imagine it vividly) for an extended period, until their anxiety decreases.

fluid intelligence Aspects of intelligence involving abstract reasoning and mental flexibility, which peak in the early 20s and decline slowly as people age.

foot-in-the-door technique A strategy designed to gain a favorable response to a small request at first, with the intent of making the person more likely to agree later to a larger request.

forebrain The largest part of the brain where cognitive functions as well as many of the motor functions of the brain are carried out.

forgetting The inability to bring to mind information that was previously remembered.

formal concept A concept that is clearly defined by a set of rules, a formal definition, or a classification system.

fovea (FO-vee-uh) A small area at the center of the retina that provides the clearest and sharpest vision because it has the largest concentration of cones.

framing The way information is presented so as to emphasize either a potential gain or a potential loss as the outcome.

free association A psychoanalytic technique used to explore the unconscious by having patients reveal whatever thoughts, feelings, or images come to mind.

frequency The number of cycles completed by a sound wave in one second, determining the pitch of the sound; expressed in the unit called the hertz.

frequency theory The theory of hearing that holds that hair cell receptors vibrate the same number of times per second as the sounds that reach them.

frontal lobes The largest of the brain's lobes, which contain the motor cortex, Broca's area, and the frontal association areas.

frustration-aggression hypothesis The hypothesis that frustration usually produces aggression.

functional fixedness The failure to use familiar objects in novel ways to solve problems because of a tendency to view objects only in terms of their customary functions.

functional MRI (fMRI) A brain-imaging technique that reveals both brain structure and brain activity more precisely and rapidly than PET.

functionalism An early school of psychology that was concerned with how humans and animals use mental processes in adapting to their environment.

fundamental attribution error The tendency to give more attention to dispositional factors than is appropriate for a situation.

g factor Spearman's term for a general intellectual ability that underlies all mental operations to some degree.

gender roles Cultural expectations about the behavior appropriate for each gender.

gender-sensitive therapy An approach to therapy that takes into account the effects of gender on both the therapist's and the client's behavior.

general adaptation syndrome (GAS) The predictable sequence of reactions (alarm, resistance, and exhaustion stages) that organisms show in response to stressors.

general slowing A process in which the reductions in the speed of neural transmission lead to a slowing of physical and mental functions.

generalization In classical conditioning, the tendency to make a conditioned response to a stimulus that is similar to the original conditioned stimulus.

generalization In operant conditioning, the tendency to make the learned response to a stimulus similar to that for which the response was originally reinforced.

generalized anxiety disorder (GAD) An anxiety disorder in which people experience chronic, excessive worry for 6 months or more.

genes The segments of DNA that are located on the chromosomes and are the basic units for the transmission of all hereditary traits.

genotype An individual's genetic makeup.

Gestalt (geh-SHTALT) A German word that roughly refers to the whole form, pattern, or configuration that a person perceives.

Gestalt psychology The school of psychology that emphasizes that individuals perceive objects and patterns as whole units and that the perceived whole is more than the sum of its parts.

Gestalt therapy A therapy that was originated by Fritz Perls and that emphasizes the importance of clients' fully experiencing, in the present moment, their feelings, thoughts, and actions and then taking responsibility for them.

glial cells (GLEE-ul) Specialized cells in the brain and spinal cord that support neurons, remove waste products such as dead neurons, and perform other manufacturing, nourishing, and cleanup tasks.

goal orientation theory The view that achievement motivation depends on which of four goal orientations (mastery/approach, mastery/avoidance, performance/avoidance, performance/approach) an individual adopts.

goal setting An approach to work motivation that involves establishing specific, difficult goals rather than simply telling people to do their best in the absence of assigned goals.

gonads The ovaries in females and the testes in males; endocrine glands that produce sex hormones.

group polarization A group member's adoption of a more extreme position about an issue than she or he originally held after participating in a discussion in which other group members strongly express agreement with her or him.

group therapy A form of therapy in which several clients (usually 7 to 10) meet regularly with one or more therapists to resolve personal problems.

groupthink The tendency for members of a tightly knit group to be more concerned with preserving group solidarity and uniformity than with objectively evaluating all alternatives in decision making.

gustation The sense of taste.

hair cells Sensory receptors for hearing that are attached to the basilar membrane in the cochlea.

hallucination An imaginary sensation.

hallucinogens (hal-LU-sin-o-jenz) A category of drugs that can alter and distort perceptions of time and space, alter mood, produce feelings of unreality, and cause hallucinations; also called *psychedelics*.

halo effect The tendency to assume that a person has generally positive or negative traits as a result of observing one major positive or negative trait.

hardiness A combination of three psychological qualities—commitment, control, and challenge—shared by people who can handle high levels of stress and remain healthy.

hassles Irritating demands that occur daily and may cause more stress than major life changes do.

health psychology The subfield within psychology that is concerned with the psychological factors that contribute to health, illness, and recovery.

heritability An index of the degree to which a characteristic is estimated to be influenced by heredity.

heuristic (yur-RIS-tik) A rule of thumb that is derived from experience and used in decision making and problem solving, even though there is no guarantee of its accuracy or usefulness.

higher-order conditioning Conditioning that occurs when conditioned stimuli are linked together to form a series of signals.

hindbrain A link between the spinal cord and the brain that contains structures that regulate physiological functions, including heart rate, respiration, and blood pressure.

hippocampal region A part of the limbic system, which includes the hippocampus itself and the underlying cortical areas, involved in the formation of semantic memories.

hippocampus (hip-po-CAM-pus) A structure in the limbic system that plays a central role in the storing of new memories, the response to new or unexpected stimuli, and navigational ability.

homeostasis The natural tendency of the body to maintain a balanced internal state in order to ensure physical survival.

homophobia An intense, irrational hostility toward or fear of homosexuals.

hormone A chemical substance that is manufactured and released in one part of the body and affects other parts of the body.

hue The dimension of light that refers to the specific color perceived.

human immunodeficiency virus (HIV) The virus that causes AIDS.

humanistic psychology The school of psychology that focuses on the uniqueness of human beings and their capacity for choice, growth, and psychological health.

humanistic therapies Psychotherapies that assume that people have the ability and freedom to lead rational lives and make rational choices.

hypnosis A procedure through which one person, the hypnotist, uses the power of suggestion to induce changes in thoughts, feelings, sensations, perceptions, or behavior in another person, the subject.

hypothalamus (HY-po-THAL-uh-mus) A small but influential brain structure that regulates hunger, thirst, sexual behavior, internal body temperature, other body functions, and a wide variety of emotional behaviors.

hypothesis A testable prediction about the conditions under which a particular behavior or mental process may occur.

hypothetico-deductive thinking The ability to base logical reasoning on a hypothetical premise.

id (ID) The unconscious system of the personality, which contains the life and death instincts and operates on the pleasure principle; source of the libido.

illusion A false perception or a misperception of an actual stimulus in the environment.

imagery The representation in the mind of a sensory experience—visual, auditory, gustatory, motor, olfactory, or tactile.

imaginary audience A belief of adolescents that they are or will be the focus of attention in social situations and that others will be as critical or approving as they are of themselves.

impression formation The mental process of developing opinions about other people.

impression management The intentional steps we take to influence others' opinions of us.

inattentional blindness The phenomenon in which we shift our focus from one object to another and, in the process, fail to notice changes in objects to which we are not directly paying attention.

incentive An external stimulus that motivates behavior (for example, money or fame).

inclusion Educating students with intellectual disabilities by placing them in classes with students who do not have disabilities for part or all of the day; also called *mainstreaming*.

independent variable In an experiment, a factor or condition that is deliberately manipulated to determine whether it causes any change in another behavior or condition.

individualism/collectivism dimension A measure of a culture's emphasis on either individual achievement or social relationships.

industrial/organizational (I/O) psychologists Psychologists who apply their knowledge in the workplace and are especially interested in work motivation and job performance.

infantile amnesia The relative inability of older children and adults to recall events from the first few years of life.

information-processing theory A framework for studying memory that uses the computer as a model of human cognitive processes.

information-processing theory An approach to the study of mental structures and processes that uses the computer as a model for human thinking.

in-group A social group with a strong sense of togetherness, from which others are excluded.

inhibitory effect Suppressing a behavior because a model is punished for displaying the behavior.

inner ear The innermost portion of the ear, containing the cochlea, the vestibular sacs, and the semicircular canals.

insight The sudden realization of the relationship between elements in a problem situation, which makes the solution apparent.

insight therapies Approaches to psychotherapy based on the notion that psychological well-being depends on self-understanding.

insomnia A sleep disorder characterized by difficulty falling or staying asleep, by waking too early, or by sleep that is light, restless, or of poor quality.

intellectual disability A condition in which an individual has scores below 70 on a standardized intelligence test and displays adaptive functioning significantly below that of others of the same age.

intelligence An individual's ability to understand complex ideas, to adapt effectively to the environment, to learn from experience, to engage in various forms of reasoning, and to overcome obstacles through mental effort.

intelligence quotient (IQ) An index of intelligence, originally derived by dividing mental age by chronological age and then multiplying by 100, but now derived by comparing an individual's score with the scores of others of the same age.

intelligence test A test of individual differences in general intellectual ability.

interference   A cause of forgetting that occurs because information or associations stored either before or after a given memory hinder the ability to remember it.

interpersonal therapy (IPT)   A brief psychotherapy designed to help people with depression better understand and cope with problems relating to their interpersonal relationships.

intrinsic motivation   The desire to behave in a certain way because it is enjoyable or satisfying in and of itself.

intuition   Rapidly formed judgments based on "gut feelings" or "instincts."

inventory   A paper-and-pencil test with questions about a person's thoughts, feelings, and behaviors, which measures several dimensions of personality and can be scored according to a standard procedure.

James–Lange theory   The theory that emotional feelings result when an individual becomes aware of a physiological response to an emotion-provoking stimulus (for example, feeling fear because of trembling).

just noticeable difference (JND)   The smallest change in sensation that a person is able to detect 50% of the time.

kinesthetic sense   The sense providing information about the position and movement of body parts.

laboratory observation   A descriptive research method in which behavior is studied in a laboratory setting.

language   A means of communicating thoughts and feelings using a system of socially shared but arbitrary symbols (sounds, signs, or written symbols) arranged according to rules of grammar.

latent content   Freud's term for the underlying meaning of a dream.

latent learning   Learning that occurs without apparent reinforcement and is not demonstrated until the organism is motivated to do so.

lateral hypothalamus (LH)   The part of the hypothalamus that acts as a feeding center to incite eating.

lateralization   The specialization of one of the cerebral hemispheres to handle a particular function.

law of effect   One of Thorndike's laws of learning, which states that the consequence, or effect, of a response will determine whether the tendency to respond in the same way in the future will be strengthened or weakened.

Lazarus theory   The theory that a cognitive appraisal is the first step in an emotional response and all other aspects of an emotion, including physiological arousal, depend on it.

learned helplessness   A passive resignation to aversive conditions that is learned through repeated exposure to inescapable or unavoidable aversive events.

learning   A relatively permanent change in behavior, knowledge, capability, or attitude that is acquired through experience and cannot be attributed to illness, injury, or maturation.

left hemisphere   The hemisphere that controls the right side of the body, coordinates complex movements, and, in most people, handles most of the language functions.

lens   The transparent disk-shaped structure behind the iris and the pupil that changes shape as it focuses on objects at varying distances.

levels-of-processing model   The memory model that describes maintenance rehearsal as "shallow" processing and elaborative rehearsal as "deep" processing.

life events approach   The view that a person's state of well-being can be threatened by major life changes.

limbic system   A group of structures in the brain, including the amygdala and hippocampus, that are collectively involved in emotional expression, memory, and motivation.

linguistic relativity hypothesis   The notion that the language a person speaks largely determines the nature of that person's thoughts.

lithium   A drug used to treat bipolar disorder, which at proper maintenance dosage reduces both manic and depressive episodes.

locus of control   Rotter's concept of a cognitive factor that explains how people account for what happens in their lives—either seeing themselves as primarily in control of their behavior and its consequences (internal locus of control) or perceiving what happens to them to be in the hands of fate, luck, or chance (external locus of control).

long-term memory (LTM)   The memory system with a virtually unlimited capacity that contains vast stores of a person's permanent or relatively permanent memories.

long-term potentiation (LTP)   An increase in the efficiency of neural transmission at the synapses that lasts for hours or longer.

low-ball technique   A strategy in which someone makes a very attractive initial offer to get a person to commit to an action and then makes the terms less favorable.

low-birth-weight baby   A baby weighing less than 5.5 pounds.

lucid dream   A dream that an individual is aware of dreaming and whose content the individual is often able to influence while the dream is in progress.

lymphocytes   The white blood cells—including B cells and T cells—that are the key components of the immune system.

maintenance rehearsal   Repeating information over and over again until it is no longer needed; may eventually lead to storage of information in long-term memory.

major depressive disorder   A mood disorder marked by feelings of great sadness, despair, and hopelessness as well as the loss of the ability to experience pleasure.

manic episode   (MAN-ik) A period of excessive euphoria, inflated self-esteem, wild optimism, and hyperactivity, often accompanied by delusions of grandeur and by hostility if activity is blocked.

manifest content   Freud's term for the content of a dream as recalled by the dreamer.

matching hypothesis   The notion that people tend to have lovers or spouses who are similar to themselves in physical attractiveness and other assets.

maturation   Changes that occur according to one's genetically determined biological timetable of development.

means–end analysis   A heuristic strategy in which the current position is compared with the desired goal and a series of steps are formulated and taken to close the gap between them.

meditation   A group of techniques that involve focusing attention on an object, a word, one's breathing, or one's body movements in an effort to block out all distractions, to enhance well-being, and to achieve an altered state of consciousness.

medulla   (muh-DUL-uh) The part of the brainstem that controls heartbeat, blood pressure, breathing, coughing, and swallowing.

memory   The process of encoding, storage, and retrieval of information.

menarche   (men-AR-kee) The onset of menstruation.

menopause   The cessation of menstruation, occurring between ages 45 and 55 and signifying the end of reproductive capacity.

mental set   The tendency to apply a familiar strategy to the solution of a problem without carefully considering the special requirements of that problem.

mere-exposure effect   The tendency to feel more positively toward a stimulus as a result of repeated exposure to it.

metabolic rate   (meh-tuh-BALL-ik) The rate at which the body burns calories to produce energy.

method   A set study of strategies that includes five steps: survey, question, read, review, and recite.

microelectrode   A small wire used to monitor the electrical activity of or stimulate activity within a single neuron.

midbrain   Area that contains structures linking the physiological functions of the hindbrain to the cognitive functions of the forebrain.

middle ear   The portion of the ear containing the ossicles, which connect the eardrum to the oval window and amplify sound waves.

Minnesota Multiphasic Personality Inventory (MMPI)   The most extensively researched and widely used personality test, which is used to screen for and diagnose psychiatric problems and disorders; revised as MMPI-2.

mirror neuron system (MNS)   A network of cells that the brain uses to interpret and produce motor actions and emotion-related behavior.

misinformation effect   Erroneous recollections of witnessed events that result from information learned after the fact.

model   The individual who demonstrates a behavior or whose behavior is imitated.

modeling effect   Learning a new behavior from a model through the acquisition of new responses.

monocular depth cues   (mah-NOK-yu-ler) Depth cues that can be perceived by one eye alone.

morphemes   The smallest units of meaning in a language.

motivated forgetting   Forgetting through suppression or repression in an effort to protect oneself from material that is painful, frightening, or otherwise unpleasant.

motivation   All the processes that initiate, direct, and sustain behavior.

motive   Need or desire that energizes and directs behavior toward a goal.

motor cortex   The strip of tissue at the rear of the frontal lobes that controls voluntary body movement and participates in learning and cognitive events.

MRI (magnetic resonance imaging)   A diagnostic scanning technique that produces high-resolution images of the structures of the brain.

multifactorial inheritance   A pattern of inheritance in which a trait is influenced by both genes and environmental factors.

myelin sheath   (MY-uh-lin) The white, fatty coating wrapped around some axons that acts as insulation and enables impulses to travel much faster.

Myers-Briggs Type Indicator (MBTI)   A personality inventory useful for measuring individual differences; based on Jung's theory of personality.

naive idealism   A type of thought in which adolescents construct ideal solutions for problems.

narcolepsy   An incurable sleep disorder characterized by excessive daytime sleepiness and uncontrollable attacks of REM sleep.

narcotics   A class of depressant drugs derived from the opium poppy that produce both pain-relieving and calming effects.

natural concept   A concept acquired not from a definition but through everyday perceptions and experiences.

naturalistic observation   A descriptive research method in which researchers observe and record behavior in its natural setting, without attempting to influence or control it.

nature–nurture debate   The debate over whether intelligence and other traits are primarily the result of heredity or environment.

need for achievement (n Ach)   The need to accomplish something difficult and to perform at a high standard of excellence.

negative punishment   A decrease in behavior that results from a removed consequence.

negative reinforcement   The termination of an unpleasant condition after a response, which increases the probability that the response will be repeated.

neodissociation theory of hypnosis   A theory proposing that hypnosis induces a split, or dissociation, between two aspects of the control of consciousness: the planning function and the monitoring function.

neonate   A newborn infant up to 1 month old.

neuron   (NEW-ron) A specialized cell that conducts impulses through the nervous system.

neuroscience   An interdisciplinary field that combines the work of psychologists, biologists, biochemists, medical researchers, and others in the study of the structure and function of the nervous system.

neurotransmitters   Specialized chemicals that facilitate or inhibit the transmission of impulses from one neuron to the next.

nondeclarative memory   The subsystem within long-term memory that stores motor skills, habits, and simple classically conditioned responses; also called implicit memory.

nondirective therapy   Any type of psychotherapy in which the therapist allows the direction of the therapy sessions to be controlled by the client; an example is person-centered therapy.

norms   Age-based averages.

NREM (non-REM) sleep   Four sleep stages characterized by slow, regular respiration and heart rate, little body movement, and blood pressure and brain activity that are at their 24-hour low points.

NREM dream   A type of dream occurring during NREM sleep that is typically less frequent and less memorable than REM dreams are.

obedience   Behaving in accordance with the rules and commands of those in authority.

obesity   BMI over 30.

object permanence   The realization that objects continue to exist, even when they can no longer be perceived.

observational learning (social-cognitive learning)   Learning by observing the behavior of others and the consequences of that behavior; learning by imitation.

obsession   A persistent, involuntary thought, image, or impulse that invades consciousness and causes great distress.

obsessive-compulsive disorder (OCD)   An anxiety disorder in which a person has recurrent obsessions and/or compulsions.

occipital lobes (ahk-SIP-uh-tul) The lobes that are involved in the reception and interpretation of visual information; they contain the primary visual cortex.

Oedipus or Elektra complex (ED-uh-pus) Occurring in the phallic stage, a conflict in which the child is sexually attracted to the opposite-sex parent and feels hostility toward the same-sex parent (Oedipus for males; Elektra for females).

olfaction (ol-FAK-shun) The sense of smell.

olfactory bulbs Two matchstick-sized structures above the nasal cavities, where smell sensations first register in the brain.

olfactory epithelium Two 1-square-inch patches of tissue, one at the top of each nasal cavity, which together contain about 10 million olfactory neurons, the receptors for smell.

operant A voluntary behavior that accidentally brings about a consequence.

operant conditioning A type of learning in which the consequences of behavior are manipulated so as to increase or decrease the frequency of an existing response or to shape an entirely new response.

opponent-process theory The theory of color vision suggesting that three kinds of cells respond by increasing or decreasing their rate of firing when different colors are present.

optic nerve The nerve that carries visual information from each retina to both sides of the brain.

outer ear The visible part of the ear, consisting of the pinna and the auditory canal.

out-group A social group made up of individuals specifically identified by the in-group as not belonging.

overextension The act of using a word, on the basis of some shared feature, to apply to a broader range of objects than is appropriate.

overregularization The act of inappropriately applying the grammatical rules for forming plurals and past tenses to irregular nouns and verbs.

pancreas The endocrine gland responsible for regulating the amount of sugar in the bloodstream.

panic attack An episode of overwhelming anxiety, fear, or terror.

panic disorder An anxiety disorder in which a person experiences recurring, unpredictable episodes of overwhelming anxiety, fear, or terror.

paraphilic disorders Sexual disorders in which recurrent sexual urges, fantasies, or behavior involve nonhuman objects, children, other nonconsenting persons, or the suffering or humiliation of the individual or his or her partner.

parasomnias Sleep disturbances in which behaviors and physiological states that normally take place only in the waking state occur while a person is sleeping.

parasympathetic nervous system The division of the autonomic nervous system that brings the heightened bodily responses back to normal following an emergency.

parathyroid glands The endocrine glands that produce PTH, a hormone that helps the body absorb minerals from the diet.

parental investment A term used by evolutionary psychologists to denote the amount of time and effort men or women must devote to parenthood.

parietal lobes (puh-RY-uh-tul) The lobes that contain the somatosensory cortex (where touch, pressure, temperature, and pain register) and other areas that are responsible for body awareness and spatial orientation.

partial reinforcement effect The typical outcome of a variable ratio of reinforcement in which a slow rate of initial learning is coupled with resistance to extinction.

participant modeling A behavior therapy in which an appropriate response to a feared stimulus is modeled in graduated steps and the client attempts to imitate the model step by step, encouraged and supported by the therapist.

participant-related bias A type of bias in which a study's participants are not representative of the population to which results will be generalized.

perception The process by which the brain actively organizes and interprets sensory information.

perceptual constancy The phenomenon that allows us to perceive objects as maintaining stable properties, such as size, shape, and brightness, despite differences in distance, viewing angle, and lighting.

perceptual set An expectation of what will be perceived, which can affect what actually is perceived.

peripheral nervous system (PNS) (peh-RIF-er-ul) The nerves connecting the central nervous system to the rest of the body.

permissive parents Parents who make few rules or demands and allow children to make their own decisions and control their own behavior.

personal fable An exaggerated sense of personal uniqueness and indestructibility, which may be the basis for adolescent risk taking.

personal space An area surrounding each person, much like an invisible bubble, that the person considers part of himself or herself and uses to regulate the level of intimacy with others.

personal unconscious In Jung's theory, the layer of the unconscious that contains all of the thoughts, perceptions, and experiences accessible to the conscious, as well as repressed memories, wishes, and impulses.

personality A person's characteristic patterns of behaving, thinking, and feeling.

personality disorder A long-standing, inflexible, maladaptive pattern of behaving and relating to others, which usually begins in early childhood or adolescence.

person-centered therapy A nondirective, humanistic therapy developed by Carl Rogers, in which the therapist creates an accepting climate and shows empathy, freeing clients to be themselves and releasing their natural tendency toward self-actualization.

persuasion A deliberate attempt to influence the attitudes and/or behavior of another person.

PET scan (positron-emission tomography) A brain-imaging technique that reveals activity in various parts of the brain, based on patterns of blood flow, oxygen use, and glucose consumption.

phenotype An individual's actual characteristics.

phobia (FO-bee-ah) A persistent, irrational fear of some specific object, situation, or activity that poses little or no real danger.

phonemes The smallest units of sound in a spoken language.

physical drug dependence A compulsive pattern of drug use in which the user develops a drug tolerance coupled with unpleasant withdrawal symptoms when the drug use is discontinued.

pineal gland The endocrine gland that secretes the hormone that controls the sleep/wakefulness cycle.

pituitary gland The endocrine gland located in the brain that releases hormones that activate other endocrine glands as well as growth hormone; often called the "master gland."

place theory The theory of hearing that holds that each individual pitch a person hears is determined by the particular location along the basilar membrane of the cochlea that vibrates the most.

placebo (pluh-SEE-bo) An inert or harmless substance given to the control group in an experiment as a control for the placebo effect.

placebo effect The phenomenon that occurs in an experiment when a participant's response to a treatment is due to his or her expectations about the treatment rather than to the treatment itself.

plasticity The capacity of the brain to adapt to changes such as brain damage.

polygenic inheritance A pattern of inheritance in which many genes influence a trait.

pons The bridgelike structure that connects the medulla and the cerebellum.

population The entire group of interest to researchers to which they wish to generalize their findings; the group from which a sample is selected.

positive bias The tendency for pleasant autobiographical memories to be more easily recalled than unpleasant ones and memories of unpleasant events to become more emotionally positive over time.

positive psychology The scientific study of psychological characteristics that enable individuals and communities to thrive in the face of adversity.

positive psychology The view that psychologists should study and promote the development of human strengths such as optimism.

positive punishment A decrease in behavior that results from an added consequence.

positive reinforcement Any pleasant or desirable consequence that follows a response and increases the probability that the response will be repeated.

postconventional level Kohlberg's highest level of moral development, in which moral reasoning involves weighing moral alternatives; "right" is whatever furthers basic human rights.

posttraumatic stress disorder (PTSD) A prolonged and severe stress reaction to a catastrophic event or to severe, chronic stress.

pragmatics The patterns of intonation and social roles associated with a language.

preconscious The thoughts, feelings, and memories that a person is not consciously aware of at the moment but that may be easily brought to consciousness.

preconventional level Kohlberg's lowest level of moral development, in which moral reasoning is based on the physical consequences of an act; "right" is whatever avoids punishment or gains a reward.

prefrontal cortex The part of the frontal lobes directly behind the forehead that controls executive processing, the coordination of multiple brain activities in pursuit of cognitive goals.

prejudice Attitudes (usually negative) toward others based on their gender, religion, race, or membership in a particular group.

prenatal development Development from conception to birth.

presbyopia (prez-bee-O-pee-uh) A condition, occurring in the mid- to late 40s, in which the lenses of the eyes no longer accommodate adequately for near vision, and reading glasses or bifocals are required for reading.

preterm infant An infant born before the 37th week and weighing less than 5.5 pounds; a premature infant.

primacy effect The tendency for an overall impression of another to be influenced more by the first information that is received about that person than by information that comes later.

primacy effect The tendency to recall the first items in a sequence more readily than the middle items.

primary appraisal A cognitive evaluation of a potentially stressful event to determine whether its effect is positive, irrelevant, or negative.

primary auditory cortex The part of each temporal lobe where hearing registers in the cerebral cortex.

primary drives States of tension or arousal that arise from a biological need and are unlearned.

primary mental abilities According to Thurstone, seven relatively distinct capabilities that singly or in combination are involved in all intellectual activities.

primary reinforcer A reinforcer that fulfills a basic physical need for survival and does not depend on learning.

primary visual cortex The area at the rear of the occipital lobes where vision registers in the cerebral cortex.

primary visual cortex The part of the brain in which visual information is processed.

proactive coping Active measures taken in advance of a potentially stressful situation in order to prevent its occurrence or to minimize its consequences.

problem solving Thoughts and actions required to achieve a desired goal that is not readily attainable.

problem-focused coping A direct response aimed at reducing, modifying, or eliminating a source of stress.

projective test A personality test in which people respond to inkblots, drawings of ambiguous human situations, or incomplete sentences by projecting their inner thoughts, feelings, fears, or conflicts onto the test materials.

prosocial behavior Behavior that benefits others, such as helping, cooperation, and sympathy.

prospective forgetting Not remembering to carry out some intended action.

prototype An example that embodies the most common and typical features of a concept.

proximity Physical or geographic closeness; a major influence on attraction.

pruning The process through which the developing brain eliminates unnecessary or redundant synapses.

psychiatrist A mental health professional who is a medical doctor.

psychoactive drug Any substance that alters mood, perception, or thought; called a controlled substance if approved for medical use.

psychoanalysis (SY-ko-ah-NAL-ih-sis) The term Freud used for both his theory of personality and his therapy for the treatment of psychological disorders; the unconscious is the primary focus of psychoanalytic theory.

psychoanalysis (SY-ko-uh-NAL-ul-sis) The first psychodynamic therapy, which was developed by Freud and uses free association, dream analysis, and transference.

psychodynamic therapies Psychotherapies that attempt to uncover repressed childhood experiences that are thought to explain a patient's current difficulties.

psycholinguistics The study of how language is acquired, produced, and used and how the sounds and symbols of language are translated into meaning.

psychological disorders Mental processes and/or behavior patterns that cause emotional distress and/or substantial impairment in functioning.

psychological drug dependence A craving or irresistible urge for a drug's pleasurable effects.

psychological perspectives General points of view used for explaining people's behavior and thinking, whether normal or abnormal.

psychologist A mental health professional who possesses a doctoral degree in psychology.

psychology The scientific study of behavior and mental processes.

psychoneuroimmunology (sye-ko-NEW-ro-IM-you-NOLL-oh-gee) A field in which psychologists, biologists, and medical researchers combine their expertise to study the effects of psychological factors on the immune system.

psychosexual stages A series of stages through which the sexual instinct develops; each stage is defined by an erogenous zone around which conflict arises.

psychosis (sy-CO-sis) A condition characterized by loss of contact with reality.

psychosocial stages Erikson's eight developmental stages for the entire life span; each is defined by a conflict that must be resolved satisfactorily for healthy personality development to occur.

psychosurgery Brain surgery performed to alleviate serious psychological disorders or unbearable chronic pain.

psychotherapy Any type of approach that uses psychological rather than biological means to treat psychological disorders.

puberty A period of rapid physical growth and change that culminates in sexual maturity.

punisher Anything that follows a response and weakens it or decreases the probability that it will occur.

punishment The removal of a pleasant stimulus or the application of an unpleasant stimulus, thereby lowering the probability of a response.

quasi-experiments Comparisons of groups that differ in exposure to a variable of interest that cannot be manipulated for ethical or practical reasons.

random assignment The process of selecting participants for experimental and control groups by using a chance procedure to guarantee that each participant has an equal probability of being assigned to any of the groups; a control for selection bias.

rational emotive behavior therapy (REBT) A directive form of psychotherapy, developed by Albert Ellis and designed to challenge clients' irrational beliefs about themselves and others.

realistic conflict theory The view that as competition increases among social groups for scarce resources, so do prejudice, discrimination, and hatred.

recall A memory task in which a person must produce required information by searching memory.

recency effect The tendency to recall the last items in a sequence more readily than those in the middle.

receptors Protein molecules on the surfaces of dendrites and cell bodies that have distinctive shapes and will interact only with specific neurotransmitters.

reciprocal determinism Bandura's concept of a mutual influential relationship among behavior, cognitive factors, and environment.

recognition A memory task in which a person must simply identify material as familiar or as having been encountered before.

recognition heuristic A strategy in which decision making stops as soon as a factor that moves one toward a decision has been recognized.

reconstruction An account of an event that has been pieced together from a few highlights.

reflexes Built-in responses to certain stimuli that neonates need to ensure survival in their new world.

rehearsal The act of purposely repeating information to maintain it in short-term memory.

reinforcement Any event that follows a response and strengthens or increases the probability that the response will be repeated.

reinforcer Anything that follows a response and strengthens it or increases the probability that it will occur.

relationship therapies Therapies that attempt to improve clients' interpersonal relationships or create new relationships to support clients' efforts to address psychological problems.

relearning method A measure of memory in which retention is expressed as the percentage of time saved when material is relearned compared with the time required to learn the material originally.

reliability The ability of a test to yield nearly the same score when the same people are tested and then retested on the same test or an alternative form of the test.

REM (rapid eye movement) sleep A type of sleep characterized by rapid eye movements, paralysis, fast and irregular heart and respiration rates, increased brain-wave activity, and vivid dreams.

REM dream A type of dream occurring almost continuously during each REM period and having a story-like quality; typically more vivid, visual, and emotional than NREM dreams.

REM rebound The increased amount of REM sleep that occurs after REM deprivation.

replication The process of repeating a study to verify research findings.

representative sample A sample that mirrors the population of interest; it includes important subgroups in the same proportions as they are found in that population.

representativeness heuristic A thinking strategy based on how closely a new object or situation is judged to resemble or match an existing prototype of that object or situation.

repression A psychological process in which traumatic memories are buried in the unconscious.

resistance stage The second stage of the general adaptation syndrome, when there are intense physiological efforts to either resist or adapt to the stressor.

resting potential The slight negative electrical potential of the axon membrane of a neuron at rest, about −70 millivolts.

restorative theory of sleep The theory that the function of sleep is to restore body and mind.

reticular formation A structure in the brainstem that plays a crucial role in arousal and attention and that screens sensory messages entering the brain.

retina The layer of tissue that is located on the inner surface of the eyeball and contains the sensory receptors for vision.

retrieval The process of bringing to mind information that has been stored in memory.

retrieval cue Any stimulus or bit of information that aids in retrieving particular information from long-term memory.

retrieval failure Not remembering something one is certain of knowing.

retrograde amnesia (RET-ro-grade) A loss of memory for experiences that occurred shortly before a loss of consciousness.

reuptake The process by which neurotransmitters are taken from the synaptic cleft back into the axon terminal for later use, thus terminating their excitatory or inhibitory effect on the receiving neuron.

reversibility The realization that any change in the shape, position, or order of matter can be reversed mentally.

right hemisphere The hemisphere that controls the left side of the body and, in most people, is specialized for visual-spatial perception.

risk/resilience model A perspective that proposes that risk and protective factors interact to produce or protect us from illness.

rods The light-sensitive receptor cells in the retina that look like slender cylinders and allow the eye to respond to as few as five photons of light.

Rorschach Inkblot Method (ROR-shok) A projective test composed of 10 inkblots that the test taker is asked to describe; used to assess personality, make differential diagnoses, plan and evaluate treatment, and predict behavior.

sample A part of a population that is studied to reach conclusions about the entire population.

saturation The purity of a color, or the degree to which the light waves producing it are of the same wavelength.

scaffolding A type of instruction in which an adult adjusts the amount of guidance provided to match a child's present level of ability.

scapegoating Displacing aggression onto members of minority groups or other innocent targets not responsible for the frustrating situation.

Schachter–Singer theory A two-factor theory stating that for an emotion to occur, there must be (1) physiological arousal and (2) a cognitive interpretation or explanation of the arousal, allowing it to be labeled as a specific emotion.

schedule of reinforcement A systematic process for administering reinforcement.

schemas Frameworks of knowledge and assumptions that we have about people, objects, and events.

schemes Plans of action, based on previous experiences, to be used in similar circumstances.

schizophrenia (SKIT-soh-FREE-nee-ah) A severe psychological disorder characterized by loss of contact with reality, hallucinations, delusions, inappropriate or flat affect, some disturbance in thinking, social withdrawal, and/or other bizarre behavior.

scientific method The orderly, systematic procedures that researchers follow as they identify a research problem, design a study to investigate the problem, collect and analyze data, draw conclusions, and communicate their findings.

secondary appraisal A cognitive evaluation of available resources and options prior to deciding how to deal with a stressor.

secondary reinforcer A reinforcer that is acquired or learned through association with other reinforcers.

secondary sex characteristics Those physical characteristics that are not directly involved in reproduction but distinguish the mature male from the mature female.

selection bias The assignment of participants to experimental or control groups in such a way that systematic differences among the groups are present at the beginning of the experiment.

self-actualization Developing to one's fullest potential.

self-actualization The pursuit of self-defined goals for personal fulfillment and growth.

self-efficacy The perception a person has of his or her ability to perform competently whatever is attempted.

self-esteem A person's sense of self-worth.

self-serving bias The tendency to attribute one's successes to dispositional causes and one's failures to situational causes.

semantic memory The type of declarative memory that stores general knowledge, or objective facts and information.

semantics The meaning or the study of meaning derived from morphemes, words, and sentences.

semicircular canals Three fluid-filled tubular canals in the inner ear that sense the rotation of the head.

sensation The process through which the senses pick up visual, auditory, and other sensory stimuli and transmit them to the brain.

sensory adaptation The process in which sensory receptors grow accustomed to constant, unchanging levels of stimuli over time.

sensory memory The memory system that holds information from the senses for a period ranging from only a fraction of a second to about 2 seconds.

sensory receptors Highly specialized cells in the sense organs that detect and respond to one type of sensory stimulus—light, sound, or odor, for example—and transduce (convert) the stimuli into neural impulses.

separation anxiety The fear and distress shown by a toddler when the parent leaves, occurring from 8 to 24 months and reaching a peak between 12 and 18 months.

serial position effect The finding that, for information learned in a sequence, recall is better for the beginning and ending items than for the middle items in the sequence.

set point The weight the body normally maintains when one is trying neither to gain nor to lose weight.

sexual dysfunctions Persistent, recurrent, and distressing problems involving sexual desire, arousal, or the pleasure associated with sex or orgasm.

sexual orientation The direction of one's sexual interest—toward members of the opposite sex (heterosexuality), toward one's own sex (homosexuality), or toward both sexes (bisexuality).

sexual response cycle The four phases—excitement, plateau, orgasm, and resolution—that make up the human sexual response in both males and females, according to Masters and Johnson.

sexually transmitted diseases (STDs) Infections that are spread primarily through intimate sexual contact.

shaping An operant conditioning technique that consists of gradually molding a desired behavior (response) by reinforcing any movement in the direction of the desired response, thereby gradually guiding the responses toward the ultimate goal.

short-term memory (STM) The component of the memory system that holds about seven (from five to nine) items for less than 30 seconds without rehearsal; also called working memory.

situation–trait debate A discussion among theorists about the relative influence of traits and situations on personality.

situational attribution Attributing a behavior to some external cause or factor operating within the situation; an external attribution.

Skinner box A soundproof chamber with a device for delivering food to an animal subject; used in operant conditioning experiments.

sleep apnea A sleep disorder characterized by periods during sleep when breathing stops and the individual must awaken briefly in order to breathe.

sleep cycle A period of sleep lasting about 90 minutes and including one or more stages of NREM sleep, followed by REM sleep.

sleep spindles Sleep Stage 2 brain waves that feature short periods of calm interrupted by brief flashes of intense activity.

slow-wave sleep Deep sleep; associated with Stage 3 and Stage 4 sleep.

social anxiety disorder (social phobia) An irrational fear and avoidance of any social or performance situation in which one might embarrass or humiliate oneself in front of others by appearing clumsy, foolish, or incompetent.

social cognition The process of attending to, interpreting, and remembering information about ourselves and others.

social facilitation Any positive or negative effect on performance that can be attributed to the presence of others, either as an audience or as coactors.

social identity A social psychological process in which individuals join with others to construct a group identity to insulate themselves from stressors.

social loafing The tendency to put forth less effort when working with others on a common task than when working alone.

social motives Motives (such as the needs for affiliation and achievement) that are acquired through experience and interaction with others.

social norms The attitudes and standards of behavior expected of members of a particular group.

social psychology The subfield that attempts to explain how the actual, imagined, or implied presence of others influences the thoughts, feelings, and behavior of individuals.

Social Readjustment Rating Scale (SRRS) Holmes and Rahe's measure of stress, which ranks 43 life events from most to least stressful and assigns a point value to each.

social roles Socially defined behaviors considered appropriate for individuals occupying certain positions within a given group.

social support Tangible and/or emotional support provided in time of need by family members, friends, and others; the feeling of being loved, valued, and cared for by those toward whom we feel a similar obligation.

social-cognitive theory The view that personality can be defined as a collection of learned behaviors acquired through social interactions.

socialization The process of learning socially acceptable behaviors, attitudes, and values.

sociocognitive theory of hypnosis A theory suggesting that the behavior of a hypnotized person is a function of that person's expectations about how subjects behave under hypnosis.

sociocultural approach The view that social and cultural factors may be just as powerful as evolutionary and physiological factors in affecting behavior and mental processing and that these factors must be understood when interpreting the behavior of others.

socioeconomic status A collective term for the economic, occupational, and educational factors that influence an individual's relative position in society.

somatic symptom disorders Disorders in which physical symptoms are present that are due to psychological causes rather than any known medical condition.

somatosensory cortex (so-MAT-oh-SENS-or-ee) The strip of tissue at the front of the parietal lobes where touch, pressure, temperature, and pain register in the cerebral cortex.

source memory A recollection of the circumstances in which you formed a memory.

source monitoring Intentionally keeping track of the sources of incoming information.

specific phobia A marked fear of a specific object or situation; a general label for any phobia other than agoraphobia and social phobia.

spinal cord An extension of the brain, from the base of the brain through the neck and spinal column, that transmits messages between the brain and the peripheral nervous system.

split-brain operation A surgical procedure, performed to treat severe cases of epilepsy, in which the corpus callosum is cut, separating the cerebral hemispheres.

spontaneous recovery The reappearance of an extinguished response (in a weaker form) when an organism is exposed to the original conditioned stimulus following a rest period.

SQ3R method A study method involving the following five steps: (1) survey, (2) question, (3) read, (4) recite, and (5) review.

stage 4 sleep The deepest stage of NREM sleep, characterized by an EEG pattern of more than 50% delta waves.

standardization Establishing norms for comparing the scores of people who will take a test in the future; administering tests using a prescribed procedure.

state-dependent memory effect   The tendency to recall information better if one is in the same pharmacological or psychological state as when the information was encoded.

stereotypes   Widely shared beliefs about the characteristic traits, attitudes, and behaviors of members of various social groups (racial, ethnic, or religious), including the assumption that the members of such groups are usually all alike.

stimulants   A category of drugs that speed up activity in the central nervous system, suppress appetite, and can cause a person to feel more awake, alert, and energetic; also called "uppers."

stimulus   (STIM-yu-lus) Any event or object in the environment to which an organism responds; plural is *stimuli*.

stimulus motives   Motives that cause humans and other animals to increase stimulation when the level of arousal is too low (examples are curiosity and the motive to explore).

storage   The process of keeping or maintaining information in memory.

stranger anxiety   A fear of strangers common in infants at about 6 months and increasing in intensity until about 12 months, and then declining in the second year.

stress   The physiological and psychological response to a condition that threatens or challenges a person and requires some form of adaptation or adjustment.

stressor   Any stimulus or event capable of producing physical or emotional stress.

stroke   An event in the cardiovascular system in which a blood clot or plug of fat blocks an artery and cuts off the blood supply to a particular area of the brain.

structuralism   The first formal school of thought in psychology, aimed at analyzing the basic elements, or structure, of conscious mental experience.

subjective night   The time during a 24-hour period when the biological clock is telling a person to go to sleep.

subliminal perception   The capacity to perceive and respond to stimuli that are presented below the threshold of awareness.

substance abuse   Continued use of a substance after several episodes in which use of the substance has negatively affected an individual's work, education, and social relationships.

substantia nigra   (sub-STAN-sha NI-gra) The structure in the midbrain that controls unconscious motor movements.

successful aging   Maintaining one's physical health, mental abilities, social competence, and overall satisfaction with life as one gets older.

successive approximations   A series of gradual steps, each of which is more similar to the final desired response.

superego   (sue-per-EE-go) The moral system of the personality, which consists of the conscience and the ego ideal.

suprachiasmatic nucleus (SCN)   A pair of tiny structures in the brain's hypothalamus that control the timing of circadian rhythms; the biological clock.

survey   A descriptive research method in which researchers use interviews and/or questionnaires to gather information about the attitudes, beliefs, experiences, or behaviors of a group of people.

symbolic function   The understanding that one thing—an object, a word, a drawing—can stand for another.

sympathetic nervous system   The division of the autonomic nervous system that mobilizes the body's resources during stress and emergencies, preparing the body for action.

synapse   (SIN-aps) The junction where the axon terminal of a sending neuron communicates with a receiving neuron across the synaptic cleft.

synesthesia   The capacity for experiencing unusual sensations along with ordinary ones.

syntax   The aspect of grammar that specifies the rules for arranging and combining words to form phrases and sentences.

systematic desensitization   A behavior therapy that is based on classical conditioning and used to treat fears by training clients in deep muscle relaxation and then having them confront a graduated series of anxiety-producing situations (real or imagined) until they can remain relaxed while confronting even the most feared situation.

tactile   Pertaining to the sense of touch.

taste aversion   The intense dislike and/or avoidance of a particular food that has been associated with nausea or discomfort.

taste buds   Structures along the sides of many of the tongue's papillae that are composed of 60 to 100 receptor cells for taste.

telegraphic speech   Short sentences that follow a strict word order and contain only essential content words.

temperament   A person's behavioral style or characteristic way of responding to the environment.

temporal lobes   The lobes that are involved in the reception and interpretation of auditory information; they contain the primary auditory cortex, Wernicke's area, and the temporal association areas.

teratogens   Harmful agents in the prenatal environment, which can have a negative impact on prenatal development or even cause birth defects.

thalamus   (THAL-uh-mus) The structure, located above the brainstem, that acts as a relay station for information flowing into or out of the forebrain.

Thematic Apperception Test (TAT)   A projective test consisting of drawings of ambiguous human situations, which the test taker describes; thought to reveal inner feelings, conflicts, and motives, which are projected onto the test materials.

theory   A general principle or set of principles proposed to explain how a number of separate facts are related.

theory of dissociated control   The theory that hypnosis weakens the control that the executive function exerts over other subsystems of consciousness.

theory of multiple intelligences   Howard Gardner's proposal that there are several independent forms of intelligence.

thymus gland   The endocrine gland that produces hormones that are essential to immune system functioning.

thyroid gland   The endocrine gland that produces thyroxine and regulates metabolism.

timbre   (TAM-burr) The distinctive quality of a sound that distinguishes it from other sounds of the same pitch and loudness.

time out   A behavior modification technique used to eliminate undesirable behavior, especially in children and adolescents, by withdrawing all reinforcers for a period of time.

tip-of-the-tongue (TOT) phenomenon   The experience of knowing that a particular piece of information has been learned but being unable to retrieve it.

token economy A behavior modification technique that rewards appropriate behavior with tokens that can be exchanged later for desired goods and/or privileges.

token economy A program that motivates socially desirable behavior by reinforcing it with tokens that can be exchanged for desired items or privileges.

top-down processing Information processing in which previous experience and conceptual knowledge are applied to recognize the whole of a perception and thus easily identify the simpler elements of that whole.

trait A personal characteristic that is stable across situations and is used to describe or explain personality.

transduction The process through which sensory receptors convert the sensory stimulation into neural impulses.

transference An emotional reaction that occurs during psycho-analysis, in which the patient displays feelings and attitudes toward the analyst that were present in another significant relationship.

triangular theory of love Sternberg's theory that three components—intimacy, passion, and commitment—singly and in various combinations produce seven different kinds of love.

triarchic theory of intelligence Sternberg's theory that there are three types of intelligence: componential (analytical), experiential (creative), and contextual (practical).

trichromatic theory The theory of color vision suggesting that three types of cones in the retina each make a maximal chemical response to one of three colors—blue, green, or red.

Type A behavior pattern A behavior pattern marked by a sense of time urgency, impatience, excessive competitiveness, hostility, and anger; considered a risk factor in coronary heart disease.

Type B behavior pattern A behavior pattern marked by a relaxed, easygoing approach to life, without the time urgency, impatience, and hostility of the Type A pattern.

Type D behavior pattern People who exhibit chronic emotional distress combined with a tendency to suppress negative emotions.

unconditional positive regard Unqualified caring and nonjudgmental acceptance of another.

unconditioned response (UR) A response that is elicited by an unconditioned stimulus without prior learning.

unconditioned stimulus (US) A stimulus that elicits a specific unconditioned response without prior learning.

unconscious (un-KON-shus) For Freud, the primary motivating force of human behavior, containing repressed memories as well as instincts, wishes, and desires that have never been conscious.

underextension Restricting the use of a word to only a few, rather than to all, members of a class of objects.

uplifts The positive experiences in life, which may neutralize the effects of many hassles.

validity The ability of a test to measure what it is intended to measure.

variable Any condition or factor that can be manipulated, controlled, or measured.

variable-interval (VI) schedule A schedule in which a reinforcer is given after the first correct response that follows a varying time of nonreinforcement, based on an average time.

variable-ratio (VR) schedule A schedule in which a reinforcer is given after a varying number of non-reinforced responses, based on an average ratio.

ventromedial hypothalamus (VMH) The part of the hypothalamus that acts as a satiety (fullness) center to inhibit eating.

vestibular sense (ves-TIB-yu-ler) The sense that provides information about the body's orientation in space.

viral STDs Sexually transmitted diseases that are caused by viruses and are considered to be incurable.

visible spectrum The narrow band of light waves that are visible to the human eye.

visual cliff An apparatus used to test depth perception in infants.

wavelength A measure of the distance from the peak of a light wave to the peak of the next.

Weber's law The law stating that the just noticeable difference (JND) for all the senses depends on a proportion or percentage of change in a stimulus rather than on a fixed amount of change.

Wernicke's aphasia Aphasia that results from damage to Wernicke's area and in which the person's speech is fluent and clearly articulated but does not make sense to listeners.

Wernicke's area (VUR-nih-keys) The language area in the left temporal lobe involved in comprehending the spoken word and in formulating coherent speech and written language.

withdrawal symptoms The physical and psychological symptoms that occur when a regularly used drug is discontinued and that terminate when the drug is taken again.

work motivation The conditions and processes responsible for the arousal, direction, magnitude, and maintenance of effort of workers on the job.

working backward A heuristic strategy in which a person discovers the steps needed to solve a problem by defining the desired goal and working backward to the current condition; also called *backward search*.

working memory The memory subsystem that we use when we try to understand information, remember it, or use it to solve a problem or communicate with someone.

Yerkes–Dodson law The principle that performance on tasks is best when the arousal level is appropriate to the difficulty of the task: higher arousal for simple tasks, moderate arousal for tasks of moderate difficulty, and lower arousal for complex tasks.

zone of proximal development A range of cognitive tasks that a child cannot yet do but can learn to do through the guidance of an older child or adult.

zygote Cell that results from the union of a sperm and an ovum.

References

AAA Foundation for Traffic Safety. (2012). *Distracted driving*. Retrieved October 29, 2012, from http://www.aaafoundation.org/multimedia/Distracteddriving.cfm.

Aaltola, E. (2005). The politics and ethics of animal experimentation. *International Journal of Biotechnology, 7,* 234–249.

Abbott, J., Cumming, G., Fidler, F., & Lindell, A. (2011). The perception of positive and negative facial expressions in unilateral brain-damaged patients: A meta-analysis. *Laterality, 17,* 629–642.

Abboud, T., Sarkis, F., Hung, T., Khoo, S., Varakian, L., Henriksen, E., Houehihed, R., & Goebelsmann, U. (1983). Effects of epidural anesthesia during labor on maternal plasma beta-endorphin levels. *Anesthesiology, 59,* 1–5.

ABC News/*Washington Post*. (2009). *ABC News/Washington Post poll: Race relations*. Retrieved February 8, 2013, from http://abcnews.go.com/images/PollingUnit/1085a2RaceRelations.pdf.

Abraham, A., Knudsen, H., & Roman, P. (2011). A longitudinal examination of alcohol pharmacology adoption in substance use disorder treatment programs: Patterns of sustainability and discontinuation. *Journal of Studies on Alcohol and Drugs, 72,* 669–677.

Abrams, D., Crisp, R., Marques, S., Fagg, E., Bedford, L., & Provias, D. (2008). Threat inoculation: Experienced and imagined intergenerational contact prevents stereotype threat effects on older people's math performance. *Psychology and Aging, 23,* 934–939.

Abrams, D., Hopthrow, T., Hulbert, L., & Firings, D. (2006). Groupdrink? The effect of alcohol on risk attraction among groups versus individuals. *Journal of Studies on Alcohol, 67,* 628–636.

Achari, K., Venu, P., & Atanu, K. (2007). Morningness-eveningness preference in Indian school students as function of gender, age and habitat. *Biological Rhythm Research, 38,* 1–8.

Adam, M., & Reyna, V. (2005). Coherence and correspondence criteria for rationality: Experts' estimation of risks of sexually transmitted infections. *Journal of Behavioral Decision Making, 18,* 169–186.

Addis, M., & Mahalik, J. (2003). Men, masculinity, and the contexts of help seeking. *American Psychologist, 58,* 5–14.

Ader, D., & Johnson, S. (1994). Sample description, reporting, and analysis of sex in psychological research: A look at APA and APA division journals in 1990. *American Psychologist, 49,* 216–218.

Ader, R. (2000). On the development of psychoneuroimmunology. *European Journal of Pharmacology, 405,* 167–176.

Adler, A. (1927). *Understanding human nature*. New York: Greenberg.

Adler, A. (1956). In H. L. Ansbacher & R. R. Ansbacher (Eds.), *The individual psychology of Alfred Adler: A systematic presentation in selections from his writings*. New York: Harper & Row.

Adler, L., Spencer, T., McGough, J., Jiang, H., & Muniz, R. (2009). Long-term effectiveness and safety of dexmethylphenidate extended-release capsules in adult ADHD. *Journal of Attention Disorders, 12,* 449–459.

Ainsworth, M. (2000). ABCs of "internet therapy." *Metanoia* [Electronic version]. Retrieved 2000 from *www.metanoia.org*

Ainsworth, M. D. S. (1973). The development of infant-mother attachment. In B. Caldwell & H. Ricciuti (Eds.), *Review of child development research* (Vol. 3). Chicago: University of Chicago Press.

Ainsworth, M. D. S. (1979). Infant-mother attachment. *American Psychologist, 34,* 932–937.

Ajdacic-Gross, V., Ring, M., Gadola, E., Lauber, C., Bopp, M., Gutzwiller, F., & Rossler, W. (2008). Suicide after bereavement: An overlooked problem. *Psychological Medicine, 38,* 673–676.

Aksan, N., & Kochanska, G. (2005). Conscience in childhood: Old questions, new answers. *Developmental Psychology, 41,* 506–516.

Al'absi, M., Hugdahl, K., & Lovallo, W. (2002). Adrenocortical stress responses and altered working memory performance. *Psychophysiology, 39,* 95–99.

Alamilla, S., Kim, B., & Lam, N. (2010). Acculturation, enculturation, perceived racism, minority status stressors, and psychological symptomatology among Latino/as. *Hispanic Journal of Behavioral Sciences, 32,* 55–76.

Alberts, A., Elkind, D., & Ginsberg, S. (2007). The personal fable and risk-taking in early adolescence. *Journal of Youth and Adolescence, 36,* 71–76.

Albrecht, K. (1979). *Stress and the manager: Making it work for you.* Englewood Cliffs, NJ: Prentice-Hall.

Ali, M., Blades, M., Oates, C., & Blumberg, F. (2009). Young children's ability to recognize advertisements in web page designs. *British Journal of Developmental Psychology, 27,* 71–83.

Allan, R. (2011). Type A behavior pattern. In R. Allan & J. Fisher (Eds.). *Heart and mind: The practice of cardiac psychology* (2nd ed.). (pp. 287–290). Washington, DC, USA: American Psychological Association.

Allebrandt, K., Teder-Laving, M., Akyol, M., Pichler, I., Muller-Myhsok, B., Pramstaller, P., Merrow, M., Meitinger, T., Metspalu, A., & Roenneberg, T. (2010). CLOCK gene variants associate with sleep duration in two independent populations. *Biological Psychiatry, 67,* 1040–1047.

Allen, B. (2008). An analysis of the impact of diverse forms of childhood psychological maltreatment on emotional adjustment in early adulthood. *Child Maltreatment, 13,* 307–312.

Allen, K. W. (1996). Chronic nailbiting: A controlled comparison of competing response and mild aversion treatments. *Behaviour Research and Therapy, 34,* 269–272.

Allport, G. W. (1954). *The nature of prejudice*. Reading, MA: Addison-Wesley.

Allport, G. W. (1961). *Pattern and growth in personality*. New York: Holt, Rinehart & Winston.

Allport, G. W., & Odbert, J. S. (1936). Trait names: A psycholexical study. *Psychological Monographs, 47*(1, Whole No. 211), 1–171.

Al-Mahtab, M. (2010). State of the globe: Helicobacter pylori and hepatitis C together hamper health. *Journal of Global Infectious Disease, 2,* 1–3.

Almeida, D. (2005). Resilience and vulnerability to daily stressors assessed with diary methods. *Current Directions in Psychological Science, 14,* 62–68.

Alpers, G. (2010). Avoiding treatment failures in specific phobias. In M. Otto & S. Hofmann (Eds.). *Avoiding treatment failures in the anxiety disorders.* (pp. 209–227). New York, NY, USA: Springer Science _ Business Media.

Alquist, J., Ainsworth, S., & Baumeister, R. (2013). Determined to conform: Disbelief in free will increases conformity. *Journal of Experimental Psocial Psychology, 49,* 80–86.

Alter, A., Aronson, J., Darley, J., Rodriguez, C., & Ruble, D. (2010). Rising to the threat: Reducing stereotype threat by reframing the threat as a challenge. *Journal of Experimental Social Psychology, 46*, 166–171.

Altermatt, E., & Pomerantz, E. (2003). The development of competence-related and motivational beliefs: An investigation of similarity and influence among friends. *Journal of Educational Psychology, 95*, 111–123.

Amado, S., & Ulupinar, P. (2005). The effects of conversation on attention and peripheral detection: Is talking with a passenger and talking on the cell phone different? *Transportation Research, 8*, 383–395.

American Cancer Society. (2009). *Cancer facts & figures.* Retrieved March 12, 2010, from *http://www.cancer.org/downloads/STT/500809web.pdf.*

American Cancer Society. (2012). *Lifetime risk of developing or dying from cancer.* Retrieved January 26, 2013, from http://www.cancer.org/cancer/cancerbasics/lifetime-probability-of-developing-or-dying-from-cancer

American Lung Association. (2010). *Smoking among older adults.* Retrieved January 8, 2013, from http://www.lung.org/stop-smoking/about-smoking/facts-figures/smoking-and-older-adults.html

American Medical Association. (1994). *Report of the Council on Scientific Affairs: Memories of childhood abuse.* CSA Report 5-A-94.

American Psychiatric Association. (1993a). *Statement approved by the Board of Trustees, December 12, 1993.* Washington, DC: Author.

American Psychiatric Association. (1994). *Diagnostic and statistical manual of mental disorders* (4th ed.). Washington DC: Author.

American Psychiatric Association. (2000a). *The Diagnostic and Statistical Manual of Mental Disorders* (4th ed., Text Revision). Washington, DC: Author.

American Psychiatric Association. (2013). *Diagnostic and statistical manual of mental disorders* (5th ed.) (*DSM-5*). Arlington, VA, USA: American Psychiatric Association Publishing, Inc.

American Psychological Association (APA). (1994). *Interim report of the APA Working Group on Investigation of Memories of Childhood Abuse.* Washington, DC: Author.

American Psychological Association (APA). (2002). Ethical principles of psychologists and code of conduct. *American Psychologist, 57*, 1060–1073.

American Psychological Association (APA). (2003b). Guidelines on multicultural education, training, research, practice, and organizational change for psychologists. *American Psychologist, 58*, 377–402.

American Psychological Association (APA). (2006a). *Practice guidelines for treatment of patients with eating disorders* (3rd edition). Retrieved October 12, 2006, from http://psych.org/psych_pract/treatg/pg/EatingDisorders3ePG_04-28-06.pdf

American Psychological Association. (2008). *2007 APA Early career psychologists survey.* Retrieved January 12, 2010 from

American Psychological Association, Ethics Committee. (2010). Report of the ethics committee, 2009. *American Psychologist, 65*, 483–492.

Amodio, D., Devine, P., & Harmon-Jones, E. (2007). A dynamic model of guilt: Implications for motivation and self-regulation in the context of prejudice. *Psychological Science, 18*, 524–530.

Anand, B. K., & Brobeck, J. R. (1951). Hypothalamic control of food intake in rats and cats. *Yale Journal of Biological Medicine, 24*, 123–140.

Anderman, E., & Patrick, H. (2012). Achievement goal theory, conceptualization of ability/intelligence, and classroom climate. In S. Christenson, A. Reschly, & C. Wylie (Eds.) *Handbook of research on student engagement.* (pp. 173–191). New York, NY, USA: Springer Science + Business Media.

Andersen, B. L., & Cyranowski, J. M. (1995). Women's sexuality: Behaviors, responses, and individual differences. *Journal of Consulting and Clinical Psychology, 63*, 891–906.

Anderson, C. A., & Anderson, K. B. (1996). Violent crime rate studies in philosophical context: A destructive testing approach to heat and southern culture of violence effects. *Journal of Personality and Social Psychology, 70*, 740–756.

Anderson, C. A., & Dill, K. E. (2000). Video games and aggressive thoughts, feelings, and behavior in the laboratory and in life. *Journal of Personality & Social Psychology, 78*, 772–790.

Anderson, C., & Carnagey, N. (2009). Causal effects of violent sports video games on aggression: Is it competitiveness or violent content? *Journal of Experimental Social Psychology, 45*, 731–739.

Anderson, R. (2002). Deaths: Leading causes for 2000. *National Vital Statistics Reports, 50*(16), 1–86.

Anderson, S., & Patrick, A. (2006). *Doctor Dolittle's delusion: Animals and the uniqueness of human language.* New Haven, CT: Yale University Press.

Anderson, G. (2010). *Chronic care: Making the case for ongoing care.* Retrieved December 15, 2012, from http://www.rwjf.org/content/dam/web-assets/2010/01/chronic-care

Andrews, G., & Erskine, A. (2003). Reducing the burden of anxiety and depressive disorders: The role of computerized clinician assistance. *Current Opinion in Psychiatry, 16*, 41–44.

Anglin, J. (1995, March). *Word learning and the growth of potentially knowable vocabulary.* Paper presented at the biennial meetings of the Society for Research in Child Development, Indianapolis, IN.

Anokhin, A., Vedeniapin, A., Sitevaag, E., Bauer, L., O'Connor, S., Kuperman, S., et al. (2000). The P300 brain potential is reduced in smokers. *Psychopharmacology, 149*, 409–413.

Aram, D., & Levitt, I. (2002). Mother-child joint writing and storybook reading: Relations with literacy among low SES kindergarteners. *Merrill-Palmer Quarterly, 48*, 202–224.

Araujo, L. (2009). Stochastic parsing and evolutionary algorithms. *Applied Artificial Intelligence, 23*, 346–372.

Arcelus, J., Mitchell, A., Wales, J., & Nielsen, S. (2011). Mortality rates in patients with anorexia nervosa and other eating disorders: A meta-analysis of 36 studies. *Archives of General Psychiatry, 68*, 724–731.

Archer, J. (1996). Sex differences in social behavior: Are the social role and evolutionary explanations compatible? *American Psychologist, 51*, 909–917.

Arendt, J. (2009). Managing jet lag: Some of the problems and possible new solutions. *Sleep Medicine Reviews, 13*, 249–256.

Arim, R., & Shapka, J. (2008). The impact of pubertal timing and parental control on adolescent problem behaviors. *Journal of Youth and Adolescence, 37*, 445–455.

Ariznavarreta, C., Cardinali, D., Villanua, M., Granados, B., Martin, M., Chiesa, J., Golombek, D., & Tresguerres, J. (2002). Circadian rhythms in airline pilots submitted to long-haul transmeridian flights. *Aviation, Space, and Environmental Medicine, 73*, 445–455.

Arnett, J. (2011). Emerging adulthood(s): The cultural psychology of a new life stage. In L. Jensen (Ed.). *Bridging cultural and developmental approaches to psychology: New syntheses in theory, research, and policy.* (pp. 255–275). New York, NY, USA: Oxford University Press.

Aronson, E. (1988). *The social animal* (3rd ed.). San Francisco: W. H. Freeman.

Aronson, E., Stephan, W., Sikes, J., Blaney, N., & Snapp, M. (1978). *Cooperation in the classroom.* Beverly Hills, CA: Sage.

Arushanyan, E., & Shikina, I. (2004). Effect of caffeine on light and color sensitivity of the retina in healthy subjects depending on psychophysiological features and time of day. *Human Physiology, 30,* 56–61.

Asch, S. E. (1955). Opinions and social pressure. *Scientific American, 193,* 31–35.

Ashkenazi, S., Rosenberg-Lee, M., Tenison, C., & Menon, V. (2012). Weak task-related modulation and stimulus representations during arithmetic problem solving in children with developmental dyscalculia. *Developmental Cognitive Neuroscience, 2,* S152–S166.

Assadi, S., Noroozian, M., Pakravannejad, M., Yahyazadeh, O., Aghayan, S., Shariat, S., et al. (2006). Psychiatric morbidity among sentenced prisoners: Prevalence study in Iran. *British Journal of Psychiatry, 188,* 159–164.

Assefi, S., & Garry, M. (2003). Absolute memory distortions: Alcohol placebos influence the misinformation effect. *Psychological Science, 14,* 77–80.

Atkinson, R. C., & Shiffrin, R. M. (1968). Human memory: A proposed system and its controlled processes. In K. W. Spence & J. T. Spence (Eds.), *The psychology of learning and motivation* (Vol. 2, pp. 89–195). New York: Academic.

Augestad, L. B. (2000). Prevalence and gender differences in eating attitudes and physical activity among Norwegians. *Eating and Weight Disorders: Studies on Anorexia, Bulimia, and Obesity, 5,* 62–72.

Austenfeld, J., & Stanton, A. (2004). Coping through emotional approach: A new look at emotion, coping, and health-related outcomes. *Journal of Personality, 72,* 1335–1363.

Autism Society of America. (2006). *Treatment.* Retrieved July 18, 2006 from http://www.autism-society.org/site/PageServer?pagename=Treatment

Avena, N., & Bocarsly, M. (2012). Dysregulation of brain reward systems in eating disorders: Neurochemical information from animal models of binge eating, bulimia nervosa, and anorexia nervosa. *Neuropharmacology, 63,* 87–96.

Axel, R. (1995, October). The molecular logic of smell. *Scientific American, 273,* 154–159.

Ayers, J., Althouse, B., Allern, J., Childers, M., Zafar, W., Latkin, C., Ribisl, K., & Brownstein, J. (2012). Novel surveillance of psychological distress during the great recession. *Journal of Affective Disorders, 142,* 323–330.

Azar, B. (2000). A web of research. *Monitor on Psychology, 31* [Online version]. Retrieved March 13, 2002, from *http://www.apa.org/monitor/*

Azrin, N. H., & Holz, W. C. (1966). Punishment. In W. K. Honig (Ed.), *Operant behavior: Areas of research and application* (pp. 380–447). New York: Appleton-Century-Crofts.

Babor, T. (2004). Brief treatments for cannabis dependence: Findings from a randomized multisite trial. *Journal of Consulting & Clinical Psychology, 72,* 455–466.

Baddeley, A. (1998). *Human memory: Theory and practice.* Boston, MA: Allyn & Bacon.

Baddeley, A. (2009). Working memory. In A., Baddeley, M., Eysenck, & M. Anderson (Eds), *Memory* (pp. 41–68). New York: Psychology Press.

Baddeley, A. (2012). Working memory: Theories, models, and controversies. *Annual Review of Psychology, 63,* 1–29.

Baer, J. (1996). The effects of task-specific divergent-thinking training. *Journal of Creative Behavior, 30,* 183–187.

Bahrick, H. P., Bahrick, P. O., & Wittlinger, R. P. (1975). Fifty years of memory for names and faces: A cross-sectional approach. *Journal of Experimental Psychology: General, 104,* 54–75.

Bahrick, H. P., Hall, L. K., & Berger, S. A. (1996). Accuracy and distortion in memory for high school grades. *Psychological Science, 7,* 265–271.

Bailey, J. M., & Pillard, R. C. (1991). A genetic study of male sexual orientation. *Archives of General Psychiatry, 48,* 1089–1096.

Bailey, B., & Konstan, J. (2006). On the need for attention-aware systems: Measuring effects of interruption on task performance, error rate, and affective state. *Computers in Human Behavior, 22,* 685–708.

Bailey, J. M., Pillard, R. C., Neale, M. C., & Agyei, Y. (1993). Heritable factors influence sexual orientation in women. *Archives of General Psychiatry, 50,* 217–223.

Baio, J. (2012). Prevalence of autism spectrum disorders—autism and developmental disabilities monitoring network, 14 sites, United States, 2008. *Surveillance Summaries, 61,* 1–19.

Baird, A. (2010). The terrible twelves. In P., Zalazo, M., Chandler, & E. Crone (Eds.), *Developmental social cognitive neuroscience,* The Jean Piaget symposium (pp. 191–207). New York: Psychology Press.

Bajic, D., & Rickard, T. (2009). The temporal dynamics of strategy execution in cognitive skill learning. *Journal of Experimental Psychology: Learning, Memory, and Cognition, 35,* 113–121.

Baker, L., Jacobson, K., Raine, A., Lozano, D., & Bezdjian, S. (2007). Genetic and environmental bases of childhood antisocial behavior: A multi-informant twin study. *Journal of Abnormal Psychology, 116,* 219–235.

Balthazart, J. (2012). *The biology of homosexuality: Behavioral neuroendocrinology.* New York, NY, USA: Oxford University Press.

Bandura, A. (1973). *Aggression: A social learning analysis.* Englewood Cliffs, NJ: Prentice-Hall.

Bandura, A. (1976). On social learning and aggression. In E. P. Hollander & R. C. Hunt (Eds.), *Current perspectives in social psychology* (4th ed., pp. 116–128). New York: Oxford University Press.

Bandura, A. (1977). *Social learning theory.* Englewood Cliffs, NJ: Prentice-Hall.

Bandura, A. (1986). *Social functions of thought and action: A social-cognitive theory.* Englewood Cliffs, NJ: Prentice-Hall.

Bandura, A. (1989). Social cognitive theory. *Annals of Child Development, 6,* 1–60.

Bandura, A. (1997a, March). Self-efficacy. *Harvard Mental Health Letter, 13*(9), 4–6.

Bandura, A. (1997b). *Self-efficacy: The exercise of control.* New York: Freeman.

Bandura, A., Adams, N. E., & Beyer, J. (1977). Cognitive processes mediating behavioral change. *Journal of Personality and Social Psychology, 35,* 125–139.

Bandura, A., Jeffery, R. W., & Gajdos, E. (1975). Generalizing change through participant modeling with self-directed mastery. *Behaviour Research and Therapy, 13,* 141–152.

Bandura, A., Ross, D., & Ross, S. A. (1961). Transmission of aggression through imitation of aggressive models. *Journal of Abnormal and Social Psychology, 63,* 575–582.

Bandura, A., Ross, D., & Ross, S. A. (1963). Imitation of film-mediated aggressive models. *Journal of Abnormal and Social Psychology, 66,* 3–11.

Barbarich, N., McConaha, C., Gaskill, J., La Via, M., Frank, G., Achenbach, S., Plotnicov, K., & Kaye, W. (2004). An open trial of olanzapine in anorexia nervosa. *Journal of Clinical Psychiatry, 65,* 1480–1482.

Bard, P. (1934). The neurohumoral basis of emotional reactions. In C. A. Murchison (Ed.), *Handbook of general experimental psychology* (pp. 264–311). Worcester, MA: Clark University Press.

Bargiel-Matusiewicz, K., Trzcieniecka-Green, A., Krupa, A., & Krzystanek, M. (2005). Reaction phases following HIV positive diagnosis. *Archives of Psychiatry and Psychotherapy, 7,* 63015069.

Barker, L. (2006). Teaching evolutionary psychology: An interview with David M. Buss. *Teaching of Psychology, 33,* 69–76.

Barnes, P., Bloom, B., & Nahin, R. (2008). Complementary and alternative medicine use among adults and children: United States, 2007. *National Health Statistics Reports, 12,* 1–24.

Barrett. D. (2007). An evolutionary theory of dreams and problem-solving. In D. Barrrett & P. McNamara (Eds.), *The new science of dreaming, Volume 3: Cultural and theoretical perspectives* (pp. 133–153). Westport, CT: Praeger Publishers.

Barrick, M., Shaffer, J., & DeGrassi, S. (2009). What you see may not be what you get: Relationships among self-presentation tactics and ratings of interview and job performance. *Journal of Applied Psychology, 94,* 1394–1411.

Barsh, G. S., Farooqi, I. S., & O'Rahilly, S. (2000). Genetics of body-weight regulation. *Nature, 404,* 644–651.

Bartlett, F. C. (1932). *Remembering: A study in experimental and social psychology.* London: Cambridge University Press.

Bartoshuk, L. M., & Beauchamp, G. K. (1994). Chemical senses. *Annual Review of Psychology, 45,* 419–449.

Bartzokis, G., Sultzer, D., Lu, P., Huechterlein, K., Mintz, J., & Cummings, J. (2004). Heterogeneous age-related breakdown of white matter structural integrity: Implications for cortical "disconnection" in aging and Alzheimer's disease. *Neurobiology of Aging, 25,* 843–851.

Basco, M. (2006). *The bipolar workbook.* New York: Guilford Press.

Bassili, J. N. (1995). Response latency and the accessibility of voting intentions: What contributes to accessibility and how it affects vote choice. *Personality and Social Psychology Bulletin, 21,* 686–695.

Bates, M., Labouvie, D., & Voelbel, G. (2002). Individual differences in latent neuropsychological abilities at addictions treatment entry. *Psychology of Addictive Behaviors, 16,* 35–46.

Bateson, G. (1982). Totemic knowledge in New Guinea. In U. Neisser (Ed.), *Memory observed: Remembering in natural contexts* (pp. 269–273). San Francisco: W. H. Freeman.

Batson, C. (2010). Empathy-induced altruistic motivation. In M. Mikulincer & P. Shaver (Eds.). *Prosocial motives, emotions, and behavior: The better angels of our nature.* (pp. 15–34). Washington, DC, USA: American Psychological Association.

Baucom, B., McFarland, P., & Christensen, A. (2010). Gender, topic, and time in observed demand-withdraw interaction in cross- and same-sex couples. *Journal of Family Psychology, 24,* 233–242.

Baucom, D., Epstein, N., & Sullivan, L. (2012). In M. Dewan, B. Steenberger, & R. Greenberg (Eds.). *The art and science of brief psychotherapies: An illustrated guide* (2nd ed.). (pp. 239–276). Arlington, VA, USA: American Psychiatric Publishing, Inc.

Bauer, J., Schwab, J., & McAdams, D. (2011). Self-actualizing: Where ego development finally feels good? *The Humanistic Psychologist, 39,* 121–136.

Baumrind, D. (1967). Child care practices anteceding three patterns of preschool behavior. *Genetic Psychology Monographs, 75,* 43–88.

Baumrind, D. (1971). Current patterns of parental authority. *Developmental Psychology Monographs, 4*(1, Pt. 2).

Baumrind, D. (1980). New directions in socialization research. *American Psychologist, 35,* 639–652.

Baumrind, D. (1991). The influence of parenting style on adolescent competence and substance use. *Journal of Early Adolescence, 11,* 56–95.

Bavelier, D., Tomann, A., Hutton, C., Mitchell, T., Corina, D., Liu, G., & Neville, H. (2000). Visual attention to the periphery is enhanced in congenitally deaf individuals. *Journal of Neuroscience, 20,* 1–6.

Bazan, S. (1998). Enhancing decision-making effectiveness in problem-solving teams. *Clinical Laboratory Management Review, 12,* 272–276.

BBC World Service. (2007). *Figure it out: Winning the lottery—probability and coincidence.* Retrieved January 27, 2007, from *http://www.bbc.co.uk/worldservice/sci_tech/features/figure_it_out/lottery.shtml*

Beare, P., Severson, S., & Brandt, P. (2004). The use of a positive procedure to increase engagement on-task and decrease challenging behavior. *Behavior Modification, 28,* 28–44.

Bureau of Labor Statistics. (2012). *Employment characteristics of families summary.* Retrieved December 16, 2012, from http://www.bls.gov/news.release/famee.nr0.htm

Beck, A. T. (1976). *Cognitive therapy and the emotional disorders.* New York: New American Library.

Beck, J. (1995). *Cognitive therapy: Basics and beyond.* New York: Guilford Press.

Becker, K., & Wallace, J. (2010). *Central sleep apnea.* Retrieved April 29, 2010 from *http://emedicine.medscape.com/article/304967-overview.*

Becker, M., Vignoles, V., Owe, E., Brown, R., Smith, P., Easterbrook, M., Herman, G., de Sauvage, I., Bourguignon, D., Torres, A., Camino, L., Lemos, F., Ferreira, M., Koller, S., González, R., Carrasco, D., Cadena, M., Lay, S., Wang, Q., Bond, M., Trujillo, E., Balanta, P., Valk, A., Mekonnen, K., Nizharadze, G., Fülöp, M., Regalia, C., Manzi, C., Brambilla, M., Harb, C., Aldhafri, S., Martin, M., Macapagal, M., Chybicka, A., Gavreliuc, A., Buitendach, J., Gallo, I., Özgen, E., Güner, Ü., & Yamakoğlu, N. (2012). Culture and the distinctiveness motive: Constructing identity in individualistic and collectivistic contexts. *Journal of Personality and Social Psychology, 102,* 833–855.

Beede, K., & Kass, S. (2006). Engrossed in conversation: The impact of cell phones on simulated driving performance. *Accident Analysis & Prevention, 38,* 415–421.

Beins, B. (2012). Jean Piaget: Theorist of the child's mind. In W. Pickren, D. Dewsbury, & M. Wertheimer (Eds.) *Portraits of pioneers in developmental psychology.* (pp. 89-107). New York, NY, USA: Psychology Press.

Beirut, L., Dinwiddie, S., Begleiter, H., Crowe, R., Hesselbrock, V., Nurnberger, J., et al. (1998). Familial transmission of substance dependence: Alcohol, marijuana, cocaine, and habitual smoking: A report from the collaborative study on the genetics of alcoholism. *Archives of General Psychiatry, 55,* 982–988.

Békésy, G. von. (1957). The ear. *Scientific American, 197,* 66–78.

Bekinschtein, T., Cardozo, J., & Manes, F. (2008). Strategies of Buenos Aires waiters to enhance memory capacity in a real-life setting. *Behavioural Neurology, 20,* 65–70.

Belcourt-Dittloff, A., & Stewart, J. (2000). Historical racism: Implications for Native Americans. *American Psychologist, 55,* 1164–1165.

Bell, A. P., Weinberg, M. S., & Hammersmith, S. K. (1981). *Sexual preference: Its development in men and women.* Bloomington: Indiana University Press.

Belsky, J., & Fearon, R. (2002). Infant-mother attachment security, contextual risk, and early development: A moderational analysis. *Development & Psychopathology, 14,* 293–310.

Bem, S. L. (1981). Gender schema theory: A cognitive account of sex typing. *Psychological Review, 88,* 354–364.

Ben-Porath, Y. S., & Butcher, J. N. (1989). The comparability of MMPI and MMPI-2 scales and profiles. *Psychological Assessment: A Journal of Consulting and Clinical Psychology, 1,* 345–347.

Benarroch, E. (2008). Suprachiasmatic nucleus and melatonin: Reciprocal interactions and clinical correlations. *Neurology, 71,* 594–598.

Benedek, M., Konen, T., & Neubauer, A. (2012). Associative abilities underlying creativity. *Psychology of Aesthetics, Creativity, and the Arts, 6,* 273–281.

Benjafield, J. G. (1996). *A history of psychology.* Boston: Allyn & Bacon.

Benjamin, L., & Crouse, E. (2002). The American Psychological Association's response to Brown v. Board of Education: The case of Kenneth B. Clark. *American Psychologist, 57,* 38–50.

Bennani, O., Bennani, D., Diouny, S., & Boumalif, O. (2012). The application of a telemedicine management system: The case of a Moroccan hospital unit. *Assistive Technology, 24,* 209–213.

Berckmoes, C., & Vingerhoets, G. (2004). Neural foundations of emotional speech processing. *Current Directions in Psychological Science, 13,* 182–185.

Berenbaum, S. A., & Snyder, E. (1995). Early hormonal influences on childhood sex-typed activity and playmate preferences: Implications for the development of sexual orientation. *Developmental Psychology, 31,* 31–42.

Berger, J., & Milkman, K. (2012). What makes online content viral? *Journal of Marketing Research, 49,* 192–205.

Bergman, O., Hakansson, A., Westberg, l., Nordenstrom, K., Belin, A., Sydow, O., Olson, L., Holmberg, B., Eriksson, E., & Nissbrandt, H. (2010). PITX3 polymorphism is associated with early onset Parkinson's disease. *Neurobiology of Aging, 31,* 114–117.

Bergström, M., Kieler, H., & Waldenström, U. (2009). Effects of a natural childbirth preparation versus standard antenatal education on epidural rates, experience of childbirth and parental stress in mothers and fathers: A randomised controlled multicentre trial. *British Journal of Obstetrics and Gynaecology, 116,* 1167–1176.

Berkowitz, L. (1990). On the formation and regulation of anger and aggression: A cognitive-neoassociationistic analysis. *American Psychologist, 45,* 494–503.

Berkowitz, L. (1988). Frustrations, appraisals, and aversively stimulated aggression. *Aggressive Behavior, 14,* 3–11.

Berndt, E. R., Koran, L. M., Finkelstein, S. N., Gelenberg, A. J., Kornstein, S. G., Miller, I. M., et al. (2000). Lost human capital from early-onset chronic depression. *American Journal of Psychiatry, 157,* 940–947.

Berndt, T. J. (1992). Friendship and friends' influence in adolescence. *Current Directions in Psychological Science, 1,* 156–159.

Bernstein, I. L. (1985). Learned food aversions in the progression of cancer and its treatment. *Annals of the New York Academy of Sciences, 443,* 365–380.

Bernstein, I. L., Webster, M. M., & Bernstein, I. D. (1982). Food aversions in children receiving chemotherapy for cancer. *Cancer, 50,* 2961–2963.

Berridge (2009). "Liking" and "wanting" food rewards: Brain substrates and roles in eating disorders. *Physiology & Behavior, 97,* 537–550.

Berry, J. W., Kim, U., Minde, T., & Mok, D. (1987). Comparative studies of acculturative stress. *International Migration Review, 21,* 491–511.

Berscheid, E., Dion, K., Walster, E., & Walster, G. W. (1971). Physical attractiveness and dating choice: A test of the matching hypothesis. *Journal of Experimental Social Psychology, 7,* 173–189.

Bessell, A. (2012). Computer-based psychosocial interventions. In N. Rumsey & D. Harcourt (Eds.), *The Oxford Handbook of the Psychology of Appearance.* (pp. 568–580). New York, NY, USA: Oxford University Press.

Beyenburg, S., Watzka, M., Clusmann, H., Blümcke, I., Bidlingmaier, F., Stoffel-Wagner, et al. (2000). Androgen receptor mRNA expression in the human hippocampus. *Neuroscience Letters, 294,* 25–28.

Bhalla, R., Moraille-Bhalla, P., & Aronson, S. (2010). *Depression.* Retrieved March 15, 2010 from *http://emedicine.medscape.com/article/286759-overview.*

Bhugra, D. (2005). The global prevalence of schizophrenia. *Public Library of Science, 5.* [Online only, no pages.] Retrieved July 18, 2006, from *http://medicine.plosjournals.org/perlserv?request=getdocument&doi=10.1371/journal.pmed.0020151.*

Bienenfeld, D. (2013). *Personality disorders.* Retrieved January 26, 2013, from http://emedicine.medscape.com/article/294307-treatment#àw2aab6b6b3

Bienvenu, O., Hettema, J., Neale, M., Prescott, C., & Kendler, K. (2007). Low extraversion and high neuroticism as indices of genetic and environmental risk for social phobia, agoraphobia, and animal phobia. *American Journal of Psychiatry, 164,* 1714–1721.

Bierman, A., Fazio, & Milkie, M. (2006). A multifaceted approach to the mental health advantage of the married: Assessing how explanations vary by outcome measure and unmarried group. *Journal of Family Issues, 27,* 554–582.

Birren, J. E., & Fisher, L. M. (1995). Aging and speed of behavior: Possible consequences for psychological functioning. *Annual Review of Psychology, 46,* 329–353.

Bissing-Olson, M., Iyer, A., Fielding, K., & Zacher, H. (2013). Relationships between daily affect and pro-environmental behavior at work: The moderating role of pro-environmental attitude. *Journal of Organizational Behavior, 34,* 156–175.

Bitter, S., Mills, N., Adler, C., Strakowski, S., & DelBello, M. (2011). Progression of amygdala volumetric abnormalities in adolescents after their first manic episode. *Journal of the American Academy of Child & Adolescent Psychiatry, 50,* 1017–1026.

Blake, K., & Davis. V. (2011). Adolescent medicine. In K. Marcdante, R. Kliegman, H. Jenson, & R. Behrman (Eds.) *Nelson essentials of pediatrics* (6th ed.). (pp. 265–284). Philadelphia, PA, USA: Saunders/Elsevier, Inc.

Blasco-Fontecilla, H., Delgado-Gomez, D., Legido-Gil, T., de Leon, J., Perez-Rodriguez, M., & Baca-Garcia, E. (2012). Can the Homes-Rahe social readjustment rating scale (SRRS) be used as a suicide risk scale? An exploratory study. *Archives of Suicide Research, 16,* 13–28.

Blatt, S. J., Sanislow, C. A., III, Zuroff, D. C., & Pilkonis, P. A. (1996). Characteristics of effective therapists: Further analyses of data from the National Institute of Mental Health Treatment of Depression Collaborative Research Program. *Journal of Consulting and Clinical Psychology, 64,* 1276–1284.

Blatt, S., Zuroff, D., & Hawley, L. (2009). Factors contributing to sustained therapeutic gain in outpatient treatments of depression. In R., Levy, & J. Ablon (Eds.), *Handbook of evidence-based psychodynamic psychotherapy: Bridging the gap between science and practice* (pp. 279–301). Totowa, NJ: Humana Press.

Blinn-Pike, L., Berger, T., Hewett, J., & Oleson, J. (2004). Sexually abstinent adolescents: An 18-month follow-up. *Journal of Adolescent Research, 19,* 495–511.

Bloom, B. S. (Ed.). (1985). *Developing talent in young people.* New York: Ballantine.

Bloom, B., & Cohen, R. (2007). Summary health statistics for U.S. children: National Health Interview Survey, 2006. *Vital Health Statistics, 10,* 1–87.

Bloomer, C. M. (1976). *Principles of visual perception.* New York: Van Nostrand Reinhold.

Bobes, J., Gibert, J., Ciudad, A., Alvarez, E., Cañas, F., Carrasco, J., Gascón, J., Gómez, J., & Gutiérrez, M. (2003). Safety and effectiveness of olanzapine versus conventional antipsychotics in the acute treatment of first-episode schizophrenic inpatients. *Progress in Neuro-Psychopharmacology & Biological Psychiatry, 27,* 473–481.

Bogen, J. E., & Vogel, P. J. (1963). Treatment of generalized seizures by cerebral commissurotomy. *Surgical Forum, 14,* 431.

Bohannon, R., Larkin, P., Cook, A., Gear, J., & Singer, J. (1984). Decrease in timed balance test scores with aging. *Physical Therapy, 64,* 1067–1070.

Bohn, C., Aderka, I., Schreiber, F., Stangier, U., & Hofmann, S. (2013). *Journal of Consulting and Clinical Psychology, 81,* 177–182.

Bohner, G & Dickel, N. (2011). Attitudes and attitude change. *Annual Review of Psychology, 62,* 391–417.

Boivin, D. B., Czeisler, C. A., Dijk, D-J., Duffy, J. F., Folkard, S., Minors, D. S., et al. (1997). Complex interaction of the sleep-wake cycle and circadian phase modulates mood in healthy subjects. *Archives of General Psychiatry, 54,* 145–152.

Bonanno, G. A., Keltner, D., Holen, A., & Horowitz, M. J. (1995). When avoiding unpleasant emotions might not be such a bad thing: Verbal-autonomic response dissociation and midlife conjugal bereavement. *Journal of Personality and Social Psychology, 69,* 975–989.

Bonnefond, A., Härmä, M., Hakola, T., Sallinen, M., Kandolin, I., & Virkkala, J. (2006). Interaction of age with shift-related sleep-wakefulness, sleepiness, performance, and social life. *Experimental Aging Research, 32,* 185–208.

Bono, J., Davies, S., & Rasch, R. (2012). Positive traits. In K. Cameron, & G. Spreitzer (Eds.). *The Oxford handbook of positive organizational scholarship.* (pp. 125–137). New York, NY, USA: Oxford University Press.

Bonson, K., Grant, S., Contoreggi, C., Links, J., Metcalfe, J., Weyl, H., et al. (2002). Neural systems and cue-induced cocaine craving. *Neuropsychopharmacology, 26,* 376–386.

Borbely, A. A., Achermann, P., Trachsel, L., & Tobler, I. (1989). Sleep initiation and initial sleep intensity: Interactions of homeostatic and circadian mechanisms. *Journal of Biological Rhythms, 4,* 149–160.

Borden, W. (2009). *Contemporary psychodynamic theory and practice.* Chicago: Lyceum Books.

Borzekowski, D., Fobil, J., & Asante, K. (2006). Online access by adolescents in Accra: Ghanaian teens' use of the Internet for health information. *Developmental Psychology, 42,* 450–458.

Bouchard, T. J., Jr. (1994). Genes, environment, and personality. *Science, 264,* 1700–1701.

Bouchard, T. J., Jr., & McGue, M. (1981). Familial studies of intelligence: A review. *Science, 212,* 1055–1058.

Boul, L. (2003). Men's health and middle age. *Sexualities, Evolution, & Gender, 5,* 5–22.

Boulenger, J., Loft, H., & Florea, I. (2012). A randomized clinical study of Lu AA21004 in the prevention of relapse in patients with major depressive disorder. *Journal of Psychopharmacology, 26,* 1408–1416.

Bourassa, M., & Vaugeois, P. (2001). Effects of marijuana use on divergent thinking. *Creativity Research Journal, 13,* 411–416.

Boutwell, B., Franklin, C., Barnes, J., & Beaver, K. (2011). Physical punishment and childhood aggression: The role of gender and gene-environment interplay. *Aggressive Behavior, 37,* 559–568.

Bowden, C., Myers, J., Grossman, F., & Xie, Y. (2004). Risperidone in combination with mood stabilizers: A 10-week continuation phase study in bipolar I disorder. *Journal of Clinical Psychiatry, 65,* 707–714.

Bowen-Reid, T., & Harrell, J. (2002). Racist experiences and health outcomes: An examination of spirituality as a buffer. *Journal of Black Psychology, 28,* 18–36.

Bower, G. H., Thompson-Schill, S., & Tulving, E. (1994). Reducing retroactive interference: An interference analysis. *Journal of Experimental Psychology: Learning, Memory, and Cognition, 20,* 51–66.

Bowers, K. S. (1992). Imagination and dissociative control in hypnotic responding. *International Journal of Clinical and Experimental Hypnosis, 40,* 253–275.

Bowers, K. S., & Woody, E. Z. (1996). Hypnotic amnesia and the paradox of intentional forgetting. *Journal of Abnormal Psychology, 105,* 381–390.

Bowers, M., Choi, D., & Ressler, K. (2012). Neuropeptide regulation of fear and anxiety: Implications of cholecystokinin, endogenous opioids, and neuropeptide Y. *Physiology & Behavior, 107,* 699–710.

Boyce, J., & Shone, G. (2006). Effects of aging on smell and taste. *Postgraduate Medical Journal, 82,* 239–241.

Boykin, S., Diez-Roux, A., Carnethon, M., Shrager, S., Ni, H., & Whitt-Glover, M. (2011). Racial/ethnic heterogeneity in the socioeconomic patterning of CVD risk factors in the United States: The multi-ethnic study of atherosclerosis. *Journal of Health Care for the Poor and Underserved, 22,* 111–127.

Bozorg, A., & Benbadis, S. (2009). *Narcolepsy.* Retrieved February 5, 2010 from *http://emedicine.medscape.com/article/1188433-overview.*

Brackbill, R., Hadler, J., DiGrande, L., Ekenga, C., Farfel, M., Friedman, S., Perlman, S., Stellman, S., Walker, D., Wu, D., Yu, S., & Thorpe, L. (2009). Asthma and posttraumatic stress symptoms 5 to 6 years following exposure to the World Trade Center terrorist attack. *JAMA: Journal of the American Medical Association, 302,* 502–516.

Brain imaging and psychiatry—Part I. (1997, January). *Harvard Mental Health Letter, 13*(7), 1–4.

Brakemeier, E., & Fraw, L. (2012). Interpersonal psychotherapy (IPT) in major depressive disorder. *European Archives of Psychiatry and Clinical Neuroscience, 262,* 117–121.

Brand, B., McNary, S., Myrick, A., Classen, C., Lanius, R., Loewenstein, R., Pain, C., & Putnam, F. (2012). *Psychological Trauma: Theory, Research, Practice, and Policy, 4,* 490–500.

Brannon, L., & Feist, J. (2010). *Health psychology: An introduction to behavior and health* (7th ed.). Wadsworth Publishing.

Brasic, J. (2012). *Tardive dyskinesia.* Retrieved January 27, 2013, from http://emedicine.medscape.com/article/1151826-overview

Brasic, R., & Kao, A. (2011). *PET scanning in autism spectrum disorder.* Retrieved October 21, 2012, from http://emedicine.medscape.com/article/1155568-overview#a1.

Brawman-Mintzer, O., & Lydiard, R. B. (1996). Generalized anxiety disorder: Issues in epidemiology. *Journal of Clinical Psychiatry, 57*(7, Suppl.), 3–8.

Brawman-Mintzer, O., & Lydiard, R. B. (1997). Biological basis of generalized anxiety disorder. *Journal of Clinical Psychiatry, 58*(3, Suppl.), 16–25.

Bray, G. A., & Tartaglia, L. A. (2000). Medicinal strategies in the treatment of obesity. *Nature, 404,* 672–677.

Bredemeier, K., & Simons, D. (2012). Working memory and inattentional blindness. *Psychonomic Bulletin & Review, 9,* 239–244.

Bremner, J., & Vermetten, E. (2007). Psychiatric approaches to dissociation: Integrating history, biology, and clinical assessment. In E. Vermetten, M. Dorahy, & D. Spiegel (Eds.). *Traumatic dissociation: Neurobiology and treatment.* (pp. 239–258). Arlington, VA, USA: American Psychiatric Publishing, Inc.

Brenner, I. (2009). A new view from the Acropolis: Dissociative identity disorder. *Psychoanalytic Quarterly, 78,* 57–105.

Brent, D. A., Bridge, J., Johnson, B. A., & Connolly, J. (1996). Suicidal behavior runs in families: A controlled family study of adolescent suicide victims. *Archives of General Psychiatry, 53,* 1145–1152.

Brent, D., Oquendo, M., Birmaher, B., Greenhill, L., Kolko, D., Stanley, B., et al. (2002). Familial pathways to early-onset suicide attempt. *Archives of General Psychiatry, 59,* 801.

Bressan, P., & Pizzighello, S. (2008). The attentional cost of inattentional blindness. *Cognition, 106,* 379–383.

Brewer, W. F. (1992). The theoretical and empirical status of the flashbulb memory hypothesis. In E. Winograd, & U. Neisser (Eds.), *Affect and accuracy in recall* (pp. 274–305). Cambridge, UK: Cambridge University Press.

Brewer, N., Weber, N., Wootton, D., & Lindsay, D. (2012). Identifying the bad guy in a lineup using confidence judgments under deadline pressure. *Psychological Science, 23,* 1208–1214.

Brighton, H., & Gigerenzer, G. (2012). How heuristics handle uncertainty. In P. Todd & G. Gigerenzer (Eds.) *Ecological rationality: Intelligence in the world.* (pp. 33–60). New York, NY, USA: Oxford University Press, ABC Research Group.

BrightRoll,Inc.(2012).*Digitalvideo2012.*RetrievedFebruary22,2013,from http://marketing.btrll.com/research/reports/agency_survey/us/2012/BrightRollUS_VideoAdvertisingReport_2012.pdf.

Britt, R. (2006). *Sound science: Pete Townshend blames headphones for hearing loss.* Retrieved December 13, 2006, from *http://www.foxnews.com/story/0,2933.180844,00.html*

Brody, L. R. (1985). Gender differences in emotional development: A review of theories and research. *Journal of Personality, 53,* 102–149.

Brooks-Gunn, J., & Furstenberg, F. F. (1989). Adolescent sexual behavior. *American Psychologist, 44,* 249–257.

Brown, G. W., Harris, T. O., & Hepworth, C. (1994). Life events and endogenous depression: A puzzle reexamined. *Archives of General Psychiatry, 51,* 525–534.

Brown, R. (1973). *A first language: The early stages.* Cambridge, MA: Harvard University Press.

Brown, R., & Kulik, J. (1977). Flashbulb memories. *Cognition, 5,* 73–99.

Brown, R., & McNeil, D. (1966). The "tip of the tongue" phenomenon. *Journal of Verbal Learning and Verbal Behavior, 5,* 325–337.

Brown, R., Cazden, C., & Bellugi, U. (1968). The child's grammar from I to III. In J. P. Hill (Ed.), *Minnesota symposium on child psychology* (Vol. 2, pp. 28–73). Minneapolis: University of Minnesota Press.

Brown, T. (2007). Relationships among dimension of temperament and DSM-IV anxiety and mood disorder constructs. *Journal of Abnormal Psychology, 116,* 313–328.

Bruch, M., Fallon, M., & Heimberg, R. (2003). Social phobia and difficulties in occupational adjustment. *Journal of Counseling Psychology, 50,* 109–117.

Brundage, S. (2002). *Preconception health care.* Retrieved November 30, 2006, from *http://www.aafp.org/afp/20020615/2507.html*

Brunetti, A., Carta, P., Cossu, G., Ganadu, M., Golosio, B., Mura, G., et al. (2002). A real-time classification system of thalassemic pathologies based on artificial neural networks. *Medical Decision Making, 22,* 18–26.

Bruno-Petrina, A. (2009). *Motor recovery in stroke.* Retrieved January 15, 2010 from *http://emedicine.medscape.com/article/324386-overview.*

Bryant, R., & Das, P. (2012). The neural circuitry of conversion disorder and its recovery. *Journal of Abnormal Psychology, 121,* 289–296.

Buchanan, N., & Fitzgerald, L. (2008). Effects of racial and sexual harassment on work and the psychological well-being of African American women. *Journal of Occupational Health Psychology, 13,* 137–151.

Buchert, S., Laws, E., Apperson, J., & Bregman, N. (2008). First impressions and professor reputation: Influence on student evaluations of instruction. *Social Psychology of Education, 11,* 397–408.

Buckingham, H. W., Jr., & Kertesz, A. (1974). A linguistic analysis of fluent aphasics. *Brain and Language, 1,* 29–42.

Buhusi, C., & Meck, W. (2002). Differential effects of methamphetamine and haloperidol on the control of an internal clock. *Behavioral Neuroscience, 116,* 291–297.

Buller, D. B., Burgoon, M., Hall, J. R., Levine, N., Taylor, A. M., Beach, B. H., et al. (2000). Using language intensity to increase the success of a family intervention to protect children from ultraviolet radiation: Predictions from language expectancy theory. *Preventive Medicine, 30,* 103–113.

Burke, A., Heuer, F., & Reisberg, D. (1992). Remembering emotional events. *Memory and Cognition, 20,* 277–290.

Burriss, R., Roberts, S., Welling, L., Puts, D., & Little, A. (2011). Heterosexual romantic couples mate assortatively for facial symmetry, but not masculinity. *Personality and Social Psychology Bulletin, 37,* 601–613.

Burton, D. (2003). Male adolescents: Sexual victimization and subsequent sexual abuse. *Child & Adolescent Social Work Journal, 20,* 277–296.

Burton, C., & Plaks, J. (2013). Lay theories of personality as cornerstones of meaning. In K. Markman, T. Proulx, & M. Lindberg,(Eds.). *The psychology of meaning.* (pp. 115–133). Washington, DC, USA: American Psychological Association.

Bushman, B. (2002). Does venting anger feed or extinguish the flame? Catharsis rumination, distraction, anger and aggressive responding. *Personality & Social Psychology Bulletin, 28,* 724–731.

Bushman, B. J. (1995). Moderating role of trait aggressiveness in the effects of violent media on aggression. *Journal of Personality and Social Psychology, 69,* 950–960.

Bushman, B., & Cantor, J. (2003). Media ratings for violence and sex: Implications for policymakers and parents. *American Psychologist, 58,* 130–141.

Bushman, B., & Huesmann, L. (2012). Effects of violent media on aggression. In D. Singer & J. Singer (Eds). *Handbook of children and the media* (2nd edition). (pp. 231–248). Thousand Oaks, CA, USA: Sage Publications, Inc.

Busnel, M. C., Granier-Deferre, C., & Lecanuet, J. P. (1992). Fetal audition. *Annals of the New York Academy of Sciences, 662,* 118–134.

Buss, D., Larsen, R., Westen, D., & Semmelroth, J. (1992). Sex differences in jealousy: Evolution, physiology, and psychology. *Psychological Science, 3,* 251–255.

Buss, D. M. (1984). Marital assortment for personality dispositions: Assessment with three different data sources. *Behavioral Genetics, 14,* 111–123.

Buss, D. M. (1994). The strategies of human mating. *American Scientist, 82,* 238–249.

Buss, D. M. (1999). *Evolutionary psychology: The new science of the mind.* Boston: Allyn & Bacon.

Buss, D. M. (2000a). *The dangerous passion: Why jealousy is as necessary as sex and love.* New York: Free Press.

Buss, D. M. (2000b). Desires in human mating. *Annals of the New York Academy of Sciences, 907,* 39–49.

Buss, D. M., Abbott, M., Angleitner, A., Asherian, A., Biaggio, A., Blanco-Villasenor, A., et al. (1990). International preferences in selecting mates: A study of 37 cultures. *Journal of Cross-Cultural Psychology, 21,* 5–47.

Buss, D. M., Shackelford, T., Kirkpatrick, L., & Larsen, R. (2001). A half century of mate preferences: The cultural evolution of values. *Journal of Marriage and the Family, 63,* 491–503.

Buss, D., & Shackelford, T. (2008). Attractive women want it all: Good genes, economic investment, parenting proclivities, and emotional commitment. *Evolutionary Psychology, 6,* 134–146.

Buss, D., & Shackelford, T. (2008). Attractive women want it all: Good genes, economic investment, parenting proclivities, and emotional commitment. *Evolutionary Psychology, 6,* 134–146.

Bussey, K., & Bandura, A. (1999). Social cognitive theory of gender development and differentiation. *Psychological Review, 106, 676–713.*

Butcher, J. N., & Graham, J. R. (1989). *Topics in MMPI–2 interpretation.* Minneapolis: Department of Psychology, University of Minnesota.

Butcher, J. N., Dahlstrom, W. G., Graham, J. R., Tellegen, A., & Kaemmer, B. (1989). *Manual for the restandardized Minnesota Multiphasic Personality Inventory: MMPI–2. An administrative and interpretive guide.* Minneapolis: University of Minnesota Press.

Butler, L., Waelde, L., Hastings, T., Chen, X., Symons, B., Marshall, J., Kaufman, A., & Nagy, T. (2008). Meditation with yoga, group therapy with hypnosis, and psychoeducation for long-term depressed mood: A randomized pilot trial. *Journal of Clinical Psychology, 64, 806–820.*

Byne, W. (1993). *Sexual orientation and brain structure: Adding up the evidence.* Paper presented at the annual meeting of the International Academy of Sex Research. Pacific Grove, CA.

Cabral, R., & Smith, T. (2011). Racial/ethnic matching of clients and therapists in mental health services: A meta-analytic review of preferences, perceptions, and outcomes. *Journal of Counseling Psychology, 58, 537–554.*

Caby'oglu, M., Ergene, N., & Tan, U. (2006). The mechanism of acupuncture and clinical applications. *International Journal of Neuroscience, 116, 115–125.*

Cahn, B., & Polich, J. (2006). Meditation states and traits: EEG, ERP, and neuroimaging studies. *Psychological Bulletin, 132, 180–211.*

Calhoun, S., & Dickerson Mayes, S. (2005). Processing speed in children with clinical disorders. *Psychology in the Schools, 42, 333–343.*

Calton, T., & Spandler, H. (2009). Minimal-medication approaches to treating schizophrenia. *Advances in Psychiatric Treatment, 15, 209–217.*

Camerer, C. (2005). Three cheers—psychological, theoretical, empirical—for loss aversion. *Journal of Marketing Research, 42, 129–133.*

Camp, D. S., Raymond, G. A., & Church, R. M. (1967). Temporal relationship between response and punishment. *Journal of Experimental Psychology, 74, 114–123.*

Campbell, F., & Ramey, C. (1994). Effects of early intervention on intellectual and academic achievement: A follow-up study of children from low-income families. *Child Development, 65, 684–698.*

Campbell, F., Pungello, E., Burchinal, M., Kainz, K., Pan, Y., Wasik, B., Barbarin, O., Sparling, J., & Ramey, C. (2012). Adult outcomes as a function of an early childhood educational program: An Abecedarian Project follow-up. *Developmental Psychology, 48, 1033–1043.*

Campbell, P., & Dhand, R. (2000). Obesity. *Nature, 404, 631.*

Cannon, T. D., Kaprio, J., Lönnqvist, J., Huttunen, M., & Koskenvuo, M. (1998). The genetic epidemiology of schizophrenia in a Finnish twin cohort: A population-based modeling study. *Archives of General Psychiatry, 55, 67–74.*

Cannon, W. B. (1927). The James-Lange theory of emotions: A critical examination as an alternative theory. *American Journal of Psychology, 39, 106–112.*

Cannon, W. B. (1929). *Bodily changes in pain, hunger, fear and rage* (2nd ed.). New York: Appleton.

Cannon, W. B. (1935). Stresses and strains of homeostasis. *American Journal of Public Health, 189, 1–14.*

Capel, B. (2000). The battle of the sexes. *Mechanisms of Development, 92, 89–103.*

Caramaschi, D., de Boer, S., & Koolhaas, J. (2008). Is hyper-aggressiveness associated with physiological hypoarousal? A comparative study on mouse lines selected for high and low aggressiveness. *Physiology & Behavior, 95, 591–598.*

Cardoso, S. H., de Mello, L. C., & Sabbatini, R. M. E. (2000). How nerve cells work. Retrieved June 10, 2007 from *http://www.cerebromente. org.br/n10/fundamentos/pot2_i.htm.org.br/cm/n09/fundamentos/ transmissao/voo_i.htm*

Carlat, D. J., Camargo, C. A., Jr., & Herzog, D. B. (1997). Eating disorders in males: A report on 135 patients. *American Journal of Psychiatry, 154, 1127–1132.*

Carlsson, I., Wendt, P. E., & Risberg, J. (2000). On the neurobiology of creativity. Differences in frontal activity between high and low creative subjects. *Neuropsychologia, 38, 873–885.*

Carnagey, N., & Anderson, C. (2004). Violent video game exposure and aggression: A literature review. *Minerva Psychiatrica, 45, 1–18.*

Carnagey, N., Anderson, C., & Bushman, B. (2007). The effect of video game violence on physiological desensitization to real-life violence. *Journal of Experimental Social Psychology, 43, 489–496.*

Carpenter, S. (2001). Sights unseen. *Monitor on Psychology, 32* [Electronic version]. Retrieved May 13, 2003, from *http://www.apa. org/monitor/apr01/blindness.html*

Carpentier, P., de Jong, C., Dijkstra, B., Verbrugge, C., & Krabbe, P. (2005). A controlled trial of methylphenidate in adults with attention deficit/hyperactivity disorder and substance use disorders. *Addiction, 100, 1868–1874.*

Carr, A. (2009). The effectiveness of family therapy and systemic interventions for child-focused problems. *Journal of Family Therapy, 31, 3–45.*

Carriba, P., Pardo, L., Parra-Damas, A., Lichtenstein, M., Saura, C., Pujol, A., Masgrau, R., & Galea, E. (2012). ATP and noradrenaline activate CREB in astrocytes via noncanonical Ca2_ and cyclic AMP independent pathways. *Glia, 60, 1330–1344.*

Carroll, M., & Perfect, T. (2002). Students' experiences of unconscious plagiarism: Did I beget or forget? In T., Perfect, & B. Schwartz (Eds.), *Applied metacognition* (pp. 146–166). New York: Cambridge University press.

Carskadon, M., Wolfson, A., Acebo, C., Tzischinsky, O., & Seifer, R. (1998). Adolescent sleep patterns, circadian timing, and sleepiness at a transition to early school days. *Sleep: Journal of Sleep Research & Sleep Medicine, 21, 871–881.*

Carson, R., Butcher, J., & Mineka, S. (2000). *Abnormal psychology and modern life* (11th ed.). Boston: Allyn & Bacon.

Carver, C. S., Pozo, C., Harris, S. D., Noriega, V., Scheier, M. F., Robinson, D. S., et al. (1993). How coping mediates the effect of optimism on distress: A study of women with early stage breast cancer. *Journal of Personality and Social Psychology, 65, 375–390.*

Cary, P. (2006). *The marijuana detection window.* Retrieved November 10, 2012, from http://www.ndci.org/sites/default/files/ndci/THC_ Detection_Window_0.pdf.

Casey, B. (2013). Individual and group differences in spatial ability. In D. Waller & L. Nadel (Eds). *Handbook of spatial cognition.* (pp. 117–134). Washington, DC, USA: American Psychological Association.

Cash, T. F., & Janda, L. H. (1984, December). The eye of the beholder. *Psychology Today,* 46–52.

Caspi, A., Lynam, D., Moffitt, T. E., & Silva, P. A. (1993). Unraveling girls' delinquency: Biological, dispositional, and contextual contributions to adolescent misbehavior. *Developmental Psychology, 29, 19–30.*

Cassell, M., Halperin, D., Shelton, J., & Stanton, D. (2006). Risk compensation: The Achilles' heel of innovations in HIV protection? *British Medical Journal, 332, 605–607.*

Castellini, G., Polito, C., Bolognesi, E., D'Argenio, A., Ginestroni, A., Mascalchi, M., Pellicanò, G., Mazzoni, L.N., Rotella, F., Faravelli, C., Pupi, A., & Ricca, V. (2013). Looking at my body. Similarities and differences between anorexia nervosa patients and controls in body image visual processing. *European Psychiatry* [in press].

Cattell, H., & Mead, A. (2008). The sixteen personality factor questionnaire (16PF). In G. Boyle, G. Matthews, & D. Saklofske (Eds.). *The Sage handbook of personality theory and assessment, Vol. 2: Personality measurement and testing.* (pp. 135–159). Thousand Oaks, CA, USA: Sage Publications.

Cattell, R. B. (1950). *Personality: A systematic, theoretical, and factual study.* New York: McGraw-Hill.

Cattell, R. B., Eber, H. W., & Tatsuoka, M. M. (1977). *Handbook for the 16 personality factor questionnaire.* Champaign, IL, USA: Institute of Personality and Ability Testing.

Cattell, R., & Schuerger, J. (2003). *Essentials of 16PF assessment.* New York: John Wiley & Sons.

Cattell, R., Cattell, A., & Cattell, H. (2003). *The 16PF select manual.* Champaign, IL: Institute for Personality and Ability Testing.

Cavanaugh, S. (2004). The sexual debut of girls in early adolescence: The intersection of race, pubertal timing, and friendship group. *Journal of Research on Adolescence, 14,* 285–312.

Centers for Disease Control (CDC). (2008). *About the childhood lead poisoning prevention program.* Retrieved May 8, 2009 from *http://www.cdc.gov/nceh/lead/about/program.htm.*

Centers for Disease Control (CDC). (2008). *Youth risk behavior surveillance: United States, 2007.* Retrieved February 27, 2010 from *http://www.cdc.gov/mmwr/PDF/ss/ss5704.pdf.*

Centers for Disease Control (CDC). (2009a). *Sexually transmitted diseases surveillance: National Profile.* Retrieved March 12, 2010 from *http://www.cdc.gov/std/stats08/surv2008-NationalProfile.pdf.*

Centers for Disease Control (CDC) (2012a). *HIV surveillance - Epidemiology of HIV infection (through 2010).* Retrieved January 7, 2013, from http://www.cdc.gov/hiv/topics/surveillance/resources/slides/general/index.htm

Centers for Disease Control (2012b). *Second-hand smoke facts.* Retrieved January 8, 2013, from http://www.cdc.gov/tobacco/data_statistics/fact_sheets/secondhand_smoke/general_facts/index.htm

Centers for Disease Control. (2012c). *Sexually transmitted disease surveillance 2011.* Retrieved January 8, 2013, from http://www.cdc.gov/std/stats11/Surv2011.pdf

Centers for Disease Control (2012d). *Genital herpes fact sheet.* Retrieved January 8, 2013, from http://www.cdc.gov/std/herpes/stdfact-herpes.htm

Centers for Disease Control (2012e). *Genital HPV infection fact sheet.* Retrieved January 8, 2013, from *http://www.cdc.gov/std/HPV/STDFact-HPV.htm*

Centers for Disease Control (2012f). *HIV surveillance report.* Retrieved January 8, 2013, from http://www.cdc.gov/hiv/surveillance/resources/reports/2010supp_vol17no3/pdf/hssr_vol_17_no_3.pdf#page=21

Centers for Disease Control and Prevention (CDC). (1999). *Physical activity and health.* Retrieved January 29, 2003, from *http://www.cdc.gov/needphp/sgr/ataglan.htm.*

Centers for Disease Control and Prevention (CDC). (2002). Nonfatal self-inflicted injuries treated in hospital emergency departments—United States, 2000. *Morbidity & Mortality Weekly Report, 51,* 436–438.

Centers for Disease Control and Prevention (CDC). (2006b). Growing stronger: Strength training for older adults. Retrieved July 7, 2006 from *http://www.cdc.gov/nccdphp/dnpa/physical/growing_stronger/index.htm.*

Centers for Disease Control and Prevention (CDC). (2006e). Quick stats: General information on alcohol use and health. Retrieved July 7, 2006 from *http://www.cdc.gov/alcohol/quickstats/general_info.htm.*

Chabris, C., & Simons, D. (2010). *The invisible gorilla: And other ways our intuitions deceive us.* New York, NY, USA: Crown Publishers/Random House.

Chaitow, L., & DeLany, J. (2002). *Clinical application of neuromuscular techniques.* London: Elsevier Science Limited.

Chamley, C., Carson, P., Randall, D., & Sandwell, M. (2005). *Developmental anatomy and physiology of children.* Edinburgh, Scotland, UK: Elsevier Churchill Livingstone.

Chamorro-Premuzic, T., & Furnham, A. (2003). Personality predicts academic performance: Evidence from two longitudinal university samples. *Journal of Research in Personality, 37,* 319–338.

Chan, J., Thomas, A., & Bulevich, J. (2009). Recalling a witnessed event increases eyewitness suggestibility: The reversed testing effect. *Psychological Science, 20,* 66–73.

Chang, F., & Burns, B. (2005). Attention in preschoolers: Associations with effortful control and motivation. *Child Development, 76,* 247–263.

Chao, R. (2001). Extending research on the consequences of parenting style for Chinese Americans and European Americans. *Child Development, 72,* 1832–1843.

Chao, R., & Aque, C. (2009). Interpretations of parental control by Asian immigrant and European American youth. *Journal of Family Psychology, 23,* 342–354.

Chaplin, W. F., Philips, J. B., Brown, J. D., Clanton, N. R., & Stein, J. L. (2000). Handshaking, gender, personality, and first impressions. *Journal of Personality and Social Psychology, 19,* 110–117.

Charles, S., Mather, M., & Carstensen, L. (2003). Aging and emotional memory: The forgettable nature of negative images for older adults. *Journal of Experimental Psychology, 132,* 310–324.

Charness, N. (1989). Age and expertise: Responding to Talland's challenge. In L. W. Poon, D. C. Rubin, & B. A. Wilson (Eds.), *Everyday cognition in adulthood and old age* (pp. 437–456). New York: Cambridge University Press.

Chart, H., Grigorenko, E., & Sternberg, R. (2008). Identification: The Aurora battery. In J., Plucker & C. Callahan (Eds.), *Critical issues and practices in gifted education: What the research says* (pp. 281–301). Waco, TX: Prufrock Press.

Chase, W. G., & Simon, H. A. (1973). Perception in chess. *Cognitive Psychology, 4,* 55–81.

Chassin, L., Presson, C., Sherman, S., & Kim, K. (2003). Historical changes in cigarette smoking and smoking-related beliefs after 2 decades in a midwestern community. *Health Psychology, 22,* 347–353.

Chee, M., Tan, J., Zheng, H., Parimal, S., Weissman, D., Zagorodnov, V., & Dinges, D. (2008). Lapsing during sleep deprivation is associated with distributed changes in brain activation. *Journal of Neuroscience, 28,* 5519–5528.

Cherry, E. (1953). Some experiments on the recognition of speech with one and two ears. *Journal of the Acoustical Society of America, 25,* 975–979.

Chilosi, A., Cipriani, P., Bertuccelli, B., Pfanner, L., & Cioni, G. (2001). Early cognitive and communication development in children with focal brain lesions. *Journal of Child Neurology, 16,* 309–316.

Chiu, C., Yeh, Y., Ross, C., Lin, S., Huang, W., & Hwu, H. (2012). Recovered memory experience in a nonclinical sample is associated with dissociation rather than with aversive experiences. *Psychiatry Research, 197,* 265–269.

Cho, K. (2001). Chronic "jet lag" produces temporal lobe atrophy and spatial cognitive deficits. *Nature Neuroscience, 4,* 567–568.

Cho, K., Ennaceur, A., Cole, J., & Kook Suh, C. (2000). Chronic jet lag produces cognitive deficits. *Journal of Neuroscience, 20,* RC66.

Cho, S., Ku, J., Park, J., Han, K., Lee, H., Choi, Y., Jung, Y., Namkoong, K., Kim, J., Kim, I., Kim, S., & Shen, D. (2008). Development and verification of an alcohol craving-induction tool using virtual reality: Craving characteristics in social pressure situations. *CyberPsychology & Behavior, 11,* 302–309.

Choca, J. (2013). *The Rorschach Inkblot Test: An interpretive guide for clinicians.* Washington, DC, USA: American Psychological Association.

Choi, H., & Smith, S. (2005). Incubatin and the resolution of tip-of-the-tongue states. *Journal of General Psychology, 132,* 365–376.

Choi, I., Dalal, R., Kim-Prieto, C., & Park, H. (2003). Culture and judgment of causal relevance. *Journal of Personality & Social Psychology, 84,* 46–59.

Choi, J., & Silverman, I. (2002). The relationship between testosterone and route-learning strategies in humans. *Brain & Cognition, 50,* 116–120.

Chollar, S. (1989). Conversation with the dolphins. *Psychology Today, 23,* 52–57.

Chomsky, N. (1957). *Syntactic structures.* The Hague: Mouton.

Chomsky, N. (1968). *Language and mind.* New York: Harcourt, Brace & World.

Chowdhury, R., Ferrier, I., & Thompson, J. (2003). Cognitive dysfunction in bipolar disorder. *Current Opinion in Psychiatry, 16,* 7–12.

Christensen, A., Atkins, D., Berns, S., Wheeler, J., Baucom, D., & Simpson, L. (2004). Traditional versus integrative behavioral couple therapy for significantly and chronically distressed married couples. *Journal of Consulting and Clinical Psychology, 72,* 176–191.

Christianson, S-Å. (1992). Emotional stress and eyewitness memory: A critical review. *Psychological Bulletin, 112,* 284–309.

Church, R. M. (1963). The varied effects of punishment on behavior. *Psychological Review, 70,* 369–402.

Cialdini, R. B., Cacioppo, J. T., Basset, R., & Miller, J. A. (1978). Low-ball procedure for producing compliance: Commitment then cost. *Journal of Personality and Social Psychology, 36,* 463–476.

Cialdini, R. B., Vincent, J. E., Lewis, S. K., Catalan, J., Wheeler, D., & Darby, B. L. (1975). Reciprocal concessions procedure for inducing compliance: The door-in-the-face technique. *Journal of Personality and Social Psychology, 31,* 206–215.

Clark, D., & Beck, A. (2010). *Cognitive therapy of anxiety disorders: Science and practice.* New York: Guilford Press.

Clark, L., Bechara, A., Damasio, H., Atiken, M., Sahakian, B., & Robbins, T. (2008). Differential effects of insular and ventromedial prefrontal cortex lesions on risky decision-making. *Brain: A Journal of Neurology, 131,* 1311–1322.

Clark, L., Watson, D., & Reynolds, S. (1995). Ciagnosis and classification of psychopathology: Challenges to the current system and future directions. *Annual Review of Psychology, 46,* 121–153.

Clark, M. (2009). Suppose Freud had chosen Orestes instead. *Journal of Analytical Psychology, 54,* 233–252.

Clay, R. (2003). Researchers replace midlife myths with facts. *APA Monitor on Psychology, 34,* 36.

Cloninger, C. R., Sigvardsson, S., Bohman, M., & von Knorring, A. L. (1982). Predispositions to petty criminality in Swedish adoptees, II. Cross-fostering analysis of gene-environment interaction. *Archives of General Psychiatry, 39,* 1242–1249.

Cloos, J., & Ferreira, V. (2009). Current use of benzodiazepines in anxiety disorders. *Current Opinion in Psychiatry, 22,* 90–95.

CNN.com. (February 16, 2003). *Fatal shooting caught on tape.* Retrieved February 17, 2003, from *http://www.cnn.com/2003/US/South/02/16/gas.shooting.ap/index.html.*

Codina, C., Pascalis, O., Mody, C., Toomey, P., Rose, J., Gummer, L., & Buckley, D. (2011). Visual advantage in deaf adults linked to retinal changes. *PLoS ONE, 6,* e20417.

Cohen, H., & Amerine-Dickens, M., & Smith, T. (2006). Early intensive behavioral treatment: Replication of the UCLA model in a community setting. *Journal of Developmental & Behavioral Pediatrics, 27,* S145–S155.

Cohen, R., & Stussman, B. (2010). *Health information technology use among men and women aged 18–64: Early release of estimates from the National Health Interview Survey, January–June 2009.* Retrieved March 12, 2010 from *http://www.cdc.gov/nchs/data/hestat/healthinfo2009/healthinfo2009.htm.*

Cohen, S., Doyle, W. J., Skoner, D. P., Rabin, B. S., & Gwaltney, J. M., Jr. (1997). Social ties and susceptibility to the common cold. *Journal of the American Medical Association, 277,* 1940–1944.

Cohen, S., Doyle, W., & Baum, A. (2006). Socioeconomic status is associated with stress hormones. *Psychosomatic Medicine, 68,* 414–420.

Cohen, S., Janicki-Deverts, D., Doyle, W., Miller, G., Frank, E., Rabin, B., & Turner, R. (2012). Chronic stress, glucocorticoid receptor resistance, inflammation, and disease risk. *Proceedings of the National Academies of Science, 109,* 5995–5999.

Colburn, H., Shinn-Cunningham, B., Kidd, G., & Durlach, N. (2006). The perceptual consequences of binaural hearing. *International Journal of Audiology, 45,* S34-S44.

Colby, A., Kohlberg, L., Gibbs, J., & Lieberman, M. (1983). A longitudinal study of moral judgment. *Monographs of the Society for Research in Child Development, 48*(1–2, Serial No. 200).

Cole, R., Smith, J., Alcala, Y., Elliott, J., & Kripke, D. (2002). Bright-light mask treatment of delayed sleep phase syndrome. *Journal of Biological Rhythms, 17,* 89–101.

Collaer, M. L., & Hines, M. (1995). Human behavioral sex differences: A role for gonadal hormones during early development. *Psychological Bulletin, 118,* 55–107.

Colwell, J., & Payne, J. (2000). Negative correlates of computer game play in adolescents. *British Journal of Psychology, 91*(Pt. 3), 295–310.

Condon, W. S., & Sander, L. W. (1974). Neonatal movement is synchronized with adult speech: Interactional participation and language acquisition. *Science, 183,* 99–101.

Coney, J., & Fitzgerald, J. (2000). Gender differences in the recognition of laterally presented affective nouns. Cognition and Emotion, 14, 325–339.

Conger, A., Dygdon, J., & Rollock, D. (2012). Conditioned emotional responses in racial prejudice. *Ethnic and Racial Studies, 35,* 298–319.

Consumer *Reports.* (1995, November) Mental health: Does therapy help?, 734–739.

Consumer Reports. (2012). *10 surprising dangers of vitamins and supplements.* Retrieved January 8, 2013, from http://www.consumerreports.org/cro/magazine/2012/09/10-surprising-dangers-of-vitamins-and-supplements/index.htm

Corenblum, B., & Meissner, C. (2006). Recognition of faces of ingroup and outgroup children and adults. *Journal of Experimental Child Psychology, 93,* 187–206.

Corker, K., Oswald, F., & Donnellan, M. (2012). Conscientiousness in the classroom: A process explanation. *Journal of Personality, 80,* 995–1028.

Costa, P. T., Jr., & McCrae, R. R. (1985). *The NEO Personality Inventory.* Odessa, FL: Psychological Assessment Resources.

Costa, P., & McCrae, R. (2009). The five-factor model and the NEO Inventories. In J. Butcher (Ed.), *Oxford handbook of personality assessment,* Oxford Library of Psychology (pp. 299–322). New York: Oxford University Press.

Courage, M. L., & Adams, R. J. (1990). Visual acuity assessment from birth to three years using the acuity card procedures: Cross-sectional and longitudinal samples. *Optometry and Vision Science, 67,* 713–718.

Coyne, S., Archer, J., & Eslea, M. (2004). Cruel intentions on television and in real life: Can viewing indirect aggression increase viewers' subsequent indirect aggression? *Journal of Experimental Child Psychology, 88,* 234–253.

Craighead, W., Craighead, L., Ritschel, L., & Zagoloff, A. (2013). Behavior therapy and cognitive-behavioral therapy. In G. Stricker, T. Widiger, & I. Weiner. (Eds). *Handbook of psychology, Vol. 8: Clinical psychology* (2nd ed.). (pp. 291–319). Hoboken, NJ, USA: John Wiley & Sons, Inc.

Craik, F., & Bialystok, E. (2010). Bilingualism and aging: Costs and benefits. In L., Bäckman & L. Nyberg (Eds.), *Memory, aging and the brain: A Festschrift in honour of Lars-Göran Nilsson* (pp. 115–131). New York: Psychology Press.

Craik, F. I. M., & Lockhart, R. S. (1972). Levels of processing: A framework for memory research. *Journal of Verbal Learning and Verbal Behavior, 11,* 671–684.

Craik, F. I. M., & Tulving, E. (1975). Depth of processing and the retention of words in episodic memory. *Journal of Experimental Psychology: General, 104,* 268–294.

Crano, W., & Prislin, R. (2006). Attitudes and persuasion. *Annual Review of Psychology, 57,* 345–374.

Crits-Christoph, P., Gibbons, M., Losardo, D., Narducci, J., Schamberger, M., & Gallop, R. (2004). Who benefits from brief psychodynamic therapy for generalized anxiety disorder? *Canadian Journal of Psychoanalysis, 12,* 301–324.

Crits-Christoph, P., Gibbons, M., Ring-Kurtz, S., Gallop, R., Stirman, S., Present, J., Temes, C., & Goldstein, L. (2008). Changes in positive quality of life over the course of psychotherapy. *Psychotherapy, Theory, Research, Practice, Training, 45,* 419–430.

Crombag, H., & Robinson, T. (2004). Drugs, environment, brain, and behavior. *Current Directions in Psychological Science, 13,* 107–111.

Crone, E., Wendelken, C., Donohue, S., van Leijenhorst, L., & Bunge, S. (2006). Neurocognitive development of the ability to manipulate information in working memory. *Proceedings for the National Academy of Sciences, 103,* 9315–9320.

Crowder, R. G. (1992) Sensory memory. In L. R. Squire (Ed.), *Encyclopedia of learning and memory.* New York: Macmillan.

Crowther, J., Kichler, J., Shewood, N., & Kuhnert, M. (2002). The role of familial factors in bulimia nervosa. *Eating Disorders: The Journal of Treatment & Prevention, 10,* 141–151.

Cruess, D., Localio, A., Platt, A., Brensinger, C., Christie, J., Gross, R., Parker, C., Price, M., Metlay, J., Cohen, A., Newcomb, C., Strom, B., & Kimmel, S. (2010). Patient attitudinal and behavioral factors associated with warfarin non-adherence at outpatient anticoagulation clinics. *International Journal of Behavioral Medicine, 17,* 33–42.

Csikszentmihalyi, M. (1996, July/August). The creative personality. *Psychology Today, 29,* 36–40.

Csikszentmihalyi et al., 2005

Cui, X-J., & Vaillant, G. E. (1996). Antecedents and consequences of negative life events in adulthood: A longitudinal study. *American Journal of Psychiatry, 153,* 21–26.

Cunningham, M. R., Roberts, A. R., Barbee, A. P., Druen, P. B., & Wu, C-H. (1995). "Their ideas of beauty are, on the whole, the same as ours": Consistency and variability in the cross-cultural perception of female physical attractiveness. *Journal of Personality and Social Psychology, 68,* 261–279.

Cummings, H., & Vandewater, E. (2007). Relation of adolescent video game play to time spent in other activities. *Archives of Pediatrics & Adolescent Medicine, 161,* 684–689.

Cupach, W. R., & Canary, D. J. (1995). Managing conflict and anger: Investigating the sex stereotype hypothesis. In P. J. Kalbfleisch & M. J. Cody (Eds.), *Gender, power, and communication in human relationships* (pp. 233–252). Hillsdale, NJ: Erlbaum.

Curci, A. (2009). Measurement issues in the study of flashbulb memory. In O., Luminet & A. Curci (Eds.), *Flashbulb memories: New issues and perspectives* (pp. 13–32). New York: Psychology Press.

Cyranowski, J. M., Frand, E., Young, E., & Shear, M. K. (2000). Adolescent onset of the gender difference in lifetime rates of major depression. *Archives of General Psychiatry, 57,* 21–27.

D'Azevedo, W. A. (1982). Tribal history in Liberia. In U. Neisser (Ed.), *Memory observed: Remembering in natural contexts* (258-268). San Francisco: W. H. Freeman.

Dadds., M., Fraser, J., Frost, A., & Hawes, D. (2005). Disentangling the underlying dimensions of psychopathy and conduct problems in childhood: A community study. *Journal of Consulting and Clinical Psychology, 73,* 400–410.

Dahloef, P., Norlin-Bagge, E., Hedner, J., Ejnell, H., Hetta, J., & Haellstroem, T. (2002). Improvement in neuropsychological performance following surgical treatment for obstructive sleep apnea syndrome. *Acta Oto-Laryngologica, 122,* 86–91.

Dale, N., & Kandel, E. R. (1990). Facilitatory and inhibitory transmitters modulate spontaneous transmitter release at cultured *Aplysia* sensorimotor synapses. *Journal of Physiology, 421,* 203–222.

Daley, T., Whaley, S,. Sigman, M., Espinosa, M., & Neumann, C. (2003). IQ on the rise: The Flynn Effect in rural Kenyan children. *Psychological Science, 14,* 215–219.

Dalgleish, T. (2004). The emotional brain. *Nature Neuroscience Reviews, 5,* 582–589.

Dalgleish, T., Dunn, B., & Mobbs, D. (2009). Affective neuroscience: Past, present, and future. *Emotion Review, 1,* 355–368.

Dalle Grave, R., Calugi, S., Doll, H., & Fairburn, C. (2013). Enhanced cognitive behavior therapy for adolescents with anorexia nervosa: An alternative to family therapy? *51,* R9–R12.

Damasio, A. (1995). On some functions of the human prefrontal cortex. *Annals of the National Academy of Sciences, 769,* 241–251.

Damasio, A. R., Grabowski, T. J., Bechara, A., Damasio, H., Ponto, L. L. B., Parvizi, J. and Hichwa, R. D. (2000). "Subcortical and Cortical Brain Activity during the Feeling of Self-Generated Emotions." *Nature Neuroscience, 3* (10), 1049–1056.

Dandy, J., & Nettelbeck, T. (2002). The relationship between IQ, homework, aspirations and academic achievement for Chinese, Vietnamese and Anglo-Celtic Australian school children. *Educational Psychology, 22,* 267–276.

Danforth, L., Olle, C., & Wester, S. (2012). *Gender-sensitive therapy with male veterans: An integration of recent research and theory.* Paper presented at the annual meeting of the American Psychological Association. Orlando, FL, USA.

Dang-Vu, T., Schabus, M., Desseilles, M., Schwartz, S., & Maquet, P. (2007). Neuroimaging of REM sleep and dreaming. In D. Barrett & P. McNamara (Eds.), *The new science of dreaming: Volume 1. Biological aspects* (pp. 95–113). Westport, CT: Praeger Publishers.

Danielides, V., Katotomichelakis, M., Balatsouras, D., Riga, M., Tripsianis, G., Simopoulou, M., & Nikolettos, N. (2009). Improvement of olfaction after endoscopic sinus surgery in smokers and nonsmokers. *Annals of Otology, Rhinology, & Laryngology, 118,* 13–20.

Dantzker, M., & Eisenman, R. (2003). Sexual attitudes among Hispanic college students: Differences between males and females. *International Journal of Adolescence & Youth, 11,* 79–89.

Darley, J. M., & Latané, B. (1968a). Bystander intervention in emergencies: Diffusion of responsibility. *Journal of Personality and Social Psychology, 8,* 377–383.

Darley, J. M., & Latané, B. (1968b, December). When will people help in a crisis? *Psychology Today*, 54–57, 70–71.

Darwin, C. (1872/1965). *The expression of emotion in man and animals.* Chicago: University of Chicago Press. (Original work published 1872).

Dasen, P. R. (1994). Culture and cognitive development from a Piagetian perspective. In W. J. Lonner & R. Malpass (Eds.), *Psychology and culture* (pp. 145–149). Boston: Allyn & Bacon.

Dattilio, F. (2010). *Cognitive-behavioral therapy with couples and families: A comprehensive guide for clinicians.* New York: Guilford Press.

Davalos, D., Kisley, M., & Ross, R. (2002). Deficits in auditory and visual temporal perception in schizophrenia. *Cognitive Neuropsychiatry, 7,* 273–282.

Davidson, J. R. T. (1997). Use of benzodiazepines in panic disorder. *Journal of Clinical Psychiatry, 58*(2, Suppl.), 26–28.

Davies, L. (2003). Singlehood: Transitions within a gendered world. *Canadian Journal on Aging, 22,* 343–352.

Davis, S., Butcher, S. P., & Morris, R. G. M. (1992). The NMDA receptor antagonist D-2-amino-5-phosphonopentanoate (D-AP5) impairs spatial learning and LTP in vivo at intracerebral concentrations comparable to those that block LTP in vitro. *Journal of Neuroscience, 12,* 21–34.

Dawood, K., Bailey, J., & Martin, N. (2009). Genetic and environmental influences on sexual orientation. In Y. Kim (Ed.) *Handbook of behavior genetics.* (pp. 269–279). New York, NY, USA: Springer Science + Business Media.

Day, S., & Schneider, P. (2002). Psychotherapy using distance technology: A comparison of face-to-face, video, and audio treatment. *Journal of Counseling Psychology, 49,* 499–503.

Dayan, P., & Huys, Q. Serotonin, inhibition, and negative mood. *Public Library of Science: Computational Biology.* Retrieved July 26, 2009, from *http://www.ploscompbiol.org/article/info:doi/10.1371/journal.pcbi.0040004.*

De Brito, S., Mechelli, A., Wilke, M., Laurens, K., Jones, A., Barker, G., Hodgins, S., & Viding, E. (2009). Size matters: Increased grey matter in boys with conduct problems and callous-unemotional traits. *Brain: A Journal of Neurology, 132,* 843–852.

De Bruin, E., Rowson, M., Van Buren, L., Rycroft, J., & Owen, G. (2011). Black tea improves attention and self-reported alertness. *Appetite, 56,* 235–240.

Deese, J. (1959). On the prediction of occurrence of particular verbal intrusions in immediate recall. *Journal of Experimental Psychology, 58,* 17–22.

de Groot, E., Verheul, R., & Trijsburg, R. (2008). An integrative perspective on psychotherapeutic treatments for borderline personality disorder. *Journal of Personality Disorders, 22,* 332–352.

de Lacoste, M., Horvath, D., & Woodward, J. (1991). Possible sex differences in the developing human fetal brain. *Journal of Clinical and Experimental Neuropsychology, 13,* 831.

Dell'Osso, B., Glick, I., Bladwin, D., & Altamura, A. (2013). Can long-term outcomes be improved by shortening the duration of untreated illness in psychiatric disorders? A conceptual framework. *Psychopathology, 46,* 14–21.

De Martino, B., Kumaran, O., Seymour, B., & Dolan, R. (2006). Frames, biases, and rational decision-making in the human brain. *Science, 313,* 684–687.

de Mello, M., Esteves, M., Pires, D., Santos, L., Bittencourt, R., & Tufik, S. (2008). Relationship between Brazilian airline pilot errors and time of day. *Brazilian Journal of Medical and Biological Research, 41,* 1129–1131.

De Raad, B., & Kokkonen, M. (2000). Traits and emotions: A review of their structure and management. *European Journal of Personality, 14,* 477–496.

De Roo, M., Klauser, P., Muller, D., & Sheng, M. (2008). LTP promotes a selective long-term stabilization and clustering of dendritic spines. *Public Library of Science: Biology, 6,* e219.

de Voogd, J., Sanderman, R., & Coyne, J. (2012). A meta-analysis of spurious associations between type D personality and cardiovascular disease endpoints. *Annals of Behavioral Medicine, 44,* 136–137.

De Vos, S. (1990). Extended family living among older people in six Latin American countries. *Journal of Gerontology: Social Sciences, 45,* S87–S94.

Deacon, B., & Olatunji, B. (2007). Specificity of disgust sensitivity in the prediction of behavioral avoidance in contamination fear. *Behaviour Research and Therapy, 45,* 2110–2120.

Deinzer, R., Kleineidam, C., Stiller-Winkler, R., Idel, H., & Bach, D. (2000). Prolonged reduction of salivary immunoglobulin (sIgA) after a major academic exam. *International Journal of Psychophysiology, 37,* 219–232.

Delgado, J. M. R., & Anand, B. K. (1953). Increased food intake induced by electrical stimulation of the lateral hypothalamus. *American Journal of Physiology, 172,* 162–168.

DeLongis, A., Folkman, S., & Lazarus, R. S. (1988). The impact of daily stress on health and mood: Psychological and social resources as mediators. *Journal of Personality and Social Psychology, 54,* 486–495.

Dement, W. (1974). *Some must watch while some must sleep.* Oxford, England, UK: W. H. Freeman.

Denollet, J. (1997). Personality, emotional distress and coronary heart disease. *European Journal of Personality, 11,* 343–357.

DePrince, A., & Freyd, J. (2004). Forgetting trauma stimuli. *Psychological Science, 15,* 488–492.

Derebery, M., Vermiglio, A., Berliner, K., Potthoff, M., & Holguin, K. (2012). Facing the music: Pre- and postconcert assessment of hearing in teenagers. *Otology & Neurology, 33,* 1136–1141.

Desler, M., Wehrle, R., Spoormaker, V., Koch, S., Holsboer, F., Steiger, A., Obrig, H., Samann, P., & Czisch, M. (2012). Neural correlates of dream lucidity obtained from contrasting lucid versus non-lucid REM sleep: A combined EEG/fMRI case study. *Sleep: Journal of Sleep and Sleep Disorders Research, 35,* 1017–1020.

DeSpelder, L., & Strickland, A. (1983). *The last dance: Encountering death and dying.* Palo Alto, CA: Mayfield.

Devine, P. G. (1989). Stereotypes and prejudice: Their automatic and controlled components. *Journal of Personality and Social Psychology, 56,* 5–18.

Dewsbury, D. A. (2000). Introduction: Snapshots of psychology circa 1900. *American Psychologist, 55,* 255–259.

DeYoung, C., Hirsch, J., Shane, M., Papademetris, X., Rajeevan, N., & Gray, J. (2010). Testing predictions from personality neuroscience: Brain structure and the Big Five. *Psychological Science, 21,* 820–828.

DeYoung, C., Peterson, J., & Higgins, D. (2002). Higher-order factors of the Big Five predict conformity: Are there neuroses of health? *Personality & Individual Differences, 33,* 533–552.

Dhar, V., & Chang, E. (2009). Does chatter matter: The impact of user-generated content on music sales. *Journal of Interactive Marketing, 23,* 300–307.

Di Fabio, A., & Palazzeschi, L. (2009). An in-depth look at scholastic success: Fluid intelligence, personality traits or emotional intelligence? *Personality and Individual Differences, 46,* 581–585.

Diaper, A., & Hindmarch, I. (2005). Sleep disturbance and its management in older patients. In S. Curran & R. Bullock (Eds.), *Practical old age psychopharmacology* (pp. 177–194). Oxon, Oxford, United Kingdom: Radcliffe Publishing.

Dickens, W., & Flynn, R. (2001). Heritability estimates versus large environmental effects: The IQ paradox resolved. *Psychological Review, 108,* 346–369.

Diefendorff, J., & Chandler, M. (2011). Motivating employees. In S. Zedeck (Ed.) *APA handbook of industrial and organizational psychology, Vol. 3: Maintaining, expanding, and contracting the organization.* (pp. 65–135) Washington, DC, USA: American Psychological Association.

Diefendorff, J., & Richard, E. (2003). Antecedents and consequences of emotional display rule perceptions. *Journal of Applied Psychology, 88,* 284–294.

Dijkstra, M., Buijtels, H., & van Raaij, W. (2005). Separate and joint effects of medium type on consumer response: A comparison of television, print, and the Internet. *Journal of Business Research, 58,* 2005.

Dillard, J., & Anderson, J. (2004). The role of fear in persuasion. *Psychology & Marketing, 21,* 909–926.

Dilorio, C., McCarty, F., DePadilla, L., Resnicow, K., Holstad, M., Yeager, k., Sharma, S., Morisky, D., & Lundberg, B. (2009). Adherence to antiretroviral medication regimens: A test of a psychosocial model. *AIDS and Behavior, 13,* 10–22.

Din-Dzietham, R., Nembhard, W., Collins, R., & Davis, S. (2004). Perceived stress following race-based discrimination at work is associated with hypertension in African-Americans. *Social Science & Medicine, 58,* 449–461.

Dion, K., Berscheid, E., & Walster, E. (1972). What is beautiful is good. *Journal of Personality and Social Psychology, 24,* 285–290.

Dobson, R., & Baird, T. (2006, May 28). "Women learn to play it like a man." *Timesonline.co.uk* Retrieved March 2, 2010 from *http://www.timesonline.co.uk/article/0,,2089-2200093.html*

Dodson, C. S., Koutstaal, W., & Schacter, D. L. (2000). Escape from illusion: Reducing false memories. *Trends in Cognitive Sciences, 4,* 391–397.

Doghramji, K., Brainard, G., & Balaicuis, J. (2010). Sleep and sleep disorders. In D. Monti & B. Beitman (Eds.), *Integrative psychiatry.* Weil integrative medicine library (pp. 195–239). New York: Oxford University Press.

Dohanich, G. (2003). Ovarian steroids and cognitive function. *Current Directions in Psychological Science, 12,* 57–61.

Doherty, W., & McDaniel, S. (2010). History. In W., Doherty, & S. McDaniel (Eds.), *Family therapy: Theories of psychotherapy* (pp. 5–27). Washington, DC: American Psychological Association.

Dohrenwend, B. (2006). Inventorying stressful life events as risk factors for psychopathology: Toward resolution of the problem of intracategory variability. *Psychological Bulletin, 132,* 477–495.

Dollard, J., Doob, L. W., Miller, N., Mowrer, O. H., & Sears, R. R. (1939). *Frustration and aggression.* New Haven: Yale University Press.

Domjan, M. (2005). Pavlovian conditioning: A functional perspective. *Annual Review of Psychology, 56,* 179–206.

Doob, L. W., & Sears, R. R. (1939). Factors determining substitute behavior and the overt expression of aggression. *Journal of Abnormal and Social Psychology, 34,* 293–313.

Downing, P., Jiang, Y., Shuman, M., & Kanwisher, N. (2001). A cortical area selective for visual processing of the human body. *Science, 293,* 2470–2473.

Doyle, J. A., & Paludi, M. A. (1995). *Sex and gender* (3rd ed.). Madison, WI: Brown & Benchmark.

Drachman, D. (2005). Do we have brain to spare? *Neurology, 64,* 2004–2005.

Draper, J. (2011). *Teratology and drug use during pregnancy.* Retrieved December 16, 2012, from http://emedicine.medscape.com/article/260725-overview#aw2aab6b4

Dreikurs, R. (1953). *Fundamentals of Adlerian psychology.* Chicago: Alfred Adler Institute.

Drevets, W. C., Price, J. L., Simpson, J. R., Jr., Todd, R. D., Reich, T., Vannier, M., et al. (1997). Subgenual prefrontal cortex abnormalities in mood disorders. *Nature, 386,* 824–827.

Drevets, W., Price, J., & Furey, M. (2008). Brain structural and functional abnormalities in mood disorders: Implications for neurocircuitry models of depression. *Brain Structure and Function, 213,* 93–118.

Drummond, S. P. A., Brown, G. G., Gillin, J. C., Stricker, J. L., Wong, E. C., & Buxton, R. B. (2000). Altered brain response to verbal learning following sleep deprivation. *Nature, 403,* 655–657.

Drummond, S., Brown, G., Salamat, J., & Gillin, J. (2004). Increasing task difficulty facilitates the cerebral compensatory response to total sleep deprivation. *Sleep: Journal of Sleep & Sleep Disorders Research, 27,* 445–451.

Dryden-Edwards., R. (2013). *Drug dependence and abuse.* Retrieved January 9, 2013, from http://www.emedicinehealth.com/drug_dependence_and_abuse/article_em.htm

Duckworth, A., & Seligman, M. (2006). Self-discipline gives girls the edge: Gender in self-discipline, grades, and achievement test scores. *Journal of Educational Psychology, 98,* 198–208.

Dudley, M., Goldney, R., & Hadzi-Pavlovic, D. (2010). Area dolescents dying by suicide taking SSRI antidepressants? A review of observational studies. *Australasian Psychiatry, 18,* 242–245.

Dunkel-Schetter, C., Feinstein, L. G., Taylor, S. E., & Falke, R. L. (1992). Patterns of coping with cancer. *Health Psychology, 11,* 79–87.

Dunn, J., Cutting, A., & Fisher, N. (2002). Old friends, new friends: Predictors of children's perspective on their friends at school. *Child Development, 73,* 621–635.

Durante, K., Griskevicius, V., Simpson, J., Cantú, S., & Li, N. (2012). Ovulation leads women to perceive sexy cads as good dads. *Journal of Personality and Social Psychology, 103,* 292–305.

Durbin, C., & Klein, D. (2006). Ten-year stability of personality disorders among outpatients with mood disorders. *Journal of Abnormal Psychology, 115,* 75–84.

Durex. (2008). *Sexual wellbeing survey 2007/2008.* Retrieved January 3, 2013, from http://www.durex.com/en-sg/sexualwellbeingsurvey/documents/swgspptv2.pdf

Duyme, M. (1988). School success and social class: An adoption study. *Developmental Psychology, 24,* 203–209.

Dwyer, K. & Davidson, M. (2012). Is public speaking really more feared than death? *Communication Researcher Reports, 29,* 99–107.

Eagly, A. H., Ashmore, R. D., Makhijani, M. G., & Longo, L. C. (1991). What is beautiful is good …: A meta-analytic review of research on the physical attractiveness stereotype. *Psychological Bulletin, 110,* 109–128.

Eagly, A. & Wood, W. (2012). Social role theory. In P. Van Lange, A. Kruglanski, & E. Higgins (Eds.) *Handbook of theories of social psychology* (Vol. 2). (pp. 458–476). Thousand Oaks, CA, USA: Sage Publications Ltd.

Earlandsson, L., & Eklund, M. (2003). The relationships among hassles and uplifts to experience of health in working women. *Women & Health, 38,* 19–37.

Eaton, D., Kann, L., Kinchen, S., Shanklin, S., Flint, K., Hawkins, J., Harris, W., Lowry, R., McManus, T., Chyen, D., Whittle, L., Lim, C., & Wechsler, H. (2012). Youth risk behavior surveillance-United States, 2011. *Morbidity and Mortality Weekly Report, 61,* 1–162.

Edwards, K., & Smith, E. E. (1996). A disconfirmation bias in the evaluation of arguments. *Journal of Personality and Social Psychology, 71,* 5–24.

Ehlers, C., Gizer, I., Vieten, C., Gilder, D., Stouffer, G., Lau, P., & Wilhelmsen, K. (2010). Cannabis dependence in the San Francisco family study: Age of onset of use, DSM-IV symptoms, withdrawal, and heritability. *Addictive Behaviors, 35,* 102–110.

Ehlers, C., Gizer, I., Gilder, D., & Yehuda, R. (2012). Lifetime history of traumatic events in an American Indian community sample: Heritability and relation to substance dependence, affective disorder, conduct disorder and PTSD. *Journal of Psychiatric Research, 47,* 155–161.

Eichenbaum, H., & Otto, T. (1993). LTP and memory: Can we enhance the connection? *Trends in Neurosciences, 16,* 163.

Eidelson, R., & Eidelson, J. (2003). Dangerous ideas. *American Psychologist, 58,* 182–192.

Eisold, B. (2005). Notes on lifelong resilience: Perceptual and personality factors implicit in the creation of a particular adaptive style. *Psychoanalytic Psychology, 22,* 411–425.

Ekman, P. (1972). Universals and cultural differences in facial expression of emotion. In J. Cole (Ed.), *Nebraska symposium on motivation* (Vol. 19). Lincoln: University of Nebraska Press.

Ekman, P. (1993). Facial expression and emotion. *American Psychologist, 48,* 384–392.

Ekman, P., & Friesen, W. V. (1975). *Unmasking the face: A guide to recognizing emotions from facial clues.* Englewood Cliffs, NJ: Prentice-Hall.

Ekman, P., Levenson, R. W., & Friesen, W. V. (1983). Autonomic nervous system activity distinguishes among emotions. *Science, 221,* 1208–1210.

Elal, G., Altug, A., Slade, P., & Tekcan, A. (2000). Factor structure of the Eating Attitudes Test (EAT) in a Turkish university sample. *Eating and Weight Disorders: Studies on Anorexia, Bulimia, and Obesity, 5,* 46–50.

Elkin, I., Gibbons, R. D., Shea, M. T., Sotsky, S. M., Watkins, J. T., Pikonis, P. A., & Hedeker, D. (1995). Initial severity and differential treatment outcome in the National Institute of Mental Health Treatment of Depression Collaborative Research Program. *Journal of Consulting and Clinical Psychology, 63,* 841–847.

Elkin, I., Shea, M. T., Watkins, J. T., et al. (1989). National Institute of Mental Health Treatment of Depression Collaborative Research Program: General effectiveness of treatments. *Archives of General Psychology, 46,* 971–982.

Elkind, D. (1967). Egocentrism in adolescence. *Child Development, 38,* 1025–1034.

Elkind, D. (1974). *Children and adolescents: Interpretive essays on Jean Piaget* (2nd ed.). New York: Oxford University Press.

Elliot, A. J., & Devine, P. G. (1994). On the motivational nature of cognitive dissonance: Dissonance as psychological discomfort. *Journal of Personality and Social Psychology, 67,* 382–394.

Elliot, A., Tracy, J., Pazda, A., & Beall, A. (2013). Red enhances women's attractiveness to men: First evidence suggesting universality. *Journal of Experimental Social Psychology, 49,* 165 –168.

Elliott, 2003

Elliott, J. (2003). Dynamic assessment in educational settings: Realising potential. *Educational Review, 55,* 15–32.

Ellis, A. (1961). *A guide to rational living.* Englewood Cliffs, NJ: Prentice-Hall.

Ellis, A. (1977). The basic clinical theory of rational-emotive therapy. In A. Ellis & R. Grieger (Eds.), *Handbook of rational-emotive therapy* (pp. 3–33). New York: Springer.

Ellis, A. (1993). Reflections on rational-emotive therapy. *Journal of Consulting and Clinical Psychology, 61,* 199–201.

Ellis, A. (2004a). Why I (really) became a therapist. *Journal of Rational-Emotive & Cognitive Behavior Therapy, 22,* 73–77.

Ellis, A. (2004b). Why rational-emotive behavior therapy is the most comprehensive and effective form of behavior therapy. *Journal of Rational-Emotive & Cognitive Behavior Therapy, 22,* 85–92.

Ellison, P., & Nelson, A. (2009). Brain development: Evidence of gender differences. In E., Fletcher-Janzen (Ed.), *The neuropsychology of women: Issues of diversity in clinical neuropsychology* (pp. 11–30). New York: Springer Science and Business Media.

Else-Quest, N., Hyde, J., Goldsmith, H., & Van Hulle, C. (2006). Gender differences in temperament: A meta-analysis. *Psychological Bulletin, 132,* 33–72.

Engen, T. (1982). *The perception of odors.* New York: Academic Press.

Epperson, C., Amin, Z., Ruparel, K., Gur, R., & Loughead, J. (2012). Interactive effects of estrogen and serotonin on brain activation during working memory and affective processing in menopausal women. *Psychoneuroendocrinology, 37,* 372–382.

Epstein, D., Willner-Reid, J., & Preston, K. (2010). Addiction and emotion: Theories, assessment techniques, and treatment implications. In J. Kassel (Ed.), *Substance abuse and emotion* (pp. 259–260). Washington, DC: American Psychological Association.

Equifax. (2006). *How lenders see you.* Retrieved November 29, 2006, from *https://www.econsumer.equifax.com/consumer/sitepage.ehtml?forward=cps_hlsysample*

Erdberg, P. (2012). Bridging the gap: Quantitative Rorschach approaches to psychodynamic constructs. *Rorschachiana, 33,* 100–107.

Erdogan, A., Kocabasoglu, N., Yalug, I., Ozbay, G., & Senturk, H. (2004). Management of marked liver enzyme increase during clozapine treatment: A case report and review of the literature. *International Journal of Psychiatry in Medicine, 34,* 83–89.

Erikson, E. (1968). *Identity, youth, and crisis.* New York: W. W. Norton & Company.

Erikson, E. H. (1980). *Identity and the life cycle.* New York: Norton.

Erikson, E., & Erikson, K. (1957). The confirmation of the delinquent. *Chicago Review, 10,* 15–23.

Erlenmeyer-Kimling, L., & Jarvik, L. F. (1963). Genetics and intelligence: A review. *Science, 142,* 1477–1479.

Eron, L. D. (1987). The development of aggressive behavior from the perspective of a developing behaviorism. *American Psychologist, 42,* 435–442.

Escorial, S., & Martin-Buro, C. (2012). The role of personality and intelligence in assortative mating. *Spanish Journal of Psychology, 15,* 680–687.

Espeland, M., Tindle, H., Bushnell, C., Jaramillo, S., Kuller, L., Margolis, K., Mysiw, W., Maldjian, J., Melhem, E., & Resnick, S., for the Women's Health Initiative Memory Study. (2009). Brain volumes, cognitive impairment, and conjugated equine estrogens. *Journals of Gerontology Series A: Biological Sciences and Medical Sciences, 64A,* 1243–1250.

Estes, W. K. (1994). *Classification and cognition.* New York: Oxford University Press.

Etcoff, N., Ekman, P., Magee, J., & Frank, M. (2000). Lie detection and language comprehension. *Nature, 405,* 139.

Evans, D., & Zarate, O. (2000). *Introducing evolutionary psychology.* New York: Totem Books.

Evans, G. W., & Lepore, S. J. (1993). Household crowding and social support: A quasiexperimental analysis. *Journal of Personality and Social Psychology, 65,* 308–316.

Evans, S., Huxley, P., Gately, C., Webber, M., Mears, A., Pajak, S., Medina, J., Kendall, T., & Katona, C. (2006). Mental health, burnout and job satisfaction among mental health social workers in England and Wales. *British Journal of Psychiatry, 188,* 75–80.

Everson, S. A., Goldberg, D. E., Kaplan, G. A., Cohen, R. D., Pukkala, E., Tuomilehto, J., et al. (1996). Hopelessness and risk of mortality and incidence of myocardial infarction and cancer. *Psychosomatic Medicine, 58,* 113–121.

Exner, J. E. (1993). *The Rorschach: A comprehensive system: Vol. 1. Basic foundations* (3rd ed.). New York: Wiley.

Eysenbach, G., Powell, J., Kuss, O., & Sa, E. (2002). Empirical studies of health information for consumers on the World Wide Web: A systematic review. *JAMA: Journal of the American Medical Association, 287,* 2691–2700.

Eysenck, H. J. (1990). Genetic and environmental contributions to individual differences: The three major dimensions of personality. *Journal of Personality, 58,* 245–261.

Eysenck, H. J. (1994). The outcome problem in psychotherapy: What have we learned? *Behaviour Research and Therapy, 32,* 477–495.

Eysenck, M., & Keane, M. (2010). *Cognitive psychology.* 6th ed. New York: Taylor & Francis.

Fagot, B. (1995). Observations of parent reactions to sex-stereotyped behavior: Age and sex effects. *Child Development, 62,* 617–628.

Falconnier, L. (2009). Socioeconomic status in the treatment of depression. *American Journal of Orthopsychiatry, 79,* 148–158.

Fallon, J., Irvine, D., & Shepherd, R. (2008). Cochlear implants and brain plasticity. *Hearing Research, 238,* 110–117.

Famighetti, R. (Ed.). (1997). *The world almanac and book of facts 1998.* Mahwah, NJ: World Almanac Books.

Fang, C., & Myers, H. (2001). The effects of racial stressors and hostility on cardiovascular reactivity in African American and Caucasian men. *Health Psychology, 20,* 64–70.

Fanous, A., Gardner, C., Prescott, C., Cancro, R., & Kendler, K. (2002). Neuroticism, major depression and gender: A population-based twin study. *Psychological Medicine, 32,* 719–728.

Fantz, R. L. (1961). The origin of form perception. *Scientific American, 204,* 66–72.

Farber, B., Khurgin-Bott, R., & Feldman, S. (2009). The benefits and risks of patient self-disclosure in the psychotherapy of women with a history of childhood sexual abuse. *Psychotherapy: Theory, Research, Practice, Training, 46,* 52–67.

Farde, L. (1996). The advantage of using positron emission tomography in drug research. *Trends in Neurosciences, 19,* 211–214.

Farrer, L. A., & Cupples, A. (1994). Estimating the probability for major gene Alzheimer disease. *American Journal of Human Genetics, 54,* 374–383.

Fasano, S., D'Antoni, A., Orban, P., Valjent, E., Putigano, E., Vara, H., Pizzorusso, T., Giusetto, M., Yoon, B., Soloway, P., Maldonado, R., Caboche, J., & Brambilla, R. (2009). Ras-guanine nucleotide-releasing factor 1 (Ras-GRF1) controls activation of extracellular signal-regulated kinase (ERK) signaling in the striatum and long-term behavioral responses to cocaine. *Biological Psychiatry, 66,* 758–768.

Fasotti, L. (2003). Executive function retraining. In J. Grafman, & I. Robertson (Eds.), *Handbook of Neuropsychology: Volume 9: Plasticity and Rehabilitation* (pp. 67–78). Amsterdam, The Netherlands: Elsevier Science.

Faunce, G. (2002). Eating disorders and attentional bias: A review. *Eating Disorders: The Journal of Treatment & Prevention, 10,* 125–139.

Fazio, R. H., & Williams, C. J. (1986). Attitude accessibility as a moderator of the attitude perception and attitude-behavior relations: An investigation of the 1984 presidential election. *Journal of Personality and Social Psychology, 51,* 505–514.

Federal Interagency Forum on Aging—Related Statistics (FIFARS). (2004). *Older Americans 2004: Key indicators of well-being.* Retrieved January 27, 2005, from *http://www.agingstats.gov/chartbook2004/default.htm*

Federal Interagency Forum on Aging Related Statistics (FIFARS). (2012). *Older Americans 2012: Key indicators of well-being.* Retrieved December 15, 2012, from http://www.agingstats.gov/agingstatsdotnet/main_site/default.aspx

Federman, R. (2012). Is bipolar II easier to live with than bipolar I? *Psychology Today.* Retrieved January 26, 2013, from http://www.psychologytoday.com/blog/bipolar-you/201210/is-bipolar-ii-easier-live-bipolar-i

Feeney, K. (2007). The legal bases for religious peyote use. In M. Winkelman, & T. Roberts (Eds.), *Psychedelic medicine: New evidence for hallucinogenic substances as treatments (Vol. 1)* (pp. 233–250). Westport, CT: Praeger Publishers.

Feingold, A. (1988). Matching for attractiveness in romantic partners and same-sex friends: A meta-analysis and theoretical critique. *Psychological Bulletin, 104,* 226–235.

Feguson, C., San Muguel, C., Garza, A., & Jerabeck, J. (2012). A longitudinal test of video game violence influences on dating and aggression: A 3-year longitudinal study of adolescents. *Journal of Psychiatric Research, 46,* 141–146.

Ferguson, C., & Kilburn, J. (2010). Much ado about nothing: The misestimation and overinterpretation of violent video game effects in Eastern and Western nations: Comment on Anderson et al. (2010). *Psychological Bulletin, 136,* 174–178.

Ferguson, S., Gitchell, J., & Shiffman, S. (2012). Continuing to wear nicotine patches after smoking lapses promotes recovery of abstinence. *Addiction, 107,* 1349–1353.

Fernald, A. (1993). Approval and disapproval: Infant responsiveness to vocal affect in familiar and unfamiliar languages. *Child Development, 64,* 637–656.

Ferrari, J., & Pychyl, T. (2012). "If I wait, my partner will do it:" The role of conscientiousness as a mediator in the relation of academic procrastination and perceived social loafing. *North American Journal of Psychology, 14,* 13–24

Ferreira, S., de Mello, M., Pompeia, S., & de Souza-Formigoni, M. (2006). Effects of energy drink ingestion on alcohol intoxication. *Alcoholism: Clinical and Experimental Research, 30,* 598.

Festinger, L. (1957). *A theory of cognitive dissonance.* Evanston, IL: Row, Peterson.

Festinger, L., & Carlsmith, J. M. (1959). Cognitive consequences of forced compliance. *Journal of Abnormal and Social Psychology, 58,* 203–210.

Festinger, L., Pepitone, A., & Newcomb, T. (1952). Some consequences of de-individuation in a group. *Journal of Abnormal and Social Psychology, 47,* 382–389.

Fiatarone, M. A., O'Neill, E. F., Ryan, N. D., Clements, K. M., Solares, G. R., Nelson, M. E., et al. (1994). Exercise training and nutritional supplementation for physical frailty in very elderly people. *New England Journal of Medicine, 330,* 1769–1775.

Field, T. (2002). Infants' need for touch. *Human Development, 45,* 100–103.

Field, T. (2009). Biofeedback. In T. Field (Ed.), *Complementary and alternative therapies research* (pp. 119–126). Washington, DC: American Psychological Association.

Field, T. (2009). Origins of complementary and alternative therapies. In T. Field (Ed.), *Complementary and alternative therapies research* (pp. 13–21). Washington, DC: American Psychological Association.

Field, T. M., Cohen, D., Garcia, R., & Greenberg, R. (1984). Mother–stranger face discrimination by the newborn. *Infant Behavior and Development, 7,* 19–25.

Field, T., Schanberg, S. M., Scfidi, F., Bauer, C. R., Vega-Lahr, N., Garcia, R., et al. (1986, May). Tactile/kinesthetic stimulation effects on preterm neonates. *Pediatrics, 77,* 654–658.

Finchbaugh, C., Moore, E., Chang, Y., & May, D. (2012). Student well-being interventions: The effects of stress management techniques and gratitude journaling in the management education classroom. *Journal of Management Education, 36*, 191–219.

Fink, B., & Penton-Voak, I. (2002). Evolutionary psychology of facial attractiveness. *Current Directions in Psychological Science, 11*, 154–158.

Fiorella, L., & Mayer, R. (2012). Paper-based aids for learning with a computer-based game. *Journal of Educational Psychology, 104*, 1074–1082.

Fischbach, G. D. (1992). Mind and brain. *Scientific American, 267*, 48–56.

Fixx, J. F. (1978). *Solve It! A perplexing profusion of puzzles*. New York: Doubleday.

Flavell, J. H. (1985). *Cognitive development*. Englewood, NJ: Prentice-Hall.

Flavell, J. H. (1992). Cognitive development: Past, present, and future. *Developmental Psychology, 28*, 998–1005.

Fleck, D., Hendricks, W., DelBellow, M., & Strakowski, S. (2002). Differential prescription of maintenance antipsychotics to African American and White patients with new-onset bipolar disorder. *Journal of Clinical Psychiatry, 63*, 658–664.

Fleming, J. D. (1974, July). Field report: The state of the apes. *Psychology Today*, pp. 31–46.

Fleshner, M., & Laudenslager, M. (2004). Psychoneuroimmunology: Then and now. *Behavioral & Cognitive Neuroscience Reviews, 3*, 114–130.

Fligor, B. (2010). Recreational noise and its potential risk to hearing. *Hearing Review, 17*, 48-55.

Florio, V., Fossella, S., Maravita, A., Miniussi, C., & Marzi, C. (2002). Interhemispheric transfer and laterality effects in simple visual reaction time in schizophrenics. *Cognitive Neuropsychiatry, 7*, 97–111.

Flynn, J. R. (1987). Race and IQ: Jensen's case refuted. In S. Modgil, & C. Modgil (Eds.), *Arthur Jensen: Consensus and controversy* (221–232). New York: Palmer Press.

Foa, E. B. (1995). How do treatments for obsessive-compulsive disorder compare? *Harvard Mental Health Letter, 12*(1), 8.

Fock, K., & Ang, T. (2010). Epidemiology of helicobacter pylori infection and gastric cancer in Asia. *Journal of Gastroenterology and Hepatology, 25*, 479–486.

Fogel, S., Smith, C., & Beninger, R. (2010). Increased GABAergic activity in the region of the pedunculopontine and deep mesencephalic reticular nuclei reduces REM sleep and impairs learning in rats. *Behavioral Neuroscience, 124*, 79–86.

Folkman, S. (1984). Personal control and stress and coping processes: A theoretical analysis. *Journal of Personality and Social Psychology, 46*, 839–852.

Folkman, S., & Lazarus, R. S. (1980). An analysis of coping in a middle-aged community sample. *Journal of Health and Social Behavior, 21*, 219–239.

Folkman, S., Chesney, M., Collette, L., Boccellari, A., & Cooke, M. (1996). Postbereavement depressive mood and its prebereavement predictors in HIV+ and HIV– gay men. *Journal of Personality and Social Psychology, 70*, 336–348.

Fontaine, D., Deudon, A., Lemaire, J., Razzouk, M., Viau, P., Darcourt, J., & Robert, P. (2013). Symptomatic treatment of memory decline in Alzheimer's Disease by deep brain stimulation: A feasibility study. *Journal of Alzheimer's Disease, 34*, 315–323.

Foran, H., & O'Leary, K. (2008). Alcohol and intimate partner violence: A meta-analytic review. *Clinical Psychology Review, 28*, 1222–1234.

Foster, R., Hankins, M., & Peirson, S. (2007). Light, photoreceptors, and circadian clocks. In E. Rosato (Ed.), *Circadian rhythms: Methods and protocols* (pp. 3–28). Totowa, NJ: Humana Press.

Fourkas, A., Bonavolonta, V., Avenanti, A., & Aglioti, S. (2008). Kinesthetic imagery and tool-specific modulation of corticospinal representations in expert tennis players. *Cerebral Cortex, 18*, 2382–2390.

Fox, N. A., & Bell, M. A. (1990). Electrophysiological indices of frontal lobe development: Relations to cognitive and affective behavior in human infants over the first year of life. *Annals of the New York Academy of Sciences, 608*, 677–698.

Francis-Smythe, J., & Smith, P. (1997). The psychological impact of assessment in a development center. *Human Relations, 50*, 149–167.

Francks, C., DeLisi, L., Fisher, S., Laval, S., Rue, J., Stein, J., et al. (2003). Confirmatory evidence for linkage of relative hand skill to 2p12-q11. *American Journal of Human Genetics, 72*, 499–502.

Francks, C., Maegawa, S., Lauren, J., Abrahams, B., Velayos-Baeza, A., Medland, S., Colella, S., Groszer, M., McAuley, E., Caffrey, T., Timmusk, T., Pruunsild, P., Koppel, I., Lind, P., Natsummoto-Itaba, N., Nicok, J., Xiong, L., Joober, R., Enard, W., Krinsky, B., Nanba, E., Richardson, A., Riley, B., Martin, N., Strittmatter, S., Miller, H., Rejuescu, D., St. Clair, D., Muglia, P., Roos, J., Fisher, S., Wade-Martins, R., Rouleau, G., Stain, J., Karayiorgou, M., Geschwind, D., Ragoussis, J., Kendler, K., Airaksinen, M., Oshimura, M., DeLisi, L., & Monaco, A. (2007). LRRTM1 on chromosome 2p12 is a maternally suppressed gene that is associated paternally with handedness and schizophrenia. *Molecular Psychiatry, 12*, 1129–1139.

Frank, E., Anderson, B., Reynolds, C. F., III, Ritenour, A., & Kupfer, D. J. (1994). Life events and the research diagnostic criteria endogenous subtype. *Archives of General Psychiatry, 51*, 519–524.

Frank, E., Kupfer, D. J., Wagner, E. F., McEachran, A. B., & Cornes, C. (1991). Efficacy of interpersonal psychotherapy as a maintenance treatment of recurrent depression: Contributing factors. *Archives of General Psychiatry, 48*, 1053–1059.

Frankenburg, W. K., Dodds, J. B., Archer, P., et al. (1992). *Denver II training manual*. Denver, CO, USA: Denver Developmental Materials.

Franklin, A., Pilling, M., & Davies, I. (2005). The nature of infant colour categorization: Evidence from eye-movements on a target detection task. *Journal of Experimental Child Psychology, 91*, 227–248.

Fratiglioni, L., & Wang, H. (2007). Brain reserve hypothesis in dementia. *Journal of Alzheimers Disease, 12*, 11–22.

Frazer, A. (1997). Antidepressants. *Journal of Clinical Psychiatry, 58*(6, Suppl.), 9–25.

Frazer, N., Larkin, K., & Goodie, J. (2002). Do behavioral responses mediate or moderate the relation between cardiovascular reactivity to stress and parental history of hypertension? *Health Psychology, 21*, 244–253.

Fredricks, J., & Eccles, J. (2002). Children's competence and value beliefs from childhood through adolescence growth trajectories in two male-sex-typed domains. *Developmental Psychology, 38*, 519–533.

Fredrickson, B. (2009). *Positivity: Groundbreaking research reveals how to embrace the hidden strength of positive emotions, overcome negativity, and thrive*. New York: Crown Publishers/Random House.

Fredrikson, M., Annas, P., Fischer, H., & Wik, G. (1996). Gender and age differences in the prevalence of specific fears and phobias. *Behaviour Research and Therapy, 34*, 33–39.

Freedman, J. L., & Fraser, S. C. (1966). Compliance without pressure: The foot-in-the-door technique. *Journal of Personality and Social Psychology, 4*, 195–202.

Freeman, E., Colpe, L., Strine, T., Dhingra, S., McGuire, L., Elam-Evans, L., & Perry, G. (2010). Public health surveillance for mental health. *Preventing Chronic Disease: Public Health Research, Practice, and Policy, 7,* 1–7.

Freeman, W. J. (1991). The physiology of perception. *Scientific American, 264,* 78–85.

Freud, S. (1900/1953a). The interpretation of dreams. In J. Strachey (Ed. and trans.), *The standard edition of the complete psychological works of Sigmund Freud* (Vols. 4 and 5). London: Hogarth Press. (Original work published 1900).

Freud, S. (1905/1953b). Three essays on the theory of sexuality. In J. Strachey (Ed. and Trans.), *The standard edition of the complete psychological works of Sigmund Freud* (Vol. 7). London: Hogarth Press. (Original work published 1905).

Freud, S. (1922). *Beyond the pleasure principle.* London: International Psychoanalytic Press.

Freud, S. (1930/1962). *Civilization and its discontents* (J. Strachey, Trans.). New York: W. W. Norton. (Original work published 1930).

Freud, S. (1933/1965). *New introductory lectures on psychoanalysis* (J. Strachey, Trans.). New York: W. W. Norton. (Original work published 1933).

Freudenberger, H., & Richelson, G. (1981). *Burnout.* New York: Bantam Books.

Frew, J., & Spiegler, M. (2013). Introduction to contemporarary psychotherapies for a diverse world. In J. Frew & M. Spiegler (Eds.). *Contemporaray psychotherapies for a diverse world.* (pp. 1–18). New York, NY, USA: Routledge/Taylor & Francis Group.

Frey, M., & Detterman, D. (2004). Scholastic assessment or *g*? The relationship between the scholastic assessment test and general cognitive ability. *Psychological Science, 15,* 373–378.

Frick, P., Cornell, A., Bodin, S., Dane, H., Barry, C., & Loney, B. (2003). Callous-unemotional traits and developmental pathways to severe conduct problems. *Developmental Psychology, 39,* 246–260.

Friedland, N., Keinan, G., & Regev, Y. (1992). Controlling the uncontrollable: Effects of stress on illusory perceptions of controllability. *Journal of Personality and Social Psychology, 63,* 923–931.

Friedman, M. I., Tordoff, M. G., & Ramirez, I. (1986). Integrated metabolic control of food intake. *Brain Research Bulletin, 17,* 855–859.

Friedman, M., & Rosenman, R. H. (1974). *Type A behavior and your heart.* New York: Fawcett.

Friedman, E., Karlamangla, A., Almeida, D., & Seeman, T. (2012). Social strain and cortisol regulation in midlife in the U.S. *Social Science & Medicine, 74,* 607–615.

Friedman, N., Sadhu, J., & Jellnick, M. (2012). DSM-5: Anticipated changes relevant to children. *Clinician's Research Digest, 30,* 13.

Frijda, N. (2012). How emotions work. In M. Eysenck, M. Fajkowska, & T. Maruszewski (Eds.) *Personality, cognition, and emotion.* Clinton Corners, NY, USA: Eliot Werner Publications.

Furdon, S. (2012). *Prematurity.* Retrieved December 16, 2012, from http://emedicine.medscape.com/article/975909-overview#a0199

Furniss, F., Biswas, A., Bezilla, B., & Jones, A. (2011). Self-injurious behavior: Overview and behavioral interventions. In J. Matson & P. Sturney (Eds.). *Autism and child psychopathology seriesi.* (pp. 437–452). New York, NY, USA: Springer Science + Business Media.

Fuzhong, L., Harmer, P., Fisher, K., & McAuley, E. (2004). Tai Chi: Improving balance and predicting subsequent falls in older persons. *Medicine & Science in Sports & Exercise, 36,* 2046–2052.

Gabora, L., Rosch, E., & Aerts, D. (2008). Toward an ecological theory of concepts. *Ecological Psychology, 20,* 84–116.

Gadea, M., Martinez-Bisbal, M., Marti-Bonmati, Espert, R., Casanova, B., Coret, F., & Celda, B. (2004). Spectroscopic axonal damage of the right locus coeruleus relates to selective attention impairment in early stage relapsing-remitting multiple sclerosis. *Brain, 127,* 89–98

Gaertner, L., Sedikides, C., & Chang, K. (2008). On pancultural self-enhancement: Well-adjusted Taiwanese self-enhance on personally valued traits. *Journal of Cross-Cultural Psychology, 39,* 463–477.

Gaggioli, A., & Riva, G. (2007). A second life for telehealth? *Annual Review of CyberTherapy and Telemedicine, 5,* 29–36.

Galambos, N., Turner, P., & Tilton-Weaver, L. (2005). Chronological and subjective age in emerging adulthood: The crossover effect. *Journal of Adolescent Research, 20,* 538–556.

Gall, T., & Guirguis-Younger, M. (2013). Religious and spiritual coping Current theory and research. In K. Pargament, J. Exline, & J. Jones (Eds.). *APA handbook of psychology, religion, and spirituality (Vol 1): Context, theory, and research.* (pp. 349–364). Washington, DC, USA: American Psychological Association.

Gallagher, M., & Rapp, P. R. (1997). The use of animal models to study the effects of aging on cognition. *Annual Review of Psychology, 48,* 339–370.

Gallagher, M., & Resick, P. (2012). Mechanisms of change in cognitive processing therapy and prolonged exposure therapy for PTSD: Preliminary evidence for the differential effects of hopelessness and habituation. *Cognitive Therapy and Research, 36,* 750–755.

Gallup, G., Jr., & Hugick, L. (1990). Racial tolerance grows, progress on racial equality less evident. *Gallup Poll Monthly, 297,* 23–32.

Galton, F. (1874). *Eglishmen of science: Their nature and nurture.* London, UK: Macmillan & Company.

Ganellen, R. J. (1996). Comparing the diagnostic efficiency of the MMPI, MCMI-II, and Rorschach: A review. *Journal of Personality Assessment, 67,* 219–243.

Garcia, J., & Koelling, A. (1966). Relation of cue to consequence in avoidance learning. *Psychonomic Science, 4,* 123–124.

Gardner, H. (1983). *Frames of mind: The theory of multiple intelligences.* New York: Basic Books.

Gardner, H. (2011). Changing minds: How the application of the Multiple Intelligences (MI) framework could positively contribute to the theory and practice of international negotiation. In F. Aguilar & M. Galluccio (Eds.) *Psychological and political strategies for peace negotiation: A cognitive approach.* (pp. 1–14). New York, NY, USA: Spring Science + Business Media.

Gardner, H., & Hatch, T. (1989). Multiple intelligences go to school: Educational implication of the theory of multiple intelligences. *Educational Researcher, 18*(8), 6.

Gardner, R. A., & Gardner, B. T. (1969). Teaching sign language to a chimpanzee. *Science, 165,* 664–672.

Garfield, C. (1986). *Peak performers: The new heroes of American business.* New York: Morrow.

Garmon, L. C., Basinger, K. S., Gregg, V. R., & Gibbs, J. C. (1996). Gender differences in stage and expression of moral judgment. *Merrill-Palmer Quarterly, 42,* 418–437.

Granier-Deferre, C., Bassereau, S., Ribeiro, A., Jacquet, A., & DeCasper, A. (2011). A melodic contour repeatedly experienced by human near-term fetuses elicits a profound cardiac reaction one month after birth. *PLoS One, 6,* e17304.

Garrett, M., Garrett, J., & Brotherton, D. (2001). Inner circle/outer circle: A group technique based on Native American healing circles. *Journal for Specialists in Group Work, 26,* 17–30.

Garrett, J. (2012). The ethics of animal research: An overview of the debate. In J. Garrett (Ed.). *The Ethics of Animal Research: Exploring the Controversy* (pp. 1–16). Cambridge, MA, USA: MIT Press.

Garry, M., & Loftus, E. F. (1994). Pseudomemories without hypnosis. *International Journal of Clinical and Experimental Hypnosis, 42,* 363–373.

Garssen, B. (2004). Psychological factors and cancer development: Evidence after 30 years of research. *Clinical Psychology Review, 24,* 315–338.

Gates, G., & Newport, F. (2012). *Special Report: 3.4% of U.S. Adults Identify as LGBT.* Retrieved January 3, 2013, from http://www.gallup.com/poll/158066/special-report-adults-identify-lgbt.aspx?utm_source=alert&utm_medium=email&utm_campaign=syndication&utm_content=morelink&utm_term=Politics

Gauchet, A., Shankland, R., Dantzer, C., et al. (2012). Clinical applications in health psychology, *Psychologie Française, 57,* 131–142.

Gawin, F. H. (1991). Cocaine addiction: Psychology and neurophysiology. *Science, 251,* 1580–1586.

Gawronski, B., Alshut, E., Grafe, J., Nespethal, J., Ruhmland, A., & Schulz, L. (2002). Processes of judging known and unknown persons. *Zeitschrift fuer Sozialpsychologie, 33,* 25–34.

Gazzaniga, M. (1970). *The bisected brain.* New York: Appleton-Century-Crofts.

Gazzaniga, M. S. (1983). Right hemisphere language following brain bisection: A 20-year perspective. *American Psychologist, 38,* 525–537.

Gazzaniga, M. (1989). Organization of the human brain. *Science, 245,* 947–952.

Geary, N. (2004). Endocrine controls of eating: CCK, leptin, and ghrelin. *Physiology & Behavior, 81,* 719–733.

Gee, D., Karlsgodt, K., van Erp, T., Bearden, C., Lieberman, M., Belger, A., Perkins, D., Olvet, D., Cornblatt, B., Constable, T., Woods, S., Addington, J., Cadenhead, K., McGlashan, T., Seidman, L., Tsuang, M., Walker, E., & Cannon, T. (2012). Altered age-related trajectories of amygdala-prefrontal circuitry in adolescents at clinical high risk for psychosis: A preliminary study. *Schizophrenia Research, 134,* 1–9.

Gee, G., Walsemann, K., & Brondolo, E. (2012). A life course perspective on how racism may be related to health inequities. *American Journal of Public Health, 102,* 967–974.

Geen, R. G. (1984). Human motivation: New perspectives on old problems. In A. M. Rogers & C. J. Scheier (Eds.), *The G. Stanley Hall lecture series* (Vol. 4, pp. 9–57). Washington, DC: American Psychological Association.

Gehart, D., & Lyle, R. (2001). Client experience of gender in therapeutic relationships: An interpretive ethnography. *Family Process, 40,* 443–458.

Gehring, D. (2003). Couple therapy for low sexual desire: A systematic approach. *Journal of Sex & Marital Therapy, 29,* 25–38.

Geiselman, R. E., Schroppel, T., Tubridy, A., Konishi, T., & Rodriguez, V. (2000). Objectivity bias in eye witness performance. *Applied Cognitive Psychology, 14,* 323–332.

Genen, L. (2012). *Cannabis compound abuse.* Retrieved November 9, 2012, from http://emedicine.medscape.com/article/286661-overview#a0104.

George, T., & Vessicchio, J. (2001). Nicotine addiction and schizophrenia. *Psychiatric Times.* Retrieved February 12, 2007, from *http://www.psychiatrictimes.com/p010239.html*

George, M. (2012). Health beliefs, treatment preferences and complementary and alternative medicine for asthma, smoking, and lung cancer self-management in diverse Black communities. *Patient Education and Counseling, 89,* 489–500.

Gerstein, P. (2011). *Emergent treatment of schizophrenia.* Retrieved January 27, 2013, from http://emedicine.medscape.com/article/815881-overview

Gerstorf, D., Ram, N., Hoppmann, C., Willis, S., & Schaie, K. W. (2011). Fluid and crystallized abilities in the Seattle Longitudinal Study: Cohort differences in cognitive aging and dying. *Developmental Psychology, 47,* 1026–1041.

Gevins, A., Leong, H., Smith, M. E., Le, J., & Du, R. (1995). Mapping cognitive brain function with modern high-resolution electroencephalography. *Trends in Neurosciences, 18,* 429–436.

Gibbons, A. (1991). Déjà vu all over again: Chimp-language wars. *Science, 251,* 1561–1562.

Gibbs, J., Basinger, K., Grime, R., & Snarey, J. (2007). Moral judgment development across cultures: Revisiting Kohlberg's universality claims. *Developmental Review, 27,* 443–500.

Gibson, E., & Walk, R. D. (1960). The "visual cliff." *Scientific American, 202,* 64–71.

Gibson, J. (1994). The visual perception of objective motion and subjective motion. *Psychological Review, 101,* 318–323.

Gigerenzer, G. (2004). Dread risk, September 11, and fatal traffic accidents. *Psychological Science, 15,* 286–287.

Gilbert, D. (2006). *Stumbling on happiness.* New York: Alfred A. Knopf.

Gilligan, C. (1982). *In a different voice: Psychological theory and women's development.* Cambridge, MA: Harvard University Press.

Gingell, C., Nicolosi, A., Buvat, J., Glasser, D., Simsek, F., Hartmann, U., et al. (2003). *Sexual activity and dysfunction among men and women aged 40 to 80 years.* Poster presented at the XVIIIth Congress of the European Association of Urology. Madrid, March, 2003.

Ginzburg, K., Solomon, Z., & Bleich, A. (2002). Repressive coping style, acute stress disorder, and post-traumatic stress disorder after myocardial infarction. *Journal of the American Psychosomatic Society, 64,* 748–757.

Girolamo, G., & Bassi, M. (2003). Community surveys of mental disorders: Recent achievements and works in progress. *Current Opinion in Psychiatry, 16,* 403–411.

Glannon, W. (2006). Neuroethics. *Bioethics, 20,* 37–52.

Glantz, L. A., & Lewis, D. A. (2000). Decreased dendritic spine density on prefrontal cortical pyramidal neurons in schizophrenia. *Archives of General Psychiatry, 57,* 65–73.

Glass, D. C., & Singer, J. E. (1972). *Urban stress: Experiments in noise and social stressors.* New York: Academic Press.

Global Fund to Fight AIDS, Tuberculosis, and Malaria (2005). *Global Fund ARV factsheet.* Retrieved July 3, 2006, from *http://www.theglobalfund.org/en/files/publications/factsheets/aids/ARV_Factsheet_2006.pdf*

Gluck, M. A., & Myers, C. E. (1997). Psychobiological models of hippocampal function in learning and memory. *Annual Review of Psychology, 48,* 481–514.

Glucksman, M., & Kramer, M. (2004). Using dreams to assess clinical change during treatment. *Journal of the American Academy of Psychoanalysis and Dynamic Psychiatry, 32,* 345–358.

Gökcebay, N., Cooper, R., Williams, R. L., Hirshkowitz, M., & Moore, C. A. (1994). Function of sleep. In R. Cooper (Ed.), *Sleep* (pp. 47–59). New York: Chapman & Hall.

Godart, N., Berthoz, S., Curt, F., Perdereau, F., Rein, Z., Wallier, J., Horreard, A., Kaganski, I., Lucet, R., Atger, F., Corcos, M., Fermanian, J., Falissard, B., Flament, M., Eisler, I., & Jeammet, P. (2012). A randomized controlled trial of adjunctive family therapy and treatment as usual following inpatient treatment for anorexia nervosa adolescents. *PLOSOne.* Retrieved January 4, 2013, from http://www.plosone.org/article/info%3Adoi%2F10.1371%2Fjournal.pone.0028249

Godden, D. R., & Baddeley, A. D. (1975). Context-dependent memory in two natural environments: On land and underwater. *British Journal of Psychology, 66,* 325–331.

Goffman, E. (1959). *The presentation of self in everyday life*. Garden City, NY: Doubleday-Anchor.

Gogtay, N., Giedd, J., Lusk, L., Hayashi, K., Greenstein, D., Vaituzis, A., et al. (2004). Dynamic mapping of human cortical development during childhood through early adulthood. *Proceedings of the National Academy of Science, 101*, 8174–8179.

Goldberg, L. (1993). The structure of phenotypic personality traits. *American Psychologist, 48*, 26–34.

Goleman, D., Kaufman, P., & Ray, M. (1992). *The creative spirit*. New York: Dutton.

Gollan, T., & Brown, A. (2006). From tip-of-the-tongue (TOT) data to theoretical implications in two steps: When more TOTs means better retrieval. *Journal of Experimental Psychology: General, 135*, 462–483.

Golz, A., Netzer, A., Westerman, S., Westerman, L., Gilbert, D., Joachims, H., & Goldenberg, D. (2005). Reading performance in children with otitis media. *Otolaryngology: Head and Neck Surgery, 132*, 495–499.

Gonsalves, B., Reber, P., Gitelman, D., Parrish, T., Mesulam, M., & Paller, K. (2004). Neural evidence that vivid imagining can lead to false remembering. *Psychological Science, 15*, 655–660.

Gonzalez, R., Ellsworth, P. C., & Pembroke, M. (1993). Response biases in lineups and showups. *Journal of Personality and Social Psychology, 64*, 525–537.

Goodin, B., Quinn, N., Kronfli, T., King, C., Page, G., Haythornthwaite, J., Edwards, R., Stapleton, L., & McGuire, L. (2012). Experimental pain ratings and reactivity of cortisol and soluble tumor necrosis factor-Ⅹ receptor II following a trial of hypnosis: Results of a randomized controlled pilot study. *Pain Medicine, 13*, 29–44.

Goodman, E., McEwen, B., Huang, B., Dolan, L., & Adler, N. (2005). Social inequalities in biomarkers of cardiovascular risk in adolescence. *Psychosomatic Medicine, 67*, 9–15.

Goodman, G., Quas, J., & Ogle, C. (2010). Child maltreatment and memory. *Annual Review of Psychology, 61*, 325–351.

Gorman, J. (2007). *The essential guide to psychiatric drugs* (4th ed.). New York: St. Martin's Press.

Gosling, S., Vazire, S., Srivastava, S., & John, O. (2004). Should we trust Web-based studies? A comparative analysis of six preconceptions about Internet questionnaires. *American Psychologist, 59*, 93–104.

Gosseries, O., Demertzi, A., Ledoux, D., Bruno, M., Vanhaudenhuyse, A., Thibaut, A., Laureys, S., & Schnakers, C. (2012). Burnout in healthcare workers managing chronic patients with disorders of consciousness. *Brain Injury, 26*, 1493–1499.

Gottesman, I. I. (1991). *Schizophrenia genesis: The origins of madness*. New York: W. H. Freeman.

Gottesmann, C. (2000). Hypothesis for the neurophysiology of dreaming. *Sleep Research Online, 3*, 1–4.

Gottfried, J. (2010). Olfaction and its pleasures: Human neuroimaging perspectives. In Kringelbach, M., & Berridge, K. (Eds.). *Pleasures of the brain*. (pp. 125–145). New York: Oxford University Press.

Gough, H. (1987). *California Psychological Inventory: Administrator's Guide*. Palo Alto: Consulting Psychologists Press.

Gougoux, F., Lepore, F., Lassonde, M., Voss, P., Zatorre, R.J. & Belin, P. (2004) Pitch discrimination in the early blind. *Nature, 430*, 309.

Gouin, J., Glaser, R., Malarkey, W., Beversdorf, D., & Kiecolt-Glaser, J. (2012). Chronic stress, daily stressors, and circulating inflammatory markers. *Health Psychology, 31*, 264–268.

Gowen, C. (2011). Fetal and neonatal medicine. In K. Marcdante, R. Kliegman, H. Jenson, & R. Behrman (Eds.) *Nelson essentials of pediatrics* (6th ed.). (pp. 213–264). Philadelphia, PA, USA: Saunders/Elsevier, Inc.

Gower, A., & Crick, N. (2011). Baseline autonomic nervous system arousal and physical and relational aggression in preschool: The moderating role of effortful control. *International Journal of Psychophysiology, 81*, 142–151.

Graham, S. (1992). "Most of the subjects were white and middle class": Trends in published research on African Americans in selected APA journals, 1970–1989. *American Psychologist, 47*, 629–639.

Graham, J., & Roemer, L. (2012). A preliminary study of the moderating role of church-based social support in the relationship between racist experiences and general anxiety symptoms. *Cultural Diversity and Ethnic Minority Psychology, 18*, 268–276.

Graham, K., Bernards, S., Osgood, D., & Wells, S. (2012). "Hotspots" for aggression in licensed drinking venues. *Drug and Alcohol Review, 31*, 377–384.

Grande, G., Romppel, M., & Barth, J. (2012). Association between type D personality and prognosis in patients with cardiovascular diseases: A systematic review and meta-analysis. *Annals of Behavioral Medicine, 43*, 299–310.

Granic, I., & Patterson, G. (2006). Toward a comprehensive model of antisocial development: A dynamic systems approach. *Psychological Review, 113*, 101–131.

Green, J. P., & Lynn, S. J. (2000). Hypnosis and suggestion-based approaches to smoking cessation: An examination of the evidence. *International Journal of Clinical Experimental Hypnosis, 48*, 195–224.

Green, J., & Shellenberger, R. (1990). *The dynamics of health and wellness: A biopsychosocial approach*. Fort Worth: Holt, Rinehart & Winston.

Green, R., MacDorman, K., Ho, C., & Vasudevan, S. (2008). Sensitivity to the proportions of faces that vary in human likeness. *Computers in Human Behavior, 24*, 2456–2474.

Green, S., Moll, J., Deakin, J., Hulleman, J., Zahn, R. (2013). Proneness to decreased negative emotions in major depressive disorder when blaming others rather than oneself. *Psychopathology, 46*, 34–44.

Greenberg, W. (2009). *Obsessive-compulsive disorder*. Retrieved March 15, 2010 from *http://emedicine.medscape.com/article/287681-overview*.

Greenberg, W. (2012). *Obsessive-compulsive disorder treatment and management*. Retrieved January 25, 2013, from http://emedicine.medscape.com/article/1934139-treatment#aw2aab6b6b4

Greenfield, S., & Hennessy, G. (2008). Assessment of the patient. In M. Galanter & H. Kleber (Eds.), *The American Psychiatric Publishing textbook of substance abuse* (4th ed., pp. 55–78). Arlington, VA: American Psychiatric Publishing.

Greenglass, E., & Fiksenbaum, L. (2009). Proactive coping, positive affect, and well-being: Testing for mediation using path analysis. *European Psychologist, 14*, 29–39.

Greenwald, A. (1992). New look 3: Unconscious cognition reclaimed. *American Psychologist, 47*, 766–779.

Greenwald, A., Spangenberg, E., Pratkanis, A., & Eskenazi, J. (1991). Double-blind tests of subliminal self-help audiotapes. *Psychological Science, 2*, 119–122.

Greer, M. (2005). Keeping them hooked in. *APA Monitor on Psychology, 36*, 60.

Gregory, R. J. (1996). *Psychological testing: History, principles, and applications* (2nd ed.). Boston: Allyn & Bacon.

Greist, J. H. (1992). An integrated approach to treatment of obsessive compulsive disorder. *Journal of Clinical Psychiatry, 53*(4, Suppl.), 38–41.

Greitmeyer, T., & Osswald, S. (2010). Effects of prosocial video games on prosocial behavior. *Journal of Personality and Social Psychology, 98*, 211–221.

Griffiths, M. (2003). Communicating risk: Journalists have responsibility to report risks in context. *British Medical Journal, 327,* 1404.

Grigorenko, E. (2003). Epistasis and the genetics of complex traits. In R. Plomin, J. DeFries, I. Craig, & P. McGuffin (Eds.), *Behavioral genetics in the postgenomic era* (pp. 247–266). Washington, DC: American Psychological Association.

Grimbos, T., Dawood, K., Burriss, R., Zucker, K., & Puts, D. (2010). Sexual orientation and the second to fourth finger length ratio: A meta-analysis in men and women. *Behavioral Neuroscience, 124,* 278–287.

Gron, G., Wunderlich, A. P., Spitzer, M., Tomczrak, R., & Riepe, M. W. (2000). Brain activation during human navigation: Gender-different neural networks as substrate of performance. *Nature Neuroscience, 3,* 404–408.

Gross, J. (2002). Emotion regulation: Affective, cognitive, and social consequences. *Psychophysiology, 39,* 281–291.

Grünbaum, A. (2006). Is Sigmund Freud's psychoanalytic edifice relevant to the 21st century? *Psychoanalytic Psychology, 23,* 257–284.

Guéguen, N., & Lamy, L. (2012). Men's social status and attractiveness: Women's receptivity to men's date requests. *Swiss Journal of Psychology, 71,* 157–160.

Guenther, K. (2002). Memory. In D. Levitin (Ed.), *Foundations of cognitive psychology.* Cambridge, MA: MIT Press.

Guilford, J. P. (1967). *The nature of human intelligence.* New York: McGraw-Hill.

Gulick, D., & Gould, T. (2009). Effects of ethanol and caffeine on behavior in C57BL/6 mice in the plus-maze discriminative avoidance task. *Behavioral Neuroscience, 123,* 1271–1278.

Gur, R. C., Turetsky, B., Mastsui, M., Yan, M. Bilker, W., Hughett, P., & Gur, R. E. (1999). Sex differences in brain gray and white matter in healthy young adults: correlations with cognitive performance. *Journal of Neuroscience, 19,* 4067–4072.

Gur, R., Gunning-Dixon, F., Bilker, W., & Gur, R. (2002). Sex differences in temporolimbic and frontal brain volumes of healthy adults. *Cerebral Cortex, 12,* 998–1003.

Gurin, J. (1989, June). Leaner, not lighter. *Psychology Today,* 32–36.

Guse, B., Falkai, P., Gruber, O., Shalley, H., Gibson, L., Hasan, A., Obst, K., Dechent, P., McIntosh, A., Suchan, B., & Wobrock, T. (2013). The effect of long-term high frequency repetitive transcranial magnetic stimulation on working memory in schizophrenia and healthy controls—A randomized placebo-controlled, double-blind fMRI study. *Behavioural Brain Research, 237,* 300–307.

Guse, B., Falkai, P., Gruber, O., Whalley, H., Gibson, L., Hasan, A., Obst, K., Dechent, P., McIntosh, A., Suchan, B., & Wobrock, T. (2013). The effect of long-term high frequency repetitive trnscranial magnetic stimulation on working memory in schizophrenia and healthy controls—A randomized placebo-controlled, double-blind fMRI study. *Behavioural Brain Research, 237,* 300–307.

Guthrie, J. P., Ash, R. A., & Bendapudi, V. (1995). Additional validity evidence for a measure of morningness. Journal of Applied Psychology, 80, 186–190.

Gwak, Y., Kang, J., Unabia, G., Hulsebosch, C. (2012). Spatial and temporal activation of spinal glial cells: Role of gliopathy in central neuropathic pain following spinal cord injury in rats. *Experimental Neurology, 234,* 362–372.

Haag, L., & Stern, E. (2003). In search of the benefits of learning Latin. *Journal of Educational Psychology, 95,* 174–178.

Haaken, J., & Reavey, P. (2010). Memory matters: Contexts for understanding sexual abuse recollections (pp. 1–13). New York: Routledge/Taylor & Francis Group.

Haber, R. N. (1980). How we perceive depth from flat pictures. *American Scientist, 68,* 370–380.

Haberlandt, D. (1997). *Cognitive psychology* (2nd ed.). Boston: Allyn & Bacon.

Hada, M., Porjesz, B., Begleiter, H., & Polich, J. (2000). Auditory P3a assessment of male alcoholics. *Biological Psychiatry, 48,* 276–286.

Hakuta, K., Bialystok, E., & Wiley, E. (2003). Critical evidence: A test of the critical-period hypothesis for second-language acquisition. *Psychological Science, 14,* 31–38.

Halaas, J. L., Gajiwala, K. S., Maffei, M., Cohen, S. L., Chait, B. T., Rabinowitz, D., et al. (1995). Weight-reducing effects of the plasma protein encoded by the obese gene. *Science, 269,* 543–546.

Halama, P., & Strízenec, M. (2004). Spiritual, existential or both? Theoretical considerations on the nature of "higher" intelligences. *Studia Psychologica, 46,* 239–253.

Halaris, A. (2003). Neurochemical aspects of the sexual response cycle. *CNS Spectrums, 8,* 211–216.

Haldeman, D. (2012). Diversity training: Multiple minority awareness. In R. Nettles & R. Balter. (Eds.). *Multiple minority identities: Applications for practice, research, and training.* (pp. 231–247). New York, NY, USA: Springer Publishing Co.

Hall, C. (1953). A cognitive theory of dream symbols. *The Journal of General Psychology, 48,* 169–186.

Hallon, S., Stewart, M., & Strunk, D. (2006). Enduring effects for cognitive therapy in the treatment of depression and anxiety. *Annual Review of Psychology, 57,* 285–316.

Hallschmid, M., Benedict, C., Born, J., Fehm, H., & Kern, W. (2004). Manipulating central nervous mechanisms of food intake and body weight regulation by intranasal administration of neuropeptides in man. *Physiology & Behavior, 83,* 55–64.

Halverson, J. (2012). *Depression.* Retrieved January 26, 2013, from http://emedicine.medscape.com/article/286759-overview#aw2aab6b2b5

Ham, P. (2003). Suicide risk not increased with SSRI and antidepressants. *Journal of Family Practice, 52,* 587–589.

Hamdy, O. (2012). *Obesity.* Retrieved January 4, 2013, from http://emedicine.medscape.com/article/123702-overview

Hamilton, B., & Ventura, S. (2012). Birth rates for U.S. teenagers reach historic lows for all age and ethnic groups. *NCHS Data Brief, 89,* 1–8.

Hampson, S., Goldberg, L., Vogt, T., & Dubanoski, J. (2006). Forty years on: Teachers' assessments of children's personality traits predict self-reported health behaviors and outcomes at midlife. *Health Psychology, 25,* 57–64.

Hancock, P., & Ganey, H. (2003). From the inverted-u to the extended-u: The evolution of a law of psychology. *Journal of Human Performance in Extreme Environments, 7,* 5–14.

Hannover, B., & Kuehnen, U. (2002). "The clothing makes the self" via knowledge activation. *Journal of Applied Social Psychology, 32,* 2513–2525.

Hanoch, Y., & Vitouch, O. (2004). When less is more: Information, emotional arousal and the ecological reframing of the Yerkes-Dodson law. *Theory & Psychology, 14,* 427–452.

Hare, R. (1998). The Hare PCL-R: Some issues concerning its use and misuse. *Legal and Criminological Psychology, 3,* 99–119.

Hargadon, R., Bowers, K. S., & Woody, E. Z. (1995). Does counterpain imagery mediate hypnotic analgesia? *Journal of Abnormal Psychology, 104,* 508–516.

Harlow, H. F., & Harlow, M. K. (1962). Social deprivation in monkeys. *Scientific American, 207,* 137–146.

Harlow, J. M. (1848). Passage of an iron rod through the head. *Boston Medical and Surgical Journal, 39,* 389–393.

Harms, P., Roberts, B., & Winter, D. (2006). Becoming the Harvard Man: Person–environment fit, personality development, and academic success. *Personality and Social Psychology Bulletin, 32,* 851–865.

Harris, J. (2005). The increased diagnosis of "Juvenile Bipolar Disorder": What are we treating? *Psychiatric Services, 56,* 529–531.

Harrold, L., Ware, C., Mason, J., McGuire, E., Lewis, D., Pagano, L., & Alley, W. (2009). *The distracted teenage driver.* Paper presented at the annual meeting of the Pediatric Academic Society. Baltimore, MD.

Harrold, J., Dovey, T., Blundell, J., & Halford, J. (2012). CNS regulation of appetite. *Neuropharmacology, 63,* 3–17.

Hart, J., Karau, S., Stasson, M., & Kerr, N. (2004). Achievement motivation, expected coworker performance, and collective task motivation: Working hard or hardly working? *Journal of Applied Social Psychology, 34,* 984–1000.

Hart, S., Petrill, S., Thompson, L., & Plomin, R. (2009). The ABCs of math: A genetic analysis of mathematics and its links with reading ability and general cognitive ability. *Journal of Educational Psychology, 101,* 388–402.

Harter, S. (2012). *The construction of the self: Developmental and sociocultural foundations* (2nd ed.). New York, NY, USA: Guilford Press.

Haslam, S., & Reicher, S. (2004). A critique of the role-based explanation of tyranny: Thinking beyond the Stanford Prison Experiment. *Revista de Psicología Social, 19,* 115–122.

Haslam, S. A., & Reicher, S. (2006). Stressing the group: Social identity and the unfolding dynamics of responses to stress. *Journal of Applied Psychology, 91,* 1037–1052.

Haslam, S., Jetten, J., Postmes, T., & Haslam, C. (2009). Social identity, health and well-being: An emerging agenda for applied psychology. *An International Review, 58,* 1–23.

Haslam, S., & Reicher, S. (2008). Questioning the banality of evil. *The Psychologist, 21,* 16–19.

Haslam, S., & Reicher, S. (2012). Contesting the "nature" of conformity: What Milgram and Zimbardo's studies really show. *PLoS Biology, 10,* e1001426.

Hatashita-Wong, M., Smith, T., Silverstein, S., Hull, J., & Willson, D. (2002). Cognitive functioning and social problem-solving skills in schizophrenia. *Cognitive Neuropsychiatry, 7,* 81–95.

Haug, T., Nordgreen, T., Öst, L., Göran, H., & Odd, E. (2012). Self-help treatment of anxiety disorders: A meta-analysis and meta-regression of effects and potential moderators. *Clinical Psychology Review, 2,* 425–445.

Hauser, M. D. (1993). Right hemisphere dominance for the production of facial expression in monkeys. *Science, 261,* 475–477.

Haxby, J., Gobbini, M., Furey, M., Ishai, A., Schouten, J., & Pietrini, P. (2001). Distributed and overlapping representations of faces and objects in ventral temporal cortex. *Science, 293,* 2425–2430.

Haywood, H., & Lidz, C. (2007). *Dynamic assessment in practice: Clinical and educational applications.* New York: Cambridge University Press.

Hazlett-Stevens, H., Craske, M., Roy-Byrne, P., Sherbourne, C., Stein, M., & Bystritsky, A. (2002). Predictors of willingness to consider medication and psychosocial treatment for panic disorder in primary care patients. *General Hospital Psychology, 24,* 316–321.

HCF Nutrition Foundation. (2003). *The benefits of fiber.* Retrieved January 29, 2003, from *http://www.hcf-nutrition.org/fiber/fiberben_article.html*

Hebb, D. O. (1949). *The organization of behavior.* New York: John Wiley & Sons.

Hecht, S., Shlaer, S., & Pirenne, M. H. (1942). Energy, quanta, and vision. *Journal of General Physiology, 25,* 819.

Heckhausen, J., & Brian, O. (1997). Perceived problems for self and others: Self-protection by social downgrading throughout adulthood. *Psychology & Aging, 12,* 610–619.

Hedges, L. B., & Nowell, A. (1995). Sex differences in mental test scores, variability, and numbers of high-scoring individuals. *Science, 269,* 41–45.

Heider, F. (1958). *The psychology of interpersonal relations.* Mahwah, NJ: Lawrence Erlbaum Associates.

Heil, M., Rolke, B., & Pecchinenda, A. (2004). Automatic semantic activation is no myth. *Psychological Science, 15,* 852–857.

Held, R. (1993). What can rates of development tell us about underlying mechanisms? In C. E. Granrud (Ed.), *Visual perception and cognition in infancy* (pp. 75–89). Hillsdale, NJ: Erlbaum.

Hellige, J. B. (1990). Hemispheric asymmetry. *Annual Review of Psychology, 41,* 55–80.

Hellstrom, Y., & Hallberg, I. (2004). Determinants and characteristics of help provision for eldery people living at home and in relation to quality of life. *Scandinavian Journal of Caring Sciences, 18,* 387–395.

Hendin, H., & Haas, A. P. (1991). Suicide and guilt as manifestations of PTSD in Vietnam combat veterans. *American Journal of Psychiatry, 148,* 586–591.

Henkel, L. A., Franklin, N., & Johnson, M. K. (2000). Cross-modal source monitoring confusions between perceived and imagined events. *Journal of Experimental Psychology: Learning, Memory, and Cognition, 26,* 321–335.

Herek, G. (2002). Gender gaps in public opinion about lesbians and gay men. *Public Opinion Quarterly, 66,* 40–66.

Hernandez, L., & Hoebel, B. G. (1989). Food intake and lateral hypothalamic self-stimulation covary after medial hypothalamic lesions or ventral midbrain 6-hydroxydopamine injections that cause obesity. *Behavioral Neuroscience, 103,* 412–422.

Herness, S. (2000). Coding in taste receptor cells: The early years of intracellular recordings. *Physiology and Behavior, 69,* 17–27.

Heron, M. (2012). Deaths: Leading causes for 2009. *National Vital Statistics Reports, 61,* 1–96.

Herpetz, S., Vloet, T., Mueller, B., Domes, G., Willmes, K., & Herpetz-Dahlmann, B. (2007). Similar autonomic responsivity in boys with conduct disorder and their fathers. *Journal of the American Academy of Child & Adolescent Psychiatry, 46,* 535–544.

Hetherington, A. W., & Ranson, S. W. (1940). Hypothalamic lesions and adiposity in the rat. *Anatomical Record, 78,* 149–172.

Heyman, G., Gee, C., & Giles, J. (2003). Preschool children's reasoning about ability. *Child Development, 74,* 516–534.

Hickman, J., & Geller, E. (2003). A safety self-management intervention for mining operations. *U.S. Journal of Safety Research, 34,* 299–308.

Higgins, E., & George, M. (2009). *Brain stimulation therapies for clinicians.* Arlington, VA: American Psychiatric Publishing.

Hilgard, E. R. (1986). *Divided consciousness: Multiple controls in human thought and action.* New York: Wiley.

Hilgard, E. R. (1992). Dissociation and theories of hypnosis. In E. Fromm & M. R. Nash (Eds.), *Contemporary hypnosis research* (pp. 69–101). New York: Guilford.

Hill, M., & Augoustinos, M. (2001). Stereotype change and prejudice reduction: Short- and long-term evaluation of a cross-cultural awareness programme. *Journal of Community & Applied Social Psychology, 11,* 243–262.

Hirsch, J. (2012). Virtual reality exposure therapy and hypnosis for flying phobia in a treatment-resistant patient: A case report. *American Journal of Clinical Hypnosis, 55,* 168–173.

Hirsch, D., & Zukowska, Z. (2012). NPY and stress 30 years later: The peripheral view. *Cellular and Molecular Neurobiology, 32*, 645–659.

Hirsh, J., Quilty, L., Bagby, R., & McMain, S. (2012). The relationship between agreeableness and the development of the working alliance in patients with borderline personality disorder. *Journal of Personality Disorders, 26*, 616–627.

Hirst, W., & Echterhoff, G. (2012). Remember in conversations: The social sharing and reshaping of memories. *Annual Review of Psychology, 63*, 55–79.

Hirst, W., Phelps, E., Buckner, R., Budson, A., Cuc, A., Gabrieli, J., Johnson, M., Lustig, C., Lyle, K., Mather, M., Meksin, R., Mitchell, K., Ochsner, K., Schacter, D., Simons, J., & Vaidya, C. (2009). Long-term memory for the terrorist attack of September 11: Flashbulb memories, event memories, and the factors that influence their retention. *Journal of Experimental Psychology: General, 138*, 161–176.

Hobson, J. A. (1988). *The dreaming brain*. New York: Basic Books.

Hobson, J. A. (1989). *Sleep*. New York: Scientific American Library.

Hobson, J. A., & McCarley, R. W. (1977). The brain as a dream state generator: An activation-synthesis hypothesis of the dream process. *American Journal of Psychiatry, 134*, 1335–1348.

Hockett, C. (1959). Animal "language" and human language. *Human Biology, 31*, 32–39.

Hofer, H., Carroll, J., Neitz, J., Neitz, M., & Williams, D. (2005). Organization of the human trichromatic cone mosaic. *Journal of Neuroscience, 25*, 9669–9679.

Hoffman, M. (2007). The origins of empathic morality in toddlerhood. In C., Brownell, & C. Kopp (Eds.), *Socioemotional development in the toddler years: Transitions and transformations* (pp. 132–145). New York: Guilford Press.

Hofstede, G. (1980). *Culture's consequences: International differences in work-related values*. Beverly Hills, CA: Sage.

Hofstede, G. (1983). Dimensions of national cultures in fifty countries and three regions. In J. Deregowski, S. Dzuirawiec, and R. Annis (Eds.), *Explications in cross-cultural psychology* (pp. 335–355). Lisse, The Netherlands: Swets and Zeitlinger.

Holden, C. (1996). Sex and olfaction. *Science, 273*, 313.

Holland, C., & Rathod, V. (2012). Influence of personal mobile phone ringing and usual intention to answer on driver error. *Accident Analysis and Prevention*, August 4, 2012.

Hollon, S., Thase, M., & Markowitz, J. (2002). Treatment and prevention of depression. *Psychological Science in the Public Interest, 3*, 39–77.

Holmes, T. H., & Masuda, M. (1974). Life change and illness susceptibility. In B. S. Dohrenwend & B. P. Dohrenwend (Eds.), *Stressful life events: Their nature and effects* (pp. 45–72). New York: Wiley.

Holmes, T. H., & Rahe, R. H. (1967). The social readjustment rating scale. *Journal of Psychosomatic Research, 11*, 213–218.

Home, S., & Biss, W. (2005). Sexual satisfaction as more than a gendered concept: The roles of psychological well-being and sexual orientation. *Journal of Constructivist Psychology, 18*, 25–38.

Hong, Y., Wyer, R., & Fong, C. (2008). Chinese working in groups: Effort dispensability versus normative influence. *Asian Journal of Social Psychology, 11*, 187–195.

Hooten, W., Wolter, T., Ames, S., Hurt, R., Viciers, K., Offord, K., & Hays, J. (2005). Personality correlates related to tobacco abstinence following treatment. *International Journal of Psychiatry in Medicine, 35*, 59–74.

Hopkins, W., & Cantalupo, C. (2004). Handedness in chimpanzees (*Pan troglodytes*) is associated with asymmetries of the primary motor cortex but not with homologous language areas. *Behavioral Neuroscience, 118*, 1176–1183.

Horberry, T., Anderson, J., Regan, M., Triggs, T., & Brown, J. (2006). Driver distraction: The effects of concurrent in-vehicle tasks, road environment complexity and age on driving performance. *Accident Analysis & Prevention, 38*, 185–191.

Horn, J. L. (1982). The theory of fluid and crystallized intelligence in relation to concepts of cognitive psychology and aging in adulthood. In F. I. M. Craik & S. Trehub (Eds.), *Aging and cognitive processes* (pp. 201–238). New York: Plenum Press.

Horney, K. (1937). *The neurotic personality of our time*. New York: W. W. Norton.

Horney, K. (1939). *New ways in psychoanalysis*. New York: W. W. Norton.

Horney, K. (1945). *Our inner conflicts*. New York: W. W. Norton.

Horney, K. (1950). *Neurosis and human growth*. New York: W. W. Norton.

Horney, K. (1967). *Feminine psychology*. New York: W. W. Norton.

Hoshi, R., Pratt, H., Mehta, S., Bond, A., & Curran, H. (2006). An investigation into the sub-acute effects of ecstasy on aggressive interpretive bias and aggressive mood—Are there gender differences? *Journal of Psychopharmacology, 20*, 291–301.

Hovland, C. I., Lumsdaine, A. A., & Sheffield, F. D. (1949). *Experiments on mass communication*. Princeton, NJ: Princeton University Press.

Howard, A. D., Feighner, S. D., Cully, D. F., Arena, J. P., Liberator, P. A., Rosenblum, C. I., et al. (1996). A receptor in pituitary and hypothalamus that functions in growth hormone release. *Science, 273*, 974–977.

Howlader, N., Noone, A., Krapcho, M., Neyman, N., Aminou, R., Altekruse, D., Kosary, C., Ruhl, J., Tatalovich, Z., Cho, H., Mariotto, A., Eisner, M., Lewis, D., Chen, H., Feuer, E., & K. Cronin. (2012). Retrieved January 8, 2013, from http://seer.cancer.gov/csr/1975_2009_pops09/

Hrushesky, W. J. M. (1994, July/August). Timing is everything. *The Sciences*, pp. 32–37.

Hsieh, P., & Colas, J. (2012). Awareness is necessary for extracting patterns in working memory but not for directing spatial attention. *Journal of Experimental Psychology: Human Perception and Performance, 38*, 1085–1090.

Hua, M., & Tan, A. (2012). Media reports of Olympic success by Chinese and American gold medalists: Cultural differences in causal attribution. *Mass Communication & Society, 15*, 546–558.

Hubel, D. H. (1963). The visual cortex of the brain. *Scientific American, 209*, 54–62.

Hubel, D. H. (1995). *Eye, brain, and vision*. New York: Scientific American Library.

Hubel, D. H., & Wiesel, T. N. (1959). Receptive fields of single neurons in the cat's striate cortex. *Journal of Physiology, 148*, 547–591.

Hubel, D. H., & Wiesel, T. N. (1979). Brain mechanisms of vision. *Scientific American, 241*, 130–144.

Huesman, L., Moise-Titus, J., Podolski, C., & Eron, L. (2003). Longitudinal relations between children's exposure to television violence and their aggressive and violent behavior in young adulthood. *Developmental Psychology, 39*, 201–221.

Hughes, J. (2008). A review of recent reports on autism: 1000 studies published in 2007. *Epilepsy & Behavior, 13*, 425–437.

Hughes, S., Levinson, G., Rosen, M., & Shnider, S. (2002). *Shnider and Levinson's anesthesia for obstetrics*. Chicago, IL: Wolters Kluwer Health.

Hull, C. L. (1943). *Principles of behavior*. New York: Appleton-Century-Crofts.

Hultsch, D. F., & Dixon, R. A. (1990). Learning and memory in aging. In J. E. Birren & K. W. Schaie (Eds.), *Handbook of the psychology of aging* (3rd ed., pp. 359–374). San Diego: Academic Press.

Hunton, J., & Rose, J. (2005). Cellular telephones and driving performance: The effects of attentional demands on motor vehicle crash risk. *Risk Analysis, 25,* 855–866.

Hupbach, A., & Fieman, R. (2012). Moderate stress enhances immediate and delayed retrieval of educationally relevant material in healthy young men. *Behavioral Neuroscience,* 819–825.

Hur, Y. (2009). Genetic and environmental covariations among obsessive-compulsive, symptoms, neuroticism, and extraversion in South Korean adolescent and young adult twins. *Twin Research and Human Genetics, 12,* 142–149.

Huttenlocher, P. (1994). Synaptogenesis, synapse elimination, and neural plasticity in human cerebral cortex. In C. Nelson (Ed.), *The Minnesota symposia on child psychology* (Vol. 27, pp. 35–54). Hillsdale, NJ: Erlbaum.

Hyde, J. (2005). The gender similarities hypothesis. *American Psychologist, 60,* 581–592.

Iacoboni, M. (2009). Neurobiology of imitation. *Current Opinion in Neurobiology, 19,* 661–665.

Intons-Peterson, M. J., & Fournier, J. (1986). External and internal memory aids: When and how often do we use them? *Journal of Experimental Psychology: General, 115,* 267–280.

Iredale, W., & van Vugt, M. (2012). Altruism as showing off: A signaling perspective on promoting green behavior and acts of kindness. In S. Roberts (Ed.). *Applied evoluationary psychology.* (pp. 173–185). New York, NY, USA: Oxford University Press.

Isaksson, K., Johansson, G., Bellaagh, K., & Sjöberg, A. (2004). Work values among the unemployed: Changes over time and some gender differences. *Scandinavian Journal of Psychology, 45,* 207–214.

Ishii, K. (2011). Mere exposure to faces increases attention to vocal affect: A cross-cultural investigation. *Cognitive Studies: Bulletin of the Japanese Cognitive Science Society, 18,* 453–461.

Izard, C.E. (1971). *The face of emotion.* New York: Appleton-Century-Crofts.

Izard, C. E. (1992). Basic emotions, relations among emotions, and emotion-cognition relations. *Psychological Review, 99,* 561–565.

Izard, C. E. (1993). Four systems for emotion activation: Cognitive and noncognitive processes. *Psychological Review, 100,* 68–90.

Jacklin, C. N. (1989). Female and male: Issues of gender. *American Psychologist, 44,* 127–133.

Jackson, J., Bogg, T., Walton, K., Wood, D., Harms, P., Lodi-Smith, J., Edmonds, G., & Roberts, B. (2009). Not all conscientiousness scales change alike: A multimethod, multisample study of age differences in the facets of conscientiousness. *Journal of Personality and Social Psychology, 96,* 446–459.

Jain, V. (2012). *Psychosocial and environmental pregnancy risks.* Retrieved December 16, 2012, from http://emedicine.medscape.com/article/259346-overview#aw2aab6b7

James, W. (1890). *The principles of psychology.* New York, NY, USA: Henry Holt and Co.

James, W. (1884). What is an emotion? *Mind, 9,* 188–205.

Janis, I. (2007). Groupthink. In R. Vecchio (Ed.), *Leadership: Understanding the dynamics of power and influence in organizations* (2nd ed.) (pp. 157–169). Notre Dame, IN: University of Notre Dame Press.

Janis, I. L. (1982). *Groupthink: Psychological studies of policy decisions and fiascoes* (2nd ed.). Boston: Houghton Mifflin.

Jansz, J. (2005). The emotional appeal of violent video games for adolescent males. *Communication Theory, 15,* 219–241.

Jansz, J., & Martens, L. (2005). Gaming at a LAN event: The social context of playing video games. *New Media & Society, 7,* 333–355.

Jarvin, L., Newman, T., Randi, J., Sternberg, R., & Grigorenko, E. (2008). Matching instruction and assessment. In J., Plucker, & C. Callahan (Eds.), *Critical issues and practices in gifted education: What the research says* (pp. 345–365). Waco, TX: Prufrock Press.

Jaynes, J. (1976). *The origin of consciousness and the breakdown of the bicameral mind.* Boston, MA, USA: Houghton Mifflin.

Jelicic, M., & Bonke, B. (2001). Memory impairments following chronic stress? A critical review. *European Journal of Psychiatry, 15,* 225–232.

Jellinek, E. M. (1960). *The disease concept of alcoholism.* New Brunswick, NJ: Hillhouse Press.

Jeltova, I., Birney, D., Fredine, N., Jarvin, L., Sternberg, R., & Grigorenko, E. (2007). Dynamic assessment as a process-oriented assessment in educational settings. *Advances in Speech Language Pathology, 9,* 273–285.

Jenike, M. A. (1990, April). Obsessive-compulsive disorder. *Harvard Medical School Health Letter, 15,* 4–8.

Jenkins, J. J., Jimenez-Pabon, E., Shaw, R. E., & Sefer, J. W. (1975). *Schuell's aphasia in adults: Diagnosis, prognosis, and treatment* (2nd ed.). Hagerstown, MD: Harper & Row.

Jewell, J., & Buehler, B. (2011). *Fragile x syndrome.* Retrieved October 23, 2012 from http://emedicine.medscape.com/article/943776-overview

Jing, L. (2004). Neural correlates of insight. *Acta Psychologica Sinica, 36,* 219–234.

John, L. (2004). Subjective well-being in a multicultural urban population: Structural and multivariate analyses of the Ontario Health Survey well-being scale. *Social Indicators Research, 68,* 107–126.

Johnson, J., Simmons, C., Trawalter, S., Ferguson, T., & Reed, W. (2003). Variation in Black anti-White bias and target distancing cues: Factors that influence perceptions of "ambiguously racist" behavior. *Personality & Social Psychology Bulletin, 29,* 609–622.

Johnson, M., Hashtroudi, S., & Lindsay, S. (1993). Source monitoring. *Psychological Bulletin, 114,* 3–28.

Johnson, M. P., Duffy, J. F., Dijk, D-J., Ronda, J. M., Dyal, C. M., & Czeisler, C. A. (1992). Short-term memory, alertness and performance: A reappraisal of their relationship to body temperature. *Journal of Sleep Research, 1,* 24–29.

Johnson, W., Bouchard, T., McGue, M., Segal, N., Tellegen, A., Keyes, M., & Gottesman, I. (2007). Genetic and environmental influences on the verbal-perceptual-image rotation (VPR) model of the structure of mental abilities in the Minnesota study of twins reared apart. *Intelligence, 35,* 542–562.

Johnson, W., Turkheimer, E., Gottesman, I., & Bouchard, T. (2009). Beyond heritability: Twin studies in behavioral research. *Current Directions in Psychological Science, 18,* 207–220.

Johnston, D. (2000). A series of cases of dementia presenting with PTSD symptoms in World War II combat veterans. *Journal of the American Geriatrics Society, 48,* 70–72.

Johnston, L. D., O'Malley, P. M., Bachman, J. G., & Schulenberg, J. E. (2010). *Monitoring the future national results on adolescent drug use: Overview of key findings, 2009* (NIH Publication No. [yet to be assigned]). Bethesda, MD: National Institute on Drug Abuse.

Joiner, T., Van Orden, K., Witte, T., & Rudd, M. (2009). Diagnoses associated with suicide. In T., Joiner, K., Van Orden, T., Witte, & M. Rudd (Eds.), *The interpersonal theory of suicide: Guidance for working with suicidal clients* (pp. 21–51). Washington, DC: American Psychological Association.

Jones, E. E., & Nisbett, R. E. (1971). *The actor and the observer: Divergent perceptions of the causes of behavior.* New York: General Learning.

Jones, M. (1924). A laboratory study of fear: The case of Peter. *Pedagogical Seminary, 31,* 308–315.

Jones, P. (2005). The American Indian Church and its sacramental use of peyote: A review for professionals in the mental-health arena. *Mental Health, Religion, & Culture, 8,* 227–290.

Jones, R. (2003). Listen and learn. *Nature Reviews Neuroscience, 4,* 699.

Jones, S. (2003). *Let the games begin: Gaming technology and entertainment among college students.* Washington, DC: Pew Internet and American Life Project. Retrieved May 17, 2006, from *http://www.pewinternet.org/PPF/r/93/report_display.asp*

Jordan, C., Logel, C., Spencere, S., & Zanna, M. (2012). Discrepancies between implicit and explicit attitudes, prejudices, and self-esteem: A model of simultaneous accessibility. In B. Gawronski, & F. Strack. (Eds.). *Cognitive consistency: A fundamental principle in social cognition.* (pp. 202–222). New York, NY, USA: Guilford Press.

Jorgensen, G. (2006). Kohlberg and Gilligan: Duet or duel? *Journal of Moral Education, 35,* 179–196.

Jorgensen, M., & Keiding, N. (1991). Estimation of spermarche from longitudinal spermaturia data. *Biometrics, 47,* 177–193.

Josephs, R., Newman, M., Brown, R., & Beer, J. (2003). Status, testosterone, and human intellectual performance. *Psychological Science, 14,* 158–163.

Josephs, L., & Weinberger, J. (2013). Psychocynamic psychotherapy. In G. Stricker, T. Wikiger, & I. Weiner. (Eds.) *Handbook of psychology, Vol. 8: Clinical psychology* (2nd ed.). (pp. 431–453). Hoboken, NJ, USA: John Wiley & Sons, Inc.

Judd, L. L., Akiskal, H. S., Zeller, P. J., Paulus, M., Leon, A. C., Maser, J. D., et al. (2000). Psychosocial disability during the long-term course of unipolar major depressive disorder. *Archives of General Psychiatry, 57,* 375–380.

Judd, L., Akiskal, H., Schettler, P., Coryell, W., Endicott, J., Maser, J., Solomon, D., Leon, A., & Keller, M. (2003). A prospective investigation of the natural history of the long-term weekly symptomatic status of bipolar II. *Archives of General Psychiatry, 60,* 261–269.

Julien, R. M. (1995). *A primer of drug action* (7th ed.). New York: W.H. Freeman.

Junco, R., & Cotton, S. (2012). The relationship between multitasking and academic performance. *Computers & Education, 59,* 505–514.

Jung, C. G. (1933). *Modern man in search of a soul.* New York: Harcourt Brace Jovanovich.

Köhler, W. (1925). *The mentality of apes* (E. Winter, Trans.). New York: Harcourt Brace Jovanovich.

Kübler-Ross, E. (1969). *On death and dying.* New York: Macmillan.

Kagan, J. (2003). Foreword: A behavioral science perspective. In R. Plomin, J. DeFries, I. Craig, & P. McGuffin (Eds.), *Behavioral genetics in the postgenomic era* (pp. xvii–xxiii). Washington, DC: American Psychological Association.

Kagan, J., & Herschkowitz, N. (2005). *A young mind in a growing brain.* Hillsdale, NJ, USA: Lawrence Erlbaum Associates.

Kahneman, D., Krueger, A., Schkade, D., Schwarz, N., & Stone, A. (2006). Would you be happier if you were richer? A focusing illusion. *Science, 312,* 1908–1910.

Kahneman, D., & Tversky, A. (1984). Choices, values, and frames. *American Psychologist, 39,* 341–350.

Kail, R. (2007). Longitudinal evidence that increases in processing speed and working memory enhance children's reasoning. *Psychological Science, 18,* 312–313.

Kaiser, C., & Pratt-Hyatt, J. (2009). Distributing prejudice unequally: Do whites direct their prejudice toward strongly identified minorities? *Journal of Personality and Social Psychology, 96,* 432–445.

Kaiser Family Foundation. (2012). *The global HIV/AIDS epidemic.* Retrieved January 7, 2013, from http://www.kff.org/hivaids/upload/3030-17.pdf

Kalidindi, S., & McGuffin, P. (2003). The genetics of affective disorders: Present and future. In R. Plomin, J. Defries, I. Craig, & P. McGuffin (Eds.), *Behavioral genetics in the postgenomic era* (pp. 481–502). Washington, DC: American Psychological Association.

Kallio, S., & Revonsuo, A. (2003). Hypnotic phenomena and altered states of consciousness: A multilevel framework of description and explanation. *Contemporary Hypnosis, 20,* 111–164.

Kaltiala-Heino, R., Rimpelae, M., Rissanen, A., & Rantanen, P. (2001). Early puberty and early sexual activity are associated with bulimic-type eating pathology in middle adolescence. *Journal of Adolescent Health, 28,* 346–352.

Kanner, A. D., Coyne, J. C., Schaefer, C., & Lazarus, R. S. (1981). Comparison of two modes of stress measurement: Daily hassles and uplifts versus major life events. *Journal of Behavioral Medicine, 4,* 1–39.

Karau, S. J., & Williams, K. D. (1993). Social loafing; a meta-analytic review and theoretical integration. *Journal of Personality and Social Psychology, 65,* 681–706.

Karlson, B., Eek, F., Ørbæk, P., & Österberg, K. (2009). Effects on sleep-related problems and self-reported health after a change of shift schedule. *Journal of Occupational Health Psychology, 14,* 97–109.

Karni, A., Tanne, D., Rubenstein, B. S., Askenasy, J. J. M., & Sagi, D. (1994). Dependence on REM sleep of overnight improvement of a perceptual skill. *Science, 265,* 679–682.

Karpicke, J., Butler, A., & Roediger, H. (2009). Metacognitive strategies in student learning: Do students practise retrieval when they study on their own? *Memory, 17,* 471–479.

Katerndahl, D., Burge, S., & Kellogg, N. (2005). Predictors of development of adult psychopathology in female victims of childhood sexual abuse. *Journal of Nervous and Mental Disease, 193,* 258–264.

Katz-Wise, S., Priess, H., & Hyde, J. (2010). Gender-role attitudes and behavior across the transition to parenthood. *Developmental Psychology, 46,* 18–28.

Katzell, R. A., & Thompson, D. E. (1990). Work motivation: Theory and practice. *American Psychologist, 45,* 144–153.

Kaufman, S. (2011). Intelligence and the cognitive unconscious. In R. Sternberg & S. Kaufman (Eds.) *Cambridge handbook of intelligence.* New York, NY, USA: Cambridge University Press.

Kawanishi, Y., Tachikawa, H., & Suzuki, T. (2000). Pharmacogenomics and schizophrenia. *European Journal of Pharmacology, 410,* 227–241.

Keating, C. R. (1994). World without words: Messages from face and body. In W. J. Lonner & R. Malpass (Eds.), *Psychology and culture* (pp. 175–182). Boston: Allyn & Bacon.

Keesey, R. (1978). Set-points and body weight regulation: Biological constants or "set-points." *Psychiatric Clinics of North America, 1,* 523–543.

Keitner, N., & Boschini, D. (2009). Electroconvulsive therapy. *Perspectives in Psychiatric Care, 45,* 66–70.

Keller, H. (2011). Culture and cognition: Developmental perspectives. *Journal of Cognitive Education and Psychology, 10,* 3–8.

Kellett, S., Newman, D., Matthews, L., & Swift, A. (2004). Increasing the effectiveness of large group format CBT via the application of practice-based evidence. *Behavioural & Cognitive Psychotherapy, 32,* 231–234.

Kelley, C., & Jacoby, L. (2012). Past selves and autobiographical memory. In S. Vazire & T. Wilson (Eds.). *Handbook of self-knowledge.* (pp. 293–309). New York, NY, USA: Guilford Press.

Kelly, C., & McCreadie, R. (2000). Cigarette smoking and schizophrenia. *Advances in Psychiatric Treatment, 6,* 327–331.

Kelly, J., Stout, R., & Slaymaker, V. (2013). Emerging adults' treatment outcomes in relation to 12-step mutual-help attendance and active involvement. *Drug and Alcohol Dependence*, Volume 129, pp. 151–157.

Kendler, K. S., & Diehl, S. R. (1993). The genetics of schizophrenia: A current genetic-epidemiologic perspective. *Schizophrenia Bulletin, 19*, 261–285.

Kendler, K., Kupfer, D., Narrow, W., Phillips, K., & Fawcett, J. (2009). *Guidelines for making changes to DSM-V*. Retrieved February 5, 2013, from http://www.dsm5.org/ProgressReports/Documents/Guidelines-for-Making-Changes-to-DSM_1.pdf

Kennedy, Q., Mather, M., & Carstensen, L. (2004). The role of motivation in the age-related positivity effect in autobiographical memory. *Psychological Science, 15*, 208–214.

Kenney-Benson, G., Pomerantz, E., Ryan, A., & Patrick, H. (2006). Sex differences in math performance: The role of children's approach to schoolwork. *Developmental Psychology, 42*, 11–26.

Kermer et al., 2006

Kermer, D., Driver-Linn, E., Wilson, T., & Gilbert, D. (2006). Loss aversion is an affective forecasting error. *Psychological Science, 17*, 649–653.

Kerr, N., & Tindale, S. (2004). Group performance and decision making. *Annual Review of Psychology, 55*, 623–655.

Kesici, S., Sahin, I., & Akturk, A. (2009). Analysis of cognitive learning strategies and computer attitudes, according to college students' gender and locus of control. *Computers in Human Behavior, 25*, 529–534.

Kessler, R. C., Stein, M. B., & Berglund, P. (1998). Social phobia subtypes in the National Comorbidity Survey. *American Journal of Psychiatry, 155*, 613–619.

Kessler, R., Adler, I., Barkley, R., Biederman, J., Conners, C., Demler, O., Faraone, S., Greenhill, L., Howes, M., Secnik, K., Spencer, T., Ustun, T., Walters, E., & Zaslavsky, A. (2006). The prevalence and correlates of adult ADHD in the United States: Results from the National Comorbidty Survey Replication. *American Journal of Psychiatry, 163*, 716–723.

Kessler, R., Angermeyer, M., Anthony, J., De Graaf, R., Demyttenaere, K., Gasquet, I., Girolamo, G., Gluzman, S., Gureje, O., Haro, J., Kawakami, N., Karam, A., Levinson, D., Mora, M., Browne, M., Posada-Villa, J., Stein, D., Tsang, C., Aguilar-Gaxiola, S., Alonso, J., Lee, S., Heeringa, S., Pennell, B., Berglund, P., Gruber, M., Petukhova, M., Chatterji, S., & Ustun, T. (2007). Lifetime prevalence and age-of-onset distributions of mental disorders in the World Health Organization's World Mental Health Survey Initiative, *World Psychiatry, 6*, 168–176.

Khaleefa, O., Abdelwahid, S., Abdulradi, F., & Lynn, R. (2008). The increase of intelligence in Sudan 1964–2006. *Personality and Individual Differences, 45*, 412–413.

Khan, A., Faucett, J., Lichtenberg, P., Kirsch, I., & Brown, W. (2012). A systematic review of comparative efficacy of treatments and controls for depression. *PLoS One, 7*, e41778.

Khanfer, R., Lord, J., & Phillips, A. (2010). Predictors of employees' early retirement intentions: An 11-year longitudinal study. *Occupational Medicine, 60*, 94–100.

Khanfer, R., Lord, J., & Phillips, A. (2011). Neutrophil fu8nciton and cortisol: DHEAS ratio in bereaved older adults. *Brain, Behavior, and Immunity, 25*, 1182–1186.

Kiecolt-Glaser, J. (2000). *Friends, lovers, relaxation, and immunity: How behavior modifies health. Cortisol and the language of love: Text analysis of newlyweds' relationship stories*. Paper presented at the annual meeting of the American Psychological Association, Washington, DC.

Kiecolt-Glaser, J. K., Fisher, L. D., Ogrocki, P., Stout, J., Speicher, C. E., & Glaser, R. (1987). Marital quality, marital disruption, and immune function. *Psychosomatic Medicine, 49*, 13–34.

Kiecolt-Glaser, J., Gouin, J., & Hantsoo, L. (2010). Close relationships, inflammation, and health. *Neuroscience and Biobehavioral Reviews, 35*, 33–38

Kihlstrom, J. (2007). Consciousness in hypnosis. In P. Zelazo, M. Moscovitch, & E. Thompson (Eds.), *The Cambridge handbook of consciousness* (pp. 445–479). New York: Cambridge University Press.

Kilbride, J. E., & Kilbride, P. L. (1975). Sitting and smiling behavior of Baganda infants. *Journal of Cross-Cultural Psychology, 6*, 88–107.

Kim, C., Redberg, R., Pavlic, T., & Eagle, K. (2007). A systematic review of gender differences in mortality after coronary artery bypass graft surgery and percutaneous coronary interventions. *Clinical Cardiology, 30*, 491–495.

Kim, H., & Chung, R. (2003). Relationship of recalled parenting style to self-perception in Korean American college students. *Journal of Genetic Psychology, 164*, 481–492.

Kim, J. J., Mohamed, S., Andreasen, N. C., O'Leary, D. S., Watkins, L., Ponto, L. L. B., et al. (2000). Regional neural dysfunctions in chronic schizophrenia studied with positron emission tomography. *American Journal of Psychiatry, 157*, 542–548.

Kim, K. H. S., Relkin, N. R., Lee, K-M., & Hirsch, J. (1997). Distinct cortical areas associated with native and second languages. *Nature, 388*, 171–174.

Kim, L., & Makdissi, A. (2009). *Hyperparathyroidism*. Retrieved January 20, 2010 from *http://emedicine.medscape.com/article/127351-overview.*

Kimber, L., McNabb, M., McCourt, C., Haines, A., & Brocklehurst, P. (2008). Massage or music for pain relief in labour: A pilot randomised placebo controlled trial. *European Journal of Pain, 12*, 961–969.

Kimura, D. (1992). Sex differences in the brain. *Scientific American, 267*, 118–125.

King, B. (2006). The rise, fall, and resurrection of the ventromedial hypothalamus in the regulation of feeding behavior and body weight. *Physiology & Behavior, 87*, 221–244.

King, D., Viney, W., & Woody, W. (2009). *A history of psychology: Ideas and context* (4th ed.). Boston, MA: Pearson Allyn & Bacon.

Kinnunen, T., Zamansky, H. S., & Block, M. L. (1994). Is the hypnotized subject lying? *Journal of Abnormal Psychology, 103*, 184–191.

Kinsey, A. C., Pomeroy, W. B., & Martin, C. E. (1948). *Sexual behavior in the human male*. Philadelphia: W. B. Saunders.

Kinsey, A. C., Pomeroy, W. B., Martin, C. E., & Gebhard, P. H. (1953). *Sexual behavior in the human female*. Philadelphia: W. B. Saunders.

Kirchner, T., & Sayette, M. (2003). Effects of alcohol on controlled and automatic memory processes. *Experimental & Clinical Psychopharmacology, 11*, 167–175.

Kirkcaldy, B., Shephard, R., & Furnham, A. (2002). The influence of Type A behavior and locus of control upon job satisfaction and occupational health. *Personality & Individual Differences, 33*, 1361–1371.

Kirsch, I., & Lynn, S. J. (1995). The altered state of hypnosis: Changes in the theoretical landscape. *American Psychologist, 50*, 846–858.

Kirshner, H., & Hoffmann, M. (2012). *Aphasia*. Retrieved October 23, 2012, from http://emedicine.medscape.com/article/1135944-clinical#a0217

Kirshner, H., & Jacobs, D. (2008). *Aphasia*. Retrieved February 3, 2009 from *http://emedicine.medscape.com/article/1135944-overview.*

Kirvan, C., Swedo, S., Snider, L., & Cunningham, M. (2006). Antibody-mediated neuronal cell signaling in behavior and movement disorders. *Journal of Neuroimmunology, 179*, 173–179.

Kitayama, S., & Markus, H. R. (2000). The pursuit of happiness and the realization of sympathy: Cultural patterns of self, social relations, and well-being. In E. Diener & E. M. Suh (Eds.), *Subjective well-being across cultures* (pp. 113–164). Cambridge, MA: MIT Press.

Kiyatkin, E., & Wise, R. (2002). Brain and body hyperthermia associated with heroin self-administration in rats. *Journal of Neuroscience, 22,* 1072–1080

Klaczynski, P., Fauth, J, & Swanger, A. (1998). Adolescent identity: Rational vs. experiental processing, formal operations, and critical thinking beliefs. *Journal of Youth & Adolescence, 17,* 185–207.

Klar, A. (2003). Human handedness and scalp hair-whorl direction develop from a common genetic mechanism. *Genetics, 165,* 269–276.

Klatzky, R. L. (1980). *Human memory: Structures and processes* (2nd ed.). New York: W. H. Freeman.

Kleinman, A., & Cohen, A. (1997, March). Psychiatry's global challenge. *Scientific American, 276,* 86–89.

Klerman, E., & Dijk, D. (2008). Age-related reduction in the maximal capacity for sleep: Implications for insomnia. *Current Biology, 18,* 1118–1123.

Kline, G., Stanley, S., Markan, H., Olmos-Gallo, P., St. Peters, M., Whitton, S., et al. (2004). Timing is everything: Pre-engagement cohabitation and increased risk for poor marital outcomes. *Journal of Family Psychology, 18,* 311–318.

Klucharev, V., Smidts, A., & Fernandez, G. (2008). Brain mechanisms of persuasion: How "expert power" modulates memory and attitudes. *Social Cognitive and Affective Neuroscience, 3,* 353–366.

Kluwer, E., & Johnson, M. (2007). Conflict frequency and relationship quality across the transition to parenthood. *Journal of Marriage and Family, 69,* 1089–1106.

Kmietowicz, Z. (2002). US and UK are top in teenage pregnancy rates. *British Medical Journal, 324,* 1354.

Knafo, D. (2009). Freud's memory erased. *Psychoanalytic Psychology, 26,* 171–190.

Knapp, C., Ciraulo, D., & Kranzler, H. (2008). Neurobiology of alcohol. In M. Galanter & H. Kleber (Eds.), *The American Psychiatric Publishing textbook of substance abuse* (4th ed., pp. 111–128). Arlington, VA: American Psychiatric Publishing.

Knipe, J. (2010). Dysfunctional positive affect: Procrastination. In M. Luber (Ed.). *Eye movement desensitization and reprocessing (EMDR) scripted protocols: Special populations* (pp. 453–458). New York: Springer Publishing Company.

Knussen, C., & Yule, F. (2008). "I'm not in the habit of recycling": The role of habitual behavior in the disposal of household waste. *Environment and Behavior, 40,* 683–702.

Knyazev, G. (2009). Is cortical distribution of spectral power a stable individual characteristic? *International Journal of Psychophysiology, 72,* 123–133.

Kobasa, S. (1979). Stressful life events, personality, and health: An inquiry into hardiness. *Journal of Personality and Social Psychology, 37,* 1–11.

Kobasa, S. C., Maddi, S. R., & Kahn, S. (1982). Hardiness and health: A prospective study. *Journal of Personality and Social Psychology, 42,* 168–177.

Koehler, T., Tiede, G., & Thoens, M. (2002). Long and short-term forgetting of word associations: An experimental study of the Freudian concepts of resistance and repression. *Zeitschrift fuer Klinische Psychologie, Psychiatrie and Psychotherapie, 50,* 328–333.

Koenig, L., & Vaillant, G. (2009). A prospective study of church attendance and health over the lifespan. *Health Psychology, 28,* 117–124.

Kohlberg, L. (1966). A cognitive-developmental analysis of children's sex-role concepts and attitudes. In E. E. Maccoby (Ed.), *The development of sex differences* (pp. 82–173). Palo Alto, CA: Stanford University Press.

Kohlberg, L. (1968, September). The child as a moral philosopher. *Psychology Today,* 24–30.

Kohlberg, L., & Ullian, D. Z. (1974). In R. C. Friedman, R. M. Richart, & R. L. Vande Wiele (Eds.), *Sex differences in behavior* (pp. 209–222). New York: Wiley.

Kolivas, E., Riordan, P., & Gross, A. (2008). Overview of behavioral treatment with children and adolescents. In M., Hersen, & D. Reitman (Eds.), *Handbook of psychological assessment, case conceptualization, and treatment, Vol. 2: Children and adolescents.* Hoboken, NJ: John Wiley & Sons.

Koltz, C. (1983, December). Scapegoating. *Psychology Today,* 68–69.

Konigsberg, R. (2011). *The truth about grief: The myth of its five stages and the new science of loss.* New York, NY: USA: Simon & Schuster.

Konstantareas, M. (2006). Social skill training in high functioning autism and Asperger's disorder. *Hellenic Journal of Psychology, 268,* 66–73.

Koob, G. (2008). Neurobiology of addiction. In M. Galanter & H. Kleber (Eds.), *The American Psychiatric Publishing textbook of substance abuse* (4th ed., pp. 3–16). Arlington, VA: American Psychiatric Publishing.

Kopelowicz, A., Liberman, R., & Zarate, R. (2007). In P. Nathan, & J. Gorman (Eds.), *A guide to treatments that work* (3rd ed.). New York: Oxford University Press.

Kopp, D., Spitzer, C., Kuwert, P., Barnow, S., Orlob, S., Lüth, H., Freyberger, H., & Dudeck, M. (2009). Psychiatric disorders and childhood trauma in prisoners with antisocial personality disorder. *Fortschiritte der Neurologie, Psychiatrie, 77,* 152–159.

Korobov, N., & Thorne, A. (2006). Intimacy and distancing: Young men's conversations about romantic relationships. *Journal of Adolescent Research, 21,* 27–55.

Korten, N., Comijs, H., Lamers, F., & Penninx, B. (2012). Early and late onset depression in young and middle aged adults: Differential symptomatology, characteristics, and risk factors? *Journal of Affective Disorders, 138,* 259–267.

Kosslyn, S., Thompson, W., & Ganis, G. (2009). *The case for mental imagery.* New York, NY, USA: Oxford University Press, USA.

Kouider, S., deGardelle, V., Dehaene, S., Dupoux, E., & Pallier, C. (2009). Cerebral bases of subliminal speech priming. *Neuroimage, 49,* 922–929.

Kounios, J., Fleck, J., Green, D., Payne, L., Stevenson, J., Bowden, E., & Jung-Beeman, M. (2008). The origins of insight in resting-state brain activity. *Neuropsychologia, 46,* 281–291.

Kovacs, D., Mahon, J., & Palmer, R. (2002). Chewing and spitting out food among eating-disordered patients. *International Journal of Eating Disorders, 32,* 112–115.

Kovas, Y., Haworth, C., Dale, P., & Plomin, R. (2007). The genetic and environmental origins of learning abilities and disabilities in the early school years. *Monographs of the Society for Research in Child Development, 72,* 1–144.

Kozak, M. J., Foa, E. B., & McCarthy, P. R. (1988). Obsessive-compulsive disorder. In C. G. Last & M. Herson (Eds.), *Handbook of anxiety disorders* (pp. 87–108). New York: Pergamon Press.

Kranzler, H. R. (1996). Evaluation and treatment of anxiety symptoms and disorders in alcoholics. *Journal of Clinical Psychiatry, 57*(6, Suppl.).

Kraus, S. J. (1995). Attitudes and the prediction of behavior: A meta-analysis of the empirical literature. *Personality and Social Psychology Bulletin, 21,* 58–75.

Krcmar, M., & Cooke, M. (2001). Children's moral reasoning and their perceptions of television violence. *Journal of Communication, 51,* 300–316.

Krebs, D., & Denton, K. (2005). Toward a more pragmatic approach to morality: A critical evaluation of Kohlberg's model. *Psychological Review, 112,* 629–649.

Krebs, N., & Primak, L. (2011). Pediatric nutrition and nutritional disorders. In K. Marcdante, R. Kliegman, H. Jensen, & R. Behrman (Eds.). *Nelson's essential of pediatrics.* (pp. 103–122). New York: Elsevier Health Publishers.

Kripke, D., Garfinkel, L., Wingard, D., Klauber, M., & Marler, M. (2002). Mortality associated with sleep duration. *Archives of General Psychiatry, 59,* 131–136.

Kripke, D., Youngstedt, S., Elliott, J., Tuunainen, A., Rex, K., Hauger, R., et al. (2005). Circadian phase in adults of contrasting ages. *Chronobiology International, 22,* 695–709.

Krueger, R., & Johnson, W. (2004). Genetic and environmental structure of adjectives describing the domains of the Big Five model of personality: A nationwide U.S. twin study. *Journal of Research in Personality, 38,* 448–472.

Kruk, M., Meelis, W., Halasz, J., & Haller, J. (2004). Fast positive feedback between the adrenocortical stress response and a brain mechanism involved in aggressive behavior. *Behavioral Neuroscience, 118,* 1062–1070.

Kubzansky, L., Cole, S., Kawachi, I., Vokonas, P., & Sparrow, D. (2006). Shared and unique contributions of anger, anxiety, and depression to coronary heart disease: A prospective study in the normative aging study. *Annals of Behavioral Medicine, 31,* 21–29.

Kucharska-Pietura, K., & Klimkowski, M. (2002). Perception of facial affect in chronic schizophrenia and right brain damage. *Acta Neurobiologiae Experimentalis, 62,* 33–43.

Kudielka, B., Federenko, I., Hellhammer, D., & Wust, S. (2006). Morningness and eveningness: The free cortisol rise after awakening in "early birds" and "night owls." *Biological Psychology, 72,* 141–146.

Kuhn, D., & Lao, J. (1996). Effects of evidence on attitudes: Is polarization the norm? *Psychological Science, 7,* 115–120.

Kumpfer, K., Alvarado, R., Smith, P., & Ballamy, N. (2002). Cultural sensitivity and adaptation in family-based prevention interventions. *Prevention Science, 3,* 241–246.

Kunkel, D., & Castonguay, J. (2012). Children and advertising: Content, comprehension, and consequences. In D. Singer & J. Singer (Eds.). *Handbook of children and the media* (2nd edition) (pp. 395–418). Thousand Oaks, CA, USA: Sage Publications, Inc.

Kunda, Z., & Oleson, K. C. (1995). Maintaining stereotypes in the face of disconfirmation: Construction grounds for subtyping deviants. *Journal of Personality and Social Psychology, 68,* 565–579.

Kunz, D., & Herrmann, W. M. (2000). Sleep-wake cycle, sleep-related disturbances, and sleep disorders: A chronobiological approach. *Comparative Psychology, 41*(2, Suppl. 1), 104–105.

Kuo, C., & Tsaur, C. (2004). Locus of control, supervisory support and unsafe behavior: The case of the construction industry in Taiwan. *Chinese Journal of Psychology, 46,* 392–405.

Kuo, W., Sjorstrom, T., Chen, Y, Wang, Y, & Huang, C. (2009). Intuition and deliberation: Two systems for strategizing in the brain. *Science, 324,* 519–522.

Kurup, R., & Kurup, P. (2002). Detection of endogenous lithium in neuropsychiatric disorders. *Human Psychopharmacology: Clinical & Experimental, 17,* 29–33.

Kwong, O. (2013). *New perspectives on computational and cognitive strategies for word sense disambiguation.* New York, NY, USA: Springer Science + Business Media.

LaFarge, L. (2012). Defense and resistance. In G. Gabbard, B. Litowitz, & P. Williams (Eds.). *Textbook of psychoanalysis* (wnd ed.). (pp. 93–104). Arlington, VA: USA: American Psychiatric Publishing, Inc.

Lafferty, K. (2008). *Toxicity, barbiturate.* Retrieved February 8, 2010 from *http://emedicine.medscape.com/article/813155-overview.*

Lahon, K., Shetty, H., Paramel, A., & Sharma, G. (2011). Sexual dysfunction with the use of antidepressants in a tertiary care mental health setting—A retrospective case series. *Journal of Pharmacology and Pharmacotherapy, 2,* 128–131.

Laitinen, H. (2005). Factors affecting the use of hearing protectors among classical music players. *Noise & Health, 7,* 21–29.

Lal, S. (2002). Giving children security: Mamie Phipps Clark and the racialization of child psychology. *American Psychologist, 57,* 20–28.

Lamberg, L. (1996). Narcolepsy researchers barking up the right tree. *Journal of the American Medical Association, 276,* 265–266.

Lamborn, S. D., Mounts, N. S., Steinberg, L., & Dornbusch, S. M. (1991). Patterns of competence and adjustment among adolescents from authoritative, authoritarian, indulgent, and neglectful families. *Child Development, 62,* 1049–1065.

Lambright, L. (2004). *Lessons from Vietnam.* Paper presented at International Intercultural Education Conference, St Louis, MO, April, 2004.

Lamplugh, C., Berle, D., Millicevic, D., & Starcevic, V. (2008). Pilot study of cognitive behaviour therapy for panic disorder augmented by panic surfing. *Clinical Psychology & Psychotherapy, 15,* 440–445.

Landers, D. (2007). The arousal-performance relationship revisited. In D., Smith & M. Bar-Eli (Eds.), *Essential readings in sport and exercise psychology* (pp. 211–218). Champaign, IL: Human Kinetics.

Laney, C., & Loftus, E. (2009). Eyewitness memory. In R. Koscis (Ed.), *Applied criminal psychology: A guide to forensic behavioral sciences* (pp. 121–145). Springfield, IL: Charles C. Thomas Publisher.

Lang, A. R., Goeckner, D. J., Adesso, V. J., & Marlatt, G. A. (1975). Effects of alcohol on aggression in male social drinkers. *Journal of Abnormal Psychology, 84,* 508–518.

Lang, A., Craske, M., Brown, M., & Ghaneian, A. (2001). Fear-related state dependent memory. *Cognition & Emotion, 15,* 695–703.

Langdon, K., & Corbett, D. (2012). Improved working memory following novel combinations of physical and cognitive activity. *Neurorehabilitation and Neural Repair, 26,* 523–532.

Lange, C. G., & James, W. (1922). *The emotions* (I. A. Haupt, Trans.). Baltimore: Williams and Wilkins.

Langer, E. J., & Rodin, J. (1976). The effects of choice and enhanced personal responsibility for the aged: A field experiment in an institutional setting. *Journal of Personality and Social Psychology, 34,* 191–198.

Langer, P., Holzner, B., Magnet, W., & Kopp, M. (2005). Hands-free mobile phone conversation impairs the peripheral visual system to an extent comparable to an alcohol level of 4–5g/100 ml. *Human Psychopharmacology: Clinical and Experimental, 20,* 65–66.

Langlois, J. H., Kalakanis, L., Rubenstein, A. J., Larson, A., Hallam, M., & Smoot, M. (2000). Maxims or myths of beauty? A meta-analytic and theoretical review. *Psychological Bulletin, 126,* 390–423.

Lao, J., & Kuhn, D. (2002). Cognitive engagement and attitude development. *Cognitive Development, 17,* 1203–1217.

LaPaglia, J., & Chan, J. (2012). Retrieval does not always enhance suggestibility: Testing can improve witness identification performance. *Law and Human Behavior, 36,* 478–487.

Larsson, H., Andershed, H., & Lichtenstein, P. (2006). A genetic factor explains most of the variation in the psychopathic personality. *Journal of Abnormal Psychology, 115,* 221–230.

Latané, B., Williams, K., & Harkins, S. (1979). Many hands make light the work: The causes and consequences of social loafing. *Journal of Personality and Social Psychology, 37*, 822–832.

Latner, J., & Wilson, T. (2004). Binge eating and satiety in bulimia nervosa and binge eating disorder: Effects of macronutrient intake. *International Journal of Eating Disorders, 36*, 402–415.

Laurent, J., Swerdik, M., & Ryburn, M. (1992). Review of validity research on the Stanford-Binet Intelligence Scale: Fourth Edition. *Psychological Assessment, 4*, 102–112.

Lauritsen, M., Pedersen, C., & Mortensen, P. (2004). The incidence and prevalence of pervasive developmental disorders: A Danish population-based study. *Psychological Medicine, 34*, 1339–1346.

Lawrence, V., Houghton, S., Douglas, G., Durkin, K., Whiting, K., & Tannock, R. (2004). Children with ADHD: Neuropsychological testing and real-world activites. *Journal of Attention Disorders, 7*, 137–149.

Laws, E., Apperson, J., Buchert, S., & Bregman, N. (2010). Student evaluations of instruction: When are enduring first impressions formed? *North American Journal of Psychology, 12*, 81–92.

Law, A., Logie, R., & Pearson, D. (2006). The impact of secondary tasks on multitasking in a virtual environment. *Acta Psychologica, 122*, 27–44.

Lawton, B. (2001). *Damage to human hearing by airborne sound of very high frequency or ultrasonic frequency.* Contract Research Report No. 343/2001. Highfield, Southampton, U.K.: Institution of Sound and Vibration Research, University of Southampton/Highfield. Retrieved December 13, 2006, from *http://www.compoundsecurity. co.uk/download/HSE.pdf*

Layton, L., Deeny, K., Tall, G., & Upton, G. (1996). Researching and promoting phonological awareness in the nursery class. *Journal of Research in Reading, 19*, 1–13.

Lazarus, R. S. (1966). *Psychological stress and the coping process.* New York: McGraw-Hill.

Lazarus, R. S. (1984). On the primacy of cognition. *American Psychologist, 39*, 124–129.

Lazarus, R. S. (1991a). Cognition and motivation in emotion. *American Psychologist, 46*, 352–367.

Lazarus, R. S. (1991b). Progress on a cognitive-motivational-relational theory of emotion. *American Psychologist, 46*, 819–834.

Lazarus, R. S. (1995). Vexing research problems inherent in cognitive-mediational theories of emotion—and some solutions. *Psychological Inquiry, 6*, 183–187.

Lazarus, R. S., & DeLongis, A. (1983). Psychological stress and coping in aging. *American Psychologist, 38*, 245–253.

Lazarus, R. S., & Folkman, S. (1984). *Stress, appraisal, and coping.* New York: Springer.

LeDoux, J. E. (2000). Emotion circuits in the brain. *Annual Review of Neuroscience, 23*, 155–184.

LeDoux, J., & Doyère, V. (2011). Emotional memory processing: Synaptic connectivity. In S. Nalbantian, P. Matthews, & J. McClelland (Eds.) *The memory process: Neuroscientific and humanistic perspectives.* (pp. 153–171). Campbridge, MA, USA: MIT Press.

Lee, S. (2010). Contemporary issues of ethical e-therapy. *Journal of Ethics in Mental Health, 5*, 1–5.

Lee, I., & Kesner, R. (2002). Differential contribution of NMDA receptors in hippocampal subregions to spatial working memory. *Nature Neuroscience, 5*, 162–168.

Lee, J., Kelly, K., & Edwards, J. (2006). A closer look at the relationships among trait procrastination, neuroticism, and conscientiousness. *Personality and Individual Differences, 40*, 27–37.

Lembke, A., & Humphreys, K. (2012). What self-help organizations tell us about the syndrome model of addiction. In H. Shaffer, D. LaPlante, & S. Nelson (Eds.). *APA addiction syndrome handbook, Vol. 2: Recovery, prevention, and other issues.* (pp. 157–168). Washington, DC, USA: American Psychological Association.

Lenhart, A., Jones, S., & Macgill, A. (2008). *Video games: Adults are players too.* Pew Internet & American Life Project. Retrieved February 11, 2010 from *http://pewresearch.org/pubs/1048/ video-games-adults-are-players-too.*

Leon, M. (1992). The neurobiology of filial learning. *Annual Review of Psychology, 43*, 337–398.

Leonardo, E., & Hen, R. (2006). Genetics of affective and anxiety disorders. *Annual Review of Psychology, 57*, 117–137.

Lerman, D. C., & Iwata, B. A. (1996). Developing a technology for the use of operant extinction in clinical settings: An examination of basic and applied research. *Journal of Applied Behavior Analysis, 29*, 345–382.

Lesch, K. (2003). Neuroticism and serotonin: A developmental genetic perspective. In R. Plomin, J. DeFries, I. Craig, & P. McGuffin (Eds.), *Behavioral genetics in the postgenomic era* (pp. 389–423). Washington, DC: American Psychological Association.

Lester, B., Hoffman, J., & Brazelton, T. (1985). The rhythmic structure of mother-infant interaction in term and preterm infants. *Child Development, 56*, 15–27.

Levashina, J., & Campion, M. (2007). Measuring faking in the employment interview: Development and validation of an interview faking behavior scale. *Journal of Applied Psychology, 92*, 1638–1656.

LeVay, S. (1991). A difference in hypothalamic structure between heterosexual and homosexual men. *Science, 253*, 1034–1037.

Levenson, R. W., Ekman, P., & Friesen, W. (1990). Voluntary facial action generates emotion-specific autonomic nervous system activity. *Psychophysiology, 27*, 363–385.

Levrini, A., & Prevatt, F. (2012). Overcoming procrastination and fear to improve time management. In A. Levrini & F. Prevatt (Eds.) *Succeeding with adult ADHD: Daily strategies to help you achieve your goals and manage your life* (pp. 55–88). Washington, DC, USA: American Psychological Association.

Levy, J. (1985). Right Brain, Left Brain: Fact and Fiction, *Psychology Today,* May, 43–44.

Lewald, J. (2004). Gender-specific hemispheric asymmetry in auditory space perception. *Cognitive Brain Research, 19*, 92–99.

Lewis, M. (2012). Exploring the positive and negative implications of facial feedback. *Emotion, 12*, 852–859.

Li, J. (2003). U.S. and Chinese cultural beliefs about learning. *Journal of Educational Psychology, 95*, 258–267.

Libby, D., Worhunsky, P., Pilver, C., & Brewer, J. (2012). Meditation-induced changes in high-frequency heart rate variability predict smoking outcomes. *Frontiers in Human Neuroscience, 6*, 54.

Lichtenberger, E., & Kaufman, A. (2012). *Essentials of WAIS-IV assessment.* New York, NY, USA: John Wiley & Sons.

Lilienfeld, S., Lynn, S., Namy, L., & Woolf, N. (2009). *Psychology: From inquiry to understanding.* Boston: Allyn & Bacon.

Lin, H., Mao, S., Chen, P., & Gean, P. (2008). Chronic cannabinoid administration in vivo compromises extinction of fear memory. *Learning & Memory, 15*, 876–884.

Linder, J., & Gentile, D. (2009). Is the television rating system valid? Indirect, verbal, and physical aggression in programs viewed by fifth grade girls and associations with behavior. *Journal of Applied Developmental Psychology 30*, 286–297.

Lindsay, D., Hagen, L., Read, J., Wade, K., & Garry, M. (2004). True photographs and false memories. *Psychological Science, 15,* 149–154.

Lishman, W. A. (1990). Alcohol and the brain. *British Journal of Psychiatry, 156,* 635–644.

Litz, B., Stein, N., Delaney, E., Lebowitz, L., Nash, W., Silva, C., & Maguen, S. (2009). Moral injury and moral repair in war veterans: A preliminary model and intervention strategy. *Clinical Psychology Review, 29,* 695–706.

Liu, B., & Lee, Y. (2006). In-vehicle workload assessment: Effects of traffic situations and cellular telephone use. *Journal of Safety Research, 37,* 99–105.

Liu, O., & Wilson, M. (2009). Gender differences and similarities in PISA 2003 mathematics: A comparison between the United States and Hong Kong. *International Journal of Testing, 9,* 20–40.

Liu, S., Liao, H., & Pratt, J. (2009). The impact of media richness and flow on e-learning technology acceptance. *Computers & Education, 52,* 599–607.

Livingston, E., Huerta, S., Arthur, D., Lee, S., De Shields, S., & Heber, D. (2002). Male gender is a predictor of morbidity and age a predictor of mortality for patients undergoing gastric bypass surgery. *Annals of Surgery, 236,* 576–582.

Loehlin, J. (2009). History of behavior genetics. In Kim, Y. (Ed.), *Handbook of behavior genetics* (pp. 3–14). New York: Spring Science + Business Media, LLC.

Loehlin, J. C., Horn, J. M., & Willerman, L. (1990). Heredity, environment, and personality change: Evidence from the Texas Adoption Project. *Journal of Personality, 58,* 221–243.

Loehlin, J. C., Lindzey, G., & Spuhler, J. N. (1975). *Race differences in intelligence.* San Francisco: Freeman.

Loehlin, J. C., Willerman, L., & Horn, J. M. (1987). Personality resemblance in adoptive families: A 10-year follow-up. *Journal of Personality and Social Psychology, 53,* 961–969.

Loehlin, J. C., Willerman, L., & Horn, J. M. (1988). Human behavior genetics. *Annual Review of Psychology, 39,* 101–133.

Loewenstein, G., Rick, S., & Cohen, J. (2008). Neuroeconomics. *Annual Review of Psychology, 59,* 647–672.

Lofquist, D., Lugaila, T., O'Connell, M., & Feliz, S. (2012). *Household and families: 2010.* Retrieved December 16, 2012, from http://www.census.gov/prod/cen2010/briefs/c2010br-14.pdf

Loftus, E. (2004). Memories of things unseen. *Current Directions in Psychological Science, 13,* 145–147.

Loftus, E. F. (1979). *Eyewitness testimony.* Cambridge, MA: Harvard University Press.

Loftus, E. F. (1993). Psychologists in the eyewitness world. *American Psychologist, 48,* 550–552.

Loftus, E. F., & Loftus, G. R. (1980). On the permanence of stored information in the human brain. *American Psychologist, 35,* 409–420.

Loftus, E., & Bernstein, D. (2005). Rich false memories: The royal road to success. In A. Healy (Ed.), *Experimental cognitive psychology and its applications* (pp. 101–113). Washington, DC: American Psychological Association.

Logothetis, N. (2008). What we can do and what we cannot do with fMRI. *Nature, 453,* 869–878.

Lohr, J., Olatunji, B., Baumeister, R., & Bushman, B. (2007). The psychology of anger venting and empirically supported alternatives that do no harm. *The Scientific Review of Mental Health Practice, 5,* 53–64.

Long, D., & Baynes, K. (2002). Discourse representation in the two cerebral hemispheres. *Journal of Cognitive Neuroscience, 14,* 228–242.

Long, G. M., & Crambert, R. F. (1990). The nature and basis of age-related changes in dynamic visual acuity. *Psychology and Aging, 5,* 138–143.

Lott, B., & Saxon, S. (2002). The influence of ethnicity, social class and context on judgments about U.S. women. *Journal of Social Psychology, 142,* 481–499.

Low, C., Bower, J., Moskowitz, J., & Epel, E. (2011). Positive psychological states and biological processes. In K. Sheldon, T. Kashdan, & M. Steger (Eds.). *Designing positive psychology: Taking stock and moving forward.* (pp. 41–50). New York, NY, USA: Oxford University Press.

Lubart, T. (2003). In search of creative intelligence. In R. Sternberg, J. Lautrey, & T. Lubart (Eds.), *Models of intelligence: International perspective* (pp. 279–292). Washington, DC: American Psychological Association.

Lubit, R., Bonds, C., & Lucia, M. (2009). *Sleep disorders.* Retrieved February 5, 2010 from *http://emedicine.medscape.com/article/ 287104-overview.*

Luchins, A. S. (1957). Experimental attempts to minimize the impact of first impressions. In C. I. Hovland (Ed.), *Yale studies in attitude and communication: Vol. 1. The order of presentation in persuasion* (pp. 62–75). New Haven, CT: Yale University Press.

Luders, E., Phillips, O., Clark, K., Kurth, F., Toga, A., & Narr, K. (2012). Bridging the hemispheres in meditation: Thicker callosal regions and enhanced fractional anisotropy (FA) in long-term practitioners. *NeuroImage, 61,* 181–187.

Luiselli, J., & Hurley, A. (2005). The significance of applied behavior analysis in the treatment of autism spectrum disorders (ASD). *Mental Health Aspects of Developmental Disabilities, 8,* 128–130.

Luo, S., & Klohnen, E. (2005). Assortative mating and marital quality in newlyweds: A couple-centered approach. *Journal of Personality & Social Psychology, 88,* 304–326.

Lustig, C., Konkel, A., & Jacoby, L. (2004). Which route to recovery? Controlled retrieval and accessibility bias in retroactive interference. *Psychological Science, 15,* 729–735.

Lydiard, R. B., Brawman-Mintzer, O., & Ballenger, J. C. (1996). Recent developments in the psychopharmacology of anxiety disorders. *Journal of Consulting and Clinical Psychology, 64,* 660–668.

Lynn, R. (2006). *Race differences in intelligence: An evolutionary analysis.* Atlanta, GA: Washington Summit Books.

Lynn, S., Lilienfeld, S., Merckelbach, H., Giesbrecht, T., & van der Kloet, D. (2012). Dissociation and dissociative disorders: Challenging conventional wisdom. *Current Directions in Psychological Science, 21,* 48–53.

Lyvers, M. (2000). "Loss of control" in alcoholism and drug addiction: A neuroscientific interpretation. *Experimental and Clinical Psychopharmacology, 8,* 225–245.

Müller, M., Regenbogen, B., Sachse, J., Eich, F., Härtter, S., & Hiemke, C. (2006). Gender aspects in the clinical treatment of schizophrenic inpatients with amisulpride: A therapeutic drug monitoring study. *Pharmacopsychiatry, 39,* 41–46.

Maccoby, E. E. (1992). The role of parents in the socialization of children: An historical overview. *Developmental Psychology, 28,* 1006–1017.

Maccoby, E. E., & Martin, J. A. (1983). Socialization in the context of the family: Parent-child interaction. In P. H. Mussen (Ed.), *Handbook of child psychology* (4th ed., Vol. 4. pp. 1–101). New York: John Wiley.

Macey, P., Henderson, L., Macey, K., Alger, J., Frysinger, R., Woo, M., et al. (2002). Brain morphology associated with obstructive sleep apnea. *American Journal of Respiratory and Critical Care Medicine, 166,* 1382–1387.

Macht, M., & Mueller, J. (2007). Immediate effects of chocolate on experimentally induced mood states. *Appetite, 49,* 667–674.

MacWhinney, B. (2005). Language development. In M. Bornstein & M. Lamb (Eds.), *Developmental science: An advanced textbook* (5th ed., pp. 359–387). Hillsdale, NJ: Lawrence Erlbaum Associates.

MacWhinney, B. (2011). Language development. In M. Bornstein & M. Lamb (Eds.), *Developmental science: An advanced textbook* (6th ed.). (pp. 389–424). New York: Psychology Press.

Maddi, S. (2013). *Hardiness: Turning stressful circumstances into resilient growth*, New York, NY: USA: Springer Science + Business Media.

Maguire, E. A., Gadian, D. G., Johnsrude, I. S., Good, C. D., Ashburner, J., Frackowiak, R. S. J., & Frith, C. D. (2000). Navigation-related structural change in the hippocampi of taxi drivers. *Proceedings of the National Academy of Science, 97*, 4398–4403.

Maguire, E., Nannery, R., & Spiers, H. (2006). Navigation around London by a taxi driver with bilateral hippocampal lesions. *Brain, 129*, 2894–2907.

Mahler, H., Kulik, J., Gibbons, F., Gerrard, M., & Harrell, J. (2003). Effects of appearance-based intervention on sun protection intentions and self-reported behaviors. *Health Psychology, 22*, 199–209.

Maier, S. F., & Laudenslager, M. (1985, August). Stress and health: Exploring the links. *Psychology Today*, 44–49.

Main, M., & Solomon, J. (1990). Procedures for identifying infants as disorganized/disoriented during the Ainsworth Strange Situation. In M. Greenberg, D. Cicchetti, & M. Cummings (Eds.), *Attachment in the preschool years: Theory, research, and intervention* (pp. 121–160). Chicago: University of Chicago Press.

Mainz, V., Schulte-Rüther, M., Fink, G., Herpertz-Dahlmann, B., & Konrad, K. (2012). Structural brain abnormalities in adolescent anorexia nervosa before and after weight recovery and associated hormonal changes. *Psychosomatic Medicine, 74*, 574–582.

Majercsik, E. (2005). Hierarchy of needs of geriatric patients. *Gerontology, 51*, 170–173.

Malle, B. (2006). The actor-observer asymmetry in attribution: A (surprising) meta-analysis. *Psychological Bulletin, 132*, 895–919.

Maltz, W. (1991). *The sexual healing journey: A guide for survivors of sexual abuse*. New York: HarperCollins.

Manderscheid, R., & Henderson, M. (2001). *Mental health, United States, 2000*. Rockville, MD: Center for Mental Health Services. Retrieved January 14, 2003, from *http://www.mentalhealth.org/publications/allpubs/SMA01-3537/*

Mandler, J. M. (1990). A new perspective on cognitive development in infancy. *American Scientist, 78*(3), 236–243.

Maner, J., Gailliot, M., & Miller, S. (2009). The implicit cognition of relationship maintenance: Inattention to attractives. *Journal of Experimental Social Psychology, 45*, 174–179.

Mangen, A. (2008). Hypertext fiction reading: Haptics and immersion. *Journal of Research in Reading, 31*, 404–419.

Manhal-Baugus, M. (2001). E-therapy: Practical, ethical, and legal issues. *CyberPsychology and Behavior, 4*, 551–563.

Manly, T., Lewis, G., Robertson, I., Watson, P., & Dalta, A. (2002). Coffee in the cornflakes: Time-of-day as a modulator of executive response control. *Neuropsychologica, 40*, 1–6.

Mantooth, R. (2010). *Toxicity, benzodiazepine*. Retrieved February 8, 2010 from *http://emedicine.medscape.com/article/813255-overview*.

Manzardo, A., Stein, L., & Belluzi, J. (2002). Rats prefer cocaine over nicotine in a two-level self-administration choice test. *Brain Research, 924*, 10–19.

Marcia, J. (2002). Identity and psychosocial development in adulthood. *Identity, 2*, 7–28.

Marcus, G. F. (1996). Why do children say "breaked"? *Current Directions in Psychological Science, 5*, 81–85.

Margulies, D., Weintraub, S., Basile, J., Grover, P., & Carlson, G. (2012). Will disruptive mood dyregulation disorder reduce false diagnosis of bipolar disorder in children? *Bipolar Disorders, 14*, 488–496.

Marks, I. (1987). The development of normal fear: A review. *Journal of Child Psychology and Psychiatry, 28*, 667–697.

Marriott, L., & Wenk, G. (2004). Neurobiological consequences of long-term estrogen therapy. *Current Directions in Psychological Science, 13*, 173–176.

Marsh, A., Elfenbein, H., & Ambady, N. (2007). Separated by a common language: Nonverbal accents and cultural stereotypes about Americans and Australians. *Journal of Cross-Cultural Psychology, 38*, 284–301.

Marshall, W. L., & Segal, Z. (1988). Behavior therapy. In C. G. Last & M. Hersen (Eds.), *Handbook of anxiety disorders* (pp. 338–361). New York: Pergamon.

Marshall, W., Marshall, L., & Serran, G. (2009). Empathy and offending behavior. In M., McMurran, & R. Howard (Eds.), *Personality, personality disorder and violence: An evidence based approach* (pp. 229–244). New York: Wiley-Blackwell.

Martin, C. L., & Little, J. K. (1990). The relation of gender understanding to children's sex-typed preferences and gender stereotypes. *Child Development, 61*, 1427–1439.

Martin, C., & Ruble, D. (2002). Cognitive theories of early gender development. *Psychological Bulletin, 128*, 903–933.

Martin, J., Hamilton, B., Sutton, P., Ventura, S., Menacker, F., & Munson, M. (2003). Births: Final data for 2002. *National Vital Statistics Reports, 52*, 1–50.

Martinez, C. (1986). Hispanics: Psychiatric issues. In C. B. Wilkinson (Ed.), *Ethnic psychiatry* (pp. 61–88). New York: Plenum.

Martinez, C. (2006). Abusive family experiences and object relation disturbances: A case study. *Clinical Case Studies, 5*, 209–219.

Martinez, I. (2002). The elder in the Cuban American family: Making sense of the real and ideal. *Journal of Comparative Family Studies, 33*, 359–375.

Maruna, S., & Mann, R. (2006). A fundamental attribution error? Rethinking cognitive distortions. *Legal and Criminological Psychology, 11*, 155–177.

Masataka, N. (1996). Perception of motherese in a signed language by 6-month-old deaf infants. *Developmental Psychology, 32*, 874–879.

Masland, R. H. (1996). Unscrambling color vision. *Science, 271*, 616–617.

Maslow, A. (1970). *Motivation and personality*. New York, NY, USA: Harper & Row.

Mason, R., & Just, M. (2004). How the brain processes causal inferences in text: A theoretical account of generation and integration component processes utilizing both cerebral hemispheres. *Psychological Science, 15*, 1–7.

Massey Cancer Center. (2006). *Familial cancer: Genetic counseling and consultation services*. Retrieved November 30, 2006, from *http://www.masseyvcu.edu/discover/?pid=1888*.

Masters, W. H., & Johnson, V. E. (1966). *Human sexual response*. Boston: Little, Brown.

Mata, I., Perez-Iglesias, R., Roiz-Santianez, R., Tordesillas-Gutierez, D., Pazos, A., Gutierrez, A., Vazquez-Barquero, J., & Crespo-Facorro, B. (2010). Gyrification brain abnormalities associated with adolescence and early-adulthood cannabis use. *Brain Research, 1317*, 297– 304.

Mather, G. (2006). *Foundations of perception*. New York, NY, USA: Psychology Press.

Mathew, R. J., & Wilson, W. H. (1991). Substance abuse and cerebral blood flow. *American Journal of Psychiatry, 148*, 292–305.

Mathur, N., & Roland, P. (2009), *Hearing loss*. Retrieved February 2, 2010, from http://emedicine.medscape.com/article/857813-overview.

Mathy, R. (2002). Suicidality and sexual orientation in five continents: Asia, Australia, Europe, North America, and South America. *International Journal of Sexuality & Gender Studies, 7*, 215–225.

Matlin, M. W., & Foley, H. J. (1997). *Sensation and perception* (4th ed.). Boston: Allyn & Bacon.

Matsunami, H., Montmayeur, J-P., & Buck, L. B. (2000). A family of candidate taste receptors in human and mouse. *Nature, 404*, 601–604.

Matthews, K. A., Shumaker, S. A., Bowen, D. J., Langer, R. D., Hunt, J. R., Kaplan, R. M., et al. (1997). Women's health initiative: Why now? What is it? What's new? *American Psychologist, 52*, 101–116.

Matthews, J., & Barch, D. (2004). Episodic memory for emotional and nonemotional words in schizophrenia. *Cognition and Emotion, 18*, 721–740.

Matz, D., & Wood, W. (2005). Cognitive dissonance in groups: The consequences of disagreement. *Journal of Personality & Social Psychology, 88*, 22–37.

Mayer, R. (2010). Fostering scientific reasoning with multimedia instruction. In H. Waters & W. Schneider (Eds.), *Metacognition, strategy use, and instruction* (pp. 160–175). New York: Guilford Press.

Mayer, R. (2012). Information processing. In K. Harris, S. Graham, T. Urdan, C. McCormick, G. Sinatra, & J. Sweller (Eds.) *APA educational psychology handbook, Vol. 1: Theories, constructs, and critical issues*. (pp. 85–99).

Mayer, R., Hegarty, M., Mayer, S., & Campbell, J. (2005). When static media promote active learning: Annotated illustraitons versus narrated animations in multimedia instruction. *Journal of Experimental Psychology: Applied, 11*, 256–265.

Mayer, R., Heiser, J., & Lonn, S. (2001). Cognitive constraints on multimedia learning: When presenting more material results in less understanding. *Journal of Educational Psychology, 93*, 187–198.

Mayer, J., Caruso, D., Panter, A., & Salovey, P. (2012). The growing significance of hot intelligences. *American Psychologist, 67*, 502–503.

Mayo Clinic. (2006b). *Sleep tips for the perpetually awake*. Retrieved December 16, 2006, from *http://mayoclinic.com/health/sleep/HQ01387*

Mayo Clinic. (2010). *Weight loss: Six strategies for success*. Retrieved January 4, 2013, from http://www.mayoclinic.com/health/weight-loss/HQ01625/NSECTIONGROUP=2

Mayur, P., Byth, K., & Harris, A. (2012). Acute antidepressant effects of right unilateral ultra-belief ECT: A double-blind randomized controlled trial. *Journal of Affective Disorders, 28*, 229–233.

Mazur, E., & Kozarian, L. (2010). Self-presentation and interaction in blogs of adolescents and young emerging adults. *Journal of Adolescent Research, 25*, 124–144.

Mazzoni, G., & Memon, A. (2003). Imagination can create false autobiographical memories. *Psychological Science, 14*, 186–188.

McCaffrey, T. (2012). Innovation relies on the obscure: A key to overcoming the classic problem of functional fixedness. *Psychological Science, 23*, 215–218.

McClelland, D. C. (1958). Methods of measuring human motivation. In J. Atkinson (Ed.), *Motives in fantasy, action and society: A method of assessment and study*. Princeton, NJ, USA: Van Nostrand.

McClelland, D. C. (1961). *The achieving society*. Princeton, NJ: Van Nostrand.

McClelland, D. C. (1985). *Human motivation*. New York: Cambridge University Press.

McClelland, D. C., Atkinson, J. W., Clark, R. W., & Lowell, E. L. (1953). *The achievement motive*. New York: Appleton-Century-Crofts.

McClelland, J. L., McNaughton, B. L., & O'Reilly, R. C. (1995). Why there are complementary learning systems in the hippocampus and neocortex: Insights from the successes and failures of connectionist models of learning and memory. *Psychological Bulletin, 102*, 419–457.

McCown, B., Blake, I., & Keiser, R. (2012). Content analyses of the beliefs of academic procrastinators. *Journal of Rational-Emotive & Cognitive Behavior Therapy, 30*, 213–222.

McCrae, R. (2011). Personality theories for the 21st century. *Teaching of Psychology, 38*, 209–214.

McCrae, R., & Costa, P. (2003). *Personality in adulthood: A five-factor theory perspective* (2nd ed.). New York: Guilford Press.

McCue, J. M., Link, K. L., Eaton, S. S., & Freed, B. M. (2000). Exposure to cigarette tar inhibits ribonucleotide reductase and blocks lymphocyte proliferation. *Journal of Immunology, 165*, 6771–6775.

McCullough, M. E., Hoyt, W. T., Larson, D. B., Koenig, H. G., & Thoresen, C. (2000). Religious involvement and mortality: A meta-analytic review. *Health Psychology, 19*, 211–222.

McDonald, J. L. (1997). Language acquisition: The acquisition of linguistic structure in normal and special populations. *Annual Review of Psychology, 48*, 215–241.

McDowell, C., & Acklin, M. W. (1996). Standardizing procedures for calculating Rorschach interrater reliability: Conceptual and empirical foundations. *Journal of Personality Assessment, 66*, 308–320.

McElwain, N., & Volling, B. (2004). Attachment security and parental sensitivity during infancy: Associations with friendship quality and false-belief understanding at age 4. *Journal of Social & Personal Relationships, 21*, 639–667.

McGaugh, J., & Cahill, L. (2009). Emotion and memory: Central and peripheral contributions. In R., Davidson, K., Scherer, & H. Goldsmith (Eds.), *Handbook of affective sciences*. Series in affective science. (pp. 93–116). New York: Oxford University Press.

McGuire, W. J. (1985). Attitudes and attitude change. In G. Lindzey & E. Aronson (Ed.), *Handbook of social psychology* (Vol. 2, 3rd ed.). New York: Random House.

McMahon, F., Akula, N., Schulze, T., Pierandrea, M., Tozzi, F., Detera-Wadleigh, S., Steele, C., Breuer, R., Strohmaier, J., Wendland, J., Mattheisen, M., Muhleisen, T., Maier, W., Nothen, M., Cichon, S., Farmer, A., Vincent, J., Holsboer, F., Preisig, M., & Reitschel, M. (2010). Meta-analysis of genome-wide association data identifies a risk locus for major mood disorders on 3p21.1. *Nature, 42*, pp. 128–131.

McNally, R. (2003). The demise of pseudoscience. *The Scientific Review of Mental Health Practice, 2*, 97–101.

McNally, R., Lasko, N., Clancy, S., Macklin, M., Pitman, R., & Orr, S. (2004). Psychophysiological responding during script-driven imagery in people reporting abduction by space aliens. *Psychological Science, 15*, 493–497.

McNamara, P., McLaren, D., & Durso, K. (2007). Representation of the self in REM and NREM dreams. *Dreaming, 17*, 113–126.

Mednick, S. A., & Mednick, M. T. (1967). *Examiner's manual, Remote Associates Test*. Boston: Houghton-Mifflin.

Mefoh, P., & Nwanosike, C. (2012). Effects of group size and expectancy of reward on social loafing. *IFE Psychologia: An International Journal, 20*, 229–239.

Meltzer, H. Y., Rabinowitz, J., Lee, M. A., Cola, P. A., Ranjan, R., Findling, R. L., et al. (1997). Age at onset and gender of schizophrenic patients in relation to neuroleptic resistance. *American Journal of Psychiatry, 154*, 475–482.

Meltzer, H., Alphs, L., Green, A., Altamura, A., Anand, R., Bertoldi, A., et al. (2003). Clozapine treatment for suicidality in schizophrenia: International suicide prevention trial. *Archives of General Psychiatry, 60*, 82–91.

Melzack, R., & Wall, P. D. (1965). Pain mechanisms: A new theory. *Science, 150*, 971–979.

Melzack, R., & Wall, P. D. (1983). *The challenge of pain.* New York: Basic Books.

Memmert, D., Simons, D., & Grimme, T. (2009). The relationship between visual attention and expertise in sports. *Psychology of Sport and Exercise, 10*, 146–151.

Mercier, H., & Landemore, H. (2012). Reasoning is for arguing: Understanding the successes and failures of deliberation. *Political Psychology, 33*, 243–258.

Merson, M. (2006). The HIV/AIDS pandemic at 25: The global response. *New England Journal of Medicine, 354*, 2414–2417.

Messer, S., Sanderson, W., & Gurman, A. (2013). Brief psychotherapies. In G. Stricker, T. Widiger, & I. Weiner. (Eds.), *Handbook of psychology, Vol. 8: Clinical Psychology* (2nd ed.). (pp. 431–453). Hoboken, NJ, USA: John Wiley & Sons Inc.

Meyer, A. (1997, March/April). Patching up testosterone. *Psychology Today, 30*, 54–57, 66–70.

Meyer, P. (1972). If Hitler asked you to electrocute a stranger, would you? In R. Greenbaum & H. A. Tilker (Eds.), *The challenge of psychology* (pp. 456–465). Englewood Cliffs, NJ: Prentice-Hall.

Mezulis, A., Abramson, L., Hyde, J., & Hankin, B. (2004). Is there a universal positivity bias in attributions? A meta-analytic review of individual, developmental, and cultural differences in the self-serving attributional bias. *Psychological Bulletin, 130*, 711–747.

Michaels, J. W., Bloomel, J. M., Brocato, R. M., Linkous, R. A., & Rowe, J. S. (1982). Social facilitation and inhibition in a natural setting. *Replications in Social Psychology, 2*, 21–24.

Miles, D. R., & Carey, G. (1997). Genetic and environmental architecture of human aggression. *Journal of Personality and Social Psychology, 72*, 207–217.

Milgram, S. (1963). Behavioral study of obedience. *Journal of Abnormal and Social Psychology, 67*, 371–378.

Milgram, S. (1965). Liberating effects of group pressure. *Journal of Personality and Social Psychology, 1*, 127–134.

Miller, B., Norton, M., Curtis, T., Hill, E., Schvaneveldt, P., & Young, M. (1998). The timing of sexual intercourse among adolescents: Family, peer, and other antecedents: Erratum. *Youth & Society, 29*, 390.

Miller, G. A. (1956). The magical number seven, plus or minus two: Some limits on our capacity for processing information. *Psychological Review, 63*, 81–97.

Miller, H., Watkins, R., & Webb, D. (2009). The use of psychological testing to evaluate law enforcement leadership competencies and development. *Police Practice & Research: An International Journal.*

Miller, J. G., Bersoff, D. M., & Harwood, R. L. (1990). Perceptions of social responsibilities in India and in the United States: Moral imperatives or personal decisions? *Journal of Personality and Social Psychology, 58*, 33–47.

Miller, J., Lynam, D., Zimmerman, R., Logan, T., Leukefeld, C., & Clayton, R. (2004). The utility of the Five Factor Model in understanding risky sexual behavior. *Personality and Individual Differences, 36*, 1611–1626.

Miller, N. E. (1941). The frustration-aggression hypothesis. *Psychological Review, 48*, 337–342.

Miller, J., Lynam, D., Zimmerman, R., Logan, T., Leukefeld, C., & Clayton, R. (2004). The utility of the Five Factor Model in understanding risky sexual behavior. *Personality and Individual Differences, 36*, 1611–1626.

Milling, L., Coursen, E., Shores, J., & Waszkiewica, J. (2010). The predictive utility of hypnotizability: The change in suggestibility produced by hypnosis. *Journal of Consulting and Clinical Psychology, 78*, 126–130.

Millman, R. (2005). Excessive sleepiness in adolescents and young adults: Causes, consequences, and treatment strategies. *Pediatrics, 115*, 1774–1786.

Milner, B. (1966). Amnesia following operation on the temporal lobes. In C. W. M. Whitty & O. L. Zangwill (Eds.), *Amnesia* (pp. 109–133). London: Butterworth.

Milner, B., Corkin, S., & Teuber, H. L. (1968). Further analysis of the hippocampal amnesic syndrome: 14-year follow-up study of H. M. *Neuropsychologia, 6*, 215–234.

Milton, J., & Wiseman, R. (2001). Does psi exist? Reply to Storm and Ertel (2001). *Psychological Bulletin, 127*, 434–438.

Mineka, S., & Oehlberg, K. (2008). The relevance of recent developments in classical conditioning to understanding the etiology and maintenance of anxiety disorder. *Acta Psychologica, 127*, 567–580.

Mischel, W. (1966). A social-learning view of sex differences in behavior. In E. E. Maccoby (Ed.), *The development of sex differences* (pp. 56–81). Palo Alto, CA: Stanford University Press.

Mischel, W. (1973). Toward a cognitive social learning reconceptualization of personality. *Psychological Review, 80*, 252–283.

Mischel, W. (1977). The interaction of person and situation. In D. Magnusson & N. S. Endler (Eds.), *Personality at the crossroads: Current issues in interactional psychology* (pp. 333–352). Hillsdale, NJ: Lawrence Erlbaum.

Mishra, R. (1997). Cognition and cognitive development. In J. Berry, P. Dasen, & T. Saraswathi (Eds.), *Handbook of cross-cultural psychology* (Vol. 2). Boston, MA: Allyn & Bacon.

Mistry, J., & Rogoff, B. (1994). Remembering in cultural context. In W. J. Lonner & R. Malpass (Eds.), *Psychology and culture* (pp. 139–144). Boston: Allyn & Bacon.

Mohan, J. (2006). Cardiac psychology. *Journal of the Indian Academy of Applied Psychology, 32*, 214–220.

Mohr, D., Goodkin, D., Nelson, S., Cox, D., & Weiner, M. (2002). Moderating effects of coping on the relationship between stress and the development of new brain lesions in multiple sclerosis. *Psychosomatic Medicine, 64*, 803–809.

Molnar, M., Potkin, S., Bunney, W., & Jones, E. (2003). MRNA expression patterns and distribution of white matter neurons in dorsolateral prefrontal cortex of depressed patients differ from those in schizophrenia patients. *Biological Psychiatry, 53*, 39–47.

Monk, T. H. (1989). Circadian rhythms in subjective activation, mood, and performance efficiency. In M. H. Kryger, T. Roth, & W. C. Dement (Eds.), *Principles and practice of sleep medicine* (pp. 163–172). Philadelphia: W. B. Saunders.

Monroe, S., & Reid, M. (2009). Life stress and major depression. *Current Directions in Psychological Science, 18*, 68–72.

Montejo, A., Llorca, G., Izquierdo, J., & Rico-Villademoros, F. (2001). Incidence of sexual dysfunction associated with antidepressant agents: A prospective multicenter study of 1022 outpatients. *Journal of Clinical Psychiatry, 62*, 10–21.

Montgomery, G., Weltz, C., Seltz, M., & Bovbjerg, D. (2002). Brief presurgery hypnosis reduces distress and pain in excisional breast biopsy patients. *International Journal of Clinical & Experimental Hypnosis, 50*, 17–32.

Montoya, E., Terburg, D., Bos, P., & van Honk, J. (2012). Testosterone, cortisol, and serotonin as key regulators of social aggression: A review and theoretical perspective. *Motivation and Emotion, 36*, 65–73.

Moore, T. (2012). *Gestational diabetes.* Retrieved December 16, 2012, from http://emedicine.medscape.com/article/127547-overview

Morales, J., Calvo, A., & Bialystok, E. (2013). Working memory development in monolingual and bilingual children. *Journal of Experimental Child Psychology, 114*, 187–202.

Morewedge, C., & Norton, M. (2009). When dreaming is believing: The (motivated) interpretation of dreams. *Journal of Personality and Social Psychology, 96*, 249–264.

Morey, L. (2013). Measuring personality and psychopathology. In J. Schinka, W. Velicer, & I. Weiner (Eds.). (pp. 395–427). *Handbook of psychology, Vol. 2: Research methods in psychology* (2nd ed.). Hoboken, NJ, USA: John Wiley & Sons, Inc.

Morgan, C. D., & Murray, H. A. (1935). A method for investigating fantasies: The Thematic Apperception Test. *Archives of Neurology and Psychiatry, 34*, 289–306.

Morgan, C. D., & Murray, H. A. (1962). Thematic Apperception Test. In H. A. Murray et al. (Eds.), *Explorations in personality: A clinical and experimental study of fifty men of college age* (pp. 530–545). New York: Science Editions.

Morgan, R., & Flora, D. (2002). Group psychotherapy with incarcerated offenders: A research synthesis. *Group Dynamics: Theory, Research, and Practice, 6*, 203–218.

Morgenthaler, T., Lee-Chiong, T., Alessi, C., Friedman, L., Aurora, R., Boehlecke, B., Brown, T., Chesson, A., Kapur, V., Maganti, R., Owens, J., Pancer, J., Swick, T., & Zak, R. (2007). Practice parameters for the clinical evaluation and treatment of circadian rhythm sleep disorders: An American Academy of Sleep Medicine report. *Sleep: Journal of Sleep and Sleep Disorders Research, 30*, 1445–1459.

Morofushi, M., Shinohara, K., Funabashi, T., & Kimura, F. (2000). Positive relationship between menstrual synchrony and ability to smell 5alpha-androst-16-en-3alpha-ol. *Chemical Senses, 25*, 407–411.

Morra, S., Gobbo, C., Marini, Z., & Sheese, R. (2008). *Cognitive development: Neo-Piagetian perspectives.* New York: Taylor & Francis Group/Lawrence Erlbaum Associates.

Morris, A., Cui, L., & Steinberg, L. (2013). Parenting research and themes: What we have learned and where to go next. In R. Larzelere, Morris, A., & A. Harrist (Eds.) *Authoritative parenting: Synthesizing nurturance and discipline for optimal child development.* (pp. 35–58). Washington, DC, USA: American Psychological Association.

Morsella, E., Krieger, S., & Bargh, J. (2010). Minimal neuroanatomy for a conscious brain: Homing in on the networks constituting consciousness. *Neural Networks, 23*, 14–15.

Moser, G., & Robin, M. (2006). Environmental annoyances: An urban-specific threat to quality of life? *European Review of Applied Psychology, 56*, 35–41.

Moss, J., Schunn, C., Schneider, W., McNamara, D., & VanLehn, K. (2011). The neural correlates of strategic reading comprehension: Cognitive control and discourse comprehension. *Neuroimage, 58*, 675–686.

Moss, T., Sacco, K., Allen, T., Weinberger, A., Vessicchio, J., & George, T. (2009). Prefrontal cognitive dysfunction is associated with tobacco dependence treatment failure in smokers with schizophrenia. *Drug and Alcohol Dependence, 104*, 94–99.

Motti-Stefanidi, F., Berry, J., Chryssochoou, X., Sam, D., & Phinney, J. Positive immigrant youth adaptation in context: Developmental, acculturation, and social-psychological perspectives. In A. Masten, K. Liebkind, & D. Hernandez (Eds.). *Realizing the potential of immigrant youth.* (pp. 117–158). New York, NY, Usa: Cambridge University Press.

Moynihan, J., Larson, M., Treanor, J., Dubersetein, P., Power, A., Shre, B., et al. (2004). Psychosocial factors and the response to influenza vaccination in older adults. *Psychosomatic Medicine, 66*, 950–953.

Mufson, L., Gallagher, T., Dorta, K., & Young, J. (2004). A group adaptation of interpersonal psychotherapy for depressed adolescents. *American Journal of Psychotherapy, 58*, 220–237.

Muller, L. (2002). Group counseling for African American males: When all you have are European American counselors. *Journal for Specialists in Group Work, 27*, 299–313.

Mumtaz, S., & Humphreys, G. (2002). The effect of Urdu vocabulary size on the acquisition of single word reading in English. *Educational Psychology, 22*, 165–190.

Munaf√≥ et al., 2008

Munafó, M., Yalcin, B., Willis-Own, S., & Flint, J. (2008). Association of the dopamine D4 receptor (DRD4) gene and approach-related personality traits: Meta-analysis and new data. *Biological Psychiatry, 63*, 197–206.

Munroe, R. H., Shimmin, H. S., & Munroe, R. L. (1984). Gender role understanding and sex role preference in four cultures. *Developmental Psychology, 20*, 673–682.

Munzar, P., Li, H., Nicholson, K., Wiley, J., & Balster, R. (2002). Enhancement of the discriminative stimulus effects of phencyclidine by the tetracycline antibiotics doxycycline and minocycline in rats. *Psychopharmacology, 160*, 331–336.

Murphy, R. (2011. *Dynamic assessment, intelligence and measurement.* New York, NY, USA: John Wiley & Sons.

Murray, B. (2002). Finding the peace within us. *APA Monitor on Psychology, 33*, 56–57.

Murray, H. (1938). *Explorations in personality.* New York: Oxford University Press.

Murray, J., Liotti, M., Ingmundson, P., Mayburg, H., Pu, Y., Zamarripa, F., et al. (2006). Children's brain activations while viewing televised violence revealed by fMRI. *Media Psychology, 8*, 24–37.

Murty, V., Labar, K., & Adcock, R. (2012). Threat of punishment motivates memory encoding via amygdala, not midbrain, interactions with the medial temporal lobe. *Journal of Neuroscience, 32*, 8969–8976.

Must, O., te Njienhuis, J., Must, A., & van Vianen, A. (2009). Comparablity of IQ scores over time. *Intelligence, 37*, 25–33.

Myers, D. G., & Bishop, G. D. (1970). Discussion effects on racial attitudes. *Science, 169*, 778–779.

Najavits, L., Highley, J., Dolan, S., & Fee, F. (2012). Substance use disorder. In J. Vasterling, R. Bryant, & T. Keane (Eds.). *PTSD and mild traumatic brain injury.* (pp. 124–145). New York, NY, USA: Guilford Press.

Narvaez, D. (2002). Does reading moral stories build character? *Educational Psychology Review, 14*, 155–171.

National Alliance for Mental Illness (NAMI). (2003). *Panic disorder.* Retrieved July 19, 2006, from *http://www.nami.org/Template.cfm?Section=By_Illness&Template=/TaggedPage/TaggedPageDisplay.cfm&TPLID=54&ContentID=23050*

National Cancer Institute. (2000). *Questions and answers about smoking cessation.* Retrieved January 29, 2003, from *http://cis.nci.nih.gov/fact/8_13.htm*

National Center for Chronic Disease Prevention and Health Promotion. (2006). *The health consequences of involuntary exposure to tobacco smoke: A report of the surgeon general.* Retrieved July 7, 2006, from *http://www.cdc.gov/TOBACCO/sgr/sgr_2006/index.htm*

National Center for Education Statistics (NCES). (2006). *Digest of Education Statistics, 2005.* Retrieved January 31, 2009 from *http://nces.ed.gov/programs/digest/d06/index.asp.*

National Center for Education Statistics (NCES). (2008). *Trends in international mathematics and science study (TIMSS): TIMSS 2007 results.* Retrieved May 9, 2009, from http://nces.ed.gov/timss/results07.asp.

National Center for Health Statistics (NCHS). (2006a). *Health, United States, 2006.* Retrieved February 12, 2007, from *http://www.cdc.gov/nchs/data/hus/hus06.pdf#046*

National Center for Health Statistics (NCHS). (2010). *Health, United States, 2009.* Retrieved March 12, 2010 from *http://www.cdc.gov/nchs/data/hus/hus09.pdf#062*

National Center for Health Statistics (NCHS). (2012). *Health, United States, 2011: With special feature on socioeconomic status and health.* Retrieved January 8, 2013, from http://www.cdc.gov/nchs/data/hus/hus11.pdf

National Center for Health Statistics (NCHS). (2012). *Prevalence of overweight, obesity, and extreme obesity among adults: United States, Trends 1960-1962 through 2009-2010.* Retrieved January 7, 2013, from http://www.cdc.gov/nchs/data/hestat/obesity_adult_09_10/obesity_adult_09_10.pdf

National Council on Alcoholism and Drug Dependence. (2013). *Alcohol and crime.* Retrieved February 8, 2013 from http://www.ncadd.org/index.php/learn-about-alcohol/alcohol-and-crime.

National Highway and Traffic Safety Administration (NHTSA). (2007). *Alcohol poisoning.* Retrieved February 7, 2007, from *http://www.nhtsa.dot.gov/PEOPLE/outreach/safesobr/15qp/web/idalc.html*

National Institute of Mental Health (NIMH). (2001). *The numbers count: Mental disorders in America (NIMH Report No. 01–4584).* Washington, DC: Author.

National Institute of Mental Health (NIMH). (2009). *Suicide in the U.S.: Statistics and prevention.* Retrieved June 11, 2009 from *http://www.nimh.nih.gov/health/publications/suicide-in-the-us-statistics-and-prevention/index.shtml.*

National Institute of Mental Health (NIMH). (2013). *Statistics.* Retrieved January 26, 2013 from http://www.nimh.nih.gov/statistics/index.shtml

National Library of Medicine. (2012). *A tutorial for evaluating internet health information.* Retrieved January 8, 2013, from http://www.nlm.nih.gov/medlineplus/webeval/webeval.html

National Science Foundation (NSF). (2002). *Science and engineering: Indicators 2002.* Retrieved January 29, 2003, from *http://www.nsf.gov/sbc/srs/seind02/toc.htm*

Nawrot, M., Nordenstrom, B., & Olson, A. (2004). Disruption of eye movements by ethanol intoxication affects perception of depth from motion parallax. *Psychological Science, 15,* 858–865.

Neisser, U., Boodoo, G., Bouchard, T. J., Jr., Boykin, A. W., Brody, N., Ceci, S. J., et al. (1996). Intelligence: Knowns and unknowns. *American Psychologist, 51,* 77–101.

Neitz, M., & Neitz, J. (1995). Numbers and ratios of visual pigment genes for normal red-green color vision. *Science, 267,* 1013–1016.

Nelson, J. (2009). Trycyclic and tetracyclic drugs. In A. Schatzberg & C. Nemeroff. (Eds.). *The American Psychiatric Publishing Textbook of Psychopharmacology* (4th ed.). (pp. 263–287). Arlington, VA, USA: American Psychiatric Publishing, Inc.

Nelson, J. C. (1997). Safety and tolerability of the new antidepressants. *Journal of Clinical Psychiatry, 58*(6, Suppl.), 26–31.

Nelson, T. (1996). Consciousness and metacognition. *American Psychologist, 51,* 102–116.

Nestor, P., Graham, K., Bozeat, S., Simons, J., & Hodges, J. (2002). Memory consolidation and the hippocampus: Further evidence from studies of autobiographical memory in semantic dementia and frontal variant frontotemporal dementia. *Neuropsychologia, 40,* 633–654.

Neumann, I. (2008). Brain oxytocin: A key regulator of emotional and social behaviours in both females and males. *Journal of Neuroendocrinology, 20,* 858–865.

Newberg, A., Alavi, A. Baime, M., Pourdehnad, M., Santanna, J. d'Aquili, E. (2001). The measurement of cerebral blood flow during the complex cognitive task of meditation: A preliminary SPECT study. *Psychiatry Research: Neuroimaging, 106,* 113–122.

Newell, B., Lagnado, D., & Shanks, D. (2007). *Straight choices: The psychology of decision making.* New York: Psychology Press.

Newell, B. (2011). Recognizing the recognition heuristic for what it is (and what it's not). *Judgment and Decision Making, 6,* 409–412.

Newman, M., & Roberts, N. (2013). *Health and social relationships: The good, the bad, and the complicated.* Washington, DC, USA: American Psychological Association.

Newton, E. (2012). *Neuroleptic agent toxicity.* Retrieved January 27, 2013, from http://emedicine.medscape.com/article/815881-overview

Nickerson, R. S., & Adams, M. J. (1979). Long-term memory for a common object. *Cognitive Psychology, 11,* 287–307.

Nicol, S. E., & Gottesman, I. I. (1983). Clues to the genetics and neurobiology of schizophrenia. *American Scientist, 71,* 398–404.

Nieto-Hernandez, R., Rubin, G., Cleare, A., Weinman, J., & Wessely, S. (2008). Can evidence change belief? Reported mobile phone sensitivity following individual feedback of an inability to discriminate active from sham signals. *Journal of Psychosomatic Research, 65,* 453–460.

Nisbett, R. E., & Wilson, T. D. (1977). The halo effect: Evidence for unconscious alteration of judgments. *Journal of Personality and Social Psychology, 35,* 250–256.

Nisbett, R., Aronson, J., Blair, C., Dickens, W., Flynn, J., Halpern, D., & Turkheimer, E. (2012). Intelligence: New findings and theoretical developments. *American Psychologist, 67,* 130–159.

Nishida, M., Pearsall, J., Buckner, R., & Walker, M. (2008). REM sleep, prefrontal theta, and the consolidation of human emotional memory. *Cerebral Cortex, 19,* 1158–1166.

Niyuhire, F., Varvel, S., Martin, B., & Lichtman, A. (2007). Exposure to marijuana smoke impairs memory retrieval in mice. *Journal of Pharmacology and Experimental Therapeutics, 322,* 1067–1075.

Noltemeyer, A., Bush, K., Patton, J., & Bergen, D. (2012). The relationship among deficiency needs and growth needs: An empirical investigation of Maslow's theory. *Child and Youth Services Review, 34,* 1862–1867.

Noriko, S. (2004). Identity development pre- and post-empty nest women. *Japanese Journal of Developmental Psychology, 15,* 52–64.

Norman, S., Norman, G., Rossi, J., & Prochaska, J. (2006). Identifying high- and low-success smoking cessation subgroups using signal detection analysis. *Addictive Behaviors, 31,* 31–41.

Norman, W. (1963). Toward an adequate taxonomy of personality attributes: Replicated factor structure in peer nomination personality ratings. *Journal of Abnormal & Social Psychology, 66,* 574–583.

North, C., & Suris, A. (2012). Psychiatric and psychological issues in survivors of major disasters. In I. Marini & M. Stebnicki (Eds.). *The psychological and social impact of illness and disability* (6th ed.). (pp. 165–177). New York, NY, USA: Springer Publishing Co.

North, F., Ward, W., Varkey, P., & Tulledge-Scheitel, S. (2012). Should you search the Internet for information about your acute symptom? *Telemedicine and e-Health, 18,* 213–218.

Noyes, R., Jr., Burrows, G. D., Reich, J. H., Judd, F. K., Garvey, M. J., Norman, T. R., et al. (1996). Diazepam versus alprazolam for the treatment of panic disorder. *Journal of Clinical Psychiatry, 57,* 344–355.

Nunn, J., Gregory, L., Brammer, M., Williams, S., Parslow, D., Morgan, M., Morris, R., Bullmore, E., Baron-Cohen, S., & Gray, J. (2002). Functional magnetic resonance imaging of synesthesia: Activation of V4/V8 by spoken words. *Nature Neuroscience, 5,* 371–375.

Nutt, D. (2000). Treatment of depression and concomitant anxiety. *European Neuropsychopharmacology, 10* (Suppl. 4), S433–S437.

O'Brien, C. P. (1996). Recent developments in the pharmacotherapy of substance abuse. *Journal of Consulting and Clinical Psychology, 64*, 677–686.

O'Leary, K. D., & Smith, D. A. (1991). Marital interactions. *Annual Review of Psychology, 42*, 191–212.

Ogawa, A., Mizuta, I., Fukunaga, T., Takeuchi, N., Honaga, E., Sugita, Y., Mikami, A., Inoue, Y., & Takeda, M. (2004). Electrogastrography abnormality in eating disorders. *Psychiatry & Clinical Neurosciences, 58*, 300–310.

Olatunji, B., Lohr, J, Sawchuk, C., & Tolin, D. (2007). Multimodal assessment of disgust in contamination-related obsessive-compulsive disorder. *Behaviour Research and Therapy, 45*, 263–276.

Olender, T., Lancet, D., & Nebert, D. (2008). Update on the olfactory receptor (OR) gene superfamily. *Human Genomics, 3*, 87-97.

Oliver, J. E. (1993). Intergenerational transmission of child abuse: Rates, research, and clinical implications. *American Journal of Psychiatry, 150*, 1315–1324.

Olson, M., Krantz, D., Kelsey, S., Pepine, C., Sopko, G., Handberg, E., Rogers, W., Gierach, G., McClure, C., & Merz, C. (2005). Hostility scores are associated with increased risk of cardiovascular events in women undergoing coronary angiography: A report from the NHLBI-sponsored WISE study. *Psychosomatic Medicine, 67*, 546–552.

Ono, H. (2003). Women's economic standing, marriage timing and cross-national contexts of gender. *Journal of Marriage & Family, 65*, 275–286.

Ophir, E., Nass, C., & Wagner, A. (2009). Cognitive control in media multitaskers. *PNAS Proceedings of the National Academy of Sciences of the United States of America, 106*, 15583–15587.

Oquendo, M., Placidi, G., Malone, K., Campbell, C., Kelp, J., Brodsky, B., et al. (2003). Positron emission tomography of regional brain metabolic responses to a serotonergic challenge and lethality of suicide attempts in major depression. *Archives of General Psychiatry, 60*, 14–22.

Orban, P., Peigneux, P., Lungu, O., Albouy, G., Breton, E., Laberenne, F., Benali, H., Maquet, P., & Doyon, J. (2009). The multifaceted nature of the relationship between performance and brain activity in motor sequence learning. *Neuroimage, 49*, 694–702.

Orenstein, W., Paulson, J., Brady, M., Cooper, L., & Seib, Katherine. (2013). Global vaccination recommendations and thimerosal. *Pediatrics, 131*, 149-151.

Orman, M. (1996). *How to conquer public speaking fear.* Retrieved February 15, 2003, from *http://www.stresscure.com/jobstress/speak.html*

Osborn, D., Fletcher, A., Smeeth, L., Sitrling, S., Bulpitt, C., Breeze, E., et al. (2003). Factors associated with depression in a representative sample of 14,217 people aged 75 and over in the United Kingdom: Results from the MRC trial of assessment and management of older people in the community. *International Journal of Geriatric Psychiatry, 18*, 623–630.

Osland, T., Bjorvatn, B., Steen, V., & Pallesen, S. (2011). *Chronobiology International, 28*, 764–770.

Ossorio, P., & Duster, T. (2005). Race and genetics: Controversies in biomedical, behavioral, and forensic sciences. *American Psychologist, 60*, 115–128.

Osterhout, C. (2011). *Bulimia nervosa treatment and management.* Retrieved January 4, 2013, from, http://emedicine.medscape.com/article/286485-treatment

Ostrom, T. M., Carpenter, S. L., Sedikides, C., & Li, F. (1993). Differential processing of in-group and out-group information. *Journal of Personality and Social Psychology, 64*, 21–34.

Overmeier, J. B., & Seligman, M. E. P. (1967). Effects of inescapable shock upon subsequent escape and avoidance responding. *Journal of Comparative and Physiological Psychology, 67*, 28–33.

Owen, M., & O'Donovan, M. (2003). Schizophrenia and genetics. In R. Plomin, J. Defries, I. Craig, & P. McGuffin (Eds.), *Behavioral genetics in the postgenomic era* (pp. 463–480). Washington, DC: American Psychological Association.

Ozcan, L., Ergin, A., Lu, A., Chung, J., Sarkar, S., Nie, D., Myers, M., & Ozcan, U. (2009). Endoplasmic reculum stress plays a central role in development of leptin resistance. *Cell Metabolism, 9*, 35–51.

Pöysti, L., Rajalin, S., & Summala, H. (2005). Factors influencing the use of cellular (mobile) phone during driving and hazards while using it. *Accident Analysis & Prevention, 37*, 47–51.

Packard, M. (2009). Anxiety, cognition, and habit: A multiple memory systems perspective. *Brain Research, 1293*, 121–128.

Page-Gould, E., Mendoza-Denton, R., & Tropp, L. (2008). With a little help from my cross-group friend: Reducing anxiety in intergroup contexts through cross-group friendshps. *Journal of Personality and Social Psychology, 95*, 1080–1094.

Paivio, S. C., & Greenberg, L. S. (1995). Resolving "unfinished business": Efficacy of experiential therapy using empty-chair dialogue. *Journal of Consulting and Clinical Psychology, 63*, 419–425.

Palinscar, A. S., & Brown, A. L. (1984). Reciprocal teaching of comprehension-fostering and comprehension-monitoring activities. *Cognition and Instruction, 1*, 117–175.

Palmer, R., McGeary, J., Francazio, S., Raphael, B., Lander, A., Heath, A., & Knopik, V. (2012). The genetics of alcohol dependence: Advancing towards systems-based approaches. *Drug and Alcohol Dependence, 125*, 179–191.

Panksepp, J. (2010). Evolutionary substrates of addiction: The neurochemistries of pleasure seeking and social bonding in the mammalian brain. In J. Kassel (Ed.), *Substance abuse and emotion* (pp. 137–167). Washington, DC: American Psychological Association.

Pansky, A. (2012). Inoculation against forgetting: Advantages of immediate versus delayed initial testing due to superior verbatim accessibility. *Journal of Experimental Psychology: Learning, Memory, and Cognition, 38*, 1792–1800.

Papolos, D., Mattis, S., Golshan, S., & Molay, F. (2009). Fear of harm, a possible phenotype of pediatric bipolar disorder: A dimensional approach to diagnosis for genotyping psychiatric syndromes. *Journal of Affective Disorders, 118*, 28–38.

Paquette, D. (2004). Dichotomizing paternal and maternal functions as a means to better understand their primary contributions. *Human Development, 47*, 237–238.

Parish, B., Richards, M., & Cameron, S. (2011). *Hallucinogens.* Retrieved November 10, 2012 from, http://emedicine.medscape.com/article/293752-overview.

Park, G., Lubinski, D., & Benbow, C. (2013). When less is more: Effects of grade skipping on adult STEM productivity among mathematically precocious adolescents. *Journal of Educational Psychology, 105*, 176–198.

Parke, R. D. (1977). Some effects of punishment on children's behavior-revisited. In E. M. Hetherington, E. M. Ross, & R. D. Parke (Eds.), *Contemporary readings in child psychology.* New York: McGraw-Hill.

Parkinson, W. L., & Weingarten, H. P. (1990). Dissociative analysis of ventromedial hypothalamic obesity syndrome. *American Journal of Physiology, 259*, 829–835.

Passaro, E. (2009). *Insomnia.* Retrieved February 5, 2010 from *http://emedicine.medscape.com/article/1187829-overview.*

Pastore, N. (1950). The role of arbitrariness in the frustration-aggression hypothesis. *Journal of Abnormal and Social Psychology, 47*, 728–731.

Paul, T., Schroeter, K., Dahme, B., & Nutzinger, D. (2002). Self-injurious behavior in women with eating disorders. *American Journal of Psychiatry, 159*, 408–411.

Paul, W. E. (1993). Infectious diseases and the immune system. *Scientific American, 269,* 90–99.

Paulhus, D., Harms, P., Bruce, M., & Lysy, D. (2003). The over-claiming technique: Measuring self-enhancement independent of ability. *Journal of Personality & Social Psychology, 84,* 890–904.

Paulus, P. B., Cox, V. C., & McCain, G. (1988). *Prison crowding: A psychological perspective.* New York: Springer-Verlag.

Pavizi, J., Jacques, C., Foster, B., Withoft, N., Rangarajan, V., Weiner, K., & Grill-Spector, K. (2012). Electrical stimulation of human fusiform face-selective regions distorts face perception. *Journal of Neuroscience, 24,* 14915–14020.

Pavlov, I. P. (1927/1960). *Conditioned reflexes: An investigation of the physiological activity of the cerebral cortex* (G. V. Anrep, Trans.). New York: Dover. (Original translation published 1927).

Payami, H., Montee, K., & Kaye, J. (1994). Evidence for familial factors that protect against dementia and outweigh the effect of increasing age. *American Journal of Human Genetics, 54,* 650–657.

Pearson, P., & Cerbetti, G. (2013). The psychology and pedagogy of reading processes. In W. Reynolds, G. Miller, & I. Wiener. (Eds.) *Handbook of psychology, Volume 7: Educational Psychology* (2nd ed.). (pp. 257–281). Hoboken, NJ, USA: John Wiley & Sons, Inc.

Pedersen, D., & Minnotte, K. (2012). Self- and spouse-reported work-family conflict and dual-earners' job satisfaction. *Marriage & Family Review, 48,* 272–292.

Pedersen, A., Zachariae, R., Jensen, A., Bovbjerg, D., Andersen, O., & von der Masse, H. (2009). Psychological stres predicts the risk of febrile episodes in cancer patients during chemotherapy. *Psychotherapy and Psychosomatics, 78,* 258–260.

Pedersen, D. M., & Wheeler, J. (1983). The Müller-Lyer illusion among Navajos. *Journal of Social Psychology, 121,* 3–6.

Pederson, S., Van Domburg, R., & Theuns, D. (2004). Type D personality is associated with increased anxiety and depressive symptoms in patients with an implantable cardioverter defibrillator and their partners. *Psychosomatic Medicine, 66,* 714–719.

Peeters, M., & Oerlemans, W. (2009). The relationship between acculturation orientations and work-related well-being: Differences between ethnic minority and majority employees. *International Journal of Stress Management, 16,* 1–24.

Penfield, W. (1969). Consciousness, memory, and man's conditioned reflexes. In K. Pribram (Ed.), *On the biology of learning* (pp. 129–168). New York: Harcourt Brace Jovanovich.

Pennisi, E. (1997). Tracing molecules that make the brain–body connection. *Science, 275,* 930–931.

Peplau, L. (2003). Human sexuality: How do men and women differ? *Current Directions in Psychological Science, 12,* 37–40.

Pepperberg, I. (2006). Grey parrot *(Psittacus erithacus)* numerical abilities: Addition and further experiments on a zero-like concept. *Journal of Comparative Psychology, 120,* 1–11.

Pepperberg, I. M. (1991, Spring). Referential communication with an African grey parrot. *Harvard Graduate Society Newsletter,* 1–4.

Pepperberg, I. M. (1994a). Numerical competence in an African grey parrot (Psittacus erithacus). *Journal of Comparative Psychology, 108,* 36–44.

Pepperberg, I. M. (1994b). Vocal learning in grey parrots (Psittacus erithacus): Effects of social interaction, reference, and context. *The Auk, 111,* 300–314.

Pereira, S., Ki, M., & Power, C. (2012). Sedentary behavior and biomarkers for cardiovascular disease and diabetes in mid-life: The role of television-viewing and sitting at work. *PLOSOne.* Retrieved January 9, 2013, from http://www.plosone.org/article/info%3Adoi%2F10.1371%2Fjournal.pone.0031132

Perez-Felkner, L., McDonald, S., Schneider, B., & Grogan, E. (2012). Female and male adolescents' subjective orientations to mathematics and the influence of those orientations on post-secondary majors. *Developmental Psychology, 48,* 1658–1673.

Perez-Navarro, J., Lawrence, T., & Hume, I. (2009). Personality, mental state and procedure in the experimental replication of ESP: A preliminary study of new variables. *Journal of the Society for Psychical Research, 73,* 17–32.

Perls, F. S. (1969). *Gestalt therapy verbatim.* Lafayette, CA: Real People Press.

Perron, H., Mekaoui, L., Bernard, C., Veas, F., Stefas, I., & Leboyer, M. (2008). Endogenous retrovirus type W GAG and envelope protein antigenemia in serium of schizophrenic patients. *Biological Psychiatry, 64,* 1019–1023.

Peters, A., Leahu, D., Moss, M. B., & McNally, J. (1994). The effects of aging on area 46 of the frontal cortex of the rhesus monkey. *Cerebral Cortex, 6,* 621–635.

Peters, M., Hauschildt, M., Moritz, S., & Jelinek, L. (2013). Impact of emotionality on memory and meta-memory in schizophrenia using video sequences. *Journal of Behavior Therapy and Experimental Psychiatry, 44,* 77–83.

Peterson, L. R., & Peterson, M. J. (1959). Short-term retention of individual verbal items. *Journal of Experimental Psychology, 58,* 193–198.

Petry, N., Tedford, J., Austin, M., Nich, C., Carroll, K., & Rounsaville, B. (2004). Prize reinforcement contingency management for treating cocaine users: How low can we go, and with whom? *Addiction, 99,* 349–360.

Pew Research Center. (2006). *Global gender gaps.* Retrieved June 29, 2006, from *http://pewglobal.org/commentary/display.php?AnalysisID=90*

Phillips, K., Fulker, D. W., Carey, G., & Nagoshi, C. T. (1988). Direct marital assortment for cognitive and personality variables. *Behavioral Genetics, 18,* 347–356.

Piaget, J. (1927/1965). *The moral judgment of the child.* New York: Free Press.

Piaget, J. (1963). *Psychology of intelligence.* Patterson, NJ: Littlefield, Adams.

Piaget, J. (1964). *Judgment and reasoning in the child.* Patterson, NJ: Littlefield, Adams.

Piffer, D. (2012). Can creativity be measured? An attempt to clarify the notion of creativity and general directions for future research. *Thinking Skills and Creativity, 7,* 258–264.

Pillow, D. R., Zautra, A. J., & Sandler, I. (1996). Major life events and minor stressors: Identifying mediational links in the stress process. *Journal of Personality and Social Psychology, 70,* 381–394.

Pinel, J. (2007). *Basics of Biopsychology.* Boston: Allyn & Bacon.

Pinel, J. P. L. (2000). *Biopsychology* (4th ed.). Boston: Allyn & Bacon.

Pinker, S. (1994). *The language instinct: How the mind creates language.* New York: Morrow.

Piper, W., & Ogrodniczuk, J. (2013). Brief group therapies for complicated grief: Interpretive and supportive approaches. In M. Stroebe, H., Schut, & J. van den Bout (Eds.). *Complicated grief: Scientific foundations for health care professionals.* (pp. 263–277). New York, NY, USA: Routledge/Taylor & Francis Group.

Pittenger, D. (2011). Cautionary comments regarding the Myers-Briggs Type Indicator. *Consulting Psychology Journal: Practice and Research, 57,* 210–221.

Plassman, B., Langa, K., Fisher, G., Heeringa, S., Weir, D., Ofstedal, M., Burke, J., Hurd, M., Potter, G., Rodgers, W., Steffens, D., Willis, R., & Wallace, R. (2007). Prevalence of dementia in the United States: The aging, demographics, and memory study. *Neuroepidemiology, 29,* 125–132.

Pletcher, M., Vittinghoff, E., Kalhan, R., Richman, J., Safford, M., Sidney, S., Lin, F., & Kertesz, S. (2012). Association between marijuana exposure and pulmonary function over 20 years. *Journal of the American Medical Association, 307,* 173–181.

Polanco-Roman, L., & Miranda, R. (2013). Culturally related stress, hopelessness, and vulnerability to depressive symptoms and suicidal ideation in emerging adulthood. *Behavior Therpay, 44,* 75–87.

Polderman, T., de Geus, E., Hoekstra, R., Bartels, M., van Leeusen, M., Verhulst, F., & Posthuman, D. (2009). Attention problems, inhibitory control, and intelligence index overlapping genetic factors: A study in 9-, 12-, and 18-year-old twins. *Neurospychology, 23,* 381–391.

Poldrack, R., & Wagner, A. (2004). What can neuroimaging tell us about the mind? Insights from prefrontal cortex. *Current Directions in Psychological Science, 13,* 177–181.

Popma, A., Vermeiren, R., Geluk, C., Rinne, T., van den Brink, W., Knol, D., Jansen, L., van Engeland, H., & Doreleijers, T. (2007). Cortisol moderates the relationship between testosterone and aggression in delinquent male adolescents. *Biological Psychiatry, 61,* 405–411.

Poponoe, D., & Whitehead, B. D. (2000). Sex without strings, relationships without rings: Today's young singles talk about mating and dating. In *National Marriage Project, The State of Our Unions, 2000.* Retrieved June 10, 2007 from *http://marriage.rutgers.edu/Publications/SOOU/NMPAR2000.pdf*

Popper, K. (1972). *Objective knowledge: An evolutionary approach.* New York: Oxford University Press.

Porjesz, B., Begleiter, H., Reich, T., Van Eerdewegh, P., Edenberg, H., Foroud, T., et al. (1998). Amplitude of visual P3 event-related potential as a phenotypic marker for a predisposition to alcoholism: Preliminary results from the COGA project. *Alcoholism: Clinical & Experimental Research, 22,* 1317–1323.

Porter, F. L., Porges, S. W., & Marshall, R. E. (1988). Newborn pain cries and vagal tone: Parallel changes in response to circumcision. *Child Development, 59,* 495–505.

Porter, S., Bellhouse, S., McGougall, A., ten Brinke, L., & Wilson, K. (2010). A prospective investigation of the vulnerability of memory for positive and negative emotional scenes to the misinformation effect. *Canadian Journal of Behavioural Science, 42,* 55–61.

Posada, G., Jacobs, A., Richmond, M., Carbonell, O., Alzate, G., Bustamante, M., et al. (2002). Maternal caregiving and infant security in two cultures. *Developmental Psychology, 38,* 67–78.

Postman, L., & Phillips, L. W. (1965). Short-term temporal changes in free recall. *Quarterly Journal of Experimental Psychology, 17,* 132–138.

Potenza, M., Hong, K., Lacadie, C., et al. (2012). Neurla correlates of stress-induced and cue-induced drug craving: Influences of sex and cocaine dependence. *American Journal of Psychiatry, 169,* 406–414.

Potts, N. L. S., Davidson, J. R. T., & Krishman, K. R. R. (1993). The role of nuclear magnetic resonance imaging in psychiatric research. *Journal of Clinical Psychiatry, 54*(12, Suppl.), 13–18.

Poulin, M., & Cohen Silver, R. (2008). World benevolence beliefs and well-being across the life span. *Psychology and Aging, 23,* 13–23.

Powell, C., & Van Vugt, M. (2003). Genuine giving or selfish sacrifice? The role of commitment and cost level upon willingness to sacrifice. *European Journal of Social Psychology, 33,* 403–412.

Powlishta, K. K. (1995). Intergroup processes in childhood: Social categorization and sex role development. *Developmental Psychology, 31,* 781–788.

Powsner, S., & Dufel, S. (2009). *Conversion disorder.* Retrieved March 17, 2010 from *http://emedicine.medscape.com/article/805361-overview.*

Prabhu, V., Porjesz, B., Chorlian, D., Wang, K., Stimus, A., & Begleiter, H. (2001). Visual P3 in female alcoholics. *Alcoholism: Clinical & Experimental Research, 25,* 531–539.

Precekl, F., Lipnevich, A., Schneider, S., & Roberts, R. (2011). Chronotype, cognitive abilities, and academic achievement: A meta-analytic investigation. *Learning and Individual Differences, 21,* 483–492.

Preda, A. (2012). *Opioid abuse.* Retrieved November 9, 2012, from http://emedicine.medscape.com/article/287790-overview#a0104.

Premack, D. (1971). Language in chimpanzees. *Science, 172,* 808–822.

Premack, D., & Premack, A. J. (1983). *The mind of an ape.* New York: Norton.

Price, D., Finniss, D., & Benedetti, F. (2008). A comprehensive review of the placebo effect: Recent advances and current thought. *Annual Review of Psychology, 59,* 565–590.

Pryke, S., Lindsay, R. C. L., & Pozzulo, J. D. (2000). Sorting mug shots: Methodological issues. *Applied Cognitive Psychology, 14,* 81–96.

Psychologists' pigeons score 90 pct. picking Picasso. (1995, May 7). *St. Louis Post-Dispactch,* p. 2A.

Public Agenda Online. (2002). *The issues: Race.* Retrieved November 13, 2002, from *http://www.publicagenda.com/issues/overview.dfm?issue_type=race*

Purves, D., Augustine, G., Fitzpatrick, D., Hall, W., LaMantia, A., & White, L. (2011). *Neuroscience* 5th ed. Sinderland, MA: Sinauer Associates, Inc.

Quaid, K., Aschen, S., Smiley, C., Nurnberger, J. (2001). Perceived genetic risks for bipolar disorder in patient population: An exploratory study. *Journal of Genetic Counseling, 10,* 41–51.

Querido, J., Warner, T., & Eyberg, S. (2002). Parenting styles and child behavior in African American families of preschool children. *Journal of Clinical Child & Adolescent Psychology, 31,* 272–277.

Quick, N., & Janik, V. (2008). Whistle rates of wild bottlenose dolphins (Tursiops truncatus): Influences of group size and behavior. *Journal of Comparative Psychology, 122,* 305–311.

Quill, T. (2007). Legal regulation of physician-assisted death: The latest report cards. *New England Journal of Medicine, 356,* 1911–1913.

Quiroga, T., Lemos-Britton, Z., Mostafapour, E., Abbott, R., & Berninger, V. (2002). Phonological awareness and beginning reading in Spanish-speaking ESL first graders: Research into practice. *Journal of School Psychology, 40,* 85–111.

Rönnqvist, L., & Domellöf, E. (2006). Quantitative assessment of right and left reaching movements in infants: A longitudinal study from 6 to 36 months. *Developmental Psychobiology, 48,* 444–459.

Raeikkoenen, K., Matthews, K., & Salomon, K. (2003). Hostility predicts metabolic syndrome risk factors in children and adolescents. *Health Psychology, 22,* 279–286.

Rahe, R. J., Meyer, M., Smith, M., Kjaer, G., & Holmes, T. H. (1964). Social stress and illness onset. *Journal of Psychosomatic Research, 8,* 35–44.

Ramey, S., Ramey, C., & Lanzi, R. (2007). In J., Jacobson, J., Mulick, & J. Rojahn (Eds.), *Handbook of intellectual and developmental disabilities: Issues in clinical child psychology* (pp. 445–463). New York: Springer Publishing Co.

Rammstedt, B., Spinath, F., Richter, D., & Schupp, J. (2013). Partnership longevity and personality congruence in couples. *Personality and Individual Differences, 54,* 832–855.

Ramsey, J., Langlois, J., Hoss, R., Rubenstein, A., & Griffin, A. (2004). Origins of a stereotype: Categorization of facial attractiveness by 6-month-old infants. *Developmental Science, 7,* 201–211.

Rangaswamy, M., Jones, K., Porjesz, B., Chorlian, D., Padmanabhapillai, A., Karajan, C., Kuperman, S., Rohrbaugh, J., O'Connor, S., Bauer, L., Schuckit, M., & Begleiter, H. (2007). Delta and theta oscillations as risk markers in adolescent offspring of alcoholics. *International Journal of Psychophysiology, 63,* 3–15.

Rasetti, R., Mattay, V., Wiedholz, L., Kolachana, B., Hariri, A., Callicott, J., Meyer-Lindenberg, A., & Weinberger, D. (2009). Evidence that altered amygdala activity in schizophrenia is related to clinical state and not genetic risk. *American Journal of Psychiatry, 166,* 216–225.

Ratty, H., Vaenskae, J., Kasanen, K., & Kaerkkaeinen, R. (2002). Parents' explanations of their child's performance in mathematics and reading: A replication and extension of Yee and Eccles. *Sex Roles, 46,* 121–128.

Raven, M., & Parry, P. (2012). Psychotropic marketing practices and problems: Implications for DSM-5. *Journal of Nervous and Mental Disease, 200,* 512–516.

Ravindran, A., & Ravindran, L. (2009). Depression and comorbid anxiety: An overview of pharmacological options. *Psychiatric Times, 26.* Retrieved June 18, 2009 from *http://www.psychiatrictimes.com/cme/display/article/10168/1421225?pageNumber=2.*

Ravindran, A., da Silva, T., Ravindran, L., Richter, M., & Rector, N. (2009). Obsessive-compulsive spectrum disorders: A review of the evidence-based treatments. *Canadian Journal of Psychiatry, 54,* 331–343.

Ray, S., & Bates, M. (2006). Acute alcohol effects on repetition priming and word recognition memory with equivalent memory cues. *Brain and Cognition, 60,* 118–127.

Raz, N., Lindenberger, U., Rodrigue, K., Kennedy, K., Head, D., Williamson, A., Dahle, C., Gerstorf, D., & Acker, J. (2006). Regional brain changes in aging healthy adults: General trends, individual differences and modifiers. *Cerebral Cortex, 15,* 1679–1689.

Razoumnikova, O. M. (2000). Functional organization of different brain areas during convergent and divergent thinking: An EEG investigation. *Cognitive Brain Research, 10,* 11–18.

Rebs, S., & Park, S. (2001). Gender differences in high-achieving students in math and science. *Journal for the Education of the Gifted, 25,* 52–73.

Reczek, C., & Umberson, D. (2012). Gender, health behavior, and intimate relationships: Lesbian, gay, and straight contexts. *Social Science & Medicine, 74,* 1783–1790.

Redish, A. & Ekstrome, A. (2013). Hippocampus and related areas: What the place cell literature tells us about cognitive maps in rats and humans. In D. Waller, & L. Nadel (Eds). *Handbook of spatial cognition.* (pp. 15–34). Washington, DC, USA: American Psychological Association.

Reeves, W., Strine, T., Pratt, L., Thompson, W., Ahlauwalia, I., Dhingra, S., McKnight-Eily, L., Harrison, L., D'Angelo, D., Williams, L., Morrow, B., Gould, D., & Safran, M. (2011). Mental illness surveillance among adults in the United States. *Morbidity and Mortality Weekly Report, 60,* 1–32.

Reinhardt, J., Boerner, K., Horowitz, A., & Lloyd, S. (2006). Good to have but not to use: Differential impact of perceived and received support on well-being. *Journal of Social and Personal Relationships, 23,* 117–129.

Reitman, D., Murphy, M., Hupp, S., & O'Callaghan, P. (2004). Behavior change and perceptions of change: Evaluating the effectiveness of a token economy. *Child & Family Behavior Therapy, 26,* 17–36.

Rescorla, R. (2008). Conditioning of stimuli with nonzero initial value. *Journal of Experimental Psychology: Animal Behavior Processes, 34,* 315–323.

Rescorla, R. A., & Wagner, A. R. (1972). A theory of Pavlovian conditioning: Variations in the effectiveness of reinforcement and nonreinforcement. In A. Black & W. F. Prokasy (Eds.), *Classical conditioning: II. Current research and theory* (pp. 64–99). New York: Appleton.

Restak, R. (1988). *The mind.* Toronto: Bantam.

Reuters News Service. (2006, June 30). *Japan elderly population ratio now world's highest.* Retrieved July 3, 2006, from *http://today.reuters. co.uk/news/newsArticle.aspx?type=worldNews&storyID=2006-06-30T084625Z_01_T83766_RTRUKOC_0_UKJAPANPOPULATION.xml&archived=False*

Reyna, V. (2004). How people make decisions that involve risk: A dual-processes approach. *Current Directions in Psychological Science, 13,* 60–66.

Reynolds, A., & Temple, J. (2008). Cost-effective early childhood development programs from preschool to third grade. *Annual Review of Clinical Psychology, 4,* 109–139.

Rhéaume, J., & Ladouceur, R. (2000). Cognitive and behavioural treatments of checking behaviours: An examination of individual cognitive change. *Clinical Psychology & Psychotherapy, 7,* 118–127.

Ricks, T., & Wiley, J. (2009). The influence of domain knowledge on the functional capacity of working memory. *Journal of Memory and Language, 61,* 519–537.

Ridderinkhof, K., Scheres, A., Oosterlaan, J., & Sergeant, J. (2005). Delta plots in the study of individual differences: New tools reveal response inhibition deficits in AD/HD that are eliminated by methylphenidate treatment. *Journal of Abnormal Psychology, 114,* 197–215.

Rideout, V., Roberts, D., & Foehr, U. (2005). *Generation M: Media in the lives of 8-18 year-olds.* Washington, DC, USA: Kaiser Family Foundation. Retrieved May 18, 2006, from http://www.kff.org/entmedia/entmedia030905pkg.dfm.

Riedel, G. (1996). Function of metabotropic glutamate receptors in learning and memory. *Trends in Neurosciences, 19,* 219–224.

Reiker, P., Bird, C., & Lang, M. (2010). Understanding gender and health: Old patterns, new trends, and future directions. In C. Bird, P. Conrad, A. Fremont, & S. Timmermans (Eds.). *Handbook of medical sociology* (6th ed.). (pp. 52–74). Nashville, TN, USA: Vanderbilt University Press.

Rini, C., Manne, S., DuHamel, K., Austin, J., Ostroff, J., Boulad, F., et al. (2004). Mothers' perceptions of benefit following pediatric stem cell transplantation: A longitudinal investigation of the roles of optimism, medical risk, and sociodemographic resources. *Annals of Behavioral Medicine, 28,* 132–141.

Rissman, J., & Wagner, A. (2012). Distributed representations in memory: Insights from functional brain imaging. *Annual Review of Psychology, 63,* 101–128.

Roan, S. (2000, March 6). *Cyberanalysis.* Retrieved June 10, 2007 from *http://www.doctorchase.com/html/cyberanalysis.html.*

Roberts, G., Treasure, D., & Conroy, D. (2007). Understanding the dynamics of motivation in sport and physical activity: An achievement goal interpretation. In G., Tenenbaum, & R. Eklund (Eds.), *Handbook of sport psychology* (3rd ed.) (pp. 3–30). Hoboken, NJ: John Wiley & Sons.

Roberts, J., & Bell, M. (2000). Sex differences on a mental rotation task: Variations in electroencephalogram hemispheric activation between children and college students. *Developmental Neuropsychology, 17,* 199–223.

Roberts, M. (2006). "IDOL" dreams: Tracy Moore's story of hope and discovery. *Schizophrenia Digest, 4,* 30–33.

Roberts, P., & Moseley, B. (1996, May/June). Fathers' time. *Psychology Today, 29,* 48–55, 81.

Robins, R. W., Gosling, S. D., & Craik, K. H. (1999). An empirical analysis of trends in psychology. *American Psychologist, 54,* 117–128.

Robins, R., & Trzesniewski, K. (2005). Self-esteem development across the lifespan. *Current Directions in Psychological Science, 14,* 158–162.

Robinson, F. (1970). *Effective study* (4th ed.). New York: Harper & Row.

Robinson, M., & Tamir, M. (2005). Neuroticism as mental noise: A relation between neuroticism and reaction time standard deviations. *Journal of Personality and Social Psychology, 89,* 107–114.

Robles, T., Glaser, R., & Kiecolt-Glaser, J. (2005). Out of balance: A new look at chronic stress, depression, and immunity. *Current Directions in Psychological Science, 14,* 111–115.

Rock, I., & Palmer, S. (1990). The legacy of Gestalt psychology. *Scientific American, 263,* 84–90.

Rodin, J., & Salovey, P. (1989). Health psychology. *Annual Review of Psychology, 40,* 533–579.

Rodin, J., Wack, J., Ferrannini, E., & DeFronzo, R. A. (1985). Effect of insulin and glucose on feeding behavior. *Metabolism, 34,* 826–831.

Roediger, H. (1980). Memory metaphors in cognitive psychology. *Memory & Cognition, 8,* 231–246.

Rogers, C. R. (1951). *Client-centered therapy: Its current practice, implications, and theory.* Boston: Houghton Mifflin.

Rogers, M., Blumberg, N., Heal, J., & Hicks, G. (2007). Increased risk of infection and mortality in women after cardiac surgery related to allogeneic blood transfusion. *Journal of Women's Health, 16,* 1412–1420.

Rogers, M., Langa, K., Kim, C., Nallamothu, B., McMahon, L., Malani, P., Fries, B., Kaufman, S., & Saint, S. (2006). Contribution of infection to increased mortality in women after cardiac surgery. *Archives of Internal Medicine, 166,* 437–443.

Rogoff, B., & Mistry, J. (1995). Memory development in cultural context. In M. Pressley & C. Brainerd (Eds.), *The cognitive side of memory development.* New York, NY, USA: Springer-Verlag.

Roiser, J., Levy, J., Fromm, S., Goldman, D., Hodgkinson, C., Hasler, G., Sahakian, B., & Drevets, W. (2012). Serotonin transporter genotype differentially modulates neural responses to emotional words following tryptophan depletion in patients recovered from depression and healthy volunteers. *Journal of Psychopharmacology, 26,* 1434–1442.

Roisman, G., Masten, A., Coatsworth, J., & Tellegen, A. (2004). Salient and emerging developmental tasks in the transition to adulthood. *Child Development, 75,* 123–133.

Roorda, A., & Williams, D. R. (1999). The arrangement of the three cone classes in the living human eye. *Nature, 397,* 520–521.

Roozendaal, B., Catello, N., Vedana, G., Barsegyan, A., & McGaugh, J. (2008). Noradrenergic activation of the basolateral amygdala modulates consolidation of object recognition memory. *Neurobiology of Learning and Memory, 90,* 576–579.

Rosch, E. & Lloyd, B. (1978). *Cognition and categorization.* Hillsdale, NJ: Erlbaum.

Rosch, E. H. (1973). Natural categories. *Cognitive Psychology, 4,* 328–350.

Rosch, E. H. (1987). Linguistic relativity. *Et Cetera, 44,* 254–279.

Rose, J. (2006). Nicotine and nonnicotine factors in cigarette addiction. *Psychopharmacology, 184,* 274–285.

Roselli, C., Larkin, K., Schrunk, J., & Stormshak, F. (2004). Sexual partner preference, hypothalamic morphology and aromatase in rams. *Physiology & Behavior, 83,* 233–245.

Rosenbloom, T. (2006). Sensation seeking and pedestrian crossing compliance. *Social Behavior and Personality, 34,* 113–122.

Rosenhan, D. L. (1973). On being sane in insane places. *Science, 179,* 250–258.

Rosenzweig, M. R. (1961). Auditory localization. *Scientific American, 205,* 132–142.

Rosenzweig, S., Greeson, J., Reibel, D., Green, J., Jasser, S., & Beasley, D. (2010). Mindfulness-based stress reduction for chronic pain conditions: Variation in treatment outcomes and role of home meditation practice. *Journal of Psychosomatic Research, 68,* 29–36.

Rosner, S., Hackl-Herrwerth, A., Leucht, S., Lehert, P., Vecchi, S., & Soyka, M. (2010). Acamprosate for alcohol dependence. *Cochrane Reviews, 8,* 4332.

Ross, J., Baldessarini, R. J., & Tondo, L. (2000). Does lithium treatment still work? Evidence of stable responses over three decades. *Archives of General Psychiatry, 57,* 187–190.

Ross, L. (1977). The intuitive psychologist and his shortcomings: Distortions in the attribution process. In L. Berkowitz (Ed.), *Advances in experimental social psychology* (pp. 173–220). New York: Academic Press.

Rossow, I., & Amundsen, A. (1997). Alcohol abuse and mortality: A 40-year prospective study of Norwegian conscripts. *Social Science & Medicine, 44,* 261–267.

Rotter, J. B. (1966). Generalized expectancies for internal versus external control of reinforcement. *Psychological Monographs, 80*(1, Whole No. 609).

Rotter, J. B. (1971, June). External control and internal control. *Psychology Today,* 37–42, 58–59.

Rotter, J. B. (1990). Internal versus external control of reinforcement: A case history of a variable. *American Psychologist, 45,* 489–493.

Rotton, J., & Cohn, E. G. (2000). Violence is a curvilinear function of temperature in Dallas: A replication. *Journal of Personality & Social Psychology, 78,* 1074–1082.

Rotton, J., Frey, J., Barry, T., Milligan, M., & Fitzpatrick, M. (1979). The air pollution experience and physical aggression. *Journal of Applied Social Psychology, 9,* 397–412.

Rouch, I., Wild, P., Ansiau, D., & Marquie, J. (2005). Shiftwork experience, age and cognitive performance. *Ergonomics, 48,* 1282–1293.

Round-the-clock baby TV channel to debut. (2006, May 11). Retrieved May 11, 2006, from http://www.news.yahoo.com.

Rowe, D. (2003). Assessing genotype-environment interactions and correlations in the postgenomic era. In R. Plomin, J. DeFries, I. Craig, & P. McGuffin (Eds.), *Behavioral genetics in the postgenomic era* (pp. 71–86). Washington, DC: American Psychological Association.

Rowe, D. C. (1987). Resolving the person-situation debate: Invitation to an interdisciplinary dialogue. *American Psychologist, 42,* 218–227.

Rowe, J., & Kahn, R. (1998). *Successful aging.* New York: Pantheon.

Rubin, D., Boals, A., & Klein, K. (2010). Autobiographical memories for very negative events: The effects of thinking about and rating memories. *Cognitive Therapy and Research, 34,* 35–48.

Rubino, T., Realini, N., Braida, Da., Guidi, S., Capurro, V., Vigano, D., Guidall, C., Pinter, M., Sala, M., Bartesaghi, R., & Parolaro, D. (2009). Changes in hippocampal morphology and neuroplasticity induced by adolescent THC treatment are associated with cognitive impairment in adulthood. *Hippocampus, 19,* 763–772.

Rubinstein, G. (2001). Sex-role reversal and clinical judgment of mental health. *Journal of Sex & Marital Therapy, 27,* 9–19.

Ruble, D., Taylor, L., Cyphers, L., Greulich, F., Lurye, L., & Shrout, P. (2007). The role of gender constancy in early gender development. *Child Development, 78,* 1121–1136.

Ruby, N., Dark, J., Burns, D., Heller, H., & Zucker, I. (2002). The suprachiasmatic nucleus is essential for circadian body temperature rhythms in hibernating ground squirrels. *Journal of Neuroscience, 22,* 357–364.

Rudebeck, P., Walton, M., Millette, B., Shirley, E., Rushworth, M., & Bannerman, D. (2007). *European Journal of Neuroscience, 26,* 2315–2326.

Rudman, L., Ashmore, R., & Gary, M. (2001). "Unlearning" automatic biases: The malleability of implicit prejudice and stereotypes. *Journal of Personality & Social Psychology, 81,* 856–868.

Ruetzler, T., Taylor, J., Reynolds, D., Baker, W., & Killen, C. (2012). What is professional attire today? A conjoint analysis of personal presentation attributes. *International Journal of Hospitality Management.*31(3), 937–943.

Ruggero, M. A. (1992). Responses to sound of the basilar membrane of the mammalian cochlea. *Current Opinion in Neurobiology, 2,* 449–456.

Rumbaugh, D. (1977). *Language learning by a chimpanzee: the Lana project.* New York: Academic Press.

Rummel, C., Goodfellow, M., Gast, H., Hauf, M., Amor, F., Stibal, A., Mariani, L., & Schindler, K. (2013). A systems-level approach to human epileptic seizures. *Neuroinformatics, 10,* Volume 11, pp. 159–173.

Ruscio, J. (2001). Administering quizzes at random to increase students' reading. *Teaching of Psycholog, 28,* 204–206.

Rushton, J. P., Fulker, D. W., Neale, M. C., Nias, D. K. B., & Eysenck, H. J. (1986). Altruism and aggression: The heritability of individual differences. *Journal of Personality and Social Psychology, 50,* 1192–1198.

Rushton, J., & Jensen, A. (2003). African–White IQ differences from Zimbabwe on the Wechsler Intelligence Scale for Children-Revised are mainly on the g factor. *Personality & Individual Differences, 34,* 177–183.

Rushton, P., & Jensen, A. (2005). Thirty years of research on race differences in cognitive ability. *Psychology, Public Policy, and Law, 11,* 235–294.

Russell, T., Rowe, W., & Smouse, A. (1991). Subliminal self-help tapes and academic achievement: An evaluation. *Journal of Counseling and Development, 69,* 359–362.

Ryan, R., Kim, Y., & Kaplan, U. (2003). Differentiating autonomy from individualism and independence: A self-determination theory perspective on internalization of cultural orientations and well-being. *Journal of Personality and Social Psychology, 84,* 97–110.

Saber, T. (2012). *Bariatric surgery treatment and management.* Retrieved January 4, 2013, from http://emedicine.medscape.com/article/197081-treatment#a1128

Sack, R., Auckley, D., Auger, R., Carskadon, M., Wright, K., Vitiello, M., & Zhdanova, I. (2007a). Circadian rhythm sleep disorders: Part I, Basic principles, shift work and jet lag disorders. An American Academy of Sleep Medicine review. *Sleep, 30,* 1460–1483.

Sackeim, H. A., Luber, B., Katzman, G. P., Moeller, J. R., Prudic, J., Devanand, D. P., et al. (1996). The effects of electroconvulsive therapy on quantitative electroencephalograms. *Archives of General Psychiatry, 53,* 814–824.

Sackeim, H. A., Prudic, J., Devanand, D. P., Nobler, M. S., Lisanby, S. H., Peyser, S., et al. (2000). A prospective, randomized, double-blind comparison of bilateral and right unilateral electroconvulsive therapy at different stimulus intensities. *Archives of General Psychiatry, 57,* 425–434.

Sackett, P., & Ryan, A. (2012). Concerns about generalizing stereotype threat research findings to operational high-stakes testing. In M. Inzlicht & T. Schmader (Eds.) *Stereotype threat: Theory, process, and application.* (pp. 249–263). New York, NY, USA: Oxford University Press.

Sacks, O. (1984). *A leg to stand on.* New York: Harper & Row.

Saczynski, J., Willis, S., & Schaie, K. W. (2002). Strategy use in reasoning training with older adults. *Aging, Neuropsychology, & Cognition, 9,* 48–60.

Safir, M., Wallach, H., & Bar-Zvi, M. (2012). Virtual reality cognitive-behavior therapy for public speaking anxiety: One-year follow-up. *Behavior Modification, 36,* 235–246.

Sagarin, B., Martin, A., Coutinho, S., Edlund, J., Patel, L., Skowronski, J., & Zengel, B. (2012). Sex differences in jealousy: A meta-analytic examination. *Evolution and Human Behavior, 33,* 595–614.

Salisch, M. (2001). Children's emotional development: Challenges in their relationships to parents, peers, and friends. *International Journal of Behavioural Development, 25,* 310–319.

Salmon, D., & Bondi, M. (2009). The neuropsychology of Alzheimer's disease. *Neurology, 72,* 521–527.

Salmon, J., Owen, N., Crawford, D., Bauman, A., & Sallis, J. (2003). Physical activity and sedentary behavior: A population-based study of barriers, enjoyment, and preference. *Health Psychology, 22,* 178–188.

Salovey, P., & Pizarro, D. (2003). The value of emotional intelligence. In R. Sternberg, J. Lautrey, & T. Lubart (Eds.), *Models of intelligence: International perspective* (pp. 263–278). Washington, DC: American Psychological Association.

Salthouse, T. (2004). What and when of cognitive aging. *Current Directions in Psychological Science, 13,* 140–144.

Sanchez, G. (1932). Scores of Spanish-speaking children on repeated tests. *The Pedagogical Seminary and Journal of Genetic Psychology, 40,* 223–231.

Sanchez, G. (1934). The implications of a basal vocabulary to the measurement of the abilities of bilingual children. *The Journal of Social Psychology, 5,* 395–402.

Sanes, J. N., & Donoghue, J. P. (2000). Plasticity and primary motor cortex. *Annual Review of Neuroscience, 23,* 393–415.

Sansone, R., & Sansone, L. (2011). Personality disorders: A nation-based perspective on prevalence. *Innovations in Clinical Neuroscience, 8,* 13–18.

Santiago-Rivera, A., & Altarriba, J. (2002). The role of language in therapy with the Spanish-English bilingual client. *Professional Psychology: Research & Practice, 33,* 30–38.

Saper, C., Scammell, T., & Lu, J. (2005). Hypothalamic regulation of sleep and circadian rhythms. *Nature, 437,* 1257–1263.

Sateia, M. J., Doghramji, K., Hauri, P. J., & Morin, C. M. (2000). Evaluation of chronic insomnia. An American Academy of Sleep Medicine review. *Sleep, 23,* 243–308.

Sattler, J. (2008). *Assessment of children: Cognitive foundations* (5th ed.). San Diego, CA: Jerome M. Sattler, Publisher.

Saudino, K. (2012). Sources of continuity and change in activity level in early childhood. *Child Development, 83,* 266–281.

Savage, M., & Holcomb, D. (1999). Adolescent female athletes' sexual risk-taking behaviors. *Journal of Youth and Adolescence, 28,* 583–594.

Savage-Rumbaugh, E. S. (1990). Language acquisition in a nonhuman species: Implications for the innateness debate. *Developmental Psychology, 26,* 599–620.

Savage-Rumbaugh, E. S., Sevcik, R. A., Brakke, K. E., & Rumbaugh, D. M. (1992). Symbols: Their communicative use, communication, and combination by bonobos (Pan paniscus). In L. P. Lipsitt & C. Rovee-Collier (Eds.). *Advances in infancy research* (Vol. 7, pp. 221–278). Norwood, NJ: Ablex.

Scarr, S., & Weinberg, R. (1976). The influence of "family background" on intellectual attainment. *American Sociological Review, 43,* 674–692.

Schachter, S., & Singer, J. E. (1962). Cognitive, social, and physiological determinants of emotional state. *Psychological Review, 69,* 379–399.

Schaie, K. (1993). Ageist language in psychological research. *American Psychologist, 48,* 49–51.

Schaie, K. (2005). *Developmental influences on adult intelligence: The Seattle longitudinal study.* New York: Oxford University Press.

Schaie, K. (2008). Historical processes and patterns of cognitive aging. In S., Hofer, & D. Alwin (Eds.), *Handbook of cognitive aging: Interdisciplinary perspectives*. (pp. 368–383). Thousand Oaks, CA: Sage Publications.

Schauer, P., Ikramuddin, S., Gourash, W., Ramanathan, R., & Luketich, J. (2000). Outcomes after laparoscopic roux-en-Y gastric bypass for morbid obesity. *Annals of Surgery, 232*, 515–529.

Schenck, C. H., & Mahowald, M. W. (2000). Parasomnias. Managing bizarre sleep-related behavior disorders. *Postgraduate Medicine, 107*, 145–156.

Scherer, K. R., & Wallbott, H. G. (1994). Evidence for universality and cultural variation of differential emotion response patterning. *Journal of Personality and Social Psychology, 66*, 310–328.

Schiff, M., & Lewontin, R. (1986). *Education and class: The irrelevance of IQ genetic studies*. Oxford, England: Clarendon.

Schizophrenia.com. (2006). *Brain disorders, smoking and nicotine addiction: A special report*. Retrieved February 12, 2007, from *http://www.schizophrenia.com/smokerreport.htm*

Schmidt, P., Murphy, J., Haq, N., Rubinow, D., & Danaceau, M. (2004). Stressful life events, personal losses, and perimenopause-related depression. *Archives of Women's Mental Health, 7*, 19–26.

Schmitt, N., Fuchs, A., & Kirch, W. (2008). Mental health disorders and work-life balance. In A. Linos & W. Kirch (Eds.), *Promoting health for working women*. (pp. 117–136). New York: Springer.

Schmitt, N., Keeney, J., Oswald, F., Pleskac, T., Billington, A., Sinha, R., & Zorzie, M. (2009). Prediction of 4-year college student performance using cognitive and noncognitive predictors and the impact on demographic status of admitted students. *Journal of Applied Psychology, 94*, 1479–1497.

Schmitt, D., Jonason, P., Byerley, G., Flores, S., Illbeck, B., O'Leary, K., & Qudrat, A. (2012). A reexamination of sex differences in sexuality: New studies reveal old truths. *Current Directions in Psychological Science, 21*, 135–139.

Schofield, J., & Ward, S. (2006). Internet use in schools: Promise and problems. In K. Sawyer (Ed.). *The Cambridge Handbook of the Learning Sciences*. (pp. 521–534). New York, NY, USA: Cambridge University Press.

Schofield, J. W., & Francis, W. D. (1982). An observational study of peer interaction in racially mixed "accelerated" classrooms. *Journal of Educational Psychology, 74*, 722–732.

Scholz, U., Dona, B., Sud, S., & Schwarzer, R. (2002). Is general self-efficacy a universal construct? Psychometric findings from 25 countries. *European Journal of Psychological Assessment, 18*, 242–251.

Schreppel, T., Egetemeir, J., Schecklmann, M., Plichta, M., Pauli, P., Ellgring, H., Fallgatter, A., & Herrmann, M. (2008). Activiation of the prefrontal cortex in working memory and interference resolution processes assessed with near-infrared spectroscopy. *Neuropsychobiology, 57*, 188–193.

Schulz, T., Whitehead, H., Gero, S., & Rendell, L. (2008). Overlapping and matching of codas in vocal interactions between sperm whales: Insights into communication function. *Animal Behavior, 76*, 1977–1988.

Schwabe, L., & Wolf, O. (2009). The context counts: Congruent learning and testing environments prevent memory retrieval impairment following stress. *Cognitive, Affective & Behavioral Neuroscience, 9*, 229–236.

Schwartz, S., & Maquet, P. (2002). Sleep imaging and the neuro-psychological assessment of dreams. *Trends in Cognitive Sciences, 6*, 23–30.

Sedikides, C., Gaertner, L., & Toguchi, Y. (2003). Pancultural self-enhancement. *Journal of Personality & Social Psychology, 84*, 60–79.

Sedlemeier, P., Eberth, J., Schwarz, M., Zimmermann, D., Haarig, F., Jaeger, S., & Kunze, S. (2012). *Psychological Bulletin, 138*, 1139–1171.

Seegert, C. (2004). Token economies and incentive programs: Behavioral improvement in mental health inmates housed in state prisons. *Behavior Therapist, 26*, 210–211.

Seeman, T., Dubin, L., & Seeman, M. (2003). Religiosity/spirituality and health. *American Psychologist, 58*, 53–63.

Segall, M. H. (1994). A cross-cultural research contribution to unraveling the nativist/empiricist controversy. In J. Lonner & R. Malpass (Eds.), *Psychology and culture* (pp. 135–138). Boston: Allyn & Bacon.

Segall, M. H., Campbell, D. T., & Herskovitz, M. J. (1966). *The influence of culture on visual perception*. Indianapolis: Bobbs-Merrill.

Seidman, S. (2002). Exploring the relationship between depression and erectile dysfunction in aging men. *Journal of Clinical Psychiatry, 63*, 5–12.

Seih, Y., Bhrmester, M., Lin, Y., Huang, C., Swann, J. (2012). Self-verification theory. In P. Van Lange, A. Kruglanski, & E. Higgins (Eds.). *Handbook of theories of social psychology*. (pp. 23–42). Thousand Oaks, CA, USA: Sage Publications Ltd.

Seijts, G., & Latham, G. (2012). Knowing when to set learning versus performance goals. *Organizational Dynamics, 41*, 1–6.

Self, M., & Zeki, S. (2005). The integration of colour and motion by the human visual brain. *Cerebral Cortex, 15*, 1270–1279.

Seligman, M. E. P. (1972). Phobias and preparedness. In M. E. P. Seligman & J. L. Hager (Eds.), *Biological boundaries of learning* (pp. 307–320). Englewood Cliffs, NJ: Prentice Hall.

Seligman, M. E. P. (1975). *Helplessness: On depression, development and death*. San Francisco: Freeman.

Seligman, M. E. P. (1991). *Learned optimism*. New York: Knopf.

Seligman, M. E. P. (1995). The effectiveness of psychotherapy: The *Consumer Reports* Study. *American Psychologist, 50*, 965–974.

Seligman, M. E. P. (1996). Science as an ally of practice. *American Psychologist, 51*, 1072–1079.

Seligman, M., & Csikszentmihalyi, M. (2000). Positive psychology: An introduction. *American Psychologist, 55*, 5–14.

Seligman, M. (2011). *Flourish: A visionary new understanding of happiness and well-being*. New York, NY, US: Free Press.

Selye, H. (1956). *The stress of life*. New York: McGraw-Hill.

Serido, J., Almeida, D., & Wethington, E. (2004). Chronic stressors and daily hassles: Unique and interactive relationships with psychological distress. *Journal of Health and Social Behavior, 45*, 17–33.

Serpell R., & Hatano, G. (1997). Education, schooling, and literacy. In J. Berry, P. Dasen, & T. Sarswthi (Eds.), *Handbook of cross-cultural psychology* (Vol. 2, pp. 339–376). Boston: Allyn & Bacon.

Shackelford, T., Voracek, M., Schmitt, D., Buss, D., Weekes-Shackelford, V., & Michalski, R. (2004). Romantic jealousy in early adulthood and in later life. *Human Nature, 15*, 283–300.

Shackelford, T., Goetz, A., Liddle, J., & Bush, L. (2012). Sexual conflict in humans. In T. Shackleford & A. Goetz (Eds.) *The Oxford handbook of sexual conflict in humans*. (pp. 3–14). New York, NY, USA: Oxford University Press.

Shargorodsky, J., Curhan, S., Curhan, G., & Eavey, R. (2010). Change in prevalence of hearing loss in US adolescents. *Journal of the American Medical Association, 304*, 772–778.

Sharma, S. (2006). Parasomnias. Retrieved December 16, 2006, from *http://www.emedicine.com/med/topic3131.html*

Shaunessy, E., Karnes, F., & Cobb, Y. (2004). Assessing potentially gifted students from lower socioeconomic status with nonverbal measures of intelligence. *Perceptual & Motor Skills, 98*, 1129–1138.

Shaw, J. I., & Steers, W. N. (2001). Gathering information to form an impression: Attribute categories and information valence. *Current Research in Social Psychology, 6*, 1–21.

Shaw, J. S., III. (1996). Increases in eyewitness confidence resulting from postevent questioning. *Journal of Experimental Psychology: Applied, 2,* 126–146.

Shaw, V. N., Hser, Y.-I., Anglin, M. D., & Boyle, K. (1999). Sequences of powder cocaine and crack use among arrestees in Los Angeles County. *American Journal of Drug and Alcohol Abuse, 25,* 47–66.

Shears, J., Robinson, J., & Emde, R. (2002). Fathering relationships and their associations with juvenile delinquency. *Infant Mental Health Journal, 23,* 79–87.

Sheets, R., & Mohr, J. (2009). Perceived social support from friends and family and psychosocial functioning in bisexual young adult college students. *Journal of Counseling Psychology, 56,* 152–163.

Sheikhiani, M., & Nair, B. (2012). Proactive coping skills and state-trait anxiety of women teacher students. *Journal of the Indian Academy of Applied Psychology, 38,* 277–286.

Shelton, J., & Richeson, J. (2005). Intergroup contact and pluralistic ignorance. *Journal of Personalty & Social Psychology, 88,* 91–107.

Sher, L. (2004a). Hypothalamic-pituitary-adrenal function and preventing major depressive episodes. *Canadian Journal of Psychiatry, 49,* 574–575.

Sher, L. (2004b). Type D personality, cortisol and cardiac disease. *Australian and New Zealand Journal of Psychiatry, 38,* 652–653.

Sherif, M. (1956). Experiments in group conflict. *Scientific American, 195,* 53–58.

Sherif, M. (1958). Superordinate goals in the reduction of intergroup conflict. *American Journal of Sociology, 63,* 349–358.

Sherif, M., & Sherif, C. W. (1967). The Robbers' Cave study. In J. F. Perez, R. C. Sprinthall, G. S. Grosser, & P. J. Anastasiou, *General psychology: Selected readings* (pp. 411–421). Princeton, NJ: D. Van Nostrand.

Shiffrin, R. (1999). Thirty years of memory. In C. Izawa (Ed.), *On human memory: Evolution, progress, and reflections on the 30th anniversary of the Atkinson-Shiffrin model* (pp. 17–33). Hillsdale, NJ: Lawrence Erlbaum Associates.

Shinar, D., Tractinsky, N., & Compton, R. (2005). Effects of practice, age, and task demands, on interference from a phone task while driving. *Accident Analysis & Prevention, 37,* 315–326.

Shiner, R. (2000). Linking childhood personality with adaptation: Evidence for continuity and change across time into late adolescence. *Journal of Personality and Social Psychology, 78,* 310–325.

Shiner, R., & Masten, A. (2012). Childhood personality as a harbinger of competence and resilience in adulthood. *Development and Psychopathology, 24,* 507–528.

Shneidman, E. (1989). The Indian summer of life: A preliminary study of septuagenarians. *American Psychologist, 44,* 684–694.

Siegel, J. (2009). Sleep viewed as a state of adaptive inactivity. *Nature Reviews Neuroscience, 10,* 747–753.

Siegel, R. (2005). *Intoxication: The universal drive for mind-altering substances.* Rochester, VT: Park Street Press.

Siegfried, N., Muller, M., Deeks, J., & Volmink, J. (2009). Male circumcision for prevention of heterosexual acquisition of HIV in men. *Cochrane Database of Systematic Reviews, 2,* Online article No. CD003362.

Siegler, R. S. (1991). *Children's thinking* (2nd ed.). Englewood Cliffs, NJ: Prentice-Hall.

Siegmund, A., Köster, L., Meves, A., Plag, J., Stoy, M., & Ströhle, A. (2011). Stress hormones during flooding therapy and their relationship to therapy outcome in patients with panic disorder and agoraphobia. *Journal of Psychiatric Research, 45,* 339–346.

Sigmon, S., Herning, R., Better, W., Cadet, J., & Griffiths, R. (2009). Caffeine withdrawal, acute effects, tolerance, and absence of net beneficial effects of chronic administration: Cerebral blood flow velocity, quantitative EEG, and subjective effects. *Psychopharmacology, 204,* 573–585.

Sikorski, C., Luppa, M., Brahler, E., Konig, H., Riedel-Heller, S. (2012). Obese children, adults and senior citizens in the eyes of the general public: Results of a representative study on stigma and causation of obesity. *PLoS ONE, 7,* e46924.

Simon, H. (1956). Rational choice and the structure of the environment. *Psychological Review, 63,* 129–138.

Simons, D., & Rensink, R. (2005). Change blindness: Past, present, and future. *Trends in Cognitive Sciences, 9,* 16–20.

Simons, J., & Carey, K. (2002). Risk and vulnerability for marijuana use problems. *Psychology of Addictive Behaviors, 16,* 72–75.

Simpson, P., & Stroh, L. (2004). Gender differences: Emotional expression and feelings of personal inauthenticity. *Journal of Applied Psychology, 89,* 715–721.

Simunovic, M. (2010). Colour vision deficiency. *Eye, 24,* 727– 755.
Singh, B. (1991). Teaching methods for reducing prejudice and enhancing academic achievement for all children. *Educational Studies, 17,* 157–171.

Singh, M., Patel., J., Gallagher, R., Childers, M., Salcido, R., & Talavera, F. (2012). *Chronic pain syndrome.* Retrieved October 28, 2012 from http://emedicine.medscape.com/article/310834-treatment#aw2aab6b6b6.

Sinke, C., Halpern, J., Zedler, M., Neufeld, J., Emrich, H., & Passie, T. (2012). Genuine and drug-induced synesthesia: A comparison. *Consciousness and Cognition: An International Journal, 21,* 1419–1434.

Skinner, B. F. (1957). *Verbal behavior.* New York: Appleton Century.

Skrabalo, A. (2000). Negative symptoms in schizophrenia(s): The conceptual basis. *Harvard Brain, 7,* 7–10.

Slawinski, E. B., Hartel, D. M., & Kline, D. W. (1993). Self-reported hearing problems in daily life throughout adulthood. *Psychology and Aging, 8,* 552–561.

Sloan, M. (2012). Controlling anger and happiness at work: An examination of gender differences. *Gender, Work, and Organization, 19,* 370–391.

Slobin, D. (1972, July). Children and language: They learn the same all around the world. *Psychology Today,* 71–74, 82.

Small, G. (2005). *Effects of a 14-day healthy aging lifestyle program on brain function.* Paper presented at the 44th Annual Meeting of the American College of Neuropsychopharmacology. December 11–15, 2005. Waikoloa, Hawaii.

Smith, M. (1978). Moral reasoning: Its relation to logical thinking and role-taking. *Journal of Moral Education, 8,* 41–49.

Smith, G., Wong, H., MacEwan, G., Kopala, L., Ehmann, T., Thornton, A., Lang, D., Barr, A., Procyshyn, R., Austin, J., Flynn, S., & Honer, W. (2009). *Schizophrenia Research, 108,* 258–264.

Smith, H., Polenik, K., Nakasita, S., & Jones, A. (2012). Profiling social, emotional and behavioural difficulties of children involved in direct and indirect bullying behaviours. *Emotional & Behavioural Difficulties, 17,* 243–257.

Smith, J., & Brennan, B. (2009). *Management of the third stage of labor.* Retrieved February 27, 2010 from *http://emedicine.medscape.com/article/275304-overview*

Smith, M. L., Glass, G. V., & Miller, T. I. (1980). *The benefits of psychotherapy.* Baltimore, MD: Johns Hopkins University Press.

Smith, S. M., Glenberg, A., & Bjork, R. A. (1978). Environmental context and human memory. *Memory & Cognition, 6,* 342–353.

Smith, Y., Stohler, C., Nichols, T., Bueller, J., Koeppe, R., & Zubieta, J. (2006). Pronociceptive and antinociceptive effects of estradiol through endogenous opioid neurotransmission in women. *The Journal of Neuroscience, 26,* 5777–5785.

Smrt, D., & Karau, S. (2011). Protestant work ethic moderates social loafing. *Group Dynamics: Theory, Research, and Practice, 15,* 267–274.

Smucny, J., Cornier, M., Eichman, L., Thomas, E., Bechtell, J., & Tregellas, J. (2012). Brain structure predicts risk for obesity. *Appetite, 59,* 859–865.

Snarey, J. R. (1985). Cross-cultural universality of social-moral development: A critical review of Kohlbergian research. *Psychological Bulletin, 97,* 202–232.

Snow, C. E. (1993). Bilingualism and second language acquisition. In J. B. Gleason & N. B. Ratner (Eds.), *Psycholinguistics* (pp. 391–416). Fort Worth, TX: Harcourt.

Snyder, D., Castellani, A., & Whisman, M. (2006). Current status and future directions in couple therapy. *Annual Review of Psychology, 57,* 317–344.

Soares-Weiser, K., & Fernandez, H. (2007). Tardive dyskinesia. *Seminars in Neurology, 27,* 159–69.

Soei, E., Koch, B., Schwarz, M., & Daum, I. (2008). Involvement of the human thalamus in relational and non-relational memory. *European Journal of Neuroscience, 28,* 2533–2541.

Sokolov, E. N. (2000). Perception and the conditioning reflex: Vector encoding. *International Journal of Psychophysiology, 35,* 197–217.

Solomon, S., Rothblum, E, & Balsam, K. (2004). Pioneers in partnership: Lesbian and gay male couples in civil unions compared with those not in civil unions and married heterosexual siblings. *Journal of Family Psychology, 18,* 275–286.

Solso, R., MacLin, O., & MacLin, M. (2008). *Cognitive psychology* (8th ed.). Upper Saddle River, NJ: Pearson Prentice-Hall.

Somers, V., White, D., Amin, R., Abraham, W., Costa, F., Culebras, A., Daniels, S., Floras, J., Hunt, C., Olson, L., Pickering, T., Russell, R., Woo, M., & Young, T. (2008). Expert consensus document: Sleep apnea and cardiovascular disease. *Journal of the American College of Cardiology, 52,* 686–717.

Sonnentag, S. (2003). Recovery, work engagement, and proactive behaviour: A new look at the interface between work and non-work. *Journal of Applied Psychology, 88,* 518–528.

Soreff, S. (2012). *Bipolar affective disorder.* Retrieved January 27, 2013, from http://emedicine.medscape.com/article/286342-medication#4

Sorkhabi, N., & Mandara, J. (2013). Are the effects of Baumrind's parenting styles culturally specific or culturally equivalent? In R. Larzelere, Morris, A., & A. Harrist (Eds.) *Authoritative parenting: Synthesizing nurturance and discipline for optimal child development.* (pp. 113–135). Washington, DC, USA: American Psychological Association.

Soto, C., John, O., Gosling, S., & Potter, J. (2011). Age differences in personality traits from 10 to 65: Big Five domains and facets in a large cross-sectional sample. *Journal of Personality and Social Psychology, 100,* 330–348.

Soussignan, R. (2002). Duchenne smile, emotional experience, and autonomic reactivity: A test of the facial feedback hypothesis. *Emotion, 2,* 52–74.

South, S., Reichborn-Kjennerud, T., Eaton, N., & Krueger, R. (2013). Genetics of personality. In H. Tennen, J. Suls, & I. Weiner. *Handbook of psychology, Vol. 5: Personality and social psychology* (2nd ed.). (pp. 3–25). Hoboken, NJ, USA: John Wiley & Sons, Inc.

Spanos, N. P. (1986). Hypnotic behavior: A social-psychological interpretation of amnesia, analgesia, and "trance logic." *Behavioral and Brain Sciences, 9,* 499–502.

Sparks, R., Patton, J., & Ganschow, L. (2012). Profiles of more and less successful L2 learners: A cluster analysis study. *Learning and Individual Differences, 22,* 463–472.

Spearman, C. (1927). *The abilities of man.* New York: Macmillan.

Spector, F., & Maurer, D. (2009). Synesthesia: A new approach to understanding the development of perception. *Developmental Psychology, 45,* 175–189.

Spence, I., & Feng, J. (2010). Video games and spatial cognition. *Review of General Psychology, 14,* 92–104.

Spencer, R., Zelaznik, H., Diedrichsen, J., & Ivry, R. (2003). Disrupted timing of discontinuous but not continuous movements by cerebellar lesions. *Science, 300,* 1437–1439.

Sperling, G. (1960). The information available in brief visual presentations. *Psychological Monographs: General and Applied 74* (Whole No. 498), 1–29.

Sperry, R. W. (1964). The great cerebral commissure. *Scientific American, 210,* 42–52.

Sperry, R. W. (1968). Hemisphere deconnection and unity in conscious experience. *American Psychologist, 23,* 723–733.

Spreen, O., Risser, A., & Edgell, D. (1995). *Developmental neuropsychology.* New York: Oxford University Press.

Squire, L. R., Knowlton, B., & Musen, G. (1993). The structure and organization of memory. *Annual Review of Psychology, 44,* 453–495.

Stabell, B., & Stabell, U. (2009). *Duplicity theory of vision: From Newton to the present.* New York: Cambridge University Press.

Steele, C., & Aronson, J. (1995). Stereotype threat and the intellectual test performance of African Americans. *Journal of Personality & Social Psychology, 69,* 797–811.

Steeves, R. (2002). The rhythms of bereavement. *Family & Community Health, 25,* 1–10.

Steffensen, M., & Calker, L. (1982). Intercultural misunderstandings about health care: Recall of descriptions of illness and treatments. *Social Science and Medicine, 16,* 1949–1954.

Stein, J., Milburn, N., Zane, J., & Rotheram-Borus, M. (2009). Paternal and maternal influences on problem behaviors among homeless and runaway youth. *American Journal of Orthopsychiatry, 79,* 39–50.

Stein, M. B., & Kean, Y. M. (2000). Disability and quality of life in social phobia: Epidemiologic findings. *American Journal of Psychiatry, 157,* 1606–1613.

Stein, N., Mills, M., Arditte, K., Mendoza, C., Borah, A., Resick, P., & Litz, B. (2012). A scheme for categorizing traumatic military events. *Behavior Modification, 36,* 787–807.

Stein-Behrens, B., Mattson, M. P., Chang, I., Yeh, M., & Sapolsky, R. (1994). Stress exacerbates neuron loss and cytoskeletal pathology in the hippocampus. *Journal of Neuroscience, 14,* 5373–5380.

Steinberg, L., & Dornbusch, S. (1991). Negative correlates of part-time employment during adolescence: Replication and elaboration. *Developmental Psychology, 27,* 304–313.

Steinberg, L., Blatt-Eisengart, I., & Cauffman, E. (2006). Patterns of competence and adjustment among adolescents from authoritative, authoritarian, indulgent, and neglectful homes: A replication in a sample of serious juvenile offenders. *Journal of Research on Adolescence, 16,* 47–58.

Steinberg, L., Elman, J. D., & Mounts, N. S. (1989). Authoritative parenting, psychosocial maturity, and academic success among adolescents. *Child Development, 60,* 1424–1436.

Sterling, K., Berg, C., Thomas, A., Glantz, S., & Ahluwalia, J. (2013). Factors associated with small cigar use among college students. *American Journal of Health Behavior, 37,* 325–333.

Stern, W. (1914). *The psychological methods of testing intelligence.* Baltimore, MD, USA: Warwick and York.

Sternberg, R. J. (1985). *Beyond IQ: A triarchic theory of human intelligence.* New York: Cambridge University Press.

Sternberg, R. J. (1986a). *Intelligence applied: Understanding and increasing your intellectual skills.* San Diego: Harcourt Brace Jovanovich.

Sternberg, R. J. (1986b). A triangular theory of love. *Psychological Review, 93,* 119–135.

Sternberg, R. J. (2000). The holey grail of general intelligence. *Science, 289,* 399–401.

Sternberg, R. J., Wagner, R. K., Williams, W. M., & Horvath, J. A. (1995). Testing common sense. *American Psychologist, 50,* 912–927.

Sternberg, R. (2012). Intelligence in its cultural context. In M. Gelfand, C. Ciu, & Y. Hong (Eds.) *Advances in culture and psychology:* Vol. II. New York, NY, USA: Oxford University Press.

Stevenson, H. W. (1992). Learning from Asian schools. *Scientific American, 267,* 70–76.

Stewart, G., Fulmer, I., & Barrick, M. (2005). An exploration of member roles as a multilevel linking mechanism for individual traits and team outcomes. *Personnel Psychology, 58,* 343–365.

Stewart, N. (2009). The cost of anchoring on credit-card minimum repayments. *Psychological Science, 20,* 39–41.

Still, C. (2001). *Health benefits of modest weight loss.* Retrieved January 29, 2003, from *http://abcnews.go.com/sections/living/Healthology/weightloss_benefits011221.html*

Stilwell, N., Wallick, M., Thal, S., & Burleson, J. (2000). Myers-Briggs type and medical specialty choice: A new look at an old question. *Teaching & Learning in Medicine, 12,* 14–20.

Stingaris, A. (2011). Irritability in children and adolescents: A challenge for DSM-5. *European Child & Adolescent Psychiatry, 20,* 61–66.

Stockhorst, U., Mayl, N., Krueger, M., Huenig, A., Schottenfeld-Naor, Y., Huebinger, A., Berreshaim, H., Steingrueber, H., & Scherbaum, W. (2004). Classical conditioning and conditionability of insulin and glucose effects in healthy humans. *Physiology & Behavior, 81,* 375–388.

Stoll, E., & Ha-Brookshire, J. (2012). Motivations for success: Case of U. S. textile and apparel small- and medium-sized enterprises. *Clothing & Textiles Research Journal, 30,* 149–163.

Stone, J. (2003). Self-consistency for low self-esteem in dissonance processes: The role of self-standards. *Personality & Social Psychology Bulletin, 29,* 846–858.

Strack, F., Martin, L. L., & Stepper, S. (1988). Inhibiting and facilitating conditions of facial expressions: A nonobtrusive test of the facial feedback hypothesis. *Journal of Personality and Social Psychology, 54,* 768–777.

Strange, B., Hurlemann, R., & Dolan, R. (2003). An emotion-induced retrograde amnesia in humans is amygdala- and b-adrenergic-dependent. *Proceedings of the National Academy of Science, 100,* 13626–13631.

Strayer, D., & Drews, F. (2004). Profiles in driver distraction: Effects of cell phone conversations on younger and older drivers. *Human Factors, 46,* 640–649.

Strohmetz, D., Rind, B., Fisher, R., & Lynn, M. (2002). Sweetening the till: The use of candy to increase restaurant tipping. *Journal of Applied Social Psychology, 32,* 300–309.

Suarez, M. G. (1983). *Implications of Spanish-English bilingualism in the TAT stories.* Unpublished doctoral dissertation, University of Connecticut.

Sucala, M., Schnur, J., Constantino, M., Miller, S., Brackman, E., & Montgomery, G. (2012). *Journal of Medical Internet Research, 14,* 175–187.

Sugita, M., & Shiba, Y. (2005). Genetic tracing shows segregation of taste neuronal circuitries for bitter and sweet. *Science, 309,* 781–785.

Sullivan, A. D., Hedberg, K., & Fleming, D. W. (2000). Legalized physician-assisted suicide in Oregon—The second year. *New England Journal of Medicine, 342,* 598–604.

Sullivan, A., Maerz, J., & Madison, D. (2002). Anti-predator response of red-backed salamanders (Plethodon cinereus) to chemical cues from garter snakes (Thamnophis sirtalis): Laboratory and field experiments. *Behavioral Ecology & Sociobiology, 51,* 227–233.

Sullman, M. (2012). An observational study of driver distraction in England. *Transportation Research Part F: Traffic Psychology and Behaviour, 15,* 272–278.

Sung, K. (2008). Serial and parallel attentive visual searches: Evidence from cumulative distribution functions of response times. *Journal of Experimental Psychology: Human Perception and Performance, 34,* 1372–1388.

Sung, K-T. (1992). Motivations for parent care: The case of filial children in Korea. *International Journal of Aging and Human Development, 34,* 109–124.

Super, C. W. (1981). Behavioral development in infancy. In R. H. Munroe, R. L. Munroe, & B. B. Whiting (Eds.), *Handbook of cross-cultural human development* (pp. 181–269). Chicago: Garland.

Super, D. (1971). A theory of vocational development. In N. H. J. Peters & J. C. Hansen (Eds.), *Vocational guidance and career development* (pp. 111–122). New York: MacMillan.

Super, D. (1986). Life career roles: Self-realization in work and leisure. In D. T. H. & Associates (Eds.), *Career development in organizations* (pp. 95–119). San Francisco: Jossey-Bass.

Susman, E., & Dorn, L. (2009). Puberty: Its role in development. In R., Lerner & L. Steinberg (Eds.), *Handbook of adolescent psychology.* Volume I: Individual bases of adolescent development (3rd ed.) (pp. 116–151). Hoboken, NJ: John Wiley & Sons.

Sutin, A., Ferrucci, L., Zonderman, A., & Terracciano, A. (2011). Personality and obesity across the adult life span. *Journal of Personality and Social Psychology, 101,* 579–592.

Swann, W. (2012). Self-verification theory. In p. Van Lange, A. Kruglanski, & E. Higgins (Eds.), *Handbook of theories of social psychology* (Vol 2). (pp. 23–42). Thousand Oaks, CA: USA: Sage Publications Ltd.

Swann, W., & Bosson, J. (2008). Identity negotiation: A theory of self and social interaction. In O., John, R., Robins, & L. Pervin (Eds.), *Handbook of personality psychology: Theory and research* (3rd ed.) (pp. 448–471). New York: Guilford Press.

Swanson, S., Crow, S., Le Grange, D., Swendsen, J., & Merikangas, K. (2011). Prevalence and correlates of eating disorders in adolescents: Results from the National Comorbidity Survey Replication Adolescent Supplement. *Archives of General Psychiatry, 68,* 714–723.

Swartz, H., Frank, E., Frankel, D., Novick, P., & Houck, P. (2009). Psychotherapy as monotherapy for the treatment of bipolar II depression: A proof of concept study. *Bipolar Disorders, 11,* 89–94.

Swartz, M., Frohberg, N., Drake, R., et al. (2012). Psychosocial therapies. In J. Lieberman (Ed.). *Essentials of schizophrenia* (pp. 207–224). Arlington, VA, USA: American Psychiatric Publishing.

Sweatt, J. D., & Kandel, E. R. (1989). Persistent and transcriptionally dependent increase in protein phosphorylation in long-term facilitation of *Aplysia* sensory neurons. *Nature, 339,* 51–54.

Swedo, S., & Grant, P. (2004). PANDAS: A model for autoimmune neuropsychiatric disorders. *Primary Psychiatry, 11,* 28–33.

Sweller, J., & Levine, M. (1982). Effects of goal specificity on means-end analysis and learning. *Journal of Experimental Psychology: Learning, Memory, and Cognition, 8,* 463–474.

Symister, P., & Friend, R. (2003). The influence of social support and problematic support on optimism and depression in chronic illness: A prospective study evaluating self-esteem as a mediator. *Health Psychology, 22,* 123–129.

Taitz, I. (2011). Learning lucid dreaming and its effect on depression in undergraduates. *International Journal of Dream Research, 4,* 117–126.

Taki, Y., Hashizume, H., Sassa, Y., et al. (2012). Correlation among body height, intelligence, and brain gray matter volume in healthy children. *Neuroimage, 16,* 1023–1027.

Talarico, J., & Rubin, D. (2009). Flashbulb memories result from ordinary memory processes and extraordinary event characteristics. In O., Luminet, & A. Curci (Eds.), *Flashbulb memories: New issues and perspectives* (pp. 13–32). New York: Psychology Press.

Tanner, J. M. (1990). *Fetus into man* (2nd ed.). Cambridge MA: Harvard University Press.

Tate, D., Paul, R., Flanigan, T., Tashima, K., Nash, J., Adair, C., et al. (2003). The impact of apathy and depression on quality of life in patients infected with HIV. *AIDS Patient Care & STDs, 17,* 117–120.

Taub, G., Hayes, B., Cunningham, W., & Sivo, S. (2001). Relative roles of cognitive ability and practical intelligence in the prediction of success. *Psychological Reports, 88,* 931–942.

Tay, C., Ang, S., & Dyne, L. (2006). Personality, biographical characteristics, and job interview success: A longitudinal study of the mediating effects of interviewing self-efficacy and the moderating effects of internal locus of causality. *Journal of Applied Psychology, 91,* 446–454.

Tchanturia, K., Serpell, L., Troop, N., & Treasure, J. (2001). Perceptual illusions in eating disorders: Rigid and fluctuating styles. *Journal of Behavior Therapy & Experimental Psychiatry, 32,* 107–115.

Teachman, B., Marker, C., & Smith-Janik, S. (2008). Automatic associations and panic disorder; Trajectories of change over the course of treatment. *Journal of Consulting and Clinical Psychology, 76,* 988–1002.

Teachman, J. (2003). Premarital sex, premarital cohabitation and the risk of subsequent marital dissolution among women. *Journal of Marriage and Family, 65,* 444–455.

Teitelbaum, P. (1957). Random and food-directed activity in hyperphagic and normal rats. *Journal of Comparative and Physiological Psychology, 50,* 486–490.

Tennant, C. (2002). Life events, stress and depression: A review of the findings. *Australian & New Zealand Journal of Psychiatry, 36,* 173–182.

Tepper, B. (2008). Nutritional implications of genetic taste variation: The role of PROP sensitivity and other taste phenotypes. *Annual Review of Nutrition, 28,* 367–388.

Tepper, B., & Ullrich, N. (2002). Influence of genetic taste sensitivity to 6-n-propylthiouracil (PROP), dietary restraint and disinhibition on body mass index in middle-aged women. *Physiology & Behavior, 75,* 305–312.

Tercyak, K., Johnson, S., Roberts, S., & Cruz, A. (2001). Psychological response to prenatal genetic counseling and amniocentesis. *Patient Education & Counseling, 43,* 73–84.

Terman, L. M. (1925). *Genetic studies of genius, Vol. 1: Mental and physical traits of a thousand gifted children.* Palo Alto, CA: Stanford University Press.

Terman, L. M., & Oden, M. H. (1947). *Genetic studies of genius, Vol. 4: The gifted child grows up.* Palo Alto, CA: Stanford University Press.

Terman, L. M., & Oden, M. H. (1959). *Genetic studies of genius, Vol. 5: The gifted group at mid-life.* Palo Alto, CA: Stanford University Press.

Terrace, H. (1979, November). How Nim Chimpski changed my mind. *Psychology Today,* 65–76.

Terrace, H. (2011). Thinking without language. In M. Gernsbacher, R. Pew, L. Hough, & J. Pomerantz (Eds.) *Psychology and the real world: Essays illustrating fundamental contributions to society* (pp. 98–106). New York, NY, USA: Worth Publishers.

Terrace, H. S. (1981). A report to an academy. *Annals of the New York Academy of Sciences, 364,* 115–129.

Terrace, H. S. (1985). In the beginning was the "name." *American Psychologist, 40,* 1011–1028.

Terrace, H. S. (1986). *Nim: A chimpanzee who learned sign language.* New York: Columbia University Press.

Thaakur, S., & Himabindhu, G. (2009). Effect of alpha lipoic acid on the tardive dyskinesia and oxidative stress induced by haloperidol in rats. *Journal of Neural Transmission, 116,* 807–814.

Thakker, J. (2013). Should group membership be considered for treatment to be effective? In J. Wood, & T. Gannon (Eds.). *Crime and crime reduction: The importance of group processes.* (pp. 177–195). New York, NY, USA: Routledge/Taylor & Francis Group.

Thapar, A., O'Donovan, M., & Owen, M. (2005). The genetics of attention deficit hyperactivity disorder. *Human Molecular Genetics, 14,* R275–R282.

Thase, M. E., & Kupfer, D. J. (1996). Recent developments in the pharmacotherapy of mood disorders. *Journal of Consulting and Clinical Psychology, 64,* 646–659.

Thirthalli, J., & Benegal, V. (2006). Psychosis among substance users. *Current Opinion in Psychiatry, 19,* 239–245.

Thomas, A., Chess, S., & Birch, H. G. (1970). The origin of personality. *Scientific American, 223,* 102–109.

Thomas, S., & Jordan, T. (2004). Contributions of oral and extra-oral facial movement to visual and audiovisual speech perception. *Journal of Experimental Psychology: Human Perception & Performance, 30,* 873–888.

Thompson, A. & O'Sullivan, L. (2012). Gender differences in associations of sexual and romantic stimuli: Do young men really prefer sex over romance? *Archives of Sexual Behavior, 41,* 949–957.

Thompson, P., Dutton, R., Hayashi, K., Toga, A., Lopez, O., Aizenstein, H., & Becker, J. (2005). Thinning of the cerebral cortex visualized in HIV/AIDS reflects CD4+ T lymphocyte decline. *Proceedings of the National Academies of Science, 102,* 15642–15647.

Thompson, P., Vidal, C., Giedd, J., Gochman, P., Blumenthal, J., Nicolson, R., et al. (2001). Mapping adolescent brain change reveals dynamic wave of accelerated gray matter loss in very early-onset schizophrenia. *Proceedings of the National Academy of Sciences, 98,* 11650–11655.

Thompson, R., Emmorey, K., & Gollan, T. (2005). "Tip of the fingers" experiences by deaf signers. *Psychological Science, 16,* 856–860.

Thompson, S. C., Sobolew-Shubin, A., Galbraith, M. E., Schwankovsky, L., & Cruzen, D. (1993). Maintaining perceptions of control: Finding perceived control in low-control circumstances. *Journal of Personality and Social Psychology, 64,* 293–304.

Thornberry, T., Knight, K., & Lovegrove, P. (2012). Does maltreatment beget maltreatment? A systematic review of the intergenerational literature. *Trauma, Violence, & Abuse, 13,* 135–152.

Thorndike, E. L. (1911/1970). *Animal intelligence: Experimental studies.* New York: Macmillan. (Original work published 1911).

Thorne, B. (2000). Extra credit exercise: A painless pop quiz. *Teaching of Psychology, 27,* 204–205.

Thornton, L., Frick, P., Crapanzano, A., & Terranova, A. (2013). The incremental utility of callous-unemotional traits and conduct problems in predicting aggression and bullying I a community sample of boys and girls. *Psychological Assessment* [in press].

Thorsteinsson, E., & Brown, R. (2009). Mediators and moderators of the stressor-fatigue relationship in nonclinical samples. *Journal of Psychosomatic Research*, 66, 21–29.

Thurstone, L. L. (1938). *Primary mental abilities.* Chicago: University of Chicago Press.

Tiedemann, J. (2000). Parents' gender stereotypes and teachers' beliefs as predictors of children's concept of their mathematical ability in elementary school. *Journal of Educational Psychology, 92,* 144–151.

Toastmasters International. (2013). *10 tips for public speaking.* Retrieved January 26, 2013, from http://www.toastmasters.org/tips.asp

Tobin, M. (2007). Psychopharmacology column: Why choose selegiline transderman system for refractory depression. *Issues in Mental Health Nursing, 28,* 223–228.

Todorov, A., & Bargh, J. (2002). Automatic sources of aggression. *Aggression & Violent Behavior, 7,* 53–68.

Tohidian, I. (2009). Examining linguistic relativity hypothesis as one of the main views on the relationship between language and thought. *Journal of Psycholinguistic Research, 38,* 65–74.

Tolman, E. C. (1932). *Purposive behavior in animals and men.* New York: Appleton-Century-Crofts.

Tolman, E. C., & Honzik, C. H. (1930). Introduction and removal of reward, and maze performance in rats. *University of California Publications in Psychology, 4,* 257–275.

Tooby, J., & Cosmides, L. (2005). Conceptual foundations of evolutionary psychology. In Buss, D. (Ed.). *Handbook of evolutionary psychology* (pp. 5–67). Hoboken, NJ: Wiley.

Topolinski, S., & Strack, F. (2009). The architecture of intuition: Fluency and affect determine intuitive judgments of semantic and visual coherence and judgments of grammaticality in artificial grammar learning. *Journal of Experimental Psychology: General, 138,* 39–63.

Torrey, E. (1992). *Freudian fraud: The malignant effect of Freud's theory on American thought and culture.* New York: Harper Collins.

Totterdell, P., & Kellett, S. (2008). Restructuring mood in cyclothymia using cognitive behavior therapy: An intensive time-sampling study. *Journal of Clinical Psychology, 64,* 501–518.

Tourangeau, R., Smith, T. W., & Rasinski, K. A. (1997). Motivation to report sensitive behaviors on surveys: Evidence from a bogus pipeline experiment. *Journal of Applied Social Psychology, 27,* 209–222.

Tovar-Murray, D., Jenifer, E., Andrusyk, J., D'Angelo, R., & King, T. (2012). Racism-related stress and ethnic identity as determinants of African American college students' career aspirations. *The Career Development Quarterly, 60,* 254–262.

Town, J., Diener, M., Abbass, A., Leichsenring, F., Driessen, E., Rabung, S. (2012). A meta-analysis of psychodynamic psychotherapy outcomes: Evaluating the effects of research-specific procedures. *Psychotherapy, 49,* 276–290.

Traverso, A., Ravera, G., Lagattolla, V., Testa, S., & Adami, G. F. (2000). Weight loss after dieting with behavioral modification for obesity: The predicting efficiency of some psychometric data. *Eating and Weight Disorders: Studies on Anorexia, Bulimia, and Obesity, 5,* 102–107.

Triandis, H. C. (1994). *Culture and social behavior.* New York: McGraw-Hill.

Triplett, N. (1898). The dynamogenic factors in pacemaking and competition. *American Journal of Psychology, 9,* 507–533.

Troglauer, T., Hels, T., & Christens, P. (2006). Extent and variations in mobile phone use among drivers of heavy vehicles in Denmark. *Accident Analysis & Prevention, 38,* 105–111.

Troxel, W., Matthews, K., Bromberger, J., & Sutton-Tyrrell, K. (2003). Chronic stress burden, discrimination, and subclinical carotid artery disease in African American and Caucasian women. *Health Psychology, 22,* 300–309.

Tsai, J., Knutson, B., & Fung, H. (2006). Cultural variation in affect valuation. *Journal of Personality and Social Psychology, 90,* 288–307.

Tsai, S., Kuo, C., Chen, C., & Lee, H. (2002). Risk factors for completed suicide in bipolar disorder. *Journal of Clinical Psychiatry, 63,* 469–476.

Tsai, W., Huang, T., & Yu, H. (2012). Investigating the unique predictability and boundary conditions of applicant physical attractiveness and non-verbal behaviours on interviewer evaluations in job interviews. *Journal of Occupational and Organizational Psychology, 85,* 60–79.

Tullett, A., Prentice, M., Teper, R., Nash, K., Inzlicht, M., & McGregor, I. (2013). Neural and motivational mechanics of meaning and threat. In K. Markman, T. Proulx, & M. Lindberg (Eds.) *The psychology of meaning.* (pp. 401–419). Washington, DC, USA: American Psychological Association.

Tulving, E. (1995). Organization of memory: Quo vadis? In M. S. Gazzaniga (Ed.), *The cognitive neurosciences* (pp. 839–847). Cambridge, MA: MIT Press.

Tulving, E., & Thompson, D. M. (1973). Encoding specificity and retrieval processes in episodic memory. *Psychological Review, 80,* 352–373.

Tuminello, E., & Davidson, D. (2011). What the face and body reveal: In-group emotion effects and stereotyping of emotion in African American and European American children. *Journal of Experimental Child Psychology, 110,* 258–274.

Turner, J. C., Hogg, M. A., Oakes, P. J., Reicher, S. D., & Wetherell, M. S. (1987). *Rediscovering the social group: A self-categorization theory.* Oxford, England: Blackwell.

Turner, R., Hewstone, M., Voci, A., & Vonofakou, C. (2008). A test of extended intergroup contact hypothesis: The mediating role of intergroup anxiety, perceived ingroup and outgroup norms, and inclusion of the outgroup in the self. *Journal of Personality and Social Psychology, 95,* 843–860.

Tversky, A. (1972). Elimination by aspects: A theory of choice. *Psychological Review, 79,* 281–299.

Tversky, A., & Kahneman, D. (1974). Judgment under uncertainty: Heuristics and biases. *Science, 185,* 1124–1130.

Tweed, R., & Lehman, D. (2002). Learning considered within a cultural context: Confucian and Socratic approaches. *American Psychologist, 57,* 89–99.

U. S. Cancer Statistics Working Group. (2013). *United States cancer statistics: 1999–2009* **incidence and mortality Web-based report.** Retrieved January 26, 2013, from www.cdc.gov/uscs. *http://apps. nccd.cdc.gov/uscs/cancersbyraceandethnicity.aspx*

U.S. Census Bureau. (2010). *Estimated median age at first marriage, by sex: 1890 to the present.* Historical Time Series. Retrieved February 27, 2010, from *http://www.census.gov/population/www/socdemo/hh-fam.html#ht*

United States Census Bureau. (2012). *Statistical abstract of the United States, 2012.* Retrieved January 8, 2013, from http://www.census.gov/compendia/statab/

U.S. Department of Energy. (2009). *Human genome project information.* Retrieved January 17, 2010 from

United States Department of Energy. (2012). *Human genome project information.* Retrieved October 23, 2012, from http://www.ornl.gov/sci/techresources/Human_Genome/home.shtml.

U.S. Department of Justice. (1999). *Eyewitness evidence: A guide for law enforcement.* Retrieved February 22, 2010 from *http://www.ncjrs.gov/pdffiles1/nij/178240.pdf.*

U.S. Food and Drug Administration (FDA). (2004, October 15). *Suicidality in children and adolescents being treated with antidepressant medication.* Retrieved May 12, 2005, from *http://www.fda.gov/cder/drug/antidepressants/SSRIPHA200410.htm.*

U.S. Food and Drug Administration (FDA). (2006a, April 20). Interagency advisory regarding claims that smoked marijuana is a medicine. Retrieved May 15, 2006, from *http://www.fda.gov/bbs/topics/NEWS/2006/NEW01362.html*

U.S. Food and Drug Administration (FDA). (2006b). *Prozac patient information sheet*. Retrieved July 26, 2006, from *http://www.fda.gov/cder/drug/InfoSheets/patient/fluoxetinePIS.htm*

Uchida, Y., Norasakkunkit, V., & Kitayama, S. (2004). Cultural constructions of happiness: Theory and empirical evidence. *Journal of Happiness Studies, 5*, 223–239.

Uchiumi, O., Kasahara, Y., Fukui, A., Hall, F., Uhl, G., & Sora, I. (2013). Serotonergic involvement in the amelioration of behavioral abnormalities in dopamine transporter knockout mice by nicotine. *Neuropharmacology, 64*, 348–356.

Uman, L., Chambers, C., McGrath, P., & Kisely, S. (2008). A systematic review of randomized controlled trials examining psychological interventions for needle-related procedural pain and distress in children and adolescents: An abbreviated Cochrone review. *Journal of Pediatric Psychology, 33*, 842–854.

Umberson, D., Williams, K., Powers, D., Liu, H., & Needham, B. (2006). You make me sick: Marital quality and health over the life course. *Journal of Health and Social Behavior, 47*, 1–16.

Umeh, K. (2012). Does a credible source also need a fearful audience? *Journal of Applied Social Psychology, 42*, 1716–1744.

UNAIDS. (2011). *World AIDS day report*. Retrieved January 7, 2013, from http://www.unaids.org/en/media/unaids/contentassets/documents/unaidspublication/2011/jc2216_worldaidsday_report_2011_en.pdf

Underwood, B. J. (1957). Interference and forgetting. *Psychological Review, 64*, 49–60.

Underwood, B. J. (1964). Forgetting. *Scientific American, 210*, 91–99.

University of Michigan Transportation Research Institute (UMTRI). (2003). Ready for the road: Software helps teens drive safely. *UMTRI Research Review, 34*, 1–2.

Ushikubo, M. (1998). A study of factors facilitating and inhibiting the willingness of the institutionalized disabled elderly for rehabilitation: A United States–Japanese comparison. *Journal of Cross-Cultural Gerontology, 13*, 127–157.

Utsey, S., Chae, M., Brown, C., & Kelly, D. (2002). Effect of ethnic group membership on ethnic identity, race-related stress and quality of life. *Cultural Diversity & Ethnic Minority Psychology, 8*, 367–378.

Vaccarino, V., Abramson, J., Veledar, E., & Weintraub, W. (2002). Sex differences in hospital mortality after coronary artery bypass surgery: Evidence for a higher mortality in younger women. *Circulation, 105*, 1176.

Valadez, J., & Ferguson, C. (2012). Just a game after all: Violent video game exposure and time spent playing effects on hostile feelings, depression, and visuospatial cognition. *Computers in Human Behavior, 28*, 608–616.

Valeo, T. (2008). Role of sleep in memory and learning elucidated in new studies. *Neurology Today, 8*, 16.

Valipour, A., Lothaller, H., Rauscher, H., Zwick, H., Burghuber, O., & Lavie, P. (2007). Gender-related differences in symptoms of patients with suspected breathing disorders in sleep: A clinical population study using the Sleep Disorders Questionnaire. *Sleep: Journal of Sleep and Sleep Disorders Research, 30*, 312–319.

Valtonen, H., Suominen, K., Haukka, J., Mantere, O., Arvilommi, P., Leppämäki, S., & Isometsä, E. (2009). Hopelessness across phases of bipolar I or II disorder: A prospective study. *Journal of Affective Disorders, 115*, 11–17.

Van Assema, P., Martens, M., Ruiter, A., & Brug, J. (2002). Framing of nutrition education messages in persuading consumers of the sdvantages of a healthy diet. *Journal of Human Nutrition & Dietetics, 14*, 435–442.

van Beest, I., Carter-Sowell, A., van Dijk, E., & Williams, K. (2012). Groups being ostracized by groups: Is the pain shared, is recovery quicker, and are groups more likely to be aggressive? *Group Dynamics: Theory, Research, and Practice, 16*, 241–254.

Van der Elst, W., Van Boxtel, M., Van Breukelen, G., & Jolles, J. (2006). The Stroop color-word test: Influence of age, sex, and education; and normative data for a large sample across the adult age range. *Assessment, 13*, 62–79.

van der Kloet, D., Giesbrecht, T., Lynn, S., Merckelbach, H., de Zutter, A. (2012). Sleep normalization and decrease in dissociative experiences: Evaluation in an inpatient sample. *Journal of Abnormal Psychology, 121*, 140–150.

van Eijk, J., Demirakca, T., Frischknecht, U., Hermann, D., Mann, K., & Ende, G. (2013). Rapid partial regeneration of brain volume during the first 14 days of abstinence from alcohol. *Alcoholism: Clinical & Experimental Research, 37*, 67–74.

Van Lommel, S., Laenen, A., & d'Ydewalle, G. (2006). Foreign-grammar acquisition while watching subtitled television programmes. *British Journal of Educational Psychology, 76*, 243–258.

VanRyzin, M., Fosco, G., & Dishion, T. (2012). Family and peer predictors of substance use from early adolescence to early adulthood: An 11-year prospective analysis. *Addictive Behaviors, 37*, 1314–1324.

van Schoor, G., Bott, S., & Engels, R. (2008). Alcohol drinking in young adults: The predictive value of personality when peers come around. *European Addiction Research, 14*, 125–133.

Varley, A., & Blasco, M. (2003). Older women's living arrangements and family relationships in urban Mexico. *Women's Studies International Forum, 26*, 525–539.

Vasterling, J., Duke, L., Brailey, K., Constans, J., Allain, A., & Sutker, P. (2002). Attention, learning, and memory performances and intellectual resources in Vietnam veterans: PTSD and no disorder comparisons. *Neuropsychology, 16*, 5–14.

Vaux, K. (2012). *Fetal alcohol syndrome*. Retrieved December 16, 2012, from http://emedicine.medscape.com/article/974016-overview

Verdejo-García, A., López-Torrecillas, F., Aguilar de Arcos, F., & Pérez-García, M. (2005). Differential effects of MDMA, cocaine, and cannabis use severity on distinctive components of the executive functions in polysubstance users: A multiple regression analysis. *Addictive Behaviors, 30*, 89–101.

Verhaeghen, P., Aikman, S., & Van Gulick, A. (2011). Prime and prejudice: Co-occurrence in the culture as a source of automatic stereotype priming. *British Journal of Social Psychology, 50*, 501–518.

Verissimo, M., Santos, A., Vaughn, B., Torres, N., Monteiro, L., & Santos, O. (2011). *Early Child Development and Care, 181*, 27–38.

Vermeersch, H., T'Sjoen, G., Kaufman, J., & Vincke, J. (2008). The role of testosterone in aggressive and non-aggressive risk-taking in adolescent boys. *Hormones and Behavior, 53*, 463–471.

Vernon, L., Relationships among proactive coping posttrauma gratitude, and psychopathology in a traumatized college sample. *Journal of Aggressioin, Maltreatment & Trauma, 21*, 114–130.

Verwijk, E., Cornijs, H., Kok, R., Spaans, H., Stek, M., & Scherder, E. (2012). Neurocognitive effects after brief pulse and ultrabrief pulse unilateral electroconvulsive therapy for major depression: A review. *Journal of Affective Disorders, 140*, 233–243.

Victor, T., Furey, M., Fromm, S., Bellgowan, P., Ohman, A., & Drevets, W. (2012). The extended functional neuroanatomy of emotional processing biases for masked faces in major depressive disorder. *PLoS ONE, 7*, e46439.

Viding, E., Blair, R., Moffitt, T., & Plomin, R. (2005). Evidence of substantial genetic risk for psychopathy in 7-year-olds. *Journal of Child Psychology and Psychiatry, 46*, 592–597.

Vieta, E. (2003). Atypical antipsychotics in the treatment of mood disorders. *Current Opinion in Psychiatry, 16*, 23–27.

Villani, S. (2001). Impact of media on children and adolescents: A 10-year review of the research. *Journal of the American Academy of Child & Adolescent Psychiatry, 40*, 392–401.

Villegas, A., Sharps, M., Satterthwaite, B., & Chisholm, S. (2005). Eyewitness memory for vehicles. *Forensic Examiner, 14*, 24–28.

Violari, A., Cotton, M., Gibb, D., Babiker, A., Steyn, J., Madhi, S., Jean-Philippe, P., & McIntyre, J. (2008). Early antiretroviral therapy and mortality among HIV-infected infants. *New England Journal of Medicine, 359*, 2233–2244.

Visser, P. S., & Krosnick, J. A. (1998). Development of attitude strength over the life cycle: Surge and decline. *Journal of Personality & Social Psychology, 75*, 1389–1410.

Vitousek, K., & Manke, F. (1994). Personality variables and disorders in anorexia nervosa and bulimia nervosa. *Journal of Abnormal Psychology, 103*, 137–147.

Volkow, N., Wang, G., Kollins, S., Wigal, T., Newcorn, J., Telang, F., Fowler, J., Zhu, W., Logan, J., Ma, Y., Pradhan, K., Wong, C., & Swanson, J. (2009). Evaluating dopamine reward pathway in ADHD: Clinical implications. *JAMA: Journal of the American Medical Association, 302*, 1084–1091.

Volpato, V., Macchiarelli, R., Guatelli-Steinberg, D., et al. (2012). Hand to mouth in a Neandertal: Right-handedness in Regourdou. *PLoS One, 7*, e43949.

von Bonsdorff, M., Huuhtanen, P., Tuomi, K., & Seitsamo, J. (2010). Predictors of employees' early retirement intentions: An 11-year longitudinal study. *Occupational Medicine, 60*, 94–100.

Von Dras, D. D., & Siegler, I. C. (1997). Stability in extraversion and aspects of social support at midlife. *Journal of Personality and Social Psychology, 72*, 233–241.

Votruba, S., Horvitz, M., & Schoeller, D. (2000). The role of exercise in the treatment of obesity. *Nutrition, 16*, 179–188.

Vroomen, J., Driver, J., & deGelder, B. (2001). Is cross-modal integration of emotional expressions independent of attentional resources? *Cognitive, Affective & Behavioral Neuroscience, 1*, 382–387.

Vyas, M., Garg, A., Iansayichus, A., et al. (2012). Shift work and vascular events: Systematic review and meta-analysis. *British Medical Journal, 345*, e4800.

Vygotsky, L. (1926/1992). *Educational psychology*. Boca Raton, FL: St. Lucie Press.

Vygotsky, L. S. (1936/1986). *Thought and language* (A. Kozulin, Trans.). Cambridge, MA: MIT Press. (Original work published 1936).

Wade, T., & DiMaria, C. (2003). Weight halo effects: Individual differences in personality evaluations as a function of weight. *Sex Roles, 48*, 461–465.

Wadey, R., Evans, L., Hanton, S., & Neil, R. (2012a). An examination of hardiness throughout the sport injury process. *British Journal of Health Psychology, 17*, 103–128.

Wadey, R., Evans, L., Hanton, S., & Neil, R. (2012b). An examination of hardiness throughout the sport-injury process: A qualitative follow-up study. *British Journal of Health Psychology, 17*, 872–893.

Wagner, S., & Martin, C. (2012). Can firefighters' mental health be predicted by emotional intelligence and proactive coping? *Journal of Loss and Trauma, 17*, 56–72.

Wald, G., Brown, P. K., & Smith, P. H. (1954). Iodopsin. *Journal of General Physiology, 38*, 623–681.

Walker, L. (1989). A longitudinal study of moral reasoning. *Child Development, 60*, 157–166.

Walker, E., Kestler, L., Bollini, A., & Hochman, K. (2004). Schizophrenia: Etiology and course. *Annual Review of Psychology, 55*, 401–430.

Walker, E., Mittal, V., & Tessner, K. (2008). Stress and the hypothalamic pituitary adrenal axis in the developmental course of schizophrenia. *Annual Review of Clinical Psychology, 4*, 189–216.

Walker, I., & Crogan, M. (1998). Academic performance, prejudice and the jigsaw classroom: New pieces to the puzzle. *Journal of Community & Applied Social Psychology, 8*, 381–393.

Walker, M., & Stickgold, R. (2006). Sleep, memory, and plasticity. *Annual Review of Psychology: 57*, 139–166.

Wallentin, M. (2009). Putative sex differences in verbal abilities and language cortex: A critical review. *Brain and Language, 108*, 175–183.

Walster, E., & Walster, G. W. (1969). The matching hypothesis. *Journal of Personality and Social Psychology, 6*, 248–253.

Wang, J., Keown, L., Patten, S., Williams, J., Currie, S., Beck, C., Maxwell, C., & El-Guebaly, N. (2009). A population-based study on ways of dealing with daily stress: Comparisons among individuals with mental disorders, with long-term general medical conditions and healthy people. *Social Psychiatry and Psychiatric Epidemiology, 44*, 666–674.

Warburton, J., McLaughlin, D., & Pinsker, D. (2006). Generative acts: Family and community involvement of older Australians. *International Journal of Aging & Human Development, 63*, 115–137.

Ward, C. (1994). Culture and altered states of consciousness. In W. J. Lonner & R. Malpass (Eds.), *Psychology and culture* (pp. 59–64). Boston: Allyn & Bacon.

Wark, G. R., & Krebs, D. L. (1996). Gender and dilemma differences in real-life moral judgment. *Developmental Psychology, 32*, 220–230.

Warmerdam, L., van Straten, A., Jongsma, J., Twisk, J., & Cuijpers, P. (2010). Online cognitive behavioral therapy and problem-solving therapy for depressive symptoms: Exploring mechanisms of change. *Journal of Behavior Therapy and Experimental psychiatry, 41*, 64–70.

Warshaw, M. G., & Keller, M. B. (1996). The relationship between fluoxetine use and suicidal behavior in 654 subjects with anxiety disorders. *Journal of Clinical Psychiatry, 57*, 158–166.

Warzak, W., Floress, M., Kellen, M., Kazmerski, J., & Chopko, S. (2012). Trends in time-out research: Are we focusing our efforts where our efforts are needed? *The Behavior Therapist, 35*, 30–33.

Washington University School of Medicine. (2003). *Epilepsy surgery* [Online factsheet]. Retrieved September 29, 2003, from *http://neurosurgery.wustl.edu/clinprog/epilepsysurg.htm*

Waterman, A. (1985). Identity in the context of adolescent psychology. *Child Development, 30*, 5–24.

Watson, D. (2002). Predicting psychiatric symptomatology with the Defense Style Questionnaire-40. *International Journal of Stress Management, 9*, 275–287.

Watson, J. (1913). Psychology as the behaviorist view it. *Psychological Review, 20*, 158–177.

Watson, J. B., & Rayner, R. (1920). Conditioned emotional reactions. *Journal of Experimental Psychology, 3*, 1–14.

Weaver, M., & Schnoll, S. (2008). Hallucinogens and club drugs. In M. Galanter & H. Kleber (Eds.), *The American Psychiatric Publishing Textbook of Substance Abuse* (4th ed., pp. 191–200). Arlington, VA: American Psychiatric Publishing, Inc.

Webb, W. (1995). The cost of sleep-related accidents: A reanalysis. *Sleep, 18*, 276–280.

Wechsler, D. (1939). *The measurement of adult intelligence*. Baltimore: Williams & Wilkins.

Weigman, O., & van Schie, E. G. (1998). Video game playing and its relations with aggressive and prosocial behaviour. *British Journal of Social Psychology, 37*(Pt. 3), 367–378.

Weikel, W. (2011). The "telephone" technique. In H. Rosenthal (Ed.) *Favorite counseling and therapy techniques* (2nd ed.). (pp. 329–330) New York, NY, USA: Routledge/Taylor & Francis Group.

Weiner, I. (2004). Monitoring psychotherapy with performance-based measures of personality functioning. *Journal of Personality Assessment, 83*, 323–331.

Weiner, I. B. (1997). Current status of the Rorschach Inkblot Method. *Journal of Personality Assessment, 68*, 5–19.

Weinstock, M., Assor, A., & Broide, G. (2009). Schools as promoters of moral judgment: The essential role of teachers' encouragement of critical thinking. *Social Psychology of Education, 12*, 137–151.

Weisberg, M. (2008). 50 years of hypnosis in medicine and clinical health psychology: A synthesis of cultural crosscurrents. *American Journal of Clinical Hypnosis, 51*, 13–27.

Weiss, P., & Weiss, W. (2011). Criterion-related validity in police psychological evaluations. In J. Kitaeff (Ed.). (pp. 125–133). *Handbook of police psychology*. New York, NY, USA: Routledge/Taylor & Francis Group.

Wells, K. (2007). The short- and long-term medical effects of methamphetamine on children and adults. In H. Covey (Ed.) *The methamphetamine crisis: Strategies to save addicts, families, and communities*. (pp. 57–74). Westport, CT, USA: Praeger Publishers.

Wells, B., & Twenge, J. (2006). Changes in young people's sexual behavior and attitudes, 1943–1999: A cross-temporal meta-analysis. *Review of General Psychology, 9*, 249–261.

Wells, D. L., & Hepper, P. G. (2000). The discrimination of dog odours by humans. *Perception, 29*, 111–115.

Wells, G. L. (1993). What do we know about eyewitness identification? *American Psychologist, 48*, 553–571.

Wells, G. L., Malpass, R. S., Lindsay, R. C., Fisher, R. P., Turtle, J. W., & Fulero, S. M. (2000). From the lab to the police station. A successful application of eyewitness research. *American Psychologist, 55*, 6581–6598.

Welsh, D. (2009). Predictors of depressive symptoms in female medical-surgical hospital nurses. *Issues in Mental Health Nursing, 30*, 320–326.

Wertheimer, M. (1912). Experimental studies of the perception of movement. *Zeitschrift fuer Psychologie, 61*, 161–265.

Weschke, S., & Niedeggen, M. (2012). Differential effects of moderate alcohol consumption on motion and contrast processing. *Psychophysiology, 49*, 833–841.

West, A., Schenkel, L., & Pavuluri, M. (2008). Early childhood temperament in pediatric bipolar disorder and attention deficit hyperactivity disorder. *Journal of Clinical Psychology, 64*, 402–421

West, A., & Weinstein, S. (2012). Bipolar disorder: School-based cognitive-behavioral interventions. In R. Mennuti, R. Christner, & A. Freeman. (Eds.) *Cognitive-behaviorral interventions in educational settings: A handbook for practice* (2nd ed.). (pp. 239–274). New York, NY, USA: Routledge/Taylor & Francis Group.

Westerhof, G., Katzko, M., Dittmann-Kohli, F., & Hayslip, B. (2001). Life contexts and health-related selves in old age: Perspectives from the United States, India and Congo-Zaire. *Journal of Aging Studies, 15*, 105–126.

Westling, E., Andrews, J., Hampson, S., & Peterson, M. (2008). Pubertal timing and substance use: The effects of gender, parental monitoring, and deviant peers. *Journal of Adolescent Health, 42*, 555–563.

Wheeler, M., & McMillan, C. (2001). Focal retrograde amnesia and the episodic-semantic distinction. *Cognitive, Affective & Behavioral Neuroscience, 1*, 22–36.

Wheeler, M., Stuss, D., & Tulving, E. (1997). Toward a theory of episodic memory: The frontal lobes and autonoetic consciousness. *Psychological Bulletin, 121*, 331–354.

Whisenhunt, B. L., Williamson, D. A., Netemeyer, R. G., & Womble, L. G. (2000). Reliability and validity of the Psychosocial Risk Factors Questionnaire (PRFQ). *Eating and Weight Disorders: Studies on Anorexia, Bulimia, and Obesity, 5*, 1–6.

Whisman, M., Johnson, D., Be, D., & Li, A. (2012). Couple-based interventions for depression. *Couple and Family Psychology: Research and practice, 1*, 185–198.

Whitam, F. L., Diamond, M., & Martin, J. (1993). Homosexual orientation in twins: A report on 61 pairs and three triplet sets. *Archives of Sexual Behavior, 22*, 187–296.

White, S. D., & DeBlassie, R. R. (1992). Adolescent sexual behavior. *Adolescence, 27*, 183–191.

Whitehead, B., & Popenoe, D. (2005). *The state of our unions: The social health of marriage in America: 2005: What does the Scandinavian experience tell us?* Retrieved June 15, 2006, from *http://marriage.rutgers.edu/Publications/SOOU/TEXTSOOU2005.htm*

Whitehurst, G. J., Fischel, J. E., Caulfield, M. B., DeBaryshe, B. D., & Valdez-Menchaca, M. C. (1989). Assessment and treatment of early expressive language delay. In P. R. Zelazo & R. Barr (Eds.), *Challenges to developmental paradigms: Implications for assessment and treatment* (pp. 113–135). Hillsdale, NJ: Erlbaum.

Whorf, B. L. (1956). Science and linguistics. In J. B. Carroll (Ed.), *Language, thought, and reality: Selected writings of Benjamin Lee Whorf* (pp. 207–219). Cambridge, MA: MIT Press.

Wickelgren, I. (1996). For the cortex, neuron loss may be less than thought. *Science, 273*, 48–50.

Wicker, A. W. (1969). Attitudes versus action: The relationship of verbal and overt behavioral responses to attitude objects. *Journal of Social Issues, 25*, 41–78.

Widom, C. S., & Morris, S. (1997). Accuracy of adult recollections of childhood victimization: Part 2. Childhood sexual abuse. *Psychological Bulletin, 9*, 34–46.

Wiederhold, B., & Wiederhold, M. (2008). Virtual reality with fMRI: A breakthrough cognitive treatment tool. *Virtual Reality, 12*, 259–267.

Wigboldus, D., Dijksterhuis, A., & Van Knippenberg, A. (2003). When stereotypes get in the way: Stereotypes obstruct stereotype-inconsistent trait inferences. *Journal of Personality & Social Psychology, 84*, 470–484.

Wilcox, D., & Hager, R. (1980). Toward realistic expectation for orgasmic response in women. *Journal of Sex Research, 16*, 162–179.

Wilde, D. (2011). *Jung's personality theory quantified*. New York, NY, USA: Springer-Verlag Publishing.

Wilhelm, K., Kovess, V., Rios-Seidel, C., & Finch, A. (2004). Work and mental health. *Social Psychiatry & Psychiatric Epidemiology, 39*, 866–873.

Wilken, J. A., Smith, B. D., Tola, K., & Mann, M. (2000). Trait anxiety and prior exposure to non-stressful stimuli: Effects on psychophysiological arousal and anxiety. *International Journal of Psychophysiology, 37*, 233–242.

Wilkinson, R. (2004). The role of parental and peer attachment in the psychological health and self-esteem of adolescents. *Journal of Youth & Adolescence, 33*, 479–493.

Williams, J. (2003). Dementia and genetics. In R. Plomin, J. de Fries, I. Craig, & P. McGuffin (Eds.), *Behavioral genetics in the postgenomic era* (pp. 503–528). Washington, DC: APA.

Williams, L. M. (1994). Recall of childhood trauma: A prospective study of women's memories of child sexual abuse. *Journal of Consulting and Clinical Psychology, 62*, 1167–1176.

Williams, R. (1987). Refining the Type A hypothesis: Emergence of the hostility complex. *The American Journal of Cardiology, 60,* 27J–32J.

Willoughby, T., Anderson, S., Wood, E., Mueller, J., & Ross, C. (2009). Fast searching for information on the Internet to use in a learning context: The impact of domain knowledge. *Computers & Education, 52,* 640–648.

Willoughby, T., Adachi, P., & Good, M. (2012). A longitudinal study of the association between violent video game play and aggression among adolescents. *Developmental Psychology, 48,* 1044–1057.

Wilson, G., & Sysko, R. (2006). Cognitive-behavioral therapy for adolescents with bulimia nervosa. *European Eating Disorders Review, 14,* 8–16.

Wilson, M. A., & McNaughton, B. L. (1993). Dynamics of the hippocampal ensemble code for space. *Science, 261,* 1055–1058.

Wilson, W., Mathew, R., Turkington, T., Hawk, T., Coleman, R. E., & Provenzale, J. (2000). Brain morphological changes and early marijuana use: A magnetic resonance and positron emission tomography study. *Journal of Addictive Diseases, 19,* 1–22.

Winograd, E. (1988). Some observations on prospective remembering. In M. M. Gruneberg, P. E. Morris, & R. N. Sykes (Eds.), *Practical aspects of memory: Current research and issues: Vol. 1* (pp. 348–353). Chichester, England: John Wiley & Sons.

Wirth, S., Yanike, M., Frank, L., Smith, A., Brown, E., & Suzuki, W. (2003). Single neurons in the monkey hippocampus and learning of new associations. *Science, 300,* 1578–1581.

Wirz-Justice, A. (2009). From the basic neuroscience of circadian clock function to light therapy for depression: On the emergence of chronotherapeutics. *Journal of Affective Disorders, 116,* 159–160.

Wise, R. (2009). Drugs addiction: Actions. In W. Squire (Ed.) *Encyclopedia of neuroscience* Vol. 4. (pp. 713–716). Waltham, MA: Elsevier Academic Press.

Wittenberg, M., Bremmer, F., & Wachtler, T. (2008). Perceptual evidence for saccadic updating of color stimuli. *Journal of Vision, 8,* 1–9.

Wolf, O. (2009). Stress and memory in humans: Twelve years of progress? *Brain Research, 1293,* 142–154.

Wolford, G., Miller, M. B., & Gazzaniga, M. (2000). The left hemisphere's role in hypothesis formation. *Journal of Neuroscience, 20,* 1–4.

Wolk, D., & Budson, A. (2010). Memory systems. *CONTINUUM: Lifelong Learning in Neurology,* 15–28.

Wolpe, J. (1958). *Psychotherapy by reciprocal inhibition.* Palo Alto, CA: Stanford University Press.

Wolpe, J. (1973). *The practice of behavior therapy* (2nd ed.). New York: Pergamon.

Wolsko, P., Eisenberg, D., Davis, R., & Phillips, R. (2004). Use of mind-body medical therapies: Results of a national survey. *Journal of General Internal Medicine, 19,* 43–50.

Wolters, C. (2003). Understanding procrastination from a self-regulated learning perspective. *Journal of Educational Psychology, 95,* 179–187.

Wolters, C. (2004). Advancing achievement goal theory using goal structures and goal orientations to predict students' motivation, cognition, and achievement. *Journal of Educational Psychology, 96,* 136–250.

Wood, J. M., Nezworski, M. T., & Stejskal, W. J. (1996). The Comprehensive System for the Rorschach: A critical examination. *Psychological Science, 7,* 3–10.

Wood, J., Cowan, P., & Baker, B. (2002). Behavior problems and peer rejection in preschool boys and girls. *Journal of Genetic Psychology, 163,* 72–88.

Wood, W., & Conway, M. (2006). Subjective impact, meaning making, and current and recalled emotions for self-defining memories. *Journal of Personality, 75,* 811–846.

Wood, W., & Eagly, A. (2007). Social structure origins of sex differences in human mating. In S. Gangestad, & J. Simpson (Eds.), *The evolution of mind: Fundamental questions and controversies* (pp. 383–390). New York: Guilford Press.

Wood, W., Lundgren, S., Ovellette, J., Busceme, S., & Blackstone, T. (1994). Minority influence: A meta-analytic review of the social influence processes. *Psychological Bulletin, 115,* 323–345.

Woodman, G., & Luck, S. (2003). Serial deployment of attention during visual search. *Journal of Experimental Psychology: Human Perception and Performance, 29,* 121–138.

Woodward, A. L., Markman, E. M., & Fitzsimmons, C. M. (1994). Rapid word learning in 13- and 18-month-olds. *Developmental Psychology, 30,* 553–566.

Woody, E. Z., & Bowers, K. S. (1994). A frontal assault on dissociated control. In S. J. Lynn & J. W. Rhue (Eds.), *Dissociation: Clinical, theoretical and research perspectives* (pp. 52–79). New York: Guilford.

World Health Organization. (2010). *Gender and women's mental health.* Retrieved March 18, 2010 from *http://www.who.int/mental_health/ prevention/genderwomen/en/.*

Wozniak, J., Biederman, J., Kwon, A., Mick, E., Faraone, S., Orlovsky, K., Schnare, L., Cargol., C., & van Grondelle, A. (2005). How cardinal are cardinal symptoms in pediatric bipolar disorder? An examination of clinical correlates. *Biological Psychiatry, 58,* 583–588.

Wright, J. C., & Mischel, W. (1987). A conditional approach to dispositional constructs: The local predictability of social behavior. *Journal of Personality and Social Psychology, 53,* 1159–1177.

Wright, K. (2002, September). Times of our lives. *Scientific American,* 58–65.

Wyrobek, A., Eskenazi, B., Young, S., Arnheim, N., Tiemann-Boege, I., Jabs, E., et al. (2006). Advancing age has differential effects on DNA damage, chromatin integrity, gene mutations, and aneuploidies. *Proceedings of the National Academies of Sciences, 103,* 9601–9606.

Yackinous, C., & Guinard, J. (2002). Relation between PROP (6-n-propylthiouracil) taster status, taste anatomy and dietary intake measures for young men and women. *Appetite, 38,* 201–209.

Yale-New Haven Hospital. (2003). *Making the right choice: Speak up about complementary and alternative therapies.* Retrieved August 6, 2003, from *http://www.ynhh.org/choice/cam.html*

Yanagita, T. (1973). An experimental framework for evaluation of dependence liability in various types of drugs in monkeys. *Bulletin of Narcotics, 25,* 57–64.

Yasui-Furukori, N., Saito, M., Nakagami, T., Kaneda, A., Tateishi, T., & Kaneko, S. (2006). Association between multidrug resistance 1 (MDR1) gene polymorphisms and therapeutic response to bromperidol in schizophrenic patients: A preliminary study. *Progress in Neuro-Psychopharmacology & Biological Psychiatry, 30,* 286–291.

Yates, W. (2008). *Anxiety disorders.* Retrieved March 15, 2010, from *http://emedicine.medscape.com/article/286227-overview.*

Yeh, S., & Lo, S. (2004). Living alone, social support, and feeling lonely among the elderly. *Social Behavior & Personality, 32,* 129–138.

Yip, S., Sacco, K., George, T., & Potenza, M. (2009). Risk/reward decision-making in schizophrenia: A preliminary examination of the influence of tobacco smoking and relatioship to Wisconsin Card Sorting Task performance. *Schizophrenia Research, 110,* 156–164.

Yolken, R., & Torrey, E. (2008). Are some cases of psychosis caused by microbial agents? A review of the evidence. *Molecular Psychiatry, 13,* 470–479.

Young, G. (2009). Coma. In Schiff, N., & Laureys, S. (Eds.), *Disorders of consciousness. Annals of the New York Academy of Sciences* (pp. 32–47). New York: Wiley-Blackwell.

Yovell, Y., Bannett, Y., & Shalev, A. (2003). Amnesia for traumatic events among recent survivors: A pilot study. *CNS Spectrums, 8,* 676–685.

Zajonc, R. B. (1980). Feeling and thinking: Preferences need no inferences. *American Psychologist, 35,* 151–175.

Zajonc, R. B. (1984). On the primacy of affect. *American Psychologist, 39,* 117–123.

Zajonc, R. B., & Sales, S. M. (1966). Social facilitation of dominant and subordinate responses. *Journal of Experimental Social Psychology, 2,* 160–168.

Zaragoza, M. S., & Mitchell, K. J. (1996). Repeated exposure to suggestion and the creation of false memories. *Psychological Science, 7,* 294–300.

Zatorre, R., Belin, P., & Penhune, V. (2002). Structure and function of the auditory cortex: Music and speech. *Trends in Cognitive Sciences, 6,* 37–46.

Zentner, M., & Mitura, K. (2012). Stepping out of the caveman's shadow: Nations' gender gap predicts degree of sex differentiation in mate preferences. *Psychological Science, 23,* 1176–1185.

Zhang, D., Li, Z., Chen, X., Wang, Z., Zhang, X., Meng, X., et al. (2003). Functional comparison of primacy, middle and recency retrieval in human auditory short-term memory: An event-related fMRI study. *Cognitive Brain Research, 16,* 91–98.

Zhang, X., Liang, J., Chen, D., Xiu, M., He, J., Cheng, W., Wu, Z., Yang, F., Haile, C., Sun, H., Lu, L., Kosten, & Kosten, T. (2013). Cigarette smoking in male patients with chronic schizophrenia in a Chinese population: Prevalence and relationship to clinical phenotypes. *PLoS One.* Retrieved February 4, 2013, from http://www.plosone.org/article/info%3Adoi%2F10.1371%2Fjournal.pone.0030937

Zhang, Y., Goonetilleke, R., Plocher, T., & Liang, S. (2005). Time-related behavior in multitasking situations. *International Journal of Human-Computer Studies, 62,* 425–455.

Zimbardo, P. (1969). The human choice: Individuation, reason, and order versus deindividuation, impulse, and chaos. *Nebraska Symposium on Motivation, 17,* 237–307.

Zimbardo, P. G. (1972). Pathology of imprisonment. *Society, 9,* 4–8.

Zimmerman, M., Posternak, K., & Chelminski, I. (2002). Symptom severity and exclusion from antidepressant efficacy trials. *Journal of Clinical Psychopharmacology, 22,* 610–614.

Zinbarg, R., & Griffith, J. (2008). Behavior therapy. In J. Lebow (Ed.), *Twenty-first century psychotherapies: Contemporary approaches to theory and practice* (pp. 8–42). Hoboken, NJ: John Wiley & Sons.

Zubieta, J., Bueller, J., Jackson, L., Scott, D., Xu, Y., Koeppe, R., Nichols, T., & Stohler, C. (2005). Placebo effects mediated by endogenous opioid activity on μ-opioid receptors. *Journal of Neuroscience, 25,* 7754–7762.

Zucker, A., Ostrove, J., & Stewart A. (2002). College-educated women's personality development in adulthood: Perceptions and age differences. *Psychology & Aging, 17,* 236–244.

"48% say Obama's inauguration signals new era of race relations." (January 20, 2009). Retrieved February 14, 2009 from *http://www.rasmussenreports.com/public_content/politics/obama_administration/january_2009/48_say_obama_s_inauguration_signals_new_era_of_race_relations.*

Credits

COVER: mikiekwoods/Fotolia

CHAPTER 1 UNFIG CO-01, p. 1: unscrew/Fotolia. CO-01, p. 1: Andres Rodriguez/Alamy. Photo 1.10, p. 4: Pearson Education. Figure 1.5, p. 24: Data from Lang et al. (1995). Photo 1.1, p. 7: Joggie Botma/Shutterstock. Photo 1.2, p. 8: Archives of the History of American Psychology The University of Akron. Photo 1.3, p. 9: With permission of the University Archives, Columbia University in the City of New York. Photo 1.4, p. 11: Lon C. Diehl/PhotoEdit, Inc. Photo 1.5, p. 12: Ariel Skelley/Blend/Glow Images. Photo 1.6a, p. 13: Swissmacky/Shutterstock. Photo 1.6b, p. 13: Blue Jean Images/Alamy. Photo 1.7, p. 18: Nancy DeVore/Anthro-Photo. Photo 1.8, p. 19: Wavebreakmedia Ltd./Shutterstock. Photo 1.9, p. 21: Skjold Photographs/PhotoEdit, Inc. Photo 1.11, p. 22: Pearson Education.

CHAPTER 2 UNFIG CO-02, p. 38: Tom Grill/Corbis. Photo 2.9, p. 39: Barbara Penoyar/Stockbyte/Getty Images. Photo 2.1, p. 40: xpixel/Shutterstock. Photo 2.2, p. 40: Alexander Tsiaras/Science Source/Photo Researchers. Photo 2.3, p. 43: 20th Century Fox/Album/Newscom. Photo 2.4, p. 44: Biophoto Associates/Photo Researchers. Photo 2.5, p. 45: Bill Aron/PhotoEdit, Inc. Figure 2.2, p. 44: Adapted from Lilienfeld, Lynn, Namy, & Wolf (2009). Figure 2.5, p. 48: Lilienfeld, Lynn, Namy, & Woolf (2009). Figure 2.6, p. 49: Adapted from Lilienfeld, S., Lynn, S., Namy, L., & Woolf, N. (2009). Photo 2.7, p. 50: Jason Moore/ZUMA Press/Newscom. Photo 2.10, p. 55: Pearson Education. Text, p. 55: President John F. Kennedy. Figure 2.11, p. 56: Based on Gazzaniga, M. (1983). Photo 2.6a, p. 59: BSIP/Photo Researchers, Inc. Photo 2.6b, p. 59: BSIP/Photo Researchers, Inc. Photo 2.8, p. 66: Dann Tardif/LWA/Corbis/Bridge/Glow Images.

CHAPTER 3 UNFIG CO-03, p. 75: Juice Images/Alamy. Figure 3.3, p. 80: Science Source/Photo Researchers. Text, p. 85: Alien Twentieth Century Fox. Figure 3.5, p. 85: Jon Barlow/Pearson Education Ltd. Figure 3.9, p. 89: Dr. Goran Bredberg/Science Source/Photo Researchers, Inc. Figure 3.9.1, p. 89: Dr. Goran Bredberg/Science Source/Photo Researchers, Inc. Figure 3.10, p. 90: Eric Limon/Shutterstock. Figure 3.12, p. 92: Science Source/Photo Researchers, Inc. Figure 3.12a, p. 92: Pearson Education. Figure 3.13, p. 98: Highlights for Children (May, 1995). Figure 3.15, p. 101: Pearson Education. Figure 3.16, p. 102: Anton Levitski/Age Fotostock. Figure 3.17a, p. 103: Kent Meireis/The Image Works. Figure 3.17b, p. 103: James Randklev/Stone/Getty Images. Figure 3.17c, p. 103: sanderstock/Fotolia. Figure 3.17d, p. 103: S.R.Lee Photo Traveller/Shutterstock. Figure 3.17e, p.103: vvoe/Shutterstock. Figure 3.17f, p 103: AlexQ/Fotolia. Figure 3.17g, p. 103: Pete Turner/Riser/Getty Images. Photo 3.1, p. 77: ArenaCreative/Fotolia. Photo 3.2a, p. 84: Shutterstock. Photo 3.3, p. 92: Hideo Haga/Haga/The Image Works. Photo 3.4, p. 94: Purestock/Getty Images. Photo 3.4.1, p. 96: Pearson Education. Photo 3.5, p. 97: Sciencephotos/Alamy. Photo 3.6, p. 105: Richard Lord Enterprises, Inc./Image Works.

CHAPTER 4 UNFIG CO-04, p. 115: David Burch/UpperCut Images/Alamy. Figure 4.2, p. 122: Foley, Ancoli-Israel, Britz, & Walsh, 2004; Iglowstein, Jenni, Molinari, & Largo, 2003; Hansen, Janssen, Schiff, & Zee, 2005; Millman, 2005; Mindell, 1999; Ohayan, Carskadon, Guilleminault, & Vitiello, 2004. Photo 4.1, p. 119: Pixel974/Fotolia. Photo 4.2, p. 121: Russ Curtis/Science Source/Photo Researchers. Photo 4.3, p. 123: WavebreakmediaMicro/Fotolia. Photo 4.1.1, p. 124: Pearson Education. Photo 4.4, p. 124: Emmanuel Mignot/Stanford University School of Medicine. Photo 4.5, p. 127: Pictorial Press Ltd/Alamy. Photo 1.2.1, p. 128: Pearson Education. Photo 4.7, p. 129: Chris Rout/Bubbles Photolibrary/Alamy. Photo 4.8, p. 132: Pablo Paul/Alamy. Photo 4.9, p. 133: TopFoto/The Image Works. Photo 4.10, p. 136: Noah Berger/AP Photo.

CHAPTER 5 UNFIG CO-05, p. 144: Henry Westheim Photography/Alamy. Figure 5.5, p. 150: Professor Ben Harris, University of New Hampshire. Figure 5.6, p. 157: From Tolman & Honzik (1930). Figure 5.8 p. 171: Data from Lenhart, A., Jones, S., & Macgill, A. (2008). Photo 5.1, p. 151: Kevin Laubacher/Taxi/Getty Images. Photo 5.2, p. 152: Zcb Wenn Photos/Newscom. Photo 5.3, p. 154: Nina Leen/Contributor/Time & Life Pictures/Getty Images. Photo 5.4, p. 156: Roy Mehta/Riser/Getty Images. Photo 5.5, p. 157: Jack Sullivan/Alamy. Photo 5.6, p. 160: Illene MacDonald/PhotoEdit, Inc. Photo 5.7, p. 163: Rachel Epstein/PhotoEdit, Inc. Photo 5.7.1, p. 163: Pearson Education. Photo 5.8a, p. 169: From A. Bandura & R. Walters/Photo Courtesy of Albert Bandura. Photo 5.8b, p. 169: From A. Bandura & R. Walters/Photo Courtesy of Albert Bandura. Photo 5.8c, p. 169: From A. Bandura & R. Walters/Photo Courtesy of Albert Bandura. Photo 5.9, p. 170: Richard Drew/AP Photo. Photo 5.10, p.171: Pond Stephen/Newsteam/SIPA/Newscom. Photo 5.11, p. 171: Fred Prouser/Reuters/Corbis.

CHAPTER 6 UNFIG CO-06, p. 178: Andersen Ross/Blend Images/Getty Images. Photo 6.1, p. 181: Ocean/Corbis. Photo 6.2, p. 186: Randy Faris/Corbis. Photo 6.3, p. 190: Louis Lanzano/AP Images. Photo 6.4, p. 192: Eye Ubiquitous/Glow images. Photo 6.8, p. 194: Photo 6.7, p. 199: Adapted from Maguire et al. (2000), Proceedings of the National Academy of Sciences. Bettmann/Corbis. Photo 6.5, p. 201: Jiri Rezac/Polaris/Newscom. Photo 6.6, p. 203: Kayte Deioma/PhotoEdit, Inc. Text, p. 204: Maltz, W. (1991). The sexual healing journey: A guide for survivors of sexual abuse. New York: HarperCollins.

CHAPTER 7 CO-07, p. 212: Bill Aron/PhotoEdit . Photo 7.1, p. 214: Premack, D. (1971). Language in chimpanzees? Science, 172, 808–822. Reprinted by permission from AAAS. Bill Aron/PhotoEdit. Jacques Brinon/AP Images. Photo 7.2a, p. 215: visceralimage/Fotolia. Photo 7.2b, p. 215: Silver/Fotolia. Photo 7.1.1, p. 217: Pearson Education. Photo 7.3, p. 218: Jeff Greenberg/PhotoEdit, Inc. Photo 7.4, p. 220: TopFoto/The Image Works. Photo 7.2.1, p. 220: Pearson Education. Photo 7.5, p. 221: Adam Nadel/AP Photo. Photo 7.6a/b, p. 223: Mike Margol/PhotoEdit, Inc. Photo 7.7, p. 224: Frans Lanting/Corbis. Figure 7.1, p. 224: Premack, D. (1971). Language in chimpanzees? Science, 172, 808–822. Reprinted by permission from AAAS. Photo 7.8, p. 226: Charlie Riedel/AP Images. Figure 7.3, p. 229: Campbell, Linda C.; Campbell, Bruce; Dickinson, Dee, Teaching and Learning Through Multiple Intelligences, 3rd Ed., (c) 2004. Reprinted and Electronically reproduced by permission of Pearson Education, Inc., Upper Saddle River, New Jersey. Figure 7.4a, p. 230: Floresco Productions/OJO Images/Getty Images. Figure 7.4b, p. 230: Custom Medical Stock Photo/Alamy. Figure 7.4b, p. 230: Rafael Macia/Photo Researchers, Inc. Figure 7.4c, p. 230: Louise Murray/Alamy Photo 7.9, p. 233: National Library of Medicine. Figure 7.7, p. 236: Based on data from Bouchard & McGue (1981); Erlenmeyer-Kimling & Jarvik (1963). Figure 7.8, p. 238: Campbell, F., & Ramey, C. (1994). Effects of achievement: A follow-up study of children from low-income families. Child Development, 65, 684–698. Figure 1, p. 690.

CHAPTER 8 CO-08, p. 251: Blend Images/SuperStock. Photo 8.1.1, p. 254: Pearson Education. Photo 1, p. 257: Angela Hampton Picture Library/Alamy. Photo 2, p. 257: Jaimie Duplass/Shutterstock. Photo 3, p. 257: Spencer grant/PhotoEdit, Inc. Photo 4, p. 257: Will Hart/PhotoEdit, Inc. Figure 8.2, p. 261: Colby, A., Kohlberg, L., Gibbs, J., & LIeberman, M. (1983). A longitudinal study of moral judgment. Monographs of the Society for Research in Child Development, 48, pp. 1–124. Photo 8.1, p. 258: SW Productions/Digital Vision/Getty Images. Photo 8.2a, p. 266: Francis Leroy/Biocosmos/Science Source. Photo 8.2b, p. 266: Gary Retherford/Photo Researchers. Photo 8.2c, p. 266: Biophoto Associates/Science Source/Photo Researchers, Inc. Photo 8.3, p. 267: Mark Richards/PhotoEdit, Inc. Figure 8.3a, p. 269: BSIP/Photo Researchers, Inc/Science source. Figure 8.3b, p. 269: Leila Cutler/Alamy. Figure 8.3c, p. 269: Robert Dant/Alamy. Figure 8.3d, p. 269: Kozlovskaya Ksenia/Shutterstock. Figure 8.3e, p. 269: Jaroslaw Grudzinski/Shutterstock. Figure 8.3f, p. 269: Marina Raith/Picture Press/Alamy. Figure 8.3g, p. 269: Brigitte Sporrer/Cultura/Getty Images. Figure 8.3h, p. 269: Kwame Zikomo/Purestock/Alamy. Figure 8.3i, p. 269: Isabelle Zelonka/Alamy. Figure 8.3j, p. 269: Valerie Garner/Alamy. Figure 8.3k, p. 269: Sally and Richard Greenhill/Alamy. Photo 8.4, p. 269: Martin Rogers/Stone/Getty Images. Figure 8.3l, p. 269: Masterfile. Photo 8.5, p. 270: Vanessa Davies/Dorling Kindersley, Ltd. Photo 8.6, p. 273: Christina Kennedy/PhotoEdit, Inc. Photo 8.7, p. 275: Peter Cade/Stone/Getty Images. Photo 8.2.1, p. 278: Pearson Education. Photo 8.8, p. 281: Liam Norris/Cultura/Getty Images. Photo 8.3.1, p. 282: Pearson Education. Photo 8.9, p. 284: Jim Craigmyle/Corbis. Figure 8.5, p. 286: http://www.agingstats.gov/agingstatsdotnet/Main_Site/Data/2012_Documents/Docs/EntireChartbook.pdf.

CHAPTER 9 CO-09, p. 294: Janis Miglavs/Danita Delimont/Alamy. Photo 9.2, p. 296: Ethan Miller/Getty Images Entertainment/Getty Images. Figure 9.1, p. 297: Phase4Photography/Fotolia. Photo 9.2, p. 299: Andrey Bandurenko/Fotolia. Figure 9.4, p. 305: National Center for Health Statistics (2012). Photo 9.3, 306: Custom Medical Stock Photo/Alamy. Photo 9.4, p. 307: Jackson Lee/Splash News/Newscom. Photo 9.5, p. 312: Lane Oatey/Blue Jean Images/Getty Images. Photo 9.6, p. 314: Jim Bourg/Reuters/Corbis. Figure 9.6, p. 317: James Cavallini / Science Source. Photo 9.7, p. 318: Monkey Business/Fotolia. Photo 9.8a, p. 319: Paul Ekman Group. Photo 9.8b, p. 319: Paul Ekman Group. Photo 9.8c, p. 319: Paul Ekman Group. Photo 9.8d, p. 319: Paul Ekman Group. Photo 9.8e, p. 319: Paul Ekman Group. Photo 9.8f, p. 319: Paul Ekman Group. Photo 9.9, p. 320: bikeriderlondon/Shutterstock.

Name Index

Subject Index

A

ABC theory, 434–435
Abnormal behavior, 393–394
  criteria for, 393–394
    causing personal distress, 394
    danger to self or others, 394
    legal responsibility for one's own acts, 394
    maladaptive behavior, 393–394
    strange within the person's culture, 394
    unusual for age group, 394
Absolute threshold, 76–77
Acamprosate, 351
Acceptance stage, death and dying, 286
Accommodation, 80, 253
Accountability, 333
Acculturative stress, 335
Acetylcholine (Ach), 45, 46, 61
Achievement motivation, 296, 300–301, 466
Achievement tests, 231
Acquired immune deficiency syndrome (AIDS), 352–355
Acrophobia, 400
Action potential, 43, 44
Activation phase, of motivation, 295
Activation-synthesis hypothesis of dreaming, 127
Active euthanasia, 287
Active listening, 428
Actor-observer effect, 456
Acupuncture, 94
Adaptive theory of sleep, 120
Addiction, 152. *See also* Substance abuse and addiction
Additive strategy, 215, 216
ADHD. *See* Attention-deficit/hyperactivity disorder (ADHD)
Adolescence, 276–279
  emerging adulthood, 278–279
  puberty, 276–277
  sexual behavior, 276–277
  sleep patterns in, 122
  social relationships, 277–278
Adolescent egocentrism, 255
Adolescent growth spurt, 276
Adoption studies, 68, 237–238, 376, 377, 474–475
Adrenal glands, 65, 312
Adrenalin, 199
Adulthood
  early and middle, 279–283
  emerging, 278–279
  late, 283–287
Adult-onset genetic disorders, 67
Aerial perspective, 102, 103
Aerobic exercise, 355
Affective neuroscience, 317–318
Afferent (sensory) neurons, 41, 49
African Americans
  culturally sensitive therapy and, 445
  health and illness in, 347–348
  racism experienced by, 334
Afterimage, 83–84
Age/aging, 285
  brain and, 61–62, 76
  sleep patterns and, 122
  successful aging, 285
  suicide rates and, 406
Ageism, 28

Aggression, 474–477
  alcohol and, 475
  biological factors in, 474–475
  crowding and, 476
  frustration-aggression hypothesis, 475
  media and, 169–170
  against outsiders, 476
  pain and, 476
  scapegoating, 476
  social learning theory of, 476–477
  testosterone and, 475
Agoraphobia, 398
Agreeableness, 375
AIDS. *See* Acquired immune deficiency syndrome (AIDS)
AIDS-related dementia, 355
Alarm stage, 338
Alcohol, 131, 134, 137
  abuse, 132, 350–351
  aggression and, 475
  poisoning, 350
  during pregnancy, 266
Alcoholic Anonymous (AA), 351, 429
Alertness, 118–119
Algorithms, 220
All-or-none law, 43
All-or-nothing thinking, 436
Alpha waves, 120–121
Altered states of consciousness, 117
Alternative medicine, 356–357
Altruism, 473
Alzheimer's disease, 200, 201
Amacrine cells, 81
Ambiguous figures, 104
Amenorrhea, 307
American College Testing Program (ACT), 231
American Psychological Association (APA), ethics code, 442–443
Amnesia, 200–201
  anterograde, 200
  dissociative, 412
  infantile, 204
  retrograde, 200
Amphetamines, 131, 133–134, 137, 417–418
Amplitude, 86
Amygdala, 51, 317
Anal retentive personality, 366
Analogy heuristic, 219
Anchoring, 218–219
Androgens, 65, 275, 312
Anecdotal evidence, 17
Anemia, 355
Anger, 318, 319, 345
Animal language, 223–225
  arbitrariness, 223
  cultural transmission, 223
  displacement, 223
  duality of patterning, 223
  interchangeability, 223
  prevarication, 223
  productivity, 223
  reflexiveness, 223
  specialization, 223
Animals, used in research, 29–30
Anorexia nervosa, 307–308
Antabuse, 433

Anterior cingulate cortex (ACC), 318
Anterograde amnesia, 200–201
Antianxiety drugs, 439–440
Antibodies, 337, 338
Anticonvulsant drugs, 439, 440
Antidepressant drugs, 438–439
Antigens, 337
Antipsychotics, 437–438
Antiretroviral drugs, 352
Antisocial personality disorder, 414
Anvil, 86–87
Anxiety, 393, 398
Anxiety disorders, 395, 397–402
  agoraphobia, 398
  explanations for, 400–401
  generalized anxiety disorder, 399
  obsessive-compulsive disorder, 401–402
  panic attacks, 398
  panic disorder, 399
  performance anxiety, 399
  phobias, 400, 401
  social anxiety disorder, 399–400
APA code of ethics, 28–29
Aphasia, 59, 60
Applied research, 6
Approach-approach conflict, 332
Approach-avoidance conflict, 332
Aptitude tests, 231
Arbitrariness, 223
Archetypes, 369
Armed Services Vocational Aptitude Battery (ASVAB), 231
Arousal, 298
Arousal theory, 298, 299, 303
Arthritis, 94, 283–284
Artificial intelligence, 221
Artificial neural networks (ANNs), 221
Artistic personality type, 282
Asian Americans, 347
Asperger's Syndrome, 416–417
Assimilation, 253
Assisted suicide, 287
Association areas, 53
Asthma, 348
Atkinson-Shiffrin model, 188
Atmospheric perspective, 103
Atmospheric perspective, 102, 268–271
Attachment
  avoidant attachment, 270
  contact comfort, 269
  disorganized/disoriented attachment, 270
  father-child, 270–271
  infant-caregiver attachment, 268–271
  resistant attachment, 270
  secure attachment, 270
  separation anxiety, 270
  stranger anxiety, 270
Attention, 95–97
  cocktail party phenomenon, 96–97
  cross-modal perception, 97
  inattentional blindness, 95–96
Attention-deficit/hyperactivity disorder (ADHD), 46, 348, 417–418
  in adulthood, 418
  explanations for, 417
  treatment of, 417–418